Trial
Handbook
for
New York
Lawyers

Third Edition

by

Aaron J. Broder, Esq.

1996

TM **The Lawyers Cooperative Publishing Co.**
Rochester, New York 14694

ABOUT THE AUTHOR

Aaron J. Broder

Aaron J. Broder has won wide recognition for his success before juries in personal injury and wrongful death cases. In recent years, he has obtained unprecedented recoveries for victims of well-publicized disasters. These have included $20 million in wrongful death lawsuits arising from the Soviet destruction of a Korean Airlines plane in 1983, and a $19 million verdict in 1995 for the wife of an executive killed in the bombing of Pam Am 103 over Lockerbie, Scotland, in 1988.

Mr. Broder is a past president of the New York State Trial Lawyers Association and the recipient of numerous commendations from bar associations, legal academies and law publications. He has made a specialty of seeking compensation for seriously injured victims of defective products, automobile accidents, medical malpractice, and mass disasters. His successes have expanded the scope of the law to allow a wider range of recovery and a broader measure of damages in tort cases, including pre-impact terror in airline cases. His cases have also contributed to greater tort accountability by industry and by municipal, state and federal governments.

Mr. Broder's numerous articles on legal subjects have been collected in a book entitled *Aaron J. Broder on Trial: Reflections of a Master Litigator*, edited by George M. Gold and published by Lawyers Cooperative Publishing Co. He has also lectured before many medical, legal and government forums. He practices from offices in Manhattan and is a graduate of New York University Law School.

INTRODUCTION TO THE THIRD EDITION

Users of previous editions of the *Trial Handbook for New York Lawyers* will find that the focus of this third edition has been sharpened to concentrate on providing guidance and support to the practitioner of civil litigation, and personal injury litigation in particular.

We have sought to broaden the coverage of problems frequently encountered in civil trials, while eliminating subjects applicable solely to criminal trials. Citations to criminal cases are included only where they provide precedent on evidentiary issues governed by the same rules as civil cases.

We hope that you, the practitioner, will find this edition a valuable courtroom companion in meeting the never-ending challenge of civil trial practice.

ACKNOWLEDGEMENTS

There are many people to thank for their invaluable help, but most of all I am indebted to my esteemed colleague, David Schuller, who is also appellate counsel to our firm, for his dedication to the task of bringing this third edition of the *Trial Handbook for New York Lawyers* to fruition. The many long hours he spent were an inspiration to our entire staff. Many staff members also contributed to the effort, in particular Paul Zilberfein and Adam Polo, who assisted in researching cases, and Meryl Schwartz, the managing attorney of our firm, and Deborah Broder, my partner, who oversee the smooth operation of our office.

I would be remiss not to express my thanks to Howard Angione of Lawyers Cooperative, without whose gentle prodding this book might not have been completed.

I also wish to gratefully acknowledge Bernard Able's many years of association with this project. His extraordinary assistance and scholarly attention to detail contributed to the success of the first and second editions and the yearly supplements upon which this edition is based.

Finally, I am grateful for the many contributions of Alice Broder:

> Blessed are you little lady,
> Mistress of my universe,
> Who have kept us alive,
> Sustained us and brought us
> To this time.

Aaron J. Broder
New York City, 1996

FOREWORD

After three decades of trials (not without tribulations), I am happy to report that both the rules of evidence and I are alive and well. We are both reborn at the commencement of each trial, and the excitement is heightened with the first witness.

I still believe that, to win, trial counsel must view each case as one of life or death. Counsel must take command in opening, hold the initiative throughout the course of the trial, and, with a steady forward pace, take on every point at issue. The most critical factors are to master the facts and law, then govern the direction of the testimony and evidence with the same forcefulness and urgency as the adrenalin coursing through counsel's body.

Because counsel believes in the justice of the cause at issue, careful preparation of the trial represents the attainment of a nobel objective. The rules of evidence must be viewed, not in the light of trickery or artifice, but rather as the vehicle that enables the search for truth to find fulfillment.

As a practical matter, counsel should demonstrate through the presentation of the case that the principles of evidence are both sound and consonant with common understanding. This philosophy underlies the use of the rules of evidence and, without this philosophy, they may appear to be stale and artificial. Whether I am attempting to project the *prima facie* facts upon which my cases depends, or whether I am trying to demonstrate the lack of substance in my adversary's case, I never seek to win a point that would appear artificial, parochial or contrary to a common-sense appraisal. It is my conviction that a wall of silence resulting from an unduly technical application of rigid rules more often that not causes a high degree of speculation and perhaps a verdict based not upon evidence, but upon what the trier of fact thought the precluded matter would have established.

I do not mean to imply that the rules governing the trial are not based upon a sound formulation of principles calculated to reduce the impact of human frailty on the search for truth. But the rules must be understood in their common-sense application. For example, there is good reason to exclude hearsay; there is good reason to weigh the interest of a party; there is good reason for the application of the Dead Man's Statute, etc. But common sense and the rules also give the trial judge wide discretion in many crucial aspects of the trial.

The purpose of this book is to provide a short and concise reference that enables counsel to be better equipped to master the movement of a trial. Where there is an absolute exclusionary rule, counsel should be careful to avoid its transgression. Where, during the course of trial, questions arise that involve the discretion of the court, counsel should be equipped to persuade the court that the interest of justice would be better served if counsel were permitted to move forward. This necessarily requires ready reference to the case law, because the first principle of fairness requires that counsel carefully present to the trial judge a clear position supported by an accurate statement of the law. As an officer of the court, counsel owes the presiding judge no less; for the client, counsel can do no more.

Regrettably, the material here cannot, by itself, inspire the verve, veracity and tenaciousness that must characterize the proper presentation of a cause. That must be left to the artistry and hard work of the trial lawyer. We hope this work will come to life when the lawyer finds citations of authority to substantiate the common-sense presentation that he or she has carefully fashioned.

Aaron J. Broder

TABLE OF CONTENTS

CHAPTER 1

THE CONDUCT OF THE TRIAL

CHAPTER 2

MOTIONS DURING TRIAL, DEFAULT AND DISMISSAL

CHAPTER 3

CONTEMPT OF COURT

CHAPTER 4

SELECTION OF JURY

CHAPTER 5

OPENING STATEMENTS

CHAPTER 6

ORDER OF PROOF

Table of Contents

CHAPTER 7

BURDEN OF PROOF

CHAPTER 8

PROOF OF FACTS

CHAPTER 9

WITNESSES

CHAPTER 10

IMPEACHMENT OF WITNESSES

CHAPTER 11

COMPETENCY OF A WITNESS TO TESTIFY

CHAPTER 12

DEAD MAN STATUTE

Table of Contents

CHAPTER 13

EXAMINATION OF WITNESSES

CHAPTER 14

CROSS-EXAMINATION

CHAPTER 15

REDIRECT AND RECROSS EXAMINATION

CHAPTER 16

PRIVILEGED COMMUNICATIONS

CHAPTER 17

JUDICIAL NOTICE

CHAPTER 18

PRESUMPTIONS

CHAPTER 19

REAL AND DEMONSTRATIVE EVIDENCE

CHAPTER 20

THE VIEW

CHAPTER 21

DOCUMENTARY EVIDENCE

Table of Contents

CHAPTER 22

OPINION EVIDENCE

CHAPTER 23

HEARSAY EVIDENCE

CHAPTER 24

ADMISSIONS

Table of Contents

CHAPTER 25

ADMISSIBILITY OF OTHER TYPES OF EVIDENCE

CHAPTER 26

OBJECTIONS TO EVIDENCE

CHAPTER 27

MISTRIAL

CHAPTER 28

DIRECTED VERDICT

CHAPTER 29

DAMAGES

Table of Contents

CHAPTER 30

CLOSING ARGUMENTS

CHAPTER 31

INSTRUCTIONS TO THE JURY

CHAPTER 32

CONDUCT OF THE JURY

CHAPTER 33

THE VERDICT

CHAPTER 34

THE JUDGMENT

CHAPTER 1

THE CONDUCT OF THE TRIAL

§ 1:1   CONDUCT OF THE TRIAL, IN GENERAL — Every litigant has a right to a fair and impartial trial before an unbiased tribunal. *Whitehead v Mutual Life Ins. Co.* (1942) 264 AD 647, 37 NYS2d 261. The rights of litigants to a fair trial and to a verdict uninfluenced by appeals to passion and to prejudice must be protected. *Chertok v Effremoff* (1929) 226 AD 388, 235 NYS 246, affd 253 NY 523, 171 NE 765.

It is the duty of the court, to the extent that this is within its power, to see that any testimony on any trial before it is presented under conditions that are most conducive to veracity, in an atmosphere in which witnesses will be free from duress and in which they may testify to the truth with impunity. *Bator v Hungarian Commercial Bank* (1949) 194 Misc 232, 87 NYS2d 700, mod 196 Misc 157, 90 NYS2d 34 and mod 275 AD 826, 90 NYS2d 35.

A party is entitled to a fair trial, but a fair trial is not necessarily a perfect one. *Evans v Newark-Wayne Community Hospital, Inc.* (1970, 4th Dept) 35 AD2d 1071, 316 NYS2d 447.

The trial court has broad discretion in regulating the conduct of a trial in order to achieve a speedy and unprejudiced disposition of the matters at issue, including the granting of adjournments. *Gombas v Roberts* (1984, 3d Dept) 104 AD2d 521, 479 NYS2d 592.

The development of facts in the presence of the jury should be uncomplicated by personalities and acrimony. *Rudnik v Norwich Pharmacal Co.* (1970, 1st Dept) 34 AD2d 912, 311 NYS2d 363. Where a trial was held solely on the issue of damages due to personal injury and the attorney for the plaintiff was placed under undue pressure to present his evidence and complete his case, the parties did not have a fair and proper trial and a new trial should have been ordered in the interest of justice. The trial was started at 3:35 p.m. and the case was submitted to the jury at 4:35 p.m. that same afternoon. *Soto v Correa* (1964, 1st Dept) 20 AD2d 694, 246 NYS2d 744.

Where an ordained Roman Catholic priest who was also an attorney admitted to practice, appeared for defendant in his clerical garb, the trial court properly directed that he remove his clerical collar. *La Rocca v Lane* (1975) 37 NY2d 575, 376 NYS2d 93, 84 ALR3d 1131, cert den 424 US 968, 47 L Ed 2d 734, 96 S Ct 1464.

It was error to require defendant in a civil trial, a devout adherent of the Jewish faith, who sincerely believed that wearing a skull cap was a mandatory part of his religion, to choose between removal of the skull cap and exclusion from the court room. *Close-It Enterprises, Inc. v Weinberger* (1978, 2d Dept) 64 AD2d 686, 407 NYS2d 587. The court distinguished this case from *La Rocca v Lane* (1975, 2d Dept) 47 AD2d 243, 366 NYS2d 456, affd 37 NY2d 575, 376 NYS2d 93, 84 ALR3d 1131, cert den 424 US 968, 47 L Ed 2d 734, 96 S Ct 1464.

While the judiciary has traditionally been more tolerant of *pro se* litigants and generally will allow them greater leeway in the presentation of their cases, they, like the professionally-represented litigant, must be prepared to comply with the calendar requirements and procedures of the court. *Re Bales* (1983, 2d Dept) 93 AD2d 861, 461 NYS2d 365.

Although on a motion to recuse the trial judge the decision is generally a matter of personal conscience, where the trial judge, who had formerly been an Assistant District Attorney, had prosecuted defendant on drug-related charges, he should have recused himself in the current prosecution, based on his former role. *People v Smith* (1986, 2d Dept) 120 AD2d 753, 503 NYS2d 72.

It is error for a court to advise a jury at length as to its reasons for dismissing a particular cause of action; the trial court must be cautious in providing instructions that do not influence the jury in some way with respect to the party remaining in the case. *Harding v Noble Taxi Corp.* (1992, 1st Dept) 182 AD2d 365, 582 NYS2d 1003.

§ 1:2 BIFURCATION — Although the decision whether to order a bifurcation of the liability and damages issues rests within the sound discretion of the trial court, trial judges are encouraged to order a bifurcation in any personal injury action where "bifurcation may assist in a clarification of issues and a fair and more expeditious resolution of the action." 22 NYCRR § 202.42(a).

Bifurcation may be an abuse of the trial court's discretion "where the nature of the injuries has an important bearing on the issue of liability." *Schwartz v Binder* (1982, 2d Dept) 91 AD2d 660, 457 NYS2d 109.

Where the plaintiff had minimal recollection, and the nature of the injuries would tend to establish the force of impact and the speed of the vehicle, a bifurcated trial was inappropriate. *Addesso v Belting Associates* (1987, 2d Dept) 128 AD2d 489, 512 NYS2d 416.

Where a bifurcated trial is ordered, and it is expected that the issues of liability and damages will be tried before the same jury, counsel may, during *voir dire*, question prospective jurors on the issues of liability and damages as if the trial were not to be bifurcated. 22 NYCRR § 202.42 (c).

During opening statements in the liability phase, counsel may not discuss the issue of damages. If there is a verdict on liability, however, then counsel must be afforded an opportunity to make a further opening statement on the issue of damages at the commencement of the damages phase. 22 NYCRR § 202.42(d).

Where practical, the damages phase should proceed immediately after a successful liability verdict, before the same jury. If the trial court finds that this is impractical, the trial court is directed to state on the record its reasons for disbanding the jury and ordering a delay in proceeding to the damages phase. 22 NYCRR § 202.42(e).

§ 1:3   PRESENCE OF PARTIES AND COUNSEL — Although a party has a right to counsel at a trial, it has been held that the right to be advised of this right does not deprive a person of his right to elect to proceed without counsel. *Silvestris v Silvestris* (1965, 1st Dept) 24 AD2d 247, 265 NYS2d 173. The right to counsel must be exercised in conformity with orderly procedure. When an election to go to trial without counsel has been intelligently made, and where the right to counsel is asserted after proceedings have begun, it is within the discretion of the trial judge to determine whether to grant such a request. *Silvestris v Silvestris, supra*.

The trial court erred in requiring a party to proceed to trial, without counsel, after her counsel had withdrawn, on the first day that the case appeared on the calendar for trial, and in denying her a 30-day adjournment to obtain new counsel. *McCoy v Woodcraft Homes, Inc.* (1973, 2d Dept) 42 AD2d 846, 346 NYS2d 711.

In the absence of express waiver or unusual circumstances, a party has a constitutional right to be present at all stages of the trial. *Lunney v Graham* (1982, 1st Dept) 91 AD2d 592, 457 NYS2d 282.

Where there were no unusual circumstances, it was error for the trial court to exclude an officer of a corporate defendant from the courtroom during a portion of the trial. *American Printing Converters, Inc. v JES Label & Tape, Inc.* (1984, 2d Dept) 103 AD2d 787, 477 NYS2d 660.

Where plaintiff, who had been married at the time of the accident, divorced her husband and was remarried at the time of the trial, it was error for the trial court to direct that plaintiff be represented by her former husband's attorney, even though her counsel was permitted to sit at the counsel table to confer with the ex-husband's attorney, because counsel for plaintiff could not cross-examine the several witnesses remaining, nor sum up on her behalf. *Schulman v Consolidated Edison Co.* (1982, 1st Dept) 85 AD2d 186, 447 NYS2d 722.

Where plaintiffs brought a lawsuit against defendants for the reasonable value of legal services rendered, and defendants counterclaimed for legal malpractice, and where the counterclaim was intimately related to the claim asserted in the complaint, plaintiffs were not entitled to separate attorneys to represent them in the main action and on the counterclaim. *Sirlin & Sirlin v Fusco* (1981, 2d Dept) 81 AD2d 884, 439 NYS2d 57.

In the absence of clear and convincing evidence that the father, who was a respondent in a proceeding brought by the mother for upward modification of child support provisions, had waived the right to counsel and elected to proceed *pro se*, the respondent had a right to counsel at a support hearing. *Smith v Smith* (1986, 4th Dept) 122 AD2d 546, 504 NYS2d 893. Although adjournments are within the discretion of the trial court, the range of that discretion is narrowed when a fundamental right such as the right to counsel is involved. *Patricia L. v Steven L.* (1986, 2d Dept) 119 AD2d 221, 506 NYS2d 198. It was error for the court to compel a mother to proceed without counsel at a child custody hearing after her attorney had not appeared on the morning of the hearing. *Patricia L. v Steven L., supra.*

While every litigant has a fundamental right, guaranteed by the due process clause of both the federal and state constitutions, to be present at every stage of the trial, a balancing of the respective interests of the parties justified the Family Court's exercise of its statutory responsibility to protect the child by excluding the respondent during the child's testimony. The exclusion was in any event not prejudicial because the respondent's counsel was permitted to be present while the child testified and he was also given the right to cross-examine her. *Re Donna K.* (1987, 4th Dept) 132 AD2d 1004, 518 NYS2d 289.

The Surrogate properly determined that appellant could no longer represent himself in any proceeding in connection with the administration of his father's estate, where the record amply showed the appellant's disrespect for the court and demonstrated that in seeking to represent himself he was not acting in good faith, but was rather attempting to disrupt the proceedings. *Re*

Estate of Rappaport (1989, 2d Dept) 150 AD2d 779, 542 NYS2d 215.

The trial court did not commit error in excluding plaintiff from the courtroom during the liability phase of the trial; although the physical condition of a plaintiff, in and of itself, is not enough to justify his involuntary exclusion from any phase of the trial, when a plaintiff is both physically and mentally incapable and his mental incapacity prevents him from assisting counsel in any meaningful way, then the decision to exclude the plaintiff from the liability phase of a trial lies within the sound discretion of the trial court. *Caputo v Joseph J. Sarcona Trucking Co.* (1994, 2d Dept) 204 AD2d 507, 611 NYS2d 655.

§ 1:4   THE DEMEANOR OF THE JUDGE — No matter how strongly a trial judge may feel about the lack of merit of a case, he is not justified in denying plaintiff a fair trial so as to lead to a verdict that is consistent with the views of the judge. *Habenicht v R.K.O. Theatres, Inc.* (1965, 1st Dept) 23 AD2d 378, 260 NYS2d 890. Conduct of the trial, which created the impression of the judge's disbelief in the defense, precluded a fair trial. *Livant v Adams* (1962, 1st Dept) 17 AD2d 784, 232 NYS2d 641. Plaintiffs in an injury case were denied a fair trial where the trial judge unnecessarily criticized plaintiffs' counsel for wasting time with objections, gratuitously commented on the credibility of a witness, found fault with counsel because of his refusal to stipulate to certain evidence, improvidently interfered with summation by plaintiff, and erroneously excluded evidence. *Salzano v New York* (1964, 1st Dept) 22 AD2d 656, 253 NYS2d 138. Where the record did not require clarification by questions from the trial justice, and counsel were experienced, frequent interference by the trial justice with direct examination of defendant's witnesses followed by undue cross-examination was unwarranted. *Marchant v Fred F. French Management Co.* (1949, Sup App T) 90 NYS2d 5.

The conduct of the trial court in indicating on numerous occasions that counsel for plaintiffs was really wasting the court's time by his manner of presenting his case, that some of counsel's evidence was useless except for clouding the issues, and that counsel was worthy of being held in contempt, was so excessive as to irremediably prejudice the jury against plaintiffs. *Dicker v Wald-baum's, Inc.* (1977, 2d Dept) 56 AD2d 621, 391 NYS2d 677.

Although a trial judge has a right and an obligation to clarify matters that may be unclear to a jury, he should never do so in a manner that may possibly lead the triers of the facts to conclude that he has a view of the facts that they should adopt, and where the court, by the questions asked in an endeavor to keep the record clear, may well have caused the jury to believe the defendant's position, reversal and a new trial was warranted. *Kingsley v Mandell Food Stores* (1977, 2d Dept) 57 AD2d 944, 395 NYS2d 86.

A new trial was required in the interests of justice where the judge in charging the jury referred to a party as "stupid, careless and an idiot to permit a child of that age to wander off" because such comments, coming from an impartial and guiding source, may very well have influenced the jury in determining the issue of credibility. *Samuel v Porchia* (1972, 2d Dept) 40 AD2d 697, 336 NYS2d 387.

A trial judge should at all times exercise a high degree of patience and forbearance. *Soto v Correa* (1964, 1st Dept) 20 AD2d 694, 246 NYS2d 744. The duty of a trial judge to expedite the business of his court and to utilize fully the court time should not be performed in a manner to prejudice a party in the fair and orderly presentation of his case or defense. *Soto v Correa, supra.*

There was no undue participation by the trial court where the questions asked by the trial court appear to have been asked in the interest of clarification and expedition and with no indication of partiality. *Bumstead v Sweeney* (1965, 3d Dept) 24 AD2d 674, 261 NYS2d 199. Although the trial judge injected himself into an action for personal injuries sustained by an infant, and such conduct constituted error, the error did not require reversal of a judgment for the defendant where it was clear that on the facts plaintiff could not and should not prevail. *London v Smith-Cairns Motor Sales Co.* (1965, 1st Dept) 23 AD2d 657, 257 NYS2d 877, affd 17 NY2d 497, 267 NYS2d 216. Where the presiding justice participates in the examination of witnesses during the course of the trial in the furtherance and expedition of the trial and for the purpose of clarifying the testimony, there is no ground for reversal where the court's participation cannot be said to have indicated partiality. *Levine v Ross* (1966) 25 AD2d 718, 269 NYS2d 682. (See briefs and record on appeal.)

Where plaintiff's medical witness testified that it was bad practice to leave a person of plaintiff's age unattended in an examining room, and defendant's medical expert testified that there was no such absolute rule, that it depended upon the circumstances and that, under the circumstances of the case, he did not see anything medically wrong with defendant's having left plaintiff unattended in the examining room, and the trial court told the jury in the course of marshaling the evidence that both plaintiff's and defendant's medical experts had testified that they would not leave a patient of this lady's age and condition in an examining room unattended, this was error and the court's charge was the equivalent of a directed verdict. *Roma v Blaustein* (1974, 2d Dept) 44 AD2d 576, 353 NYS2d 44.

Reversal and a new trial were required in a malpractice action where not only was the court's marshalling of facts confusing and inaccurate with regard to certain important details, but where in addition the court manifested mistrust, skepticism, and bias with respect to the credibility of decedent's treating physician, and the testimony of defendant's two other medical witnesses. *Theodoropoulos v New York City Health & Hospitals Corp.* (1982, 2d Dept) 90 AD2d 792, 455 NYS2d 401. Although a trial court is granted wide latitude in controlling the conduct of a trial, it was held that the court exercised its discretion improvidently in that it: (1) affirmatively placed its credibility at direct odds with that of defense counsel concerning the physical observation of an occurrence during the trial, (2) argued with defense counsel several times and then asked plaintiff's counsel whether he agreed with the court, (3) insisted that defense counsel produce another witness or rest its case, in apparent violation of its own rule that the jury was to be let out at 4:00 P.M., (4) refused to permit immediate argument of objections by defense counsel who attempted to place the time of day on the record, (5) refused to permit counsel to take an exception, going so far as to threaten him with contempt if he should do so, (6) refused to permit defense counsel to make any objections during plaintiff's counsel's summation, and

(7) refused to allow defense counsel to converse with defendant at the luncheon recess between direct and cross-examination of defendant. *Roma v Blaustein, supra.*

Repeated references in the court's charge to possible financial ruin of the City if it were required to repair every crack in its sidewalks or respond in damages in every case in which an injury was sustained, the court's comment that a photograph of the defect tended to exaggerate the condition of the sidewalk, and its innuendo that a visit by the plaintiff's lawyer to the home of the two principal witnesses on the eve of trial to discuss the case was improper, tended to discredit the plaintiff's evidence and may have substantially influenced the outcome. *Coneys v New York* (1975, 2d Dept) 48 AD2d 651, 367 NYS2d 559.

Threats against counsel made in the presence of the jury, and manifested bias outside the presence of the jury, required reversal and a new trial before a different justice. *Millington v New York City Transit Authority* (1976, 1st Dept) 54 AD2d 649, 387 NYS2d 865.

The trial court committed reversible error requiring a new trial where it never charged plaintiff's theory of excessive speed, charging instead that sudden stops, lurches, and jerks were not sufficient proof of negligence, and that estimates of speed were only guesses. The trial court had also consistently rehabilitated defendant's witnesses after cross-examination, and in other ways belittled plaintiff's counsel and his case. *Mendez v Manhattan & Bronx Surface Transit Operating Authority* (1977, 1st Dept) 57 AD2d 823, 395 NYS2d 28.

Where the trial court routinely interrupted counsel to question the witnesses, often in detail, in a manner that was at times facetious, and at other times pedantic, the gratuitous nature of these intrusions, particularly on cross-examination, the manner in which they were made and their frequency, deprived the municipal appellants of a fair trial. *Lopez v Linden General Hospital* (1982, 2d Dept) 89 AD2d 1010, 454 NYS2d 452.

It is error for the trial court to permit an attorney for one of the parties to read statutes to the jury rather than embodying them in its charge or additional charge; it is also error for the trial court to pass on to the attorney and then to the jury the question of the pertinency of a statute. Each constitutes an abdication of the judicial function. *Petru v Hertz Corp.* (1969, 1st Dept) 33 AD2d 755, 305 NYS2d 828, later app (1st Dept) 36 AD2d 704, 319 NYS2d 199.

The contention of trial counsel for plaintiffs that the trial court was hostile and biased did not constitute sufficient justification for his refusal to participate further in the case. He should have continued to present whatever additional evidence was available to him, and then, if the decision was adverse, he could have advanced his arguments of hostility and bias to the Appellate Court for review. *Roberts v Great Neck* (1978, 2d Dept) 63 AD2d 967, 405 NYS2d 507.

The defendants were not deprived of a fair trial by the trial judge's occasional questioning of witnesses, which was intended to aid the jury in evaluating the evidence, was done in an even-handed non-prejudicial manner, and did not impart any views of the trial judge. *Vialva v New York* (1986, 2d Dept) 118 AD2d 701, 499 NYS2d 977.

It was error for the trial court to force defendant's counsel to make her objections to the jury charge in the presence of the jury, and this, together with the numerous hostile and demeaning comments made by the court in response to defense counsel's request for additional charges, prejudiced the fairness of the trial. *Cummings v Consolidated Edison Co.* (1986, 1st Dept) 125 AD2d 224, 509 NYS2d 29.

A wrongful death judgment against a hospital was properly reversed where the trial court severely undermined the hospital's case on the issue of the cause of death of a psychiatric patient, by striking the opinion of the defense expert as to cause of death, by engaging in questioning that indicated the disbelief of the trial judge in the defense case, and by permitting counsel for plaintiffs to impermissibly impeach the credibility of the defense experts. *Serota v Kaplan* (1987, 2d Dept) 127 AD2d 648, 511 NYS2d 667.

The trial court's comment expressing its belief in the veracity of one of the defendants was improper. *Hardy v Sicuranza* (1987, 2d Dept) 133 AD2d 138, 518 NYS2d 812.

In a medical malpractice case the trial court cannot be said to have erred in failing to advise plaintiff's counsel regarding a reasonable sum he could suggest to the jury, where the record established that the plaintiff's counsel refused to suggest a reasonable figure to the court; under the circumstances the trial court was not obligated to provide plaintiff's counsel with a reasonable figure. *Smith v Catholic Medical Center, Inc.* (1989, 2d Dept) 155 AD2d 435, 547 NYS2d 96.

The trial court's criticism of defense counsel for interrupting the beginning of its charge to the jury was, while perhaps excessive, warranted, because counsel's interjection at this point was totally improper in view of his repeated failure to comply with the court's instructions to provide timely written requests to charge. *Thoda v Arcoleo* (1992, 1st Dept) 179 AD2d 508, 579 NYS2d 30.

The plaintiff failed to demonstrate that he was prejudiced by the court's failure in marshaling the evidence to address the testimony of two of the doctors who testified for the plaintiff. *Raney v Suffolk Obstetrical & Gynecological Assocs., P.C.* (1994, 2d Dept) 200 AD2d 612, 606 NYS2d 729.

§ 1:5 CONDUCT OF COUNSEL — Where the conduct of counsel affects the fairness of the trial, reversal is warranted. Where, although the trial court permitted a witness on redirect to state that he was a minister for the limited purpose of explaining why he had refused to repeat an obscenity, it was error for the court to characterize as "fair comment" a statement by counsel in summation that the witness was an ordained minister and very active in his work as an ordained minister, because that implicitly suggested to the jury that it was more likely that the witness was telling the truth because he was a clergyman. *Taggart v Alexander's, Inc.* (1982, 2d Dept) 90 AD2d 542, 455 NYS2d 117.

The grossly improper conduct of defense counsel who: suggested that there was a mystery and a web of deception underlying the plaintiffs' case; insinuated that plaintiffs used various spellings of their names for different purposes and that one plaintiff at times used her maiden name for purposes of deception; suggested that he did not know whether plaintiff's husband was a criminal, or whether he was claiming welfare under six different names at five different addresses; referred to a chiropractor whom claimant had visited as a "quack"; called plaintiff's attorney "a very, very clever lawyer from a very prestigious New York City law firm in the Empire State Building"; elaborated unnecessarily on the question of the religion of plaintiff, a member of the Christian Science Church, and elicited testimony from his medical expert to the effect that an injury known as "green poultice syndrome" is one that is cured by a "nice big insurance check," was cumulatively so prejudicial, inflammatory and totally irrelevant to any legitimate issue presented at trial as to require reversal of the judgment. *Giuamara v O'Donnell* (1983, 2d Dept) 96 AD2d 1049, 466 NYS2d 692.

Calling of plaintiff's attorney as a witness and cross-examining him as to the name of a person who defendant's attorney claimed was a witness to the accident in a manner that made it appear to the jury that plaintiff's attorney was deliberately withholding the name of a witness who was not shown by the record to be in existence, was highly prejudicial, requiring a new trial. *Popplewell v Clark* (1964, 4th Dept) 22 AD2d 1014, 254 NYS2d 882.

In a bifurcated trial where proof of injury was not at issue, defense counsel's statement which created the impression that plaintiff had sustained no injury resulted in a prejudice that was not cured despite the fact that the trial court sustained the objection of plaintiff's counsel, and despite insufficient and untimely curative instructions by the trial court. *Boyd v Blessey* (1983, 2d Dept) 96 AD2d 816, 465 NYS2d 563.

The unfair, prejudicial and inflammatory remarks made by defense counsel in summation with respect to plaintiff's medical expert, among which was a statement that the doctor was a "pro," not in the sense of medical expertise, but in being "the best doctor money could buy," required a new trial. *La Russo v Pollack* (1982, 2d Dept) 88 AD2d 584, 449 NYS2d 794. It was improper for defense counsel to inject racial issues into the trial, particularly after the trial court's express prohibition on this matter. *Serpe v Rappaport* (1984, 2d Dept) 103 AD2d 771, 477 NYS2d 403.

The Appellate Court was unable to say whether an inflammatory and improper summation that had as its continuing theme a personal attack on defendant's attorney, unsubstantiated charges of perjury and subornation of perjury, racial overtones, and assertions of personal knowledge and personal opinion as to the case and the credibility of witnesses, did or did not influence the jury's verdict. Therefore, reversal and a new trial were required. *Caraballo v New York* (1982, 1st Dept) 86 AD2d 580, 446 NYS2d 318.

The conduct of defense counsel during the trial, involving not just an isolated remark during questioning or summation, but a seemingly continual and deliberate effort to divert the attention of the jurors and the court from the issues to be determined, created an atmosphere that deprived the plaintiffs of a fair trial, and resulted in reversal and a new trial. *Mercurio v Dunlop, Ltd.* (1980, 2d Dept) 77 AD2d 647, 430 NYS2d 140.

A new trial was ordered where plaintiff's counsel, in summation, referred to one of the defense's medical experts as "here comes Howie," implied that he would offer any desired testimony for a price, and accused the defendant and his attorney of having perjured themselves because of an apparent inconsistency between defendant's pleadings and the trial testimony. *Taormina v Goodman* (1978, 2d Dept) 63 AD2d 1018, 406 NYS2d 350.

Because loss of enjoyment of sexual relations was properly compensable in a personal injury action, it was highly prejudicial for defense counsel to make inflammatory reference to the testimony of plaintiffs concerning their diminished sexual activity, which allegedly resulted from their injuries. *Vassura v Taylor* (1986, 2d Dept) 117 AD2d 798, 499 NYS2d 120, app dismd 68 NY2d 643, 505 NYS2d 74. It was also prejudicial error, requiring reversal, for defense counsel to make numerous references to other persons who allegedly had suffered worse injuries than had plaintiff, an apparent device by defense counsel to minimize the seriousness of plaintiff's injuries, where there was no testimony at the trial concerning any injuries other than plaintiff's. *Vassura v Taylor, supra*.

Introduction of unduly prejudicial evidence, which was withheld by the movant's opponent and which the movant could not have anticipated in the exercise of due diligence, constituted unfair surprise. *Hannon v Dunkirk Motor Inn, Inc.* (1990, 4th Dept) 167 AD2d 834, 562 NYS2d 248.

It was error for the court to allow plaintiff's counsel to comment upon a magazine article during summations; the article was not admitted into evidence and counsel's suggestion that the substance of the article would support plaintiff's testimony as to the structural integrity of his car was improper and highly prejudicial. *Aurnou v Craig* (1992, 4th Dept) 184 AD2d 1048, 584 NYS2d 249.

§ 1:6 PUBLICITY OF PROCEEDINGS — The proceedings of every court in the New York State shall be public, and every citizen may freely attend the same, except that in all proceedings and trials and in cases for divorce, seduction, rape, assault with intent to commit rape, sodomy, bastardy or affiliation, the court may, in its discretion, exclude all persons who are not directly interested in the matter with the exception of jurors, witnesses and officers of the court. Judiciary Law § 4.

Although it is essential to a public trial that there be access to spectators, any particular spectator is quite dispensable, as are all spectators, if they are disorderly. *Katz v Murtagh* (1971) 28 NY2d 234, 321 NYS2d 104.

The problem of publicity of proceedings has also been dealt with by the U.S. Supreme Court. In *Sheppard v Maxwell* (1966) 384 US 333, 16 L Ed 2d 600, 86 S Ct 1507, the Court laid down a number of rules governing publicity that bear on the right of a defendant to a fair trial and violation of these rules in a state court may constitute deprivation of due process.

Included in such rules are the following:

1. The conclusions reached in the case are to be induced only by evidence and argument in open court and not by outside influence, whether such outside influence constituted private talks or public print.

2. The trial court must not only suggest that the jury refrain from following the trial in the press, radio and television; it must also take strong steps to ensure that the jurors are, in fact, shielded from those influences.

3. There cannot be a fair trial if the jurors become celebrities because of the judge's failure to insulate them from the press.

4. A defendant may be deprived of a fair trial because of pretrial publicity about the trial, such as televising of an inquest.

5. A trial should not take place in the heated atmosphere

that results when the prosecutor and/or the judge are involved in a hotly contested election.

6. The judge must take charge of the proceedings to avoid having representatives of the various news media obtain control of the proceedings.

7. Media must not provide such a large amount of sensational material that it becomes clear that at least some of this has reached the jury.

8. It is the power and the duty of the trial judge to restrict prejudicial news accounts of the trial.

9. Where it is apparent that a defendant may otherwise be prejudiced or disadvantaged, the presence of the press at judicial proceedings must be limited.

10. The court should limit the number of reporters in the courtroom, at the first sign that their presence will disrupt the trial.

11. Newsmen should not be permitted to handle and photograph trial exhibits lying on the counsel table during recesses.

12. Where a trial is a heated one, the court should insulate witnesses, so that the news media may not interview them at will, disclosing their testimony in advance.

13. Where a trial attracts great attention, the court should try to control the release of leads, information and gossip to the press by police officers, witnesses and counsel for both sides.

14. If the court has reason to believe that publicity is false or misleading, it is under a duty to warn the media to check the accuracy of their accounts.

15. The judge should, where necessary, impose control over the statements made to news media by counsel, witnesses and officials, particularly because it is important to avoid giving the news media information that is not admissible in evidence.

16. The court should warn reporters who have written or broadcasted prejudicial material as to the impropriety of this type of action.

17. Where a reasonable likelihood exists that prejudicial news preceding the trial will prevent a fair trial, the case should be adjourned until the threat has ended or it should be transferred to another county not so permeated with publicity.

18. Where the fairness of the trial is threatened because of publicity during the trial, the court should order a new trial.

19. Courts should take whatever steps are necessary, by rule and regulation, to protect their processes from prejudicial outside interference.

20. There should be no collaboration between counsel and the press with respect to information that affects the fairness of the criminal trial, and such collaboration is not only subject to regulation, but is highly censurable and deserves disciplinary measures.

When a trial court is concerned about pretrial publicity, it may properly exclude the public from a hearing to determine the admissibility of certain evidence. *Poughkeepsie Newspapers, Inc. v Rosenblatt* (1984) 61 NY2d 1005, 475 NYS2d 370.

The fundamental precept that trials and judicial proceedings generally shall be open to public view and the mandate of Judiciary Law § 4 which provides that court sessions shall be public, does not preclude a court's exclusion of the public when such exclusion is necessary or appropriate to protect confidential trade information. *Crain Communications, Inc. v Hughes* (1987, 1st Dept) 135 AD2d 351, 521 NYS2d 244, 14 Media L R 1951, app dismd without op 71 NY2d 993, 529 NYS2d 277.

§ 1:7 TRANSCRIBING THE TESTIMONY — Full stenographic notes of the testimony and all other proceedings in each cause tried or heard must be taken by an official court stenographer. Judiciary Law § 295. In jury trials, the stenographer must take each and every remark or comment by the judge during the trial when requested to do so by either party, together with each and every exception taken to any ruling and decision, remark, or comment by or on behalf of any party to the action. Although frequently such passing remarks may be of no moment, trial counsel has a statutory right, on request, to have them taken down. *Paffen* *v New York* (1917) 176 AD 423, 162 NYS 723. A party is entitled to have the summation of counsel recorded, and refusal of such a request is an improvident exercise of discretion. *Croix v New York City Transit Authority* (1967, 2d Dept) 28 AD2d 691, 281 NYS2d 224.

In light of the proclivity of plaintiff's attorney for making prejudicial comments, it was error for the trial judge to deny defendant's request to record plaintiff's closing statement to the jury. *Bergen Street Properties Corp. v New York Property Ins. Underwriting Asso.* (1981, 2d Dept) 82 AD2d 817, 439 NYS2d 439.

While it was proper for the presiding judge to conduct conferences for negotiation of a settlement in chambers without the presence of a stenographer, the settlement allegedly made as a result of the conference was not the equivalent of an oral stipulation in open court. *Accarino v Hirsch* (1958, 2d Dept) 6 AD2d 795, 175 NYS2d 435.

§ 1:8 JUDGE AS TRIER OF THE FACTS — Generally, the rules applicable to a non-jury trial are the same as those that apply to jury trials. In a non-jury trial, however, the court is both the trier of the facts and the judge of the law. *Belkin v Playdium, Inc.* (1949) 194 Misc 950, 87 NYS2d 813.

Where the trial is by the court without a jury, a decision is required and it must state the facts that the court deems essential. *Salzman v Sakofsky* (1949) 195 Misc 166, 89 NYS2d 39. Where the court dismisses a complaint, if such action is deemed a non-suit, findings of fact are not necessary, but if the decision is one on the merits, such findings of fact are necessary. *Ten Eyck v Lombard* (1937) 162 Misc 517, 296 NYS 49.

§ 1:9 JUDGE AS DETERMINER OF THE LAW — The trial judge is the sole determiner of the law. *Marquart v Yeshiva Machezikel Torah D'Chasidei Belz* (1976, 2d Dept) 53 AD2d 688, 385 NYS2d 319. The decision holds that it was error for the trial court to allow an expert witness to usurp the court's function as the sole determiner of the law.

RESEARCH REFERENCES

American Law Reports

90 ALR4th 1033, Measure and elements of damages recoverable for attorney's negligence in preparing or conducting litigation–Twentieth Century cases

90 ALR4th 621, Liability in tort for interference with attorney-client relationship

90 ALR4th 326, Authority of attorney to compromise action–modern cases

86 ALR4th 1071, Appointment of counsel for attorney facing disciplinary charges

85 ALR4th 846, Attorney's liability in tort for interference with contract to which client was party

85 ALR4th 700, Judge's previous legal association with attorney connected to current case as warranting disqualification

82 ALR4th 886, Attorney's argument as to evidence previously ruled inadmissible as contempt

82 ALR4th 567, Disciplinary action against judge for engaging in ex parte communication with attorney, party, or witness

70 ALR4th 1119, Small claims; jury trial rights in, and on appeal from, small claims court proceeding

70 ALR4th 1033, Necessity or propriety of appointment of independent guardian for child who is subject of paternity proceedings

69 ALR4th 131, Prejudicial effect of bringing to jury's attention fact that plaintiff in personal injury or death action is entitled to workers' compensation benefits

68 ALR4th 954, Counsel's argument or comment stating or implying that defendant is not insured and will have to pay verdict himself as prejudicial error

66 ALR4th 256, Attorney's personal liability for expenses incurred in relation to services for client

65 ALR4th 73, Disqualification of judge because of political association or relation to attorney in case

64 ALR4th 323, Incompetence of counsel as ground for relief from state court civil judgment

61 ALR4th 1216, Attorney's misrepresentation to court of his state of

health or other personal matter in seeking trial delay as ground for disciplinary action

57 ALR4th 1049, Court reporter's death or disability prior to transcribing notes as grounds for reversal or new trial

52 ALR4th 1063, Court appointment of attorney to represent, without compensation, indigent in civil action

48 ALR4th 747, Jury trial waiver as binding on later state civil trial

38 ALR4th 1170, Deafness of juror as ground for impeaching verdict, or securing new trial or reversal on appeal

37 ALR4th 751, Propriety of attorney acting as both counsel and class member or representative

34 ALR4th 1186, Applicability of judicial immunity to acts of clerk of court under state law

27 ALR4th 583, Physical condition of plaintiff in personal injury action as affecting right to be present at trial

14 ALR4th 121, Validity, propriety, and effect of allowing orprohibiting media's broadcasting, recording, or photographing court proceedings

9 ALR4th 191, Validity, construction, and effect of contract providing for contingent fee to defendant's attorney

6 ALR4th 951, Manner or extent of trial judge's examination of witnesses in civil case

87 ALR3d 238, Propriety and prejudicial effect of permitting non-party to be seated at counsel table

84 ALR3d 1143, Right of clergyman in court as professional attorney to be in clerical garb

79 ALR3d 401, Propriety of exclusion of press or other media representatives from civil trial

75 ALR3d 1021, Membership in fraternal or social club or order affected by a case as ground for disqualification of judge

73 ALR3d 353, Power of court to impose standard of personal appearance or attire

72 ALR3d 375, Disqualification of judge, justice of the peace, or similar judicial officer for pecuniary interest in fines, forfeitures, or fees payable by litigants

25 ALR3d 1331, Disqualification of judge because of his or another's holding or owning stock in corporation involved in litigation

25 ALR3d 637, Absence of judge from courtroom during trial of civil case

23 ALR3d 1416, Disqualification of judge for bias against counsel for litigant

22 ALR3d 1198, Disqualification of judge on ground of being a witness in the case

ALR Quick Index: Attorneys; Judge; Presence or Absence

American Jurisprudence 2d

75A Am Jur 2d, Trial §§ 497-512

75 Am Jur 2d, Trial §§ 87-123, 192-201

75 Am Jur 2d, Trial §§ 180-230

7 Am Jur 2d, Attorneys at Law §§ 91-152, 167-308

American Jurisprudence Pleading and Practice

23 Am Jur Pl & Pr Forms (Rev) , Trial, Forms 1-64

American Jurisprudence Proof of Facts

48 Am Jur Proof of Facts 2d 635, Medicolegal Malpractice: Attorney's Negligence in Selecting and Using Expert Medical Consultant

American Jurisprudence Trials

52 Am Jur Trials 1, Civil Litigation

51 Am Jur Trials 1, Managing Litigation

47 Am Jur Trials 145, Handling Tractor Rollover Cases for the Plaintiff

47 Am Jur Trials 1, Environmental Law Litigation Under CERCLA

46 Am Jur Trials 325, Avoiding Legal Malpractice Claims in Litigation

43 Am Jur Trials 1, Constitutional Employment Litigation: Trial of the Political Discharge Case

41 Am Jur Trials 683, Computer Research for the Trial Lawyer

41 Am Jur Trials 445, Computer Technology in Civil Litigation

3 Am Jur Trials 681, Tactics and Strategy of Pleading

1 Am Jur Trials 303, Controlling Trial Publicity

Other Resources

Auto-Cite®: Any case citation herein can be checked for form, parallel references, later history and annotation references through the Auto-Cite computer research system.

CHAPTER 2

MOTIONS DURING TRIAL, DEFAULT AND DISMISSAL

§ 2:1 MOTIONS DURING TRIAL, IN GENERAL — For purposes of this work, the term "motions" refers only to matters arising during the course of the trial. It does not include pretrial motions or motions subsequent to judgment.

A motion is an application for an order. CPLR 2211. During the course of a trial, a variety of motions may be made, including a motion for judgment during trial, CPLR 4401; a motion for a continuance or a new trial, CPLR 4402; a motion for a new trial or to confirm or reject or grant other relief after reference to report or after the verdict of an advisory jury, CPLR 4403; and a post-trial motion for judgment or for a new trial, CPLR 4404.

CPLR 4401(a) requires that a motion for judgment at the end of the plaintiff's case be granted on a cause of action for medical malpractice based solely on lack of informed consent if the plaintiff has failed to present expert medical testimony to support the alleged qualitative insufficiency of consent. CPLR 4401(a) applies to medical, not to dental, malpractice cases. *Carrasquillo v Roths-child* (1981) 110 Misc 2d 758, 443 NYS2d 113.

Other motions made during the course of the trial include motions for a continuance, for a voluntary dismissal, for an involuntary dismissal, and for a default judgment.

§ 2:2 CONTINUANCES — Although the question of continuances generally arises before the day a case is scheduled for trial, the problem may arise on the day a case is to be tried or during the course of the trial. Ordinarily, a motion to adjourn is addressed to the discretion of the trial court. Only in exceptional cases will the court's exercise of discretion be reviewed. *Zirn v Bradley* (1946) 270 AD 829, 60 NYS2d 114, app den 270 AD 897, 61 NYS2d 926.

The court should have granted a short adjournment where defendant's trial counsel was engaged in another court, no other member of his firm qualified to try the case appeared to be available, and the defense counsel had offered to pay the necessary expenses of plaintiff's out-of-country witnesses whose appearance was required. *Fitzgerald v American Trading & Production Corp.* (1976, 1st Dept) 51 AD2d 700, 380 NYS2d 651.

The court erred when it entered a default against defendant whose attorney was actually involved in another trial and who had no available replacement. The attorney would be unavailable only as long as the other case required his attention, there was no indication of bad faith or an attempt at undue delay, and there was no demonstration that the plaintiff would be prejudiced. *Desai v New York* (1981, 1st Dept) 81 AD2d 797, 439 NYS2d 124.

The court abused its discretion in denying an adjournment to petitioner who learned only fifteen minutes before the hearing that the doctor whose testimony was necessary had been called on an emergency. *Re Commissioner of Social Services on behalf of White v Thornton* (1983, 4th Dept) 94 AD2d 974, 464 NYS2d 99.

Having permitted counsel to withdraw on the eve of trial, the court should have granted plaintiff an adjournment for a reasonable period of time to retain new counsel. *A-1 Syracuse Commercial Painting Co. v Allied Chemical Corp.* (1985, 4th Dept) 115 AD2d 268, 495 NYS2d 849.

The trial court abused its discretion in refusing to grant counsel a continuance to enable him to ascertain the availability of an essential witness. The hearing would have been short, there was no showing of inconvenience to anyone, and counsel had been diligent. *Re Application of Allstate Ins. Co.* (1985, 1st Dept) 114 AD2d 796, 495 NYS2d 49.

The court did not abuse its discretion in denying the defendant Transit Authority's requested adjournment of the trial in a personal injury action brought by a subway passenger. The record did not support the defendant's contention that it had tried diligently to secure the presence of a medical expert whose testimony it contended was necessary. *Cromartie v New York City Transit Authority* (1985, 2d Dept) 113 AD2d 915, 493 NYS2d 818.

The trial court did not err in denying defense counsel's application for a continuance to call a social worker who had interviewed plaintiff at the hospital. Although both sides had been informed two months earlier of the trial date, counsel had not attempted to arrange for the witness's appearance and could not assure the court that the witness would be present on the requested adjourned date. *Vogelhut v Waldbaum's Supermarket* (1987, 2d Dept) 127 AD2d 590, 511 NYS2d 647.

Where the record demonstrated that a witness essential to plaintiff's ability to establish a *prima facia* case had recently become unavailable, the court erred in denying plaintiff's application for an adjournment. Counsel for plaintiff had attempted to contact the witness, and the defendant did not object to an adjournment or raise any claim of prejudice. *Rodriguez v Pisa Caterers, Inc.* (1989, 2d Dept) 146 AD2d 686, 537 NYS2d 50. Additionally, the trial court erred by dismissing plaintiff's case immediately following the denial of her application for an adjournment. *Rodriguez v Pisa Caterers, Inc., supra.*

Although applications for continuances are ordinarily left to the trial court's discretion, continuances to obtain material evidence and to prevent miscarriages of justice should be liberally granted. It is well settled that it is an abuse of the court's discretion to deny a continuance when the application complies with all requirements of the law and is not made merely for delay, the evidence is material, and the need for a continuance does not result from failure to exercise due diligence. *Cirino v St. John* (1989, 3d Dept) 146 AD2d 912, 536 NYS2d 901.

When plaintiffs obtained their files from their former counsel only three days prior to jury selection, the trial court erred in refusing to grant them a reasonable adjournment to obtain substitute counsel. Nothing in the record suggested that plaintiffs were attempting to delay the case, and none of the defendants had moved for dismissal. *Blunt v Northern Oneida County Landfill (NOCO)* (1988, 4th Dept) 145 AD2d 913, 536 NYS2d 295.

In a divorce action in which child custody was an issue, the court improvidently refused to grant even a one-day adjournment to the father's counsel to bring the father's brother and sister from Florida to testify. There were clear indications that the mother may have had a history of drug and alcohol abuse, which she did not acknowledge or seek treatment for. The proffered testimony might have substantiated the allegations of her drug and alcohol abuse, which the court had specifically found were unsubstantiated. *Satalino v Satalino* (1987, 2d Dept) 152 AD2d 661, 544 NYS2d 154.

The court did not improvidently deny plaintiff's request at mid-trial for an adjournment so lengthy it would necessitate a mistrial, because she had previously been granted numerous adjournments on the assertion that her unidentified medical expert was unavailable, including two adjournments after the attorneys had been sent out for jury selection. *Scarola v St. Vincent's Medical Center* (1989, 2d Dept) 154 AD2d 364, 545 NYS2d 840.

The trial court abused its discretion when it dismissed plaintiff's action after denying her motion for a continuance. Plaintiff needed a short continuance because her medical witnesses were unavailable, a circumstance she had no control over. The defendant neither objected to a continuance nor moved to dismiss. Furthermore, the plaintiff had been ready to proceed to trial on 13 prior court dates between 1983 and March 1989 when the defendant was granted adjournments, even after the case had been marked "final." *Stabler v Manhattan & Bronx Surface Transit Operating Authority* (1989, 1st Dept) 155 AD2d 390, 548 NYS2d 17.

The Supreme Court did not abuse its discretion in denying defendant's motion for an adjournment, because defense counsel was aware when he took over the case that the matter had been certified as ready for trial for over three years. *Gallagher's Stud, Inc. v Fishman* (1990, 3d Dept) 156 AD2d 50, 553 NYS2d 561.

The trial court abused its discretion in denying the defense counsel's motion for a continuance to obtain the presence of two eye witnesses to the accident who had not responded to subpoenas. The testimony of the two proposed witnesses was critical to the issue of defendant motorist's speed, the need for the continuance was not the result of failure to exercise due diligence, and the application was not intended merely to delay the proceedings. *Hoffner v County of Putnam* (1990, 3d Dept) 167 AD2d 755, 562 NYS2d 891.

In a wrongful death case, the trial court did not err in refusing to grant a two-hour continuance to await the arrival of the funeral director who had embalmed the decedent's body, because the funeral director's proposed testimony was irrelevant and not essential to plaintiff's case. *Dunleavy v Samuel* (1991, 2d Dept) 177 AD2d 540, 576 NYS2d 44.

The court improvidently exercised its discretion by not allowing plaintiff's counsel a reasonable time to travel from his office to the courthouse before imposing the drastic sanction of dismissal. There was no indication in the record that plaintiffs had wilfully engaged in dilatory tactics or abandoned the action, and the defendant had consented to the short adjournment requested. *Bauer v Claridge at Park Place, Inc.* (1992, 1st Dept) 181 AD2d 566, 581 NYS 2d 55.

The trial court improvidently refused to honor counsel's affirmation of engagement, when there was no reason to believe that plaintiff's counsel had misrepresented the situation, the merits of plaintiff's action were sufficiently apparent, and it did not appear that any of the parties to the litigation would have been prejudiced by an adjournment. *Mayo v New York Tel. Co.* (1991, 3d Dept) 175 AD2d 390, 572 NYS2d 99.

Defendant's request for a two-week adjournment of the trial was properly denied, because he intentionally failed to appear to continue his testimony at trial in violation of a judicial subpoena and had previously been held in contempt for similar conduct. *Dorkin v Spodek* (1994, 2d Dept) 201 AD2d 529, 607 NYS2d 951.

The trial court did not improperly exercise its discretion in denying defendant's application for an adjournment, given defendant's condition and the ambiguity in his treating physician's affidavit concerning the defendant's ability to assist in his defense after an adjournment of three to five months. The physician's affidavit indicated that the defendant would not be able to participate in the defense of the action for at least the next three to five months. *Bay Ridge Fed. Sav. & Loan Ass'n v Morano* (1993, 2d Dept) 199 AD2d 354, 605 NYS2d 377, app den 84 NY2d 801.

§ 2:3   MOTION FOR JUDGMENT DURING TRIAL — After the close of the evidence presented by an opposing party with respect to a cause of action or issue, or at any time on the basis of admissions, any party may move for judgment with respect to the cause of action or issue on the ground that the moving party is entitled to judgment as a matter of law. CPLR 4401. The grounds for the motion must be specified. CPLR 4401.

If there is a question of fact and credibility for the jury, the trial court may not direct a verdict. *Callery v Lyons* (1944) 292 NY 15; *Shapiro v Lahne* (1939) 258 AD 811, 15 NYS2d 1010.

A motion to dismiss at the close of the entire case is substantially the equivalent of a motion for a directed verdict made at that point. *Farrell v Lavine* (1962) 37 Misc 2d 497, 236 NYS2d 323. A motion for a directed verdict is in the nature of a demurrer to the evidence. It concedes the truth of the evidence introduced by the adverse party and the inferences the jury would be warranted in making from the evidence. *Ford v Snook* (1923) 205 AD 194, 199 NYS 630, affd 240 NY 624, 148 NE 732.

The court may dismiss a complaint after a verdict or even after the discharge of the jury without a verdict. *Baxter v Baxter* (1957) 11 Misc 2d 69, 169 NYS2d 871. In considering a motion to direct a verdict, the test to be applied is whether the trial court could find that by no rational process could the trier of facts base a finding in favor of the party moved against on the evidence presented. *Wearever Upholstery & Furniture Corp. v Home Ins. Co.* (1955) 286 AD 93, 141 NYS2d 107.

If a verdict in defendant's favor would have to be set aside as a matter of law for lack of credible evidence supporting it, a directed verdict for the plaintiff would be proper. *Bank of United States v Manheim* (1934) 264 NY 45, 189 NE 776, reh den 264 NY 511, 191 NE 540.

When the complaint stated a cause of action but the evidence showed that the facts gave no right of action, the judgment should have been one of nonsuit for failure of proof. *Woodruff v Germansky* (1922) 233 NY 365, 135 NE 601.

Where the evidence at the close of plaintiff's case was sufficient to put the defendant to his proofs, it was reversible error to dismiss the complaint. *Matovich v Weiss* (1948, App Tm) 80 NYS2d 539. If the evidence introduced by the plaintiff establishes a *prima facie* case, the complaint may not be dismissed at the close of the plaintiff's evidence. *Re Mulderig* (1949) 196 Misc 527, 91 NYS2d 895.

A motion to dismiss may be made at the close of an opposing party's case or at any time on the basis of admissions. *Cass v Broome County Co-operative Ins. Co.* (1983, 3d Dept) 94 AD2d 822, 463 NYS2d 312. A dismissal prior to the close of the opposing party's case will be reversed as premature, even if the ultimate success of the opposing party in the motion is improbable. *Cass v Broome County Co-operative Ins. Co., supra.*

A trial court should direct a verdict only when the jury could not reach a contrary result by any rational process. *Pekar v Tax* (1974, 2d Dept) 43 AD2d 957, 352 NYS2d 39.

Where plaintiff's version of the accident was corroborated by an independent witness and was not incredible as a matter of law, a question of fact was presented for the jury to determine. It was error for the trial court to direct a verdict. *Del Cerro v New York* (1974, 2d Dept) 46 AD2d 898, 361 NYS2d 707.

Where the trial court had doubts as to the merits of the plaintiff's proof, the proper procedure on a motion to dismiss was to reserve decision on the motion and submit the case to the jury. *Slusarczyk v Slusarczyk* (1973, 4th Dept) 41 AD2d 593, 340 NYS2d 250.

§ 2:4 MOTION FOR CONTINUANCE OR NEW TRIAL DURING THE TRIAL

§ 2:4 **MOTION FOR CONTINUANCE OR NEW TRIAL DURING THE TRIAL** — At any time during the trial, the court, on motion of any party, may order a continuance or a new trial in the interest of justice on such terms as may be just. CPLR 4402.

Generally, in civil cases the trial court has wide discretion to declare a mistrial, but such discretion is not absolute. *Murphy v New York* (1948) 273 AD 492, 78 NYS2d 191. The court erred in refusing defendant's request for a mistrial in an action for personal injuries in which the plaintiff's evidence was completely at variance with the claims stated in the complaint and specified in the bill of particulars and the defendant pleaded surprise. *Amato v Galleja* (1947) 272 AD 295, 70 NYS2d 758.

Granting a motion for a mistrial made after the verdict was error, because it permitted defendant's counsel to speculate on the verdict. *Collins v Ward* (1933) 240 AD 985, 268 NYS 142.

When counsel for defendant was taken ill and was unable to proceed with the trial, defendant was entitled to a new trial. *Flanzer v Annette Manor Realty Corp.* (1929) 228 AD 666, 238 NYS 300.

Where witnesses were excluded from the courtroom and plaintiff's attorney made a statement reflecting on the propriety of defense counsel's consultation with defendant's witnesses, the granting of a mistrial to defendant was warranted. The statements by plaintiff's counsel carried a strong and highly prejudicial implication of wrongdoing, which may have unjustly influenced the jury in arriving at a verdict. *Capitol Cab Corp. v Anderson* (1949) 194 Misc 21, 85 NYS2d 767, affd 197 Misc 1035, 100 NYS2d 39.

It was an improvident exercise of the trial court's discretion to deny defendant a reasonable adjournment to engage other trial counsel, because, as the court was aware, the current counsel's testimony was crucial to defendant's case. Additionally, the matter had been on the trial calendar for only three months and had been adjourned only twice, there was no evidence of prejudice to plaintiff, and plaintiff's attorney did not oppose the adjournment. *Ninth Federal Sav. & Loan Asso. v Quote Me, Inc.* (1980, 1st Dept) 78 AD2d 619, 432 NYS2d 623. The law favors the resolution of cases on the merits. *Ninth Federal Sav. & Loan Asso. v Quote Me, Inc., supra.*

It was error for the court in a non-jury trial to refuse to allow appellant the few days needed to produce a witness whose testimony was important on its own and also because it would have corroborated a significant portion of another witnesses's testimony, which the trial court found to be totally unworthy of belief. *Bohan v Auto Parts of Jamaica, Inc.* (1980, 2d Dept) 74 AD2d 834, 425 NYS2d 395.

Generally, counsel's deliberate attempt to convey to the jury that defendant is insured constitutes grounds for a mistrial. *Brand v Mangust Holding Corp.* (1945, Sup) 53 NYS2d 882. A codefendant's intimation to the jury that he is inadequately insured is prejudicial to the other defendant and requires a new trial. *Brennan v Felter* (1975, 2d Dept) 48 AD2d 846, 369 NYS2d 175.

In the absence of prejudice, the trial court improvidently denied a party's motion made at the close of her case to reopen the case in order to offer medical proof that she was mentally incompetent to testify. *Iulio v Ford Motor Co.* (1969, 2d Dept) 31 AD2d 820, 298 NYS2d 33.

When defendant's expert physician was in court before the summations began and defendant made application at that time for the doctor to be permitted to testify, the request should have been granted. A new trial was ordered in the interest of justice. *Raphael v Booth Memorial Hospital* (1974, 2d Dept) 46 AD2d 894, 361 NYS2d 704.

The court ordered a new trial when it determined that the jury could have become confused by the prolixity of acrimonious colloquy permeating the record. *Armocida v Misiti* (1974, 2d Dept) 43 AD2d 858, 351 NYS2d 441.

Although the decision to grant a mistrial in a civil case is generally a discretionary matter for the trial court, certain events are so extraordinarily prejudicial that a mistrial is required as a matter of law. *Reome v Cortland Memorial Hospital* (1989, 3d Dept) 152 AD2d 773, 543 NYS2d 552. In a medical malpractice action, a mistrial was required when a juror collapsed during a recess and suffered what appeared to be a stroke or heart attack; the defendant doctor, his attorney, and one or more jurors carried the stricken juror to an open area near the jury box; the doctor administered aid to the stricken juror, including a blow to the chest; and the jurors, including the alternate, observed this activity. The court subsequently informed the jury that the ill juror had not been admitted to the hospital and apparently was fine. Although the jurors indicated that they were not biased by this incident and, indeed, found the defendant doctor liable, the unconsciona- bly low award suggested that the jury was subliminally influenced to view the defendant doctor favorably at plaintiff's expense. *Reome v Cortland Memorial Hospital, supra.*

§ 2:5 ACTION BY ADVISORY JURY OR REFEREE — Upon the motion of any party or on his own initiative, the judge who is required to decide the issue may confirm or reject, in whole or in part, the verdict of an advisory jury or the report of a referee; may make new findings with or without taking additional testimony and may order a new trial or hearing. The motion shall be made within fifteen days after the verdict or the filing of the report and prior to further trial in the action. Where no issues remain to be tried, the court shall render decision directing judgment in the action. CPLR 4403.

§ 2:6 POST-TRIAL MOTION FOR JUDGMENT AND NEW TRIAL — After the trial of a cause of action or issue triable of right by a jury, upon the motion of any party or on its own initia- tive, the court may set aside a verdict or any judgment entered thereon and direct that judgment be entered in favor of a party entitled to judgment as a matter of law, or it may order a new trial of a cause of action or separable issue where the verdict is contrary to the weight of evidence, in the interest of justice, or where the jury cannot agree after being kept together for as long as is deemed reasonable by the court. CPLR 4404(a).

After a trial which is not triable of right by a jury, upon the motion of any party or on its own initiative, the court may set aside its decision or any judgment entered thereon. The court may make new findings of fact or conclusions of law, with or without taking additional testimony, render a new decision and direct entry of judgment, or it may order a new trial of a cause of action or separable issue. CPLR 4404(b).

Judgment notwithstanding a jury's verdict may be granted only when the court concludes that the verdict was "utterly irrational."

Cohen v Hallmark Cards, Inc. (1978) 45 NY2d 493, 410 NYS2d 282, later proceeding (1st Dept) 70 AD2d 509, 415 NYS2d 657.

A motion to set aside the verdict as against the weight of the evidence and for a new trial should not be granted unless the jury could not have reached its verdict on any fair interpretation of the evidence. *Bent v Andersen Corp.* (1994, 2d Dept) 207 AD2d 370, 615 NYS2d 700, app dismd, in part, app den, in part 85 NY2d 901, 627 NYS2d 315; *Olmstead v Federated Department Stores, Inc.* (1994, 3d Dept) 208 AD2d 979, 617 NYS2d 225.

The trial court properly denied plaintiff's motion for judgment notwithstanding the verdict or for a new trial, because the preponderance of evidence in plaintiff's favor was not so great that the verdict could not have been reached by any fair interpretation of the evidence. *Cone v Williams* (1992, 4th Dept) 585 NYS2d 243, later proceeding (4th Dept) 585 NYS2d 322, app den 80 NY2d 758, 589 NYS2d 309.

The trial court abused its discretion in setting aside a verdict and ordering a new trial where the verdict was not palpably incorrect. *Loughman v A.W. Flint Co.* (1987, 1st Dept) 132 AD2d 507, 518 NYS2d 389, app den 70 NY2d 613, 524 NYS2d 432.

A motion pursuant to CPLR 4401 to dismiss for failure to establish a *prima facie* case should be granted if there is no rational basis by which a trier of fact could find for a plaintiff and against a defendant on the evidence presented. *Royal Ins. Co. of Am. v Mercy Hospital* (1994, 1st Dept) 204 AD2d 219, 612 NYS2d 137.

When plaintiffs failed to move pursuant to CPLR 4401 for judgment at the close of evidence on the issue of negligence, they conceded that the issue was for the trier of fact. Thus, they had not preserved for appeal the question of whether they were entitled to judgment notwithstanding the verdict. *Torrillo v Command Bus Co.* (1994, 2d Dept) 206 AD2d 520, 614 NYS2d 756. Where there was evidence that the bus driver attempted to gradually slow the bus to a stop and the bus hit the rear of an automobile after slipping on a slick roadway surface, the verdict for the defendant bus company was not against the weight of the evidence. *Torrillo v Command Bus Co., supra.*

On a motion for judgment notwithstanding the verdict or for a new trial based on the weight of the evidence, the evidence must be viewed in the light most favorable to the prevailing party. *Johnson v Oval Pharmacy* (1991, 1st Dept) 165 AD2d 587, 569 NYS2d 49, app den 78 NY2d 859, 575 NYS2d 455.

All questions of witness credibility must be resolved in favor of the prevailing party. *Lipsius v White* (1983, 2d Dept) 91 AD2d 271, 458 NYS2d 928; *Niewierski v National Cleaning Contractors* (1987, 1st Dept) 126 AD2d 424, 510 NYS2d 127, app den 70 NY2d 602, 518 NYS2d 1024.

§ 2:7 VOLUNTARY DISMISSAL — When a trial has commenced, any party may discontinue it without an order by filing with the clerk of the court, before the case has been submitted to the court or jury, a stipulation in writing signed by the attorneys of record for all parties, provided that no party is an infant, incompetent person for whom a committee has been appointed or conservatee and no person not a party has an interest in the subject matter of the action. CPLR 3217(a)(2). Where the parties have not so stipulated, an action shall not be discontinued by a party asserting a claim except upon order of the court and upon terms and conditions, as the court deems proper. CPLR 3217(b).

After the cause has been submitted to the court or jury to determine the facts, the court may not order an action discontinued except upon the stipulation of all parties appearing in the action. CPLR 3217(b).

Unless otherwise stated in the notice, stipulation or order of discontinuance, the discontinuance is without prejudice, except that a discontinuance by means of a notice operates as an adjudication on the merits if the party has once before discontinued, by any method, an action based on or including the same cause of action in a court of any state or the United States. CPLR 3217(c).

It was error to deny plaintiff's application for leave to discontinue the action, which was made before the plaintiff had completed its proofs. *Consolidated Const. Corp. v Board of Education* (1935) 155 Misc 586, 280 NYS 87. Generally, a plaintiff may discontinue an action or submit to a voluntary nonsuit at any time before the issues have been submitted to the court. *Piedmont Hotel Co. v A. E. Nettleton Co.* (1934) 241 AD 562, 272 NYS 573.

Plaintiff cannot submit to a voluntary nonsuit after the case has been submitted to the jury, but the court may grant a motion to withdraw a juror after the case has been submitted to the jury. *Re Taylor's Will* (1947) 271 AD 947, 67 NYS2d 823.

Where there was no counterclaim or other pleading entitling the defendant to affirmative relief and the plaintiff made a timely motion to discontinue the action before she rested and before the issues of fact were submitted to the trier of facts, plaintiff was entitled to a discontinuance upon appropriate terms. *Hayes v 255-79th Realty Corp.* (1939) 257 AD 1048, 13 NYS2d 605.

Although the court reserved decision after trial and asked counsel to submit proposed findings and judgment and six months passed without any submission, the plaintiff was not entitled to her own cause discontinued, absent a stipulation of all parties. *Farkas v Farkas* (1965) 47 Misc 2d 827, 263 NYS2d 214.

An order discontinuing the plaintiff's previous action against defendants annulled all proceedings held in connection with the action and rendered the pleadings ineffective. *Mahon v Remington* (1939) 256 AD 889, 9 NYS2d 47. When an action is discontinued, all further proceedings are arrested and all that has been done is annulled, so that the action is as if it had never been commenced. *Radin v Harper* (1946, Sup) 82 NYS2d 121.

Because the plaintiff made no representation, express or implied, that he would not reassert his claim, his voluntary dismissal of his action did not prevent him from bringing a second action. *Secklir v Penney* (1933) 148 Misc 807, 266 NYS 327, affd 244 AD 830, 280 NYS 1009.

A discontinuance was improperly granted in a divorce action where the sole apparent reason the husband sought the discontinuance was to inconvenience the wife and to cause her potential economic detriment. *Kane v Kane* (1990, 2d Dept) 163 AD2d 568, 558 NYS2d 627.

In the absence of special circumstances, such as particular prejudice or other improper consequences, a party's application for voluntary discontinuance should be granted. *Commissioner of Franklin County Dep't of Social Services on behalf of Carla L. v Terry M.* (1991, 3d Dept) 178 AD2d 881, 577 NYS2d 735.

The determination of plaintiff's motion for discontinuance rests within the sound discretion of the court, and the motion is ordinarily granted absent prejudice to a substantial right of the defendant. *Conte v Getty Petroleum Corp.* (1994, 2d Dept) 202 AD2d 621, 609 NYS2d 332.

§ 2:8 DEFAULT AND INVOLUNTARY DISMISSAL — When a plaintiff or defendant fails to proceed to trial of an action reached and called for trial, a default judgment may be entered against such party. CPLR 3215(a).

When defendant's attorneys walked out of the courtroom after being directed to proceed to trial on a case that had been marked "peremptorily against defendants," their action constituted a wilful abandonment and not a mere default. *Nussbaum v Schwager* (1961) 33 Misc 2d 450, 228 NYS2d 995.

When plaintiff's attorney failed to appear in the special "crash part" of the court designated to proceed quickly from trial to trial, the presiding justice properly exercised his discretion in restoring the case. The record showed that the case had merit and that the attorney, who had accepted a previous engagement, had honestly believed that the case in the crash part would not be reached for trial because another case was under way in that part and because one of the attorneys for the numerous codefendants was actually engaged in another trial. *Sicuranza v United States Steel Corp.* (1972, 1st Dept) 39 AD2d 1020, 334 NYS2d 597.

When counsel failed to appear for trial on several occasions, the imposition of costs on him personally was a more appropriate remedy than the dismissal of the case, because the last non-appearance was apparently not wilful and there was no indication of undue prejudice to the defendants. *Moscatiello v Savarese* (1973, 1st Dept) 42 AD2d 519, 344 NYS2d 285.

The trial court did not err in refusing to extend a stay of the dismissal of judgment. Approximately one year earlier, the court had dismissed the complaint because of the lack of the executor's capacity to sue. On the plaintiff's representation that the will would be admitted to probate imminently, the court had stayed entry of the dismissal judgment for sixty days or until commencement of a new action by a duly named representative of the estate, whichever occurred first. Thereafter, the court agreed to extend the stay several times, each time accepting plaintiff's claims that the contested probate proceedings would shortly be resolved and a representative named. *Estate of Salerno v Estate of Salerno* (1989, 2d Dept) 154 AD2d 430, 546 NYS2d 8.

The Supreme Court lacks the power to dismiss a complaint for "general delay." *Bauernfeind v Albany Medical Center Hosp.* (1989, 3d Dept) 154 AD2d 754, 546 NYS2d 201. Although the court had granted the plaintiff's attorneys 10 days to make a motion to be relieved as counsel on the condition that the complaint would be dismissed if the motion was not timely made, the trial court did not have authority to dismiss the complaint on the merits for alleged failure to prosecute. The plaintiff was not in default and had not been given notice of her attorneys' request. *Bauernfeind v Albany Medical Center Hosp., supra.*

Plaintiff's refusal to go forward with selection of a jury on the appointed date for commencement of the trial constituted an abandonment of her claims against the institutional defendants. *Osipova v New York University* (1990, 1st Dept) 157 AD2d 487, 549 NYS2d 674.

In an action brought to recover damages for personal injury and wrongful death resulting from an automobile engine fire, the court had no viable sanction alternative and, therefore, properly dismissed the complaint. The court had issued an order directing plaintiffs to preserve the car for inspection by defendants' experts, but on examination, defendants' experts found that several parts had been removed. On renewed inspection, defendants found that many of the missing parts were still not produced, while those that were tendered did not belong to the subject car. *Hughes v Atlantic Oldsmobile* (1994, 2d Dept) 202 AD2d 392, 608 NYS2d 522.

RESEARCH REFERENCES

American Law Reports

57 ALR4th 1049, Court reporter's death or disability prior to transcribing notes as grounds for reversal or new trial

34 ALR4th 778, Construction, as to terms and conditions, of state statute or rule providing for voluntary dismissal without preju-

dice upon such terms and conditions as state court deems proper

32 ALR4th 840, What constitutes bringing an action to trial or other activity in case sufficient to avoid dismissal under state statute or court rule requiring such activity within stated time

32 ALR4th 212, Dismissal of state court action for failure or refusal of plaintiff to appear or to answer questions at deposition or oral examination

30 ALR4th 9, Judgment in favor of plaintiff in state court action for defendant's failure to obey request or order to answer interrogatories or other discovery questions

27 ALR4th 61, Dismissal of state court action for failure or refusal of plaintiff to obey request or order for production of documents or other objects

26 ALR4th 849, Judgment in favor of plaintiff in state court action for defendant's failure to obey request or order for production of documents or other objects

9 ALR4th, Continuance of civil case as conditioned upon applicant's payment of costs or expenses incurred by other party

4 ALR4th 1274, Propriety of court's dismissing indictment or prosecution because of failure of jury to agree after successive trials

75 ALR3d 894, Right to a jury trial on motion to vacate judgment

70 ALR3d 797, Affidavit or motion for disqualification of judge as contempt

31 ALR3d 449, What amounts to "final submission" or "retirement of jury" within statute permitting plaintiff to take voluntary dismissal or nonsuit without prejudice before submission or retirement of jury

24 ALR3d 768, Voluntary dismissal of replevin action by plaintiff as affecting defendant's right to judgment for the return or value of the property

ALR Quick Index: Continuance and Adjournment; Default; Dismissal or Discontinuance; Motions

American Jurisprudence 2d

24 Am Jur 2d, Dismissal, Discontinuance, and Nonsuit §§ 1 et seq.

21 NY Jur 2d, Continuances §§ 1 et seq.

17 Am Jur 2d, Continuance §§ 1 et seq.

American Jurisprudence Pleading and Practice

23 Am Jur Pl & Pr Forms (Rev), Trial, Forms 41-75

8A AM JUR PL & PR FORMS (Rev), Dismissal, Discontinuance, and Non-suit Forms 1 et seq.

American Jurisprudence Proof of Facts

24 AM JUR PROOF OF FACTS 2d 705 "Excusable Neglect" Warranting Relief from Default Judgment

10 AM JUR PROOF OF FACTS 2d 427, Fraud in Obtaining Default Judgment

American Jurisprudence Trials

34 AM JUR TRIALS 1, Representing Sex Offenders and the "Chemical Castration Defense"

4 AM JUR TRIALS 223, Motions for Production and Inspection

3 AM JUR TRIALS 681, Tactics and Strategy of Pleading

Other Resources

CARMODY-WAIT 2d, §§ 47:1 et seq.

Auto-Cite®: Any case citation herein can be checked for form, parallel references, later history and annotation references through the Auto-Cite computer research system.

CHAPTER 3

CONTEMPT OF COURT

§ 3:1 POWER OF COURT TO PUNISH FOR CONTEMPT —

The court has power to punish for criminal contempt, Judiciary Law § 750, as well as for civil contempt, Judiciary Law § 753.

The power to punish for civil contempt is much broader than the power to punish for criminal contempt and includes the power to punish a party for any abuse of a mandate or proceeding of the court. *Gabrelian v Gabrelian* (1985, 2d Dept) 108 AD2d 445, 489 NYS2d 914, app dismd 66 NY2d 741, 497 NYS2d 365.

Applications to punish for civil contempt may be commenced by ordinary notice of motion. *Mayfair Nursing Home v Neidhardt* (1991, 2d Dept) 173 AD2d 794, 571 NYS2d 30; Judiciary Law § 756.

Designated housing judges who preside in the Housing Part of Civil Court are officers of that court and are expressly authorized by statute to punish for contempt in the same manner as Civil Court judges. *Department of Hous. Preservation & Dev. v 24 W. 132 Equities, Inc.* (1987, App Term) 137 Misc 2d 459, 524 NYS2d 324, affd without op (1989, 1st Dept) 150 AD2d 181, 540 NYS2d 711, appeal dismissed without op (1989) 74 NY2d 841, 546 NYS2d 558, cert denied (1990) 493 US 1078.

Contempt is a drastic remedy that should not be granted absent a clear right for such relief. *Usina Costa Pinto, S. A. v Sanco Sav*

Co. (1991, 1st Dept) 174 AD2d 487, 571 NYS2d 264. If there are factual disputes regarding the alleged contemnor's wilfulness in disobeying the prior order that cannot be resolved on the papers, a hearing must be held before a party or its attorney can be adjudicated in contempt. Contempt is to be proven: (a) beyond a reasonable doubt, as is the case with criminal contempt, or (b) with reasonable certainty, as in the case of civil contempt. *Usina Costa Pinto, S. A. v Sanco Sav Co., supra.*

§ 3:2   CIVIL AND CRIMINAL CONTEMPT — Civil contempt involves an injury or wrong done to a party who is a suitor before the court and has established a claim on the court's protection. Civil contempt results in a money indemnity to the litigant or a compulsory act or omission enforced for his benefit. *People ex rel. Munsell v Court of Oyer & Terminer* (1886) 101 NY 245, 4 NE 259. Criminal contempts involve violations of the rights of the public, as represented by their constituted legal tribunals. Punishment is in the interest of public justice, not in the interest of an individual litigant. If a fine is imposed, its maximum is limited by a fixed general law and not by the needs of individuals. Its proceeds, when collected, go into the public treasury, not into the purse of an individual suitor. *People ex rel. Munsell v Court of Oyer & Terminer, supra.* An essential element of criminal contempt is intent to defy the dignity and authority of the court, as, for example, by wilful disobedience of the order of the court. *Sheridan v Kennedy* (1961, 1st Dept) 12 AD2d 332, 212 NYS2d 296.

Various acts constituting criminal contempt are set forth in § 750 of the Judiciary Law. Section 753 of the Judiciary Law indicates various acts constituting civil contempt.

Although the line between civil and criminal contempt may be difficult to draw in a given case and the same act may be punishable as both a civil and a criminal contempt, the element that elevates a contempt from civil to criminal is the degree of wilfulness of the conduct. *McCormick v Axelrod* (1983) 59 NY2d 574, 466 NYS2d 279, as amended (1983) 60 NY2d 652, 467 NYS2d 571.

A trustee who failed to comply with court orders directing him to file a proper accounting was in civil contempt. *Kelly v Sassower* (1980, 1st Dept) 78 AD2d 502, 431 NYS2d 819.

A party may be found in civil or criminal contempt for failing to obey a court order. *Callanan Industries, Inc. v White* (1986, 3d Dept) 123 AD2d 56, 510 NYS2d 230. Civil contempt occurs when disobedience of a court order, regardless of motive, defeats, impairs, impedes, or prejudices the rights of the other party. *Callanan Industries, Inc. v White, supra.* A party is guilty of criminal contempt if the court order has been wilfully disobeyed. *Callanan Industries, Inc. v White, supra.*

Judiciary Law § 753(A)(1) provides that a court may punish for contempt, the neglect or violation of a duty or other misconduct constituting disobedience of a lawful mandate of the court or judge, with the result that the right of a party in a civil action or special proceeding is defeated, impeded, impaired, or prejudiced. *Re Bonnie "H"* (1988, 3d Dept) 145 AD2d 830, 535 NYS2d 816, app dismd without op 74 NY2d 650, 542 NYS2d 520. It is not necessary that the disobedience be deliberate. The mere act of disobedience by a county commissioner of social services, regardless of motive, was sufficient to sustain a finding of civil contempt where the disobedience defeated, impaired, impeded, or prejudiced the rights of a party. *Re Bonnie "H", supra.*

In the context of a contempt motion, an ambiguity should be resolved in favor of the alleged contemnor. *Virgil v Ford* (1992, 3d Dept) 184 AD2d 901, 585 NYS2d 559.

§ 3:3   PROCEDURE IN CIVIL CONTEMPT — Although a proceeding to punish for civil contempt is a civil proceeding, it is quasi-criminal in character. *Hynes v Hartman* (1978, 1st Dept) 63 AD2d 1, 406 NYS2d 818. For a court to hold a respondent in civil contempt, petitioner must establish an affirmative case by more than a fair preponderance of the evidence. He must demonstrate with reasonable certainty that respondent failed to comply with a subpoena or order of the court. *Hynes v Hartman, supra; Callanan Industries, Inc. v White,* (1986, 3d Dept) 123 AD2d 56, 510 NYS2d 230.

Because Article 19 of the Judiciary Law does not expressly require personal service of an application to punish for civil contempt, service of an application may be made by regular mail. *New York Higher Education Assistance Corp. v Cooper* (1978, 3d Dept) 65 AD2d 906, 410 NYS2d 687.

The record amply established civil contempt on the part of defendant's parents, who were non-party witnesses, for failure to comply with court orders and subpoenas served on them and on various corporations under their control. *Frankel v Frankel* (1985, 3d Dept) 111 AD2d 447, 488 NYS2d 825.

In order for a court to hold a party in civil contempt for failing to obey a lawful mandate of the court, the mandate must be clearly expressed, and it must appear with reasonable certainty that it has been violated. *Gordon v Janover* (1986, 2d Dept) 121 AD2d 599, 503 NYS2d 860. The act of disobedience need not be deliberate; the mere act of disobedience, regardless of its motive, is sufficient to sustain a finding of civil contempt if such disobedience defeats, impairs, impedes, or prejudices the rights of a party. *Gordon v Janover, supra*

An application to punish respondents for contempt did not contain the warning legend required by § 756 of the Judiciary Law, which sets forth the procedure for an application to punish for a civil contempt. The absence of the required warning was fatal, because the requirements of § 756 are jurisdictional. *Re Estate of Devine* (1987, 1st Dept) 126 AD2d 491, 511 NYS2d 231.

A motion to punish for civil contempt is fatally defective if it fails to include the statutorily required notice that the purpose of the hearing is to punish the accused for contempt of court and that the punishment may consist of a fine, imprisonment, or both, according to law. *Mente v Wenzel* (1993, 3d Dept) 192 AD2d 862, 596 NYS2d 520, app dismd, in part, app den, in part 82 NY2d 843, 606 NYS2d 593.

An attorney's intentional use of conflicting court appearances to avoid a prompt hearing on the charge of contempt is equivalent to an outright refusal to attend the contempt hearing and constitutes a waiver, particularly since the attorney did not proffer any testimony or documentary evidence that he had attempted to avoid or reschedule the conflicting court appearances so that he could attend his contempt hearing. *People ex rel. Sassower v Sheriff of Suffolk County* (1987, 2d Dept) 134 AD2d 641, 521 NYS2d 536.

The court is vested with broad discretion to determine appropriate conditions for a contemnor to purge the contempt. *Midlar-*

sky v D'Urso (1987, 2d Dept) 133 AD2d 616, 519 NYS2d 724. Where the court had held defendant in contempt for failing to comply with the Supreme Court order directing him to deposit cash into a brokerage account, the court did not abuse its discretion in permitting the defendant to purge the contempt by providing the plaintiff with alternative security, because the purpose of the order was to provide security for the underlying action. *Midlarsky v D'Urso, supra*.

The Family Court erred when it found the Monroe County Department of Social Services in civil contempt, because the order to show cause served on the department failed to give notice that the purpose of the proceeding was to determine whether the department should be punished for contempt. Moreover, the court had no basis to hold the department in contempt, because the petition in support of the motion did not allege evidentiary facts showing that the department was guilty of contempt. *Hernandez v Hernandez* (1989, 4th Dept) 148 AD2d 1011, 539 NYS2d 240.

The purpose of a civil contempt fine is not deterrence or punishment but rather the compensation or indemnification of the complainant. *Re v Beiny* (1990, 1st Dept) 164 AD2d 233, 562 NYS2d 58, as amended (1990) 177 AD2d 463, 576 NYS2d 501.

Punitive damages may not be imposed for a civil contempt. If a fine imposed is punitive in nature rather than compensatory, the fine must be set aside. *St. Regis Mohawk Dev. Corp. v Cook* (1992, 3d Dept) 181 AD2d 964, 581 NYS2d 877.

If no actual damages have been demonstrated in an action to punish for civil contempt, the court may impose on the offending party the other party's reasonable costs and expenses, including attorney's fees. *Glennon v Mayo* (1991, 2d Dept) 174 AD2d 599, 571 NYS2d 307.

The court erred in providing in its contempt order that future noncompliance would be punished by additional $250 fines, without further application to the court. A subsequent contempt finding by the Supreme Court is required. *Commissioner of Community Dev. v Gray* (1992, 4th Dept) 186 AD2d 1076, 588 NYS2d 689.

§ 3:4   PROCEDURE IN CRIMINAL CONTEMPT — At common law, the power to punish for contempt by summary conviction was deemed to be inherent in the courts of justice and in legislative assemblies. *Re Barnes* (1912) 204 NY 108, 97 NE 508. Now contempt proceedings are purely statutory. *Re Depue* (1906) 185 NY 60, 77 NE 798.

Except as provided in subdivisions (2), (3) and (4) of § 751 of the Judiciary Law, punishment for a contempt specified in § 750, may be by fine, not to exceed $1,000, by imprisonment, not to exceed thirty days in the jail of the county where the court is sitting, or both, in the discretion of the court. Judiciary Law § 751(1).

If a person is committed to jail for nonpayment of a fine imposed under § 751 of the Judiciary Law, he must be discharged at the end of 30 days. If, however, he is also committed for a definite time, the 30 days must be computed from the expiration of the definite time. Judiciary Law § 751 (1).

When the punishment for contempt is based on a violation of an order of protection issued under § 530.12 or § 530.13 of the Criminal Procedure Law, imprisonment may be for a term not exceeding three months. Judiciary Law § 751 (1).

When an employee organization defined in § 201 of the Civil Service Law wilfully disobeys a lawful mandate of a court of record or wilfully offers resistance to such lawful mandate in a case involving or growing out of a strike in violation of Civil Service Law § 210(1), the punishment for each day that the contempt persists may be a fine fixed in the discretion of the court. Judiciary Law § 751 (2)(a).

A judgment debtor who wilfully failed to obey two court orders directing him to appear for examination was adjudicated to be in criminal contempt and was fined $250 for each contempt, the fine to be cumulative. He was also sentenced to 30 days in jail on each contempt, with the sentences to run concurrently. *James v Powell* (1966) 52 Misc 2d 1054, 277 NYS2d 962, mod (1st Dept) 32 AD2d 517, 298 NYS2d 840. A teachers' union and its president committed criminal contempt by wilfully disobeying for seventeen days the Supreme Court order enjoining the teachers from striking. A fine was levied against the union in the sum of $150,000 and the union's president was fined the sum of $250 and sentenced to jail for a period of 15 days. *Board of Education v Shanker* (1967) 54 Misc 2d 941, 283 NYS2d 548, affd (1st Dept 1967) 29 AD2d 634, 286 NYS2d 453.

The Supreme Court may punish a person who is in contempt of its order by putting him in jail and may permit the person to purge himself of contempt by any manner deemed advisable by the court. *Greenzang v Greenzang* (1938) 169 Misc 516, 8 NYS2d 257.

As a general rule, a contemnor will be allowed to purge the contempt by performing the act required or by undoing the act constituting the contempt. *January 1979 Grand Jury etc. v Doe* (1981, 3d Dept) 84 AD2d 588, 444 NYS2d 201.

If a criminal contempt has been committed in the immediate view and presence of the court, it can be punished summarily, without proof, if the acts constituting the contempt are seen or heard by the presiding judge and the judge can assert of his own knowledge the facts constituting the contempt in the mandate of commitment. *Douglas v Adel* (1935) 269 NY 144, 199 NE 35, remittitur den (1936) 271 NY 528.

It was inappropriate for the trial court to conduct a summary proceeding to punish for contempt a subpoenaed witness for the defense in a murder trial who appeared in court wearing a T-shirt that contained offensive language. Even though the witness knew that the T-shirt was inappropriate attire for a courtroom and the witness's wearing the T-shirt disrupted the criminal proceeding, other than wearing the T-shirt, the witness engaged in no contemptuous or disruptive behavior. Although Judiciary Law § 755 authorizes the use of a summary proceeding whenever the offense is committed in the immediate view of and presence of the court, the court's summary contempt power is limited to exceptional and necessitous circumstances, when the court reasonably believes that a prompt adjudication of contempt may help in maintaining and/or restoring proper order and decorum. *Doyle v Aison* (1995, 3d Dept) ___ AD2d ___, 627 NYS2d 485.

A statute providing for commitment for criminal contempt not committed in the immediate presence of the court that did not provide notice to the party accused and an opportunity to be heard in his defense would violate his constitutional rights, because it might deprive him of liberty or property without due process of law. *People ex rel. Roache v Hanbury* (1914) 162 AD 337, 147 NYS 851. When acts constituting a contempt are not committed within the hearing of the presiding judge or he does not see them and cannot so state in the mandate of commitment, the offender must be given an opportunity to be heard after notice. *Douglas v Adel, supra.*

The publication of a false and grossly inaccurate report on a proceeding in the court is a contempt committed out of the court, and the party charged must be notified of the accusation. *People ex rel. Barnes v Court of Sessions* (1895) 147 NY 290, 41 NE 700. What constitutes sufficient notice and a reasonable time to make a defense within the meaning of § 751 of the Judiciary Law depends on the particular circumstances of each case. *Spector v Allen* (1939) 281 NY 251.

In a prosecution of two defendants for assault, a verbal directive by the court that police officers appear at a preliminary hearing was not a proper basis for a charge against them of contempt committed within the immediate view and presence of the court, when they failed to appear. There was no notice to the officers that their failure to appear would subject them to a charge of contempt. *Waterhouse v Celli* (1972) 71 Misc 2d 600, 336 NYS2d 960.

In criminal contempt proceedings, proof of guilt must be established beyond a reasonable doubt. *Yorktown Cent. School Dist. v Yorktown Congress of Teachers* (1973, 2d Dept) 42 AD2d 422, 348 NYS2d 367.

When the crime of contempt is prosecuted by indictment, a court may not permit the contempt to be purged. *People v Leone* (1978) 44 NY2d 315, 405 NYS2d 642. Indictment for the crime of contempt as defined in the Penal Law, like any other crime, entitles the defendant to a plenary trial. *People v Leone, supra.*

Defendant-appellant had been directed by judgment to turn over to plaintiff-respondent corporation certain shares of stock but claimed inability to comply because the stock had been pledged against a loan and was not under his control. After he was adjudicated in contempt and repeated under oath that he was unable to comply, giving the reason he could not, the burden was on respondent to prove appellant's ability to comply. *Penn-Dixie Industries, Inc. v Castle* (1980, 1st Dept) 77 AD2d 844, 431 NYS2d 34.

By contesting the contempt application on the merits and failing to object in a timely manner to the omission of the notice and warning required by Judiciary Law § 756, respondent waived the protections afforded by the statute. *Re Estate of Rappaport* (1982) 58 NY2d 725, 458 NYS2d 911.

A trial judge who had demonstrated a personal animosity toward the attorney whom he sought to hold in contempt, as shown both in the stenographic record and in the affidavit submitted in the contempt proceeding, should not have sat in judgment, but should have referred the matter elsewhere for adjudication. *Garber v Soden* (1981, 1st Dept) 82 AD2d 725, 439 NYS2d 384.

If the terms of an order are vague and indefinite as to whether a particular action by a party is required or prohibited, then an alleged disobedience of those terms cannot be the basis of a criminal contempt. *Department of Environmental Protection v Department of Environmental Conservation* (1987) 70 NY2d 233, 519 NYS2d 539.

Both civil and criminal contempt determinations require a finding that the court order said to be defied expressed its mandate clearly and unequivocally. *Spinnenweber v New York State Dep't of Environmental Conservation* (1990, 3d Dept) 160 AD2d 1138, 554 NYS2d 346.

A criminal contempt mandate can be rendered only in a special proceeding, which requires personal service with equal dignity to that required of a summons. Failure to serve the alleged contemnor personally is a jurisdictional defect requiring reversal. *Re Grand Jury Subpoena Duces Tecum Served Upon Morano's of Fifth Avenue, Inc.* (1988, 1st Dept) 144 AD2d 252, 533 NYS2d 869, lv den, 73 NY2d 1009, 541 NYS2d 762.

As with any other criminal charge, each element of criminal contempt must be proven beyond a reasonable doubt. *Gouiran Holdings, Inc. v McCormick* (1990, 1st Dept) 163 AD2d 44, 558 NYS2d 18, app dismd without op 76 NY2d 851, 560 NYS2d 991.

The requirement that the court set forth the particular circumstances of the offense applies to all judicial criminal contempts, whether or not committed in the court's presence. *Gouiran Holdings, Inc. v McCormick, supra*.

When any member of the news media wilfully disobeys a lawful mandate of a court issued pursuant to Judiciary Law § 751, the punishment for each day that the contempt persists may be by a fine fixed at the court's discretion but not to exceed $5,000 per day, imprisonment not to exceed 30 days in jail in the county where the court is sitting, or both, in the discretion of the court. Judiciary Law § 751(5).

In order to adjudge a party in criminal contempt, the court mandate allegedly violated must be clearly expressed. *County of Westchester v O'Neill* (1993, 2d Dept) 191 AD2d 556, 594 NYS2d 814.

§ 3:5 ACTS CONSTITUTING CRIMINAL CONTEMPT — A number of acts are defined by statute as coming within the power of the court to punish for criminal contempt. Among them are disorderly, contemptuous, or insolent behavior committed during the court's sitting, in its immediate view and presence, and directly tending to interrupt the court proceedings or to impair the respect due its authority, Judiciary Law § 750(1); breach of the peace, noise, or other disturbance directly tending to interrupt the court proceedings, Judiciary Law § 750(2); wilful disobedience of its lawful mandate, Judiciary Law § 750(3); resistance wilfully offered to its lawful mandate, Judiciary Law § 750(4); contumacious and unlawful refusal to be sworn as a witness, or after being sworn, to answer any legal and proper questions, Judiciary Law § 750(5); or publication of a false or grossly inaccurate report of the court proceedings, Judiciary Law § 750(6). A court cannot, however, punish as a contempt the publication of a true, full, and fair report of a trial, argument, decision, or other proceeding therein. Judiciary Law § 750(6).

Criminal contempt may be committed by acts of omission or comission. *People v Solomon* (1934) 150 Misc 873, 271 NYS 136.

The unlawful practice of law is punishable as a contempt by Juciciary Law § 750(B).

The giving of advice to the public by a person who has not been duly admitted to the bar of the state and who holds himself out to be a "consultant in the law of his specialty" constitutes the unlawful practice of law punishable as contempt. *Application of New York County Lawyers Asso.* (1955) 207 Misc 698, 139 NYS2d 714.

There was no contempt of court against an attorney who was absent from the courtroom for 10 minutes after the court had been convened and after the court had unsuccessfully sent messengers to order the attorney to return. Following an unsuccessful attempt in chambers to settle the case, the attorney had gone directly to the telephone to inform an expert witness that his appearance in court was required. *Re Walker* (1949) 275 AD 688, 86 NYS2d 726, affd 299 NY 686.

Although tardiness by counsel following recesses and adjournments is not to be condoned, such conduct is not a willful wrong warranting punishment by contempt. *People ex rel. Hughes v Capoccia* (1980, 3d Dept) 76 AD2d 1024, 429 NYS2d 494.

Refusal by counsel to produce certain photographs that had previously been discovered and copied was not contemptuous, because the photographs in question had previously been discovered and the court has the power to issue a subpoena. Nevertheless, the court indicated that it did not look kindly on the refusal. *People ex rel. Hughes v Capoccia, supra.*

The failure of a judgment debtor to appear for an examination pursuant to an order of the trial court was criminal contempt of court. *James v Powell* (1966) 52 Misc 2d 1054, 277 NYS2d 962, mod (1st Dept) 32 AD2d 517, 298 NYS2d 840. A deliberate and wilful disobedience of subpoenaes issued by a court rendered the defendant subject to punishment for criminal contempt. *Re Katzenstein* (1961, 2d Dept) 12 AD2d 806, 210 NYS2d 354, motion gr (2d Dept) 13 AD2d 517, 212 NYS2d 710 and motion gr (2d Dept) 13 AD2d 541, 214 NYS2d 681.

An attorney's conduct constituted a criminal contempt, when he interrupted the remarks of the court with loud and boisterous declamation and, ignoring the court's admonition to desist, persisted his contemptuous conduct in a high-pitched and assertive voice and a rude and offensive manner. *Waldman v Churchill*

(1933) 262 NY 247, 186 NE 690. A profane observation regarding a witness's testimony at an examination before trial, which was made in a loud voice and interrupted the hearing, constituted criminal contempt. *Sewards v Rubin* (1953) 204 Misc 172, 125 NYS2d 776.

The mandate of commitment, which stated that petitioner, an attorney, continually interrupted, criticized, and made statements to the presiding judge during the course of the trial, despite repeated orders and warnings to desist from doing so, was not sufficient to satisfy the statutory requirements for criminal contempt. The trial transcript indicated that the statements of petitioner for which he was found to be in contempt were misunderstood by the court, and there was no showing that they were made for any reason other than to protect the record in the best interests of his client. *Sickmen v Goldstein* (1977, 2d Dept) 59 AD2d 731, 398 NYS2d 583.

Although remarks by counsel could be considered provocative, his continuous questioning of a witness about the circumstances of the evidentiary issue before the court was not "disorderly," "insolent," or "willful," as required by Judiciary Law § 750. *Thau v Fitzer* (1979, 1st Dept) 69 AD2d 800, 415 NYS2d 430.

An order adjudging petitioner-attorney guilty of criminal contempt committed in the immediate presence of the court was annulled, because there was no showing that she acted for any reason other than to protect the record in the best interests of her client. Additionally, she was never afforded an opportunity to make a statement in her defense or in extenuation of her conduct, as is required by § 701.2(c) of the Rules of the Appellate Division, Second Department. *Marino v Burstein* (1979, 2d Dept) 72 AD2d 814, 421 NYS2d 904.

The mandate of the trial judge, which required defendant to furnish voice exemplars, could not form the predicate for the crime of contempt, because no prior notice of the prosecution's intention to apply for that relief was given to the defendant and the necessity for the relief was not established on any papers served on the defendant. Furthermore, the defendant was not afforded the opportunity to controvert the grounds for the application, and compelling him to submit to the taking of a voice exemplar constituted a denial of due process. *People v Giglio* (1980, 2d Dept) 74 AD2d 348, 428 NYS2d 27.

False statements made by the petitioner on two occasions to the trial judge, indicating that he had spoken to the defendant and that the defendant needed an interpreter to testify, constituted contempt of court. *Zols v Lakritz* (1973) 74 Misc 2d 322, 344 NYS2d 626.

Where the alleged contempt consisted of having failed to carry out the provisions of an agreement entered into under the auspices of the Family Court and the provisions of the agreement were not implemented by an order of the court, the failure to carry out the provisions cannot provide the basis for an adjudication of contempt. *Gingold v Gingold* (1975, 1st Dept) 48 AD2d 623, 367 NYS2d 791.

If a court of general jurisdiction has subject matter jurisdiction in an action, it has power to issue an injunction or to enforce its decree and to punish the breach thereof by a process of contempt. *People ex rel. Davis v Sturtevant* (1853) 9 NY 263. Where, however, a justice of the Supreme Court has no power to grant an injunction, he has no power to punish the person to whom it was directed for contempt for failing to obey it. *Re Holle* (1914) 160 AD 369, 145 NYS 388.

A juror may not be punished in contempt proceedings for his attitude in the jury room and for any matter relating to a proposed verdict. *People v Diefendorf* (1953) 281 AD 465, 865, 119 NYS 469, affd 306 NY 818. In a criminal prosecution, however, a juror was guilty of criminal contempt for failing to disclose, when asked, that he knew one of the defendants. *Re Bassett* (1939) 172 Misc 613, 15 NYS2d 737, affd 258 AD 929, 16 NYS2d 699, app den 259 AD 788, 18 NYS2d 751.

The acts of a deputy sheriff in charge of jurors who secretly purchased liquor for the jurors and became personally drunk while guarding the jury would constitute disorderly, contemptuous, and insolent behavior directly tending to impair the respect due the authority of the court within the meaning of the statute governing contempt. *People v Higgins* (1939) 173 Misc 96, 16 NYS2d 302. Sexual intercourse with a woman juror by a deputy sheriff while he was in charge of the jury would likewise constitute disorderly, contemptuous, and insolent behavior directly tending to impair the respect due to the authority of the court. *People v Higgins, supra.*

A reporter who conceals himself in a jury room and listens to the deliberation taking place among the jurors is guilty of criminal contempt. *People ex rel. Choate v Barrett* (1890) 56 Hun 351, 9 NYS 321, affd 121 NY 678, 24 NE 1095.

Petitioner had been banned by the trial justice from the courtroom, the corridor, and the courthouse while court was in progress because of his disrespectful and disruptive behavior and abusive language. When he returned to the courtroom during the course of a criminal trial and refused in a calculatedly contemptuous manner to obey the court's order to leave, using unbridled and provocative language to the trial justice in open court, his acts warranted punishment for contempt committed in the immediate presence of the court. *Gumbs v Martinis* (1972, 1st Dept) 40 AD2d 194, 338 NYS2d 817.

Contempt is committed when a defendant's response is so false and evasive as to be equivalent to no answer at all. *People v Didio* (1978, 4th Dept) 60 AD2d 978, 401 NYS2d 640. However, even if testimony regarding the residence of a witness was false, it is not summarily punishable as a criminal contempt without a showing that the perjury obstructed the court in the performance of its duty. *Tamberg v Waltemade* (1963, 1st Dept) 19 AD2d 874, 244 NYS2d 193.

Perjury alone is not the test of whether a contempt of court is committed. *Re Kamell* (1939) 170 Misc 868, 11 NYS2d 479, affd 258 AD 723, 15 NYS2d 141. For perjury to constitute criminal contempt, there must also be deliberate obstruction. *Re Shapolsky* (1959, 1st Dept) 8 AD2d 122, 185 NYS2d 639.

The answers of defendant, who appeared before a grand jury, were not contemptuous, because they were sufficiently explicit to provide a basis for a perjury charge in the event they were shown to be false. *People v Yacovelli* (1985, 1st Dept) 113 AD2d 718, 493 NYS2d 473.

A Supreme Court justice was empowered to hold a defendant in contempt and punish him therefor based on his refusal to answer routine questions about his income and assets directed toward the satisfaction of a judgment. The defendant did not demonstrate that he had invoked the Fifth Amendment in good faith because of a real danger or reasonable possibility that the answer to the questions might actually tend to incriminate him. *Federal Deposit Ins. Corp. v Salesmen Unlimited Agency Corp.* (1984, 2d Dept) 101 AD2d 876, 475 NYS2d 1020, later proceeding (2d Dept) 101 AD2d 877, 475 NYS2d 1023.

The general rule with respect to contempt for failure to answer proper questions is that if the witness's conduct shows beyond any doubt whatever that he is refusing to tell what he knows, he is in contempt of court, and the proper test is whether on its mere face and without collateral inquiry the testimony is not a *bona fide* effort to answer the questions at all. *Ruskin v Detken* (1973) 32 NY2d 293, 344 NYS2d 933.

False and evasive claims of an inability to recall events or details that were significant and, therefore, memorable are punishable as criminal contempt. *People v Arnette* (1983) 58 NY2d 1104, 462 NYS2d 817. Evidence, which showed that a state official gave equivocal answers when called to testify about allegations that while in office he had used state employees to repair the roof of his home during working hours and had used state building materials, was sufficient to sustain his conviction of criminal contempt. *People v Arnette, supra.*

Defendant, an active business woman all her life, was unable to recall or testify consistently about recent business transactions involving large sums of money. The court held that her conduct was so evasive or falsely equivocal and contradictory that it amounted to no answer at all, thereby justifying her conviction for criminal contempt in the first degree. *People v Schenkman* (1978) 46 NY2d 232, 413 NYS2d 284.

Where a witness was granted immunity in connection with a grand jury inquiry related to the commission of serious crimes within the county, she had a duty to answer the questions she was asked, which were material to the inquiry. By refusing to do so, she was guilty of contempt, even though she would be required to violate the tenets of her religion by testifying, because the testimony would harm others. *People v Woodruff* (1966, 2d Dept) 26

AD2d 236, 272 NYS2d 786, app dismd 20 NY2d 879, 285 NYS2d 622 and affd 21 NY2d 848, 288 NYS2d 1004.

A witness's refusal to testify because she feared for her life and that of her child was not a defense to a charge of contempt for such refusal. *People v Clinton* (1973) 42 AD2d 815, 346 NYS2d 345.

The trial court lawfully and properly directed the defendant to remove his eyeglasses for identification purposes so that a prosecution witness could observe him without his glasses. The defendant's refusal to obey the court's direction constituted criminal contempt committed in the immediate view and presence of the court. *People v Sanders* (1977, 1st Dept) 58 AD2d 525, 395 NYS2d 190.

It was not appropriate to adjudge defense counsel in contempt of court after he had asserted in open court but not within the hearing of the jury that the trial judge was improperly holding *ex parte* conferences with the prosecutor. The court proceedings were not disrupted by his allegation, the court was able to conduct its normal business despite his comments, and the deferral of imposition of sanctions until the end of the trial indicated that the immediacy required for summary contempt adjudication was not present. *Breitbart v Galligan* (1988, 1st Dept) 135 AD2d 323, 525 NYS2d 219.

A *pro se* petitioner was guilty of criminal contempt after he moved to vacate, for the fourth time, in clear defiance of the court's instructions that his proper remedy was to review the court's decision by appeal, not by a motion to vacate. The court had warned petitioner that another motion to vacate seeking the same relief would result in a finding and a fine for criminal contempt. *Hunter v Murray* (1987, 3d Dept) 130 AD2d 836, 515 NYS2d 160, cert den and app dismd 484 US 1038, 98 L Ed 2d 854, 108 S Ct 767.

An attorney is not relieved of his obligation to maintain a respectful attitude toward the court by what he may regard as a deficiency in the conduct or ruling of a judge. *Brostoff v Berkman* (1991, 1st Dept) 170 AD2d 364, 566 NYS2d 927, affd (1992) 79 NY2d 938, 582 NYS2d 989. The trial judge was justified in finding that an assistant district attorney was in criminal contempt of court. The attorney refused to remove himself from the well after the judge had directed him to do so, deliberately disobeyed the court's command, and behaved in a manner derisive of the court's authority. *Browstoff v Berkman, supra.*

An attorney who has been disbarred and continues to practice law after being personally served with an order of disbarment is guilty of criminal contempt. *Re Michalek* (1992, 4th Dept) 180 AD2d 67, 582 NYS2d 892.

Justification for a court's power to punish summarily a contempt committed in its immediate view and presence is based on the need to preserve order in the courtroom so that the court can conduct its normal business. *Kunstler v Galligan* (1991, 1st Dept) 168 AD2d 146, 571 NYS2d 930. The transcript of the courtroom proceedings unequivocally indicated that petitioner attorney had been informed by the justice that there would be neither oral argument nor an evidentiary hearing concerning the motion before the court and that the clerk had been directed to call the next case. The petitioner wilfully disobeyed that court order by stating to the respondent justice: "You have exhibited what your partisanship is. You shouldn't be sitting in court. You are a disgrace to the bench." The Supreme Court justice was justified in finding that the criminal defense attorney was in contempt. The attorney's conduct constituted disorderly, contemptuous, and insolent behavior displayed in open court in the immediate view and presence of the respondent justice. *Kunstler v Galligan, supra.*

§ 3:6 ACTS CONSTITUTING CIVIL CONTEMPT — In determining whether to grant an application to punish for civil contempt pursuant to Judiciary Law § 753, the court need not find wilful or intentional conduct on the part of the contemnor, nor is the court required to find that the contemnor benefited from his act of disobedience. The mere act of disobedience, regardless of its motive, is sufficient to sustain a finding of civil contempt if such disobedience defeats, impairs, impedes, or prejudices the rights of a party. *Campanella v Campanella* (1989, 2d Dept) 152 AD2d 190, 548 NYS2d 279. When a bank failed to restrain the defendant's funds in his bank accounts, impairing and impeding plaintiff's ability to obtain her court ordered award of maintenance and counsel fees *pendente lite*, the bank was held liable in civil contempt. *Campanella v Campanella, supra.*

To sustain a finding of civil contempt based on violation of a court order, it is necessary to establish that a lawful court order clearly expressing an unequivocal mandate was in effect and that the person alleged to have violated that order had actual knowledge of its terms. *Graham v Graham* (1989, 2d Dept) 152 AD2d 653, 543 NYS2d 735. Although it is not necessary that an order has actually been served on the party, actual notice is an essential predicate for a contempt order. *Graham v Graham, supra.*

The requirements for civil contempt are: (1) a lawful order, (2) an unequivocal mandate, (3) a reasonable certainty that the order has been disobeyed, (4) the alleged contemnor's knowledge of the court order, and (5) prejudice to the right of a party. *Waldman v United Talmudical Academy* (1990) 147 Misc 2d 529, 558 NYS2d 781.

RESEARCH REFERENCES

American Law Reports

82 ALR4th 886, Attorney's argument as to evidence previously ruled inadmissible as contempt

81 ALR4th 1008, Contempt: state court's power to order indefinite coercive fine or imprisonment to exact promise of future compliance with court's order–anticipatory contempt

76 ALR4th 982, Abuse or misuse of contempt power as ground for removal or discipline of judge

61 ALR4th 1216, Attorney's misrepresentation to court of his state of health or other personal matter in seeking trial delay as ground for disciplinary action

46 ALR4th 238, Intoxication of witness or attorney as contempt of court

38 ALR4th 563, Failure to rise in state courtroom as constituting criminal contempt

37 ALR4th 1004, Disqualification of judge in state proceedings to punish contempt against or involving himself in open court and in his actual presence

36 ALR4th 978, Contempt based on violation of court order where another court has issued contrary order

31 ALR4th 1279, Attorney's use of objectionable questions in examination of witness in state judicial proceeding as contempt of court

30 ALR4th 155, Oral communications insulting to particular state judge, made to third party out of judge's physical presence, as criminal contempt

26 ALR4th 950, Contempt finding as precluding substantive criminal charges relating to same transaction

13 ALR4th 122, Attorney's failure to attend court, or tardiness, as contempt

8 ALR4th 1181, Attorney's conduct in delaying or obstructing discovery as basis for contempt proceeding

7 ALR4th 893, Violation of state court order by one other than party as contempt

100 ALR3d 889, Oral court order implementing prior written order or decree as independent basis of charge of contempt within contempt proceedings based on violation of written order

88 ALR3d 1089, Acquittal of criminal charges other than contempt as precluding contempt proceedings relating to same transaction

85 ALR3d 895, Right of injured party to award of compensatory damages or fine in contempt proceedings

84 ALR3d 1047, Contempt for violation of compromise and settlement, the terms of which were approved by the court but not incorporated in court order, decree, or judgment

70 ALR3d 797, Affidavit or motion for disqualification of judge as contempt

68 ALR3d 273, Addressing allegedly insulting remarks to court during course of trial as contempt

43 ALR3d 793, Allowance of attorneys' fees in civil contempt proceedings

33 ALR3d 589, Contempt adjudication or conviction as subject to review, other than by appeal or writ of error

33 ALR3d 448, Appealability of contempt adjudication or conviction

29 ALR3d 1399, Prejudicial effect of holding accused in contempt of court in presence of jury

24 ALR3d 650, Appealability of acquittal from or dismissal of charge of contempt of court

27 ALR Fed 915, Failure to rise in federal courtrooms as constituting criminal contempt

3 ALR Fed 420, Construction of provision in Federal Criminal Procedure Rule 42(b) that if contempt charges involve disrespect to or criticism of judge, he is disqualified from presiding at trial or hearing except with defendant's consent

ALR QUICK INDEX: Contempt

American Jurisprudence 2d

17 AM JUR 2d, Contempt §§ 1-115

American Jurisprudence Pleading and Practice

7 AM JUR PL & PR FORMS (Rev), Contempt, Forms 1 et seq.

Other Resources

22 CARMODY-WAIT 2d, Contempt Proceedings §§ 140:1 et seq.

21 NY JUR 2d, Contempt §§ 1 et seq.

Auto-Cite®: Any case citation herein can be checked for form, parallel references, later history and annotation references through the Auto-Cite computer research system.

CHAPTER 4

SELECTION OF JURY

§ 4:1 CLASSIFICATION OF CHALLENGES — A challenge may be directed to an individual juryman or to an entire panel. A challenge directed to an individual juryman is either a peremptory challenge, CPLR 4109, or a challenge for cause, CPLR 4110.

Challenges for cause are either challenges for principal cause or challenges to the favor. A challenge for principal cause arises when the proposed juror is shown not to be indifferent between the parties. *Greenfield v People* (1878) 74 NY 277. A challenge to the favor arises when there is only a suspicion or inference that the juror is not indifferent between the parties. *People v Bodine*, 1 Denio 281.

An objection to the qualifications of a juror must be made by challenge unless he is excluded by stipulation of the parties. CPLR 4108.

§ 4:2   PEREMPTORY CHALLENGES — Peremptory challenges are a matter of right and can be exercised arbitrarily without any reason being given for their use with any one or more jurors. *People v Bodine*, 1 Denio 281. Even though an attorney has tentatively selected a juror, he may peremptorily challenge that juror at any time before the jury is sworn. *Sorensen v Hunter* (1945) 268 AD 1078, 52 NYS2d 872, reh den, app dismd 269 AD 808, 56 NYS2d 404. Thus, plaintiff's counsel states he is satisfied with the jury, and defendant's counsel peremptorily challenges two jurors without first requesting that plaintiff's counsel exhaust his peremptory challenges. When the places of the two excused jurors are filled, plaintiff's counsel may then challenge one of the other jurors on the panel. *Dorman v Broadway R. Co.* (1889, City Ct) 5 NYS 769, revd on other grounds 117 NY 655, 23 NE 162.

Each party has three peremptory challenges plus one peremptory challenge for each alternate juror. CPLR 4109; *Sorensen v Hunter, supra.* When there are more parties on one side than the other, the court has discretion to grant additional challenges to the side with fewer peremptory challenges. CPLR 4109.

§ 4:3   CHALLENGES FOR PRINCIPAL CAUSE — A challenge for principal cause is an assertion that the proposed juror is biased as a matter of law. *Butler v Glen Falls, S. H. & F. E. S. R. Co.* (1890) 121 NY 112, 24 NE 187. In such case, there is a legal presumption that the case could not be tried fairly by the challenged juror. *Greenfield v People* (1878) 74 NY 277.

Persons related within the sixth degree of consanguinity or affinity to a party are disqualified from sitting as jurors. CPLR 4110(b); *Maiello v Johnson* (1966) 18 NY2d 826, 275 NYS2d 835.

A prospective juror was challenged for cause after he stated that he had worked for the last three years as a part-time police officer in a town in Rensselaer County; that he not only knew the presenting prosecutor but had worked professionally with him and with the Rensselaer County District Attorney's Office; and that he had socialized with the presenting prosecutor on several occasions. He stated, however, that his job as a part-time police officer as well as his personal relationship with the prosecutor would not interfere with his exercise of impartiality or cause him to decide the issues of guilt or innocence in any manner other than by a fair interpretation of all the evidence. In this situation, the trial court erred by disallowing the defendant's challenge for cause. *People v Branch* (1977, 3d Dept) 59 AD2d 459, 399 NYS2d 930, affd 46 NY2d 645, 415 NYS2d 985.

It was not error for the trial court to deny defendant's challenge for cause to two prospective jurors, one of whom was excused peremptorily by the defense, because the court could not have concluded, on the statements of each juror in question, that the juror's state of mind was likely to preclude the rendering of an impartial verdict. *People v Fox* (1975, 3d Dept) 47 AD2d 699, 364 NYS2d 592.

§ 4:4 CHALLENGES TO THE FAVOR — A challenge to the favor is similar to one for principal cause, but of lesser degree. *People v Bodine,* 1 Denio 281. Here, the juror's bias is a question of fact, not of law, and it is for the court to determine, based on the evidence given on the challenge. *Butler v Glen Falls, S. H. & F. E. S. R. Co.* (1890) 121 NY 112, 24 NE 187. Thus, when there is a challenge to the favor based on the juror's acquaintance with a party or with counsel, the trial judge's exercise of discretion is required. *Scott v Rues,* (1899) 26 Misc 834, 56 NYS 1057. A showing of more than mere acquaintance or prior business relations with one of the attorneys at some time in the past would be necessary to disqualify the juror. *Scott v Rues, supra.*

By statute, it is a ground for a challenge to the favor if the juror is employed by a party to the action, or in the case of a corporate party, is a shareholder or stockholder of the corporation, or in an action for personal injury or property damage, is a shareholder, officer, director, stockholder, or employee of any insurance company issuing policies for protection against liability damage. CPLR 4110(a).

The fact that a prospective juror resides in, or is liable to pay taxes to, a city, town, village, or county that is a party to the action is not grounds for challenge to the favor to that juror. CPLR 4110(a).

It is improper to order counsel to refrain from asking prospective jurors, individually or as a panel, anything about insurance or insurance companies except the items enumerated in CPLR 4110(a), because this limits the *voir dire* examination and counsel's right to determine whether he should exercise a peremptory challenge. *Graham v Waite* (1965, 4th Dept) 23 AD2d 628, 257 NYS2d 629. If a prospective juror comes within any of the classifications enumerated in CPLR 4110(a) (formerly CPA § 452), a good ground of challenge is presented. *Lindboe v Syracuse Transit Co.* (1940) 175 Misc 396, 23 NYS2d 667. When plaintiff's attorney asked if a juror was a shareholder, stockholder, officer, director, or employee of any insurance company issuing liability policies for personal injury or property damage, defendant's attorney stated that in view of the question, he would inform the jury that defendants were not insured. The court had discretion to grant a mistrial, because the defendant's lack of insurance was immaterial. *Lindboe v Syracuse Transit Co., supra.* A party has a right to waive the provisions of CPLR 4110(a) permit an agent of an insurance company to serve on the jury. *Halper v Broadmain Const. Corp.* (1945, Sup) 60 NYS2d 533.

§ 4:5   THE RIGHT TO A FAIR AND IMPARTIAL JURY — The right to a fair and impartial jury is guaranteed in both civil and criminal cases. New York State Constitution Art 1, § 2. Expediency alone does not warrant denial of the fundamental right to a jury trial, *Kaminsky v Kahn* (1967) 20 NY2d 573, 285 NYS2d 833, and efficiency and low cost cannot be allowed to curtail constitutionally guaranteed rights such as trial by jury. *People v Bowdoin* (1968) 57 Misc 2d 536, 293 NYS2d 748.

The Sixth Amendment of the U.S. Constitution guarantees the right to a trial by an impartial jury in all criminal prosecutions, and, under the Seventh Amendment, in civil suits at common law when the value in controversy exceeds $20. The jury must be impartial at the beginning of the trial and should be influenced only by legal and competent evidence during the trial. *People v Lashkowitz* (1938) 166 Misc 640, 3 NYS2d 98.

A jury in a civil case shall be composed of six persons. CPLR 4104. The first six persons who appear as their names are drawn and called must be sworn and constitute the jury to try the issue if they are approved as indifferent between the parties and are not discharged or excused. CPLR 4105.

Where a fair and impartial person has been sworn in as a juror, he cannot be dismissed at plaintiff's insistence because his business partner is a friend of the defendant's attorney. Dismissal is reversible error. *Santee v Standard Pub. Co.* (1899) 36 AD 555, 55 NYS 361. The error is not obviated merely because the adverse party did not exhaust his peremptory challenges and the jury that tried the case was in fact impartial. *Santee v Standard Pub. Co., supra*.

§ 4:6 METHOD OF SUMMONING JURORS — The lists of citizens qualified to serve as jurors are compiled by the officials authorized by statute. Judiciary Law §§ 502, 509. The various officials required to compile the lists of jurors, conduct drawings of names, notify those selected, and see to attendance are set forth in various statutes. Judiciary Law §§ 502, 506-508, 509.

The term "jury" implies a body of competent and disinterested people. *Blair v McCormack Constr. Co.* (1907) 123 AD 30, 107 NYS 750, affd 195 NY 521, 88 NE 1114.

Although they are taken from a class of people whose qualifications may be arbitrarily fixed by law, jurors are selected by a process that, while constantly changing in form, is designed to obtain the services of intelligent and impartial citizens, *People v Cosmos* (1912) 205 NY 91, 98 NE 408, and to protect parties to lawsuits from the possible prejudices of jurors. *Dulberger v Gimbel Bros.* (1912) 76 Misc 225, 134 NYS 574.

§ 4:7 DISCRIMINATION BECAUSE OF SEX, RACE, ETC. — An intentional, planned, and deliberate exclusion of or discrimination against members of a particular political or economic group, religious faith, race, ancestry, or sex by officers in charge of selecting and summoning a jury violates the due process and equal protection clauses of the Fourteenth Amendment to the U.S. Constitution. *Whitus v Georgia* (1967) 385 US 545, 17 L Ed 2d 599, 87 S Ct 643, conformed to 223 Ga 127, 153 SE2d 446. However, there is no duty on the part of the state to provide a jury made up of a cross-section of the population. *People v Chestnut* (1970) 26 NY2d 481, 311 NYS2d 853. The party challenging the makeup of the jury has the burden of proving the existence of purposeful discrimination. *People v Wright* (1969) 60 Misc 2d 59, 301 NYS2d 825.

There is no constitutional right to a jury drawn from uneducated and unintelligent citizens and no right to a jury chosen only from people at the lower end of the economic and social scale. *People v Cohen* (1967) 54 Misc 2d 873, 283 NYS2d 817. A jury of peers does not mean a jury of persons of identical race or similar background but rather a random selection of persons reflecting a normal cross-section of the community. It is not sufficient to show that a particular class of people is not represented. A party may show, however, that the exclusion of a particular class was deliberate. *People v Henry* (1967) 55 Misc 2d 134, 284 NYS2d 726.

Under *Batson v Kentucky* (1986) 476 US 79, 90 L Ed 2d 69, 106 S Ct 1712, to make a *prima facie* case of discrimination based on the prosecutor's use of peremptory challenges, a criminal defendant must establish that he is a member of a cognizable racial group and any other relevant circumstances that create an inference of discrimination, such as a pattern of strikes against black jurors or the prosecutor's questions and comments during *voir dire*. If defendant meets this burden, the burden shifts to the prosecutor to provide neutral explanations for the use of his peremptory challenges. If the prosecutor fails to do so, the conviction must be reversed. *People v James* (1987, 4th Dept) 132 AD2d 932, 518 NYS2d 266.

The *Batson* rule applies equally in civil cases, and a civil litigant has standing to object to his or her adversary's use of peremptory challenges to exclude persons from the jury on the basis of race. *Edmonson v Leesville Concrete Co.* (1991) 500 US 614, 114 L Ed 2d 660, 111 S Ct 2077, on remand 943 F2d 551 (5th Cir 1991).

The defendants in a civil suit jointly employed nine peremptory challenges to excuse six black and three Latino venirepersons, so that at the time of plaintiff's objection, the only two jurors who had been selected were white. The court found that a *prima facie* showing of racially motivated exclusion had been satisfied. The court then directed defense counsel to offer race neutral explanations for their challenges. The court interviewed the three challenged venirepersons who were still available and, finding no reason to question their assertion that they could and would fairly try the action, ordered that they be seated on the jury. It is not required that the party making the objection be of the same race or heritage as the potential jurors on whose behalf the objection is made. In this case, for example, the plaintiff was white and of Italian ancestry. *Siriano v Beth Israel Hosp. Ctr.* (1994) 161 Misc 2d 512, 614 NYS2d 700.

The court found discrimination in a podiatric malpractice case in which plaintiffs were black and defense counsel used all three of his peremptory challenges to exclude the only potential black jurors. Even though defense counsel offered race neutral explanations for exercising the challenges, the only excuse offered that had any direct bearing on the case was that one of the jurors had undergone extensive podiatric treatment. Even with respect to that juror, however, there was no indication that the juror's experience with treatment had been negative. Because jury selection in civil cases is generally conducted without the presence of a judge, the usual deference given the trial judge's evaluation of non-pretextual, race neutral explanations in criminal cases, where there is a record and the trial judge has had the benefit of observing the demeanor of the attorney exercising the challenge, will not be afforded. Defendant's verdict was reversed and a new trial ordered. *Ancrum v Eisenberg* (1994, 1st Dept) 206 AD2d 324, 615 NYS2d 14, *app dsmd* (1995) 85 NY2d 853, 624 NYS2d 367.

The *Batson* rule also prohibits the exercise of peremptory challenges on the basis of gender. *People v Irizarry* (1990, 1st Dept) 165 AD2d 715, 560 NYS2d 279; *People v Blunt* (1990, 2d Dept) 162 AD2d 86, 561 NYS2d 90, supp op (2d Dept) 176 AD2d 741, 574 NYS2d 812. A male party has standing to object to the exclusion of female jurors. *People v Irizarry, supra.* The fact that not all women were excluded did not vitiate the challenge. *People v Irizarry, supra.*

During *voir dire*, a defendant objected to the prosecutor's use of peremptory challenges. The trial court asked the prosecutor to provide a race-neutral explanation for his challenges, disallowed one of his challenges, and seated a black person on the jury. Because the defendant never moved for a mistrial and did not object to the court's corrective measures, the issue was not properly preserved for appellate review. Nevertheless, the court invoked its interest of justice jurisdiction, and held that the trial judge's actions were appropriate. *People v Steans (Rudy)* (1991, 2d Dept) 174 AD2d 582, 571 NYS2d 85, app den (1991) 78 NY2d 1015, 575 NYS2d 823.

The mere fact that some black persons had not been peremptorily challenged did not establish that there was no *prima facie* showing of discrimination. *People v Jenkins* (1990) 75 NY2d 550, 555 NYS2d 39. The court properly considered that two of the blacks who were not challenged would probably have been challenged by the other side for different reasons. *People v Jenkins, supra.* Even though the jury reflected a statistical cross-section of the community despite improper challenges, the court found that the Equal Protection Clause had been violated, because some blacks had been excluded improperly. *People v Jenkins, supra.*

The prosecutor's explanation for challenging the only two black members of the panel and another member, apparently of Hispanic extraction, was racially neutral, even though the prosecutor conceded that defendant had presented a *prima facie* case of discrimination with respect to the jurors involved. The prosecutor explained that he had excused the minority members because each failed to meet a profile of Ulster County residents with children near the victim's age that had been designed for the case. The record also showed that the prosecution had challenged on a fairly consistent basis other jurors who were single or had children much older than the victim. *People v Gregory ZZ.* (1987, 3d Dept) 134 AD2d 814, 521 NYS2d 873, app den 71 NY2d 905, 527 NYS2d 1014.

Defendant, a black man, established a *prima facie* case that the prosecutor had purposefully discriminated in using peremptory

66

challenges against all four prospective black jurors. None of the excused jurors exhibited signs of bias favoring the defendant, and their backgrounds and knowledge of the case suggested that any bias they might have would favor the prosecution. *People v Mack* (1988, 2d Dept) 143 AD2d 280, 532 NYS2d 161.

The prosecution satisfied its burden of providing a racially neutral explanation for its rejection of two prospective jurors, who were fluent in Spanish and indicated that they would try to respect as authoritative the official court interpreter's translation of evidence given by Spanish-speaking witnesses, but did not state unequivocally that they would rely *only* on the court interpreter's version of the testimony. *People v Hernandez* (1990) 75 NY2d 350, 553 NYS2d 85, affd (1991) 500 US 352, 114 L Ed 2d 395, 111 S Ct 1859.

The defendant's contention that the prosecutor's use of peremptory challenges to strike the only four black venirepersons from the jury was sufficient to make a *prima facie* case of racial discrimination and to require the prosecutor to articulate racially neutral explanations for the exclusion of these individuals. *People v Dove* (1989, 2d Dept) 154 AD2d 705, 546 NYS2d 686.

In light of all the facts of the case and the fact that the prosecutor peremptorily removed more white prospective jurors than black prospective jurors, the defendant failed to make a *prima facie* showing of discriminatory intent in the prosecutor's exercise of peremptory challenges. *People v Smith* (1993, 2d Dept) 196 AD2d 559, 601 NYS2d 142, app den 82 NY2d 903, 610 NYS2d 170

In a prosecution for sexual abuse and incest, the prosecution's use of more than 90% of its peremptory challenges to strike males was sufficient to establish a *prima facie* case of discrimination based on gender and to shift the burden to the prosecution to provide non-discriminatory explanations for its challenges. *People v Allen* (1993, 3d Dept) 199 AD2d 781, 605 NYS2d 503, revd on other grounds (1995) 86 NY2d 101, 629 NYS2d 1003.

§ 4:8 CONDUCT OF *VOIR DIRE* EXAMINATION — A judge must be present at the examination of jurors for a civil trial if one party so requests. CPLR 4107. Counsel for each side examines prospective jurors in order to make peremptory challenges, CPLR 4109, or challenges for cause, CPLR 4110.

The statutory requirement that a party has a right to have a judge present at the examination of jurors if it so requests was not satisfied when the trial court denied defendant's application to continue jury selection in the presence of the court, then later assigned a law assistant to supervise the *voir dire*, and still later presided in person at the selection. *Guarnier v American Dredging Co.* (1988, 1st Dept) 145 AD2d 341, 535 NYS2d 705.

In 1995, the Chief Administrator of the Courts issued new rules governing the conduct of *voir dire* examinations. 22 § NYCRR 202.33. The rules require the judge to establish time limitations for the questioning of prospective jurors. The judge is also to preside at the commencement of the *voir dire* proceeding and determine whether continued judicial supervision is appropriate.

The rules also require the judge to determine which of three accepted methods of jury selection will be used – "White's Method," the "Struck Method," or the "Strike and Replace Method." Standards for the first two methods are set forth in the rules. Use of the Strike and Replace Method is allowed in districts where the specifics of it have been approved by the Chief Administrator, based on experience indicating the method is efficient and orderly.

§ 4:9 QUESTIONING OF JURORS, GENERALLY — Although it is not absolute, the right to examine prospective jurors is conferred by statute, and while the statutes remain in force, all parties may insist on the right. *N. Wagman & Co. v Schafer Motor Freight Service, Inc.* (1938) 167 Misc 681, 4 NYS2d 526.

The right of counsel to question prospective jurors is an important part of a trial, and it is the method by which counsel determines whether a juror is indifferent between the parties. *Fortune v Trainor* (1892, Sup) 19 NYS 598, affd 141 NY 605, 36 NE 740. Any appropriate question designed to elicit the prospective juror's state of mind concerning either the parties or the subject of the action may properly be asked of the individual members of the panel or the entire body. *Fortune v Trainor, supra.* Counsel is entitled to great latitude in examining prospective jurors so that he can determine whether to exercise a peremptory challenge. *Dresch v Elliott* (1910) 137 AD 252, 122 NYS 14. A question involving propositions law is improper. *People v McLaughlin* (1896) 150 NY 365, 44 NE 1017. Information properly elicited would include any possible feeling against the plaintiff or in favor of the defendant. Where a juror had feelings against a plaintiff, it was held to be his duty to have disclosed this fact during the course of his examination as a juror. *Payne v Burke* (1932) 236 AD 527, 260 NYS 259, motion den 262 NY 630, 188 NE 96.

In a suit against a city, plaintiff's counsel asked if any member of the panel had business relations with the city attorney's office either presently or in the past. When no one replied, the attorney stated he would take the failure to reply to mean that no one had any such relations. The subsequent discovery that one juror had business relations with the city attorney's office resulted in a new trial. *McGarry v Buffalo* (1893, Sup) 24 NYS 16. When a member of the panel denied on *voir dire* that plaintiff's counsel had ever done any legal work for him, defendant's counsel was entitled to know that seven years earlier plaintiff's attorney had made a plea for leniency in his behalf. Defendant was entitled to a new trial, even without a claim that the juror was biased or corrupt. *Trafton v New York State Electric & Gas Corp.* (1950) 277 AD 1013, 100 NYS2d 375.

Plaintiff, a paraplegic, had an absolute right to be present during selection of the jury, and that right was not affected by the fact that he was represented by competent counsel. *Carlisle v County of Nassau* (1978, 2d Dept) 64 AD2d 15, 408 NYS2d 114.

§ 4:10 QUESTIONING OF JURORS REGARDING INSURANCE — Although in personal injury and property damage actions it is grounds for mistrial to disclose that defendant is insured, *Herald Nathan Press v Bourges* (1936) 161 Misc 208, 291 NYS 650, or not insured, *Lindboe v Syracuse Transit Co.* (1940) 175 Misc 396, 23 NYS2d 667, it is proper to ask jurors whether they are stockholders, officers, directors, or employees of any insurance company issuing liability policies for damage to property or injury to person. CPLR 4110(a); *Blair v McCormack Constr. Co.* (1907) 123 AD 30, 107 NYS 750, affd 195 NY 521, 80 NE 1114. These relationships constitute grounds for challenge to the favor. CPLR 4110(a). A party is entitled to pursue this type of inquiry fully. *Wood v New York State Electric & Gas Corp.* (1939)

257 AD 172, 12 NYS2d 947, affd 281 NY 797. Thus, it was an improvident exercise of discretion to direct counsel that on a subsequent trial he limit his *voir dire* questions about insurance to those items specifically set forth in CPLR 4110(a), because this limitation would curtail counsel's right to determine if there was any basis for the exercise of a peremptory challenge. *Graham v Waite* (1965, 4th Dept) 23 AD2d 628, 257 NYS2d 629. The right to this inquiry should not be denied merely because it might cause the jury to infer from the questions that the defendant is insured. *Blair v McCormack Constr. Co.* (1907) 123 AD 30, 107 NYS 750, affd 195 NY 521, 88 NE 1114.

A deliberate attempt by plaintiff to convey to the jury the idea that the defendant is insured is ground for reversal, *Goodman v Guida* (1934) 150 Misc 677, 269 NYS 811; counsel has no right to attempt to convey to the jury the fact that defendant is covered by insurance. *Loughlin v Brassil* (1907) 187 NY 128, 79 NE 854.

§ 4:11   SELECTION OF ALTERNATE JURORS — Occasionally, a juror may be become unavailable after the trial has started because of illness or other reason. To avoid the resultant delay, the CPLR provides for the selection of one or two alternate jurors. CPLR 4106. The alternates are drawn at the same time, from the same panel, and in the same manner as the regular jurors and have the same qualifications. CPLR 4106. They are subject to the same *voir dire* examination and to the same types of challenges. CPLR 4106.

The alternates selected are seated with the regular jurors, are given the oath with them, and are treated in the same manner, except that the alternate jurors are discharged by the court after the case is submitted to the jury. CPLR 4106.

If a regular juror dies, becomes ill, or is otherwise unavailable prior to final submission of the case, the court may order him discharged and draw the name of an alternate. The alternate then replaces the discharged juror in the jury box and becomes one of the regular jurors. CPLR 4106.

§ 4:12   NUMBER OF PEREMPTORY CHALLENGES — In a civil case, each party is entitled to three peremptory challenges plus one for each alternate juror. CPLR 4109. When there are more parties on one side than the other, before *voir dire* examination begins, the court may grant additional challenges to the side with the smaller number of challenges. CPLR 4109.

§ 4:13   NO EXEMPTIONS FROM JURY SERVICE — Judiciary Law § 512 formerly exempted from jury service lawyers, doctors, police officers, sole proprietors of businesses, parents who cared at home for children under age 16, and various other categories of individuals. It was repealed in 1995, however, by Chapter 188 of the 1995 Session Laws. Effective January 1, 1996, no otherwise eligible individual is exempt from jury service.

An estimated one million New York residents had been exempt under the law, including 100,000 in Manhattan.

The legislation abolishing the exemptions also expanded Judiciary Law § 517 to allow an automatic postponement of jury service for any prospective juror who has not previously received a postponement, provided the postponement is to a date certain not more than six months from the date service would otherwise have begun. Judiciary Law § 517(a)(2).

Provision was also made for court officials to grant additional postponements in hardship cases. Judiciary Law §517(c). Under regulations issued by the Chief Administrator of the Courts, 22 NYCRR § 128.6a, any subsequent request for a postponement requires a written application, together with documentation showing that jury duty "would result in hardship that was unanticipated at the time of the prior postponement." Unless "extraordinary circumstances" are shown, each prospective juror is limited to three postponements for a maximum of 18 months.

Commissioners may excuse prospective jurors for as long as two years if can show medical incapacity to serve or that service "would cause undue hardship or extreme inconvenience to the prospective juror, a person under his or her care or supervision, or the public."

Provision was also made for prospective jurors to seek exemption "based upon matters of conscience." Decisions on these requests are to be made by a judge rather than a jury commissioner.

§ 4:14 PASSING UPON CHALLENGES FOR CAUSE — A
challenge to an individual juror or to the panel or array of jurors
shall be tried and determined by the court. CPLR 4108; *People v
Decker* (1898) 157 NY 186, 51 NE 1018. The court may require
more evidence to enable it to rule on a challenge. *Butler v Glen
Falls, S. H. & F. E. S. R. Co.* (1890) 121 NY 112, 24 NE 187.

A challenge for principal cause is sufficient by itself to result in
the juror's exclusion, and the court has discretion in the matter,
People v Bodine, 1 Denio 281, because the juror is asserted to be
biased as a matter of law. *Butler v Glens Falls, S. H. & F. E. S. R.
Co., supra.* The court must set the juror aside. *People v Bodine,
supra.* On the other hand, because a challenge to the favor does
not involve bias as a matter of law, the trial court has discretion to
determine whether the juror is indifferent between the parties.
Butler v Glens Falls, S. H. & F. E. S. R. Co., supra.

If the trial judge finds that the juror is not entirely indifferent,
the court has a duty to reject him. *Butler v Glens Falls, S. H. & F.
E. S. R. Co., supra.* The court has discretion to excuse a juror for
good cause at any time before evidence is given and even after the
juror has been sworn but before the taking of evidence. The court
may reject a juror on its own motion if it deems the juror not
competent or not indifferent between the parties. *People v Little*
(1968) 57 Misc 2d 1059, 294 NYS2d 25. The power of the court
is not, however, unlimited, and it may not arbitrarily excuse a
proposed juror who is in all respects qualified to serve. *De Puy v
Quinn* (1891) 61 Hun 237, 16 NYS 708.

An objection made to the court's ruling on a challenge to a juror
is reviewable on appeal. CPLR 5501(a)(3). But if the court determines that the juror is incompetent, its decision should not be
disturbed on appeal unless it is clear that the evidence cannot in
any possible view support the ruling. *Butler v Glens Falls, S. H. &
F. E. S. R. Co., supra.*

Generally, unless an appellant shows that he has been prejudiced because a party to the action was a member of the jury
panel, a judgment will not be reversed on that ground. *Verdow
Chevrolet, Inc. v Dean* (1954) 284 AD 517, 132 NYS2d 202, app
den 284 AD 860, 133 NYS2d 557. Thus, the court held that the
record, in a contract action, disclosed that the defendant had not

been prejudiced by the fact that a nominal plaintiff had been a member of the jury panel. The denial of a new trial on that ground was warranted. *Verdow Chevrolet, Inc. v Dean, supra.*

During a side-bar conference in the course of a criminal trial, one of the jurors made an approving gesture with her hand to the arresting officer who was then on the witness stand. The court erred in not discharging the juror. *People v Sellers* (1979, 2d Dept) 73 AD2d 697, 423 NYS2d 222.

The court erred in denying defendant's challenge for cause of a juror who stated that a year and a half before the trial he had served on a federal grand jury, because Judiciary Law § 511(5) specifically disqualifies a juror on that ground. *People v O'Hare* (1986, 2d Dept) 117 AD2d 757, 498 NYS2d 478.

Judiciary Law § 510(2) requires that a person be less than 76 and not less than 18 years of age to qualify as a juror. The trial court's failure to excuse for cause a prospective juror who was 77 years old denied the defendant a fair trial and under the circumstances constituted reversible error. *People v Anderson* (1986, 1st Dept) 118 AD2d 488, 500 NYS2d 2.

A juror's prior relationship with a witness who testifies at the trial does not automatically disqualify the juror, although it may in a particular case require that the juror be excused. *People v Rentz* (1986) 67 NY2d 829, 501 NYS2d 643. In one case, for example, a juror was acquainted with two prosecution witnesses on an essentially professional basis. Nevertheless, according to the juror's own assessment, the relationship with one of the witnesses was also somewhat intimate. Under those circumstances, the court should have found the juror unqualified to serve. *People v Rentz, supra.*

Most, if not all, jurors bring with them some predispositions of varying intensity when they enter the jury box. Only when it is shown, however that there is a substantial risk that those predispositions will affect the juror's ability to discharge his responsibilities should he be excused for cause. *People v Williams* (1984) 63 NY2d 882, 483 NYS2d 198. The trial court did not err in denying the application of defendant, a black man, to excuse two jurors who had indicated that although they did not associate with blacks and although they did not approve of marriages between blacks and whites and the defendant had a white girlfriend with whom he had a child, they could render a fair and impartial verdict. *People v Williams, supra.*

§ 4:15   NUMBER OF JURORS — A trial jury in a civil case is composed of six persons. CPLR 4104.

§ 4:16   SWEARING THE JURY — The point at which jurors are to be sworn is not controlled by statute, and the trial court may determine whether to swear in each juror individually as he is examined and accepted or to swear in the panel as a body. *People v Fromen* (1954) 284 AD 576, 132 NYS2d 376, app dismd 308 NY 324.

§ 4:17   THE RIGHT OF A PARTY TO BE PRESENT AT *VOIR DIRE* — Jury selection is such a vital and crucial aspect of any trial and the right to an impartial jury is so fundamental that the right to be present during the jury selection process cannot be abrogated except for substantially compelling reasons. *Liquori v Barrow* (1990, 2d Dept) 160 AD2d 843, 554 NYS2d 278.

§ 4:18   JUROR'S DISABILITY AS A DISQUALIFICATION — A hearing-impaired juror was not incapable of serving, because he could speak English fluently, read lips and communicate readily in signed English, and the court was satisfied that his interpreter was competent and could abide by ethical constraints and the court's instructions prohibiting the interpreter from participating in the jury deliberations. *People v Guzman* (1990) 76 NY2d 1, 556 NYS2d 7.

RESEARCH REFERENCES

American Law Reports

12 ALR5th 508, Right to jury trial in action under state civil rights law

9 ALR5th 102, Prospective juror's connection with insurance company as ground for challenge for cause

66 ALR4th 509, Effect of juror's false or erroneous answer on voir dire regarding previous claims or actions against himself or his family

57 ALR4th 1260, Jury: who is lawyer or attorney disqualified or exempt from service, or subject to challenge for cause

52 ALR4th 964, Professional or business relations between proposed juror and attorney as ground for challenge for cause

48 ALR4th 1154, Jury: visual impairment as disqualification

48 ALR4th 747, Jury trial waiver as binding on later state civil trial

39 ALR4th 450, Propriety of asking prospective female jurors questions on voir dire not asked of prospective male jurors, or vice versa

38 ALR4th 267, Effect of juror's false or erroneous answer on voir dire in personal injury or death action as to previous claims or actions for damages by himself or his family

97 ALR3d 434, Validity of statutory classification based on population-jury selection statutes

95 ALR3d 172, Religious belief, affiliation, or prejudice of prospective juror as proper subject of inquiry or ground for challenge on voir dire

86 ALR3d 781, Trial jurors as witnesses in same state court or related case

80 ALR3d 869, Validity of requirement or practice of selecting prospective jurors exclusively from list of registered voters

79 ALR3d 14, Use of peremptory challenge to excuse from jury persons belonging to race or class

78 ALR3d 1147, Validity of enactment requiring juror to be an elector or voter or have qualifications thereof

69 ALR3d 1269, Competency of juror as affected by his membership in co-operative association interested in the case

15 ALR3d 1101, Propriety and prejudicial effect of reference by counsel in civil case to result of former trial of same case, or amount of verdict therein

ALR QUICK INDEX: Jury and Jury Trial

American Jurisprudence 2d

47 AM JUR 2d, Jury §§ 1 et seq.

American Jurisprudence Pleading and Practice

15 AM JUR PL & PR FORMS (Rev), Jury, Forms 1 et seq.

American Jurisprudence Proof of Facts

9 AM JUR PROOF OF FACTS 2d 407, Discrimination in Jury Selection-Systematic Exclusion or Under Representation of Identifiable Group

American Jurisprudence Trials

5 AM JUR TRIALS 143, Selecting the Jury-Plaintiff's View

5 AM JUR TRIALS 247, Selecting the Jury-Defense View

Other Resources

40 L Ed 2d 846, Supreme Court's construction of Seventh Amendment's guaranty of right to trial by jury

8 CARMODY-WAIT 2d, Selection and Impanelment of Jury, §§ 55:1-55:17

Auto-Cite®: Any case citation herein can be checked for form, parallel references, later history and annotation references through the Auto-Cite computer research system.

CHAPTER 5

OPENING STATEMENTS

§ 5:1 OPENING STATEMENTS, IN GENERAL — While strictly speaking this chapter deals with opening statements, the right to open first is inextricably linked with the right to close last. To this extent, the right to sum up last will also be discussed.

§ 5:2 DISMISSAL ON THE OPENING STATEMENT — Dismissals at the conclusion of plaintiff's opening statement are not favored and should be granted only where it is clear that (1) the complaint does not state a cause of action, (2) the cause of action is conclusively defeated by an admitted defense, or (3) counsel has subverted his cause of action by admissions or statements of fact. *O'Leary v American Airlines* (1984, 2d Dept) 100 AD2d 959, 475 NYS2d 285.

A complaint may not be dismissed on counsel's opening unless the facts as alleged and presented by counsel preclude any possibility of plaintiffs' recovery. *DiPasquale v Baker-Roos, Inc.* (1989, 4th Dept) 156 AD2d 941, 548 NYS2d 827.

In a civil case, the court will not grant a motion to dismiss based on the opening statement without first giving plaintiff's attorney an opportunity to correct any defect in the opening statement by making an offer of proof. *De Vito v Katsch* (1990, 2d Dept) 157 AD2d 413, 556 NYS2d 649.

Although dismissing a complaint at the conclusion of counsel's opening statement is clearly not favored, if it becomes obvious on the opening that the action cannot be maintained because it lacks a legal basis or, when taken in its strongest light, cannot succeed, the trial court has the power to dismiss the action. *Giroux v Snedecor* (1991, 3d Dept) 178 AD2d 802, 577 NYS2d 699.

The dismissal of the complaint following the opening statement was affirmed because the allegation that city officials supervised the demolition of buildings adjacent to a section of sidewalk where plaintiff fell did not satisfy the city's written notice requirement. *Jackson v City of Mount Vernon* (1995, 3d Dept) 213 AD2d 292, 623 NYS2d 658, app den 85 NY2d 812, 631 NYS2d 288.

§ 5:3   RIGHT TO MAKE AN OPENING STATEMENT — Before any evidence is offered, counsel for each plaintiff having a separate right and for each defendant having a separate right may make an opening statement. CPLR 4016. At the conclusion of the evidence, counsel for each such party may make a closing statement in inverse order to the opening statements. CPLR 4016.

Where several parties appear separately and each has separate and distinct interests, each may make an opening and closing statement to permit counsel to explain the nature of the action and to indicate what he expects to prove in the course of the trial. *Lyman v Fidelity & Casualty Co.* (1901) 65 AD 27, 72 NYS 498.

For the plaintiff, who has the affirmative on all issues of fact raised by denials in the answer, the right to open and close is a substantial one. *Gibbs v Sokol* (1926) 216 AD 260, 214 NYS 533. This right is not dependent on the trial judge's discretion; a party who is deprived of this right by an erroneous ruling is entitled to a new trial. *Elwell v Chamberlin* (1864) 31 NY 611.

The purpose of the opening address is to clarify the issues for the jury. *Tisdale v Delaware & Hudson Canal Co.* (1889) 116 NY 416, 22 NE 700.

§ 5:4   CONTENT OF THE OPENING STATEMENTS — The plaintiff's opening is a brief statement of the nature of the action, the issues to be tried, and the facts he expects to prove. *Kley v Healy* (1891) 127 NY 555, 28 NE 593. Defendant's opening should be limited to answering plaintiff's case and indicating the evidence he proposes to introduce. *Ayrault v Chamberlain*, 33 Barb 229.

While the court may restrain undue license on counsel's part in addressing the jury, *Walsh v People* (1882) 88 NY 458, whether the court will interfere with counsel in his opening address is generally a matter within the trial judge's discretion. *Walsh v People, supra.*

§ 5:5 ORDER OF OPENING — The right of a party to open first and close last is governed by the pleadings. *Lake Ontario Nat'l Bank v Judson* (1890) 122 NY 278, 25 NE 367. Ordinarily plaintiff is entitled to open if he has anything whatsoever to prove on the issue of damages, *Huntington v Conkey*, 33 Barb 218, even if he seeks exemplary damages, because damages are an integral part of plaintiff's case. *Parrish v Sun Printing & Publishing Ass'n* (1896) 6 AD 585, 39 NYS 540.

One rule for ascertaining which party has the right to open first and close last is to determine which party will have the verdict if no evidence is produced. *Heilbronn v Herzog* (1900) 165 NY 98, 58 NE 759. If the plaintiff is entitled to recover on the pleadings without giving any evidence, the defendant has the right to open and close. *Heilbronn v Herzog, supra.* If, however, the plaintiff must prove anything whatsoever in order to prevent a verdict against him, he has the right to open and close. *Lake Ontario Nat. Bank v Judson, supra.*

The test of a plaintiff's right to open first and close last is whether he is entitled to recover on all the causes of action alleged in the complaint without submitting any proof. *Burke v National Liberty Ins. Co.* (1925) 212 AD 738, 209 NYS 608. If a defendant admits all the essential allegations of the complaint and interposes an affirmative defense, he may be able to deprive the plaintiff of the right to open first and close last. *Conselyea v Swift* (1886) 103 NY 604, 9 NE 489. Thus, it is possible for a defendant to obtain the right to open first and close last by framing his answer in such a way that it leaves no triable issue as to any of the essential allegations in the complaint, *Burke v National Liberty Ins. Co., supra*, leaving defendant the burden of proof or requiring no evidence from the plaintiff. *Lake Ontario Nat. Bank v Judson, supra.*

The order of opening cannot, however, be determined by admissions or withdrawal of denials made at the trial, unless all issues are admitted in favor of the party with the affirmative. *Parrish v Sun Printing & Publishing Ass'n, supra.* The issues may be changed only by amending the pleadings. *Lake Ontario Nat. Bank v Judson, supra.*

When an issue of release is tried separately in a negligence action, defendant has the burden of proof and, therefore, has the right to open first and close last. *Flaherty v Wunsch* (1941, Sup) 28 NYS2d 178.

In an action to recover the proceeds of a life insurance policy, the defendant insurance company effectively denied an essential allegation of plaintiff's *prima facie* case that was specifically pleaded in the complaint, that is, that all conditions had been performed and that the policy was in full force and effect. By interposing the affirmative defense of material misrepresentation, the defendant thereby gave plaintiff the ultimate burden of establishing that a valid contract existed that was binding on the defendant and gave plaintiff the consequent right to open first and close last to the jury. *Di Filippi v Equitable Life Assurance Soc.* (1978, 2d Dept) 61 AD2d 168, 401 NYS2d 532, rev'd on other grounds 45 NY2d 939, 411 NYS2d 562.

If two parties each have the right to open first and close last on different affirmative issues and each party claims it, the court has discretion to determine which party has the right. *Re Brown's Estate* (1932) 144 Misc 440, 259 NYS 275. Only an abuse of the court's discretion would be error. *Re Brown's Estate, supra.*

In a consolidated case, the right to open first and close last is ordinarily given to the plaintiff in the action first begun. *Brink's Express Co. v Burns* (1930) 230 AD 559, 245 NYS 649. This is true even if the first action was begun in a court of lesser jurisdiction. *Rothman v Universal Sportwear, Inc.* (1945, Sup) 52 NYS2d 876, affd 269 AD 743, 54 NYS2d 706. A plaintiff who moves to consolidate subsequent actions commenced against him by the defendant does not thereby waive his right to open first and close last. *Van Devort v K. & H. Evaporating Co.* (1937) 252 AD 8, 297 NYS 277.

While the general rule is that in consolidated actions the right to open first and close last goes to the party who commenced the first action, there are exceptions when justice requires. *Lee v*

Schmeltzer (1930) 229 AD 206, 242 NYS 34. Thus, by evading service, a defendant was able to commence an action against the plaintiff one day before the latter started his suit. Nevertheless, the plaintiff was given the right to open first and close last. *Phil-Or Textile Shrinking Corp. v Monarch Textile Shrinking Corp.* (1936) 160 Misc 610, 290 NYS 377.

The right to open and close may be waived. *Bender v Terwilliger* (1900) 48 AD 371, 63 NYS 269, affd (1901) 166 NY 590, 59 NE 1118. If the party who has this right fails to claim it and permits the other party to open and carry the burden of presenting the evidence, he may not claim the right to close last. *Bender v Terwilliger, supra*.

Defendants waived any right they might have had to open first by failing to object or even request that they be permitted to do so pending the court's decision on which side had the burden of proof. Indeed, they affirmatively agreed with the court that the decision could be postponed until the close of the evidence. *Koo v Robert Koo Wine & Liquor* (1994, 1st Dept) 203 AD2d 180, 611 NYS2d 4.

RESEARCH REFERENCES

American Law Reports

71 ALR4th 130, Propriety of trial court order limiting time for opening or closing argument in civil case–state cases

ALR QUICK INDEX: Argument of Counsel

American Jurisprudence 2d

75A AM JUR 2d, Trial §§ 513-532

75 AM JUR 2d, Trial §§ 68-71, 202-210

Other Resources

8 CARMODY-WAIT 2d, Presentation of the Case §§ 56:2-56:7

Auto-Cite®: Any case citation herein can be checked for form, parallel references, later history and annotation references through the Auto-Cite computer research system.

CHAPTER 6

ORDER OF PROOF

§ 6:1 RIGHT TO OPEN AND CLOSE — The party holding the affirmative of the issues joined in the pleadings has the right to open and close. *Lake Ontario Nat. Bank v Judson* (1890) 122 NY 278, 25 NE 367. That party is ordinarily the plaintiff, for if the plaintiff must prove anything whatsoever, no matter how slight, he has the right to open and close. *Lake Ontario Nat. Bank v Judson, supra.* If, however, the plaintiff is entitled to recover on the pleadings without giving any evidence, defendant is entitled to open and close, *Heilbronn v Herzog* (1900) 165 NY 98, 58 NE 759, because the affirmative of the issue then rests with the defendant. *Heilbronn v Herzog, supra.* If both parties have a burden of proof, as, for example when defendant has interposed an affirmative defense, plaintiff has the right to open and close. But if defendant admits the entire cause of action and pleads an affirmative defense, he has the right to open and close. *Lake Ontario Nat. Bank v Judson, supra.*

The right to open and close is a substantial right and is not dependent on the court's discretion. *Goldberg v Alois* (1956) 3 Misc 2d 154, 154 NYS2d 273. In other words, the trial court has no discretion to change the proper order of opening and closing. *Goldberg v Alois, supra.* The right to open and close may, however, be waived. *Bender v Terwilliger* (1900) 48 AD 371, 63 NYS 269, affd 166 NY 590, 59 NE 1118.

§ 6:2 ORDER OF PRODUCING TESTIMONY — The party having the right to open and close normally puts in all his evidence before he rests. *Seguin v Berg* (1940) 260 AD 284, 21 NYS2d 291. He may not put in merely enough evidence to make out a *prima facie* case and reserve the rest for a later stage of trial. *Seguin v Berg, supra*. The adversary then produces all of his proof. *Seguin v Berg, supra*. After the adversary has put in his proof, evidence in rebuttal is heard. *Seguin v Berg, supra*.

Ordinarily, the party bearing the burden of proof is obligated to complete his *prima facie* case before the opposing party must present his proof. *Roberts v St. Francis Hospital* (1983, 3d Dept) 96 AD2d 272, 470 NYS2d 716.

Plaintiff may not reopen his case after defendant has closed and under the guise of rebuttal, present evidence in support of his burden of proof under the pleadings. *Seguin v Berg, supra*. Despite the general rule, however, the court has the discretion to allow a departure from the rule and to permit a party to reopen and correct defects in evidence that have inadvertently occurred. *Seguin v Berg, supra*.

Appellant's expert physician was present in court before the summations commenced, and appellant applied at that time to have the doctor testify. The court should have granted the application, particularly since appellant's case on the issue of liability rested mainly on the testimony of her expert medical witness. *Raphael v Booth Memorial Hospital* (1974, 2d Dept) 46 AD2d 894, 361 NYS2d 704.

In negligence actions, bifurcation of trials on the issues of liability and damages has become the preferred procedure in appropriate cases. 22 NYCRR § 202.42; *Caputo v Joseph J. Sarcona Trucking Co.* (1994, 2d Dept) 204 AD2d 507, 611 NYS2d 655. However, separate trials on the issues of liability and damages should not be held when the nature of the injuries has an important bearing on the issue of liability. *Schwartz v Binder* (1982, 2d Dept) 91 AD2d 660, 457 NYS2d 109.

The general rule is that neither party has the right to introduce his own evidence when cross-examining the other's witnesses. *Neil v Thorn* (1882) 88 NY 270. Nevertheless, the trial judge has discretion to admit such evidence on cross-examination. *Neil v*

Thorn, supra. To the extent the court does permit such questions, the cross-examiner makes the witness his own and is limited by the rules governing direct examination. *People ex rel. Phelps v Court of Oyer & Terminer* (1881) 83 NY 436.

The trial court may in its discretion vary the order of proof. *People v Reeves* (1989, 1st Dept) 156 AD2d 305, 548 NYS2d 690, app den 76 NY2d 741, 558 NYS2d 903.

§ 6:3 REBUTTAL TESTIMONY — Rebuttal evidence may contradict the witnesses produced by the adversary, corroborate those introduced by a party on his case in chief, or negative some affirmative fact that the answering party has attempted to prove. *Marshall v Davies* (1879) 78 NY 414. After a party rests his case, he has no legal right to reopen it and put in evidence that might have been produced before he rested. *Marshall v Davies, supra*. A party holding the affirmative is required to produce all the evidence before he closes. He must exhaust all testimony in support of the issue on his side before the opposite side has been heard. *Marshall v Davies, supra*.

Reception of rebuttal testimony is a matter for the trial court's discretion. *Lisanti v William F. Kenny Co.* (1928) 225 AD 129, 232 NYS 103, affd 250 NY 621, 166 NE 347. A party may not introduce evidence in support of his case in chief under the pretense of introducing rebuttal evidence, *Gibson v Johnson* (1897) 21 Misc 59, 46 NYS 870. Such evidence is properly excluded. *Gibson v Johnson, supra*. Evidence offered in rebuttal is admissible, not to establish the party's case, but to defeat that which the adversary asserts against him. *Seguin v Berg* (1940) 260 AD 284, 21 NYS2d 291.

Thus, evidence that plaintiff could have offered as part of his affirmative case but may not offer after defendant has rested may still be introduced by plaintiff if it tends to impeach or discredit defendant's testimony. Where, therefore, evidence would have been proper as part of a plaintiff's affirmative case, even though he has no right to offer this after defendant has rested, he may still offer such evidence if it tends to impeach or discredit defendant's testimony, *Seguin v Berg, supra*. Additionally, the trial judge, in the exercise of discretion, may allow a departure from the rule and permit a party to reopen and supply evidence that has been inadvertently omitted. *Seguin v Berg, supra.*

In an action based on negligence, the court abused its discretion in refusing to permit plaintiff to testify in rebuttal following the close of defendant's evidence, because it appeared that her testimony would have contradicted, impeached, or discredited defendant's testimony. *Eisner v Daitch Crystal Dairies, Inc.* (1967, 1st Dept) 27 AD2d 921, 279 NYS2d 247. It was error to exclude testimony offered in rebuttal that would have answered the defendant's contention. *Odell v McGrath* (1897) 21 AD 252, 47 NYS 601. However, in a wrongful death action based on the statute providing for recovery if injury or death is caused by the illegal sale of liquor to an intoxicated person, on plaintiff's case in chief, plaintiff had established only inferentially and by circumstantial evidence that a bartender had served decedent liquor. The trial court improvidently exercised its discretion in permitting a witness offered by plaintiff in rebuttal to testify unequivocally that defendant's bartender had served beer to the decedent while the latter was drunk. *Kerfein v Bruno* (1965, 4th Dept) 23 AD2d 961, 261 NYS2d 240.

The question of whether to permit the introduction of rebuttal evidence rests within the sound discretion of the trial court. The court's decision in that regard should not be disturbed on appeal absent a clear abuse or improvident exercise of discretion. *Capone v Gannon* (1989, 2d Dept) 150 AD2d 749, 542 NYS2d 199.

The trial court did not abuse its discretion in allowing the plaintiff to call a rebuttal witness to respond to the contention of defendants' expert that cranioplasty is a cosmetic procedure and has no effect on speech or seizure disorders. When and in what order evidence should be introduced are matters within the trial court's discretion. *Rigatti v Leventhal* (1992, 2d Dept) 181 AD2d 726, 581 NYS2d 354.

The trial court did not improvidently exercise its discretion in denying the request of plaintiff's decedent to present rebuttal evidence, because the evidence could have been presented during her direct case and would merely have served to bolster her case. *Harvin v New York City Transit Auth.* (1993, 2d Dept) 198 AD2d 401, 603 NYS2d 893.

At the trial, any party may rebut any relevant evidence contained in a deposition, whether introduced by that party or by any other party. CPLR 3117(d).

§ 6:4 RIGHT TO INTRODUCE TESTIMONY AT LATER STAGE — Ordinarily, a party who rests his case may not as a matter of right reopen his case and present evidence in support of his claim or defense that could have been introduced before he rested. *Marshall v Davies* (1879) 78 NY 414. Thus, in an action for injuries resulting from an allegedly defective condition of a highway, when plaintiff rested without proving that the city had notice of the defect, the court did not abuse its discretion in refusing to permit plaintiff to recall a witness. *MacCormack v Brooklyn & Queens Transit Corp.* (1943) 266 AD 735, 40 NYS2d 718. Parties who have rested will ordinarily be compelled by the court to abide by their decision to do so, particularly when they have had an adequate opportunity to present evidence. *Mohawk Carpet Mills, Inc. v State* (1940) 173 Misc 319, 17 NYS2d 780. However, a motion to reopen the case for further proof after the case has been completed but before judgment is rendered is addressed to the discretion of the court. If the proffered evidence may aid materially in the determination of the case, even though it is cumulative, the motion should be granted, provided there has been no inexcusable default or delay by the party making the motion. *Mohawk Carpet Mills, Inc. v State, supra.*

The trial court erred in refusing to grant a short adjournment when the defendant's expert witness in a medical malpractice case was en route to court but arrived late because the cross-examination of prior witnesses was much shorter than had been anticipated. The court also erred by refusing to reopen the case when the witness arrived after counsel had begun his summation "under protest." *Castro v Beekman Downtown Hospital* (1973, 1st Dept) 43 AD2d 537, 349 NYS2d 683. See also *M. Schottenfeld & Sons, Inc. v Kasabali* (1956) 5 Misc 2d 562, 158 NYS2d 814.

The order of introducing evidence and the time when it may be introduced are matters generally within the sound discretion of the trial court. *Feldsberg v Nitschke* (1980) 49 NY2d 636, 427 NYS2d 751. The trial court has the power to permit the introduction of evidence after the close of the offeror's case or to prohibit its introduction. *Feldsberg v Nitschke, supra.*

After the case has been closed and the jury dismissed, the court has no power to reopen the case for further taking of testimony. *Kram v Manufacturers' Trust Co.* (1933) 238 AD 680, 265 NYS2d 541, motion den 240 AD 812, 266 NYS 942. Thus, in a replevin action in which plaintiff failed to prove the value of part of the stock sued for and the jury returned a verdict "for the plaintiff in full" without fixing the value, the case had to be retried. *Kram v Manufacturers Trust Co., supra.*

The court erred in imposing conditions for the reopening of hearings, because the inability to procure testimony was not the fault of the moving party. *Morgenbesser v Tartasky* (1932) 235 AD 697, 255 NYS 501. In a hearing to determine if damages were sustained by vendors because of an attempted wrongful rescission by purchasers of a contract for purchase of realty, a motion to reopen was made after both sides had rested but before the issue of damages was decided. The court had the discretion to allow the hearing to be reopened for further proof to complete the record. *Mayer v Manufacturers Trust Co.* (1957) 11 Misc 2d 359, 170 NYS2d 43.

During the argument of a motion for nonsuit and before the jury was recalled to the courtroom, the attorney for plaintiffs stated he had inadvertently failed to elicit certain testimony regarding the speed of an automobile just prior to the accident. Because the testimony would have raised a question of fact for the jury if it had been admitted, the court should have granted plaintiffs' motion to reopen the case, and a new trial was ordered. *Hollenbeck v Hollenbeck* (1955) 286 AD 937, 142 NYS2d 911, reh den 286 AD 977, 144 NYS2d 722. In an appropriate case, the court must, in the interests of justice, grant an application to reopen the trial for the taking of pertinent testimony or for receiving relevant documents if the application is made after summation but before the charge to the jury. *Engelberg v Putter* (1955, App Tm) 146 NYS2d 291.

A plaintiff's motion to reopen and present additional proof made immediately after he has rested and before any offer of proof by the defendant should be granted in the absence of a showing of prejudice to the defendant. *Salzman v Alan S. Rosell, D.D.S., P.C.* (1987, 3d Dept) 129 AD2d 833, 513 NYS2d 846.

The trial court did not abuse its discretion when it refused to permit plaintiff to present a rebuttal witness at the close of all the evidence. The evidence that plaintiff sought to present on rebuttal could have been presented during his direct case and the exclusion of that evidence was not fatal. *Gobbelet v Hit Cycle Corp.* (1986, 2d Dept) 121 AD2d 682, 504 NYS2d 55.

The trial court erred in dismissing the complaint against defendant doctors at the conclusion of plaintiff's case. The court should have exercised its power to do substantial justice by permitting the plaintiff to reopen his case, thus affording him an opportunity to introduce testimony the court found lacking and thereby insuring his right to have his case adjudicated on the merits. *Kennedy v Peninsula Hospital Center* (1987, 2d Dept) 135 AD2d 788, 522 NYS2d 671.

Even if the trial court had been correct in its determination that plaintiff failed to establish causation, the court erred in denying her motion to reopen so that further testimony could be introduced on this issue. *Harding v Noble Taxi Corp.* (1992, 1st Dept) 182 AD2d 365, 582 NYS2d 1003.

RESEARCH REFERENCES

American Law Reports

79 ALR Fed 812, Propriety of ordering separate trials as to liability and damages, under Rule 42(b) of Federal Rules of Civil Procedure, in contract actions

79 ALR Fed 220, Propriety of ordering separate trials as to liability and damages, under Rule 42(b) of Federal Rules of Civil Procedure, in civil rights actions

78 ALR Fed 890, Propriety of ordering separate trials as to liability and damages, under Rule 42(b) of Federal Rules of Civil Procedure, in actions involving personal injury, death, or property damage

ALR QUICK INDEX: Evidence

American Jurisprudence 2d

75 AM JUR 2d, Trial §§ 145-161

American Jurisprudence Pleading and Practice

23 Am Jur Pl & Pr Forms (Rev), Trial, Forms 76-78

American Jurisprudence Trials

52 Am Jur Trials 1, Commonsense Principles of Civil Litigation

5 Am Jur Trials 695, Courtroom Semantics §§ 112-114

5 Am Jur Trials 505, Mapping the Trial-Order of Proof

Other Resources

8 Carmody-Wait 2d, Presentation of the Case §§ 56:104- 56:107

Auto-Cite®: Any case citation herein can be checked for form, parallel references, later history and annotation references through the Auto-Cite computer research system.

CHAPTER 7

BURDEN OF PROOF

§ 7:1 BURDEN OF PROOF AND BURDEN OF GOING FOR-WARD — The burden of proof is the duty of a party to establish the truth of a given proposition by that quantum of evidence demanded by the law in the type of case on trial. *Anderson v Material Co-ordinating Agency, Inc.* (1946, Sup) 63 NYS2d 324. In a civil case, the party must satisfy this burden by a preponderance of the evidence. *Parker v Culler Furniture Co.* (1951) 278 AD 135, 103 NYS2d 710, reh and app den 278 AD 808, 104 NYS2d 798. This burden rests with the party who, based on the pleadings, must convince the trier of the facts that the proposition is true. *Whitlatch v Fidelity & Casualty Co.* (1896) 149 NY 45, 43 NE 405, reh den 149 NY 600, 44 NE 1129.

The burden of proof, in the sense of establishing the truth of a given proposition, remains from first to last on the party on whom the law placed it at the start of the trial. *Doheny v Lacy* (1901) 168 NY 213, 61 NE 255. The burden of proof never shifts during the course of the trial regardless of any presumptions that

91

shift the burden of going forward. *Plumb v Richmond L. & R. Co.* (1922) 233 NY 285, 135 NE 504, 25 ALR 685.

Unlike the burden of proof, the burden of going forward with the evidence may shift from party to party throughout the trial. *Re Braunfeld's Estate* (1936) 159 Misc 687, 288 NYS 367, affd 249 AD 805, 293 NYS 509. At any given stage of the trial, the burden of going forward will be on the party who is required to meet a *prima facie* case of his adversary, *Coler v Corn Exchange Bank* (1928) 250 NY 136, 164 NE 882, 65 ALR 879, affd 280 US 218, 74 L Ed 378, 50 S Ct 94, or to overcome a presumption. *Plumb v Richmond L. & R. Co., supra.*

In a case involving *res ipsa loquitur,* if the defendant offers a satisfactory explanation, plaintiff must rebut it with evidence of negligence. *Plumb v Richmond L. & R. Co., supra.*

A presumption arising after some evidence has been presented may help a party to satisfy the ultimate burden of proof and will shift to his adversary the burden of going forward with the evidence. *Plumb v Richmond L. & R. Co., supra.* Thus, where a passenger proves he delivered merchandise in good condition to a carrier and the loss of the merchandise is unexplained, the passenger has made out a *prima facie* case. *Saleeby v Central R. Co.* (1904) 99 AD 163, 90 NYS 1042, affd 184 NY 597, 77 NE 1196.

In some cases, the burden of proof is determined by statute. Thus, in a hearing on a complaint that challenged a dismissal or a finding of ineligibility based on subversive activities pursuant to Civil Service Law § 105, the party who dismissed the employee or made the order of ineligibility has the burden of proof. Civil Service § 105(2). Similarly, Multiple Dwelling Law § 37 provides that the owner of a building who wishes to avoid liability arising from the failure to provide artificial lighting in hallways and vestibules by claiming that the light was extinguished without his knowledge or consent has the burden of proving such lack of knowledge or consent. Multiple Dwelling Law § 37(2).

The rules providing that the burden of proof rests on a party's adversary constitute a substantial right. *Anderson v Material Co-ordinating Agency, Inc.* (1946, Sup) 63 NYS2d 324.

Where the instrumentality that was the proximate cause of the accident was identified as belonging to the defendant, it was appropriate to infer that it was under the defendant's operation and control, and the defendant was required to rebut the inference by more than a mere denial. *Demogenes v Village Carting Co.* (1974, 1st Dept) 44 AD2d 155, 354 NYS2d 7.

A defendant that failed to produce two of its employees at the trial bore the burden of showing that it was unable to produce one or both of these witnesses. *Grun v Sportsman, Inc.* (1977, 2d Dept) 58 AD2d 802, 396 NYS2d 250.

Although the inference created by *res ipsa loquitur* does not mandate that defendants come forward with rebuttal proof, defendants have the burden of explanation and should present evidence for the jury to weigh against the inference of negligence. *Loeffler v Rogers* (1988, 3d Dept) 136 AD2d 824, 523 NYS2d 660.

In a slip-and-fall case in which defendant presents evidence that no foreign substance or residue could conceivably have been on the floor because no wax was used, plaintiff must then show that a slippery foreign substance was in fact present or that the floor was improperly maintained. Absent such a showing, the complaint should be dismissed as a matter of law. *Katz v New York Hosp.* (1991, 1st Dept) 170 AD2d 345, 566 NYS2d 46.

In a case based on Labor Law § 240(1), if plaintiff shows that a scaffold collapsed without any apparent cause, the burden shifts to the defendant to submit evidentiary facts that would raise a factual issue on liability. *Bras v Atlas Constr. Corp.* (1990, 2d Dept) 166 AD2d 401, 560 NYS2d 467.

In an action arising out of a slip and fall on broken eggs on the floor of a store, defendants made a *prima facie* showing that they neither created the condition causing the fall nor had actual or constructive notice of its existence. The burden then shifted to plaintiffs to come forward with evidentiary proof sufficient to raise triable issues of fact. *Salty v Altamont Assocs.* (1993, 3d Dept) 198 AD2d 591, 603 NYS2d 352.

§ 7:2 BURDEN OF PROOF, GENERALLY — In a civil case, the plaintiff has the burden of proving his case by a fair preponderance of the evidence. *Kennealy v Westchester E. R. Co.* (1903) 86 AD 293, 83 NYS 823, affd 181 NY 582, 74 NE 1119. This means that if the evidence is equal on both sides, the verdict should be for the defendant. *Kennealy v Westchester E. R. Co., supra*.

Preponderance of proof requires that the evidence offered by one side shall outweigh in probability the evidence offered to contradict it. *Commissioner of Public Welfare v Ryan* (1933) 238 AD 607, 265 NYS 286. Preponderance of proof not hinge merely on the number of witnesses, because the jury may believe one witness over a number of witnesses, even where the one witness is a party. *Devonshire v Stubbs* (1930) 135 Misc 886, 238 NYS 707.

In a civil action for the intentional tort of fraud, however, all the elements of fraud must be established by clear and convincing evidence. *Simcuski v Saeli* (1978) 44 NY2d 442, 406 NYS2d 259; *Stephenson v Lord* (1979, 3d Dept) 72 AD2d 857, 421 NYS2d 730.

When a defendant claims release as a defense and the plaintiff claims the release is void because it was induced by false representation, the defendant has the burden of proof in a separate trial on the issue. *Boxberger v New York, N. H. & H. R. Co.* (1923) 237 NY 75, 142 NE 357.

Ordinarily, a party defending a suit on the basis of a release has a presumption in his favor that there have been no irregularities in the execution of the release. This presumption is sufficient to establish a *prima facie* case if the party can also prove the authenticity of the signature on the document. *Fleming v Ponziani* (1969) 24 NY2d 105, 299 NYS2d 134. The proof of authenticity shifts the burden of going forward to the plaintiff to show fraud, duress, or some other fact sufficient to void the release. *Fleming v Ponziani, supra*. Once the latter puts in some evidence, the presumption is no longer in the case, and the burden is on the party defending the action and claiming a release. *Fleming v Ponziani, supra*.

The plaintiff has the burden of proving that a release was based on a mutual mistake of fact, because she is the party seeking to set the release aside. *Elson v Delaney* (1975, 4th Dept) 47 AD2d 708, 365 NYS2d 572.

One seeking to overturn the generality of a release has the burden of establishing that he did not intend more than a limited release, that he did not know of later revealed injuries, and that different injuries are involved rather than unanticipated consequences of known injuries. *Mangini v McClurg* (1969) 24 NY2d 556, 301 NYS2d 508. The burden of persuasion has been held to be on the party who seeks to set the release aside on grounds of mutual mistake. *Mangini v McClurg, supra*. When a release is obtained in violation of a statute prohibiting entering a hospital within 15 days after the patient is injured to obtain a general release from the patient, the burden of proof is on the party seeking to use the release defensively. *Fleming v Ponziani, supra*.

The burden of proving the allegations necessary to warrant imposition of a constructive trust were on the plaintiff. *Cassidy v Cassidy* (1955) 309 NY 332, motion den 309 NY 966. When plaintiff demonstrates a *prima facie* case of fraud and undue influence, although the burden of proof does not shift, the burden of going forward with the evidence shifts to defendant. *Cassidy v Cassidy, supra*.

Plaintiff has the burden of proving damages. *Kauders v Gorki* (1957) 8 Misc 2d 948, 160 NYS2d 975. However, in order to prevent a recovery of full consequential damages on the ground that the injured party failed to minimize damages, the burden is on the wrongdoer to prove failure to mitigate. *Consolidated Box Co. v Penn* (1958) 15 Misc 2d 705, 180 NYS2d 831.

An agent who has a duty to account has the burden of showing proper disposition of all monies paid to him if he admits receiving the funds and commingling them with his own. *Aircheck, Inc. v Felder* (1954, Sup) 133 NYS2d 790.

When a property owner claims the right to exemption from property taxes, the burden is on the party seeking the exemption. *People ex rel. Watchtower Bible & Tract Soc. v Mastin* (1948) 191 Misc 899, 80 NYS2d 323.

When a qualified privilege has been shown to exist in a libel action, the burden of proof shifts to the plaintiff to demonstrate that the communication was not made in good faith but was solely the product of malice. Mere conclusory allegations or charges based on conjecture, surmise, and suspicion are insufficient to defeat the qualified privilege defense. *Paskiewicz v NAACP* (1995, 2d Dept) ___ AD2d ___, 628 NYS2d 405; *Kamerman v Kolt* (1994, 2d Dept) 210 AD2d 454, 621 NYS2d 97.

In a false arrest case, the defendant has the burden of proving legal justification as an affirmative defense. *Gebbie v Gertz Div. of Allied Stores*, Inc. (1983, 2d Dept) 94 AD2d 165, 463 NYS2d 482. On the other hand, in an action for malicious prosecution, the plaintiff has the burden of proving the absence of probable cause for the criminal proceeding. *Gebbie v Gertz Div. of Allied Stores, Inc., supra*.

Although a party breaching a contract bears the risk of any uncertainty regarding the amount of damages, the plaintiff must first establish that he has, in fact, suffered loss of profits. *Kenford Co. v County of Erie* (1985, 4th Dept) 108 AD2d 132, 489 NYS2d 939, affd, in part 67 NY2d 257, 502 NYS2d 131.

In an action on an insurance policy, the insured has the burden of proving that a valid insurance policy was in full force and effect and that the loss incurred was within the policy's coverage. The insurer then bears the burden of demonstrating that an exclusion contained in the policy defeats the claim. *Moneta Dev. Corp. v Generali Ins. Co.* (1995, 1st Dept) 212 AD2d 428, 622 NYS2d 930.

A liability insurance carrier that seeks to defeat coverage by claiming a lack of cooperation by the insured bears the burden of showing that the circumstances support the inference that the insured's failure to cooperate was deliberate. *Mount Vernon Fire Ins. Co. v 170 E. 106th St. Rlty. Corp.* (1995, 1st Dept) 212 AD2d 419, 622 NYS2d 758, app den 86 NY2d 707, 632 NYS2d 500.

In order to maintain a claim of duress, the aggrieved party must demonstrate that threats of an unlawful act compelled him or her to perform an act that he or she had the legal right to abstain from performing. *Polito v Polito* (1986, 2d Dept) 121 AD2d 614, 503 NYS2d 867, app dismd 68 NY2d 981, 510 NYS2d 564. Evidence that a wife had signed a release of her interest in the marital residence as a result of threats and violence against her sufficiently established that she had executed the release as a result of duress rather than of her own free will. Therefore, she was entitled to rescission of the release and to reformation of the deed to the property to reflect her ownership of the property as a joint tenant. *Polito v Polito, supra*.

Defendant who sets forth an affirmative defense in his answer preserves his right to present evidence on the issue raised by the defense, but that has no effect on the plaintiff's burden of proof. She must still establish her case by a preponderance of the credible evidence. *Palmier v United States Fidelity & Guaranty Co.* (1987, 3d Dept) 135 AD2d 1057, 523 NYS2d 192.

In an action brought by the purchaser of realty against the vendor-contractor for breach of contract and/or breach of warranty, the plaintiffs had the burden of demonstrating the extent of the damages incurred based on the reasonable cost of replacing or completing the defective work. *Cotazino v Basil Dev. Corp.* (1990, 3d Dept) 167 AD2d 632, 562 NYS2d 988.

Because defendants did not submit evidence of collateral source payments for the court's consideration, the court did not err in failing to reduce the award pursuant to CPLR 4545. *Hill v Muchow* (1991, 4th Dept) 178 AD2d 954, 579 NYS2d 254.

The defendant bears the burden of proof on an affirmative defense, including one that asserts that the plaintiff is not the real party in interest. *Brignoli v Balch, Hardy & Scheinman, Inc.* (1991, 1st Dept) 178 AD2d 290, 577 NYS2d 375.

A defense based on documentary evidence can succeed if the documents submitted resolve all factual issues as a matter of law. *Gaphardt v Morgan Guar. Trust Co.* (1993, 1st Dept) 191 AD2d 229, 594 NYS2d 248, app den 82 NY2d 656.

§ 7:3 BURDEN OF PROOF IN NEGLIGENCE CASES — Labor Law § 240(1) imposes a non-delegable duty on owners, general contractors, and their agents to provide proper protection to persons working on elevated structures. A subcontractor may be deemed an agent under the statute and held liable if the agent is delegated the supervision and control over the specific work area involved or the work that gives rise to the injury. The plaintiff has the burden of presenting evidence of the particular defendants' supervision and control of the activity that resulted in his injury. *Headen v Progressive Painting Corp.* (1990, 1st Dept) 160 AD2d 319, 553 NYS2d 401.

To establish a *prima facie* case of negligence based wholly on circumstantial evidence, it is enough that plaintiff shows facts and conditions from which the defendant's negligence and the causation of the accident by that negligence may be reasonably inferred. *Secof v Greens Condominium* (1990, 2d Dept) 158 AD2d 591, 551 NYS2d 563.

In a negligence action for a slip and fall in defendant's store, there was no evidence that defendant had notice of any slippery condition before plaintiff fell, and the testimony showed at most that defendant's manager learned of a slippery condition from the fall. Consequently, the evidence was insufficient to establish the element of notice. *Fasolino v Charming Stores, Inc.* (1991) 77 NY2d 847, 567 NYS2d 640.

The use of *res ipsa loquitur* does not relieve plaintiff of the burden of proof and the defendant is under no obligation to offer any countervailing proof in rebuttal. *Nesbit v New York City Transit Authority* (1991, 1st Dept) 170 AD2d 92, 574 NYS2d 179. Submission of a case on the theory of *res ipsa loquitur* is generally warranted only when plaintiff has established that (1) the event was a kind that ordinarily does not occur in the absence of someone's negligence, (2) it was caused by an agency or instrumentality within the exclusive control of defendant, and (3) it was not due to any voluntary action or contribution on the part of plaintiff. *Nesbit v New York City Transit Authority, supra.*

Proximate cause may be inferred from the facts and circumstances surrounding the event. *Kerrick v Finger Lakes Racing Ass'n.* (1992, 4th Dept) 181 AD2d 984, 581 NYS2d 944.

In elevator accident cases, the doctrine of *res ipsa loquitur* can be used where more than one defendant is in a position to exercise exclusive control. *Myron v Millar Elevator Industries, Inc.* (1992, 1st Dept) 182 AD2d 558, 582 NYS2d 201.

By submitting proof that a scaffold collapsed or broke, a plaintiff establishes a *prima facie* violation of Labor Law § 240(1), and the burden of going forward then shifts to the defendant to submit evidence that would raise a factual issue or evidence of an acceptable excuse for its failure to provide the proper protection. *Davis v Pizzagalli Constr. Co.* (1992, 3d Dept) 186 AD2d 960, 589 NYS2d 211.

In order to make out a *prima facie* case in an action based on a slip-and-fall accident, is required to show defendant's actual or constructive notice of the condition causing the fall. This requires proof that defendant created the condition or had a reasonable opportunity to remedy the situation. *Grimes v Golub Corp.* (1992, 3d Dept) 188 AD2d 721, 590 NYS2d 590.

Notice of violation is material to recovery under General Municipal Law § 205-a, which imposes liability when a fireman is injured as a direct or indirect result of the defendant's failure to comply with a statutory or regulatory provision respecting safety and maintenance of the premises. *Lusenskas v Axelrod* (1992, 1st Dept) 183 AD2d 244, 592 NYS2d 685, app dismd, motion dismd 81 NY2d 300, 598 NYS2d 166. However, while notice of a violation is an essential element of recovery, it may be inferred. *Lusenskas v Axelrod, supra.*

Where the comparative negligence doctrine was applicable in a negligence case, the trial court erred in charging the jury that the plaintiff had the burden of proof regarding defendant's negligence and plaintiff's lack of contributory negligence. That instruction clearly contravened the requirement of CPLR 1412 that a defendant plead and prove plaintiff's culpable conduct if it is asserted in diminution of damages. *Gonzalez v Medina* (1979, 1st Dept) 69 AD2d 14, 417 NYS2d 953.

Although the plaintiff must generally prove that the defendant's negligence was a substantial cause of the events that produced the injury, it is not necessary that he demonstrate that the precise manner in which the accident happened was foreseeable. *Derdiarian v Felix Contracting Corp.* (1980) 51 NY2d 308, 434 NYS2d 166.

An epileptic motorist who failed to take his medication on time lost control of his vehicle when he suffered an epileptic seizure. The vehicle crashed through a barricade striking a subcontractor's employee, who was thrown into the air and on landing was splattered by boiling liquid enamel from a kettle that was also struck by the vehicle. The issue of whether the inadequate safety precautions taken by the contractor on the work site constituted a proximate cause of the accident was a question of fact for the jury. *Derdiarian v Felix Contracting Corp., supra.*

Claimant in a negligence case is not required to exclude all other possible causes of the accident. *Humphrey v State* (1983) 60 NYS2d 742, 469 NYS2d 661 (superseded by statute on other grounds as stated in *Barker v Kallash*, 63 NY2d 19, 479 NYS2d 201).

An issue in a personal injury action was whether plaintiff's present complaints resulted from the automobile accident or were caused by a chronic pre-existing back problem. Plaintiff bore the burden of showing that the doctor who had treated him prior to the accident was not within his power to call. *Griffin v Nissen* (1982, 4th Dept) 89 AD2d 808, 453 NYS2d 277.

In a malpractice action plaintiff has the burden of proving that defendant departed from accepted practice and procedure. *Weinstein v Prostkoff* (1959) 23 Misc 2d 376, 191 NYS2d 310, revd (2d Dept) 13 AD2d 539, 213 NYS2d 571. The doctrine of *res ipsa loquitur* could not be invoked based on the administration of a barium enema in the course of which barium perforated the wall of the bowel. *George v New York* (1964, 1st Dept) 22 AD2d 70, 253 NYS2d 550, affd 17 NY2d 561, 268 NYS2d 325. Only when common sense suggests that the condition discovered is incompatible with proper surgery or medical treatment does the defendant have the burden of going forward with an explanation. *Charlton v Montefiore Hospital* (1965) 45 Misc 2d 153, 256 NYS2d 219. In a malpractice action, an unexplained injury in an area remote from the operation occurring while the patient is anesthetized permits the application of the doctrine of *res ipsa loquitur* to establish a *prima facie* case against the doctors and the hospital, individually or jointly, where concurrent control had been exercised by the defendants. *Fogal v Genesee Hospital* (1973, 4th Dept) 41 AD2d 468, 344 NYS2d 552.

For a doctor to be found liable for failure to obtain a patient's informed consent to a procedure, the plaintiff must sustain the burden of proof on three issues: (1) the doctor failed to apprise her of a reasonably foreseeable risk of the procedure, (2) having been informed of the risks and alternatives, a reasonable person in her condition would have opted against the procedure, and (3) the procedure was the proximate cause of her injury. *Bernard v Block* (1991, 2d Dept) 176 AD2d 843, 575 NYS2d 506; Public Health Law § 2805-d. Plaintiff must adduce expert medical testimony in support of the alleged qualitative insufficiency of the consent. CPLR 4401-a.

In an action for dental malpractice, the burden of proving causation remains with the plaintiff, and defendant does not have to offer an explanation for other possible causes of the plaintiff's injury. *DeCicco v Roberts* (1994, 1st Dept) 202 AD2d 165, 607 NYS2d 946.

§ 7:4　BURDEN OF PROOF IN WRONGFUL DEATH CASES

— A plaintiff in a wrongful death action is not held to as high a degree of proof as a plaintiff in a personal injury action and is entitled to benefit from every favorable inference that can be reasonably drawn from the evidence in determining whether a *prima facie* case has been made out. *Locker v Ford Motor Co.* (1982, 1st Dept) 91 AD2d 510, 456 NYS2d 379; *Hanna v State* (1989, 3d Dept) 152 AD2d 881, 544 NYS2d 85. This rule is based on necessity, because, unlike a plaintiff in a personal injury action, a decedent cannot take the stand and give his version of how the accident happened. *Noseworthy v New York* (1948) 298 NY 76. However, notwithstanding the lesser standard of proof afforded plaintiffs in a death action, the case must be based on more than speculation. *Friedman v Sandy Sirulnick Realty Corp.* (1982, 2d Dept) 90 AD2d 479, 454 NYS2d 548. There must be some showing of negligence before the lesser standard of proof can be invoked. *Mildner v Wagner* (1982, 3d Dept) 89 AD2d 638, 453 NYS2d 100.

If there is no direct or circumstantial evidence of negligence or some breach of duty by the defendant or an employee, a *prima facie* case has not been established, even under the favorable rules applicable to death cases. *Christian v New York City Transit Authority* (1980, 1st Dept) 74 AD2d 751, 425 NYS2d 586, affd 52 NY2d 920, 437 NYS2d 663.

Although a plaintiff in a wrongful death case has the burden of proving that the alleged negligence was a substantial factor in producing the injury, he is not held to as high a degree of proof as the plaintiff in a personal injury action. In establishing his *prima facie* case, a plaintiff need not eliminate entirely all possibility that a defendant's conduct was not the cause; it is enough that he offer sufficient evidence from which reasonable men might conclude that it is more probable than not that the injury was caused by the defendant. *Natale v Niagara Mohawk Power Corp.* (1987, 3d

Dept) 135 AD2d 955, 522 NYS2d 364, app den 71 NY2d 804, 528 NYS2d 829.

Although the *Noseworthy* doctrine is applied to benefit amnesia victims, it was held to be inapplicable where plaintiff contended that his injuries were caused by a fall down stairs and sought to use the doctrine to assist in satisfying the burden of proving that the allegedly defective stairway was a proximate cause of the fall. Because the defendant did not witness the accident, the parties were on an equal footing with respect to knowledge of the occurrence. *Lynn v Lynn* (1995, 1st Dept) ___ AD2d ___, 628 NYS2d 667.

The lower standard of proof established for victims who have died as a result of defendant's negligence is inapplicable where the case involved is not a wrongful death action and the death of plaintiff's decedent was not caused by the accident. *Jordan v Parrinello* (1988, 2d Dept) 144 AD2d 540, 534 NYS2d 686.

Although plaintiff in a wrongful death case is not held to as high a degree of proof of the cause of action as is an injured plaintiff who can describe the occurrence himself, to invoke this rule, plaintiffs must make a showing of facts from which negligence can be inferred. *Pierson v Dayton* (1991, 4th Dept) 168 AD2d 173, 572 NYS2d 142.

Where a wrongful death claim was withdrawn during trial and only a personal injury cause of action remained, the trial court erred in charging that, as in a wrongful death, the estate of the deceased plaintiff had a lesser burden of proof. *Clarke v New York City Transit Authority* (1992, 1st Dept) 174 AD2d 268, 580 NYS2d 221.

§ 7:5 CLAIMS AGAINST ESTATES — Claims against estates present a number of unusual problems, including both the allowance of rightful claims and the defense against false or exaggerated claims after the person who knows the most about their merits is dead and can do nothing to protect his estate against raids of the greedy. Claimants against an estate should not be permitted to prevail except upon clear and convincing proof, and the evidence pertaining thereto must be carefully scrutinized. *Re Shepard's Estate* (1939) 257 AD 1031, 13 NYS2d 679, reh den 258 AD 779, 14 NYS2d 1010. This is particularly so when the claim is being asserted against the estate for the first time after the death of decedent. *Re Lochmuller's Estate* (1946, Sur) 67 NYS2d 598, affd 273 AD 759, 75 NYS2d 653. Even where the estate representative cannot produce a single witness, the trial court is not required to accept the claimant's proof. *Re Kempf's Estate* (1931, Sur Ct) 138 Misc 204, 248 NYS 247.

Although evidence in support of a claim against an estate of a decedent must be clear and convincing, *Re Finnegan's Estate* (1951, Sur) 109 NYS2d 210, such a claim need only be established by a fair preponderance. *Re O'Beirne's Estate* (1940) 259 AD 1047, 21 NYS2d 97, affd 287 NY 791. Stale demands are presumed to have been paid during the lifetime of the testator. *Re Saxe's Estate* (1948, Sur) 82 NYS2d 738.

A person asserting a claim against an estate for services rendered to a decedent has the burden of establishing such a claim. *Re Bluford's Estate* (1951) 201 Misc 138, 108 NYS2d 742. The executor has the burden of proof regarding the alleged payment of a claim against the estate for services rendered to the decedent. *Re Fee's Estate* (1934) 151 Misc 410, 271 NYS 608.

Generally, in a proceeding to recover from an estate for services rendered to the decedent by a claimant, proof that the services were in fact rendered raises a presumption that they were rendered in the expectation of compensation by the estate. *Re Estate of Wilson* (1991, 4th Dept) 178 AD2d 996, 579 NYS2d 779. When the parties are related, however, particularly where the relationship is that of parent and child, the presumption is reversed. In that case, it is presumed that the services were rendered in consideration of love and affection without any expectation of payment. *Re Estate of Wilson, supra.*

Many other special problems enter into the proof of claims against an estate. The Dead Man's Act governs the admission of testimony in favor of the claim. CPLR 4519. It has been held, however, that where a specific contract to compensate for services rendered cannot be shown because of either the statute relating to personal transactions with a decedent or some other the compensation payable is the reasonable value of the services. *Re Mulderig* (1949) 196 Misc 527, 91 NYS2d 895.

§ 7:6   PROCEEDINGS TO RECOVER ASSETS — In the probate of an estate, the personal representative may bring proceedings to recover property of the estate held by others. In such proceedings, the petitioner has the burden of establishing a *prima facie* case. *Re Buckler* (1929) 227 AD 146, 237 NYS 242. The burden of proving a gift is on the alleged donee. *Re Booth's Will* (1926) 215 AD 516, 213 NYS 684, later app 130 Misc 332, 224 NYS 371, revd 224 AD 363, 231 NYS 218, resettled 224 AD 616, 231 NYS 564. Where the respondent claimed that the property was a gift from decedent, respondent had the burden of proof on this issue. *Re Carraher's Estate* (1931) 142 Misc 675, 255 NYS 434.

Given the fiduciary or confidential relationship that existed between decedent and the executrix, her daughter, the fact that decedent was elderly and could neither read nor write, and the fact that decedent entrusted her financial affairs to her daughter, the burden clearly shifted to the executrix to show that her mother knowingly and willfully intended to make a gift to her of assets in a bank account. *Re Estate of Camarda* (1978, 4th Dept) 63 AD2d 837, 406 NYS2d 193.

In an action by executrix against defendants to recover property belonging to the decedent on the grounds of fraud and undue influence, it was claimed that one of the defendants had induced decedent to live as a "guest" in defendant's home. Although evidence of two prior judgments against defendant involving findings of undue influence was not admissible to show a common scheme or plan, it was admissible for the purpose of negating the owner's innocent state of mind. *Re Estate of Brandon* (1982) 55 NY2d 206, 448 NYS2d 436.

§ 7:7   CONSTRUCTIVE TRUST CASES — A constructive trust requires either a confidential relationship or a fiduciary relationship and entails the trustee's unjust enrichment by something passing from the beneficiary or from someone else on the beneficiary's behalf. *White v White* (1952, Sup) 119 NYS2d 306. A constructive trust may be imposed even though there is no fiduciary relationship, such as that between attorney and client or principal and agent. It is sufficient that there is a family relationship or a relationship of such a character that the transferor is justified in

104

believing that the transferee will act in the transferor's interest. *Powell v Powell* (1953) 205 Misc 14, 126 NYS2d 182. However, the mere fact that the relationship is that of parent and child is not, in and of itself, sufficient to create a trust and the mere reposing of confidence in a blood relative does not create a trust or make him a trustee. *Wojtkowiak v Wojtkowiak* (1947, Sup) 85 NYS2d 198, affd 273 AD 1052, 81 NYS2d 171.

Where a religious leader was the spiritual adviser to a follower, that relationship placed on him the burden of explaining and justifying his acceptance and retention of his follower's money and chattels. *Brown v Father Divine* (1940) 173 Misc 1029, 18 NYS2d 544, affd 260 AD 443, 23 NYS2d 116, reh and app den 260 AD 1006, 24 NYS2d 991.

The burden of proving the allegations necessary to warrant imposition of a constructive trust is on the plaintiff. *Cassidy v Cassidy* (1955) 309 NY 332, motion den 309 NY 966. Thus, in an action by two children against the mother's executor based on a claim that wages they turned over to the mother in excess of a sum for room and board created an express or implied trust, the children had the burden of proof to establish such a trust. *Wojtkowiak v Wojtkowiak, supra.*

Unjust enrichment does not require the performance of any wrongful act by the one to be enriched. *Ptachewich v Ptachewich* (1983, 2d Dept) 96 AD2d 582, 465 NYS2d 277. Generally, it requires that a party hold property under such circumstances that in equity and good conscience he ought not to retain it. *Ptachewich v Ptachewich, supra.* The court imposed a constructive trust on investments that were purchased with moneys from the parties' joint bank accounts, which were funded by the efforts of both parties. *Ptachewich v Ptachewich, supra.*

In an action by a decedent's wife to impose a constructive trust on the proceeds of a life insurance policy in which the decedent's mother was the named beneficiary, the wife's assertion that the decedent had told her he intended to name her beneficiary and had so informed his mother was not sufficient to support the action, particularly since no change of beneficiary had been made in the office of the insurer. *Hunnell v Hunnell* (1974, 4th Dept) 45 AD2d 521, 359 NYS2d 926, affd 37 NY2d 931, 379 NYS2d 841.

There was a fiduciary relationship between the defendant husband and the plaintiff, his wife, that placed on him the burden of proving that her consent to surrender her half interest in the marital home was freely and knowingly given. *Bonarrigo v Bonarrigo* (1975, 2d Dept) 47 AD2d 642, 363 NYS2d 839.

Plaintiff brought an action for her share of the assets she and her former husband acquired as wedding gifts and savings from their earnings, which the defendant had placed in his individual bank account. The court created a constructive trust in favor of the wife for her share of the gifts because of the confidential relationship of the parties and determined that plaintiff was entitled to an accounting. *Darlagiannis v Darlagiannis* (1975, 2d Dept) 48 AD2d 875, 369 NYS2d 475.

The relationship of husband and wife by itself is not adequate to support the imposition of a constructive trust on the marital home. *Marrone v Marrone* (1979, 2d Dept) 69 AD2d 898, 415 NYS2d 892. The spouse who seeks the constructive trust must show that there has been a transfer of property in reliance on the marriage relationship that subsequently results in the unjust enrichment of the other spouse. *Marrone v Marrone, supra.*

Plaintiff wife's payment of household expenses from December 1969 to the commencement of the action in 1976 cannot be considered a transfer to defendant that would entitle her to impose a constructive trust on defendant's bank account. Nevertheless, deposits into defendant's saving account of monies withdrawn from the parties' joint checking account may constitute transfers that would entitle plaintiff to an increase in the amount of the constructive trust to the extent of her interest in the those sums. *Warren v Warren* (1982) 55 NY2d 874, 448 NYS2d 467, on remand (2d Dept) 95 AD2d 807, 463 NYS2d 855.

To impress a constructive trust on a property interest, the plaintiff must prove (1) a confidential or fiduciary relationship, (2) a promise, (3) a transfer in reliance on the promise, and (4) unjust enrichment. *Ladone v Ladone* (1986, 2d Dept) 121 AD2d 512, 503 NYS2d 831. To establish that there was a transfer in reliance on a promise to reconvey, it must be shown that the party seeking to impose the constructive trust had an interest in the property prior to obtaining the promise that the property would be conveyed. *Ladone v Ladone, supra.*

Based on all the evidence, the Surrogate properly found that a confidential relationship had existed between the father and the son. In view of that relationship, the father's gratuitous conveyance of the subject property to the son's children was presumptively fraudulent, and therefore the son had the burden of proving that the transfer constituted a legitimate gift. *Laurenzano v Laurenzano* (1989, 2d Dept) 156 AD2d 430, 548 NYS2d 547.

Where two parties had lived together, a cause of action to impose a constructive trust on an apartment owned by defendant could not stand, because the plaintiff failed to establish that she had a property interest in the apartment, nor did she establish all of the elements necessary for the imposition of a constructive trust. *Jennings v Hurt* (1990, 1st Dept) 160 AD2d 576, 554 NYS2d 220, app den 77 NY2d 804, 568 NYS2d 347.

The court refused to impose a constructive trust on the marital residence because plaintiff wife had no prior interest in the marital residence, which had been acquired by her husband, the defendant, before the parties' marriage. Additionally, her allegations were insufficient to establish that the defendant's failure to fulfill his alleged oral promise to convey an interest in the marital residence had resulted in his unjust enrichment. *Davidman v Davidman* (1991, 2d Dept) 175 AD2d 232, 572 NYS2d 363.

In a matrimonial action, the court properly imposed a constructive trust on assets as a remedy to defendant husband's effort to place marital property out of plaintiff's reach. *Elkaim v Elkaim* (1991, 1st Dept) 176 AD2d 116, 574 NYS2d 2.

§ 7:8 BURDEN OF PROVING FRAUD — It is essential to the establishment of fraud that the person charged has knowledge of the falsity of his statement and, hence, an intent to deceive the other party. *Clark v Standard Rock Asphalt Corp.* (1931) 233 AD 536, 253 NYS 730, affd (1932) 259 NY 595, 182 NE 195. In actual fraud, there must be an intent to deceive and to defraud. *Tompkins v Board of Regents* (1948) 274 AD 354, 85 NYS2d 140, revd 299 NY 469. Because it is impossible to look into a person's mind to ascertain intent, it may be determined from the surrounding circumstances. *Gafco, Inc. v H. D. S. Mercantile Corp.* (1965) 47 Misc 2d 661, 263 NYS2d 109.

Plaintiff has the burden of proving fraud. *Finsilver v Still* (1934) 240 AD 87, 269 NYS 9. In a civil action for fraud, the proof required to sustain the cause of action is more demanding than that needed to prove a breach of contract. *Jo Ann Homes at Bellmore, Inc. v Dworetz* (1969) 25 NY2d 112, 302 NYS2d 799. Fraud is only established when facts are proven from which fraud is an unavoidable inference. *Altman v Casale* (1966, 2d Dept) 25 AD2d 877, 270 NYS2d 509. Fraud will not be presumed, *Allstate Ins. Co. v Altman* (1959) 21 Misc 2d 162, 191 NYS2d 270, and cannot be based on suspicion, conjecture, or doubtful inference. It must be established by clear and convincing proof. *Allstate Ins. Co. v Altman, supra; Stephenson v Lord* (1979, 3d Dept) 72 AD2d 857, 421 NYS2d 730.

To recover for fraud, plaintiff must prove that he relied on the false representations. *Allied Financial Corp. v Duo Factors, Inc.* (1966, 1st Dept) 26 AD2d 538, 271 NYS2d 402, affd 19 NY2d 865, 280 NYS2d 668. Moreover, the person asserting that he relied to his detriment on a fraudulent misrepresentation must establish his right to rely thereon. He may not enter into a transaction closing his eyes to available information and then charge that he has been deceived by the words or conduct of the other party. *Feliton v Chismore* (1949) 194 Misc 715, 86 NYS2d 867. The right of a person to rely on the representations made to him depend on all the circumstances surrounding the transaction. If by exercising ordinary prudence he had ample opportunity to determine the truth of the representations before acting but failed to so do, he is charged with knowledge and may not then claim that his loss was due to the deceit of another. *Feliton v Chismore, supra.* With the opportunity to obtain knowledge of the facts, one cannot sit idly by to reap the harvest, if plentiful, but in the event of scarcity, charge fraud. *Hartford Acci. & Indem. Co. v Kranz* (1959, 3d Dept) 7 AD2d 604, 184 NYS2d 918.

A party cannot claim to have been defrauded into doing that which it was already legally bound to do. *New York State Urban Dev. Corp. v Marcus Garvey Brownstone Houses, Inc.* (1983, 2d Dept) 98 AD2d 767, 469 NYS2d 789.

It was held, however, that a purchaser of land does not have equal knowledge with the vendor and hence could rely on his representations about acreage. *Hall v Grays* (1929) 227 AD 337, 238 NYS 67. Reliance may be placed on a representation of law by one having superior knowledge of the law. *Belkin v Belkin* (1963) 40 Misc 2d 984, 243 NYS2d 995. Where the developers of a housing project had exclusive knowledge of the facts regarding the payment of sewer assessment costs and they wilfully misrepresented those facts, the failure of purchasers of property in the project to ascertain the truth when inspecting the public records was not fatal to their action for fraud. *Todd v Pearl Woods, Inc.* (1964, 2d Dept) 20 AD2d 911, 248 NYS2d 975, affd 15 NY2d 817, 257 NYS2d 937.

To sustain an action for fraud, plaintiff must prove by clear and convincing evidence that a representation of a material fact was made, that such representation was false and known to be false by the party making it or was recklessly made, that such representation was made to deceive and to induce the other party to act on it, and that the party to whom the representation was made relied on it to its injury or damage. *Orbit Holding Corp. v Anthony Hotel Corp.* (1986, 1st Dept) 121 AD2d 311, 503 NYS2d 780.

A purported misrepresentation that plaintiff would receive a return of $850,000 as a result of the sale of property does not support a claim for fraud, because the oral promise was not enforceable and no justifiable reliance could be placed thereon. *Highland Sec. Co. on behalf of Georgetown Hospitality Associates, L. P. v Hecht* (1988, 1st Dept) 145 AD2d 393, 536 NYS2d 67.

Without damages there can be no action for fraud. *Dunkin' Donuts, Inc. v HWT Assoc., Inc.* (1992, 2d Dept) 181 AD2d 711, 581 NYS2d 363.

Proof of active concealment alone will not support a fraud action brought by purchasers of a home against the vendors and the broker where the vendee should have known of the defect. *George v Lumbrazo* (1992, 4th Dept) 184 AD2d 1050, 584 NYS2d 704, app dismd 81 NY2d 759, 594 NYS2d 719, reconsideration den 81 NY2d 835, 595 NYS2d 397.

§ 7:9   BAILMENT CASES — When the bailor has shown that the goods were received by the bailee in good condition and were not returned to the bailor on demand, the bailor has made out a *prima facie* case of negligence against the bailee. The bailee must then show that the loss or damage was caused without his fault. *Jay Howard, Inc. v Rothschild* (1962, 1st Dept) 16 AD2d 628, 226 NYS2d 769. In showing that care was exercised, bailee must explain the loss or damage and not simply point to a mystery for which he has no better explanation than the bailor. Uniform Commercial Code § 7-403; *National Dairy Products Corp. v Lawrence American Field Warehousing Corp.* (1965, 1st Dept) 22 AD2d 420, 255 NYS2d 788, revd 16 NY2d 344, 266 NYS2d 785, 21 ALR3d 1320. The effect of this rule is not to shift the burden of proof from plaintiff to the defendant but to shift only the burden of proceeding. *Textile Overseas Corp. v Riveredge Warehouse Corp.* (1949) 275 AD 236, 88 NYS2d 429. When the bailor makes out a *prima facie* case of negligence against the bailee by showing that the goods have not been returned on demand, the resultant presumption of the bailee's negligence disappears if the defendant presents any evidence that the loss was caused by some means other than his negligence. The bailor then continues to have the onus of proving want of care by the bailee. *Textile Overseas Corp. v Riveredge Warehouse Corp., supra.*

Plaintiffs established a *prima facie* case for negligence and conversion by establishing that two diamond rings were left in the defendant's possession to be remodeled and that thereafter defendants failed to return the rings on proper demand. *Damast v New Concepts in Jewelry, Ltd.* (1982, 2d Dept) 86 AD2d 886, 447 NYS2d 530. After plaintiffs established a *prima facie* case in either conversion or negligence, it became incumbent on defendants to present evidence to explain what happened to the two rings. *Damast v New Concepts in Jewelry, Ltd., supra.*

The general rule is that if a bailee fails to return a bailor's property, there is a presumption of liability, and if the property cannot be found, a *prima facie* case of negligence exists. *Maisel v Gruner & Jahr USA, Inc.* (1982, 1st Dept) 89 AD2d 503, 452 NYS2d 192. However, if it appears that the cause of the loss was not within the bailee's control, the *prima facie* case is overcome and the bailor must prove negligence by the bailee. *Maisel v Gruner & Jahr USA, Inc., supra.*

A bailor who delivered leather goods to a bailee for processing made out a *prima facie* case in negligence by establishing that the goods were delivered to defendant and were returned in a damaged condition. This merely placed the burden of going forward with an explanation for the damage on the defendant, who accomplished this by proof of fire. Plaintiff then had the burden of demonstrating that the skins were damaged due to the defendant's failure to exercise ordinary and reasonable care to safeguard them, which mere proof of the fire did not accomplish. *Feuer Hide & Skin Corp. v Kilmer* (1981, 3d Dept) 81 AD2d 948, 439 NYS2d 704.

In the case of a gratuitous bailee, however, a plaintiff complaining of theft from such a bailee has the burden of going forward with the evidence regarding the defendant's gross carelessness. *J. W. Mays, Inc. v Hertz Corp.* (1961, 1st Dept) 15 AD2d 105, 221 NYS2d 766.

The operator of a self-service unattended parking lot at an airport is not liable for the unexplained disappearance of a car without proof of negligence, because the motorist parked the vehicle herself after receiving a ticket from an automatic machine that stated that the lot was unattended, that parking was at the motorist's risk, and that the motorist should lock the car and retain the keys. *Ellish v Airport Parking Co.* (1973, 2d Dept) 42 AD2d 174, 345 NYS2d 650, app dismd 33 NY2d 764, 350 NYS2d 411 and affd 34 NY2d 882, 359 NYS2d 280.

§ 7:10 BURDEN OF PROVING NEGATIVE AVERMENTS — If a negative allegation is averred in a pleading or a party's case depends on the establishment of a negative, the burden of proof is on the party alleging the negative. *Sasmor v V. Vivaudou, Inc.* (1951) 200 Misc 1020, 103 NYS2d 640.

RESEARCH REFERENCES

American Law Reports

9 ALR5th 826, Sufficiency of evidence to raise last clear chance doctrine in cases of automobile collision with pedestrian or bicyclist–modern cases

84 ALR4th 531, Sufficiency of evidence of nonrevocation of lost will where codicil survives

82 ALR4th 598, Burden of proof in civil action for using unreasonable force in making arrest as to reasonableness of force used

78 ALR4th 154, Burden of proving feasibility of alternative safe design in products liability action based on defective design

73 ALR4th 1093, Unemployment compensation: burden of proof as to voluntariness of separation

72 ALR4th 132, Sufficiency of showing, in establishing boundary by parol agreement, that boundary was uncertain or in dispute before agreement

70 ALR4th 323, Sufficiency of evidence of nonrevocation of lost will not shown to have been inaccessible to testator–modern cases

67 ALR4th 544, Applicability of res ipsa loquitur in case of multiple medical defendants–modern status

64 ALR4th 10, Products liability: sufficiency of evidence to support product misuse defense in actions concerning commercial or industrial equipment and machinery

63 ALR4th 18, Products Liability: sufficiency of evidence to support product misuse defense in actions concerning automobiles, boats, aircraft, and other vehicles

61 ALR4th 156, Products liability: sufficiency of evidence to support product misuse defense in actions concerning building components and materials

60 ALR4th 678, Products liability: sufficiency of evidence to support product misuse defense in actions concerning agricultural implements and equipment

59 ALR4th 201, Applicability of res ipsa loquitur in case of multiple, nonmedical defendants–modern status

59 ALR4th 102, Products liability: sufficiency of evidence to support product misuse defense in actions concerning weapons and ammunition

59 ALR4th 73, Products liability: sufficiency of evidence to support product misuse defense in actions concerning ladders and scaffolds

58 ALR4th 131, Products liability: sufficiency of evidence to support product misuse defense in actions concerning gas and electric appliances

58 ALR4th 76, Products liability: sufficiency of evidence to support product misuse defense in actions concerning paint, cleaners, or other chemicals

58 ALR4th 40, Products liability: sufficiency of evidence to support product misuse defense in actions concerning cosmetics and other personal care products

58 ALR4th 7, Products liability: sufficiency of evidence to support product misuse defense in actions concerning food, drugs, and other products intended for ingestion

55 ALR4th 1062, Products liability: sufficiency of evidence to support product misuse defense in actions concerning lawnmowers

54 ALR4th 746, Libel and slander: sufficiency of identification of allegedly defamed party

52 ALR4th 276, Products liability: sufficiency of evidence to support product misuse defense in actions concerning wearing apparel

50 ALR4th 1226, Products liability: sufficiency of evidence to support product misuse defense in actions concerning athletic, exercise, or recreational equipment

89 ALR3d 87, Sufficiency of evidence to prove future medical expenses as result of injury to head or brain

86 ALR3d 980, Sufficiency of evidence that will was not accessible to testator for destruction, in proceeding to establish lost will

35 ALR3d 289, Conflict of laws as to presumptions and burden of proof concerning facts of civil case

32 ALR3d 1303, Race or color of child as admissible in evidence on issue of legitimacy or paternity, or as basis of rebuttal or exception to presumption of legitimacy

30 ALR3d 571, Presumptions and burden of proof as to time of alteration of deed

24 ALR3d 1434, Applicability and application, in civil case, of presumption of addressee's receipt of telegram

94 ALR Fed 101, Burden and sufficiency of proof under "first sale" doctrine in prosecution for copyright infringement

86 ALR Fed 230, Nature and burden of proof in Title VII action alleging favoritism in promotion or job assignment due to sexual or romantic relationship between supervisor and another

ALR QUICK INDEX: Evidence

American Jurisprudence 2d

29 AM JUR 2d, Evidence §§ 123-158

American Jurisprudence Pleading and Practice

9A AM JUR PL & PR FORMS (Rev), Evidence, Forms 71-78

American Jurisprudence Proof of Facts

50 Am Jur Proof of Facts 2d 1, Proving Significant Disability from Mild Head Injury

49 Am Jur Proof of Facts 2d 293, Products Liability: Proof That Defect Was Not Cause of Injury

American Jurisprudence Trials

39 Am Jur Trials 1, Automobile Warranty Litigation

38 Am Jur Trials 231, All-Terrain Vehicle Litigation

6 Am Jur Trials 963, Predicting Personal Injury Verdicts and Damages

5 Am Jur Trials 505, Mapping the Trial-Order of Proof §§ 42-45

Other Resources

34 NY Jur 2d, Criminal Law §§ 2481, 2482

Auto-Cite®: Any case citation herein can be checked for form, parallel references, later history and annotation references through the Auto-Cite computer research system.

CHAPTER 8

PROOF OF FACTS

§ 8:1 SITUATIONS WHERE PROOF IS EXCUSED BEFORE TRIAL — Under certain conditions, some elements of the case or defense do not require proof. The failure to deny an allegation in a pleading constitutes an admission. CPLR 3018(a).

When a party admits an allegation in a pleading, it is conclusive and no proof is required. *Ward v Davega City Radio* (1937) 163 Misc 335, 297 NYS 361. An admission that is made pursuant to a notice to admit is binding upon the party making the admission. It eliminates the necessity for proof at the trial. CPLR 3123(a); *Nader v General Motors Corp.* (1967) 53 Misc 2d 515, 279 NYS2d 111, affd 29 AD2d 632, 286 NYS2d 209.

When a case is submitted on an agreed state of facts, no proof is necessary. CPLR 3222(a); *Nott v Klein* (1935) 159 Misc 35, 285 NYS 1025. Additionally, no proof is needed as to matters that have been agreed upon pursuant to stipulation. Such agreement is binding upon the courts. CPLR 2104; *Di Donato v Rosenberg* (1930) 230 AD 538, 245 NYS 675, affd 256 NY 412, 176 NE 822.

An admission made during a deposition is not conclusive and may be explained away. However, an admission in response to a notice to admit, unless amended or withdrawn by court order, is

115

conclusive. *Groeger v Col-Les Orthopedic Associates, P.C.* (1988, 4th Dept) 136 AD2d 952, 524 NYS2d 950.

Generally, a notice to admit facts as to which there is no genuine dispute, including the authenticity of documents, may be used to avoid the necessity (1) of presenting evidence of uncontested facts, and (2) of laying foundations for documents that are admitted to be authentic. If the party upon whom a notice to admit fails to respond within 20 days, the facts asserted in the notice are deemed to be admitted. CPLR 3123. However, a defendant's failure to respond to a notice to admit, with respect to contested facts that go to the very essence of the dispute, does not transform the unanswered requests into admissions. Such requests are palpably improper. *Burnside v Foglia* (1994, 3d Dept) 208 AD2d 1085, 617 NYS2d 921.

An admission in a pleading in one action is admissible against the pleader in another suit, provided that it can be shown that the facts were alleged with the pleader's knowledge or under his direction. Such an admission, however, is open to explanation and is not conclusive. *Jack C. Hirsch, Inc. v North Hempstead* (1991, 2d Dept) 177 AD2d 683, 577 NYS2d 75.

§ 8:2 SITUATIONS WHERE PROOF IS EXCUSED DURING TRIAL — Matters of which a court takes judicial notice need not be proved. *Pfleuger v Pfleuger* (1952) 304 NY 148. Likewise, if a party or his attorney admits a fact in open court, in the course of a trial, that fact need not be proved. *People v Brady* (1965) 16 NY2d 186, 264 NYS2d 361.

§ 8:3 METHODS OF PROVING FACTS — Where proof of facts has not been dispensed with, various methods of proof may be employed. A fact may be proved by a party's own witnesses; this includes the testimony of the party himself. CPLR 4512.

A party may call an adverse party as his witness. *McDermott v Manhattan Eye, Ear & Throat Hospital* (1964) 15 NY2d 20, 255 NYS2d 65. The plaintiff in a medical malpractice action may compel a defendant physician to give expert testimony as part of plaintiff's proof. *McDermott v Manhattan Eye, Ear & Throat Hospital, supra*. This rule is not limited to medical malpractice cases.

Lingener v State Farm Mut. Auto Ins. Co. (1993, 3d Dept) 195 AD2d 838, 600 NYS2d 395.

Facts may be proved by the use of real and demonstrative evidence, such as diagrams, maps and sketches, *People v Johnson* (1893) 140 NY 350, 35 NE 604, photographs, *People v Webster* (1893) 139 NY 73, 34 NE 730, and motion pictures. *Boyarsky v G. A. Zimmerman Corp.* (1934) 240 AD 361, 270 NYS 134. Facts may be proved by direct evidence, *Pease v Smith* (1875) 61 NY 477, or by circumstantial evidence, *People v Travato* (1955) 309 NY 382.

There was testimony that a photograph of a hole in a basement floor, taken the day after the accident, was a fair and accurate representation of the scene of the accident as of the time it occurred. It was held not to be unreasonable for a jury to infer from the condition of the defect, as indicated by the discoloration of the concrete-like substance shown in the photograph, that the hole had been there a sufficiently long time for the landlord to have known of the defect. *Batton v Elghanayan* (1978) 43 NY2d 898, 403 NYS2d 717.

Under CPLR 4533-a, an itemized bill or invoice that is receipted or marked paid for services or repairs of an amount not in excess of $2,000 is admissible in evidence and is *prima facie* evidence of the reasonable value and necessity of such services or repairs. The bill or invoice must be certified by the person rendering the services. It also must contain a verified statement that no part of the payment received will be refunded and that the amounts itemized are the usual and customary rates charged for such services. A true copy of such itemized bill or invoice, together with a notice of intention to introduce such bill or invoice into evidence, must be served upon each party at least 10 days before trial. No more than one invoice from the same person or firm is admissible in evidence.

§ 8:4 USE OF STIPULATIONS TO EXCUSE PROVING FACTS — Generally, the parties to an action are free to stipulate to any matter in an action. A stipulation will be enforced if it is made in open court, or in writing and subscribed by the parties or counsel, or is reduced to the form of an order and entered. CPLR 2104.

A stipulation arrived at in open court is the equivalent of a contract. *Storman v New York* (1953, Sup) 120 NYS2d 569. When a controversy has been submitted to the court pursuant to an agreed statement of facts, the court is bound by the facts as submitted by the parties. *Ng v Simons* (1985, 2d Dept) 114 AD2d 1019, 495 NYS2d 456.

A written stipulation constitutes a judicial admission and a substitute for evidence, thus eliminating the need for evidence. *Davies v Lynch* (1957, 4th Dept) 4 AD2d 1008, 167 NYS2d 849. A stipulation may be written, CPLR 2104, or it may be oral. *Royal Globe Ins. Co. v Dinan* (1964) 42 Misc 2d 595, 248 NYS2d 469. An oral stipulation arrived at in chambers may be binding upon the parties. *Royal Globe Ins. Co. v Dinan, supra.*

An attorney by his stipulation may bind his client. *Campbell v Bussing* (1948) 274 AD 893, 82 NYS2d 616. If an attorney has entered into a stipulation, the court has acted upon it, and the client has had the benefit of it, it is too late for the client to repudiate the attorney's authority to make the stipulation. *Ives v Ives* (1894) 80 Hun 136, 29 NYS 1053.

The parties may determine a variety of matters by stipulation. Counsel for the parties may stipulate to a set of facts and such stipulation is the equivalent of testimony that supports a decision. *Place v Place* (1950, Dom Rel Ct) 99 NYS2d 266.

When a case is submitted on an agreed statement of facts, the court is bound to restrict itself to consideration of the submitted facts and inferences to be drawn from them. It is error for the court to depart from the stipulated facts in arriving at its decision. *Goldfarb v State* (1980, 3d Dept) 73 AD2d 1027, 424 NYS2d 745.

If parties enter into a stipulation fixing the value of property, the need to prove the value at trial is eliminated. *Hunt Aylmer Corp. v Landy* (1934) 241 AD 682, 269 NYS 465.

By entering into stipulations, the parties to an action may chart the course of a trial. *Axelrod v Axelrod* (1956) 2 Misc 2d 79, 150 NYS2d 633. The parties may determine for themselves which matters are the subject of dispute and on which matters proof may be required. *Queck-Berner v Macy* (1925) 240 NY 341, 148 NE 543.

It was proper for parties to an Article 78 proceeding to agree by stipulation that they would put aside whatever had occurred in a prior proceeding and any law of the case that may have been the result of such proceeding. They could further stipulate that they would submit to the court only the question of whether petitioner's appointment had become permanent. *Albano v Kirby* (1975) 36 NY2d 526, 369 NYS2d 655.

In the absence of a strong countervailing public policy, parties to a civil litigation may consent formally or by their conduct to the law to be applied. *Martin v Cohoes* (1975) 37 NY2d 162, 371 NYS2d 687, on remand (3d Dept) 50 AD2d 1035, 377 NYS2d 757, app dismd 39 NY2d 740, 384 NYS2d 774, motion den 39 NY2d 910, 386 NYS2d 401; *Greer v Ferrizz* (1986, 2d Dept) 118 AD2d 536, 499 NYS2d 758.

The parties may, by stipulation, shape the facts to be determined at trial and thus circumscribe the relevant issues for the court to the exclusion of disputed matters that otherwise would be available to the parties. *Deitsch Textiles, Inc. v New York Property Ins. Underwriting Asso.* (1984) 62 NY2d 999, 479 NYS2d 487. When a stipulation is used to limit the issues in a case, the courts are to consider only those issues so stipulated. *Ardrey v 12 West 27th Street Associates* (1986, 1st Dept) 117 AD2d 538, 498 NYS2d 814.

In the absence of any affront to public policy, the parties to a civil dispute have the right to chart their own litigation course. In disposing of such litigation in this fashion, parties may stipulate away statutory and even constitutional rights. *Trump v Trump* (1992, 1st Dept) 179 AD2d 201, 582 NYS2d 1008; *Re Malloy's Estate* (1938) 278 NY 429.

Where the parties had stipulated that counsel fees would be fixed by the trial court upon submission of affirmations, the court properly awarded plaintiff counsel fees without conducting an evidentiary hearing. *Burns v Burns* (1993, 4th Dept) 193 AD2d 1104, 598 NYS2d 888.

An agreed stipulation of facts pursuant to CPLR 3222 must cover all points in dispute so as to permit determination of the legal issue without resort to evidence outside the stipulation. *Coccio v Parisi* (1989, 3d Dept) 151 AD2d 817, 542 NYS2d 405.

§ 8:5 CONSTRUCTION AND ENFORCEMENT OF STIPULA-
TIONS — Stipulations entered into in open court are not treated lightly. They have the same force as written agreements, with the added power of the court to enforce their provisions summarily. *De Santolo v La Porte* (1949, City Ct) 89 NYS2d 114. Where an agreement proposed by a plaintiff fairly represented the terms of a stipulation made between the parties in open court, the trial court's refusal to grant plaintiff's motion to compel execution of the proposed agreement was error. *Cost v Benetos* (1950) 277 AD 880, 97 NYS2d 799, reh and app den 277 AD 900, 98 NYS2d 590.

A stipulation signed by attorneys for plaintiff's predecessor is valid and binding on the plaintiff. *Wells v Wells* (1975, 2d Dept) 49 AD2d 771, 372 NYS2d 735, app dismd 38 NY2d 825, 382 NYS2d 45.

A stipulation concerning any matter in an action is not binding unless it is made in open court between counsel, contained in a writing subscribed by the party or his attorney, or reduced to the form of an order and entered. *Klein v Mt. Sinai Hospital* (1984) 61 NY2d 865, 474 NYS2d 462. See also CPLR 2104.

A written stipulation discontinuing a third-party action by a compensation claimant was good as between the parties. It could be enforced as a contract, even though no formal order of discontinuance had been signed and entered. *Burmester v De Lucia* (1934) 263 NY 315, 189 NE 231.

An ambiguity in a stipulation must be resolved most strongly against the litigant whose attorney prepared it. *Re Will of Mintzer* (1968, 3d Dept) 29 AD2d 792, 286 NYS2d 879.

Where the parties had entered into a valid stipulation that limited the court's review to a particular question of law, the court's determination contrary to the stipulation was error. *Trustees of Union College v Board of Assessment Review* (1982, 3d Dept) 91 AD2d 713, 457 NYS2d 971.

The appraiser was mutually selected by the parties and clearly met the experience requirements of the stipulation of the parties with respect to the division of the marital property. The stipulation should be enforced by requiring the plaintiff to sell her interest in the marital home to defendant at the appraised market value of the house. *Williams v Williams* (1982, 2d Dept) 88 AD2d 993, 451 NYS2d 831.

When acting under a stipulation, the court cannot go beyond its terms. *Twin Realty Corp. v Glens Falls Portland Cement Co.* (1929) 225 AD 515, 234 NYS 217. The court is a party to a stipulation and is bound to enforce its provisions when the stipulation has been made in open court. *Stein v Severino* (1963) 41 Misc 2d 209, 245 NYS2d 634.

As an incident to its power to exercise supervisory control over all phases of pending actions and proceedings, a trial court possesses discretionary power to relieve parties from the consequences of a stipulation effected during litigation. *Teitelbaum Holdings, Ltd. v Gold* (1979) 48 NY2d 51, 421 NYS2d 556. A court has the power to relieve a party from the terms of a stipulation where the parties can be placed in *status quo* and where there is a showing of good cause, such as a mistake, *Huie v Payuk* (1972, 3d Dept) 39 AD2d 982, 333 NYS2d 251, fraud, collusion or other similar grounds. *Matinzi v Joy* (1983, 1st Dept) 96 AD2d 780, 465 NYS2d 731, affd 60 NY2d 835, 470 NYS2d 131.

In general, a party is bound by stipulations made in open court by his attorney. However, the rule may be relaxed in the interest of elementary fairness when it is evident, on the face of the record, that the attorney's understanding of the stipulated terms differs so obviously and radically from the perception of his opponent and of the Court as to warrant the conclusion that there was in effect no stipulation at all. *Way v Poughkepsie* (1980, 2d Dept) 75 AD2d 602, 426 NYS2d 810.

Plaintiff chose to bring an independent action to set aside a stipulation of settlement and judgment of divorce. Plaintiff was required to make a *prima facie* showing of extrinsic fraud in the procurement of either the stipulation or the judgment of divorce. *Miller v Miller* (1983, 2d Dept) 96 AD2d 1073, 466 NYS2d 722.

If a stipulation does not represent the intent of the parties, the aggrieved party's remedy is to move in the court wherein it was entered to vacate it. *Re Estate of Horton* (1976, 4th Dept) 51 AD2d 856, 379 NYS2d 569.

When the parties enter into a stipulation recorded in the minutes of the court, the settlement agreement terminates all of the claims of the parties made in the action. The agreement becomes enforceable as a contract binding on all parties to it. *Ianielli v North River Ins. Co.* (1986, 2d Dept) 119 AD2d 317, 506 NYS2d 970, app den 69 NY2d 606.

Stipulations are favored by the courts and are not lightly to be cast aside. *Lynch v Lynch* (1986, 4th Dept) 122 AD2d 572, 505 NYS2d 739. Although an unauthorized stipulation of settlement is a nullity, a stipulation of settlement made by counsel may bind the client even where it exceeds counsel's actual authority if counsel had apparent authority to enter into the stipulation. A mistaken understanding between defendant and his former counsel as to the meaning of defendant's words, "let's get it on paper this afternoon," is not of a character sufficient to invalidate the settlement agreement. *Lynch v Lynch, supra.*

In a medical malpractice case, plaintiff stipulated at trial to limit the issue to whether the defendant prescribed medication for the plaintiff on a specified date. Thus, plaintiff was barred from raising the issue of whether the medical malpractice statute of limitations was tolled based upon alleged prior medical treatment by defendant doctor. *Nouri v Reich* (1993, 1st Dept) 198 AD2d 116, 603 NYS2d 827.

§ 8:6   AGREEMENTS EXEMPTING CERTAIN TORTFEASORS FROM LIABILITY — By statute, agreements exempting certain types of tortfeasors from liability for negligence are void. General Obligations Law § 5-326 renders void and unenforceable any agreement exempting from tort liability the owners or operators of places of amusement, pools, gymnasiums or recreational and similar establishments, and pursuant to which such owner or operator receives a fee or other compensation. Agreements exempting caterers and catering establishments from liability for negligence are also void and unenforceable. General Obligations Law § 5-322.

Operators of garages, parking lots or similar establishments having capacity for housing, storage, parking, repair or servicing of four or more motor vehicles, may not exempt themselves, by agreement, from liability for injury to person or property resulting from their negligence. However, by agreement with the person storing the vehicle, they may limit the liability to an amount not less than $25,000 or, in the alternative, provide for a larger liability in which event increased rates may be charged based upon such increased liability. General Obligations Law, § 5-325.

The statute renders void, as against public policy and wholly unenforceable, agreements in connection with or collateral to a lease of real property that exempt the lessor from liability for damages for injuries to personal property resulting from the negligence of the lessor, his agents, servants or employees. General Obligations Law, § 5-321.

The statute also renders void, as against public policy and unenforceable, agreements exempting building service or maintenance contractors from liability for negligence as a result of work or services rendered in connection with construction, maintenance and repair of real property or its appurtenances. General Obligations Law § 5-323.

General Obligations Law § 5-322.1 deems against public policy and renders void and unenforceable a covenant, promise, agreement or understanding in, or in connection with or collateral to a contract or agreement relative to the construction, alteration, repair or maintenance of a building, structure, appurtenances and appliances, including moving, demolition and excavating connected therewith, purporting to indemnify or hold harmless the promisee against liability for damage arising out of bodily injury to persons or damage to property contributed to, caused by or resulting from the negligence of the promisee, his agents or employees or indemnity, whether such negligence be theirs in whole or in part. Section 5-322.1 does not preclude a promisee from requiring indemnification for damages arising out of bodily injury to persons or damage to property caused by or resulting from the negligence of a party other than a promisee, whether or not the promisee is partially negligent.

Exemption of a lessor from liability from his own acts of negligence is specifically prohibited by General Obligations Law § 5-321. *Pellegrino v Walker Theatre, Inc.* (1987, 2d Dept) 127 AD2d 574, 511 NYS2d 372. However, a clause in a lease which provided for exemption of the lessor from liability caused or occasioned by the use or occupancy of the premises arising from negligence or otherwise did not come within the prohibition of General

Obligations Law § 5-321. The parties were sophisticated and had negotiated at arm's length to enter into a lease containing an indemnification clause, which in any event was valid because the parties had allocated the risk of liability to third parties between themselves, *La Vack v National Shoes, Inc.* (1986, 3d Dept) 124 AD2d 352, 507 NYS2d 293, such as by requiring one party to procure insurance for their mutual benefit, *Jensen v Chevron Corp.* (1990, 2d Dept) 160 AD2d 767, 553 NYS2d 485.

A contractual provision purported to hold a general contractor harmless from all claims and damages arising through the execution of the subcontractor's work under the contract. Such a provision is unenforceable as against public policy only insofar as it may be interpreted to require the subcontractor to indemnify the contractor against the contractor's own negligence. *Magrath v J. Migliore Constr. Co.* (1988, 4th Dept) 139 AD2d 893, 527 NYS2d 892.

A clause in a contract required that a contractor indemnify the building owner regardless of whether injuries to the contractor's employees were caused by the building owner. That clause was void as a matter of public policy pursuant to General Obligations Law § 5-322.1, no matter how slight the building owner's liability may be. *Arbusto v Fordham University* (1990, 1st Dept) 160 AD2d 191, 554 NYS2d 2.

Although General Obligations Law § 5-322.1 prohibits and renders unenforceable any promise to hold harmless and indemnify a promisee who is a construction contractor or land owner against its own negligence, the language of the statute makes clear that it was not intended to preclude a promisee from requiring indemnification for damages caused by or resulting from the negligence of a party other than the promisee. *Kilfeather v Astoria 31st Street Assoc.* (1989, 2d Dept) 156 AD2d 428, 548 NYS2d 545.

General Obligations Law § 5-322.1 does not prohibit indemnification of a land owner by a contractor pursuant to their contract, whereby the contractor is required to indemnify the land owner against liability arising in connection with the work performed under the contract, if there is no showing that the land owner has been negligent in whole or in part. *Connolly v Brooklyn Union Gas Co.* (1990, 2d Dept) 168 AD2d 477, 562 NYS2d 718.

An indemnity agreement between a subcontractor and a contractor provided that the subcontractor would indemnify the general contractor and owner for all claims for injuries sustained at a construction site, regardless of whether the accident was caused as a result of the fault of the contractor or owner. Because the parties stipulated that the subcontractor was 100% at fault, General Obligations Law § 5-322.1 was not applicable. *Hawthorne v South Bronx Community Corp.* (1990, 1st Dept) 165 AD2d 652, 560 NYS2d 30, app gr 77 NY2d 807, 569 NYS2d 610.

A general contractor, which had been held liable for the death of a subcontractor's employee resulting from the collapse of a scaffold, had no claim for contractual indemnity against the subcontractor. Under General Obligations Law § 5-322.1, the promise to indemnify regardless of the general contractor's fault is unenforceable as a matter of public policy. *Public Adm'r of Bronx County v Trump Village Constr. Corp.* (1991, 1st Dept) 177 AD2d 258, 575 NYS2d 843.

Although public policy prohibits indemnification of punitive damages, it does not prohibit indemnification for compensatory damages. *Holyoke Mut. Ins. Co. v Jason B.* (1992, 2d Dept) 184 AD2d 550, 585 NYS2d 61.

The provisions of General Obligations Law § 5-322.1, which provide that any agreement in a construction contract that purports to indemnify or hold harmless the promisee against liability for damage arising out of bodily injury to persons or damage to property caused by or resulting from the sole negligence of the promisee is against public policy and void and unenforceable, are not applicable retroactively to any contractual indemnification obligations undertaken before the effective date of the statute's amendment. *Sapper v Saint Vincent's Hosp. & Medical Ctr.* (1993, 1st Dept) 190 AD2d 549, 593 NYS2d 507.

The indemnification clause executed by a subcontractor was inapplicable where the injuries allegedly sustained by the injured plaintiff did not arise out of or result from the performance of the subcontractor's work under the subcontract. *Leone v Columbia Sussex Corp.* (1994, 2d Dept) 203 AD2d 430, 610 NYS2d 586.

General Obligations Law § 5-322.1 does not preclude enforcement of an indemnification clause as to the liability of a subcontractor to indemnify a general contractor where the liability of the general contractor arises under Labor Law § 240(1), which imposes absolute liability. *Schelble v ADF Constr. Corp.* (1993, 4th Dept) 199 AD2d 973, 608 NYS2d 25, related proceeding (4th Dept) 199 AD2d 974, 608 NYS2d 131.

General Obligations Law § 5-326 did not vitiate an exculpatory clause where defendant's private swimming pool was used for instructional purposes, and the fee paid by plaintiff was for tuition and was not a use fee for recreational facilities contemplated by statute. *Baschuk v Diver's Way Scuba, Inc.* (1994, 2d Dept) 209 AD2d 369, 618 NYS2d 428.

In medical a malpractice action, plaintiff allegedly suffered injuries as a result of defendant's failure to diagnose and treat. As a condition of releasing the infant against medical advice, defendant hospital required the mother to sign a purported release of it from infant's malpractice claims. The release was held to be a nullity, violative of public policy, as to infant's cause of action. A hospital cannot demand, as a condition to do what it is obligated to do, a promise to save it from its own wrongdoing. The purported release is further inoperative because it seeks to deny the infant's claim based on a release by another. *Dedely by Dedely v Kings Highway Hosp. Ctr., Inc.* (1994) 162 Misc 2d 444, 617 NYS2d 445.

RESEARCH REFERENCES

American Law Reports

15 ALR5th 119, Admissibility of evidence of repairs, change of conditions, or precautions taken after accident–modern state cases

10 ALR5th 371, Admissibility of evidence of absence of other accidents or injuries at place where injury or damage occurred

8 ALR5th 860, Liability of public or private agency or its employees to prospective adoptive parents in contract or tort for failure to complete arrangement for adoption

8 ALR5th 177, Liability for injury or death from collision with guy wire

8 ALR5th 1, Liability for personal injury or death allegedly caused by defect in church premises

7 ALR5th 1, Liability of hospital, physician, or other medical personnel

for death or injury to mother or child caused by improper diagnosis and treatment of mother relating to and during pregnancy

2 ALR5th 396, Liability of travel publication, travel agent, or similar party for personal injury or death of traveler

2 ALR5th 286, Hospital's liability for injury resulting from failure to have sufficient number of nurses on duty

2 ALR5th 1, Liability for injury or death allegedly caused by spoilage, contamination, or other deleterious condition of food or food product

1 ALR5th 243, Liability of hospital, physician, or other medical personnel for death or injury from use of drugs to stimulate labor

1 ALR5th 1, Liability for injury or death allegedly caused by foreign object in food or food product

80 ALR4th 337, Adverse presumption or inference based on party's failure to produce or examine family member other than spouse–modern cases

79 ALR4th 1044, Admissibility of evidence of reputation as to land boundaries or customs affecting land, under Rule 803(20) of Uniform Rules of Evidence and similar formulations

79 ALR4th 779, Adverse presumption or inference based on party's failure to produce or examine friend–modern cases

79 ALR4th 694, Adverse presumption or inference based on party's failure to produce or examine spouse–modern cases

78 ALR4th 616, Adverse presumption or inference based on party's failure to produce or examine witness who was occupant of vehicle involved in accident–modern cases

78 ALR4th 571, Adverse presumption or inference based on party's failure to produce or examine that party's attorney–modern cases

77 ALR4th 463, Adverse presumption or inference based on party's failure to produce or question examining doctor–modern cases

41 ALR4th 877, Admissibility of visual recording of event or matter other than that giving rise to litigation or prosecution

16 ALR4th 967, Validity and effect of stipulation in contract to effect that it shall be governed by law of particular state which is neither place where contract is made nor place where it is to be performed

15 ALR4th 213, Validity of agreement, by stipulation or waiver in state civil case, to accept verdict by number of proportion of jurors less than that constitutionally permitted

9 ALR4th 494, Products liability: sufficiency of proof of injuries resulting from "second collision"

86 ALR3d 1089, Answers to interrogatories as limiting answering party's proof at state trial

75 ALR3d 177, Pleading and proof of law of foreign country

71 ALR3d 232, Proof of public records kept or stored on electronic computing equipment

7 ALR3d 1394, Effectiveness of stipulation of parties or attorneys, notwithstanding its violating form requirements

ALR Quick Index: Evidence; Judicial Notice; Stipulations

American Jurisprudence 2d

73 Am Jur 2d, Stipulations §§ 1 et seq.

29 Am Jur 2d, Evidence §§ 14-122

American Jurisprudence Pleading and Practice

23 Am Jur Pl & Pr Forms (Rev), Stipulations, Forms 1 et seq.

American Jurisprudence Proof of Facts

28 Am Jur Proof of Facts 3d 87, Proof of Unsuitable and Unauthorized Trading by Securities Brokers

26 Am Jur Proof of Facts 3d 395, Water Pollution: Proof of Water Quality Under the Clean Water Act

25 Am Jur Proof of Facts 3d 473, Liability for Dioxin Contamination

24 Am Jur Proof of Facts 3d 123, Proof of Unauthorized Disclosure of Confidential Patient Information by a Psychotherapist

23 Am Jur Proof of Facts 3d 71, Proving A Claim Under The National Vaccine Injury Compensation Program

23 Am Jur Proof of Facts 3d 1, Optician's Negligence: Proof That An Optician Negligently Dispensed An Optical Device

17 Am Jur Proof of Facts 3d 685, Tortious Interference by Parent Corporation With Subsidiary's Contract With Third Party

17 Am Jur Proof of Facts 3d 121, Pleura Injuries

16 Am Jur Proof of Facts 3d 115, Nerve Injury from Exposure to Industrial Agents

15 Am Jur Proof of Facts 3d 259, Proof of Damages for Sexual Assault

15 Am Jur Proof of Facts 3d 105, Nerve Injury from Exposure to Drugs

14 Am Jur Proof of Facts 3d 241, Coronary Episode, Heart Attack as Result of Physical Trauma

14 Am Jur Proof of Facts 3d 1, Nerve Injury from Exposure to Toxic Metals

13 Am Jur Proof of Facts 2d 505, Client's Ratification of Stipulation

Made by Counsel

11 AM JUR PROOF OF FACTS 3d 343, "Lemon Law" Litigation–Existence of Substantial Defect

10 AM JUR PROOF OF FACTS 3d 757, Peripheral and Cranial Nerve Injury Due to Trauma

9 AM JUR PROOF OF FACTS 3d 459, Proof and Disproof of Alcohol-Induced Driving Impairment Through Evidence of Observable Intoxication and Coordination Testing

9 AM JUR PROOF OF FACTS 3d 307, The Psychological Effects of Physical Disfigurement

7 AM JUR PROOF OF FACTS 3d 523, Habit of Person

35 AM JUR PROOF OF FACTS 2d 589, Routine Business Practice

21 AM JUR PROOF OF FACTS 2d 1, Law of Foreign Jurisdiction

American Jurisprudence Trials

47 AM JUR TRIALS 271, Clergy Malpractice for Negligent Counseling

45 AM JUR TRIALS 637, Trying the Portable Kerosene Heater Liability Case

45 AM JUR TRIALS 1, Determining Preliminary Facts Under Federal Rule 104

5 AM JUR TRIALS 577, Using Blackboards and Related Visual Aids

5 AM JUR TRIALS 553, Introducing and Marking Exhibits

5 AM JUR TRIALS 505, Mapping the Trial-Order of Proof

Other Resources

8 CARMODY-WAIT 2d, Presentation of the Case §§ 56:18-56:20

Auto-Cite®: Any case citation herein can be checked for form, parallel references, later history and annotation references through the Auto-Cite computer research system.

CHAPTER 9

WITNESSES

§ 9:1 COMPELLING ATTENDANCE OF WITNESSES — Generally, a person may be compelled to give evidence at a trial, either verbal or documentary, and his personal convenience or preference is immaterial. *Re Ebbets' Will* (1935) 155 Misc 870, 280 NYS 710. Such attendance may be compelled, even though the witness objects that the testimony to be elicited would be immaterial or irrelevant. The materiality or relevance of the evidence often cannot be estimated until heard in the context of all other evidence. *Re Edge Ho Holding Corp.* (1931) 256 NY 374, 176 NE 537. It is only where the subpoena clearly and inevitably cannot produce anything legitimate can there be a "halt upon the threshold." *Re Ebbets' Will, supra.*

The means by which a person is compelled to testify is a subpoena. *Application of Remy Sportswear, Inc.* (1959) 16 Misc 2d 407, 183 NYS2d 125. A subpoena requires the attendance of a person to give testimony. CPLR 2301. A subpoena *duces tecum* requires the production of books and/or documents. CPLR 2301.

A subpoena is a process issued in the name of a judge or court and disobedience may be punishable as contempt. Judiciary Law § 750; *Application of Remy Sportswear, Inc.* (1959) 16 Misc 2d 407,

183 NYS2d 125. Subpoenas may be issued without a court order, by a clerk of the court; by a judge; by an attorney of record for a party to an action, administrative hearing or arbitration; by an arbitrator; or by a referee or a member of a board, commission or committee authorized to hear, try or determine a matter or act in any official capacity with regard to which proof may be taken or the attendance of a witness required. However, a subpoena to compel production of a patient's clinical record maintained pursuant to the provisions of § 33.13 of the Mental Hygiene Law must be accompanied by a court order. CPLR 2302(a).

Where an officer or employee of the Department of Motor Vehicles has conducted a hearing with regard to the owner or operator of a motor vehicle, such officer or employee cannot be required to testify in a civil action in which the same owner or operator is a party except pursuant to a subpoena signed by a judge of a court of record or of the court in which the case is pending, issued upon application, after at least one day's notice to the Commissioner or a Deputy Commissioner of Motor Vehicles. Vehicle and Traffic Law § 204.

A witness who has been subpoenaed is required to attend court on the date indicated in the subpoena and on any adjourned date. No additional process is required to compel his attendance on the subsequent date. CPLR 2305(a). At the end of the day's attendance, the witness can demand his fee for the next additional day of attendance. CPLR 2305(a).

When a subpoena is issued by a judge, clerk or officer of the court, disobedience is punishable as a contempt of court. If the witness is a party, the court may strike his pleadings. CPLR 2308(a). The court also has the power to direct the sheriff to bring a witness to court by the issuance of a warrant. CPLR 2308(a). If a person who has been subpoenaed disobeys, whether or not the subpoena is one issued by a court, he may be liable to the person on whose behalf the subpoena was issued for a penalty of up to $50 plus damages sustained by virtue of his failure to comply. CPLR 2308(a).

Statutes dealing with compulsory attendance of witnesses must be strictly construed. *Application of Combs* (1963) 38 Misc 2d 242, 237 NYS2d 857. A person who disobeys a subpoena does so at the risk of being held in contempt if he is wrong. *Application of Remy Sportswear, Inc.* (1959) 16 Misc 2d 407, 183 NYS2d 125. It is for the court, not the person served, to determine the propriety of the subpoena. *Application of Remy Sportswear, Inc. supra.* If the person served has wrongfully disobeyed a subpoena, his disobedience will not be excused even if it is committed on advice of counsel. *Application of Remy Sportswear, Inc., supra.*

To hold a party in civil contempt for disobeying a subpoena, it is not necessary that such disobedience be deliberate. Regardless of motive, the mere act of disobedience is sufficient to sustain a finding of civil contempt if such disobedience defeats, impairs, impedes or prejudices the rights of a party. *Yalkowsky v Yalkowsky* (1983, 2d Dept) 93 AD2d 834, 461 NYS2d 54.

The proper way to challenge the propriety of a subpoena is by a motion to quash. *Application of Remy Sportswear, Inc., supra.*

Although personal injury defendant knew that plaintiff suffered from a heart condition, he was not guilty of abuse of process or negligence in issuing subpoena to compel appearance of plaintiff. Plaintiff had been uncooperative, refused to be deposed at bedside, and had not sought to extricate himself from compulsion of subpoena by moving to quash; plaintiff's potential testimony was important to the case; and plaintiff's physician had not indicated that a court appearance would pose a grave health risk. *Miller v Boland* (1994, 2d Dept) 208 AD2d 508, 616 NYS2d 793.

A corporation doing business in the State of New York may be subpoenaed to testify as a witness about a corporate transaction through its officers and employees who have knowledge of the transaction. *Standard Fruit & S.S. Co. v Waterfront Com. of New York Harbor* (1977) 43 NY2d 11, 400 NYS2d 732. If the person who participated in the questioned corporate activity is an officer or employee of the corporation or is under its control or direction, it is the responsibility of the corporation to produce that person pursuant to a subpoena served upon the corporation, even though the officers and employees who participated in the corporate transaction in question are not within the jurisdiction or refuse to appear or testify in New York. *Standard Fruit & S.S. Co. v Waterfront Com. of New York Harbor, supra.*

In a medical malpractice action arising out of the allegedly negligent implantation of artificial breasts by defendant, it was an abuse of discretion by the trial court to refuse to issue a warrant for a subpoenaed doctor who had failed to appear. The testimony of that doctor or his office manager was required to lay a foundation for evidence directly relevant to a key issue in the plaintiff's case. *Hefte v Bellin* (1988, 1st Dept) 137 AD2d 406, 524 NYS2d 42.

A party in a civil suit may be called as a witness by his adversary. *Guillen v New York City Transit Auth.* (1993, 2d Dept) 192 AD2d 506, 596 NYS2d 88.

§ 9:2   COMPELLING OF ATTENDANCE OF CONVICTS — If a person is confined in a penitentiary or jail, a subpoena to compel his attendance must be issued by the court. Unless it is ordered otherwise, a motion for such a subpoena must be made on at least one day's notice to the person in whose custody the prisoner is confined. CPLR 2302(b).

A subpoena to produce a prisoner so confined must be issued by a judge to whom a petition for habeas corpus could be made pursuant to CPLR 7002(b), or by a judge of the Court of Claims, of the Surrogate's Court or of the Family Court, if the matter is pending before that particular court. CPLR 2302(b).

§ 9:3   WITNESSES FROM OUT OF STATE — The attendance of a non-resident who remains outside the state cannot be compelled in any action pending in the state. *Thermoid Co. v Fabel* (1958) 4 NY2d 494, 176 NYS2d 331. If such non-resident voluntarily enters the state to appear in court as a party or witness, he is immune to service of civil process while attending court and for a reasonable time before and after to enable him to come to court and return home. *Thermoid Co. v Fabel, supra.* Such non-resident is protected from service of a subpoena and any other process in addition to a summons. *Application of Robinson* (1963, 1st Dept) 18 AD2d 449, 240 NYS2d 82, motion den 13 NY2d 725, 241 NYS2d 854.

The doctrine of immunity from service protects non-domiciliaries of New York State from civil process when they voluntarily appear in the state to participate in legal proceedings of any kind, whether as parties or as mere witnesses. That doctrine applies to any action sought to be commenced against the voluntary participant whether or not related to the proceedings for which he is in the state. *Moreo v Regan* (1988, 2d Dept) 140 AD2d 313, 527 NYS2d 547.

§ 9:4 SUBPOENA *DUCES TECUM* — A subpoena *duces tecum* requires the production of books, papers, or other things. CPLR 2301. It may be employed in the examination of any witness, whether or not he is a party and whether he is examined at the trial or prior to it. *Smith v Macdonald*, 1 Abb NC 350, 50 How Pr 519, republished 52 How Pr 117. A subpoena *duces tecum* required production of all papers, books, documents, records and things referring to certain affairs, and more particularly those items listed on the attached schedule "if any." Such a subpoena has been held not so broad and indefinite as to be improper, despite the fact that no schedule was attached. *Falcone v Joint Legislative Committee* (1957) 8 Misc 2d 693, 168 NYS2d 543.

The court must issue a subpoena to compel production of an original document or record when a certified transcript or copy is admissible in evidence. Unless otherwise ordered, a motion for such subpoena must be made on one day's notice to the person having custody of such document or record. CPLR 2302(b). The power to compel the production of books and papers is subject to the limitation that the book or paper have some materiality or relevancy to the matter under consideration. *Barr v Dolphin Holding Corp.* (1955, Sup) 141 NYS2d 906.

A person who has been served with a subpoena *duces tecum* must comply in person or through a subordinate. If he appears personally, his attendance is not necessarily voluntary. *Sebring v Stryker* (1894) 10 Misc 289, 30 NYS 1053. A person may comply with a subpoena *duces tecum* by having the requisite documents produced by a person who can identify them and give the necessary testimony as to their origin, purpose and custody. CPLR 2305(b). Therefore, to obtain the testimony of the specific person named in the subpoena *duces tecum* and avoid the appearance of a substitute, an ordinary witness subpoena must be served in addition to the subpoena *duces tecum*. CPLR 2301.

In a proceeding, the wife was seeking increased child support from the husband, in addition to other relief. It was error for Special Term to quash a subpoena *duces tecum* issued by the husband's attorney upon the wife's employer, when such subpoena sought information as to the wife's salary along with other benefits and income. *Stern v Stern* (1977, 1st Dept) 59 AD2d 857, 399 NYS2d 125.

A subpoena *duces tecum* that was framed in general, rather than specific terms, was held to be improper. It sought a wholesale fishing expedition of the files and records of three non-party witnesses and it was overly broad as well as lacking in specificity. *International Brotherhood of Teamsters, Welfare Fund v Trans World Life Ins. Co.* (1982, 1st Dept) 88 AD2d 509, 449 NYS2d 728.

A physician had been served with a subpoena *duces tecum*. Initially, through counsel, the physician raised various dilatory defenses, including that the subpoena was burdensome and in violation of the physician-patient relationship. The physician's counsel subsequently contended that the physician did not have possession, custody or control of the subpoenaed documents. The physician's counsel should have raised the latter contention initially; the physician was held in contempt. *Kuriansky v Weinberg* (1986, 1st Dept) 121 AD2d 991, 505 NYS2d 412.

An untimely subpoena for production of documents, not served until the date scheduled for a hearing, was properly held to be a nullity. *Merschrod v Cornell University* (1988, 3d Dept) 139 AD2d 802, 527 NYS2d 109.

The standard to be applied on a motion to quash a subpoena *duces tecum* is whether the requested information is utterly irrelevant to any proper inquiry. *Ayubo v Eastman Kodak Co.* (1990, 2d Dept) 158 AD2d 641, 551 NYS2d 944. The burden of establishing that the requested documents and records are irrelevant is on the person being subpoenaed. *Abrams v Thruway Food Market & Shopping Center, Inc.* (1989, 2d Dept) 147 AD2d 143, 541 NYS2d 856, companion case (1989, 2d Dept) 150 AD2d 679, 541 NYS2d 860.

When a motion to quash is granted, it results in completely voiding the process. Accordingly, the court properly precluded the plaintiff from presenting any evidence at the trial derived from the materials that had been produced in response to the quashed subpoenas. *Uhler v Stix* (1990, 2d Dept) 167 AD2d 388, 561 NYS2d 803.

A subpoena is not rendered invalid merely because it requires production of a substantial number of documents. Relevancy, rather than quantity, is the test of the validity of a subpoena. *Riggi v Riggi* (1991, 3d Dept) 177 AD2d 788, 576 NYS2d 399.

§ 9:5 COMPENSATION OF WITNESSES — Regardless of whether testimony is taken, a witness who attends court under compulsion of a subpoena will receive $15 for each day's attendance, as well as 23 cents per mile to the place of attendance from the place where he was served, and return. However, there is no mileage fee for travel entirely within a city. CPLR 8001(a).

Mileage for attendance of a witness can only be allowed for the most direct route from the place of trial to the residence of the witness. *Hinton v Scharoun Industries, Inc.* (1943, Sup) 41 NYS2d 595. Without any specific agreement, a physician who is subpoenaed as an expert witness is only entitled to witness fees. *Potter v Austin* (1921, App Term) 190 NYS 712.

§ 9:6 EXCLUSION OF WITNESSES — In its discretion, the court may grant an order for the exclusion of witnesses, *Publishers' Book Bindery Inc. v Ziegelheim* (1945) 184 Misc 559, 54 NYS2d 798, or the sequestration of witnesses. *Capitol Cab Corp. v Anderson* (1949) 194 Misc 21, 85 NYS2d 767, affd 197 Misc 1035, 100 NYS2d 39.

The rule permitting the exclusion of witnesses does not apply to a party, who has a right to be present at all times. *Leed v Robert Joshua, Ltd.* (1947, App Term) 72 NYS2d 3. In an action against a corporation, the court should exercise caution in considering an application for the exclusion from the courtroom of the corporate officers or of a representative in charge of the matters being litigated. *Sherman v Irving Merchandise Corp.* (1941, App Term) 26 NYS2d 645.

A witness is not incompetent to testify because he has violated an order for the exclusion of witnesses from the courtroom. He may, however, be subject to punishment for contempt. *People v*

Gifford (1956, 3d Dept) 2 AD2d 634, 151 NYS2d 980. It was not error to receive the testimony of a witness who apparently misunderstood, and therefore disobeyed, an order for exclusion of witnesses from the courtroom. The jury was permitted to take into its consideration the fact that the witness had remained in the courtroom on the question of his credibility. *People v Gifford, supra.*

The determination as to whether a non-party witness should be excluded from the courtroom is normally left to the discretion of the trial court. However, it was error for the trial court to refuse to exclude the attorney who had represented both parties during the drafting of a separation agreement and whose role with respect to this matter was therefore the crux of the case. *Levine v Levine* (1981, 2d Dept) 83 AD2d 606, 441 NYS2d 299, revd on other grounds 56 NY2d 42, 451 NYS2d 26.

Although a motion to exclude non-party witnesses is usually granted, expert witnesses may be permitted to remain in the courtroom. In certain circumstances, it may be an abuse of discretion to exclude an expert witness from the courtroom if the expert's assistance to counsel during the testimony of other witnesses is crucial. *People v Santana* (1992) 80 NY2d 92, 587 NYS2d 570; *see also, Brignola v Pei-Fei Lee, M.D., P.C.* (1993, 3d Dept) 192 AD2d 1008, 597 NYS2d 250.

§ 9:7 USE OF INTERPRETER — An interpreter should be sworn, even for the purpose of administering an oath to a witness. *People v Fisher* (1918) 182 AD 301, 169 NYS 729, revd on other grounds 223 NY 459, 119 NE 845. An interpreter who knowingly translates falsely is guilty of perjury. *People v Fisher, supra.*

If it is impossible to secure the services of a competent interpreter and there is no serious delinquency on the part of the party requiring the services of the interpreter, the trial should be suspended and the case returned to the calendar. *Menella v Metropolitan S. R. Co.* (1904) 43 Misc 5, 86 NYS 930.

An interpreter should not be appointed unless it is necessary to conduct the case. *People v Jean-Charles* (1986, 2d Dept) 122 AD2d 166, 504 NYS2d 544. The defendant was attending college and had taken two courses taught in English in which he had received a "B" and a "D." Defendant's counsel assured the court that the defendant was capable of understanding English. Additionally, at no time during his testimony did the defendant indicate that he did not understand the proceedings. Under those circumstances, it was not necessary to have an interpreter appointed. *People v Jean-Charles, supra.*

The authority of the court to appoint interpreters under Judiciary Law § 387 extends beyond language interpreters and applies to interpreters for witnesses or parties with physical or mental disabilities. *People v Miller* (1988) 140 Misc 2d 247, 530 NYS2d 490.

A party may waive the right to an interpreter by failing to inform the court that he does not have a sufficient understanding of the English language to enable him to understand the court proceedings. *People v Calizaire* (1993, 2d Dept) 190 AD2d 857, 593 NYS2d 879.

RESEARCH REFERENCES

American Law Reports

4 ALR5th 403, Divorce: spouse's right to order that other spouse pay expert witness fees

82 ALR4th 1038, Propriety and prejudical effect of third party accompanying or rendering support to witness during testimony

77 ALR4th 927, Admissibility of hypnotically refreshed or enhanced testimony

63 ALR4th 712, Propriety of allowing state court civil litigant to call non-expert witness whose name or address was not disclosed during pretrial discovery proceedings

61 ALR4th 1155, Closed-circuit television witness examination

50 ALR4th 1188, Deaf-mute as witness

45 ALR4th 602, Propriety and prejudicial effect of comments by counsel vouching for credibility of witness–state cases

6 ALR4th 158, Disqualification, for bias, of one offered as interpreter of testimony

86 ALR3d 633, Judge as witness in cause not on trial before him

71 ALR3d 119, Right in eminent domain proceeding to call as witness expert engaged but not called as witness by opposing party

ALR QUICK INDEX: Subpoenas; Witnesses

American Jurisprudence 2d

81 Am Jur 2d, Witnesses §§ 1-1045

American Jurisprudence Pleading and Practice

25 Am Jur Pl & Pr Forms (Rev), Witnesses, Forms 1 et seq.

American Jurisprudence Proof of Facts

35 Am Jur Proof of Facts 2d 665, Qualifying Child Witness to Testify

American Jurisprudence Trials

40 Am Jur Trials 629, Using the Human Factors Expert in Civil Litigation

38 Am Jur Trials 711, Cross-Examination of Key Witness in Auto Product Liability Case

5 Am Jur Trials 807, Handling Perception and Distortion in Testimony

2 Am Jur Trials 229, Locating and Interviewing Witnesses

Other Resources

7 Carmody-Wait 2d, Subpoenas; Notice to Produce §§ 54:1 et seq.

Auto-Cite®: Any case citation herein can be checked for form, parallel references, later history and annotation references through the Auto-Cite computer research system.

CHAPTER 10

IMPEACHMENT OF WITNESSES

§ 10:1 THE IMPEACHMENT OF WITNESSES, IN GENERAL

— "Impeachment of a witness" is any action taken at a trial that tends to impair a witness's credibility. It includes a wide variety of developments.

A witness may be impeached by showing his interest, *Noseworthy v New York* (1948) 298 NY 76; bias, *Brink v Stratton* (1903) 176 NY 150, 68 NE 148; or hostility, *Garnsey v Rhodes* (1893) 138 NY 461, 34 NE 199. He may also be impeached by showing prior inconsistent statements, *Nappi v Falcon Truck Renting Corp.* (1956) 1 NY2d 750, 152 NYS2d 297, or by evidence that his reputation for truth and veracity is bad. *People v Hinksman* (1908) 192 NY 421, 85 NE 676.

The CPLR provides that a witness may be impeached by showing he has been convicted of a crime. CPLR 4513. An adverse witness may also be impeached by cross-examination as to any previous criminal or immoral act of his life. *People v Webster* (1893) 139 NY 73, 34 NE 730.

A party may not ordinarily impeach his own witness. *Jacob & Emil Leitner, Inc. v Scalzo* (1940, City Ct) 22 NYS2d 910, affd (App Tm) 26 NYS2d 572. However, the CPLR permits such impeachment of one's own witness by prior inconsistent statements, sworn to or subscribed. CPLR 4514. It was reversible error for the trial court to refuse to permit defense counsel to cross-examine his own witness regarding his signed prior inconsistent statement. *Johnson v New York City Transit Authority* (1981, 2d Dept) 79 AD2d 982, 434 NYS2d 477.

A party may impeach its own witness if such witness' testimony on a material fact tends to disprove the party's position or affirmatively damages the party's case. *People v Saez* (1987) 69 NY2d 802, 513 NYS2d 380.

Statements made during hypnotic procedure are generally inadmissible for purposes of impeachment. *People v Hults* (1990) 76 NY2d 190, 557 NYS2d 2707.

In an action for assault and battery, false arrest and malicious prosecution, plaintiff called the arresting officer as a witness and was not permitted to introduce civilian complaints against that officer for impeachment purposes. *Kourtalis v City of New York* (1993, 2d Dept) 191 AD2d 480, 594 NYS2d 325.

The issue of the admissibility of a prior inconsistent statement for the purpose of impeaching a witness is addressed to the sound discretion of the trial court. The trial court's determination will not be set aside absent an improvident exercise of that discretion. *People v Santano* (1992, 2d Dept) 187 AD2d 618, 590 NYS2d 113, app den 81 NY2d 847, 595 NYS2d 746.

§ 10:2   IMPEACHMENT ON COLLATERAL ISSUES — A witness may be cross-examined as to immaterial or collateral matters to which he has testified. *People v McCormick* (1952) 303 NY 403. However, a witness may not be contradicted as to such matters by another witness who testifies merely to impeach him, without giving evidence material to any issue in the case. *People v Sellinger* (1934) 265 NY 149, 191 NE 868.

Although the cross-examiner may not use other, contradictory testimony to contradict the witness as to collateral matters, he is not necessarily bound by the witness' first answer. The cross-examiner may continue the inquiry for the purpose of obtaining a more favorable answer. *People v McCormick, supra.* Although a cross-examiner cannot contradict the witness as to collateral matters by producing extrinsic, impeaching evidence, evidence is admissible if it is relevant to some material issue in the case, other than credibility, or if it is independently admissible in the case. *People v Schwartzman* (1969) 24 NY2d 241, 299 NYS2d

817, remittitur amd 24 NY2d 914, 301 NYS2d 644 and cert den 396 US 846, 24 L Ed 2d 96, 90 S Ct 103.

A witness may be cross-examined with regard to any criminal, immoral or vicious act in his life. *Hyman v Dworsky* (1933) 239 AD 413, 267 NYS 539. The cross-examiner is, however, bound by the witness' denial that he has committed the act, and he may not introduce other evidence that the witness has in fact committed the act in question. *People v McCormick, supra.* A witness who answers in the negative when cross-examined as to previous conviction of a crime may, however, be impeached by introducing the judgment of conviction in evidence. CPLR 4513. This statutory provision is an exception to the rule. *People v McCormick, supra.*

If a witness admits having been convicted of a crime or crimes, it is permissible to examine him as to the particular crime or crimes for which he has been convicted. *Moore v Leventhal* (1952) 303 NY 534. The witness, however, has a right to explain the circumstances attending the conviction. *People v Tait* (1932) 234 AD 433, 255 NYS 455, affd 259 NY 599, 182 NE 197.

The cross-examiner is not concluded by the answers of the witness as to acts indicating hostility, bias or interest. *People v McCormick* (1951) 278 AD 410, 105 NYS2d 571, affd 303 NY 403. These are not collateral matters. *Hoag v Wright* (1903) 174 NY 36, 66 NE 579; *Re Edward F.* (1989, 2d Dept) 154 AD2d 464, 546 NYS2d 630. Cross-examination of an expert witness as to his competency is not a collateral matter, and the examiner is not concluded by the answer of the witness. *Hoag v Wright, supra.*

Further cross-examination of the witness was properly refused when the witness had already testified on both direct and cross-examination that he was an inmate of Attica on a narcotics conviction; that he had been convicted of assault, promoting prostitution and various traffic charges; that he used hard drugs and took money from prostitutes; that he had lied on a bail application; and that he did not believe in working for a living. Under those circumstances, the defendant was given ample opportunity to destroy the credibility of the witness and introduction of further material would have little if any effect. *People v Rizzo* (1973, 4th Dept) 41 AD2d 691, 342 NYS2d 877.

A matter is not collateral when it is relevant to impeach a witness by showing the witness has a motive to lie. *People v Gilland* (1985, 4th Dept) 110 AD2d 1078, 488 NYS2d 935.

Evidence of complainant's interest in the successful prosecution of defendant arising out of complainant's having taken some action in contemplation of the commencement against defendant of a civil law suit, based upon the same conduct for which defendant was being prosecuted, is probative of a motive to lie, and is not collateral. It was therefore error for the trial court to refuse to allow defendant to counter complainant's denial thereof with extrinsic evidence. *People v Bruno* (1980, 2d Dept) 77 AD2d 922, 431 NYS2d 106.

In a personal injury action brought for injury to an infant plaintiff, the mother testified on cross-examination that she did not receive monies from the Social Services Department to which she was not entitled. It was error to permit defense counsel to produce a confession of judgment, extrinsic evidence of the fact which the mother had denied, because the issue was a collateral one. *Badr v Hogan* (1990) 75 NY2d 629, 555 NYS2d 249.

Plaintiff pedestrian claimed to have been injured on Housing Authority property and had filed a notice of claim, which listed a different address from which plaintiff claimed at trial as location of accident. Plaintiff could be impeached with the prior inconsistent statement contained in the notice of claim, even though she claimed that she could not read the notice of claim because she did not understand English, and that no one had read it to her; these factors go to the weight rather than the admissibility of the notice of claim. The exclusion of this evidence was reversible error, and the verdict for plaintiff was set aside and a new trial ordered. *Rodriguez v New York City Hous. Auth.* (1995, 2d Dept) ___ AD2d ___, 626 NYS2d 240.

In a medical malpractice action, the trial court did not abuse its discretion in refusing to allow defendant hospital to call plaintiff for the purpose of impeaching the credibility of her surgeon, a non-party witness, on a collateral matter. *Pipitone v Zweig* (1992, 1st Dept) 186 AD2d 73, 588 NYS2d 16.

The rule prohibiting the use of extrinsic evidence to impeach a witness on a matter that is merely collateral has no application where the issue to which the evidence relates is material in the sense that it is relevant to the very issues the jury must decide. *People v Knight* (1992) 80 NY2d 845, 587 NYS2d 588.

Although proof aimed at establishing a motive to fabricate is never collateral and may not be excluded on that ground, a trial court may, in the exercise of its discretion, properly exclude such proof where it is too remote or speculative. *People v Rodriguez* (1993, 2d Dept) 191 AD2d 723, 595 NYS2d 799, app den 81 NY2d 1079, 601 NYS2d 599.

§ 10:3 LAYING THE FOUNDATION FOR IMPEACHING A WITNESS — Under some circumstances, it is necessary to lay a foundation for the impeachment of a witness. Under other circumstances, no foundation is necessary.

It is not necessary to lay a foundation before showing by extrinsic evidence that a witness is biased or hostile. *People v Michalow* (1920) 229 NY 325, 128 NE 228.

A foundation must be laid before impeaching a witness with a prior inconsistent statement. *Larkin v Nassau E. R. Co.* (1912) 205 NY 267, 98 NE 465. If the witness admits making the statement, without any qualification or explanation, that is the end of the inquiry. *Hanlon v Ehrich* (1904) 178 NY 474, 71 NE 12. If the witness denies making the statement or does not recall having done so, he may be impeached by proof that the inconsistent statement was made. *Morton v Smith Hoisting Co.* (1914) 161 AD 939, 145 NYS 1134, later app 166 AD 436, 151 NYS 1087.

In the case of a written and subscribed statement, it must first be shown to the witness and he must be asked if the signature is his. *Larkin v Nassau E. R. Co., supra.* If the witness admits the signature is his, the document may be put in evidence. If the witness denies he signed the document, this may be proved by any legally competent method. *Larkin v Nassau E. R. Co., supra.* If the witness is a party, it is not necessary first to ask the witness whether the statement was made if the statement qualifies as admission against interest. *Blossom v Barrett* (1868) 37 NY 434.

When a party makes an extra-judicial admission, this is admissible not only for impeachment purposes, but also as proof of the facts admitted. *Burns v Dixon* (1974, 3d Dept) 46 AD2d 943, 362 NYS2d 245.

§ 10:4 CREDIBILITY OF WITNESSES, GENERALLY — The
credibility of a witness is ordinarily for the jury to decide. *Elwood
v Western Union Tel. Co.* (1871) 45 NY 549. The jury determines
the weight to give the statements of the witnesses. *McFall v
Compagnie Maritime Belge (Lloyd Royal) S.A.* (1952) 304 NY 314
(ovrld on other grounds *Dole v Dow Chemical Co.* (1972) 30
NY2d 143, 331 NYS2d 382, 53 ALR3d 175, as stated in
D'Ambrosio v New York (1982) 55 NY2d 454, 450 NYS2d 149).

When policemen testified that their sirens were sounded during
a police chase, their credibility is for the jury to decide when other
persons present at the scene testified that they did not hear the
siren. *Thain v New York* (1970, 2d Dept) 35 AD2d 545, 313
NYS2d 484, affd 30 NY2d 524, 330 NYS2d 67.

Assessment of the weight of the evidence and the credibility of
witnesses is a function of the finder of fact. It is generally not relevant to the question of sufficiency of evidence. *Dominguez v
Manhattan & Bronx Surface Transit Operating Authority* (1979)
46 NY2d 528, 415 NYS2d 6341, on remand (1st Dept) 71 AD2d
555, 418 NYS2d 411.

In considering the testimony of a witness, the jury may take
into consideration his interest, bias, or prejudice; his appearance;
his manner in testifying; his opportunity for observing the facts
concerning which he testifies; and the probability or improbability
of his testimony, in the light of all the evidence. New York Pattern Jury Instructions, §§ 1:20-1:21. The jury may properly consider the age of the witness in weighing his testimony. New York
Pattern Jury Instructions §§ 1:20-1:21. The jury may consider the
appearance, attitude and demeanor of the witness in determining
the weight to be given to his testimony. *Re Nowakowski's Estate*
(1954) 284 AD 655, 133 NYS2d 842, adhered to (4th Dept) 1
AD2d 250, 149 NYS2d 489, affd 2 NY2d 618, 162 NYS2d 19.

The trier of the facts is not required, merely because evidence is
uncontradicted, to believe such evidence. *Thomas v New York*
(1941) 285 NY 496. The trier of the facts need not believe the testimony of an interested witness even if it is the only evidence as
to a particular issue. *Piwowarski v Cornwell* (1937) 273 NY 226.

When the testimony of a party to the action is uncontradicted,
his interest in the outcome leaves a question of credibility for the

jury. *Wohlfahrt v Beckert* (1883) 92 NY 490. The mere fact, however, that a witness is interested does not mean that a jury is required to disregard his testimony; its credibility is determined by the trier of the facts. *Coutant v Mason* (1917) 221 NY 49, 116 NE 866.

Credibility is not necessarily an issue for the jury where the testimony of a party to an action is not contradicted by direct evidence or by any legitimate inferences from the evidence, is not opposed to the probabilities, and is not surprising or suspicious. *Re Carney's Will* (1934) 150 Misc 590, 271 NYS 123, revd 242 AD 650, 273 NYS 371.

On the other hand, statements of a party or other witness may be so inherently improbable as to induce the trier to disregard his evidence. *Tosto v Marra Bros., Inc.* (1949) 275 AD 686, 86 NYS2d 549, affd 299 NY 700.

When a party's testimony on a second trial is irreconcilable with his testimony on a prior trial, this is a question of credibility and, therefore, the evidence is for the jury. *Cannon v Fargo* (1918) 222 NY 321, 118 NE 796; *People v Stavris* (1980, 1st Dept) 75 AD2d 507, 426 NYS2d 741.

The principle of "falsus in uno, falsus in omnibus" permits the trier to reject all the testimony of a witness who has knowingly and intentionally testified falsely. *Harris v Rabinowitz* (1928) 133 Misc 507, 231 NYS 654. Although the trier has the right to reject all such testimony, it is not bound to do so. *Re Martin's Estate* (1934) 151 Misc 94, 273 NYS 123, affd 243 AD 513, 276 NYS 796. Such falsehood must have been on a material point. *Re Martin's Estate, supra*. If the false statement was made through mistake or misapprehension, the jury should not disregard his testimony altogether. *Lee v Smith* (1936) 161 Misc 43, 291 NYS 47.

Where plaintiff's version of the incident was corroborated by an independent witness and was not incredible as a matter of law, it was error for the trial court to direct a verdict for defendant. Under these circumstances, the defendant was not entitled to judgment as a matter of law. *Del Cerro v New York* (1974, 2d Dept) 46 AD2d 898, 361 NYS2d 707.

The mere employer/employee relationship existing between an employee and a defendant, either at the time of the incident or the trial, does not necessarily make the employee an interested witness. However, it is firmly established that an actor in the incident, with a motive to shield himself from blame, is an interested witness, even though he is not a party to the action. *Adams v Supermarkets General Corp.* (1988, 1st Dept) 138 AD2d 253, 525 NYS2d 208; *Coleman v New York City Transit Authority* (1975) 37 NY2d 137, 371 NYS2d 663. When there was an issue as to whether the store manager had notice of an unsafe condition, he was an interested witness. *Adams v Supermarkets General Corp., supra.*

Whether a witness is interested in the outcome of a case is ordinarily a question of fact to be determined by the jury. *People v Romero* (1988, 2d Dept) 136 AD2d 659, 523 NYS2d 890.

The trial court properly declined to charge that a passenger in an automobile involved in an accident was an interested witness, even though the automobile had been provided by the employer of the driver and the passenger. The passenger was not an actor in the transaction at issue and had no reason to shield herself from blame. *Deutsch v Horizon Leasing Corp.* (1988, 2d Dept) 145 AD2d 405, 535 NYS2d 383.

Drug abuse by a witness does not, by itself, discredit his testimony as a matter of law. *People v Streeter* (1991, 1st Dept) 169 AD2d 636, 564 NYS2d 769, app den 77 NY2d 967, 570 NYS2d 501.

§ 10:5 PARTICULAR MATTERS AFFECTING CREDIBILITY
— As previously discussed, no witness is rendered incompetent to testify because of his interest in the case, but such interest may be shown for the purpose of affecting his credibility. *Ryan v Dwyer* (1969, 4th Dept) 33 AD2d 878, 307 NYS2d 565. It is error to charge a jury that a disinterested witness is entitled to greater credibility than an interested one. *People v Gerdvine* (1914) 210 NY 184, 104 NE 129. However, the bias of a witness toward a party against whom he is called to testify is always pertinent on the question of his credibility. *Garnsey v Rhodes* (1893) 138 NY 461, 34 NE 199.

It is proper to bring out the witness' hostility toward a party. *Schultz v Third A. R. Co.* (1882) 89 NY 242. While the extent of cross-examination to prove hostility is at least to some degree in the discretion of the trial judge, he may not exclude all evidence offered for this purpose. *Garnsey v Rhodes* (1893) 138 NY 461, 34 NE 199.

Many different kinds of facts may be brought out to show interest or bias. It is permissible for plaintiff's counsel to ask a passenger who testified for defendant, whether he had settled his case with the defendant. *Keet v Murrin* (1932) 260 NY 586, 184 NE 104. He may also ask a witness whether he is an adjuster retained by defendant, *Young v Sonking* (1949) 275 AD 871, 88 NYS2d 392, or whether he is an employee. *Noseworthy v New York* (1948) 298 NY 76.

Although the jury could properly consider that private detectives who testified were paid for their services, there is no presumption that they would not tell the truth. It was error to instruct the jury that their testimony should be regarded with suspicion and distrust. *Schwartz v Prudential Ins. Co.* (1940) 259 AD 1052, 21 NYS2d 68. Also deemed proper as bearing on the credibility of the witness are his relations with the plaintiff and with his counsel, *Marshall v New York* (1950, Sup) 100 NYS2d 388, affd 278 AD 812, 105 NYS2d 399, and interest in the outcome of the suit. *Ryan v People* (1880) 79 NY 593.

It is improper to attempt to impeach a witness by showing he was charged with a crime. *Landt v Kingsway Equipment Leasing Corp.* (1956, Sup) 159 NYS2d 453, affd (2d Dept) 4 AD2d 785, 165 NYS2d 715. The trial court properly precluded the defendant from cross-examining a police officer as to acts underlying criminal charges against the officer where those charges had resulted in acquittal. *People v Booker* (1987, 4th Dept) 134 AD2d 949, 521 NYS2d 953, app den 70 NY2d 953, 525 NYS2d 836.

The credibility of a witness is not impaired by conviction of a traffic infraction. *Ando v Woodberry* (1960) 8 NY2d 165, 203 NYS2d 74.

A conviction for resisting arrest goes to credibility because it evidences a tendency to place personal above societal interests.

People v Dare (1988, 3d Dept) 137 AD2d 866, 524 NYS2d 547, app den 71 NY2d 967, 529 NYS2d 78.

A court refused to allow the jury to know that the plaintiff's witness, the sole claimed eyewitness to identify defendant's truck as the offending vehicle in a hit-and-run accident, had an extensive history of criminal convictions (including trespass, prostitution, attempted larceny, and attempted burglary) or even that he was deposed in a penitentiary, or that he was, at the time of trial, serving a three- to six-year sentence in state prison. Thus, the court permitted the jury to believe that there was no reason whatsoever to doubt the witness' veracity. This constituted reversible error. *Sansevere v United Parcel Service, Inc.* (1992, 1st Dept) 181 AD2d 521, 581 NYS2d 315.

During a podiatric malpractice trial, it was error to allow plaintiff to impeach the defendant podiatrist on direct examination by raising a prior criminal conviction and by attacking his qualifications; however, the error did not prejudice a substantial right of the defendant. Defendant's counsel had stated at the outset of the trial that he intended to call defendant as a witness. *Skerencak v Fischman* (1995, 4th Dept.) ___ AD2d ___, 626 NYS2d 337.

It is improper to bring out that there are outstanding unpaid judgments against a party for office rent, merchandise, money lent and for work and services, *Theodore v Daily Mirror, Inc.* (1940) 282 NY 345, 130 ALR 353, or that he has been expelled from a church or society, *People v Dorthy* (1898) 156 NY 237, 50 NE 800. The financial condition of a witness is not relevant. *Theodore v Daily Mirror, Inc., supra.*

It was improper to cross-examine a personal injury plaintiff with respect to his personal bankruptcy in order to impeach his credibility. Under the circumstances of the case, however, the error could not have affected the verdict. *Catalan v Empire Storage Warehouse, Inc.* (2d Dept. 1995) ___ AD2d ___, 623 NYS2d 311.

A witness may be impeached by proof he is a drug addict. *People v Williams* (1959) 6 NY2d 18, 187 NYS2d 750, cert den 361 US 920, 4 L Ed 2d 188, 80 S Ct 266. However, such a witness could not be impeached by the testimony of a doctor that he is not entitled to credibility, because this conclusion, if drawn, was to be drawn solely by the jury. *People v Williams, supra.*

In a medical malpractice action, on cross-examination of plaintiff's expert witness, it was proper to inquire into the expert's alleged drug addiction which, it was contended, caused suspension of the expert's clinical activities. Questions were asked in good faith, based on a letter by the expert's employer, and were used to cross-examine the expert regarding inconsistent statements and his character in general. *Winant v Carras* (1994, 2d Dept) 208 AD2d 618, 617 NYS2d 487.

Generally, evidence of narcotic addiction is admissible to impeach a witness' credibility if it tends to show that she was under the influence of drugs while testifying or at the time of the events to which she testified, or that her powers of perception or recollection were actually impaired by the habit. *People v Freeland* (1975) 36 NY2d 518, 369 NYS2d 649.

A court's refusal to allow any cross-examination of a witness with regard to his mental condition, which might have had a bearing on his capacity to perceive and recall, was error. A showing was made that the witness had a lengthy history of psychiatric problems, including confinement in mental hospitals on several occasions in the recent past and had been diagnosed as paranoiac. *People v Knowell* (1987, 2d Dept) 127 AD2d 794, 512 NYS2d 190.

Although evidence of repairs made after an accident is not admissible as an admission of negligence or culpability in causing the injury, subsequent acts of repair may be shown for any other relevant purpose, such as impeaching the credibility of a defendant. *Schechtman v Lappin* (1990, 1st Dept), 161 AD2d 118, 554 NYS2d 846. Where plaintiff tripped over an oil filler cap in the sidewalk adjoining defendant's building, evidence of repairs to the sidewalk made by defendants during the weekend immediately following the accident was admissible to impeach the credibility of defendants who claimed that they knew nothing about the accident until months later. *Schechtman v Lappin, supra.*

It was error to admit evidence that the defendant's driver's license had been suspended, and that he had received a citation for disorderly conduct as a result of an argument he had with the police officer who responded to the scene. These improper lines of inquiry could have had no purpose other than to influence prejudicially the jurors on the issue of the defendant's percentage of fault. *White v Molinari* (1990, 1st Dept), 160 AD2d 302, 553 NYS2d 396.

Although a cross-examiner is bound by the answers of a witness to questions concerning matters inquired into solely to affect credibility, such answers may be proven false by the testimony of other witnesses. When a plaintiff in a personal injury action testifies both on cross-examination and redirect that he has not worked since the accident, it is not error for the trial court to allow defendants to introduce testimony of an investigator to prove that plaintiff worked after the accident. *Osnato v New York City Transit Authority* (1991, 2d Dept), 172 AD2d 597, 568 NYS2d 821.

RESEARCH REFERENCES

American Law Reports

11 ALR5th 1, Propriety of questioning expert witness regarding specific incidents or allegations of expert's unprofessional conduct or professional negligence

73 ALR4th 691, Admissibility of traffic conviction in later state civil trial

69 ALR4th 298, Discovery, in civil proceeding, of records of criminal investigation by state grand jury

45 ALR4th 602, Propriety and prejudicial effect of comments by counsel vouching for credibility of witness–state cases

28 ALR4th 647, Permissibility of impeaching credibility of witness by showing verdict of guilty without judgment of sentence thereon

14 ALR4th 828, Admissibility of affidavit to impeach witness

7 ALR4th 468, Conviction by court-martial as proper subject of cross-examination for impeachment purposes

97 ALR3d 1150, Use of unrelated misdemeanor conviction (other than for traffic offense) to impeach general credibility of witness in state civil case

75 ALR3d 539, Propriety and prejudicial effect of impeaching witness by reference to religious belief or lack of it

65 ALR3d 705, Use of drugs as affecting competency or credibility of witnesses

ALR QUICK INDEX: Impeachment

American Jurisprudence 2d

81 AM JUR 2d, Witnesses §§ 518-631, 656-669

81 AM JUR 2d, Witnesses §§ 862-1000

American Jurisprudence Pleading and Practice

23 AM JUR PL & PR FORMS (Rev), Trial, Forms 181-197

American Jurisprudence Proof of Facts

49 AM JUR PROOF OF FACTS 2d 649, General Reputation of Person in Community

36 AM JUR PROOF OF FACTS 2d 747, Impeachment of Witness by Prior Criminal Conviction

31 AM JUR PROOF OF FACTS 2d 443, Contradiction of Expert Witness Through Use of Authoritative Treatise

21 AM JUR PROOF OF FACTS 2d 73, Impeachment of Expert Witness-Financial Interest

21 AM JUR PROOF OF FACTS 2d 101, Impeachment of Witness-Prior Inconsistent Statements

American Jurisprudence Trials

38 AM JUR TRIALS 711, Cross-Examination of Key Witness in Auto Product Liability Case

6 AM JUR TRIALS 201, Cross-examination of Plaintiff and Plaintiff's Witnesses §§ 47-57

Other Resources

8 CARMODY-WAIT 2d, Presentation of the Case §§ 156:121-156:126

Auto-Cite®: Any case citation herein can be checked for form, parallel references, later history and annotation references through the Auto-Cite computer research system.

CHAPTER 11

COMPETENCY OF A WITNESS TO TESTIFY

§ 11:1 COMPETENCY OF WITNESS IN GENERAL — A person interested in the event is, with one exception, not disqualified from testifying by reason of his interest, or because he is a party or the spouse of a party to the action or proceeding. CPLR 4512. *Re Bluford's Estate* (1951) 201 Misc 138, 108 NYS2d 742. The chief exception is found in the provision that, when appearing on his own behalf or on behalf of his predecessor in interest, a person or party interested in the event or the person through whom such person or party derives his interest may not testify to a personal transaction with a decedent or mentally ill person against the representative, survivor or successor of such decedent or mentally ill person. CPLR 4519.

The common law rule prohibiting persons convicted of infamous crimes from testifying was long ago removed by statute. CPLR 4513 and predecessor statutes. The testimony of a witness may, however, be impeached by reason of his conviction. CPLR 4513.

A party may, when called as a witness by the adverse party, be required to testify as to all relevant matters, even if such testimony should aid his opponent's case. *McDermott v Manhattan Eye, Ear & Throat Hospital* (1964) 15 NY2d 20, 255 NYS2d 65.

It is presumed that anyone offered as a witness is competent to testify. *People v Rensing* (1964) 14 NY2d 210, 250 NYS2d 401. When objection is made to the competency of a witness to testify, it is the duty of the court to determine his competency before testimony is taken. To do so, the court will conduct a *voir dire* examination, and, if necessary, hear other evidence on the issue. *People v Rensing, supra.*

All adults are presumed to be competent to testify. Commitment to a mental institution does not, by itself, result in an automatic disqualification. *People v Parks* (1976) 41 NY2d 36, 390 NYS2d 848.

The witness's use of drugs and her condition at the time of the crime did not render her testimony incompetent. However, they were factors to be considered by the jury on the issue of her credibility. *People v Goddard* (1989, 2d Dept) 153 AD2d 758, 545 NYS2d 42, app den 74 NY2d 896, 548 NYS2d 429.

§ 11:2   COMPETENCY OF A FELON TO TESTIFY — A person is not disqualified to testify by reason of a previous conviction and sentence for the commission of a crime, CPLR 4513, regardless of the nature of the crime. This is contrary to the common law rule. However, the conviction may be shown for the purpose of affecting the witness' credibility. CPLR 4513.

§ 11:3   COMPETENCY OF A CHILD TO TESTIFY — A child is not disqualified to testify merely because of age. *Rittenhouse v North Hempstead* (1960, 2d Dept) 11 AD2d 957, 205 NYS2d 564, reh den (2d Dept) 11 AD2d 1071, 207 NYS2d 1019, reh and app den (2d Dept) 12 AD2d 490, 210 NYS2d 493. It is for the court, upon preliminary examination, to determine the capacity of an infant to testify. *Stoppick v Goldstein* (1916) 174 AD 306, 160 NYS 947. Upon appeal, there will be no interference with the court's discretion in making this determination, unless a clear abuse is shown. *Gehl v Bachmann-Bechtel Brewing Co.* (1913) 156 AD 51, 141 NYS 133, app den 156 AD 915, 141 NYS 1120.

The proper practice is for the court to make a preliminary interrogation of a child to determine his competency to testify as a witness. *Rittenhouse v North Hempstead, supra.* A child as young as 9½ years has been held to be old enough to testify, if qualified under that test. It was error for the trial court to exclude his testimony solely because of age without first inquiring as to his capacity and knowledge. *Rittenhouse v North Hempstead, supra.*

A child over 12 years of age is presumed competent to testify. *Olshansky v Prensky* (1918) 185 AD 469, 172 NYS 856.

In a matrimonial action, it was prejudicial error for the trial court to exclude the testimony of the 14-year-old son of the parties on the basis of "his age and immaturity," without conducting an adequate examination to determine his capacity and the extent of his knowledge. *Kapuscinski v Kapuscinski* (1980, 2d Dept) 75 AD2d 576, 426 NYS2d 582.

A child's unsworn testimony is not admissible in a civil action. *Stoppick v Goldstein* (1916) 174 AD 306, 160 NYS 947.

The fact that a child was non-verbal, had been diagnosed as autistic, and classified as retarded did not preclude her from testifying. She could testify provided that she understood the nature and obligations of the oath and provided also that she possessed the capacity to give a correct account of what she had seen or heard in reference to the question at issue. *In re Luz P.* (1993, 2d Dept) 189 AD2d 274, 595 NYS2d 541.

§ 11:4 COMPETENCY OF A SPOUSE TO TESTIFY FOR OR AGAINST OTHER SPOUSE —With certain exceptions, the husband or the wife of a party is a competent witness. CPLR 4512.

If an action is founded on adultery, a husband or a wife is not competent to testify against the other except for certain limited purposes. CPLR 4502(a). A spouse may testify in such an action only to prove the marriage, disprove adultery, or disprove a defense after evidence has been introduced tending to prove such a defense. CPLR 4502(a). However, it was held in a divorce action that a husband's testimony which tended to show adultery by his wife was competent on the issue of custody, even though it was not competent on the issue of adultery. *Johnson v Johnson* (1966, 2d Dept) 25 AD2d 672, 268 NYS2d 403.

A husband or wife may not be required to disclose a confidential communication made by one to the other during the marriage. CPLR 4502(b). If the other spouse is living, the husband or wife is not allowed to disclose such confidential communication. CPLR 4502(b). This privilege may be waived. *Grobin v Grobin* (1945) 184 Misc 996, 55 NYS2d 32. The presence of the daughter at a conversation between a husband and wife, which might otherwise have been inadmissible, destroyed any confidential character the conversation may have had. *Re Bourne's Estate* (1954) 206 Misc 378, 133 NYS2d 192.

In a matrimonial suit based on cruel and inhuman treatment, a spouse may give testimony of adultery. Such testimony is permissible notwithstanding CPLR 4502 which, with certain exceptions, prohibits a husband or wife from testifying against the other in an action for adultery or from divulging confidential communications of the other. *Lee v Lee* (1976, 2d Dept) 51 AD2d 576, 378 NYS2d 459.

In an action instituted against a husband and wife to recover the proceeds of stolen securities, the trial court properly declined to quash a subpoena duces tecum directed to the wife. No marital privilege would attach to the ordinary business records sought and to the testimony as to ordinary business matters of a spouse. *Securities Settlement Corp. v Johnpoll* (1987, 1st Dept) 128 AD2d 429, 512 NYS2d 814.

§ 11:5 COMPETENCY OF A JUDGE, JUROR OR ATTORNEY TO TESTIFY

— A judge, presiding at a trial, is not a competent witness at that trial. *People v Dohring* (1874) 59 NY 374. However, he may be a witness in subsequent or different proceedings. *Huff v Bennett* (1852) 6 NY 337. A judge should not be required to testify for or against litigants who appeared before him. *Herald Cos. v Geddes* (1983) 122 Misc 2d 236, 470 NYS2d 81.

It has been held that a juror may be sworn and testify in a trial in which he participates. *People v Dohring, supra*. The testimony and affidavits of a juror are admissible to prove an illegal view of the scene. *People v De Lucia* (1967) 20 NY2d 275, 282 NYS2d 526.

§ 11:6 COMPETENCY OF ATHEIST, ADDICT, DEAF MUTE, OR INCOMPETENT TO TESTIFY

— The common law prohibition against testifying by atheists has been removed. New York State Constitution Art 1 § 3. No person is incompetent to testify as a witness because of any opinions he may have on matters of religious belief. New York State Constitution Art 1 § 3. A witness may be sworn either by oath or by affirmation in accordance with his religious or ethical beliefs. CPLR 2309(b). It is improper to show his religious belief or the lack of it in order to impeach his credibility. *Toomey v Farley* (1956) 2 NY2d 71, 156 NYS2d 840.

A deaf mute may testify if he has sufficient mental capacity to observe and understand the nature of his oath, and is capable of communicating his testimony either through writing or through an interpreter who is able to translate for him. *Cowley v People* (1881) 83 NY 464.

A person who is incompetent, insane or mentally ill may testify if he understands the nature of his oath, and is able to observe, recollect and communicate the facts. *People v Rensing* (1964) 14 NY2d 210, 250 NYS2d 401. Moreover, such capacity is presumed. If objection is made that he is incompetent, his mental capacity to testify is for the judge to determine in the exercise of his discretion. *People v Rensing, supra*.

A commitment to a mental institution or an adjudication of incompetency does not render a witness incompetent as a matter of law. *Brown v Ristich* (1975) 36 NY2d 183, 366 NYS2d 116. However, it has been held that an adjudication of insanity is *prima facie* evidence of incompetency as a witness. *Hoyt v Adee*, 3 Lans 173.

The mere fact that a person was adjudged an idiot some years ago and incapable of managing his own affairs did not necessarily disqualify him as a witness. *Barker v Washburn* (1911) 200 NY 280, 93 NE 958. Such a person may possess sufficient intelligence to qualify him as a witness. *Barker v Washburn, supra*. It is within the discretion of the trial court, after interrogation, to determine the competency of the proffered witness. *Barker v Washburn, supra*.

An adjudged incompetent may be called as a witness. After interrogation by the court and counsel, such individual may be sworn as a witness if he is determined to be reasonably competent. *Hayes v State* (1975) 80 Misc 2d 498, 363 NYS2d 986, revd on other grounds (3d Dept) 50 AD2d 693, 376 NYS2d 647, affd 40 NY2d 1044, 392 NYS2d 282.

A person may be so intoxicated that the court is justified in refusing to allow him to testify. *Hartford v Palmer,* 16 Johns 143. Ordinarily, this determination is for the trial judge in the exercise of his discretion. *Hartford v Palmer, supra.*

RESEARCH REFERENCES

American Law Reports

35 ALR4th 810, Attorney as witness for client in civil proceedings–modern state cases

31 ALR4th 1239, Fact that witness undergoes hypnotic examination as affecting admissibility of testimony in civil case

15 ALR4th 1043, Admissibility of testimony regarding spontaneous declarations made by one incompetent to testify at trial

71 ALR3d 119, Right in eminent domain proceeding to call as witness expert engaged but not called as witness by opposing party

65 ALR3d 705, Use of drugs as affecting competency or credibility of witnesses

37 ALR3d 420, Malpractice testimony: competency of physician or surgeon from one locality to testify, in malpractice case, as to standard of care required of defendant practicing in another locality

33 ALR3d 1405, Competency of nonexpert's testimony, based on sound alone, as to speed of motor vehicle involved in accident

ALR Quick Index: Witnesses

American Jurisprudence 2d

81 Am Jur 2d, Witnesses §§ 69-140

American Jurisprudence Proof of Facts

35 Am Jur Proof of Facts 2d 665, Qualifying Child Witness to Testify

American Jurisprudence Trials

5 Am Jur Trials 807, Handling Deception and Distortion in Testimony

Other Resources

8 Carmody-Wait 2d, Presentation of the Case §§ 56:70-56:74

Auto-Cite®: Any case citation herein can be checked for form, parallel references, later history and annotation references through the Auto-Cite computer research system.

CHAPTER 12

DEAD MAN STATUTE

§ 12:1 DISQUALIFICATION UNDER DEAD MAN STATUTE, IN GENERAL — Ordinarily in the absence of statute, the fact that a witness is an interested one will not affect his competency to testify although it may affect his credibility. *Re Fitzpatrick's Will* (1929) 252 NY 121, 169 NE 110. A statutory exception to this rule is found in the so-called "Dead Man Statute," which deals with personal transactions between the witness and a decedent or a mentally ill person. CPLR 4519.

At a trial or at a hearing upon the merits of a special proceeding, a party or person interested in the event, or any person through whom such party or interested witness derives his interest, may not testify on his own behalf or on behalf of the successor to his title or interest against the executor, administrator or survivor of a decedent or the committee of a mentally ill person, or a person whose title or interest is derived from, through or under a decedent or mentally ill person, whether by assignment or otherwise, concerning a personal transaction or communication between the decedent or mentally ill person and the witness, unless the committee, executor, administrator, survivor or person so deriving his interest testifies on his own behalf, or the testimony of the decedent or mentally ill person is given in evidence concerning the same transaction or communication. CPLR 4519. A party or person who is interested in the event, but otherwise competent to testify, will not be disqualified from testifying because costs may possibly be imposed against him or awarded to him. CPLR 4519.

A party or interested person, or a person from, through or under whom such a party or interested person derives his interest, whether by assignment or otherwise, is not qualified to testify on his own behalf or interest, or on behalf of the party succeeding to his title or interest, to personal transactions or communications with the donee of a power of appointment in an action or proceeding for the probate of a will, which exercises or attempts to exercise a power of appointment granted by the will of a donor of such power, or in an action or proceeding involving the construction of the will of the donee after its admission to probate. CPLR 4519.

For purposes of the statute, a person is not deemed interested by virtue of being a stockholder or officer of any banking corporation which is a party to the action or proceeding or interested in the event. CPLR 4519.

CPLR 4519 does not render a person incompetent to testify as to the facts or results of an accident where the proceeding involves a claim of negligence or contributory negligence in an action in which one or more parties is the representative of a decedent or mentally ill person. Such an action may arise out of the operation of a motor vehicle upon the highways of New York State or the ownership of such motor vehicle, or the operation or ownership of aircraft being operated over the air space over this state, or the ownership or operation of a vessel on any of the lakes, rivers, streams, canals or other waters of this state. CPLR 4519. However, in such proceedings which involve claims of negligence or contributory negligence, testimony as to conversations with a deceased person is not permitted. CPLR 4519.

The purpose of the statute and its predecessor, § 347 of the Civil Practice Act, was to prevent a person who might be a partisan witness from testifying to a transaction with a person who was dead and could not speak. *Re Christie's Estate* (1938) 167 Misc 484, 4 NYS2d 484. The "Dead Man Statute" applies only to testimony given on trial, not to preliminary proceedings prior to trial. *Colaci v Pagano* (1954, Sup) 130 NYS2d 801.

Thus, in an action to set aside a conveyance from a decedent to a defendant, plaintiffs were entitled to examine defendant before trial, as an adverse party, regarding transactions with the decedent. *Colaci v Pagano, supra.* Where plaintiff served a notice to take her own deposition before trial, the court held that the possibility that at the trial plaintiff might be incompetent to testify to a personal transaction with a decedent did not affect her right to an examination before trial as to such transaction. *Lemlich v Lemlich* (1943) 266 AD 748, 41 NYS2d 81, app den 266 AD 787, 41 NYS2d 955.

Although acts of intercourse and cohabitation are transactions within the meaning of the statute, testimony as to such acts between a putative father and the deceased mother were admissible. The Dead Man Statute was designed to protect a decedent's estate from the prejudice of uncontroverted or perjured testimony when a pecuniary or property interest is involved. In the instant case, no such pecuniary or property interest was involved. *People ex rel. Blake v Charger* (1974) 76 Misc 2d 577, 351 NYS2d 322.

The Dead Man Statute did not apply to a proceeding instituted by the family of the decedent to have the body disinterred. The proceeding did not involve a claim by or against a decedent's estate. It also did not involve any property right or pecuniary interest. *Re Estate of Conroy* (1988, 3d Dept) 138 AD2d 212, 530 NYS2d 653, app dismd without op 73 NY2d 810, 537 NYS2d 497.

A party claiming that a witness is a person interested in the event carries the burden of proving that the witness's testimony is subject to the statutory exclusion. *Stay v Horvath* (1991, 3d Dept) 177 AD2d 897, 576 NYS2d 908.

§ 12:2 PERSONS ENTITLED TO PROTECTION OF DEAD MAN STATUTE — Those who are entitled to the protection of CPLR 4519 are the executor, administrator, or survivor of a deceased person, or the committee of a mentally ill person, or the successor in interest of any of them. A party or person interested in the event of the trial or proceeding or his predecessor is not incompetent unless he testifies on his own behalf against one of them. CPLR 4519.

The protection of CPLR 4519 extends to all persons succeeding to the interest of the decedent or mentally ill person concerning testimony as to communications and transactions between the witness and the decedent or mentally ill person. *Carpenter v Romer & Tremper S.B. Co.* (1900) 48 AD 363, 63 NYS 274. This language includes the successor in office of a deceased trustee or personal representative. *Brundige v Bradley* (1945) 294 NY 345. Included within the meaning of the term "survivor" are heirs and next of kin, *Roberts v Mack* (1904) 98 AD 485, 90 NYS 526, as well as a surviving partner. *Clift v Moses* (1889) 112 NY 426, 20 NE 392.

The title or interest referred to in the statute as derived from a deceased person contemplates property or an interest belonging to the decedent during his lifetime and to which title has passed from the decedent to the party protected by the statute. *Ward v New York Life Ins. Co.* (1919) 225 NY 314, 122 NE 207. Persons who claim money directly from an insurance company by virtue of a designation under a policy do not claim "from, through or under" the insured. Testimony against such persons as to personal transactions with the decedent is not rendered inadmissible. *Ward v New York Life Ins. Co., supra.*

Where a will devised a life estate in realty with an absolute power of disposition, the remainderman was not a survivor of the deceased life tenant and did not derive his interest through him within the meaning of the statute. *Agluzzi v Aluzzo* (1955) 286 AD 399, 143 NYS2d 51. Where a defendant's claim was based upon a deed that was clearly executed 15 years after decedent's death, the deed was obviously null and defendant was not protected by the statute. *Diers v Heckelman* (1958) 16 Misc 2d 872, 181 NYS2d 722, affd (2d Dept) 12 AD2d 952, 212 NYS2d 1010, app den 13 AD2d 799, 217 NYS2d 533. If the testimony is not against the interest of the representative or survivor of the decedent, it is not inadmissible by virtue of the statute. *Home Ins. Co. v Aurigemma* (1965) 45 Misc 2d 875, 257 NYS2d 980.

§ 12:3 PERSONS BARRED FROM TESTIFYING UNDER DEAD MAN STATUTE — If a person is not a party to the action or proceeding, he is a competent witness unless he has a legal interest in the event. *Croker v New York Trust Co.* (1927) 245 NY 17, 156 NE 81. A person with such a legal interest is one who will gain or lose by the direct legal operation of the judgment or against whom the record would constitute legal evidence. *Friedrich v Martin* (1945) 294 NY 588, 163 ALR 1210. The interest of the witness must be present, certain and vested, and not remote or contingent. *Re Bluford's Estate* (1951) 201 Misc 138, 108 NYS2d 742.

Where a payee brought an action on a note, his brother was held competent to testify as to conversations between the payee and the decedent who was the maker of the note. The witness had no interest in the event. *Frieder v Fuchs* (1956, 2d Dept) 2 AD2d 772, 154 NYS2d 483. Additionally, where a woman brought an action for services rendered to a decedent, her husband could testify to conversations and transactions with the deceased since he had no interest in the outcome. *Estenes v McCaughin* (1958) 11 Misc 2d 748, 174 NYS2d 629.

In an action brought by or against a personal representative of a decedent, a party examined on his own behalf is incompetent to testify as to payment or non-payment of the claim sued upon. *Lerche v Brasher* (1887) 104 NY 157, 10 NE 58. Moreover, it is immaterial that the witness has only a small interest. *Re Radley's Will* (1930) 228 AD 119, 239 NYS 44. Where the committee of an incompetent brought an action to compel defendant to account for the incompetent's money, the defendant could not testify as to the creation of a trust. *Re McCulloch's Will* (1934) 263 NY 408, 189 NE 473, 91 ALR 1440, reh den 264 NY 598, 191 NE 583.

An interest in the question involved is not the same as an interest in the event. In the former situation the witness is not disqualified. *Eisenlord v Clum* (1891) 126 NY 552, 27 NE 1024. Where decedent contracted to pay the plaintiff for the care and

165

support of decedent's illegitimate child, the mother, who was not a party to the action, was competent to testify. *Connolly v O'Connor* (1889) 117 NY 91, 22 NE 753. However, the grandmother of an illegitimate child has been held incompetent to testify against the estate of the putative father as to his promise to pay for the child's support. The claim was made that she contracted with the decedent and the child's interest was derived through her. *Duncan v Clarke* (1955) 308 NY 282, 49 ALR2d 1287.

A stockholder in a non-banking corporation may not testify on behalf of the corporation to a personal transaction with a decedent. The statute only makes exceptions in the case of stockholders and officers of banking corporations. *Andrews v Reiners* (1906) 112 AD 378, 98 NYS 658, adhered to 115 AD 909, 101 NYS 1111. However, where such a stockholder transfers his stock, even during trial, he is then competent to testify to a transaction with a decedent. *Friedrich v Martin* (1945) 294 NY 588, 163 ALR 1210. The bookkeeper of a corporation may testify as to the accuracy of the corporate books, even though he is a stockholder. He is not testifying about a personal transaction with a decedent. *William L. Mantha Co. v De Graff* (1935) 266 NY 581, 195 NE 209.

When the witness will in no way be bound by the judgment rendered in the case upon which he is called to testify, the witness's testimony with respect to transactions with the deceased is not foreclosed by the mere fact that there is a remote, contingent and uncertain possibility that another lawsuit upon another theory growing out of the same set of facts may possibly implicate the witness in liability. *Franklin v Kidd* (1916) 219 NY 409, 114 NE 839.

Where the administrator of the payee brought an action on a note, the wife of the maker was competent to testify as to payment by her husband, even though the money was borrowed by both the husband and the wife, in the name of the husband, to make payment on property jointly owned by both of them. *Laka v Krystek* (1933) 261 NY 126, 184 NE 732, 88 ALR 243. The mere fact that the husband is the agent of the wife, who is a party to the action, does not render him incompetent to testify on her behalf. *Whitman v Foley* (1891) 125 NY 651, 26 NE 725, remittitur den (NY) 27 NE 411.

In an action by the mortgagee of chattels against the personal representative of a deceased person for the alleged conversion of the chattel by the decedent prior to his death, the mortgagor is incompetent to testify as to the transfer of the chattel to the decedent by the mortgagor. The mortgagee is a party to the action and derives his title through the mortgagor. *Beck v Cooke* (1899) 27 Misc 185, 57 NYS 653, later proc 31 Misc 808, 62 NYS 1132, affd 31 Misc 833, 65 NYS 1127.

Legatees named in a will or codicil are patently interested in the action and are therefore not competent witnesses to prove a conversation taking place at its preparation. *Re Will of Sheehan* (1976, 4th Dept) 51 AD2d 645, 378 NYS2d 141.

The children of a deceased testator brought an action seeking to compel the executor to deliver certain works of art to them. It was error for the Surrogate to hold that the estranged wife of the decedent was incompetent to testify that the decedent had made a gift of the paintings to the children. She was not a person from, through or under whom the children would take the contested paintings if her testimony were credited, even though she increased the children's share of the estate by waiving her rights as a surviving spouse and creditor of the estate to any property that might be recovered from the estate by the children. *Re Estate of Lefft* (1978) 44 NY2d 915, 408 NYS2d 1.

In a medical malpractice action that a patient brought against the estate of the doctor, the testimony of the patient's wife was not barred with respect to certain conversations she had with the doctor. The patient's wife had dropped her derivative action against the estate of the doctor. *Bechard v Eisinger* (1984, 3d Dept) 105 AD2d 939, 481 NYS2d 906.

Plaintiff, a building resident, and her mother were barred by the Dead Man Statute from testifying against the wife of the deceased owner of the corporation which owned the building. The barred testimony was to the effect that the decedent had agreed to give the plaintiff a 50% interest in the corporation in exchange for a small contribution and the assistance of her mother in managing three brownstones. The wife, as a survivor of the deceased, derived her interest in the corporate assets from, through or under the decedent. *Kwoh v Delum Builders & Suppliers, Inc.* (1991, 1st Dept) 173 AD2d 326, 575 NYS2d 465.

§ 12:4 RULES APPLIED IN DETERMINING INCOMPETENCY

— Objection is directed to the competency of the witness, not the competency of the testimony. *Hoag v Wright* (1903) 174 NY 36, 66 NE 579. The proper objection is that the witness is not competent to answer a question involving a personal transaction between himself and a decedent because the statute prohibits this. *Russell v Hitchcock* (1905) 105 AD 315, 93 NYS 950.

The disqualification of the witness must appear clear; it is not a matter of inference. *Riegle v Bratt* (1894) 78 Hun 532, 29 NYS 400. The objecting party has the burden of showing the incompetency of the witness. *Riegle v Bratt, supra.* Because CPLR 4519 only prohibits a party or interested person from testifying on his own behalf or interest or that of a party succeeding to his title or interest, it follows that the statute does not bar his testimony except where such party or interested person testifies on his own behalf or interest or that of his successor in interest. *Re Potter's Will* (1899) 161 NY 84, 55 NE 387; *Albany County Sav. Bank v McCarty* (1896) 149 NY 71, 43 NE 427.

The statute does not apply to a witness who offers to testify against his own interest. *Harrington v Schiller* (1921) 231 NY 278, 132 NE 89, reh den 231 NY 646, 132 NE 923. In such a case, the evidence can be received. *Albany County Sav. Bank v McCarty* (1896) 149 NY 71, 43 NE 427. Thus, a residuary beneficiary under the terms of a will may testify as to an *inter vivos* gift by the testator to a third party, because this effectively precludes him from sharing in any portion of the property at issue. *Re Estate of Tremaine* (1989, 3d Dept) 156 AD2d 862, 549 NYS2d 857.

A witness may be called to testify on behalf of a party whose interests are opposed to his own. *Re Hayden's Will* (1941) 261 AD 103, 24 NYS2d 608. Where a witness is examined on behalf of the adverse party, rather than on his own behalf, the prohibition of the statute is not applicable. *Re Anna's Estate* (1928) 248 NY 421, 162 NE 473.

When a party examines a witness as to part of a transaction or communication, the other party may prove the entire transaction or communication. *Re Booth's Will* (1926) 215 AD 516, 312 NYS

684, later app 130 Misc 332, 224 NYS 371, revd 224 AD 363, 231 NYS 218, resettled 224 AD 616, 231 NYS 564.

The granting of temporary administration to the defendant to conserve the estate of his son who had been absent for three years is an insufficient adjudication of death to satisfy the application of the exclusionary statutory rule of CPLR 4519, which applies only to a deceased or mentally ill person. The plaintiff, an attorney suing for legal fees, was, therefore, not an incompetent witness. *Jacobs v Stark* (1975) 83 Misc 2d 605, 373 NYS2d 758.

§ 12:5   TIME AT WHICH INCOMPETENCY IS DETERMINED

— It is interest in the event at the time of the testimony that disqualifies the witness. *Hobart v Hobart* (1875) 62 NY 80. In an action by a corporation against the administrators of a decedent's estate, the controlling stockholder of plaintiff corporation was disqualified as a witness. The controlling stockholder sold his stock to his sister during a recess, resigned his offices in the corporation, and was declared competent to testify. *Friedrich v Martin* (1945) 294 NY 588, 63 ALR 1210.

The rationale for retention of the "Dead Man Statute" is that there is no one who can confront and cross-examine a witness as to conversations with a deceased party. *Siegel v Waldbaum* (1977, 2d Dept) 59 AD2d 555, 397 NYS2d 144. However, in an action brought by plaintiff against his former partner who died subsequent to the institution of the action, and who while still alive took a deposition of the plaintiff, that deposition should have been admitted into evidence. *Siegel v Waldbaum, supra.*

§ 12:6   STATEMENT OF DECEASED PARTNERS OR JOINT CONTRACTORS

— In an action by an administratrix, who claimed there was a partnership between her decedent and the defendant, testimony by defendant relating to transactions or communications with a deceased person was properly excluded. *Ellis v Ellis* (1921) 196 AD 896, 187 NYS 316. In an action against surviving partners, evidence of statements made to plaintiff by the deceased partner in the presence of a surviving partner was not admissible, despite the fact that plaintiff did not participate in the conversation. *Brimo v Revillon* (1931) 139 Misc 416, 247 NYS 698, affd 235 AD 781, 256 NYS 978.

A partner brought an action against an executor for conversion of a check that was payable to the members of the firm, consisting of the plaintiff, the decedent and the executor. It was held proper for plaintiff to testify as to the terms of his partnership with the decedent, based on an oral agreement. Plaintiff's action was against the defendant individually rather than the estate of the deceased partner. *Gratwick v Smith* (1922) 202 AD 600, 195 NYS 568.

§ 12:7   STATEMENTS OF DECEASED AGENTS — The prohibition of the statute does not apply to conversations with an agent who is dead at the time of the trial. *Carmen v Shore Cleaners & Dyers, Inc.* (1946) 270 AD 945, 62 NYS2d 362. A party is not prevented from testifying as to transactions with the deceased agent of the adversary. *Masone v Ferino* (1961) 32 Misc 2d 15, 221 NYS2d 472.

§ 12:8   WAIVER OF INCOMPETENCY — The prohibition of the statute as to the testimony of a party or interested witness does not apply when the executor, administrator, survivor, committee or successor is examined on his own behalf or the testimony of a decedent or mentally ill person is introduced into evidence with respect to the same transaction or communication. CPLR 4519.

Thus, when the plaintiff, who is the personal representative of the decedent, testifies on his own behalf as to a personal transaction between the defendant and the decedent, the defendant is competent to testify on his own behalf as to that transaction only, not to other transactions. *Rogers v Maguire* (1897) 153 NY 343, 47 NE 452; *Re Estate of Wood* (1981) 52 NY2d 139, 436 NYS2d 850. In a discovery proceeding, a son is competent to testify as to the details of a gift where the petitioner has testified on direct examination as to the same transaction. *Re Berardini's Will* (1933) 238 AD 433, 264 NYS 479, affd 263 NY 627, 189 NE 730. To the same effect is *Re Bodker's Estate* (1945, Sur) 72 NYS2d 237.

Testimony of the decedent means sworn testimony on some prior occasion. *Re Callister's Estate* (1897) 153 NY 294, 47 NE 268. Thus, a promissory note executed by the decedent, although evidence, was not the testimony of the deceased. Its introduction in evidence did not constitute such a waiver of the protection of the statute as would permit the interested party to testify about the circumstances surrounding the execution of the note. *Re Callister's Estate, supra.*

Although the protection of the statute is waived when the personal representative of the deceased testifies on his own behalf as to a personal transaction between the deceased and defendant, CPLR 4519, there is no waiver when the plaintiff executor proves by the testimony of a witness that certain conversations took place between the decedent and the defendant at a particular place. *Pinney v Orth* (1882) 88 NY 447.

Although the rule interdicts the testimony of a party in interest with respect to a personal transaction or communication with the deceased, nevertheless he may testify as to such extraneous matters such as whether the testimony given at the trial with respect to such transaction is true. He may also testify about any other facts that tend to show that a witness has testified falsely regarding such transaction. *Pinney v Orth, supra.*

The reading of a pretrial deposition of an adverse party effectuates a waiver of the protection accorded by this statute. *Re Estate of Sylvestri* (1977, 2d Dept) 57 AD2d 558, 393 NYS2d 82.

Even though plaintiff proved statements of decedent made at a different time than the transaction between decedent and defendant, such statements were not the statements of a decedent given in evidence within the meaning of the statute. Such statements did not make admissible testimony that was otherwise clearly incompetent. *Lyon v Ricker* (1894) 141 NY 225, 36 NE 189.

The rule that when an executor elicits testimony from an interested party as to a personal transaction with the decedent, he waives the protection of the statute and renders otherwise incompetent testimony of his adversary admissible to explain fully the disputed personal transaction, applies only when the executor forces another interested party to testify. It does not apply when the testimony is given in an unrelated proceeding in which representatives of the estate are not parties. *Estate of Sternberg v Sternberg* (1981, 4th Dept) 81 AD2d 1010, 440 NYS2d 96.

When the personal representative examines the adverse party as a witness with respect to a transaction or communication with the decedent, that witness may testify on his own behalf as to the entire communication or transaction relating to the part as to which he was examined. *Cole v Sweet* (1907) 187 NY 488, 80 NE 355. Plaintiff sued to recover for merchandise sold and called defendant to testify as to his purchase of such merchandise. The statute did not render defendant incompetent to testify on cross-examination that he paid plaintiff's intestate for the merchandise, despite the fact that the sale and the payments took place on different days and constituted different transactions within the meaning of the statute. *Mahoney v Jones* (1898) 35 AD 84, 54 NYS 488.

The protection of the statute may be waived by the committee of an incompetent, subject to obtaining the consent of the court. *Dean v Halliburton* (1925) 241 NY 354, 150 NE 141, reh den 242 NY 506, 152 NE 403. The failure to object in the trial court to the competency of the witness was held to constitute a waiver of the statute. *Re Levine's Estate* (1936) 247 AD 19, 286 NYS 513. An executor suing to recover the amount of a check cross-examined the widow of decedent with respect to the transactions concerning the check. That opened the door for direct examination of the widow as to the circumstances under which she received the check. *Kings County Trust Co. v Hyams* (1926) 242 NY 405, 152 NE 129.

When the executor produced evidence of the opening of bank accounts and the withdrawals from them, he did not open the door to testimony by the respondents concerning what they did with the cash following the withdrawals. The executor did not waive the protection of the Dead Man Statute. *Re Estate of Wood* (1981) 52 NY2d 139, 436 NYS2d 850.

By introducing the testimony of one of the persons with an interest in the event that she received money from the decedent following each of his withdrawals from his savings accounts, the executor opened the door to otherwise incompetent testimony of the interested party at trial. *Re Radus* (1988, 2d Dept) 140 AD2d 348, 527 NYS2d 840.

In a malpractice case, the testimony of defendant doctor that the plaintiff-decedent was suffering from a hormonal mass did not violate the Dead Man Statute. *Nigro v Benjamin* (1989, 4th Dept) 155 AD2d 872, 547 NYS2d 710. By testifying on her own behalf concerning defendant's examination of her mother, the plaintiff-administratrix waived the protection of the statute and opened the door to this limited testimony. *Nigro v Benjamin, supra*.

§ 12:9   STATUTORY EXCEPTIONS — Certain exceptions are contained within the statute. A stockholder or officer of a banking corporation that is a party to an action or proceeding is not, by virtue of his status, interested in the event. CPLR 4519. The possible imposition of costs against the witness or the possible award of costs to him does not render him incompetent. CPLR 4519. Thus, the statute does not bar testimony as to conversations between officials of a mortgagee bank and the decedent mortgagor with respect to banking transactions. *Domestic Finance Corp. v Tinney Cadillac Corp.* (1960) 23 Misc 2d 153, 197 NYS2d 693.

When negligence is involved in an action based on ownership or operation of a motor vehicle, vessel or aircraft, the statute no longer bars a witness from testifying as to the facts or results of the accident, even though one or more of the parties to the lawsuit is a representative of the decedent or incompetent. CPLR 4519. This exception, however, does not permit the witness to testify as to conversations with the decedent. CPLR 4519. A defendant may testify as to who was driving the automobile, because this is one of the facts of the accident. *Rost v Kessler* (1944) 267 AD 686, 49 NYS2d 97.

An executor brought an action on behalf of his deceased father to recover stock and a claimed share of profits allegedly due the decedent as a result of the decedent's efforts in obtaining building maintenance contracts for defendant's decedent. The plaintiff-executor read into evidence the examination before trial of defendant's decedent, taken while the latter was still alive and subsequent to the commencement of the action. It was proper to permit plaintiff executor to testify as to conversations with the deceased defendant under the exception to CPLR 4519 involving testimony of a decedent that has been given in evidence. *Tepper v Tannenbaum* (1978, 1st Dept) 65 AD2d 359, 411 NYS2d 588, reh den

(1st Dept) 67 AD2d 882, 413 NYS2d 1019 and later app (1st Dept) 83 AD2d 541, 441 NYS2d 470.

§ 12:10   WHAT TESTIMONY IS BARRED — Because the statute bars the testimony of a person or party interested in the event only when he is being examined concerning a personal transaction or communication with a decedent or mentally ill person, it follows that if the evidence does not pertain to a personal transaction with a decedent or mentally ill person, the witness is competent to testify. *Hamlin v Stevens* (1901) 59 AD 522, 59 NYS 255.

An attorney is permitted to testify as to advice he gave the testator's widow with respect to her rights in her husband's estate when the decedent had not been a participant in the conversations. *Re French's Will* (1959, 3d Dept) 8 AD2d 660, 185 NYS2d 132. A witness may testify as to a conversation that took place in his presence between a decedent and another person, when he himself took no part in the conversation. *Griswold v Hart* (1912) 205 NY 384, 98 NE 918.

It has been held that officers of a religious congregation were not barred from testifying as to conversations with the deceased concerning a gift to the congregation. The officers served without pay and had no personal pecuniary interest in the issue involved in the lawsuit. *Re Kladneve's Estate* (1929) 133 Misc 766, 234 NYS 246, affd 228 AD 772, 239 NYS 851.

"Transactions" and "communications" embrace every variety of affairs that can form the subject of negotiation, interviews or actions between two persons. They also include every method by which one person can derive impressions or information from the conduct, condition or language of another. *Holcomb v Holcomb* (1884) 95 NY 316. It was error to receive in evidence plaintiff's book of account in which was contained an itemized statement of services purportedly rendered to decedent, when the executrix objected and the only evidence as to the authenticity of the book was that of plaintiff herself. *Eby v Grieves* (1934) 153 Misc 428, 275 NYS 90.

Plaintiffs were barred from testifying as to decedent's alleged deathbed designation of plaintiffs as additional beneficiaries under a pension plan that had vested in decedent during his lifetime. *Poslock v Teachers' Retirement Bd. of the Teachers Retirement*

Sys. (1995, 1st Dept) 209 AD2d 87, 624 NYS2d 574. However, plaintiffs were competent to testify that decedent expressed the desire to provide for his family and friends with regard to the component of the same benefit package consisting of a group term life insurance policy that had no cash value and could not be invaded during decedent's lifetime. *Poslock v Teachers' Retirement Bd., supra.*

A witness is not barred from testifying as to acts that took place after a person's death, such as where she went and what she did on the night her father died, when his papers were entrusted to her after his death. *Re Abwender's Estate* (1934) 241 AD 566, 272 NYS 569.

The statute bars not only testimony that a communication did take place, but also testimony that a decedent failed to make a communication. Plaintiffs were thus incompetent to testify as to things that decedent did not say or do when they sought to show that by failing to inform or act, the decedent had committed fraud. *Endervelt v Slade* (1994) 162 Misc 2d 975, 618 NYS2d 520, affd (1995, 1st Dept) 214 AD2d 456, 625 NYS2d 210.

The statute does more than merely bar direct testimony by the witness that a personal transaction did or did not take place. It also bars every attempt at proving the same thing indirectly. *Boyd v Boyd* (1900) 164 NY 234, 58 NE 118. Thus, it is improper to attempt to negative the doing of a given act by someone other than the decedent, or to isolate a given act from the circumstances surrounding it, or to have the survivor testify to a seemingly independent fact, *Boyd v Boyd, supra,* when other evidence shows that it originated in or resulted from a personal transaction. *Clift v Moses* (1889) 112 NY 426, 20 NE 392.

When the claim was made that a decedent had given a note to his son, the son may not testify that the note was not given to him by any other person. *Grey v Grey* (1872) 47 NY 552. It has, however, been held that when a witness has sworn to a conversation between the surviving party and the decedent, the former may testify that the witness was never present during any conversation that took place between the survivor and the deceased. *Pinney v Orth* (1882) 88 NY 447. The statute does not prohibit an alleged surviving spouse from testifying that neither he nor decedent ever instituted a matrimonial action against each other. *Estate of Lancaster* (1960) 30 Misc 2d 7, 209 NYS2d 395.

An interested witness may not testify that he saw the decedent write so as to enable him to express an opinion with respect to the decedent's handwriting when the signature is in dispute. *Wilber v Gillespie* (1908) 127 AD 604, 112 NYS 20.

A wife claimed her elective share against her deceased husband's estate and the estate sought to bar her by virtue of the provisions of an antenuptial agreement. The wife contended that an oral agreement had been made between her and the husband to the effect that the antenuptial agreement would only be of one year's duration. There was no waiver of the protection of the Dead Man Statute merely because the attorney for the estate had cross-examined the wife as to whether she had signed the antenuptial agreement. *Re Estate of Miller* (1983, 3d Dept) 97 AD2d 581, 467 NYS2d 922.

RESEARCH REFERENCES

American Law Reports

50 ALR4th 1238, Dead man's statutes as affected by Rule 601 of the Uniform Rules of Evidence and similar state rules

67 ALR3d 970, Statutes excluding testimony of one person because of death of another as applicable to attorneys

35 ALR3d 955, Personal representative's loss of rights under dead man statute by prior institution of discovery proceedings

23 ALR3d 389, Taking deposition or serving interrogatories in civil case as waiver of incompetency of witness

18 ALR3d 606, Statute excluding testimony of one person because of death of another as applied to testimony in respect of lost or destroyed instrument

13 ALR3d 404, Competency of interested witness to testify to signature or handwriting of deceased

77 ALR2d 676, Competency of witness in wrongful death action as affected by dead man statute

ALR QUICK INDEX: Dead Man's Statute

American Jurisprudence 2d

81 AM JUR 2d, Witnesses §§ 303-412

American Jurisprudence Proof of Facts

4 AM JUR PROOF OF FACTS 185, Conversations and Transactions With Deceased

American Jurisprudence Trials

19 AM JUR TRIALS 1, Actions by or Against a Decedent's Estate §§ 7-11

Other Resources

8 CARMODY-WAIT 2d, Presentation of the Case §§ 56:76-56:83

Auto-Cite®: Any case citation herein can be checked for form, parallel references, later history and annotation references through the Auto-Cite computer research system.

CHAPTER 13

EXAMINATION OF WITNESSES

§ 13:1 MATERIALITY OF QUESTIONS ASKED ON DIRECT EXAMINATION

§ 13:1 **MATERIALITY OF QUESTIONS ASKED ON DIRECT EXAMINATION** — A question that is asked on direct examination must be material. Evidence is material when it has an effective influence or bearing on the question in issue. *Barr v Dolphin Holding Corp.* (1955, Sup) 141 NYS2d 906.

Even though evidence is material, it may be excluded if it is too remote. *Bashaw v Bouvia* (1961, 3d Dept) 14 AD2d 640, 218 NYS2d 194. The determination of whether specific facts are relevant or too remote is for the discretion of the trial judge. *Christie v Mitchell* (1960, 4th Dept) 10 AD2d 52, 197 NYS2d 206.

In a civil suit for assault and battery, the suspicions of an investigating officer that defendant may have been the perpetrator were probative of nothing. That testimony was improperly admitted. *O'Connell v Jacobs* (1992, 4th Dept) 181 AD2d 1064, 583 NYS2d 61.

§ 13:2 **RELEVANCY OF QUESTIONS ASKED ON DIRECT EXAMINATION** — The testimony sought to be elicited by a question must be relevant. A fact is relevant to another fact when the existence of one renders the existence of the other probable, according to the common course of events. *People v Nitzberg* (1941) 287 NY 183, 138 ALR 1253, reh den 287 NY 754 138 ALR 1266.

Circumstantial evidence, to be admissible, should tend to create in the trier of the facts a reasonable persuasion or belief as to the existence or non-existence of the facts in issue. *People v Steele* (1942) 179 Misc 587, 37 NYS2d 199. Any evidence that logically tends to prove or disprove one of the principal facts in issue is relevant and admissible, unless the admission of the evidence would violate some exclusionary rule. *Oliver v England* (1965) 48 Misc 2d 335, 264 NYS2d 999.

Relevance is not always enough. Even if the evidence is proximately relevant, it may be rejected if its probative value is outweighed by the danger that its admission would prolong the trial to an unreasonable extent without any corresponding advantage, confuse the main issue and mislead the jury, unfairly surprise a party, or create undue prejudice to one of the parties. *People v Davis* (1977) 43 NY2d 17, 400 NYS2d 735, cert den 435 US 998,

56 L Ed 2d 88, 98 S Ct 1653 and cert den 438 US 914, 57 L Ed 2d 1160, 98 S Ct 3143.

In a civil action, where character is not in issue, evidence of character or reputation of a party to the action is generally inadmissible. *Beach v Richtmyer* (1949) 275 AD 466, 90 NYS2d 332. If general reputation has not been attacked, evidence of general reputation for chastity or good character is not admissible. *Booth v Booth* (1929) 135 Misc 350, 238 NYS 193. Although the character of a party may not be shown in a civil action to raise an inference that he either did or did not do the act in question, such evidence is admissible in a civil case where character is directly in issue, such as a defamation or malicious prosecution action. *Goberman v McNamara* (1974) 76 Misc 2d 791, 352 NYS2d 369.

Testimony may be relevant because it explains facts already in evidence or inferences to be drawn from such facts. Thus, the court erred in rejecting testimony offered in explanation of facts that could have rendered innocuous an inference with which opposing counsel improperly dealt in his summation. *Leonard v Home Owners' Loan Corp.* (1946) 270 AD 363, 270 AD 785, 270 AD 867, 60 NYS2d 78, affd 297 NY 103.

In an action against a motorist for injuries sustained by a 9-year-old girl as a result of a contact between the defendant's vehicle and the plaintiff, questions from which the jury might infer that the plaintiffs had Americanized their name were irrelevant. *Sandy v Wicks* (1940) 260 AD 1046, 24 NYS2d 424.

Testimony as to the condition of an automobile at the time of an accident constituted some evidence of its value in an action for damages. *Schwartz v Fletcher* (1933) 238 AD 554, 265 NYS 277. The cost of an automobile when new is some evidence of its value in determining the loss to its owner. *Henderson v Parks Cent. Motors Service Inc.* (1930) 138 Misc 183, 244 NYS 409.

In determining the true value of corporate stock, its book value is entitled to little, if any, weight. *Diston v Loucks* (1941, Sup) 62 NYS2d 138, affd 264 AD 758, 35 NYS2d 715, app den 264 AD 838, 35 NYS2d 763. There must be a consideration of the record of the corporation, its prospects for the future, the investment value as determined by the rate of return, the selling price of stocks of like character, the appraised and sale value of the assets, the market conditions, and any other relevant evidentiary facts relating to the property that may be reflected in the worth of the stocks. *Diston v Loucks, supra.*

Rent reserved, *i.e.*, recited in a lease, is some evidence of the rental value of the premises. *Goelet v National Surety Co.* (1928) 249 NY 287, 164 NE 101, 62 ALR 425. Alterations made on leased premises to make them suitable for neighborhood and general business purposes were held to be material in determining the rental value of a lease assigned by the administratrix. *Re Schlossman's Adm'x* (1930) 136 Misc 893, 242 NYS 417.

In determining the value of a condemned parcel of land, the prior sale price was entitled to significant, even if not overbearing, consideration. *Re James Madison Houses* (1962, 1st Dept) 17 AD2d 317, 234 NYS2d 799. However, the price allegedly paid in a foreign country 25 years ago for an article of personal property is not, in and of itself, competent evidence of its present market value in this country. *Sand v Standard Acci. Ins. Co.* (1954, App Term) 136 NYS2d 755.

An arm's-length sale of subject property can be the best evidence of market value for tax purposes. *Seneca Grape Juice Corp. v Board of Assessors* (1970, 3d Dept) 33 AD2d 951, 306 NYS2d 537. This is particularly true if the sale is recent and is not explained away as abnormal in any fashion. *Lane Bryant, Inc. v Tax Com. of New York* (1964) 21 AD2d 669, 249 NYS2d 994, affd 19 NY2d 715, 279 NYS2d 175.

The assessed valuation of real estate is some evidence of its fair market value and must be considered along with other factors in determining such value, but it is not conclusive. *North Hornell v Rauber* (1943) 181 Misc 546, 40 NYS2d 938.

The net profit that a developer might obtain in the future after subdividing property into a number of residential lots is not relevant to the fair market value at the time when the defendant breached his agreement to purchase the land as a single lot. *Deeb v Drake* (1992, 3d Dept) 184 AD2d 947, 584 NYS2d 940.

Where proof of an oral contract was properly excluded, it was improper to admit proof of damages based on such a contract. *Halloran v N. & C. Contracting Co.* (1928) 249 NY 381, 164 NE 324.

In an action by a shipper against a trucking company and against the agent engaged to arrange for the shipment of goods, evidence as to the custom in the business and the course of dealing between the shipper and the agent was relevant. Such evidence bore upon the issue of whether the agent had acted with due care, within the knowledge of the shipper and within the agent's customary practice and authority in effecting the wishes of the shipper. The exclusion of such evidence was an error sufficiently substantial to warrant a new trial. *Universal Ltd. v S. Stern & Co.* (1970, 1st Dept) 34 AD2d 770, 311 NYS2d 317.

In an action for personal injuries, defendant's co-employee testified that immediately after the accident, while plaintiff was lying in the eastbound lane of the highway with his feet extending into the westbound lane, the defendant-driver of a truck stated: "Get his feet out of the way. I want to get out of here." It was error to receive this statement in evidence, because it was unrelated to the happening of the accident and highly prejudicial. *Zipay v Benson* (1975, 3d Dept) 47 AD2d 233, 365 NYS2d 920, later app (3d Dept) 57 AD2d 683, 393 NYS2d 825, app dismd 42 NY2d 1052, 399 NYS2d 214.

Even though evidence is logically and technically relevant, it is not necessarily admissible. It will be excluded if it is too slight, remote, or conjectural to have any legitimate influence in determining the fact in issue. *Dermatossian v New York City Transit Authority* (1986) 67 NY2d 219, 501 NYS2d 784.

Plaintiff may not adduce evidence tending to demonstrate that a person alleged to have committed a negligent act has previously committed similar acts or was generally negligent. *Feaster v New York City Transit Authority* (1991, 1st Dept) 172 AD2d 284, 568 NYS2d 380.

The trial court can properly permit testimony, on behalf of the defense, as to plaintiff's character, reputation and professional misconduct, if it is relevant and probative to a determination of issues in a case. Thus, such testimony was properly permitted in determining whether the plaintiff had, in fact, forged his wife's name to a variety of important financial documents, as well as whether his employers improperly fired him and cited forgery as the reason therefor. *Burdick v Shearson American Express, Inc.*

(1990, 1st Dept) 160 AD2d 642, 559 NYS2d 506, app den 76 NY2d 706, 560 NYS2d 988.

In an action by an insured building owner against his fire insurance company, the trial court properly permitted evidence with respect to plaintiff's relationship with his wife, his delinquency in mortgage payments, cancellation of his insurance coverage, his place of residence at the time of the fire, and facts relating to a loan application made by him after the fire. This evidence was relevant to the issues of motive, opportunity and financial status. *Torian v Reliance Ins. Co.* (1991, 3d Dept) 171 AD2d 971, 567 NYS2d 913.

The determination of issues of relevancy are matters resting largely in the discretion of the trial court. *Rhoades v Niagara Mohawk Power Corp.* (1994, 3d Dept) 202 AD2d 762, 608 NYS2d 733.

§ 13:3 ADMISSIBILITY OF NEGATIVE EVIDENCE — There may be an issue in a case as to whether a given act did or did not occur. To prove the non-occurrence of such act, evidence may be offered by witnesses who did not see or hear the given occurrence. This has been described as negative evidence. If otherwise relevant, negative evidence is admissible.

Testimony, based on negative knowledge, that a fact which the witness failed to hear or to see did not occur, is admissible, if the witness was so situated that in the ordinary course of events he would have heard or seen the fact had it occurred. *Latourelle v New York C. R. Co.* (1950) 301 NY 103, reh den 301 NY 677. Thus, a witness's negative evidence that he heard no whistle was admissible where the fact in issue was a railroad engineer's alleged negligence in failing to blow a whistle as the train approached a road crossing at which it struck an automobile. *Latourelle v New York C. R. Co., supra.*

In a criminal prosecution for negligent homicide that resulted from a fatal collision between defendant's truck and another vehicle, the trial court properly permitted, as admissible negative evidence, the testimony of an accident reconstruction expert to the effect that he found no evidence that the truck stopped. The fact that he did not visit the scene of the accident until seven weeks after it occurred, and therefore might not have discovered any such existing evidence in the ordinary course of his investigation, merely goes to the weight to be accorded his testimony, not to its admissibility. *People v Moore* (1989, 3d Dept) 155 AD2d 725, 547 NYS2d 685, app den 75 NY2d 773, 551 NYS2d 915.

§ 13:4 RELEVANCE OF THE CONDUCT OF A PARTY OR OF CONDITIONS SHORTLY BEFORE AN ACCIDENT — A difficult question is presented with respect to the relevance of testimony regarding a person's actions or the conditions prevailing sometime before an accident when such testimony is offered to show the person's conduct or the conditions prevailing at the time of the accident. In an action to recover for a fall on a slippery ramp, testimony to the effect that snow, ice, and slush had collected on the ramp on the previous day was admissible when the temperature and weather conditions on the two days were similar. *Madalina v Wegman's Food Markets, Inc.* (1943, Sup) 41 NYS2d 631, affd 272 AD 957, 72 NYS2d 678.

In a negligence action, where the prior condition of a radiator cover was not in issue, evidence thereof was properly excluded. *Bellefeuille v City & County Sav. Bank* (1976) 40 NY2d 879, 389 NYS2d 345.

In one case, the loose condition of a railing was measured by a witness five months after the accident, and it was shown that the condition five months after the accident was the same as it had been before the accident. The evidence taken five months afterwards was admissible. *Wiener v Board of Education* (1975, 2d Dept) 48 AD2d 887, 369 NYS2d 207.

§ 13:5 COMPETENCY OF QUESTIONS ASKED ON DIRECT EXAMINATION — A question asked on direct examination must be of such a nature that the testimony sought to be elicited in response is competent. This means that the testimony is not barred by any exclusionary rule of evidence.

Thus, for example, the exclusionary rule bars evidence obtained by an illegal search and seizure by public officials; this applies to official proceedings such as one to determine the suspension of a license for permitting gambling on the premises, *Malik v New York State Liquor Authority* (1968, 4th Dept) 30 AD2d 1040, 294 NYS2d 948, affd 24 NY2d 647, 301 NYS2d 584, motion den 25

NY2d 777, 303 NYS2d 526 and cert den 396 US 840, 24 L Ed 2d 91, 90 S Ct 103, and to civil proceedings. *Chmielewski v Rosetti* (1969) 59 Misc 2d 335, 298 NYS2d 875. Where evidence has been obtained by a private litigant by use of lawless force, such evidence is not inadmissible. *Sackler v Sackler* (1964) 15 NY2d 40, 255 NYS2d 83, 5 ALR3d 664.

A hotel guest alleged that she had slipped and fallen on food on the floor of the hotel nightclub and testified that, after the accident, an unidentified purported employee of defendant made an admission to a busboy: "I told you . . . before . . . to clean up." That testimony was inadmissible because the oral statement did not qualify as an admission or under the *res gestae* exception to the hearsay rule. *Sherman v Tamarack Lodge* (1989, 2d Dept) 146 AD2d 767, 537 NYS2d 249.

The trial court erred in refusing to admit hearsay testimony of statements made by defendant's employees following an accident. The hearsay statements, to the effect that an employee had been directed to drive the car into the garage, were admissible against the defendant as excited utterances. *Simmons v Ricks* (1989, 4th Dept) 149 AD2d 914, 540 NYS2d 49.

An automobile driver stated to her passenger: "I cannot control the car. It's a sheet of ice." The statement was an excited utterance and, therefore, admissible in a civil suit arising out of the accident. *Deutsch v Horizon Leasing Corp.* (1988, 2d Dept) 145 AD2d 405, 535 NYS2d 383.

§ 13:6   FORM AND CONTENT OF QUESTIONS ON DIRECT EXAMINATION — A question should in fact be a question rather than a statement to the witness as to the nature of the testimony desired from him. Questions are improper if they suggest to the witness the specific tenor of the reply that the examiner desires, so that an answer is likely to be given irrespective of an actual memory. *People v Hamilton* (1941, Gen Sess) 30 NYS2d 155. A leading question is one that instructs the witness how to answer on material points or puts into his mouth the words to be echoed back. *People v Hamilton, supra.*

If a question is in the form of an assertion or assumes material facts in issue, it is ordinarily objectionable. *People v Slover* (1921) 232 NY 264, 133 NE 633. A question calling for a witness's conclusion is ordinarily an improper one. *Psota v Long Island R. Co.* (1927) 246 NY 388, 159 NE 180, 62 ALR 1163.

Another type of improper question is one that requires the witness to characterize an act or conduct. For example, where a witness has testified with respect to her acts and the purpose of her visit to a doctor's office, it is improper to ask the witness whether she went to the doctor's office for the purpose of trapping him. The question called for a characterization of her act. *Friedel v Board of Regents* (1947) 296 NY 347, remittitur amd 297 NY 585.

§ 13:7　LEADING QUESTIONS — A leading question puts words into the mouth of the witness and suggests the answer to be given by the witness. *People v Hamilton* (1941, Gen Sess) 30 NYS2d 155. The trial court appropriately sustained objection to counsel leading his own witness, where the witness was not the adverse party or otherwise hostile. *Cohen v St. Regis Paper Co.* (1985, 4th Dept) 109 AD2d 1048, 487 NYS2d 406.

If a witness is hostile, it is permissible to use leading questions on the direct examination of that witness. *Zilver v Robert Graves Co.* (1905) 106 AD 582, 94 NYS 714. It is also permissible to lead a witness as to preliminary matters. *Cope v Shibley*, 12 Barb 521. In addition, leading questions are permissible if the witness is somewhat slow-witted, *Strnad v William Messer Co.* (1913, App Term) 142 NYS 314, or too illiterate, weak, sick or young to testify declaratively. *Nicoletti v Dieckmann* (1915, Sup) 89 Misc 131, 151 NYS 520.

The extent to which leading questions are permitted on direct examination is within the discretion of the trial court. *Downs v New York C. R. Co.* (1871) 47 NY 83.

§ 13:8　AIDING A WITNESS BY REFRESHING MEMORY — Ordinarily, a witness takes the stand and tells his story from his own memory with no help from the examining attorney other than the asking of proper questions. A witness is, however, under certain conditions, permitted to refresh his memory.

Before the memory of a witness may be refreshed by documents or other extraneous means, it must ordinarily be shown that the present recollection of the witness is exhausted. *People v Reger* (1961, 1st Dept) 13 AD2d 63, 213 NYS2d 298. The document must actually serve the purpose of refreshing the recollection of the witness. *People v Betts* (1947) 272 AD 737, 74 NYS2d 791, affd 297 NY 1000. When the memory of the witness has been stimulated, he must thereafter testify to the facts of his own knowledge. *Brown v Western Union Tel. Co.* (1966, 4th Dept) 26 AD2d 316, 274 NYS2d 52.

A memorandum used by a witness to refresh his recollection need not have been made by the witness. *Levenson v Commonwealth Syndicate, Inc.* (1940, App Term) 24 NYS2d 781. It is the testimony of the witness whose memory has been refreshed that goes into evidence, not the writing used to refresh the recollection. *Brown v Western Union Tel. Co. supra; Levenson v Commonwealth Syndicate, Inc., supra.*

In an automobile collision case, a police officer was properly permitted to testify to an independent recollection of defendant's admissions and also properly allowed to refer to a memorandum made by another policeman from the testifying police officer's notes on his conversation with the defendant. *Paulo v Kaiser* (1957, 3d Dept) 5 AD2d 746, 168 NYS2d 651. It was error for the trial court to prevent plaintiff from refreshing the recollection of defendant's assistant manager about the accident with an accident report supplied to plaintiff by defendant. *Newman v Great Atlantic & Pacific Tea Co.* (1984, 2d Dept) 100 AD2d 538, 473 NYS 231.

Although a writing is not admissible solely because it revives a witness's recollection, opposing counsel has the right to inspect it. *People v Brown* (1956, 4th Dept) 2 AD2d 202, 153 NYS2d 744. Opposing counsel also has a right to use the writing to cross-examine the witness. *Patchogue Oil Terminal Corp. v Sambach* (1958) 15 Misc 2d 266, 178 NYS2d 659.

In a medical malpractice action, it was reversible error to deny defendant physician's request to review plaintiff's personal diary in which he kept notes regarding his contacts with defendant. During cross-examination, plaintiff testified that he had "looked at" and "read" the diary immediately prior to trial. It was clear that plaintiff's sole purpose in reading the diary was to refresh his memory, even though plaintiff never explicitly stated that he had used the diary to "refresh his recollection." Accordingly, the defendant was entitled to inspect the diary and use it for cross-examination of plaintiff. *Chabica v Schneider* (1995, 2d Dept) 213 AD2d 579, 624 NYS2d 271.

The writing used to refresh the recollection of the witness may not be shown to the jury by the party using it. *Tarulli v Salanitri* (1970, 2d Dept) 34 AD2d 962, 312 NYS2d 55.

A witness could not use records to refresh his recollection, where he had no knowledge or memory of any facts that could be refreshed. *Munro Athletic Products Co. v Universal Carloading & Distributing Co.* (1944, App Term) 53 NYS2d 170. If a witness has no independent recollection of the memorandum or the facts that it recites and his memory is not refreshed thereby, the memorandum may not be used as a basis for his testimony. *Brown v Western Union Tel. Co., supra.*

§ 13:9   QUESTIONS THAT IMPEACH ONE'S OWN WITNESS

— A party may not ordinarily ask his own witness a question that tends to impeach him. *Hanrahan v New York Edison Co.* (1924) 238 NY 194, 144 NE 499. A party who calls a witness vouches for him, and the witness's honesty and integrity may not be questioned by that party. *Rosati v H. W. E., Inc.* (1948, Sup) 81 NYS2d 412.

Although a party may not impeach his witness, he is free to contradict him or to challenge the accuracy of his recollection. *Rosati v H. W. E., Inc., supra.* Thus, a party may present contradictory evidence. *Re Tessitore's Estate* (1950, Sur) 99 NYS2d 776.

When a party cross-examines a witness as to matters not brought out on the direct examination, to that extent the examination becomes a direct one and the cross-examiner is then bound by the answers and may not impeach the witness. *Tarulli v Salanitri* (1970, 2d Dept) 34 AD2d 962, 312 NYS2d 55.

If the witness is the adverse party, there is an exception to the general rule that one may not impeach one's own witness. *Re Tessitore's Estate* (1950, Sur) 99 NYS2d 776. By calling an adverse party as a witness, a party is not bound by the witness's version of the facts. It may not be said that the party who called the adverse witness has adopted his version of the facts. *Spampinato v A. B. C. Consol. Corp.* (1974) 35 NY2d 283, 360 NYS2d 878.

§ 13:10 TESTIMONY THAT TENDS TO INCRIMINATE THE WITNESS — A witness cannot be compelled to give testimony that will incriminate him. This applies to testimony that may incriminate him directly or furnish a link in the chain of incrimination. *Triangle Publications, Inc. v Ferrare* (1957, 3d Dept) 4 AD2d 591, 168 NYS2d 128. If the witness's answer furnishes a lead from which incriminating evidence may be obtained, the privilege applies. *Bradley v O'Hare* (1956, 1st Dept) 2 AD2d 436, 156 NYS2d 533.

The privilege against self-incrimination is guaranteed by the Fifth Amendment of the U.S. Constitution and by Article 1 § 6 of the New York State Constitution. The privilege against self-incrimination has been enacted into statute as well. CPLR 4501.

The privilege against self-incrimination is a personal one. *Bradley v O'Hare* (1956, 1st Dept) 2 AD2d 436, 156 NYS2d 533. In the case of a non-party witness, neither a party nor the counsel for a party to the action may raise the objection. *June Fabrics, Inc. v Teri Sue Fashions, Inc.* (1948) 194 Misc 267, 81 NYS2d 877. When a non-party witness is ordered to testify, the privilege is exclusively between the court and the witness and a party has no right to object to the testimony on the ground of the privilege. *People v Kozer* (1969, 3d Dept) 33 AD2d 617, 304 NYS2d 793. The privilege against self-incrimination may be claimed for a witness by his counsel; it may not be claimed by another person's counsel or on behalf of another person. *Gullo v Courtright* (1970) 62 Misc 2d 721, 309 NYS2d 735.

Because the privilege against self-incrimination is personal and individual, officers of a corporation cannot claim it on behalf of the corporation or refuse to produce the books of the corporation, which may disclose individual criminality. *State v Brooklyn Trade Waste Asso.* (1975) 81 Misc 2d 174, 363 NYS2d 793.

Although the privilege against self-incrimination is applied more frequently in criminal cases, the rule is equally applicable to civil actions or proceedings. *Berner v Schlesinger* (1957) 11 Misc 2d 1024, 178 NYS2d 135, affd (1st Dept) 6 AD2d 781, 175 NYS2d 579. The privilege against self-incrimination in New York extends not only to a trial in court, but also to an investigation in the legislature. *Doyle v Hofstader* (1931) 257 NY 244, 177 NE

489, 87 ALR 418. An administrative body cannot compel a witness to testify in violation of his constitutional privilege. *Oleshko v New York State Liquor Authority* (1967, 1st Dept) 29 AD2d 84, 285 NYS2d 696, stay gr 21 NY2d 728, 287 NYS2d 693 and affd 21 NY2d 778, 288 NYS2d 474.

A defendant may not be compelled to testify against himself in a criminal contempt proceeding. *State University of New York v Denton* (1970, 4th Dept) 35 AD2d 176, 316 NYS2d 297.

Protection against self-incrimination applies not only to a trial but also to all pretrial stages, including examinations before trial and pleadings. *Gullo v Courtright* (1970) 62 Misc 2d 721, 309 NYS2d 735. Because a verified pleading is testimony within the meaning of the constitutional provision against self-incrimination, a party cannot be compelled to verify an answer that tends to implicate himself in a crime. *Sunley v Badler* (1942, Sup) 33 NYS2d 642; CPLR 3020(a).

The privilege against self-incrimination cannot be asserted in advance of the questions actually propounded on the examination or hearing in a civil case. *Wilman v Miller* (1942) 178 Misc 549, 35 NYS2d 352, affd 264 AD 850, 36 NYS2d 187.

A non-party witness at a deposition has a right to invoke the privilege against self-incrimination with respect to any questions to be asked or any documents required to be produced in response to a judicial subpoena *duces tecum*. He should be required to raise his privilege at the deposition with respect to each question to be asked and each document required to be produced by him. *Flushing Nat'l Bank v Transamerica Ins. Co.* (1987, 2d Dept) 135 AD2d 486, 521 NYS2d 727.

§ 13:11 EXTENT OF PRIVILEGE AGAINST SELF-INCRIMINATION

— The privilege against self-incrimination is not limited to answers that directly connect the witness with the commission of a crime. It also extends to those answers that may furnish evidence from which it may be ascertained that the witness has committed a crime. *Doyle v Hofstader* (1931) 257 NY 244, 177 NE 489, 87 ALR 418.

A witness has a right to refuse to furnish even a single link in a chain of facts that may result in his incrimination. *American Blue Stone Co. v Cohn Cut Stone Co.* (1916) 97 Misc 428, 161 NYS

667, affd 177 AD 952, 164 NYS 1085. If the testimony may provide a clue that will result in establishing the guilt of the witness, he has a right to refuse to answer. *Haftel v Appleton* (1964) 42 Misc 2d 292, 247 NYS2d 967, app dismd (1st Dept) 21 AD2d 651, 249 NYS2d 437.

The privilege against self-incrimination does not apply to answers that may render a witness civilly liable. *Taylor v Jennings* (1867) 30 NY Super Ct 581.

When a prosecution has been barred by the statute of limitations, the privilege against self-incrimination does not apply. *Meyer v Mayo* (1916) 173 AD 199, 159 NYS 405. The privilege does not apply when immunity has been granted. *June Fabrics, Inc. v Teri Sue Fashions, Inc.* (1948) 194 Misc 267, 81 NYS2d 877. However, it did not constitute sufficient immunity to warrant non-application of the privilege where the coroner, a chief of police, and a district attorney stated to a defendant in a wrongful death action that he would not be prosecuted criminally. *Owen v Fisher* (1947) 189 Misc 69, 66 NYS2d 856.

The privilege applies only when there is a real danger of prosecution. It does not extend to mere remote possibilities. *Brill v Dodd* (1942, Sup) 36 NYS2d 975.

The Fifth Amendment privilege that exists as to private papers cannot be asserted with respect to records that are required by law to be kept and that are subject to governmental regulation and inspection. *People v Doe* (1983) 59 NY2d 655, 463 NYS2d 405.

In one case, the testimony of the president of a teachers' association in no way incriminated him as an individual, and the Association itself was the only defendant against whom his identification of the records and leaflets was directed. There was no denial to the association president of his privilege against self-incrimination in requiring him to identify the records and leaflets of the association for purposes of entry into evidence. *Orchard Park Cent. School Dist. v Orchard Park Teachers Asso.* (1976, 2d Dept) 50 AD2d 462, 378 NYS2d 511, app dismd 38 NY2d 911, 382 NYS2d 756.

Because the sole purpose of the privilege against self-incrimination is to shield a witness against the incriminating effect of his testimony, the court will not permit its use as a weapon to prejudice unfairly an adversary. *Lagin v Lagin* (1977, 1st Dept) 57 AD2d 774, 394 NYS2d 432.

The rule that defendant's invocation of the privilege against self-incrimination is not to be considered in weighing the evidence against him applies only in criminal cases. The rule does not apply in civil cases where the parties are on an equal footing and the only disadvantage threatened is liability to compensate an adversary for damages. *Marine Midland Bank v John E. Russo Produce Co.* (1980) 50 NY2d 31, 427 NYS2d 961. The rule also does not apply in administrative proceedings. *Terra v Department of Health* (1993, 3d Dept) 199 AD2d 577, 604 NYS2d 644.

Invocation of the privilege against self-incrimination is not a basis for precluding civil discovery. *Stuart v Tomasino* (1989, 1st Dept) 148 AD2d 370 539 NYS2d 327.

In an action for the wrongful deaths of homicide victims, defendant, who was acquitted of homicide, and who invoked his privilege against self-incrimination as the basis for non-disclosure, could be compelled to answer questions at an examination before trial. Although defendant had previously given a statement to the state police and was concerned that he might contradict that statement at any examination before trial, the statute of limitations for perjury had run at the time of the examination before trial and there was no exposure to prosecution for perjury. *Brahm v Hatch* (1991, 3d Dept) 169 AD2d 263, 572 NYS2d 395.

§ 13:12   INVOKING THE PRIVILEGE AGAINST SELF-INCRIMINATION — Before a witness may be protected by the privilege against self-incrimination, he must invoke the privilege at the time the question is asked. *Radin v Kornreich* (1943) 17 Misc 2d 860, 41 NYS2d 638. By denying guilt and asserting facts in a verified answer and affidavit that are contrary to the allegations of the plaintiff, a person does not waive the privilege against self-incrimination. *Southbridge Finishing Co. v Golding* (1955) 208 Misc 846, 143 NYS2d 911, affd (1st Dept) 2 AD2d 882, 157 NYS2d 898.

A witness may not claim the privilege before the questions have actually been asked. *Wilman v Miller* (1942) 178 Misc 549, 35 NYS2d 352, affd 264 AD 850, 36 NYS2d 187.

The privilege against self-incrimination does not embrace a privilege against being required to claim the privilege, *i.e.*, a witness cannot refuse to take the stand, even if upon doing so the witness's only response is to plead the Fifth Amendment. *Cunningham v Nadjari* (1976) 39 NY2d 314, 383 NYS2d 590.

A judgment debtor was properly held to have waived the privilege by failing to invoke it at the time he did not answer information subpoenas. The judgment debtor had declined to respond to the information subpoenas of the judgment creditor and had invoked the privilege against self-incrimination only after contempt proceedings had been commenced. *Chase Manhattan Bank, Nat'l Ass'n v Federal Chandros, Inc.* (1989, 2d Dept) 148 AD2d 567, 539 NYS2d 36.

§ 13:13   INSPECTION OF PERSON OF ACCUSED OR WITNESS — Under both the Fifth and Fourteenth Amendments to the U.S. Constitution, the privilege against self-incrimination guarantees the right to remain silent unless the individual chooses to speak. It does not extend to situations where testimonial compulsion is not involved. The Supreme Court of the United States has held, for example, that there is no violation of the privilege when a blood sample is taken from the accused and discloses sufficient alcohol in the blood to indicate intoxication. *Schmerber v California* (1966) 384 US 757, 16 L Ed 2d 908, 86 S Ct 1826.

A hearing was held before the Commissioner of Motor Vehicles to determine whether or not to revoke the license of a motorist who refused to submit to a chemical analysis of his urine for alcoholic content after being arrested for driving while intoxicated. The hearing was not a criminal proceeding. It was an opportunity afforded petitioner by law to be heard on the question of whether or not he was entitled to a continuation of the privilege of operating a motor vehicle upon the public highway. Therefore, the constitutional right against self-incrimination had no application. *Combes v Kelly* (1956) 2 Misc 2d 491, 152 NYS2d 934.

§ 13:14   RULING UPON THE EXISTENCE OF PRIVILEGE AGAINST SELF-INCRIMINATION — Ordinarily, the witness is permitted to judge for himself whether his answer will result in subjecting him to liability for criminal punishment. *Re Grae* (1940) 282 NY 428, 127 ALR 1276. However, the court will exercise discretion in determining whether to accept the witness's mere conclusion that his answer will tend to incriminate him. *Doyle v Hofstader* (1931) 257 NY 244, 177 NE 489, 87 ALR 418.

The trial court must decide whether there is any substance or merit to the witness's claim that he has a right to refuse to answer questions on the ground that his answers might incriminate him. *People ex rel. McKinney v Richter* (1943) 182 Misc 96, 43 NYS2d 114. Although the court may not compel a witness to say more than that which asserts the privilege against self-incrimination, the court will determine whether his silence is justified. *Slater v Slater* (1974) 78 Misc 2d 13, 355 NYS2d 943.

Where the witness's refusal to testify is a clear device to protect some person other than herself, the court has discretion to determine whether the testimony that is requested of the witness will in fact degrade or incriminate her. *Burdy v Conroy* (1944) 182 Misc 476, 48 NYS2d 871.

§ 13:15 WHEN PRIVILEGE AGAINST SELF-INCRIMINATION IS LOST — A party who voluntarily testifies on his own behalf waives the privilege against self-incrimination. *Berner v Schlesinger* (1957) 11 Misc 2d 1024, 178 NYS2d 135, affd (1st Dept) 6 AD2d 781, 175 NYS2d 579. Waiver that results from a party testifying on his own behalf applies equally in civil proceedings and in criminal ones. *Berner v Schlesinger, supra.*

Once a party has taken the stand on his own behalf, the waiver is complete and he may not then reassert the privilege. *Berner v Schlesinger, supra.*

The waiver does not apparently extend to collateral matters affecting credibility. It is confined only to matters relevant to the issue. *People v Shapiro* (1955) 308 NY 453, 51 ALR2d 515.

It has been held that a witness does not waive the privilege by voluntarily testifying about the subject matter in issue but only by giving testimony that is actually incriminating. *Application of Newark Morning Ledger Co.* (1961, Sup) 215 NYS2d 929. In a filiation proceeding, where a putative father was called by petitioner to testify and the court committed error in compelling him to testify, the putative father did not waive the privilege by taking the stand at the close of the petitioner's evidence. *Schreck v Long* (1966, 3d Dept) 25 AD2d 599, 266 NYS2d 1017.

Defendant's denial of guilt and assertion of facts in a verified answer and affidavit, in contradiction of plaintiff's allegations, are not a waiver of the privilege against self-incrimination. *Southbridge Finishing Co. v Golding* (1955) 208 Misc 846, 143 NYS2d 911, affd (1st Dept) 2 AD2d 882, 157 NYS2d 898. A mere denial of wrongdoing and a mere failure to deny an allegation in a complaint cannot serve as a basis for the claim of waiver of the right to remain silent. *Steinbrecher v Wapnick* (1969) 24 NY2d 354, 300 NYS2d 555.

§ 13:16   EFFECT OF INVOKING THE PRIVILEGE AGAINST SELF-INCRIMINATION — In an action brought by a surety against debtors under an indemnification agreement, a negative inference could be drawn from the invocation by the debtors of their Fifth Amendment right; such negative inferences can be drawn in a civil action. *Indemnity Ins. Co. v Levine* (1990, 1st Dept) 168 AD2d 323, 563 NYS2d 811.

Where assertion of the Fifth Amendment privilege results in plaintiffs' failure to provide disclosure, the I.A.S. court properly dismiss the complaint. Plaintiffs offered, as a deposition witness, a principal of the plaintiff corporation who refused to answer any substantive questions on the assertion of his privilege pursuant to the Fifth Amendment. They did not offer any other knowledgeable witness. *Federal Chandros, Inc. v Silverite Constr. Co.* (1990, 1st Dept) 167 AD2d 315, 562 NYS2d 64, app den 77 NY2d 893, 568 NYS2d 910

§ 13:17   USE OF LIE DETECTOR (POLYGRAPH) TESTS — In a proceeding brought to seek dismissal of a police officer as a result of his alleged misconduct, it was proper to consider the results of a polygraph test and admit them into evidence. There was substantial evidence of the reliability of the machine used, its proper functioning on the day in question, and the qualifications of the test administrator. *May v Shaw* (1981, 2d Dept) 79 AD2d 970, 434 NYS2d 284.

§ 13:18   REQUIREMENTS OF THE WITNESS'S ANSWER — A witness who is asked a question should answer it in a manner that is responsive. *O'Hagan v Dillon* (1879) 76 NY 170. For example, if the issue in question revolves around the sanity of a person and a lay witness is asked whether particular acts of a person had impressed him as being irrational, it is unresponsive to state that the person was in fact irrational. *Re Myer's Will* (1906) 184 NY 54, 76 NE 920.

A witness is permitted to answer that a fact is or is not true to the best of his knowledge. *Blake v People* (1878) 73 NY 586. However, a witness who had been asked to describe an event and answered "I should judge he struck a stone" was held to have given an answer that was unresponsive and a mere guess. *Ryan v People* (1880) 79 NY 593.

§ 13:19 TESTIMONY CONCERNING TELEPHONE CONVERSATIONS — A witness may testify with respect to a telephone conversation, if he is able to identify the person with whom he is speaking. *Murphy v Jack* (1894) 142 NY 215, 36 NE 882. Evidence of the conversation has been held to be admissible even where the witness was not acquainted with the speaker at the time of the telephone conversation and therefore did not recognize his voice, but met the speaker subsequent to the conversation and then recognized his voice as the one he had heard over the telephone. *Walker Discount Corp. v Sapin* (1965) 48 Misc 2d 277, 264 NYS2d 841.

Where a witness testified that he could not recognize defendant's voice on the telephone, that he had called the defendant, that the person to whom he talked said he was the defendant, and there was no evidence to confirm the identity of the other person as the defendant, it was improper to admit the evidence of the telephone conversation. *Mankes v Fishman* (1914) 163 AD 789, 149 NYS 228.

It has been held that circumstantial evidence is permissible to authenticate a voice that is heard over the telephone when the conversation indicates that the speaker at the other end of the line knew facts that only the party sought to be identified would be likely to know, or when other confirmatory circumstances make it likely that the party was the speaker. *Dave Levine & Co. v Wolf's Package Depot, Inc.* (1955) 29 Misc 2d 1085, 138 NYS2d 427, affd (1st Dept) 1 AD2d 874, 150 NYS2d 543, app den (1st Dept) 1 AD 2d 949, 151 NYS2d 601.

§ 13:20   TESTIMONY REFRESHED BY HYPNOSIS OR DRUGS

— In a personal injury action, the infant plaintiff was precluded from testifying as to her hypnotically enhanced recollection of the event. The court restricted her testimony to her prehypnotic recollection. The court noted that, in parallel circum-stances in criminal cases, the rule that has evolved is that testimony based upon hypnotically enhanced recollection is inadmissible *per se*, and is not subject to a case-by-case approach. *Bennett v Saeger Hotels* (1994, 4th Dept) 209 AD2d 946, 619 NYS2d 424.

RESEARCH REFERENCES

American Law Reports

56 ALR4th 402, Admissibility of evidence of pertinent trait under Rule 404(a) of the Uniform Rules of Evidence

32 ALR4th 774, Failure to object to improper questions or comments as to defendant's pretrial silence or failure to testify as constituting waiver of right to complain of error-modern cases

27 ALR4th 1167, Propriety and prejudicial effect of questions or comments as to witness' religious beliefs or standards designed to enhance credibility

6 ALR4th 951, Manner or extent of trial judge's examination of witnesses in civil cases

80 ALR3d 1212, Propriety of allowing absent witness to be examined over closed-circuit television

American Jurisprudence 2d

81 Am Jur 2d, Witnesses §§ 416-458

American Jurisprudence Pleading and Practice

25 Am Jur Pl & Pr Forms (Rev), Witnesses, Form 1 et seq.

American Jurisprudence Proof of Facts

17 Am Jur Proof of Facts 166-282, Unintentional Errors in Testimony

American Jurisprudence Trials

6 Am Jur Trials 263, Direct Examination of Defendant

5 Am Jur Trials 807, Handling Perception and Distortion in Testimony

5 Am Jur Trials 611, Presenting Plaintiff's Case

Other Resources

8 CARMODY-WAIT 2d, Presentation of the Case §§ 56:69, 56:108-56:11

Auto-Cite®: Any case citation herein can be checked for form, parallel references, later history and annotation references through the Auto-Cite computer research system.

CHAPTER 14

CROSS-EXAMINATION

§ 14:1 RIGHT TO CROSS-EXAMINE WITNESSES — Cross-examination of adverse witnesses is a matter of right. *Ziehm v State* (1946) 270 AD 876, 61 NYS2d 99. The right to cross-examine is an intrinsic aspect of the right to due process. *Re Greenebaum* (1911) 201 NY 343, 94 NE 853.

Cross-examination, for the purpose of weakening the effect of direct examination, may not be denied unless it is waived. *Sullivan v Sullivan* (1935) 246 AD 55, 284 NYS 119. A party must be permitted to cross-examine. *Young v Valentine* (1904) 177 NY 347, 69 NE 643. It is therefore reversible error for the court unnecessarily to limit cross-examination. *Sees v Massachusetts Bonding & Ins. Co.* (1935) 243 AD 400, 277 NYS 198. However, if a party has been given a full opportunity to cross-examine but

201

elects not to do so, the right has been waived. *Re White's Will* (1957) 2 NY2d 309, 160 NYS2d 841, 70 ALR2d 484.

If the right of cross-examination is denied without fault on the part of the party who was denied the right, introduction into evidence of the direct testimony was error. *People v Cole* (1871) 43 NY 508. Thus, where testimony has been given in an action, it may not be used in another action against a party who did not have the opportunity to cross-examine the witness in the previous action. *Re Lynch* (1930) 227 AD 477, 238 NYS 482.

Once the right of cross-examination has been accorded, the extent of such cross-examination rests largely with the court. The court's exercise of such discretion is not reviewable unless abused. *Friedel v Board of Regents* (1947) 296 NY 347, remittitur amd 297 NY 585.

§ 14:2   EFFECT OF DENIAL OF RIGHT TO CROSS-EXAMINE
— A person may not be deprived of liberty or property without an opportunity to cross-examine adverse witnesses. *Sullivan v Sullivan* (1935) 246 AD 55, 284 NYS 119. Denial of the right of cross-examination is an error of law, reviewable on appeal. *Friedel v Board of Regents* (1947) 296 NY 347, remittitur and 297 NY 585.

§ 14:3   THE SCOPE OF CROSS-EXAMINATION — The scope and extent of the cross-examination rests largely in the discretion of the court. *Friedel v Board of Regents* (1947) 296 NY 347, remittitur amd 297 NY 585. A reviewing court will interfere with the trial court's ruling only in the case of clear abuse of discretion, resulting in manifest prejudice to the complaining party. *Langley v Wadsworth* (1885) 99 NY 61, 1 NE 106.

The court should keep the cross-examination within fair and reasonable limits. *Friedel v Board of Regents, supra.* The extent to which inquiry may be made as to collateral matters, solely to impeach the credibility of the witness, is within the discretion of the trial judge and he may keep it within reasonable limits. *Third Great Western Turnpike Road Co. v Loomis* (1865) 32 NY 127.

A witness may be cross-examined as to past criminal acts in order to discredit his testimony; however, the examiner may not multiply such questions in order to implant suspicion in the minds of the jurors. *People v Slover* (1921) 232 NY 264, 133 NE 633. Although it is proper to discredit a witness by showing that he has been convicted of a crime, it is improper to bring out that he has been charged with a criminal offense. *Landt v Kingsway Equipment Leasing Corp.* (1956, Sup) 159 NYS2d 453, affd (2d Dept) 4 AD2d 785, 165 NYS2d 715.

The court may not deprive a party of the right to inquire into matters directly relevant to the principal issue of the case against him. However, the court may, in the proper exercise of discretion, restrict inquiry into collateral matters or prohibit unnecessarily repetitive examination. *Feldsberg v Nitschke,* (1980) 49 NY2d 636, 427 NYS2d 751.

Failure to permit the fullest cross-examination of the plaintiff was held to be erroneous, in an action for fraudulent representations as to the value of corporate stock. *O'Hara v Derschug* (1934) 241 AD 513, 272 NYS 189. However, it was reversible error to allow cross-examination of a plaintiff, who was a taxi driver, as to prior accidents mentioned in connection with his application for renewal of his hack license. *Powell v Beskin* (1961, 2d Dept) 13 AD2d 683, 213 NYS2d 868.

Where a party's witnesses have been excluded from the courtroom pursuant to the rule permitting such exclusion, and the party's trial attorney consults with such witnesses during a recess, his adversary has a right to cross-examine the witnesses as to the consultation, to the extent allowable in the judge's discretion. *Capitol Cab Corp. v Anderson* (1949) 194 Misc 21, 85 NYS2d 767, affd 197 Misc 1035, 100 NYS2d 39.

By going beyond the subject matter of the direct examination, the cross-examining counsel makes the witness his own to that extent. *Cavalier v Bittner* (1946) 186 Misc 848, 60 NYS2d 355. A defendant may not go beyond the scope of the direct examination and thereby attempt to put his theory of the case before the trier of the facts. *Cavalier v Bittner, supra.*

It is improper to permit cross-examination of a plaintiff concerning a prior accident. *Hartley v Szadkowski* (1969, 2d Dept) 32 AD2d 550, 300 NYS2d 82. However, it was proper to cross-examine plaintiff as to whether he had ever commenced an action to recover for an injury to his right shoulder. The cross-examination was intended to determine whether plaintiff had sustained or claimed to have sustained the same injury under circumstances not related to those in the case at bar. *Bowers v Johnson* (1966, 2d Dept) 26 AD2d 552, 271 NYS2d 106.

It was proper to cross-examine defendant as to special equipment on his automobile because this was relevant on the question of his ability to stop his vehicle in time to avoid the accident. *Kirkpatrick v Fesinger* (1963, 4th Dept) 18 AD2d 1132, 239 NYS2d 395. It was prejudicial, however, to cross-examine him as to his using his automobile in racing and drag racing shortly before the trial but more than two years after the accident. *Kirkpatrick v Fesinger, supra.*

Bias of a witness may always be exposed to affect his credibility, This may be accomplished in various ways, including the demonstration of a business or close social relationship of the witness to one of the parties. *Luce v St. Peter's Hospital* (1982, 3d Dept) 85 AD2d 194, 448 NYS2d 855. Wide latitude should be allowed for the purpose of establishing bias. *Young v Sonking* (1949) 275 AD 871, 88 NYS2d 392.

When an adverse party is called as a witness, it may be assumed that such adverse party is a hostile witness. In the discretion of the court, direct examination may assume the nature of cross-examination by the use of leading questions. However, a party may not impeach the credibility of a witness whom he calls unless the witness made a contradictory statement either under oath or in writing. *Jordan v Parrinello* (1988, 2d Dept) 144 AD2d 540, 534 NYS2d 686.

When the opposing party elicits testimony on cross-examination not touched upon in the direct examination, a party has the right to examine more fully on that topic. The extent of redirect examination is, for the most part, governed by the discretion of the trial court. *People v Bailey* (1990, 3d Dept) 159 AD2d 862, 553 NYS2d 512.

In a divorce action, where evidence had been brought out regarding a relationship between the wife and "her lover," the trial court should have permitted the wife's attorney to question the housekeeper and cross-examine the husband concerning parallel activities on the husband's part. *Linda R. v Richard E.* (1990, 2d Dept) 561 NYS2d 29.

In an action for assault and battery brought by plaintiff against a hospital and a guard employed by the hospital, it was not an improvident exercise of the trial court's discretion to refuse to permit plaintiff's counsel to cross-examine the guard regarding another civil action arising out of an incident similar to the one involved in the case at bar. *De Gregorio v Lutheran Medical Center* (1988, 2d Dept) 142 AD2d 543, 529 NYS2d 903.

In a civil action against a New York City Transit Authority police officer to recover for assault and battery, false arrest, and malicious prosecution, the police officer was asked questions regarding inadmissible civilian complaints against him. A new trial was necessary because such questions were extremely prejudicial, considering that the prior alleged conduct involved abusive behavior similar to that alleged in the case at bar. *Kourtalis v City of New York* (1993, 2d Dept) 191 AD2d 480, 594 NYS2d 325.

§ 14:4   CROSS-EXAMINATION BY COURT — The trial court consistently and unnecessarily injected itself into the proceedings with questions that tended either to rehabilitate respondent's expert witnesses or to blunt the testimony of appellant's expert. The totality of the court's intercessions had the effect of depriving appellant of an impartial jury verdict on the issue of damages. *Gerichten v Ruiz* (1981, 2d Dept) 80 AD2d 578, 435 NYS2d 783.

§ 14:5   FORM OF QUESTIONS ON CROSS-EXAMINATION — Unlike the attorney on direct examination, a cross-examiner is not bound by the rule prohibiting leading questions. As a general rule, he may elicit testimony on cross-examination by asking leading questions. *Becker v Koch* (1887) 104 NY 394, 10 NE 701.

It is permissible to examine a witness further on the chance he may change his testimony or answer. *Brown v Western Union Tel. Co.* (1966, 4th Dept) 26 AD2d 316, 274 NYS2d 52.

§ 14:6   PRIOR INCONSISTENT STATEMENT — The witness may be cross-examined as to prior inconsistent statements. *Patchin v Astor Mut. Ins. Co.* (1855) 13 NY 268. Any oral or written statement made by a witness out of court may be introduced in evidence if it contradicts a material part of the witness's testimony and if it is properly proven. Such statement may be introduced not as substantive proof of its truth, but for the purpose of discrediting the witness. *Larkin v Nassau E. R. Co.* (1912) 205 NY 267, 98 NE 465. A prior inconsistent statement, admissible for the purpose of discrediting the witness, is not evidence of any fact contained in such statement. *Fallon v American Sugar Refining Co.* (1953) 282 AD 910, 124 NYS2d 897; *Jeffries v Long Island R. R. Co.* (1962, 1st Dept) 15 AD2d 356, 224 NYS2d 497. The jury should be clearly instructed to that effect. *People v Tisdale* (1963, 4th Dept) 18 AD2d 274, 239 NYS2d 226.

It was error to exclude proof of a witness's prior inconsistent statements that pertained to the subject matter of the action and were inconsistent with his testimony. *Joseph v Griesman Trucking Co.* (1943) 265 AD 590, 40 NYS2d 200. An allegedly inconsistent statement by a city employee, called as a witness on behalf of the New York City, was competent on the issue of the credibility of the witness but was not binding on the city as an admission. *Aldridge v New York* (1943) 266 AD 652, 40 NYS2d 129.

The witness or the party in whose behalf he has testified may produce evidence that denies or explains the alleged inconsistent statements. *Ryan v Dwyer* (1969, 4th Dept) 33 AD2d 878, 307 NYS2d 565.

The prior inconsistent statement need not be a direct and positive contradiction of the testimony of the witness. It is sufficient if the statement either proves different facts or is inconsistent with such testimony. *McCoy v Gorenstein* (1953) 282 AD 984, 125 NYS2d 683.

A witness for defendant who testified that plaintiff ran out in front of defendant's vehicle could be impeached by a written statement the witness had given to plaintiff's attorney, which did not mention plaintiff running across the street. *Kesten v Forbes* (1948) 273 AD 646, 78 NYS2d 769. A bill of particulars, verified by a parent acting in a representative capacity, does not constitute a prior inconsistent statement when the infant is the witness sought to be impeached. *Arestivo v Matusewitz* (1969) 60 Misc 2d 236, 303 NYS2d 139.

A prior inconsistent statement of a witness cannot be read to a jury or used as a basis for cross-examination until it is in evidence. *Kesten v Forbes, supra.*

The deposition of a party may be used to impeach him and it may be put in evidence. CPLR 3117(a); *Jobse v Connolly* (1969) 60 Misc 2d 69, 302 NYS2d 35. The same is true for the deposition of anyone who was an officer, director, member, or managing or authorized agent of a party at the time when the deposition was taken. CPLR 3117(a)(2). In addition, any adversely interested party may use, for any purpose, the deposition of an employee of a party produced by that party at the taking of the deposition. CPLR 3117(a)(2).

Because the prior inconsistent statements of a witness have no value as evidence in chief, they are insufficient, standing alone, to raise a triable issue of fact. *Egleston v Kalamarides* (1982, 4th Dept) 89 AD2d 777, 453 NYS2d 489, mod 58 NY2d 682, 458 NYS2d 530.

A party may impeach his own witness by showing that the witness made a prior contradictory statement if the statement is either subscribed by the witness sought to be impeached or was made under oath by him. CPLR 4514; *Brown v Western Union Tel. Co.* (1966, 4th Dept) 26 AD2d 316, 274 NYS2d 52. The statutory provision permitting impeachment of one's own witness is in derogation of common law and must therefore be strictly construed. *Jenkins v 313-321 W. 37th Street Corp.* (1940) 284 NY 397, reh den 285 NY 614.

When impeaching one's own witness, it is not permissible to use oral contradictory statements or statements that are not signed or under oath. *Jenkins v 313-321 W. 37th Street Corp., supra.* Where a trial counsel represented a defendant and also his insurance carrier, he could not impeach his client of record by an inconsistent written statement when that client insisted on admitting liability to protect his other client, the insurer. *Friedman v Berkowitz* (1954) 206 Misc 889, 136 NYS2d 81.

Where a husband testified in his divorce action that his wife had locked him out of the marital apartment, it was improper to exclude Family Court records of the wife's prior support action, showed that the husband had not claimed a lock-out. *Walden v Walden* (1973, 2d Dept) 41 AD2d 664, 340 NYS2d 709.

A prior inconsistent statement made by a witness to a police officer over the telephone shortly after the accident was not rendered inadmissible simply because the police officer was unable to identify the witness's voice. The identity of a party to a telephone conversation can be proven by circumstantial evidence and, in this case, the substance of the conversation served to confirm the witness's identity. *Noskewicz v New York* (1989, 2d Dept) 155 AD2d 646, 548 NYS2d 237.

§ 14:7   LAYING A FOUNDATION FOR PRIOR INCONSISTENT STATEMENTS — A witness cannot be impeached by statements alleged to have been made by him before or after he has testified until he has been adequately warned by the cross-examination that those statements will be later offered against him. Thus, the witness or the party calling him can correct the testimony given or prepare a denial or an explanation of the statements. *Larkin v Nassau E. R. Co.* (1912) 205 NY 267, 98 NE 465. In the case of oral statements, the warning is given by asking the witness, in substance and effect, if he did not at a given time and place, in the presence of or to a person or persons specified, make the alleged contradictory statements. *Larkin v Nassau E. R. Co., supra*. If the witness admits, without explanation or qualification, having made the statement, that is the end of the inquiry. The witness has discredited himself and there is no need for contradiction. *Hanlon v Ehrich* (1904) 178 NY 474, 71 NE 12. On the other hand, if the witness denies having made the statement, or does not remember having made it, he may then be contradicted by any person who heard him make it. *Hanlon v Ehrich, supra*.

The trial court properly excluded evidence offered by the plaintiff as to a prior inconsistent statement because no proper foundation had been laid for the introduction of the allegedly inconsistent statement. *Morris v Palmier Oil Co.* (1983, 3d Dept) 94 AD2d 911, 463 NYS2d 631, later proceeding (3d Dept) 104 AD2d 517, 479 NYS2d 884, app gr, ques certified (3d Dept) 108 AD2d 944, 486 NYS2d 706.

§ 14:8   IMPEACHMENT BY PROOF OF PRIOR CONVICTION

— At common law, a person who had been convicted of a crime could not testify. This disqualification has been removed by statute and such a person is now competent as a witness. CPLR 4513. However, the conviction may be proved for the purpose of affecting the weight to be given to the testimony. CPLR 4513.

On cross-examination, a witness may be asked, for purposes of impeachment, whether he has been convicted of a crime, *Perham v Noel* (1897) 20 AD 516, 47 NYS 100. The cross-examiner is not bound by the answer of the witness. CPLR 4513.

The type of conviction contemplated by the statute is one arrived at in a court of law before a judge or jury. *People v Sullivan* (1898) 34 AD 544, 54 NYS 538. The decision of a police commissioner, finding a policeman guilty of certain crimes, is not a conviction within the meaning of the statute. *People v Sullivan, supra*. The action of the commissioner of motor vehicles in suspending or revoking an operator's license for reckless driving is not a conviction within the contemplation of the statute. *Tryon v Willbank* (1932) 234 AD 335, 255 NYS 27.

In a negligence action, plaintiff could not be required to disclose a previous conviction for a driving infraction. *De Stasio v Janssen Dairy Corp.* (1939) 279 NY 501. Imprisonment for breach of military discipline is not a conviction. *People v Joyce* (1922) 233 NY 61, 134 NE 836. An adjudication of juvenile delinquency is not admissible to impeach the credibility of a party to a civil action or his witnesses. *Murphy v New York* (1948) 273 AD 429, 78 NYS2d 191. A proceeding to compel a witness to furnish an undertaking to keep the peace is not a criminal one; therefore, it is prejudicial to permit a cross-examiner to ask a witness if he has been put under a bond to keep the peace. *McWharf v Webber* (1927) 222 AD 347, 225 NYS 761.

A judgment in a civil action to recover a fine imposed by a city ordinance for keeping a house of ill fame is not a conviction that may be used to cross-examine the witness. *Arhart v Stark* (1894) 6 Misc 579, 27 NYS 301. In an action for the reasonable value of the legal services rendered by an attorney prior to his disbarment, the order and opinion of the court in the disbarment proceeding were properly excluded; the order and opinion set forth various acts for which the witness had been disbarred. *Shabbona Creston Oil & Gas Corp. v Doherty* (1942) 264 AD 909, 35 NYS2d 839, app den 264 AD 918, 36 NYS2d 426, and reh den 265 AD 812, 37 NYS2d 831. Conviction for public intoxication was not conviction of a crime and it was error, in a personal injury action, to permit cross-examination of the plaintiff along such lines. Its obvious purpose was to permit the jury to infer from the fact that plaintiff was intoxicated on other occasions, that he was intoxicated at the time of the accident. *McQuage v New York* (1954) 285 AD 249, 136 NYS2d 111.

In one case, part of infant plaintiff's demand for damages rested on a claim that the accident had caused him to change from a well-behaved boy to one who became violent, struck his mother and otherwise displayed a vicious temper. Infant plaintiff's mother had previously testified that her other children were all well-behaved. It was proper to test her credibility through cross-examination regarding whether another son, not a party to the action, had been adjudged a juvenile delinquent. The questions asked were not violative of the Children's Court Act (predecessor of the Family Court Act) section providing that a child's appearances before Children's Court shall never be admissible as evidence against him or his interests in any other court. *Murello v Lustig* (1952, Sup) 114 NYS2d 632, affd 282 AD 712, 122 NYS2d 895.

Exclusion of evidence that the plaintiff in a civil action and his principal witness had been convicted of bookmaking was error. *Diodato v Rosetti* (1959) 19 Misc 2d 780, 195 NYS2d 865.

The credibility of a witness at a civil trial may be impeached by inquiry into the nature of the crime rather than just the fact of the conviction. There are no exceptions for a crime for which a witness has obtained a certificate of relief from disability, which removes certain restrictions that otherwise apply to convicted felons. *Able Cycle Engines, Inc. v Allstate Ins. Co.* (1981, 2d Dept) 84 AD2d 140, 445 NYS2d 469.

A witness may not be cross-examined as to whether or not he has ever been impeached. *Hall v United States Radiator Co.* (1902) 76 AD 504, 78 NYS 549.

Matters as to which a party may be examined to discredit him must show moral turpitude. *Seventh Ave. Delicatessen v Manhat-*

tan Provision Co. (1955, Sup) 146 NYS2d 25, affd (2d Dept) 1 AD2d 1037, 153 NYS2d 572.

Where the general character of the witness for truth and veracity are impeached by evidence of his conviction, this may be answered by evidence of general good character. *Derrick v Wallace* (1916) 217 NY 520, 112 NE 440.

If a witness is impeached by showing his conviction of a crime, he may explain the facts surrounding his conviction. *People v Tait* (1932) 234 AD 433, 255 NYS 455, affd 259 NY 599, 182 NE 197. He may even assert that he is innocent, despite the fact that he has been convicted of the particular crime. *Sims v Sims* (1878) 75 NY 466.

In an action for the wrongful death of the patron of a cocktail lounge, there was evidence that employees of the lounge had been convicted of assault, third degree, arising out of an attack by the employees on the patron. Such evidence was admissible on the issue of the credibility of the lounge employee who testified, particularly on the issue of what occurred the morning the patron was injured and as evidence that the assault on the patron took place in the cocktail lounge and not as the result of an attack by a street gang. *Brereton v McEvoy* (1974, 2d Dept) 44 AD2d 594, 353 NYS2d 512.

§ 14:9   MANNER OF PROVING A CONVICTION — When a witness denies that he has been convicted of a crime, his denial does not conclude the cross-examiner; the cross-examiner may then proceed to prove the conviction. CPLR 4513; *People v McCormick* (1951) 278 AD 410, 105 NYS2d 571, affd 303 NY 403. The cross-examiner may show the conviction even though it has been admitted by the witness. *McQuage v New York* (1954) 285 AD 249, 136 NYS2d 111. The prior conviction of the witness may be shown by the record of conviction, as well as by cross-examination. CPLR 4513.

§ 14:10   ADDITIONAL MATTERS PROPER ON CROSS-EXAMINATION — In addition to matters brought out on direct examination, there are a number of areas about which the cross-examiner may question the witness. For instance, if the witness testified as to only a part of a transaction, statement, or conversation on direct examination, he may be asked to give the rest or the whole of such matter on cross-examination. *Stephenson v Southerland* (1912) 150 AD 275, 134 NYS 774. When a memorandum is used to refresh the recollection of a witness, the adverse counsel may inspect the memorandum and employ it to cross-examine the witness. *Patchogue Oil Terminal Corp. v Sambach* (1958) 15 Misc 2d 266, 178 NYS2d 659. However, a writing cannot be read to the jury and it may not be used for cross-examination as to its contents unless it is in evidence. *Blackwood v Chemical Corn Exchange Bank* (1957, 1st Dept) 4 AD2d 656, 168 NYS2d 335, reh and app den (1st Dept) 5 AD2d 768, 170 NYS2d 504, app dismd 4 NY2d 802, 173 NYS2d 33.

Cross-examination that elicited evidence of the racial origin of the witness was error. *Leonard v Home Owners' Loan Corp.* (1946) 270 AD 363, 270 AD 785, 270 AD 867, 60 NYS2d 78, affd 297 NY 103.

Plaintiff in a personal injury action testified that he had been in very good health prior to the accident. In the absence of any claim of privilege, it was proper to introduce records of prior hospital treatment of plaintiff for chronic alcoholism and to cross-examine him with respect to such treatment. *Miller v New York* (1955) 286 AD 1033, 145 NYS2d 295. However, it was reversible error, in an automobile negligence action, to permit cross-examination of the plaintiff motorist as to his prior accidents, particularly in view of the sharp conflict of testimony between plaintiff and defendant who were the only witnesses. *Lizzo v O'Connor* (1955) 286 AD 1021, 145 NYS2d 101.

A party may impeach an opponent's witness by asking whether the witness was a plaintiff in another action pending against the party. *Thompson v Korn* (1975, 4th Dept) 48 AD2d 1007, 368 NYS2d 923.

A plaintiff in a medical malpractice action may call as a witness the doctor against whom she brought the action and question him as a medical expert. Such doctor may be cross-examined as a hostile witness and an expert witness. *Segreti v Putnam Community Hospital* (1982, 2d Dept) 88 AD2d 590, 449 NYS2d 785.

The court properly permitted the respondent in a paternity action to use records of petitioner's confinement for mental illness for purposes of cross-examination; petitioner did not raise the physician-patient privilege. *Delia v Spina* (1987, 4th Dept) 132 AD2d 1006, 518 NYS2d 292, app den 70 NY2d 609, 522 NYS2d 109.

§ 14:11 MANNER OF CONDUCTING CROSS-EXAMINA-TION — The court should not permit questions that are designed to humiliate and degrade the witness and are not asked for the purpose of impeaching or discrediting the witness's account of what happened. Thus, it was error to permit counsel to cross-examine witnesses as to their racial origin in order to show, inferentially, bias on the part of the witnesses or to arouse prejudice either against the witnesses or against the party on whose behalf they testified. *Abbate v Solan* (1939) 257 AD 776, 15 NYS2d 332, reh den 258 AD 886, 16 NYS2d 704.

It was held improper to show by cross-examination, for the purpose of discrediting a witness, that the witness had been expelled from a church, *People v Dorthy* (1897) 20 AD 308, 46 NYS 970, affd 156 NY 237, 50 NE 800, or that he had been expelled from a social organization. *Lindsley v Miller* (1896) 3 AD 127, 39 NYS 393. It was also improper to cross-examine a witness as to whether he had been expelled from the fire department. *Nolan v Brooklyn C. & N. R. Co.* (1881) 87 NY 63.

A witness may be asked on cross-examination whether he has been disbarred as an attorney, without being questioned as to the reasons for his disbarment. *Hyman v Dworsky* (1933) 239 AD 413, 267 NYS 539. He may not be cross-examined as to the specific criminal acts on which the disbarment proceedings were based. *People v Dorthy, supra.*

Where a witness testified that he sometimes drove horses on racetracks, it was improper to cross-examine him as to whether he had ever been charged with crooked driving. *Lindsley v Miller, supra.*

§ 14:12 TESTING THE WITNESS'S KNOWLEDGE AND ACCU-RACY — The witness may be cross-examined to show his lack of knowledge. *Wells v Kelsey* (1867) 37 NY 143. He may also be cross-examined to show that his knowledge is based upon hearsay or any condition that would interfere with his perception, memory or judgment, such as his drug addiction. *People v Webster* (1893) 139 NY 73, 34 NE 730.

The fact that a witness is a narcotics addict is an important consideration in passing on the credibility of that witness. It is proper to show that his way of life makes him unworthy of belief. *People v Williams* (1959) 6 NY2d 18, 187 NYS2d 750, cert den 361 US 920, 4 L Ed 2d 188, 80 S Ct 266.

RESEARCH REFERENCES

American Law Reports

11 ALR5th 1, Propriety of questioning expert witness regarding specific incidents or allegations of expert's unprofessional conduct or professional negligence

31 ALR4th 1279, Attorney's use of objectionable questions in examination of witness in state judicial proceeding as contempt of court

7 ALR4th 468, Conviction by court-martial as proper subject of cross-examination for impeachment purposes

99 ALR3d 934, Denial of recollection as inconsistent with prior statement so as to render that statement admissible

98 ALR3d 1060, Right to cross-examine prosecuting witness as to his pending or contemplated civil action against accused for damages arising out of same transaction

88 ALR3d 74, Use of unrelated traffic offense conviction to impeach general credibility of witness in state civil case

85 ALR3d 541, Right to cross-examine witness as to his place of residence

27 ALR3d 1304, Right to cross-examination of witnesses in hearings before administrative zoning authorities

55 ALR Fed 742, Propriety of court's failure or refusal to strike direct testimony of government witness who refuses, on grounds of self-incrimination, to answer questions on cross-examination

ALR QUICK INDEX: Discovery; Witnesses

American Jurisprudence 2d

81 AM JUR 2d, Witnesses §§ 463-517

81 AM JUR 2d, Witnesses §§ 800-861

American Jurisprudence Proof of Facts

31 AM JUR PROOF OF FACTS 2d 443, Contradiction of Expert Witness

Through Use of Authoritative Treatise

21 AM JUR PROOF OF FACTS 2d 101, Impeachment of Witness-Prior Inconsistent Statements

American Jurisprudence Trials

38 AM JUR TRIALS 711, Trial Report: Effective Cross-Examination of Key Witnesses in an Auto Product Liability Case

6 AM JUR TRIALS 423, Collateral Cross-Examination of Medical Witness

6 AM JUR TRIALS 297, Cross-Examination of Defendant

6 AM JUR TRIALS 201, Cross-Examination of Plaintiff and Plaintiff's Witness

Other Resources

8 CARMODY-WAIT 2d, Presentation of the Case §§ 56:112-56:126

Auto-Cite®: Any case citation herein can be checked for form, parallel references, later history and annotation references through the Auto-Cite computer research system.

CHAPTER 15

REDIRECT AND RECROSS EXAMINATION

§ 15:1 SCOPE OF REDIRECT EXAMINATION — The right to re-examine a witness, and the extent of redirect examination, are matters that rest largely in the discretion of the trial court. *People v Fay* (1945) 270 AD 261, 59 NYS2d 127, affd 296 NY 510, affd 332 US 261, 91 L Ed 2043, 67 S Ct 1613, reh den 332 US 784, 92 L Ed 367, 68 S Ct 27; *People v Melendez* (1982) 55 NY2d 445, 449 NYS2d 946.

The purpose of redirect examination is to enable the witness to explain any inconsistent or otherwise discrediting facts elicited on cross-examination, thereby rehabilitating the witness. *Kings County Trust Co. v Hyams* (1926) 242 NY 405, 152 NE 129. Thus, in an action by an executor to recover the amount of a check claimed to have been forged and wrongfully cashed by the widow of a decedent, cross-examination of the widow by the executor as to transactions concerning the check were held to have opened the door for direct examination of the widow as to the circumstances under which she received the check. *Kings County Trust Co. v Hyams, supra*.

When the opposing party opens the door on cross-examination to matters not touched upon during the direct examination, a party has the right on redirect to explain, clarify and fully elicit the question only partially explored on cross-examination. *People*

217

v Peoples (1988, 2d Dept) 143 AD2d 780, 533 NYS2d 311, app den 73 NY2d 925, 539 NYS2d 309.

Defense counsel directed a question at a police officer to the effect, "Did you see the defendant do anything illegal?" That opened the door to redirect on the issue of marihuana that had been discovered on the defendant at the time of his arrest. *People v Bailey* (1993, 2d Dept) 193 AD2d 689, 598 NYS2d 33, app den 81 NY2d 1069, 601 NYS2d 589.

A party holding an affirmative of an issue is bound to present all of his evidence before he closes his proof and may not add to it by use of rebuttal evidence. *Yeomans v Warren* (1982, 3d Dept) 87 AD2d 713, 448 NYS2d 889.

§ 15:2 EXPLAINING AND CORRECTING TESTIMONY ON REDIRECT EXAMINATION — If only a part of a conversation or transaction has been brought out on cross-examination, it is proper to bring out the balance of it on redirect examination. *People v Jelke* (1956) 1 NY2d 321, 152 NYS2d 479. The redirect examination should be strictly limited to those parts of the conversation that qualify, limit or explain the part previously brought out. *People v Lewis* (1963, 4th Dept) 18 AD2d 277, 239 NYS2d 408.

In a prosecution for inducing and attempting to induce females to live a life of prostitution, defense counsel referred, on cross-examination, to material in the prostitute's life story as told to tabloids after the first trial. Such referrence warranted the prosecutor's action on redirect in calling attention to other portions of her life story as told to other papers or magazines in which she had said the opposite. *People v Jelke, supra.*

A witness to an accident gave a written statement to the police at the scene of the occurrence. The cross-examination of that witness emphasized that the witness had spoken with the attorney prior to trial. The statement was admissible on redirect examination on the ground that the witness's direct testimony had been assailed as a recent fabrication. *Abrams v Gerold* (1971, 1st Dept) 37 AD2d 391, 326 NYS2d 1.

A witness was cross-examined on the subject of a certain conversation with another person at the scene of an accident. It was error for the court to deny an opportunity upon redirect to go into the full facts concerning that conversation. The cross-examiner had "opened the door" to this line of questions, and the conversation contradicted the version of the accident given by one of the parties. *Feblot v New York Times Co.* (1973) 32 NY2d 486, 346 NYS2d 256, 63 ALR3d 881.

In a personal injury action, the trial court erred in not allowing the plaintiff to testify on redirect examination that certain statements made by him at his examination before trial may have been the result of his misunderstanding the questions due to a language barrier. *Sitaras v James Ricciardi & Sons, Inc.* (1989, 2d Dept) 154 AD2d 451, 545 NYS2d 937, app den 75 NY2d 708, 554 NYS2d 833.

Where the opposing party opens the door and brings out on cross-examination apparent inconsistencies or contradictions in a witness's statements or acts to discredit his testimony, a party has the right on redirect to rehabilitate that witness by explaining to the jury the relevant surrounding circumstances. *People v Rogers* (1992, 4th Dept) 179 AD2d 1014, 579 NYS2d 278.

In a prosecution for arson, defendant, by inquiring into a portion of a statement of a fire marshal on cross-examination, opened the door for admission of the entire statement on redirect examination. *People v Richards* (1992, 1st Dept) 184 AD2d 222, 584 NYS2d 804, app den 80 NY2d 1029, 592 NYS2d 679.

§ 15:3   REHABILITATING A WITNESS — A witness may be rehabilitated on redirect examination by permitting him to explain testimony that was brought out on cross-examination. *Friedman v New York City Omnibus Corp.* (1947) 272 AD 265, 70 NYS2d 628. In an action for wrongful death that arose out of injuries sustained by the decedent when he was struck either by defendant's bus or by a truck, the expressman on the truck was entitled to explain on redirect examination his statement at a hearing by the Commissioner of Motor Vehicles that the decedent contacted the corner of a bus, by stating that anything that he may have testified to at the hearing which tended to qualify the apparent contradiction in his testimony. *Friedman v New York City Omnibus Corp., supra.*

Redirect examination as a matter of right is limited to new matters that have been brought out on cross-examination. *Ander-*

son v Brown (1950) 276 AD 450, 95 NYS2d 711, amd 276 AD 1057, 96 NYS2d 310 and affd 302 NY 773. Nevertheless, on redirect examination, the court may, in its discretion, permit a party to bring out such matters as he should have, but failed to, elicit on direct examination. *Gleason v Metropolitan S. R. Co.* (1904) 99 AD 209, 90 NYS 1025.

If the testimony of a witness is assailed on cross-examination either directly or inferentially as a recent fabrication, the witness may be rehabilitated with prior consistent statements that pre-date the motive to falsify. *People v McDaniel* (1993) 81 NY2d 10, 595 NYS2d 364.

§ 15:4   RECROSS EXAMINATION — It was error for the trial court to deny defendant the right of recross examination of a police officer with respect to a weapons charge, in view of the fact that for the first time on redirect, the prosecutor developed testimony thereon from the police officer. *People v Russo* (1978, 2d Dept) 60 AD2d 853, 400 NYS2d 584.

RESEARCH REFERENCES

American Law Reports

ALR QUICK INDEX: Redirect Examination

American Jurisprudence 2d

81 AM JUR 2d, Witnesses §§ 424, 425, 508

American Jurisprudence Trials

6 AM JUR TRIALS 297, Cross-Examination of Defendant § 25

6 AM JUR TRIALS 263, Direct Examination of Defendant § 35

6 AM JUR TRIALS 109, Basis of Medical Testimony §§ 60, 61

Other Resources

8 CARMODY-WAIT 2d, Presentation of the Case § 56:127

Auto-Cite®: Any case citation herein can be checked for form, parallel references, later history and annotation references through the Auto-Cite computer research system.

CHAPTER 16

PRIVILEGED COMMUNICATIONS

§ 16:1 THE NATURE OF PRIVILEGED COMMUNICATIONS
— For reasons of public policy, in certain specified instances, where one person acquires information from another by reason of

the confidential relationship existing between the parties, the communication is deemed to be privileged. These relationships are: husband and wife, CPLR 4502; attorney and client, CPLR 4503; physician, dentist, nurse, chiropractor, or podiatrist and patient, CPLR 4504; clergyman and penitent, CPLR 4505; psychologist and client, CPLR 4507; and social worker and client, CPLR 4508.

Under CPLR 4504, the relationship of physician and patient exists between a university faculty practice corporation organized under § 1412 of the Not-For-Profit Corporation Law to practice medicine and dentistry and the patients to whom they render professional services. It also exists between patients and a medical corporation as defined in Article 44 of the Public Health Law and a professional service corporation organized under Article 15 of the Business Corporation Law to practice medicine.

It was formerly held that a communication made to a journalist was not privileged against being used in evidence. *People ex rel. Mooney v Sheriff of New York County* (1936) 269 NY 291, 199 NE 415, 102 ALR 769. Section 79-K of the Civil Rights Law now protects journalists who refuse to disclose news or the source of news coming into their possession.

§ 16:2 COMMUNICATIONS BETWEEN HUSBAND AND WIFE — Confidential communications between husband and wife were protected at common law. Such communications could not be revealed by either on the witness stand unless the other had consented. *People v Hayes* (1894) 140 NY 484, 35 NE 951. This privilege has been codified as CPLR 4502.

A husband or wife may not be required, or, without the consent of the other if living, may not be permitted, to disclose a confidential communication made by one to the other during the marriage. CPLR 4502(b). In addition, a husband or wife is not competent to testify against the other in an action based on adultery, except to prove the marriage, disprove the adultery, or to disprove a defense after evidence has been introduced tending to prove such a defense. CPLR 4502(a).

In a divorce action, the husband's testimony which tended to establish adultery on the part of the wife was not admissible, even in the absence of an objection thereto. *Bolognino v Bolognino*

(1930) 136 Misc 656, 241 NYS 445, affd 231 AD 817, 246 NYS 883. The incompetency to testify where the issue is adultery cannot be waived, and testimony does not become admissible by a failure to object to it. *Admire v Admire* (1943) 180 Misc 68, 42 NYS2d 755.

In a divorce action, evidence of non-access, from which the further inference of adultery is to be established on proof that defendant gave birth to a child during the absence, is incompetent. No objection to the competency of the evidence is necessary. *Taylor v Taylor* (1908) 123 AD 220, 108 NYS 428.

In an action for divorce by a husband, it was competent for the wife to show that the plaintiff had brought the wife and the correspondent together and encouraged their intimacy to establish a defense to the adultery claim. *Parsons v Parsons* (1920) 191 AD 545, 181 NYS 642. In a divorce action by a wife against the husband, she was not permitted to give testimony identifying her husband's handwriting in a letter to her purportedly confessing his adultery. *Grobin v Grobin* (1945) 184 Misc 996, 55 NYS2d 32.

One spouse, may, however, in a divorce action identify the other to a process server in order to obtain jurisdiction. *Walsh v Walsh* (1960) 25 Misc 2d 441, 208 NYS2d 380.

The marital privilege against self-incrimination is an extension of the Fifth Amendment right. It is grounded upon the theory that just as one may not be convicted by his own compelled testimony, so he may not be convicted by the testimony of his spouse as to a communication uttered in reliance upon the sanctity of the marital relationship. *Lewis v Hynes* (1975) 82 Misc 2d 256, 368 NYS2d 738, affd (2d Dept) 51 AD2d 550, 379 NYS2d 374.

Where the petitioners, a husband and wife, moved to quash a subpoena for the production of records in connection with the investigation of nursing home and health care abuses, the court held that the marital privilege did not apply. The privilege is no greater than the right not to incriminate oneself, and it has been held that no such right exists in such a case because the records are those of a separate business entity. *Lewis v Hynes, supra.* In addition, the entries and records of a nursing home are not communications from one spouse to the other, and there was no indication that any entry or record was made in reliance upon and in respect of the marital relationship. *Lewis v Hynes, supra*.

A husband recorded a tape and delivered it to his wife outside the presence of any third parties. The tape, which was unknown to anyone outside the marriage, remained confidential for purposes of the marital privilege. The fact that the tape passed through the hands of third parties with no justifiable interest in becoming privy to its contents did not destroy that privilege. *Re Vanderbilt* (1982) 57 NY2d 66, 453 NYS2d 662. The privilege falls only when the substance of a communication, and not the mere fact of its occurrence, is revealed to third parties. *Re Vanderbilt, supra*.

Although acts as well as words may be communications, they are not subject to the privilege between husband and wife unless they are confidential. The privilege is designed to protect not all the daily and ordinary exchanges between the spouses but merely those which were induced by and would not have been made but for the absolute confidence in the marital relationship. *People v Wilson* (1984) 64 NY2d 634, 485 NYS2d 40.

A communication between spouses is presumed to have been conducted under the mantle of confidentiality. *People v Fediuk* (1985) 66 NY2d 881, 498 NYS2d 763. This presumption is not rebutted by the fact that the parties are not living together at the time of the communication or that their marriage has deteriorated; even in a stormy separation, disclosures to a spouse may be induced by absolute confidence in the marital relationship. *People v Fediuk, supra*.

§ 16:3 REQUIREMENTS FOR PRIVILEGE TO EXIST BETWEEN HUSBAND AND WIFE — Privilege extends only to those communications between a husband and wife that are of a strictly confidential nature. *Pardee v Mutual Ben. Life Ins. Co.* (1933) 148 Misc 860, 265 NYS 833, mod on other grounds 238 AD 294, 265 NYS 837. The communication must have been induced by the marital relationship. *Symington v Symington* (1926) 215 AD 553, 214 NYS 307.

Whether a communication is actually confidential and, therefore, privileged, is a preliminary question of fact to be determined by the trial judge. *People v Dudley* (1969) 24 NY2d 410, 301

NYS2d 9. Thus, where evidence showed that a defendant had held a marriage together solely by fear and domination and had threatened to kill his wife if she disclosed what she observed, the defendant's words and acts relating to the offense with which he was charged were not confidential and privileged. *People v Dudley, supra.*

If a communication is made by one spouse to another in the presence of a third person, the communication loses its confidential character. *Re Bourne's Estate* (1954) 206 Misc 378, 133 NYS2d 192. The presence of a daughter at a conversation between a husband and a wife destroyed any confidential character that the conversation might otherwise have had that would have rendered it inadmissible. *Re Bourne's Estate, supra.*

There is a clear public policy to permit the testimony of one spouse against the other when child abuse is the subject of a judicial proceeding. The testimony of the wife was admissible concerning deliberate injuries inflicted on the child of the marriage by the husband. The injuries were inflicted in the presence of the wife and resulted in the beating-death of the child. *People v Allman* (1973, 2d Dept) 41 AD2d 325, 342 NYS2d 896.

Where the wife of decedent brought an action for his wrongful death, she waived any confidential privilege as to communications between herself and her husband. If the decedent had been alive, he could not have asserted this privilege. *Prink v Rockefeller Center, Inc.* (1979) 48 NY2d 309, 422 NYS2d 911.

A police officer who did not report her husband's known illegal drug activities, as required under the Patrol Guide, was not protected by the spousal privilege. Whatever communications were involved had been made in the presence of third parties. *Colon v Ward* (1990, 1st Dept) 160 AD2d 587, 554 NYS2d 231.

Communications that include threats are not protected by the marital privilege. The threats indicate that the communication is not being made in reliance upon the marital relationship. *People v Edwards* (1989, 4th Dept) 151 AD2d 987, 542 NYS2d 425, app den 74 NY2d 808, 546 NYS2d 566.

Defendant's second wife was not barred by the marital privilege from testifying that during a visit with defendant at the Queens House of Detention, he admitted having killed his first wife. At the time that defendant married his second wife, his first wife was still alive and they had not been divorced. Therefore the second marriage was void and no marital privilege existed. *People v Mulgrave* (1990, 2d Dept) 163 AD2d 538, 558 NYS2d 607, app den 76 NY2d 989, 563 NYS2d 777.

Acts as well as words may be communications, but they are not privileged unless they are confidential. The testimony of defendant's wife that defendant had his gun with him on the day of the robbery was not confidential. *People v Beard* (1993, 2d Dept) 197 AD2d 582, 602 NYS2d 430, app den 82 NY2d 891, 610 NYS2d 158.

§ 16:4   CLAIMING AND WAIVING THE PRIVILEGE — To the extent that the statute provides that a husband or a wife is not competent to testify against each other with respect to adultery, this cannot be waived. *Bolognino v Bolognino* (1930) 136 Misc 656, 241 NYS 445, affd 231 AD 817, 246 NYS 883.

The portion of the statute that provides that a husband or a wife shall not be compelled, or without the other's consent permitted, to disclose confidential communications made by one of them to the other during the marriage confers a privilege that may be waived. *Grobin v Grobin* (1945) 184 Misc 996, 55 NYS2d 32. Such a waiver requires the consent of both husband and wife. *People v Wood* (1891) 126 NY 249, 27 NE 362.

§ 16:5   PRIVILEGED COMMUNICATIONS BETWEEN ATTORNEY AND CLIENT — The privileged nature of communications made by a client to an attorney in the course of the attorney-client relationship was recognized at common law. *Bacon v Frisbie* (1880) 80 NY 394. This privilege is now statutory. CPLR 4503.

Unless the client waives the privilege, an attorney or his employee, or any person who obtains without the client's knowledge evidence of a confidential communication between the attorney or his employee and the client in the course of professional employment, is prohibited from disclosing or being allowed to disclose such communication. The client cannot be compelled to disclose such confidential communication, in any action, disciplinary trial or hearing or administrative action, proceeding or hearing conducted by or on behalf of any state, municipal or local governmental agency or by the legislature or any of its committees or other bodies. Evidence of such confidential communication obtained by any such person, and evidence resulting from it, cannot be disclosed by any state, municipal or local governmental agency or by the legislature or any of its committees or other bodies. CPLR 4503(a).

The relationship of attorney and client exists between a professional service corporation organized under Article 15 of the Business Corporation Law to practice as an attorney and the clients to whom it renders legal services. CPLR 4503(a).

In any action involving the probate, validity or construction of a will, an attorney or his employee can be required to disclose information regarding the preparation, execution or revocation of any will or other relevant instrument. However, he is not permitted to disclose any communication privileged under CPLR 4503(a) which would tend to disgrace the decedent's memory. CPLR 4503(b).

An attorney may not refuse to testify unless his client asserts the privilege. *Packer v Rapoport* (1949, Sup) 88 NYS2d 118, revd on other grounds 275 AD 820, 89 NYS2d 703 and affd 277 AD 1116, 101 NYS2d 936 and affd 278 AD 649, 103 NYS2d 127. By moving to vacate subpoenas *duces tecum* that had been served on his present and former attorneys as witnesses, defendant claimed the attorney-client privilege. *Beach v Oil Transfer Corp.* (1960) 23 Misc 2d 47, 199 NYS2d 74.

The privilege belongs to the client, survives him and may be claimed by his personal representatives. *Pearsall v Elmer*, 5 Redf 181.

A protected communication may be oral, written or consist of papers that have been shown by the client to the attorney. *Kellogg v Kellogg*, 6 Barb 116.

If two or more persons consult an attorney regarding a matter of common interest, and an action subsequently arises between the parties or their personal representatives, no attorney-client privilege may be invoked to exclude the testimony of the attorney. Nothing that is said by the parties or the attorney is deemed confidential under those circumstances. *Re Estate of Friedman* (1978, 2d Dept) 64 AD2d 70, 407 NYS2d 999. This is especially the case when an insured and his insurer initially have a common interest in defending an action against the insured, and there is a possibility that those communications might play a role in a subsequent action between the insured and his insurer. *Goldberg v American Home Assurance Co.* (1981, 1st Dept) 80 AD2d 409, 439 NYS2d 2.

The husband in a divorce action had previously consulted with the wife's attorney in connection with a prior action between the husband and his former wife, which might bear a substantial relationship to the present divorce litigation. The husband's motion to disqualify the wife's attorney was granted. *Leisman v Leisman* (1994, 2d Dept) 208 AD2d 688, 617 NYS2d 807.

Not all communications to an attorney are privileged. To make a valid claim of privilege, it must be shown that the information sought to be protected from disclosure was a confidential communication made to the attorney for the purpose of obtaining legal advice or services. *Priest v Hennessy* (1980) 51 NY2d 62, 431 NYS2d 511.

The fee arrangement between attorney and client does not ordinarily constitute a confidential communication and, thus, is not privileged in the usual case. *Priest v Hennessy, supra.* When certain attorneys who had previously represented particular prostitutes were called before a grand jury investigating prostitution in the county, the attorneys could not claim privilege when asked to testify as to who had paid them for their representation. *Priest v Hennessy, supra.*

Confidentiality has been held not to apply to fee arrangements between an attorney and his client, because this is considered not to be directly relevant to legal advice that may be given. It is simply a collateral matter. *Oppenheimer v Oscar Shoes, Inc.* (1985, 1st Dept) 111 AD2d 28, 488 NYS2d 693.

The identity of the client is likewise not privileged. *Oppenheimer v Oscar Shoes, Inc., supra.* However, where an injured person sought, through a pre-action motion under CPLR 3102(c), to compel an attorney to divulge the identity of the person who had consulted the attorney following a hit-and-run accident, the privilege was held to attach to the potential client's identity. Disclosure of the identity itself would have revealed the potential client's possible involvement in a crime. *D'Alessio v Gilberg* (1994, 2d Dept) 205 AD2d 8, 617 NYS2d 484.

For the attorney-client privilege to apply to a communication between an attorney and a client, the communication must be made in the course of professional employment for the purpose of obtaining legal services, or to enable the attorney to act in a professional capacity as attorney. *Broun v Equitable Life Assurance Soc.* (1984, 1st Dept) 101 AD2d 783, 476 NYS2d 141. A letter written by decedent to an attorney, which was of a type that could equally have been written to any other person that decedent trusted, was not privileged and should have been received in evidence. *Broun v Equitable Life Assurance Soc., supra.*

A letter written by the client to the attorney, concerning a waiver of invalid service, was properly excluded from evidence, because it was clearly a confidential communication for the purpose of obtaining legal services. *Bleier v Heschel* (1987, 2d Dept) 128 AD2d 662, 512 NYS2d 902.

Where it is alleged that an insurer has breached its fiduciary duty to its insured, the insurer may not use the attorney-client or work product privilege as a shield to prevent disclosure that is relevant to the insured's bad faith action. The same rule applies when an excess liability insurer brings an action against the primary insurer for bad faith refusal to settle a claim. *Zurich Ins. Co. v State Farm Mut. Auto. Ins. Co.* (1988, 1st Dept) 137 AD2d 401, 524 NYS2d 202.

The trial court did not abuse its discretion in denying defendant's motion to compel disclosure of the communications between plaintiff and his former attorneys where plaintiff had not waived the attorney-client privilege. The defendant's allegations of fraud on the part of the plaintiff were not substantiated by the record and were therefore insufficient to overcome the attorney-client privilege. *Escalera v Van Dorn Plastic Machinery Co.* (1987, 2d Dept) 134 AD2d 562, 521 NYS2d 462.

The New York statutory attorney-client privilege is not absolute. Because it constitutes an obstacle to the truth-finding process, its invocation should be cautiously observed to ensure that its application is consistent with its purpose. *Hoopes v Carota* (1988, 3d Dept) 142 AD2d 906, 531 NYS2d 407, affd 74 NY2d

716. Merely because a communication occurs between a lawyer and a client is not enough. The information must be a confidential communication for the purpose of obtaining legal advice. *Hoopes v Carota, supra.*

The privilege may also yield to a strong public policy requiring disclosure. For that reason, the burden of bringing the information sought within the privilege is upon the party asserting it. *Hoopes v Carota, supra.* In an action brought by beneficiaries of a trust, which held stock in a corporation their family had founded, against the corporation's president, who was also a trustee, the defendant was not entitled to shield absolutely from the beneficiaries the communications between him and his attorneys with respect to pertinent affairs of the trust and of the corporation. *Hoopes v Carota, supra.*

Corporations as well as other clients may avail themselves of the attorney-client privilege. *Rossi v Blue Cross & Blue Shield* (1989) 73 NY2d 588, 542 NYS2d 508. As long as the communication is primarily or predominantly of a legal character, the privilege is not lost merely because it also refers to certain non-legal matters. *Rossi v Blue Cross & Blue Shield, supra.*

The attorney-client privilege extends only to communications and not facts. *Spectrum Systems Int'l Corp. v Chemical Bank* (1990, 1st Dept) 157 AD2d 444, 558 NYS2d 486, mod on other grounds (1991) 78 NY2d 371, 575 NYS2d 809. Information that the attorney receives from other persons and sources while acting on behalf of a client does not come within the attorney-client privilege. *Spectrum Systems Int'l Corp. v Chemical Bank, supra.*

The attorney-client privilege applies to communications with attorneys, whether such attorneys are on the corporate staff or are outside counsel. It extends to the attorney's communications to the client. *Nicolo v Greenfield* (1990, 4th Dept) 163 AD2d 837, 558 NYS2d 371; *Quail Ridge Assoc. v Chemical Bank* (1991, 3d Dept) 174 AD2d 959, 571 NYS2d 648.

The reports of a hospital's Law Committee, one of whose functions was to address such issues as the legality of any charges against a member of the medical staff, were privileged. They were made in order to render legal services or advice to the hospital. Confidential internal memoranda between in-house counsel and employees are protected by the attorney-client privilege. *Kraus v Brandstetter* (1992, 2d Dept) 185 AD2d 300, 586 NYS2d 270, later proceeding (2d Dept) 185 AD2d 302, 586 NYS2d 269.

Letters exchanged between a state commission and its attorneys with respect to the progress of litigation are not subject to disclosure. They are protected by the attorney-client privilege. *Mahoney v Staffa* (1992, 3d Dept) 184 AD2d 886, 585 NYS2d 543, app dismd without op 80 NY2d 972.

Where the plaintiff in an action took an adversary's privileged confidential documents from the counsel table at a pretrial proceeding, it was a proper exercise of the trial court's discretion to dismiss the complaint for abuse of the discovery process, pursuant to CPLR 3103(c). Suppression of either the documents or the information contained in them was not a realistic alternative remedy. Disqualification of counsel would not ameliorate the prejudice since it was plaintiff herself who engaged in the misconduct and then had the knowledge of the confidential information. *Lipin v Bender* (1994) 84 NY2d 562, 620 NYS2d 744.

§ 16:6 EXISTENCE OF ATTORNEY AND CLIENT RELATION-SHIP — For the communication to acquire its confidential character, the relation of attorney and client must exist and the communication must be regarded by the parties as confidential. *Rousseau v Bleau* (1892) 131 NY 177, 30 NE 52. A formal retainer of the attorney by the client is not required to create the privileged relationship contemplated by the statute. *Gage v Gage* (1897) 13 AD 565, 43 NYS 810. The privilege between attorney and client does not apply merely because such a relationship exists. *Beard v Ames* (1983, 4th Dept) 96 AD2d 119, 468 NYS2d 253.

The privilege will attach to information provided at a preliminary consultation with an attorney. Whether the attorney is actually retained to represent the client is not critical in determining whether the communication was confidential. *Leisman v Leisman* (1994, 2d Dept) 208 AD2d 688, 617 NYS2d 807; *see also*, *D'Alessio v Gilberg* (1994, 2d Dept) 205 AD2d 8, 617 NYS2d 484.

If a communication is made to an attorney in his character as a friend or social acquaintance, the communication is not confidential and the privilege does not attach. *Haulenbeek v McGibbon* (1891) 60 Hun 26, 14 NYS 393.

An attorney was employed as house counsel for a corporation and participated actively in certain corporate litigation. He qualified as an attorney for the corporation for purposes of the privilege, even though he was not admitted to practice law in the state. *Georgia-Pacific Plywood Co. v United States Plywood Corp.* (1956, DC NY) 18 FRD 463.

Generally, a corporation's attorney represents the corporation and not its employees. Where a former employee had communicated information to the corporate employer's attorney, the employee could not successfully claim the privilege in subsequent litigation against the former employer. There was no expectation of confidentiality at the time the communication was made to the attorney. *Talvy v American Red Cross* (1994, 1st Dept) 205 AD2d 143, 618 NYS2d 25.

When the attorney acts in a capacity which renders the relationship one that is not attorney and client, there is no privilege. *Gallagher v Akoff Realty Corp.* (1950) 197 Misc 460, 95 NYS2d 796. Thus, when an attorney acts in a dual capacity both professionally and as a negotiator, the rules applicable to agents govern his actions as negotiator and the attorney-client privilege does not preclude his examination as a witness. *Gallagher v Akoff Realty Corp., supra.*

Privilege applied to prevent a law guardian from testifying regarding statements made by the child at an *in camera* interview and the law guardian's opinions concerning the veracity of child's statements. An attorney-client relationship existed and the record did not reflect any willingness on the part of the child to waive her privilege. *In re Angelina AA* (1995, 3d Dept) 211 AD2d 951, 622 NYS2d 336.

Written statements obtained by a County Attorney in the course of his investigation are not shielded by the attorney-client privilege. *Civil Service Employees Asso. v Ontario County Health Facility* (1984, 4th Dept) 103 AD2d 1000, 478 NYS2d 380, later proceeding (4th Dept) 103 AD2d 1001, 478 NYS2d 583, app dismd 64 NY2d 816, 486 NYS2d 926.

§ 16:7 CONFIDENTIAL NATURE OF THE COMMUNICATION

— When a communication has not been made in confidence, the attorney is not privileged from disclosing it. *Yachnin v Bedford Home Builders, Inc.* (1930) 228 AD 795, 240 NYS 44. A communication that is not intended to be confidential is not privileged. *Dunn v Bloom* (1962, 3d Dept) 15 AD2d 687, 223 NYS2d 709.

A communication is not privileged if a client makes it to an attorney for an illegal purpose, such as to obtain his advice as to the method of committing a crime or to ask for the attorney's assistance in the commission of a crime. *People v Farmer* (1909) 194 NY 251, 87 NE 457.

If a communication by a client to an attorney was intended to be confidential, the fact that it may have been overheard by a third person does not necessarily destroy this privilege. *People v Decina* (1956) 2 NY2d 133, 157 NYS2d 558, 63 ALR2d 970. However, statements that are knowingly made in the presence of a third party are not privileged. *Re Luckenbach's Estate* (1962) 35 Misc 2d 122, 228 NYS2d 649.

Where the client was a 76-year-old defendant who had lost control of her vehicle, mounted a curb and caused at least a dozen people to be injured, her daughter's presence at her consultations with her attorney did not negate the confidential nature of the communications. The client had been required to recall and perhaps relive the most traumatic experience of her life, and the daughter had selected the law firm for her mother, had transported her to the law office, and had put the client sufficiently at ease to communicate effectively with counsel. Under those circumstances, the daughter was acting as the client's agent and the client had a reasonable expectation of confidentiality. *Stroh v General Motors Corp.* (1995, 1st Dept) 213 AD2d 267, 623 NYS2d 873.487

If an attorney gains knowledge as a result of representing an executor, it constitutes privileged information. The attorney may not petition for the removal of the executor, even though the relationship had been terminated at the time of the removal petition. *Re Estate of Howard* (1975) 80 Misc 2d 754, 363 NYS2d 711.

Although communications made between a defendant and counsel in the presence of a third party are generally not privileged, an exception exists for statements made by the client to the attorney's employees or in their presence. Clients have a reasonable expectation that such statements will be used solely for their benefit and remain confidential. *People v Osorio* (1989) 75 NY2d 80, 550 NYS2d 612. A party does not enjoy a confidential privilege when communicating with counsel in the presence of another co-party, unless the co-parties are mounting a common position and the exchange is for that purpose. *People v Osorio, supra.*

Although typically arising in the context of a client's communication to an attorney, the privilege extends as well to communications from attorney to client. *Spectrum Systems Int'l Corp. v Chemical Bank* (1991) 78 NY2d 371, 575 NYS2d 809. The privilege is limited to communications; it does not extend to underlying facts. *Spectrum Systems Int'l Corp. v Chemical Bank, supra.*

§ 16:8   CLAIMING AND WAIVING THE ATTORNEY-CLIENT PRIVILEGE — The attorney-client privilege is intended for the benefit of the client, and the client may waive this privilege. *Re Hart's Estate* (1967) 53 Misc 2d 555, 279 NYS2d 119, affd 30 AD2d 781, 292 NYS2d 1017, app dismd 24 NY2d 158, 299 NYS2d 182. However, an attorney cannot testify to communications with the client other than those relating to matters concerning which the client has waived the privilege. *Hamlin v Hamlin* (1928) 224 AD 168, 230 NYS 51.

When the client voluntarily testifies with respect to the confidential communication, there is a waiver of the privilege. *People v Patrick* (1905) 182 NY 131, 74 NE 843, reh den 183 NY 52, 75 NE 963 and remittitur den 183 NY 537, 76 NE 1102. However, the mere fact that a party testifies generally on his own behalf does not constitute a waiver of the privilege, provided the party does not testify with respect to any privileged communication with his counsel. *People v Shapiro* (1955) 308 NY 453, 51 ALR2d 515.

A client is deemed to have impliedly waived the privilege if he voluntarily testifies to a privileged matter, publicly discloses such matter or permits his attorney to testify regarding the matter. *Jakobleff v Cerrato, Sweeney & Cohn* (1983, 2d Dept) 97 AD2d 834, 468 NYS2d 895. Waiver of the attorney-client privilege by injecting an issue occurs only if the privileged material is placed in issue by the party who enjoys the protection of the privilege. *Manufacturers & Traders Trust Co. v Servotronics, Inc.* (1987, 4th Dept) 132 AD2d 392, 522 NYS2d 999.

In a matrimonial action, where the former wife moved to set aside portions of a separation agreement and a judgment of divorce based thereon, the attorney who represented her at the signing of the separation agreement was questioned as to whether she indicated that she was aware of defendant's actual financial situation and the reasons for entering into the agreement. It was error for the court to permit the plaintiff to assert the attorney-client privilege regarding those communications. That privilege was waived when the plaintiff placed the subject matter of the communications in issue. Invasion of the privilege was required to determine the validity of the plaintiff's claim. *Paruch v Paruch* (1988, 2d Dept) 140 AD2d 418, 528 NYS2d 119.

Any attorney-client privilege was waived when the plaintiff used his written statement prior to his deposition to refresh his recollection as to the events of the occurrence and when plaintiff's witness reread her statement prior to the trial for the same purpose. The defendant was entitled to have the statements made available to him and to use them in cross-examination. *Grieco v Cunningham* (1987, 2d Dept) 128 AD2d 502, 512 NYS2d 432.

A bank sued to recover losses resulting from a loan that was made in reliance on defendant company's letter to the effect that it held collateral belonging to the borrower valued at $10 million. The bank's president stated that plaintiffs had relied on the advice of its attorneys who informed it that "we had a good security." The attorney-client privilege was waived by placing the subject matter of counsel's advice in issue and by making selective disclosure of such advice. *Orco Bank N. V. v Proteinas Del Pacifico, S. A.* (1992, 1st Dept) 179 AD2d 390, 577 NYS2d 841.

§ 16:9 TERMINATION OF THE ATTORNEY-CLIENT PRIVILEGE — The privilege is not terminated by the termination of the attorney-client relationship. *Myers v Dorman* (1884) 34 Hun 115. Even after the termination of the professional relationship, the attorney is bound to maintain silence as to any communications between himself and his former client. *Myers v Dorman, supra.*

§ 16:10 EXISTENCE OF PHYSICIAN-PATIENT PRIVILEGE

— At common law, information acquired by a physician in the course of his treatment of a patient was not privileged. *Munzer v State* (1943, Ct Cl) 41 NYS2d 98. By statute, however, unless a patient waives the privilege, a person authorized to practice medicine, dentistry, or chiropractic, or a registered professional or licensed practical nurse may not disclose any information that he or she acquired in attending a patient in a professional capacity and which was necessary to enable him or her to act in that capacity. CPLR 4504(a).

The foregoing professionals are required, however, to disclose information indicating that a patient under the age of 16 has been the victim of a crime. Dentists are required to disclose information necessary to identify a patient. CPLR 4504(b).

The relationship of physician and patient also exists between a patient and a medical corporation defined in Article 44 of the Public Health Law, a professional service corporation organized under Article 15 of the Business Corporation Law, or a university faculty practice corporation organized under § 1412 of the Not-for-Profit Corporation Law to practice medicine or dentistry.

If a physician actually treats a person, regardless of whether the person requested treatment or gave consent, the physician-patient relationship arises. *People v Decina* (1956) 2 NY2d 133, 157 NYS2d 558, 63 ALR2d 970. Whether actual treatment was undertaken is not decisive. *People v Decina, supra.*

The burden of proving that evidence falls within the physician-patient privilege rests upon the party seeking to invoke the privilege. *People v Hedges* (1983, 4th Dept) 98 AD2d 950, 470 NYS2d 61.

Not all matters are privileged. The privilege does not apply when information is readily ascertainable, such as the dates on which the physician saw the patient, the fees charged and whether he referred the patient to a particular attorney. *Re Judicial Inquiry* (1959, 2d Dept) 8 AD2d 842, 190 NYS2d 406. In an action to recover on a life insurance policy, a physician may testify as to the fact that he attended the deceased insured professionally, as well as to the dates and frequencies of his professional visits to his office. *Hindin v Mutual Trust Life Ins. Co.* (1959, Sup) 195 NYS2d 457, affd (1st Dept) 12 AD2d 763, 210 NYS2d 969.

The physician-patient privilege is not intended to prohibit a person from testifying to such ordinary incidents and facts as are plain to the observation of anyone without expert or professional knowledge. *Hughson v St. Francis Hospital* (1983, 2d Dept) 93 AD2d 491, 463 NYS2d 224 (disagreed with on other grounds Williams v Roosevelt Hospital (1st Dept) 108 AD2d 9, 487 NYS2d 767, affd 66 NY2d 391, 497 NYS2d 348 (1985). A physician is not prohibited by the privilege from testifying that an individual was his patient, that he attended him as a patient, how many times he attended the patient, whether he attended the patient daily or hourly, that the patient visited him and made certain payments to him, that he referred the patient to an attorney, and that the patient was sick, provided that such condition of sickness was plainly observable by anyone. *Hughson v St. Francis Hospital, supra.* However, the physician may not be asked questions that are obviously designed to elicit the character of the disease or ailment for which the patient was being treated. *Hughson v St. Francis Hospital, supra.*

A physician observed that there was a strong odor of alcohol on defendant's breath, that the defendant's speech was slurred and disjointed, and that the defendant was extremely intoxicated. Those observations were of such a nature that they could have been made by a lay person, did not depend upon any confidential communication by the defendant, and were therefore not privileged. *People v Hedges* (1983, 4th Dept) 98 AD2d 950, 470 NYS2d 61.

Photographs of all of a hospital's patients who meet a particular description may be subpoenaed without violating CPLR 4504(a). The same is true of the names and addresses of a particular doctor's patients. These are facts that are plain to the observation of anyone without expert or professional knowledge and are not within the physician-patient privilege. *Re Grand Jury Investigation* (1983) 59 NY2d 130, 463 NYS2d 758

The privilege protects only the information that a physician obtains in his professional capacity and is needed to diagnose and treat a condition. *Henry v Lewis* (1984, 1st Dept) 102 AD2d 430,

478 NYS2d 263. It is only when a doctor attends a patient professionally for the purpose of giving medical advice and treatment that the privilege applies, and not otherwise. *Meyer v Supreme Lodge K. P.* (1904) 178 NY 63, 70 NE 111, affd 198 US 508, 49 L Ed 1146, 25 S Ct 754.

Testimony by a physician as to how an accident happened was based upon information acquired by the physician from the injured party while the physician attended him in a professional capacity as a surgeon. Such testimony does not come within the physician-patient privilege in the absence of any evidence that the information was necessary to enable the physician to act in a professional capacity. *Green v Metropolitan S. R. Co.* (1902) 171 NY 201, 63 NE 958.

Hospital records are privileged communications within the meaning of the statute. *La Plante v Garrett* (1953) 282 AD 1096, 126 NYS2d 470, reh den 283 AD 987, 130 NYS2d 910. However, records of a state hospital relating to an inmate who made a sexual assault on an infant claimant, who was also an inmate, were not privileged except as to certain entries relating to the inmate's propensities, diagnosis and prognosis. Claimants were entitled to have the records made available to them in an action against the State. *Boykin v State* (1958, 3d Dept) 7 AD2d 819, 180 NYS2d 884.

An affidavit by a former family physician could be considered in a proceeding on a petition for the appointment of a commission to inquire into the alleged incompetency of the respondent and for the appointment of a committee of her person and property. The affidavit was not inadmissible on the ground of violation of the privilege. *Re Allen* (1960) 24 Misc 2d 763, 204 NYS2d 876, app dismd (1st Dept, 1960) 13 AD2d 473, 217 NYS2d 478.

In an action on a life insurance policy containing a double indemnity clause, a certificate issued by the insured's physician to another insurance company, wherein the physician stated that he believed that the insured had a cardiac condition, was inadmissible. *Epstein v Metropolitan Life Ins. Co.* (1937) 250 AD 854, 294 NYS 919.

Communications to a druggist and prescriptions given to him by his customer are not confidential communications protected from disclosure. Such communications and prescriptions, under proper circumstances, may be received in evidence. *Re Miner's Will* (1954) 206 Misc 234, 133 NYS2d 27.

A medical examiner autopsy report is not a privileged document relating to physician-patient privilege. It is a proper subject for inspection in a civil action. *Walsh v Beckman* (1961) 29 Misc 2d 591, 215 NYS2d 398.

A physician or nurse may be required to disclose information as to the mental or physical condition of a deceased patient which is privileged under the statute, except such information as would tend to disgrace the memory of the decedent, either in the absence of an objection by a party to the litigation or when the privilege has been waived. The privilege may be waived: (1) by the personal representative or surviving spouse or next of kin of the decedent, or (2) by any party in interest, in any litigation where the trial judge deems the interests of the personal representative to be adverse to those of the estate of the decedent, or (3) by the executor named in the will or the surviving spouse, or any heir at law, or any next of kin or any other party in interest, if the validity of decedent's will is in question. CPLR 4504(c).

Where the Public Health Law requires attending physicians to furnish to the Commissioner of Health the names and addresses of the parents of aborted fetuses, the physician-patient privilege does not apply. *State v Jacobus* (1973) 75 Misc 2d 840, 348 NYS2d 907.

When plaintiff brought an action for malpractice against a physician, she placed her physical condition in controversy by the commencement of the action. She thereby waived the physician-patient privilege with regard to matters relating to such condition. *Josephs v Oliver* (1975, 2d Dept) 48 AD2d 688, 367 NYS2d 836.

In a malpractice action against a physician and hospital, records and inquiry concerning medical procedures performed on persons other than the plaintiff are privileged confidential communications that the hospital may not divulge without an express waiver from the third parties affected thereby. *Boddy v Parker* (1974, 2d Dept) 45 AD2d 1000, 358 NYS2d 218.

In a wrongful death action, where defendant sought to establish that decedent died as a result of an attempted suicide rather than defendant's negligence, disclosure could be compelled as to decedent's conversations with his psychiatrist. If decedent had been alive to bring the action himself, he could not have successfully resisted defendant's demand for disclosure. *Prink v Rockefeller Center, Inc.* (1979) 48 NY2d 309, 422 NYS2d 911.

The provision by the state of a central facility for storing and retrieving statistics that involve in-patients and out-patients of institutions and facilities owned or operated by the state did not, on the record, violate the physician-patient privilege. *Volkman v Miller* (1977) 41 NY2d 946, 394 NYS2d 631.

The physician-patient privilege is a purely statutory creation, in derogation of the common law rule that a physician could be compelled to disclose information acquired in the treatment of a patient. *Camperlengo v Blum* (1982) 56 NY2d 251, 451 NYS2d 697. A physician could not avail himself of the physician-patient privilege with respect to a subpoena by the New York State Department of Social Services with respect to treatment of Medicaid patients. *Camperlengo v Blum, supra.*

The physician-patient privilege belongs to the patient, but the physician may assert it for the patient's protection where the patient has not waived the privilege. *Re Grand Jury Proceedings* (1982) 56 NY2d 348, 452 NYS2d 361. A hospital that was being investigated for possible criminal activity in connection with the death of two elderly patients did not have the standing to assert the constitutional rights, if any, of its patients. *Re Grand Jury Proceedings, supra.*

A plaintiff who sues only in her representative capacity as mother and natural guardian of an infant does not thereby place her own medical history in issue and waive her physician-patient privilege. *Herbst v Bruhn* (1984, 2d Dept) 106 AD2d 546, 483 NYS2d 363. However, where medical negligence was claimed in connection with prenatal care, the plaintiff mother was held to have waived her privilege to the extent of the period of time the child was *in utero. Napoleoni v Union Hosp.* (1994, 1st Dept) 207 AD2d 660, 616 NYS2d 38.

A defendant charged with vehicular manslaughter had a blood test was performed by a physician in the course of attending the defendant in a professional capacity. He was entitled to have the results of that test suppressed, because there was no evidence that the defendant at any time waived the privilege. *People v Petro* (1986, 3d Dept) 122 AD2d 309, 504 NYS2d 67.

Communications between a defendant and his physician that are not related to diagnosis or treatment are not protected by the physician-patient privilege. *Litwak v Crown Beverages Corp.* (1987, 2d Dept) 133 AD2d 742, 520 NYS2d 29; *Rubin v Alamo Rent-A-Car* (1993, 2d Dept) 190 AD2d 661, 593 NYS2d 284.

A party does not waive the physician-patient privilege whenever forced to defend an action in which his or her mental or physical condition is in controversy. To effect a waiver, the party must do more than simply deny the allegations in the complaint. He or she must affirmatively assert the condition either by way of counterclaim or to excuse the conduct complained of in the complaint. *Dillenbeck v Hess* (1989) 73 NY2d 278, 539 NYS2d 707.

In an action seeking monetary damages for physical and psychological injuries sustained by plaintiff in a motor vehicle collision, the Supreme Court properly directed disclosure of psychiatric reports regarding plaintiff's hospitalization for attempted suicide. Plaintiff clearly waived his physician-patient privilege by affirmatively placing his psychological condition in issue. *Levine v Morris* (1990, 1st Dept) 157 AD2d 567, 550 NYS2d 289.

The information revealed by the infant plaintiff's parents during the course of their depositions, which had previously been revealed to the infant plaintiff's physicians, constituted mere facts and incidents of the medical history of plaintiff's siblings and thus did not constitute privileged material. By voluntarily revealing the medical history information that was not privileged, the infant plaintiff's parents cannot be said to have waived the physician-patient privilege as to the medical records in issue. *Wepy v Shen* (1991, 2d Dept) 175 AD2d 124, 571 NYS2d 817.

In an action brought against a hospital resulting from a fall in the lobby of a hospital, disclosure of the identity of a non-party witness who had fallen in the lobby 13 days previously does not violate the physician-patient privilege. *Gechoff v Our Lady of Victory Hosp.* (1993, 4th Dept) 190 AD2d 1060, 593 NYS2d 682.

The guardian of an infant plaintiff does not put her mental or physical condition in controversy. Disclosure of the medical records of the guardian, who was a half-sibling of the infant plaintiff, was properly denied. *Muniz v Preferred Assocs.* (1993, 1st Dept) 189 AD2d 738, 592 NYS2d 734.

In a wrongful death action, the personal representative of the decedent waives any privilege relating to decedent's actual condition of health immediately before his death. The representative does not waive his or her own physician-patient privilege. *Scalone v Phelps Memorial Hosp. Center* (1992, 2d Dept) 184 AD2d 65, 591 NYS2d 419.

In a matrimonial action, by actively contesting custody, a party may waive the physician-patient privilege concerning his or her mental or physical condition. There must first be a showing beyond mere conclusory statements that resolution of the custody issue requires revelation of protected material. *McDonald v McDonald* (1994, 2d Dept) 196 AD2d 7, 608 NYS2d 477.

A patient authorized a friend to use her influence with a hospital to determine whether the patient was getting a particular level of care. The patient also authorized the friend to inquire of the patient's physician as to the patient's condition and concerns. Under those circumstances, the patient was found to have waived confidentiality. *Heidi E. v Wanda W.* (1994, 4th Dept) 210 AD2d 918, 620 NYS2d 665.

§ 16:11   DENTIST-PATIENT PRIVILEGE — Persons asserting the existence of a dentist-patient privilege bear the burden of establishing that the dentist, whose testimony is sought to be excluded, acquired such information while attending to the patient in a professional capacity, that the information was necessary to enable him to act in that capacity, and that the information was intended to be confidential. *Polsky v Union Mut. Stock Life Ins. Co.* (1981, 1st Dept) 80 AD2d 777, 436 NYS2d 744.

Where the decedent had discussed suicide with his dentist and personal friend, the information supplied by the decedent about his mental condition was unnecessary for the dentist to treat his patient's mouth. Such information was, therefore, not privileged when the insurer asserted a defense of suicide in an action by the widow to recover accidental death benefits under life insurance policies. *Polsky v Union Mut. Stock Life Ins. Co.* (1981, 1st Dept) 80 AD2d 777, 436 NYS2d 744.

A dentist is required to disclose information needed to identify a patient, as well as information that may indicate whether a patient under the age of 16 has been the victim of a crime. CPLR 4504(b).

§ 16:12 PRIVILEGED COMMUNICATIONS TO CLERGY —

By statute, unless the person confiding or confessing waives the privilege, a clergyman or other minister of any religion is not allowed to disclose a confession made to him in his professional character as a spiritual adviser. CPLR 4505.

A confession made by a penitent to a clergyman for spiritual advice, aid or comfort is privileged, even though the penitent is not a member of the church from which she seeks advice. *Kohloff v Bronx Sav. Bank* (1962) 37 Misc 2d 27, 233 NYS2d 849. It did not amount to a waiver of the privilege when none of the parties objected to an order for the examination of a rabbi as a witness in a separation action. *Kruglikov v Kruglikov* (1961) 29 Misc 2d 17, 217 NYS2d 845, app dismd (4th Dept) 16 AD2d 735, 226 NYS2d 931.

Other than the statutory privilege which protects only confidential communications or confessions made by a penitent to a clergyman or spiritual adviser, there is no privilege, common law or statutory, which invests a clergyman's ministry with an immunity against disclosure. *Deputy Attorney-General v Gigante* (1978, 1st Dept) 64 AD2d 585, 407 NYS2d 163, affd 47 NY2d 160, 417 NYS2d 226, cert den 444 US 887, 62 L Ed 2d 118, 100 S Ct 181.

Not every communication made to a clergyman is entitled to the protection of the privilege. The law endeavors to protect only confidential communications made to a clergyman in his spiritual capacity. *People v Drelich* (1986, 2d Dept) 123 AD2d 441, 506 NYS2d 746. The defendant's communications to his rabbi were made for the secular purposes of seeking assistance in the retention of counsel, in negotiating with the prosecutor's office, and in securing other assistance in connection with the preparation of his defense to criminal charges. The defendant did not make the communications in confidence to his rabbi in his professional character as spiritual advisor and, accordingly, the communications were not privileged. *People v Drelich, supra.*

The privilege was properly asserted by an ordained minister, who was also a detective employed by the New York City Housing Authority, with respect to the identity of an individual who surrendered a gun to the clergyman at the church at a time when the clergyman was off duty and presiding over a church function. *Lewis v New York City Housing Authority* (1989, 1st Dept) 151 AD2d 237, 542 NYS2d 165, app den 75 NY2d 705, 552 NYS2d 927.

The trial court correctly allowed a clergyman to testify that defendant had told him to tell the victim that defendant was sorry. The apology, as an admission intended to be passed on to a third party, was not excluded by the clergyman-penitent privilege. *People v Dixon* (1993, 2d Dept) 199 AD2d 332, 604 NYS2d 604, app den 83 NY2d 851, 612 NYS2d 383.

§ 16:13   PSYCHOLOGISTS AND CLIENTS — By statute, the confidential relations and communications between a psychologist registered under the provisions of Article 153 of the Education Law and his client are placed on the same basis as those provided by law between an attorney and client. Nothing in that Article may be construed to require the disclosure of any such privileged communication. CPLR 4507.

The defendant husband in a matrimonial action waived his right to the privilege by actively contesting custody, thereby putting his mental and emotional well-being into issue. *Baecher v Baecher* (1977, 2d Dept) 58 AD2d 821, 396 NYS2d 447.

§ 16:14   SOCIAL WORKER AND CLIENT — A person duly registered as a certified social worker is not required to disclose a communication made by his or her client to him or her, or his or her advice given thereon, in the course of professional employment. Any clerk, stenographer or other person working for the certified social worker or for the same employer as the certified social worker is not allowed to disclose any such communications or advice given thereon. CPLR 4508.

There are four exceptions to the prohibition on disclosure: (1) a certified social worker may disclose such information as the client may authorize, (2) a certified social worker is not required to treat as a confidential communication such communication by a client which reveals the contemplation of a crime or harmful act, (3) where the client is a child under the age of 16 and the certified social worker acquires information which indicates that the client has been the victim or subject of a crime, the certified social worker may be required to testify fully about it upon any examination, trial or other proceeding in which the commission of such crime is a subject of inquiry, and (4) where the client waives the privilege by bringing charges against the certified social worker and such charges involve confidential communications between the client and the certified social worker. CPLR 4508.

A client who, for the purpose of obtaining insurance benefits, authorizes the disclosure of any privileged communication to any person is not deemed to have waived the privilege created by CPLR 4508.

A parole officer who is also a certified social worker, who interviews a prisoner or parolee at the direction of the Board of Parole, is required to report thereon to the Board of Parole and is not bound by the disclosure restrictions of this section that are applicable to certified social workers. Op Atty. Gen. Jan. 26, 1969.

Communications made in confidence are not protected purely because of their confidentiality, but may be kept secret only if premised upon a public policy expressed by statute or in furtherance of an overriding public concern of constitutional dimension. *Perry v Fiumano* (1978, 4th Dept) 61 AD2d 512, 403 NYS2d 382.

A certified social worker is not required to treat as confidential a communication that reveals the contemplation of a harmful act. *Perry v Fiumano, supra.* Statements to a social worker were not privileged and would not be suppressed on the trial of defendant for assaulting his 10-week-old son. *Re Easter* (1979, 3d Dept) 71 AD2d 762, 419 NYS2d 327.

§ 16:15 PRIVILEGED COMMUNICATIONS TO JOURNAL-ISTS — There was formerly no privilege that permitted a newspaperman to refuse to divulge the source of his information. *People ex rel. Mooney v Sheriff of New York County* (1936) 269 NY 291, 199 NE 415, 102 ALR 769. A journalist could formerly be required to testify as to communications made to him. *People ex rel. Mooney v Sheriff of New York County, supra.* Journalists are now protected from disclosing news or the sources of news by the provisions of Civil Rights Law § 79-h.

This statute replaces a body of case law that had developed on the issue. It provides an absolute privilege with respect to confidential news and sources, and a qualified privilege with respect to non-confidential news and sources.

Section 79-h(b) provides:

"Exemption of professional journalists and newscasters from contempt: Absolute protection for confidential news. Notwithstanding the provisions of any general or specific law to the contrary, no professional journalist or newscaster presently or having previously been employed or otherwise associated with any newspaper, magazine, news agency, press association, wire service, radio or television transmission station or network or other professional medium of communicating news or information to the public shall be adjudged in contempt by any court in connection with any civil or criminal proceeding, or by the legislature or other body having contempt powers, nor shall a grand jury seek to have a journalist or newscaster held in contempt by any court, legislature or other body having contempt powers for refusing or failing to disclose any news obtained or received in confidence or the identity of the source of any such news coming into such person's possession in the course of gathering or obtaining news for publication or to be published in a newspaper, magazine, or for broadcast by a radio or television transmission station or network or for public dissemination by any other professional medium or agency which has as one of its main functions the dissemination of news to the public, by which such person is professionally employed or otherwise associated in a news gathering capacity notwithstanding that the material or identity of a source of such material or related material gathered by a person described above performing a function described above is or is not highly relevant to a particular inquiry of government and notwithstanding that the information was not solicited by the journalist or newscaster prior to disclosure to such person."

Section 79-h(c) provides:

"Exemption of professional journalists and newscasters from contempt: Qualified protection for nonconfidential news. Notwithstanding the provisions of any general or specific law to the contrary, no professional journalist or newscaster presently or having previously been employed or otherwise associated with any newspaper, magazine, news agency, press association, wire service, radio or television transmission station or network or other professional medium of communicating news to the public shall be adjudged in contempt by any court in connection with any civil or criminal proceeding, or by the legislature or other body having contempt powers, nor shall a grand jury seek to have a journalist or newscaster held in contempt by any court, legislature, or other body having contempt powers for refusing or failing to disclose any unpublished news obtained or prepared by a journalist or newscaster in the course of gathering or obtaining news as provided in subdivision (b) of this section, or the source of any such news, where such news was not obtained or received in confidence, unless the party seeking such news has made a clear and specific showing that the news: (i) is highly material and relevant; (ii) is critical or necessary to the maintenance of a party's claim, defense or proof of an issue material thereto; and (iii) is not obtainable from any alternative source. A court shall order disclosure only of such portion, or portions, of the news sought as to which the above-described showing has been made and shall support such order with clear and specific findings made after a hearing. The provisions of this subdivision shall not affect the availability, under appropriate circumstances, of sanctions under section thirty-one hundred twenty-six of the civil practice law and rules."

§ 16:16 NON-PRIVILEGED RELATIONSHIPS — There is no common law or statutory privilege regarding information communicated between an architect or engineer and his client. *Pickard & Anderson v YMCA* (1986, 4th Dept) 119 AD2d 976, 500 NYS2d 874.

Under certain circumstances there may be a parent-child privilege, that is, where a minor, under arrest for a serious crime seeks the guidance and advice of a parent in the unfriendly environment of a police precinct. If these circumstances are not present, no privileges attaches. *People v Edwards* (1987, 2d Dept) 135 AD2d 556, 521 NYS2d 778, app den 71 NY2d 968, 529 NYS2d 79.

**§ 16:17   RECORDS OF PARTICIPATION IN A SUBSTANCE
ABUSE PROGRAM** — Mental Hygiene Law § 23.05(a) prohibits
the introduction of evidence of a person's participation in a substance abuse program against such person in any action or proceeding in any court. *People v Simms* (1991, 4th Dept) 174 AD2d
979, 572 NYS2d 138.

§ 16:18   THE PUBLIC INTEREST PRIVILEGE — The public
interest privilege developed as part of New York State's decisional
law. It provides generally that official information in the hands of
government agencies has been deemed privileged in certain con-
texts. *Martin A. v Gross* (1993, 1st Dept) 194 AD2d 195, 605
NYS2d 742.

Statements made by a witness to the District Attorney's office
are protected by the public interest privilege, which is qualified.
Sanchez v City of New York (1994, 1st Dept) 201 AD2d 325, 607
NYS2d 321. Where the privilege exists, the test to be applied for
disclosure requires a balancing of the litigant's need for production
of the information against the potential harm to the public from
disclosure. *Sanchez v City of New York, supra.*

RESEARCH REFERENCES

American Law Reports

87 ALR4th 845, Liability for interference with physician-patient relationship

86 ALR4th 1024, Existence, nature, and application to medical professional disciplinary board of privilege against disclosure of identity
of informer

84 ALR4th 15, Discoverability of traffic accident reports and derivative
information

44 ALR4th 649, Validity, construction, and application of statute limiting physician-patient privilege in judicial proceedings relating to
child abuse or neglect

39 ALR4th 480, Presence of child at communication between husband
and wife as destroying confidentiality of otherwise privileged communication between them

33 ALR4th 539, Privileged communications between accountant and client

32 ALR4th 1177, Applicability of marital privilege to written communications between spouses inadvertently obtained by third person

31 ALR4th 1226, Privilege as to communications between lay representative in judicial or administrative proceeding as contempt of court

31 ALR4th 458, Attorney-client privilege as extending to communications relating to contemplated civil fraud

27 ALR4th 568, Work product privilege as applying to material prepared for terminated litigation or for claim which did not result in litigation

24 ALR4th 144, Defamation: loss of employer's qualified privilege to publish employee's work record or qualification

23 ALR4th 932, Libel and slander: attorneys' statements, to parties other than alleged defamed party or its agents, in course of extrajudicial investigation or preparation relating to pending or anticipated civil litigation as privileged

20 ALR4th 576, Libel and slander: reports of pleadings as within privilege for reports of judicial proceedings

14 ALR4th 594, Applicability of attorney-client privilege to communications made in presence of or solely to or by third person

13 ALR4th 1305, Existence of spousal privilege where marriage was entered into for purpose of barring testimony

10 ALR4th 552, Physician-patient privilege as extending to patient's medical or hospital records

10 ALR4th 355, Construction and application, under state law, of doctrine of "executive privilege"

9 ALR4th 807, Testimony before or communications to private professional society's judicial commission, ethics committee, or the like, as privileged

6 ALR4th 544, Testimonial privilege for confidential communications between relatives other than husband and wife-state cases

5 ALR4th 730, Confidentiality of proceedings or reports of judicial inquiry board or commission

4 ALR4th 765, Applicability of attorney-client privilege to evidence or testimony in subsequent action between parties originally represented contemporaneously by same attorney, with reference to communication to or from one party

4 ALR4th 422, Communication between unmarried couple living together as privileged

3 ALR4th 1104, Spouse's betrayal or connivance as extending marital

communications privilege to testimony of third person

99 ALR3d 37, Privilege of newsgatherer against disclosure of confidential sources or information

98 ALR3d 1285, Effect, on competency to testify against spouse or on marital communication privilege, of separation or other marital instability short of absolute divorce

85 ALR3d 1196, Physician-patient privilege as applied to physician's testimony concerning wound required to be reported to public authority

85 ALR3d 1161, Privileged nature of communications between insurer and insured

85 ALR3d 1137, Privileged nature of statements or utterances by member of school board in course of official proceedings

83 ALR3d 749, Restricting access to records of disciplinary proceedings against attorneys

82 ALR3d 19, Validity, construction, and application of statutory provisions relating to public access to police records

71 ALR3d 794, Matters to which privilege covering communications to clergyman or spiritual advisor extends

59 ALR3d 441, Admissibility of defense communication made in connection with plea bargaining

55 ALR3d 1322, Applicability of attorney-client privilege to communications relating to drafting of documents

34 ALR3d 1106, Communications by corporation as privileged in stockholders' action

34 ALR3d 775, Propriety and prejudicial effect of comment or instruction by court with respect to party's refusal to permit introduction of privileged testimony

31 ALR3d 557, Power of trustee in bankruptcy to waive privilege of communications available to bankruptcy

81 ALR Fed 904, "Scholar's privilege" under Rule 501 of Federal Rules of Evidence

ALR QUICK INDEX: Privileged and Confidential Communications

American Jurisprudence 2d

81 AM JUR 2d, Witnesses §§ 141-556

American Jurisprudence Pleading and Practice

25 AM JUR PL & PR FORMS (Rev), Witnesses, Form 172

American Jurisprudence Proof of Facts

48 AM JUR PROOF OF FACTS 2d 525, Existence of Attorney-Client Relationship

47 AM JUR PROOF OF FACTS 2d 721, Psychotherapist and Patient Privilege

46 AM JUR PROOF OF FACTS 2d 373, Existence of Physician and Patient Relationship

45 AM JUR PROOF OF FACTS 2d 595, Protected communication between physician and patient

19 AM JUR PROOF OF FACTS 2d 335, Interference with Attorney-Client Relationship

17 AM JUR PROOF OF FACTS 785, Privileged Communications Between Physician and Patient

Other Resources

8 CARMODY-WAIT 2d, Presentation of the Case §§ 56:85-56:95

Auto-Cite®: Any case citation herein can be checked for form, parallel references, later history and annotation references through the Auto-Cite computer research system.

CHAPTER 17

JUDICIAL NOTICE

§ 17:1 PROOF EXCUSED IF FACT IS JUDICIALLY NOTICED

— Judicial notice is a method by which a court ascertains matters that are of universal knowledge, without the necessity of introducing evidence with respect to such matters in the particular case. *People v Goldberger* (1916, Sp Sess) 163 NYS 663. Judicial notice of a fact is a substitute for evidence. *Burr v Carvel Dari-Freeze Stores, Inc.* (1962, Sup) 224 NYS2d 804.

Although the court is ordinarily informed of facts by means of witnesses and evidence offered by the contending parties, many facts do not have to be proved because they are judicially noticed by the court and by the jury. *Viemeister v White* (1904) 179 NY 235, 72 NE 97.

The power to take judicial notice should be exercised with caution, and due care should be taken to see that the subject comes within the limits of common knowledge. With that in mind, the courts will take notice of whatever is generally known within the limits of their jurisdiction, *Viemeister v White, supra,* or whatever should be known, if pertinent to the issue being tried. *McGovern v New York* (1923) 234 NY 377, 138 NE 26, 25 ALR 1442, reh den, remittitur amd 236 NY 508, 142 NE 262.

The test is whether the fact sought to be judicially noticed is sufficiently well known to permit the court to assume its existence without proof. If there is any doubt either as to the truth of the fact or as to the fact being a matter of common knowledge, evidence must be presented. *Ecco High Frequency Corp. v Amtorg Trading Corp.* (1948, Sup) 81 NYS2d 610, reh den (Sup) 81 NYS2d 897, affd 274 AD 982, 85 NYS2d 304, reh and app den 274 AD 1056, 86 NYS2d 465. Simply put, judges are not necessarily to be ignorant in court of those facts with which everyone else and they themselves out of court are familiar. *Keefe v O'Brien* (1952) 203 Misc 113, 116 NYS2d 286.

Courts are not bound to take judicial notice of matters of fact. *Hunter v New York, O. & W. R. Co.* (1889) 116 NY 615, 23 NE 9. Whether or not they will do so depends on the nature of the subject, the issue involved and the apparent justice of the case. *Hunter v New York, O. & W. R. Co., supra.* If a matter is one of common knowledge in the state, it is a proper subject for judicial notice by the Court of Appeals, even though the matter is not the subject of universal knowledge. *Viemeister v White, supra.*

By statute, the court is now required to take judicial notice of various matters of law. CPLR 4511.

§ 17:2 JUDICIAL NOTICE OF LAWS — Every court will take judicial notice, without request, of the common law; constitutions and public statutes of the United States and of every state, territory and jurisdiction of the United States; the official compilation of codes, rules and regulations of the state, except those that relate solely to the organization or internal management of an agency of the state; and of all local laws and county acts. CPLR 4511(a).

Every court may take judicial notice, without request, of private acts and resolutions of the United States Congress and of the legislature of the states; ordinances and regulations of officers, agencies or governmental subdivisions of the state or of the United States; and the laws of foreign countries or their political subdivisions. Judicial notice will be taken of those matters if a party requests it, furnishes the court sufficient information to enable it to comply with the request, and has given each adverse party notice of his intention to request it. Notice will be given in the pleadings or prior to the presentation of any evidence at the trial, but a court may require or permit other evidence. CPLR 4511(b).

Whether a matter is judicially noticed or proof is taken, every matter specified in CPLR 4511 will be determined by the judge or referee and will be included in his findings or charged to the jury. Such findings or charge will be subject to review on appeal as a finding or charge on a matter of law. CPLR 4511(c).

In considering whether a matter of law should be judicially noticed and in determining the matter of law to be judicially noticed, the court may consider any testimony, document, information or argument on the subject, whether it is offered by a party or discovered through its own research. Whether or not judicial notice is taken, a printed copy of a statute or other written law or a proclamation, edict, decree or ordinance by an executive contained in a book or publication, purporting to have been published by a government or commonly admitted as evidence of the existing law in the judicial tribunals of the jurisdiction where it is enforced, is *prima facie* evidence of such law. The unwritten or common law of a jurisdiction may be proved by witnesses or printed reports of cases of the courts of the jurisdiction. CPLR 4511(d).

The court must take judicial notice of the law of New York. *Souveran Fabrics Corp. v Virginia Fibre Corp.* (1969, 1st Dept) 32 AD2d 753, 301 NYS2d 273. This applies to the statutes of the state, *Methodist Episcopal Union Church v Pickett* (1859) 19 NY 482, as well as to the common law that is found in court decisions. *People v Herkimer*, 4 Cow 345.

The court must take judicial notice of the relevant common and statutory laws of a sister state, even though neither has been pleaded or proved. *Martens v Bethel* (1966) 51 Misc 2d 202, 273 NYS2d 137. It was held that the trial court was required to take judicial notice of the New York City traffic regulations in an action for injuries sustained when infant plaintiff came into the path of defendant's motor vehicle and was injured. *Sansivero v Garz* (1964, 2d Dept) 20 AD2d 723, 247 NYS2d 596.

The courts must take judicial notice of federal statutes. *Scheinzeit v Kelly* (1948) 192 Misc 300, 80 NYS2d 509. The court may, in its discretion, take judicial notice of the laws of a foreign country. *Silberfeld v Swiss Bank Corp.* (1944) 183 Misc 234, 50 NYS2d 838, affd 268 AD 984, 52 NYS2d 583.

The common law in a sister state is presumed to be the same as that of New York, in the absence of proof on the subject. *Hopkins v Amtorg Trading Corp.* (1942) 265 AD 278, 38 NYS2d 788. Similarly, in the absence of contrary proof, foreign law will be presumed to be the same as the law of this state. *Re Dumarest's Estate* (1933) 146 Misc 442, 262 NYS 450.

The law of a sister state must be accorded judicial notice whether or not it is pleaded and whether or not advance notice is given. *Gevinson v Kirkeby-Natus Corp.* (1966, 1st Dept) 26 AD2d 71, 270 NYS2d 989. Although the law of foreign countries should be stated in substance in the pleading that relies on it, the court retains discretion to apply the law of foreign countries notwithstanding the absence of a request to do so or some advance notice. *Gevinson v Kirkeby-Natus Corp., supra.*

The taking of judicial notice of foreign law is permissive, not mandatory. *Earl S. Peed Organization, Inc. v Gray* (1963) 40 Misc 2d 471, 243 NYS2d 111. A party who seeks to have the substance of the litigation governed by Austrian law rather than New York law must plead and prove the foreign law if he intends to establish a rule different from that of the forum. Failure to meet this burden permits the court to proceed under the assumption that the law of the foreign jurisdiction accords with that of New York on the subject. *Stein v Siegel* (1975, 2d Dept) 50 AD2d 916, 377 NYS2d 580.

The court was required to take judicial notice of regulations of the Thruway Authority. *Cruise v New York State Thruway Authority* (1967, 3d Dept) 28 AD2d 1029, 283 NYS2d 779, affd 26 NY2d 1037, 311 NYS2d 924. The court must take judicial notice of the official Compilation of Codes, Rules and Regulations of New York State Offices & Agencies. *People v Wiley* (1969) 59 Misc 2d 519, 299 NYS2d 704. All courts must take judicial notice of the Constitution of the United States. *Ingersoll-Rand Co. v United States Shipping Bd. Emergency Fleet Corp.* (1921) 195 AD

838, 187 NYS 695. Courts must likewise take judicial notice of the public and general acts of Congress. *Benner v Atlantic Dredging Co.* (1892) 134 NY 156, 31 NE 328.

Judicial notice could be taken of the fact that an action is begun by the service of process. *Keene v Newark Watch Case Mfg. Co.* (1903) 81 AD 48, 80 NYS 859.

The courts have taken judicial notice that the law making it a crime to operate a motor vehicle on the highway while intoxicated was intended to protect persons lawfully on the highway from the threat posed by persons who operate a motor vehicle while intoxicated as a result of consumption of alcoholic beverages. *People v Koch* (1937) 250 AD 623, 294 NYS 987.

The court took judicial notice of the fact that the Metropolitan Transit Authority took over ownership of all stock of the Long Island Railroad under powers granted to it by the Public Authorities Law. *Bujosa v Metropolitan Transp. Authority* (1974, 2d Dept) 44 AD2d 849, 355 NYS2d 800.

A treaty such as the Warsaw Convention, although written in French, is a treaty of the United States and is the supreme law of the land. The New York courts are required to take judicial notice of such a treaty. *Rosman v Trans World Airlines, Inc.* (1974) 34 NY2d 385, 358 NYS2d 97, 72 ALR3d 1282. The Appellate Division must take judicial notice of an extradition treaty between the United States and Canada because it is a public law of the United States. *People v Jackson* (1982, 3d Dept) 89 AD2d 697, 453 NYS2d 875.

Lower courts are entitled to take judicial notice of any potentially applicable foreign law, even in the absence of a request from the parties. If such a request is not made, it cannot be said that the lower courts abused their discretion as a matter of law in declining to take judicial notice. *Lerner v Karageorgis Lines, Inc.* (1985) 66 NY2d 479, 497 NYS2d 894.

In a negligence action brought by a pedestrian who was hit by a barricade at a construction site after the barricade had been hit by a passing car, the trial court should have taken judicial notice of sections of the Administrative Code with respect to construction site safety and should have instructed the jury concerning their meaning and application. The failure of the trial court to do so deprived plaintiff of a fair trial. *Chanler v Manocherian* (1989, 1st Dept) 151 AD2d 432, 543 NYS2d 671.

§ 17:3 JUDICIAL NOTICE OF FACTS CONCERNING THE COURT — A court has knowledge of its own administrative structure. *Moskowitz v La Guardia* (1944) 183 Misc 33, 48 NYS2d 174, affd 268 AD 918, 51 NYS2d 758, affd 294 NY 830. A Surrogate's Court takes judicial notice of its own proceedings. *Re Hatlee's Estate* (1939) 171 Misc 1032, 14 NYS2d 763. Judicial notice would be taken of the existence of a process for passing judicial opinions through the clerk's office to the publisher who had contracted with the court for publication of opinions. *Bradford v Pette* (1953) 204 Misc 308. Judicial notice can be taken of the expense of litigation and the inadequacy of ordinary costs. *East India Trading Co. v Dada Haji Ebrahim Halari* (1952) 280 AD 420, 114 NYS2d 93, affd 305 NY 866.

The court may take judicial notice of its own records. *Edgar A. Levy Leasing Co. v Cohen* (1932) 145 Misc 810, 261 NYS 145. The Surrogate's Court may take judicial notice of a document on file in the court itself. *Re Blake's Will* (1933) 146 Misc 780, 263 NYS 310.

In a proceeding brought under the Agriculture and Markets Law to ascertain whether two dogs allegedly owned by respondent were dangerous, the court took judicial notice of its own records indicating respondent's 38 prior convictions, including several recent convictions, for violations of leash-law ordinances. *Re Fugazy* (1974) 82 Misc 2d 135, 368 NYS2d 652.

The Appellate Division took judicial notice of an acquisition agreement that was not part of the record on appeal before it. The agreement was contained in the record on appeal in another case currently pending before the same court. *Schmidt v Magnetic Head Corp.* (1983, 2d Dept) 97 AD2d 151, 468 NYS2d 649, later proceeding (2d Dept) 97 AD2d 244, 468 NYS2d 663, later proceeding (2d Dept) 101 AD2d 268, 476 NYS2d 151.

Although a court may take judicial notice of its own records, such as a process server's affidavit of service on file with the court, it cannot take judicial notice of a "fact" that has been controverted, such as whether service of the summons was properly effected. *Weinberg v Hillbrae Builders, Inc.* (1977, 1st Dept) 58 AD2d 546, 396 NYS2d 9.

§ 17:4 JUDICIAL NOTICE OF FACTS ABOUT GOVERN- MENT, OFFICERS, AND POLITICAL SUBDIVISIONS — The court will take judicial notice as to who are the only elected offi- cials of the various political subdivisions of the state. *William J. Sheldrick Asso. v Robert B. Blaikie Regular Democratic Organiza- tion, Inc.* (1954) 17 Misc 2d 238, 134 NYS2d 218.

The Supreme Court, Westchester County, could take judicial notice of the fact that the Town of Yorktown is located in Westchester County. *Johnson v Westall* (1955) 208 Misc 360, 144 NYS2d 633, affd 286 AD 966, 146 NYS2d 475. Special Term could take judicial notice of the budgetary problems encountered by the Board of Estimate of the City of New York. *Kaufman v Board of Elections* (1958) 14 Misc 2d 197, 178 NYS2d 193. The court took judicial notice of the fact that much rezoning in com- munities in the Rochester area had followed a piecemeal pattern. *Place v Hack* (1962) 34 Misc 2d 777, 230 NYS2d 583.

The Appellate Division could take judicial notice of problems facing all cities as a result of constantly increasing traffic conges- tion. *Comereski v Elmira* (1954) 283 AD 556, 128 NYS2d 913, affd 308 NY 248.

Historically and as a matter of common knowledge, fire depart- ments have been recognized as agencies of municipal govern- ments. Their organization, operation and administrative control have been deemed matters of local control. *Holland v Bankson* (1984) 290 NY 267.

A tenant sought review of a determination of the Commis- sioner of Housing and Development Administration that the ten- ant's apartment was vacancy-decontrolled. The Appellate Divi- sion would take judicial notice with respect to the tenant's Civil Court action by which he sought recovery for rent overcharges, even though that action was *dehors* the record. *Hartman v Joy* (1975, 1st Dept) 47 AD2d 624, 365 NYS2d 182.

In an Article 78 proceeding, the petitioner, who had been indicted for second-degree murder, sought to obtain an order of prohibition against both the trial justice and the prosecution. The order was sought on the ground that the grand jury which had returned the indictment against him was drawn from a grand jury pool which was in violation of due process by reason of a systematic exclusion of students and the deliberate discrimination in the exclusion of women. For the purpose of determining the questions of law raised in the petition, the Appellate Division took judicial notice of testimony in a previous case in which the jury pool was held to be invalid. *Paciona v Marshall* (1974, 4th Dept) 45 AD2d 462, 359 NYS2d 360, affd 35 NY2d 289, 360 NYS2d 882.

Judicial notice may be taken of a Memorandum of the Department of Civil Service that is concerned with the enforcement of a statute and the regulations adopted under it. *Albano v Kirby* (1975) 36 NY2d 526, 369 NYS2d 655.

The Appellate Division took judicial notice of the appropriate resolution of the Board of Estimate, not the one initially and erroneously relied upon by the defendant. *Kleiman v New York* (1990, 1st Dept) 162 AD2d 363, 557 NYS2d 30.

§ 17:5   MATTERS OF PUBLIC RECORD — Data culled from public records is a proper subject of judicial notice. *Siwek v Mahoney* (1976) 39 NY2d 159, 383 NYS2d 238. Dates of birth, death, marriage and lack of heirs are matters of public record that may be judicially noticed for the first time on appeal. *Re Will of Wilhelm* (1978, 4th Dept) 62 AD2d 1155, 405 NYS2d 157, affd 46 NY2d 947, 415 NYS2d 413.

In a proceeding brought by the Medical Malpractice Insurance Association to annul the determination of the Superintendent of Insurance establishing rates, the Court of Appeals could take judicial notice of the Regulatory Impact Statement that the Superintendent filed while the case was pending before the Supreme Court. *Medical Malpractice Ins. Asso. v Superintendent of Ins.* (1988) 72 NY2d 753, 537 NYS2d 1, cert den (US) 104 L Ed 2d 661, 109 S Ct 2100.

§ 17:6   OTHER FACTS JUDICIALLY NOTICED — Generally, a court may take judicial notice of those facts that are universally known and recognized. *Re Buszta's Estate* (1959) 18 Misc 2d 716, 186 NYS2d 192. A matter may be judicially noticed even though not widely known, if it is commonly known within the particular jurisdiction. Thus, the Supreme Court of Nassau County will take judicial notice of the character and physical appearance of the Village of North Hills as a rural high-class residential community. *Elbert v North Hills* (1941, Sup) 28 NYS2d 317, revd 262 AD 856, 28 NYS2d 172, reh den 262 AD 872, 29 NYS2d 152.

Courts will take judicial notice of the course and laws of nature. Thus, a court will take judicial notice that the gestation period of 280 days was normal, but recognize that a gestation in excess of or less than the normal period was possible. *Re Niles' Will* (1950, Sur) 99 NYS2d 238. A court will also take judicial notice that a child born to petitioner was a full-term baby only if the period of gestation had been around 280 days. *J v K* (1974, 3d Dept) 46 AD2d 935, 362 NYS2d 37.

It is common knowledge that on September 21 at about 8:20 p.m. Daylight Saving Time, before night has fully set in, visibility is difficult at best. *Fitzgerald v State* (1950) 198 Misc 39, 96 NYS2d 452.

A court will take judicial notice of the operation and effect of natural forces. Thus, a court would take judicial notice of the fact that implements wear out. *Re Colliton's Estate* (1934) 150 Misc 616, 271 NYS 163. It would also take judicial notice of the fact that the blowout of automobile tires can affect the direction of the car. *Kemp v Stephenson* (1931) 139 Misc 38, 247 NYS 650.

A court may take judicial notice of geographical facts, *Salamon v Koninklijke Luchtvaart Maatschappij, N. V.* (1950) 198 Misc 780, 100 NYS2d 702, such as the location of a road. *Northeastern Shares Corp. v International Ins. Co.* (1934) 240 AD 80, 269 NYS 351, affd 265 NY 574, 193 NE 326.

A court may take judicial notice of a historical fact, such as that the years 1935 through 1938 were Depression years. *People ex rel. Rubin v Tax Com.* of New York (1959, 3d Dept) 9 AD2d 47, 189 NYS2d 784, affd 8 NY2d 922, 204 NYS2d 165. The court would take judicial notice of the fact that in 1905 the automobile industry was in its early infancy. *Pelletier v Brown Bros. Chevrolet & Oldsmobile, Inc.* (1956, Sup) 164 NYS2d 249. The Surrogate's Court judicially noticed the commencement of brutality in the Nazi invasion of Lithuania. *Re Frankel's Estate* (1949) 196 Misc 268, 92 NYS2d 30. Judicial notice may properly be taken of historical events that involved catastrophes which resulted in the death of massive numbers of people. *Re Estate of Regas* (1974) 79 Misc 2d 170, 359 NYS2d 857.

The court would take judicial notice of facts with respect to human life and health. It is common knowledge that many persons are allergic to conditions that do not affect the normal individual. *Cleary v John M. Maris Co.* (1940) 173 Misc 954, 19 NYS2d 38. It is also common knowledge that a person who is afflicted with a progressive organic disease may have sufficient mental strength to make a will up to a relatively short time before death. *Re Lindsay's Estate* (1930) 136 Misc 555, 241 NYS 513, affd 234 AD 841, 254 NYS 921.

Judicial notice may be taken of language, words, phrases, and the uses thereof. The court could take judicial notice of generally accepted definitions of the mental disease schizophrenia. *Becker v Becker* (1954) 207 Misc 17, 138 NYS2d 397. The court would not, however, take judicial cognizance of the meaning of foreign languages, *Re Will of Tomljenovich* (1956, Sur) 154 NYS2d 327, or the meaning of a term such as "rubber check." *Ostro v Safir* (1937) 165 Misc 647, 1 NYS2d 377.

The court was required to take judicial notice of matters of time, days and dates. Thus, it was held that a court erred in not taking judicial notice of the time of sunset on the day of an accident. *Auerbach v Stein* (1936) 162 Misc 102, 293 NYS 545.

Courts will take judicial notice of matters of general custom and usage. *Rothstein v Monette* (1940, City Ct) 17 NYS2d 369. It is common knowledge that a custom or practice exists of giving cash discounts between wholesalers and retailers. *Bristol-Myers Co. v Picker* (1952) 302 NY 61, 22 ALR2d 1203.

Where an apparatus consisted of bars extending seven feet above the ground and situated above a hard, black-top surface and was intended to be climbed upon by children, the nature and use of such apparatus was one of common knowledge. *Hunt v Board of Education* (1974, 3d Dept) 43 AD2d 397, 352 NYS2d 237.

In holding that sexual status could be considered for purposes of evaluating an applicant for appointment to a civil service position, where it could be shown that such sexual status was reasonably related to the ability to perform the job, the court took judicial notice of the fact that the searching of female prisoners would be better performed by female State troopers. *Button v Rockefeller* (1973) 76 Misc 2d 701, 351 NYS2d 488.

The court took judicial notice of the fact that Social Services liens are sometimes still enforced against infant tort recoveries in New York State, resulting in unequal protection for the children whose funds are thus depleted. *Marsh v La Marco* (1973) 75 Misc 2d 139, 351 NYS2d 253, affd (2d Dept) 46 AD2d 888, 361 NYS2d 691, affd 39 NY2d 397, 384 NYS2d 128.

In an action arising out of a fall by plaintiff in defendant's store, the trial court did not err in taking judicial notice of the fact that a customer entering a store may have his attention focused on merchandise on prominent display in the store. The court also did not err in concluding that it would be unreasonable to expect that every customer should be watching the floor as he moves down the entry aisle. *Miller v Food Fair Stores, Inc.* (1978, 3d Dept) 63 AD2d 766, 404 NYS2d 740.

Despite the presumption against suicide, it is a matter of common knowledge, of which the Court of Appeals could take judicial notice, that many apparently accidental deaths are in fact suicides and that a wrongful death complaint predicated upon an alleged accidental fall from a 36th story window is sufficiently equivocal to put in issue decedent's mental condition. *Prink v Rockefeller Center, Inc.* (1979) 48 NY2d 309, 422 NYS2d 911.

The Appellate Division took judicial notice of the uninsured motorist endorsement in automobile policies that is mandated by statute. *Avila v Motor Vehicle Acci. Indemnification Corp.* (1979, 1st Dept) 71 AD2d 582, 418 NYS2d 437.

In an action brought by passengers in an automobile that was involved in a collision with a train, it was error for the trial court to take judicial notice of the stopping distance of an automobile traveling at a certain rate of speed, particularly when it was not clearly indicated to the jury that it was an average distance for automobiles operating under favorable conditions. *Murray v Donlan* (1980, 2d Dept) 77 AD2d 337, 433 NYS2d 184.

However, it has been recognized as common knowledge that a normal walking speed is two and one-half to three miles per hour. *Wood v Woodlawn Improv. Ass'n Trans. Corp.* (1926, 3d Dept) 215 AD 628, 214 NYS 398, *affd* (1928) 247 NY 598.

A court may take judicial notice of the fact that after 20 minutes to one-half hour, the water or the combination of water and coolant in the radiator of an overheated car will cool down so that there will be no escaping steam and hot water. *Myers v Fir Cab Corp.* (1984, 1st Dept) 100 AD2d 29, 473 NYS2d 413, revd on other grounds, summary judgment den, in part 64 NY2d 806, 486 NYS2d 922.

Judicial notice can be taken of the common knowledge that oil can seep through the ground into surface and groundwater near a highway and cause ecological damage. *Merrill Transport Co. v State* (1983, 3d Dept) 94 AD2d 39, 464 NYS2d 249; *Domermuth Petroleum Equipment & Maintenance Corp. v Herzog & Hopkins, Inc.* (1985, 3d Dept) 111 AD2d 957, 490 NYS2d 54.

The Appellate Division may take judicial notice that the metropolitan New York area, including northern New Jersey, contains a great many full-time Yeshivahs and Jewish day schools. *Gruber v Gruber* (1982, 1st Dept) 87 AD2d 246, 451 NYS2d 117.

It was not error for the trial judge to take judicial notice of facts within her personal knowledge that were derived from an unrelated case previously before her. She advised both attorneys of the fact and gave the party adversely affected an opportunity to clarify any factual inconsistencies concerning the surrounding circumstances. *Sam & Mary Housing Corp. v Jo/Sal Market Corp.* (1984, 2d Dept) 100 AD2d 901, 474 NYS2d 786, app dismd 62 NY2d 941, 479 NYS2d 215 and affd 64 NY2d 1107, 490 NYS2d 185.

The court took judicial notice of the fact that Tennessee Williams' name is far better known than his photograph. *Southeast Bank, N.A. v Lawrence* (1984, 1st Dept) 104 AD2d 213, 483 NYS2d 218, revd on other grounds (1985) 66 NY2d 910, 498 NYS2d 775 (1985).

The court took judicial notice of the fact that most individuals suffer emotional trauma from the loss of any body part, whether it be a finger, an ear, a testicle or a breast. *Re Shirley C.* (1987) 136 Misc 2d 843, 519 NYS2d 328.

It is common knowledge that tackling injuries incurred in a game of football can occur even when players are professionally trained and equipped. *Locilento v John A. Coleman Catholic High School* (1987, 3d Dept) 134 AD2d 39, 523 NYS2d 198.

In an action on a debt incurred in Canada, where the complaint asked for a money judgment based on Canadian currency, the trial court took judicial notice of the exchange rates for the applicable period. The court converted the demand in the complaint from $7,315.07 Canadian currency to $5,270.22 United States currency and, of its own motion, amended the plaintiff's complaint to conform to the proof. *Air Canada v Golowaty* (1989) 142 Misc 2d 259, 536 NYS2d 962.

The trial court took judicial notice of the fact that the virus generally known as Acquired Immune Deficiency Syndrome is spread from person to person by the transmission of body fluids, including sexual fluids, and by a person's exposure to the AIDS virus; that the virus may be detected by an analysis of blood, conducted by trained medical-scientific experts, commonly known as the AIDS antibody test; and that such exposure may not be detectable for several months or years after the incident or exposure. *People v Thomas* (1988) 139 Misc 2d 1072, 529 NYS2d 429. The court also took judicial notice of the fact that AIDS exposure is markedly more prevalent among the state prison population than among the general population. *People v Thomas, supra.* Additionally, a court took judicial notice of the fact that there was no cure for AIDS at the time. *People v Juan R.* (1992, Sup) 153 Misc 2d 400, 589 NYS2d 256.

It was proper for the court to take judicial notice of government inflation statistics in allocating a portion of the appreciation of the marital residence to plaintiff as her separate property. *Sommers v Sommers* (1994, 4th Dept) 611 AD2d 971, 611 NYS2d 971.

§ 17:7 FACTS NOT JUDICIALLY NOTICED — The courts will not take judicial notice of matters that are unascertainable without proof. *Polley v Plainshun Corp.* (1959, 2d Dept) 8 AD2d 638, 186 NYS2d 295.

In a personal injury action involving an automobile that had been stolen from its rightful owner, judicial notice would not be taken that a directory book under which defendant hid a key to the automobile was a particularly desirable article, especially attractive to a thief. *Banellis v Yackel* (1979, 4th Dept) 69 AD2d 1013, 416 NYS2d 151, affd 49 NY2d 882, 427 NYS2d 941.

It would be improper for the court to take judicial notice of a letter when its contents are neither of common knowledge nor determinable by resort to sources of indisputable accuracy. *Crater Club, Inc. v Adirondack Park Agency* (1982, 3d Dept) 86 AD2d 714, 446 NYS2d 565, affd 57 NY2d 990, 457 NYS2d 244.

Plaintiff showed *prima facie* that a hysterosalpingogram was potentially dangerous. In the absence of medical affidavits or citations to medical tests refuting this showing, there was no basis for the court to take judicial notice that the test is without danger to the plaintiff. *Lefkowitz v Nassau County Medical Center* (1983, 2d Dept) 94 AD2d 18, 462 NYS2d 903.

The New York State Highway Design Manual is not a public record subject to judicial notice. *Kissinger v State* (1987, 3d Dept) 126 AD2d 139, 513 NYS2d 275.

Papers filed in support of a stay application are not a viable alternative to a proper record on appeal. The Appellate Division would not take judicial notice of such papers. *Gintell v Coleman* (1988, 1st Dept) 136 AD2d 515, 523 NYS2d 830.

The viciousness of German shepherds is not an appropriate subject of judicial notice. *De Vaul v Carvigo, Inc.* (1988, 2d Dept) 138 AD2d 669, 526 NYS2d 483, app dismd without op 72 NY2d 914, 532 NYS2d 848 and app den 72 NY2d 806, 532 NYS2d 847.

Plaintiffs moved to vacate a default judgment entered for failure to prosecute and did not submit a statement of the merits by a proper party. They were not entitled to have the court take judicial notice of a statement of the merits by a proper party submitted in a related case that the plaintiffs were attempting to consolidate with the case at bar. *Sutton v Lavezzo* (1990, 1st Dept) 160 AD2d 292, 553 NYS2d 386.

A court will not take judicial notice of the status and authority of a particular kind of ecclesiastical officer. *Ingham v Town of Dickinson* (1993, 3d Dept) 192 AD2d 813, 597 NYS2d 173, app den 82 NY2d 653, 601 NYS2d 583.

In a personal injury action, ownership of the property that abutted the area of the sidewalk where the plaintiff sustained her injury was not a proper subject for judicial notice. *Truden v Town of Oyster Bay* (1994, 2d Dept) 204 AD2d 434, 611 NYS2d 647.

RESEARCH REFERENCES

American Law Reports

74 ALR4th 969, Necessity of expert evidence in proceeding for revocation or suspension of license of physician, surgeon, or dentist

86 ALR3d 484, Judicial notice as to location of street address within particular political subdivision

75 ALR3d 177, Pleading and proof of law of foreign country

45 ALR3d 1169, Reception of evidence to contradict or rebut matters judicially noticed

42 ALR3d 1439, Judicial notice as to assessed valuations

23 ALR3d 1437, Uniform judicial notice of Foreign Law Act

ALR QUICK INDEX: Judicial Notice

American Jurisprudence 2d

29 AM JUR 2d, Evidence §§ 14-122

American Jurisprudence Pleading and Practice

9 AM JUR PL & PR FORMS (Rev), Evidence, Form 1

American Jurisprudence Proof of Facts

21 AM JUR PROOF OF FACTS 2d 1, Law of Foreign Jurisdiction

5 AM JUR PROOF OF FACTS 539, Habit and Custom

4 AM JUR PROOF OF FACTS 3d 439, Unreliability of the Horizontal Gaze Nystagmus Test

4 AM JUR PROOF OF FACTS 3d 229, Proof and Disproof of Alcohol-Induced Driving Impairment Through Breath Alcohol Testing

Other Resources

8 CARMODY-WAIT 2d, Presentation of the Case §§ 56:18-56:20

Auto-Cite®: Any case citation herein can be checked for form, parallel references, later history and annotation references through the Auto-Cite computer research system.

CHAPTER 18

PRESUMPTIONS

§ 18:1   THE NATURE OF PRESUMPTIONS — A presumption is a rule of law that attaches definite probative value to specific facts, *Leask v Hoagland* (1912) 205 NY 171, 98 NE 395, reh den 205 NY 594, 98 NE 1106, or draws an inference as to the existence of one fact, not actually known, from its connection with other known or proven facts. *George Foltis, Inc. v New York* (1941) 287 NY 108, 153 ALR 1122.

Subject to constitutional restrictions, the legislature may, without infringing on the judiciary, provide by statute that a certain fact may be *prima facie* or presumptive evidence of another fact, provided reason and human experience so connect the ultimate fact with the fact proved that the existence of one may be fairly inferred from the other. To have force and validity, the inference of the existence of the ultimate fact from the fact proved must not be purely arbitrary, unreasonable or unnatural. Additionally, the evidentiary fact must have some fair relation or natural connection with the fact to be proved and some tendency to prove it. *People ex rel. Woronoff v Mallon* (1918) 222 NY 456, 119 NE 102, 4 ALR 463.

Proof of a fact will result in a presumption only if there is a rational connection between the fact proved and the fact presumed. *McFarland v American Sugar Refining Co.* (1916) 241 US 79, 60 L Ed 899, 36 S Ct 498. The inference drawn must, on the basis of human experience, be the natural or probable conclusion to be drawn from the fact proved. *Engel v United Traction Co.* (1911) 203 NY 321, 96 NE 731.

A presumption is not evidence, but rather a substitute for evidence. It disappears when the opposing party produces proof to rebut it. *People ex rel. Wallington Apartments, Inc. v Miller* (1942) 288 NY 31, 141 ALR 1036, reh den 288 NY 672.

It has been held that a presumption cannot be based on another presumption. *Lamb v Union R. Co.* (1909) 195 NY 260, 88 NE 371. Similarly, an inference cannot be based on another inference. *People v Van Aken* (1916) 217 NY 532, 112 NE 380.

However, parallel inferences may be derived from a given set of circumstantial facts in evidence. For example, in a death case, there was no direct evidence of impact. It was held that by reason of the extent of physical damage done to the vehicle and the position of the body, it could be inferred that the vehicle came into contact with the deceased and had been operated at an excessive speed. *Allen v Stokes* (1940) 260 AD 600, 23 NYS2d 443, reh and app den 260 AD 1007, 24 NYS2d 994.

§ 18:2 IRREBUTTABLE PRESUMPTIONS — The law recognizes certain presumptions which, on grounds of public policy, may not be rebutted. They are sometimes known as presumptions of law, or conclusive presumptions of law, or conclusive presumptions. These are not presumptions, properly speaking, but are rules of substantive law.

A child under four is conclusively presumed to be incapable of contributory negligence. *Chandler v Keene* (1957, 3d Dept) 5 AD2d 42, 168 NYS2d 788.

§ 18:3   REBUTTABLE PRESUMPTIONS — A second class of presumptions comprises those that are rebuttable. These are sometimes known as presumptions of fact. A rebuttable presumption is a substitute for testimony or evidence. It has the force of proof until it is overcome by contradictory evidence. Such presumptions may be rebutted either by evidence that tends to disprove the facts upon which the presumption has been based or by evidence that tends to disprove the presumed fact itself.

When the presumption has been rebutted, it ordinarily vanishes entirely. *Re Goldman's Estate* (1935) 156 Misc 817, 282 NYS 787. In the face of evidence, the presumption ceases to exist and cannot be weighed in the balance against evidence to establish a fact. *Castellani v Castellani* (1941) 176 Misc 763, 28 NYS2d 879, affd 263 AD 984, 34 NYS2d 400.

A few rebuttable presumptions, such as the presumption against suicide, are overcome only by proof characterized as "clear and convincing." *Mandi v Metropolitan Life Ins. Co.* (1932) 143 Misc 771, 257 NYS 71.

The formula applied to parental income for purposes of determining child support, codified in the Child Support Standards Act (Dom. Rel. L. § 240, Fam. Ct. Act § 413), creates a rebuttable presumption that the guidelines will yield the correct amount of child support. Where the father failed to rebut the presumption, the Family Court correctly increased the Hearing Examiner's award to the statutory guideline amount. *Keay v Menda* (1994, 2d Dept) 210 AD2d 483, 620 NYS2d 472.

§ 18:4   INFERENCES — A third class of presumptions is the weakest of all three forms. They permit the jury to draw an inference from a fact in evidence. They are not a substitute for testimony or evidence.

Thus, it was held that if an adversary withholds evidence in his possession or control that would likely support his version of the case, the strongest inference may be drawn against him that the opposing evidence in the record permits. *Noce v Kaufman* (1957) 2 NY2d 347, 161 NYS2d 1. When an attorney commits subornation of perjury, this is admissible even though the subornation was not authorized by the client. *Nieves v New York* (1951, Sup) 109 NYS2d 556, affd 280 AD 972, 116 NYS2d 927. Such evidence is competent for the jury's consideration in weighing the case. *Millington v New York City Transit Authority* (1976, 1st Dept) 54 AD2d 649, 387 NYS2d 865.

In an action for wrongful death where it was contended that the decedent was already dead when the accident occurred, the presumption against death runs in favor of the plaintiff. *Rodak v Fury* (1969, 2d Dept) 31 AD2d 816, 298 NYS2d 50. The presumption against death is merely an inference that can be rebutted by evidence. When the testimony failed to establish that the deceased was dead prior to being struck by the automobile, the presumption against death operated to create a question for the jury on that issue. *Rodak v Fury, supra.*

In the absence of proof of a negligent application of wax or polish, the fact that a floor is slippery by reason of its smoothness or polish does not give rise to a cause of action or an inference of negligence. *Katz v New York Hosp.* (1991, 1st Dept) 170 AD2d 345, 566 NYS2d 46.

Violation of a statute does not give rise to an inference of negligence without proof that the party has sustained an injury proximately caused by the breach. *Azzue v Galore Realty, Inc.* (1991, 1st Dept) 172 AD2d 467, 568 NYS2d 955, app den 78 NY2d 856, 574 NYS2d 937.

Any inference that the lettuce which caused plaintiff to fall had been on the floor of the supermarket for an appreciable length of time due to plaintiff's characterization of it as "wilted" is mere speculation. *Browne v Big V Supermarkets, Inc.* (1992, 3d Dept) 188 AD2d 798, 591 NYS2d 223, app den 81 NY2d 708, 598 NYS2d 767.

§ 18:5   *RES IPSA LOQUITUR* — An accident itself affords reasonable evidence that it arose from want of proper care when, in the absence of an explanation by the party charged with negligence, a thing that caused the injury is shown to be under the control or management of the party so charged and the occurrence is such as in the ordinary course of things would not have happened if that party had used proper care. *Galbraith v Busch* (1935) 267 NY 230, 196 NE 36.

The purpose of the *res ipsa loquitur* doctrine is to allow proof of negligence by circumstantial evidence when the direct evidence concerning cause of injury is primarily within the knowledge and control of the defendant. The *res ipsa loquitur* doctrine, where applicable, establishes a *prima facie* case of negligence. *Courtney v Gainsborough Studios* (1919) 186 AD 820, 174 NYS2d 855.

The doctrine is applied as a matter of necessity and is based on the theory that defendant has, within his knowledge and control, evidence that the plaintiff does not possess and cannot conveniently obtain. *Slater v Barnes* (1925) 241 NY 284, 149 NE 859. The presumption of negligence is a permissive presumption of fact and is circumstantial evidence to be considered by the jury. *Maslenka v Brady* (1919) 188 AD 661, 176 NYS 842.

Res ipsa loquitur is essentially a rule of evidence which permits, but does not require, the jury to infer on the basis of circumstantial evidence that an unusual occurrence resulted from defendant's negligence. *Chisholm v Mobil Oil Corp.* (1974, 3d Dept) 45 AD2d 776, 356 NYS2d 699. Even where the defendant offers no proof, it is still for the jury to decide, on plaintiff's proof, whether liability has been established. *Chisholm v Mobil Oil Corp., supra.*

Liability in a *res ipsa loquitur* case, like any other, must rest on more than speculation, guess, or surmise. *Cooke v Bernstein* (1974, 1st Dept) 45 AD2d 497, 359 NYS2d 793. A condition precedent to the application of the doctrine requires proof that the event was caused by an instrumentality within the exclusive control of the defendant. *Cooke v Bernstein, supra.*

Exclusive control is a concept that is not "absolutely rigid." It implies such possession and control by the defendant that the probability that the negligent act was caused by someone other than the defendant is so remote that it is fair to permit an inference that the defendant is the negligent party. *Chisholm v Mobil Oil Corp., supra.*

Thus, the rigid requirement of "exclusive control" has been relaxed by the application of a more flexible common-sense approach to the doctrine of *res ipsa loquitur. Lindenauer v State* (1974, 3d Dept) 45 AD2d 73, 356 NYS2d 366. It must be shown that the defendant is correctly identified with probability as the party responsible for the negligent conduct. *Lindenauer v State, supra.*

It has been held that proof of specific acts of negligence deprives plaintiff of the benefit of the doctrine of *res ipsa loquitur. Fischer v John A. Johnson & Sons, Inc.* (1955) 20 Misc 2d 891, 198 NYS2d 470. However, the rule would appear to be that the introduction of such evidence by the plaintiff, when it does not provide a complete explanation of the accident, does not deprive him of the right to invoke the doctrine. *McKenna v Allied Chemical & Dye Corp.* (1959, 4th Dept) 8 AD2d 463, 188 NYS2d 919. Furthermore, the mere fact that the plaintiff seeks to bolster his case by introducing specific evidence of negligence does not deprive the plaintiff of the right to rely upon *res ipsa loquitur,* unless the proof produced actually refutes or negates the inference that might otherwise have been drawn from the application of that rule. *Abbott v Page Airways, Inc.* (1969) 23 NY2d 502, 297 NYS2d 713, 35 ALR3d 696.

More than one defendant may be held liable under the doctrine in certain circumstances. It is nevertheless plaintiff's burden to establish the negligence of each of the defendants against whom the doctrine is sought to be invoked. *Cooke v Bernstein* (1974, 1st Dept) 45 AD2d 497, 359 NYS2d 793.

When more than one defendant is in control, which makes the doctrine applicable, each defendant is required to explain his conduct. *Covey v State* (1951) 200 Misc 340, 106 NYS2d 18. Thus, in a case where contiguous landowners shared a dual responsibility for a board that was erected partly on the property of each, the doctrine was held properly applicable against either or both owners. *Corcoran v Banner Super Market, Inc.* (1967) 19 NY2d 425, 280 NYS2d 385, remittitur amd 21 NY2d 793, 288 NYS2d 484.

The doctrine is particularly applicable in medical malpractice cases in which an injury to an area remote from the operative site occurs to an anesthetized patient during surgery. *Ceresa v Karakousis* (1994, 4th Dept) 210 AD2d 884, 620 NYS2d 646. For example, plaintiff sustained an unusual compression injury to his shoulder and arm during an operation on the lower spine. Plaintiff's medical expert testified that the complications would not have occurred had he been properly positioned. The trial court erred in denying plaintiff's request for a *res ipsa* charge. *Ceresa v Karakousis, supra.*

In a medical malpractice case, *res ipsa loquitur* was properly applied against the hospital, surgeon and anesthesiologist, individually or jointly, when the instrumentality was within the exclusive control of the defendants. They each, individually or jointly, owed an independent duty to the patient and exercised concurrent control over the operation and the equipment. *Fogal v Genesee Hospital* (1973, 4th Dept) 41 AD2d 468, 344 NYS2d 552.

During the course of surgery for treatment of rectal cancer, a patient suffered third degree burns on the side of her left thigh. She could properly rely on the doctrine of *res ipsa loquitur* in her medical malpractice action. The surgeon had full control of the instrumentality which caused the plaintiff patient's injury, the burning of her thigh was an unusual occurrence, and she was unconscious during the entire procedure. *Mack v Lydia E. Hall Hospital* (1986, 2d Dept) 121 AD2d 431, 503 NYS2d 131.

In a medical malpractice action brought by a patient whose front teeth were knocked out during foot surgery, the *res ipsa loquitur* doctrine was applicable to the facts of the case because: (1) a patient's teeth are not ordinarily knocked out during foot surgery in the absence of someone's negligence; (2) the injury must have been caused by an agency or instrumentality in the operating room which was within the exclusive control of defendants; (3) plaintiff was under general anesthesia and could not have contributed to the injury; and (4) evidence of the cause of the injury is more readily available to defendants than to the plaintiff. *Kerber v Sarles* (1989, 4th Dept) 151 AD2d 1031, 542 NYS2d 94, later proceeding (4th Dept) 151 AD2d 1032, 544 NYS2d 522.

Shortly after undergoing surgery for a condition in his left leg, a plaintiff suffered problems with his right leg and required further surgery that purportedly rendered him unable to function normally. Plaintiff was not entitled to the benefit of the *res ipsa loquitur* doctrine. That doctrine did not apply because the event was not one of a kind that can be said ordinarily not to occur in the absence of negligence. *Jones v Society of New York Hosp.* (1989, 1st Dept) 155 AD2d 338, 547 NYS2d 309, app den 75 NY2d 709, 555 NYS2d 692.

To recover under the *res ipsa loquitur* doctrine, plaintiff is not required to disprove every alternative hypothesis suggesting a cause other than negligence. *Barker v State* (1962) 32 Misc 2d 191, 224 NYS2d 838.

If a satisfactory explanation is offered by defendant, plaintiff must rebut it by evidence of negligence or lose his case. *Plumb v Richmond L. & R. Co.* (1922) 233 NY 285, 135 NE 504, 25 ALR 685.

It is incumbent on defendant to furnish an explanation of the occurrence consistent with due care on his part, if he can. Whether the evidence introduced by defendant in explanation of the occurrence is sufficient to rebut the presumption of negligence is a question of fact for the jury. *Kay v Metropolitan S. R. Co.* (1900) 163 NY 447, 57 NE 751.

If the evidence is equally consistent with causation of the accident by defendant's negligence and with lack of such causal connection, the rule of *res ipsa loquitur* may not be invoked. *Mercatante v New York* (1955) 286 AD 265, 142 NYS2d 473, reh and app den 286 AD 964, 144 NYS2d 914.

Even if defendant introduces no evidence, the court may not ordinarily direct a verdict for plaintiff. *Calhoun v Northeast Airlines, Inc.* (1959, DC NY) 180 F Supp 532.

The doctrine of *res ipsa loquitur* may be applicable with regard to the operation of a ski lift and injuries which, upon an appropriate record, can only reasonably be attributable to the operation of such lift. *Lawrence v Davos, Inc.* (1974, 3d Dept) 46 AD2d 41, 360 NYS2d 730. However, the doctrine was not applicable where the record established that the defendant had provided a chain obviously intended to be fastened by patrons for the purpose of holding them in their chair; the plaintiff was aware that such chains were generally provided by the defendant as a safety device but did not use them; plaintiff made no claim that his chain was not usable or was in any way defective; and there was no evidence in the record that the accidental injuries would probably have been sustained even if the plaintiff had fastened his safety chain. *Lawrence v Davos, Inc., supra.*

Where a patient was burned in the shower room in a hospital and thereafter contracted pneumonia and died, the doctrine of *res ipsa loquitur* was properly applied. However, the trial court erred in excluding testimony of the attending physician that the deceased had admitted that he had slipped in the shower, accidentally turning off the cold water. *Mikel v Flatbush General Hospital* (1975, 2d Dept) 49 AD2d 581, 370 NYS2d 162.

Damage in a restaurant was determined to stem from "ignition of grease in exhaust duct by gas and flame" and the cause remained a mystery. There was no basis for invocation of the doctrine unless the conflagration was one that could not ordinarily occur without negligence. *Schultheis v Pristouris* (1974, 2d Dept) 45 AD2d 864, 358 NYS2d 551.

Where there was no evidence that identified the instrumentality causing the fire, there was no showing that the instrumentality was in the exclusive control of defendant. Therefore, there was no circumstantial link between the accident and the conduct of the defendant leading to the logical inference that the accident probably was caused by defendant's negligence. The trial court correctly declined to apply the doctrine of *res ipsa loquitur. Archer v Suburban Propane Gas Co.* (1979, 4th Dept) 69 AD2d 993, 416 NYS2d 129.

Res ipsa loquitur does not create a presumption in favor of the plaintiff. It merely permits the inference of negligence to be drawn from the circumstances of the occurrence. The rule has the effect of creating a *prima facie* case of negligence sufficient for submission to the jury and the jury may, but is not required to, draw the permissible inference. *Dermatossian v New York City Transit Authority* (1986) 67 NY2d 219, 501 NYS2d 784. Thus, in New York, it is the general rule that submission of the case on the theory of *res ipsa loquitur* is warranted only when the plaintiff can establish: (1) the event must be of a kind that ordinarily does not occur in the absence of someone's negligence; (2) it must be caused by an agency or instrumentality within the exclusive control of the defendant; and (3) it must not have been due to any voluntary action or contribution on the part of the plaintiff. *Dermatossian v New York City Transit Authority, supra.*

The trial court properly instructed the jury as to the doctrine of *res ipsa loquitur* in a personal injury action brought against the operator of an elevator; the inference of negligence was justified by evidence of prior, similar malfunctions. *Liebman v Otis Elevator Co.* (1987, 2d Dept) 127 AD2d 745, 512 NYS2d 136.

In elevator accident cases, *res ipsa loquitur* can be applied where more than one defendant is in a position to exercise exclusive control. *Duke v Duane Broad Co.* (1992, 1st Dept) 181 AD2d 589, 581 NYS2d 767, appeal dismssd without op 79 NY2d 977, 583 NYS2d 195 (1992), leave denied 81 NY2d 703, 594 NYS2d 717 (1993).

A passenger in an elevator testified that he sustained an injury when the elevator fell nine floors and then abruptly stopped. If found credible by the trier of the facts, such testimony was sufficient to support an inference of both negligence and causation under the doctrine of *res ipsa loquitur. Williams v Swissotel New York, Inc.* (1989, 1st Dept) 152 AD2d 457, 542 NYS2d 651.

Where a claimant used defendant's lifeguard stand without authorization to execute a backflip, the doctrine of *res ipsa loquitur* did not apply to the facts of the case. Claimant failed to establish that the lifeguard stand was within the exclusive control of defendant or that the fracturing of the stand's footrest was not due to any voluntary action or contribution on the part of claimant. *Florin v State* (1988, 2d Dept) 137 AD2d 581, 524 NYS2d 472.

Assuming that plaintiff was entitled to rely on the doctrine of *res ipsa loquitur* to establish a *prima facie* case from which negligence could be inferred, plaintiff still bore the burden of proving the defendant's negligence by a fair preponderance of the evidence. *DeFoe Corp. v Semi-Alloys, Inc.* (1989, 2d Dept) 156 AD2d 634, 549 NYS2d 133. An action brought by a corporation against a neighboring corporation that manufactured electric components was based upon a claim that a scrubber used by defendant corporation malfunctioned, causing emission of considerable quantities of sodium hydroxide. Defendant offered evidence as to its maintenance of the scrubber. Plaintiff offered no evidence upon which the court could conclude that such maintenance was inadequate to safeguard against the emission of sodium hydroxide. The court was free to reject a permissible inference of negligence based upon *res ipsa loquitur. DeFoe Corp. v Semi-Alloys, Inc., supra.*

A passerby was injured by a glass storm window falling from an apartment building and brought an action against the owner of the building and the lessee of the apartment from which the glass had come. The doctrine of *res ipsa loquitur* was not applicable against either defendant. The owner was not in actual possession of the apartment from which the window fell and the defendant lessee asserted that he played no role in the installation or cleaning of the windows. *Veltri v Stahl* (1989, 1st Dept) 155 AD2d 287, 547 NYS2d 49.

Even though a burst water pipe is unexplained, it is not the type of occurrence which, by itself and unattended by other exceptional circumstances, creates an inference of negligence so strong as to leave no serious doubt that it could have been avoided by the exercise of due care. *Shinshine Corp. v Kinney System, Inc.* (1991, 1st Dept) 173 AD2d 293, 569 NYS2d 686.

Plaintiff's expert testified that the wooden deck was improperly designed and constructed prior to defendant's ownership and control. Such testimony rendered inappropriate any inference based on *res ipsa loquitur* that the defendant was responsible for the accident. *Duncan v Corbetta* (1991, 2d Dept) 178 AD2d 459, 577 NYS2d 129.

The proof showed that several subcontractors other than the named defendants had access to and performed extensive construction work in the area where the plaintiff tripped. Defendants lacked exclusive control and the theory of *res ipsa loquitur* was inappropriate. *McCluskey v West Bradford Corp.* (1991, 3d Dept) 177 AD2d 744, 575 NYS2d 981.

There was evidence that decedent, who was walking on the street, was struck on the head by a bar and chain that fell from a train passing overhead. Such evidence was sufficient to send the case to the jury on the theory of *res ipsa loquitur. Nesbit v New York City Transit Authority* (1991, 1st Dept) 170 AD2d 92, 574 NYS2d 179.

For purposes of application of the *res ipsa loquitur* rule, the requirement of exclusive control is intended to eliminate, within reason, all explanations for the accident other than defendant's negligence. However, this does not mean that all other possible causes must be altogether eliminated, but only that their likelihood must be so reduced that the greater probability lies at defendant's door. *Finocchio v Crest Hollow Club at Woodbury, Inc.* (1992, 2d Dept) 184 AD2d 491, 584 NYS2d 201.

While filling his own gas tank, plaintiff was injured when the hose burst. He was not entitled to a *res ipsa* charge. The hose was continuously available for use by defendant's customers and, thus, was not under defendant's exclusive control. Additionally, the occurrence was not of a kind that ordinarily does not occur in the absence of negligence. *Troisi v Merit Oil Co.* (1994, 2d Dept), 208 AD2d 615, 617 NYS2d 347.

Where plaintiff was injured when his grandstand race track seat collapsed, the operator of the track was not subject to a *res ipsa* charge. The access of thousands of patrons daily did not exclude the chance that the seat had been damaged by other patrons. *Raimondi v New York Racing Ass'n* (1995, 2d Dept), 213 AD2d 708, 624 NYS2d 273, app den 86 NY2d 207, 632 NYS2d 500.

§ 18:6   PRESUMPTION OF DEATH AFTER THREE YEARS ABSENCE

— Under the former rule, a person could be presumed dead when he was absent from home and not heard from for seven years by those who would naturally hear from him if he were alive. *Butler v Mutual Life Ins. Co.* (1919) 225 NY 197, 121 NE 758. This rule was also found in a statute. Decedent Estate Law § 80. By later statutory enactment, this period was reduced to five years, and then further reduced to three years. Estates, Powers and Trusts Law (EPTL) § 2-1.7(a).

Ordinarily, it will be presumed that the decedent died at the end of three years. EPTL § 2-1.7(a)(1). If a person was exposed to a specific peril of death, however, this fact may be the basis for determining that he died in less than three years after the absence began. EPTL § 2-1.7(a)(1).

The presumption of death will not be invoked without a showing by the person seeking adjudication that he has conducted a thorough and exhaustive search for the missing person. *Re Layh's Estate* (1967) 55 Misc 2d 92, 284 NYS2d 511. The inquiry should be directed not only to the place from which the last information of the absentee came, but also to every locality to which his known inclinations, habits and associations might reasonably be supposed to have led him. *Re Layh's Estate, supra.*

If the person who disappeared was then unmarried, there is a presumption that he died intestate and without issue. *Re Harrison's Will* (1947) 190 Misc 215, 73 NYS2d 162.

The presumption of death from absence does not arise when facts or circumstances may exist that reasonably account for the party's absence or where disappearance occurred under circumstances indicating communication was unlikely. *Gardner v Northwestern Mut. Life Ins. Co.* (1934) 152 Misc 873, 274 NYS 256, affd 242 AD 886, 275 NYS 996. Such circumstances preventing an inference of death from unexplained absence include a desire to conceal identity, improbability that the missing person would have communicated with his home or family, existence of a cloud on his character, or the fact that he was a fugitive from justice. *Gardner v Northwestern Mut. Life Ins. Co., supra.*

In Smyrna, Turkey, during September and October of 1922, as a result of genocidal slaughter and fire, a substantial portion of the Greek population of the Smyrna area died. Those not slaughtered by violence, drowning or fire were expatriated to Greece. After 1922, the objectants' family established contact with the expatriates but never again heard from their Greek relatives who did not escape to Greece. It was not unreasonable to presume the death of the individuals who were at the scene of the genocide and were members of the victimized group. *Re Estate of Regas* (1974) 79 Misc 2d 170, 359 NYS2d 857.

Normally the question whether the statutory presumption of death should arise from the evidence presented is one of fact for the jury. However, the question is one of law for the trial justice to decide when the evidence is without contradiction and incapable, whether with or without contradiction, of creating conflicting inferences in reasonable minds. *Kutner v New England Mut. Life Ins. Co.* (1977, 4th Dept) 57 AD2d 697, 395 NYS2d 540.

§ 18:7 PRESUMPTION OF VALIDITY OF MARRIAGE —
When a marriage is shown, the law raises a presumption of its validity. *Fisher v Fisher* (1929) 250 NY 313, 165 NE 460, 61 ALR 1523. The burden of proving its invalidity is upon the objecting

party. *Fleming v People* (1863) 27 NY 329. When the celebration of a marriage is shown, everything necessary to the validity of the marriage is presumed, including the contract and the capacity of the parties, in the absence of proof to the contrary. CPLR 4526; *Appelbaum v Appelbaum* (1957) 9 Misc 2d 677, 168 NYS2d 970.

In conflicting marriages, there is a presumption of validity in favor of the last marriage. *Re Will of Fuller* (1959) 9 AD2d 565, 189 NYS2d 287, reh den (3d Dept) 9 AD2d 854, 194 NYS2d 454. If the celebration of a marriage is shown and also a prior marriage, the death of the former spouse will be presumed and the burden of proof is on the party asserting the invalidity of the last marriage. *Re Tompkins' Estate* (1923) 207 AD 166, 201 NYS 696.

There is an extremely strong presumption of validity when there is a ceremonial marriage. A stranger to the marital relationship has a heavy burden to establish its invalidity. *Meltzer v McAnns Bar & Grill* (1981, 3d Dept) 85 AD2d 826, 445 NYS2d 655.

Normally, proof of the existence of a marital relationship gives rise to a strong presumption that it is valid and continuing. *Seidel v Crown Industries* (1987, 3d Dept) 132 AD2d 729, 517 NYS2d 310. If two competing marriages have been proved, the presumption favoring the validity of the second marriage is stronger than the presumption that the prior marriage is continued. Moreover, when the party actually challenging the validity of the marriage is a total stranger to the marital relationship, the presumption becomes even stronger. *Seidel v Crown Industries, supra.*

A divorce judgment, which established that the decedent and another person were still married to one another on the date that the decedent went through a marriage ceremony with his alleged wife at death, was sufficient to rebut the presumption of the validity of the later marriage. *Re Estate of Warren* (1987, 2d Dept) 131 AD2d 681, 516 NYS2d 759, app dismd, in part, app den, in part 70 NY2d 950, 524 NYS2d 674.

The State of Rhode Island recognizes common law marriages where the relationship commences at a time when each is married to another. However, a presumption arises that what was meretricious in its origins continues so in the absence of clear and convincing proof that the parties' conduct was of such a character as to lead to a belief in the community that they were married. *In re Estate of Gates* (1993, 3d Dept) 189 AD2d 427, 596 NYS2d 194, app dismd, app den 82 NY2d 679, 601 NYS2d 568 and app dismd, app den 82 NY2d 680, 601 NYS2d 568.

§ 18:8 PRESUMPTIONS ARISING FROM THE CONDUCT OF A PARTY — If a party has relevant evidence under his control and fails to produce such evidence, the inference is permissible that such evidence would not be favorable to him. *Wholesale Service Supply Corp. v State* (1951) 201 Misc 56, 103 NYS2d 820. If a party fails or refuses to produce books or papers at the trial after due notice, it may be presumed that such failure or refusal is because such evidence, if produced, would operate against his claim and in favor of the claim of the opposing party. *Feingold v Walworth Bros., Inc.* (1924) 238 NY 446, 144 NE 675. Additionally, if a party intentionally destroys evidence relevant to his case, the jury may draw an inference unfavorable to him. *Re Eno's Will* (1921) 196 AD 131, 187 NYS 756.

A defendant failed to produce crucial reports and did not produce anyone who directly testified that the reports could not be found despite a complete search. The failure of the trial court to charge as to defendant's failure to produce the reports was prejudicial error requiring reversal and a new trial. *Cusumano v New York City Transit Authority* (1980, 2d Dept) 75 AD2d 801, 427 NYS2d 644.

The defendant in a negligence action failed to produce certain reports that its supervising employee testified were kept in the regular course of the defendant's business. The plaintiff was entitled to a jury charge that inferences contrary to the witness's testimony may be drawn where there was opposing evidence because of defendant's failure to provide evidence in his possession or control. *Levine v Ross* (1966) 25 AD2d 718, 269 NYS2d 682. (See briefs and record on appeal.)

A husband failed to produce his recent tax records and his family-owned business failed to produce the business financial records in compliance with subpoenas. Thus, the court was entitled to draw an inference that these records would not support the husband's claim that he was not an owner of the business. *Scheer v Scheer* (1987, 2d Dept) 130 AD2d 479, 515 NYS2d 61.

When a party to a civil action fails to testify as to matters that are or should be within his knowledge, the trier of facts has a right to infer that his testimony would be contrary to his own interest. *Eraser Co. v Kaufman* (1955, Sup) 138 NYS2d 743. Although a dismissed patrolman could not be compelled to incriminate himself, his failure to testify was subject to an unfavorable inference in a proceeding, not penal in nature, to review his dismissal from the police force. *Semerad v Schenectady* (1967, 3d Dept) 27 AD2d 673, 276 NYS2d 357, affd 22 NY2d 923, 295 NYS2d 51.

If a party attempts to bribe a witness to testify falsely, there is a presumption against that party. *Nowack v Metropolitan S. R. Co.* (1901) 166 NY 433, 60 NE 32.

§ 18:9 PRESUMPTION OF DELIVERY OF LETTER — Upon proof that a letter or communication was deposited in the post office or some subdivision of the postal department, properly stamped with sufficient postage and properly addressed to the addressee, there is a presumption of due receipt thereof. *Trusts & Guarantee Co. v Barnhardt* (1936) 270 NY 350. The letter must, however, have been properly addressed and sealed and the full postage paid. *Roxbury Light & Power Co. v Dimmick* (1922, Co Ct) 196 NYS 320.

The presumption of delivery may be rebutted by evidence that the letter or communication was not in fact received. *Curry v Mackenzie* (1925) 239 NY 267, 146 NE 375. It is for the jury to determine whether the presumption of receipt has been overcome by the rebuttal evidence. *Austin v Holland* (1877) 69 NY 571.

Thus, as a general rule of evidence, proof that an item was properly mailed gives rise to a rebuttable presumption that the item was received by the addressee. A conclusory denial of receipt by the addressee, coupled with speculation that the transmission was lost in the mail, is ordinarily insufficient to rebut the presumption of delivery. *Rosa v Board of Examiners* (1988, 2d Dept) 143 AD2d 351, 532 NYS2d 307.

It has been held that there is a presumption that a letter mailed in the same city to which it is addressed has been delivered the following day. *Dulberg v Equitable Life Assurance Soc.* (1938) 277 NY 17. However, one may question whether that presumption still exists. It is also presumed that when a letter is received in the mail, it was sent by the person indicated in the letter as the sender. *Re Seymour* (1920) 113 Misc 421, 185 NYS 373.

Before an insurance company may have the benefit of the presumption that a notice of cancellation was delivered to the insured who died of injuries incurred in the automobile accident in which plaintiff was also injured, proof of mailing must be adduced. *Thomas v Government Employees Ins. Co.* (1978, 2d Dept) 61 AD2d 1044, 403 NYS2d 121.

If the proof exhibits an office practice and procedure followed by an insurer in the regular course of its business which shows that notices of cancellation have been duly addressed and mailed, a presumption arises that those notices have been received by the insureds. That presumption is not rebutted by denial of receipt by the insureds. *Nassau Ins. Co. v Murray* (1978) 46 NY2d 828, 414 NYS2d 117. In addition to a claim of no receipt, there must be a showing that the office practice was not followed, or was so careless that it would be unreasonable to assume that the notice was mailed. *Nassau Ins. Co. v Murray, supra.*

However, evidence of interoffice mailing procedure may be insufficient to prove that notice of cancellation has been mailed. Such evidence was insufficient when there was no proof that the envelopes, which were ostensibly mailed or perhaps were in fact mailed, were sent to the same addressees whose names appeared on the computer printout list. *Ackler v Nationwide Mut. Ins. Co.,* (1983, 3d Dept) 87 AD2d 730, 449 NYS2d 334.

Proof by an automobile insurer with respect to its office practice and procedure as to mailing of notices of cancellation was held to be insufficient. The proof consisted of testimony that a computer printed out a notice of cancellation for each name on a mailing list; that an inserter machine placed the notices of cancellation into envelopes by opening the flap of an envelope, inserting the cancellation notice, and sealing and stamping the envelope; that neither the witness nor anyone else checked the names appearing on the envelopes with the names on the mailing list; and that after the machine had inserted the cancellation notices into the envelopes and sealed and stamped them, she tied the envelopes and put them into a United States Government mail bag. *Manning v Boston Old Colony Ins. Co.* (1975, 2d Dept) 48 AD2d 838, 368 NYS2d 284.

Although the State's witnesses could not testify that a specific letter had in fact been properly mailed, they did testify to a course of business and office practice according to which it naturally would have been mailed. This gave rise to a presumption that the letter in fact had been mailed. The mere denial of receipt was not sufficient evidence to rebut this presumption. *A. & B. Service Station, Inc. v State* (1975, 3d Dept) 50 AD2d 973, 376 NYS2d 656.

For the presumption of delivery of a letter once mailed to arise, the office practice must be geared so as to ensure the likelihood that the mailing is always properly addressed and mailed. *Re Claim of Feinerman* (1983, 3d Dept) 97 AD2d 920, 470 NYS2d 762.

Evidence that a letter is properly addressed, stamped and mailed is ordinarily presumptive evidence of delivery, provided that an adequate foundation is laid to show that the letter was actually mailed or that customary office practice in the mailing of such correspondence was followed. *Ray v Blum* (1982, 4th Dept) 91 AD2d 822, 458 NYS2d 105. If no witnesses are produced who have personal knowledge that the letter has actually been sent or that the usual practices of the office in sending such letters were followed, the presumption does not arise. *Ray v Blum, supra.*

A duly executed and notarized affidavit of service by mail is usually sufficient to create a presumption that a document was mailed and delivered. *Watt v New York City Transit Authority* (1983, 2d Dept) 97 AD2d 466, 467 NYS2d 655. However, that presumption was rebutted by a subsequent admission by the person who had prepared the affidavit of service that routine office practice was not followed or was so careless that it would be unreasonable to assume that the complaint was mailed. *Watt v New York City Transit Authority, supra.*

An affidavit of service executed by defendant's attorney with respect to a conditional order of preclusion with notice of entry was sufficient to establish a presumption that it was mailed. The affidavit was also sufficient to form a basis for the granting of summary judgment, when plaintiff's counsel did not comply with the preclusion order. The mere denial by plaintiff's counsel of receipt of the preclusion order was not sufficient to rebut the presumption of mailing. *Engel v Lichterman* (1983, 2d Dept) 95 AD2d 536, 467 NYS2d 642, affd 62 NY2d 943, 479 NYS2d 188.

Tax Law § 1147(a)(1) provides that the mailing of a tax notice is presumptive evidence of its receipt by the addressee. That presumption arises upon the presentation of proof by the sender that it has a routine office practice and procedure for mailing the tax notices, which demonstrates that the notices were in fact properly addressed and mailed. *T. J. Gulf, Inc. v New York State Tax Com.* (1986, 3d Dept) 124 AD2d 314, 508 NYS2d 97. Testimony amounting to no more than mere denials of receipt, even the testimony of three witnesses, is insufficient to rebut the presumption. *T.J. Gulf, Inc. v New York State Tax Com., supra.*

Certified mailing receipts created a presumption that a mailing was in fact made by the insured to the insurance company. This presumption was not overcome by testimony by a casualty claim adjuster that the insurance company's file did not contain any notice of the accident or claim prior to a given date. *Allstate Ins. Co. v Patrylo* (1988, 1st Dept) 144 AD2d 243, 533 NYS2d 436.

A bare denial of receipt of an overcharge order was insufficient to rebut the presumption of receipt raised by the sworn statements of respondent's mail room personnel as to the routine office procedures followed in mailing such orders. *H.C. Black Realty Co. v State Div. of Hous. & Community Renewal* (1994, 1st Dept) 201 AD2d 432, 607 NYS2d 944.

§ 18:10 PRESUMPTION OF DELIVERY OF TELEGRAM — Upon proof that a telegram, properly addressed with the necessary fee therefor, was delivered to the telegraph office, there is a presumption that it was delivered to the addressee. *Oregon S.S. Co. v Otis* (1885) 100 NY 446, 53 NE 485, error dismd 116 US 548, 29 L Ed 719, 6 S Ct 523. This presumption may, however, be rebutted. *Oregon S.S. Co. v Otis, supra.*

§ 18:11 PRESUMPTIONS ABOUT INDIVIDUALS — There are a number of presumptions about people covering a great many varieties of conduct.

Each person is presumed to be sane. *Re Preston's Will* (1906) 113 AD 732, 99 NYS 312. It is for the party alleging incompetency to rebut the presumption. *Re Preston's Will, supra*. Persons of mature age are presumed sane and mental incompetency cannot be inferred merely from old age or physical illness. *Curran v Hosey* (1912) 153 AD 557, 138 NYS 910. No presumption of mental deterioration arises from physical infirmity. *Curran v Hosey, supra*. The presumption is that the grantor in a deed was of sound mind. The burden of showing that he was mentally incapable is on the complaining party. *Curran v Hosey, supra*. Proof of suicide is not sufficient to overcome the presumption of sanity. *Weed v Mutual Ben. Life Ins. Co.* (1877) 70 NY 561.

A party's competence is presumed and the party asserting incapacity bears the burden of proving incompetence. *Feiden v Feiden* (1989, 3d Dept) 151 AD2d 889, 542 NYS2d 860. Persons suffering from a disease such as Alzheimer's are not presumed incompetent and they may execute a valid deed. *Feiden v Feiden, supra*.

There is a presumption against suicide. In any case where death is an issue and there is nothing to show that it was caused by suicide, there is a presumption that it was caused by an accident. *Bruning v Sheffield Farms Co.* (1959, 3d Dept) 8 AD2d 241, 187 NYS2d 666.

The presumption against suicide arises in recognition of the fact that self-destruction is contrary to the general conduct of mankind. It is a judicial recognition authorizing a jury to take heed of the truth, drawn from general human experience, that death by suicide is an improbability and that most men cling to life. *Schelberger v Eastern Sav. Bank* (1983, 1st Dept) 93 AD2d 188, 461 NYS2d 785, affd 60 NY2d 506, 470 NYS2d 548.

The presumption against suicide vanishes only when no reasonable inference other than suicide may be drawn from the evidence. *Wellisch v John Hancock Mut. Life Ins. Co.* (1944) 293 NY 178. The presumption was held to be overcome by the evidence in the record furnished by the Medical Examiner that the decedent had committed suicide. *Leib v Paparo* (1981, 2d Dept) 84 AD2d 538, 443 NYS2d 98.

A child under four years of age is conclusively presumed to be incapable of negligence. *Chandler v Keene* (1957, 3d Dept) 5 AD2d 42, 168 NYS2d 788.

There is a presumption that every person is capable of managing his own affairs. *Schneidman v Steckler* (1958) 12 Misc 2d 946, 173 NYS2d 89, affd (2d Dept) 5 AD2d 990, 173 NYS2d 654.

A person is presumed to intend the natural and probable consequences of his voluntary acts. *Quinones v Quinones* (1955, Sup) 139 NYS2d 607.

In the absence of evidence to the contrary, it is presumed that all people act fairly, honestly and in good faith. *Fraser v Kent* (1921) 194 AD 742, 185 NYS 746.

There is a strong presumption that a child born in wedlock is legitimate. *Re Findlay* (1930) 253 NY 1, 170 NE 471. In a suit in which paternity is at issue, that presumption is overcome if the court finds that all the experts' blood tests show that the husband is not the father of the child. *Anonymous v Anonymous* (1956, 2d Dept) 1 AD2d 312, 150 NYS2d 344. It may also be overcome by proof of non-access. Family Court Act § 436.

Although the presumption of legitimacy is one of the strongest and most persuasive presumptions known to the law, it is not conclusive. It may be rebutted where to do otherwise would outrage common sense and reason. *Re Estate of Fay* (1978) 44 NY2d 137, 404 NYS2d 554, app dismd 439 US 1059, 59 L Ed 2d 25, 99 S Ct 820, reh den 440 US 968, 59 L Ed 2d 784, 99 S Ct 1521. *See also, Queal v Queal* (1992, 4th Dept) 179 AD2d 1070, 579 NYS2d 527; *Elizabeth A.P. v Paul T. P.* (1993, 4th Dept) 199 AD2d 1030, 605 NYS2d 614.

Where petitioner in a paternity action did not negate access by her husband during the time when conception occurred and thus failed to overcome the presumption of legitimacy, she did not establish paternity on the part of the putative father by clear and conclusive evidence. *D. v B.* (1978, 2d Dept) 65 AD2d 592, 409 NYS2d 260.

There is a presumption, not conclusive, that a woman over 50 years of age cannot bear children. *Washington v Bank for Sav.* (1901) 65 AD 338, 72 NYS 752, affd 171 NY 166, 63 NE 831.

It has sometimes been held that one is presumed to know the law. *Garlen v Glens Falls* (1962) 35 Misc 2d 363, 230 NYS2d 965, affd (3d Dept) 17 AD2d 277, 234 NYS2d 564, affd 12 NY2d 1025, 239 NYS2d 349. However, there is in fact no presumption that all persons know the law. *Municipal Metallic Bed Mfg. Corp. v Dobbs* (1930) 253 NY 313, 171 NE 75, 68 ALR 1376. The "presumption" exists only in the sense that in passing on the character of their acts, all persons are treated as if they knew the law, and ignorance of the law does not excuse persons so as to exempt them from the consequences of their acts, such as punishment for crime. *Municipal Metallic Bed Mfg. Corp. v Dobbs, supra.*

It is, however, presumed that a business person knows what is essential to a valid merchandise sales contract. *Re Huxley* (1945) 294 NY 146, 169 ALR 194. A debtor is legally bound to know that the attorney has no authority to accept a sum less than the full amount of the judgment, and that the attorney's acceptance of such a lesser sum does not bind the client unless such act is subsequently ratified and approved by the client. *Farmer v Schneider* (1945) 269 AD 1043, 58 NYS2d 587.

It is presumed that trade union members know what the laws of the union's existence declare as binding upon them. *O'Connell v O'Leary* (1938) 167 Misc 324, 3 NYS2d 833. There also is a conclusive presumption that a common carrier has knowledge of the lawful rates filed with the Interstate Commerce Commission. *Kelleher Car-Loading & Distributing Co. v Muller Paper Goods Co.* (1954, App Tm) 134 NYS2d 659.

There is a presumption that a person knows the truth with respect to facts within his own special means of knowledge. *Guild v Herrick* (1944, Sup) 51 NYS2d 326. Thus, when a person had access to the books and records of a company, there was a presumption that he knew their contents. *Guild v Herrick, supra.*

If a record kept in the ordinary course of business contains the name of a party, a presumption arises that the recorded name refers to that party. *Douler v Prudential Ins. Co.* (1911) 143 AD 537, 128 NYS 396.

Identity of name creates a presumption of identity of person. *McCabe v Union Dime Sav. Bank* (1934) 150 Misc 157, 268 NYS 449.

A testator is presumed to know the law and the impact of estate taxes. *Re Will of Miller* (1974) 76 Misc 2d 1092, 353 NYS2d 379.

A property owner is chargeable with knowledge that taxes will be levied against the property regularly and that a default may result in forfeiture of the land. *McCann v Scaduto* (1986, 2d Dept) 123 AD2d 111, 510 NYS2d 149, revd (1987) 71 NY2d 164, 524 NYS2d 398.

The failure to produce proof of financial security upon request raises a presumption that a vehicle was not insured. However, it does not raise a presumption that the operator had knowledge that the vehicle was uninsured. The Vehicle and Traffic Law does not require each non-owner-operator to inquire of the owner concerning insurance coverage. *People v Hakimi-Fard* (1987) 137 Misc 2d 116, 519 NYS2d 766.

An owner of property is charged with knowledge of statutory provisions affecting the control or disposition of his or her property. *D & Z Holding Corp. v New York Dep't of Finance* (1992, 2d Dept) 179 AD2d 796, 579 NYS2d 694, app den 79 NY2d 758, 584 NYS2d 446.

§ 18:12 PRESUMPTIONS OF CONTINUANCE OF A CONDITION — There are a number of separate presumptions based upon the general rule that a condition once proved to exist will be presumed to continue until the contrary is shown. Such presumptions operate prospectively rather than retrospectively, so that proof of a condition as of a certain date does not create any presumption that the same condition existed earlier. *Bromley v Mollnar* (1942) 179 Misc 713, 39 NYS2d 424.

Once the existence of a person, personal relation, or state of things is established by proof, the law presumes that it continues to exist as before until the contrary is shown. *Carlson v New York* (1912) 150 AD 264, 134 NYS 661. Such relation or state of things is presumed to continue to exist for a reasonable period, *Young v Shulenberg* (1901) 165 NY 385, 59 NE 135, at least in the absence of a contrary showing. *Currie v International Magazine Co.* (1931) 256 NY 106, 175 NE 530.

Although the presumption of continuity does not ordinarily apply retrospectively, it may occasionally be applied backward. *Larsen Baking Co. v New York* (1968, 2d Dept) 30 AD2d 400, 292 NYS2d 145, affd 24 NY2d 1036, 303 NYS2d 80. For example, it was shown that one corporation had a surplus equal to 21 times its capital 13 months after organization, and another had a surplus 28 times its capital two months after organization. In the absence of a contrary demonstration, it was a legitimate deduction that these corporations were at all times solvent in the intervening time. *Re Auditore's Estate* (1930) 136 Misc 664, 240 NYS 502, affd 233 AD 740, 250 NYS 902, app dismd 257 NY 554, 178 NE 792.

The rule that the presumption of continuance does not flow backwards should be confined in its application to cases where, as a matter of logic, no inference as to the past condition can be drawn from the evidence of the present one. *Bailey v Baker's Air Force Gas Corp.* (1975) 50 AD2d 129, 376 NYS2d 212.

The presumption that conditions once existing may be presumed to continue until they are shown to have changed is no more than a common sense inference, as strong or as weak as the nature of the surrounding circumstances permits. *Hynes v Sloma* (1977, 4th Dept) 59 AD2d 1014, 399 NYS2d 745. Proof of the existence of a condition at a given time raises a presumption that it can continue for as long as is usual with things of that nature. *Cummins v County of Onondaga* (1993, 4th Dept) 198 AD2d 875, 605 NYS2d 694, related proceeding (4th Dept) 198 AD2d 879, 605 NYS2d 982.

There is a presumption that title or ownership continues. *Re Cofer's Estate* (1923) 121 Misc 292, 200 NYS 906. Once established, the following facts are also presumed to continue: (1) employer-employee relationship, *Re Napoli's Will* (1952, Sur) 110 NYS2d 406, mod on other grounds 282 AD 814, 123 NYS2d 10; (2) marriage, *Re Pinder's Estate* (1946) 271 AD2d 302, 65 NYS2d 274; (3) relationship of principal and agent, *Currie v International Magazine Co.* (1931) 256 NY 106, 175 NE 530; (4) foreign law, *Re Gehrig's Estate* (1891) 126 NY 537, 27 NE 784; (5) encumbrances, *Bryan L. Kennelly, Inc. v Shapiro* (1928) 222 AD 488, 226 NYS 692, affd 250 NY 523, 166 NE 309; (6) knowledge, *Re Rogers' Will* (1937) 250 AD 26, 293 NYS 626; (7) the condition of premises. *Mansfield v New York* (1907) 119 AD 199, 104 NYS 386.

A person shown to be of sound or unsound mind is presumed to continue to be in the same condition until the contrary is shown. *Quarterman v Quarterman* (1943) 179 Misc 759, 39 NYS2d 737. The burden of proving sanity in a *habeas corpus* proceeding is upon the party who seeks the release of a person from commitment in a state hospital. *Rosario v State* (1964) 42 Misc 2d 699, 248 NYS2d 734.

When an attorney appears for litigants, his employment is presumed to continue until the contrary is shown. *Thomas v Thomas* (1942) 178 Misc 349, 34 NYS2d 320.

§ 18:13 PRESUMPTION OF CONSTITUTIONALITY OF A STATUTE — A legislative enactment carries with it a strong presumption of constitutionality. *Lincoln Bldg. Associates v Barr* (1956) 1 NY2d 413, 153 NYS2d 633, app dismd 355 US 12, 2 L Ed 2d 20, 78 S Ct 12; *Mancuso v Levitt* (1994, 1st Dept) 201 AD2d 386, 607 NYS2d 353, app dismd without op 83 NY2d 952, 615 NYS2d 876. This presumption can be upset only by proof that is persuasive beyond a reasonable doubt. *Hotel Dorset Co. v Trust for Cultural Resources* (1978) 46 NY2d 358, 413 NYS2d 357; *Medical Soc'y of State v Sobol* (1993, 3d Dept) 192 AD2d 78, 600 NYS2d 177, app dismd without op 82 NY2d 802, 604 NYS2d 558, reconsideration den, app den 82 NY2d 917, 610 NYS2d 145 and cert den (US) 128 L Ed 2d 902, 114 S Ct 2183; *Abwilda V. v Thomas W.* (1986, 2d Dept) 122 AD2d 950, 505 NYS2d 969.

A statute should be construed so as to avoid doubts concerning its constitutionality. *Re C.* (1980) 49 NY2d 161, 424 NYS2d 395. Whenever possible, a statute should be interpreted so as to uphold its constitutionality. *Wittenberg v New York* (1988, 1st Dept) 135 AD2d 132, 523 NYS2d 1003, affd 73 NY2d 753, 536 NYS2d 57.

The substantial burden of proving unconstitutionality beyond a reasonable doubt rests with a statute's antagonist. *People v Scalza* (1990) 76 NY2d 604, 562 NYS2d 14.

The Court of Appeals is required to avoid interpreting a statute in a way that would render it unconstitutional if such a construction can be avoided. The Court is also required to uphold the legislation if any uncertainty about its validity exists. *Alliance of American Insurers v Chu* (1991) 77 NY2d 573, 569 NYS2d 364.

A statute, which is presumed to be constitutional, must be construed so as to uphold its constitutionality if there is a rational basis for doing so. *Saratoga Water Servs. v Sarasota County Water Auth.* (1993, 3d Dept) 190 AD2d 40, 596 NYS2d 872, affd 83 NY2d 205, 608 NYS2d 952.

§ 18:14   OTHER PRESUMPTIONS CREATED BY LAW — In

the absence of proof to the contrary, there is a strong presumption
that public officers have properly discharged the duties of their
office and have performed faithfully those matters with which
they are charged. *Stupnicki v Southern New York Fish & Game
Asso.* (1962) 41 Misc 2d 266, 244 NYS2d 558, affd (3d Dept) 19
AD2d 921, 245 NYS2d 333.

A public official is presumed to act legally. *Richmond R. Co. v
Gilchrist* (1929) 225 AD 371, 233 NYS 184. It is presumed that
county authorities will act in a proper manner. *Irondequoit v
Monroe County* (1939) 171 Misc 125, 11 NYS2d 933.

The presumption of regularity of procedures only shifts the burden of going forward to the party claiming that normal procedures
were not followed. *Dougherty v Rye* (1984) 63 NY2d 989, 483
NYS2d 999.

A determination by an administrative agency is presumed to be
correct. *Syracuse v Hueber* (1976, 4th Dept) 52 AD2d 341, 383
NYS2d 774.

In the absence of any showing that the Town Board did not validly exercise its legislative powers, the specifications adopted by it
upon the recommendation of its engineer are entitled to the strongest presumption of validity. *Ludlow's Sand & Gravel Co. v La
Bella* (1974) 80 Misc 2d 997, 364 NYS2d 669.

The presumption of regularity attaching to the acts of a Commissioner of Deeds as a public officer should not be inapplicable,
as a matter of law, to statements of a Commissioner of Deeds
who is the candidate named in the designating petition in which
his statements appear. *Rittersporn v Sadowski* (1979) 48 NY2d
618, 421 NYS2d 49.

It is presumed that the law of a foreign state is the same as that
of the forum, in the absence of proof to the contrary. *Gaines v
Jacobsen* (1954) 308 NY 218, 48 ALR2d 312. There is a presumption that the common law of a sister state is the same as that of
New York, in the absence of evidence to the contrary. However,
the presumption does not apply to those states that have inherited
or adopted the civil law, such as Louisiana. *Strain v Seven Hills
Associates* (1980, 1st Dept) 75 AD2d 360, 429 NYS2d 424.

There is a statutory presumption that one spouse contracting for improvements on property owned by either or both is the agent of the other, in the absence of notice to the contractor. Lien Law § 3.

It is presumed that a written instrument expresses the intention of the parties. *Eastern Air Lines, Inc. v Trans Caribbean Airways, Inc.* (1968, 1st Dept) 29 AD2d 379, 288 NYS2d 317, affd 23 NY2d 709, 296 NYS2d 153. There is a presumption that a check was drawn and executed on the date it bears. *News Syndicate Co. v Gatti Paper Stock Corp.* (1931) 256 NY 211, 176 NE 169, reh den 256 NY 678, 177 NE 190.

A rebuttable presumption of ownership arises from possession of chattels. *Manhattan Co. v Morgan* (1922) 199 AD 767, 192 NYS 239. A similar presumption arises from possession of real property under a claim of right. *Schick v Wolf* (1924) 207 AD 652, 202 NYS 601. If the possession is open, notorious and uninterrupted for 10 years, legal title is acquired by adverse possession. CPLR 212.

At common law, if two or more persons die in a common disaster, there is no presumption as to survivorship. *Re Fowles' Will* (1918) 222 NY 222, 118 NE 611. When persons die in a common disaster and it cannot be determined who survived, certain statutory provisions apply. EPTL § 2-1.6.

Where the title to property or the devolution thereof depends upon which of two or more persons died first, and no sufficient proof exists that death was other than simultaneous, the property of each person shall be disposed of as if he had survived, except as otherwise provided in the governing statutory section. EPTL § 2-1.6. The statutory provisions are subordinate to those in any will, living trust, deed or life insurance policy which provide for disposition in a manner different from that provided for in the statute. EPTL § 2-1.6(e).

Where a testamentary disposition of property depends upon the time of death of two or more beneficiaries designated to take alternatively because of survivorship, and there is no sufficient evidence that death was other than simultaneous, the property thus disposed of shall be divided into as many equal shares as there are alternative beneficiaries and such shares shall be distributed respectively to those who would have taken the whole property in the event the designated beneficiary through whom they take had survived. EPTL § 2-1.6(b).

Where there is no sufficient evidence that two joint tenants or tenants by the entirety have died otherwise than simultaneously, the property shall be distributed one-half as if one had survived and one-half as if the other had survived. If there are more than two such joint tenants and all of them have died simultaneously, the property shall be distributed in the proportion that one bears to the whole number of joint tenants. EPTL § 2-1.6(c).

Where the insured and beneficiary of a life insurance policy or accident insurance policy die and there is no evidence other than that of simultaneous death, the proceeds of the policy shall be distributed as if the insured had survived the beneficiary. EPTL § 2-1.6(d).

A person is presumed solvent until shown to be insolvent. *Gifford v O'Conner* (1889) 117 NY 275, 22 NE 1036.

Section 388 of the Vehicle and Traffic Law creates a rebuttable presumption that the operator of a vehicle was using the vehicle with the owner's express or implied permission. This presumption was held not to have been rebutted when there was no convincing evidence that the leased vehicle had been either converted or stolen. *Banner Casualty Co. v Lazar* (1975) 81 Misc 2d 360, 366 NYS2d 314.

§ 18:15 CONFLICTING PRESUMPTIONS — It is clear from a reading of the foregoing sections that the law of evidence has given rise to a rather substantial number of presumptions. A given case may involve two conflicting presumptions. When this occurs, one presumption or both must yield. *Re Pinder's Estate* (1946) 271 AD2d 302, 65 NYS2d 274. In such a case, the stronger presumption prevails over the weaker one. *Re Pinder's Estate, supra.*

Presumptions of equal weight cancel each other out and neither one is considered. *Palmer v Palmer* (1900) 162 NY 130, 56 NE 501. If the facts are equally consistent with either of two conflicting presumptions, neither prevails. *Re Brown's Ex'r* (1927) 130 Misc 865, 226 NYS 1, mod on other grounds 225 AD 759, 232 NYS 371, mod on other grounds, 252 NY 366, 169 NE 612.

Each particular case must be determined on the basis of its own particular circumstances, which vary from one proceeding to another. Precedents are seldom helpful. *Re Pinder's Estate, supra.*

In a conflict between the presumption of continuance of a prior marriage and the presumption of legitimacy of a child of the second marriage, the latter is stronger and will prevail over the former. *Castellani v Castellani* (1941) 176 Misc 763, 28 NYS2d 879, affd 263 AD 984, 34 NYS2d 400.

§ 18:16 INFERENCE ARISING FROM FAILURE TO PRO-DUCE A WITNESS — If a party fails to call a witness on a material issue, the jury may draw the inference that the testimony would be adverse to such party. *Cushman v De Mallie* (1899) 46 AD 379, 61 NYS 878. However, the witness must be one whom the party would be expected to call and within the ability of the party to produce. The witness must be friendly rather than hostile. His testimony must be material rather than unimportant or merely cumulative. *Reehil v Fraas* (1908) 129 AD 563, 114 NYS 17, revd on other grounds (1909) 197 NY 64.

The rule does not apply if the witness is a stranger to the party against whom the inference is sought, particularly if the witness is in court and equally subject to call by both sides. *Longacre v Yonkers R. Co.* (1923) 236 NY 119, 140 NE 215, 28 ALR 1030. Neither is the presumption applicable where a reasonable explanation has been shown for failure to call a witness, *Estatio v O'Hara* (1919, App Tm) 174 NYS 608. Thus, the presumption is not applicable in the case of a witness confined in an insane asylum, *Metallurgical Sec. Co. v Mechanics & Metals Nat'l Bank* (1916) 171 AD 321, 157 NYS 321, or where the testimony of the witness is merely cumulative or corroborative. *Sugarman v Brengel* (1902) 68 AD 377, 74 NYS 167. The presumption does not apply where the testimony of the witness has been excluded. *Costigan v Third A. R. Co.* (1924) 124 Misc 165, 207 NYS 216.

The presumption or inference resulting from failure to call a witness does not constitute substantive proof and, consequently, cannot take the place of such proof. *Eldridge v Terry & Tench Co.* (1911) 145 AD 560, 129 NYS 865. It can, however, corroborate a *prima facie* case already made. *Eldridge v Terry & Tench Co., supra.*

In summation in a negligence action to recover damages for personal injuries, the plaintiff's attorney should be permitted to comment on the failure of the defendant to take the stand. *Sky v Kahan-Frankl* (1975, 2d Dept) 47 AD2d 939, 367 NYS2d 84, later app (2d Dept) 54 AD2d 587, 387 NYS2d 163.

In an action to set aside allegedly fraudulent conveyances by a judgment debtor to a corporation controlled by his wife, the wife failed to appear and testify. Such failure warranted the trial court in drawing the strongest inferences against her and the corporation that the opposing evidence in the record might permit. *Scola v Morgan* (1979, 1st Dept) 66 AD2d 228, 412 NYS2d 893.

Plaintiff had been treated for a back problem prior to the accident. An issue developed at trial as to whether plaintiff's present complaints resulted from the automobile accident or were caused by the pre-existing problem. It was not error for the court to charge the jury as to the effect of plaintiff's failure to produce the doctor who had treated him for the prior condition. *Griffin v Nissen* (1982, 4th Dept) 89 AD2d 808, 453 NYS2d 277.

Although equally accessible to both parties, the witness was favorable to one party, her husband, and hostile to the other. It was error for the court to refuse to charge that defendant's failure to call his wife as a witness would entitle the jury to draw the inference that her testimony would not have been favorable to him with regard to the manner of the happening of the accident, even though the wife was in the courtroom and available to both sides. *Rosa v Blander* (1975, 2d Dept) 47 AD2d 865, 366 NYS2d 36. The principle of equal availability is not applicable under those circumstances. *Rosa v Blander, supra*. Relatives are generally considered under the control of a party. *Ausch v St. Paul Fire & Marine Ins. Co.* (1987, 2d Dept) 125 AD2d 43, 511 NYS2d 919.

A "missing witness charge" should be given when the witness, who has not been called, is under a party's control and is in a position to give substantial, not merely cumulative, evidence. Proof that a witness is beyond the jurisdiction of the court is ordinarily sufficient to bar the inference as a matter of law. *Zeeck v Melina Taxi Co.* (1991, 2d Dept) 177 AD2d 692, 576 NYS2d 878.

An unfavorable inference may ordinarily arise when a doctor has examined the plaintiff and is not called to testify. If the testimony would not have constituted material evidence, the inference may not be drawn. *Kushner v Mollin* (1992, 2d Dept) 181 AD2d 866, 581 NYS2d 836.

When a doctor who examined plaintiff on defendant's behalf does not testify at the trial, an inference generally arises that the testimony of such witness would be unfavorable to defendant. To rebut the inference, defendant must demonstrate that the testimony would be merely cumulative, the witness was unavailable or not under his control, or the witness would address matters not in dispute. *Arroyo v New York* (1991, 1st Dept) 171 AD2d 541, 567 NYS2d 257.

RESEARCH REFERENCES

American Law Reports

81 ALR4th 939, Adverse presumption or inference based on partys failure to produce or examine transferor, transferee, broker, or other person allegedly involved in transaction at issue–modern cases

80 ALR4th 405, Adverse presumption or inference based on partys failure to produce or examine witness with employment relationship to party–modern cases

80 ALR4th 337, Adverse presumption or inference based on partys failure to produce or examine family member other than spouse–modern cases

79 ALR4th 779, Adverse presumption or inference based on partys failure to produce or examine friend–modern cases

79 ALR4th 694, Adverse presumption or inference based on party's failure to produce or examine spouse–modern cases

77 ALR4th 463, Adverse presumption or inference based on party's failure to produce or question examining doctor–modern cases

36 ALR4th 843, Presumptions and evidence respecting identification of land on which property taxes were paid to establish adverse possession

25 ALR4th 1237, Res ipsa loquitur in aviation accidents

21 ALR4th 929, Res ipsa loquitur as to cause of or liability for real-property fires

19 ALR4th 919, Refusal of defendant in "public figure" libel case to identify claimed sources as raising presumption against existence of
source

94 ALR3d 608, Unexplained gratuitous transfer of property from one relative to another as raising presumption of gift

93 ALR3d 897, Applicability of res ipsa loquitur doctrine in action for
injury to patron of beauty salon

93 ALR3d 776, Application of res ipsa loquitur doctrine to accidents
incurred by passenger while boarding or alighting from a carrier

92 ALR3d 726, Establishment of "family" relationship to raise presumption that services were rendered gratuitously, as between persons
living in same household but not related by blood or affinity

91 ALR3d 186, Res ipsa loquitur as applicable in actions for damage to
property by overflow or escape of water

90 ALR3d 1032, Who may dispute presumption of legitimacy of child
conceived or born during wedlock

88 ALR3d 622, Amnesiac party as entitled to presumption of due care

87 ALR3d 949, Statutory presumption of possession of weapon by occu-
pants of place or vehicle where it was found

84 ALR3d 495, Proof of husband's impotency or sterility as rebutting presumption of legitimacy

79 ALR3d 346, Res ipsa loquitur as applied to accident resulting from
wheel or part thereof becoming detached from motor vehicle

69 ALR3d 1311, Presumption of payment as applicable to bank deposit

69 ALR3d 1285, Presumption of payment of bank, deposit 46 ALR3d
158, Presumption of legitimacy of child born after annulment,
divorce, or separation

44 ALR3d 171, Presumption and burden of proof where subject of bailment is destroyed by fire

43 ALR3d 607, Presumption and burden of proof where subject of bailment is destroyed or damaged by windstorm or other meteorologi-
cal phenomena

35 ALR3d 289, Conflict of laws as to presumption and burden of proof
concerning facts of civil case

13 ALR3d 381, Presumption or inference of undue influence from testamentary gift to relative, friend, or associate of person preparing will
or procuring its execution

5 ALR3d 100, Modern status of rules against basing an inference or a
presumption upon a presumption

ALR Quick Index: Presumptions and Burden of Proof; Res Ipsa Loquitur

American Jurisprudence 2d

29 Am Jur 2d, Evidence §§ 159-248

American Jurisprudence Pleading and Practice

23 Am Jur Pl & Pr Forms (Rev), Trial Forms 154-156

9A Am Jur Pl & Pr Forms (Rev), Evidence, Forms 51-65

American Jurisprudence Proof of Facts

19 Am Jur Proof of Facts 2d 377, Circumstances Warranting Inference of Death

18 Am Jur Proof of Facts 2d 187, Circumstances Rebutting Presumption of Payment of Savings Account

14 Am Jur Proof of Facts 2d 409, Husband's Sterility as Rebutting Presumption of Legitimacy

American Jurisprudence Trials

51 Am Jur Trials 1, Managing Litigation

49 Am Jur Trials 171, Defense of Claim Brought Under The Americans With Disabilities Act

5 Am Jur Trials 505, Mapping the Trial-Order of Proof §§ 43, 44

Other Resources

8 Carmody-Wait 2d, Presentation of the Case §§ 56:16, 56:17

Auto-Cite®: Any case citation herein can be checked for form, parallel references, later history and annotation references through the Auto-Cite computer research system.

CHAPTER 19

REAL AND DEMONSTRATIVE EVIDENCE

§ 19:1 REAL AND DEMONSTRATIVE EVIDENCE, IN GENERAL — The term "real evidence" is sometimes used interchangeably with demonstrative evidence. It refers to objects or persons exhibited to the jury. Real evidence involves primarily the exhibition to the jury of objects that are relevant to the issues. *Mulhado v Brooklyn C. R. Co.* (1864) 30 NY 370. For example, the exhibition of an injured arm to the jury may make the description of the injury more intelligible. *Mulhado v Brooklyn C. R. Co., supra*.

§ 19:2 TANGIBLE ARTICLES WITH SOME BEARING ON THE TRANSACTION IN QUESTION — Tangible articles relating to the issues in the case may ordinarily be admitted in evidence if they are material and relevant. *Smith v Lehigh V. R. Co.* (1904) 177 NY 379, 69 NE 729. Their admissibility lies within the discretion of the court. *Clark v Brooklyn H. R. Co.* (1904) 177 NY 359, 69 NE 647. However, a flagrant abuse of discretion will call for a reversal. *Boyarsky v G. A. Zimmerman Corp.* (1934) 240 AD 361, 270 NYS 134.

The record contained testimony that the bottle and cap were the ones in question and that their condition was basically the same as it was at the time of the happening of the incident. It was error for the trial court to exclude them because a sufficient foundation for their admissibility had been laid. *Hansen v Coca Cola Bottling Co.* (1980, 2d Dept) 78 AD2d 848, 432 NYS2d 723.

It is not always necessary that the witness identify the objects sought to be introduced in evidence with absolute certainty as being identical to those in issue. *People v Levia* (1956, 3d Dept) 3 AD2d 42, 158 NYS2d 448, later app (3d Dept) 6 AD2d 961, 176 NYS2d 427. Thus, in a civil action to recover penalties for alleged violations of the Conservation Law, it was held that the witnesses were not required to identify positively the three fish as being the same three that they had seen caught. The connection was so close that it rendered the exhibit competent evidence; the absence of direct and positive proof went to the weight, not to the competency. *People v Levia, supra*.

In an action for the death of a window cleaner, stone fragments were improperly admitted in evidence in the absence of proof indicating the time when they had become detached from the window ledge. *Andross v Trustees of Columbia University* (1940) 260 AD 941, 23 NYS2d 285. In an automobile collision case, it was error to admit a whiskey bottle found near the accident when it was offered to show that the defendant was drunk. *Wurtzman v Kalinowski* (1931) 233 AD 187, 251 NYS 328.

In an action for malpractice, it was error to refuse to permit the jury to examine the plaintiff's throat to determine the result of defendant's operation for the removal of tonsils, by comparison with a diagram in evidence of a throat conceded to be normal. *Dictz v Aronson* (1935) 244 AD 746, 279 NYS 66.

A police officer drove defendant's automobile to the police station and a subsequent search at the police station revealed the presence of marijuana and marijuana paraphernalia in the automobile. The failure of the prosecution to call the officer who drove defendant's car to the station house broke the chain of evidence linking defendant to the contraband later found therein. *People v Bennett* (1975, 1st Dept) 47 AD2d 322, 366 NYS2d 639.

§ 19:3   TANGIBLE ARTICLES IN THE SAME CONDITION — Before an item of real evidence may be deemed admissible, it must be shown to be in the same condition as it was at the time of the occurrence that is the subject of the case. *People v Flanigan* (1903) 174 NY 356, 66 NE 988. Defendants sought to defeat plaintiff's action for the purchase price of a machine by claiming that fraudulent representations had been made regarding the ability of the machine to do its work in a certain manner. The court properly refused the defendant's offer to produce the machine in court, unless it could be proven that the machine was in the same condition as when it was delivered to the defendant. *American Multigraph Sales Co. v Fred R. Jones & Co.* (1909, App Tm) 119 NYS 1087.

§ 19:4   ADMISSIBILITY OF PHOTOGRAPHS — Photographs are admissible in evidence. *Saporito v New York* (1964) 14 NY2d 474, 253 NYS2d 985. Such photographs may help the jury to better understand the evidence. *Saporito v New York, supra.*

The photograph must be shown to be a true representation. *English v Genovese* (1966) 49 Misc 2d 321, 267 NYS2d 283. Of course, the matter contained in the photograph must be relevant. *Overend v New York* (1947) 271 AD 975, 67 NYS2d 625.

In a personal injury action, the trial court properly excluded photographs from evidence where they did not show the accident site under conditions that were substantially the same as those at the time of the accident. *Calandriello v New York Racing Ass'n* (1994, 2d Dept) 203 AD2d 503, 611 NYS2d 247.

Photographs of the plaintiff's vehicle were taken three weeks after the accident and were received in evidence without proper foundation. They were prejudicial to the defendant. *McNamara v Iannaci* (1974, 2d Dept) 45 AD2d 861, 358 NYS2d 543.

For a photograph to be admissible, the person who took it is not required to verify it. *Stiasny v Metropolitan S. R. Co.* (1901) 58 AD 172, 68 NYS 694, affd 172 NY 656, 65 NE 1122. Because the purpose of verification of a photograph is the establishment of its accuracy, any person having the required knowledge may verify it. *Stiasny v Metropolitan S. R. Co., supra.*

When a photograph shows a hole in the pavement, a sufficient foundation for its admission is established by testimony to the effect that the photograph correctly shows the condition of the pavement at the time of the accident. It is no bar to its admissibility that it shows the presence of rubbish on the sidewalk or buildings in the vicinity which are at a more advanced state of completion than at the time of the accident. *Saporito v New York, supra.* Photographs showing the street signs are admissible to show the physical characteristics of an intersection, if this is relevant. *People v Hausen* (1959) 20 Misc 2d 113, 193 NYS2d 61.

When offered in evidence in a negligence action, photographs of subsequent repairs are not admissible on the issue of negligence. *Frummer v Hilton Hotels International, Inc.* (1969) 60 Misc 2d 840, 304 NYS2d 335. However, evidence of subsequent repairs may be shown to establish control, if this is an issue. *Scudero v Campbell* (1942) 288 NY 328.

A photograph showing that railings had been subsequently erected about a platform was properly excluded. *Anneberg v First Nat. City Bank* (1975) 49 AD2d 827, 373 NYS2d 353.

The fact that a photograph is admitted in evidence does not mean that it is the exclusive evidence of the conditions it purports to represent. *Huston v Chenango County* (1937) 253 AD 56, 1 NYS2d 252, affd 278 NY 646. It is permissible to receive evidence regarding what a witness can see at a particular point even though photographs in evidence indicate that the witness could not see that to which he has testified. *Havecker v Weiss* (1932) 237 AD 856, 261 NYS 494, resettled 238 AD 787, 262 NYS 907.

Photographs are admissible to identify a person and to show his physical condition and appearance and the extent of injuries to the part of the body photographed. *Alberti v New York, L. E. & W. R. Co.* (1889) 118 NY 77, 23 NE 35, reh den (NY) 23 NE 1146. In an action for wrongful death based on medical malpractice, it was error to admit photographs of the decedent into evidence. However, the court held that the error was not so prejudicial that it required unconditional reversal of the judgment. *Mayes v County of Nassau* (1968, 2d Dept) 31 AD2d 638, 295 NYS2d 989.

A posed photograph may be admissible if a proper foundation has been laid by preliminary testimony showing that the matters portrayed are faithfully represented. *People v Veld* (1913) 154 AD 752, 139 NYS 788. However, in an action against a city and police officer for injuries sustained by plaintiff, it was held to be prejudicial to the plaintiff when obviously "staged" photographs were offered in evidence showing a police officer and one or both of the defendant's witnesses re-enacting their version of the accident. *Torres v Geneva* (1969, 4th Dept) 33 AD2d 880, 307 NYS2d 602.

Under proper conditions, photographic copies of handwriting are admissible. *Hoffman v Prussian Nat. Ins. Co.* (1918) 181 AD 412, 168 NYS 841. Thus, admittedly genuine and allegedly spurious writings may be admitted for comparison purposes by means of photographically enlarged copies of them. *Hoffman v Prussian Nat. Ins. Co., supra.* To be received in evidence, however, the photograph must be shown to be a fair, accurate and truthful representation of the writing. *Hynes v McDermott* (1880) 82 NY 41.

A photograph is not rendered inadmissible by the presence of marks on it. *Wilson v Kenyon* (1953, Co Ct) 120 NYS2d 638. Thus, photographs previously marked during the taking of a deposition were admitted during the trial. *Wilson v Kenyon, supra.*

In an action for personal injuries that resulted when the plaintiff's foot caught in a hole, photographs of the condition had been taken the day after the accident. The accuracy of the photographs had not been challenged and plaintiff testified that they were a fair and accurate representation of the scene of the accident at the time of the accident. The photographs were held to be sufficiently clear and precise to permit a jury reasonably to infer from the condition of the defect, as indicated by discoloration of a concrete-like substance shown on the photographs, that the hole in the basement floor had been there a sufficiently long time for the defendant to have known of the defect. *Batton v Elghanayan* (1978) 43 NY2d 898, 403 NYS2d 717; *Davis v County of Nassau* (1990, 2d Dept) 166 AD2d 498, 560 NYS2d 696; *Ferlito v Great South Bay Assoc.* (1988, 2d Dept) 140 AD2d 408, 528 NYS2d 111.

Photographs may be used to prove constructive notice of an alleged defect shown in the photographs if they are taken reasonably close to the time of the accident and there is testimony to show that the condition at the time of the accident was substantially as shown in the photographs. However, the trial court properly refused to admit in evidence several photographs for the purpose of showing constructive notice of the defect when the photographs were taken four years after the accident. *Anis v Associated Restaurant Management Corp.* (1994, 2d Dept) 202 AD2d 459, 609 NYS2d 51.

In a products liability action arising out of injuries that rendered the plaintiff a quadriplegic, it was proper to introduce color photographs of plaintiff with Crutchfield tongs on a Stryker frame. The photographs were not inflammatory and they assisted the jury in understanding the medical evidence. *Caprara v Chrysler Corp.* (1979, 3d Dept) 71 AD2d 515, 423 NYS2d 694, affd 52 NY2d 114, 436 NYS2d 251.

A photograph of a "sister tractor" to the one completely destroyed in the accident was properly admitted in evidence. It was admitted on the basis of testimony that the photograph, although not of the tractor involved in the accident, was nonetheless a fair and accurate representation of that tractor. *Moore v Leaseway Transp. Corp.* (1980) 49 NY2d 720, 426 NYS2d 259.

In an action for personal injuries, it was proper to permit the introduction into evidence of photographs purporting to show the tires on plaintiff's vehicle. *De Francisci v Baron* (1983, 2d Dept) 97 AD2d 453, 467 NYS2d 419.

Photographs of the accident site taken the day after the accident were not erroneously admitted into evidence. A witness testified that the photographs accurately depicted the condition of the roadway immediately after the accident with certain minor exceptions. In addition, there was no evidence that the road's condition was altered by reason of the accident. *Schuster v Hempstead* (1987, 2d Dept) 130 AD2d 481, 515 NYS2d 64, app den 70 NY2d 613, 524 NYS2d 431.

In a medical malpractice action against a hospital, there was no error in admitting three photographs that the hospital had taken of the infant plaintiff's feet a few days after the incident. The photographs were not inflammatory and they aided the members of the jury in assessing both the medical testimony and the infant plaintiff's pain and suffering. *Rivera v New York* (1990, 2d Dept) 160 AD2d 985, 554 NYS2d 706.

The trial court did not improvidently exercise its discretion in declining to admit a photograph of the plaintiff's injury taken some two years prior to trial. On the record before it, the court could reasonably have concluded that the admission of a single, two-year-old photograph created a potentially unbalanced representation of the plaintiff's injury and would tend to confuse, rather than assist, the jury in its deliberations. *Marchiano v Mason* (1992, 2d Dept) 179 AD2d 739, 578 NYS2d 646.

The trial court did not abuse its discretion in denying plaintiff's motion seeking to admit into evidence certain photographs allegedly depicting plaintiff's injuries under the following circumstances: the record revealed and the trial court specifically found that the plaintiff violated a preliminary conference order by failing to exchange the photographs in question on or before a specified date; the photographs were concededly first offered as evidence on the eve of trial, to the surprise of defense counsel; and the plaintiff failed to lay a proper foundation for their admission by establishing through testimony or otherwise that the photographs fairly and accurately represented the condition of the plaintiff's body and the injuries sustained by the plaintiff as a direct result of the assault. *Khalil v Marion* (1994, 1st Dept) 200 AD2d 500, 606 NYS2d 652.

§ 19:5 ADMISSIBILITY OF MOTION PICTURES — When relevant and properly authenticated, motion pictures are admissible in evidence. *Boyarsky v G. A. Zimmerman Corp.* (1934) 240 AD 361, 270 NYS 134. Thus, it has been held to be an abuse of discretion and therefore reversible error for the court to exclude motion pictures that are properly authenticated and relevant. *Boyarsky v G. A. Zimmerman Corp., supra.* If there is no proper authentication, including a showing of the manner in which the motion picture film was prepared, the motion picture will be excluded. *Gibson v Gunn* (1923) 206 AD 464, 202 NYS 19, adhered to 208 AD 745, 202 NYS 927.

In a products liability action arising out of an accident in which plaintiff was rendered a quadriplegic, the trial court did not abuse its discretion in allowing plaintiff to show a silent motion picture, narrated by plaintiff's brother, which purported to show a portion of the daily routine of plaintiff being tended to at his parents' home. The film illustrated in an informative manner the impact the injury had on the plaintiff's life. *Caprara v Chrysler Corp.* (1979, 3d Dept) 71 AD2d 515, 423 NYS2d 694, affd 52 NY2d 114, 436 NYS2d 251.

§ 19:6 ADMISSIBILITY OF X-RAY PHOTOGRAPHS — X-rays are admissible in evidence when verified and properly identified. *Brady v Comprehensive Omnibus Corp.* (1938, App Tm) 5 NYS2d 781. It is proper, if not essential, to have the testimony of an expert in aid of the x-ray plates. *Marion v B. G. Coon Const. Co.* (1915) 216 NY 178, 110 NE 444. Although ordinarily the testimony of an expert is required, it is permissible by statute to have x-rays admitted in evidence without the testimony of an expert provided the procedure outlined in the statute is followed. CPLR 4532-a. The same rule applies to magnetic resonance images, computed axial tomographs, positron emission tomographs, electromyograms, sonograms and fetal heart rate monitor strips.

An x-ray report, sought to be admitted into evidence at the trial, is inadmissible without the introduction of the underlying x-ray, unless the proponent of the evidence establishes an excuse for its non-production. *Schozer v William Penn Life Ins. Co.* (1994) 84 NY2d 639, 620 NYS2d 797.

§ 19:7 ADMISSIBILITY OF VIDEOTAPE RECORDINGS — Videotape is nothing more than a motion picture synchronized with a sound recording. It is descriptive, corroborative and physical evidence. Compliance with standard rules of evidence regarding admission of underlying testimonial evidence should be a sufficient basis for admission of a videotape that records the event. *People v Higgins* (1977) 89 Misc 2d 913, 392 NYS2d 800. In the absence of a proper foundation exhibiting to the court's satisfaction that the movie or videotape offered is a true, fair and accurate representation of the events, people or scene depicted, it should be excluded. *People v Higgins, supra.*

A property owner brought a lawsuit against two nursing homes and a city for damages allegedly caused by flooding, which was allegedly the result of improper maintenance of the sewer by the city and improper disposal of diapers in the sewer by the nursing homes. The trial court properly excluded a videotape purporting to show that the diapers flowed into the sewers. The videotape was made at least three years after the flooding incidents for which damages were sought and, therefore, was too remote and not probative of any issue. *Merritt v Long Beach* (1988, 2d Dept) 139 AD2d 574, 527 NYS2d 74.

The question of whether a videotape should be viewed by the jury depends upon the facts and circumstances of each case and lies within the sound discretion of the trial court. *Austin v Bascaran* (1992, 3d Dept) 185 AD2d 474, 585 NYS2d 859. In an action brought by plaintiff against defendant dog owners to recover damages for injuries sustained by plaintiff who was allegedly attacked by a dog, it was error to admit a videotape produced by defendants exclusively for trial more than three years after the incident. The videotape consumed approximately 20 minutes and depicted defendants walking around the farm pointing out various landmarks and showing the dog in question herding sheep and following commands. *Austin v Bascaran, supra.*

The trial court did not improvidently exercise its discretion by admitting into evidence a videotape of the execution of the will. The videotape was not offered in an attempt to probate the document as a will; it was offered as evidence of the decedent's testamentary capacity. A proper foundation was laid because the three witnesses to the will and the attorney who supervised its execution testified that the videotape was a fair and accurate depiction of the events that were filmed. The attorney who supervised the will execution also testified extensively regarding the chain of custody of the videotape and testified that it did not appear that there had been any tampering with the tape. *Re Estate of Burack* (1994, 2d Dept) 201 AD2d 561, 607 NYS2d 711.

§ 19:8 ADMISSIBILITY OF SOUND RECORDINGS IN EVIDENCE — Sound recordings on tape, wire, or other material may be admitted in evidence if otherwise competent, material and relevant, provided a proper foundation is laid. *Frank v Cossitt Cement Products, Inc.* (1950) 197 Misc 670, 97 NYS2d 337. It was held that a proper foundation had been laid for the admissibility of the recording where the witness testified that the machine on which the recording was made was his, that he took care of the mechanical operation of the machine at the time the recording was made, that he had had possession of the wire spool since the making of the recording, that he had played it back before the trial, and that the recording constituted an accurate reproduction of the sounds he had heard coming from defendant's plant. *Frank v Cossitt Cement Products, Inc., supra.*

Before a sound recording is offered in evidence, it is necessary to identify sufficiently the voice recorded as that of the party against whom it is offered in evidence. *Epstein v Epstein* (1955) 285 AD 593, 139 NYS2d 451, app den 285 AD 1128, 141 NYS2d 819.

Typewritten transcripts of recordings are also admissible in evidence. *Applebaum v Applebaum* (1948, Sup) 84 NYS2d 505. A telephone conversation was recorded and the recording was sufficiently audible to permit the stenographer, by the use of earphones, to transcribe the conversation. The court properly permitted the transcribed notes to be read to the jury, after the stenographer laid the proper foundation by testifying about hearing, understanding and transcribing the conversation as played back from the tape, as well as testifying about the steps connecting the telephone conversation to the recording. *Applebaum v Applebaum, supra.*

When the tape recordings have been made by a participant in the conversation, proof of a chain of custody is not required for the introduction of tape recordings into evidence. *People v McGee* (1979) 49 NY2d 48, 424 NYS2d 157, cert den 466 US 942, 64 L Ed 2d 797, 100 S Ct 2166. A foundation may be established by a participant in the conversation who testifies that the conversation has been accurately and fairly reproduced and that the evidence has not been altered. *People v McGee, supra.* When the participant in a recorded conversation is available to testify that it was fairly and accurately reproduced on tape and that it has not been altered, a foundation is established and chain-of-custody evidence is not necessary. *People v Tayeh* (1983, 2d Dept) 96 AD2d 1045, 466 NYS2d 458.

The trial court did not err in refusing to admit into evidence a tape recording of a purported telephone conversation between the sex abuse victim and her stepfather. Neither participant testified about whether the conversation had been accurately and fairly reproduced. Although the individual who operated the tape recorder did testify, it was established that he did not hear the conversation while it was taking place. He was thus unable to establish that the recording constituted a complete, accurate and fair reproduction of the conversation. *Re Nicole T.* (1991, 3d Dept) 178 AD2d 849, 577 NYS2d 906.

A redacted "911" tape was properly admitted in evidence under the "prompt outcry" exception to the hearsay rule. *People v Smith* (1994, 1st Dept) 202 AD2d 366, 610 NYS2d 190.

§ 19:9 ADMISSIBILITY OF MAPS, DRAWINGS, DIAGRAMS, AND DISPLAYS — Maps, drawings, sketches and diagrams, illustrating the scenes of a transaction and the relative location of objects, may be admissible if material and relevant. *Poulos v Ferraiolo* (1962, 3d Dept) 17 AD2d 1006, 233 NYS2d 800. It must be demonstrated that they show with reasonable accuracy and correctness what they are alleged to depict. *Camden v New York* (1907) 119 AD 84, 103 NYS 971.

The diagrammatic representations do not always have to be of the particular object that is the subject of the testimony. They may be of such objects generally or of other objects of the same type and are used for illustrating testimony and indicating the principles involved. *Golden Eagle Farm Products, Inc. v Approved Dehydrating Co.* (1945, CA2 NY) 147 F2d 359, cert den 325 US 868, 89 L Ed 1987, 65 S Ct 1407.

The trial court properly excluded a transparent overlay that purportedly represented the distances at the accident scene but whose measurements were made by pacing the distances. It did not present accurate figures for the jury's consideration. *Feldsberg v Nitschke* (1980) 49 NY2d 636, 427 NYS2d 751.

The trial court properly excluded the police officer's diagram of the purported location of the vehicles at the time of the impact. The evidence showed that the vehicles had been moved prior to the time the officer arrived, the sole source of information on which the diagram was based was the bus driver, and the police officer took no measurements and made no independent investigation. *Campbell v Manhattan & Bronx Surface Transit Operating Auth.* (1981, 1st Dept) 81 AD2d 529, 438 NYS2d 87.

§ 19:10   ADMISSIBILITY OF MODELS AND CASTS — A model or cast may be admitted in evidence if it is material and relevant, and subject to establishing that it is an accurate depiction of what it purports to show. *Coolidge v New York* (1904) 99 AD 175, 90 NYS 1078, affd 185 NY 529, 77 NE 1192.

A witness testified to an accident that allegedly had been caused by the breaking of tongs. It was held proper to admit into evidence an artificial reproduction, in the form of a model, of a broken pin in the tongs. *McKeon v Proctor & Gamble Mfg. Co.* (1914) 162 AD 784, 147 NYS 1012.

It is proper to employ a human skull for the purpose of explaining to the jury the nature of the plaintiff's injury. *McNaier v Manhattan R. Co.* (1889, Sup) 4 NYS 310, affd 123 NY 664, 26 NE 750. A sculptured model prepared from photographs of a decedent was held inadmissible for the purpose of proving the resemblance between the decedent and a party who claimed to be his relative. *Re Wendel's Estate* (1933) 146 Misc 260, 262 NYS 41.

§ 19:11   EFFECT OF MARKS OR NOTATIONS ON DEMONSTRATIVE EVIDENCE —Photographs, pictures, casts, models, maps or diagrams otherwise admissible are not necessarily rendered inadmissible because of marks, memoranda, legends or other extraneous matter. *Clegg v Metropolitan S. R. Co.* (1896) 1 AD 207, 37 NYS 130, affd 159 NY 550, 54 NE 1089. Thus, when the party who has made the mark or writing explains it, or some other witness familiar with the facts testifies to the correctness of the item, it is not rendered inadmissible. *Clegg v Metropolitan S. R. Co., supra.*

§ 19:12   DISPLAYING PERSONAL INJURIES TO THE JURY

— If the plaintiff's physical condition is an issue, the plaintiff may be exhibited to the jury when this tends to make the physician's testimony more understandable. *Mulhado v Brooklyn C. R. Co.* (1864) 30 NY 370. If such an exhibition is intended to prejudice the minds of the jurors, however, it should not be permitted. *Clark v Brooklyn H. R. Co.* (1904) 177 NY 359, 69 NE 647.

It was unfair to permit a plaintiff who claimed to have sustained a nervous condition from an injury to act out the condition after he and his physicians testified about it, because the demonstration could be controlled by the witness. *Clark v Brooklyn H. R. Co., supra.* The display at trial of a child's amputated foot has been held improper. It was not necessary for the jury to understand the injury or the circumstances surrounding it, and it was intended only to arouse the prejudice and inflame the passions of the jury. *Rost v Brooklyn H. R. Co.* (1896) 10 AD 477, 41 NYS 1069.

However, the trial court did not err in permitting a plaintiff, who sustained a brachial plexus palsy, to partially disrobe and redress in the presence of the jury to demonstrate the limiting effect of his disabled arm and hand. The value of this evidence outweighed its potential for prejudice. In addition, there was no indication in the record that the plaintiff "faked" or otherwise exaggerated his limitations in this regard. *Sutherland v County of Nassau* (1993, 2d Dept) 190 AD2d 664, 593 NYS2d 287, app den 81 NY2d 710, 599 NYS2d 804.

A subject whose condition is relevant to the issue may be presented in open court to afford the trier of fact an opportunity to evaluate the alleged condition by the direct use of his senses. *Harvey v Mazal American Partners* (1992, 1st Dept) 179 AD2d 1, 581 NYS2d 748. For the purpose of showing the nature and extent of plaintiff's brain damage, the trial court properly permitted the plaintiff to be exhibited and questioned before the jury without being sworn as a witness. *Harvey v Mazal American Partners, supra.*

§ 19:13   BLOOD TESTS IN PATERNITY CASES — The determination of paternity or non-paternity by means of blood grouping tests is authorized by statute. Family Court Act § 418.

315

An exclusionary result is conclusive in regard to non-paternity. *Clark v Rysedorph* (1953) 281 AD 121, 118 NYS2d 103. However, the weight to be given such a result depends upon a showing that precautions were taken to ensure accurate results and that a scientific basis existed for the tests. *Commissioner of Welfare ex rel. Tyler v Costonie* (1950) 277 AD 90, 97 NYS2d 804.

CPLR 4518(c),(d) provide that all records, writings and other things referred to in CPLR 2306 and 2307, and any records or reports relating to the administration and analysis of a blood genetic marker test or a DNA test administered pursuant to Family Court Act §§ 418 and 532 are admissible in evidence and are *prima facie* evidence of the facts contained in them. They must bear a certification or authentication by the head of the hospital, laboratory, department or bureau of a municipal corporation or of the state or by an employee delegated for that purpose or by a qualified physician. CPLR 4518 (c), (d).

When a hospital record is in the custody of a warehouse or warehouseman, pursuant to a plan approved in writing by the state Commissioner of Health, admissibility under the statute may be established by a certification made by the manager of the warehouse. The certification must set forth: (1) the authority by which the record is held, including but not limited to a court order or order of the Commissioner or order or resolution of the governing party or official of the hospital, and (2) that the record has been in the exclusive custody of such warehouse or warehouseman since its receipt from the hospital or, if another has access to it, the name and address of such person and the date on which and the circumstances under which such person had access. Any warehouseman providing a certification required by the statute will have no liability for acts or omissions relating thereto except for intentional misconduct. CPLR 4518(c).

The human leucocyte antigen blood test is highly accurate on the issue of paternity. The court held that it should be accorded great weight in a proceeding to establish paternity. *Bowling on behalf of Morgan v Coney* (1983, 4th Dept) 91 AD2d 1195, 459 NYS2d 183. Although HLA test results are not conclusive on the issue of paternity, they are highly probative. *Utah ex rel. Pamela "WW" v Robert "XX"* (1994, 3d Dept) ___ AD2d ___, 609 NYS2d 703.

In a paternity proceeding, the evidence showed that petitioner and respondent had sexual intercourse only 259 days before the child was born, the results of a blood test were inconclusive, and the respondent raised the possibility that another had had access to the mother. The petitioner wholly failed to adduce any medical proof explaining the apparent shortness of her gestation period. The court could not say that petitioner had met her burden of proof, establishing the respondent to be the father of the child, by clear, convincing and satisfactory evidence. Accordingly, the court reversed and remitted for further proceedings. *L v M* (1974, 3d Dept) 46 AD2d 935, 361 NYS2d 741, later app (3d Dept) 50 AD2d 1009, 377 NYS2d 225.

Even in a case where a third-party has had intercourse with the mother during the critical time of conception, the human leucocyte antigen blood tissue test may establish paternity on the part of the putative father. *Amy J. v Brian K.* (1990, 3d Dept) 161 AD2d 1022, 557 NYS2d 595.

Respondent's paternity was established by clear and convincing evidence, even though the mother admitted to having sexual intercourse with two other men during the possible period of conception. The HLA test excluded the possibility that either of the other two was the child's father and the HLA test result established a 97.5% probability that respondent was the child's father. *Cattaraugus County Dept. of Social Services v Brown* (1991, 4th Dept) 176 AD2d 1205, 576 NYS2d 703.

Where a blood grouping test resulted in the exclusion of the respondent as the father of the child, the court denied the motion of the mother for a second test. The court also ruled that she would be given the opportunity to rebut this evidence. *Brian v Johns* (1974) 78 Misc 2d 219, 358 NYS2d 593. Where there were obvious discrepancies between the results of two human leucocyte antigen tests administered to the putative father, a retest was ordered to resolve the obvious discrepancy between the two results. *Shepherd v Skeete* (1991, 1st Dept) 169 AD2d 626, 564 NYS2d 760.

The trial court properly refused to consider the results of the party's privately arranged DNA test. There was no evidence of the procedures followed by the laboratory conducting the test. In addition, the reliability of this test depended heavily on the father's assurance that he did not tamper with the blood samples when he personally delivered them to the laboratory. *Barbara A. M. v Gerard J. M.* (1991, 2d Dept) 178 AD2d 412, 577 NYS2d 110.

The petitioner introduced the results of a human leucocyte antigen test that indicated a high probability of paternity on the part of the putative father. Although the results were probative, they were not conclusive. The mother's testimony did not convincingly demonstrate that she was engaged in a sexual relationship with the putative father during the period of conception. She also admitted that she was in a continuing sexual relationship with a former boyfriend during the period of time when her child was conceived. *Sherry G. v George F.* (1992, 2d Dept) 183 AD2d 825, 584 NYS2d 316.

The trial court properly concluded that the human leukocyte antigen test was only a factor which, when combined with the mother's testimony that during the time of conception she had sexual relations with no one other than respondent, supplied the clear and convincing evidence needed to establish paternity. *Helen NN v Daniel OO* (1992, 3d Dept) 187 AD2d 860, 589 NYS2d 718.

A human leucocyte antigen blood test that indicates a 99.98% probability that respondent is the child's father is entitled to great weight. *Stone v Ilardo* (1993, 4th Dept) 191 AD2d 965, 595 NYS2d 265.

The mother testified that she had intercourse with the putative father during the period of conception without using birth control and a human leucocyte antigen blood test revealed the probability of respondent's paternity at 99.94%. The fact that the mother admitted that she had protected intercourse with another man on one occasion near the period of conception was not necessarily fatal to the paternity proceeding. *Otsego County Dep't of Social Servs. on behalf of Debby UU v John VV* (1993, 3d Dept) 196 AD2d 918, 602 NYS2d 228.

§ 19:14   EXHIBITING THE CHILD IN PATERNITY CASES —
In paternity cases, the child may not be exhibited to demonstrate an alleged resemblance to the putative father. *Bilkovie v Loeb* (1913) 156 AD 719, 141 NYS 279. Thus, in an action to recover

damages for a carnal assault as a result of which it is claimed that the plaintiff gave birth to a child, it was improper to exhibit the child to the jury for the purpose of showing resemblance to the alleged father. *Beuschel v Manowitz* (1934) 151 Misc 899, 271 NYS 277, revd 241 AD 888, 272 NYS 165, motion den 265 NY 509, 193 NE 295.

§ 19:15   EXPERIMENTS AND TESTS — The result of an experiment or test is admissible if it appears that the test was conducted under such conditions that the evidence will be reliable. *Thomas v Central Greyhound Lines, Inc.* (1958, 1st Dept) 6 AD2d 649, 180 NYS2d 461.

It was proper to receive in evidence a patch test of a substance the defendant had used in his beauty shop in the course of treating the plaintiff. *Gualtieri v Ferraro* (1946) 270 AD 1067, 63 NYS2d 40. Exclusion of a medical witness's testimony regarding the conditions for which an electroencephalogram is a test was held to be error. *Mayole v B. Crystal & Son, Inc.* (1943) 266 AD 1008, 44 NYS2d 411. The exclusion of the electroencephalogram was likewise held to be error when a proper foundation had been laid. *Mayole v B. Crystal & Son, Inc., supra.*

Although the conditions under which the experiment is conducted need not be identical with those at the time of the occurrence, there must be a substantial similarity. *Green v Long Island R. Co.* (1909) 131 AD 277, 115 NYS 590. The existence of some variation between conditions at the time of experiment and those at the time of the occurrence affects the weight of the testimony but will not result in its exclusion. *Washington v Long Island R. R. Co.* (1961, 2d Dept) 13 AD2d 710, 214 NYS2d 115.

However, if the conditions are substantially dissimilar from those prevailing at the time of the occurrence in question, the evidence is not admissible. *Kratche v New York C. R. Co.* (1930) 228 AD 820, 240 NYS 443. The test for determining the extent to which variations in conditions are permissible is whether such variation will confuse or mislead the jury. *People v Fiori* (1908) 123 AD 174, 108 NYS 416.

An experiment or test may be conducted during the course of a trial, in the discretion of the trial court. *MacMahon v Brooklyn & N. Y. Ferry Co.* (1896) 10 AD 376, 41 NYS 1026, reh den 18 AD

626, 48 NYS 1109 and app den 153 NY 667, 48 NE 1105 and error dismd 166 US 718, 41 L Ed 1186, 17 S Ct 992. Thus, it is permissible to test the eyesight of a witness by directing his attention to printed characters and figures in the courtroom. *MacMahon v Brooklyn & N. Y. Ferry Co., supra.* However, it has been held improper to test the accuracy of a stenographer. *Underhill v Waite* (1880) 9 NY Week Dig 438, 9 Daly 83.

The result of an experiment is admissible only if the conditions under which it is conducted are sufficiently similar to those existing at the time in question to make the result achieved by the test relevant to the issue. *Weinstein v Daman* (1987, 2d Dept) 132 AD2d 547, 517 NYS2d 278, app dismd without op 70 NY2d 872, 523 NYS2d 497 In a medical malpractice action, plaintiff claimed that he was unable to see defendant doctor's attorney because of the loss of vision in his right eye. It was error to permit defense counsel to test the plaintiff's credibility by asking each juror to sit in the witness chair, cover his or her right eye and determine whether the defense attorney could be seen with the other eye. There was no assurance that the vision of each juror was similar to that of plaintiff. In addition, the court took no measures to assure that each juror sat in the same position as the plaintiff had and looked in the same direction. *Weinstein v Daman, supra.*

A products liability action was brought against the distributor and manufacturer of a motorcycle for injuries allegedly caused by negligent and defective design. Plaintiff had sold his motorcycle for scrap shortly after the accident. Defendants offered evidence of the impact experiments conducted by their expert, using a similar gas tank but one that had been manufactured three years earlier than the one involved in the accident. It was error for the trial court to exclude evidence of the result. The fact that the tanks were manufactured in different years went to the weight to be given to the evidence, not its admissibility. *Bolm v Triumph Corp.* (1979, 4th Dept) 71 AD2d 429, 422 NYS2d 969.

A polygraph test was administered by a detective who had taken a course in the use of the machine for six weeks but had no prior training in such work. It was held that he was not sufficiently trained and expert to justify the use of the test in a court of law. In addition, the testimony of an expert who was not present when the tests were given was not sufficient to remedy the deficiency. *Pereira v Pereira* (1974) 35 NY2d 301, 361 NYS2d 148.

The trial court properly ruled a laboratory report on a blood sample inadmissible. The doctor who drew the blood sample gave it to a Fire Department chauffeur whose name he could not recall and who was not produced at the trial. There was no accounting for the custody of the blood sample for more than 36 hours. No testimony was adduced to indicate who received the sample at the laboratory, its condition on receipt, the size of the vial containing the specimen, whether it was refrigerated during the long interval, how the vial was labeled or identified, or the quantity or condition of its contents upon arrival. Moreover, there could be no reasonable assurance of the unchanged condition of the blood sample. *Amaro v New York* (1976) 40 NY2d 30, 386 NYS2d 19.

In an automobile personal injury action, the trial court properly excluded evidence of a breathalyzer test administered to a defendant. No evidence was presented to establish that the chemicals used in the test were of the proper kind and mixed in the proper proportions. *Miller v Farina* (1977, 4th Dept) 58 AD2d 731, 395 NYS2d 867.

Neither expert testimony nor detailed findings by the scientific community are essential before scientific tests or procedures are recognized. The court may find scientific tests reliable based on the general acceptance of the procedures as shown through legal writings and judicial opinions. *Lahey v Kelly* (1987) 71 NY2d 135, 524 NYS2d 30.

In a personal injury action arising out of an automobile accident, it was error for the trial court to prevent plaintiffs from introducing evidence of defendant's refusal to submit to a breathalyzer test after the accident. *Bazza v Banscher* (1988, 2d Dept) 143 AD2d 715, 533 NYS2d 285. Although evidence of refusal may be of limited probative force, the refusal may be regarded as conduct inconsistent with defendant's position on trial that he was not intoxicated at the time of the accident. *Bazza v Banscher, supra.*

RESEARCH REFERENCES

American Law Reports

15 ALR5th 119, Admissibility of evidence of repairs, change of conditions, or precautions taken after

10 ALR5th 663, Admissibility of evidence of polygraph test results, or offer or refusal to take test, in action for malicious prosecution

84 ALR4th 313, Admissibility of DNA identification evidence

82 ALR4th 980, Permissibility of in-court demonstration to show effect of injury in action for bodily injury

79 ALR4th 576, Admissibility of lie detector test results, or of offer or refusal to take test, in attorney disciplinary proceeding

70 ALR4th 984, Intentional spoliation of evidence, interfering with prospective civil action, as actionable

58 ALR4th 160, Products liability: sufficiency of evidence to support product misuse defense in actions concerning bottles, cans, storage tanks, or other containers

58 ALR4th 131, Products liability: sufficiency of evidence to support product misuse defense in actions concerning gas and electric appliances

58 ALR4th 76, Products liability: sufficiency of evidence to support product misuse defense in actions concerning paint, cleaners, or other chemicals

58 ALR4th 40, Products liability: sufficiency of evidence to support product misuse defense in actions concerning cosmetics and other personal care products

58 ALR4th 7, Products liability: sufficiency of evidence to support product misuse defense in actions concerning food, drugs, and other products intended for ingestion

57 ALR4th 1111, Admissibility of school records under hearsay exceptions

56 ALR4th 1105, Thermographic tests: admissibility of test results in personal injury suits

55 ALR4th 1062, Products liability: sufficiency of evidence to support product misuse defense in actions concerning lawnmowers

55 ALR4th 1010, Products liability: sufficiency of evidence to support product misuse defense in actions concerning electrical generation

and transmission equipment

52 ALR4th 276, Products liability: sufficiency of evidence to support product misuse defense in actions concerning wearing apparel

50 ALR4th 1226, Products liability: sufficiency of evidence to support product misuse defense in actions concerning athletic, exercise, or recreational equipment

47 ALR4th 1202, Admissibility of voice stress evaluation test results or of statements made during test

43 ALR4th 579, Admissibility and weight of blood-grouping tests in disputed paternity cases

41 ALR4th 877, Admissibility of visual recording of event or matter other than that giving rise to litigation or prosecution

41 ALR4th 812, Admissibility of visual recording of event or matter giving rise to litigation or prosecution

37 ALR4th 510, Admissibility of results of computer analysis of defendant's mental state

37 ALR4th 167, Admissibility, weight and sufficiency of Human Leukocyte Antigen (HLA) tissue typing tests in paternity cases

11 ALR4th 1245, Propriety of discovery order permitting "destructive testing" of chattel in civil case

97 ALR3d 1220, Measure of damages where vendor, after execution of contract for sale but before conveyance of property, removes part of property contracted for

97 ALR3d 294, Admissibility and weight of voice print evidence

66 ALR3d 637, Use of videotape to take deposition for presentation at civil trial in state court

58 ALR3d 598, Admissibility in evidence of sound recording as affected by hearsay and best evidence rule

57 ALR3d 746, Omission of inaudibility of portions of sound recording as affecting its admissibility in evidence

23 ALR3d 825, Eminent domain: admissibility of photographs or models of property condemned

11 ALR3d 1015, Admissibility of expert evidence to decipher illegible document

9 ALR3d 976, Admissibility in evidence, in automobile negligence action, of charts showing braking distance, reaction times, etc.

5 ALR3d 303, Preliminary proof, verification, or authentication of x-rays requisite to their introduction in evidence in civil cases

ALR QUICK INDEX: Demonstrative Evidence; Experiments or Tests; Motion Pictures; Photographs; Models; Pictures and Photographs; Sound Recordings; Videotape; Voice; X-rays

American Jurisprudence 2d

29 AM JUR 2d, Evidence §§ 769-833

American Jurisprudence Proof of Facts

27 AM JUR PROOF OF FACTS 3d 213, Use of Statistical Evidence in Proving Churning Of Securities Accounts

26 AM JUR PROOF OF FACTS 3d 395, Water Pollution: Proof of Water Quality Under The Clean Water Act

18 AM JUR PROOF OF FACTS 3d 515, Intentional Spoliation of Evidence

16 AM JUR PROOF OF FACTS 3d 493, Foundation for Contemporaneous Videotape Evidence

15 AM JUR PROOF OF FACTS 3d 595, Questioned Document Examination–Identification of Handwriting on Document

9 AM JUR PROOF OF FACTS 3d 115, Reconstruction of Traffic Accidents

8 AM JUR PROOF OF FACTS 3d 145, Use of CAT Scans in Litigation

4 AM JUR PROOF OF FACTS 3d 73, Admissibility and Reliability of Electrocardiogram

49 AM JUR PROOF OF FACTS 2d 293, Products Liability: Proof That Defect Was Not Cause of Injury

44 AM JUR PROOF OF FACTS 2d 707, Foundation for admission of map, diagram, or chart

43 AM JUR PROOF OF FACTS 2d 217, Footprint Identification

40 AM JUR PROOF OF FACTS 2d 1, Blood Typing

38 AM JUR PROOF OF FACTS 2d 377, Hair Analysis

38 AM JUR PROOF OF FACTS 2d 145, Foundation for Admissibility of Hospital Records and X-rays

10 AM JUR PROOF OF FACTS 2d 365, Nondestructive Testing of Material-X-ray, Gamaray, and Neutron Radiography

American Jurisprudence Trials

140 AM JUR TRIALS 249, Using or Challenging a "Day-in-the-Life" Documentary in a Personal Injury Law Suit

51 AM JUR TRIALS 493, Structural Damage to Residential Buildings

48 AM JUR TRIALS 1, Audio Recordings: Evidence, Experts, and Technology

42 AM JUR TRIALS 313, Uses, Techniques, and Reliability of Polygraph Testing

39 AM JUR TRIALS 261, Planning and Producing a "Day-in-the-Life" Video-tape in a Personal Injury Lawsuit

3 AM JUR TRIALS 507, Preparing and Using Diagrams

3 AM JUR TRIALS 427 Preparing and Using Experimental Evidence

3 AM JUR TRIALS 377, Preparing and Using Models

3 AM JUR TRIALS 1, Preparing and Using Photographs in Civil Cases

2 AM JUR TRIALS 669, Preparing and Using Maps

Other Resources

8 CARMODY-WAIT 2d, Presentation of the Case §§ 56:13-56:15

Auto-Cite®: Any case citation herein can be checked for form, parallel references, later history and annotation references through the Auto-Cite computer research system.

CHAPTER 20

THE VIEW

§ 20:1 VIEW OF PREMISES — In an action for waste, the referee, or the judge if the case is tried without a jury, may in his discretion view the premises and direct attorneys for the parties to attend accordingly. If the case is tried with a jury, the court may in its discretion direct a view by the jury. Real Property Actions and Proceedings Law § 821. Before any judgment may be rendered in the Court of Claims for appropriation of land, the value of which exceeds $5,000, the judge rendering or one of the judges concurring in the judgment is required to visit the premises affected thereby. Court of Claims Act § 12(4).

CPLR 4110-c permits viewing of the premises during a civil trial. Section 4110-c(1) of the CPLR provides that during the course of a trial, when the court is of the opinion that it will be helpful to the jury, in determining any material factual issue, to have a viewing or observation of the premises or place where alleged injuries to the person or property were sustained in an accident or occurrence claimed to have been the cause of such injuries, or any other premises or place involved in the case, the court may in its discretion, at any time before the commencement of summations, order that the jury be conducted to such premises or place.

CPLR 4110-c(2) provides that in such a case, the jury must be kept together throughout, under the supervision of an appropriate public servant or servants appointed by the court, and the court itself also must be present throughout. Subdivision (2) further provides that the parties to the action and counsel for them may

327

as a matter of right be present throughout, but they may waive such right.

CPLR 4110-c(3) provides that the purpose of such an inspection is solely to permit a visual observation by the jury of the premises or place in question. Neither the court, the parties, counsel nor the jurors may engage in discussion or argumentation concerning the significance or implications of anything under observation or concerning any issue in the case.

The trial court did not abuse its discretion in denying the jury a view of the scene of the accident. There was no significant dispute regarding the appearance of a filler cap involved and the surrounding concrete. In addition, the jury was apprised of the nature of the scene by the graphic photographs introduced into evidence by each side and referred to in the expert testimony. *Schechtman v Lappin* (1990, 1st Dept) 161 AD2d 118, 554 NYS2d 846.

§ 20:2   UNAUTHORIZED VIEW — One of the primary dangers of unauthorized viewings by a juror is that evidence may be considered by the jury against a party who has no opportunity to confront the "witness" or to rebut his evidence. Where the sole juror who made the unauthorized visit and viewed the scene of the accident was the only juror voting for the party seeking to overturn the verdict, there was no prejudice requiring reversal. *Alford v Sventek* (1981) 53 NY2d 743, 439 NYS2d 339.

RESEARCH REFERENCES

American Law Reports

11 ALR3d 918, Prejudicial effect of unauthorized view by jury in civil case of scene of accident or premises in question

85 ALR2d 512, Propriety of permitting view by jury in civil personal injury or death action as affected by claimed change of conditions since accident or incident

77 ALR2d 548, Right to view by jury in condemnation proceedings

ALR QUICK INDEX: View by Jury

American Jurisprudence 2d

75 AM JUR 2d, Trial §§ 72-86

American Jurisprudence Pleading and Practice

23 Am Jur Pl & Pr Forms (Rev), Trial, Forms 91-95

Other Resources

Auto-Cite®: Any case citation herein can be checked for form, parallel references, later history and annotation references through the Auto-Cite computer research system.

CHAPTER 21

DOCUMENTARY EVIDENCE

§ 21:1   DOCUMENTARY EVIDENCE, IN GENERAL — Documentary evidence may be any written instrument to which a party did or did not affix his signature and from which written instrument evidence material to the issues is supplied. *Woltin v Metropolitan Life Ins. Co.* (1938) 167 Misc 382, 4 NYS2d 296. Such evidence is in the form of a writing or writings; it is such evidence as is furnished by written instruments, inscriptions and documents of all kinds. *Ticknor v Ticknor* (1960) 23 Misc 2d 257, 200 NYS2d 661.

To the extent that a document establishes facts in issue, it is admissible. *Diamond v Davis* (1942, Sup) 38 NYS2d 93, affd 265 AD 919, 39 NYS2d 412, affd 292 NY 552. Documentary evidence must be competent under all the rules of evidence. Thus, a document that is otherwise inadmissible does not become admissible simply because it is made in the regular course of business. *Poses v Travelers' Ins. Co.* (1935) 245 AD 304, 281 NYS 126.

An action was brought against a seller of a tent for personal injury and wrongful death resulting from a tent fire. A laboratory report prepared by an employee of the tent producer who was deceased at the time of the trial was properly held not to qualify as an exception to the hearsay rule under records kept in the ordinary course of business. A notation appeared in the report regarding the composition of the material, but the source of the notation was undisclosed. *Rush v Sears, Roebuck & Co.* (1983, 3d Dept) 92 AD2d 1072, 461 NYS2d 559.

In addition, a document must ordinarily be authenticated before it is admissible; that is, there must be some proof that the document is genuine. This requirement applies whether the document is private, *People ex rel. Bruckner v Wyner* (1955) 207 Misc 673, 142 NYS2d 393, or public, *Lash, Inc. v A. C. Ogden Milk Co.* (1937) 163 Misc 407, 297 NYS 1008.

Certain business records may be received in evidence without having been authenticated by their maker, if they are certified in accordance with CPLR 4518(c). However, the admission into evidence of an FS-25 form and a police report, without the benefit of any testimony establishing their authenticity or accuracy and without proper certification, was error. *Peerless Ins. Co. v Milloul* (1988, 2d Dept) 140 AD2d 346, 527 NYS2d 838.

A physician's office records are admissible in evidence under the business record exception to the hearsay rule. These records may be received in evidence whether the physician is available to testify regarding the substance and content of the records, *Napolitano v Branks* (1988, 2d Dept) 141 AD2d 705, 529 NYS2d 824, or fails to appear and testify, provided that the proper foundation is made that the records are authentic and were the physician's regular office records made and kept in the ordinary course of business. *Wilson v Bodian* (1987, 2d Dept) 130 AD2d 221, 519

NYS2d 126. All legible entries germane to diagnosis and treatment contained in the physician's office records will be received, including medical opinions and conclusions. *Wilson v Bodian, supra.*

However, if the physician who made the records does not testify, any personal abbreviations or symbols that are beyond the ken of the jury should not be received, in the absence of medical testimony that such abbreviations have a well-known and accepted meaning. *Wilson v Bodian, supra.* Physician's day-to-day office records must be distinguished from medical reports prepared for attorneys, which are generated for purposes of litigation and are not made in the ordinary course of patient care. *Wilson v Bodian, supra.*

§ 21:2   WHEN AUTHENTICATION IS EXCUSED — Although documentary evidence must be authenticated before it can be admissible, such proof of genuineness may be excused by some action of the adversary.

Authentication is not required if a party admits the genuineness of the document pursuant to a demand served by his adversary. CPLR 3123. If a document is acknowledged, proved or certified in the manner provided by statute, authentication is not necessary. CPLR 4538. Thus, it was held that a corporate acknowledgment by a religious corporation on each of the bonds sued upon was *prima facie* proof of proper execution of the instrument. It could be overthrown only on proof so clear and convincing that it amounted to a moral certainty. *Bernstein v Friedlander* (1968) 58 Misc 2d 492, 296 NYS2d 409.

When a party fails to interpose a denial in a required responsive pleading, this may be an admission of the genuineness of a document, thereby waiving the requirement of authentication. CPLR 3018(a).

Even though x-rays contained in plaintiff's medical records were not authenticated pursuant to CPLR 4532-a, they were nevertheless admissible as business records under CPLR 4518 and CPLR 2306. The last sentence of CPLR 4532-a expressly provides that nothing contained in the section will prohibit the admissibility of an x-ray in evidence in a personal injury action if it is otherwise admissible. *Hoffman v New York* (1988) 141 Misc 2d 893, 535 NYS2d 342.

It was proper for the trial court to consider a letter submitted by plaintiff's counsel at oral argument when there was no objection to consideration of the document. *Akivis v Drucker* (1991, 1st Dept) 177 AD2d 349, 576 NYS2d 119.

§ 21:3 AUTHENTICATION OF PRIVATE WRITINGS — All written documents and instruments, other than public records, are private writings. This includes such instruments as deeds, commercial paper, invoices, bills of sale, bank statements, leases, contracts and mortgages. Such writings must be authenticated; that is, their genuineness must be established. *People ex rel. Bruckner v Wyner* (1955) 207 Misc 673, 142 NYS2d 393.

The genuineness of a signature may be established by the testimony of competent witnesses. *Re Seaman's Will* (1949) 275 AD 484, 90 NYS2d 336, affd 300 NY 756. The testimony of a handwriting expert is admissible to prove the genuineness of a signature. *Re Burbank* (1905) 104 AD 312, 93 NYS 866, affd 185 NY 559, 77 NE 1183. However, the party identifying the handwriting need not be an expert. *People v Corey* (1896) 148 NY 476, 42 NE 1066.

§ 21:4 AUTHENTICATION OF ATTESTED DOCUMENTS — Under the common law rule, it was necessary to prove the execution of every attested instrument by producing the subscribing witness when that was possible. *Jones v Underwood* (1858) 28 Barb 481. Although the production of the subscribing witness was required, it was not necessary that such witness remember the circumstances of the execution of the instrument. It was sufficient that the witness recognize his signature and, from that, be able to state his belief that the document had been executed in his presence. *Merrill v Ithaca & O. R. Co.* (1837) 16 Wend 586.

This rule no longer applies. It is not necessary to call the subscribing witness unless a writing requires a subscribing witness for its validity. CPLR 4537.

In the case of a will, it is necessary to prove its execution by the production of the subscribing witnesses unless their absence is satisfactorily explained. Surrogate's Court Practice Act (SCPA) §

1404. In the latter event, it is possible to prove the will by other methods. SCPA § 1405.

The testimony of any subscribing witness may also be unnecessary if such witness has executed an affidavit, during the testator's lifetime or after the testator's death, stating such facts as would, if uncontested, establish the genuineness of the will, the validity of its execution, and that the testator at the time of execution of the will was in all respects competent to make the will and not under any restraint. SCPA § 1406. The simplified procedure may not be employed, however, if any person entitled to process in the proceedings objects or if the court, for any other reason, requires that the subscribing witness appear. SCPA § 1406.

§ 21:5 AUTHENTICATION OF RECORDED DOCUMENTS —
It is provided by statute that the certificate of the acknowledgment or the proof of a conveyance, or the record, or the transcript of the record of such a conveyance, is not conclusive. It may be rebutted and the effect thereof may be contested by a party affected thereby. Real Property Actions and Proceedings Law (RPAPL) § 301(1).

If it appears that the acknowledgment or the proof was taken upon the oath of an interested witness or an incompetent one, the conveyance, or the record or transcript of the record thereof, will not be received in evidence until its execution is established by other competent proof. There is an exception in a case where title to the land conveyed or affected by such a conveyance or instrument has passed to a subsequent purchaser for a valuable consideration. RPAPL § 301(2).

§ 21:6 AUTHENTICATION OF STATUTE — The courts must
take judicial notice of the statutes of the United States and of every state, territory and jurisdiction of the United States. CPLR 4511(a). The courts may take judicial notice of the laws of foreign countries or their political subdivisions. CPLR 4511(b).

No proof is necessary for matters that must be judicially noticed by the court. With respect to matters of which the court may take judicial notice, such as the law of a foreign jurisdiction, it has been held that a photostatic copy of statutes and the book from which the photostatic copies were made was sufficient evidence. *Lady Nelson, Ltd. v Creole Petroleum Corp.* (1961, CA2 NY) 286 F2d 684.

A published or printed copy of a law of New York State is entitled to be read into evidence if it is: (1) contained in a book or pamphlet published under the direction of the temporary president of the senate and speaker of the assembly pursuant to the provisions of Legislative Law § 44; or (2) certified to be a slip copy of a session law printed under the direction of the temporary president of the senate and speaker of the assembly; or (3) contained in a book or pamphlet, or supplement thereto, and certified by the temporary president of the senate and speaker of the assembly to be a correct transcript of the text of such law as last amended; or (4) certified as a correct transcript of the text of such law by the Secretary of State. New York Public Officers Law § 70-b.

§ 21:7 AUTHENTICATION OF CODE, RULE OR REGULATION OF NEW YORK STATE —Any code, rule or regulation of the State of New York may be read in evidence from the official compilation or supplement to it. Executive Law § 106. To entitle any copy of a code, rule or regulation published in a publication other than the official compilation or supplement to it to be read in evidence, the same book or pamphlet must contain a printed certificate of the secretary of state that such copy is a correct transcript of the text of the code, rule or regulation as published in such official compilation or supplement thereto. Executive Law § 106.

§ 21:8 AUTHENTICATION OF NEW YORK CITY ADMINISTRATIVE CODE — A published or printed copy of the New York City administrative code will be entitled to be read into evidence if it is contained in a book or pamphlet or supplement thereto and certified by the temporary president of the senate and the speaker of the assembly to be a correct transcript of the text of such code as last amended. Whenever the provisions of such code contain amendments, additions or repeals effected by passage of local laws by the New York City council, certification by the temporary president of the senate and the speaker of the assembly will not be made unless prior thereto certified or official copies of such local laws have been transmitted by the city clerk of New York City to the New York state legislative bill drafting commission at its office in Albany. New York Public Officers Law § 70-b(2).

§ 21:9 AUTHENTICATION OF COURT PAPERS AND RECORDS
— Ordinarily, judicial records are proved by certified copy. CPLR 4540; CPLR 4541.

If the record to be proved is that of a New York State court, it must be accompanied by a certificate signed by or with a facsimile of the signature of the clerk of a court having legal custody of a record and, except when the copy is used in the same court or before one of its officers, with the seal of the court affixed. CPLR 4540(b).

When the copy is attested by an officer of another jurisdiction, it must be accompanied by a certificate that such officer has legal custody of the record and that his signature is believed to be genuine. Such certificate will be made by a judge of a court of record of the district or political subdivision in which the record is kept, with the seal of the court affixed. The certificate may also be made by any public officer having a seal of office and having official duties in that district or political subdivision with respect to the subject matter of the record, with the seal of his office affixed. CPLR 4540(c).

§ 21:10 AUTHENTICATION OF RECORDS OF CORPORA-TIONS
— Corporate records and minutes, properly authenticated, may be admitted in evidence to prove the acts of a corporation, persons who are its stockholders, proceedings of stockholders' meetings and meetings of the board of directors, and, when the solvency of the corporation is in issue, its financial condition. *Rudd v Robinson* (1891) 126 NY 113, 26 NE 1046.

The record of corporate acts contained in the regular books, the correctness of which is authenticated by the officer in charge, usually renders the record admissible in evidence. *Diamond v Davis* (1942, Sup) 38 NYS2d 93, affd 265 AD 919, 39 NYS2d 412, affd 292 NY 552.

§ 21:11 AUTHENTICATION OF A LETTER
— If parties to a transaction subsequently engage in litigation, written communications between them are competent evidence of the terms of the

transaction. *Eppens, Smith & Wiemann Co. v Littlejohn* (1900) 164 NY 187, 58 NE 19.

The mere fact that a letter purports to have been written and signed by a particular person does not necessarily establish its authenticity and genuineness for the purpose of rendering it admissible in evidence. *Material Men's Mercantile Ass'n v Material Men's Credit Agency, Inc.* (1920) 191 AD 73, 180 NYS 801. Such letter must be authenticated. *Re Clarke* (1932) 145 Misc 660, 260 NYS 750, revd on other grounds 240 AD 728, 240 AD 766, 265 NYS 1035. However, when a letter is received by mail and purports to be an answer from a party to whom a prior letter has been sent, authentication is not required. *Todd Protectograph Co. v Wells Fargo & Co. Express* (1920) 111 Misc 282, 181 NYS 128.

§ 21:12 AUTHENTICATION OF A FAMILY BIBLE AND CHURCH RECORDS — A family Bible is admissible in evidence even if it has not been authenticated. *Hunt v Johnson* (1859) 19 NY 279. However, entries in a family Bible are not admissible as proof of the matters recorded if better evidence is available. For example, if the party making the entries is alive and able to testify, that would constitute better evidence. *Leggett v Boyd* (1829) 3 Wend 376.

Church registers and records are likewise admissible in evidence if made *ante litem motam*, in the course of the business of the party making the entries. *Hartshorn v Metropolitan Life Ins. Co.* (1900) 55 AD 471, 67 NYS 13. A party applied for letters of administration, claiming to be the son of the decedent. The church record of his baptism on its face showed him not to be the son of decedent. Such record was competent evidence on the question of pedigree on behalf of the opposing party. *Re Greco's Estate* (1915) 90 Misc 241, 154 NYS 306. A baptismal record is not, however, admissible as proof of a party's age. *Syrowik v Foster* (1924) 210 AD 816, 206 NYS 966.

§ 21:13 AUTHENTICATION OF ANCIENT DOCUMENTS — For a document to be admissible in evidence under the ancient document exception to the hearsay rule, it must be properly authenticated. It must be free of any indication of fraud or invalidity. *Fairchild v Union Ferry Co.* (1923) 121 Misc 513, 201 NYS

295, affd 212 AD 823, 207 NYS 835, affd 240 NY 666, 148 NE 750. In addition, it must be shown to be more than 30 years of age. *Fairchild v Union Ferry Co., supra.*

To show that the document is free of suspicion of fraud or illegality, it must be shown to have been in such custody that such suspicion will not attach to the document. *Coleman v Bruch* (1909) 132 AD 716, 117 NYS 582. When documents are found in the custody of people who might be naturally and reasonably expected to have them in their possession or in the possession of persons who have an interest in such documents, they are considered to be in the type of custody that gives them authenticity as ancient documents. *Dodge v Gallatin* (1891) 130 NY 117, 29 NE 107. Thus, the records of a county board of supervisors were in the proper custody for the purposes of having them admitted as ancient documents. The records were more than 30 years old and were in the custody of the county clerk. *Re Webster* (1905) 106 AD 360, 94 NYS 1050, affd 186 NY 549, 79 NE 1118.

Occasionally, records claimed to be ancient documents have been denied admissibility on the ground that they were not shown to have been in the custody of a proper custodian. *Longworth v East River Nat'l Bank* (1914) 160 AD 737, 145 NYS 1051, affd 220 NY 718, 116 NE 1058.

Plaintiff brought an action for damages, claiming encroachment on her real property. A paper survey by a certified surveyor was held not to be admissible as an ancient document. There was no proof that the survey had been recorded. Additionally, the survey was dated June 30, 1972, and the alleged encroachment had begun in 1969 or 1970. *Greenberg v Manlon Realty, Inc.* (1974, 2d Dept) 43 AD2d 968, 352 NYS2d 494.

RESEARCH REFERENCES

American Law Reports

7 ALR4th 638, Admissibility in evidence of professional directories

7 ALR4th 8, Admissibility of computerized private business records

84 ALR3d 598, Restricting public access to judicial records of state courts

83 ALR3d 824, Restricting access to judicial records of pending adoption

proceedings

83 ALR3d 800, Restricting access to judicial records of concluded adoption proceedings

80 ALR3d 456, Admissibility under state law of hospital record relating to intoxication or sobriety of patient

80 ALR3d 405, Requirement of notice as condition for admission in evidence of summary of voluminous records

72 ALR3d 1243, Construction and effect of § 1-202 of the Uniform Commercial Code dealing with documents which are prima facie evidence of their own authenticity and genuineness

71 ALR3d 232, Proof of public records kept or stored on electronic computing equipment

69 ALR3d 104, Admissibility under uniform business records as evidence act or similar statutes of medical report made by consulting physician to treating physician

84 ALR Fed 668, Admissibility of depositions under Federal Evidence Rule 804(b)(1)

83 ALR Fed 554, Federal Rules of Evidence: Admissibility, pursuant to Rule 1004(1), of other evidence of contents of writing, recording, or photograph, where originals were allegedly lost or destroyed

ALR QUICK INDEX: Documentary Evidence

American Jurisprudence 2d

29 AM JUR 2d, Evidence §§ 834-913

American Jurisprudence Proof of Facts

29 AM JUR PROOF OF FACTS 3d 549, The Effects of Alterations to Documents

27 AM JUR PROOF OF FACTS 3d 213, Use of Statistical Evidence in Proving Churning of Securities Accounts

23 AM JUR PROOF OF FACTS 3d 621, Examination and Identification of Photocopies and Photocopiers

23 AM JUR PROOF OF FACTS 3d 315, Foundation for Audio Recording As Evidence

16 AM JUR PROOF OF FACTS 3d 493, Foundation for Contemporaneous Videotape Evidence

15 AM JUR PROOF OF FACTS 3d 595, Questioned Document Examination-Identification of Handwriting on Document

50 AM JUR PROOF OF FACTS 2d 321, Ancient Documents

44 AM JUR PROOF OF FACTS 2d 707, Foundation for Admission of Map,

Diagram, or Chart

38 Am Jur Proof of Facts 2d 145, Foundation for Admissibility of Hospital Records and X-rays

34 Am Jur Proof of Facts 2d 509, Foundation for Offering Business Records in Evidence

1 Am Jur Proof of Facts 2d 285, Authentication of Copies

American Jurisprudence Trials

44 Am Jur Trials 171, Videotape Evidence

40 Am Jur Trials 249, Using or Challenging a "Day-in-the-Life" Documentary in a Personal Injury Lawsuit

2 Am Jur Trials 409, Locating Public Records

Other Resources

8 Carmody-Wait 2d, Presentation of the Case §§ 56:41-56:68

Auto-Cite®: Any case citation herein can be checked for form, parallel references, later history and annotation references through the Auto-Cite computer research system.

CHAPTER 22

OPINION EVIDENCE

§ 22:1 REQUIREMENT THAT A WITNESS TESTIFY AS TO FACTS

— Generally, an ordinary witness, as opposed to an expert witness, may only testify as to fact and may describe the conditions and surrounding circumstances. *Hartley v Szadkowski* (1969, 2d Dept) 32 AD2d 550, 300 NYS2d 82. When witnesses testify to facts, they may be specifically contradicted, and if they testify falsely, they are liable to punishment for perjury. On the other hand, if they give false opinions, they may do so without punishment. *Ferguson v Hubbell* (1884) 97 NY 507.

An expert's opinion is only as sound as the facts on which it is based, and opinion testimony may be properly excluded if it does not rest on facts in evidence or those personally known and testified to by the expert. *People v Bellini* (1990, 2d Dept) 162 AD2d 693, 557 NYS2d 407, app den 76 NY2d 937, 563 NYS2d 66.

§ 22:2　FACTS DISTINGUISHED FROM OPINIONS — There is no clear distinction between facts and opinions. What appears at first glance to be a statement of fact may actually be a combination of fact and opinion or even pure opinion. Thus, a complainant's statement that he saw intoxicating liquor sold on particular premises was held to be opinion rather than fact because the complainant had not shown facts from which his competency to judge that the liquor was intoxicating might be inferred. *Re Liquors Seized at Auto Inn* (1923) 204 AD 185, 197 NYS 758.

An examination of some cases will indicate the difficulty in making the distinction between fact and opinion. An officer's assertion that what he did in taking plaintiffs into custody was not an arrest merely amounted to the conclusion of a layman as to what the law considered his conduct to be. *Martin v Orange County Publications, Inc.* (1965) 49 Misc 2d 84, 266 NYS2d 875, affd (3d Dept) 25 AD 471, 266 NYS2d 348. An answer to a question about which of two engines discharged the most sparks was held to be a statement of fact. *People v Deacons* (1888) 109 NY 374, 16 NE 676. Testimony that a bathing beach was not open to the public was held to be conclusory. *Brito v New York* (1938) 254 AD 896, 5 NYS2d 519. Testimony that the superintendent of insurance had approved a rate manual and experience rating plan was held to be incompetent as a conclusion. *Metropolitan Casualty Ins. Co. v Rochester Fruit & Vegetable Co.* (1931) 232 AD 321, 249 NYS 572.

Although a witness cannot be compelled to give his opinion as an expert against his will, the line between an expert's opinion testimony and fact testimony can be difficult to draw. *Re Estate of Atkinson* (1984, 3d Dept) 103 AD2d 960, 479 NYS2d 805, appeal after remand (3d Dept) 117 AD2d 843, 498 NYS2d 543.

§ 22:3　ADMISSIBILITY OF OPINIONS IN GENERAL — For various policy reasons, the rules of evidence permit witnesses to state opinions to particular matters under certain circumstances. In some cases, no special skill, training, or experience is required of the witness. In others of a more complex nature, the witness must have some special skill, training, and experience. The latter type witness is commonly known as an expert witness.

Expert testimony is admissible when the conclusions to be drawn by a jury depend on the existence of facts that are not common knowledge and that are peculiarly within the knowledge of men whose experience or study enables them to speak with authority upon the subject, *Dougherty v Milliken* (1900) 163 NY 527, 57 NE 757, or when the conclusions to be drawn from the facts as stated, as well as the knowledge of the facts themselves, depend on professional or scientific knowledge or skill not within the range of ordinary training or intelligence. *Dougherty v Milliken, supra*.

Although expert testimony must be based on facts supported by the evidence, the facts need only be fairly inferable from the evidence. *Cross v Board of Education* (1975, 3d Dept) 49 AD2d 67, 371 NYS2d 179.

Expert testimony must have a proper foundation in the record and be based on established facts relevant to the controversy. *Hugelmaier v Sweden* (1988, 4th Dept) 144 AD2d 934, 534 NYS2d 253, app den, app dismd 74 NY2d 699, 543 NYS2d 387. When plaintiff's expert admitted that his opinion was based on his conclusion that the car left the road on the right and travelled on to the right shoulder before it veered to the left and there was no evidence that the car left the road on the right, the expert's opinion was without value. *Hugelmaier v Sweden, supra*.

In a personal injury action against the owner of premises, the trial court erred in permitting the plaintiff to attempt to prove negligence through expert testimony regarding the meaning and applicability of statutes and regulations requiring the maintenance of premises in safe condition. The expert was permitted to testify about matters beyond the scope of his expertise and by stating an opinion about the meaning and applicability of law, to usurp the function of the court. *Rodriquez v New York City Hous. Auth.* (1994, 1st Dept) 209 AD2d 260, 618 NYS2d 352.

§ 22:4 OPINIONS CONCERNING THE ULTIMATE ISSUE —
Generally, opinion evidence of an inference or judgment regarding ultimate facts to be determined by the jury is excluded. *Clark v Iceland S.S. Co.* (1958, 1st Dept) 6 AD2d 544, 179 NYS2d 708, reh and app den (1st Dept) 7 AD 837, 182 NYS2d 295. It is the

province of the jury to draw inferences from facts. *Hartley v Szadkowski* (1969, 2d Dept) 32 AD2d 550, 300 NYS2d 82.

In an automobile accident case, the court erred in permitting defense counsel over objection to elicit on cross-examination of plaintiff an opinion that the highway was dangerous. *Hartley v Szadkowski, supra.* When a patron of a restaurant was injured while leaving the restaurant through its revolving door, the court erred in permitting an expert witness appearing on behalf of plaintiff to give his opinion as to whether the revolving door was in a dangerous or unsafe condition, because this opinion practically decided the matter. *Bearss v Westbury Hotel, Inc.* (1969, 1st Dept) 33 AD2d 47, 304 NYS2d 894. It was held to be error to permit defendants' experts to give their opinion that a shirt was of merchantable quality and that its material made it reasonably fit for use as a shirt, because these conclusions embraced the very issues that were to be decided by the jury. *Feldberg v Howard Fulton Street, Inc.* (1963, 2d Dept) 20 AD2d 555, 245 NYS2d 168, later app 44 Misc 2d 218, 253 NYS2d 291, affd 24 AD2d 704, 261 NYS2d 1012, app dismd 16 NY2d 1041, 266 NYS2d 115. In an infant's action for personal injuries sustained in a municipal playground, the court held that opinion evidence was incompetent to show that more than one playground attendant was required for adequate supervision of the playground. *Storms v Fulton* (1942) 263 AD 927, 32 NYS2d 395. In a pedestrian's action against a motorist for injuries arising from an automobile accident, expert testimony on the question of whether a motorist gave a pedestrian the right of way is not admissible. *Skoller v Short* (1942, City Ct) 35 NYS2d 68. In an action for injuries sustained when a plaintiff fell at the entrance to a hotel, the testimony of an expert with respect to whether the witness would consider it good practice for the hotel to maintain a steel plate in the entrance way such as the witness had observed at the entrance to the hotel was inadmissible. *Jean v Algonquin Hotel Co.* (1938) 255 AD 279, 7 NYS2d 412.

The court committed reversible error in allowing an expert on behalf of an injured plaintiff to testify that a particular basketball practice drill was dangerous. There was no testimony as to the custom and practice of such drills and no evidence as to a departure from custom and practice. A mere opinion of an expert that a given procedure is dangerous and improper may not be presented to the triers of the facts, because it usurps their fact-finding function. *Strauch v Hirschman* (1972, 2d Dept) 40 AD2d 711, 336 NYS2d 678.

When the county coroner and chief of police gave opinion evidence in support of the finding that the decedent was a hit-and-run victim, the evidence was not objectionable on the ground that they were improperly testifying as to the ultimate issue to be decided by the trier of fact. *General Acci. Fire & Life Assurance Corp. v Krieghbaum* (1974, 3d Dept) 46 AD2d 713, 360 NYS2d 310.

§ 22:5 OPINIONS ON THE ULTIMATE ISSUE IN NEGLIGENCE CASES — A witness may not give his opinion as to the cause of an accident. *Sessa v Shevers Ice Cream Co.* (1926) 215 AD 390, 213 NYS 697. On the other hand, when two automobiles collided, the court erred in excluding evidence offered by the plaintiffs that defendant's automobile had been going "fast" at the time of the collision and that plaintiff passenger had exclaimed just prior to the impact that the defendant was coming too fast. *Hansell v Galvani* (1955) 286 AD 1019, 144 NYS2d 852, reh and app den 286 AD 1104, 146 NYS2d 926.

A witness will not be permitted to state that a thing was bad, defective, and dangerous, because this is a matter of opinion. *Gorman v New York* (1945) 184 Misc 785, 55 NYS2d 49. A woman who slipped and fell on the floor of defendant's store brought an action for personal injuries. An inspector for the manufacturer of the preparation defendant used to treat the floor made a report indicating that the floor was safe. The report was properly excluded from evidence, because it really expressed the inspector's opinion on a matter that was for the jury to decide. *Vogel v Montgomery Ward, Inc.* (1949) 275 AD 727, 86 NYS2d 817, app den 275 AD 872, 89 NYS2d 888. In an action arising out of a head-on automobile collision, it was improper to ask a passenger whether he had any complaints concerning the manner in which the automobile was driven, because this called for an expression of an opinion by the witness concerning the driver's conduct rather than what was said or done. *Dougherty v Braddock Automatic*

Music Corp. (1950) 277 AD 923, 98 NYS2d 514. A witness for defendant was not permitted to testify that based on the appearance of the front wheel of defendant's machine, it appeared as if he had lost control. *Zimmerman v Ullmann* (1916) 173 AD 650, 160 NYS 81. The statement of a janitor who said that the construction at the top of a stairway was faulty and constituted a fire trap was inadmissible, *Oppenheimer v Harrisetta Holding Co.* (1919) 188 AD 472, 176 NYS 716, as was a statement by the witness asserting that the accident could have been avoided by the use of a guard. *Schmahl v Albany Brush Co.* (1908) 61 Misc 316, 113 NYS 768.

A witness's opinion that a saw was not safely constructed was held inadmissible. *Schmahl v Albany Brush Co., supra.* However, in an action for the wrongful death of plaintiff's intestate, a lineman employed by a telephone company who was electrocuted, a witness stated that he saw another person attach one end of the wire to an iron pole, forming a current for electricity to the ground, and touch the other end to an iron brace on an adjoining telegraph pole and that the contact of the wire with the brace caused the flash that occurred. That statement was held to be competent as a statement of fact. *Dwyer v Buffalo General Electric Co.* (1897) 20 AD 124, 46 NYS 874.

No expert is permitted to testify that a party was negligent, because the determination of that issue is the exclusive function of the trier of fact. *Roman v Vargas* (1992, 1st Dept) 182 AD2d 543, 582 NYS2d 1020.

Plaintiff in an action for personal injuries arising out of an automobile accident was required to prove that the injuries sustained qualified as "serious" under the no-fault insurance statute. The trial court properly allowed experts to answer questions that tracked statutory language. The test is one of need as applied to the unique circumstances of each case, and if the jury requires the benefit of an expert's specialized knowledge, the opinion should be allowed even if it bears on the ultimate question. *Dufel v Green* (1995) 84 NY2d 795, 622 NYS2d 900.

§ 22:6   OPINION ON THE ULTIMATE ISSUE IN WILL CASES

— Although lay witnesses may state their impressions regarding the rationality or irrationality of the conversation or the conduct of the testatrix, they may not express an opinion on the question of her mental capacity. *Re Coddington's Will* (1954) 307 NY 181. Such witnesses may testify that the act and declarations of a person impressed them as rational, but they are not competent to testify regarding the mental capacity of that person. *Weinberg v Weinberg* (1938) 255 AD 366, 8 NYS2d 341. However, a subscribing witness to a will may testify to his opinion concerning the testamentary capacity of a testator as evidenced by his conduct at the time he executed the will, because the subscribing witness had been chosen by the testator for that purpose. *Re Will of Nogueira* (1961) 32 Misc 2d 446, 223 NYS2d 334.

§ 22:7   WHEN OPINION EVIDENCE ON THE ULTIMATE ISSUE IS ADMISSIBLE —Opinion is permitted on an ultimate issue in a few types of cases. This exception arises from the necessities of the case. Such situations may be found in cases in which the value of property or services is an ultimate issue. It was permissible to admit opinion evidence as to the value of a television program format created by plaintiff and allegedly taken by defendant. *Robbins v Frank Cooper Associates* (1964) 14 NY2d 913, 252 NYS2d 318. Testimony as to whether a specified document is in a particular person's handwriting is admissible, even though this may be the ultimate issue. *Ely v Stone* (1940) 173 Misc 117, 17 NYS2d 266.

When the ultimate issue of fact requires technical testimony, the expert is entitled to draw his conclusions. *Miller v Food Fair Stores, Inc.* (1978, 3d Dept) 63 AD2d 766, 404 NYS2d 740. It is only when the subject is one within the common knowledge of a jury that the expert may not give such opinions. *Miller v Food Fair Stores, Inc., supra.*

For example, although a jury may be familiar with dents caused by vehicular accidents, it is unlikely that they would be able to determine from photographs in evidence the extent of damage that would be caused by a 72,000- pound tractor trailer colliding with an ordinary vehicle under the circumstances of the accident. *Sitaras v James Ricciardi & Sons, Inc.* (1989, 2d Dept) 154 AD2d 451, 545 NYS2d 937, app den 75 NY2d 708, 554 NYS2d 833. In such a case, an expert in accident reconstruction may draw conclusions from the evidence, notwithstanding that such opinions may reach the ultimate issues in the case. *Sitaris v James Ricciardi & Sons, supra. See also, Kravitz v Long Island Jewish-Hillside Medical Center, Community Health Program, Inc.* (1985, 2d Dept) 113 AD2d 577, 497 NYS2d 51.

The opinion of an expert on the ultimate issue of fact is admissible when it concerns a matter requiring professional or skilled knowledge, such as medical conditions. *Robillard v Robbins* (1990, 3d Dept) 168 AD2d 803, 563 NYS2d 940.

§ 22:8 NON-EXPERT OPINION IN GENERAL — Under proper circumstances, an ordinary lay witness may give his opinion about a wide variety of matters. For example, testimony by a lay witness as to pain and suffering is admissible. *McSwyny v Broadway & S. A. R. Co.* (1889, Sup) 7 NYS 456.

A lay witness may testify to his own physical condition, *Vincent-Wilday, Inc. v Strait* (1948) 273 AD 1054, 79 NYS2d 811, and he may also give an opinion regarding the state of a person's health. *Rawls v American Mut. Life Ins. Co.* (1863) 27 NY 282. A witness may testify about the state of a person's health before and after an accident. *Staring v Western Union Tel. Co.* (1890, Sup) 11 NYS 817. A witness may testify to the age of a person after giving the facts and circumstances on which the opinion is based and after describing as far as practicable the appearance of the person whose age is in question. *Hartshorn v Metropolitan Life Ins. Co.* (1900) 55 AD 471, 67 NYS 13. A non-expert witness may testify about whether a person appeared to be intoxicated. *People v Eastwood* (1856) 14 NY 562.

A lay witness may testify regarding the identification of a person by his voice. *Walker Discount Corp. v Sapin* (1965) 48 Misc 2d 277, 264 NYS2d 841. Such a witness may also identify substances such as whiskey. *People v Marx* (1908) 128 AD 828, 112 NYS 1011.

§ 22:9 NON-EXPERT OPINION ON SANITY — Although a lay witness is not always permitted to testify that a person impressed him as irrational, *People v Pekarz* (1906) 185 NY 470, 78 NE 294, in one case, a lay witness has been held competent to testify as to whether in his opinion a particular person was rational or irrational. *People v Packenham* (1889) 115 NY 200, 21 NE 1035.

After describing the conduct of a person, he may also testify as to whether that person's acts impressed him as rational or irrational. *People v Pekarz, supra; People v Youngs* (1896) 151 NY 210, 45 NE 460.

A lay witness may not express an opinion on the question of mental capacity but may only state whether the conversation or conduct testified to seemed rational or irrational. *Gomboy v Mitchell* (1977, 2d Dept) 57 AD2d 916, 395 NYS2d 55.

An ordinary witness may describe the acts of a person whose sanity is in question and state whether those acts impressed her as rational or irrational, but other than a subscribing witness to the will, an ordinary witness may not render an opinion as to whether the testatrix was of sound mind. *Re Estate of Vickery* (1990, 4th Dept) 167 AD2d 828, 561 NYS2d 937.

§ 22:10   OPINION AS TO SPEED — Any person of ordinary ability and intelligence who has the means or opportunity of observation is competent to testify regarding the rate of speed of a vehicle. *Marcucci v Bird* (1949) 275 AD 127, 88 NYS2d 333. An estimate of the speed at which an automobile is moving at a given time is a matter of common observation rather than one calling for an expert opinion. *Marcucci v Bird, supra.*

The question of the opportunity of the witness to judge the speed of the motor vehicle under particular conditions goes to the weight of the testimony rather than to its admissibility. *Marcucci v Bird, supra.* Thus, where the vehicle of a motorist was struck from behind by a skidding truck, the plaintiff's opportunity to judge the speed of the truck that was following him was a matter that went to the weight of his testimony rather than to its admissibility. *Krug v Nathanson* (1963, 2d Dept) 18 AD2d 1078, 239 NYS2d 371.

When two automobiles collided, the court erred in excluding evidence offered by the plaintiffs that defendant's automobile had been going "fast" at the time of the collision and that plaintiff passenger had exclaimed just prior to the impact that the defendant was coming too fast. *Hansell v Galvani* (1955) 286 AD 1019, 144 NYS2d 852, reh and app den 286 AD 1104, 146 NYS2d 926. However, a police officer's testimony "reconstructing" an accident, in which he gave his opinion on the direction an automobile was traveling and on the speeds of automobiles before the collision, was held inadmissible as being speculative. *Lopez v Yannotti* (1965, 2d Dept) 24 AD2d 758, 263 NYS2d 523, motion to dismiss app den 17 NY2d 577, 268 NYS2d 334 and app dismd 17 NY2d 787, 270 NYS2d 637. Testimony about the speed of a vehicle does not have to take a particular form. It is sufficient if the witness characterizes the vehicle as "coming too fast." *Hansell v Galvani, supra.*

It was proper to permit the testimony of two part-time police officers regarding their opinion of the speed of a motorcycle prior to the accident, because their testimony was offered not as expert opinion, but as lay opinion. *Callaghan v Giuffre* (1974, 3d Dept) 44 AD2d 631, 353 NYS2d 577. On the other hand, the court subsequently held that although a witness will ordinarily be allowed to testify concerning the estimated speed of an automobile, this rule is premised on the prevalence of automobiles in our society and the frequency with which most people view them at various speeds. The same may not be said about motorcycles. *Larsen v Vigliarolo Bros., Inc.* (1980, 2d Dept) 77 AD2d 562, 429 NYS2d 273.

The trial court properly excluded the testimony of a witness regarding the speed of a motorcycle because his estimate of the speed was based only on the sound of the engine. *Grant v New York Tel. Co.* (1985, 2d Dept) 114 AD2d 350, 493 NYS2d 871.

In the absence of any testimony by a lay witness that he had any experience in estimating the speed of motorcycles, he should not have been permitted to testify that plaintiff's motorcycle was travelling between 60 and 65 miles per hour prior to the collision, despite the fact that he testified that he had been driving for 31 years and had estimated the speed of undefined moving objects. *Swoboda v We Try Harder, Inc.* (1987, 2d Dept) 128 AD2d 862, 513 NYS2d 781.

A driver and his passenger whom defendant had passed just prior to colliding with an oncoming vehicle and who had been driving for 11 and 7 years, respectively, were adequately qualified to give opinions regarding the estimated speed of defendant's vehicle. *People v Racine* (1987, 3d Dept) 132 AD2d 899, 518 NYS2d 458.

§ 22:11 NON-EXPERT OPINION ON HANDWRITING — A lay witness may testify as to the genuineness of handwriting. *Ely v Stone* (1940) 173 Misc 117, 17 NYS2d 266. The witness must have some knowledge of the handwriting of the person whose signature is in question. *Farrell v Manhattan R. Co.* (1903) 83 AD 393, 82 NYS 334, affd 178 NY 596, 70 NE 1098. It is sufficient if the witness has seen the party in question write at least once. *Hammond v Varian* (1873) 54 NY 398. A lay witness need not, however, prove familiarity with the handwriting in question by direct means. Familiarity may be proven by a course of correspondence during which letters are written and answered. *Dunklin v Reigelmann* (1915, App Tm) 155 NYS 561. In addition to showing his knowledge of the questioned handwriting, the witness must show that the knowledge has been obtained *ante litem motam*. *Hynes v McDermott* (1880) 82 NY 41.

The testator's daughter was competent to challenge the genuineness of the testator's disputed signature. *Re Estate of Fertig* (1992, 4th Dept) 184 AD2d 1015, 584 NYS2d 354.

§ 22:12 NON-EXPERT OPINION ON THE VALUE OF PERSONAL PROPERTY — A lay witness may testify about the value of personal property. *Cutler-Hammer, Inc. v Troy* (1953) 283 AD 123, 126 NYS2d 452. The price paid for the property is admissible, because this constitutes some evidence of its value. *Goldman v Omaha Estates, Inc.* (1955, Mun Ct) 139 NYS2d 854.

If a lay witness's testimony about the value of personal property is to be admissible, it must be shown that he is familiar with the market price thereof. *Klein's Auto Delivery, Inc. v Super Garage, Inc.* (1949, App Tm), 91 NYS2d 425. The amount of knowledge required, however, is discretionary with the trial court. *Cutler-Hammer, Inc. v Troy, supra*. Thus, in an action for conversion in which the goods in controversy had no market value, the witness giving an opinion as to the evidence of the value of the goods was not required to be an expert to any intensive degree. *Cutler-Hammer, Inc. v Troy, supra*.

The president of a company that rented tuxedos had peculiar knowledge regarding the value of tuxedos that had been stolen and could therefore give competent testimony concerning their value. *Irv-Bob Formal Wear, Inc. v Public Service Mut. Ins. Co.*

(1975) 81 Misc 2d 422, 366 NYS2d 596, affd 86 Misc 2d 1006, 383 NYS2d 832. The fact that the witness had not seen the particular tuxedos that were stolen may affect the weight of his testimony but not its admissibility. *Irv-Bob Formal Wear, Inc. v Public Service Mut. Ins. Co., supra.*

The trial court erred in excluding the testimony offered by the plaintiff and his expert witness, by which plaintiff sought to establish the reasonable value of the literary character created by him and misappropriated by the defendants. *Gilroy v American Broadcasting Co.* (1975, 1st Dept) 47 AD2d 728, 365 NYS2d 193, later app (1st Dept) 58 AD2d 533, 395 NYS2d 658, app dismd 43 NY2d 825, 402 NYS2d 572.

In a matrimonial action, the wife could properly testify concerning the current value of various household furnishings and other items taken from the home by the husband, and the weight to be accorded her testimony was within the discretion of the trial court. *Fassett v Fassett* (1984, 3d Dept) 101 AD2d 604, 475 NYS2d 154.

In an action to recover the value of grinding machinery and equipment, the trial court did not err in permitting the testimony regarding the value of the equipment given by plaintiff's witness, who, according to the record, was an experienced contractor conversant with the type of machinery in question and had personally seen plaintiff's equipment at a previous construction site. *Trode v Omnetics, Inc.* (1984, 3d Dept) 106 AD2d 808, 484 NYS2d 197. The fact that the witness's observations were made two to four years prior to the time when the equipment was due to be returned merely went to the weight of the testimony and not its admissibility. *Trode v Omnetics, Inc., supra.*

§ 22:13 NON-EXPERT OPINION ON THE VALUE OF REAL ESTATE — The qualification of a witness giving opinion testimony regarding real property values need not be very great. *Broward Nat'l Bank v Starzec* (1968, 3d Dept) 30 AD2d 603, 290 NYS2d 112. The witness need not be a professional broker. As long as he has some knowledge of the value of property in the general area, even his failure to possess experience regarding actual sales in the vicinity does not disqualify him as an expert but bears only on the weight to be given his testimony. *King v Daru* (1937) 252 AD 767, 298 NYS 982.

The owner may be permitted to testify as to the value of his property, but ownership alone does not qualify him if he has no knowledge of the value or is not familiar with the location, quality, and value of his real estate. *Besen v State* (1959) 17 Misc 2d 119, 185 NYS2d 495. In a condemnation case, the trial court must determine if the witness is sufficiently qualified to express an opinion. *Besen v State, supra*. It is generally understood that the opinion of the owner is so far affected by bias that it amounts to little more than a definite statement of the figure of his contention. *Besen v State, supra*.

§ 22:14 LAY TESTIMONY AS TO BODILY APPEARANCE OR CONDITION — In an automobile negligence action in which defendant filed a counterclaim, he was competent to testify about his past and present condition and about his inability to work without being caused pain. *Vincent-Wilday, Inc. v Strait* (1948) 273 AD 1054, 79 NYS2d 811. The court improperly excluded testimony of lay witnesses concerning what they observed with respect to epileptic seizures suffered by an insured. *Hochberg v Travelers Ins. Co.* (1946) 270 AD 857, 60 NYS2d 630. However, the court held that a nurse was not competent to say that a patient had tuberculosis. *Williams v Buffalo General Hospital* (1967, 3d Dept) 28 AD2d 777, 280 NYS2d 699. In an action against the telephone company for injuries allegedly resulting from electric shock, the plaintiff as a layman could not express an opinion as to what had caused his paralysis. *Manley v New York Tel. Co.* (1951) 303 NY 18.

A lay witness may testify about a person's general strength, vigor, feebleness, and illness and his comparative condition from day to day. *Stanley v Ford Motor Co.* (1975) 49 AD2d 979, 374 NYS2d 370.

A lay witness is competent to express his opinion as to whether he or any other person was intoxicated. *Allan v Keystone Nineties, Inc.* (1980, 4th Dept) 74 AD2d 992, 427 NYS2d 107.

§ 22:15 MATTERS AS TO WHICH AN EXPERT WITNESS MAY OR MUST TESTIFY —Ordinarily, expert testimony is required regarding matters that are not within the common knowledge and experience of ordinary people. *Meiselman v Crown Heights Hospital* (1941) 285 NY 389. If the facts are of such a nature that they require no special knowledge or skill, the opinion of experts is unnecessary. *Meiselman v Crown Heights Hospital, supra.* When the inquiry is into a subject of science or skill, common knowledge is inadmissible and expert testimony is required. *Goldstein v Equitable Life Assurance Soc.* (1936) 160 Misc 364, 289 NYS 1064. The nature of osteomyelitis and its cause and probable effect were proper subjects for the testimony of a competent medical witness. *Meiselman v Crown Heights Hospital, supra.* And in an action against the operator of a barber shop for injuries to the eye allegedly caused by the negligent use of an electric vibrator, expert testimony concerning the likelihood of retinal detachment in the eye from a direct blow, pressure, or vibration was admissible. *Cornbrooks v Terminal Barber Shops, Inc.* (1940) 282 NY 217, later proceeding 259 AD 375, 19 NYS2d 390.

CPLR 4401-a provides that a motion for judgment at the end of the plaintiff's case must be granted as to any cause of action for medical malpractice based solely on lack of informed consent if the plaintiff has failed to adduce expert medical testimony in support of the alleged qualitative insufficiency of the consent.

When expert testimony is required, an expert may give his opinion, but his opinion must be based on facts in evidence or facts properly assumed. *Di Filippo v Gargiulo* (1951) 278 AD 172, 104 NYS2d 149. An expert may give his opinion on the basis of facts proved by other witnesses or on facts assumed and embraced within the case. *Ley v State* (1967, 3d Dept) 28 AD2d 943, 281 NYS2d 685, affd 25 NY2d 876, 303 NYS2d 887. Thus, the opinion testimony of a physician regarding the causal relationship between an accident and the injury in response to a fair and accurate hypothetical question is acceptable as a reasonable basis on which to predicate the right to recover. *McGrath v Irving* (1965, 3d Dept) 24 AD2d 236, 265 NYS 2d 376.

Hypothetical questions, however, are not the sole manner in which the expert's opinion may be elicited. CPLR 4515 provides that unless the court orders otherwise, questions calling for the opinion of an expert witness need not be hypothetical in form, and the witness may state his opinion and the reasons without first specifying the data on which the opinion is based. On cross-examination, he may be required to specify the data and other criteria supporting the opinion.

Where plaintiff's expert testifies that there is a design deficiency within a piece of machinery, there is a question of fact for the jury and it is error for the court to decide the issue. *Belle v Printers Machinery Maintenance, Inc.* (1972, 2d Dept) 39 AD2d 759, 332 NYS2d 470. However, opinion testimony that is not supported by evidence is without probative force. *Snyder v Lawrence Warehouse Co.* (1967, 3d Dept) 28 AD2d 589, 279 NYS2d 839.

Where the future prospects of a decedent are not a matter within the general knowledge of the jurors, expert testimony is admissible on that point. *Bartkowiak v St. Adalbert's Roman Catholic Church Soc.* (1973, 4th Dept) 40 AD2d 306, 340 NYS2d 137.

Where the plaintiff sustained injuries in a fall through a sidewalk grate, the trial court properly permitted an expert to testify about the grate, its deterioration, and the way the deterioration could and should have been prevented. This information was outside the experience and knowledge of the average juror. *Ferguson v Mantell* (1995, 1st Dept) ___ AD2d ___, 628 NYS2d 286.

Expert opinion was properly admitted on the issue of the cause of a roof collapse, although the expert had not examined the roof until after repairs had been completed. A proper foundation had been laid, including examination by the expert of photographs taken immediately after the roof collapsed. *Gary v Country Club Acres, Inc.* (1975, 3d Dept) 47 AD2d 788, 366 NYS2d 57.

In an action by a child who was injured while attempting to board a moving train, the trial court erred in excluding expert testimony regarding the custom, practice, and feasibility of closing a train's doors prior to leaving the station, and regarding the speed of the train. *Miller v Long Island R.R.* (1995, 2d Dept) 212 AD2d 515, 622 NYS2d 305.

Where the Administrative Code of the City of New York specifically provided that it was applicable to structures constructed after 1938, the court erred in permitting an expert to testify that the code was applicable to structures built before 1938. And in the absence of more definite proof, it was likewise error to permit the expert to testify that the structure in question had been built after 1938. *Marquart v Yeshiva Machezikei Torah D'Chasidei Belz* (1976, 2d Dept) 53 AD2d 688, 385 NYS2d 319.

Whether a particular witness is telling the truth is a conclusion to be drawn solely by the jury, and an opinion by a psychiatrist that a particular witness lied on the witness stand is improper as an invasion of the jury's province. *People v Kampshoff* (1976, 4th Dept) 53 AD2d 325, 385 NYS2d 672, cert den 433 US 911, 53 L Ed 2d 1096, 97 S Ct 2979.

In an action against an insurance carrier for failure to settle a tort liability claim within policy limits, plaintiff may properly introduce expert testimony to identify considerations relative to the assessment of personal injury claims in general and describe the materiality and weight ascribed to such considerations. Plaintiff may also introduce testimony that is descriptive of the practice in settlement of claims followed by insurers in general. However, such testimony may not focus on the particular case and may not apply general experience to the particulars of the individual case because this trespasses upon the jury's domain. Furthermore, the expert may not voice an opinion regarding the significance to be attached to the testimony of a given witness in the particular case. *Kulak v Nationwide Mut. Ins. Co.* (1976) 40 NY2d 140, 386 NYS2d 87.

The probative force of an opinion is not to be defeated by semantics if it is reasonably apparent that a medical witness intends to signify a probability supported by some rational basis. *O'Neill v Cross County Hospital* (1978, 2d Dept) 61 AD2d 1008, 402 NYS2d 633. The use of the word "possible" by plaintiff's medical expert did not destroy the probative value of his testimony, because his opinion was accompanied by detailed explanations based on the evidence. *O'Neill v Cross County Hospital, supra.*

In an action brought by plaintiffs who sustained injuries when the vehicle in which they were riding was struck by a speeding automobile being pursued by the police, expert testimony was admissible to clarify the proper police practice expected in a given police emergency despite the lack of specific departmental rules or formal guidelines and despite the jury's common understanding of driving standards generally. *Selkowitz v County of Nassau* (1978) 45 NY2d 97, 408 NYS2d 10.

In an action to recover for personal injuries based on the alleged use of unreasonable force by police officers in arresting plaintiff, whether the police officers acted in accordance with proper police practice during the arrest was clearly relevant and beyond the scope of an ordinary juror's knowledge. The trial court erred in ruling that plaintiff would not be permitted to produce an expert witness on this question. *Dier v New York* (1980, 2d Dept) 79 AD2d 596, 433 NYS2d 510.

The trial court did not err in allowing plaintiff's expert to testify regarding reasonableness and propriety of police action or inaction in providing protection to bar patrons following death threats where special relationship imposing duty of protection existed. *Thomas v City of Auburn* (1995, 4th Dept) ___ AD2d ___, 629 NYS2d 585.

The trial court erred in setting aside the verdict and dismissing the complaint and discrediting plaintiff's expert witness, whose testimony must have been found credible by the jury. *Brown v New York* (1978, 1st Dept) 63 AD2d 635, 405 NYS2d 253, later app 47 NY2d 927, 419 NYS2d 491.

An expert witness improperly testified about the design and construction of a walkway by assuming facts that he admittedly had no personal knowledge of and that were not supported by the record. *Corelli v New York* (1982, 1st Dept) 88 AD2d 810, 450 NYS2d 823.

The trial judge properly struck from the record testimony of plaintiff's expert witness that the installation of a stop sign at a given location was improper, not only because it was speculative and not based on sound judgment but also because it was insufficient to establish that the installation of the stop sign was improper. *De Francisci v Baron* (1983, 2d Dept) 97 AD2d 453, 467 NYS2d 419.

The trial court erred in permitting an expert witness to testify about matters shown on X-rays when the X-rays were not in evidence and no explanation was given for their absence. *See Chang Chiu v Garcia* (1980, 2d Dept) 75 AD2d 594, 426 NYS2d 803.

A witness with a background in engineering and automobile accident reconstruction who was not a designer of ball joints and had never participated in constructing one was properly held qualified by the trial court to testify with respect to whether a plastic insert would have made a difference in the functioning of the ball joint that produced the accident in a products liability case. The witness had served as a consultant to almost every major American automotive manufacturer, and his practical experience included actual disassembling and analysis of some 100 ball joints. *Caprara v Chrysler Corp.* (1981) 52 NY2d 114, 436 NYS2d 251.

Plaintiff in a products liability action was injured when a two-and-a-half-year-old teapot manufactured by defendant burst while she was using it to boil water. An expert witness testifying on behalf of defendant stated that it was his opinion that the accident resulted from a weakening of the structure of the teapot caused by impact with another object. Although plaintiff denied that such an impact had occurred, she presented no expert or other testimony on her behalf regarding the cause of the accident. Consequently, the judgment for plaintiff was properly reversed, because it was based on pure conjecture regarding the cause of the accident. *Fox v Corning Glass Works, Inc.* (1981, 2d Dept) 81 AD2d 826, 438 NYS2d 602.

Any improper assumptions used by the accident reconstruction expert in establishing an impact point for the accident and the motorcycle's rate of speed affected the weight to be accorded the expert's testimony and not its admissibility. *People v Boice* (1982, 3d Dept) 89 AD2d 33, 455 NYS2d 859.

Failure to use an available seat belt and expert testimony regarding the failure to use it is a factor that the trier of the fact may consider in the light of all other factors received in evidence in determining whether a party has exercised due care, not only to avoid injury to himself, but to mitigate any injury he would likely sustain. *Cordts v State* (1986, 3d Dept) 125 AD2d 746, 509 NYS2d 166.

The trial court erred in refusing to permit the testimony of a retired police officer with respect to proper police safety procedures in a situation in which a police officer encounters a disabled vehicle on a highway. The fact that the expert witness had left the police department prior to the time of the accident affects only the weight, not the admissibility, of his testimony. *Anderson v Muniz* (1986, 2d Dept) 125 AD2d 281, 508 NYS2d 567.

The defendant, the operator of a roller skating rink, had provided instruction in the use of roller skates to the plaintiff, a novice, for a fee. Where the issue was whether the defendant had given the plaintiff inadequate and unsafe instruction, the trial court should not have stricken the testimony of plaintiff's expert, who held a doctorate in physical education and had instructed novice roller skaters on the college level for 40 years. *Doukas v America on Wheels, Inc.* (1989, 2d Dept) 154 AD2d 426, 545 NYS2d 928.

A partner in an accounting firm and a securities lawyer were qualified as experts to testify with respect to the reasonable amount of the legal fee for services rendered in a public offering of securities. *Larkin v Present Co.* (1989, 4th Dept) 152 AD2d 1005, 544 NYS2d 696, app den 74 NY2d 615, 549 NYS2d 961.

In an action brought by a pedestrian who was hit by a barricade at a construction site after the barricade was hit by a passing car, the trial court erred in disallowing expert testimony regarding the common standards and requirements applicable to the placement of barriers in a public highway. *Chanler v Manocherian* (1989, 1st Dept) 151 AD2d 432, 543 NYS2d 671.

The trial court did not abuse its discretion in admitting into evidence the testimony of a defense witness, an expert on accident reconstruction, on the issue of whether the impact of the crash in question could have caused plaintiff's knee injury. *Bravo v Victor's Cafe, Inc.* (1991, 1st Dept) 172 AD2d 297, 568 NYS2d 606.

The trial court properly permitted plaintiff's accident reconstruction expert to testify regarding the unusual configuration and traffic patterns at the intersection where the infant plaintiff was struck in order to help the jury understand whether the child was contributorily negligent in attempting to cross the street where he did. *Sullivan v LoCastro* (1991, 2d Dept) 178 AD2d 523, 577 NYS2d 631, app den 81 NY2d 701, 594 NYS2d 715.

In a custody hearing based on a claim of abuse by the father in which the mother testified that she and the child had been abused but she had not told anyone and had not sought medical treatment, the Family Court erred in excluding the testimony of an expert in the field of domestic violence regarding the battered wife syndrome. Psychological and behavioral characteristics of victims of abuse were not generally known by the average person, and the error was prejudicial because Family Court found the mother's testimony to be incredible. *In re Pratt v Wood* (1994, 3d Dept) 210 AD2d 741, 620 NYS2d 551.

§ 22:16 QUALIFICATIONS REQUIRED OF AN EXPERT WITNESS

— An expert is a person who has some special, particular, or practical knowledge in relation to the special department of the affairs of men as would qualify him to stand as an expert skilled enough to teach others. *Ellis v Thomas* (1903) 84 AD 626, 82 NYS 1064. An expert witness may qualify as such as a result of long observation and actual experience, though without actual study of the subject. *Meiselman v Crown Heights Hospital* (1941) 285 NY 389. A physician may qualify himself as an expert witness from study of the subject alone. *Meiselman v Crown Heights Hospital, supra.* An engineer who had extensive academic and practical training in heating and radiation but had never installed a heating plant as a contractor was not disqualified from stating an opinion regarding the adequacy of a heating plant installed by a plumber. *Delair v Gaudet* (1957, 3d Dept) 4 AD2d 736, 163 NYS 2d 685.

The determination of whether a witness is qualified to testify as an expert on a particular subject lies in the reasonable discretion of the trial court. *Karasik v Bird* (1984, 1st Dept) 98 AD2d 359, 470 NYS2d 605, later app (1st Dept) 104 AD2d 758, 480 NYS2d 491.

The special expertise of a witness may stem from experience, observation, or knowledge, and the qualification of a witness to testify as an expert is left to the discretion of the trial court. *McGovern v Riverdale Country School Realty Co.* (1976, 1st Dept) 51 AD2d 894, 380 NYS2d 687. Plaintiff's expert, a teacher and basketball coach by profession, sought to testify regarding unsafe physical conditions on a basketball court at which plaintiff was injured. His lack of experience in advising or assisting in the construction of basketball courts gave the trial court sufficient grounds to exercise its discretion to exclude the testimony. *McGovern v Riverdale Country School Realty Co., supra.*

Possession of a license is not determinative of the expert's qualifications to testify. The court erred in excluding the testimony of a medical witness and a hospital record made at his direction solely on the ground that he was not licensed to practice medicine in New York at the time of the accident and the making of the record. *Black v Ackerman* (1946, App Tm) 63 NYS2d 445.

Whether the expert is qualified to testify is a matter to be determined by the trial court in its discretion, which is not reviewable unless the trial court has made a serious mistake, committed an error of law, or abused its discretion. *Meiselman v Crown Heights Hospital, supra.* This determination is ordinarily made by the court as a preliminary issue on *voir dire. Masocco v Schaaf* (1931) 234 AD 181, 254 NYS 439. The extent of the expert witness's qualification is for the jury to determine on the question of the weight to be given his testimony. *Meiselman v Crown Heights Hospital, supra.* The party who introduces the expert witness is entitled to introduce evidence regarding the qualification of the expert. *Counihan v J. H. Werbelovsky's Sons, Inc.* (1957, 1st Dept) 5 AD2d 80, 168 NYS2d 829. This right cannot be defeated because the adversary concedes the qualifications of the witness. *Counihan v J. H. Werbelovsky's Sons, Inc., supra.* However, in the exercise of discretion, the trial court may curtail unnecessarily protracted qualification of an expert witness when the concession has been made by the adverse party. *Counihan v J. H. Werbelovsky's Sons, Inc., supra.* An expert witness must be qualified with respect to the particular subject he testifies about. *Tarrock v Kingston* (1951) 279 AD 693, 108 NYS2d 16. A chiropractor is competent to give his opinion concerning the nature of the chiropractic ailment and regarding its probable cause and duration. *Badke v Barnett* (1970, 2d Dept) 35 AD2d 347, 316 NYS2d 177. The licensed chiropractor who had examined and treated a plaintiff was permitted to testify that plaintiff was suffering from a particular condition, that an automobile accident was the competent producing cause of plaintiff's injuries, and that the injuries were permanent in nature. *Badke v Barnett, supra.*

However, a professional nurse was not qualified to give an opinion regarding the value of the services rendered by a non-professional nurse. *Schou v Blum* (1907) 119 AD 825, 104 NYS 887, later app 136 AD 592, 121 NYS 122. An attorney was not considered qualified to testify regarding the value of property. *Ribak v State* (1942, Ct Cl) 38 NYS2d 869. A witness who admitted that he had no knowledge as to how anyone other than himself constructed chimneys was not competent to testify as to standard and improved practices in the construction of chimneys. *Lubin v One Gramercy Park, Inc.* (1955, App Tm) 142 NYS2d 734.

The expert witness does not have to be a specialist in a particular field. A doctor experienced in the taking and reading of X-rays is qualified to give his opinion about what X-rays reveal despite the fact that he is not a specialist in that area. *Honsberger v Wilmot* (1949) 276 AD 884, 93 NYS2d 762.

An architect was competent to testify as an expert in a building owner's negligence action against consulting engineers regarding the nature and adequacy of services performed, notwithstanding that the witness was not an engineer. Dismissal of the complaint for failure of proof was reversed, and the case remanded for retrial. *Edgewater Apartments, Inc., v Flynn* (1995, 1st Dept) ___ AD2d ___, 627 NYS2d 385.

In two apparently conflicting decisions, it was held that only an alienist could testify as to the mental competency of a decedent, *Re Lindou's Will* (1934) 241 AD 819, 270 NYS 771, and that a doctor was not incompetent to testify about an insured's mental disability even though he was not a psychiatrist, although this had a bearing on the weight to be given his testimony. *Citarella v Equitable Life Assurance Soc.* (1945, App Term) 59 NYS2d 215.

The testimony of an appraiser employed by the state was not rendered incompetent by virtue of his employment, and his experience or lack thereof would affect only the weight to be accorded to his testimony and not its admissibility. *Nash v State* (1978, 3d Dept) 61 AD2d 852, 401 NYS2d 923.

In an action to recover damages based on the malpractice of a chiropractor, plaintiff's proof at the trial did not include the testimony of any chiropractic expert but rather medical doctors, whose knowledge of chiropractic was admittedly quite limited. Such testimony only served to establish defendant's deviation from a medical standard of care in his treatment of the plaintiff. Accordingly, there was no competent trial evidence on which the jury could have predicated its finding that defendant had failed to exercise that degree of care that a reasonably prudent chiropractor would exercise under the circumstances. *Taormina v Goodman* (1978, 2d Dept) 63 AD2d 1018, 406 NYS2d 350.

In a lawsuit brought against a bank claiming that the bank had cashed a check over the payee's unauthorized forged signature and was liable for the full face amount of the check, to demonstrate defendant's violation of reasonable commercial standards, plaintiff could use the deposition testimony of an officer and authorized agent of defendant bank. His testimony established that he was a professional banker, having obtained the vice presidency of both defendant and its predecessor bank, and he affirmed his familiarity with reasonable standards of commercial banking practice. *Heffernan v Norstar Bank of Upstate New York* (1986, 3d Dept) 125 AD2d 887, 510 NYS2d 248.

In an action brought to recover for personal injuries resulting from a fall on a watercap on a sidewalk, a special education teacher and evaluator was qualified to testify as an expert with regard to the infant plaintiff's coordination problems. *Bowe v New York* (1987, 2d Dept) 128 AD2d 495, 512 NYS2d 422.

The testimony of a defense expert witness who stated that he was between 95 and 99% sure that a prosecution witness had been hypnotized was without foundation where the same expert admitted that there were no thoroughly reliable criteria that can consistently be relied on to determine in all instances whether the person is actually hypnotized. *People v York* (1987, 2d Dept) 133 AD2d 130, 518 NYS2d 665, app den 70 NY2d 932, 524 NYS2d 684.

Plaintiff's expert witness testified that a guardrail should have been constructed between a parking area and the sidewalk to prevent vehicles from endangering sidewalk pedestrians or storefronts and that such a rail would not have prevented a vehicle traveling at 50 miles per hour from crashing into a store but that it would deter a car moving at 30 miles per hour from striking the building. The court determined that his testimony was without factual basis, wholly speculative, and not admissible, because he conceded that he would need to know the force of the vehicle but had made no calculations or determinations of that force. In addition, he conceded that he had made no analysis of the capacity of the proposed barricade to restrain any particular force. *Jackson v Corgan & Balestriere, P.C.* (1987, 4th Dept) 132 AD2d 960, 518 NYS2d 592, app den 70 NY2d 611, 523 NYS2d 495.

The trial court did not err by precluding the plaintiff's counsel from questioning his expert witness with regard to certain skidmarks located at the scene of the accident, because the plaintiff's expert was not qualified to testify with regard to accident reconstruction. Additionally, there was no proof that the skidmarks were made by any of the vehicles involved in the collision. *Coffey v Callichio* (1988, 2d Dept) 136 AD2d 673, 523 NYS2d 1011.

The trial court did not abuse its discretion in limiting the scope of the testimony of plaintiff's expert witness, a mechanical engineer who, while he had extensive work experience in the specialized area of the safety engineering of vehicles, was not an expert with respect to the design or development of golf courses or of any type of recreational area. *Hong v County of Nassau* (1988, 2d Dept) 139 AD2d 566, 527 NYS2d 66.

Based on her testimony about her education, training, and experience, the director of the Albany Rape Crisis Center was properly permitted to testify as an expert regarding the rape syndrome. *People v Whitehead* (1988, 3d Dept) 142 AD2d 745, 531 NYS2d 48. In a rape prosecution, the testimony of the witness that rape trauma syndrome could cause a victim to deny having been raped was clearly relevant to the evidence that defendant presented to establish that the victim had told others that she had not been raped. *People v Whitehead, supra.*

The trial court erred in instructing the jury that plaintiff's pastor was a qualified medical expert in the area of psychological injury. *Young v New York City Transit Authority* (1988, 2d Dept) 143 AD2d 656, 533 NYS2d 18, app dismd without op 73 NY2d 871, 537 NYS2d 495.

It was not necessary for an accident reconstruction expert to state that his opinion was made with a reasonable degree of certainty, because it was clear from the record that he was not speculating when he gave his opinion. Rather, he exhibited a degree of confidence in his conclusions sufficient to satisfy accepted standards of reliability. *Sitaras v James Ricciardi & Sons, Inc.* (1989, 2d Dept) 154 AD2d 451, 545 NYS2d 937, app den 75 NY2d 708, 554 NYS2d 833.

The qualification of a witness as an expert is a determination within the sound discretion of the trial court. *Kwasny v Feinberg* (1990, 2d Dept) 157 AD2d 396, 557 NYS2d 381. In a malpractice action, the trial court did not improvidently exercise its discretion in accepting plaintiff's chiropractic expert. The fact that he had been a practicing chiropractor for only five years and that his review of the plaintiff's record was purportedly superficial went not to the admissibility of his testimony but rather to its weight, which was properly evaluated by the jury. *Kwasny v Feinberg, supra.*

In a divorce action, plaintiff's expert was not qualified to testify concerning the value of plaintiff's law practice where the record revealed that the expert had never valued a law practice; had valued only one professional practice, an accounting practice; and had never visited plaintiff's law office or reviewed the office books. The receipt of his opinion was an abuse of the trial court's discretion. *Wells v Wells* (1991, 3d Dept) 177 AD2d 779, 576 NYS2d 390.

In an action brought against an insurer who refused to pay for a fire loss, an investigator's experience of investigating fires for more than 35 years was sufficient to qualify him as an expert witness with respect to the cause and origin of the fire. The fact that he lacked a license from the state to investigate fires did not affect his ability to testify but affected only the weight to be afforded his testimony. *Eagle Pet Service Co. v Pacific Employers Ins. Co.* (1991, 3d Dept) 175 AD2d 471, 572 NYS2d 623.

A police detective was qualified to render his opinion concerning an accident, based on his 21 years of training and experience. *Miller v Alagna* (1994, 2d Dept) 203 AD2d 264, 609 NYS2d 650, app den 84 NY2d 805, 618 NYS2d 7.

§ 22:17 FRAUDULENT TESTIMONY AS TO EXPERT'S QUALIFICATIONS — After a purported expert witness testified fraudulently, exaggerating his qualifications, the trial court's denial of a mistrial on discovering the fraud was an abuse of discretion. Merely instructing the jury to disregard such testimony, without informing them of the reason, was prejudicial to the defendant. *Santos v New York* (1987, 1st Dept) 135 AD2d 426, 522 NYS2d 538, app den 71 NY2d 806, 530 NYS2d 109.

§ 22:18 THE WEIGHT TO BE GIVEN EXPERT TESTIMONY — An expert witness's interjection of words like "could produce," "it is possible," or similar expressions does not by itself destroy the probative force of his testimony if the opinion is fortified by detailed explanations and other facts in the record that add to its reasonableness and probable correctness. *Miller v National Cabinet Co.* (1960) 8 NY2d 277, 204 NYS2d 129, remittitur amd 8 NY2d 1025, 206 NYS2d 795. However, a medical witness is permitted to offer general expressions of opinion in relation to cause and effect only if they are directed to showing that the particular plaintiff or claimant's condition indicated that it was caused by the injury or injurious exposure claimed. *Miller v National Cabinet Co., supra.*

The weight and credibility of witnesses' testimony are for the jury, not the court. The jury may entirely reject the testimony of experts. *Lipson v Bradford Dyeing Ass'n* (1943) 266 AD 595, 42 NYS2d 577. Although under ordinary circumstances, a trier of fact need not credit a medical expert's testimony, the opinion should be given great weight if it is not contradicted by direct evidence, opposed to the probabilities, or surprising or suspicious in its nature. *Barker v Bice* (1982, 3d Dept) 87 AD2d 908, 449 NYS2d 369.

The conclusory testimony of plaintiff's expert that the infant plaintiff's injuries were probably secondary to an injection of a particular substance and that a bad vaccine would cause neurological shock was not of sufficient credibility to sustain a finding of causal relationship. *Vincent v Thompson* (1975, 2d Dept) 50 AD2d 211, 377 NYS2d 118.

The admission of the speculative and erroneous testimony of an engineer was prejudicial error. *Marquart v Yeshiva Machezikei*

Torah D'Chasidei Belz (1976, 2d Dept) 53 AD2d 688, 385 NYS2d 319.

Opinion evidence must be based on facts in the record or facts personally known to the witness. The expert cannot reach his conclusion by assuming facts not supported by evidence. *Cassano v Hagstrom* (1959) 5 NY2d 643, 187 NYS2d 1. Although an expert witness may offer an opinion even though he has not personally viewed the items on which the opinion is based, he may not speculate or guess. His opinion must be supported either by facts disclosed by the evidence or by facts known to him personally. *Aetna Casualty & Surety Co. v Barile* (1982, 1st Dept) 86 AD2d 362, 450 NYS2d 10. Based solely on photographs, an expert witness testified about the appearance and condition of flagstones as well as about the design and construction of a walkway. As his testimony was not based either on personal knowledge or on facts in the record, his testimony was prejudicial, requiring a new trial. *Corelli v New York* (1982, 1st Dept) 88 AD2d 810, 450 NYS2d 823. However, the expert testimony of an economist who provides statistical background and a fair amount of reliability in his projections does not invite "sheer speculation" on the jury's part, but only such speculation as is based on a firm foundation and logic. *Dennis v Dachs* (1982, 1st Dept) 85 AD2d 223, 88 AD2d 511, 448 NYS2d 1.

The trial judge's refusal to charge the jury that if it rejected the testimony of plaintiff's medical witness, its verdict must be in favor of defendant constituted reversible error. *Leiman v Long Island Jewish Hillside Medical Center-South Shore Div.* (1978, 2d Dept) 60 AD2d 908, 401 NYS2d 562.

The Appellate Division erred by relying on the testimony of defendant's expert to determine the value of defendant's dental practice. The witness was admittedly unfamiliar with the criteria for assessing the value of this type of professional practice, and the $100,000 figure testified to by the witness was wholly speculative under the circumstances. *Arvantides v Arvantides* (1985) 64 NY2d 1033, 489 NYS2d 58.

The weight to be accorded to the conflicting testimony of experts is a matter peculiarly within the province of the jury. *Jones v Schockett* (1985, 2d Dept) 109 AD2d 821, 486 NYS2d

336. The testimony of a physician who reviewed the medical records of the testatrix but who did not see or examine her and did not discuss her condition with any of her attending physicians or nurses is the weakest and most unreliable kind of evidence. *Re Will of Slade* (1984, 4th Dept) 106 AD2d 914, 483 NYS2d 513. When such opinion testimony is contradicted by the facts, the facts must prevail. *Re Will of Slade, supra.*

The testimony of an engineer, viewed most favorably to the plaintiffs, was sufficient to establish *prima facie* that the defendant's failure to design a railing in such a manner as to preclude persons from sitting on it constituted a breach of duty. *Cruz v New York City Transit Auth.* (1988, 2d Dept) 136 AD2d 196, 526 NYS2d 827, appeal after remand, complaint dismd (2d Dept) 190 AD2d 651, 593 NYS2d 69, app den 82 NY2d 654, 602 NYS2d 803.

There is no absolute duty to rebut expert testimony. A jury is free to reject an expert's testimony even if it is uncontradicted. *Mechanick v Conradi* (1988, 3d Dept) 139 AD2d 857, 527 NYS2d 586.

The trial court properly set aside a verdict for the plaintiff where the opinion of plaintiff's expert was too speculative to support the verdict because it was either unsupported by or contrary to the evidence. *Skipper v New York* (1992, 1st Dept) 186 AD2d 439, 589 NYS2d 21, app den 81 NY2d 702, 594 NYS2d 716.

The trial court properly struck the testimony of plaintiff's expert witness and dismissed the action where the factual assumptions made by the expert did not correspond to the evidence in the case. *Tucker v Elimelech* (1992, 2d Dept) 184 AD2d 636, 584 NYS2d 895.

Even though the court has appointed an expert witness, it is not required to accept the opinion of that expert. *Alanna M. v Duncan M.* (1994, 2d Dept) 611 NYS2d 886.

Experts' recommendations as to which party in a divorce action should have custody of the child is merely one factor in awarding custody and is not determinative. *Prete v Prete* (1993, 2d Dept) 193 AD2d 804, 598 NYS2d 79.

Although the recommendations of court-appointed experts are but one factor to be considered in making any custody determination, those recommendations are entitled to some weight, as are the recommendations and findings of the court-appointed law guardian, unless such opinions are contradicted by the record. Denial of custody application reversed and remitted where both the court-appointed psychiatrist and law guardian recommended granting application. *Young v Young* (1995, 2d Dept) ___ AD2d ___, 628 NYS2d 957.

§ 22:19   MEDICAL EXPERTS — A physician need not be a specialist in a particular field if he otherwise possesses the requisite knowledge to make a determination of the issues presented. *Forte v Weiner* (1994, 1st Dept) 200 AD2d 421, 606 NYS2d 220; *Farkas v Saary* (1993, 1st Dept) 191 AD2d 178, 594 NYS2d 195. A doctor experienced in taking and reading X-rays is qualified to give his opinion as to what X-rays reveal, even though he is not a specialist in that area. *Honsberger v Wilmot* (1949) 276 AD 884, 93 NYS2d 762.

The trial court erred in permitting expert medical testimony regarding certain tissue slides, because they were not admitted in evidence. The testimony did not come within either of the limited exceptions to the general rule that opinion evidence must be based on facts in the record or facts personally known to the witness. *Kosiorek v Bethlehem Steel Corp.* (1988, 4th Dept) 145 AD2d 935, 536 NYS2d 614.

An expert witness is not precluded from stating his medical opinion if he has examined the injured party and a review of the records supports his conclusion. *Easley v City of New York* (1993, 1st Dept) 189 AD2d 599, 592 NYS2d 690. However, a non-treating physician hired only as an expert witness by plaintiff cannot testify about the history of an accident as related to him by the plaintiff, nor can he testify concerning plaintiff's medical complaints. *Easley v City of New York, supra.*

The court erred by permitting an orthopedic surgeon who had treated plaintiff to testify regarding permanency, based on the report of a neurologist to whom he had referred plaintiff for evaluation. *Borden v Brady* (1983, 3d Dept) 92 AD2d 983, 461 NYS2d 497.

The conclusion of the plaintiff's expert witness that the defendant doctor had acted negligently when he cut the palmar cutaneous branch of the median nerve was not supported by the record. The expert's opinion was based solely on his post-operative evaluation of symptoms that could clearly have been attributable to other factors, such as the wrist injury the plaintiff had sustained approximately one year after the operation. *Lipsius v White* (1983, 2d Dept) 91 AD2d 271, 458 NYS2d 928.

A cardiac specialist who was a treating physician and not an expert retained solely for the purposes of trial was properly permitted to testify to the history that he received from the patient before treating him. *Kruly v Eastman Kodak Co.* (1980, 4th Dept) 77 AD2d 806, 430 NYS2d 756.

The court abused its discretion as a matter of law by excluding the testimony of a physician that decedent's death was a suicide. Although the jury may have been able to evaluate some of the evidence presented, whether the number of pills required to reach the level of toxicity found in decedent's body could have been taken inadvertently and whether the circumstances surrounding the body were consistent with general patterns of behavior exhibited by other suicide victims were not matters within their knowledge. *Broun v Equitable Life Assurance Soc.* (1986) 69 NY2d 675, 512 NYS2d 12.

The treating physician of the proposed conservatee was an expert in geriatric medicine and qualified to evaluate her mental aberrations, even though he was not a psychiatrist or a psychologist, and Special Term committed error in refusing to entertain his opinion. *Re Steinberg* (1986, 1st Dept) 121 AD2d 872, 503 NYS2d 795.

In a wrongful death action, the trial court improperly precluded the plaintiff from eliciting the medical examiner's testimony that had the decedent been wearing a seat belt, he would have died anyway or would have suffered some injuries, because the precluded testimony was pertinent and relevant to the jury's determination of mitigation of damages. *Stein v Penatello* (1992, 2d Dept) 185 AD2d 976, 587 NYS2d 37.

A physician who has examined plaintiff at the request of a defendant, formulated his findings, and conveyed the findings to the parties should not be barred from relating the substance of his report when called as a witness by the plaintiff. Assuming that the expert's report has been made available to the parties, the plaintiff should be permitted to call the expert to testify about the content of the report. *Gilly v City of New York* (1987) 69 NY2d 509, 516 NYS2d 166; *Bevilacqua v Gilbert* (1988, 2d Dept) 143 AD2d 213, 532 NYS2d 15.

The trial court improvidently exercised its discretion when it precluded the plaintiff's expert, an ophthalmologist, from testifying regarding the standard of care applicable to the treatment of age-related macular degeneration by laser photo-coagulation, including the informed consent to be obtained from a patient before such treatment is administered. The expert testified that he was familiar with the standard of care utilized in laser surgery, although he himself had never performed the procedure. The expert's lack of personal experience in performing laser photo-coagulation was a factor to be evaluated by the jury and went to the weight to be given to its testimony, not to its admissibility. *Ariola v Long* (1993, 2d Dept) 197 AD2d 605, 602 NYS2d 666, app dismd without op 82 NY2d 920, 610 NYS2d 154.

The testimony of plaintiff's expert that the injured party would require observation and treatment of symptoms by bracing, by medication, or by manipulation was so vague, and his estimate of the probable cost of the injured party's hospitalization was so speculative, that no award could be based on it. *Liebman v Otis Elevator Co.* (1988, 2d Dept) 145 AD2d 546, 536 NYS2d 100.

In a medical malpractice case, the jury finding that the surgeon was negligent in failing to remove a sponge following debridement of plaintiff's surgical wound, but that this negligence was not the proximate cause of plaintiff's injuries, was supported by the evidence, despite the testimony by plaintiff's experts that plaintiff's infection, which existed before the placement of the sponge, was aggravated by the presence of the sponge. The testimony of defendant's medical experts that the sponge did not affect the course of the infection provided ample support for the jury verdict. *Patterson v Cardio-Thoracic Assoc., P. C.* (1991, 4th Dept) 177 AD2d 934, 577 NYS2d 980.

The record contained sufficient evidence for a factual finding that defendant's malpractice was a substantial and proximate cause of plaintiff's injuries. Plaintiff's medical expert testified that the removal of excessive temporal lobe during the operation in an attempt to get at the source of several recurring seizures was medically unnecessary and caused plaintiff to develop hemiplegia and become permanently disabled. Defendant's medical witnesses' contrary opinion regarding the cause of plaintiff's injuries was not a ground for setting aside the verdict. *Ayoung v Epstein* (1991, 1st Dept) 177 AD2d 460, 576 NYS2d 556.

A nurse's opinion concerning the type of post-surgery restraint that should have been ordered for the patient went beyond her professional and educational experience and could not be considered competent evidence of malpractice by a physician. *Douglass v Gibson* (1995, 3d Dept) ___ AD2d ___, 630 NYS2d 401.

§ 22:20 EXPERT TESTIMONY ON MATTERS OF BUSINESS
— A properly qualified witness may testify about matters of business. An expert witness could testify regarding the standard and established practice in the window cleaning industry with regard to passage space in windows to be cleaned from the outside. It was proper to receive expert testimony that such standard practice was violated by defendants. *Gonzalez v Concourse Plaza Syndicates, Inc.* (1969, 1st Dept) 31 AD2d 401, 298 NYS2d 167, later app (1st Dept) 37 AD2d 822, 324 NYS2d 962. The effects of inflation on investments is a proper subject for expert testimony. *Re Muller's Will* (1935) 155 Misc 748, 280 NYS 345. An expert witness has been held qualified to testify about the methods of operation of bookmakers. *People v Busco* (1942, Sp Sess) 46 NYS2d 859.

§ 22:21 EXPERT TESTIMONY ON THE VALUE OF SERVICES
— A properly qualified expert witness may testify concerning the value of services. Testimony includes the value of professional services, *MacEvitt v Maass* (1901) 33 Misc 552, 67 NYS 817, affd 64 AD 382, 72 NYS 158, as well as non-professional services, *Application of La Manna* (1965, 4th Dept) 23 AD2d 957, 259 NYS2d 987. Thus, expert testimony is admissible as to the value of a lawyer's services. *Re D'Adamo's Estate* (1916) 94 Misc 1, 157 NYS 374. In an action for room, board, and care rendered to a decedent, the court erred when it excluded proof offered by experts

to fix the value of personal services rendered. *Application of La Manna, supra.*

A physician may testify as an expert to the reasonable value of the services rendered by another physician. *Izzi v Dolgin* (1970) 64 Misc 2d 742, 315 NYS2d 1005, reinstated (2d Dept) 42 AD2d 966, 347 NYS2d 971. A professional may also testify to the reasonable value of his own services, *MacEvitt v Maass, supra,* as may any party. *Mercer v Vose* (1876) 67 NY 56.

A qualified economist may testify concerning the effect of the projection of past wage increments on lost future earnings. *Dennis v Dachs* (1982, 1st Dept) 85 AD2d 223, 88 AD2d 511, 448 NYS2d 1.

§ 22:22 TESTIMONY BY AN ACCIDENT RECONSTRUCTION EXPERT — Although a jury may be familiar with dents caused by vehicular accidents, it is unlikely that they would be able to determine from photographs in evidence the extent of damage that would be caused by a 72,000-pound tractor trailer colliding with an ordinary vehicle under the circumstances of the accident. *Sitaris v James Ricciardi & Sons, Inc.* (1989, 2d Dept) 154 AD2d 451, 545 NYS2d 937. In such a case, an expert in accident reconstruction may draw conclusions from the evidence, notwithstanding that such opinions may reach the ultimate issues in the case. *Sitaris v James Ricciardi & Sons, supra.*

The trial court did not err in precluding the plaintiffs' accident reconstruction expert from testifying, because he testified that he did not inspect the intersection where the accident occurred until almost three years after the accident and that he was not familiar through other sources with the condition of the intersection at the time of the accident. *Dulin v Maher* (1994, 2d Dept) 200 AD2d 707, 607 NYS2d 67.

§ 22:23 EXPERT TESTIMONY BY AN ECONOMIST — The expert testimony of an economist is acceptable when offered by a qualified individual who is able to express the present value of future losses based on plaintiff's economic history and projected earnings if there had been no injury. *Testa v Seidler* (1981, 3d Dept) 81 AD2d 715, 439 NYS2d 469. Because such a process and the conclusions to be derived therefrom are not matters within the general knowledge of the average juror, they are proper subjects for expert testimony. *Testa v Seidler, supra.*

A qualified economist may testify about the effect of the projection of past wage increments on lost future earnings. *Dennis v Dachs* (1982, 1st Dept) 85 AD2d 223, 88 AD2d 511, 448 NYS2d 1.

In a wrongful death action, the court did not abuse its discretion by permitting the expert testimony of an economist about the monetary value of the types of services performed by the average housewife. *De Long v County of Erie* (1983) 60 NY2d 296, 469 NYS2d 611.

The testimony of economic experts regarding the effect of inflation is admissible. *Stanley v Ford Motor Co.* (1975) 49 AD2d 979, 374 NYS2d 370.

Expert economic testimony regarding the present value of an award for loss of future earnings is generally admissible in actions to recover damages for personal injuries, provided a proper foundation is laid. *Hanratty v New York* (1987, 2d Dept) 132 AD2d 596, 517 NYS2d 757.

§ 22:24 EXPERT TESTIMONY ON THE VALUE OF REAL ESTATE — A lay witness who is familiar with real estate values may testify about the value of land. *Robertson v Knapp* (1866) 35 NY 91. The witness must have some peculiar means of forming an intelligent and correct judgment concerning the value of the property in question. *Cole v Ackerson* (1941) 261 AD 1041, 25 NYS2d 891, reh den 262 AD 805, 28 NYS2d 750.

The qualification of a witness giving opinion testimony regarding property values does not have to be very great. He need not be a broker. Even lack of experience related to actual sales in the vicinity does not disqualify him so long as he has some knowledge of the value of property in the general area. His lack of experience merely affects the weight of his testimony. *Broward Nat. Bank v Starzec* (1968, 3d Dept) 30 AD2d 603, 290 NYS2d 112. A witness need not have made any actual sales of realty in the neighborhood. *King v Daru* (1937) 252 AD 767, 298 NYS 982. A witness who described himself as a real estate broker and operator and builder of garages and gasoline stations was *prima facie* qualified to state an opinion concerning the value of a gasoline station and the factors that might be expected to affect its value. *Rein v Mottola* (1958, 1st Dept) 6 AD2d 793, 174 NYS2d 714.

The mere fact that one is a real estate broker does not necessarily qualify him as an expert witness. *Semple School for Girls v Boyland* (1955) 308 NY 382. In a proceeding by a private school that claimed an exemption from taxation on the ground that the school was used exclusively for educational purposes, a real estate broker was not qualified to testify as an expert with respect to the reproduction cost or the depreciation of a building. *Semple School for Girls v Boyland, supra.* A lawyer was not qualified to testify concerning the value of real property simply because he was a lawyer. *Ribak v State* (1942, Ct Cl) 38 NYS2d 869.

Without precise dollar adjustments, an appraiser's bald opinions represent nothing but conclusory estimates and are entitled to no probative weight. *County Dollar Corp. v Yonkers* (1983, 2d Dept) 97 AD2d 469, 467 NYS2d 666.

Where considerable testimony was given on the injury that property sustained when recreational facilities for fishing and swimming were damaged as a result of the diversion of the Delaware River by New York City, expert testimony was properly received and considered on what the value of the properties would have been but for the taking. *Re Maguire* (1975, 3d Dept) 48 AD2d 958, 370 NYS2d 680.

A real estate appraiser who testified concerning the reproduction cost approach was not qualified to do so, because he was not an architect, engineer, or builder. *Northville Industries Corp. v Board of Assessors* (1988, 2d Dept) 143 AD2d 135, 531 NYS2d 592.

When experts for both parties testified that the highest and best use of the property was as a multi-family efficiency apartment complex, which was the use of the property at the time of condemnation, the hearing court properly rejected the valuation testimony of the town's expert, who relied on the market data approach to reach his final valuation. *Riverhead v Saffals Associates, Inc.* (1988, 2d Dept) 145 AD2d 423, 535 NYS2d 389.

The plaintiff's expert testified that defendants' encroachment was on 4.48 acres and that the commercial appraised rental value of the property was $1,000 a month. The Supreme Court properly accepted this valuation. *Rose Valley Joint Venture v Appollo Plaza Assoc.* (1991, 3d Dept) 178 AD2d 695, 576 NYS2d 943.

§ 22:25 EXPERT TESTIMONY ON HANDWRITING — The CPLR expressly provides that comparison of a disputed writing with any other writing proved to the satisfaction of the court to be the handwriting of the person claimed to have made the disputed writing shall be permitted. CPLR 4536.

The basis for the use of handwriting experts is that every person's writing has a peculiar prevailing characteristic that distinguishes it from the handwritings of every other person. Therefore, by studying characteristics as they appear in the writings of the person, an expert may be able to determine with some degree of certainty whether a writing sought to be proved contains any of the characteristics of the writing he has examined and studied. *Re Hopkins' Will* (1902) 172 NY 360, 65 NE 173, reh den 176 NY 595, 68 NE 1113.

A handwriting expert may express an opinion as to whether a disputed writing appears to be in a natural or simulated hand compared with other writings conceded to be genuine. *Sudlow v Warshing* (1888) 108 NY 520, 15 NE 532. When the issue was whether a signature was genuine or forged, other signatures properly proven by common law evidence to have been written by the claimed signatory and the purported forger were admissible as standards for the purpose of comparison by experts. *Turnure v Breitung* (1921) 195 AD 200, 186 NYS 620, affd 233 NY 649, 135 NE 955.

When a defendant introduced exhibits "to show signatures only" and testified on cross-examination that they were genuine, the plaintiff was permitted to use them as standards of comparison for the same purpose. *Shaw v Bryant* (1895) 90 Hun 374, 35 NYS 909, affd 157 NY 715, 53 NE 1132. In the probate of a will, the issue was whether the testator had canceled his signature in order to revoke the will by drawing 14 nearly perpendicular marks across the letters of his signature. A handwriting expert was not competent to testify based on an examination of the testator's signature on the will that the marks were not made by the same person who wrote the signature to the will, because the marks were not "writings" within the provisions permitting comparison of writings by experts. *Re Hopkins' Will* (1902) 172 NY 360, 65 NE 173, reh den 176 NY 595, 68 NE 1113.

Because a mark is not considered to be handwriting, expert testimony as to the genuineness of a mark is properly excluded. *Re Caffrey's Will* (1916) 95 Misc 466, 159 NYS 99, affd 174 AD 398, 161 NYS 277, affd 221 NY 486, 116 NE 1038.

When the genuiness of a writing is in issue, another writing will not be admitted in evidence for the purpose of comparison with the writing at issue unless the genuineness of the writing offered is so clear that if it were one of the issues in the case, a verdict would be directed in favor of its genuineness. *Clark v Douglass* (1896) 5 AD 547, 40 NYS 769. The court erred by placing in evidence specimens of the plaintiff's signature made on the witness stand so that the jury could compare them with disputed signatures. Signatures made under these conditions are in the nature of self-serving acts, admissible only at the instance of the adverse party. *Nelson v Brady* (1944) 268 AD 226, 50 NYS2d 582.

The genuineness of a writing may be proved in one of several ways. It may be proved by the testimony of the person who is familiar with the handwriting of the person alleged to have executed the disputed writing. *Turnure v Breitung, supra*. A witness who saw the standard written may testify. *People v Molineux* (1901) 168 NY 264, 61 NE 286. The person who purportedly executed the writing may acknowledge or admit it. *People v Molineux, supra*.

The testimony of a handwriting expert is not so inherently suspect, weak, or unreliable that it is considered evidence having an impaired or restricted probative worth, and it may not be discounted as a matter of law. But like other oral and documentary proof, it must be weighed in the light of the opposing proof in the particular case. *Re Estate of Sylvestri* (1978) 44 NY2d 260, 405 NYS2d 424.

A handwriting expert was not competent to testify about the decedent's mental capacity based merely on the decedent's signature. *Re Palmentiere* (1991, 2d Dept) 171 AD2d 871, 567 NYS2d 797.

§ 22:26 EXPERT TESTIMONY BY A SOCIAL WORKER — The trial court did not improvidently exercise its discretion by permitting a social worker to testify at the trial as an expert witness with respect to whether the children involved suffered from sexually abused child syndrome. *People v Henderson* (1990, 2d Dept) 156 AD2d 92, 554 NYS2d 924, app den 76 NY2d 736, 558 NYS2d 898.

§ 22:27 EXPERT TESTIMONY BY A PSYCHIATRIST — In an action involving the custody of children, the court did not abuse its discretion by crediting the testimony of a psychiatrist who was paid to testify by one party over the testimony of a court-appointed psychiatrist. The psychiatrist paid by one of the parties had treated both parents and their children to varying degrees over the previous eight years, while the court-appointed psychiatrist had only a few hours experience with them. *Merl v Merl* (1987, 2d Dept) 128 AD2d 685, 513 NYS2d 184.

§ 22:28 EXPERT TESTIMONY BY A PSYCHOLOGIST — The testimony of plaintiff's expert, a clinical psychologist, was not based on speculation and therefore was properly admitted. The record revealed that she based her opinion on a number of tests administered to the infant plaintiff and not merely on a comparison of intelligence quotient test results. And in view of her qualifications, her opinion was entitled to such consideration as the jury chose to give it. *Campolo v Yonkers* (1988, 2d Dept) 137 AD2d 480, 524 NYS2d 229.

The trial court properly permitted testimony by a clinical psychologist with respect to the psychological effects of marriage on the wife. The witness based his testimony on the treatment of the plaintiff over the course of 30 sessions, plaintiff's history of being otherwise free of psychological problems and treatment before her marriage, and her improvement after separation from the defendant. *McKilligan v McKilligan* (1989, 3d Dept) 156 AD2d 904, 550 NYS2d 121.

§ 22:29 QUESTIONED DOCUMENTS — In addition to questions relating to handwriting, experts possessing sufficient qualifications on the subject may testify regarding questioned documents. It is proper for them to state their opinion as to whether a document was typed on a particular typewriter. *People v Storrs* (1912) 207 NY 147, 100 NE 730.

§ 22:30   TESTS FOR INTOXICATION — The result of a drunkometer test or a blood test is admissible on the issue of intoxication, provided a proper foundation is established. *People v Seger* (1970) 63 Misc 2d 921, 314 NYS2d 240. There should be testimony showing the scientific principle on which the machine is based. *People v Seger, supra.* No witness was called to explain how the breathalyzer worked and no scientific principle was presented. The sole evidence of the alleged qualifications of the officer who conducted the test on the motorist was the number of times he conducted the test and his schooling. Under these circumstances, the court would not accept the results of the breathalyzer test. *People v Seger, supra.* In addition, the officer who administers the test should be shown to possess the qualifications necessary to conduct the test. *People v Davidson* (1956) 5 Misc 2d 699, 152 NYS2d 762. Where the proper testimony was introduced concerning the scientific principles on which the machine operates and the competency of the detective to conduct the test, a conviction based on the use of the Harger Drunkometer was upheld. *People v Kovacik* (1954) 205 Misc 275, 128 NYS2d 492. The court has held, however, that because of the long usage and wide acceptance of the breathalyzer as an instrument for making a chemical analysis of alcohol in the blood, it is no longer necessary to require expert testimony to establish the general reliability of the machine. *People v Donaldson* (1971, 4th Dept) 36 AD2d 37, 319 NYS2d 172.

The trial court did not abuse its discretion by refusing to permit plaintiff's expert, a toxicologist, to respond to a hypothetical question about the alcoholic content in the blood of the driver of a vehicle when he left a bar, because there was not sufficient evidence to show what the driver had done from the time he left the bar until the time of the accident. *Scheu v High-Forest Corp.* (1987, 3d Dept) 129 AD2d 366, 517 NYS2d 798.

§ 22:31   CONTENTS OF A HYPOTHETICAL QUESTION — The testimony of an expert may be based on facts that are not within the personal knowledge of the witness. *People v Samuels*

(1951) 302 NY 163. Formerly, the opinion of the expert was elicited by means of a hypothetical question that assumed the facts necessary to form the opinion. *Weibert v Hanan* (1911) 202 NY 328, 95 NE 688.

This was changed in 1963 by statutory enactment. CPLR 4515. The statute provides that unless the court orders otherwise, questions calling for the opinion of an expert witness need not be in hypothetical form, and the witness may state his opinion and reasons without first specifying the data on which it is based. CPLR 4515. On cross-examination, the witness may be required to specify the data and other criteria supporting the opinion. CPLR 4515.

The enactment of CPLR 4515 has not eliminated the use of the hypothetical question. *McGrath v Irving* (1965, 3d Dept) 24 AD2d 236, 265 NYS2d 376. The court has held that the opinion testimony of a physician regarding causal relationship between an accident and the injury in response to a fair and accurate hypothetical question is generally acceptable as the only reasonable basis on which to predicate the right to recover. *McGrath v Irving, supra*.

When a hypothetical question is based on facts not supported by evidence, it is error to permit the witness to answer. *Begley v Prudential Ins. Co.* (1958, 2d Dept) 6 AD2d 869, 177 NYS2d 577.

An expert's lack of direct knowledge concerning the subject matter of his testimony is no bar to his testimony. The expert may base his opinion on facts proven by, or reasonably inferable from, the testimony of other witnesses. *Rodolitz v Boston-Old Colony Ins. Co.* (1980, 2d Dept) 74 AD2d 821, 425 NYS2d 353. The trial court erred when it precluded plaintiff's expert witness, called for the purpose of establishing the value of repairs made to an automobile, because the witness had not actually observed the vehicle. The cost of repairs could be established by posing hypothetical questions detailing the repairs to which other witnesses had testified. *Rodolitz v Boston-Old Colony Ins. Co., supra*.

§ 22:32　HYPOTHETICAL QUESTIONS ASKED OF A PHYSICIAN OR SURGEON — The proper method of establishing the causal relation between an accident and an injury is by a fair and accurate hypothetical question asked of a physician. *McGrath v Irving* (1965, 3d Dept) 24 AD2d 236, 265 NYS2d 376. In a malpractice action, the trial court erred in refusing to permit the plaintiff to qualify the doctor as a medical expert and to permit him to answer various hypothetical questions propounded to him. *Moss v Winkler* (1957, 4th Dept) 4 AD2d 852, 166 NYS2d 485. A licensed physician who had examined the plaintiff some time after the accident was qualified to give an opinion bearing on the causal relation, and it was error to sustain objections to the hypothetical question put to him. *Siefring v Marion* (1964, 1st Dept) 22 AD2d 765, 253 NYS2d 619. Absolute knowledge of exactly what occurred medically is not necessary to support an expert's opinion, and an educated medical theory may support the opinion of causal relationship. *Normile v Thomas P. Spagnoletti Constr. Co.* (1967, 3d Dept) 27 AD2d 169, 277 NYS2d 155.

§ 22:33   CROSS-EXAMINATION OF THE EXPERT WITNESS
— Most of the general rules relating to cross-examination of witnesses apply to cross-examination of expert witnesses as well. As a preliminary matter, an expert may be cross-examined regarding his qualifications. *Masocco v Schaaf* (1931) 234 AD 181, 254 NYS 439. An expert witness may be cross-examined about his knowledge, skill, and understanding. Thus, in a condemnation proceeding, it was proper to cross-examine an expert regarding specific sales of comparable property. *Massena v 55500 Square Feet of Land, etc.* (1959, 3d Dept) 9 AD2d 980, 195 NYS2d 733.

The expert may be cross-examined concerning the facts that form the basis for his opinion. The court erred in refusing to permit the cross-examiner to ask the expert for the basis of his conclusion. *Schwab v McElligott* (1941) 175 Misc 840, 26 NYS2d 364. When a doctor was permitted to state his general conclusion that a particular patient was an addict, it was proper to permit defense counsel to cross-examine the doctor regarding his interpretation of addiction and regarding the weight he gave to each fact or criterion in reaching his conclusion. *People v Fuller* (1969) 24 NY2d 292, 300 NYS2d 102. It is error to call the attention of the jury to the contents of a medical article that has been rejected by an expert who is being cross-examined. The contents of the article are hearsay. *Zeleznik v Jewish Chronic Disease Hospital* (1975, 2d Dept) 47 AD2d 199, 366 NYS2d 163.

On cross-examination, an expert witness may be confronted with a passage from a treatise or book that contradicts the opinion he has expressed only after the witness has accepted the treatise or book as authoritative. *Labate v Plotkin* (1993, 2d Dept) 195 AD2d 444, 600 NYS2d 144. The books themselves are not admissible in evidence, because they are hearsay. *People v Riccardi* (1941) 285 NY 21, reh den 285 NY 775. Where, however, the medical witness has not accepted a particular textbook as authoritative and the trial court permitted cross-examination based on that work, there was a violation of the hearsay rule, which constituted prejudicial error. *Roveda v Weiss* (1960, 2d Dept) 11 AD2d 745, 204 NYS2d 699.

The requirement for a concession regarding authoritativeness applies with respect to the *Physicians' Desk Reference (PDR)*. The trial court correctly precluded questioning of the defendant doctors in a medical malpractice case on direct examination and of defendants' expert on cross-examination regarding the contents of *PDR*, because the witnesses had not testified that the *PDR* was authoritative. *Winant v Carras* (1994, 2d Dept) 208 AD2d 618, 617 NYS2d 487. *See also, Rosario v New York City Health & Hospitals Corp.* (1982, 1st Dept) 87 AD2d 211, 450 NYS2d 805; *Nicolla v Fasulo* (1990, 3d Dept) 161 AD2d 966, 557 NYS2d 539. (Note: Although *PDR* is hearsay when offered against any party other than the manufacturer of the medication, who provides the information for inclusion in *PDR* and against whom the information is admissible as an admission, if appropriate evidence is presented regarding the manufacturer's suggested dosages, or other clear and explicit instructions regarding contra-indications or warnings, departure from the manufacturer's recommendations may qualify as *prima facie* evidence of departure from accepted standards of medical conduct. When coupled with appropriate expert medical testimony to establish causation, the *prima facie* evidence of departure from accepted standards will constitute a *prima facie* case of medical malpractice. *Compare, Paul v Boschenstein* (1984, 2d Dept) 105 AD2d 248, 482 NYS2d 870, *and Gatto v Cooper* (1994, 2d Dept) 201 AD2d 455, 607 NYS2d 372, *with Rosario v NYCHHC, supra and Nicolla v Fasulo, supra).*

Where an engineer who testified as an expert witness admitted that he was familiar with the general literature on the subject, he could be cross-examined with respect to such literature as he recognized as authoritative for the purpose of testing the validity of the opinions he expressed. It was prejudicial error to refuse to permit such cross-examination, particularly in view of the sharply contested issues and the important role played by expert testimony. *Hastings v Chrysler Corp.* (1948) 273 AD 292, 77 NYS2d 524. Because the statements contained in scientific books and treatises are not received as evidence of the facts or opinions stated therein, a reading from such books or treatises in connection with cross-examination of an alleged medical expert may be justified only as a means of testing his knowledge and qualifications and probing into his credibility. The trial court has a right and duty to control in a reasonable manner the reading of statements from such books or treatises in cross-examination. *O'Connell v Williams* (1958) 17 Misc 2d 296, 181 NYS2d 434.

The extent of cross-examination of a physician regarding medical authorities who have expressed opinions different from that given by the physician is discretionary with the trier of the fact. *Sutkowski v Prosperity Co.* (1958, 3d Dept) 7 AD2d 660, 179 NYS2d 166.

A witness may be contradicted and impeached on cross-examination. Thus, when a physician testified on direct examination that the first time a particular insured had ever consulted him was in 1932, a statement signed by the physician that the first time that he had seen the insured was in 1926 and that he had continued to take care of the patient up to the present time was pertinent for the purpose of impeaching the testimony of the physician. *New York Life Ins. Co. v White* (1940) 260 AD 901, 23 NYS2d 57, affd 285 NY 714. Like other witnesses, expert witnesses may be impeached and contradicted by the use of prior testimony. *Wachs v Commercial Travelers Mut. Acci. Ass'n* (1953) 283 AD 29, 125 NYS2d 857.

A condemnor's expert could not be cross-examined about an appraisal he had not made. *Re Brooklyn Bridge Southwest Urban Renewal Project* (1966) 50 Misc 2d 478, 270 NYS2d 703.

In evaluating the worth of a psychiatrist's opinion, the jury should be informed of his sources and how he evaluated those sources in arriving at his conclusion. *People v Stone* (1974) 35 NY2d 69, 358 NYS2d 737. On cross-examination, the validity of the psychiatrist's reasoning process may be probed and any "shaky factual basis" of his opinion may be exposed. *People v Stone, supra.*

The trial court erred in refusing to permit the plaintiff's counsel to cross-examine defendant's medical expert regarding his conclusion, based on the hospital X-rays of the patient's left arm, that there was a fracture dislocation of the elbow. The only diagnosis listed in the emergency room record when the defendant first treated the patient was "supracondylar fracture of the left humerus," and neither the hospital record nor the doctor's office record mentioned a dislocation of the patient's elbow. *Vanden Wel v Palazzo* (1989, 1st Dept) 155 AD2d 387, 548 NYS2d 14.

It was severely prejudicial to permit plaintiff's counsel to impeach defendant's engineering expert on cross-examination by eliciting that he had previously testified as defendant's expert in a similar case in which the jury returned a $6,000,000 verdict against the defendant. The only possible purpose of such testimony was to impeach the witness because he was on the losing side in another, factually distinguishable case. *Feaster v New York City Transit Authority* (1991, 1st Dept) 172 AD2d 284, 568 NYS2d 380.

In a medical malpractice action, once the plaintiff's expert denied that an electronystagmography test was warranted to determine whether the infant's deafness was caused by the drug gentamicin, the trial court properly allowed defense counsel to cross-examine the plaintiff's expert on his prior recommendation, in another case, that the same procedure should be conducted to determine whether gentamicin caused that child's deafness. *Garces v Hip Hosp.* (1994, 2d Dept) 201 AD2d 614, 608 NYS2d 237.

Because the report of plaintiff's consulting surgeon was evidence of a kind accepted in the medical profession as reliable in forming a professional opinion, defense counsel's reference to the report in cross-examining plaintiff's treating physician and counsel's use of the findings contained therein to propound hypothetical questions to one of defendant's medical experts was proper. *Munoz v 608-610 Realty Corp.* (1993, 1st Dept) 194 AD2d 496, 599 NYS2d 565, app den 82 NY2d 661, 605 NYS2d 6.

§ 22:34 CALLING THE ADVERSARY'S EXPERT AS A WITNESS — A doctor who has examined the plaintiff on behalf of defendant, formulated his findings, and had them conveyed to both parties in litigation should not be barred from testifying regarding the substance of his report when called as a witness by the plaintiff. *Gilly v City of New York* (1987) 69 NY2d 509, 516 NYS2d 166. Once a physician's report has been reduced to writing and been served on the adversary, it ceases to be for the exclusive use of the defendant. At that point both sides have access to this probative evidence, and there is no basis for withholding it from the trier of the fact. *Gilly v New York, supra.*

In a dental malpractice action, plaintiffs failed to demonstrate that the court abused its discretion in permitting defense counsel to make plaintiffs' expert witness defendant's own witness on cross-examination. *Nicolla v Fasulo* (1990, 3d Dept) 161 AD2d 966, 557 NYS2d 539.

§ 22:35 EXPERT TESTIMONY IN MATRIMONIAL CASES — In a divorce action, the trial court properly placed a value of $178,000 on the husband's medical practice, where that valuation was based on a review of the husband's business records, tax returns, and deposition testimony and included such factors as earnings, tangible assets, goodwill, and expenses. *Rosenberg v Rosenberg* (1989, 2d Dept) 155 AD2d 428, 547 NYS2d 90.

RESEARCH REFERENCES

American Law Reports

20 ALR5th 1, Necessity of expert testimony on issue of permanence of injury and future pain and suffering

11 ALR5th 1, Propriety of questioning expert witness regarding specific incidents or allegations of expert's unprofessional conduct or professional negligence

89 ALR4th 456, Admissibility of testimony of expert, as to basis of his

opinion, to matters otherwise excludible as hearsay–state cases of

77 ALR4th 927, Admissibility of hypnotically refreshed or enhanced testimony

66 ALR4th 213, Compelling testimony of opponent's expert in state court

60 ALR4th 1273, Right of voluntary disclosure of privileged proceedings of hospital medical review or doctor evaluation processes

52 ALR4th 1232, Necessity of expert testimony to show standard of care in negligence action against insurance agent or broker

50 ALR4th 680, Right of independent expert to refuse to testify as to expert opinion

46 ALR4th 291, Admissibility of police officer's testimony at state trial relating to motorist's admissions made in or for automobile accident report required by law

39 ALR4th 742, Propriety of cross-examining expert witness regarding his status as "professional witness"

26 ALR4th 377, Products liability: admissibility of expert or opinion evidence as to adequacy of warning provided to user of product

18 ALR4th 1153, Admissibility of expert or opinion testimony on battered wife or battered woman syndrome

16 ALR4th 666, Admissibility of expert testimony as to whether accused had specific intent necessary for conviction

14 ALR4th 170, Admissibility and necessity of expert evidence as to standards of practice and negligence in malpractice action against attorney

4 ALR4th 651, Products liability: admissibility of expert or opinion evidence that product is or is not defective, dangerous, or unreasonably dangerous

3 ALR4th 1023, Necessity of expert testimony to show malpractice of architect

1 ALR4th 837, Admissibility of social worker's expert testimony on custody issue

89 ALR3d 783, Admissibility of opinion evidence as to employability on issue of disability in health and accident insurance and workmen's compensation cases

75 ALR3d 9, Admissibility of expert medical testimony as to future consequences of injury as affected by expression in terms of probability or possibility

71 ALR3d 1119, Right in eminent domain proceeding to call as witness

expert engaged but not called as witness by opposing party

56 ALR3d 575, Admissibility of nonexpert opinion testimony as to weather conditions

56 ALR3d 300, Modern status of the rules regarding use of hypothetical questions in eliciting opinion of expert witness

55 ALR3d 551 Admissibility on issue of insanity of expert opinion based partly on medical, psychological or hospital reports

36 ALR3d 440, Locality rule as governing hospital's standard of care to patient and expert's competence to testify thereto

31 ALR3d 1163, Competency of general practitioner to testify as expert witness in action against specialist for medical malpractice

29 ALR3d 248, Opinion testimony as to speed of motor vehicle based on skid marks and other facts

ALR QUICK INDEX: Expert and Opinion Evidence

American Jurisprudence 2d

31 AM JUR 2d, Expert and Opinion Evidence §§ 1 et seq.

American Jurisprudence Pleading and Practice

23 AM JUR Pl & Pr Forms (Rev), Trial, Form 188

American Jurisprudence Proof of Facts

48 AM JUR PROOF OF FACTS 2d 635, Medicolegal Malpractice: Attorney's Negligence in Selecting and Using Expert Medical Consultant

33 AM JUR PROOF OF FACTS 2d 179, Qualification of Medical Expert Witness

31 AM JUR PROOF OF FACTS 2d 443, Contradiction of Expert Witness Through Use of Authoritative Treatise

21 AM JUR PROOF OF FACTS 2d 73, Impeachment of Expert Witness-Financial Interest

19 AM JUR PROOF OF FACTS 2d 45, Trustee's Representation that it Possessed Expert Knowledge or Skill

18 AM JUR PROOF OF FACTS 2d 305, Admissibility of Opinion Survey

17 AM JUR PROOF OF FACTS 2d 345, Forensic Economics-Use of Economists in Cases of Dissolution of Marriage

10 AM JUR PROOF OF FACTS 2d 365, Nondestructive Testing of Material-X-ray, Gamaray, and Neutron Radiography

American Jurisprudence Trials

71 AM JUR TRIALS 287, Defense Use of Economist

52 AM JUR TRIALS 473, Toxic Experts

50 AM JUR TRIALS 471, Use And Examination of Experts In Environmental Litigation

48 AM JUR TRIALS 1, Audio Recordings: Evidence, Experts, and Technology

46 AM JUR TRIALS 631, The Use of Biomechanical Experts in Products Liability Litigation

40 AM JUR TRIALS 629, Using the Human Factors Expert in Civil Litigation

6 AM JUR TRIALS 555, Use of Engineers as Experts

5 AM JUR TRIALS 675, Using Hypothetical Questions

2 AM JUR TRIALS 585, Selecting and Preparing Expert Witnesses

2 AM JUR TRIALS 357, Locating Medical Experts

2 AM JUR TRIALS 293, Locating Scientific and Technical Experts

Other Resources

8 CARMODY-WAIT 2d, Presentation of the Case §§ 56:25, 56:26, 56:107

Auto-Cite®: Any case citation herein can be checked for form, parallel references, later history and annotation references through the Auto-Cite computer research system.

CHAPTER 23

HEARSAY EVIDENCE

§ 23:1   ADMISSIBILITY OF HEARSAY EVIDENCE — Ordinarily hearsay evidence is not competent or admissible to prove any fact that may be relevant or material to the issues in the case. *Carroll v Knickerbocker Ice Co.* (1916) 218 NY 435, 113 NE 507.

A principal objection to the reception of hearsay evidence is rooted in the belief that when the party whose statement is offered is not in court and may not be cross-examined, an important tool for testing the veracity of the witness is lacking and the testimony is therefore less reliable. *Burns v New York* (1958, 1st Dept) 6 AD2d 30, 174 NYS2d 192. In addition, hearsay deprives the court and jury of the ability to observe the demeanor of the person making the declaration while he is speaking. *Donnelly v United States* (1913) 228 US 243, 57 L Ed 820, 33 S Ct 449, reh den 228 US 708, 57 L Ed 1035, 33 S Ct 1024.

Although the fact that the statement offered was not made under oath has been given as an objection to the reception of hearsay evidence, *Donnelly v United States, supra,* hearsay statements are rejected even when made under oath. *Bookman v Stegman* (1887) 105 NY 621, 11 NE 376.

It was error to permit a plaintiff to testify regarding what she had been told by her physician concerning her physical condition. *Dolan v United Casualty Co.* (1940) 259 AD 784, 18 NYS2d 387. Similarly, in an action for personal injuries allegedly sustained by a customer while leaving defendant's store, it was error to permit a policeman to testify to statements made by plaintiff who could not speak the English language, where the interpreter was not called to testify at the trial. *Scotto v Dilbert* (1942) 263 AD 1016, 33 NYS2d 835.

Where the police officer who responded to the scene of an accident and made out an "aided" card testified that he had no present recollection of the facts, did not recall the position of the injured parties when he arrived, and could not recall from whom he had obtained the information, the police aided card should not have been received in evidence to prove that the decedent was a passenger in the defendant's vehicle. *Prado v Onor Oscar, Inc.* (1974, 2d Dept) 44 AD2d 604, 353 NYS2d 789.

The trial court committed reversible error when it allowed the investigating police officer to testify, over the objection of plaintiff's counsel, that defendant told him at the scene of the accident that plaintiff had ridden through the stop sign; the statement was self-serving hearsay and the record did not establish that the statement was within any exception to the hearsay rule. *Bazza v Banscher* (1988, 2d Dept) 143 AD2d 715, 533 NYS2d 285.

In a wrongful death action, it was error to permit a friend and former neighbor to testify that decedent had told her that he had been given a stress test involving climbing stairs, bending and stooping, and complained of tiredness and pain in the days following that test; these alleged statements, possibly made weeks after the administration of the stress test, were hearsay and should have been excluded by the trial court. *Rosenberg v Equitable Life Assurance Soc.* (1989, 1st Dept) 148 AD2d 337, 538 NYS2d 551, appeal after remand (1st Dept) 169 AD2d 533, 564 NYS2d 386, app gr 77 NY2d 810, 571 NYS2d 913, 78 NY2d 995, 575 NYS2d 273, complaint dismd 79 NY2d 663, 584 NYS2d 765, reh dismd 82 NY2d 825, 605 NYS2d 3

§ 23:2 DEFINITION OF HEARSAY EVIDENCE — When a witness testifies to the utterance of a statement that has been made outside of court, and the statement is offered for the truth of the facts contained therein, this is hearsay and therefore objectionable. *Blackwood v Chemical Corn Exchange Bank* (1957, 1st Dept) 4 AD2d 656, 168 NYS2d 335, reh and app den (1st Dept) 5 AD2d 768, 170 NYS2d 504 and app dismd 4 NY2d 802, 173 NYS2d 33.

The hearsay exclusion applies to written as well as to oral matter. *People v Lammes* (1924) 208 AD 533, 203 NYS 736. Where, however, the extra-judicial statement is offered not as proof of the truth of the facts asserted therein, but only for the proposition that the statement was made, the hearsay exclusion does not apply. *Duncan v 1502 Brook Ave. Realty Corp.* (1956, 1st Dept) 2 AD2d 677, 152 NYS2d 987. Thus, where a plaintiff testified to what her lawyer had told her and the statement was not offered as evidence of the truth of anything contained therein but rather as evidence that the statement had been made by the attorney, it was not inadmissible as hearsay. *Duncan v 1502 Brook Ave. Realty Corp., supra.*

Testimony regarding a particular person's silence may constitute hearsay. *James K. Thomson Co. v International Compositions Co.* (1920) 191 AD 553, 181 NYS 637. Thus, in an action for breach of warranty, it was held to be error to permit the defendant to testify that customers other than the plaintiff had not complained about the quality of the goods. *James K. Thomson Co. v International Compositions Co., supra.*

Newspaper articles are hearsay, and associated photographs are not competently identified by the description contained in the article. *Pedro v Burns* (1994, 3d Dept) 210 AD2d 782, 620 NYS2d 524. Where the defendant in a medical malpractice action moved to vacate a subpoena, and his treating physician testified that, due to defendant's heart condition, compelling him to testify could be life-threatening, the trial court abused its discretion in denying the motion, based on a photograph and accompanying newspaper article purporting to depict the defendant's recent presence at a town meeting. *Pedro v Burns, supra.*

The testimony of a police officer characterizing an area as a drug-prone location was not hearsay, as it was based upon the officer's personal knowledge and experience. *People v Riviezzo* (1986, 2d Dept) 124 AD2d 837, 508 NYS2d 566.

The testimony of two police officers that they responded to a radio transmission about a dispute with a gun constituted inadmissible hearsay. *People v Beckford* (1988, 2d Dept) 138 AD2d 613, 526 NYS2d 197.

The trial court erred by admitting into evidence a "technical assessment" report purporting to constitute the opinion of four experts that plaintiff's vehicle was rendered structurally unsound and a total loss as a result of the accident; since only one of the four experts testified, and the remaining three who signed the report did not testify, the report constituted hearsay and should not have been admitted. *Aurnou v Craig* (1992, 4th Dept) 184 AD2d 1048, 584 NYS2d 249.

§ 23:3 INAPPLICABILITY OF THE HEARSAY RULE TO CERTAIN SITUATIONS

— The hearsay rule does not operate to exclude all testimony where a witness offers the statement made by another person. It does not operate to exclude evidence where the out-of-court statement is offered not to prove its truth, but merely to show that the statement was made. *Ferrara v Galluchio* (1958) 5 NY2d 16, 176 NYS2d 996, 71 ALR2d 331, reh den 5 NY2d 793; *DeLuca v Ricci* (1993, 1st Dept) 194 AD2d 457, 599 NYS2d 267.

If the fact that a conversation took place is of itself relevant, then the testimony regarding the utterance of this fact is original evidence, and does not come within the hearsay exclusion. *Pakas v Hurley* (1908) 61 Misc 228, 114 NYS 142. In such a case the purpose of the testimony is not to prove what was said, but rather to establish the fact that the statement was made. *Loetsch v New York City Omnibus Corp.* (1943) 291 NY 308. Such a statement is considered to be a "verbal act." *Loetsch v New York City Omnibus Corp., supra.*

In an action for fraud brought by the purchaser of realty against the vendor, based upon the theory that the vendor had falsely represented that the property had river frontage, the real estate broker's listing was properly admitted in evidence; it was not hearsay because plaintiff did not offer the listing for the truth of the matter asserted, but rather to show that the statement was made, and it was admissible for this purpose. *Welch v Shiffman* (1984, 3d Dept) 101 AD2d 948, 475 NYS2d 929.

When a witness's state of mind is relevant, the witness may testify to out-of-court statements made by others that would indicate circumstantially what the witness believed at the time. *Bergstein v Board of Education* (1974) 34 NY2d 318, 357 NYS2d 465. Where the issue in an Article 78 proceeding was the denial of tenure to a teacher, it was relevant for some of the board members to testify that they had relied on out-of-court statements concerning the petitioner, and the truth of these statements upon which the board members relied was not at issue at the trial. *Bergstein v Board of Education, supra.*

In a false arrest suit, it was permissible for a police officer of the defendant city to testify about statements made by an investigator for plaintiff's employer, because the testimony was admissible not for its truth, but rather to show what was said to the police and how it provided them with information sufficient for a belief that a crime had been committed, thereby justifying an arrest. *Veras v Truth Verification Corp.* (1982, 1st Dept) 87 AD2d 381, 451 NYS2d 761, affd 57 NY2d 947, 457 NYS2d 241.

A statement that accompanies the delivery of personal property, such as a life insurance policy, and explains the intent behind the act of the donor has been held to be admissible for its mere utterance. *Mutual Life Ins. Co. v Holley* (1939) 280 NY 330.

In a products liability action against a drug company, it was proper to admit the hearsay statement of the doctor who administered a certain drug to his patient, notwithstanding that such statement was hearsay insofar as the drug company was concerned, because the doctor was present in court subject to the oath and to cross-examination and the jury had ample opportunity to assess his credibility. *Vincent v Thompson* (1975, 2d Dept) 50 AD2d 211, 377 NYS2d 118.

It was error for the trial court to exclude testimony by plaintiff about what his ex-wife, a nurse, and his daughter, a medical doctor who was not treating him, advised him regarding the possible complications inherent in a laminectomy. The appellate court found that this proposed testimony was not inadmissible hearsay, but rather had a direct bearing on one of the principle issues in the case – whether plaintiff's decision not to undergo the surgery, and thus possibly mitigate his future damages – was reasonable. *Piehnik v Graff* (1990, 3d Dept) 158 AD2d 863, 551 NYS2d 656.

Where a negligence action was brought against a hotel as a result of a rape, the hotel logbook entries containing reports of burglaries and thefts on the premises were not hearsay, because they were offered not for the truth of the matters asserted but to show that the hotel had received the information and was therefore on notice of criminal activity. *Splawn v Lextaj Corp.* (1993, 1st Dept) 197 AD2d 479, 603 NYS2d 41, app den 83 NY2d 753, 612 NYS2d 107, motion gr (NY) 1994 NY LEXIS 296, motion gr (NY) 1994 NY LEXIS 290.

§ 23:4 EXCEPTIONS TO THE HEARSAY RULE, IN GENERAL

— The hearsay rule is subject to a great many exceptions. In fact, the exceptions seem to be more extensively applied than the rule. A statement, despite its hearsay character, will be admissible if it falls within one of the exceptions.

Certain of these exceptions will be considered in succeeding sections of this chapter. Other rules of evidence that permit the use of hearsay evidence are considered in other chapters of this work under appropriate headings. These rules involve admissions against interest, the admission of self-serving declarations under the recent fabrication rule, and the admission of prior inconsistent statements. These may be regarded as exceptions to the hearsay rule.

Thus, a self-serving declaration in a police report is inadmissible because it is hearsay. *Needle v New York R. Corp.* (1929) 227 AD 276, 237 NYS 547. However, where the testimony of the witness is assailed as a recent fabrication, a prior consistent statement, although hearsay, may be admitted into the evidence to bolster the testimony of the witness. *Abrams v Gerold* (1971, 1st Dept) 37 AD2d 391, 326 NYS2d 1. Furthermore, admissions against interest made by a party are admissible even though such admissions may be hearsay. *Yeargans v Yeargans* (1965, 1st Dept) 24 AD2d 280, 265 NYS2d 562. Likewise prior inconsistent statements, although hearsay, are properly admissible to impeach the witness. CPLR 4514.

The prior consistent statements of a witness are inadmissible unless there is a claim that the testimony of the particular witness was a recent fabrication. *Fishman v Scheuer* (1976) 39 NY2d 502, 384 NYS2d 716.

In civil cases, where hearsay evidence is offered and no objection is raised, it is admissible. *Re Findlay* (1930) 253 NY 1, 170 NE 471. However, continued offerings of hearsay in the face of objection by adversary counsel will result in a mistrial because admonition by the court will not suffice to overcome prejudice. *Doyle v New York* (1953) 281 AD 821, 119 NYS2d 71.

Actions brought in the Small Claims Court do not require the application of the rules of evidence, such as the hearsay rule, except for the statutory provisions relating to privileged communications and personal transactions with a decedent or a mentally ill person. New York City Civil Court Act § 1804; Uniform District Court Act § 1804. However, a judgment may not be supported on the basis of hearsay evidence alone. *Levins v Bucholtz* (1956, 1st Dept) 2 AD2d 351, 155 NYS2d 770.

Administrative agencies are not bound by the rules of evidence that apply at a trial, and hearsay evidence is therefore admissible in such a hearing. *Carroll v Knickerbocker Ice Co.* (1916) 218 NY 435, 113 NE 507. However, the rule requiring a residuum of legal evidence to support a determination that is largely based on hearsay has been abrogated. *300 Gramatan Ave. Associates v State Div. of Human Rights* (1978) 45 NY2d 176, 408 NYS2d 54, 96 ALR3d 488; *People ex rel. Walker v New York State Board of Parole* (1983, 2d Dept) 98 AD2d 33, 469 NYS2d 780.

In an administrative hearing before the Department of Motor Vehicles, hearsay proof, of itself, may constitute substantial evidence provided that it is trustworthy and probative and furnishes a rational basis for the conclusion reached, and the residual evidence rule, if it ever had validity in this State, no longer obtains. *Triple A Auto Driving School, Inc. v Foschio* (1985, 1st Dept) 107 AD2d 641, 484 NYS2d 566, affd 65 NY2d 755, 492 NYS2d 24.

Hearsay consisting of a written memorandum by a judge who had witnessed a deputy sheriff asleep in court while on duty was admissible in an administrative proceeding that resulted in termination for dereliction of duty. *In Grossman v Krolik* (1995, App Div, 2d Dept) 629 NYS2d 467.

In any action brought under the New York simplified procedure for court determination of disputes authorized by CPLR 3031, and 3033, the technical rules of evidence are dispensed with other than those rules that relate to privileged communications, except where the court otherwise directs. CPLR 3035, 3036. Where a matter is submitted to arbitration by the parties thereto, the rules of evidence do not apply unless the parties specify otherwise. *Application of Spectrum Fabrics Corp.* (1955) 285 AD 710, 139 NYS2d 612, affd 309 NY 709.

When seeking to have a hearsay statement admitted for the truth of the matter asserted under one of the exceptions, the burden is on the proponent of the evidence to establish that the statement comes within one of the exceptions to the rule and therefore satisfies the threshold admissibility test applicable to the exception. *People v Norton* (1990, 1st Dept) 164 AD2d 343, 563 NYS2d 802, app gr 77 NY2d 909, 569 NYS2d 941.

§ 23:5   DYING DECLARATIONS — Dying declarations are not admissible in civil cases. *Waldele v New York C. & H. R. Railroad* (1884) 95 NY 274. Thus, a so-called dying declaration was held not to be admissible in a civil action for libel. *Nunnally v Mail & Express Co.* (1906) 113 AD 831, 99 NYS 647.

§ 23:6   TESTIMONY AT FORMER TRIAL — The admissibility of the testimony of a witness at a former trial or hearing is a rule of necessity that the common law has recognized in cases where the second proceeding involves the same parties or their representatives and the same issues, because of the unavailability of the witness through death, insanity, or absence from the jurisdiction, *Shaw v New York E. R. Co.* (1907) 187 NY 186, 79 NE 984; *Re White's Will* (1957) 2 NY2d 309, 160 NYS2d 841, 70 ALR2d 484, and because there was an opportunity at the former trial to cross-examine the witness. *Young v Valentine* (1904) 177 NY 347, 69 NE 643.

By statute, when the testimony of a witness is not available because of privilege, death, physical or mental illness, absence beyond the jurisdiction of the court to compel appearance by process, or absence because the proponent of his statement does not know and with diligence has been unable to ascertain his whereabouts, the witness's testimony taken or introduced at a former trial may be introduced in evidence by any party upon any trial of the same subject matter in the same or another action between the same parties or their representatives, subject to any objection regarding its admissibility other than hearsay. CPLR 4517. Such testimony may not be used if the unavailability of the witness was the result of any culpable neglect or wrongdoing of the proponent of his statement. CPLR 4517. CPLR 4517 is largely declaratory of the common law. *Shaw v New York E. R. Co., supra.*

The statutory rule regarding former testimony applies to the testimony of an expert witness in the same fashion as it does to the testimony of any other witness. *Wallach v Manhattan E. R. Co.* (1905) 105 AD 422, 94 NYS 574.

Although physical or mental illness is one of the grounds stated in the statute as justifying the admissibility in evidence of testimony at a former trial, a commitment to a mental institution or an adjudication of incompetency does not render a witness incompetent to testify as a matter of law. *Aquilar v State* (1951) 279 AD 103, 108 NYS2d 456, amd 279 AD 1121, 112 NYS2d 779, and app withdrawn 304 NY 616. Where it was not competently proved that a witness was out of the state, there was no basis for ruling on whether the witness's testimony in Magistrate's Court could be admitted. *Turner v Sunshine Taxi Corp.* (1945) 269 AD 997, 58 NYS2d 422. It was improper to allow a wife to prove alleged adultery of her husband in her divorce action by reading the stenographic minutes of her husband's criminal trial in which a witness testified to spending several nights at a hotel with her husband, where the issue at the criminal trial was not related to the alleged adulterous relationship, and defense counsel in the criminal trial did not therefore have the same motive to expose any falsehood and inaccuracy of the allegations of adultery as would the husband's attorney at the divorce action. *Monahan v Monahan* (1968, 4th Dept) 29 AD2d 1046, 289 NYS2d 812.

Under CPLR 4517, which provides that the prior testimony of a witness at a former trial, who is absent beyond the jurisdiction of the court, may be introduced into evidence in a subsequent trial of the same subject matter in the same or another action between the same parties, it is not required that diligent efforts or any efforts be made to secure the attendance of such a witness. *Buffalo v J. W. Clement Co.* (1974, 4th Dept) 45 AD2d 620, 360 NYS2d 362.

The testimony of unavailable witnesses was not admissible where it was taken in prior proceedings in which decedent was not a party, and where defendant did not have an opportunity to cross-examine the witnesses. *In re Eighth Judicial Dist. Asbestos Litig.* (1993, 4th Dept) 190 AD2d 1008, 595 NYS2d 574.

§ 23:7 ESTABLISHING THE RIGHT TO USE TESTIMONY FROM FORMER TRIAL — The burden is on the party who seeks to introduce testimony from a former trial to show that he is entitled to introduce such testimony. *Turner v Sunshine Taxi Corp.* (1945) 269 AD 997, 58 NYS2d 422.

A defendant who refused to testify on her own behalf, invoking her Fifth Amendment rights was not thereby rendered unavailable to testify for purposes of permitting her to introduce testimony from a prior trial. *People v Ely* (1990, 3d Dept) 164 AD2d 442, 563 NYS2d 890, app den 77 NY2d 905, 569 NYS2d 937.

§ 23:8 MANNER OF PROVING TESTIMONY FROM FORMER TRIAL — When testimony from a former trial is admissible, there are several ways to establish such testimony. The testimony of a witness given at a former trial may be established from the notes of the trial judge made by him during the trial or from the recollection of anyone present at the trial who heard the witness testify and can swear to the accuracy of his recollection. *People v Scharaga* (1943, Co Ct) 45 NYS2d 343.

The stenographer's minutes are not the "best evidence" in the sense that all other evidence is "secondary." *Harmon v Matthews* (1941, Sup) 27 NYS2d 656. The original stenographic notes of the testimony, taken by a stenographer who has since died or become incompetent, may be read in evidence by any person whose competency to read them accurately is established to the satisfaction of the court. CPLR 4517.

§ 23:9 PAST RECOLLECTION RECORDED — This is to be distinguished from circumstances where a witness's recollection is refreshed by a document. Under those circumstances, the document is generally not received in evidence unless otherwise admissible, and the witness testifies from his refreshed recollection, without reference to the document. *Huff v Bennett* (1852) 6 NY 337. When such writing fails to refresh the witness's recollection, the proponent of the evidence may seek to have the writing itself received as a past recollection recorded.

In order to ensure the accuracy and reliability of the writing for testimonial purposes, certain conditions must be met. The writing must have been made at about the time of the events to which it refers or shortly thereafter. *Howard v McDonough* (1879) 77 NY 592. As a foundation for the use of the writing, the witness must testify that the writing is an accurate report of the events to which it refers. *Downs v New York C. R. Co.* (1871) 47 NY 83. There must be a necessity for the use of the writing arising from the fact that it fails to refresh the recollection of the witness. *Pardo v Sender Bros. Trucking Co.* (1932) 144 Misc 68, 257 NYS 798.

The witness must be able to assert that the record accurately represented his knowledge and recollection at the time the writing was made. *People v Fields* (1989, 2d Dept) 151 AD2d 598, 542 NYS2d 356.

It was error for the court to admit into evidence as a past recollection recorded the entire police accident report prepared by an officer who arrived at the scene of the accident shortly after it occurred; the report necessarily contained information that was not based upon the then-existing impression of the entrant, and the description of how the accident occurred may well have reflected statements made by various unnamed bystanders. *Muth v J & T Metal Products Co.* (1980, 2d Dept) 74 AD2d 898, 425 NYS2d 858, app dismd 51 NY2d 745, 432 NYS2d 365.

The testimony of plaintiff's employee and the notes of water main breaks and their proximity to sewer lines were probative on the issues of injury and causation; the notes were properly admitted as memoranda of past recollection. *Bethpage Water Dist. v Hendrickson Bros., Inc.* (1988, 2d Dept) 138 AD2d 660, 526 NYS2d 476.

A bill of particulars was not admissible as a past recollection recorded because it was not prepared contemporaneously with the occurrence of the events recited. *White Plains Towing Corp. v State* (1992, 2d Dept) 187 AD2d 503, 589 NYS2d 908.

§ 23:10   BUSINESS RECORDS — Business records are admissible in evidence as an exception to the hearsay rule. CPLR 4518. "Any writing or record, whether in the form of an entry in a book or otherwise, made as a memorandum or record of any act, transaction, occurrence or event, shall be admissible in evidence in proof of that act, transaction, occurrence, or event, if the judge finds that it was made in the regular course of any business and that it was in the regular course of such business to make it, at the time of the act, transaction, occurrence, or event, or within a reasonable time thereafter. All of the circumstances of the making of a memorandum or record, including lack of personal knowledge by the maker, may be proved to affect its weight, but they shall not affect its admissibility. The term business includes a business, profession, occupation, and calling of every kind." CPLR 4518(a).

A hospital bill is admissible in evidence under this rule and is *prima facie* evidence of the facts contained, provided it bears a certification by the head of the hospital or by a responsible employee in the controller's or accounting office that the bill is correct, that each of the items was necessarily supplied, and that the amount charged is reasonable. This subdivision does not apply to any proceeding in a Surrogate's Court or in any action instituted by or on behalf of a hospital to recover payment for accommodations or supplies furnished or for services rendered in such a hospital, except that in a proceeding pursuant to Lien Law § 189 to determine the validity and extent of a lien of a hospital, such certified hospital bills are *prima facie* evidence of the fact of services and of the reasonableness of any charges that do not exceed the comparable charges made by the hospital in the care of workmen's compensation patients. CPLR 4518(b).

All records, writings and other things referred to in CPLR 2306 and CPLR 2307, pertaining to hospital and library records of a department or bureau of a municipal corporation or of the state, or the books, papers or other things of a library, department or bureau of a municipal corporation or of the State, or any record and report relating to the administering and analysis of a blood grouping test or human leucocyte antigen test administered pursuant to §§ 418 and 532 of the Family Court Act are admissible and are *prima facie* evidence of the facts contained, if properly authenticated. CPLR 4518(c).

To be admissible, the entry must have been made in the regular course of business. *Erecto Corp. v State* (1968, 3d Dept) 29 AD2d 728, 286 NYS2d 562. Although hospital records are admissible in evidence, *Del Toro v Carroll* (1969, 1st Dept) 33 AD2d 160, 306 NYS2d 95, the history portion of a hospital record stating the manner in which an accident occurred that resulted in the injury, is not admissible where not related to diagnosis or treatment. *Williams v Alexander* (1955) 309 NY 283.

For the writing or record to be admissible, the information must have been procured from a person who is under a duty to impart the information. *Johnson v Lutz* (1930) 253 NY 124, 170 NE 517. Thus, the report of a policeman who did not witness the accident, but based his report upon hearsay statements of other people, was inadmissible as an entry made in the regular course of business. *Needle v New York R. Corp.* (1929) 227 AD 276, 237 NYS 547. However, the Westchester County Parkway Police Department's blotter was competent evidence in an action against the county and the County Park Commission for injuries sustained in an automobile that allegedly skidded on an accumulation of ice on the parkway, insofar as the blotter related to reports of officers concerning general surface conditions prevailing in the area of the accident at or about the time of the accident, if made in accordance with the rules, regulations, and requirements of the Department. *Francies v County of Westchester* (1962) 36 Misc 2d 1062, 234 NYS2d 362. Exclusion of the report of a driver to the Department of Motor Vehicles, in which it was noted that the other vehicle was stationary at the time of the accident, was error because the statement was material to the issue of the driver's credibility and was an admission against interest. *Grassie v Brown* (1971, 2d Dept) 36 AD2d 720, 318 NYS2d 812.

It was error to admit a police report that contained no entry indicating who the information had come from, and the police officer who had prepared the report, but was not an eyewitness to the accident, had died before the trial and thus was unavailable to elucidate the source of the information, which was not identifiable. *Gagliano v Vaccaro* (1983, 2d Dept) 97 AD2d 430, 467 NYS2d 396.

To be admissible, a record must be properly authenticated. *Brady v Comprehensive Omnibus Corp.* (1938, App Tm) 5 NYS2d 781. Thus, it was prejudicial error to admit into evidence, in an action in the City Court of the City of New York, minutes that were taken in another action between the same parties in the Municipal Court, without proper authentication. *Hofstetter v Goldenberg* (1928) 132 Misc 772, 230 NYS 353.

A medical examiner's autopsy report is admissible in evidence. *Walsh v Beckman* (1961) 29 Misc 2d 591, 215 NYS2d 398. Findings contained in an autopsy report are admissible in evidence in a murder prosecution. *People v Higgins* (1960) 21 Misc 2d 94, 196 NYS2d 222. However, an opinion in a medical examiner's report on the cause of death is inadmissible if it is hearsay. *Schelberger v Eastern Sav. Bank* (1983, 1st Dept) 93 AD2d 188, 461 NYS2d 785, affd 60 NY2d 506, 470 NYS2d 548. The records of a deceased doctor, contained on office cards that were identified by his widow as having been written in his handwriting each time he saw the patient, were admissible as records kept in the ordinary course of business. *Jezowski v Beach* (1968) 59 Misc 2d 224, 298 NYS2d 360. However, the opinions and diagnoses of the doctor, which were written in his own handwriting on the backs of electroencephalograms, were not admissible. *Jezowski v Beach, supra.*

The statute, which permits the admission in evidence of business records, makes no exception for records that are self-serving. *Bishin v New York C. R. Co.* (1964, 2d Dept) 20 AD2d 921, 249 NYS2d 778. In an action on an account, plaintiff's written records pertaining to the account on which he brought the action were properly admitted in evidence. *Perry v De Forest* (1944) 267 AD 925, 46 NYS2d 593.

Essentially, the business entry exception to the hearsay rule is based on the concept that the routineness of the entry in the usual course of business tends to guarantee its truthfulness because of the absence of motivation to falsify. *Ed Guth Realty, Inc. v Gingold* (1974) 34 NY2d 440, 358 NYS2d 367, 71 ALR3d 224 (superseded by statute on other grounds as stated in *Central Buffalo Project Corp. v Buffalo* (4th Dept, 1980) 74 AD2d 336, 428 NYS2d 102, affd 52 NY2d 986, 438 NYS2d 79.

The duly recorded minutes of a meeting of the Board of Directors of a corporation, signed by the corporate Secretary, are *prima facie* evidence of action taken by the corporation. *DFI Communications, Inc. v Greenberg* (1977) 41 NY2d 602, 394 NYS2d 586.

In an action brought by a fabric dealer against a seller for damage resulting from the failure of the seller to fill an order, as a result of which plaintiff's customer canceled an order with consequent loss of profits, the trial court properly received the customer's purchase order in evidence as a record made in the regular course of business and a record systematically kept. *Prestige Fab-*

rics, Inc. v Novik & Co. (1977, 1st Dept) 60 AD2d 517, 399 NYS2d 680, app after remand (1st Dept) 70 AD2d 843, 418 NYS2d 906; CPLR 4518(a).

Where nieces and nephews of the decedent brought an action to recover the proceeds of three life insurance policies, which the insurance company had destroyed in keeping with its internal procedures, and the nieces and nephews claimed that under the terms of the insurance policies they were to receive the proceeds on the death of decedent's widow, a certificate that was purportedly prepared by the insurance company in conformity with the policies and the applicable settlement agreement therein, which the insurance company sought to introduce in refutation of the testimony adduced on behalf of the plaintiffs, should have been admitted into evidence under the business records rule. *Rachlin v New York Life Ins. Co.* (1974, 2d Dept) 45 AD2d 884, 358 NYS2d 16.

Reports of an independent investigating agency that had been hired by an insurance company, which contained the wholly-conclusory assertion to the effect that "Your insured adamantly refused to cooperate," were clearly hearsay and should not have been received into evidence. *Empire Mut. Ins. Co. v Stroud* (1974, 1st Dept) 43 AD2d 931, 353 NYS2d 184, affd 36 NY2d 719, 367 NYS2d 972.

A police report, introduced by defendants for the purpose of showing that one of plaintiff's witnesses at the trial was not listed as a witness thereon, was properly admissible as a business record. *Leonick v New York* (1986, AD, 2d Dept) 120 AD2d 573, 502 NYS2d 60 app den 69 NY2d 611, 517 NYS2d 1025, reconsideration den 70 NY2d 748, 519 NYS2d 1034.

A document was properly admitted in evidence as a business record through the testimony of a witness who authenticated the document designated as a summary of tax liability and testified that it was the duty of plaintiff's accounting department to prepare such documents in the regular course of its business and that this document was prepared in the regular course of the plaintiff's business. *Flour City Architectural Metals Corp. v John Gallin & Son, Inc.* (1987, 2d Dept) 127 AD2d 559, 511 NYS2d 362.

Reports concerning the accident, prepared by defendant's employees, were properly received in evidence because the reports were admissible as business records. *Singh v New York City Transit Authority* (1988, 2d Dept) 143 AD2d 1001, 533 NYS2d 603.

Financial summaries that were not prepared in the ordinary course of business, but rather in anticipation of an inquest on damages, were not admissible under the business record exception to the hearsay rule. *Equidyne Corp. v Vogel* (1990, 1st Dept) 160 AD2d 389, 554 NYS2d 19.

In an action brought for breach of an oral and implied contract, the trial court properly excluded from evidence the personnel records from plaintiff's prior employment because the witness did not become a custodian of the records until several years after the events transpired, had no conversations with her predecessor, and had no knowledge of when and by whom the notations in question were made. *Parrotta v J.F. Hartfield & Co.* (1990, 1st Dept) 159 AD2d 453, 553 NYS2d 133.

Business records that have been subpoenaed to court do not lose their character as business records by virtue of the fact that the person who fed the original data into the computer is not the person who caused them to be produced. *Briar Hill Apartments Co. v Teperman* (1991, 1st Dept) 165 AD2d 519, 568 NYS2d 50.

In a personal injury action arising out of a subway accident, the trial court committed reversible error when it excluded the report of a fire marshal from evidence and did not admit the report as a business record exception to the hearsay rule. *Clarke v New York City Transit Authority* (1992, 1st Dept) 174 AD2d 268, 580 NYS2d 221.

The trial court erred when it received into evidence a police report, prepared by a civilian employee of the police department who was not at the scene of the accident, containing a statement that the witness stated that the truck was from UPS; the report did not qualify as a business record, because the witness was under no business duty to report the accident to the police. *Sansevere v United Parcel Service, Inc.* (1992, 1st Dept) 181 AD2d 521, 581 NYS2d 315.

In an action brought by a security guard against a union for personal injuries, which resulted when the guard was struck by a brick thrown by a union member as the guard escorted a truck across the picket line, the security company's log was properly admitted as a business record prepared in the ordinary course of its business: the entries in the log were prepared by the security guard company personnel contemporaneously with the strike, and recorded all incidents relating to it that were reported by its other personnel at various locations. *Browne v International Bhd. of Teamsters, Local Union 851* (1994, 1st Dept) 203 AD2d 13, 609 NYS2d 237.

§ 23:11 OFFICIAL RECORDS, GENERALLY — Official records are often admissible to prove the contents thereof, as an exception to the hearsay rule. Such records, dealing as they do with official actions and activities, are required by statute as reasonably necessary for the performance of the duties of the various officials, and are admissible for the truth of the matters contained therein. The reliability of such records is based primarily on the fact that the official making the entry has no motive or reason to misrepresent or falsify it. *Re Kennedy* (1913) 82 Misc 214, 143 NYS 404.

Public Health Law § 4103(3) provides that, in addition to a certified copy of the record of a birth or a death, a certification of birth or death, a transcript of a birth or death certificate, a certification of birth or certificates of registration of birth data, when properly certified by the commissioner or persons authorized to act for him, shall be *prima facie* evidence in all courts and places of the facts therein stated. It has been held that death certificates are admissible only to prove the fact of death. *Ursaner v Metropolitan Life Ins. Co.* (1948) 274 AD 77, 79 NYS2d 760, affd 299 NY 730. However, it has been held that the statute making a death certificate *prima facie* evidence of the facts stated therein was enacted for the very purpose of providing an exception to the hearsay rule and that a death certificate was admissible on behalf of a plaintiff suing on an accidental death policy to establish the cause of death. *Regan v National Postal Transport Asso.* (1967) 53 Misc 2d 901, 280 NYS2d 319. It has also been held that an official death certificate that stated the cause of death of a hospital patient to be asphyxiation by strangulation while temporarily insane was presumptive evidence of the facts alleged therein when the administrator of the estate brought a claim against the state for wrongful death. *Gioia v State* (1964, 4th Dept) 22 AD2d 181, 254 NYS2d 384.

There have, however, been contrary holdings. Thus, it was held that a certificate issued pursuant to the statutory requirement that state officials certify to the state all particulars relating to a birth proves only the fact of birth and not parentage. *Re Meyer's Estate* (1954) 206 Misc 368, 132 NYS2d 825. And the statute making death certificates *prima facie* evidence of the facts stated therein, has been held not to apply in cases of private controversies between adverse parties. *Re Curtiss' Will* (1931, Sur Ct) 140 Misc 185, 250 NYS 146.

An original marriage certificate made by the person by whom it is solemnized within the state, or the original entry thereof made pursuant to law in the office of the clerk of the city or town within the state, is *prima facie* evidence of the marriage. CPLR 4526.

Any record of the observations of the weather taken under the direction of the U.S. Weather Bureau is *prima facie* evidence of the facts stated. CPLR 4528. An inspection certificate issued by authorized agents of the U.S. Department of Agriculture on file with the U.S. Secretary of Agriculture is *prima facie* evidence of the facts stated. CPLR 4529.

When a public officer is required or authorized by special provision of law to make a certificate or affidavit to a fact ascertained or an act performed by him in the course of his official duties and to file or deposit it in a public office of the state, the certificate or affidavit so filed or deposited is *prima facie* evidence of the facts stated. CPLR 4520.

Entries that are not based upon the personal knowledge of the official making them are ordinarily inadmissible. *Greenberg v Prudential Ins. Co.* (1943) 266 AD 685, 40 NYS2d 494. Thus, a statement contained in a medical examiner's report that the decedent was said to have "fallen on subway platform" was held to be inadmissible. *Welz v Commercial Travelers Mut. Acc. Ass'n* (1943) 266 AD 668, 40 NYS2d 128.

A conviction in a criminal proceeding is admissible in evidence against a party in a subsequent civil suit based on the same facts, as conclusive proof of the facts contained in the certificate. *S. T. Grand, Inc. v New York* (1973) 32 NY2d 300, 344 NYS2d 938.

A certified copy of a motor vehicle accident report has been held to be an official record, admissible without any preliminary proof of the authenticity of the purported signature of the maker thereof, absent proof of lack of authenticity. *Welde v Wolfson* (1969, 2d Dept) 32 AD2d 973, 302 NYS2d 906.

The printed copy of a utility company's rate schedule, although uncertified, showed a Public Service Commission number of this state and an effective date. It was held to be *prima facie* evidence of the filed original tariff or classification, and it was error for the trial court to refuse to admit it into evidence. *Newman v Consolidated Edison Co.* (1973) 79 Misc 2d 153, 360 NYS2d 141.

In a negligence case, a certified copy of an autopsy report is properly admissible into evidence under CPLR 4518(c). *Nau v Ferrante* (1976, 1st Dept) 52 AD2d 523, 381 NYS2d 512.

The portion of a defendant driver's motor vehicle accident form containing her admission that she was travelling in a westbound direction at the time of the accident was properly admitted into evidence. *Dempsey v National Car Rental System, Inc.* (1982, 2d Dept) 87 AD2d 835, 449 NYS2d 270.

In an action by an attorney against former clients to recover fees, the trial court properly refused to admit into evidence an affidavit of the calendar clerk showing the number of times the case was marked "ready." *Levine v Threshman* (1982, 3d Dept) 91 AD2d 789, 458 NYS2d 75.

In a wrongful death suit arising out of decedent's suicide in jail, a report prepared by the Medical Review Commission of the State Commission of Corrections, pursuant to the Corrections Law concerning decedent's death, was at the very least admissible under the public documents common law exception to the hearsay rule because the report was prepared pursuant to a statutory mandate. *Kozlowski v Amsterdam* (1985, 3d Dept) 111 AD2d 476, 488 NYS2d 862.

§ 23:12 POLICE REPORTS — The report of a police officer who has not witnessed an accident and has based the report on hearsay statements is inadmissible as an entry made in the regular course of business. *Needle v New York R. Corp.* (1929) 227 AD

276, 237 NYS 547. Where, however, the police officer testifies at trial that he spoke to the plaintiff and the plaintiff described to him how the accident happened, the policeman's report is admissible in evidence as a record made in the regular course of business where its introduction is sought by an adverse party. *Zaulich v Thompkins Square Holding Co.* (1960, 1st Dept) 10 AD2d 492, 200 NYS2d 550. Where a policeman's report related to conditions observed by him in the general area of an accident at or about the time of the accident, the report was admissible. *Francies v County of Westchester* (1962) 36 Misc 2d 1062, 234 NYS2d 362.

Reports made by police officers based on their own observations while carrying out their police duties are admissible in evidence. *Yeargans v Yeargans* (1965, 1st Dept) 24 AD2d 280, 265 NYS2d 562.

Police records in the form of youth investigation cards completed by the officers who were eyewitnesses to the events described, pursuant to their duty in accordance with official procedure, were admissible as business records to prove the acts described therein without the necessity of calling the individual officers. *Re Anonymous* (1964) 44 Misc 2d 691, 254 NYS2d 967.

It was error for the trial court, over objections, to admit into evidence the police-aided card stating that decedent had been a passenger in a taxicab. *Prado v Onor Oscar, Inc.* (1974, 2d Dept) 44 AD2d 604, 353 NYS2d 789.

A police memorandum is admissible upon issue of existence of a stop sign under CPLR 4518(a). *Schlobohm v Command Trucking Corp.* (1976, 2d Dept) 52 AD2d 844, 382 NYS2d 816.

It was not error for the court to admit into evidence portions of two police accident reports containing diagrams purporting to represent the position of the parties' vehicles at the conclusion of the accident, because the police officer testified that the diagrams were based on his observations at the scene, not on statements made to him by others. *Heiney v Pattillo* (1980, 2d Dept) 76 AD2d 855, 428 NYS2d 513.

A police complaint report that contained an admission by a defendant that his car had been parked in front of his house, unlocked, with the keys in the ignition when it was stolen, was admissible as evidence in chief in a personal injury action brought by plaintiff against defendant as a result of a collision between defendant's vehicle, which was operated by a thief, and the vehicle in which plaintiffs were riding. *Shea v Johnson* (1984, 4th Dept) 101 AD2d 1018, 476 NYS2d 706.

If a recorder is under a business duty to record information supplied to him, while his informant is not duty-bound to supply that information, a writing created as a result of such a transaction would not be admissible in evidence under the statutory business record rule as a hearsay exception. *Murray v Donlan* (1980, 2d Dept) 77 AD2d 337, 433 NYS2d 184. Thus, a police report containing an opinion on the speed of the defendant's car and its failure to yield the right of way, not credited to anyone, is excludable under the hearsay rule as a recorded statement made by someone whose duty to make such a statement was unproven. *Murray v Donlan, supra.*

A reconstructed police accident report that was based on the personal observations of the scene by the police officer, not on hearsay statements, and was made by a person under a business duty to make the report was admissible under the CPLR 4518(a), so long as it was made within a reasonable time of the event. *D'Arienzo v Manderville* (1984, 3d Dept) 106 AD2d 686, 484 NYS2d 171.

The admission into evidence of a police report was erroneous because the identification of a particular vehicle as the one involved in the accident in question, contained in that report, was based solely on the hearsay declaration of an anonymous non-party bystander. *Peerless Ins. Co. v Milloul* (1988, 2d Dept) 140 AD2d 346, 527 NYS2d 838. *See also, Flores v Pharmakitis* (1994, 1st Dept) 209 AD2d 205, 618 NYS2d 293.

The trial court properly excluded a police report, offered to show the time of accident, where: the officer did not testify; the declarant was not identified; and there was no indication of how the time of accident was ascertained. *Cadieux v D.B. Interiors, Inc.* (1995, 1st Dept) 214 AD2d 323, 624 NYS2d 582.

In an action brought for dental malpractice, arising out of dental bridgework entailing root canal therapy, it was error for the trial court to strike plaintiff's dental history from the hospital records before they were admitted into evidence; where the question of the origin and type of infectious bacteria was pertinent to the proper diagnosis and treatment of plaintiff's condition, the dental history, expressly including the history that she developed extensive root canal work with abscesses and purulent discharge, should have been allowed in evidence by the trial court, because the court's ruling to the contrary inhibited the plaintiff's proper efforts to present the theory of the case. *Moran v Demarinis* (1989, 2d Dept) 152 AD2d 546, 543 NYS2d 480.

An uncertified clinic record relied on by an insurer as proof of the insured's longtime drug use, was nothing more than hearsay and therefore did not constitute competent proof that the insured was, as claimed, a drug user. *Botway v American International Assurance. Co.* (1989, 1st Dept) 151 AD2d 288, 543 NYS2d 651.

In a civil action brought against the New York City Transit Authority and its police officer for assault and battery, false arrest and malicious prosecution, it was error for the trial court to permit plaintiff to introduce into evidence the substance of five civilian complaints, because they constituted unsubstantiated hearsay. *Kourtalis v City of New York* (1993, 2d Dept) 191 AD2d 480, 594 NYS2d 325.

§ 23:13　HOSPITAL RECORDS — Records kept by a hospital in diagnosing and treating the ills of its patients are admissible as records kept in the ordinary course of business. *Williams v Alexander* (1955) 309 NY 283. Nurses' notes contained in a hospital record with respect to the patient and made in the regular course of business are admissible in the patient's automobile negligence action. *Spoar v Fudjack* (1965, 4th Dept) 24 AD2d 731, 263 NYS2d 340.

However, if memoranda contained in hospital records with respect to the history of an accident and the causes thereof are not relevant to diagnosis or treatment, they are not admissible as an entries made in the regular course of business. *Williams v Alexander, supra*.

Where the hopsital record kept at a state psychiatric hospital was so inadequate that it failed to conform to the standards of record-keeping in the community, it was found to have been a contributing factor that militated against proper and competent psychiatric and ordinary medical care being given to the plaintiff at that hospital. *Whitree v State* (1968) 56 Misc 693, 290 NYS2d 486.

The diagnosis contained in a hospital record should have been admitted into evidence. *Pekar v Tax* (1974, 2d Dept) 43 AD2d 957, 352 NYS2d 39.

Hospital intern's notation that patient tried to jump from window was admissible to establish the patient's state of mind in wrongful death action notwithstanding that the intern had not observed the incident. *Eady v Alter* (1976, 2d Dept) 51 AD2d 991, 380 NYS2d 737.

In a proceeding brought by the state to involuntarily admit a mentally retarded person to a school for the mentally retarded, while the recorded conclusions of physicians and others attending to petitioner's needs during a former commitment at a school for the mentally retarded would be admissible were they germane to treatment and could be utilized by court experts as the basis of their opinions, many of the entries included statements and remarks made by third persons who were not under a business duty to report to the entrant or were not otherwise admissible under an independent exception to the hearsay rule, and consequently such portions should have been excluded. *Re Harry M.* (1983, 2d Dept) 96 AD2d 201, 468 NYS2d 359.

A hospital record containing a report that the person admitted to the hospital was intoxicated upon admission is admissible, because such condition is pertinent to the diagnosis and treatment of the patient. *Campbell v Manhattan & Bronx Surface Transit Operating Auth.* (1981, 1st Dept) 81 AD2d 529, 438 NYS2d 87.

It was error for the trial court to exclude the blood test portion of the plaintiff's hospital record, on the purported ground that the foundation was insufficient, because the defendant offered unrebutted testimony that the blood test was needed for care and treatment and the record was certified pursuant to CPLR 4518(c), thus was *prima facie* evidence of the facts contained therein. *LaDuke v State Farm Ins. Co.* (1990, 4th Dept) 158 AD2d 137, 557 NYS2d 221.

When statements are made to hospital personnel and recorded in the hospital record, the statement must fall within an exception to the hearsay rule, or a two-part test must be satisfied for those statements to be admissible: (1) the statement must be within the scope of the entrant's duty to record, and (2) the declarant must be under a business duty to report the statement. *In re Commissioner of Social Servs, Alex K v Ligia K* (1994, 2d Dept) 207 AD2d 488, 615 NYS2d 923. In this decision, a neglect proceeding, entries in the mother's hospital record reflecting statements by the children that the mother had hit and bitten them were ruled admissible. Although the children were not under a business duty to report the mother's behavior to the hospital, the statements were admissible under Family Court Act § 1046(a)(iv), permitting admission of any writing made as a memorandum or record of any condition, act, transaction, occurrence or event relating to a child in an abuse or neglect proceeding.

The trial court, over plaintiff's objection, improperly admitted into evidence a hearsay statement in the hospital's records to the effect that plaintiff had fallen at home. The statement attributed to plaintiff was not germane to diagnosis or treatment, and was therefore not admissible as an integral part of the hospital's records; and since the source of the statement remained at best, unclear, the defendants failed to establish that the records contained an admission that would otherwise justify the disclosure of the statement to the jury. *Echeverria v City of New York* (1990, 2d Dept) 166 AD2d 409, 560 NYS2d 473.

§ 23:14 DOCTORS' RECORDS — The office cards of a deceased doctor, written in his own handwriting each time he saw the patient and properly identified as such by his widow, were admissible in evidence. *Jezowski v Beach* (1968) 59 Misc 2d 224, 298 NYS2d 360. In this decision, the court also found that electroencephalograms the doctor had administered to the plaintiff were admissible, after the doctor's widow identified them and testified that she worked in her husband's office. However, the deceased doctor's opinions and the diagnosis written in his own handwriting on the backs of the encephalograms were not admissible.

The records of a deceased doctor, who was not the attending physician, were not admitted into evidence, because the court held that they contained opinions that were not the records of an act, transaction, occurrence, or event made in the course of the doctor's profession. *Goodkin v Brooklyn & Queens Transit Corp.* (1934) 241 AD 737, 269 NYS 809, affd 265 NY 638, 193 NE 422.

When a doctor treats a person involved in an accident and prepares a medical report, he has an obligation to appear and give testimony. Therefore, when the doctor is in a position to testify but declines to do so unless paid an outrageous fee, his medical records covering the patient's visits – including the treatment rendered, the patient's complaints, the physical examination of the patient, whether the doctor took x-rays, the doctor's medicinal prescriptions, laboratory reports, progress record and discharge record – are admissible in evidence under CPLR 4518, but are not admissible in regard to any medical opinion. *Hessek v Roman Catholic Church of Our Lady of Lourdes* (1975) 80 Misc 2d 410, 363 NYS2d 297.

The trial court properly excluded from evidence the reports of two doctors, which contained their diagnoses and opinions relative to plaintiff's condition, because neither doctor was called to testify and no proper foundation was otherwise laid for their admission. *Sabatino v Turf House, Inc.* (1980, 3d Dept) 76 AD2d 945, 428 NYS2d 752. These reports were not admissible as records kept in the ordinary course of business by the doctors in question, because the doctor through whom plaintiff attempted to establish the business practices and procedures of the doctors who had made the reports, obviously had no knowledge of such practices and procedures, and therefore was unable to lay the necessary foundation. *Sabatino v Turf House, Inc., supra.*

Physicians' reports prepared for litigation are generally inadmissible in evidence under the business records exception to the hearsay rule. *Wilson v Bodian* (1987, 2d Dept) 130 AD2d 221, 519 NYS2d 126. However, a physician's office records containing entries germane to diagnosis and treatment are admissible, including medical opinions and conclusions. *Wilson v Bodian, supra.*

A physician's office records are admissible in evidence under the business record exception to the hearsay rule, and these records may be received as evidence despite the fact that a physician is unable to testify regarding the substance and contents of the records. *Napolitano v Branks* (1988, 2d Dept) 141 AD2d 705, 529 NYS2d 824.

§ 23:15 MEDICAL HISTORY — A treating physician may testify to the history obtained from the patient if it is germane to diagnosis and treatment. *Scott v Mason* (1989, 2d Dept) 155 AD2d 655, 547 NYS2d 889. The limited history testified to by the treating physician, that plaintiff's van was struck by some form of motor vehicle, was medically relevant to the diagnosis and treatment and was therefore admissible. *Scott v Mason, supra.*

§ 23:16 PEDIGREE — Evidence of pedigree declarations are admissible as an exception to the hearsay rule. *Eisenlord v Clum* (1891) 126 NY 552, 27 NE 1024. Matters of pedigree embrace not only descent and relationship, but birth, marriage, and death, and the times when these events occurred. *Eisenlord v Clum, supra.* Admissibility of such evidence arises from the necessity of the case since frequently it is the only evidence obtainable. Declarations that are admissible are those of deceased declarants that were made in the presence of living witnesses. *Eisenlord v Clum, supra.*

Proof may be admissible either as to an affirmative issue or as to a negative issue. *Washington v Bank for Sav.* (1902) 171 NY 166, 63 NE 831. Of course, it may be shown through pedigree evidence that a person died without issue. *Washington v Bank for Sav., supra.* Before a pedigree declaration may be admitted, the declarant must be deceased, *Re Findlay* (1930) 253 NY 1, 170 NE 471, incompetent, beyond the jurisdiction of the court, or unavailable for some other reason so that there is no way of obtaining his testimony directly. *Young v Shulenberg* (1901) 165 NY 385, 59 NE 135. The declaration must have been made before the existence of a controversy, so that there would have been no motive on the part of the declarant to either falsify or distort. *Re Findlay, supra.* There must be a family tie, either by blood or by affinity, between the declarant and the family involved. *Aalholm v People* (1914) 211 NY 406, 105 NE 647.

The matters that may be proved by pedigree declarations include such matters as family history, *Re Powers' Estate* (1950) 96 NYS2d 25, whether a particular person is a member of the family involved or related thereto, *Aalholm v People, supra*, whether a person was treated or regarded as a member of the family, *Re Kennedy* (1913) 82 Misc 214, 143 NYS 404, matters of legitimacy and paternity, *Re Monty's Estate* (1941) 32 NYS2d 705, revd 264 AD 7, 34 NYS2d 1011, revd 89 NY 685, and matters pertaining to births and marriages, *Young v Shulenberg, supra*, as well as deaths. *People v Miller* (1900) 30 Misc 355, 63 NYS 949.

Although hearsay declarations regarding pedigree are open to suspicion, they are not rejected on this ground alone. *Johnson v La Sala Mason Corp.* (1963, 3d Dept) 19 AD2d 925, 244 NYS2d 31.

For the pedigree exception to apply, one's pedigree must be directly in issue in the case. *Eisenlord v Clum, supra*. It is not sufficient that questions of birth, parentage, or relationship are involved incidentally. *Eisenlord v Clum, supra*. The declarations need not be those of the declarant, but may be based on evidence that a deceased member of a family stated that he heard certain facts. *Eisenlord v Clum, supra*.

§ 23:17   MORTALITY AND ANNUITY TABLES — Standard and recognized mortality and life expectancy tables are admissible in evidence as an exception to the hearsay rule. Mortality tables are admissible in permanent injury cases to show the length of time that a plaintiff will suffer from the effects of an injury. *Barone v Forgette* (1955) 286 AD 588, 146 NYS2d 63, reh and app den 1 AD2d 792, 149 NYS2d 235. Such tables are evidence of the average life expectancy among the class of persons in question. *Hartley v Eagle Ins. Co.* (1918) 222 NY 178, 118 NE 622, 3 ALR 1379.

The court, in charging the life expectancy of the decedent, must also charge that of the widow, *Briscoe v United States* (1933, CA2 NY) 65 F2d 404, or the expectancy of the surviving next of kin. *Bishin v New York C. R. Co.* (1964, 2d Dept) 20 AD2d 921, 249 NYS2d 778.

§ 23:18   CHURCH RECORDS AND FAMILY BIBLES — While ordinarily pedigree evidence relates to the admission of all declarations of deceased persons, it is also permissible to introduce into evidence facts and entries made without intent to deceive; such as entries in a family bible, inscriptions on a tombstone, pedigrees hung up in a family mansion, or recitals in deeds. *Layton v Kraft* (1906) 111 AD 842, 98 NYS 72. Written or printed family trees are also admissible, *Commonwealth Water Co. v Brunner* (1916) 175 AD 153, 161 NYS 794, as well as genealogies. *Re Floyd-Jones' Estate* (1955, Sur Ct) 154 NYS2d 668.

§ 23:19 ANCIENT DOCUMENTS — An ancient document, under the proper circumstances, and after a proper foundation has been laid, may be admitted into evidence to prove the truth of the statements contained therein as an exception to the hearsay rule. It must be shown that the writing is more than 30 years old, has been in the possession of the natural custodian, and is free from indications of fraud or invalidity. *Fairchild v Union Ferry Co.* (1923) 121 Misc 513, 201 NYS 295, affd 212 AD 823, 207 NYS 835, affd 240 NY 666, 148 NE 750. If the document satisfies the foregoing requirements, no other evidence of its authenticity need be presented. *Fairchild v Union Ferry Co., supra.*

All maps, surveys, official records affecting real property that have been on file with the state in the office of the registrar of any county, county clerk, court of record, or any department of the City of New York for more than 10 years are *prima facie* evidence of their contents. CPLR 4522.

§ 23:20 *RES GESTAE* — The term *res gestae* is somewhat confusing. In one sense, it refers to the admissibility of evidence under an exception to the hearsay rule based on the theory that the statement is so connected in point of time with an occurrence, that its very spontaneity gives it evidentiary value in determining the issues. In a different sense, the term refers to declarations that are admitted not for the truth of the facts asserted, but for their legal significance in characterizing the particular act or transaction. In this sense, such declarations are not within the hearsay rule and it is therefore not necessary to find still another exception to the hearsay rule for the purpose of rendering them admissible.

In some cases, the declarations of agents have been held to be admissible or inadmissible, depending upon whether or not they were part of the *res gestae. Luby v Hudson R. R. Co.* (1858) 17 NY

131. The admissions of an agent are inadmissible against his principal unless he has been expressly authorized to make such statements and they were made with respect to some act done in the course of his agency, so as to form part of the *res gestae. Taylor v Commercial Bank* (1903) 174 NY 181, 66 NE 726. In an action for services rendered for doing certain printing, where an issue arose regarding the authority of defendant's attorney to order the work, admissions and declarations made to plaintiff while the work was in progress, by an officer of defendant, were competent evidence as a part of the *res gestae. Livingston- Middleditch Co. v New York College of Dentistry* (1900) 31 Misc 259, 64 NYS 140. It has been held that a conversation between a broker and a prospective customer is admissible against the principal in an action to recover for commission as part of the *res gestae* of the employment. *Jaffe v Nagel* (1909, App Tm) 114 NYS 905.

Where facts and circumstances tend to show the financial, mental and physical condition of a deceased person just before the time of his death, they have been held to be admissible as part of the *res gestae* where an action on insurance policy involves issues regarding a possible intentional suicide. *Goldschmidt v Mutual Life Ins. Co.* (1909) 134 AD 475, 119 NYS 233.

When a declaration is offered to establish the state of mind, rather than the truth of any objectively verifiable underlying fact, then that declaration, although technically hearsay, is admissible as part of the *res gestae. Re Eichner on behalf of Fox* (1980, 2d Dept) 73 AD2d 431, 426 NYS2d 517, mod on other grounds 52 NY2d 363, 438 NYS2d 266, cert den 454 US 858, 70 L Ed 2d 153, 102 S Ct 309.

Where a co-employee of the plaintiff testified that, immediately after the accident and while plaintiff was lying in the eastbound lane of the highway with his feet extending into the westbound lane, the driver of defendant's truck made the following statement: "Get his feet out of the way. I want to get out of here," over the objection of this defendant, the statement should not have been received into evidence since it was unrelated to the happening of the accident and was highly prejudicial. *Zipay v Benson* (1975, 3d Dept) 47 AD2d 233, 365 NYS2d 920, later app (3d

Dept) 57 AD2d 683, 393 NYS2d 825, app dismd 42 NY2d 1052, 399 NYS2d 214.

To be admissible against a principal as part of the *res gestae*, the declaration of an agent must be contemporaneous with the event at issue, made in and as part of the business entrusted to the agent, and calculated to unfold its nature and characterize its action so that the acts and declarations combine to form one transaction. *Loschiavo v Port Authority of New York & New Jersey* (1982, 2d Dept) 86 AD2d 624, 446 NYS2d 358, affd 58 NY2d 1040, 462 NYS2d 440.

§ 23:21 SPONTANEOUS DECLARATIONS — Certain declarations of a spontaneous nature are admissible, under proper circumstances, as an exception to the hearsay rule. Three elements are necessary to give a spontaneous declaration admissibility under this exception to the hearsay rule: (1) there must be an occurrence sufficiently startling to produce a spontaneous and unreflecting statement, *Swensson v New York Albany Despatch Co.* (1956) 309 NY 497, (2) there must be no time to fabricate, *Swensson v New York Albany Despatch Co., supra*, and (3) the statement must relate to the circumstances of the occurrence, *People v Del Vermo* (1908) 192 NY 470, 85 NE 690.

Spontaneous declarations are admitted on the theory that spontaneity bars an opportunity for fabrication. *Swensson v New York Albany Despatch Co., supra*. Thus, where the brakes on a tractor-trailer failed while the vehicle was on a hill, and the driver of the vehicle was killed and his rider injured, the statement of the driver at the top of the hill to the effect that the air from his air-brakes was gone was held to be a classic example of the admissibility of a spontaneous declaration as part of the *res gestae*. *Swensson v New York Albany Despatch Co., supra*.

In order for testimony to be admissible under the spontaneous declaration exception to the hearsay rule, it must be made while the speaker is under the stress resulting from the startling event, although there is no fixed period of time within which the declaration shall have been made. *Saturno v Yanow* (1977, 4th Dept) 58 AD2d 968, 397 NYS2d 250. Testimony by the defendant driver that following the accident, at the scene, a passenger in plaintiff's vehicle had stated that he kept shouting to stop and that the

plaintiff had not done so, was properly received under the spontaneous declaration exception to the hearsay rule. *Saturno v Yanow,
supra.*

The question whether a spontaneous declaration conforms to
the spontaneity requirements of the rule is a preliminary question
to be determined by the trial judge, not the jury. The test used to
determine the reliability of the statement is whether it was
uttered at a time when the declarant was so influenced by the
excitement and shock of the event that it is probable he or she
spoke impulsively and without reflection, rather than with calm
deliberation after reflection. *People v Caviness* (1975) 38 NY2d
227, 379 NYS2d 695.

Excited utterances are a form of spontaneous declaration and
are admissible as an exception to the hearsay rule. *People v Del
Vermo, supra.* This exception to the hearsay rule allows proof of
statements by an injured person that were made somewhat after
the event; thus it is not accurate to say that the excited utterance
must constitute a part of the event. *People v Del Vermo, supra.*
However, this does not mean that the time when the utterances
were made in relation to the event is immaterial with regard to
the question of its admissibility. There is obviously a clear distinction between an utterance that is made immediately following
an event at a time when the declarant is still responding to the
event, and an utterance made so long after the event that it is
merely a narrative. A statement made under the latter circumstances, is not part of the *res gestae* and is inadmissible even if it
is made soon after the event. *Carroll v Knickerbocker Ice Co.*
(1916) 218 NY 435, 113 NE 507. Where there has been an opportunity for the declarant to formulate the contents of the statement
so that the statement no longer forms a part of the main event,
the courts reject the statement as hearsay. *Greener v General
Electric Co.* (1913) 209 NY 135, 102 NE 527.

When a declaration of past pain is offered for the truth of the
statement made, it is ordinarily inadmissible because the element
of spontaneity is lacking. *Davidson v Cornell* (1892) 132 NY 228,
30 NE 573. Where, however, such a declaration is made to a physician for purposes of treatment, its reliability is likely to be

greater and it should be admissible. *Meaney v United States* (1940, CA2 NY) 112 F2d 538, 130 ALR 973.

It was error to admit testimony that five minutes after a boy was hurt during basketball practice, the physical education director came on the scene and scolded the coach for ordering the drill. *Strauch v Hirschman* (1972, 2d Dept) 40 AD2d 711, 336 NYS2d 678.

The former rule that spontaneous declarations made by persons not participating in the act, such as a bystander, were excluded, is no longer valid; the spontaneous declaration of a non-participant, who has sufficient proximity to the occurrence and adequate opportunity to observe, which otherwise qualifies, is admissible. *People v Caviness* (1975) 38 NY2d 227, 379 NYS2d 695.

The statement made by a heavily bleeding accident victim, almost immediately after the accident, that he had been hit by the bus was a spontaneous declaration, admissible as an exception to the hearsay rule. *Flynn v Manhattan & Bronx Surface Transit Operating Authority* (1983, 1st Dept) 94 AD2d 617, 462 NYS2d 17, affd 61 NY2d 769, 473 NYS2d 154.

The testimony of plaintiff with respect to a conversation between a co-plaintiff and another person, which was obviously made under the stress of the moment without time for reflection or deliberation, qualified as a properly admissible spontaneous declaration. *Schiaroli v Ellenville* (1985, 3d Dept) 111 AD2d 947, 490 NYS2d 43.

In a prosecution for sodomy, the trial court properly admitted as an excited utterance the statement of the 5-year-old victim, because it was given within 15 minutes of the incident and made under the impetus of a startling event. *People v Kulakowski* (1987, 4th Dept) 135 AD2d 1119, 523 NYS2d 288, app den 70 NY2d 1007, 526 NYS2d 942. However, where approximately 45 minutes to one hour elapsed from the time that the victim had been beaten until the time she called a neighbor to tell her of the occurrence, the neighbor's testimony was inadmissible hearsay rather than an excited utterance in the absence of any evidence that the victim lacked the capacity for reflection during the interval between the occurrence and her call to the neighbor. *People v*

Clark (1987, 4th Dept) 135 AD2d 1097, 523 NYS2d 315, app den 71 NY2d 894, 527 NYS2d 1003.

The statements of a mortally wounded shooting victim made approximately 30 minutes after the occurrence in the emergency room to a police officer, were admissible as excited utterances, where they were made under the influence of the stress and excitement of being shot three times and fatally wounded, the pain was unabating, and the victim's condition steadily deteriorating. *People v Brown* (1987) 70 NY2d 513, 522 NYS2d 837.

A statement made by an automobile driver to a passenger just before the accident, that the ramp leading to an underpass was covered with ice, and that she was unable to control her automobile, was an excited utterance and therefore the statement was admissible in a civil suit arising out of the accident. *Deutsch v Horizon Leasing Corp.* (1988, 2d Dept) 145 AD2d 405, 535 NYS2d 383.

The spontaneous declaration exception to the hearsay rule applies to statements made by bystanders as well as participants, and the bystander need not be identified as long as the statements are sufficiently corroborated by other evidence. *Taft v New York City Transit Auth.* (1993, 1st Dept) 193 AD2d 503, 597 NYS2d 374.

§ 23:22 DECLARATIONS EVIDENCING INTENTION AND STATE OF MIND — Where a declarant's state of mind is an issue, statements he made that evidence his state of mind should not be excluded. *Provenzo v Sam* (1968) 23 NY2d 256, 296 NYS2d 322. In an action for personal injuries that occurred when plaintiff stopped his truck and crossed the highway to aid defendant motorist, whom plaintiff thought had suffered an illness, the plaintiff was struck by an approaching vehicle operated by a second defendant. Plaintiff's statement, made when he observed the wayward course of the first defendant's vehicle, that the defendant must have suffered illness, was admissible to shed light on why the plaintiff had crossed the highway. *Provenzo v Sam, supra.*

Declarations of intention are admissible to assist in interpreting "an equivocation," which is language that when applied to external objects, fits two or more equally. *Re Blodgett's Estate* (1938, Sur Ct) 168 Misc 898, 7 NYS2d 364. Evidence of what was said to a sheriff when a summons in an action on a fire policy was delivered to him within the time provided for bringing an action, was held to be admissible to show an intent that it should be served, in view of the statute regarding commencement of an action to avoid the statute of limitations. *Cohoes Bronze Co. v Georgia Home Ins. Co.* (1935) 243 AD 224, 276 NYS 619. In an executor's discovery proceeding to reach a fund that the testator unknowingly transferred to a legatee shortly before his death, declarations made by the testator after the date of the transfer were inadmissible. *Re Landau's Estate* (1937) 163 Misc 894, 298 NYS 150. Under certain circumstances, delivery and acceptance of an *inter vivos* gift may be proved by the declarations of the donor. *Re Earley's Will* (1950, Sur Ct) 198 Misc 727, 96 NYS2d 716. In an action for the wrongful death of parents, the wills of the parents should have been admitted to help assess the pecuniary burden that would have been assumed by them with respect to their Mongoloid child. *Zaninovich v American Airlines, Inc.* (1966, 1st Dept) 26 AD2d 155, 271 NYS2d 866.

Where a witness's state of mind is relevant, the witness may testify to out-of-court statements made by others that would indicate circumstantially what the witness believed at the time. *Bergstein v Board of Education* (1974) 34 NY2d 318, 357 NYS2d 465.

Declarations of a donor are competent evidence to establish a gift. *Re Rinchiuso's Estate* (1964, 4th Dept) 20 AD2d 254, 246 NYS2d 798, affd 15 NY2d 865, 258 NYS2d 108.

A testator's utterances, acts, and expressions, whether before or after the making of a will, are competent to show the testator's state of mind and affection for or dislike of, specific persons as well as his general testamentary attitude toward them. *Re Frank's Estate* (1937, Sur Ct) 165 Misc 411, 1 NYS2d 482, mod 253 AD 706, 1 NYS2d 860.

Where the domicile of a person is in issue, his declarations evidencing his intent to stay are admissible, because intent is an element of domicile. *Re Newcomb's Estate* (1908) 192 NY 238, 84 NE 950. Intent, however, does not have to be at issue in order for a declaration of intent to be admissible. *Stokes v People* (1873) 53 NY 164.

In a prosecution for sexual abuse, the trial court properly admitted testimony of the victim's mother about statements made by the victim during a nightmare; the statement was not hearsay because it was not admitted for the truth of any fact but solely to show the mental state of the victim, and moreover, the statement did not contain any facts accusing defendant of the commission of a crime. *People v DiFabio* (1991, 4th Dept) 170 AD2d 1028, 566 NYS2d 172.

§ 23:23   DECLARATIONS AGAINST INTEREST — Declarations against interest under the proper circumstances are admissible as an exception to the hearsay rule.

A declaration against interest is admissible even though made by a person who is not a party to or in privity with a party to the action. *Tompkins v Fonda Glove Lining Co.* (1907) 188 NY 261, 80 NE 933, reh den 188 NY 635, 81 NE 1177. For a declaration against interest to be admissible: (1) it was required that the declarant must be deceased, *Kittredge v Grannis* (1926) 244 NY 168, 155 NE 88, or absent from the jurisdiction, *Jamison v Walker* (1975, 2d Dept) 48 AD2d 320, 369 NYS2d 469; (2) the declaration must be against the pecuniary interest of the declarant at the time it was made, *Gottwald v Medinger* (1939) 257 AD 107, 12 NYS2d 241; (3) the declarant must have competent knowledge of the matter about which the declaration was made, *Livingston v Arnoux* (1874) 56 NY 507; and (4) the declarant must have no motive to falsify such declaration, *Mills v Davis* (1889) 113 NY 243, 21 NE 68.

The hearsay statement of a minor was not admissible as an admission against interest because it was not established that the declarant was unavailable or that when the declarant made the statement he knew it was against his interest. *Ellis v Allstate Ins. Co.* (1983, 4th Dept) 97 AD2d 970, 468 NYS2d 776.

To qualify for admission into evidence as a declaration against the maker's penal interest: (1) the declarant must be unavailable as a witness at trial, (2) when the statement was made, the declarant must have been aware that it was adverse to his penal interest, (3) the declarant must have competent knowledge of the facts underlying the statement, and (4) and most important, supporting circumstances independent of the statement itself must be present to attest to the trustworthiness and reliability of the statement. *People v Settles* (1978) 46 NY2d 154, 412 NYS2d 874.

Declarations made by an insured after she had taken poison indicating that she did not care to live, were admissible in a beneficiary's action on a life insurance policy. *Martorella v Prudential Ins. Co.* (1933) 238 AD 532, 264 NYS 751. A decedent's declarations that tend to sustain a claim against the estate are competent as admissions against interest. *Re Kempf's Estate* (1931, Sur Ct) 138 Misc 704, 248 NYS 247. Declarations of an alleged donor, since deceased, that she had given her bonds to her niece were admissible and constituted some evidence that a gift was made. *Re Gallagher's Will* (1943 Sur Ct) 46 NYS2d 275.

§ 23:24 CHILD PROTECTIVE PROCEEDINGS — Family Court Act § 1046(a)(vi) provides a hearsay exception for prior statements that children make in relation to allegations of abuse and neglect. *Le Favour v Koch* (1986, 3d Dept) 124 AD2d 903, 508 NYS2d 320. The Family Court properly credited the testimony regarding the out-of-court statements of the two children regarding abuse and neglect by their father. *Le Favour v Koch, supra; see also, In re Commissioner of Social Servs. ex rel. Tanya C. v Evelyn R.* (1995, 2d Dept) ___ AD2d ___, 630 NYS2d 338.

RESEARCH REFERENCES

American Law Reports

10 ALR5th 371, Admissibility of evidence of absence of other accidents or injuries at place where injury or damage occurred

89 ALR4th 456, Admissibility of testimony of expert, as to basis of his opinion, to matters otherwise excludible as hearsay–state cases

75 ALR4th 199, Residual hearsay exception where declarant unavailable; Uniform Evidence Rule 804(b)(5)

57 ALR4th 1111, Admissibility of school records under hearsay exceptions

54 ALR4th 746, Libel and slander: sufficiency of identification of allegedly defamed party

51 ALR4th 999, Uniform Evidence Rule 803(24): the residual hearsay exception

31 ALR4th 913, Admissibility in state court proceedings of police reports under official record exception to hearsay rule

15 ALR4th 1043, Admissibility of testimony regarding spontaneous declarations made by one incompetent to testify at trial

14 ALR4th 802, Admissibility of evidence concerning words spoken while declarant was asleep or unconscious

94 ALR3d 975, Evidence: admissibility of memorandum of telephone conversation

92 ALR3d 1138, Admissibility of former testimony of nonparty witness, present in jurisdiction, who refuses to testify at subsequent trial without making claim of privilege

80 ALR3d 456, Admissibility under state law of hospital record relating to intoxication or sobriety of patient

80 ALR3d 414, Admissibility, under public records exception to hearsay rule, of record kept by public official without express statutory direction or authorization

36 ALR3d 12, Comment note-Hearsay evidence in proceedings before state administrative agencies

19 ALR3d 1008, Admissibility, as against hearsay objection, of report of tests or experiments carried out by independent third party

ALR Quick Index: Hearsay

American Jurisprudence 2d

29 Am Jur 2d, Evidence §§ 493-522, 674-682, 708-768

American Jurisprudence Proof of Facts

49 Am Jur Proof of Facts 2d 649, General Reputation of Person in Community

36 Am Jur Proof of Facts 2d 605, Foundation for Telephone Conversation

35 Am Jur Proof of Facts 2d 589, Routine Business Practice

35 Am Jur Proof of Facts 2d 147, Foundation for Admission of Secondary Evidence

34 Am Jur Proof of Facts 2d 509, Foundation for Offering Business Records in Evidence

28 Am Jur Proof of Facts 2d 1, Foundation for Offering Deposition or Other Former Testimony in Evidence

22 Am Jur Proof of Facts 2d 1, Medical Malpractice-Use of Hospital Records

18 Am Jur Proof of Facts 2d 305, Admissibility of Opinion Survey

14 Am Jur Proof of Facts 2d 173, Admissibility of Computerized Business Records

Other Resources

8 Carmody-Wait 2d, Presentation of the Case §§ 56:27-56:29

Auto-Cite®: Any case citation herein can be checked for form, parallel references, later history and annotation references through the Auto-Cite computer research system.

CHAPTER 24

ADMISSIONS

§ 24:1 ADMISSIONS BY A PARTY OPPONENT — In a civil action, the admissions by a party of any fact material to the issue are always competent evidence against him, whenever, wherever, and to whomever made. *Reed v McCord* (1899) 160 NY 330, 54 NE 737. Proof of contradictory statements need not be direct and positive contradiction; it is enough that the testimony and statements are inconsistent and tend to prove different facts. *Nappi v Falcon Truck Renting Corp.* (1955) 286 AD 123, 141 NYS2d 424, affd 1 NY2d 750, 152 NYS2d 297.

Personal knowledge on the part of the party making the extrajudicial admissions is not necessary so long as the statements are inconsistent with his cause of action or defense. *Anthus v Rail Joint Co.* (1920) 193 AD 571, 185 NYS 314, affd 231 NY 557, 132 NE 887. Admissions by a party are held to be competent evidence on the theory that it is highly improbable that a party will admit or state anything against himself or even against his own interest unless it is true. *Reed v McCord, supra.*

Admissions are admissible for impeachment purposes and as evidence of the fact admitted. *Gangi v Fradus* (1920) 227 NY 452, 125 NE 677; *Burns v Dixon* (1974) 46 AD2d 943, 362 NYS2d 245. Such statements, inconsistent with a party's cause of action or defense, are not open to the objection of hearsay when offered in evidence. *Koester v Rochester Candy Works* (1909) 194 NY 92, 87 NE 77.

The defendant's negligence was conclusively established by her own uncontested admission that while driving in heavy traffic, she took her eyes off the road to search for something in her purse and drove directly into the car in front of her. *Andre v Pomeroy* (1974) 35 NY2d 361, 362 NYS2d 131.

A defendant testified that he had an unobstructed view of oncoming traffic for a distance of 150 feet but did not see an oncoming car until it was 30 feet away and the defendant had begun to make a left turn. This was an admission that he had not seen what he should have seen with the proper use of his senses and that he had violated the Vehicle and Traffic Law by making a left turn without carefully looking down the highway. *Pickard v Koenigstreuter* (1979, 3d Dept) 70 AD2d 693, 416 NYS2d 399, app dismd 48 NY2d 652, 421 NYS2d 202.

The fact that there is no opportunity for cross-examination of the person making the declaration is not a basis for excluding admissions as hearsay. *Koester v Rochester Candy Works, supra.* Such admissions are original evidence of the fact or facts admitted. *Koester v Rochester Candy Works, supra.*

A foundation is not required for the admissibility of an admission against a party in a civil action. *Keating v United States Light & Heating Co.* (1910, App Tm) 125 NYS 512. Because admissions are admissible not merely as impeaching evidence but as original evidence, it is not necessary to direct the attention of a witness to any inconsistent statements he made as a foundation to introducing proof of such statements. *Mindlin v Dorfman* (1912) 197 AD 770, 189 NYS 265.

The rules of *Miranda v Arizona* (1966) 384 US 436, 16 L Ed 2d 694, 86 S Ct 1602, 10 ALR3d 974, do not apply to admissions sought to be admitted in a civil action for damages for false imprisonment, assault, and battery. *Dixson v State* (1968, 3d Dept) 30 AD2d 626, 290 NYS2d 682. A defendant in a civil action for damages made a written statement in which he admitted an embezzlement. The written statement was not inadmissible on ground of the *Miranda* rule, because the criminal aspects of defendant's alleged wrongful acts had previously been resolved and defendant's statement constituted an admission against interest. *Greece Volunteer Ambulance Service, Inc. v Smith* (1969) 59 Misc 2d 1065, 301 NYS2d 865.

An admission may be made through an interpreter. *Ambrosino v Cie De Navagacao Lloyd Brasileiro* (1944) 267 AD 910, 47 NYS2d 61, reh den 267 AD 961, 48 NYS2d 439. Thus, an injured party who took an interpreter with him to the doctor's office made the interpreter his agent. Any statements made by the claimant to the doctor regarding the cause of the accident resulting in the injuries could be proven in evidence without the production of the interpreter to verify the accuracy of his translation. *Ambrosino v Cie De Navagacao Lloyd Brasileiro, supra*.

The unusual interest shown by a defendant in a filiation proceeding in obtaining an abortion for the complainant could be regarded as an admission against interest. *People ex rel. Quinlivan v Mendel* (1960, 3d Dept) 10 AD2d 767, 197 NYS2d 484, app den (3d Dept) 11 AD2d 605, 204 NYS2d 110, reh and app den (3d Dept) 11 AD2d 962, 207 NYS2d 250. A party's statement that is not an acknowledgement of a particular fact but rather is made in hypothetical, conditional, or tentative form or uttered without prejudice is not an admission and cannot be received in evidence. *White v Empire Mut. Ins. Co.* (1969) 59 Misc 2d 527, 299 NYS2d 998. However, a trooper's testimony that an insured voluntarily came to the state police barracks for a polygraph test and asked the trooper, "Suppose I did set the fire? What would I get out of it? Would there be any publicity? What fine or jail sentence would there be?" was admissible in an action on a fire policy, because the questions did constitute "admissions." *Terpstra v Niagara Fire Ins. Co.* (1970) 26 NY2d 70, 308 NYS2d 378, 43 ALR3d 1369.

Plaintiff, a high school student injured in the course of exercise in a gymnasium, executed an affidavit stating that the facts contained in his father's affidavit were true and correct. The father's affidavit, which purported to state the facts and circumstances of the accident, omitted a material fact claimed by the plaintiff. Nevertheless, the father's statement was admissible as plaintiff's admission, and the omission in the father's affidavit constituted an admission by the plaintiff. The exclusion of the father's affidavit was held to be error. *Cherney v Board of Education* (1969, 2d Dept) 31 AD2d 764, 297 NYS2d 668.

When a certificate of an attending physician is delivered as part of the proofs of death in connection with a claim on a life insurance policy, the certificate is an admission by the claimant as to the cause of death. *Carmichael v John Hancock Mut. Life Ins. Co.* (1904) 45 Misc 597, 90 NYS 1033.

The form of an admission, that is, whether it is oral or written, does not affect its admissibility, provided it is definite, certain, and unequivocal. *Laidlaw v Sage* (1899) 158 NY 73, 52 NE 679.

A hospital emergency room record indicated that the accident had occurred in a manner different from that testified to by the plaintiff at the trial. Even though the physician was unable to recall the incident individually, the record was admissible as an admission against interest, because the physician testified that he prepared the report in his own handwriting and signed it based on the history given to him by the plaintiff at the time of her treatment. *Argenziano v R. D. J. Holding Corp.* (1973, 2d Dept) 42 AD2d 970, 348 NYS2d 12.

The trial court erred in refusing to allow a defense witness to testify to an alleged declaration by plaintiff that was entirely inconsistent with his position at the trial. The fact that the witness was a medical doctor was irrelevant. *Ross v Schwartz* (1975, 2d Dept) 48 AD2d 844, 368 NYS2d 293.

A letter written by an unsuccessful candidate for the United States Senate in which he undertook personal responsibility for the costs of filming certain television commercials and sworn statements filed under the Federal Election Law stating that he had agreed to pay plaintiff the amounts contested constituted admissions. *Columbia Pictures Industries, Inc. v Stein for Senator Committee* (1980, 1st Dept) 77 AD2d 836, 431 NYS2d 23.

A party's testimony, which constitutes the statements of a layman in the stress of examination, generally cannot with justice be given the conclusiveness of a judicial admission in a pleading or stipulation, which is deliberately drafted by counsel for the express purpose of limiting and defining the facts in issue. *Skelka v Metropolitan Transit Authority* (1980, 2d Dept) 76 AD2d 492, 430 NYS2d 840.

In a proceeding to stay arbitration, a police report containing a statement by the insured establishing that there had been no contact between the insured's vehicle and a "hit-and-run" vehicle could be used by the insurer, because the statement qualified as an admission. *State Farm Mut. Auto. Ins. Co. v Bermudez* (1985, 2d Dept) 111 AD2d 858, 490 NYS2d 595.

The defendant driver's claim that he did not see the pedestrian until he was 10 feet or less away from her and that he did not see plaintiff prior to hitting her was an admission that he had failed to properly look out for the safety of pedestrians. *Avila v Mellen* (1987, 2d Dept) 131 AD2d 408, 515 NYS2d 856.

Plaintiff, who was shot by a fellow bar patron, could not maintain a cause of action based on the Dram Shop Act, because he admitted that he did not observe any visible signs that his attacker was intoxicated. *Campbell v Step/Lind Restaurant Corp.* (1988, 2d Dept) 143 AD2d 111, 531 NYS2d 576.

The driver who struck from behind a vehicle stopped for a red light made an admission in a statement accompanying the motor vehicle accident report that he was driving in the rain at 40 miles per hour in a 30-miles-per-hour zone. In a personal injury action arising out of the rear-end collision, the admission, which the driver did not subsequently challenge, conclusively established his negligence as a matter of law. *Benyarko v Avis Rent A Car System, Inc.* (1990, 2d Dept) 162 AD2d 572, 556 NYS2d 761.

In a personal injury action arising out of the explosion of a canister of swimming pool chemicals, the trial court improperly permitted the introduction of certain hospital records in which the swimming pool owner was reported to have said that the explosion occurred after she pulled the canister out of the pool. Since the nurse who recorded the statement could not say with certainty whether it was made by the swimming pool owner or one of several other individuals who were present in the emergency room during treatment, the origin of the statement was unclear, and the proponent of the admission of the hospital records into evidence failed to establish that they contained an admission by the swimming pool owner. *Castro v Alden Leeds, Inc.* (1988, 2d Dept) 144 AD2d 613, 535 NYS2d 73.

A bus passenger brought an action against the transit authority claiming that he was injured when the bus doors closed on his foot as he was attempting to board the bus, causing him to be dragged about 15 feet. Statements plaintiff made to a police officer and to an ambulance attendant regarding the cause of the accident were attributable to him and properly admitted into evidence. *Sanchez v Manhattan & Bronx Surface Transit Operating Auth.* (1991, 1st Dept) 170 AD2d 402, 566 NYS2d 287, appeal after remand 203 AD2d 128, 610 NYS2d 507. However, it was error to admit in evidence a statement contained in the hospital report that purportedly contradicted plaintiff's version of the accident, because no foundation was laid that plaintiff was the source of this information. Therefore, the statement was inadmissible either as a prior inconsistent statement or as an admission against interest. *Sanchez v Manhattan & Bronx Surface Transit Operating Auth., supra.*

In an action brought by the owner of films against a distributor, an admission by defendant's president that his company had been paid by television cable stations and others for licensing certain films but did not pay plaintiff, who owned the films, was sufficient to entitle plaintiff to summary judgment on its causes of action for breach of fiduciary duty, conversion, and tortious interference. *Jaywyn Video Productions, Ltd. v Servicing All Media, Inc.* (1992, 1st Dept) 179 AD2d 397, 577 NYS2d 847.

In an action on an insurance policy, statements of plaintiff and her husband contained in an examination under oath were properly received in evidence as statements of a party to a lawsuit and as extrajudicial admissions of a party. *Dlugosz v Exchange Mut. Ins. Co.* (1991, 3d Dept) 176 AD2d 1011, 574 NYS2d 864.

Plaintiff brought an action against her former husband to set aside transfers of property as fraudulent. An affidavit of the former husband indicating that the property he transferred was worth between $40,000 and $50,000 and that he transferred this to his brother for $1.00 to keep it out of the hands of his creditors, including the former wife, constituted an admission by a party and was not excluded under the hearsay rule. *Ede v Ede* (1993, 3d Dept) 193 AD2d 940, 598 NYS2d 90.

§ 24:2 ADMISSION BY AGENT, EMPLOYEE, OR PARTNER OF PARTY — The hearsay statement of an agent is admissible against his employer under the admissions exception to the hearsay rule only if the making of the statement is an activity within the scope of his authority. *Loschiavo v Port Authority of New York & New Jersey* (1983) 58 NY2d 1040, 462 NYS2d 440. Thus, the statement of an airline gate agent that other persons had tripped and fallen at the place where plaintiff fell was not admissible against his employer as an admission. His duties involved meeting flights, assisting passengers in embarking and debarking from aircraft, and reporting accidents and dangerous conditions to his superiors, but it was not his job to discuss prior accidents with passengers or the general public. *Loschiavo v Port Authority of New York & New Jersey, supra.*

Generally speaking, an agent's admissions are not binding on his principal, but if the agent was expressly or impliedly authorized to make admissions on behalf of his principal, they are admissible against the latter as proof of the truth of the facts asserted therein. *Prado v Onor Oscar, Inc.* (1974, 2d Dept) 44 AD2d 604, 353 NYS2d 789. The question is one of agency, and the agent's authority to make the admissions or declarations must first be shown. *Schner v Simpson* (1955) 286 AD 716, 146 NYS2d 369.

A declaration by an agent without authority to speak for the principal is not an admission receivable against the principal, even where the agent is authorized to act in the matter as to which his declaration relates. *Nordhauser v New York City Health & Hosp. Corp.* (1991, 2d Dept) 176 AD2d 787, 575 NYS2d 117; *Risoli v Long Island Lighting Co.* (1993, 2d Dept) 195 AD2d 543, 600 NYS2d 497, app den 82 NY2d 661, 605 NYS2d 7. In a malpractice action, a statement given by the triage nurse to the plaintiff was admissible against the nurse, not against the hospital. *Nordhauser v New York City Health & Hosp. Corp., supra.*

The trial court erred in permitting plaintiff's daughter to testify to a statement defendant's service manager allegedly made to her following an accident. Even though the manager's testimony had been taken on an examination before trial, the plaintiff adduced no proof at the trial regarding the type or scope of the agent's duties or responsibilities, and there was no proof that he had been authorized to make statements on defendant's behalf. *Maggio v Mid-Hudson Chevrolet, Inc.* (1970, 2d Dept) 34 AD2d 567, 310 NYS2d 40.

In wrongful death action arising out of an alleged pursuit of vehicle by police, an officer's statement to decedent's wife was not admissible against the city. The officer was not a party and was not authorized to speak for the city. *Brkani v City of New York* (1995, 2d Dept) 211 AD2d 740, 621 NYS2d 696.

The trial court correctly ruled inadmissible the purported admissions of a former teacher, who was not present at the trial, that he had closed the door on plaintiff's hand, since there was no showing that the teacher was authorized to make any admissions or other statements. *Robinson v New York* (1975, 2d Dept) 50 AD2d 915, 377 NYS2d 576.

Where the duties of the agent include making statements on behalf of his principal, the agent's statements may be received against the principal if made within the scope of the agent's authority. *Spett v President Monroe Bldg. & Mfg. Corp.* (1967) 19 NY2d 203, 278 NYS2d 826. Such authority may include the making of admissions regarding the liability of his principal for injuries sustained by others if the agent's responsibility extends that far. *Spett v President Monroe Bldg. & Mfg. Corp., supra.*

Where an agent's responsibilities included making statements on his principal's behalf, the agent's statements within the scope of his authority were receivable against the principal, even though the admission was derived wholly from hearsay. *Georges v American Export Lines, Inc.* (1980, 1st Dept) 77 AD2d 26, 432 NYS2d 165.

The negligence of a street railway company could not be established by the motorman's declaration made after the event. *Menkelunas v New York* (1946) 270 AD 827, 60 NYS2d 97. However, the statutory accident report by an authorized agent binds the employer with respect to any admissions contained therein. *Craciola v Lewis* (1931) 233 AD 437, 253 NYS 752.

Although the fact of agency does not have to be proved by direct evidence, *Nowack v Metropolitan S. R. Co.* (1901) 166 NY 433, 60 NE 32, the agent's declarations are not admissible as evidence of his authority. *Taylor v Commercial Bank* (1903) 174 NY 181, 66 NE 726.

Admissions by counsel, as by any other agent, are admissible against a party, provided that the statements were made by the attorney while acting in his authorized capacity. *Bellino v Bellino Constr. Co.* (1980, 2d Dept) 75 AD2d 630, 427 NYS2d 303.

Evidence of an attorney's subornation of perjury has been held to be admissible against his client, even without evidence that the client has authorized the attorney's acts. *Nieves v New York* (1951, Sup) 109 NYS2d 556, affd 280 AD 972, 116 NYS2d 927. If an honest man mistakenly employs a dishonest one to look up witnesses for him and the latter resorts to bribery, even though his employer never thought of it, the court has held that it is better for cleanliness and purity in the administration of justice that the facts be shown with the fullest opportunity for explanation than that the evidence of evil acts be excluded on the ground that they were not authorized. Authority may properly be inferred from the nature of the employment. *Nowack v Metropolitan S. R. Co.*, *supra*.

The court found the trial record to be insufficient to make a positive determination on the issue of whether the principal would be bound by admissions made by its agent. Nevertheless, it postulated the rule that where the agent was in effect the defendant's general manager, so that if he had operated the institution as an individual venture he could make an admission, then the agent's statements are admissible, even though they are hearsay and not part of the *res gestae*. The rationale was that an agent speaking about a transaction within his authority to perform is more likely to be telling the truth about it at that time than later when he is summoned and asked to give testimony against his employer's interest. *Kasper v Buffalo Bills of Western New York* (1973, 4th Dept) 42 AD2d 87, 345 NYS2d 244.

The admission of the general manager of a blood station, made hours after a negligent injection of blood that resulted in plaintiff's acute allergic reaction, was properly received in evidence against his employer, even though he intended to and did leave defendant's employ a week after the accident. *Fiedler v Mirsa, Inc.* (1975, 4th Dept) 49 AD2d 1009, 374 NYS2d 173.

A customer was injured when an exercise bicycle on which she sat collapsed in the store. A statement that the bicycle was dangerous, made shortly after the accident by defendant's store manager, was admissible as a statement against interest in an action brought by the customer. *Steinmetz v Caldor, Inc.* (1991, 3d Dept) 170 AD2d 935, 566 NYS2d 766.

The trial court erred when it instructed the jury that the deposition of the defendant's driver, his motor vehicle report, and the information he gave defendant's dispatcher could not be considered legal proof of the facts stated in them. The statements were admissions that contradicted the driver's trial testimony and could be considered evidence-in-chief. *Rosario v New York City Transit Authority* (1980, 2d Dept) 73 AD2d 912, 423 NYS2d 254.

In a personal injury action against a restaurant company, testimony that after the accident the defendant's assistant manager had told a busboy, "I thought I told you to take care of those stairs," was held to be inadmissible, because the assistant manager had no power to bind the defendant. *Golden v Horn & Hardart Co.* (1935) 244 AD 92, 278 NYS 385, affd 270 NY 544, 200 NE 309.

But where a statement was made by a grocery store's president-treasurer, the only person vested with complete managerial control, the statement was admissible against the corporate owner of the store. *Johnson v Hallam Enters. Ltd.* (1994, 3d Dept) 208 AD2d 1110, 617 NYS2d 405.

Declarations by one partner on the firm's New York State Partnership Income Tax Return that the partnership had no New York State income and that the losses the partnership sought to deduct were not derived from or connected with New York sources were not competent against a limited partner in the conduct of his personal affairs. *Vogt v Tully* (1981) 53 NY2d 580, 444 NYS2d 441.

An employee brought an action against his employer to recover for accumulated nonscheduled overtime work. A statement by the employer's payroll clerk in a telephone conversation indicating that the employee had accumulated 6,612 hours of non-scheduled overtime was an admission made by an agent within the scope of her authority and was receivable against the employer as an exception to the hearsay rule. *Falcone v EDO Corp.* (1988, 2d Dept) 141 AD2d 498, 529 NYS2d 123.

The trial court did not err in refusing to admit into evidence two letters that were written by plaintiff's attorney to appellant's attorney prior to the commencement of the lawsuit. A plaintiff's pre-litigation speculations concerning whom he might sue have no relevance to and are not inconsistent with the liability of the defendant who is actually sued. *Farina v Nastasi* (1991, 2d Dept) 173 AD2d 520, 570 NYS2d 121.

§ 24:3 ADMISSIONS BY OTHERS — Admissions of the president and active head of a corporation are binding on the corporation. *Geletucha v 222 Delaware Corp.* (1959, 4th Dept) 7 AD2d 315, 182 NYS2d 893, reh den (4th Dept) 8 AD2d 999, 188 NYS2d 980. The statements of an attorney and former president concerning a sale, which were made while they were acting for a corporation and the trustees in liquidation, constituted proof of sale in a broker's action for commissions. *Gaillard Realty Co. v Manhattan Brass Co.* (1933) 238 AD 84, 263 NYS 397.

Where there was evidence that the city attorney had authority to write a letter concerning a contract by the city to build a clubhouse and install a water system for the plaintiff, the letter was properly admitted in evidence against the city. *Beechwood Gun Club v Beacon* (1934) 153 Misc 358, 275 NYS 249, affd 242 AD 761, 275 NYS 219. Declarations of a principal made during the transaction of the business for which the surety was bound were competent evidence against the surety, but declarations made after the transaction were not competent. *John T. Stanley Co. v National Surety Corp.* (1943) 179 Misc 493, 39 NYS2d 509. Where a settlor of a trust made admissions in the form of entries regarding funds received from the trust, the admissions constituted evidence of the estate's liability to the beneficiaries of the trust. *Re Anyon's Estate* (1930) 137 Misc 582, 244 NYS 244. The general rule applicable to admissions by an agent against a principal applies to admissions made by an administrator of an estate. *Strang v Prudential Ins. Co.* (1933) 263 NY 71, 188 NE 161. Admissions made by an executor in the line of duty are admissible in proceedings to establish a gift of stock claimed to be part of the estate. *Re Brady's Estate* (1930) 228 AD 56, 239 NYS 5, affd 254 NY 590, 173 NE 879.

If an actual conspiracy between defendants is established, all conversations and writings by one or more of the conspirators in the course of the conspiracy and in furtherance of its purposes are admissible against all members of the conspiracy on the ground that whatever is done or said by any one of the defendants in furtherance of the conspiracy is part of the *res gestae*. *Blaustein v Pan American Petroleum & Transport Co.* (1940) 174 Misc 601, 21 NYS2d 651, affd in part and revd in part 263 AD 97, 31 NYS2d 934, affd 293 NY 281, reh den 293 NY 763. Admissions of one conspirator after the common design has been accomplished are inadmissible against the others. *Petition of Orans* (1965) 45 Misc 2d 616, 257 NYS2d 839, affd 15 NY2d 339, 258 NYS2d 825, app dismd 382 US 10, 15 L Ed 2d 13, 86 S Ct 75, reh den 382 US 934, 15 L Ed 2d 346, 86 S Ct 311. Acts and declarations of one co-conspirator that occur while the conspiracy is in progress and that are in furtherance of the common scheme are admissible and provable as to all other conspirators as part of the *res gestae* and are a recognized exception to the hearsay rule. However, a party seeking to fit within the co-conspirator exception to the hearsay rule must come forward with *prima facie* evidence that there is a conspiracy and that a particular defendant is a conspirator. *People v Salko* (1979) 47 NY2d 230, 417 NYS2d 894, reh den, remittitur amd 47 NY2d 1010, 420 NYS2d 223.

In a proceeding to determine whether respondent was a person in need of supervision, a partial admission from the law guardian that respondent had been guilty of curfew violations was insufficient. This "admission" from one who had no personal knowledge of the facts could not serve as legally competent evidence sufficient to prove the acts complained of beyond a reasonable doubt. *Re Application of Diallo H.* (1983, 4th Dept) 94 AD2d 976, 464 NYS2d 102.

An insurer's payment of a no-fault claim cannot be deemed an admission in the claimant's subsequent action for damages. *Dermatossian v New York City Transit Authority* (1986) 67 NY2d 219, 501 NYS2d 7840.

§ 24:4 JUDICIAL ADMISSIONS — A party's admissions, whether judicial or extrajudicial, are admissible. *Vicherek v Papanek* (1953) 281 AD 498, 120 NYS2d 197, app den 281 AD 1020, 121 NYS2d 271 and motion to dismiss app den 305 NY 927. A defendant's prior plea of guilty to a traffic offense may be introduced as evidence of his carelessness in a civil action for damages. *Ando v Woodberry* (1960) 8 NY2d 165, 203 NYS2d 74. A plea of guilty to a charge of driving while intoxicated in violation of the statute constitutes an admission against interest admissible on the trial of a personal injury lawsuit arising out of the same vehicular accident and involving the same issue. *Knibbs v Wagner* (1961, 4th Dept) 14 AD2d 987, 222 NYS2d 469.

A default judgment that granted the tenant's husband a divorce on the ground of her adultery in a case in which the tenant chose to default was not admissible as an admission on tenant's part in subsequent proceedings by the Municipal Housing Authority to evict her on the ground of her adultery, since she had merely remained silent and chosen not to answer the complaint. *Johnson v New Rochelle Municipal Housing Authority* (1964) 39 Misc 2d 138, 253 NYS2d 39. A stipulation in a partition suit that established an equitable lien on proceeds was held to be an admission of the existence of the lien prior thereto and therefore admissible to show the lien in surplus proceedings. *Bennis v Conley* (1928, App Tm) 231 NYS 635.

Plaintiff's testimony at the first trial of an action was admissible at the second trial as an informal judicial admission and as affirmative evidence, not solely as impeachment evidence. *Simmons v Westwood Apartments Co.* (1965) 46 Misc 2d 1093, 261 NYS2d 736, affd (4th Dept) 26 AD2d 764, 271 NYS2d 731, app dismd 18 NY2d 786, 275 NYS2d 271.

An offer of compromise is not admissible to raise an inference of liability. *Emery v Litchard* (1930) 137 Misc 885, 245 NYS 209. Offers of compromise are considered merely as evidence of a desire to avoid litigation or seek an end of litigation on the defendant's part. They are not accepted as evidence of admissions of liability or to measure the value of an admitted liability. *Quillen v Board of Education* (1952) 203 Misc 320, 115 NYS2d 122.

In a law suit by an architect against owners who had retained him, the owners' sworn statements regarding the amount of money they owed the plaintiff, made before the Board of Standards and Appeals in an effort to obtain a building permit, were informal judicial admissions and could be used by plaintiff in his motion for summary judgment. *Saltzman v Liebman* (1978, 1st Dept) 63 AD2d 621, 403 NYS2d 671.

Admissions by counsel are admissible against the client, provided that the statements were made while counsel was acting in that capacity. *Tai Wing Hong Importers, Inc. v King Realty Corp.* (1994, 2d Dept) 208 AD2d 710, 617 NYS2d 793.

In opposing a motion for summary judgment by one defendant, plaintiff's counsel made an admission that allegations of the complaint asserted against a second defendant were untrue and that the proximate cause of his client's injury was solely the act or acts of the first defendant. The admission constituted a judicial admission binding upon the plaintiff and served to exculpate the second defendant from any fault. *Pok Rye Kim v Mars Cup* Co. (1984, 2d Dept) 102 AD2d 812, 476 NYS2d 381.

When defendant conceded at the trial that he had given both oral and written statements to the police falsely charging that plaintiff had committed a crime punishable by imprisonment, plaintiff's cause of action for libel and slander *per se* was established. *Bishop v Chirico* (1985, 3d Dept) 108 AD2d 1061, 485 NYS2d 630.

A concession "arguendo" contained in a brief on a motion for summary judgment is not a formal judicial admission that binds the party making it to the very result he is arguing against. *1014 Fifth Ave. Realty Corp. v Manhattan Realty Co.* (1986) 67 NY2d 718, 499 NYS2d 936.

In an action brought by injured parties against asbestos manufacturers, plaintiffs' answers to interrogatories listing various companies that had contributed to their asbestos exposure constituted admissions of a party and were admissible as evidence. *Bigelow v Acands, Inc.* (1993, 1st Dept) 196 AD2d 436, 601 NYS2d 478.

§ 24:5 JUDICIAL ADMISSIONS IN PLEADINGS — The contents of a sworn statement in defendant's pleadings are competent as admissions. *Standard Oil Co. v Boyle* (1930) 231 AD 101, 246 NYS 142. Where the president of defendant railroad company executed an affidavit that was filed by the defendant on a motion for a bill of particulars and the affidavit contained an admission that plaintiff had rendered services for the defendant, the affidavit was competent evidence against the defendant. *Bogart v New York & L. I. R. Co.* (1907) 118 AD 50, 102 NYS 1093, affd 191 NY 550, 85 NE 1106.

A party under a mental disability was in no condition to authorize the statements contained in a pleading or to know the contents of a pleading. Therefore, his unverified pleading was not admissible as an admission binding on his personal representative in an action for personal injuries sustained by him. *Fischbach v Auto Boys, Inc.* (1952) 279 AD 1035, 112 NYS2d 283 639. An admission made by defendant in his answer is admissible in evidence. *Coraci v Yurkin* (1957) 12 Misc 2d 619, 174 NYS2d 540. Each material allegation of the complaint that is not controverted by the answer is also deemed an admission for purposes of the action. CPLR 3018(a). Therefore, failure to controvert any of the allegations in the complaint has the effect of a formal admission and is binding on the parties as well as on the court. *Fleischmann v Stern* (1882) 90 NY 110. A party that was impleaded as a third-party defendant made admissions in an answer that it claimed were erroneous. This claim would not preclude the use of the admissions, but the party making them would be afforded an opportunity upon the trial to explain the making of the admissions. *De Lany v Allen* (1951) 200 Misc 734, 105 NYS2d 635. An amendment would not affect the admissibility of the original answer as evidence of admissions. *American Tobacco Co. v Riggio Tobacco Corp.* (1962) 37 Misc 2d 23, 234 NYS2d 51.

Allegations contained in a defense and counterclaim that were stricken out on a former appeal constituted sworn admissions that were nevertheless available to the plaintiff on a motion for a judgment on the pleadings. *Rifkin v Ed Zit Holding Corp.* (1929) 227 AD 795, 237 NYS 161, revd 254 NY 352, 173 NE 219, remittitur amd 255 NY 565, 175 NE 315.

An alleged admission in a pleading made upon information and belief does not constitute a formal or informal judicial admission. *Scolite International Corp. v Vincent J. Smith, Inc.* (1979, 3d Dept) 68 AD2d 417, 418 NYS2d 191.

In an action against a retail seller of an air pellet pistol for injuries sustained when a 14-year-old discharged the pistol at the victim, the retailer's third-party complaint against the manufacturer contained an allegation that the pellet gun was not of merchantable quality and not safe for use by the general public. The allegation did not constitute an admission of fact, even though the seller had denied in its answer to the plaintiff's complaint that the pistol was unsafe and not of merchantable quality, and the court did not err in refusing to allow into evidence the allegations in the third-party complaint. *Collins v Caldor of Kingston, Inc.* (1979, 3d Dept) 73 AD2d 708, 422 NYS2d 524.

Statements made in a verified bill of particulars constitute informal judicial admissions, and although they do not conclusively establish the facts that they set forth, they are generally admissible pursuant to an exception to the hearsay rule. *Payne v New Hyde Park Dodge* (1990, 2d Dept) 163 AD2d 285, 557 NYS2d 152.

An admission in a pleading in one action is admissible against the pleader in another suit, provided it can be shown that the facts were alleged with the pleader's knowledge or under his direction. *Jack C. Hirsch, Inc. v North Hempstead* (1991, 2d Dept) 177 AD2d 683, 577 NYS2d 75. Although such an admission is open to explanation and is not conclusive, if the facts were alleged with the pleader's knowledge, the pleading was verified, and the allegations were not made upon information and belief, the admissions will support the granting of summary judgment. *Jack C. Hirsch, Inc. v North Hempstead, supra.*

A notice of claim filed by plaintiff in an action for negligent maintenance of roadway was admissible in a separate action against a vehicle manufacturer. *Cramer v Kuhns* (1995, 3d Dept) ___ AD2d ___, 630 NYS2d 128.

Statements contained in a bill of particulars that defendant served on the third-party defendant in its third-party action constituted informal judicial admissions that were not conclusive but were evidence of the facts admitted. *Hill v King Kullen Grocery Co.* (1992, 2d Dept) 181 AD2d 812, 581 NYS2d 378.

§ 24:6 ADMISSIBILITY OF A CRIMINAL JUDGMENT IN A SUBSEQUENT CIVIL SUIT —A plea of guilty to a traffic offense may be introduced as evidence of defendant's negligence in a civil action for damages. *Di Bone v Gambucci* (1967) 54 Misc 2d 446, 282 NYS2d 855. A fact that is formally admitted in open court by virtue of a guilty plea in a criminal case is a formal judicial admission and is conclusive in the subsequent civil action. *Di Bone v Gambucci, supra.* A conviction of a crime after a trial is likewise admissible in a subsequent civil action based on the same facts as conclusive evidence of the facts on which the conviction is based. *S. T. Grand, Inc. v New York* (1973) 32 NY2d 300, 344 NYS2d 938.

The doctrine of collateral estoppel permits the insured's criminal conviction to determine conclusively liability in the civil action. *Re Nassau Ins. Co.* (1990, 1st Dept) 161 AD2d 146, 554 NYS2d 551; *Kramer v Griffin* (1989, 4th Dept) 156 AD2d 973, 549 NYS2d 264; *Cunningham v L.P.T.G. Farragut Realty Corp.* (1994, 2d Dept) 200 AD2d 651, 606 NYS2d 776.

However, a conviction of a traffic infraction after a trial is not admissible in a subsequent civil action against the defendant. *Walther v News Syndicate Co.* (1949) 276 AD 169, 93 NYS2d 537. An acquittal in a criminal prosecution is not admissible in a subsequent civil action. *Farley v Patterson* (1915) 166 AD 358, 152 NYS 59.

In a civil suit against a municipality for assault arising from an altercation that led to the plaintiff's arrest, the trial judge erred in admitting evidence that the plaintiff had been found not guilty of assault with a weapon in a related criminal proceeding. The verdict in the criminal trial signified only that the prosecution had failed to prove the use of a knife beyond a reasonable doubt, which was not the standard at the civil trial. *Ramirez v New York* (1979, 2d Dept) 70 AD2d 904, 417 NYS2d 302.

A driver's plea of guilty to an infraction of the Vehicle and Traffic Law is admissible against him on the issue of his negligence in a civil action brought against him by a person injured in the collision. Explanations, for example, that the plea was a matter of expediency, go to the weight to be ascribed to the admission by the trier of the fact. *Ando v Woodberry* (1960) 8 NY2d 165, 203 NYS2d 74; *Canfield v Giles* (1992, 4th Dept) 182 AD2d 1075, 585 NYS2d 242, later proceeding (4th Dept) 182 AD2d 1075, 585 NYS2d 322; *Alexander v Eldred* (1984, 3d Dept) 100 AD2d 666, 473 NYS2d 864, affd 63 NY2d 460, 483 NYS2d 168.

A criminal conviction may serve as the basis for collateral estoppel insofar as the same issues are revived in subsequent civil litigation. *Davis v Hanna* (1983, 4th Dept) 97 AD2d 943, 468 NYS2d 729. However, judgments of conviction based on pleas of guilty to a federal charge of aiding and abetting transportation of stolen property in interstate commerce are insufficient to establish defendant's civil liability for conversion where the plea minutes did not establish that defendant had converted the property of plaintiff's decedents. *Davis v Hanna, supra.*

Because the wife's criminal conviction for killing her husband conclusively established that the killing was not an accident, was not committed in self-defense, and was not committed while she was insane, she was collaterally estopped from raising these defenses in a hearing to determine whether she might take under the decedent's will. *Re Will of Wells* (1973) 76 Misc 2d 458, 350 NYS2d 114. *See also Estate of Strouse* (1986, 2d Dept) 121 AD2d 549, 504 NYS2d 32.

Defendant's conviction for manslaughter in the first degree conclusively established for purposes of a subsequent action for wrongful death brought by decedent's administratrix that the decedent was struck by the bullet from a shotgun intentionally fired by the defendant, that the decedent died as a result of the injuries he thereby sustained, and that the defendant's act was neither accidental, excusable nor justifiable. This was sufficient to establish defendant's liability as a matter of law with respect to the plaintiff's causes of action for wrongful death, conscious pain and suffering, the cost of caring for the decedent as a result of his injury, and funeral expenses. *Kollin v Shaff* (1974) 79 Misc 2d 49, 359 NYS2d 515.

The fact that employees of a cocktail lounge were convicted of third-degree assault of a patron was not *res judicata* as to the lounge and its owners in a civil suit for wrongful death, because the lounge and its owners were not parties to the underlying criminal action. *Brereton v McEvoy* (1974, 2d Dept) 44 AD2d 594, 353 NYS2d 512.

In an action by a plaintiff against defendant's insurance company to recover "excess liability" for bad faith breach of an insurance contract, the plaintiff, as defendant's assignee, was collaterally estopped from denying the version of the facts established by defendant's perjury conviction, because the conviction was based on his false statement under oath that he was in the course of employment when the accident happened, and this prompted the plaintiff to bring into the case the sole "deep pocket" defendant, which in turn effectively eliminated any reasonable prospect of settlement of the case. *Brennan v Mead* (1981, 2d Dept) 81 AD2d 821, 438 NYS2d 821, affd 54 NY2d 811, 443 NYS2d 652.

Defendant's conviction for the petty offense of harassment could not later be used to preclude him from disputing the merits of a civil suit against him for assault involving the same incident and seeking a quarter of a million dollars in damages. *Gilberg v Barbieri* (1981) 53 NY2d 285, 441 NYS2d 49.

A motorist who was convicted for leaving the scene of a traffic accident without reporting it was not collaterally estopped from arguing in a related civil lawsuit that he was not the driver, where "the realities" of the criminal litigation against the defendant indicate that he pleaded guilty in return for a promise that he would not be sentenced to a period of incarceration. *Sullivan v Breese* (1990, 2d Dept) 160 AD2d 997, 554 NYS2d 937.

Because culpability for assault in the second degree can arise out of either an intentional or a reckless act, if a defendant pleads guilty to that charge in a criminal proceeding, it cannot be said that in a subsequent civil proceeding based on the same act the question of defendant's intent to assault or batter the plaintiff was

451

necessarily decided in the related criminal action. *Almeyda v Zambito* (1991, AD, 2d Dept) 171 AD2d 633, 567 NYS2d 272.

The insured's wife brought an action against the insurer to recover the proceeds of a homeowner's policy for a fire loss. The insured's guilty plea to arson charges did not collaterally estop the wife, because she was not a party to her husband's prior criminal prosecution and subsequent plea and cannot be said to have been in legal privity with him so as to render the criminal judgment conclusively binding on her in the civil action. *Fernandez v Cigna Property & Casualty Ins. Co.* (1992, 3d Dept) 188 AD2d 700, 590 NYS2d 925.Plaintiff had previously been convicted of trespass based on a finding that no easement existed in his favor. He was collaterally estopped from claiming such an easement in a subsequent civil action for declaration that he had an easement enabling him to cross the property in question. *Hudson v Varney* (1993, 2d Dept) 196 AD2d 856, 602 NYS2d 176, app dismd without op 82 NY2d 888, 610 NYS2d 153, reconsideration den 83 NY2d 801, 611 NYS2d 136 and cert den (US) 1994 US LEXIS 5467.

Although a husband's criminal conviction for murdering his wife was abated due to his subsequent death, the abatement did not deprive the husband's conviction of all probative significance. Thus, in collateral civil litigation arising out of a contest of the decedent wife's will, the murder conviction constituted a *prima facie* showing that the husband had intentionally taken the wife's life. *Will of Pikul* (1993, 1st Dept) 192 AD2d 259, 601 NYS2d 113.

A plea of *nolo contendere* in a criminal proceeding cannot be relied on in a subsequent civil or administrative action as proof of the facts alleged in the indictment. *Longo v Dolce* (1993, 2d Dept) 192 AD2d 157, 600 NYS2d 962, app dismd, app den 82 NY2d 836, 606 NYS2d 589.However, when an experienced attorney was charged with wilful evasion of income taxes, his plea of *nolo contendere* was an admission of professional misconduct. *Adel v Bar Asso. of Erie County* (1973, 4th Dept) 41 AD2d 509, 344 NYS2d 110.

§ 24:7 SILENCE OF A PARTY AS AN ADMISSION IN CIVIL CASES

— Silence may be construed as an admission if the statements or acts are such as to call for some response or act by the interested party. *O. G. Orr & Co. v Fireman's Fund Ins. Co.* (1932) 235 AD 1, 256 NYS 79. The rule, however, applies only in cases where a reasonable inference is that of an admission. *Devonshire v Stubbs* (1930) 135 Misc 886, 238 NYS 707. Before a party may be bound by his silence in the face of a statement, he must have fully heard and understood the statement that he has allegedly admitted. *Devonshire v Stubbs, supra.*

In an action arising out of a collision between a motorcycle operated by plaintiff and an automobile driven by defendant, the crucial issue was whether defendant's act had been justified by an emergency situation. Because the defendant claimed that he had been forced to veer to the left to avoid a bicyclist who had darted out into the street from between parked cars, the court erred in refusing to permit plaintiff to ask the police officer to whom defendant claimed to have given a complete narrative of the occurrence whether the defendant had mentioned a bicyclist. *Hoberman v Lane* (1981, 2d Dept) 85 AD2d 595, 444 NYS2d 704.

In a products liability lawsuit arising from the explosion of a light bulb allegedly manufactured by defendant, the plaintiff's failure to controvert the defendant's factual assertion that the filament configuration of the bulb plaintiff produced was different from the filament configuration that would be present in the same bulbs defendant produced constituted an admission of the fact by the plaintiff. *Whelan v GTE Sylvania Inc.* (1992, 1st Dept) 182 AD2d 446, 582 NYS2d 170.

§ 24:8 FAILURE TO REPLY TO WRITTEN STATEMENTS AS AN ADMISSION

— Failure to deny a written statement is not an admission. *Burns v Blidberg Rothchild Co.* (1949) 195 Misc 625, 91 NYS2d 55. Thus, where a seaman who had overstayed his shore leave did not contradict an entry in a log book that he agreed to have the expense of his transportation by air to rejoin the vessel in another port charged against his wages, his failure to deny the entry could not be accepted as an admission against him. *Burns v Blidberg Rothchild Co., supra.*

A person is not obligated to enter into correspondence with another regarding a matter in dispute between them. *Re Estate of Barnes* (1962) 37 Misc 2d 833, 237 NYS2d 183. Silence under these conditions is not an admission against the party to whom the letter was addressed. *Re Estate of Barnes, supra.*

§ 24:9   CONDUCT OF A PARTY AS AN ADMISSION — The conduct of a party may amount to an admission. *Seidenspinner v Metropolitan Life Ins. Co.* (1903) 175 NY 95, 67 NE 123. Thus, a party who accepts sick benefits by implication admits his illness. *Seidenspinner v Metropolitan Life Ins. Co., supra.* A person who applies for reinstatement of a policy is held to admit certain statements contained within the policy. *Ludmerer v New York Life Ins. Co.* (1940, Sup) 19 NYS2d 272.

A recall notice by an automobile manufacturer is admissible against the manufacturer. *Iadicicco v Duffy* (1978, 2d Dept) 60 AD2d 905, 401 NYS2d 557. When a defendant offered to marry the girl who charged him with rape, he was held to have a state of mind evidencing guilt. *People v Elston* (1919) 186 AD 224, 174 NYS 1. Where a bar patron claimed to have been assaulted on the premises and the bar owners made payments to the patron, not to settle the patron's claim but to avoid difficulty with the A.B.C. Board, the evidence of the payment was admissible in a subsequent negligence action brought by the patron. *Schwartz v Cohen* (1953) 204 Misc 142, 119 NYS2d 124.

In a civil action arising out of an accident, defendant's refusal to submit to a breathalyzer test after the accident was admissible as conduct inconsistent with defendant's position on trial that he was not intoxicated at the time of the accident. *Bazza v Banscher* (1988, 2d Dept) 143 AD2d 715, 533 NYS2d 285.

§ 24:10   OFFERS OF COMPROMISE AS ADMISSIONS — Offers of compromise do not constitute admissions of liability. *Re Estate of Steigerwald* (1956) 2 Misc 2d 389, 150 NYS2d 862. The fact that the plaintiff's insurance company made a payment in settlement of defendant's claim and received a release did not constitute an admission or bar a subsequent recovery for damages sustained by plaintiff in an automobile collision. *Emery v Litchard* (1930) 137 Misc 885, 245 NYS 209. An offer of settlement cannot be considered either an admission of liability or an admission of fact. *Universal Carloading & Distribution Co. v Penn Cent. Transp. Co.* (1984, 1st Dept) 101 AD2d 61, 474 NYS2d 502.

CPLR 3219 contains a provision for the making or tender of an offer of compromise by depositing a sum of money with the clerk of the court for the purpose of limiting the plaintiff's entitlement to interest. The statute expressly provides that such a tender or offer shall not be made known to the jury.

While an offer of settlement is inadmissible, admissions made in the course of settlement negotiations are admissible. *Bellino v Bellino Constr. Co.* (1980, 2d Dept) 75 AD2d 630, 427 NYS2d 303.

When the New York City Transit Authority settled with plaintiff and continued its third-party action against third-party defendants, the settlement with the plaintiff should not have been reported to the jury. The information could only have suggested to the jury that the Transit Authority was the sole culpable party. *Pellegrino v New York City Transit Authority* (1991, 2d Dept) 177 AD2d 554, 576 NYS2d 154.

§ 24:11 ACTIONS OF A PARTY AFTER AN ACCIDENT AS ADMISSIONS — Repairs or remedial measures taken by a defendant after the incident that has caused the lawsuit are not admissible as evidence of negligence. *Corcoran v Peekskill* (1888) 108 NY 151, 15 NE 309. Subsequent repairs may, however, be shown for the purpose of demonstrating control, where this is an issue. *Scudero v Campbell* (1942) 288 NY 328.

In a products liability action, evidence of post-accident changes in a manufacturer's manual is admissible for the limited purpose of proving the feasibility of using a different system. *Opera v Hyva, Inc.* (1982, 4th Dept) 86 AD2d 373, 450 NYS2d 615.

In a negligence action, proof of a defendant's post-accident repair or improvement ordinarily is not admissible. *Caprara v Chrysler Corp.* (1981) 52 NY2d 114, 436 NYS2d 251. This rule, however, does not apply in a strict products liability action, and evidence regarding a manufacturer's post-accident design change of ball joints was held admissible as supportive of the manufacturing and assembly defect theory on which the trial court sent the case to the jury. *Caprara v Chrysler Corp., supra.*

§ 24:12   OTHER TYPES OF ADMISSIONS — The husband in a matrimonial action had previously made a representation to a bank in connection with a loan application regarding the appraised value and mortgage encumbrances of certain commercial properties. For purposes of establishing the value of those properties for division between the spouses in the matrimonial action, the husband's earlier representation constituted an admission of the value of the properties. *Capasso v Capasso* (1986, 1st Dept) 119 AD2d 268, 506 NYS2d 686, later app 129 AD2d 267, 517 NYS2d 952.

RESEARCH REFERENCES

American Law Reports

46 ALR4th 291, Admissibility of police officer's testimony at state trial relating to motorist's admissions made in or for automobile accident report required by law

38 ALR4th 583, Products liability: admissibility of evidence of postinjury warning measures undertaken by defendant

25 ALR4th 419, Sufficiency of showing that voluntariness of confession or admission was affected by alcohol or other drugs

14 ALR4th 802, Admissibility of evidence concerning words spoken while declarant was asleep or unconscious

8 ALR4th 728, Formal sufficiency of response to request for admissions under state discovery rules

4 ALR4th 829, Admissibility and effect, on issue of party's credibility or merits of his case, of evidence of attempts to intimidate or influence witness in civil action

90 ALR3d 1173, Admissibility, as against interest, in civil case of declaration of commission of criminal act

74 ALR3d 1001, Admissibility of evidence of subsequent repairs or remedial measures in product liability cases

43 ALR3d 1375, Admissibility, in civil action, of confession or admission which could not be used against party in criminal prosecution because obtained by improper police methods

27 ALR3d 966, Admissibility and probative value of admissions of fault by agent on issue of principal's secondary liability, where both are sued

ALR QUICK INDEX: Admissions

American Jurisprudence 2d

29 AM JUR 2d, Evidence §§ 597-707

American Jurisprudence Pleading and Practice

23 AM JUR PL & PR FORMS (Rev), Trial, Forms 165-168

American Jurisprudence Trials

4 AM JUR TRIALS 215, Request for Admissions by Defendant

4 AM JUR TRIALS 185, Request for Admissions by Plaintiff

Other Resources

Auto-Cite®: Any case citation herein can be checked for form, parallel references, later history and annotation references through the Auto-Cite computer research system.

CHAPTER 25

ADMISSIBILITY OF
OTHER TYPES OF EVIDENCE

§ 25:1 ADMISSIBILITY OF CIRCUMSTANTIAL EVIDENCE
— Circumstantial evidence consists of proof of facts and circumstances from which the trier of the facts may infer facts at issue that reasonably flow therefrom. However, a fact is admissible as the basis of an inference only when the desired inference is a prob-

able or natural explanation of the fact, and a more probable or natural one than the other explanations, if any. *Engel v United Traction Co.* (1911) 203 NY 321, 96 NE 731.

Circumstantial evidence is sufficient if it supports a particular inference, even though it does not negate the existence of remote possibilities that are inconsistent with such inference. *Delacy v Ettrich* (1995, 3d Dept) ___ AD2d ___, 629 NYS2d 521.

Circumstantial evidence is competent to prove any fact that may be an issue in a civil case, and may be as compelling as direct testimony. *Wittemann v Sands* (1924) 238 NY 434, 144 NE 671, 37 ALR 1216. Circumstantial evidence is admissible to make the inferences from other testimony more plausible. *Skoller v Short* (1942, City Ct) 35 NYS2d 68. Circumstantial evidence must, of course, be material and relevant to the issues in the case. *Engel v United Traction Co., supra.*

Where plaintiff was living with a person who was a drug addict, evidence to this effect was inadmissible for the purpose of showing that plaintiff was also a drug addict. *Doyle v New York* (1953) 281 AD 821, 119 NYS2d 71.

In tort actions, it is permissible to introduce evidence of the relevant conditions and circumstances that surround the alleged tortious acts, so that the jury may draw whatever inferences they create. *Fagan v Atlantic C. L. R. Co.* (1917) 220 NY 301, 115 NE 704.

Under certain conditions, evidence may be introduced of other similar accidents at or near the place of the accident in question, involving the use of the same mechanism by persons other than the plaintiff, and at prior times not too remote from the time of the particular accident. *Webb v Rome, W. & O. R. Co.* (1872) 49 NY 420. This may be relevant on the issue of negligence. *Webb v Rome, W. & O. R. Co., supra.*

A subsequent accident occurring under conditions similar to those at the time of the accident complained of may be shown and may be evidence on the question of whether a dangerous condition existed, but such evidence cannot be shown for the purpose of charging the defendant with notice. *Galieta v YMCA* (1969, 3d Dept) 32 AD2d 711, 300 NYS2d 170.

While it is proper to admit evidence of other similar prior accidents for the purpose of showing the defendant had notice of the condition, it is error to admit such evidence where the prior conditions are not substantially the same as the ones prevailing in the accident that is the subject of the action. *Gallagher v New York* (1968, 2d Dept) 30 AD2d 688, 292 NYS2d 139.

In an action for injuries received from a fall down an elevator shaft, plaintiff's evidence concerning two accidents that had happened under similar circumstances some 10 years before at the same locality, was held to be competent. *Heimer v Stento* (1946) 270 AD 665, 63 NYS2d 29, reh and app den 271 AD 757, 64 NYS2d 917.

Where plaintiff contends he contracted a particular disease as a result of drinking contaminated water, he may properly show the number of cases of such disease in the district in which the water was contaminated, compared with the total number of cases shown in the statistical table prepared by the Department of Health for such district. *Stubbs v Rochester* (1919) 226 NY 516, 124 NE 137, 5 ALR 1396.

While a defendant's compliance with a statute is some evidence of the exercise of due care, it does not preclude a conclusion that he was negligent. *Phillips v Roux Laboratories, Inc.* (1955) 286 AD 549, 145 NYS2d 449. Thus it was held in a case where the manufacturer followed the flammability-testing method prescribed by law that the jury could find that notwithstanding such compliance, the fabric was dangerously flammable, thereby implicating the manufacturer for negligence. *Sherman v M. Lowenstein & Sons, Inc.* (1967, 2d Dept) 28 AD2d 922, 282 NYS2d 142.

Where notice of a defective condition in a roadway is required to be proved, circumstantial evidence, including proof of the presence of the defendant's inspector in a nearby construction area and complaints received by the city with respect to the defects in and about the area involved in the accident, are factors that may be sufficient to establish notice. *Procida v New York* (1971) 28 NY2d 681, 320 NYS2d 737.

Where the injured plaintiff, while shopping in defendant's store, fell backward, did not come into contact with the shelves, but hit her head directly on the floor where "a lot of broken jars" of baby food lay; and there was testimony that the baby food was dirty and messy; and a witness in the immediate vicinity of the accident did not hear any jars falling from the shelves or otherwise breaking during the 15 or 20 minutes prior to the accident; and there was testimony that the aisle had not been cleaned or inspected for at least 50 minutes prior to the accident; it could not be said as a matter of law that the circumstantial evidence was insufficient to permit the jury to draw the necessary inference that a slippery condition was created by jars of baby food that had fallen and broken a sufficient length of time before the accident to allow defendant's employees to discover the condition and remedy it, and plaintiffs had therefore made out a *prima facie* case. *Negro v Stop & Shop, Inc.* (1985) 65 NY2d 625, 491 NYS2d 151, on remand (2d Dept) 115 AD2d 529, 496 NYS2d 692.

Evidence of a person's specific acts of carelessness or carefulness on other occasions is generally inadmissible even when the underlying circumstances of the prior or subsequent conduct were similar to the one in contention. *Glusaskas v Hutchinson* (1989, 1st Dept) 148 AD2d 203, 544 NYS2d 323.

§ 25:2   PROOF OF USE OF DRUGS — Where no attempt was made to show that plaintiff in a negligence case had been under the influence of drugs at the time of the accident, it was substantial and prejudicial error to permit defense counsel to question plaintiff on prior use. *Goodstein v Ankor Leasing, Inc.* (1976, 2d Dept) 51 AD2d 722, 379 NYS2d 153.

§ 25:3   EVIDENCE THAT WILL PREJUDICE THE JURY — Where evidence is relevant, however prejudicial it may be, it is never inadmissible for prejudice alone. *Guilianelle v Brownell* (1958, 3d Dept) 7 AD2d 691, 179 NYS2d 344.

A plaintiff in a civil action for personal injuries is permitted to exhibit his injuries to the jury. *Perry v Metropolitan S. R. Co.* (1902) 68 AD 351, 74 NYS 1. It was held permissible for a plaintiff who claimed to have sustained a hole in his leg to show this to the jury. *Looram v Second Avenue R. Co.* (1887, City Ct) 11 N.Y.S.R. 652. Where, however, the purpose of the exhibition is solely to arouse prejudice and there is no evidentiary value, the evidence is not admitted. Thus, it was held to be error to permit the display of a child's amputated foot to the jury, where the fact of the amputation had already been conceded. *Rost v Brooklyn H. R. Co.* (1896) 10 AD 477, 41 NYS 1069. It was likewise held prejudicial to permit the introduction into evidence of the photograph of a dead boy lying in a coffin. *Allen v Stokes* (1940) 260 AD 600, 23 NYS2d 443, reh and app den 260 AD 1007, 24 NYS2d 994. However, the holding in *Allen v Stokes, supra*, was not based solely on the highly prejudicial nature of the evidence, but more significantly upon its lack of probative value.

In a products liability action against a drug manufacturer, one of 12 such manufacturers who cooperated in the distribution of a drug that plaintiff ingested, where plaintiff could not identify the particular drug manufacturer who had sold the product but based her theory on concerted action, there was no prejudice to the defendant in the introduction at trial of an assessment as to the size of its market share, and testimony to the effect that it dominated the market. *Bichler v Eli Lilly & Co.* (1981, 1st Dept) 79 AD2d 317, 436 NYS2d 625, affd 55 NY2d 571, 450 NYS2d 776, 22 ALR4th 171. These comments could not be considered as showing defendant's ability to pay damages, which would have been improper. *Bichler v Eli Lilly & Co., supra.*

In a dental malpractice action, the trial court appropriately received evidence of defendant's inhalation of nitrous oxide, and properly permitted plaintiff's counsel to cross-examine the defendant concerning recreational use of cocaine. As to the former, the jury may have believed that the substance, a sedative, contributed to the malpractice; as to the latter, a witness may be impeached by proof of any specific immoral, vicious or criminal acts that may have a bearing on credibility. *Simon v Indursky* (1995, 1st Dept) 211 AD2d 404, 630 NYS2d 2.

§ 25:4 ADMISSIBILITY OF EVIDENCE ON COLLATERAL ISSUES — Evidence on collateral issues may be excluded in the discretion of the court. *Lawrence v Greenwood* (1949) 300 NY 231.

However, under certain conditions such evidence may have a bearing on the matter in issue. It has been held that in a civil action, evidence tending to show that a party to that action or his agent has attempted to influence a witness, is admissible. *Nowack* v *Metropolitan S. R. Co.* (1901) 166 NY 433, 60 NE 32. Thus, the fact that an agent of a corporation attempted to bribe a witness was admissible, even in the absence of proof that there was any corporate act authorizing the agent to tamper with the witness. *Nowack v Metropolitan S. R. Co., supra.*

§ 25:5   ADMISSIBILITY OF EVIDENCE OF SIMILAR ACTS OR OCCURRENCES —Evidence of a similar act or occurrence may, under certain conditions, be admissible in a civil case. To be admissible, however, such similar acts, occurrences, or transactions must be related to the case on trial. *Linzer v Amon Frock Co.* (1948, App Tm) 80 NYS2d 86. Where acts, other than the one involved in the case at bar, are sufficiently related in character, time, and place of occurrence, as tend to support the conclusion that they were part of a plan or system, or to show the existence of such a plan or system, such other acts are admissible. *Altman v Ozdoba* (1923) 237 NY 218, 142 NE 591, 33 ALR 422.

The admissibility of evidence of similar occurrences in negligence cases depends on the particular circumstances involved and the purpose for which the evidence is offered. Thus, if such evidence is offered for the purpose of showing that the conduct of the defendant on the occasion in question was the same as that on the prior occasion, it is held to be inadmissible. *Masciarelli v Delaware & H. R. Co.* (1941) 178 Misc 458, 34 NYS2d 550. However, where it is sought to show the prior existence of the same condition that allegedly caused the accident in question, other similar prior accidents may be shown for the purpose of showing the previous existence of the condition. *Hynes v Railway Express Agency, Inc.* (1944) 267 AD 835, 46 NYS2d 18.

Where a transaction is claimed to be a fraudulent one, evidence of other similar fraudulent transactions is admissible where such similar transactions are contemporaneous. *Hammer v Eisner-Mendelson Co.* (1951, App Tm) 152 NYS 1003. Where it is claimed that one party has acquired the property of another through a fraudulent device, it is permissible to support the charge by proof that such other party contemporaneously committed acts of the same character. *Boyd v Boyd* (1900) 164 NY 234, 58 NE 118. Such transactions are admissible to show intent, on the ground that they are part of a common scheme or plan.

Ettlinger v Weil (1904) 94 AD 291, 87 NYS 1049, revd 184 NY 179. Where an action is based upon the claim that the sale of stock was effected by means of false representation made by defendant's husband and agent who were authorized to sell the stock, evidence that similar representations were made by him to other purchasers at or about the same time is admissible as bearing on the question of intent. *Chisholm v Eisenhuth* (1902) 69 AD 134, 74 NYS 496.

Where the claim is made that a particular condition has caused an accident, it is permissible for the defendant to show an absence of accidents during the time that such condition was in existence prior to the accident in question. *Roy v F. W. Woolworth Co.* (1939) 257 AD 831, 11 NYS2d 1013. Thus, where plaintiff brought an action for injuries sustained when she caught her foot in a hook attached to the door in defendant's store, defendant was entitled to show that no similar accident had occurred during the time that such condition prevailed, because this was relevant on the issue of whether defendant was negligent in failing to anticipate that someone would be injured in the manner claimed by the plaintiff. *Roy v F. W. Woolworth Co., supra; see also, Cassar v Central Hudson Gas & Electric Corp.* (1987, 3d Dept) 134 AD2d 672, 521 NYS2d 337, later proceeding (3d Dept) 188 AD2d 946, 592 NYS2d 104.

While proof of prior accidents may be admissible to show that a condition is dangerous or that defendant had notice of this condition, it must be shown that the circumstances attending the prior accidents were sufficiently similar to the relevant conditions prevailing at the time of the accident in question. *Vega v Jacobs* (1981, 2d Dept) 84 AD2d 813, 444 NYS2d 132; *Price v Alfieri Concrete, Inc.* (1979, 2d Dept) 70 AD2d 932, 417 NYS2d 527; *Kaplan v New York* (1958, 1st Dept) 6 AD2d 489, 179 NYS2d 885, reh den (1st Dept) 7 AD2d 845, 182 NYS2d 331. Where the conditions existing during both accidents are shown to be sufficiently similar, the length of the span of time between the two accidents will not bar the evidence. *Heimer v Stento* (1946) 270 AD 665, 63 NYS2d 29, reh and app den 271 AD 757, 64 NYS2d 917. Thus, where the action was brought for injuries received from a fall down an elevator shaft, the plaintiff's evidence concerning two accidents that happened under similar conditions some 10 years before the accident in question at the same location was competent. *Heimer v Stento, supra.* Where a woman brought an action for injuries sustained as a result of slipping and falling on the floor in a department store and the defendant claimed that the preparation used in treating the floor for eight years prior to the accident prevented it from becoming slippery or unsafe, testimony that a particular witness had slipped on the floor during such period was competent. *Vogel v Montgomery Ward, Inc.* (1949) 275 AD 727, 86 NYS2d 817, app den 275 AD 872, 89 NYS2d 888.

In a civil action brought by an executrix to recover property obtained by a nursing home from a decedent by means of fraud and undue influence, evidence of two prior judgments decreeing that one of the defendants had engaged in fraud and undue influence in obtaining property from two other elderly individuals was admissible. *Re Estate of Brandon* (1982) 55 NY2d 206, 448 NYS2d 436.

Where the contract in question was unclear as to whether the territory involved was exclusive, it was not error for the court to refuse to allow admission into evidence of contracts between the manufacturer and agents other than the plaintiff, where these contracts were stated by their terms to be non-exclusive and therefore had no bearing on the meaning of the contract between the parties. *Mister Filters, Inc. v Weber Environmental Systems* (1974, 3d Dept) 44 AD2d 639, 353 NYS2d 835.

In an automobile collision case, where road conditions are relevant, in applying the rule allowing proof of a prior happening, it is only necessary that the relevant conditions be shown to be similar to those existing at the time of the accident in question. *Tomassi v Union* (1977, 3d Dept) 58 AD2d 670, 395 NYS2d 747, app dismd 43 NY2d 793, 402 NYS2d 393 and mod 46 NY2d 91, 412 NYS2d 842.

Where the complaint and bill of particulars alleged faulty construction of a parking lot, as well as negligent maintenance, proof of the absence of prior accidents covering a reasonable length of time was admissible, if the trial court charged that such evidence was only a factor for consideration and not conclusive. *Wozniak v*

110 South Main Street Land & Dev. Improv. Corp. (1978, 3d Dept) 61 AD2d 848, 402 NYS2d 69.

Proof of a prior accident, whether offered as proof of the existence of a dangerous condition or as proof of notice thereof, is admissible only upon a showing that the relevant conditions of the subject accident and the previous one were substantially the same. *Hyde v County of Rensselaer* (1980) 51 NY2d 927, 434 NYS2d 984. The trial court properly permitted the testimony of a New York State Trooper that he had been present at the scene of another accident at the same location in 1973, at which time he observed its physical condition, for the purpose of showing the condition of the road shoulder and the delineator posts, on the issue of constructive notice. *Hyde v County of Rensselaer, supra.*

Although evidence of prior similar accidents may be admissible to show notice of a defect, and both prior and subsequent accidents may be proffered to demonstrate that a product is dangerous or defective, a showing that the incidents were similar, at least in their relevant details, is a prerequisite to admissibility. *Facci v General Elec. Co.* (1993, 3d Dept) 192 AD2d 991, 596 NYS2d 928.

In an action for damages for injuries sustained in a fight involving patrons of a tavern in its parking lot, proof of prior disturbances at the tavern may be relevant on the issue of foreseeability, because such proof tends to establish that the owner has notice of danger to his patrons, the extent of the danger to be guarded against, and thus the nature of his duty. *Stevens v Kirby* (1982, 4th Dept) 86 AD2d 391, 450 NYS2d 607. Whether the circumstances attending the earlier incidents are sufficiently similar to the relevant conditions prevailing at the time plaintiff was injured, is to be determined by the issues presented in each case, and this determination rests in the sound discretion of the trial judge. *Stevens v Kirby, supra.*

In an action against a municipality arising out of the alleged failure to properly maintain the roadway upon which the accident occurred, it was not error for the trial court to permit the introduction of evidence that various city agencies and officials had been notified before the accident with respect to prior accidents and near misses that had occurred at the intersection in question;

this evidence was offered on the issue of notice to the city. *Grcic v New York* (1988, 2d Dept) 139 AD2d 621, 527 NYS2d 263, motion den 73 NY2d 702, 536 NYS2d 743 and motion den 73 NY2d 702, 536 NYS2d 743 and motion den 73 NY2d 702, 536 NYS2d 743 and motion den 73 NY2d 702, 536 NYS2d 743.

In an action brought by the mother of a student who was shot to death outside a junior high school, it was error to preclude evidence of prior incidents involving altercations and the presence of weapons in or on the school. *Maness v City of New York* (1994, 1st Dept) 201 AD2d 347, 607 NYS2d 325.

In an action for assault and battery brought against a hospital, based on the acts of a guard employed by the hospital, it was not an improvident exercise of the trial court's discretion to refuse to permit plaintiff's counsel to cross-examine the guard regarding another civil action arising out of an incident similar to the one involved in the case in question. *De Gregorio v Lutheran Medical Center* (1988, 2d Dept) 142 AD2d 543, 529 NYS2d 903.

A plaintiff may not adduce evidence tending to demonstrate that a person alleged to have committed a negligent act has previously committed similar acts or was generally negligent, and it was therefore reversible error, in an action brought by a plaintiff who fell to the subway tracks and was run over by a train, to permit the plaintiff to read the motorman's deposition testimony in which he acknowledged that on two prior occasions he had operated a train that had struck a person on or near the tracks. *Feaster v New York City Transit Authority* (1991, 1st Dept) 568 NYS2d 380.

Evidence of other acts or transactions is admissible when sufficiently connected with the act or transaction at issue as tending to support the inference that they were part of a plan or system. *Re New York County DES Litigation* (1991, 1st Dept) 171 AD2d 119, 575 NYS2d 19.

In an asbestos product liability action, evidence of successful Workers' Compensation claims made by asbestos plant workers during the 1940's to the 1960's for asbestos-related pulmonary diseases, as well as evidence of pulmonary diseases among asbestos plant workers, was properly admitted on the issue of defendant corporation's knowledge of the risks of asbestos exposure and the reasonableness of its failure to warn the end users of its product of those risks. *In re Eighth Judicial Dist. Asbestos Litig.* (1993, 4th Dept) 190 AD2d 1008, 595 NYS2d 574.

§ 25:6 PROOF OF HABITS — Evidence of habit may be, in certain cases, admissible. It is permissible to show that a party followed a given course of conduct with regularity, for the purpose of showing that on a particular occasion under particular conditions he followed the same course of conduct. *Re Will of Kellum* (1873, Sur Ct) 52 NY 517. Thus, where an attorney has forgotten the particular circumstances surrounding the execution of a will, he may testify to the care with which he habitually drew wills and that he followed the provisions of the statute with respect to their execution. *Re Will of Kellum, supra.*

The testimony of a witness who appeared in his own behalf to the effect that it was his custom to be at home on the 20th of every month, was admissible on the question of whether a letter was mailed on the 20th of the month. *Beakes v Da Cunha* (1891) 126 NY 293, 27 NE 251.

However, proof of intoxication on occasions prior to the accident is not admissible to prove that the plaintiff was intoxicated at the time of the accident. *McQuage v New York* (1954) 285 AD 249, 136 NYS2d 111.

It is not competent for plaintiff to introduce evidence tending to show that the person by whom the negligent act is alleged to have been committed previously committed similar acts or that he was generally negligent, and the failure to exclude such testimony was reversible error. *Grenadier v Surface Transp. Corp.* (1946) 271 AD 460, 66 NYS2d 130. Where plaintiff's counsel developed on cross-examination of a bus driver that he had stated in a report of the accident to the Motor Vehicle Bureau that he had had two previous accidents, it was error to permit further cross-examination to show that the driver had had other accidents than those mentioned in the report. *Grenadier v Surface Transp. Corp., supra.*

Where plaintiff brought an action to recover for injuries sustained when a streetcar ran over his foot, evidence that the plaintiff was in the habit of jumping on streetcars was inadmissible. *Eppendorf v Brooklyn C. & N. R. Co.* (1877) 69 NY 195. In a negligence action, it was held error to permit evidence that a driver of a vehicle was convicted two times for speeding, because this had no bearing on the issue of whether he was careful on the occasion in question. *Flannagan v Brown* (1925) 211 AD 694, 208 NYS 211.

In an action for wrongful death that allegedly occurred while the victim was driving over a crossing, evidence that on prior occasions when driving over the same crossing it had been his habit to stop and look up and down the track, was inadmissible. *Parsons v Syracuse, B. & N. Y. R. Co.* (1909) 133 AD 461, 117 NYS 1058, later app 145 AD 900, 129 NYS 1141, mod 203 NY 167, 96 NE 431, reh den 203 NY 608, 96 NE 1127 and remittitur den 206 NY 636, 99 NE 1116.

§ 25:7   CUSTOM AND USAGE — Where a custom is relied upon to take the place of a separate principle of law, such custom must be ancient, certain, and require time to receive universal acceptance. *People v Smith* (1955) 286 AD 466, 144 NYS2d 554. A custom and usage, to be binding, must be so general that a presumption of law will arise that everyone knows of it. *Shaw v Dreyfus & Co.* (1969) 64 Misc 2d 122, 314 NYS2d 372. Thus, the rules and regulations of a membership corporation that supervises the activities of broker-members, and of which a stock brokerage company was a member, were neither a custom or a usage that could be imposed on the stock brokerage company's customer who sought to recover from the company money paid for stock he never received. *Shaw v Dreyfus & Co., supra.* What is done by one or more contractors in a section does not establish a general custom. *George Colon Contracting Corp. v Morrison* (1954, Sup) 162 NYS2d 841, affd (4th Dept) 2 AD2d 869, 157 NYS2d 927, app den (4th Dept) 3 AD2d 690, 158 NYS2d 797.

If a custom or usage is to be read into a contract to ascertain the intention of the parties, there must be proof that it was general, uniform, and unvarying. *Belasco Theatre Corp. v Jelin Productions, Inc.* (1945) 270 AD 202, 59 NYS2d 42, app den 270 AD 760, 59 NYS2d 924. A custom or trait cannot create a contract where there has been no agreement by the parties and none is implied by law, nor can it give validity to a contract that the law declares void. *Grombach Productions, Inc. v Waring* (1944) 293 NY 609, reh den 294 NY 697.

Legal contracts are interpreted in accordance with the intent of the parties entering into it, and where custom or usage is reasonable, uniform, well settled, not in opposition to fixed rules of law, and not in contradiction of the express terms of the contract, it is deemed to form a part of the contract and to enter into the intention of the parties. *Frye v State* (1948) 192 Misc 260, 78 NYS2d 342. A note or memorandum that is sufficient to satisfy the statute of frauds may be subject to a custom or a trade usage that is not inconsistent with the terms of the writing. *Richard L. Rosenthal Corp. v Burnside* (1947, Sup) 77 NYS2d 282.

Parties may contract either in accordance with custom, contrary to custom, or in the absence of custom, and it is the express agreement that governs, and the existence or absence of custom in such cases is immaterial. *R. L. Rothstein Corp. v Kerr S.S. Co.* (1964, 1st Dept) 21 AD2d 463, 251 NYS2d 81, affd 15 NY2d 897, 258 NYS2d 427.

Usages of a limited character in a particular field of litigation, in the absence of proof that the parties had knowledge thereof, cannot be held to have formed part of the agreement of the parties. *Bregoff v St. Mary's Home for Working Girls, Inc.* (1941, App Tm) 32 NYS2d 446, affd 264 AD 882, 36 NYS2d 428. Where it was not shown that one of the parties to a contract knew of an alleged trade custom as to the meaning of an expression used in a publication contract, the purported custom was held not to be binding on this party. *Duffield & Co. v Ellsworth* (1932) 143 Misc 40, 255 NYS 716.

Parol evidence is admissible to explain the meaning that a particular custom or usage has given words or terms used in any particular trade or business or in any particular locality. *Horby Realty Corp. v Yarmouth Land Corp.* (1946) 270 AD 696, 62 NYS2d 173. Not only is parol evidence of usage admissible to explain ambiguities and technical terms in a contract, but also to explain ordinary words and even to annex collateral agreements otherwise barred by the Parol Evidence Rule. *Lucisano v Paratore* (1949) 195 Misc 45, 88 NYS2d 715, affd 198 Misc 193, 98 NYS2d 608.

Custom may be proved to explain an ambiguity in a contract. *Heimerdinger v Schnitzler* (1931) 231 AD 649, 248 NYS 597. Custom cannot, however, be proved to vary the terms of an unambiguous contract. *Kasper v Metropolitan Life Ins. Co.* (1935) 244 AD 508, 279 NYS 810.

It was held that in the absence of a contract between a lithographer and his customer with respect to the ownership and disposition of plates that the lithographer had prepared for the customer, the plates belonged to the lithographer in accordance with the custom of the trade. *Universal Map Co. v Lutz & Sheinkman* (1949) 194 Misc 938, 86 NYS2d 795.

While custom or usage may be employed to help ascertain legislative intent when this is not sufficiently clear, it cannot control plain language nor can usage or custom create or take the place of positive law. *Garramone v Simmons* (1941) 177 Misc 330, 30 NYS2d 465. While custom and practice cannot override a clear rule of law, it may help to define the scope and clarify the outlines of such rule. *O'Connor v Bankers Trust Co.* (1936) 159 Misc 920, 289 NYS 252, affd 253 AD 714, 1 NYS2d 641, affd 278 NY 649.

In a negligence action, although general usage or practice is competent to show either ordinary care or the failure to exercise such care, *Garthe v Ruppert* (1934) 264 NY 290, 190 NE 643, reh den 265 NY 502, 193 NE 291, *Miller v Long Island R.R.* (1995, 2d Dept) 212 AD2d 515, 622 NYS2d 305, such evidence is not conclusive or controlling. *Trembley v Coca-Cola Bottling Co.* (1955) 285 AD 539, 138 NYS2d 332; *Capital Mut. Ins. Co. v Niagara Mohawk Power Corp.* (1988, 3d Dept) 137 AD2d 877, 524 NYS2d 561, app den 71 NY2d 806, 530 NYS2d 109; *Marus v Central R. Co.* (1916) 175 AD 783, 161 NYS 546. Such evidence is received for what it is worth in view of all the circumstances of the particular case, and under proper instruction from the court as to its inconclusive nature, the jury has the right to give it such consideration as they think it should receive in connection with all the other facts. *Shannahan v Empire Engineering Corp.* (1912) 204 NY 543, 98 NE 9; *Saglimbeni v West End Brewing Co.* (1948) 274 AD 201, 80 NYS2d 635, affd 298 NY 875. When evidence of custom and usage is admitted in a negligence case it should be received with great caution. *Rothstein v Monette* (1940, City Ct)

17 NYS2d 369. The limited value that the courts have given to such evidence is based on the consideration that under any other rule incorporated employers by their general custom or habit of acting, could create a rule of law to govern their own standard of conduct. *Marus v Central R. Co., supra.*

In a negligence action brought by a business guest for injuries allegedly sustained because of a fall due to wax on the floor of the Telephone Company's place of business, evidence with respect to the manner in which other parties apply wax to the floors in their business was not admissible. *Rainville v New York Tel. Co.* (1940) 260 AD 881, 22 NYS2d 877. In an action for personal injuries based upon an allegedly dangerous condition of the premises, although general usage or custom may be shown to establish a standard of construction as tending to show what is reasonable care, such evidence is not a controlling test. *Radin v State* (1948) 192 Misc 247, 80 NYS2d 189. Where plaintiff was injured on a moving platform of the Ford pavilion of the World's Fair, it was error for the court to dismiss where the proof demonstrated that on prior occasions the defendant had posted an attendant to assist persons alighting therefrom. *Iulio v Ford Motor Co.* (1969, 2d Dept) 31 AD2d 820, 298 NYS2d 33.

Only general custom or usage in a particular trade or industry is admissible. Thus, evidence showing that in a brewery other than that owned by the defendant, work was done in a more satisfactory manner and that waste was discharged and carried away without dust and moisture was held to be inadmissible, where it was not shown to be part of the custom or general usage in the industry. *Garthe v Ruppert, supra.*

Where a contract requires that the seller shall give and the purchaser shall accept such title as a designated title company will approve and insure, the seller assumes the burden of delivering a title that the title company will approve and insure unconditionally and without exceptions, and the existence of an alleged custom and usage not to furnish title insurance where the land in question is washed by tidal waters does not excuse the failure of the vendors to perform the undertaking in the contract. *Newmark v Weingrad* (1974, 2d Dept) 43 AD2d 983, 352 NYS2d 660, affd 35 NY2d 832, 362 NYS2d 863.

Where plaintiff's expert witness testified that the safety standard as promulgated by the National Board of Fire Underwriters represented the accepted standard in the locality, it was proper to admit said publication into the evidence, as it constituted some evidence of negligence, although not conclusive. *Bailey v Baker's Air Force Gas Corp.* (1975) 50 AD2d 129, 376 NYS2d 212.

A hospital's failure to abide by its own internal rules is evidence of negligence sufficient to raise a *prima facie* case. *Haber v Cross County Hospital* (1975) 37 NY2d 888, 378 NYS2d 369, on remand (2d Dept) 50 AD2d 885, 377 NYS2d 168, app dismd 38 NY2d 1001, 384 NYS2d 440. However, a defendant's internal rules are not admissible to the extent that they impose a higher duty than that imposed by law. *Rivera v New York City Transit Authority* (1991) 77 NY2d 322, 567 NYS2d 629; *Banayan v F.W. Woolworth Co.* (1995, 1st Dept) 211 AD2d 591, 622 NYS2d 24.

A power company may be held liable notwithstanding its compliance with the National Electric Safety Code and with the rules of the Board of Standards and Appeals, as these provisions are minimum requirements. *Miner v Long Island Lighting Co.* (1976) 40 NY2d 372, 386 NYS2d 842. Where the evidence disclosed circumstances that required a higher factor of safety than the minimum requirements, liability lies, and compliance with customary usage or industry practices is not dispositive of the issue of due care, but constitutes merely some evidence thereof. *Miner v Long Island Lighting Co., supra.*

In an action brought on an indemnification agreement, where there was no claim that the language of that agreement was ambiguous, any references to custom and practice in the local bonding market were irrelevant. *Travelers Indem. Co. v Buffalo Motor & Generator Corp.* (1977) 58 AD2d 978, 397 NYS2d 257.

When proof of an accepted practice is accompanied by evidence that the defendant conformed to it, this may establish due care; conversely, when proof of a customary practice is coupled with a showing that it was ignored and that this departure was a proximate cause of the accident, it may serve to establish liability. *Trimarco v Klein* (1982) 56 NY2d 98, 451 NYS2d 52.

The trial court erred in precluding the plaintiff's expert from testifying that it was common practice to use pressure-treated lumber in the construction of stairways such as the one involved, even though the non-pressure-treated lumber used was permissible under the applicable building code; proof of a general custom and usage is admissible because it tends to establish a standard by which ordinary care may be judged, even where an ordinance prescribes certain minimum safety requirements that the custom exceeds. *Duncan v Corbetta* (1991, 2d Dept) 178 AD2d 459, 577 NYS2d 129.

Exclusion of proof by plaintiff's expert witness who offered to testify to the customary and usual practice of having a chimney inspected before hook-up with a heating system constituted reversible error. *French v Ehrenfeld* (1992, 3d Dept) 180 AD2d 895, 579 NYS2d 480.

In an action to recover brokerage fees under an agreement with property owners, where no fee is stated, the courts may not calculate a fee without custom and usage evidence to establish an extrinsic standard that is fixed and invariable in the industry. *Cooper Square Realty, Inc. v A.R.S. Management, Ltd.* (1992, 1st Dept) 181 AD2d 551, 581 NYS2d 50.

In an action brought by a former employee to recover sales commissions, which he claimed were earned but not paid before his resignation, evidence of a trade custom or usage, by which it was determined when such commissions were earned, was properly admitted because such custom was relevant. *Edelman v Robert A. Becker, Inc.* (1993, 1st Dept) 194 AD2d 507, 599 NYS2d 578.

§ 25:8 PROOF OF INTOXICATION — Intoxication implies undue or abnormal excitation of the passions or feelings, or the impairment of the capacity to think and act correctly and efficiently, and suggests a loss of the normal control of one's faculties. *People v Weaver* (1919) 188 AD 395, 177 NYS 71.

Where a defendant in a civil action has previously pleaded guilty to driving while intoxicated, this conviction alone does not afford a basis for summary judgment against the said defendant without proof of proximate cause. *Prince v McKee* (1965, 2d Dept) 24 AD2d 455, 260 NYS2d 386. However, proof of such conviction upon a plea of guilty is admissible in evidence at the trial for such consideration as the trier of the facts may deem warranted. *Prince v McKee, supra*.

Evidence of defendant's plea of guilty to a charge of driving while intoxicated is admissible in an automobile accident case. *O'Neill v Hamill* (1964, 2d Dept) 22 AD2d 691, 253 NYS2d 289. Defendant's driving a vehicle while intoxicated constitutes negligence. *O'Neill v Hamill, supra*.

In a wrongful death action, evidence of decedent's intoxication clearly was competent and relevant, and the autopsy report and blood analysis were properly admitted into evidence pursuant to CPLR 4518(c). *Tinao v New York* (1985, 2d Dept) 112 AD2d 363, 491 NYS2d 814.

In an action brought pursuant to § 240 of the Labor Law, based upon plaintiff's fall from a ladder, plaintiff's alleged intoxication would be admissible only as proof that such intoxication was the sole proximate cause of the accident. *Hodge v Crouse Hinds Div.* (1994, 4th Dept) 207 AD2d 1007, 616 NYS2d 822; *Tate v Clancy-Cullen Storage Co.* (1991, 1st Dept) 171 AD2d 292, 575 NYS2d 832.

§ 25:9   EVIDENCE OF CHARACTER AND REPUTATION —

The terms character and reputation are related but are not synonymous. Character refers to a person's actual traits; reputation is a person's character as seen through the eyes of the public. When evidence of character is relevant, it is admissible in the form of testimony as to a person's reputation. *People v Van Gaasbeck* (1907) 189 NY 408, 82 NE 718.

In a civil case, the general reputation in the community of a party to the action is inadmissible when the character of the party is not at issue. *Schneider v Bytner* (1984, 3d Dept) 105 AD2d, 498, 481 NYS2d 777.

The character of a party may not be shown in a civil case to raise an inference that he acted in conformity therewith on the occasion in question. *O'Connell v Jacobs* (1992, 4th Dept) 181 AD2d 1064, 583 NYS2d 61. The trial court improperly admitted testimony that based upon an analysis of defendant's writings, defendant possessed personality traits of sadism, narcissism and self-centeredness and that he was capable of committing the assault. *O'Connell v Jacobs, supra*.

§ 25:10 PROOF OF CHARACTER IN CIVIL CASES — In civil cases, evidence of the character or reputation of a party is ordinarily not admissible because this is ordinarily not relevant. *Morningstar v Lafayette Hotel Co.* (1914) 211 NY 465, 105 NE 656. Evidence of character may not be shown for the purpose of proving or disproving the act with which a party is charged. *Noonan v Luther* (1912) 206 NY 105, 99 NE 178; *Liberto v Worcester Mut. Ins. Co.* (1982, 2d Dept) 87 AD2d 477, 452 NYS2d 74. However, where there has been evidence introduced attacking the character of one party, evidence of good character on behalf of that party is thereby rendered competent. *Inman v Foster*, 8 Wend 602. Thus, where the defendant has introduced evidence attacking the reputation of the plaintiff, it was competent to present proof of plaintiff's general character for honesty. *Inman v Foster, supra*.

The rule against permitting evidence of character in civil cases applies even in an action where moral turpitude is involved, such as a divorce on the ground of adultery, and a defendant has been held not to be able to prove her good character. *Booth v Booth* (1929) 135 Misc 350, 238 NYS 193. There have been some exceptions to this rule too. In a civil action for assault, defendant was permitted to prove plaintiff's bad reputation for being quarrelsome. *Silliman v Sampson* (1899) 42 AD 623, 59 NYS 923.

Evidence of a person's reputation for carefulness has been held inadmissible to show lack of negligence. *Gibson v Casein Mfg. Co.* (1913) 157 AD 46, 141 NYS 887.

In defamation actions, because it is an injury to a person's reputation that is involved, defendant is allowed to show plaintiff's bad reputation in order to mitigate or negate damages. If plaintiff's reputation before the publication was a bad one, he will have sustained no injury to it. *Douglass v Tousey*, 2 Wend 352. However, such proof of reputation may not be demonstrated by proof of specific acts of misconduct. *Theodore v Daily Mirror, Inc.* (1940) 282 NY 345, 130 ALR 353.

In a medical malpractice case, evidence of the plaintiff's alleged alcoholism, offered to show that he tended to exercise poor judgment, and the introduction of opinion evidence by doctors to the effect that plaintiff exhibited a so-called "denial syndrome," which would allegedly tend to make him disregard competent medical advice and thus choose to undergo a contra-indicated surgical procedure, was akin to evidence of character and habit, which is generally inadmissible in civil cases to raise the inference that a party acted in a particular way on the occasion in issue. The prejudice created by the introduction of such evidence required a new trial. *Davis v Blum* (1979, 2d Dept) 70 AD2d 583, 416 NYS2d 57.

Evidence of bad character is normally admissible in a civil case to impeach a witness, and may also be used in those cases in which a person's character is directly in issue as a matter of substantive law. *Kravitz v Long Island Jewish-Hillside Medical Center Community Health Program, Inc.* (1985, 2d Dept) 113 AD2d 577, 497 NYS2d 51.

§ 25:11   REPUTATION FOR TRUTH AND VERACITY — In both civil and criminal cases the credibility of a witness, whether a party or not, may be impeached by showing that his reputation for truth and veracity is bad. *Spira v Holoschutz* (1902) 38 Misc 754, 78 NYS 1138.

The person testifying as to the reputation for truthfulness of the witness must be familiar with such reputation, and it is not sufficient that he knows the witness. *Sturmwald v Schreiber* (1902) 69 AD 476, 74 NYS 995. It is not requisite that the person whose testimony is being introduced for the purpose of impeaching the reputation of the witness reside in the same community, so long as he is in a position to know what the reputation of the witness is. *People v Loris* (1909) 131 AD 127, 115 NYS 236.

§ 25:12   EVIDENCE OF LIABILITY INSURANCE — Whether defendant does or does not have liability insurance should have no weight in proving defendant's liability, thus evidence of such insurance is irrelevant and inadmissible. No hint of insurance protection of a defendant may be given in an action. *Van Romapaye Trucking Corp. v Heebner* (1948, Sup) 85 NYS2d 347.

Generally, a deliberate attempt by counsel to convey to the jury the idea that defendant is insured constitutes grounds for a mistrial. *Brand v Mangust Holding Corp.* (1945, Sup) 53 NYS2d 882. After a jury rendered a verdict in favor of the plaintiff, the trial court properly declared a mistrial and directed a retrial, where a witness had made reference during the trial to a specific insurer, and where there was some evidence suggesting that this reference influenced the amount of the plaintiff's verdict. *O'Connell v Consolo* (1969, 2d Dept) 32 AD2d 820, 302 NYS2d 319.

In a close case involving an automobile accident, comment by the plaintiff's attorney as to the adequacy of insurance coverage and his obvious and inflammatory appeal to the sympathy of the jury must be deemed to have resulted in substantial prejudice requiring reversal of a judgment for the plaintiff. *Depelteau v Ford Motor Co.* (1967, 3d Dept) 28 AD2d 1178, 284 NYS2d 490.

Evidence of lack of insurance on the part of a defendant is considered equally irrelevant and equally prejudicial. Thus, a statement by a defense counsel during the course of summation in a civil action that if plaintiff recovered a large sum, defendants would be required to work for the rest of their lives to pay the judgment, was an obvious reference to the lack of insurance coverage on the part of the defendants, and the refusal to instruct the jury to disregard such remarks upon timely objection was prejudicial error. *Rendo v Schermerhorn* (1965, 3d Dept) 24 AD2d 773, 263 NYS2d 743.

Remarks as to source of payment of a judgment made by the plaintiff's attorney in a personal injury action after his objection to reference in defendant's summation to taking money out of a man's pocket to pay for such injuries had been sustained, were clearly improper as a palpable attempt to bring the existence of insurance to the jury's attention, and in a close case must be deemed to have resulted in substantial prejudice and required reversal of a judgment for the plaintiff and a new trial. *Wisniewski v Jem Novelty Corp.* (1964, 1st Dept) 22 AD2d 10, 253 NYS2d 418.

The fact that inadequate insurance coverage on the part of one defendant was made known to the jury was extremely prejudicial to the other defendant, requiring a new trial. *Brennan v Felter* (1975, 2d Dept) 48 AD2d 846, 369 NYS2d 175.

It was improper for defendants in an action for wrongful death to show that the plaintiff was entitled to Workmen's Compensation. *Swanson v Evans Oil, Inc.* (1961, 4th Dept) 12 AD2d 875, 209 NYS2d 860.

Where an automobile had been registered in New York two years after the effective date of the Compulsory Insurance Law, a single inadvertent reference to insurance in a personal injury accident case involving the said automobile did not justify a mistrial, particularly since the answers of jurors in response to a poll of the jury indicated that the mention of insurance had no effect on their determination. *Halstead v Sanky* (1965) 48 Misc 2d 586, 265 NYS2d 426.

The giving of a statement to the jury from which an inference may be drawn that the defendant is either wealthy or is insured is error. *Freeman v Manhattan Cab Corp.* (1956) 1 Misc 2d 601, 150 NYS2d 674.

Reference to insurance is condemned only where the fact of its existence is irrelevant to the issues and where such reference is, in all likelihood, made for the purpose of improperly influencing the jury. *Oltarsh v Aetna Ins. Co.* (1965) 15 NY2d 111, 256 NYS2d 577. Where the fact of insurance or its existence is properly or legitimately in the case, there can be no grounds for complaint. *Oltarsh v Aetna Ins. Co., supra.* While the question of defendant's insurance is ordinarily irrelevant, prejudicial and therefore inadmissible in a negligence action, such evidence cannot be excluded as prejudicial if it is relevant to a material issue. *Leotta v Plessinger* (1960) 8 NY2d 449, 209 NYS2d 304, remittitur amd 9 NY2d 686, 212 NYS2d 421.

In an action for wrongful death, the defendant could not complain of the admission of evidence that revealed that defendant carried public liability insurance, where the attorney for the defendant had himself possibly opened the door for the receipt of such testimony in the course of cross-examination of a defendant who had been called as a witness for the plaintiff. *Levatino v Rochester Sav. Bank* (1942, Sup) 38 NYS2d 182. In an action for the death of an employee that involved an issue of whether, at the time of the accident, the employee was in the employ of a general or special employer, reference by the plaintiff's attorney to insurance was held not to be error where the insurance involved was Workmen's Compensation Insurance, which had been injected into the case by the defendant to prove that the insured employee was not its employee and that it was liable with the general employer under the Workmen's Compensation Law. *Lisanti v William F. Kenny Co.* (1928) 225 AD 129, 232 NYS 103, affd 250 NY 621, 166 NE 347.

The injection of evidence of insurance into an action for personal injuries sustained in an automobile accident is not reversible error where such testimony was not responsive to a question asked of the witness by plaintiff's counsel. *Gelfond v Kirschenbaum* (1937) 249 AD 894, 292 NYS 568.

In a death action brought against the seller of a tent as a result of a tent fire, the court correctly denied a defense motion for a mistrial as a result of the mention of insurance, because the answer was inadvertently volunteered, and the other evidence in the case clearly supported the jury's finding of liability on the part of the defendant. *Rush v Sears, Roebuck & Co.* (1983, 3d Dept) 92 AD2d 1072, 461 NYS2d 559.

Where the owner of a vehicle entered into a contract with a transport company that agreed to arrange to have the vehicle transported to Florida, and while en route the owner's vehicle was involved in an accident with a second vehicle which it struck and in which plaintiffs were riding, the conduct of plaintiffs' counsel in commenting, during summation, upon the ability of the owner to pay and to recover such damages from the transport company was sufficient, by itself, to require a new trial where the case was a close one. *Carey v AAA Con Transport, Inc.* (1978, 3d Dept) 61 AD2d 113, 401 NYS2d 1015.

In a negligence action, where the plaintiff's attorney referred to no-fault insurance, and the subject was raised only to clarify the setting of the trial, with no prejudice resulting, there was no error. *Shumalski v Leone* (1978, 3d Dept) 63 AD2d 764, 404 NYS2d 744.

In a personal injury action, where evidence was introduced that a doctor on behalf of one of the insurance companies examined the plaintiff, such an isolated, indirect reference to insurance coverage cannot be said to have influenced the jury and where other evidence clearly established the defendants' liability as a matter of law, a mistrial was not required. *Allen v Harrington* (1989, 3d Dept) 156 AD2d 854, 550 NYS2d 79, app den 75 NY2d 708, 554 NYS2d 833.

In a medical malpractice action, the trial court properly limited the scope of cross-examination of defendant doctor's expert witness by precluding inquiry into the expert's employment as a consultant for the doctor's insurance company; the trial court achieved a fair balance between plaintiff's right to attack the expert witness's credibility and the prejudicial effect of introducing the fact of the doctor's insurance coverage by permitting the plaintiffs to show the witness's prior medical review services for law firms. *Cerasuoli v Brevetti* (1990, 2d Dept) 166 AD2d 403, 560 NYS2d 468.

§ 25:13   USE OF DEPOSITIONS ON TRIAL — On the trial of a civil action, any witness whose testimony has previously been taken by deposition, may be impeached by the use of that deposition. CPLR 3117(a)(1).

The deposition of any person may be used by any party for any purpose against any other party who was present or represented at the taking of the deposition or who had the requisite notice, if the court finds that the proposed witness is dead, or that the witness is at a greater distance than 100 miles from the place of trial, or is out of the state, unless it appears that the absence of the witness was procured by the party seeking the deposition, or that the witness is unable to attend or testify because of age, sickness, infirmity or imprisonment, or that the party offering the deposition has been unable to procure the attendance of the witness by diligent efforts, or upon motion or notice that exceptional circumstances exist such as make its use desirable in the interest of justice and with due regard to the importance of presenting the testimony of the witness orally in open court. CPLR 3117(a)(3).

If only a part of a deposition is read at the trial by a party, then any other party may read any other part of the deposition. CPLR 3117(b). Where a party uses a deposition he is not deemed to have made the person whose deposition is employed his own witness. CPLR 3117(b). At the trial any party may rebut any evidence contained in a deposition whether introduced by him or by any other party. CPLR 3117(b).

The deposition of a party or of any person who at the time of the taking of the deposition was an officer, director, member or managing or authorized agent of a party, or the deposition of an employee of a party who has been produced by that party may be used for any purpose by any adversely interested party. CPLR 3117(a)(2). CPLR 3117(a)(4) provides that the deposition of a person authorized to practice medicine may be used by any party without the necessity of showing unavailability or special circumstances, subject to the right of any party to move pursuant to 3103 CPLR to prevent abuse.

A deposition may always be used to impeach the deponent. *Jobse v Connolly* (1969) 60 Misc 2d 69, 302 NYS2d 35. In addition, the deposition of a party may always be put into evidence by the adverse party. *Jobse v Connolly, supra.*

In a will contest it was held to be error to exclude portions of the proponent's deposition taken before trial that were inconsistent with the proponent's testimony at the trial. *Re Gallo's Will* (1937) 252 AD 861, 299 NYS 497.

It was held to be error for the trial court to refuse to allow plaintiff in a personal injury action to read from defendant motorist's examination before trial. *Rodford v Sample* (1968, 3d Dept) 30 AD2d 588, 290 NYS2d 30.

Under CPLR 3117, a party deponent may not himself read all or a part of his own pretrial deposition when the party at whose insistence it was taken has refused to do so. *Wojtas v Fifth Ave. Coach Corp.* (1965, 2d Dept) 23 AD2d 685, 257 NYS2d 404.

Where a plaintiff takes a defendant's deposition prior to trial, the plaintiff may use all of the deposition or a part of it and is not compelled to put the defendant on the witness stand, and the rule is similar where the defendant takes the plaintiff's deposition. *Schimmel v Spigal* (1956) 4 Misc 2d 406, 157 NYS2d 404.

Where the trial judge found that the illness of one defendant precluded his attendance at the trial, defendant's trial counsel could read his deposition into evidence although plaintiffs had not offered any part thereof at the trial. *Wojtas v Fifth Ave. Coach Corp., supra.*

Counsel for an 82-year-old plaintiff who was physically unable to come to court was improperly deprived of the right to testify as to the nature of plaintiff's condition as a basis for introducing her deposition. *Hill v Hudson View Gardens, Inc.* (1961, 1st Dept) 13 AD2d 730, 214 NYS2d 477.

A party may use his adversary's pretrial deposition as evidence in chief, and in so doing does not make the witness his own. *Spampinato v A. B. C. Consol. Corp.* (1974) 35 NY2d 283, 360 NYS2d 878.

The trial court committed reversible error when it held that plaintiff was bound by the defendant's denial, during an examination before trial, of personal service, because that denial was read into the record by plaintiff's attorney; plaintiff should have been given the opportunity to refute the defendant's denial and to have the issue of fact raised by defendant's affirmative defense of lack of personal jurisdiction determined by the jury. *Schiffrin v Meranchik* (1975, 2d Dept) 50 AD2d 877, 377 NYS2d 157.

A deposition, elicited in May, 1979, in an unrelated trial, previous to the one in which the deposition was introduced, in which deponent identified himself as vice president of the defendant corporation, was admissible in the current trial, because it flatly contradicted the contentions of defendant corporation that it had existed no earlier than 1981 or 1982, and in addition raised an issue as to whether the defendant corporation had supervised and trained ground service personnel and directed ground service maintenance at John F. Kennedy International Airport in 1979; the fact that the testimony was elicited in another lawsuit did not preclude its consideration in the current action. *Harris v Triangle Aviation Services, Inc.* (1985, 2d Dept) 110 AD2d 882, 488 NYS2d 434.

In a personal injury action, the trial court abused its discretion by refusing to permit defendant to present the deposition testimony of plaintiff-husband (who died before the trial) and plaintiff-wife concerning plaintiff-husband's affair with his assailant's wife. *Viscomi v S.S. Kresge Co.* (1990, 4th Dept) 159 AD2d 979, 552 NYS2d 761, leave denied 76 NY2d 708, 560 NYS2d 990.

The trial court committed reversible error by precluding plaintiff from calling a defendant as a witness on the ground that plaintiff had already read that defendant's deposition. *Perkins v New York Racing Asso.* (1976, 2d Dept) 51 AD2d 585, 378 NYS2d 757. Conversely, it was also reversible error to preclude plaintiff from reading from defendant's deposition on the ground that the defendant had already testified, and was no longer in court. *Gonzalez v Medina* (1979, 1st Dept) 69 AD2d 14, 417 NYS2d 953.

Where plaintiff reads a portion of defendant's deposition on plaintiff's direct case, the appropriate time for defense counsel to exercise the right to read other portions of the deposition is on the defendant's direct case. *Villa v Vetuskey* (1975, 4th Dept) 50 AD2d 1093, 376 NYS2d 359; *Gonzalez v Medina, supra.* However, where a witness is confronted with his or her deposition on cross-examination, other portions may be used on redirect examination of the witness for purposes of rehabilitation. *Hallock v State* (1983, 3d Dept) 98 AD2d 856, 470 NYS2d 844, revd (1984) 64 NY2d 224, 485 NYS2d 510.

§ 25:14 SELF-SERVING DECLARATIONS — Generally, self-serving declarations are inadmissible. *Sitrin Bros., Inc. v Deluxe Lines, Inc.* (1962) 35 Misc 2d 1041, 231 NYS2d 943. In a personal injury action it was held to be error to permit defendant to place in evidence his own written report of the accident. *Newcomb v Frink* (1951) 278 AD 998, 105 NYS2d 704, application den 278 AD 1028, 106 NYS2d 904 and app dismd 303 NY 669.

The self-serving declarations of a savings bank depositor were not admissible for the purpose of negativing an intention to create a joint tenancy by a deposit in the names of both the depositor and another person payable to either or to his survivor. *Re Porianda's Estate* (1931) 256 NY 423, 176 NE 826.

Evidence of declarations the donor made after the gift, was improperly received and was ineffective for the purpose of defeating the donee's claim of title. *Re Voges' Will* (1950) 276 AD 982, 95 NYS2d 207, affd 301 NY 617.

The declarations of a deceased person in his own favor are no more competent than those of a living person. *Rawlings v Prudential Ins. Co.* (1939) 256 AD 284, 9 NYS2d 979. A testator's declarations that were inconsistent with a claim for services rendered to the testator at his request were held to be inadmissible as self-serving. *Meehan v Keenan* (1929) 226 AD 812, 234 NYS 365.

It was error to receive defendant's written self-serving statement in evidence. *Rupp v Christofolo* (1947) 272 AD 856, 70 NYS2d 383. The written report to the Motor Vehicle Bureau of one of the defendants in a death action was held to be a self-serving declaration erroneously received in evidence. *Trampusch v Kastner* (1934) 242 AD 803, 274 NYS 771.

The entry made in decedent's checkbook indicating that the check, which had been made to the order of decedent's son-in-law, was a loan, was a self-serving one and was incompetent to establish a loan by the decedent. *Re Purdy's Will* (1947, Sur) 73 NYS2d 38, mod 275 AD 786, 88 NYS2d 2, affd 300 NY 688.

In a personal injury action against the city, the admission of plaintiff's sworn statement before an agent of the city was error, because the statement was a self-serving declaration, even though sworn. *Wagner v New York* (1937) 250 AD 381, 294 NYS 456.

§ 25:15 PHYSICAL AND MENTAL EXAMINATIONS — After commencement of an action in which the mental or physical condition of a party, an agent, employee or person under the custody or legal control of the party is in controversy, any party may serve notice upon the other party to submit to a physical or mental examination by a designated physician or to produce for such examination his agent, employee or the person under his custody or legal control. CPLR 3121(a). If the physical or mental examination that is sought pursuant to CPLR 3121 is not obtained, the party so seeking the examination may apply to the court to compel such examination. CPLR 3124.

Where there is no claim that the plaintiff is in such a physical condition that a blood test would be injurious to her, the defendant as part of a physical examination for trial preparation purposes should be permitted to obtain plaintiff's blood for testing. *Evens v Denny's, Inc,* (1985) 129 Misc 2d 767, 494 NYS2d 67.

The defendant's physical condition was not placed in controversy by plaintiff's unsupported allegations that defendant was intoxicated at the time of the accident, nor was it placed in controversy by the testimony of defendant at an examination before trial that he had no recollection of the circumstances surrounding the accident. Special Term properly denied those portions of plaintiff's motion that sought to obtain certain of defendant's hospital and medical records and to conduct a physical examination of him. *Gaglia v Wells* (1985, 2d Dept) 112 AD2d 138, 490 NYS2d 829.

There is no restriction in CPLR 3121(a) limiting the number of examinations to which a party or person in the custody of a party may be subjected in actions involving a dispute as to physical or mental condition. A subsequent examination is permissible where the party seeking the examination demonstrates the necessity for it. *Radigan v Radigan* (1985, 2d Dept) 115 AD2d 466, 495 NYS2d 703.

§ 25:16 PAROL EVIDENCE — The parol evidence rule is an important rule of substantive law, that is designed to permit a party to a written contract to protect himself against perjury, infirmity of memory or death of witnesses. *Fogelson v Rackfay Const. Co.* (1950) 300 NY 334, reh den 301 NY 552. The rule forbids proof of extrinsic evidence to contradict or vary the terms of a written instrument. *Sabo v Delman* (1957) 3 NY2d 155, 164 NYS2d 714.

Parol evidence may not be received to vary the clear and unambiguous terms of a solemn written agreement as between the parties, although matters may be proved that tend to show fraud, mistake, illegality, want of consideration, lack of capacity, or any other matter affecting the validity of the writing or to establish the existence of any separate oral agreement as to any other matter on which the document is silent, and which is not inconsistent with its terms, where from the circumstances of the case the court infers that the parties did not intend the document to be a complete and final statement of the whole of the transaction between them, or to establish a condition precedent to the attaching of an obligation under the contract. *Newburger v American Surety Co.* (1926) 242 NY 134, 151 NE 155. The rule excludes proof of alleged oral transactions no matter how cogent, material or relevant such proof may be. *Freund v Happiness Estates, Inc.* (1945, Sup) 55 NYS2d 410. Where a written contract is clear in its terms and purports to express the entire arrangement of the parties and to direct upon all the questions under consideration, it conclusively determines the rights of the parties and can neither be contradicted, varied nor explained. *Lese v Lamprecht* (1909) 196 NY 32, 89 NE 365.

Although parol evidence is inadmissible to vary the terms of a written contract, *Gulickson v Seglin Constr. Co.* (1934) 152 Misc

624, 273 NYS 908, such evidence is admissible without violating the rule for the purpose of showing that an instrument purporting to be a contract is in fact not a contract. *Rubin v Whitney* (1937) 162 Misc 821, 295 NYS 255. Although a contract that is complete on its face cannot be extended by the inclusion of additional terms, *William H. Waters, Inc. v March* (1934) 240 AD 120, 269 NYS 420, where the writing does not contain, on its face, the entire agreement between the parties, parol evidence that is not inconsistent with the terms thereof may be received in evidence, not for the purpose of contradicting the contract but to show the entire contract. *Merrick v New York Subways Advertising Co.* (1958) 14 Misc 2d 456, 178 NYS2d 814.

Where parol evidence is received for the purpose of showing that there is in fact no contract, such evidence is received not for the purpose of varying a written agreement but to avoid or destroy its legal force or effect. *Bowen v Merdinger* (1949) 196 Misc 987, 92 NYS2d 566, affd 279 AD 1060, 113 NYS2d 282.

Fraud may be shown by parol evidence. *J. Henry Schroder Bank & Trust Co. v Metropolitan Sav. Bank* (1986, 1st Dept) 117 AD2d 515, 497 NYS2d 931; *Salt Springs Nat'l Bank v Hitchcock* (1933) 238 AD 150, 263 NYS 55. Although generally parol evidence may not be received to vary the terms of a written instrument, where there is created any suspicion of fraud or usurious dealings, such testimony is received not for the purpose of varying the terms of a written instrument, but rather to nullify its legal effect. *Re Reif's Will* (1941, Sur Ct) 30 NYS2d 47. The parol evidence rule does not apply to an action brought to rescind on the ground of fraud, and in such a case, evidence of alleged fraudulent oral misrepresentation may be introduced to avoid the agreement. *Sabo v Delman, supra*.

The fact that a contract appears perfectly valid on its face does not preclude a defendant who is sued thereon from showing the illegality of the contract. *97 Fifth Ave. Corp. v Schatzberg* (1954) 283 AD 407, 128 NYS2d 264. Parol evidence may be admitted to show that a written contract, while lawful on its face, is either illegal or is part of an illegal transaction. *Liberty Pipe & Boiler Covering Co. v Zichlin & Fischer, Inc.* (1953, App Tm) 127 NYS2d 83. In an action on a note, evidence that the note was given for a loan of money to be used in bookmaking at a racetrack was admissible. *Chapin v Austin* (1937) 165 Misc 414, 300 NYS 932. Parol evidence is admissible for the purpose of showing that the consideration for a written contract is illegal. *97 Fifth Ave. Corp. v Schatzberg, supra.*

Parol evidence may be introduced against a written instrument for the purpose of showing that the instrument was obtained by the exercise of duress. *Schweig v Fincke* (1961, Sup) 219 NYS2d 369. Duress in obtaining a note could be shown in spite of a letter to the contrary signed by the maker when delivering the note. *Jules E. Brulatour, Inc. v Garsson* (1930) 229 AD 466, 242 NYS 583. Extrinsic evidence of the invalidity of a separation agreement because of fraud, duress or illegality would not be excluded under the parol evidence rule or by virtue of the general merger clause in a separation agreement entered into by the husband and wife prior to the husband's Mexican divorce and remarriage, in the wife's action to set aside the decree and the agreement. *Harges v Harges* (1965) 46 Misc 2d 994, 261 NYS2d 713.

Where not inconsistent with the terms of an instrument, parol evidence is admissible for the purpose of showing that the instrument was not intended to be binding until the completion of a condition precedent not contained in the writing. *Bintz v Hornell* (1945) 268 AD 742, 53 NYS2d 803, affd 295 NY 628. Although an oral condition precedent may be shown, *Clipper v Goldstein* (1931) 234 AD 85, 254 NYS 60, an oral condition subsequent may not be shown. *Jamestown Business College Ass'n v Allen* (1902) 172 NY 291, 64 NE 952. Furthermore, parol evidence is not admissible for the purpose of showing that a deed or contract for the sale of realty was delivered subject to a condition precedent. *Hamlin v Hamlin* (1908) 192 NY 164, 84 NE 805. However, it may be shown that a conditional or escrow delivery was made to one not a party to the agreement or that no delivery took place. *Frantz v Gatto* (1948) 274 AD 1003, 84 NYS2d 560.

An oral agreement that is inconsistent with a written contract is not admissible. *Smith v McCullaugh* (1932) 234 AD 490, 255 NYS 497. Before an oral agreement may be admitted to vary a written contract, it must appear that the agreement in form is a collateral one, it does not contradict the express or implied conditions of the written contract and it must be one that the parties would not ordinarily be expected to embody in the writing. *B. H. Krueger, Inc. v Hearn Dep't Stores* (1943) 265 AD 791, 40 NYS2d 923, app den 266 AD 775, 42 NYS2d 922. An oral agreement to the effect that the indemnitor on a written indemnity, which was given as surety on an appeal bond, would be released in the event of a reversal in an intermediate court was held to be inadmissible. *Consolidated Indem. & Ins. Co. v Dein* (1931) 233 AD 380, 253 NYS 162. Where a wife sued to recover from her husband the difference between the weekly amount due under a separation agreement and the amount actually paid by the husband, the parol evidence rule prohibited proof of the husband's claim that there was a prior oral agreement to pay less than the amount called for by the writing. *Kominos v Kominos* (1957) 12 Misc 2d 524, 170 NYS2d 526, affd (2d Dept) 9 AD2d 938, 196 NYS2d 572.

The parol evidence rule precludes evidence of negotiations that preceded or conversations that accompanied the making of a contract. *Campbell v Marquand* (1954, Sup) 54 NYS2d 873, affd 270 AD 756, 59 NYS2d 925, affd 295 NY 972. Testimony of a collateral agreement may be received, and an incomplete contract may be completed by parol evidence that is not inconsistent with the written terms. *Federal Brush Corp. v A. Zerega's Sons, Inc.* (1956, Co Ct) 149 NYS2d 374. Where a writing specifically states that it contains the whole contract or provides that no other oral agreement shall qualify its terms, oral testimony will not be received to contradict, vary, add to or subtract from the terms of the writing, *V. Valente, Inc. v Mascitti* (1937) 163 Misc 287, 295 NYS 330.

Where a written agreement contains no ambiguities, either latent or patent, neither the parties nor their privies may testify to what the parties meant but failed to state. *Oxford Commercial Corp. v Landau* (1963) 12 NY2d 362, 239 NYS2d 865, 13 ALR3d 309. Where, however, the language of a deed is ambiguous, parol evidence is admissible to show the parties' intent. *Cordua v Guggenheim* (1937) 274 NY 51. Where a written agreement is, in any respect, uncertain, all circumstances leading to its execution may be shown for the purpose of clarification, but not for contradiction or modification. *Tobin v Union News Co.* (1963, 4th Dept) 18 AD2d 243, 239 NYS2d 22, affd 13 NY2d 1155, 247

NYS2d 385. Resort may be had to surrounding circumstances only when the words of an instrument create an ambiguity that requires interpretation. *Harding v O'Malley* (1929) 226 AD 586, 236 NYS 172. In the absence of such an ambiguity, no extrinsic evidence is receivable to vary the terms of a written contract. *277 Park Ave. Corp. v New York C. R. Co.* (1951, Sup) 106 NYS2d 338.

The principle that parol evidence may be introduced to show that it was the intention of the parties not to enter into an enforceable contract is predicated upon proof of the intention of the parties that the entire contract was to be a nullity, and does not apply to a situation where certain provisions of the contract were to be enforceable and others were not. *Bersani v General Acci. Fire & Life Assurance. Corp.* (1975) 36 NY2d 457, 369 NYS2d 108.

Parol evidence is admissible to prove the privity of the claims of the plaintiffs and their predecessors, where plaintiffs sought to establish title to realty by adverse possession. *Brand v Prince* (1973, 3d Dept) 43 AD2d 638, 349 NYS2d 222, affd 35 NY2d 634, 364 NYS2d 826.

In an action by one cosignatory of a defaulted note to recover the amount paid thereon, while ordinarily plaintiff could only proceed against the others for contribution as to the amount he paid greater than his proportionate share, parties whose names appear on a note can show by parol evidence their respective liabilities and relationships. *Brown v Arcuri* (1974, 3d Dept) 43 AD2d 993, 352 NYS2d 254.

Where a sales agreement called for a partnership to "use its best efforts and energy" in representing a party, it was error for the trial court to refuse to accept proof concerning the parties' understanding of the meaning of the quoted phrase. *Epstein v Paganne, Ltd.* (1974, 1st Dept) 44 AD2d 520, 353 NYS2d 190, app dismd 34 NY2d 855, 359 NYS2d 70.

If several reasonable constructions are possible, the court can look to the surrounding facts and circumstances to determine the intent of the parties. *67 Wall Street Co. v Franklin Nat'l Bank* (1975) 37 NY2d 245, 371 NYS2d 915; *Bakas Restaurant, Inc. v Charos* (1985, 2d Dept) 111 AD2d 360, 490 NYS2d 17.

An agreement that any renewal notes would be endorsed by all of the original endorsers is provable by the use of parol evidence, and, if proved, would make the note unenforceable against the guarantors whose delivery was conditional upon procurement of all such endorsements. *Long Island Trust Co. v International Institute for Packaging Education, Ltd.* (1976) 38 NY2d 493, 381 NYS2d 445.

The presence of a general merger clause does not bar parol evidence of fraudulent representations in an action to rescind a contract for the sale of realty. *Fata v Troyanos* (1978, 2d Dept) 61 AD2d 828, 402 NYS2d 226.

Where the complaint states a cause of action for fraud, the parol evidence rule is not a bar to showing the fraud despite an omnibus statement that the written instrument embodies the whole agreement, or that no representations have been made. *O'Keeffe v Hicks* (1980, 2d Dept) 74 AD2d 919, 426 NYS2d 315. However, a specific disclaimer destroys allegations that the agreement was executed in reliance on a contrary oral representation. *Cohan v Sicular* (1995, 2d Dept) 214 AD2d 637, 625 NYS2d 278.

Parol evidence is admissible to show that the consideration for a contract is illegal. *Atkin v Union Processing Corp.* (1980, 4th Dept) 77 AD2d 790, 430 NYS2d 735, later app (4th Dept) 90 AD2d 332, 457 NYS2d 152, affd 59 NY2d 919, 466 NYS2d 293, cert den (US) 79 L Ed 2d 712, 104 S Ct 1316.

Parol evidence was admissible to show that what purported to be a contract was in fact not a contract at all. *Re Application of Austern* (1982, 1st Dept) 91 AD2d 505, 456 NYS2d 368.

When the issue involved is whether the parties intended to create a legal relationship or enter into a binding contract, the parol evidence rule has no application and does not bar the admission of extrinsic evidence to establish that a writing which appears to be a contract is not a contract because it was never intended to operate as such. *Arner v Arner* (1982, 2d Dept) 89 AD2d 899, 453 NYS2d 716.

Where a tenant and landlord entered into a lease stating that the premises leased were residential, the tenant could not rely upon any alleged representation by the landlord that unobtrusive commercial use was a use permitted by the lease or by law. *Corpo-*

rate Graphics, Inc. v Mehlman Management Corp. (1981, 1st Dept) 81 AD2d 767, 438 NYS2d 805.

Where parties to a loan have reduced their agreement to a writing, that rule operates to exclude evidence of any prior or contemporaneous oral agreement when offered to contradict, vary, add to, or subtract from the terms of the writing. *Conn Organ Corp. v Walt Whitman Music Studios, Inc.* (1979, 2d Dept) 67 AD2d 995, 413 NYS2d 725. Where the delivery of the note was unconditional but was subject to an oral agreement that the debt would be forgiven upon the happening of a future event, that agreement may not be proven by parol evidence. *Conn Organ Corp. v Walt Whitman Music Studios, Inc. supra*. Where, however, a different loan that formed the basis for an additional cause of action was entirely oral, parol evidence was admissible with respect thereto. *Conn Organ Corp. v Walt Whitman Music Studios, Inc. supra*.

Where the signature of an agent on a note does not show whether he signed in a representative capacity, parol evidence will be permitted to establish that the signature was made in a representative capacity. *Citibank Eastern, N.A. v Minbiole* (1975, 3d Dept) 50 AD2d 1052, 377 NYS2d 727.

Subdivision (1) of § 3-302 of the Uniform Commercial Code specifically provides, in conjunction with two other sections thereof, that a holder of a note that is unconditional on its face is not a holder in due course if he has not taken the note for value, in good faith, and without notice of claim or defenses to it, and consequently the introduction of evidence for the purpose of showing that a holder has not satisfied one or more of these three requirements is contemplated by the Code. *First International Bank, Ltd. v L. Blankstein & Son, Inc.* (1983) 59 NY2d 436, 465 NYS2d 888.

In order to determine what the parties intended at the time they executed the modification of their separation agreement so as to state that support payments were to continue until the youngest child completed four years of college, provided that she would continue to maintain full-time residence with the wife during the period, it was necessary for the court to interpret the language "full-time residence," because this was ambiguous and susceptible of either interpretation offered by the contending parties; thus, intent could not be ascertained from the document itself, and extrinsic evidence could be considered to aid in resolving the ambiguity. *Canter v Canter* (1983, 4th Dept) 91 AD2d 1180, 459 NYS2d 153.

Evidence of what the parties may have agreed to orally before the execution of an integrated written guaranty instrument cannot be received to vary the terms of the writing, because the oral agreement contradicts the provisions of the guaranty agreement, and because it is so clearly connected with the guaranty agreement that the parties could have been expected to embody it in that writing. *Braten v Bankers Trust Co.* (1983) 60 NY2d 155, 468 NYS2d 861.

The court properly excluded evidence offered by a surviving spouse that contravened the terms of an antenuptial agreement she had entered into with her now-deceased husband, because in the absence of fraud or mutual mistake, once an agreement has been reduced to an unambiguous writing, evidence of prior or contemporaneous oral agreements that are offered to contradict or vary the writing must be excluded, particularly where the agreement contains an integration clause specifically stating that the agreement embodies the entire understanding of the parties. *Re Estate of Miller* (1983, 3d Dept) 97 AD2d 581, 467 NYS2d 922.

Proof as to an oral agreement concerning the time when payment of promissory notes would be demanded was inadmissible, because it would tend to vary the plain and unambiguous terms of the notes. *Bowne & Co. v Scileppi* (1984, 1st Dept) 99 AD2d 440, 470 NYS2d 618.

The parol evidence rule applies when the written understanding is clear and unambiguous and the rule is intended to prevent proof of an oral agreement to add or vary the writing. *Shah v Eastern Silk Industries, Ltd.* (1985, 1st Dept) 112 AD2d 870, 493 NYS2d 150, affd 67 NY2d 632, 499 NYS2d 681.

The existence of directly contradictory provisions in a separation agreement between the parties gives rise to an ambiguity that may be resolved under the parol evidence rule through consideration of extrinsic evidence. *Katz v Katz* (1986 2d Dept) 118 AD2d 626, 499 NYS2d 778.

Where the contract was unambiguous, the intent of the parties could be gleaned from the contract itself and evidence extrinsic to the contract could not be considered. *Brooklyn Union Gas Co. v John Shields Detective Bureau, Inc.* (1986, 2d Dept) 121 AD2d 587, 503 NYS2d 852, app den 69 NY2d 610.

The contention by the prospective vendor that his obligations under the contract were contingent upon payment and satisfaction of the debt of a third person to him amounted, essentially, to an oral modification of a written contract, and was thus impermissible under the terms of that contract as well as under the parol evidence rule. *Fourteen Sharot Place Realty Corp. v Miceli* (1986, 2d Dept) 125 AD2d 634, 510 NYS2d 168.

Even though promissory notes executed in connection with a sale contained language to the effect that the obligation of the buyer was "absolute and unconditional," this did not rule out the use of parol evidence that fraudulent representations had induced the obligation. *GTE Automatic Electric, Inc. v Martin's, Inc.* (1987, 1st Dept) 127 AD2d 545, 512 NYS2d 107.

Although ordinarily the interpretation of written agreements poses a question of law for the court to resolve on the basis of the writing alone without resort to extrinsic evidence, where the court determines as a threshold issue that the terms of the agreement are ambiguous and the intent of the parties becomes a matter of inquiry, parol evidence is permitted. *Posh Pillows, Ltd. v Hawes* (1988, 2d Dept) 138 AD2d 472, 525 NYS2d 877.

Where a defendant signed 10 notes twice, once in a representative capacity and once in an individual capacity, his allegation that he did not know at the time that he was signing individually constituted parol evidence which varied the plain and unambiguous terms of the notes. *Hackensack Cars, Inc. v Beverly* (1988, 1st Dept) 140 AD2d 254, 528 NYS2d 383, app dismd without op 72 NY2d 1041, 534 NYS2d 939, reconsideration den 73 NY2d 872, 537 NYS2d 497.

The parol evidence rule does not bar a party from showing that a written agreement was obtained by fraudulent inducement; however, to defeat a motion for summary judgment, such evidence must be genuine and based upon proof, not conclusory assertions. *Fine Arts Enterprises, N.V. v Levy* (1989, 3d Dept) 149 AD2d 795, 539 NYS2d 827.

In cases of mutual mistake, the parol evidence rule is unavailable to bar evidence of the parties' prior oral agreement. *Intershoe, Inc. v Bankers Trust Co.* (1990, 1st Dept) 160 AD2d 520, 554 NYS2d 514, revd on other grounds 77 NY2d 517, 569 NYS2d 333.

The trial court properly admitted parol evidence of the party's intent and conduct to clarify the objective of the partnership agreement and the purposes of the parties in entering into that agreement. *Sandler v Fishman* (1990, 2d Dept) 157 AD2d 708, 549 NYS2d 808.

In a divorce action, where the parties entered into a stipulation of settlement as to the value of each party's pension, and the stipulation was unclear and ambiguous as to whether the parties intended the court to consider the tax consequences in its evaluation, extrinsic evidence was admissible to ascertain the intent of the parties in this regard. *Ackerberg v Ackerberg* (1989, 2d Dept) 154 AD2d 414, 545 NYS2d 926.

Although a separation agreement contained a clause prohibiting oral modification, this fact did not preclude proof of an executed oral modification. *Scally v Scally* (1989, 3d Dept) 151 AD2d 869, 542 NYS2d 844.

When the language of an insurance policy is ambiguous and susceptible of two reasonable interpretations, the parties may submit extrinsic evidence as an aid in construction, and the resolution of the ambiguity is for the trier of fact. *Campanile v State Farm General Ins. Co.* (1990, 3d Dept) 161 AD2d 1052, 558 NYS2d 203, affd 78 NY2d 912, 573 NYS2d 463.

Where consideration of a contract as a whole resolves the ambiguity created by one clause, there is no occasion to consider extrinsic evidence of the parties' intent. *Hudson-Port Ewen Assocs., L.P. v Chien Kuo* (1991) 78 NY2d 944, 573 NYS2d 636.

The parol evidence rule bars proof of an oral condition precedent that is expressly contradicted by the written loan agreement. *Glenfed Financial Corp., Commercial Finance Div. v Aeronautics & Astronautics Services, Inc.* (1992, 1st Dept) 181 AD2d 575, 581 NYS2d 62.

Oral declarations or secret agreements between a mortgagor and an assigning mortgagee made prior to the assignment are inadmissible against the assignee to establish a defense to the action brought by the assignee to enforce the mortgage. *Kolbe v Projects & Joint Ventures Int'l, Inc.* (1992, 4th Dept) 186 AD2d 988, 588 NYS2d 451.

§ 25:17 EVIDENCE OF WRONGDOING BY A PARTY OR ATTORNEY — A party's attempt to procure false testimony or to corrupt a witness, although collateral to the issues, is competent as an admission by acts and conduct that the party's case is weak and its evidence dishonest. *People v Davis* (1977) 43 NY2d 17, 400 NYS2d 735, cert den 435 US 998, 56 L Ed 2d 88, 98 S Ct 1653 and cert den 438 US 914, 57 L Ed 2d 1160, 98 S Ct 3143. Such evidence is not conclusive, even when believed by the jury, because a party may think he has a bad case when in fact he has a good one, but it tends to discredit his witness and to cast doubt upon his position. *Nowack v Metropolitan S. R. Co.* (1901) 166 NY 433, 60 NE 32.

The fact that evidence was fabricated is admissible, even though the evidence itself was not used. *People v Davis* (1977) 43 NY2d 17, 400 NYS2d 735, cert den 435 US 998, 56 L Ed 2d 88, 98 S Ct 1653 and cert den 438 US 914, 57 L Ed 2d 1160, 98 S Ct 3143. Where it appears that on one side there has been forgery or fraud in some material parts of the evidence, and they are discovered to be the contrivance of a party to the proceeding, it affords a presumption against the whole of the evidence on that side of the question, and has the effect of gaining a more ready admission to the evidence of the other party. *Nowack v Metropolitan S. R. Co.*, *supra*.

It was error for the trial court to deny admission of defendant's evidence that plaintiff's representatives had persuaded an eyewitness who was to have testified for the defendant at the first trial to stay away from the trial, and that on the second trial plaintiff's representatives had paid the witness money and bought him an airline ticket with the request that he not appear. *Millington v New York City Transit Authority* (1976, 1st Dept) 54 AD2d 649, 387 NYS2d 865.

RESEARCH REFERENCES

American Law Reports

64 ALR4th 125, Products liability: admissibility of experimental or test evidence to disprove defect in motor vehicle

59 ALR4th 1000, Admissibility of impeached witness' prior consistent statement–modern state civil cases

59 ALR4th 971, Admissibility of evidence summaries under Uniform Evidence Rule 1006

56 ALR4th 402, Admissibility of evidence of pertinent trait under Rule 404(a) of the Uniform Rules of Evidence

39 ALR4th 775, Admissibility of evidence of accused's membership in gang

36 ALR4th 598, Admissibility of evidence as to linguistics or typing style, forensic linguistics as basis of identification of typist or author

21 ALR4th 472, Modern status of rules as to admissibility of evidence of prior accidents or injuries at same place

14 ALR4th 802, Admissibility of evidence concerning words spoken while declarant was asleep or unconscious

12 ALR4th 1016, Admissibility of testimony concerning extrajudicial statements made to, or in presence of, witness through an interpreter

10 ALR4th 1243, Propriety, in medical malpractice case, of admitting testimony regarding physician's usual custom or habit in order to establish nonliability

5 ALR4th 1194, Evidence of automobile passenger's blood alcohol level as admissible in support of defense that passenger was contributorily negligent or assumed risk of automobile accident

4 ALR4th 829, Admissibility and effect, on issue of party's credibility or merits of his case, of evidence of attempts to intimidate or influence witness in civil action

100 ALR3d 569, Admissibility of evidence of character or reputation of party in civil action for sexual assault on issues other than impeachment

91 ALR3d 718, Admissibility of evidence of character or reputation of party in civil action for assault on issues other than impeachment

89 ALR3d 1012, Admissibility in personal injury action of hospital or other medical bill which includes expenses for treatment of condition unrelated to injury

88 ALR3d 926, Admissibility of evidence of, or propriety of comment as to, plaintiff-spouse's remarriage, or possibility thereof, in action for damages for death of other spouse

84 ALR3d 1220, Admissibility, against manufacturer, of product recall letter

83 ALR3d 1294, Exceptions to rule that oral gifts of land are unenforceable under statute of frauds

82 ALR3d 1285, Municipal corporation's safety rules and regulations as admissible in evidence in action by private party against municipal corporation or its officers or employees for negligent operation of vehicle

82 ALR3d 525, Admissibility of testimony as to general reputation at place of employment

79 ALR3d 79, Sufficiency of identification of participants as prerequisite to admissibility of telephone conversation in evidence

75 ALR3d 177, Pleading and proof of law of foreign country

74 ALR3d 1001, Admissibility of evidence of subsequent repairs or remedial measures in product liability cases

71 ALR3d 1051, Application of parol evidence rule of UCC § 2-202 where fraud or misrepresentation is claimed in sale of goods

70 ALR3d 1276, Admissibility of parol evidence to show whether guaranty of corporation's obligation was signed in officer's representative or individual capacity

69 ALR3d 1326, Application of parol evidence rule in action for contract for architect's services

64 ALR4th 567, Habit or routine practice evidence under Uniform Evidence Rule 406

53 ALR3d 1005, Admissibility of lie detector test taken upon stipulation that the result will be admissible in evidence

ALR QUICK INDEX: Character and Reputation; Circumstantial Evidence; Parol Evidence

American Jurisprudence 2d

29, 30 AM JUR 2d, Evidence, §§ 264-354, 1016-1079

American Jurisprudence Pleading and Practice

23 AM JUR PL & PR FORMS (Rev), Trial, Forms 152, 153

American Jurisprudence Proof of Facts

35 AM JUR PROOF OF FACTS 2d 589, Routine Business Practice

19 AM JUR PROOF OF FACTS 423-454, Spectrogram Voice Identification

American Jurisprudence Trials

44 AM JUR TRIALS 171, Videotape Evidence

Other Resources

Auto-Cite®: Any case citation herein can be checked for form, parallel references, later history and annotation references through the Auto-Cite computer research system.

CHAPTER 26

OBJECTIONS TO EVIDENCE

§ 26:1. Right to Object to Improper Testimony

§ 26:2. Necessity for Objection to Improper Evidence

§ 26:3. The Timeliness of the Objection

§ 26:4. Stating the Grounds for the Objection

§ 26:5. The Offer of Proof

§ 26:1   RIGHT TO OBJECT TO IMPROPER TESTIMONY — It is fundamental, of course, that when one counsel asks a question that calls for an answer inadmissible under the rules of evidence, opposing counsel has the right to object to the question.

To preserve a point for consideration by a reviewing court, a proper objection must be made thereto. *Re Levine's Estate* (1936, Sur Ct) 247 AD 19, 286 NYS 513. It has been held, however, that in the interest of justice, the Appellate Division has a right to reverse a judgment and grant a new trial where there is a fundamental error in the trial, even in the absence of an objection taken thereto at the trial. *Alexander v State* (1971, 3d Dept) 36 AD2d 777, 319 NYS2d 219, later app 43 AD2d 664, 349 NYS2d 334.

Under ordinary conditions, a question that is excluded upon objection nevertheless has the effect of suggesting matter to the jury that it has no right to consider, but will not ordinarily be grounds for reversal because the jury is presumed not to consider such matter. *Stouter v Manhattan R. Co.* (1891) 127 NY 661, 27 NE 805. Where a party believes that the thinking of the jury may be affected by matter that is outside the case, counsel should ask that the jury be instructed to disregard such matter. *Holmes v Moffat* (1890) 120 NY 159, 24 NE 275. However, where the trial court or the Appellate Division is of the opinion that such matter has affected the jury verdict, the verdict may and should be set aside. *Cosselmon v Dunfee* (1902) 172 NY 507, 65 NE 494.

Where a party offers evidence that is objectionable, to which his adversary does not object, the party offering that evidence opens the door to the introduction of similar evidence by his adversary, *Wallis v Randall* (1880) 81 NY 164. Where evidence is received over the objection of defendant, and the court attempts to cure the error by subsequently instructing the jury to disregard such error, the error is not cured where it may have affected the verdict, and defendant is entitled to a new trial. *Erben v Lorillard* (1859) 19 NY 299.

§ 26:2   NECESSITY FOR OBJECTION TO IMPROPER EVIDENCE — When a timely objection is not made, the testimony is presumed to have been unobjectionable and any alleged error is considered waived. *Horton v Smith* (1980) 51 NY2d 798, 433 NYS2d 92; *Simon v Indursky* (1995, 1st Dept) 211 AD2d 404, 630 NYS2d 2.

Where evidence is not objected to by either party, the trial court has a right to assume that such evidence is competent. *New York Life Ins. Co. v Guttenplan* (1940, Sup) 30 NYS2d 430, affd 259 AD 1004, 20 NYS2d 724, affd 284 NY 805.

Where defendant was represented by an experienced trial counsel in the trial of a death action, and speculative evidence was received on the question of the future earning ability of the decedent, the error was not reviewable because of the failure of counsel to object to it. *Ryan v Samarco* (1968, 4th Dept)) 30 AD2d 767, 292 NYS2d 319.

As a result of statutory enactment, a formal exception to the ruling of the court on a stated objection or motion is no longer required. CPLR 4017. At the time a ruling or order of the court is requested or made, a party shall make known the action that he requests the court to take, or if he has not already indicated, his objection to the action of the court. CPLR 4017. At any time before the jury retires to consider its verdict, a party shall make known his objection to a charge to the jury or a failure or refusal to charge as requested. CPLR 4110(b).

Upon appeal from a final judgment, any rulings and any remarks made by the judge, to which the appellant had objected, are brought up for review. CPLR 5501(a)(3) and (4).

Even when no objection has been taken, the Appellate Divisions may correct errors in the exercise of their power to act "in the interest of justice." *Martin v Cohoes* (1975) 37 NY2d 162, 371 NYS2d 687, on remand (3d Dept) 50 AD2d 1035, 377 NYS2d 757, app dismd 39 NY2d 740, 384 NYS2d 774, motion den 39 NY2d 910, 386 NYS2d 401.

Where the alleged error is fundamental, the Appellate Division may reverse in the interest of justice even if there was no objection to the error at the trial, and this is true with respect to the question of whether the amount of damages awarded should stand. *Graham v Murphy* (1988, 3d Dept) 135 AD2d 326, 525 NYS2d 414.

The failure of defendant to object to the use at trial of the testimony of a witness who was not sworn, constitutes a waiver of any objection. *People v Muka* (1979, 3d Dept) 72 AD2d 649, 421 NYS2d 438.

In a negligence action, where the medical doctor who had examined the plaintiff at defendant's request was called to testify by plaintiff, and defendant did not object until long after the conclusion of the testimony, when defendant moved to strike it, it was not error for the trial court to refuse to strike the doctor's testimony. *Liddy v Frome* (1981, 2d Dept) 85 AD2d 716, 445 NYS2d 841.

An objection that evidence is inadmissible as hearsay cannot be offered for the first time on appeal unless there is no viable purpose for which the evidence was admissible. *Schiaroli v Ellenville* (1985, 3d Dept) 111 AD2d 947, 490 NYS2d 43.

The objection of defendants to the second of two expert witnesses offered by the plaintiff was preserved for review even though no objection was made on the record, where defendants promptly voiced their objections to the testimony of the first expert on grounds that were applicable to the testimony of the second expert witness; because the improper evidence was of the same sort as that already received over objection, another objection to the testimony of the second expert was not necessary to preserve the issue for appellate review. *Nissen v Rubin* (1986, 1st Dept) 121 AD2d 320, 504 NYS2d 106.

A defendant who did not challenge the ruling of the court, did not allow his expert to give testimony on a certain issue, did not preserve this issue for review. *Property Owners Asso. v Ying* (1988, 2d Dept) 137 AD2d 509, 524 NYS2d 252.

A defendant who failed to raise the inadequacy of the foundation for introduction of doctor's records by objection thereto waived the "foundation" objection. *Wilson v Bodian* (1987, 2d Dept) 130 AD2d 221, 519 NYS2d 126.

Defendant's attack upon the professional qualifications of plaintiff's medical expert was not preserved for appellate review, because the defendant did not advance any legal challenge to the sufficiency of the expert's credentials in the trial court. *De Luca v Kameros* (1987, 2d Dept) 130 AD2d 705, 515 NYS2d 819; *see also, Kwasny v Feinberg* (1990, 2d Dept) 157 AD2d 396, 557 NYS2d 381.

While the Appellate Division has jurisdiction to address unpreserved issues in the interest of justice, the Court of Appeals may not address such issues in the absence of objection in the trial court. *Merrill v Albany Medical Center Hospital* (1988) 71 NY2d 990, 529 NYS2d 272.

Because the plaintiffs failed to object to the allegedly prejudicial comment made by defendant's medical expert, or to move for a mistrial, they could not claim on appeal that they were denied a fair trial as a matter of law; when a timely objection is not made, the testimony offered is presumed to have been unobjectionable and any alleged error of law considered waived. *Laniado v The New York Hosp.* (1990, 1st Dept) 168 AD2d 341, 562 NYS2d 662, app den 78 NY2d 853; *Picciallo v Norchi* (1989, 2d Dept) 147 AD2d 540, 537 NYS2d 837.

Although defendant's counsel did not specifically object to the admission into evidence of sets of internal rules, based upon the record, indicating that defendant's counsel made a number of objections to the questions of plaintiff's counsel, which dealt with particular rules, the objections were sufficiently precise to serve to alert the trial court to the problem. *Clarke v New York City Transit Authority* (1992, 1st Dept) 174 AD2d 268, 580 NYS2d 221.

By failing to object, defendant failed to preserve its contention that the court erred in allowing references to defendant's insurance company during the examination of defendant's witnesses. *Jones v Brilar Enterprises, Inc.* (1992, 4th Dept) 184 AD2d 1077, 585 NYS2d 272.

Plaintiff, who failed to object at the trial to defendant's cross-examination of her expert witness, effectively waived appellate review of that issue. *Beck v Albany Medical Ctr. Hosp.* (1993, 3d Dept) 191 AD2d 854, 594 NYS2d 844.

The issue of the court's alleged improper admission into evidence of a photograph was not preserved for appellate review where the plaintiff failed to make a timely objection to the admission of the subject photograph. *Weidemann v Knights of Columbus* (1993, 3d Dept) 199 AD2d 838, 606 NYS2d 342.

§ 26:3 THE TIMELINESS OF THE OBJECTION — An objection to a question should be made as soon as it is asked and before the witness has answered it. *Le Coulteux De Caumont v Morgan* (1887) 104 NY 74, 9 NE 861. Counsel may not wait until he ascertains whether the witness gives a favorable or unfavorable answer to the question before raising the objection. *Le Coulteux De Caumont v Morgan, supra.* When the question is improper, however, and the witness answers so quickly that the attorney does not have time to raise the objection until the question has been answered, an objection made immediately after the answer to the question is nevertheless timely. *Pratt v New York C. & H. R. R. Co.* (1894) 77 Hun 139, 28 NYS 463.

The proper time for making objections to the admission of documentary evidence is when the exhibit is offered in evidence. *Re D* (1970, Sur Ct) 63 Misc 2d 1012, 314 NYS2d 230.

§ 26:4 STATING THE GROUNDS FOR THE OBJECTION — An objection may be general or specific. By a general objection, the objecting party merely challenges the admissibility of the evidence, without stating the reason or ground therefor. An attorney who makes a specific objection points out the grounds on which he challenges the admissibility of the evidence. An objection to the effect that an answer to the question would violate the parol evidence rule is, for example, a specific objection.

Where a general objection to a question is made, a ruling sustaining that objection will be upheld if there is any specific ground that makes the question improper. *Bloodgood v Lynch* (1944) 293 NY 308. When evidence is excluded under a general objection the ruling will likewise be upheld on appeal where the evidence is essentially incompetent. *Tooley v Bacon* (1877) 70 NY 34. Counsel who is posing the question to the witness has a right to have the objections specifically stated, and if he does not ask for such specific objections he is presumed to have understood them. *Height v People* (1872) 50 NY 392. Where a specific objection is made, and the ground asserted is not the true one, the true ground for objection is waived by the specific objection. *Height v People, supra.*

Where a specific objection is made to evidence, and the objection is sustained, such a ruling will be held to be error where the evidence is not in fact objectionable upon the ground asserted even though it would have been objectionable upon some other specific ground, unless the evidence was not in any event competent or could not be made competent. *Tooley v Bacon, supra.*

Where testimony was objected to on the ground that it was immaterial, irrelevant and incompetent, the court held that the mention of these grounds of objection excluded other grounds, which must be deemed waived. *Lessler v De Loynes* (1912) 150 AD 868, 135 NYS 948, adhered to 153 AD 903, 138 NYS 503, affd 215 NY 745, 109 NE 1082.

A general objection presents an obvious advantage, if sustained, since such a ruling will be upheld on appeal if any ground of objection whatsoever exists that would make the question improper. However, if a general objection is overruled, the ruling will be sustained unless the evidence is not admissible and the party posing the question could not have overcome the objection and made the evidence admissible. *Levin v Russell* (1870) 42 NY 251.

The party asking the question is entitled to the opportunity to meet the objection to the question by reframing it, or to overcome the objection by whatever means are necessary, and a general objection deprives him of this opportunity, whereas a specific objection permits the examining attorney, if possible, to overcome the objection and render the evidence admissible. *Ward v Kilpatrick*

(1881) 85 NY 413. Where a general objection is made and overruled, and is followed by a specific objection, this will serve to call to the attention of the court and the examining attorney the reason for the objection to the question, and the ruling denying the objection will then be appealable. *Wallace v Vacuum Oil Co.* (1891) 128 NY 579, 27 NE 956.

Where evidence is objected to on the ground that it is incompetent and immaterial, this objection, if overruled, is not sufficient to raise on appeal the contentions that the evidence is inadmissible under the allegations made in the pleadings. *Voorhees v Burchard* (1873) 55 NY 98. The ground that evidence offered is not within the pleadings must be stated, so that the pleader may avoid the variance, if possible, by an amendment. *Dowly v State* (1947) 190 Misc 16, 68 NYS2d 573.

Where a general objection is overruled, the claim may not be raised on appeal that the witness was incompetent to testify concerning a personal transaction with a deceased person, because the objection, if raised at the trial on the specific ground, could have given the examining attorney an opportunity to prove the same fact by other witnesses. *Hoag v Wright* (1903) 174 NY 36, 66 NE 579. In an action for defamation, where incompetent evidence was offered to show malice, and a general objection was made and overruled, this ruling, although erroneous, was not grounds for reversal, because a specific objection would have put the examining attorney on notice and given him an opportunity to prove malice by other means. *Daly v Byrne* (1879) 77 NY 182.

Where the defect is incapable of being remedied even where specified, as for example, where the evidence is essentially incompetent, a general objection that is overruled will be appealable despite the fact that the specific ground has not been pointed out. *Wallace v Vacuum Oil Co., supra.*

A specific objection waives all other grounds of objection that could have been available if urged, even though a specific objection that was not urged would have been appropriate, and the ruling of the trial judge will not be reversed. *Gurski v Doscher* (1906) 112 AD 345, 98 NYS 588, affd 190 NY 536, 83 NE 1125. An objection that evidence is immaterial concedes that the evidence is competent, and on appeal the objection may not be made that the opinion of the witness on the particular point was incompetent. *Ward v Kilpatrick* (1881) 85 NY 413. In an action on a contract, an objection to the admission of evidence of a change of contract on the ground that it was incompetent, immaterial and irrelevant and that it tended to vary a contract that had already been executed, did not permit the raising on appeal of the point that there was no consideration for the new agreement. *Gurski v Doscher, supra.*

Where defendants argued that the statements of plaintiff, who had been exhibited and questioned before the jury, were testimonial and not merely demonstrative, the argument was not properly preserved for review by the Court of Appeals, because the general objections taken at trial to questioning of the plaintiff did not alert the court to this particular issue, and it was therefore beyond the review powers of the Court of Appeals. *Harvey v Mazal American Partners* (1992) 79 NY2d 218, 581 NYS2d 639.

Although defendants argued that it was error for the trial court to allow plaintiff's medical expert to express opinions on the very questions to be resolved by the jury, their general objections were insufficient to preserve the issue for review by the Court of Appeals. *Robillard v Robbins* (1991) 78 NY2d 1105, 578 NYS2d 126.

The plaintiff's argument that it was improper for the trial court to sustain defendant's objection to the introduction of evidence was not preserved for appellate review, because the plaintiff did not place any arguments in favor of denying the objection on the record, and apparently made no further attempt to admit the evidence. *Hamilton v Raftopoulos* (1991, 2d Dept) 176 AD2d 916, 575 NYS2d 531.

Where admission of a report was objected to at trial on the ground of irrelevancy, an objection that the report is hearsay cannot be raised for the first time on appeal. *Re New York City Asbestos Litig.* (1993, 1st Dept) 188 AD2d 214, 593 NYS2d 43, app gr 81 NY2d 707, 597 NYS2d 938, related proceeding (1st Dept) 194 AD2d 396, 599 NYS2d 953, app den 604 NYS2d 47.

Defendants, who at trial unsuccessfully urged that handwritten notes should be admitted under the hearsay exception of past recollection recorded, could not argue for the first time on appeal that the exhibit should have been admitted as a prior inconsistent statement. Because the ground urged on appeal was different than the one urged at trial, the issue was not preserved for appellate review. *Isler v Sutter* (1993, 1st Dept) 198 AD2d 68, 603 NYS2d 442, app den 83 NY2d 751, 611 NYS2d 133.

§ 26:5 THE OFFER OF PROOF — Where an objection has been sustained, it is proper for counsel to make an offer of proof to show what he expects to prove by the question and the subsequent questions of the same nature. Such an offer must be made formally in court, so that one's adversary will have the opportunity to know what is being offered and to make a timely objection to it. *Re Estate of Meyer* (1969) 59 Misc 2d 507, 299 NYS2d 731.

It has been held that a trial court is not bound to rule upon an offer of testimony, but that this is a matter within its discretion. *Re Potter's Will* (1899) 161 NY 84, 55 NE 387. In a landlord's action against tenants, however, an offer of proof by the tenants, for the purpose of showing that the installation of pipes in an apartment authorized by the lease could have been made without depriving tenants of the space in the linen closet and kitchen, should have been accepted. *Metropolitan Life Ins. Co. v McCarthy* (1939, App Tm) 13 NYS2d 550.

A mere assertion by a party that she intended to offer evidence showing that the assignee of a retail installment contract did not realize a fair price on the resale of her mobile home after default by the buyer did not constitute an evidentiary showing. *Albany Discount Corp. v Basile* (1969, 3d Dept) 32 AD2d 723, 300 NYS2d 464. In a proceeding for construction of a will and a cross-petition for construction and enforcement of a contract, the court could not rule upon the admissibility of evidence to prove the contract until it was formally offered at a hearing. *Re Estate of Atran* (1955, Sur Ct) 145 NYS2d 543.

An offer of proof was held to be insufficient where it did not establish the relevancy of the excluded evidence. *Naclerio v Naclerio* (1961, 1st Dept) 13 AD2d 331, 216 NYS2d 413, reh den (1st Dept) 14 AD2d 671, 219 NYS2d 944, affd 11 NY2d 1091, 230 NYS2d 718.

RESEARCH REFERENCES

American Law Reports

40 ALR4th 514, Former testimony used at subsequent trial as subject to ordinary objections and exceptions

32 ALR4th 774, Failure to object to improper questions or comments as to defendant's pretrial silence or failure to testify as constituting waiver of right to complain of error-modern cases

81 ALR3d 249, Modern status of rules governing legal effect of failure to object to admission of extrinsic evidence violative of parol evidence rule

68 ALR3d 314, Conduct of attorney in connection with making objections or taking exceptions as contempt of court

55 ALR Fed 726, When does trial court's noncompliance with requirement of Rule 30, Federal Rules of Criminal Procedure, that opportunity shall be given to make objection to instructions upon request, out of presence of jury, constitute prejudicial error

ALR QUICK INDEX: Evidence Rules Objections

American Jurisprudence 2d

75 AM JUR 2d, Trial §§ 162-187

American Jurisprudence Pleading and Practice

23 AM JUR PL & PR FORMS (Rev) Trial, Forms 71-78

American Jurisprudence Trials

6 AM JUR TRIALS 605, Making and Preserving the Record-Objections

Other Resources

8 CARMODY-WAIT 2d, Presentation of the Case §§ 56:128-56:137

Auto-Cite®: Any case citation herein can be checked for form, parallel references, later history and annotation references through the Auto-Cite computer research system.

CHAPTER 27

MISTRIAL

§ 27:1 THE NATURE OF A MISTRIAL — A mistrial motion is directed to the sound discretion of the trial court. However, the denial of a mistrial motion may, given the facts of a particular case, constitute reversible error if it appears that the motion should have been granted to prevent a substantial possibility of injustice. *Cohn v Meyers* (1986, 2d Dept) 125 AD2d 524, 509 NYS2d 603.

In a civil action for assault and battery, the defense counsel's inaccurate remarks to the effect that the plaintiff was responsible for the wrongful arrest and incarceration of the defendant created a substantial possibility of injustice. Instructions in the case did not adequately serve to eliminate the prejudice engendered by the remarks, and a mistrial was warranted. *Cohn v Meyers, supra.*

§ 27:2 WAIVER OF RIGHT TO MISTRIAL — A motion for a mistrial should be made before the jury returns its verdict. Plaintiffs were held to have waived their right to seek a mistrial by not moving for that relief until after the jury had returned a verdict against them. *Moore v Huntington* (1972, 2d Dept) 39 AD2d 764, 332 NYS2d 184.

A party's failure to move for a mistrial on grounds that are subsequently claimed to constitute prejudicial and reversible error amounts to a waiver of this objection. *Kamen v New York* (1991, 2d Dept) 169 AD2d 705, 564 NYS2d 190; *De Leon v New York*

City Transit Authority (1979, 2d Dept) 70 AD2d 926, 417 NYS2d 753, revd on other grounds 50 NY2d 176, 428 NYS2d 625, later app (2d Dept) 85 AD2d 593, 444 NYS2d 711; *Reilly v Wright* (1976, 1st Dept) 55 AD2d 544, 390 NYS2d 1.

A trial court's authorization to grant a mistrial is conditioned upon a motion being made by a party; the parties have a right to decide whether the harm, if any, occurring is great enough or prejudicial enough to outweigh the benefits and convenience of completing the trial. *Muka v Cohn* (1989, 3d Dept) 146 AD2d 826, 536 NYS2d 569. The trial court did not have authority to grant a mistrial of its own motion despite the *pro se* plaintiff's disregard of the court's rulings. *Muka v Cohn, supra.*

§ 27:3 GROUNDS FOR DECLARING A MISTRIAL — It was not error for the trial court to decline to declare a mistrial after the death of plaintiff, who had already testified and been cross-examined, and where the trial court had polled the jurors individually, determining that there was no possibility of prejudice to the defendant. *Maidman v Stagg* (1981, 2d Dept) 82 AD2d 299, 441 NYS2d 711.

In view of the mid-trial major change of evidentiary law, the trial court in an assessment proceeding should have *sua sponte* granted a mistrial in the interest of justice, which would have enabled the petitioner to present evidence under the select parcel or actual sales methods, should he be so advised, especially because the trial court denied petitioner's mid-trial discovery motion. *Brigham Park Cooperative Apartments, Inc. v Finance Adm'r. of New York* (1981, 2d Dept) 83 AD2d 551, 441 NYS2d 102.

A mistrial was required upon discovery that plaintiff's expert witness, whose testimony was highly credible and concerned the central issues in the case, was a fraud, who had grossly exaggerated his qualifications; it was therefore an abuse of discretion for the trial judge to merely strike his testimony and instruct the jury to disregard it without informing them of the reason. *Santos v New York* (1987, 1st Dept) 135 AD2d 426, 522 NYS2d 538, app den 71 NY2d 806, 530 NYS2d 109.

In a medical malpractice action, the trial court properly denied defendant hospital's motion for a mistrial and/or to disqualify codefendant's trial counsel. To the extent that the motion was predicated upon the fact that counsel had a prior relationship with the codefendant, that relationship was unrelated in any way to the present litigation, and the fact that the motion came midway through trial, and some eight years after commencement of the action, clearly demonstrated tactical, rather than substantive, motives. *Harnett v Long Island Jewish-Hillside Medical Ctr.* (1995, 2d Dept) ___ AD2d ___, 627 NYS2d 82.

Defense counsel's attempt, in a medical malpractice action, to pursue questioning of plaintiff's expert regarding his alleged drug addiction on recross-examination, after the witness had given rehabilitative testimony, did not warrant a mistrial, because prompt, curative instructions were administered by the court. *Winant v Carras* (1994, 2d Dept) 208 AD2d 618, 617 NYS2d 487.

§ 27:4 DISCLOSURE OF LIABILITY INSURANCE — A defendant's liability in a personal injury action must rest solely on a determination of whether or not he is at fault and legally responsible, uninfluenced by the fact that for his own protection he has insured himself against loss from his own negligence. *Gebo v Findlay* (1939) 257 AD 66, 11 NYS2d 950. In an action against the owner of an automobile for personal injuries, it was held to be error for counsel to suggest the possibility that the owner of the automobile was insured. No hint of insurance protection of a defendant may be given in an action. *Van Romapaye Trucking Corp. v Heebner* (1948, Sup) 85 NYS2d 347.

Generally, deliberate attempts by counsel to convey the idea to the jury that defendant is insured constitutes grounds for a mistrial. However, reference by plaintiff's counsel, in a suit for the death of an employee, to Workmen's Compensation Insurance that had been introduced into the case by defendant's counsel to prove liability under the Compensation Act was held not to be error. *Lisanti v William F. Kenny Co.* (1928) 225 AD 129, 232 NYS 103, affd 250 NY 621, 166 NE 347.

When a defendant injects the immaterial question that defendant is not insured, it is sound judicial discretion to declare a mistrial early in the action, while the jury is being impanelled, rather than to await a possible reversal of a verdict on that ground. *Lindboe v Syracuse Transit Co.* (1940) 175 Misc 396, 23 NYS2d 667.

In a wrongful death action, defendant could not complain of the admission of evidence to the jury that defendant carried public liability insurance, where defendant's attorney had possibly opened the door for the receipt of such testimony on cross-examination of a defendant who was called as a witness for the plaintiff. *Levatino v Rochester Sav. Bank* (1942, Sup) 38 NYS2d 182.

Reference to insurance is condemned only where the fact of its existence is irrelevant to the issues and such reference is in all likelihood made to improperly influence a jury. *Oltarsh v Aetna Ins. Co.* (1965) 15 NY2d 111, 256 NYS2d 577. When the fact of insurance or the existence of an insurer is properly or legitimately in the case, there can be no ground for complaint. *Oltarsh v Aetna Ins. Co., supra; Hennings v Power Authority of New York* (1961) 30 Misc 2d 732, 217 NYS2d 831.

Thus, a letter sent by defendant's insurance carrier to plaintiff was properly used to cross-examine defendant with regard to possibly inconsistent statements. *Galuska v Arbaiza* (1984, 2d Dept) 106 AD2d 543, 482 NYS2d 846.

The fact of inadequate insurance coverage on the part of one defendant being made known to the jury was extremely prejudicial to the other defendant and required a new trial. *Brennan v Felter* (1975, 2d Dept) 48 AD2d 846, 369 NYS2d 175. Repeated reference by plaintiffs' counsel during summation to the inability of a codefendant to pay a judgment that might be rendered against it was prejudicial to the other defendant. *Adams v Acker* (1977, 1st Dept) 57 AD2d 741, 394 NYS2d 8, on reh (1st Dept) 58 AD2d 754, 396 NYS2d 329 and app dismd 42 NY2d 965, 398 NYS2d 147 and app dismd 42 NY2d 1050, 399 NYS2d 212.

In a product liability action, an isolated, unexpected, inadvertent statement, volunteered by a defense witness and promptly followed with curative instructions by the trial court, was nonprejudicial and did not require reversal. *Manchester v Bankhead Corp., Div. of Bankhead Enterprises, Inc.* (1986, 3d Dept) 125 AD2d 740, 509 NYS2d 434.

Evidence that the alleged tortfeasor carries liability insurance is not admissible because it is potentially prejudicial. *Allen v Harrington* (1989, 3d Dept) 156 AD2d 854, 550 NYS2d 79, app den 75 NY2d 708, 554 NYS2d 833. Where the evidence introduced was that a doctor on behalf of one of the insurance companies had examined plaintiff, such isolated, indirect reference to insurance coverage can hardly be said to have influenced a jury, and where the other evidence clearly established the defendant's liability as a matter of law, a mistrial was not required. *Allen v Harrington, supra.*

§ 27:5 DISCHARGE FOR INABILITY OF JURY TO ARRIVE AT VERDICT — In a civil case, when five-sixths of the jurors constituting a jury cannot agree after being kept together for as long as is deemed reasonable by the court, the court shall discharge the jury and direct a new trial before another jury. CPLR 4113(b).

When the first trial results in a hung jury, direction of a new trial is mandatory. *Tannenbaum v Hoar* (1966, 3d Dept) 26 AD2d 980, 274 NYS2d 710. When the jury disagreement relates to one or more but not to all of the issues submitted, the court may direct a retrial of the issues upon which the jury disagreed and entry of a verdict upon the other issues. *Daggett v Keshner* (1956) 14 Misc 2d 154, 149 NYS2d 422, affd in part and revd in part (1st Dept) 6 AD2d 503, 179 NYS2d 428, affd 7 NY2d 981, 199 NYS2d 41.

RESEARCH REFERENCES

American Law Reports

71 ALR4th 1025, Propriety and prejudicial effect of trial counsel's reference or suggestion in medical malpractice case that defendant is insured

69 ALR4th 131, Prejudicial effect of bringing to jury's attention fact that plaintiff in personal injury or death action is entitled to workers' compensation benefits

68 ALR4th 954, Counsel's argument or comment stating or implying that defendant is not insured and will have to pay verdict himself as prejudicial error

98 ALR3d 997, Double jeopardy as bar to retrial after grant of defendant's motion for mistrial

93 ALR3d 556, Counsel's appeal in civil case to self-interest or prejudice of jurors as taxpayers, as ground for mistrial, new trial, or reversal

64 ALR3d 126, Juror's voir dire denial or nondisclosure of acquaintance or relationship with attorney in case, or with partner or associate of such attorney, as ground for new trial or mistrial

25 ALR3d 1149, Juror's reluctant, equivocal, or conditional assent to verdict, on polling, as ground for mistrial or new trial in criminal case

ALR QUICK INDEX: Mistrial

American Jurisprudence 2d

76 AM JUR 2d, Trial §§ 1072-1110

75B AM JUR 2d, Trial §§ 1706-1749

American Jurisprudence Pleading and Practice

23 AM JUR PL & PR FORMS (Rev), Trial, Forms 251-288

American Jurisprudence Proof of Facts

24 AM JUR PROOF OF FACTS 2d 633, Jury Misconduct Warranting New Trial

Other Resources

Auto-Cite®: Any case citation herein can be checked for form, parallel references, later history and annotation references through the Auto-Cite computer research system.

CHAPTER 28

DIRECTED VERDICT

§ 28:1 RIGHT OF COURT TO DIRECT VERDICT — In a civil case, any party may move for judgment with respect to a cause of action or issue on the ground that the moving party is entitled to judgment as a matter of law, after the close of evidence presented by an opposing party with respect to such cause of action or issue, or at any time on the basis of admissions, and the grounds for the motion shall be specified. CPLR 4401.

Section 4401(a) of the CPLR provides that a motion for judgment at the end of the plaintiff's case must be granted as to any cause of action for medical malpractice based solely on lack of informed consent if the plaintiff has failed to adduce medical testimony in support of the alleged qualitative insufficiency of the consent.

Where plaintiff in an action for damages did not move for a directed verdict, thereby plainly conceding that there was an issue of fact for the jury on the question of damages, he thereby consented to the submission of such issue to the jury and the trial court improperly directed a verdict for plaintiff in a specified sum upon its own motion. *Billig v Don Allen Midtown Chevrolet, Inc.* (1951, App Tm) 110 NYS2d 162.

Orderly procedure required that plaintiffs be permitted to complete their case, because even in a case where it seems that plaintiffs' ultimate success in the action would be improbable, the dismissal of the complaint before plaintiffs have concluded their case would be unduly precipitate. *Goldstein v C. W. Post Center of Long Island University* (1986, 2d Dept) 122 AD2d 196, 504 NYS2d 734.

§ 28:2   PROCEDURE IN MOVING FOR DIRECTED VERDICT

— A motion to dismiss at the close of the entire case is substantially equivalent to a motion for a directed verdict made at that point. *Farrell v Lavine* (1962) 37 Misc 2d 497, 236 NYS2d 323.

Admissions contained in a bill of particulars may be considered on a motion for judgment. *Rosenzweig v Schmitt* (1931) 232 AD 131, 249 NYS 266. On a motion for judgment the court cannot weigh evidence, and may not direct a verdict merely because it would set aside a contrary verdict as against the weight of evidence. *Tirschwell v Dolan* (1964, 3d Dept) 21 AD2d 923, 251 NYS2d 91. The trial judge has the right to reserve decision on a motion for judgment during the trial. *622 West 113th Street Corp. v Chemical Bank New York Trust Co.* (1966) 52 Misc 2d 444, 276 NYS2d 85.

On a motion for a directed verdict the court may not substitute its judgment for that of the jury. *Endelman v Palmer* (1946, DC NY) 65 F Supp 436. When a trial judge grants a motion for the direction of the verdict he should state the reason therefor. *F. A. MacCluer, Inc. v Distribuidores Industriales S. De R. L.* (1947) 271 AD 987, 68 NYS2d 349.

On a motion for a directed verdict of no cause of action, plaintiff is entitled to the most favorable view of, and inferences from, the evidence. *Magnoli v John Hancock Mut. Life Ins. Co.* (1948) 192 Misc 344, 78 NYS2d 130. On a motion to dismiss a counterclaim, defendants' evidence would be interpreted most favorably to them. *Town Taxi Service Corp. v Green Cab & Brokerage Co.* (1942, Sup) 38 NYS2d 529. In directing a verdict for the plaintiff, the court resolved every material disputed fact in defendant's favor. *Stiles v Annabel* (1930) 138 Misc 811, 246 NYS 524.

§ 28:3 DETERMINING THE RIGHT TO A DIRECTED VERDICT

DICT — The standard in deciding a motion for a directed verdict is whether the jury could find for the non-moving party by any rational process, and the evidence is reviewed in a light most favorable to the non-moving party, as are all questions of witness credibility. *Gendalia v Gioffre* (1993, 2d Dept) 191 AD2d 476, 594 NYS2d 322; *Ampolini v Long Island Lighting Co.* (1992, 2d Dept) 186 AD2d 772, 589 NYS2d 65; *Hylick v Halweil* (1985, 2d Dept) 112 AD2d 400, 492 NYS2d 57; *Van Syckle v Powers* (1984, 3d Dept) 106 AD2d 711, 483 NYS2d 756; *Flick v Town of Steuben* (1993, 4th Dept) 199 AD2d 970, 605 NYS2d 602.

Where a verdict, if in the defendant's favor, would necessarily have to be set aside as a matter of law for lack of credible evidence supporting it, a directed verdict for the plaintiff would be proper. *Bank of United States v Manheim* (1934) 264 NY 45, 189 NE 776, reh den 264 NY 511, 191 NE 540.

In a probate proceeding, where the contestant was unable to show any evidence of undue influence so that, had evidence on this issue been submitted to the jury and a verdict returned in favor of the contestants it would have been necessary to set it aside, the Surrogate was authorized to direct a verdict. *Re Will of Richards* (1956, 3d Dept) 1 AD2d 502, 151 NYS2d 744.

A directed verdict for the plaintiff is warranted only where the plaintiff's case is established beyond any question, or, in other words where the evidence presents no question of fact for the jury. *Van Cleef v Maxfield* (1921) 196 AD 734, 188 NYS 322.

Where, following a first trial, at which the trial judge directed a verdict in favor of plaintiff as to liability, the Appellate Division unanimously reversed, holding that there were issues of fact that required submission to the jury, and at a second trial before the same judge who had presided at the first, and on essentially the same evidence, a directed verdict was again granted in favor of plaintiff, judgment was reversed and a new trial directed. *Shramko v Hills Wrecking Corp.* (1977, 1st Dept) 56 AD2d 764, 392 NYS2d 436.

A court may not properly direct a verdict in a case where the right to a jury trial exists and an actual issue of fact is presented by the evidence. *Cohen v Hallmark Cards, Inc.* (1978) 45 NY2d

493, 410 NYS2d 282, later proceeding (1st Dept) 70 AD2d 509, 415 NYS2d 657.

A scintilla of evidence is insufficient to constitute a substantial conflict that would preclude direction of a verdict for the defendant, where the evidence at the trial conclusively establishes that plaintiff's cause of action is barred by the statute of limitations. *Duval v Skouras* (1947, Sup) 70 NYS2d 150.

Where no issue of fact was presented, a verdict should have been directed for the employee. *Mavian v Majestic Photo Engraving Co.* (1940, App Tm) 19 NYS2d 677. A verdict may be directed by the court on the uncontradicted testimony of an interested witness. *Pierson & Co. v Mitsui & Co.* (1920) 111 Misc 388, 181 NYS 273.

The plaintiff was entitled to the direction of a verdict if the evidence was wholly insufficient in point of law to sustain a counterclaim of the defendant, and the evidence was insufficient if it was incredible as a matter of law. *Blum v Fresh Grown Preserve Corp.* (1944) 292 NY 241. Evidence is incredible as a matter of law only where no reasonable man could accept it and base an inference upon it. *Blum v Fresh Grown Preserve Corp., supra.* Insufficient evidence is equivalent to no evidence, and authorizes the dismissal of a complaint or the direction of a verdict. *Soma v Handrulis* (1937) 252 AD 332, 299 NYS 850, revd on other grounds 277 NY 223, reh den 278 NY 481.

A motion for non-suit or for direction of a verdict may not be granted where facts are in dispute, or where the evidence is such that reasonable men may draw different inferences from undisputed facts, or where the issue depends upon the credibility of witnesses. *Sadowski v Long Island R. Co.* (1944) 292 NY 448, later app 268 AD 777, 50 NYS2d 171. Where at the end of the plaintiff's case, the evidence was sufficient to put the defendant to his proofs, the dismissal of the complaint was reversible error. *Matovich v Weiss* (1948, App Tm) 80 NYS2d 539. The probability or improbability of the story of a witness and his credibility because of his interest as a result of relationship were matters for the jury in weighing the testimony, and not grounds for a directed verdict. *Karten v Tabachnik* (1922, App Tm) 192 NYS 335.

Where plaintiffs had made out a *prima facie* case, the court was without power to direct a verdict. *Reisner v New York Kosher Provisions, Inc.* (1966, 1st Dept) 25 AD2d 511, 267 NYS2d 70.

Where a question of fact and credibility was presented to the jury, the trial court could not direct a verdict. *Callery v Lyons* (1944) 292 NY 15.

The question whether plaintiff had sought to suborn perjured testimony, a charge that plaintiff denied, related to the credibility of plaintiff and did not constitute a reason for directing a verdict for the defendant. *Migdalski v Arcadian Lounge, Inc.* (1980, 2d Dept) 73 AD2d 960, 424 NYS2d 264.

Whether the issue is negligence of the defendant, or the contributory negligence of the plaintiff, the test for determining whether the facts pose a question for resolution by the jury is whether there is a valid line of reasoning and permissible inferences that could possibly lead rational men to the conclusion of negligence on the basis of the evidence presented at the trial. *Nallan v Helmsley-Spear, Inc.* (1980) 50 NY2d 507, 429 NYS2d 606.

Because questions concerning what is foreseeable and what is normal may be the subject of varying inferences, as is the question of negligence itself, these issues are generally for the fact-finder to resolve. *Muhaymin v Negron* (1982, 1st Dept) 86 AD2d 836, 447 NYS2d 457.

A motion for a directed verdict made after the court's charge was timely, where plaintiff reserved her rights by reserving her motion for a directed verdict with the consent of the court. *Thompson v New York* (1983) 60 NY2d 948, 471 NYS2d 50.

Dismissal of a complaint as a matter of law is warranted when on the evidentiary materials before the court no issue of fact remains for decision by the trier of fact. *Maddox v New York* (1985) 66 NY2d 270, 496 NYS2d 726.

Because on a motion for a directed verdict, the court must view the evidence and inferences reasonably to be drawn therefrom, most favorably to the non-moving party, and determine whether the jury could find for the non-movant by any rational process, the motion should not be granted if the facts are in dispute, or if different inferences could be drawn from undisputed facts, or where resolution of an issue depends upon the credibility of witnesses. *Petrovski v Fornes* (1986, 4th Dept) 125 AD2d 972, 510 NYS2d 366.

Although proximate cause is usually a question for the jury, when only one conclusion may be drawn from the established facts, the question of legal cause may be decided as a matter of law. *Kingsland v Industrial Brown Hoist Co.* (1988, 4th Dept) 136 AD2d 901, 524 NYS2d 929.

On a motion for judgment as a matter of law, the trial court's function is not to weigh the evidence, but rather, in taking the case from the jury, to determine that by no rational process could the trier of the facts base a finding in favor of the party moved against. *Dooley v Skodnek* (1988, 2d Dept) 138 AD2d 102, 529 NYS2d 569.

The trial court properly found that there was no contract, and therefore correctly dismissed the cause of action for tortious interference with contract. *Feeley v Midas Properties, Inc.* (1989, 2d Dept) 154 AD2d 505, 546 NYS2d 131.

Where the circumstantial evidence as to the placement of boxes was equally consistent with the absence as with the presence of a wrongful act on the part of the defendant's employee, the rule was applied that the meaning must be ascribed which accords with the absence of a wrongful act. Accordingly, the trial court was justified in granting defendant's motion to dismiss the complaint at the close of the plaintiff's case. *Kerr v United Parcel Service* (1990, 2d Dept) 160 AD2d 675, 554 NYS2d 38.

Because it is inappropriate to dismiss a case for failure of proof before the plaintiff rests and in the absence of a properly grounded motion by the defendant for that relief, the Supreme Court's dismissal of the plaintiff's case before completion of plaintiff's evidence was unauthorized where the trial court's dismissal was premised primarily on the failure of the plaintiff's counsel to produce the plaintiff, whose absence had already apparently delayed the proceedings. *Canteen v White Plains* (1990, 2d Dept) 165 AD2d 856, 560 NYS2d 320.

§ 28:4   DIRECTING A VERDICT FOR A VARIANCE — Pleadings may be amended before or after judgment to conform them to the evidence, upon such terms as may be just, including the granting of costs and continuances. CPLR 3025(c). The trial court has wide discretion to grant or withhold relief under the rule permitting the amendment of pleadings to conform to the evidence. *Dittmar Explosives, Inc. v A. E. Ottaviano, Inc.* (1967) 20 NY2d 498, 285 NYS2d 55.

Where a cause of action is imperfectly stated, or on trial a variance is disclosed between the pleadings and the proof, not affecting the essential nature of the claim asserted, the court has the power to grant relief without turning a party out of court. *McCarthy v Troberg* (1949) 275 AD 139, 88 NYS2d 436, app withdrawn 300 NY 632. However, where an allegation in the complaint is unproved, not in some particulars alone but in its entire scope, no judgment can be rendered on the pleading as it stands. *McCarthy v Troberg, supra*.

Where an amendment of the pleadings to conform to the proof would lead to injustice when the theory of the decision is not one contemplated by the parties, it should be denied. *Pfeil Constr. Corp. v Moley* (1958) 14 Misc 2d 379, 179 NYS2d 443. However, denying defendant's motion to amend the answer to conform to the proof in an action upon an indemnity contract was held to be error in the absence of a claim of surprise or prejudice. *Road Garage Corp. v Marcus* (1930) 229 AD 150, 241 NYS 149.

Where a particular defense was not pleaded but some evidence was offered and received without objection tending to support such defense, a motion to conform the pleadings to the proof if made would have been granted. *Goldberg v Lama Country Club, Inc.* (1947, Sup) 67 NYS2d 765.

Under the rule permitting an amendment of the pleadings to conform to the proof, a proposed amendment may not state a new and entirely different cause of action. *Bessant v State* (1948) 192 Misc 42, 77 NYS2d 752. Where plaintiff pleaded that her injuries had been caused by a taxicab being hit from the rear, but at the trial she tried to prove that the cause was the taxicab making a short stop, plaintiff was not entitled to amend the pleadings to conform to the proof. *Du Bose v Velez* (1970) 63 Misc 2d 956, 313 NYS2d 881.

Even on appeal, the Appellate Division may amend pleadings to conform to the proof if it is convinced that no prejudice results or that the proof so warrants. *Dampskibsselskabet Torm A/S v P. L.*

Thomas Paper Co. (1966, 1st Dept) 26 AD2d 347, 274 NYS2d 601. A motion to permit the petition to be amended to conform to the evidence should be granted only if the proof adduced at the trial establishes the cause of action, and it may be conditioned so as to avoid surprise and prejudice to the adverse party as, for example, granting him a continuance to prepare to meet the new theory. *Re Will of Lipsit* (1966, Sur Ct) 50 Misc 2d 289, 269 NYS2d 989.

An increase of the *ad damnum* clause, granted by the court at the moment of trial, on oral application based solely on service of a notice of intention to move to amend at the trial, was not error. *Mykulak v New York Journal American* (1974, 1st Dept) 44 AD2d 791, 355 NYS2d 386.

Where the absence of a dollar amount in the *ad damnum* clause of a defendant's counterclaim was adequately explained as a typographical oversight, especially when the amount involved was elsewhere stated in the pleading, and defendant's motion to cure that defect was timely made without prejudice to the plaintiff, it was well within the discretion of the trial court to permit such a correction under the circumstances. *Serena Constr. Corp. v Valley Drywall Service, Inc.* (1974, 3d Dept) 45 AD2d 896, 357 NYS2d 214.

In an action by a tenant against a landlord, where the complaint alleged that the premises constituted a multiple dwelling, the court erred in denying a motion to conform the pleadings to the proof to show that the building was a two-family house, because there was no surprise to the defendants, who owned the building. *Princiotto v Materdomini* (1974, 2d Dept) 45 AD2d 883, 358 NYS2d 13.

Where the uncontradicted testimony established that the infant plaintiff was injured when defendant struck him in the face with his fist, and plaintiff framed the complaint solely on the theory of negligence, the trial court should have dismissed the complaint. *Andres v Perry* (1981, 2d Dept) 81 AD2d 848, 438 NYS2d 852, affd 54 NY2d 795, 443 NYS2d 610.

Where plaintiff's complaint, which was based upon negligence only, had never been amended, either by motion addressed to Special Term or by motion to conform the pleadings to the proof at the end of the trial, plaintiff could not recover on a conversion theory that he never pleaded. *Weinberg v D-M Restaurant Corp.* (1981) 53 NY2d 499, 442 NYS2d 965.

Although generally, in the absence of surprise or prejudice, plaintiff should be granted leave to conform his pleadings to the proof, even if a new theory of recovery is presented, when an express contract exists between the parties concerning the same subject matter, there may be no recovery on a theory of implied contract, and under such circumstances it is an abuse of discretion for the court to grant plaintiff's motion to conform the pleadings to state a cause of action in implied contract. *Nixon Gear & Machine Co. v Nixon Gear, Inc.* (1982, 4th Dept) 86 AD2d 746, 447 NYS2d 779.

Where evidence is introduced in support of a theory that has not been pleaded, this is prejudicial to the defendant, because the latter has had no opportunity to investigate the matter involved and to prepare a defense, particularly where there is a general verdict and the Appellate Court is unable to determine what reliance the jury placed upon the unpleaded element of proof. *Wallace v New York* (1982, 1st Dept) 86 AD2d 510, 445 NYS2d 742.

In a malpractice suit against a neurosurgeon where the only evidence tending to establish his liability was based on a theory of vicarious liability, and that theory was never raised in the plaintiffs' complaint, the action against the neurosurgeon was properly dismissed. *Cornacchia v Mt. Vernon Hospital* (1983, 2d Dept) 93 AD2d 851, 461 NYS2d 348.

A plaintiff in a personal injury action is bound by the specifications in his bill of particulars. *Solomon v Stroler* (1981, 1st Dept) 82 AD2d 756, 440 NYS2d 200. Where the bill of particulars alleged lumbar spine and disc injuries, it was error for the trial court to permit proof of sexual incapacity, urinary incontinence, stuttering, a nervous condition and a limp, requiring a new trial on damages. *Solomon v Stroler* (1981, 1st Dept) 82 AD2d 756, 440 NYS2d 200.

Where the bill of particulars failed to set forth those injuries claimed to be permanent, it was error to allow plaintiff's expert witness to testify with respect to the injuries claimed to be permanent, requiring a new trial on damages. *Fricker v New York* (1983, 2d Dept) 97 AD2d 832, 468 NYS2d 718.

Although permission to amend a complaint should be freely given, a motion for this relief should be made promptly after discovery or awareness of the facts upon which such an amendment is predicated. Where plaintiff gave the same testimony at an examination before trial as he gave at the trial, and this was at variance with the facts alleged in the pleadings, the trial court properly denied the motion for leave to amend, even though defendant conceded that he would incur neither prejudice nor surprise if the amendment were allowed. *Olden v Bolton* (1988, 3d Dept) 137 AD2d 878, 524 NYS2d 562.

It could not be said that the trial court improperly exercised its discretion in denying plaintiff's motion to amend the complaint, where the proposed amendment to the complaint was patently insufficient on its face. *Goldberg v Linden Towers Coop. No. 5, Inc.* (1989, 2d Dept) 147 AD2d 672, 538 NYS2d 282.

A variance between the pleadings and the proof will be disregarded unless it has misled a party's adversary and occasioned prejudice. *Van Derzee v Knight-Ridder Broadcasting, Inc.* (1992, 3d Dept) 185 AD2d 1011, 586 NYS2d 839.

§ 28:5 NEGLIGENCE AND CONTRIBUTORY NEGLIGENCE AS QUESTIONS OF LAW OR FACT — The law does not require every negligence action, without regard to the evidence presented, to be determined by a jury, and it is just as much error to submit a case to the jury where no question of fact is involved as it is to deny a litigant his right to a determination by the jury where a question of fact has been presented. *Conroy v Saratoga Springs Authority* (1940) 259 AD 365, 19 NYS2d 538, affd 284 NY 723. Where the evidence made out a *prima facie* case of negligence, the case should not have been dismissed at the close of the plaintiff's case. *Inkelis v Lehman* (1956) 2 Misc 2d 398, 155 NYS2d 929. In an action against a warehouse for injuries to a trucker who was struck by a bag of almonds that was slid down a chute from the warehouse to a truck, whether the truckman assumed the risk of injury was a question of fact for the jury. *McNulty v Sunset Warehouses, Inc.* (1939) 256 AD 821, 8 NYS2d 703.

Where plaintiff's evidence is as consistent with absence of negligence as with its existence, the evidence is insufficient to take the case to the jury. *Frellesen v Colburn* (1935) 156 Misc 254, 281 NYS 471. Where plaintiff fails to make out a *prima facie* case of negligence, it is improper to deny the company's motion to dismiss the complaint. *Russell v Union R. Co.* (1939, App Tm) 9 NYS2d 925.

The statute adopting the standard of comparative negligence in place of contributory negligence is not retroactive. *Binder v Supermarkets General Corp.* (1975, 2d Dept) 49 AD2d 562, 370 NYS2d 184.

In an action brought against New York State for the death of one claimant and the blindness of another, both of whom had been confined to a state-operated narcotics rehabilitation center, where the death and blindness resulted from the drinking of a fluid containing methyl alcohol, it was held that one may retain the power to intend, to know and yet to have an irresistible impulse to act and therefore be incapable of voluntary conduct, and it was therefore error for the Appellate Division to conclude that the conduct of both inmates constituted contributory negligence. *Padula v State* (1979) 48 NY2d 366, 422 NYS2d 943.

Non-use of an available seat belt, coupled with expert testimony with regard thereto as a causative factor, may be considered in mitigation of damages in a personal injury action. *Spier v Barker* (1974) 35 NY2d 444, 363 NYS2d 916, 80 ALR3d 1025.

A parent's negligent failure to supervise his child is not actionable as a tort by the child, nor may negligent supervision form the basis of a third party claim against the parent. *Holodook v Spencer* (1974) 36 NY2d 35, 364 NYS2d 859.

The question of an infant's contributory negligence is ordinarily one for the jury, upon consideration of the evidence and evaluation of the child's age, experience and intelligence. *Egan v Tambone* (1981, 2d Dept) 81 AD2d 604, 437 NYS2d 713. Thus, the contributory negligence of a 10-year-old boy, who knew that the thoroughfare was used by automobiles, but in the course of playing ball dashed out into the street without looking to see if any cars were coming, was for the jury. *Egan v Tambone, supra.*

Because it is fundamental that to recover in a negligence action a plaintiff must establish that the defendant owed him a duty to use reasonable care and that defendant breached that duty, in a professional sporting contest, if a participant makes an informed estimate of the risks involved in the activity, and willingly undertakes them, there can be no liability if he is injured as a result of those risks. *Turcotte v Fell* (1986) 68 NY2d 432, 510 NYS2d 49.

A plaintiff's own conduct may be a superseding force absolving a negligent defendant from liability, however, to be a superseding cause, a plaintiff's negligence must be more than mere contributory negligence; such conduct, in addition to being unforeseeable, must rise to such a level of culpability as to replace the defendant's negligence as the legal cause of the accident. *Mesick v State* (1986, 3d Dept) 118 AD2d 214, 504 NYS2d 279.

Unlike a violation of the explicit provisions of a statute proper, a breach of an administrative rule does not establish negligence as a matter of law because it lacks the force of a legislative enactment and is merely some evidence to be considered on the question of a defendant's negligence. *Marcellino v Nigro* (1989, 3d Dept) 149 AD2d 775, 539 NYS2d 820.

Contributory negligence on the part of the worker is not a defense to a violation predicated under Labor Law § 240(1), which imposes absolute liability on an owner or contractor for failing to provide or erect safety devices necessary to give proper protection to a worker who sustains injuries proximately caused by that failure; a plaintiff must prove only that the statute was violated and that the violation was a proximate cause of the injuries he sustained. *Squicciarini v Park Ridge Assocs.* (1993, 2d Dept) 199 AD2d 376, 605 NYS2d 372; *Gandley v Prestige Roofing & Siding Co.* (1989, 2d Dept) 148 AD2d 666, 539 NYS2d 416.

In an action for violation of Labor Law § 240(1), a jury question was presented concerning whether violation of statute was a proximate cause of the worker's injuries, in light of testimony that: the worker fell when he missed a rung while descending a ladder; the worker was facing away from the ladder and not holding on to it; and he was carrying a cup of coffee in one hand and his breakfast in the other. *Anderson v Schul/Mar Constr. Corp.* (1995, 2d Dept) 212 AD2d 493, 622 NYS2d 310.

A violation of the duty imposed by Labor Law § 240, which is designed to protect employees working on scaffolding and other elevated structures, imposes absolute liability on an owner or contractor regardless of the degree of its control over the work. *Klien v General Foods Corp.* (1989, 4th Dept) 148 AD2d 968, 539 NYS2d 604.

Breach of a duty pursuant to Labor Law § 240(1) to provide proper scaffolding will result in the imposition of absolute liability regardless of any contributory negligence on the part of the employee. *Pritchard v Murray Walter, Inc.* (1990, 3d Dept) 157 AD2d 1012, 550 NYS2d 500.

A worker's negligence in contributing to the accident, such as the failure to wear an available hard hat, does not diminish the absolute duty of the owner/general contractor under Labor Law § 240(1). While this does not mean that there is an affirmative duty to compel a worker who refuses to use available safety equipment to do so, in the absence of an evidentiary showing that claimant deliberately refused to use a hard hat, summary judgment on the issue of liability against defendant is warranted. *Koumianos v State* (1988, 3d Dept) 141 AD2d 189, 534 NYS2d 512.

Where the actual cause of the injury is undisputed, the question of whether the defendant's negligence was a proximate cause of plaintiff's injury is a question of law for the court. *Ziecker v Orchard Park* (1989, 4th Dept) 147 AD2d 974, 538 NYS2d 671, revd on other grounds 75 NY2d 761, 551 NYS2d 898.

Whether a special duty assumed by police officers toward a member of the public has been breached is generally a question of fact. *Kenyon v Van Vorce* (1988, 4th Dept) 144 AD2d 925, 534 NYS2d 244.

Generally, resolutions of the question of the foreseeability of danger is for the trier of the facts. *Forrester v Port Authority of New York & New Jersey* (1988, 1st Dept) 139 AD2d 449, 527 NYS2d 224.

A plaintiff who sustained a back injury when she hit her head after diving into the shallow end of a swimming pool was not guilty of reckless conduct as a matter of law, where she testified that she had never been in the pool before and did not know the depth of the water in it. *Johnson v Cherry Grove Island Management, Inc.* (1991, 2d Dept) 175 AD2d 827, 573 NYS2d 187.

The Weigand doctrine, that a plaintiff is bound to see what by the proper use of his senses he should have seen, will not be applied to absolve a defendant from his own negligence where there is evidence that the condition causing the injury was inherently dangerous. *Jimenez v Urban Universal Structures, Inc.* (1991, 2d Dept) 174 AD2d 604, 571 NYS2d 311.

In an action arising out of a single car accident, the issues of the City's negligence in failing to post adequate signs warning of a curve, and the motorist's negligence in failing to heed speed limits were properly a question of fact for the jury that properly apportioned liability among the defendants. *Nowlin v City of New York* (1992, 1st Dept) 182 AD2d 376, 582 NYS2d 669.

Although the court, as a threshold matter, must decide whether one party owes a duty of care to another, where the facts are undisputed and only one inference may be drawn, the question of duty is not for the court as a matter of law where the facts are disputed. *Gordon v Muchnick* (1992, 2d Dept) 180 AD2d 715, 579 NYS2d 745.

In a personal injury action arising out of an accident, that occurred on the Whitestone Bridge when a motorist collided with a Triborough Bridge and Tunnel Authority Towing vehicle almost immediately after changing lanes, the jury apportionment of liability charging the Triborough Bridge and Tunnel Authority with 65% of the fault based on the failure of the tow truck driver to set cones behind his vehicle and to illuminate a directional arrow on his truck to alert traffic that he was stopped, and 35% against the driver of the vehicle that collided with the tow truck, was based upon a fair appraisal of all the evidence presented to it. *Ramos v Triborough Bridge and Tunnel Authority* (1992, 1st Dept) 179 AD2d 471, 578 NYS2d 181.

§ 28:6 COMPARATIVE NEGLIGENCE — All causes of action for personal injury, wrongful death or conscious pain and suffering, accruing on and after September 1, 1975, are governed by the statute that provides for comparative negligence rather than the heretofore-applied doctrine of contributory negligence. Thus, culpable conduct attributable to the plaintiff or to the decedent, whether denominated contributory negligence or assumption of risk, no longer bars a recovery, but the amount of damages otherwise recoverable is diminished in the proportion that the culpable conduct attributable to the plaintiff or decedent bears to the culpable conduct that caused the damages. Culpable conduct claimed in diminution of damages is an affirmative defense to be pleaded and proved by the party asserting the defense. (Article 14-A; CPLR 1411, 1412, 1413; EPTL §§ 5-4.2, 11-3.2(b)). For actions accruing before September 1, 1975, the law with respect to contributory negligence remains intact and is applicable. *Binder v Supermarkets General Corp.* (1975, 2d Dept) 49 AD2d 562, 370 NYS2d 184.

The enactment of the comparative negligence statute has not abrogated the rule that no one shall be permitted to profit by his own wrong. *Barker v Kallash* (1983, 2d Dept) 91 AD2d 372, 459 NYS2d 296, affd 63 NY2d 19, 479 NYS2d 201. An infant plaintiff over the age of 14 could not recover on the theory of comparative negligence from defendants who had allegedly furnished him with gun powder. *Barker v Kallash, supra.*

In a case arising under § 240 of the Labor Law, and involving a scaffold, contributory negligence was not a defense, and therefore comparative negligence was not available as a partial defense to the contractors. *Evans v Nab Constr. Corp.* (1981, 2d Dept) 80 AD2d 841, 436 NYS2d 774, app dismd 54 NY2d 785, 443 NYS2d 369; *see also, Wright v State* (1985, 4th Dept) 110 AD2d 1060, 488 NYS2d 917, affd 66 NY2d 452, 497 NYS2d 880.

In order for CPLR 1411 to operate, plaintiff's conduct must be a cause in fact of his or her injury; when it is, the statute requires that the culpable conduct attributable to the decedent or claimant be compared with the total culpable conduct that caused the damages. *Arbegast v Board of Education* (1985) 65 NY2d 161, 490 NYS2d 751.

Claims pursuant to Labor Law §§ 200 and 241(6) are subject to the defense of comparative negligence, and require inquiry into the correlation of negligence and comparative negligence in causing the injuries complained of. *Siragusa v State* (1986, 4th Dept) 117 AD2d 986, 499 NYS2d 533; *see also, McLean v Wical Realty Corp.* (1992, 1st Dept) 182 AD2d 554, 582 NYS2d 423; *Kelleher v First Presbyterian Church* (1990, 4th Dept) 158 AD2d 946, 551 NYS2d 708, app dismd without op 75 NY2d 947, 555 NYS2d 694.

In an action brought by a motorist injured when her motor vehicle struck a guard rail, on the theory that the state was negligent in fabricating the guard rail, the verdict against the state should have been reduced based on the comparative negligence of the claimant in veering off the road, which in fact caused the impact and the injuries that resulted therefrom. *Clark v State* (1986, 3d Dept) 124 AD2d 879, 508 NYS2d 648.

When a plaintiff's culpable conduct does not cause the accident but merely aggravates the injury, the conduct is pertinent only to the issue of mitigation of damages; the trial court should not have permitted the jury to consider the issue of plaintiff's comparative liability. *State University Constr. Fund v Kipphut & Neuman Co.* (1990, 4th Dept) 159 AD2d 1003, 552 NYS2d 471.

The fact that a deceased motorist was intoxicated did not exonerate the state from liability for having created a dangerous condition, and under the circumstances the court's apportionment of fault of 50% to each party was correct. *Cappadona v State* (1989, 2d Dept) 154 AD2d 498, 546 NYS2d 124, remittitur den (2d Dept) 156 AD2d 505, 548 NYS2d 778.

Comparative negligence is not a defense available to reduce recovery by a firefighter who brings a special statutory action for injuries allegedly resulting from a property owner's failure to comply with statutes or ordinances, pursuant to General Municipal Law § 205(a) . *Johnson v Riggio Realty Corp.* (1989, 1st Dept) 153 AD2d 485, 544 NYS2d 589, app dismd without op 74 NY2d 945, 550 NYS2d 279.

The fact that the law did not require plaintiff to wear his seat belt at the time of the accident is of no moment; a jury should be allowed to consider a plaintiff's failure to wear an available seat belt in assessing damages. *Ruiz v Rochester Tel. Co.* (1993, 4th Dept) 195 AD2d 981, 600 NYS2d 879.

§ 28:7   MOTION BY BOTH PARTIES FOR DIRECTED VERDICT — A motion for a directed verdict, even when made by both parties, is not a waiver of the right to trial by jury or to present further evidence. CPLR 4401. A motion made by all parties for a directed verdict without reservation of right, or request to go to the jury on submissions of fact, was held not to be a submission to the trial court of all questions both of law and of fact and a waiver of the right to a jury trial. *McTiernan v Little Falls* (1954) 284 AD 79, 130 NYS2d 214.

§ 28:8   ASSUMPTION OF RISK — There are two distinct doctrines involving assumption of the risk, the first of which is embraced within CPLR 1411 and as used in this sense does not bar recovery but diminishes recovery in the proportion to which it contributed to the injuries; as used in this sense it is merely another name for comparative negligence. *Cohen v Heritage Motor Tours, Inc.* (1994, 2d Dept) 205 AD2d 105, 618 NYS2d 387; *Lamey v Foley* (1993, 4th Dept) 188 AD2d 157, 594 NYS2d 490, CCH Prod Liab Rep ¶ 13558. The second category of assumption of a risk, sometimes called "primary" assumption of the risk, if applicable, is a measure of defendant's duty of care and eliminates or reduces the tortfeasor's duty of care to plaintiff; in the latter case it constitutes a complete bar to recovery notwithstanding CPLR 1411. *Lamey v Foley, supra.* Primary assumption of risk arises from activities involving an elevated risk of danger, such as sporting and entertainment events, where the risks are incidental to a relationship of free association between the plaintiff and defendant in the sense that either party is perfectly free to engage in the activity or not as one sees fit. *Rodriguez v New York City Hous. Auth.* (1995, 1st Dept) 211 AD2d 328, 628 NYS2d 82.

Those who voluntarily participate in a sporting activity may be held to have consented, by their participation, to those injury-causing events that are known, apparent or reasonably foreseeable consequences of the participation. *Pascucci v Oyster Bay* (1992, 2d Dept) 186 AD2d 725, 588 NYS2d 663.

To assume a risk, a person must know and fully appreciate such risk; the failure to use reasonable care to discover the risk may constitute contributory negligence, but not assumption of risk. *Smith v Lebanon Valley Auto Racing* (1993, 3d Dept) 194 AD2d 946, 598 NYS2d 858.

RESEARCH REFERENCES

American Law Reports

82 ALR3d 974, Propriety of direction of verdict in favor of fewer than all defendants at close of plaintiff's case

55 ALR3d 272, Comment note-Power of court sitting as trier of fact to dismiss at close of plaintiff's evidence, notwithstanding plaintiff has made out prima facie case

36 ALR3d 1113, Right to voluntary dismissal of civil action as affected by opponent's motion for summary judgment, judgment on the pleadings, or directed verdict

10 ALR3d 1330, Propriety and prejudicial effect of counsel's argument or comment as to trial judge's refusal to direct verdict against him

5 ALR3d 1405, Dismissal, nonsuit, judgment, or direction of verdict on opening statement of counsel in civil action

92 ALR2d 522, Res ipsa loquitur as ground for direction of verdict in favor of plaintiff.

ALR QUICK INDEX: Direction of Verdict

American Jurisprudence 2d

75 AM JUR 2d, Trial §§ 463-558

American Jurisprudence Pleading and Practice

23 AM JUR PL & PR FORMS (Rev) Trial Forms 301-315

Other Resources

Auto-Cite®: Any case citation herein can be checked for form, parallel references, later history and annotation references through the Auto-Cite computer research system.

CHAPTER 29

DAMAGES

§ 29:1   DAMAGES, IN GENERAL — Damages in the legal sense are compensation for an injury done or a loss sustained. They are intended to put the injured party in the position he was before the injury. *Delehanty v Walzer* (1945, Sup) 59 NYS2d 777, revd 271 AD 886, 67 NYS2d 25, affd 298 NY 820.

The difficulty of ascertaining damages does not excuse the determination, and the uncertainty about the amount does not preclude recovery. *Tobin v Union News Co.* (1963, 4th Dept) 18 AD2d 243, 239 NYS2d 22, affd 13 NY2d 1155, 247 NYS2d 385. Mathematical certainty is not necessary in ascertaining damages, and a reasonable basis for computation of the approximate result is the only requirement. *Tobin v Union News Co., supra.*

Damages cannot be awarded on the basis of conjecture and guesswork. *Schanbarger v Edward Dott's Garage, Inc.* (1979, 3d Dept) 72 AD2d 882, 421 NYS2d 937. *Harsco Corp. v Rodolitz Realty Corp.* (1969) 61 Misc 2d 644, 307 NYS2d 531. A claim for damages based on sheer speculation cannot be sustained. *Suburban Club of Larkfield, Inc. v Huntington* (1968) 57 Misc 2d 1051, 294 NYS2d 4, affd 31 AD2d 718, 297 NYS2d 893.

A person violating a contract should not be permitted entirely to escape liability because the amount of damages that he has caused is uncertain, so that if it is certain that the damages have resulted from the breach of contract, and the only uncertainty is about their amount, there is rarely a good reason for excusing any damages for breach. *Randall-Smith, Inc. v 43rd St. Estates Corp.* (1966) 17 NY2d 99, 268 NYS2d 306.

Unliquidated damages recoverable for a breach of contract must be reasonable, certain and definite in amount and not speculative, problematical or resting on conjecture. *Strough v Conley* (1937) 164 Misc 248, 298 NYS 516, affd 251 AD 487, 297 NYS 785, app dismd 283 NY 631.

A plaintiff who seeks compensatory damages has the burden of proof, and should present to the court a proper basis for ascertaining the damages sought; the damages must be susceptible of ascertainment in some manner other than by mere conjecture. *Dunkel v McDonald* (1947) 272 AD 267, 70 NYS2d 653, affd 298 NY 586 and ovrld on other grounds *I. H. P.Corp v 210 Cent. Park South Corp*(1962, 1st Dept) 16 AD2d 461, 228 NYS2d 883, affd 12 NY2d 329, 239 NYS2d 547). However, damages caused by a wrong will not be denied on account of uncertainty about the amount. *Dunkel v McDonald, supra.* A wrongdoer may not escape liability for damages simply because the ordinary standards for proving damages are not available; the law will resort to some practical means that will be just to the parties. *Dunkel v McDonald, supra.*

When a plaintiff is able to establish the exact amount of his loss by competent proof and fails to do so, the jury is not permitted to speculate on the amount of damages to be awarded. *Slater v Kane* (1949) 275 AD 648, 92 NYS2d 640, reh den 276 AD 835, 93 NYS2d 725.

No single rule of damages fits every case because the rule differs with the circumstances. *Ehrenworth v George F. Stuhmer & Co.* (1920) 229 NY 210, 128 NE 108.

The court is required to instruct the jury on the factors to be considered in fixing damages. *Lesniak v Chant* (1957, 4th Dept) 4 AD2d 1007, 167 NYS2d 767 In this decision, involving a breach of contract, the appellate court said it was improper for the jurors to have been told, without any explanation of what the measure of damages should be, that if they found for the plaintiff, they should award whatever damages they thought the plaintiff was entitled to receive.

Because it is fundamental to the law of damages that a party complaining of injury has the burden of proving the extent of the harm suffered, a contractor claiming to be wrongfully delayed by his employer must establish the extent to which costs were increased by the improper acts, because recovery will be limited to damages actually sustained. *Berley Industries, Inc. v New York* (1978) 45 NY2d 683, 412 NYS2d 585.

To be recoverable, damages may not be merely speculative, possible, and imaginary, they must be reasonably certain. When it is certain that damages have been caused by a breach of contract, and the only uncertainty involves their amount, there is rarely good reason to refuse any damages for the breach because of the uncertainty about the amount of the damages. In such circumstances, it is usually the right of the person complaining of the breach of contract to prove the nature of his contract, the circumstances surrounding and following its breach, and the consequences naturally and plainly traceable to it. *Najjar Industries, Inc. v New York* (1982, 1st Dept) 87 AD2d 329, 451 NYS2d 410.

As a general rule, a party's exclusive remedy for recovery of damages caused by delay in the completion of a construction contract is the provision contained in the contractor's liquidated damage clause. *Babylon Associates v County of Suffolk* (1984, 2d Dept) 101 AD2d 207, 475 NYS2d 869. However, where the delays are caused by mutual fault of the parties, the liquidated damage clause is abrogated and the party must resort to recovery for actual damages. *Babylon Associates v County of Suffolk, supra*.

A litigant may not recover damages for the amounts expended in the successful prosecution of his rights. *Lavorato v Bethlehem Steel Corp.* (1983, 4th Dept) 91 AD2d 1184, 459 NYS2d 170.

A claim by defendant that a different measure of damages would yield a lesser award presents a mitigation issue, and the burden falls on the defendant to prove that a lesser amount than that claimed by plaintiffs would sufficiently compensate them for their loss. *Alford v Niagara Mohawk Power Corp.* (1985, 3d Dept) 115 AD2d 924, 496 NYS2d 820.

When a case is submitted to the jury under two separate theories of liability, a plaintiff is entitled to only one recovery with respect to an identical damage claim. *Leighty v Brunn* (1986, 2d Dept) 125 AD2d 648, 510 NYS2d 174.

A defendant whose answer is stricken as a result of a default, admits all traversable allegations in the complaint including the basic allegation of liability, but does not admit plaintiff's conclusion as to damages; when a default judgment is entered against a defendant, after application to the Court, the defendant is entitled to a full opportunity to cross-examine witnesses, give testimony and offer proof in mitigation of damages. *Napolitano v Branks* (1987, 2d Dept) 128 AD2d 686, 513 NYS2d 185.

§ 29:2 AMOUNT DEMANDED IN COMPLAINT — A motion made by a plaintiff to increase the amount of relief requested in the *ad damnum* clause of the complaint, whether made before or after the verdict, may be granted in the absence of prejudice to the defendant. *Loomis v Civetta Corinno Constr. Corp.* (1981) 54 NY2d 18, 444 NYS2d 571, reh den 55 NY2d 801, 447 NYS2d 436.

An application for leave to amend a complaint to increase the *ad damnum* clause rests in the sound discretion of the court. While leave to amend the *ad damnum* clause should be liberally granted, it is not automatic. A motion to amend must be supported by a proper showing by the plaintiff regarding the merits of a request for the amendment, and an explanation for the failure to initially assert the amount of damages now sought. *Century Resources Corp. v Weir* (1987, 2d Dept) 134 AD2d 398, 521 NYS2d 28.

Although a motion to amend the *ad damnum* clause, even after the verdict has been rendered, is addressed to the discretion of the trial court, in the absence of a formal motion to amend the *ad damnum* clause, damages must be limited to the amount sought in the complaint. *Reid v Weir-Metro Ambulance Serv., Inc.* (1993, 1st Dept) 191 AD2d 309, 595 NYS2d 40.

The Departments of the Appellate Division are divided on the question of the extent of counsel's right to request or suggest specific dollar amounts in summation arguments in personal injury actions. Traditionally, counsel has been permitted to request a specific dollar amount, so long as the amount requested was within the amount stated in the *ad damnum* clause. *Tate v Colabello* (1983) 58 NY2d 84, 459 NYS2d 422. The split in authority arises from the question of whether the right derives from the presence of a specific dollar amount in an *ad damnum* clause, or counsel's right to make fair comment on the evidence, or both.

In actions where *ad damnum* clauses have been prohibited by CPLR 3017(c), *i.e.*, actions for medical or dental malpractice and actions against municipal corporations, the First Department holds that the trial court may permit counsel to suggest an amount, but must bar counsel from referring to the pleadings in so doing. *Garcia v New York* (1991, 1st Dept) 173 AD2d 175, 569 NYS2d 27. The Second Department holds that counsel must be permitted to request a reasonable amount, and that the trial court's denial of that right constitutes reversible error. *Braun v Ahmed* (1987, 2d Dept) 127 AD2d 418, 515 NYS2d 473. The Third Department holds the opposite, that is, that reference to a specific amount in a case controlled by CPLR 3017(c) constitutes reversible error. *Bechard v Eisinger* (1984, 3d Dept) 105 AD2d 939, 481 NYS2d 906; *Bagailuk v Weiss* (1985, 3d Dept) 110 AD2d 284, 494 NYS2d 205. The Court of Appeals has declined to resolve this split in authority, in an appeal from the First Department, where the issue had not been raised in the Appellate Division. *McDougald v Garber* (1989) 73 NY2d 246, 538 NYS2d 937.

§ 29:3   NOMINAL DAMAGES — Nominal damages are damages in name only, having no substance, but which nevertheless vindicate the plaintiff's right. *Walters v Geheran* (1959, Sup) 192 NYS2d 23.

In equity, a judgment awarding nominal damages may be granted where necessary to preserve rights and to prevent possible breaches in the future. *Henry Hof, Inc. v Noll* (1948) 273 AD 361, 77 NYS2d 484, affd 299 NY 588.

Because the plaintiff has the burden of proving the extent of the injury and the amount of damages, *Burke, Kuipers & Mahoney, Inc. v Dallas Dispatch Co.* (1938) 253 AD 206, 1 NYS2d 674, if the plaintiff fails to sustain this burden of proof by competent evidence, recovery will be confined to nominal damages, even though the plaintiff has a good cause of action. *Walters v Geheran, supra.*

Despite the purchaser's failure to establish damages, the purchaser is still entitled to nominal damages to vindicate its rights derived from the fraud and breach of warranty practiced upon it. *Clearview Concrete Products Corp. v S. Charles Gherardi, Inc.* (1982, 2d Dept) 88 AD2d 461, 453 NYS2d 750.

Nominal damages imply the existence of actual damages. *Hunt v State* (1986, 4th Dept) 117 AD2d 1005, 499 NYS2d 294.

§ 29:4　LIQUIDATED DAMAGES AND PENALTIES — Liquidated damages constitute compensation that the parties to a contract have agreed should be paid to satisfy any loss or injury flowing from a breach of the contract. *Truck Rent-A-Center, Inc. v Puritan Farms 2nd, Inc.* (1977) 41 NY2d 420, 393 NYS2d 365.

In effect, a liquidated damages provision is an estimate by the parties, when they make their agreement, of the extent of the injury likely to be sustained if the agreement is breached. *Truck Rent-A-Center, Inc. v Puritan Farms 2nd, Inc., supra.* However, a provision requiring, in the event of a breach, the payment of a sum of money grossly disproportionate to the amount of actual damages is a penalty and cannot be enforced. *Truck Rent-A-Center, Inc. v Puritan Farms 2nd, Inc., supra.*

Parties to a contract may agree among themselves on the amount in damages that would be suffered on a breach of the contract, and this stipulation will normally be enforced unless it is unconscionable or contrary to public policy. *M. Viaggio & Sons, Inc. v New York* (1985, 2d Dept) 114 AD2d 939, 495 NYS2d 680.

For a liquidated damages clause to be enforceable, the amount of the actual loss needs to be difficult to ascertain, the stipulated sum should be a reasonable pre-estimate of the damages as interpreted from the date of the making of the contract, and the disproportion between the stipulated sum and the actual damages must not be so large that it is inequitable. *Cole v Lawas* (1986, 3d Dept) 116 AD2d 936, 498 NYS2d 512.

A liquidated damage provision normally precludes recovery of the actual damages. *Mars Associates, Inc. v Facilities Dev. Corp.* (1986, 3d Dept) 124 AD2d 291, 508 NYS2d 87.

A plaintiff, who purchased a boat pursuant to a contract allowing the manufacturer of the boat to retain the cash deposit as liquidated damages if the contract was canceled for any reason other than an increase in price, was entitled to the return of the downpayment when the manufacturer increased the price during construction. *Rogers v Maiorano* (1988, 2d Dept) 140 AD2d 596, 528 NYS2d 861.

When there is doubt about whether a provision constitutes an unenforceable penalty or a proper liquidated damage clause, it should be resolved in favor of a construction that holds the provision to be a penalty. *Willner v Willner* (1989, 2d Dept) 145 AD2d 236, 538 NYS2d 599.

Causes of action for liquidated damages based on contractual provisions lacking a reasonable relationship to the potential losses the plaintiff may have sustained are, in substance, seeking a penalty and should be dismissed. *Propoco, Inc. v Birnbaum* (1990, 2d Dept) 157 AD2d 774, 550 NYS2d 901; *see also, Mid-Atlantic Autec v Keeler Motor Car Co.* (1993, 3d Dept) 199 AD2d 732, 605 NYS2d 447.

In an action brought by a medical group against a former employee based on a restrictive covenant in the employment agreement, in light of the permanent injunction granted to the employer, an award of one year's gross medical fees as liquidated damages pursuant to the employment agreement would be so disproportionate to the employer's loss that it would have constituted an unenforceable penalty. *Novendstern v Mt. Kisco Medical Group* (1991, 2d Dept) 177 AD2d 623, 576 NYS2d 329.

A contract provision for liquidated damages controls the rights of the parties in the event of breach, notwithstanding that the stipulated sum may be less than the actual damages allegedly sustained. *Smith v Putnam* (1988, 1st Dept) 145 AD2d 383, 535 NYS2d 725.

Even if liquidated damages clauses are unenforceable as constituting a penalty, plaintiff is permitted to prove and recover its actual damages if it establishes that the contracts were breached. *AP Propane, Inc. v Sperbeck* (1990, 3d Dept) 157 AD2d 27, 555 NYS2d 211, affd 77 NY2d 886, 568 NYS2d 908.

In an action arising out of a $630,000 contract for the sale of a cooperative apartment, where the purchasers breached the contract, the seller was entitled to retain the down payment of $63,500; because the sellers sold the same apartment some seven months later for $625,000, liquidated damages in the amount of $63,500 could not be deemed unreasonably large. *Wojciechowski v Birnbaum* (1993, 1st Dept) 191 AD2d 247, 595 NYS2d 3.

§ 29:5 DUTY TO MINIMIZE DAMAGES — An injured person is under a duty to make reasonable efforts to do what an ordinarily prudent person would do toward minimizing damages. *Coyle v Serafini Constr. Co.* (1957) 8 Misc 2d 807, 167 NYS2d

680. The plaintiff must show that he has done all he reasonably could to reduce or minimize consequential damages. *Consolidated Box Co. v Penn* (1958) 15 Misc 2d 705, 180 NYS2d 831.

All that is required, however, is that the injured person do what is reasonable under the circumstances. *Architector Co. v Slomon* (1948) 192 Misc 318, 80 NYS2d 590. The injured party is under no obligation to take extraordinary or costly measures, the efficacy of which is doubtful. *Consolidated Box Co. v Penn, supra.* The failure of an injured party to make a reasonable effort to minimize damages that result from negligence does not completely bar recovery but results in preventing recovery of those damages that might have been avoided by a reasonable effort on the part of the injured party. *Consolidated Box Co. v Penn, supra.*

When a plaintiff's background indicated that he was capable of obtaining non-physical employment, damages for impairment of earning capacity should have been calculated on the basis of a partial impairment of earning capacity. *Senko v Fonda* (1976, 2d Dept) 53 AD2d 638, 384 NYS2d 849.

The duty of an injured party to minimize damages does not require that he point out to the wrongdoer ways to soften the blow that are available only to the wrongdoer, and that are as well known and obvious to the wrongdoer as to the injured party. *Gonzales v Colonial Trust Co.* (1957) 7 Misc 2d 508, 162 NYS2d 754, affd (1st Dept) 6 AD2d 679, 174 NYS2d 444, reh and app den (1st Dept) 6 AD2d 790, 175 NYS2d 567 and motion den (1st Dept) 6 AD2d 790, 175 NYS2d 568 and app dismd 5 NY2d 779, 180 NYS2d 300.

To prevent a recovery of full consequential damages on the ground that the injured party willfully or negligently failed to minimize the damages, the burden is on the wrongdoer to prove the willful or negligent failure to mitigate damages, and it is incumbent on the wrongdoer to show that the damages would in fact have been diminished if certain measures had been taken. *Consolidated Box Co. v Penn, supra.*

The duty to minimize damages requires that an effort be made in good faith, it must be conducted with reasonable skill, prudence and efficiency, it must be reasonably warranted by and proportioned to the injury and consequences to be avoided, and it must be made under a reasonably justified belief that it will avoid or reduce the damages otherwise to be apprehended from the wrong. *Den Norske Ameriekalinje Actiesselskabet v Sun Printing & Publishing Ass'n* (1919) 226 NY 1, 122 NE 463. The injured party is not bound to commit fraud or trespass or to do what, under the given circumstances, would be imprudent. *People's Gas & Electric Co. v State* (1919) 189 AD 421, 179 NYS 520, affd 231 NY 520, 132 NE 871.

Although a plaintiff, who sustained a loss when art works belonging to him were stolen, was entitled to recover the amount paid as a reward in order to procure the return of most of the stolen merchandise, he had a duty to minimize damages by paying the smallest reward possible. *Kraut v Morgan & Bro. Manhattan Storage Co.* (1974, 1st Dept) 46 AD2d 19, 360 NYS2d 889, affd 38 NY2d 445, 381 NYS2d 25, 80 ALR3d 249.

A person is not under an absolute obligation to follow the advice of a physician in order to minimize damages, but rather, his duty in this respect is only to use ordinary care in following the advice. *Fafard v Ajamian* (1978, 2d Dept) 60 AD2d 853, 400 NYS2d 856.

Expenditures incurred by an insured in mitigation of damages must be made in the reasonable expectation of reducing the amount of the loss; expenditures that result in an increased loss cannot be justified. *Howard Stores Corp. v Foremost Ins. Co.* (1981, 1st Dept) 82 AD2d 398, 441 NYS2d 674, affd 56 NY2d 991, 453 NYS2d 682.

A plaintiff who failed to seek vocational rehabilitation for his injured knee was entitled to only $300,000 and not the $600,000 that the jury awarded him, in the absence of a showing that the failure to seek rehabilitation was reasonable. *Bell v Shopwell, Inc.* (1986, 2d Dept) 119 AD2d 715, 501 NYS2d 129.

A party injured by a breach of contract is required to make a reasonable effort to mitigate its damages, and the question of whether that party acted reasonably to mitigate its damages is a question of fact. *Tynan Incinerator Co. v International Fidelity Ins. Co.* (1986, 2d Dept) 117 AD2d 796, 499 NYS2d 118.

Plaintiff, who was struck by a tractor trailer, had a duty to mitigate damages by endeavoring to seek alternate employment, and, therefore, an award for $600,000 for lost earnings was excessive to the extent that it exceeded $360,000. *McLaurin v Ryder Truck Rental* (1986, 2d Dept) 123 AD2d 671, 507 NYS2d 41.

The plaintiff's jury award for future medical, nursing and custodial expenses in the amount of $9,915,927.25 for 20.2 years of anticipated life expectancy did not warrant a reduction, where 24-hour nursing care estimated at a yearly cost of $349,073 would be required and plaintiff had sustained chronic subdural hematomas, severe cerebral encephalopathy, fractures of the twelfth thoracic, sixth and seventh cervical vertebrae and fractures of the tenth, eleventh and twelfth left ribs, was in a comatose state for nine weeks following admission to the hospital, underwent a tracheotomy and a gastrostomy and in addition was diagnosed as suffering from incomplete paraplegia and incontinency of the bowel and bladder and had to be fed, clothed and diaper-changed. *Harvey v Mazal American Partners* (1992, 1st Dept) 179 AD2d 1, 581 NYS2d 748.

In the case of a plaintiff who sustained an injury to her oscalcis, a bone in the area of the heel, as a result of an automobile accident, an award of $40,000 for future pain and suffering was not inadequate where the testimony indicated that the pain associated with plaintiff's injury could have been greatly relieved, if not eliminated, by a surgical procedure, which plaintiff declined. *Florsz v Ogruk* (1992, 2d Dept) 184 AD2d 546, 585 NYS2d 220.

Failure to use an available seat belt is to be considered in mitigation of damages, and should not be considered by the triers of fact in resolving the issue of liability. *Stein v Penatello* (1992, 2d Dept) 185 AD2d 976, 587 NYS2d 37.

There is no duty to mitigate damages in a commercial lease setting. *11 Park Place Assocs. v Barnes* (1994, 1st Dept) 202 AD2d 292, 608 NYS2d 664.

§ 29:6 DAMAGES FOR FUTURE EFFECTS OF AN INJURY
— Those consequential damages that may reasonably be anticipated to flow from an injury may be included in a recovery for the original injury, even though not existing at the time of the trial. *Schmidt v Merchants Despatch Transp. Co.* (1936) 270 NY 287, 200 NE 824, 104 ALR 450, reh den 271 NY 531.

In an infant's action for personal injuries, future medical expenses are recoverable, *Capasso v Square Sanitarium* (1956) 3 Misc 2d 273, 155 NYS2d 313, and the jury may estimate the damages to the parent for the prospective loss of services of the infant during the child's minority. *Capasso v Square Sanitarium, supra.*

A claim for damages for diminution in the amount of milk produced from a dairy is too speculative and conjectural to be included as an item of damages for the failure of a village to provide water to farm buildings and to the premises of an owner pursuant to a contract. *Strough v Conley* (1939) 257 AD 1057, 13 NYS2d 606, affd 283 NY 631. A prospective borrower was held not entitled under the circumstances to recover as damages for breach of contract to make a loan, the estimated expenses including a bonus paid for obtaining a loan. *Avalon Const. Corp. v Kirch Holding Co.* (1931) 256 NY 137, 175 NE 651.

Damages for the prospective consequences of a tortious injury are recoverable only if the prospective consequences may with reasonable probability be expected to flow from the past harm. Consequences that are contingent, speculative or merely possible are not properly considered in ascertaining damages. *Askey v Occidental Chemical Corp.* (1984, 4th Dept) 102 AD2d 130, 477 NYS2d 242.

To the extent that the award, in the case of a plaintiff whose legs were severed by a New York City Transit Authority subway train after he fell from the station platform, exceeded $1,300,000 for plaintiff's past and future pain and suffering the award was excessive. *Young Chung v New York City Transit Authority* (1992, 2d Dept) 183 AD2d 741, 583 NYS2d 476.

Where, as a result of an automobile accident, the plaintiff developed a dark spot or scotoma in the center of the field of vision of his left eye, and the injury to the eye was permanent, a verdict awarding the plaintiff $20,000 for past pain and suffering and nothing for future damages, deviated materially from what would be reasonable compensation. *Irizarry v Raybern Bus Service, Inc.* (1992, 2d Dept) 183 AD2d 872, 584 NYS2d 591.

An award of $800,000 for past and future pain and suffering associated with the comminuted fracture of plaintiff's arm, and for the resulting 10-inch keloidal scar, shortening of the arm, and atrophy, although perhaps on the high side, did not constitute a material deviation from what would be reasonable compensation. *Martinez v Gouverneur Gardens Housing Corp.* (1992, 1st Dept) 184 AD2d 264, 585 NYS2d 23, app den 80 NY2d 759, 591 NYS2d 137.

§ 29:7 LIABILITY FOR AGGRAVATION OF AN INJURY — A tortfeasor is liable for the enhancement or aggravation of an injury that was caused by, or a physical impairment that is due to, the original tort. *Rasa v New York* (1950, Sup) 95 NYS2d 291, mod 277 AD 780, 97 NYS2d 520. A person whose negligence caused an injury is liable for damages that result therefrom even though the mistake or the negligence of a physician who treated the injury increased the amount of damages. *Milks v McIver* (1934) 264 NY 267, 190 NE 487.

When a person is injured by the negligence of another and, despite the exercise of ordinary diligence in the treatment of injuries, the individual is involved in another accident because of the injuries sustained in the first accident, the tortfeasor in the first accident is also responsible for the subsequent injuries. *Daliendo v Johnson* (1989, 2d Dept) 147 AD2d 312, 543 NYS2d 987.

Where a plaintiff sustained a brain concussion as the result of a fall due to the defendant's negligence, and as a result of the fall she had dizzy spells, one of which caused her to have a second fall that injured her again, the defendant was liable to her for the injuries sustained in the second fall. *Enslein v Hudson & M. R. Co.* (1957) 8 Misc 2d 87, 165 NYS2d 630, affd in part and revd in part (2d Dept) 6 AD2d 833, 176 NYS2d 70, affd 6 NY2d 723, 185 NYS2d 810.

A person who injures another is not a joint tortfeasor with a physician whose negligence thereafter aggravates the original injury. Instead, the malpractice coalesces with the original injury and the two independent wrongs have become concurrent causes of the ultimate result, and the original wrongdoer may then be held responsible for the entire damage. *Kropp v De Angelis* (1955, Sup) 138 NYS2d 188.

One who negligently injures another, and the physician whose negligence thereafter aggravates the original injury, are successive rather than joint tortfeasors, and a plaintiff has a separate cause of action against each of them. *Abernethy v Azzoni* (1974) 78 Misc 2d 832, 358 NYS2d 264. However, a plaintiff may not obtain a double recovery. *Abernethy v Azzoni, supra.*

The owner and driver of the automobile that injured the plaintiff were liable not only for the negligent operation of their vehicle, but also for the reasonably foreseeable aggravation of plaintiff's condition by subsequent acts of malpractice. *Dubicki v Maresco* (1978, 2d Dept) 64 AD2d 645, 407 NYS2d 66.

When the negligent act of defendant is the reasonable and proximate cause of the injury, he is liable for all the harm and suffering that his negligent act has brought on, even though the injuries were aggravated by the plaintiff's predisposition or weakness or by the intervening mistake or negligence of the physician who treated the original injury. *Poplar v Bourjois, Inc.* (1948) 298 NY 62, 80 NE2d 334.

When the defendant's negligence does not cause a diseased condition but only aggravates the severity of a condition that existed at the time of the injury, the plaintiff may recover only for the portion of increased suffering that is the natural and probable consequence of the defendant's acts. *Beaudoin v State* (1960) 24 Misc 2d 962, 207 NYS2d 348. Where the negligence of a bus operator was the reasonable and proximate cause of the aggravation of plaintiff's injuries, the owner of the bus was liable for all the harm and suffering caused by the negligent act, including the aggravation of plaintiff's prior injuries. *Gonzalez v New York City Omnibus Corp.* (1956, Sup) 150 NYS2d 722, affd (1st Dept) 2 AD2d 963, 158 NYS2d 739.

Aggravation of a pre-existing condition is an element of special damages, and must be both pleaded and proven before recovery can be allowed. *Behan v Data Probe International, Inc.* (1995, 2d Dept) 213 AD2d 439, 623 NYS2d 886.

§ 29:8   LIABILITY FOR EXEMPLARY DAMAGES — The primary purpose of exemplary damages is not compensation of the victim, but to punish the wrongdoer and to provide an example to others. Such damages may be awarded only when and to the extent that the wrongdoer has acted wantonly, maliciously or with a recklessness that betokens improper motive or vindictiveness. *Douglas v Tomkins Realty Corp.* (1960) 28 Misc 2d 192, 210 NYS2d 550. Punitive damages are generally granted as punishment to the defendant and as protection for society against the violation of personal rights and social order. *De Marasse v Wolf* (1955, Sup) 140 NYS2d 235.

An award of compensatory damages depends on the commission of a wrongdoing, whereas the award of punitive damages depends on the object or the purpose of the wrongdoing. *James v Powell* (1967) 19 NY2d 249, 279 NYS2d 10. It is not the form of the action that gives the jury the right to award punitive damages, but the moral culpability of the defendant. *Walker v Sheldon* (1961) 10 NY2d 401, 223 NYS2d 488. Although an award of exemplary damages is punitive, it is a private remedial measure rather than a public criminal sanction. *Soucy v Greyhound Corp.* (1967, 3d Dept) 27 AD2d 112, 276 NYS2d 173. Although it was formerly held that equity functions went no further than to award damages as an incident to other relief and that punitive damages would not be awarded in an equity case, *Fullerton v Kennedy* (1959) 19 Misc 2d 502, 187 NYS2d 213, this rule forbidding the combination of equitable relief with punitive damages, has been overruled. *I. H. P. Corp. v 210 Cent. Park South Corp.* (1962, 1st Dept) 16 AD2d 461, 228 NYS2d 883, affd 12 NY2d 329, 239 NYS2d 547.

A claim for punitive damages does not constitute a separate cause of action. *Clifton Park v Rivercrest Sewerage Disposal Corp.* (1981, 3d Dept) 81 AD2d 982, 440 NYS2d 85. Punitive damages are but an incident of damages. *Isaacs v Interboro Mut. Indem. Ins. Co.* (1980, 1st Dept) 73 AD2d 850, 423 NYS2d 191.

Punitive damages ordinarily may be awarded only in cases where the wrong complained of is morally culpable, or is actuated by evil or reprehensible motives, not to punish the defendant, but to deter him, as well as others, who might otherwise be so prompted, from indulging in similar conduct in the future. *H & R Hats & Novelties, Inc. v Citibank, N.A.* (1984, 1st Dept) 102 AD2d 742, 477 NYS2d 9, later app (1st Dept) 104 AD2d 775, 481 NYS2d 310.

There is no necessary relationship between compensatory and punitive damages, and punitive damages may be granted even though compensatory damages are denied. *Cherno v Bank of Babylon* (1967) 54 Misc 2d 277, 282 NYS2d 114, 4 UCCRS 505, affd 29 AD2d 767, 288 NYS2d 862. Neither the fact that only nominal damages are awarded nor the amount of those damages prevents an award of exemplary damages as a deterrent against a repetition of improper conduct and as a warning to others. *Underwriters' Laboratories, Inc. v Smith* (1964) 41 Misc 2d 756, 246 NYS2d 436. When a defendant has acted maliciously, the jury may award damages that express indignation at the defendant's wrong rather than a value set on the plaintiff's loss. *Gostkowski v Roman Catholic Church of Sacred Hearts of Jesus & Mary* (1933) 262 NY 320, 186 NE 798. Unless wrongful motive exists or there was intentional wrong doing or reckless indifference amounting thereto, there is no basis for an award of punitive damages. *Gordon v Nationwide Mut. Ins. Co.* (1970) 62 Misc 2d 689, 309 NYS2d 420, affd (2d Dept) 37 AD2d 265, 323 NYS2d 550, revd on other grounds 30 NY2d 427, 334 NYS2d 601, cert den 410 US 931, 35 L Ed 2d 593, 93 S Ct 1374. When an intentional offense has not been committed but the party has done only what he believes to be his duty, punishment is not deserved and there is no basis for punitive damages. *De Marasse v Wolf* (1955, Sup) 140 NYS2d 235.

Punitive damages are inappropriate where plaintiff has not made a showing that the wrong complained of is morally culpable or is actuated by evil and reprehensible motives. *Hollender v Trump Village Cooperative* (1983, 2d Dept) 97 AD2d 812, 468 NYS2d 683.

Punitive damages generally are not recoverable where the alleged wrong was a private wrong as opposed to one aimed at the public generally. *H & R Hats & Novelties, Inc. v Citibank, N.A.* (1984, 1st Dept) 102 AD2d 742, 477 NYS2d 9, later app (1st Dept) 104 AD2d 775, 481 NYS2d 310.

Punitive damages are properly awarded where the tortious act complained of involves a wanton or reckless disregard of plaintiff's rights and may be awarded against corporations as well as against individuals. *Giblin v Murphy* (1983, 3d Dept) 97 AD2d 668, 469 NYS2d 211.

A parent cannot recover punitive damages when the injury is primarily to the infant. *Pickle v Page* (1929) 225 AD 454, 233 NYS 461, affd 252 NY 474, 169 NE 650, 72 ALR 842. The state is not subject to punitive damages. *McCandless v State* (1956) 6 Misc 2d 391, 166 NYS2d 272, mod in part and revd in part (3d Dept) 3 AD2d 600, 162 NYS2d 570, affd 4 NY2d 797, 173 NYS2d 30. *Sharapata v Islip* (1981, 2d Dept) 82 AD2d 350, 441 NYS2d 275, affd 56 NY2d 332, 452 NYS2d 347.

The publishers of a book in which the nude photograph of a professional model appeared without her consent were held to have knowingly published the photograph within the meaning of the Civil Rights Law so as to be liable for punitive damages, where the publishers merely assumed that the permission for the publication of the photograph had been obtained from the model by the agency from whom the publishers purchased the photograph. *Myers v U. S. Camera Publishing Corp.* (1957) 9 Misc 2d 765, 167 NYS2d 771; Civil Rights Law §§ 50, 51.

In an action between a landlord and a tenant, the death of the latter precludes the recovery of punitive damages against his personal representative. *Gordon v Nathan* (1974, 1st Dept) 43 AD2d 917, 352 NYS2d 464.

The prohibition against the award of punitive damages by an arbitrator renders such an award void because it is in violation of public policy, even if the "malicious" conduct would have permitted the imposition of punitive damages by a court or jury. *Garrity v Lyle Stuart, Inc.* (1976) 40 NY2d 354, 386 NYS2d 831, 83 ALR3d 1024.

Punitive damages are not available for a mere breach of contract because there, only a private wrong and not a public right is involved. *M. S. R. Associates, Ltd. v Consolidated Mut. Ins. Co.* (1977, 2d Dept) 58 AD2d 858, 396 NYS2d 684.

A defendant who resists a claim for punitive damages may show his or its lack of wealth. *Hartford Acci. & Indem. Co. v Hempstead* (1979) 48 NY2d 218, 422 NYS2d 47.

Exemplary damages should not be awarded where the record, taken as a whole, fails to demonstrate that defendant exhibited the high degree of moral turpitude that would justify the award of such damages. *O'Connor v Lempicky* (1981, 2d Dept) 81 AD2d 860, 438 NYS2d 868.

In a defamation action brought by a village building inspector resulting from publication in a newspaper of an accusation that the plaintiff had solicited a bribe, defendant's claim that punitive damages were inappropriate was without merit, because defendant acknowledged several times during the trial that there was a "feud" going on between officials of the village and himself. *Dattner v Pokoik* (1981, 2d Dept) 81 AD2d 572, 437 NYS2d 425, app dismd 54 NY2d 750, 442 NYS2d 996.

Defendant's use in a commercial of an actor's performance after expiration of the period during which the actor had consented to its use, justified punitive damages under a statute that permits the award of such damages in the discretion of the jury if the defendant has knowingly used plaintiff's name, portrait or picture in such a manner as is declared unlawful by the statute. *Welch v Mr. Christmas, Inc.* (1982, 1st Dept) 85 AD2d 74, 447 NYS2d 252, affd 57 NY2d 143, 454 NYS2d 971.

While it is true that, in a proper case, exemplary damages may be awarded as punishment by reason of the aggravated nature of a wrongful act, to prevent repetition by serving as a warning to others and to protect the public, multiple or treble damages are not allowable in the absence of a statute. *Springer v Viking Press* (1982, 1st Dept) 90 AD2d 315, 457 NYS2d 246, affd 60 NY2d 916, 470 NYS2d 579.

Punitive damages are not recoverable for a private breach of contract where a public right is not sought to be vindicated or morally culpable conduct deterred. *Niagara Falls v Hartford Fire Ins. Co.* (1986, 4th Dept) 116 AD2d 1019, 498 NYS2d 714.

In a wrongful death action, where the trial court explicitly found that the punitive damages of $45,000 awarded by the jury were not excessive nor the result of passion, it was improper for the court to set the damages aside because it concluded that it would be unfair to the defendant to let them stand because he had not adequately understood his exposure to uninsured liability; this is not an appropriate remedy for that problem. *Wittman v Gilson* (1986, 4th Dept) 120 AD2d 964, 503 NYS2d 214, affd (1988) 70 NY2d 970, 525 NYS2d 795.

An award of punitive damages against a defendant in a civil action following a criminal conviction arising out of the same drunk driving incident does not violate the constitutional prohibition against double jeopardy; while punitive damages and criminal sanctions share a common purpose of punishing misconduct, there are significant distinctions between the two. Unlike the sanction imposed on behalf of all the people of the State in a criminal case, punitive damages in a civil case context afford the injured party a personal monetary recovery over and above the compensatory loss. The procedures and standards of proof are very different for each, and a civil verdict directing payment of punitive damages does not carry the same heavy societal stigma that is stamped by a criminal conviction no matter what sentence is imposed. *Wittman v Gilson* (1988) 70 NY2d 970, 525 NYS2d 795.

A valid cause of action for compensatory damages is a necessary predicate to a demand for punitive damages; it is improper to interpose a claim for punitive damages as a separate cause of action. *Bishop v Bostick* (1988, 2d Dept) 141 AD2d 487, 529 NYS2d 116.

Punitive damages are allowable in tort cases so long as the very high threshold of moral culpability is satisfied. *Giblin v Murphy* (1988) 73 NY2d 769, 536 NYS2d 54.

In a defamation action, punitive damages may be recoverable where defendant's liability is based on a showing of knowledge of falsity of remarks, or reckless disregard for the truth. *600 West 115th Street Corp. v Von Gutfeld* (1991, 1st Dept) 572 NYS2d 655.

If the acting national editor of defendant's newspaper deliberately altered a news article, misidentifying plaintiff, a former employee of defendant, as a suspected burglar, such conduct would constitute actual malice justifying imposition of punitive damages. *Kostolecki v Buffalo Courier Express Co.* (1990, 4th Dept) 163 AD2d 856, 558 NYS2d 385.

Allegations by plaintiff that defendant had been dishonest with respect to disclosure of who was driving the truck at the time of the accident, and whether another person was present in the truck, were not sufficient to support an award of punitive damages; the wrongful conduct in the course of disclosure is not connected to the underlying tort, and therefore should not be subject to an award of damages. *Levy v Bronx County Carting Co.* (1991, 1st Dept) 172 AD2d 356, 568 NYS2d 774.

It is imperative that an award for punitive damages bear a reasonable relationship to a defendant's culpability. *Parkin v Cornell University Inc.* (1992, 3d Dept) 182 AD2d 850, 581 NYS2d 914, app dismd 80 NY2d 914, 588 NYS2d 821.

Punitive damages may be awarded when the defendant's conduct has a high degree of moral culpability. The conduct need not be intentional; it is sufficient if it is so reckless or wantonly negligent as to be the equivalent of a conscious disregard of the rights of others. *Rinaldo v Mashayekhi* (1992, 3d Dept) 185 AD2d 435, 585 NYS2d 615. Although driving while intoxicated alone may not be sufficient to justify the imposition of punitive damages, where defendant operated his vehicle with a blood alcohol level of .19, almost twice the threshold level for driving while intoxicated, drove by his own admission at a speed of 35 to 40 miles per hour in a 30-mile-per-hour speed zone, did not complete the recital of the alphabet in the course of a field sobriety test, could not walk a straight line, stand on one foot or touch his finger to his nose, and had driven directly into the rear of plaintiff's vehicle without taking any action whatsoever to avoid the collision, the jury could have concluded that defendant completely disregarded the obvious presence of plaintiff and other users of the highway, and this sufficiently established wanton negligence and recklessness on defendant's part to warrant an award of punitive damages. *Rinaldo v Mashayekhi, supra.*

The evidentiary standard for approving entitlement to punitive damages is a preponderance of the evidence, not clear and convincing evidence. *Re Seventh Judicial Dist. Asbestos Litig.* (1993, 4th Dept) 190 AD2d 1068, 593 NYS2d 685.

§ 29:9   THE AMOUNT OF EXEMPLARY DAMAGES — There is no rigid formula by which the amount of punitive damages is fixed, although such damages should bear some reasonable relation to the harm caused and to the flagrancy of the conduct causing the harm. *I. H. P. Corp. v 210 Cent. Park South Corp.* (1962, 1st Dept) 16 AD2d 461, 228 NYS2d 883, affd 12 NY2d 329, 239

NYS2d 547. Where a tenant brought an action against the land-lord to restrain interference with the tenant's quiet use of the leased premises for a restaurant, an award of exemplary damages three times the amount of actual damages sustained by the tenant was held to be proper. *I. H. P. Corp. v 210 Cent. Park South Corp.,* *supra.*

The fact of a defendant's wealth is relevant in assessing puni-tive damages, even though it has no place in assessing an award for compensatory damages. *Varriale v Saratoga Harness Racing, Inc.* (1980, 3d Dept) 76 AD2d 991, 429 NYS2d 302.

No fixed measure of damages is applicable to punitive damages, but such damages must vary to suit the circumstances of each case, and ought to be reasonably proportioned to the injury done. *De Marasse v Wolf* (1955, Sup) 140 NYS2d 235.

Although the Appellate Division or the trial court judge may exercise their own discretionary authority to overturn an excessive jury award for punitive damages, the amount of such damages awarded by a jury should not be reduced by a court unless it is so grossly excessive as to show by its very exorbitance that it was actuated by passion. *Nardelli v Stamberg* (1978) 44 NY2d 500, 406 NYS2d 443. A verdict for punitive damages should be kept within reasonable bounds considering the purpose to be achieved as well as the *mala fides* of the defendant in the particular case. *Nellis v Miller* (1984, 4th Dept) 101 AD2d 1002, 477 NYS2d 72.

§ 29:10 GENERAL AND SPECIAL DAMAGES — Fundamen-tally, damages are intended to provide compensation to the victim of a wrong commensurate with the amount of the loss or injury sustained as a result thereof. *J. B. Preston Co. v Funkhouser* (1933) 261 NY 140, 87 ALR 459 reh den 261 NY 639, 87 ALR 462 and affd 290 US 163. Compensatory damages may be either special damages, which are damages that really take place but are not implied by law, *Dumont v Smith* (1947) 4 Denio 319, or gen-eral damages, which are damages naturally resulting from the wrongful act complained of, that are implied or presumed by the law to have resulted from the act. *W. C. Loftus & Co. v Bennett* (1902) 68 AD 128, 74 NYS 290.

While special damages may serve to aid the court and the jury in determining and reviewing the amount of a damage award, they are not controlling factors in circumstances where there is uncontradicted medical testimony as to an injury. *Becker v Ginsberg* (1965, 3d Dept) 23 AD2d 916, 258 NYS2d 886.

In an action that constitutes a *prima facie* tort, only special damages are recoverable. *Firester v Lipson* (1966) 15 Misc 2d 527, 270 NYS2d 844.

There is no absolute distinction between general and special damages, but damages that may be termed general with respect to one type of contract may be classified as special with respect to another. *Kerr S.S. Co. v Radio Corp. of America* (1927) 245 NY 284, 157 NE 140, 55 ALR 1139, reh den 245 NY 620, 157 NE 882 and cert den 275 US 557, 72 L Ed 424, 48 S Ct 118. Special damages may include such items as loss of prospective profits. *Hunt v Engels Tractor Co.* (1933) 238 AD 758, 261 NYS 837.

§ 29:11   PROOF OF DAMAGES — Damages must be proved and will not be presumed, even though a wrong, such as a breach of contract, is shown. *Mohawk Nat. Bank v Citizens Trust Co.* (1963) 38 Misc 2d 222, 237 NYS2d 956. The person who claims damages has the burden of proving them. *Penn Yan Urban Renewal Agency v Penn Yan Realty Corp.* (1968) 57 Misc 2d 1033, 294 NYS2d 66. The plaintiff has the burden of proving damages by competent evidence, and the jury should be instructed accordingly. *Kauders v Gorki* (1957) 8 Misc 2d 948, 160 NYS2d 975. Plaintiff, who has the burden of establishing damages must adopt and present to the court a proper method for ascertaining the amount. *Walter Janvier, Inc. v Baker* (1930) 229 AD 679, 243 NYS 173.

When one party adopts one method for establishing damages, it then becomes the obligation of the other party to establish on the basis of some other theory that the damages were less. *Mesler v Cozzolino* (1955) 208 Misc 54, 144 NYS2d 417.

A party who has breached a contract has the burden of proving that damages could have been prevented. *Losei Realty Corp. v New York* (1930) 254 NY 41, 171 NE 899.

While a plaintiff is required to mitigate damages on the breach of a contract, the burden of proving that there was a lack of diligent effort to mitigate the damages is on the defendant. *Cornell v*

T. V. Dev. Corp. (1966) 17 NY2d 69, 268 NYS2d 29, later proceeding 50 Misc 2d 422, 270 NYS2d 45.

In the absence of evidence that an infant who had been injured in an automobile accident had unreasonably resisted having an operation that would have minimized his permanent condition, he was entitled to be compensated on the basis of the resulting condition as it would permanently exist without an operation. *Beyer v Murray* (1970, 4th Dept) 33 AD2d 246, 306 NYS2d 619.

§ 29:12 DAMAGES IN PERSONAL INJURY CASES — In a personal injury case, the plaintiff should recover an amount that will fairly compensate him for the injury he has sustained, for the pain and suffering he has endured and for the physical incapacity that has resulted from the accident. *Hayes v Albany Ice Cream Co.* (1917, Sup) 165 NYS 801.

Plaintiff is also entitled to be compensated for expenses actually incurred, *Marks v Thompson* (1937, City Ct) 1 NYS2d 215, and permanence of the injury, *Barone v Forgette* (1955) 286 AD 588, 146 NYS2d 63, reh and app den 1 AD2d 792, 149 NYS2d 235.

Compensation is also appropriate for aggravation of a pre-existing injury, *Beaudoin v State* (1960) 24 Misc 2d 962, 207 NYS2d 348 (*see also* § 29:14); loss of earnings, *Ehrgott v New York* (1884) 96 NY 264; and loss of business profits, *Steitz v Gifford* (1939) 280 NY 15, 122 ALR 292 (*see also* § 29:15).

Concern, humiliation, worry, and embarrassment are elements of mental suffering that may be considered in the assessment of damages sustained by the plaintiff by reason of personal injuries, where the evidence warrants such consideration. *Webb v Yonkers R. Co.* (1900) 51 AD 194, 64 NYS 491 (*see also* § 29:13).

When the evidence discloses that the plaintiff's education had been interrupted or curtailed by reason of injury, the trier of fact may consider this as a separate item of damage. *Grayson v Irvmar Realty Co.* (1959, 1st Dept) 7 AD2d 436, 184 NYS2d 33.

When there is bodily mutilation or scarring, the trier of fact, in assessing damages, may consider that the nature of the injury alone, without other proof of loss, represents a handicap in the struggle for existence. *Sweeting v American Knife Co.* (1919) 226 NY 199, 123 NE 82, affd 250 US 596, 63 L Ed 1161, 40 S Ct 44.

The defendant is liable for all damages that flow directly from and as a result of his acts, even though such damages could not have been foreseen by him. *Steitz v Gifford, supra*. This is true even though the exact nature and extent of the ultimate injuries are more severe than was ordinarily foreseeable. *Poplar v Bourjois, Inc.* (1948) 298 NY 62, 80 NE2d 334.

The determination of just what are the natural and proximate consequences of the defendant's misconduct is ordinarily for the jury. *Ehrgott v New York* (1884) 96 NY 264. In a case against New York State involving medical malpractice arising out of the plaintiff's confinement to a state institution, it was held proper to award damages for the inordinate length of confinement and for the side effects of moral degradation and mental anguish as well as physical injury, where the proximate cause of the damage was the lack of psychiatric care provided for the patient at the state hospital. *Whitree v State* (1968) 56 Misc 2d 693, 290 NYS2d 486. When the plaintiff has not shown that he has been materially injured, the court must charge the jury that it may bring in a verdict for nominal damages. *Rosenberg v New York C. R. Co.* (1905) 107 AD 223, 94 NYS 1115.

The amount to be allowed for pain and suffering is peculiarly a question of fact for the jury. *Robison v Lockridge* (1930) 230 AD 389, 244 NYS 663. In assessing damages for pain and suffering, no standard rule is applicable, but each case sets its own standards. *Dowly v State* (1947) 190 Misc 16, 68 NYS2d 573.

The measure of recovery for pain and suffering is the reasonable compensation to be fixed by the trier of the facts based on all the evidence. *Paley v Brust* (1964, 1st Dept) 21 AD2d 758, 250 NYS2d 356.

The social position of an injured person has no bearing on the damages to be awarded for personal injury and pain and suffering. *Di Gerlando v Second Ave. R. Corp.* (1935) 155 Misc 168, 278 NYS 797, affd 246 AD 585, 284 NYS 364.

A reduced award of $14,304,042 did not deviate materially from what would be reasonable compensation for a plaintiff who sustained chronic subdural hematomas, severe cerebral encephalopathy, fractures of the twelfth thoracic, sixth and seventh cervical vertebrae and fractures of the tenth, eleventh and twelfth left ribs, was admitted to the hospital in a comatose state and remained in that condition for nine weeks, underwent a tracheotomy and a gastronomy, suffered from incomplete paraplegia and incontinence of the bowel and bladder, suffered from disorientation with severe memory deficits, echolalia (repetition of words) and immobility requiring extensive medical care, and went from being a working man who provided for himself and others to someone who needed to be fed, clothed, diaper-changed while constantly crying and suffering from a highly agitated state. *Harvey v Mazal American Partners* (1992, 1st Dept) 179 AD2d 1, 581 NYS2d 748. (*See* § 29:16 for additional material on standards for determining that an award is excessive or inadequate on grounds that it deviates materially from what would be reasonable compensation.)

A jury verdict of $12,393,130 for a 22-month-old patient who suffered severe and diffuse brain damage, with marked difficulty in intellectual and motor functions, was excessive; the verdict was conditionally reduced to $6,143,130. *Merrill v Albany Medical Center Hospital* (1987, 3d Dept) 126 AD2d 66, 512 NYS2d 519, motion to dismiss app den 70 NY2d 669.

Awards for *in utero* injuries, resulting in mental retardation and physical malformations, of $500,000 for past pain and suffering; $1.5 million for future pain and suffering; and a total of $6.7 million for future residential care and therapy, were held not excessive. *Pay v State* (1995, 4th Dept) 213 AD2d 991, 625 NYS2d 770.

A gross award of $5 million, before reduction for plaintiff's contributory negligence, was approved in the case of a plaintiff who had suffered severe damage when doused with nearly a full liter of sulfuric acid, and who required extensive skin grafts and would require even more such grafts. *Moskowitz v Massachusetts Institute of Technology* (1984, 1st Dept) 100 AD2d 810, 474 NYS2d 742.

An award of $5 million to a 16-year-old plaintiff who was rendered paraplegic was held to be excessive and conditionally reduced to $3,750,000, of which $1 million was for pain and suffering. *Poulos v New York* (1984, 1st Dept) 99 AD2d 709, 472 NYS2d 3.

A damage award of $4,152,000 was not excessive, where plaintiff was 33 years old at the time of the accident, and suffered serious and permanent injuries, including a herniated disc, nerve root compression radiculopathy, and sexual impotence. *Poole v Cosolidated Rail Corp.* (1991, 4th Dept) 178 AD2d 941, 579 NYS2d 772, revd 80 NY2d 184, 590 NYS2d 1, cert den (US) 126 L Ed 2d 37, 114 S Ct 68.

An award of $4 million to a teen-aged girl who received second and third degree burns over 42% of her body was excessive, and was reduced to $1,500,000. *Rush v Sears, Roebuck & Co.* (1983, 3d Dept) 92 AD2d 1072, 461 NYS2d 559.

An $4 million award for past and future pain and suffering could not be sustained and was reduced to $3,005,000 where plaintiff had undergone two painful and serious surgical procedures on his back and faced the probability of further surgery, but was still able to walk, drive and engage, in a limited fashion, in many of the activities he enjoys. *Eschberger v Consolidated Rail Corp.* (1991, 4th Dept) 174 AD2d 893, 572 NYS2d 539, cert den 503 US 1011, 118 L Ed 435, 112 S Ct 1778. There was no error in the trial court's determination to allow defendant to prove, at a post-trial hearing, the amount of set-off it might be entitled to for payment of plaintiff's medical expenses. *Eschberger v Consolidated Rail Corp., supra.*

A jury award of $3 million did not shock the conscience of the court in view of extensive injuries suffered by plaintiff, whose legs were severed below the knee when he was run over by a subway train. *Lucas v New York City Transit Authority* (1990, 1st Dept) 163 AD2d 21, 557 NYS2d 919, app dismd 76 NY2d 933, 563 NYS2d 58 and app den 77 NY2d 807, 569 NYS2d 611.

An award of $2.5 million to plaintiff for future pain and suffering was not excessive, where as a result of the injuries he sustained, plaintiff cannot walk, stand, sit or even lie down for long periods without experiencing pain; he sustained foot and ankle disabilities that were extreme, permanent and progressively worsening, and in addition, plaintiff sustained severe, painful and debilitating or deforming injuries to his nose, face, mouth, jaw, neck and back that affect his appearance, eating, breathing and working; the award does not deviate materially from what would be reasonable compensation. *Hill v Muchow* (1991, 4th Dept) 178 AD2d 954, 579 NYS2d 254.

An award of $2.5 million to plaintiff, a former ballerina and beauty queen, for past and future pain and suffering, was not excessive, because she was rendered a paraplegic as a result of an automobile accident. *Nowlin v City of New York* (1992, 1st Dept) 182 AD2d 376, 582 NYS2d 669. An award to the same plaintiff of a sum in excess of $6.5 million for economic loss was reduced to $5 million. *Nowlin v City of New York, supra*.

An award of $2 million to plaintiff who eventually suffered the amputation of her right leg was not excessive, where plaintiff's injuries consisted of a crushing injury to the chest wall, including a fracture of the rib cage on both sides, fracture of the sternum, fracture of the clavicle, fracture of the left wrist and forearm, and the comminuted fracture of the tibia and fibula of the right leg, and the latter injury resulted in development of necrotic tissue and osteomyelitis, resulting in some nine surgical procedures in an attempt to save the leg, which ultimately was amputated. *Warmsley v New York* (1982, 2d Dept) 89 AD2d 982, 454 NYS2d 144.

An $2 million award was warranted to compensate a 35-year-old plaintiff for the anguish caused by multiple dental, orthopedic and internal injuries sustained that resulted in permanent jaw difficulties, a one-inch leg length differential, a lumbar injury, paralysis of the bowel, and a potentially recurring pneumothorax of the lung. *Ames v City of New York* (1991, 2d Dept) 177 AD2d 528, 575 NYS2d 917.

A judgment totaling $1,895,159.96 was fair and reasonable for a claimant who sustained injuries that resulted in permanent paralysis from the waist down, total loss of control of bladder and bowel movements, loss of sexual function, shortened life expectancy, as well as multiple lacerations of the face, fractured upper and lower jaw bones, a fractured cheek bone, a ruptured spleen, bleeding in the chest cavity, a fractured clavicle and scapula, a fracture dislocation of the spine, leg spasms and increasing stiffness and calcification of the lower body. The judgment allowed for 39 years of work expectancy. *Terwilliger v State* (1983, 3d Dept) 96 AD2d 688, 466 NYS2d 792.

In a strict products liability case, an award of $1,705,000 to a 19-year-old plaintiff was reasonable where plaintiff suffered severe injuries to both hands requiring four surgeries, lost three fingers on his right hand, the index and middle fingers were totally amputated and one of the amputated fingers was fused to the side of plaintiff's right thumb, his left hand was deformed, and a State medical examiner evaluated the loss of plaintiff's right hand and arm at 85% and of his left hand at 37½%. *Stiles v Batavia Atomic Horse Shoes, Inc.* (1992, 4th Dept) 174 AD2d 287, 579 NYS2d 790, revd 81 NY2d 950, 597 NYS2d 666, reconsideration denied, 81 NY2d 1068, 601 NYS2d 586.

The sum of $1.25 million was an appropriate award for a plaintiff who was 9 years old at the time of the accident, and had to undergo several physically painful orthopedic procedures, as well as several operations during prolonged hospitalization. She also suffered a stunting of growth and a one-inch leg differential that would require additional surgery. *Ames v City of New York, supra.*

An award of $1.2 million for past pain and future pain and suffering, to a 51-year-old electrician who sustained an extensive tear of the rotator cuff, with surgery and 16 months of formal therapy, continuing home therapy, continuing pain and restricted movement, and continuing deterioration with a prognosis for further degeneration, was held not to be excessive. *Guillory v Nautilus Real Estate, Inc.* (1995, 1st Dept) 208 AD2d 336, 624 NYS2d 110.

An award of $1.2 million for pain and suffering was excessive for a plaintiff who was in an automobile accident and suffered a torn meniscus and cartilage damage after both knees struck the dashboard of her vehicle; notwithstanding the prospect for bilateral knee replacements, plaintiff did not suffer any loss of time at work or cessation of normal activities, although she did impose limits and underwent an arthroscopic procedure. Her prognosis supported an award of $600,000 rather than $1.2 million apportioned by the jury for pain and suffering. *Gonzalez v Manhattan & Bronx Surface Transit Operating Authority* (1990, 1st Dept) 160 AD2d 420, 554 NYS2d 116.

An award of $700,000 to plaintiff, a prison inmate, was adequate where the injury resulted from performance of plaintiff's duties at the correctional facility where he was serving a sentence and where, as a result of the injury, plaintiff's left hand and forearm were severed. *Lowe v State* (1993, 3d Dept) 194 AD2d 898, 599 NYS2d 639.

An award of $600,000 to an infant who lost both legs was not so shockingly inadequate as to require a new trial, even though there was a claim by the plaintiff that there was an alleged mistake by the jury in the computation of the award. *Rodriguez v Baker* (1983, 1st Dept) 91 AD2d 143, 457 NYS2d 801, app dismd 59 NY2d 751, 463 NYS2d 443 and affd 61 NY2d 804, 473 NYS2d 972.

An award of $500,000 to plaintiff whose left eye was shot with a BB gun at the age of 13 was not excessive, where: plaintiff's permanent condition of blindness in one eye deprived him of depth perception and left peripheral vision, making it difficult or impossible to engage in such activities as driving or playing sports; he had continued and frequent severe headaches, and the pain, discomfort and humiliation of the disfigurement as well as that occasioned by having to remove and clean the prosthesis, which could not be properly fitted, and gave him a "pop-eyed" look; the pellet that caused the loss of his eye was still lodged against his optic nerve; and the unrefuted medical testimony was that the plaintiff would likely require further operations and refittings for replacement prostheses over the course of his entire life. *Davis v Board of Educ.* (1990, 1st Dept) 168 AD2d 261, 562 NYS2d 496.

An award of $500,000 was excessive for a plaintiff who sustained a fractured elbow but could nevertheless extend his arm to 95% of full extension, did not claim damages for loss of wages or medical expenses, and provided only minimal evidence that the injury was permanent. The trial court properly directed a new trial unless the plaintiff consented to a reduction of the principal sum to $75,000. *Rivera v New York* (1991, 2d Dept) 170 AD2d 591, 566 NYS2d 367.

The sum of $523,000, awarded to a patient at a mental institution for loss of his right eye, which resulted from an injury inflicted by a fellow patient, was not excessive. *Goble v State* (1986, 2d Dept) 123 AD2d 664, 507 NYS2d 35.

An award of $375,000 was not excessive where plaintiff sustained serious injuries that required the services of a neurosurgeon for a spinal fusion and bone graft after removal of a herniated cervical disc. *Manchester v Bankhead Corp., Div. of Bankhead Enterprises, Inc.* (1986, 3d Dept) 125 AD2d 740, 509 NYS2d 434.

A $375,000 damage award to a tenant who sustained injuries in a boiler explosion was not excessive, where the tenant's injuries included second degree burns over 90% of his body, in addition to conscious pain and suffering. *Donohue v Walter* (1989, 1st Dept) 156 AD2d 149, 548 NYS2d 435, app den 75 NY2d 710, 556 NYS2d 532.

A $320,000 verdict in favor of a 13-year-old girl who sustained a displaced fracture of the right clavicle, with constant atrophy and drooping of the right shoulder, which was approximately one inch lower than the left shoulder, was excessive and should be reduced to $150,000. *Tate v Colabello* (1982, 1st Dept) 88 AD2d 552, 450 NYS2d 333, affd 58 NY2d 84, 459 NYS2d 422.

The sum of $25,000 was shockingly inadequate where plaintiff, 74 years of age at the time of the accident, sustained injuries including multiple fractures of the pelvis and ribs, fractures of both shoulder sockets, both clavicles and both scapulae, resulting in 122 days of hospitalization with surgery, and permanent disability from employment; it was also shockingly inadequate to award only $10,000 to his wife, whose injuries consisted of a fracture of the left patella that extended into the knee joint capsule itself, and resulted in an irregularly healed fracture line articulating on the bone knobs of the femur of the knee joint, causing permanent irritation in the left knee. *Russo v Port Authority of New York & New Jersey* (1983, 1st Dept) 98 AD2d 618, 469 NYS2d 359.

The jury properly found the owner of a supermarket liable for pain and expenses that resulted from the customer's initial injury from a slip and fall in the supermarket, but found no liability for any subsequent aggravations or for a subsequent slip and fall at the place where the customer was employed. The initial herniated disk resulted from the slip and fall in the supermarket, but in later years the customer's additional pain and expenses resulted from an injury that was aggravated by the fact that the customer, a nurse, attempted to take such actions as lifting patients. *John v Supermarket General Corp.* (1986, 2d Dept) 116 AD2d 625, 497 NYS2d 861.

A jury verdict rejecting the plaintiff's claim that he was totally and permanently disabled was supported by photographic and videotaped evidence that contradicted his claim and damaged his credibility. Because the jury's function is to assess credibility, its verdict was based on a reasonable interpretation of the evidence presented. *Brugellis v Batts* (1987, 2d Dept) 129 AD2d 545, 514 NYS2d 39.

For the purpose of showing the length of time plaintiff will continue to suffer from an injury and endure pain, mortality tables are admissible. *Barone v Forgette* (1955) 286 AD 588, 146 NYS2d 63, reh and app den 1 AD2d 792, 149 NYS2d 235.

In a medical malpractice action, plaintiff's argument of a time-unit theory for the jury requires a reversal of the judgment, because there is no mechanical method by which pain and suffering may be translated into dollars-and-cents, and the time-unit technique injects an element of false simplicity into the determination by holding out a mathematical formula by which damages may be neatly calculated. *De Cicco v Methodist Hospital of Brooklyn* (1980, 2d Dept) 74 AD2d 593, 424 NYS2d 524.

Although it is true that in a personal injury case resort to the so called "time-unit" argument in determining an award for pain and suffering ordinarily warrants reversal, it is clear that what is prohibited is an award based on an arbitrary, simplistic formula, rather than one that will justly and fairly compensate the plaintiff. *Lee v Bank of New York* (1988, 2d Dept) 144 AD2d 543, 534 NYS2d 409. The mere suggestion to the jury that they consider units of time in reaching an award without ascribing a dollar amount for each unit does not require a reversal. *Lee v Bank of New York, supra.*

The better practice in all cases when jury awards are excluded from taxation is for the jury to be instructed in substance that such awards, if any, are not subject to income taxes, and that it should not add or subtract from the award because of income taxes but should follow the ordinary, specific instructions for measuring damages. *Lanzano v New York* (1988) 71 NY2d 208, 524 NYS2d 420, reconsideration den 71 NY2d 890, 527 NYS2d 772.

Although prior verdicts are helpful to the extent that they suggest permissible areas of evaluation for particular types of injury, *Monroe v Leonard* (1969) 62 Misc 2d 463, 308 NYS2d 933, affd 62 Misc 2d 467, 309 NYS2d 642, the passage of time results in material changes in the cost of living and the date of the prior decision is therefore a circumstance to be considered in using prior verdict as a guide to the propriety of damages awarded. *Monroe v Leonard, supra.*

It was error for the trial court to charge the jury that it could award damages for permanent injuries, where the only expert to testify was the oral surgeon who treated plaintiff for a broken jaw, and his testimony indicated that plaintiff's jaw had responded to treatment and had healed properly. *Cerasani v Noelle* (1982, 3d Dept) 87 AD2d 905, 449 NYS2d 357.

In a bifurcated trial, it was error for the trial court to exclude evidence of plaintiff's injuries during the liability phase of the trial, where defendant driver testified that the vehicle was proceeding at the rate of only 10 miles per hour, and the personal injuries sustained by plaintiff and the severity of the impact were inextricably intertwined. *Naumann v Richardson* (1980, 2d Dept) 76 AD2d 917, 429 NYS2d 259.

Where a minor sustained a permanent injury, the court in awarding compensation for injuries that resulted in body malformation, properly considered the fact that the minor would not be able to engage in any of his usual physical sports, that his future vocation would be limited to one requiring little mobility, and that the minor would experience pain and discomfort as he grew older. *Hegarty v Railway Express Agency* (1953, Sup) 126 NYS2d 107, affd 282 AD 871, 124 NYS2d 924.

Plaintiff's husband was not entitled to a recovery for loss of his wife's services to the extent that the damages were sustained after the plaintiff and her husband separated; the husband's right of recovery was limited to the period of time before his separation from his wife. *Dooley v Skodnek* (1988, 2d Dept) 138 AD2d 102, 529 NYS2d 569.

In a personal injury action, where plaintiff, a manual laborer, was able to return to work about 3½ months after the accident, and acknowledged at the trial that he was able to perform substantially all of the activities that he could perform before the accident and was unaware of any limitation of motion, to the extent that the award exceeded the sum of $200,000 for future pain and suffering, it could not be sustained. *Flansburg v Merritt Meridian Constr. Corp.* (1993, 3d Dept) 191 AD2d 756, 594 NYS2d 421.

Loss of enjoyment of life is not a separate element of damages deserving a distinct award but is, instead, only a factor to be considered by the jury in assessing damages for conscious pain and suffering. *McDougald v Garber* (1989) 73 NY2d 246, 538 NYS2d 937; *Grandinetti v Rose* (1989, 1st Dept) 155 AD2d 378 548 NYS2d 8, app den 75 NY2d 711, 557 NYS2d 309.

A tort committed against the mother of a child before the conception of the child, does not give rise to a cause of action in favor of the child if the tort has caused injury to the child during gestation. *Albala v New York* (1981) 54 NY2d 269, 445 NYS2d 108.

There is no cause of action on behalf of a child for the loss of companionship, love, emotional support and services of a parent arising out of physical injuries negligently inflicted on the parent. *De Angelis v Lutheran Medical Center* (1981, 2d Dept) 84 AD2d 17, 445 NYS2d 188, affd 58 NY2d 1053, 462 NYS2d 626.

Where the plaintiff's husband allegedly sustained an injury when struck by the defendant's employee, it was not error for the trial court to refuse to allow evidence of the mental anguish of the plaintiff wife. *Brennan v Commonwealth Bank & Trust Co.* (1978, 3d Dept) 65 AD2d 636, 409 NYS2d 266.

If a plaintiff's alleged sterile condition resulted from injuries that she suffered as a consequence of defendant's malpractice, she may recover not only for the physical injuries inflicted, but also for the mental and emotional distress attending those injuries; she may not, however, recover for the effect of her alleged sterility in depriving her of children or of their companionship, because there is no recovery for loss of offspring as such. *Villa v Marciano* (1990, 4th Dept) 167 AD2d 828, 561 NYS2d 938.

§ 29:13 DAMAGES FOR EMOTIONAL INJURIES — To recover for emotional harm, there must be a duty owed to plaintiff and he must be the person directly injured by the breach of that duty. *Rainnie v Community Memorial Hospital* (1982, 3d Dept) 87 AD2d 707, 448 NYS2d 897.

A cause of action for intentional infliction of severe emotional distress is actionable *per se*, and need not allege special damages. *Henaghan v Dicuia* (1983, 2d Dept) 98 AD2d 742, 469 NYS2d 446.

To sustain a cause of action for intentional infliction of emotional distress, it is required that there be a pattern of conduct by the defendant so extreme and outrageous as to go beyond all the possible bounds of decency, and to be regarded as atrocious and utterly intolerable in a civilized community. *Fischer v Maloney* (1978) 43 NY2d 553, 402 NYS2d 991.

A plaintiff alleging intentional infliction of emotional distress is required to allege that defendant's conduct was extreme and outrageous, or that it exceeded all bounds usually tolerated by decent society. *O'Donnell v Westchester Community Service Council, Inc.* (1983, 2d Dept) 96 AD2d 885, 466 NYS2d 41.

A cause of action for intentional infliction of emotional distress was properly dismissed against all defendants where plaintiff failed to allege sufficiently extreme and outrageous conduct. *Kasachkoff v New York* (1986) 68 NY2d 654, 505 NYS2d 67.

The complaint, which asserted a claim for intentional infliction of emotional distress and alleged that plaintiff suffered serious psychological and emotional harm as a result of being forced by her employer to submit to two polygraph examinations, did not allege facts that illustrate extreme, outrageous or atrocious conduct on the part of defendant's agents, and should have been dismissed by Special Term. *Buffolino v Long Island Sav. Bank, FSB* (1987, 2d Dept) 126 AD2d 508, 510 NYS2d 628.

In an action for intentional infliction of emotional distress, based upon alleged wrongful discharge, the claim could not survive a motion to dismiss without an allegation that the conduct of the defendant has been so outrageous in character and so extreme in degree as to go beyond all the bounds of decency, and to be utterly atrocious and intolerable in a civilized community. *Mur-*

phy v American Home Products Corp. (1983) 58 NY2d 293, 461 NYS2d 232.

An allegation by an employee that before being discharged by defendant, his former employer, he was falsely accused, failed to show such extreme and outrageous conduct by the defendant to make out an action for intentional infliction of emotional distress. *Vardi v Mutual Life Ins. Co.* (1988, 1st Dept) 136 AD2d 453, 523 NYS2d 95.

The tort of intentional infliction of emotional distress predicates liability on the basis of extreme and outrageous conduct, which so transcends the bounds of decency as to be regarded as atrocious and intolerable in a civilized society. The statements by a parent that alleged incompetence on the part of the teacher did not meet this standard. *Zuber v Bordier* (1987, 2d Dept) 135 AD2d 709, 522 NYS2d 610.

When a state hospital falsely advised a daughter that her mother, a patient, had died, the false message and the events flowing from its receipt were the proximate cause of claimant's emotional harm, for which claimant could recover. *Johnson v State* (1975) 37 NY2d 378, 372 NYS2d 638, 77 ALR3d 494.

When severe mental pain or anguish is inflicted through a deliberate and malicious campaign of harassment or intimidation, a remedy is available in the form of an action for intentional infliction of emotional distress. *Carter v Andriani* (1981, 1st Dept) 84 AD2d 513, 443 NYS2d 157, later app (1st Dept) 88 AD2d 799, 450 NYS2d 494.

A plaintiff who alleged that defendant, her psychiatrist, persuaded her to have sexual relations with him in order to obtain a therapeutic benefit, and that he placed numerous harassing telephone calls to plaintiff after she terminated their sexual relationship, stated a valid cause of action for emotional distress. *Sanchez v Orozco* (1991, 1st Dept) 178 AD2d 391, 578 NYS2d 145.

Where the state police obtained a "no-knock warrant" based on information obtained merely from a telephone call to the Rochester Telephone Company, and no steps were taken to verify the information and ascertain whether they were executing the warrant on the right parties at the right house, plaintiffs were entitled to recover damages for fear, shock, depression and other mental illness. *Herman v State* (1974) 78 Misc 2d 1025, 357 NYS2d 811.

A cause of action for intentional infliction of emotional injuries was stated by allegations that defendant made repeated telephone calls to plaintiff's house only to hang up as soon as someone answered, that as a consequence of these telephone calls, defendant pleaded guilty in a local criminal court to a reduced charge of harassment, and that notwithstanding her conviction for harassment, she continued to make the same type of telephone calls. The conduct complained of was actionable notwithstanding the absence of a physical contact. *Flatley v Hartmann* (1988, 2d Dept) 138 AD2d 345, 525 NYS2d 637.

A *prima facie* case of intentional infliction of emotional distress was made out by plaintiff based on unrebutted testimony that after defendants took control of the heating plant away from the superintendent, a pattern emerged where the tenants were denied heat and hot water and other essential services. *Salvan v 127 Management Corp.* (1984, 1st Dept) 101 AD2d 721, 475 NYS2d 30.

Although damages for emotional distress of a kind normally expected to follow from a wrongful action are available in a malicious prosecution action, recovery requires proof not only of lack of probable cause but also of actual as distinct from legal malice, that is, that the defendant acted with improper motive. *Ford Motor Credit Co. v Hickey Ford Sales, Inc.* (1984) 62 NY2d 291, 476 NYS2d 791.

Statements by defendant at a public meeting of the shareholders of a cooperative, that if the court refused to dismiss plaintiff's lawsuit against her, she would have no alternative but to kill plaintiff, which were later reported to the then pregnant plaintiff, who was not present at the meeting, were insufficient to support a cause of action for intentional infliction of emotional distress; a person may recover only where severe mental pain or anguish is inflicted through a delivered and malicious campaign of harassment or intimidation. *Owen v Leventritt* (1991, 1st Dept) 174 AD2d 471, 571 NYS2d 25. Mere threats, annoyance or other petty oppressions, no matter how upsetting, are insufficient to constitute the tort of intentional infliction of emotional distress. *Owen v Leventritt, supra*.

The arrest of plaintiff, a union official, in front of his fellow workers was not sufficiently egregious to meet the standard required for stating a cause of action for intentional infliction of emotional injuries. *Navarro v Federal Paper Board Co.* (1992, 3d Dept) 185 AD2d 590, 586 NYS2d 381.

Plaintiff, a law student, failed to state a cause of action for intentional infliction of emotional distress, because the destruction of his examination, even if motivated by animus toward him, was not so outrageous as to go beyond all possible bounds of decency. *Silverman v New York Univ. School of Law* (1993, 1st Dept) 193 AD2d 411, 597 NYS2d 314, app den 82 NY2d 658, 604 NYS2d 557.

A plaintiff who sued the operator of a garage because of faulty repairs to her car, and sought as damages compensation for embarrassment, humiliation, inconvenience and mental agony when the automobile ceased operating while being driven as a result of the alleged faulty repairs, could not recover, because an essential element of this cause of action for negligent infliction of mental distress is proof of a traumatic event that caused the plaintiff to fear for her own safety. *Ford v Village Imports, Ltd.* (1983, 4th Dept) 92 AD2d 717, 461 NYS2d 108.

In the absence of a duty on which liability can be based, there is no right of recovery for mental distress resulting from a breach of a contract-related duty. *Wehringer v Standard Sec. Life Ins. Co.* (1982) 57 NY2d 757, 454 NYS2d 984.

Although there may be a recovery for mental suffering without any requirement of physical impact, *Battalla v State* (1961) 10 NY2d 237, 219 NYS2d 34, it has been held that no cause of action lies for unintended harm caused by shock and fear sustained by a plaintiff resulting from injuries inflicted on another despite any relationship between them and even though the plaintiff was an eyewitness to the infliction of the injuries. *Tobin v Grossman* (1969) 24 NY2d 609, 301 NYS2d 554. However, in *Bovsun v Sanperi* (1984) 61 NY2d 219, 473 NYS2d 357, the court held that where a defendant's conduct is negligent as creating an unreasonable risk of bodily harm to a plaintiff, and such conduct is a substantial factor in bringing about injuries to the plaintiff in consequence of shock or fright resulting from his or her contemporaneous observation of serious injury inflicted by the defendant's conduct on a member of plaintiff's immediate family in his or her presence, the plaintiff may recover damages for such injuries.

A mother was not entitled to recover damages for emotional distress that allegedly resulted from negligent performance of amniocentesis by a physician. *Tebbutt v Virostek* (1985) 65 NY2d 931, 493 NYS2d 1010. Although recovery may be had by one suffering from distress in consequence of the observation of the serious injury or death of a member of his or her immediate family from within the zone of danger, the observation must be contemporaneous with the conduct causing the injury or death. *Tebbutt v Virostek, supra*.

To recover for psychic injury, a plaintiff must contemporaneously witness the injury or death of an immediate family member and fear for his own safety as a result of being within the zone of the danger created by defendant's negligence, which created a threat of bodily harm to both the victim of the physical injury and the eye witness. *Arroyo v New York City Health & Hosp. Corp.* (1990, 1st Dept) 163 AD2d 9, 558 NYS2d 8.

A mother, who was a passenger in an elevator with her daughter who was killed when she became caught in a door while attempting to leave the elevator, could not recover for negligent infliction of emotional distress because the mother was not in the "zone of danger" that consisted of the area from the elevator doors to the wall outside the elevator, and not the interior of the elevator; she was not in imminent danger of physical harm at the time of the accident, and did not witness the event. *Gonzalez v New York City Housing Authority* (1992, 1st Dept) 181 AD2d 440, 580 NYS2d 760.

To recover for emotional harm, the plaintiff must show, in addition to a breach of duty owed to her, that she was the person directly injured by that breach. *Aquilio v Nelson* (1980, 4th Dept) 78 AD2d 195, 434 NYS2d 520. The emotional pain and suffering of a mother because of the death of her infant the day after its birth, allegedly resulting from the malpractice of physicians, is too remote to be compensable. *Aquilio v Nelson, supra.*

Defendant hospital did not owe a direct duty to plaintiffs to care for and protect their infant daughter whom they had left in its custody, and plaintiffs were not possessed of a cognizable cause of action for their psychic injuries. *Johnson v Jamaica Hospital* (1984) 62 NY2d 523, 478 NYS2d 838.

Damages for emotional injuries were recoverable by a child who observed an assault on his father by two men and who attempted to stop the assault by pushing the two men away, thus placing the infant plaintiff within the "zone of danger." The fact that the infant plaintiff did not sustain physical injuries himself did not preclude recovery. *Di Marco v Supermarkets General Corp.* (1988, 2d Dept) 137 AD2d 651, 524 NYS2d 743.

Plaintiff, who was not physically touched or injured, but who watched as the wheels of a truck ran over her aunt, killing her instantly, was not entitled to recover damages for severe emotional injuries. *Trombetta v Conkling* (1993) 82 NY2d 549, 605 NYS2d 678.

A cause of action for "cancerphobia" cannot be sustained absent evidence of actual exposure to a disease-causing agent, and likelihood of contracting the disease as a result of the exposure. *Cottonaro v Southtowns Indus., Inc.* (1995, 4th Dept) 213 AD2d 993, 625 NYS2d 773.

A patient's daughter-in-law, who had a pre-existing heart condition, and who witnessed a negligent transfusion of mismatched blood to her mother-in-law, did not establish a cause of action for infliction of emotional distress, because there was no allegation that the defendant hospital was negligent with respect to the plaintiff, as opposed to her mother-in-law. *Lafferty v Manhasset Medical Center Hospital* (1981) 54 NY2d 277, 445 NYS2d 111.

A patient may recover for physical and mental injuries, including emotional upset suffered as a consequence of a doctor's breach of duty to that patient. *Hahn v Taefi* (1985, 4th Dept) 115 AD2d 946, 497 NYS2d 522. Thus, if the patient's sterile condition has resulted from injuries suffered by her as a consequence of the doctor's breach of duty to her, she is entitled to recover not only for the physical injuries inflicted on her but also for the mental and emotional distress attending those injuries. *Hahn v Taefi, supra.*

Damages for emotional and psychological trauma directly resulting from a violation of the Dram Shop Act are recoverable. *Winje v Cavalry Veterans of Syracuse, Inc.* (1986, 4th Dept) 124 AD2d 1027, 508 NYS2d 768. In this case, the plaintiff successfully stated a cause of action for emotional injuries, cognizable under the Dram Shop Act, when she alleged that she had needed psychotherapy since the car she was driving struck an object and, after pulling her car to the side of the road, she saw the decapitated body of a man. She said the decedent was present in the roadway because of intoxication that resulted from having been served alcoholic beverages by the defendant in violation of the statute.

In the absence of evidence that plaintiff, a hotel guest, was abused or insulted by defendant's night clerk, he was not entitled to recover compensatory damages for allegedly suffering humiliation, indignity and distress of mind. *Pollock v Holsa Corp.* (1984, 1st Dept) 98 AD2d 265, 470 NYS2d 151.

A dentist who brought suit based on the improper repair of his anesthetic machine, which resulted in the death of a patient, was entitled to recover for his pecuniary loss resulting from his inability to carry on his professional work, but he was not entitled to recover for his claim for emotional injury. *Kennedy v McKesson Co.* (1983) 58 NY2d 500, 462 NYS2d 421.

There is no right of recovery for emotional distress occasioned merely by the contemplation of having to bear an unwanted child as a result of an unsuccessful sterilization procedure. *Miller v Rivard* (1992, 3d Dept) 180 AD2d 331, 585 NYS2d 523.

A cause of action for damages for emotional distress and anxiety occasioned by the birth of a child after an unsuccessful sterilization operation is not recognized in New York State. *Sala v Tomlinson* (1982, 3d Dept) 87 AD2d 670, 448 NYS2d 830.

A mother was held not to be entitled to recover for emotional injuries resulting from the birth of her child without limbs and with other deformities, allegedly the result of a drug marketed by one defendant and administered to the mother by defendant doctor during her pregnancy, to prevent miscarriage. *Vaccaro v Squibb Corp.* (1980) 52 NY2d 809, 436 NYS2d 871.

A mother was not entitled to recover from a physician in the hospital for psychic injuries resulting from the fact that one twin was stillborn and the other died one hour after being born, where the mother did not sustain an independent physical injury; a caesarean section that was performed on the mother was not such a physical injury as would have entitled her to maintain an action against the physician in the hospital for psychic distress. *Sceusa v Mastor* (1988, 4th Dept) 135 AD2d 117, 525 NYS2d 101, app dismd without op 72 NY2d 909.

For a mother to recover for emotional distress caused by negligent medical treatment resulting in death or injury to her child either *in utero* or *postpartum*, an independent physical injury is required, and anxiety attacks, even under the most liberal pleading standards, are not sufficient to fulfill this requirement. *Hayes v Record* (1990, 3d Dept) 158 AD2d 874, 551 NYS2d 668.

In the absence of independent physical injuries to their persons, plaintiffs could not recover for any psychic or emotional harm alleged to have resulted as a consequence of the birth of their infant in an impaired state, where the plaintiff mother experienced only moderate vaginal bleeding, a common phenomenon during childbirth. *Keselman v Kingsboro Medical Group* (1989, 2d Dept) 156 AD2d 334, 548 NYS2d 287, app dismd without op 76 NY2d 845.

A mother could not recover for emotional injuries caused by the death of her newborn son, alleged to have been caused by prolonged, futile attempts at vaginal delivery; the mother sustained no independent physical injury despite the pain of the delivery itself, and was not in the "zone of danger." *Parsons v Chenango Memorial Hosp.* (1994, 3d Dept) 210 AD2d 847, 620 NYS2d 604, app dismd without op 86 NY2d 778, 631 NYS2d 610.

Although there may be recovery for emotional harm to one subjected directly to the negligence of another as long as the psychic injury is genuine, substantial and proximately caused by the defendant's conduct, the parents of a child born with Tay-Sachs disease, who ultimately died of the ailment, were not entitled to recover from the physician for their mental and emotional pain on the claim that had he informed them during pregnancy of the risk that the child would be born with such a disease, they would have taken tests and upon learning that the fetus was afflicted would have terminated the pregnancy. *Howard v Lecher* (1977) 42 NY2d 109, 397 NYS2d 363.

Plaintiffs, the parents of abnormal children, who sued on their own behalf for damages accruing as a consequence of the birth of their infants, in the one case born retarded and brain-damaged, and in the other suffering from polycystic kidney disease, and who alleged negligence on the part of defendant physicians in allegedly failing to inform the parents accurately of the risks involved in the particular pregnancies, with the result that the parents in one case decided to conceive and in the other not to terminate a pregnancy; pleaded a valid cause of action for pecuniary damages resulting from the birth. *Becker v Schwartz* (1978) 46 NY2d 401, 413 NYS2d 895. However, plaintiffs may not recover for psychic or emotional harm alleged to have occurred as a consequence of the birth of their infants in an impaired state. *Becker v Schwartz, supra.*

The improper publication by defendant hospital of the infant's photograph for advertising purposes, and its improper disclosure of confidential medical information regarding the infant, as alleged in the complaint, constituted invasions of the infant's statutory rights to privacy, rights that were personal to the infant and could not support an independent cause of action in favor of the plaintiffs, the infant's parents, for negligent infliction of emotional harm. *Smith v Long Island Jewish-Hillside Medical Center* (1986, 2d Dept) 118 AD2d 553, 499 NYS2d 167.

The publication by a newspaper of a recognizable photograph of plaintiff, a patient at a psychiatric hospital, showing plaintiff strolling with a fellow patient whose mental and physical rehabilitation was clearly newsworthy, did not furnish grounds for a claim of intentional infliction of emotional distress. *Howell v The New York Post Co.* (1992, 1st Dept) 181 AD2d 597, 581 NYS2d 330.

In an action brought for intentional infliction of emotional distress, in which there was also a cause of action for defamation, the action for emotional injuries should have been dismissed because that cause of action was redundant to the defamation action and any damages for emotional distress would be recoverable in the defamation action. *Durepo v Flower City Television Corp.* (1989, 4th Dept) 147 AD2d 934, 537 NYS2d 391.

Although a church may be held liable for intentional tortious conduct on behalf of its officers or members, even if that conduct is carried out as part of the church's religious practices, a complaint that alleged that the church subjected the decedent to a vigorous program of physical and mental training, which the complaint characterized as "brainwashing," did not state a cause of action for intentional infliction of emotional distress. *Meroni v Holy Spirit Asso. for Unification of the World Christianity* (1986, 2d Dept) 119 AD2d 200, 506 NYS2d 174.

A law firm that brought a collection action on behalf of a hospital was not liable to the persons sued for intentional infliction of emotional injuries as a result of bringing the action, even though the action was dismissed for lack of personal jurisdiction. *Crandall v Bernard, Overton & Russell* (1987, 3d Dept) 133 AD2d 878, 520 NYS2d 237, app dismd, in part, app den, in part, motion dismd 70 NY2d 940, 524 NYS2d 672.

A plaintiff could not recover damages for psychic trauma as a result of the act of a town police officer who shot plaintiff's dog, because a dog is personal property and damages may not be recovered for mental distress caused by its malicious or negligent destruction. *Fowler v Ticonderoga* (1987, 3d Dept) 131 AD2d 919, 516 NYS2d 368.

The alleged conduct of the former wife, who had remarried, who sold her engagement ring and her mink coat, and made disparaging remarks to the children concerning her former husband, did not as a matter of law, constitute a cause of action for intentional infliction of emotional injuries. *Partridge v Myerson* (1990, 2d Dept) 162 AD2d 507, 556 NYS2d 707, app den 76 NY2d 710, 563 NYS2d 61.

Public policy prohibits a claim for intentional infliction of emotional distress being brought against the state. *De Lesline v State* (1982, 3d Dept) 91 AD2d 785, 458 NYS2d 79.

§ 29:14 EFFECT OF PRE-EXISTING CONDITIONS ON DAMAGE AWARDS

§ 29:14 EFFECT OF PRE-EXISTING CONDITIONS ON DAMAGE AWARDS — A defendant must take a plaintiff as he finds him, and may be liable in damages for aggravation of a pre-existing illness. *Bartolone v Jeckovich* (1984, 4th Dept) 103 AD2d 632, 481 NYS2d 545.

Not only may the plaintiff recover where a pre-existing condition is aggravated, *Beaudoin v State* (1960) 24 Misc 2d 962, 207 NYS2d 348, he may also recover where his injuries were aggravated by a predisposition or weakness on his own part, *Seitz v Department of Fire* (1976, 4th Dept) 55 AD2d 829, 390 NYS2d 308.

A verdict in the plaintiff's favor in the sum of $500,000 was supported by the evidence indicating that before the accident he had been able to function vocationally as a carpenter, despite having suffered from a pre-existing schizophrenic illness, which had been exacerbated by the accident and had caused him, after the accident, to be in a chronic paranoid schizophrenic state that was irreversible. *Bartolone v Jeckovich, supra.*

A jury award of $800,000 for past pain and suffering and $1 million for future pain and suffering did not deviate materially from what would be reasonable in the case of the plaintiff, a diabetic on kidney dialysis, who suffered a multiple fracture of her left ankle. She experienced permanent swelling and pain in this limb, and eventually had two toes amputated from her left foot as a result of her injuries. An award of $150,000 to her husband for loss of services was also reasonable. *Dauria v City of New York* (1991, 1st Dept) 178 AD2d 289, 577 NYS2d 64.

An award of $7,454,687.50 was not excessive in the case of a 15-year-old child admitted to a psychiatric center who was self-abusive and who, as a result of defendant's failure to control claimant's self-abuse and its failure to render timely medical treatment for claimant's injuries, was rendered permanently blind. *Jones v State* (1993, 1st Dept) 198 AD2d 152, 603 NYS2d 484, app den 82 NY2d 926, 610 NYS2d 178.

§ 29:15 DAMAGES FOR LOST EARNINGS

§ 29:15 DAMAGES FOR LOST EARNINGS — Although the question of lost earnings is a question of fact for the jury, *Frey v Gerhard Lang Brewery* (1939) 256 AD 1054, 10 NYS2d 874, the issue should not be given to the jury unless there is proof of what the plaintiff's loss was. *Kane v Metropolitan S. R. Co.* (1904, App Tm) 88 NYS 162.

Even though a plaintiff was unemployed at the time of the accident, he may nevertheless prove what his prior income was and prospects of employment. *Spence v State* (1957) 6 Misc 2d 1029, 165 NYS2d 896, mod (4th Dept) 6 AD2d 1024, 178 NYS2d 45.

In addition to damages for loss of past earnings, the plaintiff in a tort case is entitled to damages for impairment of earning power, which is necessarily prospective. *Weir v Union R. Co.* (1907) 188 NY 416, 81 NE 168.

When business profits depend on the personal talents and skill of the plaintiff, those profits, when lost, are recoverable. *Steitz v Gifford* (1939) 280 NY 15, 122 ALR 292.

An award of $1,100,000 to a working-man who was 34 years old at the time he sustained an injury that precluded him from returning to his occupation, and who was earning $18,200 at the time of injury, was supported by the evidence and was not excessive. *Sullivan v Held* (1981, 2d Dept) 81 AD2d 663, 438 NYS2d 359.

An award to plaintiff, who was rendered a quadriplegic, in the sum of $1 million for lost earnings was reasonable, as were awards of $1.3 million for support services and $450,000 for future medical costs; however, an award for $1.4 million for net lost earnings was excessive, and should be reduced to $1 million. *Mesick v State* (1986, 3d Dept) 118 AD2d 214, 504 NYS2d 279.

The failure of the trial court to include the loss of earnings of plaintiff, a merchant seaman, from the five-year period between the accident and the trial as an item of special damages, was a fundamental, reversible error which, along with other errors, justified a new trial on the issue of damages despite the fact that no proper objection was made to this error. *Ostrowski v Apex Marine Corp.* (1986, 1st Dept) 123 AD2d 257, 506 NYS2d 164.

The trial court properly reduced the damage award of $6 million to $1 million where plaintiff was able to resume her career as a registered nurse some three months after her initial hospitalization, worked continuously except for an absence occasioned by the necessity for follow-up surgery, performed her job properly as evinced by her receipt of several wage increases, took up college courses subsequent to her accident in preparation for a degree in elementary education, was licensed to drive a car and continued to do so, and the testimony of plaintiff's treating physician was to the effect that the results of all surgical procedures performed were favorable with no untoward results and the post-operative course of treatment was described as uneventful. *Simon v Sears, Roebuck & Co.* (1986, 2d Dept) 124 AD2d 655, 508 NYS2d 39.

An award of $2,846,000 for lost future earnings and impairment of earning ability was largely speculative in light of a plaintiff's established work record and earnings history, even though the evidence amply demonstrated that the plaintiff had suffered severe and disabling injuries as a result of a vehicular collision. *Eichler v New York* (1993, 2d Dept) 196 AD2d 524, 601 NYS2d 318.

The trial court did not err in setting aside an award for diminution of earnings, where, although the infant plaintiff testified that she had wished to become a cosmetologist and had received some formal training in the field, and that her impairment, which involved some permanent loss of vision in her left eye, rendered her incapable of performing the tasks required of a cosmetologist, the record also revealed that plaintiff had worked at several jobs since sustaining her injury, that she had recently been employed as a receptionist for 11 months before the trial, and the testimony of an economist at the trial established that her future earnings as a receptionist would be greater than her earnings as a cosmetologist; the award for loss of earnings would therefore have operated as a windfall to her. *Alferoff v Casagrande* (1986, 2d Dept) 122 AD2d 183, 504 NYS2d 718.

Damage awards of $249,000 for economic loss and $228,381 for pain and suffering did not deviate materially from what would be reasonable compensation where, as a result of an accident, the plaintiff suffered a compound fracture of the forearm, including a fracture at the elbow level that resulted in permanent loss of motion and some degenerative arthritic changes; underwent four surgical procedures concerning his wrist; experienced daily discomfort in the forearm, elbow and wrist areas. The plaintiff, who was 25 years old at the time of the accident, testified that he had his own engine repair business, relied on his hands for a livelihood, and that his troubled arm inhibited his activities in general and in his business in particular. *Campbell v City of Elmira* (1993, 3d Dept) 198 AD2d 736, 604 NYS2d 609.

Although in a personal injury case involving a claim of lost past and future earnings resulting from an alleged permanent disability from work, evidence that plaintiff voluntarily chose to retire is often so prejudicial as to be inadmissible, it may be allowed, however, in the court's discretion in limited circumstances where it has significant probative value with respect to a validly raised question about plaintiff's malingering or motivation for not working. *Kish v Board of Educ.* (1990) 76 NY2d 379, 559 NYS2d 687.

For purposes of establishing the loss of pension sustained by a personal injury plaintiff, expert testimony is not necessary; a plaintiff who is knowledgeable about his salary and pension rights was capable of testifying to both items. *Lamot v Gondek* (1990, 3d Dept) 163 AD2d 678, 558 NYS2d 284. An award of $100,000 for lost pension benefits was reasonable in the case of a plaintiff who had been earning $45,000 per year, and was forced to retire 11 years early with a pension of $17,000. *Lamot v Gondek, supra.*

An award for past and future earnings had to be reduced as too speculative where it was based on the assumption that plaintiff would have become employed as a medical technician if not for her stroke. The plaintiff had never been employed in that position, had never obtained the necessary degree to seek the employment, and had dropped out of school after taking several courses toward the degree some 10 years earlier. *Naveja v Hillcrest General Hosp.* (1989, 2d Dept) 148 AD2d 429, 538 NYS2d 584.

CPLR 4546 provides:

"In any action for medical, dental or podiatric malpractice where the plaintiff seeks to recover damages for loss of earnings or impairment of earning ability, evidence shall be admissible for consideration by the court, outside of the presence of the jury, to establish the federal, state and local personal income taxes that the plaintiff would have been obligated by law to pay." CPLR 4546(1). "In any such action, the court shall instruct the jury not to deduct federal, state and local personal income taxes in determining the award, if any, for loss of earnings and impairment of earning ability. The court shall further instruct the jury that any reduction for such taxes from any award shall, if warranted, be made by the court." CPLR 4546(2). "In any such action, the court shall, if warranted by the evidence, reduce any award for loss of earnings or impairment of earning ability by the amount of federal, state and local personal income taxes that the court finds, with reasonable certainty, the plaintiff would have been obligated by law to pay." CPLR 4546(3).

§ 29:16   COURT REVIEW OF DAMAGE AWARDS — For all trials begun since August 1, 1988, CPLR 5501(c) provides that: "In reviewing a money judgment in an action in which an itemized verdict is required by rule forty-one hundred eleven of this chapter in which it is contended that the award is excessive or inadequate and that a new trial should have been granted unless a stipulation is entered to a different award, the appellate division shall determine that an award is excessive or inadequate if it deviates materially from what would be reasonable compensation."

A verdict may be conditionally reduced where it is excessive; *Flynn v Manhattan & Bronx Surface Transit Operating Authority* (1983, 1st Dept) 94 AD2d 617, 462 NYS2d 17, affd 61 NY2d 769, 473 NYS2d 154; it may also be conditionally increased where it is inadequate; *Protzman v State* (1982, 4th Dept) 91 AD2d 853, 458 NYS2d 408.

An award of $283,471.35 for injuries consisting of fractures of the skull, abrasions and lacerations of the face, fractured ribs, lacerations of the liver, fractured clavicle, fractures of both elbows and multiple fractures of the left leg was considered inadequate and raised to $500,000. *Protzman v State, supra*.

A jury's verdict is not necessarily excessive because of the fact that a different trier of the facts might well have arrived at a lower amount or because of the amount of special damages. *MacArthur v Coxon Real Estate, Inc.* (1967, 3d Dept) 28 AD2d 1191, 284 NYS2d 560.

A reduction of a verdict of $2.4 million by $360,000 in a personal injury case for failure to wear a seatbelt was not inadequate, as the defendant contended, because non-use of an available seatbelt and expert testimony in regard seatbelt use are merely factors that the jury may consider in light of all the other evidence when determining damages. The jury is not required to wholly adopt the opinion of an expert, even though uncontradicted. *Halvorsen v Ford Motor Co.* (1987, 3d Dept) 132 AD2d 57, 522 NYS2d 272, app den 71 NY2d 805, 529 NYS2d 76.

Although the trial court properly found that an award of $1,000 was inadequate, because it did not sufficiently compensate the plaintiff for the physical injuries she sustained, it was an abuse of discretion for the trial court to conditionally increase the verdict to $50,000, which could reflect only the trial court's determination that the accident was the cause of her claimed psychological condition, because there was ample evidence to support a finding that factors other than the accident created her psychological condition; this constituted unnecessary interference with the fact-finding function of the jury to a degree that amounted to usurpation of the jury's duty. *Compton v D'Amore* (1984, 2d Dept) 101 AD2d 800, 475 NYS2d 463.

An award of $215,000 to plaintiff a who sustained a torn rotator cuff of the shoulder, was not excessive. *Bennett v Cruz* (1990, 1st Dept) 168 AD2d 307, 562 NYS2d 638.

The trial court did not abuse its discretion in setting aside a jury award in the sum of $451,500 as shockingly low, where the child plaintiff sustained a traumatic amputation of one leg in the accident, and the medical evidence was that the child would suffer constant pain and have difficulty in using a prosthetic device because the amputation was three inches below the hip and left one inch of femur bone, with insufficient padding. *Camacho v Consolidated Rail Corp.* (1989, 1st Dept) 156 AD2d 317, 549 NYS2d 15, app dismd without op 76 NY2d 772, 559 NYS2d 985.

In an action to recover for permanent injuries sustained by an 8-year-old child, resulting from ingesting lead based paint peelings over a period of at least six months, the trial court usurped the jury's function in reducing the damage award from $1,700,000 to $200,000, where the uncontradicted medical evidence showed that the child was afflicted with a rather severe neurological impairment known as a attention deficit disorder, which manifests itself in his being hyperactive, impulsive and easily distracted, the evidence also disclosed that the infant plaintiff had serious problems with visual processing and perception, as well as significant social and emotional disorders, requires a special education program, is classified as learning disabled and has an IQ level between normal and retarded, and the prognosis with respect to the infant plaintiff is that his condition will adversely affect his employability. *Miller v Beaugrand* (1991, 1st Dept) 169 AD2d 537, 564 NYS2d 390, app den 77 NY2d 810, 571 NYS2d 913.

Although the 82-year-old plaintiff suffered a serious injury, and had to cease taking care of her husband from the time of her injury until the time she died 11 months later, an award of $25,000 to the husband for loss of services was excessive and was reduced by the Appellate Division to $10,000. *Sheinwald v Doldo* (1988, 2d Dept) 143 AD2d 129, 531 NYS2d 588.

In a strict products liability case brought against an automobile manufacturer by a plaintiff who was rendered quadriplegic, there was no abuse of discretion by the Appellate Division, which reduced a jury award of $3.6 million to $2 million. *Caprara v Chrysler Corp.* (1979, 3d Dept) 71 AD2d 515, 423 NYS2d 694, affd 52 NY2d 114, 436 NYS2d 251.

§ 29:17 DAMAGES FOR LOSS OF PERSONAL PROPERTY
— Generally speaking, the measure of damages to personal property is the difference between the market value of the property immediately before and immediately after the injury. *Gass v Agate Ice Cream, Inc.* (1934) 264 NY 141, 190 NE 323; *Atlantic Mut. Ins. Co. v Noble Van & Storage Co.* (1989, 2d Dept) 146 AD2d 729, 537 NYS2d 213.

If personal property is totally destroyed, the market value at the time and place of the destruction should be shown, and if the property is merely damaged, the difference in value immediately before and immediately after the injury should be shown. *Dubiner's Bootery, Inc. v General Outdoor Advertising Co.* (1960, 1st Dept) 10 AD2d 923, 200 NYS2d 757.

In fixing damages for the loss or destruction of personal property, the law does not recognize any purely sentimental value the property may have had. *Goor v Navilio* (1941) 177 Misc 970, 31 NYS2d 619.

The measure of damages for injury to goods held for retail sale is not the retail selling price, but the replacement costs, plus any damages sustained by reason of the absence of articles while in the process of replacement. *Dubiner's Bootery, Inc. v General Outdoor Advertising Co., supra*.

The loss to a tenant who ran an antique store of those antiques in her inventory that allegedly were damaged by construction work performed by a contractor was not limited to damages based on the cost to the tenant of such articles, because the price in the market for antiques might be high. *Penrose v Arrow Constr. Co.* (1958) 15 Misc 2d 512, 182 NYS2d 642.

In assessing the damages for water damage to personal property, a court could consider the price paid for the articles when new, together with the age and condition as well as the use to which they were put. *Goldman v Omaha Estates, Inc.* (1955, Mun Ct) 139 NYS2d 854.

An award that represented the cost of a person's destroyed clothing, personal effects, cash and small appliances, without regard to their age, use, deterioration or depreciation, could not be sustained. *Mullen v Sinclair Refining Co.* (1969, 3d Dept) 32 AD2d 1000, 301 NYS2d 716, motion gr, motion to dismiss app den 25 NY2d 679, 306 NYS2d 680.

It has been held that the basis for recovery by a utility for damage to its property consists of the actual cost of emergency expenses, together with the present-day cost of replacing the damaged or destroyed equipment less accrued depreciation and allowances for salvage. *New York State Electric & Gas Corp. v Fischer* (1965, 3d Dept) 24 AD2d 683, 261 NYS2d 310.

§ 29:18 DAMAGES TO MOTOR VEHICLES — When an automobile is totally destroyed, the measure of damages is its reasonable market value immediately before destruction, less its salvage value. *Owens v State* (1983, 3d Dept) 96 AD2d 630, 464 NYS2d 870, supp op (3d Dept) 97 AD2d 909, 471 NYS2d 21.

The damages sustained by an automobile in a collision may be established by showing the reasonable cost of repairs, but the cost of repairs must be less than the diminution in market value resulting from the injury and the repairs must not exceed the value of the automobile as it was prior to the injury. *Gass v Agate Ice Cream, Inc. supra; Schwartz v Crozier* (1991, 3d Dept) 169 AD2d 1003, 565 NYS2d 567.

If recovery for damages to an automobile that results from negligence is based on the reasonable cost of repairs, loss of use may also be added as an item of damages, even though the automobile was not used for business but only for pleasure. *Johnson v Scholz* (1949) 276 AD 163, 93 NYS2d 334.

Where an automobile owner obtained an estimate of repairs for the damages in the sum of $1,858.75, and a dealer who repossessed the automobile for default in payment repaired it at a cost to him of $1,278, the recovery of damages by the owner was limited to $1,278. *Schnitzer v Chapman* (1962, Co Ct) 236 NYS2d 103.

When an automobile is totally destroyed, the measure of damages is the reasonable market value immediately before the destruction, less the salvage value of the wreckage. Additionally, even though the vehicle constituted a total loss, plaintiff was entitled to the cost of towing, storage, insurance and loss of use of the vehicle from the date of the accident until the expiration of a reasonable time for obtaining a replacement vehicle. *Aurnou v Craig* (1992, 4th Dept) 184 AD2d 1048, 584 NYS2d 249.

An award for negligent injury to a tractor covered the aggregate of parts and labor needed for repair, including the owner's labor, plus the amount of income lost due to inability to work in a logging operation. *Weiler v Osceola* (1966) 51 Misc 2d 163, 273 NYS2d 90, affd 29 AD2d 737, 287 NYS2d 365.

§ 29:19   DAMAGES IN WRONGFUL DEATH ACTIONS — The Bill of Rights of the Constitution of the State of New York provides that the right of action for damages for injuries causing death shall never be abrogated and the amount recoverable shall not be subject to any statutory limitation. New York State Constitution Art I § 16.

By statutory enactment, the damages to be awarded to the plaintiff in a wrongful death action are such sum as the trier of fact determines would be fair and just compensation for the pecuniary injuries resulting from the decedent's death to the persons for whose benefit the action is brought. EPTL § 5-4.3 . In addition to damages recoverable by reason of pecuniary loss, the reasonable expenses of medical aid, nursing and attention incident to the injuries causing death and the reasonable funeral expenses are additional and proper elements of damage. EPTL § 5-4.3. Interest on the amount recovered by the plaintiff in a wrongful death action attaches to the award from the date of the decedent's death and is added to and becomes a part of the total sum awarded. EPTL § 5-4.3. Where the death of an individual occurs on or after September 1, 1982, in addition to any damages and expenses recoverable, punitive damages may be awarded if those damages would have been recoverable had the decedent survived. EPTL §§ 5-4.3, 11-3.2.

In any action in which the wrongful conduct is medical malpractice or dental malpractice, evidence shall be admissible to establish the federal, state and local personal income taxes the decedent would have been obligated by law to pay. EPTL § 5-4.3(c).

In assessing pecuniary loss, there is no mathematical formula for its computation. Among the factors to be considered in a wrongful death case are the decedent's age, his health, his habits, qualities, life expectancy, earning ability, income and prospective increases; and the number, age, sex, situation and condition of the dependents, as well as his disposition to support them. *Riley v Capital Airlines, Inc.* (1963) 42 Misc 2d 194, 247 NYS2d 427.

In determining the amount of damages to be awarded for the death of a father, a jury was entitled to consider the father's working habits, the amount he contributed for the support of his family, his position, his potential advancement in life, increasing earning capacity, the loss to the children of guidance, advice, care and education, as well as the constant erosion of the dollar and the spiraling cost of living. *Zaninovich v American Airlines, Inc.* (1965) 47 Misc 2d 584, 262 NYS2d 854, revd on other grounds (1st Dept) 26 AD2d 155, 271 NYS2d 866. Within the concept of pecuniary loss, the wrongful death of a mother requires an assessment of the loss of her nurture, guidance, advice, care and tender solicitude to her children and the placing of a monetary value thereon. *Zaninovich v American Airlines, Inc. supra*. In assessing the value of the pecuniary loss of a parent, the trier of fact may take into account that the loss is greater and more profound where there is no other surviving parent. *Zaninovich v American Airlines, Inc. supra*. In considering the pecuniary loss of surviving children, the trier of fact may consider that the loss sustained by them by reason of the death of a parent may continue beyond the period of their minority. *Tilley v Hudson R. R. Co.* (1862) 24 NY 471, later app 29 NY 252. The concept of "pecuniary" in the wrongful death statute is not limited in scope to the immediate loss of money but envisages all of the elements of loss for which there is a pecuniary equivalent although, of necessity, a number of these elements are prospective in nature and quality. *Zaninovich v American Airlines, Inc. supra.*

The elements of a cause of action to recover damages for wrongful death are: (1) the death of a human being, (2) the wrongful act, neglect or default of defendant by which the decedent's death was caused, (3) the survival of distributees who suffered pecuniary loss by reason of the death of decedent, and (4) appointment of a personal representative of decedent. *Chong v New York City Transit Authority* (1981, 2d Dept) 83 AD2d 546, 441 NYS2d 24.

Although a corporation that employed a decedent may suffer pecuniary injury due to his death, a corporation is not a beneficiary of the decedent and thus is not a "person ... for whose benefit" the wrongful death action is brought. *Konstantatos v County of Suffolk* (1991, 2d Dept) 174 AD2d 653.

In a wrongful death action brought by adult children for the death of their mother, damages for loss of companionship, comfort and assistance are non-pecuniary in nature, typical of a loss of consortium claim, and are not recoverable. *Bumpurs v New York City Housing Authority* (1988, 1st Dept) 139 AD2d 438, 527 NYS2d 217.

Where the decedent was a 64-year-old widow, seriously ill and living on disability benefits, no claim was made that the decedent would ever be re-employed, and her survivors were two emancipated and self-supporting children, a 43-year-old daughter and a 25-year-old son, both out-of-state residents, there was no showing of pecuniary loss. *Hartman v Dermont* (1982, 4th Dept) 89 AD2d 807, 453 NYS2d 464.

With respect to damages for loss of future potentialities, the plaintiff may introduce expert testimony as to the future prospects of the injured victim. *Zaninovich v American Airlines, Inc.*

(1966, 1st Dept) 26 AD2d 155, 271 NYS2d 866, revd on other grounds (1st Dept) 26 AD2d 155, 271 NYS2d 866.

In considering loss of future earning capacity, the trier of fact may consider the decedent's present position as well as his potential advancement in life and increased earning capacity, and to the extent that these have been destroyed an award may be made therefor. *Lucivero v Long Island R. Co.* (1960) 22 Misc 2d 674, 200 NYS2d 728.

In awarding damages for death, nothing can be allowed for sentiment or grief. *Dimitroff v State* (1939) 171 Misc 635, 13 NYS2d 458. In the absence of pecuniary injury by reason of the deceased's death, the only item of damage recoverable in a wrongful death action is funeral expenses. *Re Payne's Estate* (1961, 2d Dept) 12 AD2d 940, 210 NYS2d 925, app den (2d Dept) 13 AD2d 688, 215 NYS2d 714.

A jury verdict in favor of the mother of decedent for funeral expenses alone with respect to the wrongful death cause of action was not so low as to shock the conscience of the court, because the mother was an interested witness and the jury could reject her testimony with respect to the contribution in money and services to the household made by her daughter, as it could that of the daughter's fiancee and the economist whose testimony was based on that of the mother. *Wittman v Gilson* (1986, 4th Dept) 120 AD2d 964, 503 NYS2d 214, affd (1988) 70 NY2d 970, 525 NYS2d 795.

Although the loss sustained by the survivors of a child may be somewhat speculative, nevertheless this does not foreclose a substantial award in such a case. *Le Boeuf v Newman* (1964, 3d Dept) 21 AD2d 937, 251 NYS2d 72. Thus, in a case that involved the wrongful death of a 17-year-old child it was held that the child's talent, disposition, abilities and small part-time earnings warranted a verdict of $35,000. *Le Boeuf v Newman, supra.*

In an action for the wrongful death of a 16-year-old high school senior, who was highly intelligent, industrious and talented, and headed for a dental career, an award of $98,000 to his widowed mother was reduced to $50,000 plus $2,510.40 for medical and funeral expenses. *Gary v Schwartz* (1973, 2d Dept) 43 AD2d 562, 349 NYS2d 322.

In a wrongful death action, especially one involving a child of tender years, the absence of dollars-and-cents proof of a pecuniary loss does not relegate the distributees to the recovery of nominal damages only. *Parilis v Feinstein* (1980) 49 NY2d 984, 429 NYS2d 165.

An award of $37,500 was allowed for the wrongful death of a 5-year-old, not inclusive of funeral expenses. *Rivera v Monticello Cent. School Dist.* (1976, 3d Dept) 51 AD2d 616, 377 NYS2d 822.

An award of $51,860 was approved for the wrongful death of a 14-year-old intelligent girl with high averages in school subjects who also performed some chores on her father's farm. *Quinn v County of Sullivan* (1975, 3d Dept) 48 AD2d 965, 369 NYS2d 551.

In a death action that arose from an automobile collision, the trial court properly refused to consider the payment of insurance money, paid to the undertaker by the automobile owner's insurance carrier, in mitigation of damages or to reduce the amount of the verdict. *Petteys v Bullard, Reagan & Stafford, Inc.* (1945) 269 AD 919, 57 NYS2d 548. The cost of a cemetery lot would be awarded as part of funeral expenses. *Malvaso v State* (1959) 15 Misc 2d 585, 182 NYS2d 62, affd (4th Dept) 10 AD2d 663, 197 NYS2d 452.

The fact that the decedent's distributees were adults and not dependent on him for support is not determinative of the question of whether they suffered pecuniary injuries by reason of his death. *Gross v Abraham* (1954) 306 NY 525. Voluntary contributions by decedent to the support of the survivors may form a sufficient basis for a showing of pecuniary injury. *Walther v News Syndicate Co.* (1949) 276 AD 169, 93 NYS2d 537; *Storrs v Northern P. R. Co.* (1911) 148 AD 403, 132 NYS 954, affd 208 NY 629, 102 NE 1114; *Conklin v Central New York Tel. & Tel. Co.* (1909) 130 AD 308, 114 NYS 190. Although financial dependency is not a precondition to recovery in a wrongful death action, it is relevant in determining the amount of damages sustained. *Franchell v Sims* (1980, 4th Dept) 73 AD2d 1, 424 NYS2d 959.

However, an award of $2,500,000 deviated materially from what would be deemed reasonable compensation, where the trial testimony indicated that the 24-year-old decedent resided with her parents, was employed at a salary of $500 weekly at her last job, and contributed $100 per week to her parents' household expenses. It was unreasonable to assume that such a state of affairs would have lasted indefinitely into the future where common human experience indicates that in the normal course of events a young person would sooner or later have left home and where there was evidence that the decedent and another party were contemplating marriage. *Marigliano v City of New York* (1993, 2d Dept) 196 AD2d 533, 601 NYS2d 161.

The statute providing for interest on the verdict from the date of death is not applicable to an action for death under the Federal Employers' Liability Act. *Murmann v New York, N. H. & H. R. Co.* (1932) 258 NY 447, 180 NE 114.

In a wrongful death action, the fact that a potentially dependent distributee later marries is not admissible in evidence. *Woodard v Pancio* (1978, 4th Dept) 65 AD2d 923, 410 NYS2d 454. However, somewhat inconsistent with this principle, the fact that a dependent distributee dies before the trial of the wrongful death action may be proved, because death removes all doubt of the life expectancy of the beneficiary, which otherwise must be estimated. *Woodard v Pancio, supra.* Remarriage of a widow after the death of her husband is not taken into consideration in computing the damages recoverable for the wrongful death of the husband. *Rodak v Fury* (1969, 2d Dept) 31 AD2d 816, 298 NYS2d 50.

A 43-year-old surgeon was involved in an automobile accident, suffering a subdural contusion and cerebral concussion, followed by a period of deterioration and gradual contraction of his professional and private activities. His wife, who was partially paralyzed as a result of an old poliomyelitis, suffered "nervous exhaustion" and his mother became ill with cancer. It was for the jurors to determine whether the defendant's negligence substantially contributed to the doctor's death by suicide, and they did not have to find that it was the only cause. *Fuller v Preis* (1974) 35 NY2d 425, 363 NYS2d 568, 77 ALR3d 301.

An award of $200,000 was allowed in the wrongful death of a 46-year-old husband and father of 2 children who was earning approximately $10,000 per year in his own business. In the same case, an award of $250,000 was allowed in the wrongful death of a 32-year-old wife and mother of 3 children. *Alexander v New York* (1976, 1st Dept) 53 AD2d 846, 385 NYS2d 788, affd 43 NY2d 659, 400 NYS2d 816.

An award of $250,000 to a widow was considered inadequate where the decedent had three dependent children, one of whom was 16 years old and the other two 12 years old, a life expectancy of 31.7 years, a work expectancy of 20 years, with projected earnings of $1 million, and was conditionally raised to $500,000. *Wingerter v State* (1980, 3d Dept) 79 AD2d 817, 435 NYS2d 157, affd 58 NY2d 848, 460 NYS2d 20.

The trier of fact may not speculate as to how long a decedent would have survived had a tumor been discovered on her admission to a hospital, and speculation is no substitute for proof. *Nastasi v State* (1976, 3d Dept) 55 AD2d 724, 389 NYS2d 175.

A cause of action for pecuniary loss does not accrue to the distributees of a fetus stillborn by reason of the negligence of another. *Endresz v Friedberg* (1969) 24 NY2d 478, 301 NYS2d 65.

A claim for loss of consortium will not be recognized within a wrongful death action in the State of New York. *Liff v Schildkrout* (1980) 49 NY2d 622, 427 NYS2d 746.

Because decedent only survived for approximately eight weeks after his injury, that part of an $80,000 award for loss of services from the date of death to the date of trial, a period in excess of four years, that exceeds the sum of $2,500 is excessive, and any amount attributable to the period beyond eight weeks amounts to an award for loss of consortium, which is not compensable in a death action. *Yuet Ngor Chang v New York City Health & Hospitals Corp.* (1981, 1st Dept) 82 AD2d 764, 440 NYS2d 211. That portion of the judgment attributable to the loss of future services in the amount of $320,000 was stricken because it likewise amounted to an award for loss of consortium. *Yuet Ngor Chang v New York City Health & Hospitals Corp., supra*.

An award of $600,000 for the death of a 28-year-old housewife who was the mother of three children was not excessive. *De Long v County of Erie* (1982, 4th Dept) 89 AD2d 376, 455 NYS2d 887, affd 60 NY2d 296, 469 NYS2d 611. An award of $200,000 for conscious pain and suffering by the deceased during a period of 12 minutes was not excessive, where the evidence showed that she had received seven knife wounds and had been brutally beaten as a result of her struggle to save herself and her child from a murderous assailant, and the jury could properly have considered in its award the terror the victim must have experienced during the ultimate struggle. *De Long v County of Erie, supra.*

Plaintiff, who had been a paraplegic before the accident that resulted in his wife's death, was entitled to $305,503 to cover the cost of a health aide to replace the services the decedent had rendered. *Protzman v State* (1982, 4th Dept) 91 AD2d 853, 458 NYS2d 408.

In a wrongful death action, whether the decedent properly reported his income to the appropriate tax authorities is not controlling, but rather is merely one factor the jury may consider along with the other evidence in the case relevant to the issue of pecuniary loss to the survivors. *Spadaccini v Dolan* (1978, 1st Dept) 63 AD2d 110, 407 NYS2d 840.

Plaintiff administrator was properly permitted to offer evidence of the wages that his decedent, an alien working in the United States on an apparently illegal basis, might have earned. It is for the jury to weigh defense proof that decedent would have earned those wages, if at all, by illegal activity. *Public Adm'r v Equitable Life Assurance Soc'y* (1993, 1st Dept) 192 AD2d 325, 595 NYS2d 478.

In a wrongful death case, proof of specific acts of criminal conduct by the decedent is inadmissible where those acts do not bear upon the earning capacity of the decedent nor on his disposition to support those dependent on him. *Dobro v Sloan* (1975, 4th Dept) 48 AD2d 243, 368 NYS2d 621, app dismd 37 NY2d 804, 375 NYS2d 569.

The testimony of an economist as to the market value of the types of services performed by the average housewife in the decedent's circumstances was relevant to the issue of damages on the wrongful death cause of action. *De Long v County of Erie* (1983) 60 NY2d 296, 469 NYS2d 611.

Although plaintiff testified that her deceased husband performed certain household duties for her, and provided love, guidance and advice to the couple's adult sons, which is sufficient proof of pecuniary loss to sustain the cause of action for wrongful death, the award was excessive to the extent that it exceeded $150,000, because the decedent was 65 years old at the time of his death, had been retired for approximately six years, his only source of income was social security benefits and there was no proof that these benefits, thereafter paid to plaintiff as decedent's widow, had been reduced. *Korman v Public Service Truck Renting, Inc.* (1986, 2d Dept) 116 AD2d 631, 497 NYS2d 480.

Generally, evidence of a decedent's gross income at the time of his death is the standard to measure the value of income already lost and to measure the loss of future earnings. *Johnson v Manhattan & Bronx Surface Transit Operating Auth* (1988) 71 NY2d 198, 524 NYS2d 415.

In a wrongful death action, a jury award of $600,000 was excessive where the proof at the trial showed that decedent's projected loss of earnings would be $482,000, a figure that included neither a reduction for present value nor any reduction for personal consumption or expense, and where moreover, the mother of the decedent testified that her son made no significant monetary contribution to her household prior to his death. *Halvorsen v Ford Motor Co.* (1987, 3d Dept) 132 AD2d 57, 522 NYS2d 272, 11658, app den 71 NY2d 805, 529 NYS2d 76.

A loss of inheritance of $125,562 resulting from the loss of a federal estate tax credit the decedent would have received if he had lived longer, was not recoverable in a wrongful death action. *Farrar v Brooklyn Union Gas Co.* (1988) 73 NY2d 802, 537 NYS2d 26.

In determining whether an estate beneficiary may reasonably expect to sustain pecuniary loss as a result of decedent's death, and therefore, has a cognizable claim for compensation, it is relevant whether the decedent would have been legally obligated to support the beneficiary and, if not, whether there is any evidence that the decedent would have volunteered to do so. *Public Adm'r of Kings County v U.S. Fleet Leasing, Inc.* (1990, 1st Dept) 159 AD2d 331, 552 NYS2d 608.

A compensatory award of $250,000 in a wrongful death case was not excessive, where the evidence established that decedent was a 29-year-old talented mechanic and a loving and loyal son who had made significant contributions to his family. *James v Eber Bros. Wine & Liquor Corp.* (1990, 4th Dept) 153 AD2d 329, 550 NYS2d 972, app den 75 NY2d 711, 557 NYS2d 309.

In a wrongful death action, loss of future earnings is a legitimate item of damages, even for an infant plaintiff, and even where the computation of such damages is necessarily speculative and fraught with difficulties. *Sullivan v LoCastro* (1991, 2d Dept) 178 AD2d 523, 577 NYS2d 631, app den 81 NY2d 701, 594 NYS2d 715.

When parents' pecuniary injuries include loss of their child's services, damages are not limited to the decedent's minority. *Brown v Horn* (1992, 4th Dept) 179 AD2d 1073, 578 NYS2d 951.

An award of $6,000 as a result of the wrongful death of a 19-year-old woman who lived with her parents, was inadequate where the record showed that the parents were 41 and 42 years of age at the time of the trial, the decedent had enrolled in a training course as a nurses' aid, successfully completed the course and was certified as a nurses' aid, except for short periods of time she remained steadily employed as a nurses' aid, maintained a close and loving relationship with her parents, performed various household chores for them and regularly contributed $25 per week to her parents during the time when she was employed and lived at their home and, in addition, decedent provided care and assistance to her mother when she was incapacitated due to illness. *Brown v Horn, supra*.

Separate and apart from the wrongful death action is the so called "survival action" for personal injuries, pain and suffering sustained by the decedent during the period of his survival prior to his death. EPTL § 11-3.2. This section of the law provides that no cause of action for injury to person or property is lost because of the death of the person in whose favor the cause of action existed. For any injury, an action may be brought or continued by the personal representative of the decedent. Punitive damages may be awarded in any action brought to recover damages for personal injury where death occurs after August 31, 1982. EPTL § 11-3.2.

In determining the damages for conscious pain and suffering experienced during an interval between the injury and death, the degree of consciousness, the severity of the pain, the fear of impending death, and the duration are all elements to be considered. *Cook v Erwin* (1968, 3d Dept) 30 AD2d 579, 289 NYS2d 730. Thus, where the period of survival was three hours, notwithstanding the fact that during that brief period there were intervals of unconsciousness, the court approved an award of $10,000. *Cook v Erwin, supra.* Where the period of survival was nine hours but where the evidence disclosed severe suffering, an award of $15,000 was approved. *Ruhl v Smith* (1971, 3d Dept) 37 AD2d 1033, 326 NYS2d 78. Although no recovery for pain and suffering will be allowed where there is no evidence the decedent regained consciousness, *Alfieri v Cabot Corp.* (1962, 1st Dept) 17 AD2d 455, 235 NYS2d 753, motion gr 12 NY2d 1098, 240 NYS2d 163 and motion gr 13 NY2d 647, 240 NYS2d 760 and affd 13 NY2d 1027, 245 NYS2d 600, nevertheless, evidence that the decedent was moaning and groaning or otherwise in evident pain is sufficient to support a verdict for pain and suffering. *Kinner v Kuroczka* (1961, 3d Dept) 12 AD2d 383, 212 NYS2d 479.

An award of $300,000 for conscious pain and suffering was not excessive where decedent was a 5-year-old girl who had suffered third degree burns over almost her entire body, leading to her death 15 days later. *Rush v Sears, Roebuck & Co.* (1983, 3d Dept) 92 AD2d 1072, 461 NYS2d 559.

Mere conjecture, surmise or speculation is not enough to sustain a claim for damages, and in the absence of direct proof either of the cause of decedent's death, or that there was conscious pain and suffering in connection with that death, the evidence was insufficient to form the basis for a jury award of damages for conscious pain and suffering. *Fiederlein v New York City Health & Hospitals Corp.* (1982) 56 NY2d 573, 450 NYS2d 181.

In a wrongful death action against the state to recover for fatal injuries to a decedent who drowned as a result of an automobile accident, it was not error for the Court of Claims to dismiss the claim for conscious pain and suffering for lack of proof, where the only medical testimony was inconclusive, the physician did not state that there were agonal signs indicating that the deceased had survived for some period, and although there was no autopsy, the decedent exhibited no substantial external injuries. *Zalewski v State* (1976, 3d Dept) 53 AD2d 781, 384 NYS2d 545.

It was proper to grant summary judgment dismissing the claims for conscious pain and suffering where the decedents were killed instantly upon impact, no evidence was presented that they had suffered any conscious pain, and plaintiff was unable to show evidence from which it could be implied that decedents were aware of the danger and had suffered from pre-impact terror. *Anderson v Rowe* (1980, 4th Dept) 73 AD2d 1030, 425 NYS2d 180.

The patient's comatose and moribund condition at all the times when he may have experienced negligently-caused suffering precludes any recovery at all for conscious pain and suffering. *Jones v New York* (1977, 1st Dept) 57 AD2d 429, 395 NYS2d 10.

The damages recoverable under the survival statute are not limited to the pain and suffering endured by the decedents up until the time of death, but include other items of special damage such as loss of earnings up to the time of death and other expenses incurred during that period. *Holmes v New York* (1945) 269 AD 95, 54 NYS2d 289, affd 295 NY 615.

An award of $50,000 for decedent's pain and suffering was inadequate as a matter of law where the medical proof clearly established that until her death, 1,154 days after the accident, she endured inordinate pain and depression, with indescribable suffering and sheer agony associated with her quadriplegic, bedridden state, and in the interest of justice this award should be increased to $150,000. *Walsh v Morris* (1987, 3d Dept) 126 AD2d 911, 511 NYS2d 428. In the same case, however, the wrongful death award of $50,000 was not so disproportionate as to shock the conscience of the court where decedent's three children were 20, 19 and 18 years of age at the time of her death, she did not have any earning capacity, and there was no expert testimony as to the value of her services as a homemaker, and plaintiff, for some reason not appearing in the record, was ordered out of the home during a year of her post-accident recovery. *Walsh v Morris, supra.*

An award of $275,000 for conscious pain and suffering was not excessive where the record revealed that the 15-year-old decedent suffered burns over 75% of his body following electrocution caused by his contact with 33,000 volts of electricity in a sub-station of defendant railroad; upon electrocution, decedent became "a ball of fire" and rolled on the ground while screaming for someone to help put the flames out, and remained engulfed by flames for several minutes until reached by a bystander who extinguished the flames; and during the five days that ensued between his injury and death, aside from a brief period, the decedent was conscious and suffered extensively from his injuries and from the painful burn treatment he received while at the hospital. *Regan v Long Island R. R. Co.* (1987, 2d Dept) 128 AD2d 511, 512 NYS2d 443.

Although no recovery may be granted in a wrongful death action for loss of parental companionship, it has long been recognized that pecuniary advantage results from parental nurture and care, from physical, moral and intellectual training, and that the loss of those benefits may be considered within the calculation of pecuniary injury. *Kenavan v New York* (1986, 2d Dept) 120 AD2d 24, 507 NYS2d 193. However, an award in the sum of $250,000 for conscious pain and suffering to the estate of a deceased firefighter who was admitted to the hospital about one half hour after reaching the fire, was unconscious on arrival at the hospital and remained so until his death 24 hours later, was excessive. *Kenavan v New York, supra.*

An award of $35,000, representing damages for conscious pain and suffering during a period where the jury could reasonably have inferred from the evidence that plaintiff's decedent was conscious and suffered extensively for a period of 15 to 20 minutes before she lapsed into a coma, was not excessive, particularly in the light of the severity of her injuries, which included a crushed skull. *Coffey v Callichio* (1988, 2d Dept) 136 AD2d 673, 523 NYS2d 1011. In the same case an award of $300,000 for damages for wrongful death was excessive in view of the evidence that decedent was a 16-year-old student who did not contribute monetarily to her parents' household. *Coffey v Callichio, supra.*

In an action for wrongful death and conscious pain and suffering resulting from the drowning death of a child, where, when decedent was taken from the water, his color was described as good by one witness, another testified that he thought he detected a pulse beat, while another testified that decedent appeared to be consciously vomiting, and efforts by the paramedics at cardiopulmonary resuscitation were unsuccessful, there was sufficient evidence presented so as to permit a reasonable conclusion that decedent consciously struggled for life for as long as one hour, and an award of $100,000 for conscious pain and suffering was not excessive. *Cassar v Central Hudson Gas & Electric Corp.* (1987, 3d Dept) 134 AD2d 672, 521 NYS2d 337.

In a wrongful death action where plaintiff's expert witness in accident reconstruction testified to the ineffectiveness of seatbelts in protecting the human body against lateral impacts, concluding that it was unlikely that decedent would have survived the collision whether or not he wore a seatbelt, and defendant's medical expert stated only that decedent would not have sustained the injuries he did had he worn a seatbelt, but gave no opinion as to the likelihood of the victim's survival, failure to use a seatbelt was unavailable as an affirmative defense in mitigation of damages and the trial court correctly dismissed this defense. *Baginski v New York Tel. Co.* (1987, 1st Dept) 130 AD2d 362, 515 NYS2d 23.

Loss of enjoyment of life is not a separate element of damages deserving a distinct award but is, instead, only a factor to be considered by the jury in assessing damages for conscious pain and suffering. *Nussbaum v Gibstein* (1989) 73 NY2d 912, 539 NYS2d 289.

Although it was possible that the victim of a homicide might have been unconscious at the outset of the assault, possibly from a blow to the back of her head, the court found that the circumstantial evidence rendered it more probable that she was conscious when most of the injuries were inflicted, and that an award of $350,000 for conscious pain and suffering was not excessive. *Gonzalez v New York City Housing Authority* (1990, 1st Dept) 161 AD2d 358, 555 NYS2d 107, app gr 76 NY2d 710, 563 NYS2d 61 and affd 77 NY2d 663, 569 NYS2d 915. A wrongful death award of $100,000 to the adult grandchildren of decedent, who was 76 years old at the time of her death and had a 10 year life expectancy, was reasonable, where decedent had been a "mother" to them for many years at the time of the murder and also provided housekeeping services to the grandchildren's mother who had been under psychiatric care for over a decade. *Gonzalez v New York City Housing Authority, supra.*

Where there was considerable doubt about whether and to what extent the decedent experienced any conscious pain and suffering throughout the 19 days between injury and death, during which time he remained in varying degrees of coma, an award of $1 million for conscious pain and suffering was conditionally reduced to $300,000. *Greene v New York* (1991, 1st Dept) 170 AD2d 321, 566 NYS2d 40.

An award of $300,000 for the conscious pain and suffering of a decedent was supported by the expert testimony of a physician who established that as a result of her massive injuries, the decedent was conscious and in severe physical pain for approximately five hours before she died. *Van Norden v Kliternick* (1991, 1st Dept) 178 AD2d 167, 577 NYS2d 27.

An award of $250,000 for conscious pain and suffering was appropriate, taking into account the pre-impact fear and terror that necessarily attended the decedent's observation of the drunken motorist's automobile bearing down on him, the horrendous nature of the injuries, which included severance of the thoracic artery, and the evidence of consciousness for at least 15 minutes, and possibly as long as an hour. *Torelli v City of New York* (1991, 1st Dept) 176 AD2d 119, 574 NYS2d 5.

In the case of a 16-year-old student who drowned in a high school swimming pool, where experts from both sides indicated that a drowning victim would lose consciousness in just a few minutes, an award of $50,000 for conscious pain and suffering was proper. *Dontas v New York* (1992, 2d Dept) 183 AD2d 868, 584 NYS2d 134.

The Court of Claims could properly conclude that decedent, who was alive underwater for two or three minutes, experienced severe conscious pain and suffering, including contemplation of death for the two or three minutes, as a result of the electricity in his body that first rendered him unable to escape from the water, and then caused him to come into contact with a more intense source of electricity, eventually causing his death by electrocution. Under these circumstances, an award of $100,000 for conscious pain and suffering lasting two or three minutes was affirmed. *Higgins v State* (1993, 3d Dept) 192 AD2d 821, 596 NYS2d 479.

§ 29:20 DAMAGES FOR LOSS OF CONSORTIUM — The concept of consortium includes not only loss of support, but also such elements as love, companionship, affection, society, sexual relations, solace and more. *Millington v Southeastern Elevator Co.* (1968) 22 NY2d 498, 293 NYS2d 305, 36 ALR3d 891.

Under the former rule, an action for loss of consortium was not maintainable by a wife where personal injuries were sustained by husband as a result of defendant's negligence. *Kronenbitter v Washburn Wire Co.* (1958) 4 NY2d 524, 176 NYS2d 354. This is no longer the rule. *Millington v Southeastern Elevator Co., supra*.

A wife whose husband became completely paralyzed from the waist down as a result of an elevator accident, allegedly caused by defendant's negligence, was entitled to bring an action for loss of consortium. *Millington v Southeastern Elevator Co., supra*.

The wife of an injured harbor worker could seek recovery for loss of consortium occasioned by her husband's injury. *Alvez v American Export Lines, Inc.* (1979) 46 NY2d 634, 415 NYS2d 979, affd 446 US 274, 64 L Ed 2d 284, 100 S Ct 1673.

A wife does not have a derivative cause of action for loss of consortium with respect to breach of contract claims, because derivative claims arise from tortious conduct. *Odell v Dalrymple* (1989, 4th Dept) 156 AD2d 967, 549 NYS2d 260.

A claim for loss of consortium will not be recognized within a wrongful death action in New York State. *Liff v Schildkrout* (1980) 49 NY2d 622, 427 NYS2d 746; *Kaplan v Sparks* (1993, 4th Dept) 192 AD2d 1119, 596 NYS2d 279.

An award for loss of consortium is limited to reasonable compensation. An award of $950,000 to the plaintiff's wife did not deviate from what would be reasonable compensation, where it was shown that, as a result of an accident, her husband suffered from incomplete paraplegia and incontinency of the bowel and bladder, would require 24-hour nursing care for his life expectancy of 20.2 years, went from being a working-man who provided for himself and others to someone who needed to be fed, clothed, diaper-changed and was constantly crying and highly agitated because his condition required him to be physically restrained.

Harvey v Mazal American Partners (1991, 1st Dept) 165 AD2d 242, 566 NYS2d 242, motion gr 78 NY2d 855.

In a malpractice action, an award to a husband of $300,000 for the loss of his wife's services was excessive in that it failed to take into account the fact that the underlying disease, and the serious side effects brought about by its treatment, were, and could in the future be expected to be, the cause of much of her inability to perform her usual services. *Schneider v Memorial Hospital for Cancer & Allied Diseases* (1984, 2d Dept) 100 AD2d 583, 473 NYS2d 524.

Although plaintiffs concededly carried on a long distance marriage, being together for only a total of two or three months a year, the uncontradicted evidence established the existence of a valid and continuing marriage, and the presence of the elements of affection, companionship, society and solace and the loss thereof, which formed the basis of the consortium claim. It was error, therefore, for the trial court to fail to set aside the jury verdict awarding no damages on the claim of plaintiff wife for loss of consortium. *Rakich v Lawes* (1992, 3d Dept) 186 AD2d 932, 589 NYS2d 617.

Damages cannot be recovered under a claim for loss of consortium unless the party asserting the claim was lawfully married to the injured person at the time of the actionable conduct; where plaintiffs were living together but not married at the time the cause of action accrued, the claim for loss of consortium was properly dismissed. *Lesocovich v 180 Madison Ave. Corp.* (1990, 3d Dept) 165 AD2d 963, 561 NYS2d 851, app den 77 NY2d 804, 568 NYS2d 912; *Anderson v Eli Lilly & Co.* (1990, 3d Dept) 158 AD2d 91, 557 NYS2d 981, app gr 77 NY2d 803, 568 NYS2d 347.

In an action based on allegations that exposure of the wife to DES while *in utero* caused abnormalities in her reproductive system that left her infertile, the husband may not recover for loss of consortium based on his contention that plaintiff wife's pre-existing injury was undiscoverable at the time of the marriage and was caused by a toxic substance; consortium represents the marital partner's interest in continuance of the marital relationship as it existed at its inception, not upon some guarantee that the marital partners are free of any pre-existing latent injuries. *Anderson v Eli Lilly & Co., supra.*

A husband's cause of action for medical expenses of his wife is derivative, in the sense that it derives from the marriage relationship, which obliges the husband to provide the necessary medical care for his wife. *Rush v Bauerle* (1966) 49 Misc 2d 595, 268 NYS2d 67. If the plaintiff's husband is liable for his wife's medical expenses and the wife has a right of action against a third party, the husband may bring an action to recover such medical expenses even though no lawsuit is brought by his wife. *Rush v Bauerle supra.*

Damages for loss of consortium are not recoverable where the alleged wrongful conduct preceded the marriage. *Mehtani v New York Life Ins. Co.* (1989, 1st Dept) 145 AD2d 90, 537 NYS2d 800.

A husband cannot recover damages for the loss of his wife's services and for medical expenses that were incurred as a result of injuries negligently inflicted on her by another person before the marriage. *Rademacher v Torbensen* (1939) 257 AD 91, 13 NYS2d 124.

When no cause of action on behalf of the wife for medical malpractice is stated, the derivative claim of her husband for loss of services must fail as well. *Gastwirth v Rosenberg* (1986, 2d Dept) 117 AD2d 706, 499 NYS2d 95.

A child may not recover in a derivative action for loss of consortium against an alleged tortfeasor who inflicted disabling injuries on one of the child's parents. *De Angelis v Lutheran Medical Center* (1983) 58 NY2d 1053, 462 NYS2d 626.

§ 29:21 DAMAGES FOR INJURY TO REAL ESTATE — For an injury to real estate, the proper measure of damages is the amount that will compensate the owner for the injury sustained and restore him to his position before the commission of the wrong. *Cashin v New Rochelle* (1931) 256 NY 190, 176 NE 138.

In actions to recover damages for injuries to real estate resulting from the unlawful separation and removal of something therefrom, the courts recognize two elements of damage: (1) the value of the thing taken, after separation from the freehold, if it has any, and (2) the damage to the realty, if any, resulting from the removal. *Dwight v Elmira, C. & N. R. Co.* (1892) 132 NY 199, 30

NE 398. When the plaintiff, asserting the right to go beyond the value of the thing taken after its severance from the freehold, seeks compensation for damage to the land, the measure of damages is the difference in the value of the land before and after the injury. *Dwight v Elmira, C. & N. R. Co., supra.* Where fruit-bearing trees were destroyed by fire, the plaintiff did not have to be satisfied with a recovery based merely on the value of the trees destroyed, after separation from the realty, but could seek to obtain recovery based on the loss to the land due to the destruction of an orchard of fruit-bearing trees, which had added largely to its productive value. *Dwight v Elmira, C. & N. R. Co., supra.* Damages, in any event, are proportioned to the actual pecuniary loss sustained, and such damages may not be speculative. *Cashin v New Rochelle, supra.*

For destruction of ornamental shade trees, the measure of damages was the difference in market value of the premises immediately before and immediately after the injury complained of. *Greene v Mindon Constr. Corp.* (1959, Sup) 188 NYS2d 633, motion den 19 Misc 2d 228, 190 NYS2d 86.

A plaintiff may not recover damages he might have sustained if the property had been put to some use other than the one for which it was employed at the time of the wrongful act. *Rumsey v New York & N. E. R. Co.* (1892) 133 NY 79, 30 NE 654. Thus, where a plaintiff for about six years before the time defendant built his road, had ceased using his premises for a brickyard, it could not be said that the use as a brickyard was discontinued because of any act on the part of the defendant, and therefore damages could not be based on the rental value of the property as a brickyard. *Rumsey v New York & N. E. R. Co., supra.*

Where the plaintiff brought an action for injury resulting from unauthorized dumping of waste material, damages would be based on the difference between the value of the land before and after the fill or by the cost of removal thereof and restoration to original condition, whichever was the lesser amount. *Realty Associates, Inc. v New York* (1956, 2d Dept) 1 AD2d 1049, 152 NYS2d 766, reh den (2d Dept) 2 AD2d 812, 154 NYS2d 843.

A verdict for damage to a building may in no event exceed the value of the building. *Fagan v Pathe Industries, Inc.* (1949) 274 AD 703, 86 NYS2d 859.

Where plaintiff's hotel was damaged by fire and the furnishings of several rooms were destroyed as a result of the negligence of defendant's employee, the plaintiff was entitled to recover for the loss and damage to the furnishings upon proving their value to him, and for the loss of income during the period when a portion or all of his hotel was not available for use as such. *Turner v Reynolds* (1946) 271 AD 413, 66 NYS2d 339. Where plaintiff's dwelling was damaged, and the cost of repairs was higher than the market value, the plaintiff could not recover more than the market value of the property. *Coyle v Serafini Constr. Co.* (1957) 8 Misc 2d 807, 167 NYS2d 680.

A party who claims relief for injury to real property needs to establish the amount of damages under only one measure, although other measures may be applicable. *Jenkins v Etlinger* (1982) 55 NY2d 35, 447 NYS2d 696. Recovery for temporary injury to real property may be measured by the value of the loss of use, which is determined by the decrease in the property's rental value during the pendency of the injury. *Jenkins v Etlinger, supra.*

If the alternative measures would yield a lesser award, the burden of proving that is on the defendant. *Jaklitsch v Finnerty* (1983, 3d Dept) 96 AD2d 690, 466 NYS2d 774.

§ 29:22 DAMAGES IN EMINENT DOMAIN PROCEEDINGS
— A citizen holds his property subject to the state's exercise of the right of eminent domain. *Adamec v Post* (1937) 273 NY 250, 109 ALR 1110. Such power is inherent in every sovereign. *Board of Hudson River Regulating Dist. v Fonda, J. & G. R. Co.* (1928) 249 NY 445, 164 NE 541, remittitur amd 250 NY 559, 166 NE 324, 224. The exercise of this power is subject, however, to the restriction that the taking of property must be for an authorized public use, and just compensation must be paid to the owner. *Fifth Ave. Coach Lines, Inc. v New York* (1962) 11 NY2d 342, 229 NYS2d 400.

This right to compensation on the part of the owner when his property is taken in eminent domain proceedings is guaranteed by both the Federal and State Constitutions. *Re Bronx River Parkway*

(1940) 259 AD 552, 20 NYS2d 53, affd 284 NY 48, remittitur amd 284 NY 701 and affd 313 US 540, 85 L Ed 1508, 61 S Ct 839. The Federal and State Constitutions provide that no person shall be deprived of property without due process of law. New York State Constitution, Art I § 6. The United States Constitution, Amendment 14, and the New York State Constitution specifically provide that private property shall not be taken for public use without just compensation. New York State Constitution, Art I § 7(a).

When property is taken without just compensation, there is a deprivation of property without due process of law. *Gilman v Tucker* (1891) 128 NY 190, 28 NE 1040. The owner of property taken for public use is entitled to just compensation as a matter of right. *Pauchogue Land Corp. v Long Island State Park Com.* (1926) 243 NY 15, 152 NE 451, reh den 243 NY 542, 154 NE 597. It is the owner of the property and no one else, who may object that land is taken for a public use without due compensation. *Waterloo Woolen Mfg. Co. v Shanahan* (1891) 128 NY 345, 28 NE 358.

When a condemnation award is based on findings of value supported by substantial evidence, and the findings have been affirmed, the Court of Appeals may not review such findings. *Re Fifth Ave. Coach Lines, Inc.* (1968) 22 NY2d 613, 294 NYS2d 502, remittitur amd 24 NY2d 773, 300 NYS2d 41 and later app (1st Dept) 34 AD2d 930, 312 NYS2d 592.

Before compensation may be awarded, there must be a taking of at least a part of the land for which damages are demanded. *Re Public Beach* (1936) 248 AD 902, 290 NYS 635, affd 274 NY 536. An abutter, the value of whose land is impaired or whose easement rights are interfered with, has no right to compensation merely because there is a consequential interference with access to his land or diversion of traffic, where there has been a change of grade, unless the damages result directly from the change. *Selig v State* (1961) 10 NY2d 34, 217 NYS2d 33.

To the extent that private rights in land are invaded, lessened or destroyed, there is in a legal sense a taking of property, and that taking is in fact by its operation and effect a direct injury to the owner and his property rights and a diminution of his rights of use; but to constitute a taking, the injury must be a special one and not merely a general injury that is common to the public at large, and the damage must be peculiar to the particular property. *Re East River Drive* (1942) 264 AD 555, 35 NYS2d 990, affd 298 NY 843. A taking of riparian rights is a taking of real property with respect to condemnation proceedings. *Re East River Drive, supra.*

When property taken for public use is an integral part of a larger plot, and what is left is substantially deteriorated in value as a result of the relationship between the property taken and the entire property, there has been a partial taking. *Re Cross-Bronx Expressway* (1948) 195 Misc 842, 82 NYS2d 55. Compensation in the case of a partial taking of property is based on the difference in market value between the entire property before the taking and the market value of the property that remains after the taking. *Re Public Beach at Rockaway Beach* (1942) 288 NY 75. When part of a building is taken, the proper measure of damages is the difference between the value of a building before the taking and the value of the remaining portion after completion of the improvement. *Re Buffalo* (1910) 65 Misc 636, 120 NYS 611.

In the case of a partial taking of land, the owner is entitled to the value of the land that has been appropriated, plus any consequential damage to the remainder of property that results from the taking. *Lawrence v Greenwood* (1949) 300 NY 231. The owner is entitled to any damages he may sustain because of the use to which the acquiring party puts the land. *New York M. R. Corp. v Weber* (1919) 226 NY 70, 123 NE 68. Thus, where a railroad took land, not only could the owner be awarded the market value of the land that was taken, he was also entitled to be compensated for damages that resulted to the portion of the land he retained, as a result of the use by the railroad of the part of the land that it took. *New York M. R. Corp. v Weber, supra.*

To recover for consequential damages that result from the use to which appropriated land is put, it must be shown that the contemplated use of the property to be taken permanently interferes with and diminishes the value of the property that remains. *Culver Contracting Corp. v Humphrey* (1935) 268 NY 26, 196 NE 627, reh den 268 NY 719, 198 NE 574.

The rule that requires an award of consequential damages in the case of a partial taking applies to the property of corporations. *Re New York Water Service Corp.* (1946, Sup) 67 NYS2d 850, affd 271 AD 1019, 69 NYS2d 508, affd 296 NY 1016.

The rule on consequential damages with regard to the part retained is not applicable where under extraordinary or unusual circumstances it will result in an injustice or in the awarding of double damages. *Re Parkway in New York* (1912) 150 AD 482, 135 NYS 65.

The cost of curing a condition caused by the taking of land is a permissible item of damages, but the amount allowed may not be greater than the amount of the consequential damages. *Mobil Oil Corp. v State* (1969) 59 Misc 2d 658, 300 NYS2d 230, affd 34 AD2d 735, 313 NYS2d 353.

When a portion of property is appropriated, any consequential damages to the remaining property must be offset to the extent that such property has been benefitted by the improvement. *Esso Standard Oil Co. v State* (1959, 3d Dept) 9 AD2d 840, 192 NYS2d 823. When an entire tract of land is taken, the fundamental question in appraising the value of the condemned realty is what the owner has lost, not what the condemnor has gained. *Re Lands of P. & M. Materials Corp.* (1963) 38 Misc 2d 734, 238 NYS2d 896, mod (2d Dept) 20 AD2d 431, 248 NYS2d 539. Each condemnation case involves different facts and is to be considered by itself. General rules must yield to exceptional cases where necessary to properly compensate the owner for the land taken. *Application of Westchester County* (1953) 204 Misc 1031, 127 NYS2d 24, affd 285 AD 1169, 141 NYS2d 824.

The term "just compensation for condemnation of property" is that amount that a willing buyer would theoretically pay a willing seller. *Re Site for City-Aided Low-Rent Housing Project, etc.* (1949) 197 Misc 70, 89 NYS2d 855. The income from the business the claimant conducted on the appropriated land was an element to be considered in fixing damages. *Smith v State* (1932) 145 Misc 899, 261 NYS 169. The owners of land taken for a power site are entitled to the fair market value of the land for its highest and best available use. *Niagara, Lockport & Ontario Power Co. v Horton* (1931) 231 AD 402, 247 NYS 761. Actual rents may be looked to as a reliable index of future rents in determining the value of a condemned parcel. *Re James Madison Houses* (1962, 1st Dept) 17 AD2d 317, 234 NYS2d 799. Actual rents are, however, no absolute criterion of the rental value in eminent domain proceedings. *Re Lincoln Square Slum Clearance Project* (1961, 1st Dept) 15 AD2d 153, 222 NYS2d 786, affd 12 NY2d 1086, 240 NYS2d 30 and affd 16 NY2d 497, 260 NYS2d 439, remittitur amd 16 NY2d 828, 263 NYS2d 169. A proper percentage of what an operator could obtain as gross rental for furnished rooms was the proper standard to be applied in determining the value of a building leased to a rooming-house operator. *Re Lincoln Square Slum Clearance Project, supra.* The value of buildings could not exceed reproduction costs but could be less, because reproduction costs generally represent the highest value that can be placed on a structure. *Re Lincoln Square Slum Clearance Project, supra.*

It is proper to consider deposits of minerals that might tend to enhance the value of land in considering the question of fair market value of land taken by condemnation. *Application & Petition of Huie* (1956, 3d Dept) 1 AD2d 500, 152 NYS2d 95.

The difference in the value of land before and after a tree was cut down was the proper measure of damages to be applied in determining the loss sustained by property owners when the tree was removed by the state. *Stevens v State* (1959) 21 Misc 2d 79, 197 NYS2d 111, affd (4th Dept) 14 AD2d 823, 218 NYS2d 535. The measure of damages in an eminent domain proceeding is not the separate value of trees on the condemned land, but the value of the land as it is enhanced by them. *Comstock Foods, Inc. v State* (1959) 18 Misc 2d 519, 191 NYS2d 448, affd (4th Dept) 11 AD2d 753, 204 NYS2d 125.

Where fixtures and realty that were condemned had been custom-built or expressly adapted to fit the premises, the application of the rule of reproduction costs minus depreciation was proper. *Marraro v State* (1963) 12 NY2d 285, 239 NYS2d 105. Where electrical and plumbing connections were easily removable and had been put in by tenants solely to accommodate fixtures installed for the individual purposes of the several occupancies, the award to the tenants for such connections in condemnation proceedings was disallowed. *Marraro v State* (1963) 12 NY2d 285, 239 NYS2d 105.

A country club was specialty property, and the award for its taking should have been based on the replacement value of the golf course. *Albany Country Club v State* (1963, 3d Dept) 19 AD2d 199, 241 NYS2d 604, affd 13 NY2d 1085, 246 NYS2d 407.

Where the market value of machinery removed by the condemnee from condemned premises to a new location remained the same after removal, the condemnee was denied any compensation for loss or damage to the machinery. *Buffalo v Mollenberg-Betz Machine Co.* (1966) 53 Misc 2d 849, 279 NYS2d 842.

A award of $35,000 was held to be inadequate and was increased to $55,000 where it was shown that the city's experts valued a building at $39,500 and the claimant's expert valued the same building at $102,000. *Re Brooklyn Bridge Southwest Urban Renewal Project* (1968, 1st Dept) 30 AD2d 939, 293 NYS2d 910, affd 25 NY2d 627, 306 NYS2d 10.

An owner can recover for loss in value in a condemnation blight action caused by premature disclosure of condemnation, or any other acts of the condemnor that depreciate the value of his property. *Re Lynbrook* (1973) 75 Misc 2d 678, 348 NYS2d 115.

Where the state changed the course of a highway and thus interfered with access to the property of an abutting owner, the owner cannot recover consequential damages unless able to prove that the remaining access was not merely inadequate but also prevented the highest and best use of the property. *Cousin v State* (1972) 75 Misc 2d 1096, 348 NYS2d 806, affd (3d Dept) 42 AD2d 1016, 348 NYS2d 253.

When the state appropriates part of claimant's land, and the remaining land is enhanced in value by the taking, the benefit to the remaining land as a result of the state's appropriation may not be used as an offset against the award for direct damages for the property taken. *Chiesa v State* (1974, 3d Dept) 43 AD2d 359, 351 NYS2d 735, affd 36 NY2d 21, 364 NYS2d 848.

Where the property of a manufacturer of bicycle rims was appropriated by the state, and part of the property included a plating facility that contained an automated plating machine attached to which were plating racks, filters, cobalt and nickel anodes used to electroplate the rims, anode baskets, storage tanks, and 13 solutions used in the plating process, these items, by annexation, adaptation and intention became part of the realty. Consequently they were fixtures for which the claimants were properly compensated due to the appropriation by the state. *Wright v State* (1974, 4th Dept) 45 AD2d 919, 357 NYS2d 311.

Before a proposed appropriation by the state, the claimant had contracted to sell the subject property at a price of $10,000 per acre. This was the best and most substantial evidence of market value, and claimants were obligated to accept the sum of $10,000 per acre. *Stark v State* (1974, 3d Dept) 46 AD2d 819, 360 NYS2d 506.

Where claimant had made plans for future development involving the land taken, the trial court properly denied damages for "frustration of plans for business expansion." *Specialty Foods Corp. v State* (1974, 3d Dept) 46 AD2d 989, 362 NYS2d 266, app dismd 37 NY2d 751, 374 NYS2d 625.

A slope easement can result in fee damages if the taking actually or potentially deprives the owner of access to, or the use and enjoyment of his property. *Re Quintard Street & Additional Lands* (1975, 2d Dept) 47 AD2d 644, 363 NYS2d 962.

A property owner who has been denied an existing governmental service proves a constitutional taking when he demonstrates that such denial is economically confiscatory in effect, unreasonable in terms of necessity, and indefinite in duration. *Charles v Diamond* (1975, 4th Dept) 47 AD2d 426, 366 NYS2d 921, mod 41 NY2d 318, 392 NYS2d 594.

In determining fair market value, the condemnees are entitled to have the appraisal based on the highest and best available use of the property, regardless of whether they are so using it. *County of Suffolk v Firester* (1975) 37 NY2d 649, 376 NYS2d 458. If an increment in value must be added to the raw acreage value to reflect a property's subdivision potential, the specific increment that is selected and applied must be based on sufficient evidence and be satisfactorily explained. *County of Suffolk v Firester, supra*.

The determination of the highest and best use must be based on evidence of a use that could or would be made of the property in the near future. Where the regional shopping center proposed by the claimant was purely hypothetical and based largely upon physical possibility, rather than economic feasibility, the trial court correctly concluded that such evidence was insufficient to support a finding of highest and best use. *Consolidated Edison Co. v Neptune Assocs.* (1993, 2d Dept) 190 AD2d 669, 593 NYS2d 259.

The trial court properly rejected the claimant's appraisal where claimant failed to demonstrate that it was reasonably probable that the subject property, which was designed for use as a sanitation garage, could or would feasibly be converted for use as an air cargo facility in the near future. *City of New York v Estate of Levine* (1993, 2d Dept) 196 AD2d 654, 601 NYS2d 620, app dismd without op 84 NY2d 864, 618 NYS2d 8.

Where the income and market value of the property were substantially reduced after a portion of it was taken, the court properly concluded that the comparable sales offered by the city were not in fact comparable to the condemned property, and in addition, expenditures necessary to restore the remaining portion of the property to working condition constituted an additional loss to the owner. *Re New York* (1976) 39 NY2d 453, 384 NYS2d 402.

Where a purchaser of land acquired an easement of ingress and egress over adjacent land, which was condemned without naming the owner of the easement in the condemnation petition, the easement of ingress and egress was extinguished and its owner was entitled to compensation. *Ossining Urban Renewal Agency v Lord* (1976) 39 NY2d 628, 385 NYS2d 28, later app (2d Dept) 88 AD2d 641, 450 NYS2d 339, revd 60 NY2d 845, 470 NYS2d 134.

When the proof shows a reasonable probability that land zoned as residential would have been rezoned as the result of a court action, it was not error to award the claimant an increment above the value of the property so zoned. *Re Islip* (1980) 49 NY2d 354, 426 NYS2d 220.

Where both the county, the claimant and their respective appraisers presented proof of valuation of the rear portion of the condemned premises, then zoned as residential, on the predicate that a zoning change from residential to commercial was probable, it was error for the trial court, independently and on its own initiative, to depart from that hypothesis and fix the value of the rear portion on the basis of residential zoning without increment for probable rezoning. *County of Suffolk v Griffith* (1977) 41 NY2d 1058, 396 NYS2d 169.

When the highest and best use is the one the property currently serves, and that use is income-producing, the proper method of valuation is the capitalization of income. *Re New York (Ocean-view Terrace)* (1977) 42 NY2d 948, 398 NYS2d 134.

Plaintiffs, who were forced to abandon their homes because of the presence of explosive levels of methane gas generated on an adjoining property formerly used by defendant town as a landfill site, and who were awarded the "pre-nuisance" market value as damages, fully proved an action for "inverse condemnation" and therefore should have been required to convey title to their property to the defendant town. *Balken v Brookhaven* (1979, 2d Dept) 70 AD2d 579, 416 NYS2d 51.

Although a state or a municipality may close a street, if acting under proper statutory authority, a suitable means of access must be left to an abutting owner or he is entitled to compensation. *Gengarelly v Glen Cove Urban Renewal Agency* (1979, 2d Dept) 69 AD2d 524, 418 NYS2d 790.

In condemnation proceedings, water charges are payable by the occupant and are accorded a statutory lien in reduction of the condemnation award. *Re New York* (1980, 1st Dept) 74 AD2d 552, 425 NYS2d 118.

A *de facto* taking requires physical entry by the condemnor, a physical ouster of the owner, a legal interference with the physical use, possession or enjoyment of the property or a legal interference with the owner's power of disposition of the property. *Borntrager v County of Delaware* (1980, 3d Dept) 76 AD2d 969, 428 NYS2d 766, later app 99 AD2d 627, 472 NYS2d 182. Plaintiffs' allegations that their property was appropriated by a *de facto* condemnation when defendant entered their property and diverted and rearranged the stream, thereby altering its natural flow, depriving access to approximately 35 acres of plaintiffs' land, and destroying its value as a trout stream, set forth a cause of action in *de facto* condemnation for the permanent appropriation of plaintiffs' land. *Borntrager v County of Delaware, supra.*

Generally, if a taking renders access merely circuitous, but nevertheless adequate for the pre-taking highest and best use, a land owner is not entitled to consequential damages. If, however, the facts established at the trial of the claim show that the access involved is more than merely circuitous so that it can be characterized as "unsuitable," compensability follows. *Baan v State* (1980, 3d Dept) 75 AD2d 919, 427 NYS2d 532.

In condemnation proceedings, the constitutional requirement of just compensation necessarily includes a sum in addition to the bare value of the property to account for the delay between the taking and the ultimate payment to the property owner. *Re New York* (1983) 58 NY2d 532, 462 NYS2d 619. The property owner is entitled to receive a fair return for the deprivation of the use of the property, or the money equivalent of that use. *Re New York, supra*.

Where there was credible testimony that the extension of the claimant's driveway rendered it superior in both technology and safety to the old one, and reasonable access to the new highway was furnished, damages resulting from the alteration are *damnum absque injuria*, unless the claimant has been unlawfully saddled with the cost of preserving the extension. *Raj v State* (1986, 3d Dept) 124 AD2d 426, 507 NYS2d 770.

A condemnee using or occupying the property after acquisition for highway purposes is required to pay the condemnor the fair and reasonable value for such use and occupancy. *State v Como Meat Packers, Inc.* (1986, 3d Dept) 124 AD2d 902, 508 NYS2d 318.

A condemnee does not have a right of first refusal when a condemnor attempts to auction a leasehold in a previously condemned parcel of real property. *Mary Chamberlain Trust v Litke* (1987, 2d Dept) 135 AD2d 714, 522 NYS2d 614, app gr 72 NY2d 803.

To show that an unconstitutional taking has occurred, a landowner must prove that the land cannot yield an economically reasonable return as zoned; it is not enough to prove that the land would be more valuable under a less restrictive class. *Redco v Oyster Bay* (1990, 2d Dept) 160 AD2d 984, 554 NYS2d 705.

The court properly declined to give report by the city's appraiser any probative weight with respect to the value of the land and improvements, because it contained only conclusory estimates and failed to reflect adjustments that were made. *Re New York City Transit Authority* (1990, 2d Dept) 160 AD2d 705, 553 NYS2d 785, on remand 150 Misc 2d 917, 572 NYS2d 613.

The property taxes due and owing to the condemnor were properly deducted from the condemnation award. *County of Rockland v Kohl Industrial Park Co.* (1991, 2d Dept) 172 AD2d 607, 568 NYS2d 425.

Under Eminent Domain Procedure Law § 701, a discretionary additional allowance is permitted when the order or award is substantially exceeds the amount the state initially offered the plaintiff. *Malin v State* (1992, 2d Dept) 183 AD2d 899, 584 NYS2d 596.

Where the court's award of $47,650 was more than 200% of the condemnor's initial offer of $21,000 and the owner necessarily expended legal fees and disbursements of $9,433.32, together with appraiser's fees in the amount of $3,859.50, the award was substantially in excess of the initial offer. An award under Eminent Domain Procedure Law § 701 was necessary for the owner to receive just and adequate compensation. *County of Oswego v Maroney* (1992, 4th Dept) 186 AD2d 1031, 588 NYS2d 478.

§ 29:23 DAMAGES IN DEFAMATION ACTIONS — Two types of damages may be recoverable in a defamation action: (1) compensatory damages, for which a major portion is damage to the plaintiff's reputation as a result of the libel, and (2) punitive or exemplary damages, which result only if the publication is shown to have been made with actual malice. *Crane v New York World Tel. Corp.* (1955) 308 NY 470, 52 ALR2d 1169.

In fixing compensatory damages for libel, a jury must consider the extent of the plaintiff's injury from all circumstances. *Zator v Buchel* (1931) 231 AD 334, 247 NYS 686. Substantial compensatory damages in a libel case must be based on a finding of substantial injury, and must be commensurate with that injury. *Zator v Buchel, supra*. It was error to instruct a jury that it could find substantial compensatory damages for an attorney suing for libel even if no injury was sustained. *Zator v Buchel, supra*.

The damages recoverable in a libel action are the plaintiff's loss of reputation in the minds of people who knew him or do know about him, together with his mental suffering as a result of the libel. *Sorge v Parade Publications, Inc.* (1964, 1st Dept) 20 AD2d 338, 247 NYS2d 317.

Punitive damages cannot be awarded by a jury for libel, in the absence of express proof of malice. *Hollien v Tarrytown Daily News, Inc.* (1932) 235 AD 869, 257 NYS 543.

Actual malice that will support an award of punitive damages may be proved by showing acts or utterances or other publications of the defendant that display hatred, spite or ill will toward the plaintiff and in some cases, it may be implied from the falsity of the publication itself. *Frechette v Special Magazines, Inc.* (1954) 285 AD 174, 136 NYS2d 448. The equivalent of actual malice, for the purpose of supporting an award of punitive damages, may consist of publishing a libel with such negligence and carelessness as to indicate a wanton or reckless disregard for the rights of others. *Frechette v Special Magazines, Inc., supra; Crane v New York World Tel. Corp., supra.*

The fact that a person has such a high character that the grossest libel would not damage him is no reason for disallowing punitive damages. *Toomey v Farley* (1956) 2 NY2d 71, 156 NYS2d 840.

In an action for libel, even though plaintiffs have suffered no actual damages, they may be entitled to nominal or punitive damages. *Udell v Josephson* (1939, Sup) 11 NYS2d 866.

An award of $100 to an attorney to whom it was said, "You're no lawyer, you're a crook. You took graft," was not grossly inadequate as a matter of law, in the absence of proof of actual financial damages. *Kruglak v Landre* (1965, 2d Dept) 23 AD2d 758, 258 NYS2d 550.

An award of $4 million for humiliation, mental anguish and injury to the plaintiff's reputation was not excessive where, before the defamatory broadcast, the plaintiff, a respected business and civic leader in his community, owned four restaurants, two hotels and a meat packing business and was in the final stages of developing an airline that was to serve the tourist industry in his community, had an active social and professional life based on service to a community that relied on his good character and reputation; while after the defendant's broadcast, the plaintiff's name was tainted with a connection to organized crime and loan sharking, with the result that his customers and the investors in the airline withdrew their financial support and lost faith in his integrity. *Prozeralik v Capital Cities Communications, Inc.* (1993, 4th Dept) 188 AD2d 178, 593 NYS2d 662.

§ 29:24   DAMAGES IN CONTRACT ACTIONS — In fixing damages for breach of contract, ordinarily the object is to compensate the plaintiff by putting him in as good a position as he would have been if the defendant had abided by its agreement. *New York Water Service Corp. v New York* (1957, 1st Dept) 4 AD2d 209, 163 NYS2d 538.

Damages for breach of contract are those that ordinarily and naturally flow from the breach, the basis being indemnity to the injured party. *Tonawanda v Stapell, Mumm & Beals Corp.* (1934) 240 AD 472, 270 NYS 377, affd 265 NY 630, 193 NE 419. Thus, the value to a plaintiff of an executory contract under which he is to receive a certain compensation for doing a particular act, would ordinarily be the amount of such compensation less what it would cost him to perform. *Spitz v Lesser* (1951) 302 NY 490.

To modify the rule of damages for breach of contract, the contract itself must clearly and unequivocally so provide. *Tonawanda v Stapell, Mumm & Beals Corp., supra.* When a contract calls for work, labor and services, the amount recoverable for breach of the contract is the contract price less payments already made and less the cost of completion. *Brockhurst v Ryan* (1955) 2 Misc 2d 747, 146 NYS2d 386.

Where contractors defaulted in their performance of construction contracts, the owner had a right to terminate the contracts, complete the work and charge the contractors with his costs in excess of the contract. *Smith v Brocton Preserving Co.* (1937) 251 AD 102, 296 NYS 281.

The proper measure of damages for breach of a contract to patronize the plaintiff exclusively for one year is the loss of prospective profits for the specified period. *Sacks v Amster* (1951, App Tm) 106 NYS2d 776.

Damages for breach of covenant not to compete are limited to those losses that have been sustained, including the loss of profits and the diminution in value of the property purchased. *Present v Glazer* (1928) 225 AD 23, 232 NYS 63; *see also, Barone v Marcisak* (1983, 2d Dept) 96 AD2d 816, 465 NYS2d 561.

When a defective performance was involved and the recovery was for breach of contract, and the defects involved were so substantial that they rendered the building partially unusable or unsafe, the damages were assessed on the basis of the reasonable value of correcting the builder's performance. *Staff v Lido Dunes, Inc.* (1965) 47 Misc 2d 322, 262 NYS2d 544.

In a breach of contract action, the proper measure of damages is the loss of the entire profit; the damages may be recovered when the injured party offers some adequate basis for computing the amount. *Oneonta Dress Co. v Ozona-USA, Inc.* (1986, 3d Dept) 120 AD2d 899, 503 NYS2d 167.

The proper date for measuring damages in an action for breach of a building contract is the date of the trial, not the date of the breach. *Kaiser v Fishman* (1988, 2d Dept) 138 AD2d 456, 525 NYS2d 870.

To recover for unusual or extraordinary damages allegedly arising from a breach of contract, it must be demonstrated that such damages were brought within the contemplation of the parties, as a probable result of a breach, at the time of or before contracting. *Rourke v Fred H. Thomas Assocs. P.C.* (1994, 3d Dept) 203 AD2d 859, 611 NYS2d 57.

In an action by a landscaping contractor against a customer to recover damages for breach of contract, the loss of the entire profit as provided by the contract was a proper measure of damages, and was recoverable when the plaintiff supplied some adequate basis for computing the amount, even if that amount could not be precisely determined with absolute certainty. *Plant Planners, Inc. v Pollock* (1983) 60 NY2d 779, 469 NYS2d 675.

Although lost profits may be recovered if the injured party can establish a reasonable basis for computing the amount of damages, a new business will not be allowed to recover anticipated profits, because no basis exists upon which to estimate the amount of the lost profits. *Manniello v Dea* (1983, 3d Dept) 92 AD2d 426, 461 NYS2d 582.

In a contract for the loan of money, the borrower's damage from the breach of agreement to subscribe to bonds was the excess of the legal interest rate over the rate of interest stipulated in the bond. *Eaton v Danziger* (1930) 138 Misc 290, 246 NYS 98.

Where a contract provided that upon failure to publish a book within a specified time, the contract would terminate, all rights would revert to the author, and all payments made to him would be his without prejudice to his other remedies, the correct measure of damages for failure to publish the book was the cost of publication. *Freund v Washington Square Press, Inc.* (1973, 1st Dept) 41 AD2d 371, 343 NYS2d 401, mod 34 NY2d 379, 357 NYS2d 857.

Generally, when a contract contains a liquidated damages clause, the party seeking to repudiate that clause must show that the agreed damage is so exorbitant that it is in the nature of a penalty. *P. J. Carlin Constr. Co. v New York* (1977, 1st Dept) 59 AD2d 847, 399 NYS2d 13.

In an action for breach of lease for advertising space on the exterior wall of a building, the court should have awarded damages for the duration of a contract, not merely for lost revenues through the time of trial. *Van Wagner Advertising Corp. v S & M Enterprises* (1986) 67 NY2d 186, 501 NYS2d 628.

In an action to recover damages because of interference with contractual relations, the tortfeasor is liable for the full pecuniary loss of the benefits of the contract with which it interfered. *Wasserman v NRG Realty Corp.* (1986, 1st Dept) 118 AD2d 495, 500 NYS2d 109.

In an action to recover on an insurance policy, punitive or exemplary damages may not be obtained unless there is a showing of wanton dishonesty sufficient to imply a criminal indifference to civil obligations – morally culpable conduct directed at the general public, as opposed to a mere private wrong. *Supreme Automotive Mfg. Corp. v Continental Casualty Co.* (1987, 1st Dept) 126 AD2d 153, 512 NYS2d 820, app dismd without op 69 NY2d 1038.

§ 29:25 DAMAGES IN OTHER ACTIONS — In an action against a municipal defendant for false arrest and malicious prosecution, a damage award against the town in the sum of $31,250 was not excessive and would not be disturbed, because the record showed that the plaintiff had no prior criminal record, was a major in the Air Force Reserve and a respected employee of a large corporation. As a result of the defendant's actions, the plaintiff was arrested, handcuffed, fingerprinted, photographed, forced to undergo a strip search and held in custody at the Albany County jail, subjected to ridicule and embarrassment due to the publication in a local newspaper of his prosecution for stealing a car. *Orndorff v De Nooyer Chevrolet, Inc.* (1986, 3d Dept) 117 AD2d 365, 503 NYS2d 444.

In an action brought under the New York State Human Rights Law (Executive Law § 290 et. seq.), it was held that American Airlines was liable to one of its former managers, who was discriminated against based on her gender and a heart condition, when it denied her a promotion in favor of a younger man, and subsequently when it dismissed her. The Appellate Division upheld an award in the total sum of $2,574,389, including $400,000 for mental anguish. *Sogg v American Airlines, Inc.,* NYLJ 10/23/93 21:5 (1st Dept, 1993). In the same case, the trial court's determination striking an award for punitive damages was affirmed. *Sogg v American Airlines, Inc., supra.*

§ 29:26 DAMAGES FOR LEGAL EXPENSES INCURRED — The general rule is that legal expenses necessarily incurred in carrying on a lawsuit may not be recovered as general or special damages. *Central Trust Co. v Goldman* (1979, 4th Dept) 70 AD2d 767, 417 NYS2d 359, app dismd 47 NY2d 1008, 420 NYS2d 221.

There is, however, a well-recognized exception when the damages are the proximate and natural consequence of a tortious act by the defendant that requires plaintiff to defend or to bring an action against a third party. In such a case, reasonable attorneys' fees necessarily incurred are recoverable. *Central Trust Co. v Goldman, supra.*

§ 29:27 TREATMENT OF OTHER PAYMENTS RECEIVED BY PLAINTIFF

— In a personal injury action where the plaintiff's salary or his medical bills were voluntarily and gratuitously paid by his employer under conditions wherein the plaintiff had no obligation to repay these items, they may not be claimed as items of damage. *Drake v New York State Electric & Gas Corp.* (1937) 162 Misc 167, 294 NYS 227.

Medical expenses gratuitously paid by another party on behalf of the plaintiff are not recoverable by the latter. *Coyne v Campbell* (1962) 11 NY2d 372, 230 NYS2d 1.

The "collateral source rule" has been substantially modified by CPLR 4545. The statute essentially permits the defendant to introduce evidence to the court that all or part of medical expenses, loss of earnings, or other economic loss, past or future, has been or will be replaced or indemnified by a collateral source other than one that would be a lien against the recovery. Any reduction of the verdict is made by the court, with certain adjustments, where appropriate, for insurance premiums paid by the plaintiff for the two years preceding the accrual of the action, and the present value of future premiums. Significantly, a reduction from damages awarded for a collateral source payment that has not yet been made requires that such payment will be made "with reasonable certainty." CPLR 4545.

Plaintiff was a passenger in a vehicle that was allegedly side-swiped by an unidentified vehicle that did not stop at the scene. As a result of being hit, the vehicle in which the plaintiff was a passenger veered into a third vehicle. The plaintiff was awarded $10,000 in an arbitration proceeding brought pursuant to the Uninsured Motorist provision in the insurance policy of her host. The plaintiff then brought an action against her host and against the owner and driver of the third vehicle in the accident. The court properly granted a cross-motion by the owner and driver of the third vehicle for leave to amend the answer to the suit to include the $10,000 payment in mitigation of damages. *Brink v Killeen* (1975, 2d Dept) 48 AD2d 823, 368 NYS2d 547.

When a co-tortfeasor settles with the plaintiff in a tort action, the remaining defendants are entitled to a reduction of damages equivalent to the greatest of: (1) the amount stipulated in the release or covenant not to sue, (2) the amount actually paid, or (3) the released tortfeasor's equitable share of the damages under CPLR Article 14; General Obligations Law (GOL) § 15-108(a). The release by plaintiff relieves the settling tortfeasor from any liability for contribution to the co-tortfeasors. GOL § 15-108(b). The released tortfeasor cannot seek contribution toward his settlement from any other person. GOL § 15-108(c).

RESEARCH REFERENCES

American Law Reports

24 ALR5th 174, Failure to lose weight as basis for reduction of damages in personal injury action

23 ALR5th 75, Liability of insurer for prejudgment interest in excess of policy limits for covered loss

20 ALR5th 1, Necessity of expert testimony on issue of permanence of injury and future pain and suffering

17 ALR5th 327, Recovery of damages for expense of medical monitoring to detect or prevent future disease or condition

14 ALR5th 242, Excessiveness or inadequacy of punitive damages in cases not involving personal injury or death

9 ALR5th 63, Right to prejudgment interest on punitive or multiple damages awards

6 ALR5th 883, Release of one joint tortfeasor as discharging liability of others under Uniform Contribution Among Tortfeasors Act and other statutes expressly governing effect of release

6 ALR5th 611, Insurers liability to insurance agent or broker for damages suffered as result of insurers denial of coverage or refusal to pay policy proceeds to insured

5 ALR5th 875, Propriety of limiting to issue of damages alone new trial granted on ground of inadequacy of damages—modern cases

5 ALR5th 132, Computation of "net loss" for which fidelity insurer is liable

3 ALR5th 907, What amounts to failure or refusal to submit to medical treatment sufficient to bar recovery of workers compensation

3 ALR5th 746, Insureds recovery of uninsured motorist claim against insurer as affecting subsequent recovery against tortfeasors causing injury

3 ALR5th 721, Refusal of medical treatment on religious grounds as affecting right to recover for personal injury or death

88 ALR4th 644, Damages recoverable for wrongful dishonor of check under UCC §4-402

81 ALR4th 485, Medical malpractice: measure and elements of damages in actions based on loss of chance

78 ALR4th 542, Validity, construction, and effect of statute limiting amount recoverable in dram shop action

78 ALR4th 435, Damages and other relief under state legislation forbidding job discrimination on account of handicap

74 ALR4th 798, Recoverability of compensatory damages for mental anguish or emotional distress for tortiously causing another's birth

73 ALR4th 441, Effect of death of beneficiary, following wrongful death, upon damages

61 ALR4th 413, Excessiveness or adequacy of damages awarded for parents' noneconomic loss caused by personal injury or death of child

61 ALR4th 309, Excessiveness or adequacy of damages awarded for noneconomic loss caused by personal injury or death of spouse

61 ALR4th 251, Excessiveness or adequacy of damages awarded for noneconomic loss caused by personal injury or death of parent

58 ALR4th 878, Standard of proof as to conduct underlying punitive damage awards–modern status

58 ALR4th 844, Punitive damages: power of equity court to award

57 ALR4th 801, Emotional or mental distress as element of damages for liability insurer's wrongful refusal to settle

55 ALR4th 246, Credit life insurer's punitive damage liability for refusing payment

55 ALR4th 186, Validity of verdict awarding medical expenses to personal injury plaintiff, but failing to award damages for pain and suffering

55 ALR4th 166, Liability of successor corporation for punitive damages for injury caused by predecessor's product

54 ALR4th 998, Discovery of defendant's sales, earnings, or profits on issue of punitive damages in tort action

54 ALR4th 901, Recoverability of compensatory damages for mental anguish or emotional distress for breach of service contract

52 ALR4th 826, Recoverability of compensatory damages for mental anguish or emotional distress for breach of contract to lend money

50 ALR4th 843, Excessiveness or inadequacy of compensatory damages for malicious prosecution

50 ALR4th 787, Excessiveness or adequacy of damages awarded for personal injuries resulting in death of persons engaged in professional, white-collar, and nonmanual occupations

49 ALR4th 1158, Excessiveness or inadequacy of compensatory damages for defamation

49 ALR4th 1076, Excessiveness and adequacy of damages for personal injuries resulting in death of minor

48 ALR4th 229, Excessiveness or adequacy of damages awarded for personal injuries resulting in death of retired persons

48 ALR4th 165, Excessiveness or inadequacy of compensatory damages for false imprisonment or arrest

45 ALR4th 234, Recovery of damages for grief or mental anguish resulting from death of child–modern cases

43 ALR4th 19, Validity and construction of statute or ordinance limiting the kinds or amount of actual damages recoverable in tort action against governmental unit

39 ALR4th 1122, Evidence of defendant's rehabilitation or reformation as relevant on issue of punitive damages.

36 ALR4th 807, Proof of injury to reputation as prerequisite to recovery of damages in defamation action-post-Gertz cases

35 ALR4th 947, Provocation as basis for mitigation of compensatory damage in action for assault and battery

35 ALR4th 538, Excessiveness or inadequacy of punitive damages in cases not involving personal injury or death

35 ALR4th 441, Excessiveness or inadequacy of punitive damages awarded in personal injury or death cases

32 ALR4th 432, Necessity of determination or showing of liability for punitive damages before discovery or reception of evidence of defendant's wealth

30 ALR4th 273, Recovery of damages resulting from wrongful issuance of injunction as limited to amount of bond

27 ALR4th 318, Effect of plaintiff's comparative negligence in reducing punitive damages recoverable

26 ALR4th 396, Negligence of one parent contributing to injury or death of child as barring or reducing damages recoverable by other parent for losses suffered by other parent as result of injury or death of child

22 ALR4th 1229, Liability in damages for interference with expected inheritance or gift

21 ALR4th 21, Effect of anticipated inflation on damages for future losses-modern cases

20 ALR4th 23, Insurer's tort liability for consequential or punitive damages for wrongful failure or refusal to defend insured

19 ALR4th 801, Recovery of punitive damages by purchasers of real property charging fraud or misrepresentation

16 ALR4th 1127, Excessiveness or adequacy of damages awarded for injuries to, or conditions induced in, sensory or speech organs and systems

16 ALR4th 736, Excessiveness or adequacy of damages awarded for injuries causing particular diseases or conditions

16 ALR4th 589, Propriety of taking income tax into consideration in fixing damages in personal injury or death action

16 ALR4th 238, Excessiveness or adequacy of damages awarded for injuries to trunk or torso, or internal injuries

15 ALR4th 519, Excessiveness or adequacy of damages awarded for injuries to, or conditions induced in, respiratory system

15 ALR4th 294, Excessiveness or adequacy of damages awarded for injuries to back, neck, or spine

14 ALR4th 1335, Derivative liability of partner for punitive damages for wrongful act of copartner

14 ALR4th 539, Excessiveness or adequacy of damages awarded for injuries to, or conditions induced in, circulatory, digestive, and glandular systems

14 ALR4th 328, Excessiveness or adequacy of damages awarded for injuries to head or brain, or for mental or nervous disorders

13 ALR4th 212, Excessiveness or adequacy of damages awarded for injuries to legs and feet

13 ALR4th 183, Excessiveness or adequacy of damages awarded for injuries to, or conditions induced in, sexual organs and processes

13 ALR4th 95, Allowance of punitive damages in action against attorney for malpractice

13 ALR4th 52, Allowance of punitive damages in products liability case

12 ALR4th 891, Contractual provision for per diem payments for delay in performance as one for liquidated damages or penalty

12 ALR4th 96, Excessiveness or adequacy of damages awarded for inju-

ries to arms and hands

11 ALR4th 1261, Propriety of awarding punitive damages to separate plaintiffs bringing successive actions arising out of common incident or circumstances against common defendant or defendants ("one bite" or "first comer" doctrine)

11 ALR4th 891, Special or consequential damages recoverable, on account of delay in delivering possession, by purchaser of real property awarded specific performance

11 ALR4th 345, Right of creditor to recover damages for conspiracy to defraud him of claim

11 ALR4th 12, Proper measure and elements of damages for misappropriation of trade secret

86 L Ed 2d 816, Free speech and press clauses of Federal Constitution's First Amendment as affecting damages recoverable for defamation–Supreme Court cases

9 ALR4th 1245, Elements and measure of damages recoverable from bailee for loss, destruction, or conversion of personal papers, photographs, or paintings

9 ALR4th 494, Products liability: sufficiency of proof of injuries resulting from "second collision"

8 ALR4th 1287, Measure, elements, and amount of damages for killing or injuring cat

8 ALR4th 853, Damages recoverable for real-estate mortgagee's refusal to discharge mortgage or give partial release therefrom

7 ALR4th 1219, Allowance of punitive damages in action for slander of title or disparagement of property

5 ALR4th 833, Immediacy of observation of injury as affecting right to recover damages for shock or mental anguish from witnessing injury to another

5 ALR4th 300, Recovery for loss of consortium occurring prior to marriage

4 ALR4th 682, Measure and elements of damages for breach of contract to lend money

4 ALR4th 532, What constitutes special damages in action for slander of title

3 ALR4th 940, Per diem or similar mathematical basis for fixing damages for pain and suffering

2 ALR4th 1254, Liability of surety on private bond for punitive damages

1 ALR4th 1182, Measure of damages for landlord's breach of implied

warranty of habitability

1 ALR4th 448, Recovery of exemplary or punitive damages from municipal corporation

1 ALR4th 347, Measure and elements of damages in action against garageman based on failure to properly perform repair or service on motor vehicle

ALR QUICK INDEX: Damages; Excessive or Inadequate Damages

American Jurisprudence 2d

22 AM JUR 2d, Damages §§ 1 et seq.

American Jurisprudence Pleading and Practice

8 AM JUR PL & PR FORMS (Rev), Damages, Forms 1 et seq.

American Jurisprudence Proof of Facts

30 AM JUR PROOF OF FACTS 3d 351, Proof of Punitive Damages in Products Liability Actions

26 AM JUR PROOF OF FACTS 3d 119, Lost Profits Resulting From Tortious Injury to Business

25 AM JUR PROOF OF FACTS 3d 313, Toxic Torts: Proof of Medical Monitoring Damages for Exposure to Toxic Substances

25 AM JUR PROOF OF FACTS 3d 251, Proof of Damages in Wrongful Death or Survival Action

24 AM JUR PROOF OF FACTS 3d 393, Proof of Damages for Sexual Harassment Under the Civil Rights Act of 1991

24 AM JUR PROOF OF FACTS 3d 337, Proof of Damages for Decedents Pain and Suffering

24 AM JUR PROOF OF FACTS 3d 273, Emotional Distress Caused by Fear of Future Disease

23 AM JUR PROOF OF FACTS 3d 243, Establishing An Adequate Foundation For Proof of Medical Expenses

22 AM JUR PROOF OF FACTS 3d 137, Enforceability of Liquidated Damages Clause in Commercial Lease

22 AM JUR PROOF OF FACTS 3d 83, Brain-Damaged Infant: Damages

18 AM JUR PROOF OF FACTS 3d 323, Punitive Damages Against an Insurer for the Bad-Faith Handling of a First-Party Claim

18 AM JUR PROOF OF FACTS 3d 239, Damages for Injury to Personal Property–Motor Vehicle

18 AM JUR PROOF OF FACTS 3d 1, Punitive Damages in Motor Vehicle Litigation–Intoxicated Driver

15 AM JUR PROOF OF FACTS 3d 259, Proof of Damages for Sexual Assault

13 AM JUR PROOF OF FACTS 3d 111, Compensatory Damages for False Imprisonment

12 AM JUR PROOF OF FACTS 3d 621, Damages for Loss of Chance of Cure

12 AM JUR PROOF OF FACTS 3d 323, Damages–Traumatic Aggravation of Preexisting Mental Disorder

10 AM JUR PROOF OF FACTS 3d 97, Wife's Damages for Loss of Consortium

9 AM JUR PROOF OF FACTS 3d 207, Amputation Damages–Phantom Pain and Stump Pain

9 AM JUR PROOF OF FACTS 3d 1, Damages–Rehabilitation and Life Care Needs After a Traumatic Brain Injury

8 AM JUR PROOF OF FACTS 3d 215, Valuation of Goodwill of Professional Practice for Distribution on Divorce

5 AM JUR PROOF OF FACTS 3d 323, Intangible Damages for Injury to Elderly Person

4 AM JUR PROOF OF FACTS 3d 645, Damages for Future Medical Needs of an Injured Child

3 AM JUR PROOF OF FACTS 3d 171, Damages for Loss of Personal Property with Little or No Market Value

49 AM JUR PROOF OF FACTS 2d 191, Damages for Wrongful Death of Child

48 AM JUR PROOF OF FACTS 2d 153, Damages for Unauthorized Geophysical Exploration

41 AM JUR PROOF OF FACTS 2d 337, Damages for Breach of Contract to Lend Money

37 AM JUR PROOF OF FACTS 2d 639, Damages for Loss of or Injury to Animal

27 AM JUR PROOF OF FACTS 2d 393, Loss of Consortium in Parent-Child Relationship

24 AM JUR PROOF OF FACTS 2d 211, Wrongful Death Damages-Loss of Prospective Inheritance

23 AM JUR PROOF OF FACTS 2d 1, Pain and Suffering

22 AM JUR PROOF OF FACTS 2d 445, Aggravated Wrongful Detention-Malice Sufficient to Support Award of Punitive Damages

20 AM JUR PROOF OF FACTS 2d 115, Damages: Value of Growing Crop

16 AM JUR PROOF OF FACTS 2d 253, Forensic Economics-Valuation of Businesses and Business Losses

15 AM JUR PROOF OF FACTS 2d 209, Landlord's Reasonable Efforts to Minimize Damages After Tenant's Breach of Lease

14 AM JUR PROOF OF FACTS 2d 373, Circumstances Warranting Assess-

ment of Punitive Damages-Action for Wrongful Conversion of Automobile

14 AM JUR PROOF OF FACTS 2d 311, Forensic Economics-Death of Person Not in Labor Force

11 AM JUR PROOF OF FACTS 2d 679, Reduction or Mitigation of Damages-Employment Contract

11 AM JUR PROOF OF FACTS 2d 131, Reduction or Mitigation of Damages-Sales Contract

8 AM JUR PROOF OF FACTS 2d 399, Valuation of Structure Based on Reproduction or Replacement Cost

8 AM JUR PROOF OF FACTS 2d 1, Discount Rate for Future Damages

American Jurisprudence Trials

40 AM JUR TRIALS 317, Cost Recovery Litigation: Abatement of Asbestos Contamination

6 AM JUR TRIALS 963, Predicting Personal Injury Verdicts and Damages

Other Resources

Auto-Cite®: Any case citation herein can be checked for form, parallel references, later history and annotation references through the Auto-Cite computer research system.

CHAPTER 30

CLOSING ARGUMENTS

§ 30:1 RIGHT TO MAKE CLOSING ARGUMENT — Closing arguments are made at the close of all the evidence to discuss the evidence that has been presented in the case. CPLR 4016.

The object of summation is to give counsel an opportunity to comment on the evidence and, within reasonable limitations, to comment on those who gave the evidence. *Zemliansky v United Parcel Service, Inc.* (1940) 175 Misc 829, 24 NYS2d 672.

§ 30:2 COURT'S CONTROL OF CLOSING ARGUMENTS — The court by alert, prompt, and firm control should prevent counsel on either side from overstepping the bounds of propriety. *Bowen v Mahoney Coal Corp.* (1939) 256 AD 485, 10 NYS2d 454. When the issue on appeal is whether the statement of counsel was prejudicial, the trial court's opinion is entitled to great respect. *Bowen v Mahoney Coal Corp., supra.*

In a negligence action, the trial court did not err in precluding plaintiff from commenting during summation on defendant's failure to call as a witness the orthopedic surgeon who had examined plaintiff on defendant's behalf, because the testimony of the orthopedic surgeon on the orthopedic injuries was not relevant to the issue to be decided. *Godfrey v Dunn* (1993, 3d Dept) 190 AD2d 896, 593 NYS2d 120.

§ 30:3   RIGHT TO OPEN AND CLOSE ARGUMENTS — The right to open first and to close last in a case is an important right that is given to the party having the affirmative of an issue. *Brink's Express Co. v Burns* (1930) 230 AD 559, 245 NYS 649. A plaintiff has the affirmative on issues of fact that have been raised by denials in the answer. The plaintiff's right to open first and close last is a substantial one. *Gibbs v Sokol* (1926) 216 AD 260, 214 NYS 533.

When a motion has been made for consolidation of actions growing out of the same automobile accident, the court must exercise its discretion and consider all circumstances in determining which plaintiff has the right to open and close. *Crescent Puritan Laundry Co. v McNamara* (1938) 254 AD 646, 3 NYS2d 492.

§ 30:4   GENERAL RULES GOVERNING CLOSING ARGUMENT — At the request of either party, summations may be recorded. This is a matter of right, and the trial court's refusal to have summations recorded has been held to be reversible error. *Robinson v Ferens* (1969, 2d Dept) 33 AD2d 688, 306 NYS2d 530. Where the court directed the stenographer to record the defendant's opening address to the jury at the request of plaintiff's counsel, the court's denial of the request by defendant's counsel to direct the stenographer to record plaintiff's summation was held to be error. *Starr v Equitable Life Assurance Soc.* (1939) 257 AD 261, 12 NYS2d 953.

An attorney in summation is at liberty to utter any proper and appropriate comment so long as he confines himself to the issues. *Youngentob v Luongo* (1931) 139 Misc 840, 249 NYS 415. It is not the counsel's function to instruct the jury on the law. *Frechette v Special Magazines, Inc.* (1954) 285 AD 174, 136 NYS2d 448. Counsel may not read to the jury from medical books on which one of the experts based his opinion. *Phillips v Roux Laboratories, Inc.* (1955) 286 AD 549, 145 NYS2d 449.

An attorney may comment on the credibility of witnesses. A witness may be characterized as untruthful, as a falsifier, a liar, and even a perjurer. These comments are a matter of propriety, good taste, and judgment with which a trial court will not interfere. *Cohen v Covelli* (1950) 276 AD 375, 94 NYS2d 782, reh and app den 276 AD 1011, 95 NYS2d 905. Counsel may comment on the failure of the adverse party to call a witness who is under his control and whose testimony he could be expected to produce if it were favorable to him. *Seligson, Morris & Neuburger v Fairbanks Whitney Corp.* (1965, 1st Dept) 22 AD2d 625, 257 NYS2d 706.

The personalities of trial counsel should not receive undue emphasis during the trial. *Bowen v Mahoney Coal Corp.* (1939) 256 AD 485, 10 NYS2d 454.

Objections to the argument and conduct of counsel at the trial must be made during the trial and must be reasonably timed. *Kluchenia v Hodge* (1942, Sup) 38 NYS2d 545.

Trial counsel has a right to place before the jury the contentions of the parties as stated in the pleadings. This is distinct from the right of fair comment on the evidence. *Braun v Ahmed* (1987, 2d Dept) 127 AD2d 418, 515 NYS2d 473.

§ 30:5 ARGUMENTS ABOUT DAMAGES — Plaintiff's counsel is entitled to inform the jury of the amount of damages demanded in the complaint. *Rice v Ninacs* (1970, 4th Dept) 34 AD2d 388, 312 NYS2d 246, If he does so, however, the court should charge the jury that it must determine the amount of the verdict solely from the evidence and that the amount demanded in the complaint is not evidence and should not be so considered by the jury. *Rice v Ninacs, supra.*

Disclosure by plaintiff's counsel to the jury of the amounts demanded by plaintiff as damages in the complaint was permissible. Although such comments may have contributed to the excessiveness of the verdict, reversal was not required, because the trial judge promptly and properly instructed the jury not to use those figures in determining damages but to reach a figure based on the evidence. *Rush v Sears, Roebuck & Co.* (1983, 3d Dept) 92 AD2d 1072, 461 NYS2d 559.

In a medical malpractice action, plaintiff's argument of a time-unit theory of damages to the jury required reversal and a new trial. *De Cicco v Methodist Hospital of Brooklyn* (1980, 2d Dept) 74 AD2d 593, 424 NYS2d 524.

When in the course of his summation plaintiff's counsel referred to his client's life expectancy of 64 years and asked the jury a series of rhetorical questions concerning the value of pain over such a period of time, he did not indulge in a unit-of-time argument. Under the unit-of-time theory, small units of pain and suffering are given a specific monetary value and multiplied at this rate for the entire time for which the pain and suffering might be endured. The record disclosed that counsel suggested no specific monetary value for units of time and did not multiply them for the jury. *Tate v Colabello* (1983) 58 NY2d 84, 459 NYS2d 422.

§ 30:6 COMMENTS ON CONDUCT OF OPPOSITION — An attorney may not go outside the case and make slanderous attacks either on a party or on adverse counsel. *Youngentob v Luongo* (1931) 139 Misc 840, 249 NYS 415. While counsel may comment on the failure of the adverse party to call a witness who is under his control, *Seligson, Morris & Neuburger v Fairbanks Whitney Corp.* (1965, 1st Dept) 22 AD2d 625, 257 NYS2d 706, such comments are not proper when the witnesses are not under the control of the party who allegedly has failed to produce them. *Lyons v New York* (1968, 1st Dept) 29 AD2d 923, 289 NYS2d 2, motion gr 23 NY2d 736, 296 NYS2d 567 and affd 25 NY2d 996, 305 NYS2d 509.

A statement in defendant's summation referring to plaintiff's counsel as a liar was beyond the bounds of propriety and warranted a new trial. *Marshall v New York* (1950, Sup) 100 NYS2d 388, affd 278 AD 812, 105 NYS2d 399.

§ 30:7 IMPROPER REMARKS OF COUNSEL IN GENERAL — The issues in a trial must be presented clearly and free of any atmosphere of prejudice. *Weil v Weil* (1953) 283 AD 33, 125 NYS2d 368. Appeals to prejudice or to passion and a statement of facts that has been neither approved nor presumed have no place in a trial. *Gross v Surface Transp. Corp.* (1947) 189 Misc 165, 70

NYS2d 515, affd 190 Misc 989, 79 NYS2d 328, affd 274 AD 775, 79 NYS2d 817.

It was improper and prejudicial for counsel to make himself an unsworn witness in summation and to indulge in argument that was not founded on proof. *Bromberg v New York* (1966, 2d Dept) 25 AD2d 885, 270 NYS2d 425. In his summation in a personal injury action, plaintiff's counsel improperly referred to extraneous matters, making a new trial necessary. *Laughing v Utica Steam Engine & Boiler Works* (1962, 4th Dept) 16 AD2d 294, 228 NYS2d 44.

§ 30:8 IMPROPER REMARKS IN CIVIL CASES — When making the summation in a case in which the evidence clearly showed the town's liability for the death of an automobile driver, plaintiff's counsel appealed to the sympathy of the jury. Even though the remarks went beyond the permissible limits, they did not require reversal, because the court admonished the jury to disregard their emotions. *Bennett v Wheeler* (1924) 209 AD 283, 204 NYS 695.

In summation, plaintiff's counsel referred to defendant's efforts to help his son get an exemption from the army draft. Because these remarks were calculated to arouse in the jury's mind the most violent prejudices and to cause them to forget the issue and since the court refused to interfere, the remarks in and of themselves required a reversal. *E. A. Strout Farm Agency v De Forest* (1922) 201 AD 777, 195 NYS 101.

On summation, counsel may read to the jury the opposite party's pleadings, even though they were not introduced in evidence and no contradictions were brought to the opposite party's attention. *C. J. O'Brien, Inc. v Stokes* (1920) 192 AD 668, 183 NYS 172.

On summation, plaintiff's counsel made a statement that a witness who had given his opinion regarding the extent of plaintiff's injuries and who was concededly a highly qualified physician was "the greatest and most unmitigated rotten liar I have ever seen in a courtroom," and "a tool of the defendants." The statement exceeded permissible bounds and required the setting aside of a verdict for the plaintiff. *Zemliansky v United Parcel Service, Inc.* (1940) 175 Misc 829, 24 NYS2d 672. Where defendant's counsel in summation improperly appealed to the financial interests of the jurors and to race prejudice, defendant was not entitled to a new trial because plaintiff's counsel improperly answered these prejudicial statements. *Wood v New York State Electric & Gas Corp.* (1939) 257 AD 172, 12 NYS2d 947, affd 281 NY 797.

During summation, plaintiffs' counsel stated that the jury should not absolve the municipal defendant, because otherwise the injured plaintiffs might have no one to look to for payment of damages except a dissolved corporation. The statement was highly prejudicial and required reversal and a new trial. *Adams v Acker* (1977, 1st Dept) 57 AD2d 741, 394 NYS2d 8, on reh (1st Dept) 58 AD2d 754, 396 NYS2d 329 and app dismd 42 NY2d 965, 398 NYS2d 147 and app dismd 42 NY2d 1050, 399 NYS2d 212. In an action against a corporate defendant, plaintiff's counsel improperly stated in summation, "They're the corporations, they're the owner, they're the defendant, they've got the money, they've got the assets behind them," because allusion to a defendant's ability to pay damages is improper. *Nicholas v Island Industrial Park, Inc.* (1974, 2d Dept) 46 AD2d 804, 361 NYS2d 39.

Even if the remarks of plaintiff's counsel during summation were not so egregious as to require reversal, the cumulative effect of counsel's summation, together with error in plaintiff's expert testimony regarding the meaning and applicability of statutes and regulations requiring the maintenance of premises in safe condition, warranted reversal and a new trial. Plaintiff's counsel improperly intimated that the city housing authority's medical expert was unworthy of belief because he was compensated for his appearance at trial; disparaged another housing authority witness as a "yahoo," suggesting that he was coached; and made irrelevant reference to an alleged fraud involving records. *Rodriquez v New York City Housing Authority* (1994, 1st Dept) 209 AD2d 260, 618 NYS2d 352.

During his summation, the plaintiff's attorney made highly prejudicial remarks that one of the defendant's experts was known in the community as "here comes Howie," implying that he would offer for a price any testimony that might be desired, and that defendant and his attorney had perjured themselves, based on an apparent inconsistency between the defendant's pleadings and his testimony at the trial. *Taormina v Goodman* (1978, 2d Dept) 63 AD2d 1018, 406 NYS2d 350.

The infant plaintiff was deprived of a fair trial on the issue of damages by defense counsel's remarks that he had feigned his seizures to avoid going to Vietnam and that he was receiving a pension. *Rios v Islip* (1979, 2d Dept) 69 AD2d 855, 415 NYS2d 458, app dismd 47 NY2d 1010, 420 NYS2d 223 and app dismd, in part, app den, in part 48 NY2d 937, 425 NYS2d 94. Similarly prejudicial to the plaintiff on the issue of damages was defense counsel's remark that the individual defendant was a Marine veteran of the Vietnam War and could not afford a large judgment. *Rios v Islip, supra*.

When defense counsel stated in summation, "Believe me, there's plenty more that's not in this case and I can't say," and he vouched for the motorman's trial testimony, his remarks constituted reversible error. *Cusumano v New York City Transit Authority* (1980, 2d Dept) 75 AD2d 801, 427 NYS2d 644.

Because civil as well as criminal cases are to be tried on the merits and not by injecting matters of race, color, or creed, which can serve only to inflame the jury's passions, the deliberate endeavor by plaintiff's counsel to inject indirectly into the case the issue of religion should not be permitted. *Albarran v New York* (1981, 1st Dept) 80 AD2d 784, 437 NYS2d 4.

Where the summation of plaintiff's attorney had as its continuing theme a personal attack on defendant-appellant's attorney, unsubstantiated charges of perjury and subornation of perjury, racial overtones, as well as assertions of personal knowledge and opinion about the case and the credibility of witnesses, reversal and a new trial were ordered. *Caraballo v New York* (1982, 1st Dept) 86 AD2d 580, 446 NYS2d 318.

A new trial was required because of the unfair, prejudicial, and inflammatory remarks made by defendant's counsel in summation. He remarked that because plaintiff's two medical experts were being paid by plaintiff to testify, plaintiff's counsel may well have stated to one of them, "I paid the thousand, you voice my theories," and that the other was a "pro," not in the sense of medical expertise, but in the sense of "the best doctor money could buy." *La Russo v Pollack* (1982, 2d Dept) 88 AD2d 584, 449 NYS2d 794.

Plaintiff's counsel acted properly in attempting to comment about the absence of a defense neurologist whom the defendant did not produce at the trial, and the trial court erroneously sustained defense objections to the comments. *Grey v United Leasing, Inc.* (1983, 1st Dept) 91 AD2d 932, 457 NYS2d 823.

Repeated attacks by defendant's counsel in his summation on the integrity of plaintiff's counsel were error. The remarks were based on nothing but rhetoric and the irrelevant fact that plaintiff's counsel was a member of a large, well-known law firm. *Weinberger v New York* (1983, 2d Dept) 97 AD2d 819, 468 NYS2d 697.

In a personal injury action, defense counsel stated in summation, "Until recently, the slightest fault on the part of plaintiff would have him out of court today." The remark was clearly aimed at prejudicing the jury against the plaintiff by implying that he was the fortuitous beneficiary of a legal fad, because this was a comparative negligence case. *Berman v Hudson Bergen Trucking Co.* (1983, 2d Dept) 96 AD2d 878, 466 NYS2d 31.

Reversal was required when defense counsel took advantage of his cross-examination of plaintiff's medical witness to call to the jury's attention highly prejudicial distortions and misrepresentation of the testimony and medical records of a second doctor whom plaintiff had consulted. In addition, defense counsel reinforced the prejudicial impact of those distortions of important evidence presented to the jury when he referred repeatedly throughout his summation to the alleged findings of the second doctor and his colleagues at Downstate Medical Center. *O'Shea v Sarro* (1984, 2d Dept) 106 AD2d 435, 482 NYS2d 529.

Defense counsel's comment during summation did not require setting aside the verdict of the jury, because the court gave prompt curative instructions, to which no exception was taken. *Picciallo v Norchi* (1989, 2d Dept) 147 AD2d 540, 537 NYS2d 837.

In the course of his summation, defense counsel made a prejudicial remark comparing plaintiff's expert obstetrician-gynecologist to the television "gunman Palladin," stating that the expert's hallmark was "have opinion, will travel." Nevertheless, because this isolated comment was followed by the court's prompt curative instructions, the error was therefore harmless. *Abbott v New Rochelle Hospital Medical Center* (1988, 2d Dept) 141 AD2d 589, 529 NYS2d 352, app den 72 NY2d 808, 534 NYS2d 666.

Although the plaintiffs' attorney made improper remarks to the effect that certain expert witnesses called by defendants had been paid to say whatever the defendants wanted them to say, the remarks did not have an effect on the jury's findings and therefore constituted harmless error. *Kavanaugh v Nussbaum* (1987, 2d Dept) 129 AD2d 559, 514 NYS2d 55, mod on other grounds 71 NY2d 535, 528 NYS2d 8.

Defendants' selective presentation of isolated instances of rhetorical hyperbole used by plaintiff's counsel during his lengthy summation did not improperly reflect the overall tenor of the summation when viewed in perspective, and a new trial was not required. *Schechtman v Lappin* (1990, 1st Dept) 161 AD2d 118, 554 NYS2d 846.

In a personal injury action, reversal was not required by virtue of defendant's single reference during summation to a codefendant's arrest. While the remark was improper, it was not prejudicial, because the jury was already aware from the codefendant's own trial testimony that he had been arrested. *Parmar v Skinner* (1989, 2d Dept) 154 AD2d 444, 546 NYS2d 16.

In a medical malpractice action, defense counsel made comments that primarily referred to alternate ways in which the needle could have become embedded in the patient's abdomen. The remarks constituted a fair comment on the evidence and were well within the bounds of the wide latitude allowed to counsel in summation. *Cerasuoli v Brevetti* (1990, 2d Dept) 166 AD2d 403, 560 NYS2d 468.

The conduct of plaintiff's counsel during cross-examination and particularly during summation required reversal and a new trial. During the course of the trial, he engaged in an unfair and highly prejudicial attack on the credibility and competence of defendant's expert witnesses and attorneys. He repeatedly depicted the two physicians retained by the defense as "hired guns" who were brought into the litigation to "fluff up the case" and "fill up some time." In addition, he referred to matters not in evidence with respect to the relationship between defense counsel and the physicians they hired, and he stated that defense counsel was merely carrying out "instructions from his principals, and possibly he doesn't even believe some of the things that he said, but he has to do what he has to do." *Berkowitz v Marriott Corp.* (1990, 1st Dept) 163 AD2d 52, 558 NYS2d 511.

A bus passenger brought an action for injuries allegedly sustained when the bus doors closed on his foot as he was attempting to board the bus. In his summation, counsel for defendant improperly characterized plaintiff's case as a "bunch of crock," "bunch of bunk," and "hogwash," misstated that plaintiff's medical expert had had his privileges revoked at New York Hospital, and suggested that plaintiff's story suddenly became set once he got in touch with, and was "prepped" by, his attorney. *Sanchez v Manhattan & Bronx Surface Transit Operating Auth.* (1991, 1st Dept) 170 AD2d 402, 566 NYS2d 287, app after remand, 203 AD2d 128, 610 NYS2d 507.

In a medical malpractice action in which plaintiff produced an expert witness who was unconvincing at best, it was particularly unbecoming for the plaintiff's attorney to suggest that it was defendant's expert who was shading the truth and to accuse defendant's expert of being a hired gun. Counsel's remark that defendant's expert's idea of truth and justice is that it is a game to be played was likewise improper. *Steidel v County of Nassau* (1992, 2d Dept) 182 AD2d 809, 582 NYS2d 805.

Defendant had surveillance videotapes or films made and turned them over to plaintiff. When defendant subsequently decided not to use them at trial as a matter of trial strategy, it was improper for plaintiff to turn the strategy to advantage and comment on defendant's decision to the jury. *DiMichel v South Buffalo Ry. Co.* (1992) 80 NY2d 184, 590 NYS2d 1, reconsideration den 81 NY2d 835, 595 NYS2d 397 and cert den (US) 126 L Ed 2d 37, 114 S Ct 68.

In a personal injury case arising out of an automobile accident, the trial court erred by allowing plaintiff's counsel to comment on a magazine article during summation, because the article was not admitted into evidence. *Aurnou v Craig* (1992, 4th Dept) 184 AD2d 1048, 584 NYS2d 249.

During summation, plaintiff's counsel improperly asked the jury to consider the response of decedent's children if they were told, "We'll give you all the riches in the world but the price to you, to the children, is that we are going to poison your mother, we're going to kill your mother." *Torrado v Lutheran Medical Ctr.* (1993, 2d Dept) 198 AD2d 346, 603 NYS2d 325.

The allegedly improper summation comments of plaintiff's counsel did not require reversal where defendant did not object to several of the alleged improprieties and those comments defendant did object to were arguably within the range of fair comment or were the subject of curative action by the trial court. *Grams v Acands, Inc. (In re Eighth Judicial Dist. Asbestos Litig.)* (1993, 4th Dept) 197 AD2d 901, 602 NYS2d 452, related proceeding (4th Dept) 197 AD2d 902, 602 NYS2d 584, reh den (4th Dept) 1993 NY AD LEXIS 12791.

In summation, plaintiff's counsel referred to two items of evidence that were presented in a previous trial but were not before the jury in the case at bar. Although the reference was technically improper, it did not require reversal because defendant's objections were sustained, plaintiff's counsel was openly admonished by the trial court within the hearing of the jury, no request was made for further curative instructions, and the subjects were not mentioned again. *Warner v Village of Chatham* (1993, 3d Dept) 194 AD2d 980, 598 NYS2d 863.

§ 30:9 REMARKS IN ARGUMENT ABOUT LIABILITY INSURANCE

— No hint of the defendant's insurance protection may be given in an action. *Butera v Donner* (1942) 177 Misc 966, 32 NYS2d 633. Generally, deliberate attempts by counsel to convey to the jury the idea that the defendant is insured constitutes grounds for a mistrial. *Brand v Mangust Holding Corp.* (1945, Sup) 53 NYS2d 882.

While the question of defendant's insurance is ordinarily irrelevant, highly prejudicial, and therefore inadmissible in a negligence action, evidence of insurance cannot be excluded as prejudicial if it is relevant to a material issue. *Leotta v Plessinger* (1960) 8 NY2d 449, 209 NYS2d 304, remittitur amd 9 NY2d 686, 212 NYS2d 421. In an accident case, it is improper to suggest either the presence or the absence of insurance. *Thiele v Hickey* (1958,

3d Dept) 6 AD2d 939, 175 NYS2d 792. It is error to make any statement to the jury from which it may be inferred that the defendant is wealthy or insured. *Freeman v Manhattan Cab Corp.* (1956) 1 Misc 2d 601, 150 NYS2d 674. In a civil action, defense counsel stated on summation that if plaintiffs recovered a large sum, the defendants would be required to work for the rest of their lives to pay the judgment. This statement was an obvious reference to the defendants' lack of insurance coverage, and the court's refusal to instruct the jury to disregard the remarks on a timely objection was prejudicial error. *Rendo v Schermerhorn* (1965, 3d Dept) 24 AD2d 773, 263 NYS2d 743.

In a negligence action, evidence that defendant carried liability insurance is irrelevant and is generally considered sufficiently prejudicial to require a mistrial. Nevertheless, where the insurance carrier's name was introduced only once and without elaboration as a direct result of the dilatory, lax, and improper conduct of defendant, reversal and a new trial were not required, because the plaintiff did not intend to elicit such information, and the jury's determination of liability was not influenced by the mere mention of the company's name. *Kowalski v Loblaws, Inc.* (1978, 4th Dept) 61 AD2d 340, 402 NYS2d 681.

In an automobile negligence action, the reference by the plaintiff's attorney to no-fault insurance was not prejudicial where it was raised only to clarify the setting of the trial and no prejudice resulted. *Shumalski v Leone* (1978, 3d Dept) 63 AD2d 764, 404 NYS2d 744.

§ 30:10 USE OF CHARTS, DIAGRAMS, AND EXHIBITS IN ARGUMENT — The trial court did not abuse its discretion by permitting the counsel for an injured fireman to use a blackboard or chart during summation. *Carroll v Roman Catholic Diocese of Rockville Centre* (1966, 2d Dept) 26 AD2d 552, 271 NYS2d 7, app dismd 18 NY2d 708, 274 NYS2d 144 and affd 19 NY2d 658, 278 NYS2d 626.

It was within the trial court's discretion to refuse permission to plaintiff's attorney to display a chart to the jury during summation. *Raney v Suffolk Obstetrical & Gynecological Assocs., P.C.* (1994, 2d Dept) 200 AD2d 612, 606 NYS2d 729.

§ 30:11 CORRECTING IMPROPER CONDUCT OF COUN-

SEL — The court should have allowed objections during summations so that immediate curative action could have been taken as needed. *Van Valkenburgh v Koehler* (1990, 4th Dept) 164 AD2d 971, 559 NYS2d 766.

In the absence of timely objection or motion for a mistrial, counsel's allegedly improper remarks are generally not preserved for appellate review. *Smith v City of New York* (1995, 1st Dept) ___ AD2d ___, 629 NYS2d 411.

When plaintiff stipulated that the defense could make its objections to plaintiff's summation after it was concluded, defendant's objection to the reading of inadmissible material during plaintiff's summation was not waived. *Ginsberg by Ginsberg v North Shore Hosp.* (1995, 2d Dept) 213 AD2d 592, 624 NYS2d 257, app den 86 NY2d 701, 631 NYS2d 605.

During the course of summation, defense counsel continually disregarded the court's rulings regarding exclusion of evidence and counsel's attempts by suggestion to get before the jury matters that had been excluded. Because instructions from the trial court to disregard the comments of defendant's counsel did not correct the error, plaintiff was not obliged to move for a mistrial in order to preserve his right to a fair trial. *Nieves v New York* (1950) 277 AD 357, 100 NYS2d 221.

An improper question by counsel and an improper remark on the part of counsel during summation were not so prejudicial that they required a mistrial. The objectionable matters were not pursued after objection, and the trial court carefully instructed the jury with respect thereto. *Holly v Verrastro* (1952) 280 AD 1024, 117 NYS2d 246.

Counsel for plaintiff made a prejudicial remark in the course of summation, which was allowed to stand without a prompt judicial rebuke. The trial judge's subsequent general observation in the course of his charge to the jury that it should exclude unnecessary comments made by counsel did not cure the harm caused by the statement. *Cohen v Covelli* (1950) 276 AD 375, 94 NYS2d 782, reh and app den 276 AD 1011, 95 NYS2d 905.

In the course of summation, plaintiff's counsel improperly stated to the jury that bus drivers invariably commit perjury, implying that the practice was countenanced by the defendant. The statements went beyond the bounds of fair argument and summation and required a mistrial, even though the court sustained objections thereto, struck the improper statements from the record, and instructed the jury to disregard them. *Gross v Surface Transp. Corp.* (1947) 189 Misc 165, 70 NYS2d 515, affd 190 Misc 989, 79 NYS2d 328, affd 274 AD 775, 79 NYS2d 817.

Comments of defense counsel in a negligence action with respect to plaintiff's failure to produce certain witnesses who were not under plaintiff's control were improper. The court compounded the resulting prejudice by overruling plaintiff's objections, not issuing a proper rebuke to the defense counsel, and not properly instructing the jury. *Lyons v New York* (1968, 1st Dept) 29 AD2d 923, 289 NYS2d 2, motion gr 23 NY2d 736, 296 NYS2d 567, and affd 25 NY2d 996, 305 NYS2d 509. It has been held, however, that if counsel improperly raised in summation a corporate defendant's failure to call various witnesses who had knowledge of the facts and who were former officers or employees of the defendant, the error was cured by the court's instruction referring both to the absent witnesses by name and to the proper general rule. *Seligson, Morris & Neuburger v Fairbanks Whitney Corp.* (1965, 1st Dept) 22 AD2d 625, 257 NYS2d 706.

In summation, defense counsel in a dog-bite case emphasized that plaintiff, a 3½-year-old infant, had allegedly provoked the dog. The court should have corrected this argument by instructing the jury that the general rule that plaintiff's culpable conduct or express assumption of the risk is a defense to a claim of strict liability was not applicable to the infant plaintiff's conduct, because by virtue of his age he was not responsible for his actions. *Smith v Sapienza* (1985, 2d Dept) 115 AD2d 723, 496 NYS2d 538.

Although some of the remarks of plaintiff's counsel were better left unsaid, defendants were not prejudiced thereby, because the court immediately provided curative instructions and further provided supplemental instructions in accordance with defense counsel's request. *Kiker v Nassau County* (1991, 2d Dept) 175 AD2d 99, 571 NYS2d 804.

RESEARCH REFERENCES

American Law Reports

82 ALR4th 886, Attorney's argument as to evidence previously ruled inadmissible as contempt

71 ALR4th 1025, Propriety and prejudicial effect of trial counsel's reference or suggestion in medical malpractice case that defendant is insured

71 ALR4th 130, Propriety of trial court order limiting time for opening or closing argument in civil case–state cases

69 ALR4th 131, Prejudicial effect of bringing to jury's attention fact that plaintiff in personal injury or death action is entitled to worker's compensation benefits

68 ALR4th 954, Counsel's argument or comment stating or implying that defendant is not insured and will have to pay verdict himself as prejudicial error

93 ALR3d 556, Counsel's appeal in civil case to self-interest or prejudice of jurors as taxpayers, as ground for mistrial, new trial, or reversal

105 ALR Fed 755, Necessity of oral argument on motion for summary judgment or judgment on pleadings in federal court

ALR QUICK INDEX: Argument of Counsel

American Jurisprudence 2d

75A AM JUR 2d, Trial §§ 533-704

75 AM JUR 2d, Trial §§ 211-318

American Jurisprudence Trials

43 AM JUR TRIALS 495, Effective Summation in the Minor Back Injury Case

28 AM JUR TRIALS 599, Principles of Summation

6 AM JUR TRIALS 771, Nonjury Summations

6 AM JUR TRIALS 731, Summations for the Defense

6 AM JUR TRIALS 641, Summations for the Plaintiff

Other Resources

8 CARMODY-WAIT 2d, Presentation of the Case §§ 56:138-56:140

Auto-Cite®: Any case citation herein can be checked for form, parallel references, later history and annotation references through the Auto-Cite computer research system.

CHAPTER 31

INSTRUCTIONS TO THE JURY

§ 31:1 GENERAL REQUIREMENTS FOR JURY INSTRUCTIONS — Because the jury in a civil case determines all issues of fact, the court must instruct them with respect to the applicable law. This is done by means of the instructions given to the jury at the close of the case. The court may direct the jury to find either a general verdict or a special verdict. CPLR 4111(a).

A general verdict is one in which the jury finds in favor of one or more parties whereas a special verdict is one in which the jury finds facts only, leaving the court to determine which party is entitled to judgment. CPLR 4111(a).

When the court requires a jury to return a special verdict, it submits written questions to the jury that are susceptible of a brief answer or written forms of the several findings of fact that may be properly made, or uses any other appropriate method of submitting the issue and requiring written findings thereon. CPLR 4111(b). When the court requires the jury to return a general verdict, it may also require answers to written interrogatories submitted to the jury on one or more issues of fact, and in such case the court must give to the jurors sufficient instruction to enable them to render a general verdict and to answer the interrogatories. CPLR 4111(c).

When the charge given by the court is not clear enough on a particular point or fails to cover all phases of the case, it is the duty of counsel to request an additional charge. *Jensen v Stauffer Chemical Co.* (1956, 4th Dept) 3 AD2d 647, 158 NYS2d 197. At any time before the jury retires to consider its verdict, a party must make known his objections to a charge to the jury or to a failure or refusal to charge as requested. CPLR 4110(b).

A failure to make objections known may restrict the review on appeal. CPLR 4017. A party who fails to object to a charge at the trial is bound by it. *Commercial Casualty Ins. Co. v Roman* (1936) 269 NY 451, 199 NE 658, remittitur amd 270 NY 563, 200 NE 319. A charge, even if it is an erroneous one, is binding if no exception has been taken. *Harrington v Kedem Realty Corp.* (1961, 2d Dept) 13 AD2d 1027, 217 NYS2d 387. A charge of the trial court to which no exceptions are taken was held as the law of the case on appeal. *Pettis v New York State Electric & Gas Corp.* (1937) 249 AD 487, 293 NYS 91, affd 275 NY 507.

§ 31:2 PATTERN JURY INSTRUCTIONS — Pattern jury instructions, although prepared with the cooperation of the Judicial Conference, are primarily intended as a working tool, that may be used by counsel in preparing requests to charge, and by courts in preparation of the charge. The charges contained in New York Pattern Jury Instructions are subject to reversal on appeal or objection by counsel in the same manner as any other charges. Pattern Jury Instructions, although a useful tool, must be modified to the extent that the facts of any particular case so require. 1 New York Pattern Jury Instructions, preface, page xi.

In a medical malpractice action, there was no fundamental error in the court's failure to charge to "locality rule" where the applicable charge given in the case was taken practically verbatim from the one contained in the New York Pattern Jury Instructions. *McAteer v Arden Hill Hosp.* (1991, 3d Dept) 170 AD2d 758, 565 NYS2d 584.

§ 31:3 TIME FOR MAKING REQUESTS TO CHARGE — It is the better practice to submit to the court no later than during summation, a list of requests to charge, so the requests may be carefully read by the trial judge and each request accordingly marked "refused" or "granted." *Fallon v Mertz* (1906) 110 AD 755, 97 NYS 417.

There was no error in the trial court's refusal to charge that the defendant surgeon was an interested witness, because the plaintiff did not request this charge until after the main charge was given. *Schoch v Dougherty* (1986, 3d Dept) 122 AD2d 467, 504 NYS2d 855.

The defendants' burden to promptly notify the court that a knowledgeable witness had not been called was satisfied by their timely request for a missing witness charge at the pre-charge conference. *Dukes v Rotem* (1993, 1st Dept) 191 AD2d 35, reh den, motion gr (1st Dept) 197 AD2d 425, 604 NYS2d 699 and app dismd 82 NY2d 886, 609 NYS2d 563.

§ 31:4 REQUESTS TO CHARGE — On the trial of any action, counsel has the legal right to submit propositions of law that have a bearing on the evidence. The denial of this right is subject to review on appeal. Counsel, at the very least, has a right to have the request specifically denied by the court so that if the court is in error, counsel's exception to the denial will present an issue for review on appeal. *Chapman v McCormick*, (1881) 86 NY 479.

If counsel believes that the court has insufficiently instructed the jury, he has a right to request a charge that counsel thinks will more adequately present the issues for determination. *Hammer v Bloomingdale Bros., Inc.* (1926) 215 AD 308, 213 NYS 743.

When counsel has made a request to the court, and the court has misunderstood its meaning, counsel must call the court's attention to this fact, and failing to do so, he will be bound by the interpretation the court has given his request. *Booth v Boston & A. R. Co.* (1878) 73 NY 38.

If a party requests a charge and the court substantially gives the charge requested, that party may not complain about the language of the charge, because the court is not required to adopt the precise language requested by counsel. *Mullins v Siegel-Cooper Co.* (1905) 183 NY 129, 75 NE 1112.

If the instructions given by the court have contained an error of law, the error is not rectified by subsequent instructions that still leave the jury in doubt about the law. *Trump v Associated Transp. Inc.* (1949) 275 AD 982, 90 NYS2d 154. For the purpose of determining whether a requested charge has the effect of correcting erroneous instructions previously given, the assumption is that the construction placed upon the charge will be that of ordinary men, who are not learned in the law. *Corn Exchange Bank v American Dock & Trust Co.* (1896) 149 NY 174, 43 NE 915.

When a party is entitled to a charge on a particular point, the party is entitled to a clear and unambiguous charge that leaves the jury in no doubt as to its propriety. *Meyer v Clark* (1871) 45 NY 285. A party is entitled to a distinct charge without qualification, if entitled at all, and a court has no right to break the force of a charge by saying that while he will charge as requested, he does not believe it to be the law. *Meyer v Clark, supra.*

When a requested charge is proper and material, the refusal to grant such a charge is reversible error. *Chapman v McCormick, supra.* However, If the requested charge is legally or factually incorrect, indefinite or vague, the judge has a right to refuse to charge as requested. *Mintz v Equitable Life Assurance Soc.* (1937) 249 AD 914, 292 NYS 751, reh and app den 250 AD 813, 295 NYS 752 and affd 276 NY 546. If part of a particular request to charge is bad, the court may decline to give the entire instruction, because the court is not required to separate the bad portion of the charge from the good one. *Hamilton v Eno* (1880) 81 NY 116.

When a requested charge has already been covered in the main charge, the court may properly refuse to charge as requested. *Gaebler v Gallo* (1910) 198 NY 344, 91 NE 787. The court is not required to repeat in different words what has already been set forth in the charge. *Continental Nat'l Bank v Tradesmen's Nat'l Bank* (1903) 173 NY 272, 65 NE 1108. If counsel attempts to have favorable portions of a charge already given repeated by having them set forth in a requested charge, the court quite properly refuses such a request. *Continental Nat'l Bank v Tradesmen's Nat'l Bank, supra.*

When a court declines to charge in accordance with a request, "except as already charged on that point," this must be considered a refusal to charge in accordance with the request where the court, in fact, has not touched upon point requested in the charge. *Santiago v John E. Walsh Stevedore Co.* (1912) 152 AD 697, 137 NYS 611.

Although requests to charge should be timely made, counsel has a right to assume that the court in its charge will, without request, state the rules of evidence that are pertinent. When, therefore, at the close of the court's charge, instruction is asked on the correct rule of evidence applicable to the issue, it is error to refuse to grant this on the ground that the request should have been made along with others to be passed on before the charge was given. *Malone v Third A. R. Co.* (1896) 12 AD 508, 42 NYS 694.

Although counsel has a right to request further instructions at the conclusion of the court's charge to the jury, if counsel states that he has no further requests, he is precluded by this statement and may not complain if the court refuses to entertain any further request by him after it has given the charges requested by the adversary. *O'Neill v Dry Dock, E. B. & B. R. Co.* (1891) 129 NY 125, 29 NE 84.

In the interest of conducting the trial in an orderly manner, the court has the power to terminate the presentation of requests to charge. *Angerosa v White Co.* (1936) 248 AD 425, 290 NYS 204, affd 275 NY 524.

When a party has been given a reasonable opportunity to request instructions of the court, he cannot complain if the court, in the exercise of proper discretion, places a reasonable limitation on the exercise of the right. *O'Neill v Dry Dock, E. B. & B. R. Co., supra*.

CPLR 4110-b provides a procedure for submitting written requests to charge at the close of the evidence or at such earlier time during the trial as the court reasonably directs. When these written requests are filed, the court, out of the hearing of the jury, is required to inform counsel of its proposed action on the requests before their arguments to the jury, but the court is required to instruct the jury after arguments are completed. Under the procedure provided by CPLR 4110-b, no party may assign as error the giving or the failure to give an instruction unless he objects to it before the jury retires to consider its verdict; stating the matter to which he objects and the grounds of his objection. Counsel is to be given the opportunity to make the objection out of the hearing of the jury.

A request to charge with respect to comparative negligence, made at a charge conference before summations, was sufficient to preserve the issue for appellate review. No further request was made after the court instructed the jury and the plaintiff's counsel did not take an exception, but there was also no indication that the request was being abandoned or withdrawn. *Arbegast v Board of Education* (1985) 65 NY2d 161, 490 NYS2d 751.

The failure of the trial court to marshal the evidence in its charge did not mandate a reversal and a new trial when no request was made to marshal the evidence, nor was an exception taken to the failure of the trial court to do so, rendering the issue unpreserved for appellate review. *Brown v New York* (1989, 2d Dept) 154 AD2d 325, 545 NYS2d 801; *Green v Meyer* (1985, 2d Dept) 114 AD2d 352, 493 NYS2d 872.

§ 31:5 EXCEPTIONS OR OBJECTIONS TO INSTRUCTIONS
— At any time before the jury retires to consider its verdict, a party shall make known its objection to a charge to the jury or a failure or refusal to charge as requested. CPLR 4110-b. Failure to make known objections may restrict review upon appeal. CPLR 4017.

When a party takes no exception to a charge, the party is bound by the charge. *McCabe v Cohen* (1945) 294 NY 522. When an instruction is given and no exception is taken, the instruction becomes the law of the case. *Swensson v New York Albany Despatch Co.* (1956) 309 NY 497; *Brodeur v Cooper* (1992, 2d Dept) 182 AD2d 666, 582 NYS2d 724. This is so even though the instruction may be erroneous. *Kluttz v Citron* (1957) 2 NY2d 379, 161 NYS2d 26. Unless an exception is taken to a charge, there can be no subsequent claim that the charge was erroneous. *Bellefeuille v City & County Sav. Bank* (1976) 40 NY2d 879, 389 NYS2d 345.

If, however, the error in a charge is so fundamental that it requires a new trial in the interest of justice, it is grounds for reversal in the Appellate Division even without an exception. *Di*

Grazia v Castronova (1975, 4th Dept) 48 AD2d 249, 368 NYS2d 898. An error in the charge is fundamental only when it is so significant that the jury was prevented from fully understanding the issues at the trial. *Kilburn v Acands, Inc.* (1992, 4th Dept) 187 AD2d 988, 590 NYS2d 611.

Thus, where the court erroneously submitted a case to the jury on the theory of *res ipsa loquitur*, there was a reversal despite the failure of counsel to except to the charge. *Goodheart v American Airlines, Inc.* (1937) 252 AD 660, 1 NYS2d 288. Although counsel failed to except to the court's charge, the Appellate Division nevertheless reversed and granted a new trial in the interest of justice where the error was fundamental and the resultant injustice egregious. *Caceres v New York City Health & Hospitals Corp.* (1980, 2d Dept) 74 AD2d 619, 425 NYS2d 36; *Kazales v Minto Leasing, Inc.* (1978, 2d Dept) 61 AD2d 1039, 403 NYS2d 286. Although defendant's failure to object to the charge would ordinarily be deemed a waiver, where the error was fundamental and related to the key factual issue, the court was constrained to reverse in the interests of justice. *Antonucci v Irondequoit* (1981, 4th Dept) 81 AD2d 743, 438 NYS2d 417.

Where counsel failed to make a timely exception or request a clarifying charge, and there was no error of a fundamental character that could serve as the basis for invocation of interest of justice jurisdiction, the alleged error was not preserved for review. *Saleh v Sears, Roebuck & Co.* (1986, 2d Dept) 119 AD2d 652, 500 NYS2d 796.

Where the portions of the court's charge that were raised as issues on appeal had not been objected to in accordance with CPLR 4017 and 5501(a)(3), they were not considered on appeal because the error was not so fundamental that it required reversal of judgment and a new trial "in the interests of justice." *Jemison v Goodman* (1975, 4th Dept) 49 AD2d 1011, 373 NYS2d 926.

When counsel wishes to make an objection or take exception to a charge, it must be with respect to the specific section of the charge that counsel considers erroneous. *Gangi v Fradus* (1920) 227 NY 452, 125 NE 677. Unless the charge is incorrect in its entirety, an exception to the entire charge does not suffice. *People ex rel. Dailey v Livingston* (1879) 79 NY 279. No question of law for review is presented by an exception to the charge in its entirety. *Rapee v Beacon Hotel Corp.* (1944) 293 NY 196. The rule is a sound one, because the judge is entitled to an opportunity to correct a specific portion of the charge that is in error and he does not have this opportunity if the particular error is not made clear to him. *Gilliland v Delaware & Hudson Co.* (1924) 207 AD 509, 202 NYS 710.

If the objection the plaintiff raised to a court instruction at trial was ambiguous and failed to apprise the court explicitly of the alleged point of error, the plaintiff should be deemed to have waived the right to raise the issue on appeal. *Di Salvo v Bortle* (1977, 4th Dept) 58 AD2d 997, 396 NYS2d 943.

Plaintiff's contention that the causation instruction erroneously implied that there could be but one proximate cause of accident was not preserved for appellate review where plaintiff failed to advance that precise argument at trial, or to object to the charge on that ground. *Liebgott v City of New York* (1995, 2d Dept) 213 AD2d 606, 624 NYS2d 252.

If part of a charge to which an exception is taken is correct, so that only a modification is required, it is not sufficient to simply take an exception to the incorrect portion of the charge; instead the court's attention should be directed to the fact that a different rule is applicable. The correct procedure is for counsel to request a charge that will correct that of the court. *Rhinelander v Rhinelander* (1927) 219 AD 189, 219 NYS 548, affd 245 NY 510, 157 NE 838.

When the point at issue has already been brought to the attention of the court and the court is aware of the nature of the objection, an exception is sufficient to preserve the point for appellate review without any specific request to charge. *Bergman v Schultz* (1948) 274 AD 1001, 84 NYS2d 563.

If the entire charge consists of only one legal proposition, or if the entire charge is to be remedied, a general exception preserves the point for review and the reasons for the exception need not be stated. *Bulson v Lear* (1928) 222 AD 413, 226 NYS 479.

When the court refuses to charge as requested, in order to raise a question for appellate review regarding the ruling of the trial court, the exception must be specific and must point out the particular request to which it is intended to apply. *Newall v Bartlett* (1889) 114 NY 399, 21 NE 990. The court will be given an opportunity to correct errors rather than permitted to perpetuate them. *Holmes v Moffat* (1890) 120 NY 159, 24 NE 275. However, where the court has refused to charge with respect to a number of requests by counsel and has given counsel an exception "to the refusal to charge each of the requests by defendant," this is sufficient to preserve the requested charge for appellate review. *Kittredge v Grannis* (1923) 236 NY 375, 140 NE 730, reh den 236 NY 637, 142 NE 315.

Where the jury included damages for the mother's derivative action in the child's award for personal injuries, pursuant to court's charge, and no exception was taken, this became the law of the case and was not subject to review. *Michalek v Martyna* (1975, 4th Dept) 48 AD2d 1005, 369 NYS2d 262.

Although defendants in a medical malpractice action contended that the trial court's failure to marshal the evidence and relate the law to the facts in its charge was prejudicial, the failure of the defendant to object waived any error of law in this regard. *O'Neill v Cross County Hospital* (1978, 2d Dept) 61 AD2d 1008, 402 NYS2d 633.

In an action against defendant, which was one of four pharmaceutical companies that manufactured a drug, for injuries sustained by plaintiff from the use of that drug, defendant's claim that the instructions to the jury on concerted action were erroneous was not preserved for review by appropriate request or exception. *Bichler v Eli Lilly & Co.* (1982) 55 NY2d 571, 450 NYS2d 776, 22 ALR4th 171.

The requirement of a timely exception is not merely a technicality; its function is to give the court and the opposing party the opportunity to correct an error in the conduct of the trial. *Byrd v Genesee Hospital* (1985, 4th Dept) 110 AD2d 1051, 489 NYS2d 22. In this decision, the court found that because the appellant had failed to object to the omission of a requested charge from the court's instructions to the jury, the issue had not been preserved for appellate review. Similarly, a plaintiff who failed to object to a portion of the court's instructions on a particular issue had not preserved the issue for review. *Emmons v Country Lincoln Mercury Sales, Inc.* (1985, 2d Dept) 111 AD2d 213, 489 NYS2d 248.

Plaintiff failed to preserve her objection to the charge where, although counsel asserted a general, non-specific and ambiguous objection in a timely manner, counsel failed to clarify the objection when asked to do so by the trial court, and the clarification did not appear until the plaintiff made a post-verdict motion. *Stern v Waldbaum, Inc. # 10* (1985, 2d Dept) 109 AD2d 789, 486 NYS2d 92.

When the trial court's charge on consequential damages in an action for breach of agreement to sell manufacturer's products was not excepted to, it became the law applicable to the determination of the case, and the propriety of this instruction was not preserved for review by the Court of Appeals. *Up-Front Industries, Inc. v U.S. Industries, Inc.* (1984) 63 NY2d 1004, 484 NYS2d 505.

In an action brought to recover attorneys' fees for services rendered in a public offering of securities, although the judgment did not fully compensate the plaintiff for his disbursements, he failed to preserve that error for review by objecting to the court's instruction, the special verdict question, the jury's finding or the judgment. *Larkin v Present Co.* (1989, 4th Dept) 152 AD2d 1005, 544 NYS2d 696, app den 74 NY2d 615, 549 NYS2d 961.

Because the plaintiff failed to object to the trial court's charge, her contention that the court improperly applied the New York City Traffic Regulations instead of the Vehicle and Traffic Law to an accident that involved a pedestrian hit by a car was not preserved for appellate review. *Burke v Santoro* (1991, 2d Dept) 172 AD2d 579, 568 NYS2d 144.

Plaintiff's claim of error with respect to the court's jury instructions was not properly preserved for review, because plaintiff's counsel failed to specifically object in a timely manner when asked to do so at the pre-charge and post-charge stages of the trial. *Carrasquillo v American Type Founders Co.* (1992, 1st Dept) 183 AD2d 410, 583 NYS2d 264, app den 81 NY2d 703, 594 NYS2d 717.

§ 31:6   INSTRUCTIONS ON THE ISSUES — A party to a lawsuit has a right to have his case go to the jury on an accurate statement of the rules of law applicable thereto. *Noseworthy v*

New York (1948) 298 NY 76. A litigant is entitled to have the jury instructed with respect to all theories consistent with the evidence in the case, and such instructions cannot be confined to one theory that is consistent with the evidence while excluding another theory that is also consistent with the evidence. *Marion v B. G. Coon Const. Co.* (1915) 216 NY 178, 110 NE 444. Where elements of damage have been proved, the court may not ignore these or withdraw them from the jury. *Moore v New York E. R. Co.* (1892) 130 NY 523, 29 NE 997. There must, however, be evidence to support the instruction, and the mere fact that a theory is contained in the pleadings does not justify an instruction where no proof has been offered with respect thereto. *Lifton v Title Guarantee & Trust Co.* (1941) 263 AD 3, 31 NYS2d 94.

A party is entitled to an unambiguous instruction to the jury with respect to the applicable law, and when the charge by the court is so inconsistent or contradictory on a material proposition that it is impossible to reconcile the different versions, an appellant should be entitled to rely upon the instructions most favorable to his appeal. *Johnson v Blaney* (1910) 198 NY 312, 91 NE 721, reh den 198 NY 628, 92 NE 1087. Because the purpose of the court's instructions to the jury is to help that body, which consists of laymen, to reach a verdict, the charge should be in language that is understandable by laymen. *Stryzinski v Arnold* (1955) 285 AD 780, 141 NYS2d 11. Because the court is not writing a textbook for lawyers, but instructing a body of laymen, any technical terms employed by the court should be explained to the jurors. *Lynch v Figge* (1922) 200 AD 92, 192 NYS 873.

In a negligence action, it was reversible error for the trial judge to refuse to charge the jury that defendant could be found liable on alternate theories of creation of a hazardous condition or the failure to warn of the existence of certain potentially hazardous conditions. *Wirth v De Vito* (1982, 2d Dept) 89 AD2d 603, 452 NYS2d 463.

Where the questions of negligence and contributory negligence were close, but the trial court in its charge to the jury over-emphasized facts against plaintiffs and failed to review the conflicting evidence as to the location of the impact and the physical condition of the roadway, the judgment was reversed and a new trial granted. *Gilhooly v Piciocchi* (1974, 2d Dept) 45 AD2d 961, 359 NYS2d 336.

The doctrine of last clear chance has lost its viability since the adoption of comparative negligence, and it was therefore not error for the trial court to refuse to charge on this doctrine. *Hoyt v McCann* (1982, 2d Dept) 88 AD2d 633, 450 NYS2d 231.

The trial court's failure to charge the jury that any negligence on the part of the infant plaintiff's older brother could not be imputed to the infant plaintiff, constituted reversible error, because it precluded the jury from fairly considering the issues presented. *Avram v Haddad* (1982, 2d Dept) 88 AD2d 942, 451 NYS2d 178.

Where the issue at the trial with respect to damages was whether plaintiff's present complaints resulted from the car accident or were caused by a chronic pre-existing back problem, the trial court properly gave the jury a "failure to produce a witness" charge with respect to the doctor who had treated the plaintiff before the accident, where there was no showing that this doctor was not within the power of plaintiff to call. *Griffin v Nissen* (1982, 4th Dept) 89 AD2d 808, 453 NYS2d 277.

Because an unexcused violation of the Vehicle and Traffic Law is negligence, it is error for the trial court to refuse plaintiff's request to charge the jury with respect to the section of the law that has been violated. *Tomaselli v Goldstein* (1984, 2d Dept) 104 AD2d 872, 480 NYS2d 382.

In a will contest, where the evidence offered by the appellants was wholly circumstantial in nature, it was error for the Surrogate to deny the request of counsel for appellants to charge the jury on circumstantial evidence, because this refusal deprived the jury of the information necessary to enable it to evaluate the evidence. *Re Fodera* (1983, 2d Dept) 96 AD2d 559, 465 NYS2d 65.

Although the failure to give a requested instruction may be error, where the form of the jury verdict makes it clear that the failure to give the instruction did not influence or affect the verdict, the error will be considered harmless, and a new trial will not be required. *Young v Hackett* (1975) 49 AD2d 1013, 374 NYS2d 83.

A statute or regulation should be charged where there is evidence in the record to support a finding that the statute or regulation was violated. *Gamar v Gamar* (1985, 2d Dept) 114 AD2d 487, 494 NYS2d 402. Where defendant admitted that he failed to stop at a stop sign, plaintiffs were entitled to a specific instruction that where a traffic statute violation occurs, the jury may infer from that fact and from that fact alone that defendant driver was negligent. *Gamar v Gamar, supra.*

It is prejudicial error to charge a statute where there is no evidence to support a finding that the statute was violated. *Senn v Scudieri* (1991, 1st Dept) 165 AD2d 346, 567 NYS2d 665, app dismd without op 79 NY2d 977, 583 NYS2d 195.

In an action brought to recover for injuries sustained by a bicyclist who was struck by an automobile, the trial court did not commit reversible error when it declined to charge the jury with respect to plaintiff's violation of Vehicle and Traffic Law § 1236(b), which requires a bicycle to be equipped with a bell; assuming *arguendo* that the trial court did err in declining to charge the statutory violation, the error would not warrant reversal because no reasonable view of the evidence could support the conclusion that the lack of a bell on the plaintiff's bicycle was a proximate cause of the accident. *Cranston v Oxford Resources Corp.* (1991, 2d Dept) 173 AD2d 757, 571 NYS2d 733.

A plaintiff, who in seeking to get out of the rain had entered a vacant building that had been sealed and was awaiting demolition, was injured when the building collapsed. The plaintiff was entitled to an instruction that the Administrative Code of the City of New York, § 26-235 imposed a duty on the defendant to conduct reasonable inspections of the premises to ensure that the building remained sealed. *Watson v New York* (1992, 2d Dept) 184 AD2d 690, 585 NYS2d 100.

Because the trial court's instructions to the jury should state the law applicable to the facts of the case, the trial court committed prejudicial error when it charged the jury with respect to the proper maximum speed to be maintained while operating a motor vehicle in the City of New York where there was no evidence of a violation thereof. *Marigliano v City of New York* (1993, 2d Dept) 196 AD2d 533, 601 NYS2d 161.

Although the trial court's charge on the issue of mitigation of damages was entirely too brief and in need of elaboration, because the jurors made no request for re-reading of this or any portion of the charge or for clarification or otherwise indicated that they were confused, the error was harmless. *Zito v New York State Electric & Gas Corp.* (1986, 3d Dept) 122 AD2d 499, 505 NYS2d 464.

Although the distinction is sometimes difficult to discern, implied assumption of the risk and contributory negligence are distinct legal theories, and if the evidence introduced by a defendant supports both theories, the defendant is entitled to a jury charge on both. *McCabe v Easter* (1987, 3d Dept) 128 AD2d 257, 516 NYS2d 515.

In a medical malpractice case, a missing witness charge was not required with respect to the physician who treated the plaintiff after the surgery, because there was no indication that he was in a position to give non-cumulative evidence on any material issue in the case. *Wilson v Bodian* (1987, 2d Dept) 130 AD2d 221, 519 NYS2d 126. However, with respect to the doctor who treated plaintiff before defendant doctor's surgery, and continued to treat her for more than three years after the defendant doctor's involvement ceased, plaintiff had a burden to show that this doctor was not available or under her control to call as a witness. *Wilson v Bodian, supra*.

Plaintiffs were not entitled to a missing witness charge with respect to former employees of the defendant; no negative inference may properly be drawn from a party's failure to call a former employee, as such a person is not within the party's control. *Hershkowitz v St. Michel* (1988, 2d Dept) 143 AD2d 809, 533 NYS2d 344.

In a negligence action brought by a patron of a roller skating rink against the operators of the rink after the patron had been knocked down by rowdy teenagers, it was error for the court to refuse to give a missing witness charge with respect to a security guard employed by the rink, where there was testimony that before the occurrence the two boys who hit her were skating in a reckless and rowdy manner, interfering with other patrons, and were admonished by the guards. *Trainor v Oasis Roller World, Inc.* (1989, 1st Dept) 151 AD2d 323, 543 NYS2d 61.

In an action brought by a painter who suffered injuries and the estate of a painter who fell to his death, against a licensed rigger who had loaned his license to an unlicensed rigger, it was reversible error for the trial court to fail to give instructions, as requested, that the negligent rigging of the scaffold by an unlicensed rigger, painter's employer, did not automatically sever the causal relation between the loan of the license by the rigger and the injuries sustained by the painter. *Bjelicic v Lynned Realty Corp.* (1989, 1st Dept) 152 AD2d 151, 546 NYS2d 1020, app dismd without op 75 NY2d 947, 555 NYS2d 693.

The trial court did not commit error in refusing to charge the jury regarding the plaintiff's lack of culpable conduct, because this was not an issue in the case. *Smith v Catholic Medical Center, Inc.* (1989, 2d Dept) 155 AD2d 435, 547 NYS2d 96.

Defendant was entitled to a charge on the doctrine of comparative negligence where a reasonable view of the evidence established that plaintiff approached and attempted to pet a chained, barking dog at a time when the attention of the dog's owner was engaged by a loud altercation nearby. *Pisciotta v Parisi* (1989, 2d Dept) 155 AD2d 422, 547 NYS2d 352.

In a personal injury action arising out of a motor vehicle accident, the court properly charged with respect to a missing witness who was the driver of one of the vehicles involved in the accident and who was also the brother-in-law of the owner, and could be considered available to her, and was in a position to give substantial testimony that was not merely cumulative. *Felder v Carolina Freight Carriers* (1989, 2d Dept) 156 AD2d 540, 548 NYS2d 809.

In a medical malpractice action, the trial court did not err in refusing to give a missing witness charge with respect to two physicians, where in the case of both doctors testimony they might be expected to give was already in evidence, either by the notes and hospital records admitted into evidence, or through testimony of an expert. *Kane v Linsky* (1989, 2d Dept) 156 AD2d 333, 548 NYS2d 286.

In an action arising out of an automobile accident, the trial court erred in refusing, over counsel's objection, to give an interested witness charge as to a driver who, although no longer a party defendant in the suit, was an alleged negligent actor who would still have been liable to indemnify the vicariously liable city for any judgment recovered against it and was therefore an interested party. *Calandra v Norwood* (1981, 2d Dept) 81 AD2d 650, 438 NYS2d 381.

In a medical malpractice action, it was error for the trial court to grant plaintiff's request for a missing witness charge, with respect to the physician who had examined the plaintiff on defendant's behalf, where there was nothing to indicate that the doctor's testimony would not have been merely cumulative of the testimony of the other experts who had previously testified. *Levande v Dines* (1989, 2d Dept) 153 AD2d 671, 544 NYS2d 864.

Although the trial justice did not grant defendants' motion for a missing witness charge when plaintiff did not produce the testimony of her treating physician, the error was harmless in the absence of any indication that the testimony given by the missing witness would have covered material not already covered in testimony and voluminous documentary evidence consisting of hospital reports that were produced. *Christopher v Great Atlantic & Pacific Tea Co.* (1990, AD 1st Dept) 161 Ad2d 274, 554 NYS2d 908, app dismd 76 NY2d 1006, 564 NYS2d 716.

A missing witness charge is warranted for the failure to call a treating physician as a witness at the trial, unless the party opposing the inference shows that the witness is either unavailable, not under his control, or that the testimony of the witness would be cumulative. *Dayanim v Unis* (1991, 1st Dept) 171 AD2d 579, 567 NYS2d 673; *Arroyo v New York* (1991, 1st Dept) 171 AD2d 541, 567 NYS2d 257.

In a medical malpractice action, the jurors were erroneously instructed that the injured plaintiff had the burden of demonstrating that there was a substantial probability that the defendants' negligent conduct had caused her injuries; in so charging the jury, the court applied an improper standard of proof, thereby increasing the plaintiff's burden of proof from the usual "more probable than not" language. *Dempsey v Methodist Hosp.* (1990, 2d Dept) 159 AD2d 541, 552 NYS2d 406.

In an action based upon allegedly defective wood parquet floor-ing tiles, any error on the part of the trial court in improperly charging a manufacturing defect, as opposed to a design defect, clearly did not prejudice the defendant, even if this was error, because the evidence was overwhelming that the tiles were in fact defective. *Bellevue South Assoc. v HRH Constr. Corp.* (1990, 1st Dept) 160 AD2d 189, 553 NYS2d 159, mod on other grounds 78 NY2d 282, 574 NYS2d 165, reconsideration denied 78 NY2d 1008, 575 NYS2d 459.

The error, if any, in the language of the charge as given by the court on the issue of momentary forgetfulness could not have prejudiced the plaintiff, because the jury never reached the issue of her comparative negligence. *O'Neill v Spitzer* (1990, 1st Dept) 160 AD2d 298, 553 NYS2d 392.

The expert's testimony as to the duty of a private landowner to remove all snow within one hour after it stops falling is in conflict with the well established principle that an abutting owner or ten-ant is not liable to an injured pedestrian for failure to completely remove natural accumulations of snow and ice from the sidewalk. The trial court compounded the error by denying defendant's request to charge the jury to disregard the expert's testimony con-cerning industry standards for snow and ice removal, because such testimony conflicted with the proper standard of care to be exercised by an abutting tenant. *Nevins v Great Atlantic & Pacific Tea Co.* (1990, 1st Dept) 164 AD2d 807, 559 NYS2d 539.

The trial court properly rejected plaintiffs' request to charge the jury on inferences that may be drawn from the destruction of evi-dence, where there was in fact no showing that any evidence had been destroyed. *Lillis v D'Souza* (1991, 4th Dept) 174 AD2d 976, 572 NYS2d 136, app denied 78 NY2d 858, 575 NYS2d 454.

Where plaintiff survived the accident and died almost a year later of unrelated causes, and the wrongful death claim was with-drawn, the trial court was in error and prejudiced the defendant, by charging that the estate of the deceased plaintiff had a lesser burden of proof. *Clarke v New York City Transit Authority* (1992, 1st Dept) 174 AD2d 268, 580 NYS2d 221.

Where parties do not rely on circumstantial evidence alone, a circumstantial evidence charge is not required. *Venditto v Doody* (1992, 2d Dept) 181 AD2d 729, 581 NYS2d 82.

In an action brought by plaintiff who was injured while a guest at defendant's house, it was error for the trial court to instruct the jurors that if they found that it was plaintiff who had the duty of maintaining the premises, and his breach of that duty caused his accident, they did not have to go any further if it was the plaintiff's duty in the first place; the instructions were erroneous in that they permitted the jury to disregard the defendant's duty as a landowner to keep his land in a reasonably safe condition and obfuscated the concept of comparative negligence by implying to the jury that they could find that the plaintiff's own culpable conduct could constitute a bar to his recovery. *Farrell v Labarbera* (1992, 2d Dept) 181 AD2d 715, 581 NYS2d 226.

Because a defendant bears the burden of proof on an affirmative defense in an action for breach of contract and violation of trade secrets, including a defense that asserts that plaintiff is not the real party in interest, an erroneous charge that leaves the jury with the clear impression that the burden of proof was on plaintiff that he, and not a successor corporation, was the real party in interest, warrants a new trial. *Brignoli v Balch, Hardy & Scheinman, Inc.* (1991, 1st Dept) 178 AD2d 290, 577 NYS2d 375.

Although it was error for the court to instruct the jury that it could consider the bus's parking near a fire hydrant as some evidence of negligence, the error was harmless because the liability of the bus company was clearly established. *Sullivan v LoCastro* (1991, 2d Dept) 178 AD2d 523, 577 NYS2d 631, app den 81 NY2d 701, 594 NYS2d 715.

Unless plaintiff's conduct or her contact with a third person was so extraordinary and unforeseeable as to constitute an intervening cause, an intervening cause charge to the jury cannot be supported. *Root v Feldman* (1992, 3d Dept) 185 AD2d 409, 585 NYS2d 834.

It was error for the court to instruct the jury that if they believed plaintiff's testimony as to how the accident occurred, then, as a matter of law, the plaintiff was not negligent, because there was evidence from which the jury might have found the plaintiff comparatively negligent. *Cacciolo v Port Auth. of New York* (1992, 2d Dept) 186 AD2d 528, 588 NYS2d 350.

A party is entitled to a charge on the emergency doctrine when, viewing the proof in the light most favorable to her, there is a reasonable view of the evidence that her conduct was the product of a sudden and unforeseeable occurrence not of her own making. *Donaldson v Kilgore* (1992, 4th Dept) 187 AD2d 1018, 590 NYS2d 364.

In a medical malpractice action, in light of the fact that defendant's medical expert would have provided relevant and non-cumulative testimony at trial that was unfavorable to the defendant, specifically, testimony concerning the permanency of plaintiff's scars resulting from the surgery, and the fact that said expert would have, before accepting the patient's consent to the operative procedure, informed any patient opting for this elective surgery that permanent scars were to be expected as a result of the surgery; a missing witness charge should have been given by the trial court with respect to the defense expert. *Lee-Lu Pan v Shaw* (1994, 1st Dept) 203 AD2d 195, 611 NYS2d 158.

§ 31:7   ERRONEOUS INSTRUCTIONS — A court may commit error by giving undue prominence or emphasis in its instructions to a particular matter. Thus, where an action was brought on an accident and health policy, the court committed error that was prejudicial to the plaintiff when, in the course of its instructions to the jury it emphasized the magnitude and importance of the insurance company as a "great business organization" and as one of the largest of the old-line companies. *Dulberg v Equitable Life Assurance Soc.* (1936) 249 AD 785, 292 NYS 232.

An erroneous instruction to the jury is only deemed harmless when there is no view of the evidence under which appellant could have prevailed. *Marine Midland Bank v John E. Russo Produce Co.* (1980) 50 NY2d 31, 427 NYS2d 961.

In a negligence action, the trial court committed prejudicial error because of its emphasis on the word "substantial" in the course of its jury charge with respect to the issue of contributory negligence, especially since that portion of the charge was repeated during the deliberation of the jury in response to a request by that body. *Maggio v Mid-Hudson Chevrolet, Inc.* (1970,

2d Dept) 34 AD2d 567, 310 NYS2d 40. Undue emphasis in the court charge on the question of contributory negligence has been held to be error. *Freire v Kaupman* (1935) 245 AD 844, 281 NYS 408.

If a charge is ambiguous, inconsistent, erroneous, confusing, one-sided, incomplete or overly technical, a new trial will be ordered if prejudice has resulted to any party. *Doolittle v T.E. Conklin Brass & Copper Co.* (1984, 1st Dept) 103 AD2d 722, 478 NYS2d 625. Where a charge is so inconsistent or contradictory on a material proposition that it is impossible to reconcile the different versions, the appellant should be entitled to rely upon the construction most favorable to his appeal. *Johnson v Blaney* (1910) 198 NY 312, 91 NE 721, reh den 198 NY 628, 92 NE 1087.

Jury instructions must not contain contradictory and inadequate statements of rules of law, and when a charge confuses and creates doubt as to the principle of law to be applied, a new trial is required. *Lopato v Kinney Rent-A-Car, Inc.* (1979, 1st Dept) 73 AD2d 565, 423 NYS2d 42. A charge that is confusing and can mislead the jury requires reversal. *Spells v Foley* (1981, 2d Dept) 84 AD2d 786, 444 NYS2d 27, app dismd 55 NY2d 922, 449 NYS2d 190. Thus, it was error for the trial court to charge the jury that a plaintiff had the burden of proving his case by a preponderance of the testimony, with reasonable certainty. *Spells v Foley, supra.*

Where there were no eyewitnesses and a one-year-old child could not explain how she came to be struck by an ice cream truck, a charge to the jury that the father was not only negligent but "stupid, careless and an idiot to permit a child of that age to wander off" required a new trial, even though the court did formally instruct the jury that the father's negligence was not attributable to the child and only the defendant's negligence was in issue. *Samuel v Porchia* (1972, 2d Dept) 40 AD2d 697, 336 NYS2d 387.

The trial court erred in giving the jury a missing witness charge regarding the plaintiff's failure to produce the infant plaintiff, who was only 5 years old at the time of the underlying accident, without also instructing the jury to consider the infant's age and the circumstances surrounding the accident in determining whether or not they deemed it appropriate in this case to invoke the permissible inferences authorized in such a charge. *Crosby v Beaird* (1983, 2d Dept) 93 AD2d 852, 461 NYS2d 350.

The trial court's comments in its charge on assumption of the risk and its statement that the jury could disregard the defendant's admission that he was speeding, unduly prejudiced the plaintiff, requiring reversal and a new trial. *Haviaras v Savopoulos* (1977, 2d Dept) 59 AD2d 772, 398 NYS2d 728.

In a personal injury action, the trial court committed prejudicial error in instructing the jury that it could draw an unfavorable inference from the plaintiffs' failure to call 10 doctors as witnesses, where there was no indication that these doctors were in a position to give substantial, rather than merely cumulative evidence, where nothing in the record established that the 10 doctors concerned were under the control of the plaintiffs, and the calling of the additional 10 doctors as expert witnesses would entail substantial costs to the plaintiffs. *Oswald v Heaney* (1979, 2d Dept) 70 AD2d 653, 416 NYS2d 826.

Reversal was required because the trial court's charge to the jury as to "emergency" failed to make it clear that a change in the color of the traffic signal facing the defendant's bus driver would not be treated as creating an emergency. *Rosario v New York City Transit Authority* (1980, 2d Dept) 73 AD2d 912, 423 NYS2d 254. Because an emergency instruction is available only where a contingency could not have been anticipated and where the actor has not aggravated or created the emergency situation by his own conduct, it was error to charge the emergency doctrine in an action arising out of the shooting of a bystander by a bank guard because the possibility of a bank robbery cannot be said to be one that is not anticipated by the defendant bank. *Shaw v Manufacturer's Hanover Trust Co.* (1983, 1st Dept) 95 AD2d 738, 464 NYS2d 172.

Where a vehicular accident occurs in the City of New York, and the conduct comes within the provisions of the New York City Traffic Regulations, a charge under the state's Vehicle & Traffic Law constitutes reversible error. *Finkel v Benoit* (1995, 2d Dept)

211 AD2d 749, 622 NYS2d 295; *Eichenholtz v Livery Service Corp.* (1972, 2d Dept) 40 AD2d 990, 338 NYS2d 667.

It was error for the trial court to give the jury instructions that required it to speculate on whether or not the defendant driver, who had a fatal heart attack, knew or should have known that such attack was likely, where there was no evidence to support the charge of knowledge by the driver of any impending heart attack. *Diemer v Goad* (1980, 3d Dept) 78 AD2d 752, 432 NYS2d 740.

The trial court erred when it instructed the jury that comparative negligence was not a defense to liability based upon subdivision 6 of § 241 of the Labor Law. *Van Slyke v Niagara Mohawk Power Corp.* (1983, 4th Dept) 93 AD2d 990, 461 NYS2d 643, affd 60 NY2d 774, 469 NYS2d 674.

Where the issue involved was whether pain was a permanent injury so as to breach the threshold of the no-fault law, the failure of the court in its instructions to define permanency to include the permanent operation of a body function or system with pain, may have led the jury to believe erroneously that permanent pain did not amount to a permanent injury. *Slack v Crossetta* (1980, 2d Dept) 75 AD2d 809, 427 NYS2d 493.

Failure to properly define permanency for purposes of the serious injury requirement of the Insurance Law, constituted fundamental error because the plaintiff offered ample objective medical evidence to support a finding of persistent, permanent pain or a significant limitation of the range of motion, such that a proper charge might have resulted in a verdict in favor of the plaintiff. *Bassett v Romano* (1987, 2d Dept) 126 AD2d 693, 511 NYS2d 298.

Reversal of the jury's verdict on damages was required on the basis of the court's erroneous jury charge as to the requirements for a finding of serious injury within the meaning of Insurance Law § 5102(d), which confused the categories of serious injury set forth in the statute, and may have misled the jury into believing that one of those categories, a "significant limitation of use of a body function or system" required proof of permanence. Because this error was fundamental, the absence of a timely objection to the charge on this basis did not preclude the Appellate Division from considering the error. *Decker v Rassaert* (1987, 2d Dept) 131 AD2d 626, 516 NYS2d 710.

In a bifurcated trial, where the erroneous jury instructions tainted the liability verdict without affecting the damage finding, a new trial was ordered but limited to the issue of liability only. *Schabe v Hampton Bays Union Free School Dist.* (1984, 2d Dept) 103 AD2d 418, 480 NYS2d 328.

A missing witness charge given against a defendant was improper, where the witness in question was equally, if not more, available to plaintiff. *Houlihan Parnes Realtors v Gazivoda* (1984, 2d Dept) 106 AD2d 550, 483 NYS2d 69.

The failure of the trial court to charge the jury adequately on the principles of comparative negligence, although plaintiff's counsel specifically requested such a charge, substantially impaired plaintiff's rights, constituting reversible error and requiring a new trial. *Runfola v Bryant* (1987, 4th Dept) 127 AD2d 972, 513 NYS2d 55.

The court's charge regarding the burden of proof was inadequate in that it failed to advise the jury: (a) that it was the quality of the evidence, rather than the number of witnesses or the length of their testimony, that would determine what should constitute a preponderance of the evidence, (b) what plaintiffs were obliged to establish to sustain their burden of proof and (c) that if the evidence should weigh evenly, it would be the jury's duty to return a verdict for defendants. *Torem v 564 Cent. Ave. Rest., Inc.* (1987, 1st Dept) 133 AD2d 25, 518 NYS2d 620, resettled (1st Dept) 134 AD2d 158, 520 NYS2d 526.

In an action arising out of an accident in which a bus driver hit a utility pole, the trial court erred in giving the "sudden stop or jolt" and comparative negligence instructions, because no evidence was presented at trial to support either instruction. *Sappleton v Metropolitan Suburban Bus Authority* (1988, 2d Dept) 140 AD2d 684, 529 NYS2d 21.

§ 31:8 OTHER RULES APPLICABLE TO INSTRUCTIONS —

The court in its charge may sum up the evidence and indicate its importance to the issues to be determined. *Board of Comm'rs of Pilots v Clark* (1865) 33 NY 251. The extent of this summary of the testimony rests within the discretion of the court. *Smith v*

Gray (1897) 19 AD 262, 46 NYS 180, affd 162 NY 643, 57 NE 1124. Thus, where the evidence is complicated, the analysis of the court should be sufficient to enable the jurors to have a full understanding of the case they are to decide. This is not, however, necessary in a relatively simple case. *Smith v Gray, supra.* The court should not, however, intrude upon the province of the jury by indicating to that body how it should find on factual issues in dispute based upon the evidence. *Corrigan v Funk* (1905) 109 AD 846, 96 NYS 910.

Having chosen to marshall the evidence rather than to incorporate the factual contentions of the parties in respect to the legal principles charged, the trial court was obligated to summarize the testimony in a balanced manner. *Blaize v New York* (1981, 2d Dept) 80 AD2d 594, 436 NYS2d 34.

In a case that was of about five weeks duration and included different theories of liability and damages, together with sharply disputed issues of fact, it was error for the judge to fail to marshall the evidence despite the request to do so, by stating "I am sure both counsel will refer to those portions of the evidence that they feel best suits them." *Quigley v County of Suffolk* (1980, 2d Dept) 75 AD2d 888, 428 NYS2d 46.

Considering the complexity of the medical evidence in a malpractice case, and the sharp dispute as to proper medical procedure, the court should have marshalled the medical testimony. *Troy v Long Island Jewish-Hillside Medical Center* (1982, 2d Dept) 86 AD2d 631, 446 NYS2d 347.

The instructions to the jury should avoid undue emphasis on one or more items of evidence to the exclusion of other evidence. *Bisogno v New York R. Co.* (1920) 194 AD 316, 185 NYS 411, app dismd 233 NY 629, 135 NE 947. Where there is an issue of fact and there is evidence both ways, an instruction to the effect that there is evidence that would justify the jury in finding in favor of one of the litigants is erroneous and should be condemned. *Niemann v Cordtmeyer* (1906) 111 AD 326, 97 NYS 670. Where there is no evidence establishing a particular fact, it is proper so to charge. *Booth v Boston & A. R. Co.* (1876) 67 NY 593. Likewise, where there is evidence that a fact exists and no contrary evidence, it is proper to charge that a fact exists. *Lake v Wendt*

(1897) 21 AD 276, 48 NYS 50. Where a judge charges a jury with respect to multiple theories of liability, on the basis of any of which it may bring back a verdict for the plaintiff, and one or more of the theories is incorrect or insufficiently proved, a general verdict for the plaintiff may not be sustained, because it is impossible to determine whether the jury based its verdict on a correct or sufficiently proved theory. *Davis v Caldwell* (1981) 54 NY2d 176, 445 NYS2d 63.

Because the purpose of a charge is the instant education of the jury rather than the subsequent edification of the Appellate Division, a trial judge may not add provisions to his charge long after the jury has rendered a verdict, specifically, when the matter added, six months after the trial's end, was refused at the trial. *Petru v Hertz Corp.* (1969, 1st Dept) 33 AD2d 755, 305 NYS2d 828, later app (1st Dept) 36 AD2d 704, 319 NYS2d 199. In a civil action, the parties are entitled to have the jury adequately instructed with respect to which party has the burden of proof on particular issues and to have the terms properly defined and explained so that the jurors understand them. *Goldsmith v Morgold Garage Corp.* (1949, App Tm) 88 NYS2d 741. Where the defendant in a negligence action requested a charge that was refused by the court, to the effect that defendant was not required to call witnesses to establish the defense of contributory negligence, this was held to be error. *Shea v Danna* (1946) 270 AD 698, 62 NYS2d 81. Where defendant has asserted a counterclaim, the court should charge the jury to the effect that the defendant has the burden of proof with respect to establishing the counterclaim. *Warren v Traub* (1952) 280 AD 962, 116 NYS2d 506. Similarly, where the pleadings set up an affirmative defense, the court should charge the jury that the defendant has the burden of proof with respect to such defense. *Farmers' Loan & Trust Co. v Siefke* (1895) 144 NY 354, 39 NE 358.

In a civil case, the jury should be adequately instructed on the meaning of the term "preponderance of evidence." *McKeon v Van Slyck* (1918) 223 NY 392, 119 NE 851. In a wrongful death case, the plaintiff is entitled to have the jury instructed that the degree of proof required of him is less than it would be in a case where the plaintiff himself is alive and sues for his own injury. *Noseworthy v New York* (1948) 298 NY 76.

Where a jury, after commencing its deliberations, inquired whether the plaintiff would have to pay taxes on an award, the court should have instructed the jury that it may not consider income taxes in determining the award to be given to the plaintiff. *Towli v Ford Motor Co.* (1968, 1st Dept) 30 AD2d 319, 292 NYS2d 8. When such additional instruction is given to the jury, it should be in open court and counsel for all the contending parties should be present. *Gundersen v All America Commerce Corp.* (1949) 275 AD 572, 90 NYS2d 3, reh den 275 AD 1035, 92 NYS2d 310. Where an additional charge was given in the absence of a party and his counsel, the verdict was held to be irregular. *Schattner v Heriman* (1936) 247 AD 730, 285 NYS 343.

Where a jury requests additional instruction, counsel should be afforded an opportunity to request additional charges on the subject with respect to which the jury has inquired. *Gundersen v All America Commerce Corp., supra.*

It was error for the trial court, contrary to CPLR 4110-b, to deny the request of defendant's attorney to make objections to the charge out of the presence of the jury. *Roman v Bronx-Lebanon Hospital Center* (1976, 1st Dept) 51 AD2d 529, 379 NYS2d 81.

In light of the inadmissibility of the hospital record, the trial court erred in failing to instruct the jurors to disregard questions put to the plaintiff by defense counsel in an effort to lay a foundation for the hospital record, because these questions were highly prejudicial and may well have given the jury the impression that the plaintiff had made inconsistent statements at the hospital. *Wirth v De Vito* (1980, 2d Dept) 74 AD2d 827, 425 NYS2d 179.

If a statute is applicable, it is not error for the court to charge the substance of the statute rather than the statute itself. *Jemison v Goodman* (1975, 4th Dept) 49 AD2d 1011, 373 NYS2d 926.

Where the alleged duty of defendant, if any, exists by virtue of contract, it is essential that the trial court include in its charge instructions to aid the jury in determining whether the requisite elements of a contract were established by what the parties said and did, and where the trial court neither gave such instructions to the jury, nor instructed the jury with respect to plaintiff's burden of proving the existence of a contract, and the negligent breach of the duty created therein, reversal and a new trial was required. *Franklin v Carpinello Oil Co.* (1981, 3d Dept) 84 AD2d 613, 444 NYS2d 248.

When a juror sent the court a note, before the court's instruction as to liability, inquiring whether a car stopped on the road is required to have its brake lights or parking lights on, the court in its charge should have answered the question, because the question bore directly on the issue of liability and the failure to respond was sufficiently prejudicial to warrant a new trial. *Galuska v Arbaiza* (1984, 2d Dept) 106 AD2d 543, 482 NYS2d 846.

A charge that confuses and creates doubts as to the principles of law to be applied requires a new trial; a charge must not contain contradictory and inadequate statements of law. *Cumbo v Valente* (1986, 2d Dept) 118 AD2d 679, 500 NYS2d 30.

A trial judge should not deliver his charge to the jury by means of a tape recording device, because one of the dangers inherent in such a procedure is that jurors may fail to accord the same level of attentiveness to a recording as to the judge speaking first-hand. *Fogel v Lenox Hill Hospital* (1987, 1st Dept) 127 AD2d 548, 512 NYS2d 109, app den 69 NY2d 612.

It was not an improvident exercise of discretion for the court to grant an application for a missing witness charge, because damaging hearsay testimony was only admitted upon the plaintiffs' false representation that a doctor would be called as a witness, and plaintiffs thereafter failed to demonstrate a legitimate basis for not calling the witness. *Kronenberg v Morris* (1991, 2d Dept) 174 AD2d 610, 571 NYS2d 316.

In marshaling the evidence, the trial court could properly address inconsistencies and weaknesses in the evidence presented by any party. *Republic of Croatia v Trustee of the Marquess of Northampton 1987 Settlement* (1994, 1st Dept) 203 AD2d 167, 610 NYS2d 263.

§ 31:9 CORRECTING ERRONEOUS INSTRUCTIONS — The court may recall the jury and further charge them, or correct any error either in the charge as made or in the refusal to charge. *Phillips v New York C. & H. R. R. Co.* (1891) 127 NY 657, 27 NE 978.

A trial court has broad discretion to recall a jury to give appropriate corrective or supplemental instructions applicable to the case. *Carlino v County of Albany* (1991, 3d Dept) 178 AD2d 772, 577 NYS2d 689.

Where the jurors entertain some doubt about the law involved, they may return to the courtroom and request clarification, and the denial of such a request is reversible error. *Sansivero v Garz* (1964, 2d Dept) 20 AD2d 723, 247 NYS2d 596.

Where the court learns that the jury is considering a matter not in issue, which has not been submitted to them and that may have a decisive effect on their verdict, the court should recall the jury and instruct them properly. *Stevenson v New York Contracting Co.* (1910) 137 AD 742, 122 NYS 726.

In a product liability case, where the court neglects to give a direct answer to a question posed by the jury relating to income tax on the award, the ensuing confusion engendered by the failure of the court to properly instruct the jury requires a new trial on the issue of damages only. *Towli v Ford Motor Co.* (1968) 30 AD2d 319, 292 NYS2d 8.

When the court has committed error in its charge, it should remedy this by using explicit and strong language to insure that the jury may not be influenced by the erroneous charge; it is not enough for the court to simply reconstruct the erroneous charge. *Robinson v New York* (1958) 5 AD2d 197, 170 NYS2d 734.

The jury should be instructed in reasonable detail as to the factual issues where these are decisive in determining negligence or contributory negligence, and the mere *pro forma* recitation of law by the court is not sufficient. *Greelish v New York C. R. Co.* (1968) 29 AD2d 159, 286 NYS2d 61, affd 23 NY2d 903, 298 NYS2d 308.

In a wrongful death case, the trial court's instructions to the jury that if it found that the decedent's negligence caused or contributed to his death in a material way, the survivors may not recover, regardless of whether that negligence was great or slight, was clearly erroneous; and although the trial court in its supplemental charge instructed the jury that negligence on the decedent's part would not prevent recovery by the survivors but would only reduce the amount of damages, this did not serve to obviate the erroneous instruction, because that instruction was not withdrawn and corrected in explicit terms that would have prevented an inference that the jury might have been influenced by it. *Safdie v New York* (1988, 2d Dept) 138 AD2d 361, 525 NYS2d 650.

RESEARCH REFERENCES

American Law Reports

21 ALR5th 82, Instructions on "unavoidable accident," "mere accident," or the like, in motor vehicle cases–modern cases

9 ALR4th 897, Propriety of jury instruction regarding credibility of witness who has been convicted of a crime

99 ALR3d 901, Medical malpractice: instruction as to exercise or use of injured member

91 ALR3d 336, Propriety and prejudicial effect of sending written instructions with retiring jury in civil case

34 ALR3d 775, Propriety and prejudicial effect of comment or instruction by court with respect to party's refusal to permit introduction of privileged testimony

20 ALR3d 1081, Propriety and effect, in eminent domain proceeding, of instruction to the jury as to landowner's unwillingness to sell property

ALR Quick Index: Instructions to Jury

American Jurisprudence 2d

75 Am Jur 2d, Trial §§ 573-930

American Jurisprudence Pleading and Practice

23 Am Jur Pl & Pr Forms (Rev) Trial Forms 101-269

American Jurisprudence Trials

52 Am Jur Trials 1, Commonsense Principles of Civil Litigation

51 Am Jur Trials 1, Managing Litigation

6 Am Jur Trials 923, Instructing the Jury-Pattern Instructions

Other Resources

8 Carmody-Wait 2d, Charge to Jury §§ 57:1 et seq.

Auto-Cite®: Any case citation herein can be checked for form, parallel references, later history and annotation references through the Auto-Cite computer research system.

CHAPTER 32

CONDUCT OF THE JURY

§ 32:1 THE GENERAL CONDUCT OF THE JURY AND THOSE DEALING WITH IT — The jury is an inseparable part of our judicial system. Its conduct is governed by a highly complicated set of rules. These rules operate from the time the jurors are selected until the time they are discharged.

The verdict of the jury should be the product of proper consideration of the proceedings and careful deliberation. *Corey v Smith & Pollock, Inc.* (1943) 181 Misc 331, 43 NYS2d 250, affd 267 AD 911, 47 NYS2d 601. Thus, where the attention of the jury was distracted by the heat and humidity present during a five-day trial, and the jury did not follow the instructions of the court to give substantial damages or no damages, the verdict was set aside. *Corey v Smith & Pollock, Inc., supra.*

The only impressions the jury should receive are those in open court in the course of the trial in the presence both of the parties and their counsel, and the policy of the law is to guard the jury from any extraneous influences. *Mitchell v Carter* (1878, NY) 14 Hun 448. In this decision, the court found that the jury's verdict was improper, because the jurors had remained in the courtroom for a time after being charged, then obtained the trial judge's minutes and read a portion of them. However, a juror is not required to ignore a fact that is universally known or clearly a matter of common knowledge, *Oliver v Bereano* (1944) 267 AD 747, 48 NYS2d 142, affd 293 NY 931.

Once selected, the jurors must hear the facts involved in the case and determine the issues, and in arriving at a determination they must be indifferent and impartial, so that the verdict the reach may be a just one. *N. Wagman & Co. v Schafer Motor Freight Service, Inc.* (1938) 167 Misc 681, 4 NYS2d 526.

Because public policy requires that jurors be given the utmost freedom of debate, no juror may be punished for contempt for his part in any proceedings connected with the rendering of a verdict because of discussions had, arguments used, statements made, or the reasons given by him for his vote, or the vote itself. *Re Cochran* (1924) 237 NY 336, 143 NE 212, 32 ALR 433.

§ 32:2　CONDUCT OF JURORS DURING THE TRIAL — Because a jury must be impartial, the conduct of a juror, who accompanied the plaintiff to her home and sought to console her when she expressed fear, was a violation of his oath as a juror. *Campbell v Towber* (1965) 46 Misc 2d 891, 261 NYS2d 458.

A trial jury must evaluate the evidence presented during a trial in a completely unbiased manner. *Sheehan v Doyle* (1956, Sup) 152 NYS2d 931.

Manifested hostility of a juror toward trial counsel required reversal and a new trial. *Mark v Colgate University* (1976, 2d Dept) 53 AD2d 884, 385 NYS2d 621.

In a medical malpractice action, based on a claim of alleged failure to diagnose a condition of bacterial meningitis, the fact that a juror copied a definition of meningitis from a medical dictionary was not sufficient to warrant setting aside a verdict in favor of the defendant. The definition of meningitis was not a material issue in the action, the juror did not really read the definition through or use it as the basis for her deliberations, and testimony adduced at the hearing indicated that copies of the material were not disseminated to the other jurors. *Desmond v Nassau Hosp.* (1990, 2d Dept) 157 AD2d 828, 550 NYS2d 730, app den 75 NY2d 711, 557 NYS2d 309.

A verdict on liability was not subject to attack by defendants because two of the jurors, during deliberations, took a 10-minute smoke break. Absent any indication that an impropriety occurred, their short absences from deliberations created no defect. *Carr v U.S. Mattress Corp.* (1990, 1st Dept) 166 AD2d 172, 564 NYS2d 67.

A mistrial was not necessary as a result of a disturbance in the jury room. Although the sound of breaking glass and objects being thrown could be heard from the jury room, the jurors deliberated for approximately two hours after the incident before reaching a partial verdict, and therefore had several opportunities to communicate directly with the court if any of them felt unfairly coerced, harassed, intimidated or in physical danger. *People v Lizardi* (1990, 2d Dept) 166 AD2d 672, 561 NYS2d 261.

A juror who has not heard all the evidence in the case or the court's instructions on the applicable principles of law is grossly unqualified to render a verdict. *People v South* (1991, 2d Dept) 177 AD2d 607, 576 NYS2d 314. Where defense counsel reported to the court that a juror had been sleeping during cross-examination of a witness and again during the court's charge, the court should have conducted a probing and tactful inquiry to determine whether the particular juror was unqualified to render a verdict, based upon her apparent sleeping episodes. *People v South, supra.*

In an action brought to recover damages for injuries sustained in a construction accident, the verdict was tainted by improper outside influence when one juror spoke with the others about the benefits plaintiff would receive from Worker's Compensation. In telling the other jurors about the Worker's Compensation system and her experience with it, the juror injected significant extra-record facts into the deliberation process and thereby became an unsworn witness to non-record evidence. *Fitzgibbons v New York*

State University Constr. Fund (1991, 4th Dept) 177 AD2d 1033, 578 NYS2d 317.

Where the source of plaintiff's contention that a juror telephoned someone while deliberations were ongoing was pure hearsay, and where his attorney failed to submit any affidavits from a juror or anyone else who might have had actual knowledge of the facts, the trial court properly denied plaintiff's post-trial motion to set aside the verdict on the ground of juror misconduct. *Putchlawski v Diaz* (1993, 1st Dept) 192 AD2d 444, 597 NYS2d 10, app den 82 NY2d 654, 602 NYS2d 803.

§ 32:3 COMMUNICATIONS WITH JURORS BEFORE AND DURING TRIAL — No person should have access to the jury for any purpose, except to the extent ordered by the court. *Kaus v Barthold* (1939) 256 AD 1033, 10 NYS2d 734. There should be no contact between court officers and jurors, except to the extent authorized by the court under appropriate circumstances, because there must be no justification for arousing even suspicions as to the sanctity of jury verdicts. *Holliday v Rockwell* (1953) 282 AD 983, 125 NYS2d 629, reh den 283 AD 677, 127 NYS2d 808.

Where a colloquy took place between the court clerk and the jury in the course of deliberations without the knowledge or consent of the court or of counsel, a judgment for the plaintiff in a civil action for assault and rape was reversed in the discretion of the court, despite the fact that the clerk and the jury did not intend any wrong and the information furnished to the jury by the clerk may have been substantially correct. *Kaus v Barthold, supra.*

However, a defendant was not entitled to a mistrial where two jurors spoke with a witness for plaintiff in the courthouse elevator during a luncheon recess, because the conversation did not relate to any matter in issue before the court and the jury. *Weissman v M. & M. Transp. Co.* (1948) 191 Misc 968, 79 NYS2d 335. It was not an abuse of discretion on the part of the trial court to deny the defendant's motion for a mistrial after conversations took place in the courthouse between the plaintiff's attorney and two jurors, because the conversations were brief and casual, and followed chance encounters, and the plaintiff's attorney did not recognize the juror at the commencement of the conversation. *Sincock v Boehme* (1959, 3d Dept) 9 AD2d 579, 189 NYS2d 571.

In an action for wrongful death, the verdict was set aside on grounds that a juror had received information during the trial from one of the witnesses to the effect that, in two previous trials of the same matter, one trial resulted in a large verdict for the plaintiff and the other in a disagreement of the jury. *Johnson v Riter-Conley Mfg. Co.* (1912) 149 AD 543, 133 NYS 1004.

No communication of any kind should take place between the judge and the jury once the case has been submitted, except in open court and, wherever possible, in the presence of counsel. *Kehrley v Shafer* (1895) 92 Hun 196, 36 NYS 510. Where jurors returned to the courtroom for further instructions, and the trial court, in the absence of plaintiffs and their counsel, instructed them erroneously on a material point that was adverse to the plaintiffs, the plaintiffs could appeal the error without an exception having been taken. *Wheeler v Sweet* (1893) 137 NY 435, 33 NE 483.

Where a court stenographer, at the direction of the court but without the knowledge or consent of counsel, entered a jury room during deliberations and read a portion of the charge, this was reversible error. *Jones v S. T. Palay Textile Corp.* (1952) 279 AD 337, 110 NYS2d 170.

Although it is improper for a trial judge to enter the jury room and converse with jurors in the absence of the parties' counsel, a new trial is not warranted unless prejudice to either party's case results therefrom. *Silverman v New Rochelle Hospital* (1983, 2d Dept) 98 AD2d 774, 469 NYS2d 488.

Although an oral communication from the juror to the trial judge, and between the juror and the clerk, regarding the fact that the juror's wife wanted him to call her, should have been conveyed to counsel, in light of the undisputed nature of these communications, no prejudice resulted. *Snediker v County of Orange* (1982) 58 NY2d 647, 458 NYS2d 517.

§ 32:4   SEPARATION OF JURY DURING THE TRIAL — At early common law, jurors were kept together in a body as prisoners of the court until they reached a verdict. *Wilkins v Abbey* (1938) 168 Misc 416, 5 NYS2d 826.

It is no longer required that a jury be kept together in a body until a verdict is reached. *Hand v Hill* (1938) 255 AD 1016, 8

NYS2d 564. Where jurors were ordered to bring in a sealed verdict but failed to agree and, because it was late at night, they were permitted to return to court the next morning to continue their deliberations, their separation before reaching a verdict was not irregular and did not result in their discharge as a jury. *Hand v Hill, supra.*

Where a jury separated after formulating and sealing the verdict, and the foreman informed the court that there was unanimous agreement for the plaintiff but disagreement as to the amount, the resubmission of the case to the jury for assessment of damages was held to be proper, because the jury was still charged with the duty of completing the verdict. *Porret v New York* (1929) 252 NY 208, 169 NE 280. However, a verdict was held to be irregular and required reversal where, after a sealed verdict had been ordered and the jurors were permitted to separate for the night after they had disagreed, the court further charged the jury the next morning in the absence of defendant and his counsel. *Schattner v Heriman* (1936) 247 AD 730, 285 NYS 343.

§ 32:5   ITEMS TAKEN BY JURY TO JURY ROOM — The jurors may not take with them to the jury room books, writings and papers that have not been received in evidence. *Long v Payne* (1921) 198 AD 667, 190 NYS 803. It is an irregularity for the jurors to examine books or records that are not in evidence. When such conduct is deemed harmful, it may be sufficient ground for setting aside a verdict. *Howland v Willetts* (1853) 9 NY 170.

However, the mere fact that books or documents not in evidence are physically present in the jury room does not taint the verdict If the jurors have not read them. *Altshuler v Exeller Chemical Co.* (1943, Mun Ct) 46 NYS2d 28.

The determination whether exhibits consisting of documents or papers that are in evidence may be taken to the jury room or sent to the jury room for use during the jury's deliberations, is for the court in the exercise of its discretion. *Howland v Willetts, supra.* Where the jurors, on retiring, were told by the court that they could have whatever exhibits they wished, and the plaintiff's attorney handed a juror who had requested them two of defendant's exhibits, without the consent of defendant's attorney, there were no grounds for a new trial. *Levy v Corn* (1920) 191 AD 56,

180 NYS 794. The jurors' right to take any paper introduced in evidence into the jury room for examination and consideration while arriving at a verdict extends to a deposition that was read in evidence. *Howland v Willetts, supra.*

Where a jury has obtained documents not in evidence, even if by mistake, there may be grounds for setting aside the verdict. *Elliott v Luengene* (1896) 17 Misc 78, 39 NYS 850.

Although pleadings may be taken to the jury room with the permission of the court, where they have been admitted into evidence and marked as exhibits, *Raynolds v Vinier* (1908) 125 AD 18, 109 NYS 293, they should not be taken to the jury room over the objection of counsel where they have no evidentiary value. *Dzulvelis v Mays Fur & Ready to Wear, Inc.* (1939, App Tm) 18 NYS2d 106.

In an action involving wrongful death, personal injury and property damage, the submission to the jury of a police report that had been properly rejected when offered in evidence was prejudicial error requiring a new trial. The report, prepared by a policeman who was not a witness to the accident, contained a diagram of two vehicles colliding without anything to authenticate the diagram. *Carrier v Fruehauf Trailer Co.* (1954) 284 AD 821, 132 NYS2d 406, reh and app den 284 AD 856, 134 NYS2d 175, app dismd 307 NY 907; *see also, Stanton v New York* (1980, 2d Dept) 74 AD2d 623, 425 NYS2d 32.

In a malpractice action, where a juror who had copied the definitions of "malpractice" from several medical dictionaries read them to the other jurors and they considered these definitions rather than the court's instructions on negligence, the trial court did not err in setting aside the verdict and granting a new trial. *Maslinski v Brunswick Hospital Center, Inc.,* (1986, 2d Dept) 118 AD2d 834, 500 NYS2d 318.

The trial court did not err in granting the jury's request, during deliberations, for a magnifying glass, because the use of the magnifying glass was for the purpose of enhancing the clarity of photographs, a permissible purpose. *People v Moody* (1993, 4th Dept) 195 AD2d 1016, 600 NYS2d 581.

§ 32:6 THE RIGHT TO HAVE TESTIMONY READ BACK —

In view of uncertainty in the minds of the jurors, it was prejudicial error for the trial court to deny the jury's request to re-hear the testimony of three witnesses. *Bloch v New York* (1979, 2d Dept) 68 AD2d 932, 414 NYS2d 592.

It was prejudicial error, requiring a new trial, for the trial court to deny the jury's request for re-reading of a portion of the testimony. *Zobre v Schuttig* (1973, 3d Dept) 41 AD2d 573, 339 NYS2d 648. It was not error for the trial court to decline to have further testimony read to the jury, even though defense counsel stated that additional testimony specifically dealt with matters mentioned in a jury request, in view of the jury foreman's expressed satisfaction with the testimony that had been read, and the ambiguous nature of the testimony requested. *Marchione v McKenna* (1977, 4th Dept) 57 AD2d 729, 395 NYS2d 562.

Where the judge was not present in the courtroom when the jury requested that testimony be read, some 50 minutes elapsed before he returned to the courtroom, and during this time the jury canceled its request and reported it had reached a verdict, the delay did not result in the denial of a fair trial to defendant. The jury was polled to ensure that the delay did not taint its verdict, and there was nothing to indicate that the verdict was so tainted. *People v Chandler* (1985, 3d Dept) 110 AD2d 970, 487 NYS2d 887.

It was not an abuse of discretion for the trial court to refuse to read back opening and closing statements on the basis that they were not evidence. *People v Velasco* (1990, 1st Dept) 160 AD2d 170, 553 NYS2d 331, app gr 76 NY2d 797, 559 NYS2d 1003.

The trial court erred in permitting testimony that had been stricken to be read back to the jury. *Austin v Bascaran* (1992, 3d Dept) 185 AD2d 474, 585 NYS2d 859.

When a request is made for testimony to be read back, it is presumed to include cross-examination that impeaches that testimony. *People v Faulkner* (1993, 1st Dept) 195 AD2d 384, 600 NYS2d 231; *People v Berger* (1992, 4th Dept) 188 AD2d 1073, 592 NYS2d 173, app den 81 NY2d 881, 597 NYS2d 942.

§ 32:7 RULES GOVERNING ARRIVAL AT A VERDICT — A

trial juror is required to evaluate all the evidence produced at a trial in a completely unbiased manner. *Sheehan v Doyle* (1956, Sup) 152 NYS2d 931.

In arriving at its verdict, a jury may not consider papers or documents that are not in evidence and would tend to influence the jury verdict. *Public Operating Corp. v Weingart* (1939) 257 AD 379, 13 NYS2d 182.

The credibility of witnesses is a matter solely within the province of the jury, and it is error for the court to charge the jury in such a manner as to invade this province. *Navis v Rochester* (1951) 277 AD 667, 102 NYS2d 153, reh den 278 AD 743, 103 NYS2d 671.

The jury should not be influenced, in arriving at its verdict, by sympathy. New York Pattern Jury Instructions 1:27. In deciding whether a fact has been proved, the jury is not to equate the term "preponderance of the evidence" with the greater number of witnesses employed by one side or at the other. New York Pattern Jury Instructions 1:60.

In a civil action, the verdict need not be unanimous; the concurrence of only five out of six jurors is required. *Hazlitt v Bedient* (1958) 10 Misc 2d 283, 174 NYS2d 760. However, in the absence of a stipulation or consent on the record to receive the verdict of less than the constituted number, 12, a verdict of 11 reporting jurors was a nullity even though all 11 decided for the plaintiff and it was a case in which a verdict rendered by five out of six jurors could have been received. *Measeck v Noble* (1959) 9 AD2d 19, 189 NYS2d 748. Where the parties consented to trial of the case before 11 jurors, rather than 12, and one of the jurors who had taken part in the deliberations refused to vote, the verdict of the remaining 10 who agreed was a valid one. *Florzak v Hempstead Bus Corp.* (1941, Sup) 29 NYS2d 271. The parties in a civil case may, of course, by stipulation agree to accept a verdict of less than 5/6ths of the jury. *Neumann v Kurek* (1940) 175 Misc 238, 22 NYS2d 950, affd 264 AD 751, 35 NYS2d 264.

Although a verdict of five of six jurors is valid in a civil case, the parties are entitled to have all six jurors participate in the deliberations on all issues. Where it appeared that the dissenting juror had not actually participated in the deliberations on all issues, and the trial court failed to inquire as to that juror's participation, a new trial was required. *Sharrow v Dick Corp.* (1995) 86 NY2d 54, 629 NYS2d 980.

The verdict the jurors ultimately reached must be the result of a deliberate exercise of their best judgment. *Hamilton v Owego Waterworks* (1897) 22 AD 573, 48 NYS 106, affd 163 NY 562, 57 NE 1111. Any other method of arriving at a verdict, such as a chance verdict based upon the drawing of lots, is invalid and must be set aside. *Mitchell v Ehle* (1833) 10 Wend 595.

Where a verdict is the result of a compromise and is not based upon the evidence, it should not stand. *Ganz v Hi-Line Co.* (1951) 278 AD 761, 104 NYS2d 11. The amount, if any, for which a defendant may be liable should not be determined by a compromise involving a surrender by some jurors of their convictions. *Myers v Myers* (1903) 86 AD 73, 83 NYS 236.

Where by the nature of the case, the damages, if any, to be awarded are liquidated and certain in amount, a verdict for less than this amount is not based upon the evidence, and cannot be allowed to stand. *Friend v Morris D. Fishman, Inc.* (1951) 302 NY 389.

Retrial is mandated on all issues where there is a strong likelihood that the jury verdict resulted from a trade-off on a finding of liability in return for a compromise on damages. *Patrick v New York Bus Serv., Inc.* (1993, 1st Dept) 189 AD2d 611, 592 NYS2d 311; *see also, Sheffield v New York City Hous. Auth.* (1994, 1st Dept) 200 AD2d 369, 606 NYS2d 201.

Where the issue of liability was sharply and substantially contested and plaintiff's injuries were serious and the jury's award inexplicably low for such serious injuries, it was held that most likely the verdict was a compromise verdict. *Farmer v A & T Bus Co.* (1983, 1st Dept) 96 AD2d 783, 466 NYS2d 8. Where there is a substantial likelihood that the jury's verdict results from a trade-off on a finding of liability in return for a compromise on damages, the retrial should be on all issues, liability as well as damages. *Farmer v A & T Bus Co., supra.*

Where the award of $500 could not possibly compensate the infant plaintiff for the damages sustained, the amount awarded was the result of a compromise verdict, and there should be a new trial on the issue of liability as well as of damages. *Geisel v Flushing Hospital & Medical Center* (1979, 2d Dept) 70 AD2d 927, 417 NYS2d 760.

Where the plaintiff paid the sum of $71,000 to recover stolen art works and the jury awarded the sum of $45,000, the amount awarded was not a compromise verdict and was proper under the court's charge, to which no exception was taken. *Kraut v Morgan & Bro. Manhattan Storage Co.* (1974, 1st Dept) 46 AD2d 19, 360 NYS2d 889, affd 38 NY2d 445, 381 NYS2d 25, 80 ALR3d 249.

In an action for breach of contract to turn over box office receipts from a band concert, at which admissions were charged in the amount of $1.50, $3.00, $4.00 and $5.00, neither the fact that the verdict was for one-half of the amount requested in the complaint, nor the fact that it was in the amount of $2,189.25, rendered the verdict an impermissible compromise. *Tickner v Allen* (1979, 4th Dept) 71 AD2d 835, 419 NYS2d 368.

Where the action involves unliquidated damages, there may be differences of opinion between individual jurors that must be reconciled. Therefore, some element of compromise is required. *Hamilton v Owego Waterworks* (1897) 22 AD 573, 48 NYS 106, affd 163 NY 562, 57 NE 1111. Consequently, where an issue involving unliquidated damages has resulted in a compromise, the verdict should not be set aside on this ground. *Hamilton v Owego Waterworks, supra.* However, if the verdict represents a compromise on liability and not simply as to the amount, it will be set aside. *Sampson v Graves* (1922) 199 AD 762, 192 NYS 114.

A "quotient verdict" results where the jurors agree to write down the amount of damages that each of them thinks the party is entitled to and the total of the amount is then divided by the number of jurors, provided that the jurors agree to be bound by the quotient. *Honigsberg v New York City Transit Authority* (1964) 43 Misc 2d 1, 249 NYS2d 296. Where the jurors agree in advance to be bound by the average, the verdict is rendered illegal. *Honigsberg v New York City Transit Authority, supra.* A "quotient verdict" is not illegal where it does not affirmatively appear that there was an agreement beforehand to abide by the average of the amount. *Honigsberg v New York City Transit Authority, supra.*

The legal presumption is that there was no agreement beforehand to abide by the average judgment of all jurors, and in the absence of evidence showing or tending to show the jurors' agreement to abide by the results of any calculations concerning the total vote of individual jurors, a new trial on the theory that a quotient verdict had been rendered was precluded. *Honigsberg v New York City Transit Authority, supra.*

The jury foreman's statement that the damage figures determined by each juror were added and then divided by six to decide on the size of the awards did not require reversal. *Peters v Newman* (1985, 3d Dept) 115 AD2d 816, 495 NYS2d 774. The record in this case revealed that they collectively discussed the resultant figures after their computations, recomputing the awards if they did not agree on the sums arrived at; thus they did not render an improper quotient verdict. *Peters v Newman, supra.*

The special verdict that the testator was not competent to dispose of his property at the time of his execution of a purported will was held to be against the weight of evidence and the result of an improper compromise. *Re Estate of Donovan* (1975, 2d Dept) 47 AD2d 923, 367 NYS2d 56.

Where a verdict of $75,000 is excessive if the fracture of the hip and its associated injuries are excluded from those injuries sustained by the plaintiff for which he may recover, but inadequate if plaintiff may recover for those injuries, the award apparently was the result of an improper compromise, and therefore must be set aside in the interests of justice. *Frozzitta v Freeport* (1977, 2d Dept) 57 AD2d 827, 394 NYS2d 64.

The record did not demonstrate any indication of an impermissible compromise verdict other than the mention of the word "compromise" by a juror in describing the course the jury followed during its deliberations. In the context stated, the word "compromise" was not used as a term of art with its specific legal meaning. *Manchester v Bankhead Corp., Div. of Bankhead Enterprises, Inc.* (1986, 3d Dept) 125 AD2d 740, 509 NYS2d 434.

In a civil case, in the absence of consent by all parties, a jury made up of fewer than six persons cannot render a valid verdict. *Waldman v Cohen* (1987, 2d Dept) 125 AD2d 116, 512 NYS2d 205. In the absence of a concomitant waiver by the defendants, a plaintiff who "waived" her right to a six-person jury, did not relinquish her right to move to set aside the resultant verdict. *Waldman v Cohen, supra.*

When a jury's responses to interrogatories are inconsistent with one another and one or more conflicts with the general verdict, the trial court's only options are to either order reconsideration by the jury or a new trial. *Mars Associates, Inc. v New York City Educational Constr. Fund* (1987, 1st Dept) 126 AD2d 178, 513 NYS2d 125.

Reversal and a new trial on the sole issue of damages was required because the jury did not follow the court's instructions in reporting a special verdict with respect to the full dollar amount of damages sustained by plaintiff. *Emerson v Davis* (1989, 4th Dept) 155 AD2d 876, 548 NYS2d 955.

Where a jury issues a special finding after it has been charged by the court to deliver only a general verdict, this is regarded as surplusage and has no legal effect. *Leal v Simon* (1989, 2d Dept) 147 AD2d 198, 542 NYS2d 328.

§ 32:8 COMMUNICATIONS WITH JURORS DURING DELIBERATIONS — Public policy fosters a principle of secrecy of the jury room, to further the assurance of free, fearless and untrammeled deliberation of the evidence. For that reason, the proceedings of the jurors that precede the verdict – their talk, their discussions, their informal votes and other matters – are inviolable at all times. *Re Nunns* (1919) 188 AD 424, 176 NYS 858.

Where a reporter concealed himself in the jury room and took shorthand notes of the jury's deliberation, he violated the law and was guilty of criminal contempt. *People ex rel. Choate v Barrett* (1890) 56 Hun 351, 9 NYS 321, affd 121 NY 678, 24 NE 1095.

It was improper for the trial justice to enter the jury room, with the court reporter but in the absence of the parties or their counsel and without affording them an opportunity to be present or to consent to such procedure. Although this did not necessarily require reversal, when the trial court's answer to the jury's question with respect to one of the major issues at the trial was sparse and did not adequately answer the question posed by the jury, a new trial was required. *Blaha v Lettmoden* (1981, 2d Dept) 83 AD2d 619, 441 NYS2d 526.

Although a judge should urge the jurors to endeavor to secure a verdict, and may properly urge them to deliberate in a spirit of concession, where the jury disagrees and is not honestly of one mind, the court should not coerce a verdict, and any verdict arrived at in this manner must be set aside. *Levinson v Zipkin* (1909) 65 Misc 203, 119 NYS 680. A judge may not threaten or intimidate a jury for the purpose of affecting their deliberation. *Green v Telfair* (1853) 11 How Pr 260. Where a jury reported disagreement, and the judge instructed those in the minority to ask themselves whether they might not reasonably doubt the correctness of their stand that was not concurred in by a great majority, the instruction was held to be improperly given. *Acunto v Equitable Life Assurance Soc.* (1946) 270 AD 386, 60 NYS2d 101.

It was reversible error for a trial judge to tell jurors, who had already deliberated for 24 hours, that juries were selected not for the purpose of disagreeing but to agree, and that all the time involved had been wasted unless they came to an agreement. The judge had also said it was not likely that another jury as competent and as impartial as the one hearing the case could be assembled. These comments had the effect of improperly coercing the jurors, resulting in their agreement on a verdict in 10 minutes. *McCarthy v Odell* (1922) 202 AD 784, 195 NYS 80. Where the trial judge repeatedly advised a jury in the course of its deliberations that the minority should listen to the majority, there was reversible error. *Field v Field* (1954) 283 AD 372, 128 NYS2d 217.

A judge may, of course, urge jurors to make an honest attempt to reach a verdict. *Caldwell v New Jersey S.B. Co.* (1872) 47 NY 282. When jurors have engaged in long deliberation, it is not coercion for the judge to advise them that if they cannot agree on their verdict in a given amount of time, they may return and they will be discharged by the court. *Hill v Edinger* (1953) 281 AD 1052, 121 NYS2d 125.

A judge who receives a note from the jury indicating its inability to agree, and instructs the jury to continue its deliberations has been held not to be acting improperly. *Carolan v Altruda* (1962, 1st Dept) 17 AD2d 211, 233 NYS2d 539, app dismd 15 NY2d 621, 255 NYS2d 664 and affd 15 NY2d 1010, 260 NYS2d 21.

If an officer of the court other than the judge attempts to coerce the jury, it is equally fatal to the verdict. *Wilkins v Abbey* (1938) 168 Misc 416, 5 NYS2d 826. Thus, where a deputy sheriff in charge of the jury informed them that they had only five minutes to arrive at a verdict, the verdict could not stand. *Wilkins v Abbey, supra*.

While deliberating, a jury sent a note to the court asking for the floor plan. The court, which was presiding over another matter, did not summon the attorneys and the court stenographer so that any action taken could be a matter of record, but merely orally replied to the jury that there was no floor plan among the exhibits. Although this was improper practice, the jury's verdict was not disturbed where the record showed that the plaintiff was entitled to recover, and there was no prejudice to the defendant by the court's action. *Sands v Statler Hilton Hotel* (1972, 4th Dept) 40 AD2d 620, 336 NYS2d 529.

The trial court's *in camera* discussion with the forewoman of a jury without the presence or knowledge of counsel was improper. All instructions to the jury should be given in open court, where each party knows exactly what is being communicated to the jury and has an opportunity to note any objections, exceptions or further requests, unless consent is given. *Brown v Moodie* (1986, 4th Dept) 116 AD2d 980, 498 NYS2d 603. Although the court did not intend to influence the verdict, it may have inadvertently placed its *imprimatur* on certain possible factual determinations by inquiring into the jury's inclinations, helping the forewoman to answer the questions on the verdict sheet and actually doing the arithmetic before the jurors had reached a consensus. *Brown v Moodie, supra*.

§ 32:9　IMPROPER CONDUCT OF JURORS — Bribing a juror is a Class D felony, Penal Law § 215.19, as is the receiving of a bribe by a juror, Penal Law § 215.20.

When a person, with intent to influence the outcome of an action or proceeding, communicates with a juror in that action or proceeding, except as authorized by law, that person is guilty of tampering with a juror, a Class A misdemeanor. Penal Law § 215.25.

Misconduct by a juror, a Class A misdemeanor, occurs, when in relation to an action or proceeding pending or about to be brought before him or her, he or she agrees to give a vote, opinion, judgment, decision or report for or against any party to such action or proceeding. Penal Law § 215.30.

Misconduct by a juror may require that a verdict be set aside, but only if the misconduct is serious enough to justify the belief that it affected the decision of the jury. The fact that two jurors conversed with a witness for the plaintiff in a personal injury action in a courthouse elevator during the luncheon recess did not entitle defendants to a mistrial, where the conversation did not relate to any issue before the court and jury. *Weissman v M. & M. Transp. Co.* (1948) 191 Misc 968, 79 NYS2d 335.

However, a judgment for the plaintiff in a civil action for assault and rape was reversed where a colloquy took place between the court clerk and the jurors while they were deliberating, without the knowledge or consent of the court or of counsel. The trial court acted as a matter of discretion, despite the fact that the clerk and jury probably intended no wrong, and that the information furnished by the clerk to the jury may have been substantially correct. *Kaus v Barthold* (1939) 256 AD 1033, 10 NYS2d 734.

§ 32:10   IMPEACHMENT OF JURY VERDICTS — In most circumstances, a juror's affidavit may not be used to attack a jury verdict.

If verdicts solemnly made and publicly returned in court can be attacked and set aside on the testimony of those who took part in their publication, all verdicts could be, and many would be, followed by an inquiry in the hope of discovering something that might invalidate the finding. It is therefore well-established that, absent exceptional circumstances, juror affidavits may not be used to attack a jury verdict. *Grant v Endy* (1990, 3d Dept) 167 AD2d 807, 563 NYS2d 368. *People v Santana* (1990, 2d Dept) 163 AD2d 495, 558 NYS2d 172, affd 78 NY2d 1027, 576 NYS2d 208.

Generally, exceptional circumstances sufficient to justify departure from the rule against impeachment of a verdict involve outside influences, rather than the conduct of the jurors themselves. *See generally, People v De Lucia* (1967) 20 NY2d 275, 282 NYS2d 526.

A juror is not competent to impeach his verdict that has been made and returned into the court. *Copeland v Amboy* (1989, 4th Dept) 152 AD2d 911, 543 NYS2d 816. The jury's alleged misapprehension of a concept that was correctly charged by the court does not require reversal; setting aside the jury verdict in such circumstances would violate the rule against permitting a juror to impeach his own verdict. *Ryion v Len-Co Lumber Corp.* (1989, 4th Dept) 152 AD2d 978, 543 NYS2d 595, app den 74 NY2d 616, 549 NYS2d 961.

A juror's post-verdict allegation in a civil case that another juror had visited the accident scene could not be relied on to attack the verdict. *Careccia v Enstrom* (1995, 2d Dept) 212 AD2d 658, 622 NYS2d 770.

The court would not consider affidavits by jurors indicating that they were confused about the amount of damages to be awarded, particularly because the error alleged was not a ministerial one in reporting the verdict. *Labov v New York* (1989, 2d Dept) 154 AD2d 348, 545 NYS2d 826.

RESEARCH REFERENCES

American Law Reports

39 ALR4th 800, Impeachment of verdict by juror's evidence that he was coerced or intimidated by fellow juror

38 ALR4th 1170, Deafness of juror as ground for impeaching verdict, or securing new trial or reversal on appeal

31 ALR4th 623, Prejudicial effect of jury's procurement or use of book during deliberations in civil cases

31 ALR4th 566, Propriety of juror's tests or experiments in jury room

19 ALR4th 1209, Propriety of attorney's communication with jurors after trial

32 ALR3d 1356, Admissibility, in civil case, of juror's affidavit or testimony relating to juror's misconduct outside jury room

31 ALR3d 872, Propriety of jurors asking questions in open court during course of trial

6 ALR3d 934, Use of intoxicating liquor by jurors: civil case

ALR Quick Index: Jury and Jury Trial; Jury Room

American Jurisprudence 2d

75, 76 Am Jur 2d, Trials §§ 931-1071

American Jurisprudence Pleading and Practice

23 Am Jur Pl & Pr Forms (Rev), Trial, Form 285

American Jurisprudence Proof of Facts

24 Am Jur Proof of Facts 2d 633, Jury Misconduct Warranting New Trial

American Jurisprudence Trials

5 Am Jur Trials 123, Jury or Nonjury Trial-A Defense Viewpoint

Other Resources

Auto-Cite®: Any case citation herein can be checked for form, parallel references, later history and annotation references through the Auto-Cite computer research system.

CHAPTER 33

THE VERDICT

§ 33:1 GENERAL PROVISIONS RELATING TO VERDICTS

— A court may direct a jury to find either a general verdict or a special verdict. CPLR 4111(a). A general verdict is one in which the jury finds in favor of one or more parties. CPLR 4111(a). A special verdict is one in which the jury finds the facts only, leaving the court to determine which party is entitled to judgment thereon. CPLR 4111(a). The court has discretion to determine whether it will direct the jury to render a special or general verdict, but this discretion should not be abused by refusing to direct a special verdict where this will help the jury to determine the case intelligently. *Dore v Long I. R. R. Co.* (1965, 2d Dept) 23 AD2d 502, 256 NYS2d 425.

When a jury renders a general verdict, it means that it has resolved all disputed issues of fact in favor of the successful party and against the losing party. *Smith v Weston* (1899) 159 NY 194, 54 NE 38. When the court requires the jury to return a special verdict, it must submit to the jury written questions that are capable of brief answer, or written forms of the several findings that might properly be made, or it must use any other appropriate method of submitting the issues and requiring written findings thereon. The court must give sufficient instructions to make its findings on each issue. CPLR 4111(b).

A trial is not concluded until the jury brings in a verdict and the judge's presence is necessary when the verdict is returned. *Covaleski v Thomas* (1930) 229 AD 413, 242 NYS 174. Where the jury returned to the jury box and the foreman reported that they had not agreed, there was no verdict. *Appelt v Timpone* (1949) 195 Misc 68, 88 NYS2d 43, revd on other grounds 275 AD 1046, 91 NYS2d 869.

When a verdict is rendered, counsel for the defeated party has a right to ask for the polling of the jury in order to ascertain if the verdict announced by the foreman is the verdict of the jury. *Reed v Cook* (1951, Sup) 103 NYS2d 539. The right to poll the jury may be waived either expressly or by acts, or by failure to act. *Reed v Cook, supra*.

Until a sealed verdict is actually recorded, and the jurors have been discharged, any juror may withdraw his consent to the verdict. *Spielter v North German Lloyd S. S. Co.* (1931) 232 AD 104, 249 NYS 358.

A verdict must be responsive to the issues in the case. *Rabinowitz v 2171 Food Corp.* (1961, 1st Dept) 12 AD2d 321, 211 NYS2d 319. A verdict that is inconsistent with the allegations and with the proof may not stand. *Rabinowitz v 2171 Food Corp., supra*.

The test of rationality to support a jury verdict is not satisfied by evidence that at best would establish a fact by mere conjecture, surmise, speculation, bare possibility or a mere scintilla. *Diemer v Goad* (1980, 3d Dept) 78 AD2d 752, 432 NYS2d 740.

When multiple theories of liability have been submitted to the jury, which is instructed to return a general verdict only, a judgment entered on such a verdict in favor of plaintiff must be reversed when the proof is insufficient for submission on one or more of those theories. *Davis v Caldwell* (1981) 54 NY2d 176, 445 NYS2d 63. In such a case, a general verdict in favor of plaintiff can stand only if all theories of liability submitted to the jury are sustained by the evidence. *Caputo v Frankel* (1982, 2d Dept) 89 AD2d 595, 452 NYS2d 649. Where a case is submitted to a jury on two theories, only one of which is based upon sufficient evidence adduced at trial to support a verdict against defendant, and it is impossible to determine under which theory the jury held the defendant liable, a new trial is required. *Ryan v New York* (1981, 2d Dept) 83 AD2d 574, 441 NYS2d 136.

Where there is more than one cause of action, the court should direct the jury to return a separate verdict on each cause of action, instead of allowing a single verdict on all causes of action. *Brown v Great Atlantic & Pacific Tea Co.* (1949) 275 AD 304, 89 NYS2d 247. Where a plaintiff has established a case against two defendants, the fact that the jury fails to render a verdict on one defendant's cross-claim against his codefendant does not impair a verdict for the plaintiff. *West v New York* (1935) 155 Misc 688, 280 NYS 229.

Where the jury rendered a special verdict, finding that a red blotch on plaintiff's forehead was not sustained because hair spray sprayed onto her forehead was defective and not reasonably fit for the purpose intended, and also finding that the beauty salon's negligence in permitting hair spray to come into contact with plaintiff's forehead was a causal basis of injury, the verdict was an inconsistent one requiring reversal. *Toner v Constable* (1968) 61 Misc 2d 586, 306 NYS2d 323, mod on other grounds 61 Misc 2d 591, 307 NYS2d 231.

Where a jury fails to mention one of several defendants in its verdict, there is a verdict in favor of that particular defendant as a matter of law. *Saulsbury v Braun* (1928) 223 AD 555, 229 NYS 70, affd 249 NY 618, 164 NE 606. Where the relationship of two joint defendants is such that the liability of one is dependent upon responsibility for the acts of the second, a verdict against one defendant cannot stand where the jury fails to mention the defendant as a result of whose conduct the liability of the former arises.

Thibodeau v Gerosa Haulage & Warehouse Corp. (1937) 252 AD 615, 300 NYS 686, affd 278 NY 551. Where an employer and his employee were sued for the alleged tort committed by the employee, and the jury returned a verdict against the employer but did not mention the employee, judgment was dismissed as to each defendant. *Thibodeau v Gerosa Haulage & Warehouse Corp., supra.* Where an infant was injured in a two-car collision while a passenger in his father's automobile, a jury verdict against both drivers and owners of the respective automobiles is not inconsistent with a verdict in favor of the infant because the negligence of his parent cannot be imputed to him. *Klein v Eichen* (1970) 63 Misc 2d 590, 310 NYS2d 611.

The verdict of a jury that found an employer liable for the negligence of its employee but exonerated the employee co-tortfeasor was inconsistent, requiring reversal. *Lippes v Atlantic Bank of New York* (1979, 1st Dept) 69 AD2d 127, 419 NYS2d 505.

Where plaintiff's injuries arose out of the consumption of beer containing a partially decomposed mouse, and the roles of the wholesaler and retailer were the same in the chain of events leading to plaintiff's consumption of the beer, the jury's verdict holding the wholesaler liable and exonerating the retailer was inconsistent, requiring a new trial. *Dirsa v Martuscello* (1980, 3d Dept) 76 AD2d 1020, 429 NYS2d 483.

Judicial intervention is authorized where there are errors in reporting a verdict, or substantial confusion in reaching a verdict. *Wingate v Long Island Railroad* (1983, 1st Dept) 92 AD2d 797, 460 NYS2d 42. A verdict clothed in ambiguity and confusion should be set aside and a new trial ordered to prevent a miscarriage of justice. *Wingate v Long Island Railroad, supra.*

It is improper for a jury to apportion damages between several defendants, without an instruction to do so. *Kalmanson v Callahan* (1950) 276 AD 983, 95 NYS2d 289. However, under proper instructions, a jury has the right to apportion damages between codefendants based upon their degree of culpability, regardless of whether the alleged negligence was active-passive or primary-secondary. *Dole v Dow Chemical Co.* (1972) 30 NY2d 143, 331 NYS2d 382, 53 ALR3d 175. At the liability phase in a split trial, the only type of apportionment the jury can make is a percentage allocation. At the damage phase, the jury returns one monetary verdict and the court calculates the appropriate sums for apportionment. *Liebman v County of Westchester* (1972) 71 Misc 2d 997, 337 NYS2d 164, revd (2d Dept) 41 AD2d 756, 341 NYS2d 567.

In a civil case, a party may agree to accept a verdict from a jury that is composed of fewer members than the full number authorized, and may accept as valid a verdict that represents less than 5/6th of the jury. *Ashdown v Kluckhohn* (1977) 90 Misc 2d 618, 395 NYS2d 132, affd 62 AD2d 1137, 404 NYS2d 461.

In an action brought by plaintiff for false arrest and imprisonment and malicious prosecution, verdicts in favor of plaintiff on her cause of action for malicious prosecution and against her on her cause of action for false detention could not be reconciled and hence the cause of action for malicious prosecution was dismissed. *Feinberg v Saks & Co.* (1981, 2d Dept) 83 AD2d 952, 443 NYS2d 26, mod 56 NY2d 206, 451 NYS2d 677.

Although appellants contended that they were effectively deprived of their constitutional guarantee of a jury of six persons when after a poll a juror revealed that he neither deliberated nor voted on the issue of damages because he was the sole dissenter on the issue of liability, where they first raised this claim in connection with a post-trial motion to set aside the verdict, after the jury was discharged, they afforded the trial court no opportunity to correct the claimed error by returning the jury for additional deliberations on the issue of damages, and appellants therefore waived their objection to the juror's non-participation in deliberations or voting on the issue of damages. *Arizmendi v New York* (1982) 56 NY2d 753, 452 NYS2d 15.

In a products liability action, a defendant's failure to raise the issue of inherent inconsistencies in the jury's verdicts before the jury was discharged resulted in the issue being waived, *Halvorsen v Ford Motor Co.* (1987, 3d Dept) 132 AD2d 57, 522 NYS2d 272, app den 71 NY2d 805, 529 NYS2d 76.

§ 33:2 APPORTIONMENT OF VERDICTS — The right to apportionment of liability or to full indemnity among the parties involved in causing damage by negligence should rest on relative responsibility and be determined on the facts. *Dole v Dow Chem-*

ical Co. (1972) 30 NY2d 143, 331 NYS2d 382, 53 ALR3d 175. Apportionment of damages is permitted among joint or concurrent tortfeasors regardless of the degree or nature of the concurring fault. *Kelly v Long Island Lighting Co.* (1972) 31 NY2d 25, 334 NYS2d 851. The loss should be distributed in proportion to the allocable concurring fault. *Kelly v Long Island Lighting Co., supra.*

Contribution involves an apportionment of responsibility where wrongdoers are *in pari delicto. County of Westchester v Welton Becket Associates* (1984, 2d Dept) 102 AD2d 34, 478 NYS2d 305, app dismd 64 NY2d 734, 485 NYS2d 752. Each of the wrongdoers owes a duty to the injured party, and it is a question of fact for the jury what degree of responsibility each wrongdoer must bear for causing the injury. *County of Westchester v Welton Becket Associates, supra.* Where the jury's apportionment was found by the Appellate Division to be against the weight of the evidence, a new trial was ordered unless the parties stipulated to an apportionment in keeping with the percentage designated as proper by the Appellate Division. *Kelly v M. C. Electric Co.* (1979, 1st Dept) 68 AD2d 657, 418 NYS2d 28, app dismd 48 NY2d 634, 421 NYS2d 197.

Contribution lies not only as to joint tortfeasors, but also as to concurrent, successive, independent, alternative and even intentional tortfeasors, and applies regardless of the theory or consistency of theory upon which liability may be imposed either on the claims between them or the main claim. *Weinheimer v Hoffman* (1983, 3d Dept) 97 AD2d 314, 470 NYS2d 804.

Under principles of apportionment and comparative negligence, a tortfeasor may have a claim for proportionate liability against a third party in the absence of a duty by that third party to the injured person. *Grosshans v Rochester Gas & Electric Corp.* (1984, 4th Dept) 103 AD2d 1038, 478 NYS2d 402. If an independent obligation can be found on the part of a concurrent wrongdoer to prevent foreseeable harm, he should be held responsible for the portion of the damage attributable to his negligence, despite the fact that the duty violated was not one owing directly to the injured person. *Grosshans v Rochester Gas & Electric Corp., supra.*

When a plaintiff gives a release or covenant not to sue or to enforce a judgment to one of two or more tortfeasors, the claim of the releasing party against the remaining tortfeasors is reduced to the extent of any consideration paid for the release or covenant, or the amount of the released tortfeasor's equitable share of the damages, whichever is the greatest. General Obligations Law, § 15-108.

Where plaintiff had settled before the trial with one of two defendants, it was error for the trial court to refuse to charge the jury that it should allocate responsibility for the accident among plaintiff, the settling defendant and the remaining defendant by setting the percentage of fault, if any, attributable to each, and to instruct instead that the jury allocate responsibility between the plaintiff and the remaining defendant. *Cid v Bombardier Ltd.* (1983, 1st Dept) 91 AD2d 913, 457 NYS2d 538.

Although plaintiffs were entitled to judgment in the amount of $83,000, it was error not to afford defendant, against whom judgment had been rendered, a reduction of the verdict against him by the amount of the out-of-court settlements of his codefendants, that is, $22,500. *Chen Yan Kao v Wang* (1983, 2d Dept) 98 AD2d 709, 469 NYS2d 109.

In an action against two or more defendants, if the plaintiff discontinues against one defendant without monetary consideration, the amount of the verdict must be reduced by the equitable share of damages attributable to the released defendant, as found by the jury. *Killeen v Reinhardt* (1979, 2d Dept) 71 AD2d 851, 419 NYS2d 175.

Where, during jury deliberations, plaintiffs settled their claims against a defendant for the sum of $2,000, after which the jury returned a verdict of no cause of action as to the settling defendant, and also returned a verdict against the codefendant, the amount of the settlement paid by the settling defendant was properly applied to reduce the amount of the judgment against the codefendant. *Werner v Our Lady of Lourdes* (1977, 4th Dept) 60 AD2d 791, 400 NYS2d 659; General Obligations Law § 15-108.

A release given in good faith by an injured person to one of two or more persons claimed to be liable in tort for the same injury or wrongful death relieves the released tortfeasor of liability to any other person for contribution. *Torres v State* (1979, 4th Dept) 67 AD2d 814, 413 NYS2d 262.

A tortfeasor who has obtained a release from liability prior to a judgment is not entitled to contribution from any other person. *Mitchell v New York Hosp.* (1983, 2d Dept) 93 AD2d 832, 461 NYS2d 49, mod on other grounds 61 NY2d 208, 473 NYS2d 148.

Release given by a passenger to a promoter of a river trip before the accident did not bar a claim for contribution against the promoter by the designer and manufacturer of the boat, who had also been sued by the passenger. *Franzek v Calspan Corp.* (1980, 4th Dept) 78 AD2d 134, 434 NYS2d 288.

Section 15-108 of the General Obligations Law, which provides that a tortfeasor who has obtained his own release from liability shall not be entitled to contribution from any other person, applies only to contribution claims and has no applicability to claims for indemnification. *McDermott v New York* (1980) 50 NY2d 211, 428 NYS2d 643. A joint tortfeasor is entitled to contribution, whereas indemnification is reserved for those situations where a contract provides for it or one is held vicariously responsible solely by imputation of the law because of his relation to the actual wrongdoer, and it applies against those other tortfeasors guilty of the acts or omissions actually causing the harm. *Malette v Loblaws, Inc.* (1978, 3d Dept) 61 AD2d 1054, 402 NYS2d 474.

A defendant's right to an adjudication that his codefendant is liable for his proportionate share of the total damages is not merely an inchoate one, prior to the entry of a joint judgment against them and its payment by him, but rather is fixed and exists at the time the main action is tried. *Stein v Whitehead* (1972, 2d Dept) 40 AD2d 89, 337 NYS2d 821. A party is aggrieved by a determination dismissing the complaint against his codefendant and thus depriving him of his right to have the codefendant's *pro rata* liability for the accident and damages adjudicated by the court or jury trying the main action. *Stein v Whitehead, supra.* Even in the absence of a cross-claim, the trial court should, *sua sponte,* charge the jury that it should determine the proportionate responsibility of each defendant for the accident. *Stein v Whitehead, supra.* If all joint or concurrent tortfeasors have not been sued and the one sued has paid the full amount of the plaintiff's damages, he can bring an independent action against the other tortfeasors to recover from them their fair share of the damages, and in that independent action the court or jury will determine the proportions of the parties' liability for the damages. *Stein v Whitehead, supra.*

A counterclaim is a permissible means for raising a contribution claim. *Tierney v State* (1976, 4th Dept) 55 AD2d 158, 389 NYS2d 709; CPLR 1403.

Although a main defendant may assert his claim against a third-party defendant for contribution before any amount is paid to the plaintiff, this claim does not entitle the main defendant to contribution until such defendant has paid plaintiff an amount that is in excess of his proportionate share of the judgment. The main defendant may assert his claim for contribution where the third-party defendant's payment to plaintiff, although not in excess of his proportionate share, is in full satisfaction of the judgment. *Klinger v Dudley* (1977) 41 NY2d 362, 393 NYS2d 323.

Where a plaintiff was awarded $400,000 against a defendant, who in turn was awarded $50,000 against the third-party defendant, but before argument of the case on appeal, plaintiff settled with the defendant for $250,000, even though the third-party plaintiff had paid less than its full share of the judgment, it was entitled to recover a proportionate share of the settlement, or 12½% of $250,000. *Rock v Reed-Prentice Div. of Package Machinery Co.* (1976) 39 NY2d 34, 382 NYS2d 720; General Obligations Law § 15-108.

When the plaintiff has released a tortfeasor from liability, the settling party may not be sued for contribution by another tortfeasor. *F. W. Woolworth Co. v Southbridge Towers, Inc.* (1984, 1st Dept) 101 AD2d 434, 476 NYS2d 299.

It was improper for the trial court to charge the jury that it must apportion fault among the defendants, and that the percentage must be 100%, where a judgment-proof defendant was excluded from the apportionment. *Gannon Personnel Agency, Inc. v New York* (1977, 1st Dept) 57 AD2d 538, 393 NYS2d 915, 394 NYS2d 5, later app (1st Dept) 65 AD2d 352, 411 NYS2d 277, revd 49 NY2d 622, 427 NYS2d 746 and later proceeding 103 Misc 2d 60, 425 NYS2d 446, affd (1st Dept) 81 AD2d 755, 438

NYS2d 661, revd 58 NY2d 184, 460 NYS2d 485 and later proceeding (1st Dept) 105 AD2d 101, 483 NYS2d 228.

Although the motorists, who were the initial tortfeasors, were liable to plaintiffs not only for the injuries caused by the negligent operation of their vehicle, but also for the reasonably foreseeable aggravation of plaintiffs' conditions by subsequent acts of malpractice, an apportionment of the damages among the defendants, as requested in the cross-complaint of the motorists, should have been granted. *Dubicki v Maresco* (1978, 2d Dept) 64 AD2d 645, 407 NYS2d 66.

Where a jury found three parties liable, but apportioned the verdict against only two of them, finding the third liable in 0%, the Appellate Division held that the latter finding was against the weight of the evidence and inconsistent with the jury's finding of negligence, and modified the judgment and the apportionment accordingly. *Kelly v M. C. Electric Co.* (1979, 1st Dept) 68 AD2d 657, 418 NYS2d 28, app dismd 48 NY2d 634, 421 NYS2d 197.

Parties in a cause of action for contribution must be liable for the same injury but not necessarily on the same theory. Liability may be contractual or may arise from a breach of warranty; it need not arise from tort. *Nassau Roofing & Sheet Metal Co. v Celotex Corp.* (1980, 3d Dept) 74 AD2d 679, 424 NYS2d 786.

CPLR 1401, which provides that two or more persons who are subject to liability for damages for the same personal injury, injury to property or wrongful death, may claim contribution among them whether or not an action has been brought or a judgment has been rendered against the person from whom contribution is sought, applies not only to joint tortfeasors but also to concurrent, successive, independent, alternative or even intentional tortfeasors. *Schauer v Joyce* (1981) 54 NY2d 1, 444 NYS2d 564.

Because a claim for contribution exists only when two or more tortfeasors share in responsibility for an injury, in violation of duties they respectively owe to the injured person, and because a child has no cause of action against a sibling who is guilty of negligent supervision, it follows that a third party, whom the father of the injured child has sued, possesses no *Dole* claim for contribution against the allegedly negligent sibling. *Smith v Sapienza* (1981) 52 NY2d 82, 436 NYS2d 236.

Where one is held liable solely because of the negligence of another, indemnification, not contribution principles apply to shift the entire liability to the one who was negligent. *D'Ambrosio v New York* (1982) 55 NY2d 454, 450 NYS2d 149. When a sidewalk appurtenance negligently falls into disrepair, both the municipality and the landowner have breached their respective duties to a member of the public, and both may be made to respond in damages to those injured, so that contribution rather than indemnity applies. *D'Ambrosio v New York, supra.*

A tortfeasor may claim contribution from another person who may be subject to liability for damages for the same injury under any theory of liability that the plaintiff could have asserted against that person, but had not. *Doyle v Happy Tumbler Wash-O-Mat, Inc.* (1982, 2d Dept) 90 AD2d 366, 457 NYS2d 85.

In an action brought under the Dram Shop Act, the vendor of alcohol and the intoxicated tortfeasor are subject to liability for damages for the same personal injury, injury to property or wrongful death, and accordingly, may claim contribution among themselves with respect to compensatory damages awarded to the injured party. *Smith v Guli* (1985, 4th Dept) 106 AD2d 120, 484 NYS2d 740. Exemplary damages awarded pursuant to the Dram Shop Act are in the nature of a penalty; hence they are not subject to the principle of contribution. *Smith v Guli, supra.*

Apportionment of damages among culpable parties regardless of the degree or nature of the conferring fault is permitted under New York law, and contribution is permitted even in favor of an intentional wrongdoer if the parties are subject to liability to plaintiff for damages for the same injury. *Corva v United Services Auto. Asso.* (1985, 1st Dept) 108 AD2d 631, 485 NYS2d 264.

The conclusion that there was no liability to the plaintiff on the part of the owners of a service station for personal injuries the plaintiff sustained because of an accident occurring at the service station, necessarily defeated cross-claims for indemnification and contribution that were asserted against the owners of the service station by the owners and operator of a vehicle that struck the plaintiff. *Stone v Williams* (1984) 64 NY2d 639, 485 NYS2d 42.

In contribution the loss is distributed among tortfeasors, by requiring joint tortfeasors to pay a proportionate share of the loss to one who has discharged their joint liability, while in indemnity the party held legally liable shifts the entire loss to another. *Rosado v Proctor & Schwartz, Inc.* (1985) 66 NY2d 21, 494 NYS2d 851.

The decision in *Dole v Dow Chemical Co. (1972)*, 30 NY2d 143, 331 NYS2d 382, 53 ALR3d 175, permitted contribution among joint tortfeasors in proportion to their respective degrees of responsibility for an injury or harm they have caused. It left intact, however, the basic principles of implied indemnity, which permit one who is held vicariously liable solely due to the negligence of another to shift the entire burden of the loss to the actual wrongdoer. *Trustees of Columbia University v Mitchell/Giurgola Associates* (1985, 1st Dept) 109 AD2d 449, 492 NYS2d 371.

After settlement of a first-party action, a third-party complaint can stand only if it asserts a claim for indemnification and not one for contribution. *McHugh v International Components Corp.* (1986, 2d Dept) 118 AD2d 762, 500 NYS2d 152. The third-party complaint, which alleged only that the negligence of the third-party defendant was a cause of the injuries to the plaintiff, failed to show the nexus between the liability of the third-party plaintiff and the wrongful act of the third-party defendant that is required to support an indemnification claim. *McHugh v International Components Corp., supra*.

A successive tort-feasor may not seek apportionment of damages from a prior tort-feasor, because successive tortfeasors are only responsible for the aggravation of the original injury caused by their conduct. *Elkins v Eastern Air Lines, Inc.* (1986, 2d Dept) 122 AD2d 104, 504 NYS2d 500. However, a first tort-feasor is liable for the entire injury, and there is ample basis for holding that the first tort-feasor may maintain a claim for contribution. *Elkins v Eastern Air Lines, Inc., supra*.

Because the legislative history of CPLR Article 14 clearly shows that the sole purposes of 1401 and 1402 of the CPLR were, first, to codify the changes in the substantive law of torts for equitable contribution among joint tortfeasors, and, second, to eliminate the procedural barriers to recovery for contribution among joint

706

tortfeasors that existed under former CPLR Article 14, the statute was never intended to apply where the potential liability to the plaintiff of both the defendant and the third party defendant is purely for contractual, benefit of the bargain or loss of the value of promised performance damages. *Board of Education v Sargent, Webster, Crenshaw & Folley* (1987, 3d Dept) 125 AD2d 27, 511 NYS2d 961, motion gr 128 AD2d 1024, 513 NYS2d 651.

CPLR 1601 provides that when a verdict or decision in a personal injury action is determined in favor of a claimant and the action involves two or more tortfeasors who are jointly liable or in a claim against the State of New York and the liability of a defendant is found to be 50% or less of the total liability assigned to all persons liable, the liability of such defendant to the claimant for non-economic loss shall not be more than that defendant's equitable share determined in accordance with the relative culpability of each person causing or contributing to the total liability for non-economic loss; provided that the culpable conduct of a person who is not a party to the action is not to be considered in determining any equitable share, if the claimant proves with due diligence that he was unable to obtain jurisdiction over such person in the action. The term non-economic loss includes, but is not limited to pain and suffering, mental anguish, loss of consortium or other damages for non-economic loss. CPLR 1600.

CPLR 1602 contains a number of exceptions to the rule enunciated in CPLR 1601. CPLR 1602(6) states that the rule set forth in CPLR 1601 does not apply to automobile accidents. CPLR 1602(7) makes CPLR 1601 inapplicable to any person held liable for causing a claimant's injury by having acted with reckless disregard for the safety of others.

Generally, apportionment among tortfeasors, rather than a shifting of the entire loss through indemnification is the proper rule when two or more tortfeasors share in responsibility for an injury, in violation of duties they respectively owe to the injured person. *Guzman v Haven Plaza Housing Dev. Fund Co.* (1987) 69 NY2d 559, 516 NYS2d 451.

The basic requirement for contribution under *Dole v Dow Chemical Co.* (1972) 30 NY2d 143, 331 NYS2d 382, 53 ALR3d 175, is that the culpable parties must be subject to liability for damages for the same personal injury, injury to property or wrongful death. *Nassau Roofing & Sheet Metal Co. v Facilities Dev. Corp.* (1988) 71 NY2d 599, 528 NYS2d 516. Under *Dole*, a claim for contribution will lie whether or not the culpable parties are allegedly liable for the injury under the same or different theories and whether or not the party from whom contribution is sought is allegedly responsible for the injury as a concurrent, successive, independent, alternative, or even intentional tort-feasor. *Nassau Roofing & Sheet Metal Co. v Facilities Dev. Corp., supra.* Although the culpable party from whom contribution is sought will ordinarily have breached a duty owed directly to the injured party, this is not invariably so; in the unusual case, the right to apportionment may arise from the duty owed from the contributing party to the party seeking contribution. *Nassau Roofing & Sheet Metal Co. v Facilities Dev. Corp., supra.*

The purpose of all contribution and indemnity rules is the equitable distribution of the loss occasioned by multiple defendants. The owner of a multiple dwelling owes a non-delegable duty to persons on its premises to maintain them in a reasonably safe condition and a party injured by the owner's failure to fulfill it may recover from the owner, even though the responsibility for maintenance has been transferred to another; as between the owner and one voluntarily undertaking responsibility for maintenance, however, the party assuming the contractual duty is liable to the owner for the damages the owner must pay. *Mas v Two Bridges Assoc.* (1990) 75 NY2d 680, 555 NYS2d 669.

Because General Obligations Law § 5-322.1 prevents a party from obtaining contractual indemnification to the extent that its own negligence contributes to the accident, an airline that contracted with an engineering firm to perform certain work was entitled to contribution from the engineering firm, but not contractual indemnification for its own share of the fault. *Bishop v Port Auth. of New York & New Jersey* (1991, 2d Dept) 170 AD2d 565, 566 NYS2d 341.

Whether or not a defendant can claim the benefit of CPLR 1601 and thus limit his liability to plaintiff, he is entitled to collect from those co-defendants found liable, any amount he is required to pay plaintiffs in excess of his proportionate share of liability. *Schrader v Carney* (1992, 4th Dept) 180 AD2d 200, 586 NYS2d 687.

The remedies of contribution and indemnification are not available in actions seeking recovery for purely economic loss resulting from the breach of contractual obligations. *Lawrence Dev. Corp. v Jobin Waterproofing, Inc.* (1992, 2d Dept) 186 AD2d 634, 588 NYS2d 422.

Although the liability of an independent and successive tortfeasor is generally limited to separate injuries for the aggravation caused by his conduct, so that a claim for contribution by a subsequent tortfeasor against a prior tortfeasor is not available where the plaintiff's injury is such that it is incapable of a reasonable or practicable division or allocation between the tortfeasors, the focus shifts to the relative degree of fault of the multiple tortfeasors, and apportionment becomes appropriate. *Stathis v Jamaica Hosp.* (1992, 2d Dept) 187 AD2d 499, 589 NYS2d 606.

It was error for the trial court to allocate the bankrupt defendants' shares of liability among both settling and non-settling defendants; the percentage of fault attributed to bankrupt defendants should be allocated only among non-settling defendants. *Re New York City Asbestos Litig.* (1993, 1st Dept) 188 AD2d 214, 593 NYS2d 43, app gr 81 NY2d 707, 597 NYS2d 938, related proceeding (1st Dept) 194 AD2d 396, 599 NYS2d 953, app den 604 NYS2d 47.

An attorney sued for malpractice may bring a third-party complaint seeking indemnity or contribution against a subsequently retained attorney whose negligence has contributed to or aggravated plaintiff's damages. *Herkrath v Gaffin & Mayo, P.C.* (1993, 1st Dept) 192 AD2d 487, 597 NYS2d 34.

In a retrial on the issue of apportionment of damages, plaintiff had the burden of proof in the first instance of establishing liability on the part of the non-settling defendant, and once that liability was established, the non-settling defendant bore the burden of establishing the equitable shares attributable to the settling defendants for purposes of reducing the amount of its own responsibility for damages. *Bigelow v Acands, Inc.* (1993, 1st Dept) 196 AD2d 436, 601 NYS2d 478.

The pre-verdict "high-low" agreement between plaintiffs and third-party plaintiff general contractor, by which the third-party plaintiff guaranteed plaintiffs a minimum payment of $400,000 in exchange for plaintiff's promise not to enforce any judgment in excess of $800,000 against it, was a release within the meaning of General Obligations Law § 15-108, barring any claim for contribution by the third-party plaintiff against the third-party defendant. *Baca v HRH Constr. Corp.* (1994, 1st Dept) 200 AD2d 538, 607 NYS2d 21.

Although contribution or indemnity may be sought from one who is only vicariously liable for the injury involved, it may not be sought on behalf of the tortfeasor whose negligence is being imputed to those vicariously liable. *Maurillo v Park Slope U-Haul* (1993, 2d Dept) 194 AD2d 142, 606 NYS2d 243.

A vendor who violates the Dram Shop Act is not entitled to contribution from the deceased vendee's estate in an action brought by the vendee's dependents. *Coughlin v Barker Ave. Assocs.* (1994, 2d Dept) 202 AD2d 622, 609 NYS2d 646.

§ 33:3 VERDICTS AND WEIGHT OF EVIDENCE — On appeal, the Appellate Division is bound to assume that the jury adopted that view of the evidence most favorable to the prevailing parties. *Leone v Utica* (1979, 4th Dept) 66 AD2d 463, 414 NYS2d 412, affd 49 NY2d 811, 426 NYS2d 980.

The resolution of conflicting evidence and the credibility of the witnesses is for the jury to determine. *Boyle v Gretch* (1977, 4th Dept) 57 AD2d 1047, 395 NYS2d 797.

Assessment of the weight of the evidence and the credibility of witnesses is a function of the finder of fact, and is generally not relevant to the question of sufficiency of evidence. *Dominguez v Manhattan & Bronx Surface Transit Operating Authority* (1979) 46 NY2d 528, 415 NYS2d 634, on remand (1st Dept) 71 AD2d 555, 418 NYS2d 411.

Where the jury could not have reached its conclusion on any fair interpretation of the facts, the trial court's order setting aside the jury's determination in favor of the defendant was affirmed. *Silver v Elaine Products Co.* (1975, 2d Dept) 50 AD2d 916, 377 NYS2d 579. A jury verdict in favor of a defendant may be set aside when it plainly appears that the evidence so preponderates in favor of the plaintiff that the verdict for the defendant could not have been reached on any fair interpretation of the evidence. *Cohen v Margolin* (1979, 2d Dept) 67 AD2d 674, 412 NYS2d 183.

For a jury verdict to be set aside, it must be shown that the evidence so predominates in favor of the losing party that the jury's verdict could not have been rendered on any fair interpretation of the evidence. *Meyer v Smiley Bros., Inc.* (1988, 3d Dept) 145 AD2d 674, 535 NYS2d 217.

The trial court, which set aside a jury verdict finding that the defendant was 90% at fault did not impermissibly substitute its judgment for that of the jury; the court's judgment was supported by the testimony of a disinterested witness who confirmed the modest speed at which the automobile had been travelling, the character of the roadway where the accident occurred, and that fact that the plaintiffs stepped directly in front of the automobile. *Fuchs v Wolff* (1989, 2d Dept) 148 AD2d 665, 539 NYS2d 415.

Although a trial court has the power to set aside a jury's verdict when contrary to the weight of the evidence, the right is a limited one because a jury verdict must be accorded great deference; to justify setting the verdict aside it is necessary to first conclude that there is simply no valid line of reason and permissible inferences that could lead rational men to the conclusion reached by the jury on the basis of the evidence presented at the trial. The test is not whether the jury erred in weighing the evidence presented, but whether any viable evidence exists to support the verdict. *Lachanski v Craig* (1988, 3d Dept) 141 AD2d 995, 530 NYS2d 648.

Issues regarding credibility of witnesses and the accuracy of their testimony are primarily for the jury to determine, and its verdict should not be upset if it could have been reached by any fair interpretation of the evidence. *Jurgen v Linesburgh* (1990, 2d Dept) 159 AD2d 689, 553 NYS2d 438.

In a medical malpractice case, the verdict was not against the weight of evidence, where, in view of the conflicting evidence presented to the jury concerning the identity of the needle removed from plaintiff's abdomen and the manner in which it came to be embedded within her body, it could not be said that the verdict in defendant's favor could not have been reached by a fair interpretation of the evidence. *Cerasuoli v Brevetti* (1990, 2d Dept) 166 AD2d 403, 560 NYS2d 468.

A new trial regarding damages was required where the verdict on past and future lost earnings was both inconsistent and inadequate, and the jury awarded plaintiff only approximately one-half of his uncontested past medical expenses. *Fitzgibbons v New York State University Constr. Fund* (1991, 4th Dept) 177 AD2d 1033, 578 NYS2d 317.

If there is a valid line of reasoning and there are permissible inferences that could lead a rational person to the conclusion reached by the jury, the court should not set aside the jury's verdict as being against the weight of the evidence. *Patti v Fenimore* (1992, 2d Dept) 181 AD2d 869, 581 NYS2d 432. Where the verdict of a jury can be reconciled with a reasonable view of the evidence, the successful party is entitled to the presumption that the jury adopted that view. *Land v City of New York* (1991, 2d Dept) 177 AD2d 477, 575 NYS2d 690.

A jury's finding that a party was at fault, but that such fault was not a proximate cause of the accident, is inconsistent and against the weight of the evidence only when the issue is so inextricably interwoven that it is logically impossible to find negligence without also finding proximate cause. *Schaefer v Guddemi* (1992, 2d Dept) 182 AD2d 808, 582 NYS2d 803.

§ 33:4   OBJECTIONS TO THE FORM OF A VERDICT — Separate verdicts may be rendered with respect to two causes of action, but this may be waived by acquiescence in an instruction that the jury might return either two verdicts or a single verdict. *Helman v Markoff* (1938) 255 AD 991, 8 NYS2d 448, affd 280 NY 641. Where an action was brought for personal injuries and for wrongful death, and the plaintiff was silent as to a single verdict on two causes of action, he waived any advantage that would have accrued from a verdict in the proper form rendered separately on each cause of action, and as a result, acquiesced in the elimination of interest from the date of death. *Helman v Markoff, supra.*

Where the court charges the jury in such a manner that it permits an inconsistent verdict to be rendered, the right to challenge this is lost by failing to object to the charge. *General Exchange*

Ins. Corp. v New York City Transit Authority (1959) 20 Misc 2d 2, 189 NYS2d 555. Where a bus passenger's personal injury action against the bus company and the motorist whose vehicle collided with the bus was tried together with the motorist's property damage action against the bus company, and the jury returned inconsistent verdicts, the bus passenger should have objected when the court announced that it was ordering the jury to reconsider on both cases; in failing to object, he acquiesced in the reconsideration of his injury action. *Castanos v Lansing* (1956) 2 Misc 2d 529, 152 NYS2d 946.

Although a defendant could have requested that the jury be polled, and to see the signed answer sheets to the interrogatories before the discharge of the jury, thereby giving the court an opportunity to have the jury clarify its determinations, reconcile answers to interrogatories with the verdict, or reconsider its verdict in order to correct any obvious misunderstanding, but where defendant did not do so until after the jury had been discharged, the Appellate Division declined to hold that the verdict was constitutionally invalid. *Bichler v Eli Lilly & Co.* (1981, 1st Dept) 79 AD2d 317, 436 NYS2d 625, affd 55 NY2d 571, 450 NYS2d 776, 22 ALR4th 171.

The claim that the trial court erred by not requiring a jury to return an itemized verdict pursuant to CPLR 4111(f) was not preserved for appellate review because defendants did not object to the verdict sheet as submitted. *Tucker v Elimelech* (1992, 2d Dept) 184 AD2d 636, 584 NYS2d 895.

§ 33:5 REVISING OR AMENDING VERDICTS — The trial court has the power to correct a formal defect in the verdict. *Allan Fox Co. v Wohl* (1931) 255 NY 268, 174 NE 650, reh den 256 NY 554, 177 NE 137.

Verdicts should not be amended as a result of mere guesswork. *First International Pictures, Inc. v F. C. Pictures Corp.* (1941) 262 AD 21, 27 NYS2d 816. A party who moves to amend the verdict has the burden of showing that there is good reason for the verdict to be amended. *First International Pictures, Inc. v F. C. Pictures Corp., supra.*

Where matters of substance are involved, the intent of the jury governs and the court does not have the power to change a verdict or judgment after it is rendered. *Yablen v Thorne, Neale & Co.* (1955, Sup) 138 NYS2d 67. Where a civil court jury rendered a verdict in the amount of $12,000 and the jurisdictional limit was $10,000, the court had no power to reduce the award of its own accord to $10,000 even with the consent of the plaintiff; a defect in the verdict could have been cured only by the jury itself. *Abbey Rent A Car, Inc. v Moore* (1968, 1st Dept) 30 AD2d 952, 294 NYS2d 229. It has, however, been held that reducing the jury's verdict from $35,000 to $10,000, the jurisdictional limit of the Civil Court, without reinstructing the jury and resubmitting the case for further deliberation was not improper. *Izzi v Dolgin* (1970) 64 Misc 2d 742, 315 NYS2d 1005, reinstated (2d Dept) 42 AD2d 966, 347 NYS2d 971.

When the verdict is erroneous in form but not as a matter of substance, it may be corrected without the necessity of a new trial. *Josephson v Wibrew* (1961, 2d Dept) 15 AD2d 533, 222 NYS2d 739, affd in part and app dismd in part 12 NY2d 930, 238 NYS2d 315. When the verdict is incorrectly reported because of mistake, inadvertence or lack of familiarity with the duty of jurors, the court has the power to correct the records to express correctly what the jury intended. *Freeman v Manhattan Cab Corp.* (1956) 1 Misc 2d 601, 150 NYS2d 674. If a jury's intent is plain and the form of the verdict is improper, it is the duty of the trial court to see that the verdict is corrected to conform to the intent of the jury. *Miller v Syracuse* (1950, Sup) 101 NYS2d 346.

When a jury renders a verdict that has not been recorded, the verdict may, prior to such recording, be sent back to reconsider it, not only to correct a mistake in form or to make plain that which was not clear, but to alter it in substance as they so determined and agreed. *White v Hussey* (1948) 191 Misc 193, 76 NYS2d 924.

The power of the court to require a jury to reconsider a verdict already rendered should be exercised sparingly. *Pogo Holding Corp. v New York Property Ins. Underwriting Asso.* (1983, 2d Dept) 97 AD2d 503, 467 NYS2d 872, app dismd 61 NY2d 756, 472 NYS2d 920 and affd 62 NY2d 969, 479 NYS2d 336. It was error for the court to send the jury back for further consideration of its initial verdict, where the jury's answers were clear and required no further elucidation, and there was ample evidence in the record to support the jury's finding. *Pogo Holding Corp. v New York Property Ins. Underwriting Asso., supra.*

Where the verdict a jury rendered for one defendant and against the codefendant was irreconcilable and inconsistent, the jurors should have been advised that they could not render inconsistent verdicts and the trial judge should have directed the jurors to give further consideration to the cases. *Thorsen v Metzgar* (1951) 278 AD 421, 105 NYS2d 947.

Where at the close of the trial on liability, the jury rendered its verdict, apportioning fault to the defendant and one of the plaintiffs, and the next day, before the beginning of the trial on damages, the court received a note from the jury indicating that its verdict did not reflect its actual intentions, it was error for the trial court to deny a motion to modify the jury's special verdict to conform to its actual findings. *Reyes v 38 Sickles St. Corp.* (1992, 2d Dept) 188 AD2d 518, 591 NYS2d 469.

The trial court lacked the power to unilaterally change the jury's verdict by reducing the amount awarded for past pain and suffering from \$400,000 to \$300,000 and increasing the amount awarded for future pain and suffering from \$150,000 to \$215,000; the proper procedure for the trial court to follow was, if it found that the verdict did not deviate materially from what would be reasonable compensation, to deny the motion or, if it did deviate materially, to direct a new trial unless the parties stipulated to an appropriate *additur* or *remittitur* or both. *Fischl v Carbone* (1993, 2d Dept) 199 AD2d 463, 606 NYS2d 53.

Once a verdict is reached and the jury is discharged, it ceases to be an agency of the law. *Pache v Boehm* (1978, 2d Dept) 60 AD2d 867, 401 NYS2d 260. Once the jury is discharged, it may not be recalled. *Pache v Boehm, supra.*

§ 33:6 CONSTRUCTION OF GENERAL VERDICTS — A general verdict is a single indivisible entity and cannot be readily separated into its component parts. *Murphy v Roger Sherman Transfer Co.* (1970) 62 Misc 2d 960, 310 NYS2d 891 (disapproved on other grounds by *Schabe v Hampton Bays Union Free School Dist.* (2d Dept) 103 AD2d 418, 480 NYS2d 328).

A general verdict requires that the jury report the verdict on a combination of issues of liability and damages as a single entity.

Klein v Eichen (1970) 63 Misc 2d 590, 310 NYS2d 611. In the absence of special circumstances, a verdict in the form "for plaintiff" in an action against more than one defendant, that was silent as to whom the verdict was against, is construed as having been rendered against all defendants who have been duly served with process or who have entered an appearance. *Didchenko v Franzblau* (1962, Sup) 235 NYS2d 709, revd on other grounds (1st Dept) 19 AD2d 606, 241 NYS2d 157.

In an action for the contract price of services, a verdict for a sum less than the contract price was held to be the equivalent of a finding that the plaintiff did not fully perform. *Meriden Gravure Co. v Bedell* (1931) 232 AD 454, 251 NYS 369.

A general verdict may not be construed as based upon only one of two grounds of negligence that have been invoked. *Lo Galbo v Columbia Casualty Co.* (1932) 234 AD 510, 255 NYS 502.

In a negligence action under the former rule, a finding in favor of the plaintiff implied a finding of freedom from contributory negligence. *Elfeld v Burkham Auto Renting Co.* (1949) 299 NY 336, 13 ALR2d 370.

Where a verdict can be reconciled with a reasonable view of the evidence, the successful party is entitled to the presumption that the jury adopted that view. *Maze v Di Bartolo* (1987, 2d Dept) 130 AD2d 720, 515 NYS2d 828. A jury's verdict that both of two sets of defendants have been negligent, but that one of the two was at fault to the extent of 100% and the other to the extent of 0% was consistent with the court's charge, which distinguished between negligence and proximate cause. The jury could have found that only the negligence of one set of defendants was the proximate cause of plaintiff's injuries. *Maze v Di Bartolo, supra.*

Where negligence established by *res ipsa loquitur* was the plaintiff's sole theory of liability, as conceded by the defendant, where the trial court's charge clearly communicated plaintiff's theory to the jury, and did not charge two separate theories of recovery, a general verdict was entirely appropriate. *Nesbit v New York City Transit Authority* (1991, 1st Dept) 170 AD2d 92, 574 NYS2d 179.

§ 33:7 INCONSISTENT VERDICTS — Where a defendant, drove a vehicle across a double yellow line that separated traffic going in the direction defendant was traveling from traffic going in the opposite direction, and caused a collision with three other vehicles proceeding in the opposite direction, there was no rational basis for a finding by the jury that the defendant had proximately caused the collision with the first of three oncoming cars, but that the same defendant bore no responsibility for damages sustained by the people in the second of the three vehicles. *Capo v Desmond* (1988, 2d Dept) 137 AD2d 780, 525 NYS2d 327.

Where a jury's findings with respect to negligence and proximate cause are irreconcilably inconsistent, the judgment in favor of defendant cannot stand. *Petioni v Grisi* (1989, 1st Dept) 155 AD2d 366, 547 NYS2d 641.

Objections to a verdict on the ground of inconsistency must be raised before the jury is discharged, at which time corrective action may be taken. Where the claim of inconsistency was not raised until the jury was discharged, plaintiffs were deemed to have waived this objection. *Strauss v Huber* (1990, 2d Dept) 161 AD2d 629, 555 NYS2d 407.

In an action brought by university employees charged with theft from the university, malicious prosecution, false arrest, abuse of process, libel and slander, the jury's verdict finding the defendants not liable on the libel and slander causes of action but liable on the malicious prosecution, abuse of process and false arrest causes of action was not internally inconsistent and was improper. *Parkin v Cornell University, Inc.* (1992, 3d Dept) 182 AD2d 850, 581 NYS2d 914, app dismd 80 NY2d 914, 588 NYS2d 821.

In a malpractice action brought against a hospital and the triage nurse, where the trial court admitted into evidence a damaging statement by the triage nurse, and the jury found that the hospital was negligent but that the triage nurse was not negligent, it could not be said under any fair interpretation of the evidence that the hospital was negligent and that its negligence was the proximate cause of plaintiff's injuries, but that the conduct of the triage nurse was not negligent. *Nordhauser v New York City Health & Hosp. Corp.* (1991, 2d Dept) 176 AD2d 787, 575 NYS2d 117.

The issue of inconsistency of the verdict was preserved for appellate review where immediately after the jury's verdict was announced, there was an off-the-record conference, after which the jury was polled and discharged and thereafter, during a side bar conference the defendant moved to set aside the verdict on the ground of inconsistency. *Powell v New York City Transit Authority* (1992, 2d Dept) 186 AD2d 728, 589 NYS2d 71.

Where a jury verdict was inconsistent with regard to the damages awarded, but where the jury had not yet been discharged, the trial court correctly directed the jury to reconsider the inconsistency. *Hernandez v City of New York* (1993, 1st Dept) 194 AD2d 377, 598 NYS2d 499.

§ 33:8 SPECIAL VERDICTS — A special verdict is one in which the jury finds the facts only, while leaving the judgment to the court. *Manning v Monaghan,* (1861) 23 NY 539. In a general verdict, on the other hand, the jury pronounces generally either in favor of plaintiff or of the defendant, on all of the issues. *Manning v Monaghan, supra.*

Where different theories of negligence may be invoked, it is proper to render either a special verdict, or a general verdict accompanied by written answers to interrogatories. *Dore v Long I. R. R. Co.* (1965, 2d Dept) 23 AD2d 502, 256 NYS2d 425.

Special findings should be required of the jury by the court in cases where resolution of threshold issues can be dispositive. *Newland v Juneau* (1978, 3d Dept) 62 AD2d 1125, 404 NYS2d 701.

CPLR 4111(d) and CPLR 4111(f) mandate that in medical, dental, and podiatric malpractice actions, and in all other actions to recover for personal injuries, injury to property, and wrongful death, an award of damages must be itemized, specifying the amount awarded for each element of damages, and further specifying the amounts awarded for past and future damages in each category. The verdict must further specify the number of years for which each amount awarded for future damages is intended to provide compensation. The rule also provides that the jury shall be instructed to award the full amount of future damages, as calculated, without reduction to present value.

Where plaintiff made no request for a special verdict or for answers to interrogatories to be submitted, and took no exception to the charge, thereby indicating his apparent satisfaction with the delivered instructions, and only after the jury had rendered its verdict requested the court to ascertain from the jury whether it had applied the doctrine of comparative negligence and what determination had been made as to percentage of negligence between the parties, the court properly denied plaintiff's request. *Radtke v Yokose* (1982, 3d Dept) 87 AD2d 220, 453 NYS2d 43.

Where multiple theories of liability are involved, it is desirable to submit the case to the jury for special findings, because if one of the theories is untenable a general verdict may not stand. *Cirasuolo v Cahill* (1986, 4th Dept) 119 AD2d 986, 500 NYS2d 881.

Judicial intervention into a special verdict is authorized where there is substantial confusion in reaching the verdict; where the ambiguity in the verdict sheet was brought to the trial court's attention before the jury was discharged and could have been corrected or at least clarified at that time, a new trial was ordered. *Booth v J.C. Penney Co.* (1991, 1st Dept) 169 AD2d 663, 565 NYS2d 77.

§ 33:9 SPECIAL INTERROGATORIES — Whereas a special verdict takes the place of a general verdict and judgment is rendered upon it, *Bergman v Scottish Union & Nat'l Ins. Co.* (1934) 264 NY 205, 190 NE 409, in a case where a general verdict is rendered, the court may instruct the jury to find specifically on questions of fact that are submitted to the jury in writing. *Sherman v Leicht* (1933) 238 AD 271, 264 NYS 492. The answers to written interrogatories, as distinguished from a special verdict, are given in aid of a general verdict, or act as a substantial check upon it. *Bergman v Scottish Union & Nat'l Ins. Co., supra.*

In the trial of an action that permits recovery on the basis of different theories of liability, the court should instruct the jury to answer special questions so that the court may be advised of the theory of liability on which the verdict is based. *Deso v Albany Ladder Co.* (1966, 3d Dept) 26 AD2d 182, 271 NYS2d 823. In an action on a life insurance policy where there were questions for the jury as to whether the alleged misrepresentation was not knowingly made or on the other hand was immaterial, the court should consider submission of a special verdict or a general verdict with special findings. *Hartnett v Home Life Ins. Co.* (1963, 4th Dept) 18 AD2d 281, 239 NYS2d 308.

Special interrogatories are not proper if they present a question of law. *Socony Burner Corp. v Gold* (1929) 227 AD 369, 237 NYS 552. Where the question submitted to the jury was whether there was a breach of warranty in the sale of an oil heater, it was held to be abstract and to call for a conclusion of law. *Socony Burner Corp. v Gold, supra*.

In any given case, whether the answers to special written interrogatories are to be employed is a question to be determined by the court in the exercise of its discretion. *O'Hara v Derschug* (1934) 241 AD 513, 272 NYS 189.

Where there was no way to reconcile the jury's answer to two special interrogatories, in that the jury could not have concluded that the defendant negligently designed the override system and at the same time conclude that it was reasonably safe for its intended use, a new trial was required. *Lundgren v McColgin* (1983, 4th Dept) 96 AD2d 706, 464 NYS2d 317, later proceeding (4th Dept) 96 AD2d 707, 464 NYS2d 701 and later proceeding (4th Dept) 96 AD2d 707, 464 NYS2d 701.

Where in answer to a series of questions contained in a verdict sheet, the jury found the defendant and the third-party defendant negligent, but declared that no percentage of the fault was attributable to the former and 100% to the latter, it was error for the trial court to uphold the verdict as consistent, because the jury found that the defendant had been negligent, and any finding that the third-party defendant was solely and proximately responsible would have been against the weight of the credible evidence. *Russell v H. Friedman & Sons, Inc.* (1981, 1st Dept) 80 AD2d 768, 436 NYS2d 715.

Where multiple collisions occurred within a brief period of time, the general verdict required the trial court and the Appellate Court to speculate as to the basis of the verdict, and at the new trial the trial court should consider the advisability of requiring the jury to return a general verdict accompanied by written answers to special interrogatories. *Gandy v Wuster* (1966, 4th Dept) 25 AD2d 478, 266 NYS2d 544.

It was not error for the trial court to submit seven interrogatories to the jury in an attempt to isolate the claimed instances of malpractice, particularly since the defendant did not take exception to the use of the interrogatories. *Bell v New York City Health & Hosp. Corp.* (1982, 2d Dept) 90 AD2d 270, 456 NYS2d 787.

Although it is recommended that interrogatories involving the seatbelt defense indicate precisely what portion of the total damage award plaintiff would not have suffered if a seatbelt had been worn, resort to such interrogatories in a given case remains a matter within the sound discretion of the trial court. *Isabell v Thumm* (1985, 3d Dept) 111 AD2d 580, 489 NYS2d 645. By thoroughly charging the jury with respect to the application of the seatbelt defense, the trial court presented the issue sufficiently, and there was no impropriety in the trial court's declining to ask the jury to make separate findings of reduction in damages attributable to any failure to use the seatbelt. *Isabell v Thumm, supra*.

In an action for personal injuries brought as a result of an explosion of a canister of swimming pool chemicals, a verdict sheet submitted to the jury was unfairly suggestive in that of the 31 questions on the verdict sheet 14 asked if plaintiffs had been negligent, when in fact there was virtually no evidence to suggest that plaintiffs were remiss in their use of the defendants' product. *Castro v Alden Leeds, Inc.* (1988, 2d Dept) 144 AD2d 613, 535 NYS2d 73.

In an action arising out of a fall on a stairway, the trial court properly submitted the case to the jury with an interrogatory that limited the defendant's liability to the presence of duct tape on one of the steps, because the evidence at the trial did not support any other theory of liability. *Fallon v Damianos* (1993, 2d Dept) 192 AD2d 576, 596 NYS2d 134, app den 83 NY2d 751, 611 NYS2d 133.

Where a jury's responses to interrogatories are inconsistent with its general verdict, or are internally inconsistent absent a general verdict, the court is empowered either to resubmit the verdict or to order a new trial. *Vera v Bielomatik Corp.* (1993, 1st Dept) 199 AD2d 132, 605 NYS2d 75.

§ 33:10 SPECIAL INTERROGATORIES INCONSISTENT WITH A GENERAL VERDICT — A trial court has the power to send the jury back to deliberate further when there is a patent inconsistency in its verdicts. *Kennard v Welded Tank & Constr. Co.* (1969) 25 NY2d 324, 305 NYS2d 477.

Whether the court must, as a matter of law, send a jury back for further deliberations in any given case depends on the court's judgment as to which of the conflicting verdicts is consistent with the weight of the evidence. *Kennard v Welded Tank & Constr. Co., supra*. Thus, where general and special verdicts rendered in personal injury and wrongful death actions were inconsistent in that the general verdicts absolved the defendant of negligence while the special verdicts did not, and the trial court was of the opinion that the special verdict was in accordance with the weight of evidence, the action of the trial court in conforming the inconsistent general verdicts to the special verdicts, instead of exercising discretion to resubmit the case or order a new trial, was not error because the discretion, if exercised, would have the same result. *Kennard v Welded Tank & Constr. Co., supra*.

CPLR 4111(c) empowers the court to require the jury to return a general verdict accompanied by answers to written interrogatories on issues of fact, and when the answers to one or more of the interrogatories is in conflict with the general verdict, the court can either (1) set aside the general verdict and direct entry of judgment in accordance with the answers, (2) require the jury further to consider its answers and verdict, or (3) order a new trial. *Oakley v Rochester* (1979, 4th Dept) 71 AD2d 15, 421 NYS2d 472, affd 51 NY2d 908, 434 NYS2d 977.

To the extent that the jury's answer to a special interrogatory is inconsistent with a general verdict, the interrogatory controls. *Dreyer v Tishman Realty & Constr. Co.* (1976, 1st Dept) 52 AD2d 76, 382 NYS2d 486, revd on other grounds 42 NY2d 883, 397 NYS2d 785.

In an action for the wrongful taking of realty, the verdict on special questions, which found that the plaintiff was not entitled to possession but was nevertheless awarded a certain amount of damages, was inconsistent. The defendant's motion to set aside the verdict should have been granted. *Crawford v Hamburg* (1961, 4th Dept) 14 AD2d 482, 217 NYS2d 268.

In a medical malpractice action, where the case was submitted to the jury on 14 theories of negligence, together with 11 interrogatories, and the jury's finding was that the doctor was liable for "ordering" Nalline and the hospital was liable for administering the drug "without his order," liability turned on a mutually exclusive version of the facts. Accordingly, the verdict had to be set aside, because it could not be said that all theories submitted to the jury were sustained by the evidence. *Mertsaris v 73rd Corp.* (1984, 2d Dept) 105 AD2d 67, 482 NYS2d 792.

When a trial court has been asked to resubmit inconsistent answers of a jury to interrogatories, which are also inconsistent with the general verdict, the trial court only has the power to either ask the jury to further consider its answers and verdict or order a new trial, and it is error for a trial court to itself attempt to adjust the outcome of the litigation. *Mars Associates, Inc. v New York City Educational Constr. Fund* (1987, 1st Dept) 126 AD2d 178, 513 NYS2d 125.

§ 33:11   SEALED VERDICTS — A "sealed verdict" is simply an agreement that is reached by the jurors and does not become final until it is read into the record and the jurors are discharged. *Spielter v North German Lloyd S. S. Co.* (1931) 232 AD 104, 249 NYS 358. The trial court may direct a sealed verdict by the jury and the consent of parties is not necessary. *Fahey v South Nassau Communities Hospital* (1950) 197 Misc 490, 95 NYS2d 842, affd 277 AD 774, 97 NYS2d 711.

Where a sealed verdict was signed by 10 of 12 jurors, and one of the 10 who had signed the sealed verdict became ill during the night and was unable to attend court when the verdict was opened, plaintiff did not have the right to have the verdict set aside where the clerk reported at the poll of the jury that nine jurors present answered in the affirmative and two in the negative, and that the absent juror had signed the sealed verdict for the defendant. *Rowe v Queensborough Gas & Electric Co.* (1939) 171 Misc 395, 11 NYS2d 922, affd 258 AD 904, 16 NYS2d 832, reh den 258 AD 977, 17 NYS2d 1011.

§ 33:12   POLLING THE JURORS — After a verdict has been received and before it is entered, the party against whom it is rendered has a right to poll the jury. *Muth v J & T Metal Products Co.* (1980, 2d Dept) 74 AD2d 898, 425 NYS2d 858, app dismd 51 NY2d 745, 432 NYS2d 365.

An attorney against whose client a verdict has been rendered has a right to ask that the jury be polled for the purpose of ascertaining that the verdict announced by the foreman is the verdict of the jury. *Reed v Cook* (1951, Sup) 103 NYS2d 539. This right may be waived, either expressly or by act or by the failure to act. *Reed v Cook, supra.* Where a jury returned a verdict against two of three defendants, counsel for these defendants waived their right to poll the jury by their silence. *Reed v Cook, supra.*

When disagreement or inconsistency becomes apparent from a polling of the jury, the court has the power to send the jury back to reconsider or correct the inconsistency. *Reed v Cook, supra.*

A party against whom a verdict is declared has an absolute right to poll the jury at any time before the verdict is entered. *Brith Trumpeldor of America, Inc. v Bermil Sales & Service Co.* (1958) 16 Misc 2d 186, 174 NYS2d 725, mod 17 Misc 2d 206, 183 NYS2d 887. A jury's decision does not become final until it is recorded and until this is done, any juror has a right to withdraw his consent to a verdict and to correct a mistake. *Castanos v Lansing* (1956) 2 Misc 2d 529, 152 NYS2d 946.

While the jury was being polled one juror, when asked whether the verdicts were hers, responded "Yes, under duress, I'm saying yes," and following this the court asked the juror, "Are they your verdicts, yes or no?" to which the juror replied, "Yes." It was error for the trial court to deny the request of defense counsel to hold a hearing to make a determination on what the stated duress consisted of. *People v Pickett* (1984) 61 NY2d 773, 473 NYS2d 157.

The trial court's refusal to poll the jurors on whether they understood that the net verdict to the plaintiffs would be reduced by the 70% fault found against the plaintiff, although twice requested by plaintiff's counsel to do so, was error requiring reversal and a new trial on damages. *Luppino v Busher* (1986, 2d Dept) 119 AD2d 554, 500 NYS2d 557.

RESEARCH REFERENCES

American Law Reports

19 ALR5th 622, Propriety of reassembling jury to amend, correct, clarify, or otherwise change verdict after discharge or separation at conclusion of civil case

39 ALR4th 800, Impeachment of verdict by juror's evidence that he was coerced or intimidated by fellow juror

38 ALR4th 1170, Deafness of juror as ground for impeaching verdict, or securing new trial or reversal on appeal

15 ALR4th 213, Validity of agreement, by stipulation or waiver in state civil case, to accept verdict by number of proportion of jurors less than that constitutionally permitted

82 ALR3d 974, Propriety of direction of verdict in favor of fewer than all defendants at close of plaintiff's case

66 ALR3d 472, Validity of verdict or verdicts by same jury in personal injury action awarding damages to injured spouse but denying recovery to other spouse seeking collateral damages, or vice-versa

ALR QUICK INDEX: Verdict

American Jurisprudence 2d

76 AM JUR 2d, Trial §§ 1111-1218

75B AM JUR 2d, Trial §§ 1750-1927

American Jurisprudence Pleading and Practice

23 AM JUR PL & PR FORMS (Rev) Trial, Forms 321-480

American Jurisprudence Trials

6 AM JUR TRIALS 963, Predicting Personal Injury Verdicts and Damages

6 AM JUR TRIALS 1043, Special Verdicts

Other Resources

8 CARMODY-WAIT 2d, The Deliberations, Verdict, and Findings of the Jury §§ 58:1 et seq.

Auto-Cite®: Any case citation herein can be checked for form, parallel references, later history and annotation references through the Auto-Cite computer research system.

CHAPTER 34

THE JUDGMENT

§ 34:1 ENTRY OF THE JUDGMENT — A judgment is entered when, after it has been signed by the clerk, it is filed by him. CPLR 5016(a).

§ 34:2 DUTY OF THE CLERK TO ENTER JUDGMENT — Judgment upon the general verdict of a jury after a trial by jury as of right shall be entered by the clerk unless the court directs otherwise. CPLR 5016(b). If there is a special verdict, the court shall direct entry of an appropriate judgment. CPLR 5016(b).

The judgment must be entered by the clerk of the court in which the action is triable. CPLR 105(e).

There are no statutory provisions regarding when a judgment must be entered. *Schoen v Schechter* (1957) 9 Misc 2d 823, 175 NYS2d 77, affd (1st Dept) 5 AD2d 866, 172 NYS2d 541.

Although there are no statutory provisions regarding when a judgment must be entered, in a completed divorce proceeding where substantial property rights may be impaired, the judgment should be filed promptly. *Kennedy v Macaluso* (1982, 4th Dept) 86 AD2d 775, 448 NYS2d 276, affd 56 NY2d 630, 450 NYS2d 479.

§ 34:3 AMOUNT OF THE JUDGMENT — When a tort action results in a verdict for future damages in excess of $250,000.00, the form of the judgment, which is to be structured, is governed by Articles 50-A and 50-B of the CPLR. Article 50-A controls medical, dental, and podiatric malpractice cases, and Article 50-B controls all other actions for personal injury, injury to property, and wrongful death. The contents of the statutes are substantially equivalent, however.

Detailed analysis of these statutory provisions is outside the scope of this work. Article 50-A was enacted in 1985, and Article 50-B in 1986, and judicial construction of the arguably vague provisions contained therein, in the several departments of the Appellate Division, is in its early stages. The reader is advised to ascertain the up-to-date status of statutory interpretation whenever a judgment under these provisions is required.

The cases that follow provide general guidance on issues related to the amount of a judgment.

The amount of the judgment may not exceed that contained in the *ad damnum* clause of the complaint. *Gilliam v S. M. Johnson, Inc.* (1960, 2d Dept) 11 AD2d 769, 205 NYS2d 416. Thus, where the demand in the complaint was for the sum of $4,000, and the court properly ascertained that the damages were some $6,200, the recovery would be limited to $4,000 where there was no motion to amend the complaint. *Michalowski v Ey* (1959, 2d Dept) 8 AD2d 854, 190 NYS2d 535, affd 7 NY2d 71, 195 NYS2d 633. A motion to increase the *ad damnum* clause of the complaint will be granted on the eve of trial where it is shown that additional damages accrued to the plaintiff after the complaint had been served. *Gaeta v Rizzo* (1969, 2d Dept) 32 AD2d 653, 300 NYS2d 687 (See record and briefs on appeal.)

In the absence of prejudice to the defendant, a motion to amend the *ad damnum* clause, whether made before or after the trial, should generally be granted. *Loomis v Civetta Corinno Constr. Corp.* (1981) 54 NY2d 18, 444 NYS2d 571, reh den 55 NY2d 801, 447 NYS2d 436.

§ 34:4 INCLUSION OF INTEREST IN JUDGMENT — Interest is recoverable on a sum awarded because of a breach of contract, or because of an act or omission depriving and otherwise interfering with title to, possession or enjoyment of property, or as a civil penalty, except that in an action of an equitable nature, interest and the rate and date from which it shall be computed is in the court's discretion. CPLR 5001(a).

In an action for breach of warranty, interest was properly granted from the date that plaintiff's loss must certainly have been present. *Cohen v Bratt & Doxey Supply Co.* (1976, 2d Dept) 51 AD2d 719, 379 NYS2d 155.

Inclusion of interest in recoveries in actions of an equitable nature is left to the sound discretion of the court. *Rosenblum v Aetna Casualty & Surety Co.* (1981, 3d Dept) 81 AD2d 731, 439 NYS2d 482.

Where the action was one at law for breach of a separation agreement as a contract, rather than a matrimonial or equitable action, plaintiff was entitled to interest as a matter of right on the entire award. *Sinclair v Wieder* (1975, 2d Dept) 48 AD2d 866, 369 NYS2d 18.

The date from which interest is to be computed shall be specified in the verdict, report or decision. CPLR 5001(c). If the jury is discharged without specifying the date, the court shall, upon motion, fix the date. When the date is certain or not in dispute it may be fixed by the clerk of the court upon affidavit. CPLR 5001(c). The amount of interest shall be computed by the clerk of the court, to the date that the verdict was rendered or the report or decision made, and shall be included in the total sum awarded. CPLR 5001(c).

Interest shall be at the rate of 9% per year, except where otherwise prescribed by statute. CPLR 5004.

A plaintiff who was successful in an action for inducing a breach of contract and for unfair competition, was entitled as a matter of right to interest on the amount of the recovery, from the date of accrual of the cause of action. *De Long Corp. v Morrison-Knudsen* (1964) 14 NY2d 346, 251 NYS2d 657. In an action for damages to property as a result of negligence, the trial court properly allowed interest as a matter of law. *Harmon & Regalia Inc. v New York* (1955) 286 AD 825, 141 NYS2d 877.

In an action brought by a broker against the seller of realty for commissions, the broker was entitled to interest on the judgment from the date that he produced a buyer who was ready, willing and able to purchase at the terms set by the seller. *Smyczynski v Goeseke* (1982, 4th Dept) 88 AD2d 765, 451 NYS2d 496.

In an action against a former factor, it was error for the trial court not to award plaintiffs interest actually paid by them as a result of what the court found to be improper charge-backs, and in addition, plaintiffs were entitled to statutory interest from the date of each such improper charge-back. *Europe Craft Imports, Inc. v James Talcott, Inc.* (1982, 1st Dept) 87 AD2d 789, 449 NYS2d 498. A successful plaintiff in an action for trespass to real property is entitled as a matter of right to an award of interest from the time the cause of action accrues. *M.C.D. Carbone, Inc. v Bedford* (1983, 2d Dept) 98 AD2d 714, 469 NYS2d 117.

In an action to recover damages for breach of a stock purchase agreement, the successful plaintiff was entitled to interest from the date defendant transferred stock in violation of his purchase agreement with the plaintiff. *Levine v Joseph* (1983, 2d Dept) 98 AD2d 712, 469 NYS2d 113.

In a wrongful death action, plaintiff can recover interest on the amount awarded, from the date of decedent's death. EPTL § 5-4.3(a). In an action upon a life insurance policy, plaintiff is entitled to interest on the principal sum recovered from the date of death of the assured. Insurance Law § 3214.

There is no statutory provision for interest in a personal injury action. In a malpractice action, interest is recoverable only from the date the verdict is rendered and not from any previous period. *Glassman v Brunswick Home, Inc.* (1966) 51 Misc 2d 392, 273 NYS2d 335. In an action brought for both personal injury and wrongful death, plaintiff should ask for separate verdicts on each cause of action, because it has been held that where a lump sum is awarded for both causes of action, no basis is afforded on which interest from the date of death may be computed. *Helman v Markoff* (1938) 255 AD 991, 8 NYS2d 448, affd 280 NY 641.

Where the defendants did not delay in prosecuting their appeal from the judgment after the first trial of the action, the plaintiff was entitled to interest only from the date of the later verdict. *Brizer v City of New York* (1976, 2d Dept) 51 AD2d 791, 380

NYS2d 60 (disapproved by *Love v State*, 78 NY2d 540, 577 NYS2d 359).

Plaintiffs who obtained a verdict that was reversed on appeal and then were successful upon the retrial of the case, were not entitled to interest measured from the date of the verdict of liability at the first trial. *Barry v Manglass* (1980, 2d Dept) 77 AD2d 887, 431 NYS2d 89, affd 55 NY2d 803, 447 NYS2d 423.

Pre-verdict interest is not obtainable as of right in a libel action. *Rupert v Sellers* (1980) 50 NY2d 881, 430 NYS2d 263, cert den 449 US 901, 66 L Ed 2d 132, 101 S Ct 272.

Where the plaintiff was awarded damages because of the failure of most of a crop of red onions due to defective seeds sold to him by the defendant, he was entitled to interest as a matter of right from the earliest ascertainable date. *Arigo v Abbott & Cobb, Inc.* (1982, 4th Dept) 86 AD2d 958, 448 NYS2d 311.

After a bifurcated trial, a plaintiff is ordinarily entitled to interest from the date the interlocutory verdict is rendered, rather than the date of verdict awarding damages. *Gunnarson v State* (1986, 2d Dept) 124 AD2d 642, 507 NYS2d 896, affd (1987) 70 NY2d 923, 524 NYS2d 396; *Malkin v Wright* (1978, 1st Dept) 64 AD2d 569, 407 NYS2d 36, regardless of which party is responsible for the delay, if any, in the assessment of plaintiff's damages. *Love v State of New York* (1991) 78 NY2d 540, 577 NYS2d 359. However, in the case of a retrial, interest is properly awarded only from the date of the second verdict. *Gonzalez v New York* (1989, 2d Dept) 148 AD2d 668, 539 NYS2d 418, leave denied 74 NY2d 608, 545 NYS2d 104.

In an action brought by attorneys for unpaid contingent counsel fees under a written retainer agreement, because judgment was awarded by Special Term based on the retainer agreement between the parties, plaintiff was entitled to interest thereon as a matter of law. *Ash & Miller v Freedman* (1985, 1st Dept) 114 AD2d 823, 495 NYS2d 183. CPLR 5001(a) directs that interest be recovered upon a sum awarded because of a breach of performance of a contract, or because of an act or omission depriving or otherwise interfering with title to, or possession or enjoyment of property. *Ash & Miller v Freedman, supra*.

In litigation involving rival breach of contract actions by a general contractor and its subcontractor, it was within the court's discretion not to award interest on the equitable claims of the subcontractor at the prime rate, but at the statutory interest rate. *Louis N. Picciano & Son v Olympic Constr. Co.* (1985, 3d Dept) 112 AD2d 604, 492 NYS2d 476, app dismd 66 NY2d 854, 498 NYS2d 366.

Where the statutory interest rate on judgments was increased from 6% to 9%, the judgment creditor was entitled to 9% interest only from the effective date of the statute, and for the period prior thereto he was entitled to interest at 6%. *Chase Manhattan Bank, N.A. v Powell* (1985, 2d Dept) 111 AD2d 145, 489 NYS2d 5.

When a contract provides for interest to be paid at a specified rate until the principal is paid, the contract rate of interest, rather than the legal rate set forth in CPLR 5004, governs until payment of the principal or until the contract is merged in the judgment. *Citibank, N.A. v Liebowitz* (1985, 2d Dept) 110 AD2d 615, 487 NYS2d 368.

A title insurer's liability for a defect in title against which the policy insured accrued, and the plaintiff's cause of action existed, at the time the plaintiff acquired the defective title and the policy was issued; its right to interest on the judgment accordingly ran from that date. *L. Smirlock Realty Corp. v Title Guarantee Co.* (1984) 63 NY2d 955, 483 NYS2d 984.

A party is entitled to interest on an award for breach of contract, as a matter of right, from the date damages were incurred, and where damages were incurred at various times, interest should accrue from a single reasonable intermediate date; in the absence of a single reasonable intermediate date, interest should accrue from the date the action was commenced. *Hanover Data Services, Inc. v Arcata Nat. Corp.* (1985, 1st Dept) 115 AD2d 403, 496 NYS2d 34, app den 68 NY2d 602, 505 NYS2d 1027.

Although plaintiffs did not enter judgment for more than three years after the verdict was rendered, there was no requirement that interest on the verdict should be denied, because defendants were at liberty to file the judgement. *Walsh v Morris* (1987, 3d Dept) 126 AD2d 911, 511 NYS2d 428.

When a party successfully moves to set aside the jury's verdict, and the parties subsequently stipulate to a reduction in damages, interest should be measured from the date on which the motion is determined, rather than the date on which the original verdict was rendered. *Servidori v Mahoney* (1987, 3d Dept) 129 AD2d 944, 515 NYS2d 328.

Successful negligence plaintiffs are entitled only to interest from the date of the verdict, and not from the date of the accident. *Kurth v Wallkill Associates* (1987, 2d Dept) 132 AD2d 529, 517 NYS2d 267.

The right to interest is purely statutory. *Gross v Perales* (1987, 1st Dept) 133 AD2d 37, 518 NYS2d 624, app gr 70 NY2d 616, 526 NYS2d 436 and affd 72 NY2d 231, 532 NYS2d 68.

A teacher who was reinstated and held to be entitled to back pay, incurred damages at various times, to wit, each pay period during which she had not been reinstated or offered a full time teaching position. Under these circumstances, the interest was to be computed on each item from the date it was incurred or upon all of the damages from a single reasonable intermediate date. *Kohler v Board of Education* (1988, 2d Dept) 142 AD2d 676, 530 NYS2d 844, app den 74 NY2d 603, 543 NYS2d 396.

In the absence of evidence that defendant husband's failure to make support payments to the wife was in willful disregard of the judgment of divorce, the court did not err in failing to award interest and counsel fees to plaintiff. *Messina v Messina* (1988, 2d Dept) 143 AD2d 735, 533 NYS2d 298.

On a motion to confirm an arbitration award, if the award is silent on the question of pre-judgment interest, a court is not entitled to award such interest; rather, upon confirmation of an arbitrator's award, interest should be provided from the date of the award. *Gruberg v Cortell Group, Inc.* (1988, 1st Dept) 143 AD2d 39, 531 NYS2d 557.

Where a mortgagee of property sought to recover under a fire insurance policy and the fire insurer refused to pay the claim, the interest payable was properly awarded at the contract rate of 15% up to the date of entry of the order and judgment, and thereafter at the statutory rate of 9%. *Agriculver Profit Sharing Plan v Dry-*

den Mut. Ins. Co. (1988, 3d Dept) 145 AD2d 811, 535 NYS2d 797.

Where the husband in a matrimonial action engaged in what the court considered to be a significant amount of stonewalling, the former wife was awarded interest on her share of her former husband's pension funds at the legal rate, from the date of commencement of the action until the date of judgment, approximately seven years later. *Largiader v Largiader* (1989, 2d Dept) 151 AD2d 724, 542 NYS2d 789.

Where it was found that claimant was not entitled to recover damages for wrongful death, and was only entitled to recover the sum of $150,000 for those personal injuries that the decedent would have sustained if he had been wearing a seat belt, interest on the award was to be computed from the date of decision of the Court of Claims, not from the date of decedent's death. *Cappadona v State* (1989, 2d Dept) 156 AD2d 505, 548 NYS2d 778.

Where an action was brought by the estate of a deceased deckhand based on the Jones Act and General Maritime Law, and plaintiff prevailed only on the Jones Act wrongful death claim, he was not entitled to pre-judgment interest. *Haggerty v Moran Towing & Transp. Co.* (1990, 1st Dept) 162 AD2d 189, 556 NYS2d 314, 1990 AMC 2932.

In a maritime action, where the question of pre-judgment interest was not presented to the jury, the court was without authority to award it. *DiIorio v Gibson & Cushman, Inc.* (1990, 1st Dept) 167 AD2d 267, 561 NYS2d 767, app dismd 77 NY2d 986, 571 NYS2d 909 and cert den 502 US 868, 116 L Ed 2d 156, 112 S Ct 196.

The trial court did not abuse its discretion in awarding a plaintiff interest on its judgment from the day its contract cause of action accrued. *Dicini v William Hengerer Co.* (1991, 1st Dept) 171 AD2d 515, 567 NYS2d 241.

Although the creditor offered to waive the pre-judgment interest, it was within the trial court's discretion to calculate such interest and award it to the creditor. *British Land, Inc. v 43 West 61st Street Assoc.* (1991, 1st Dept) 177 AD2d 458, 576 NYS2d 554, app dismd without op 79 NY2d 1040, 584 NYS2d 449.

Adding pre-verdict interest to an award for post-verdict damages is contrary to the express purpose of wrongful death damages under EPTL § 5-4.3, which is to provide fair and just compensation for the pecuniary injuries resulting from decedent's death to persons for whose benefit the action is brought. *Milbrandt v A.P. Green Refractories Co.* (1992) 79 NY2d 26, 580 NYS2d 147. Prejudgment interest on future losses is no longer available under New York law. *Re New York City Asbestos Litig.* (1993, 1st Dept) 188 AD2d 214, 593 NYS2d 43, app gr 81 NY2d 707, 597 NYS2d 938, related proceeding (1st Dept), 194 AD2d 396, 599 NYS2d 953, app den 604 NYS2d 47.

Although General Municipal Law § 3-a(1) provides that the rate of interest on judgments and accrued claims against municipal corporations shall not exceed 9% a year, thereby setting a maximum upper limit without mandating 9% as the only rates that can be charged, Unconsolidated Law § 7401(5) provides that the rate of interest to be paid by the Health and Hospitals Corporation shall not exceed 3% per year; under the circumstances, the court was constrained to apply the 3% interest rate specifically applicable to the public corporation. *Carson v New York City Health & Hosp. Corp.* (1991, 1st Dept) 178 AD2d 265, 578 NYS2d 134.

In cases where maritime law applies, the award of pre-judgment interest is the rule, rather than the exception. *Escobar v Seatrain Lines, Inc.* (1991, 1st Dept) 175 AD2d 741, 573 NYS2d 498.

Where the judgment of the Appellate Division provided that defendants were to enter into a written stipulation whereby they consented to an increase in the verdict with respect to damages, and the defendants stipulated accordingly, plaintiffs were entitled to interest on the additional amount, computed from the date of the jury's verdict, and not from the date of the determination of the Appellate Division. *DePaolo v Wisoff* (1992, 2d Dept) 184 AD2d 745, 585 NYS2d 480.

Where the original order in a matrimonial action clearly awarded plaintiff wife $62,010 as her part of the marital assets, and no interest was awarded at the time, where no proper appeal was taken from the order, the wife was not entitled to interest on the award of marital assets. *Gerenstein v Gerenstein* (1992, 3d Dept) 188 AD2d 868, 591 NYS2d 269.

In an action on a promissory note, where the promissory note provided for interest at the rate of 10%, not 9%, interest on the award of damages attributable to the note should have been at the rate of 10%. *Hayduk v Rent-All Uniforms Co.* (1994, 1st Dept) 203 AD2d 104, 610 NYS2d 35.

In a divorce case, considering the five year duration of the action, the lack of evidence that either party engaged in deliberate delay tactics and the general lack of prejudice, the court's award of interest on the distributive award properly ran from the date of judgment rather than from the commencement of the action. *Basile v Basile* (1993, 3d Dept) 199 AD2d 649, 605 NYS2d 133.

Where the order granting plaintiff judgment was entered on November 26, 1984, and, due to law office failure, plaintiff did not enter judgment with the clerk until June 7, 1991, because of plaintiff's inordinate delay in entering judgment, interest commenced running from June 7, 1991. *Peerless Ins. Co. v Casey* (1993, 1st Dept) 194 AD2d 411, 599 NYS2d 542.

§ 34:5 ALLOWANCE OF COURT COSTS — The party in whose favor a judgment is entered is entitled to court costs, unless otherwise provided by statute, or unless the court determines that to allow costs would not be equitable under all of the circumstances. CPLR 8101. A plaintiff is not entitled to costs in an action brought in the Supreme Court in a county within the City of New York that could have been brought, except for the amount demanded, in the Civil Court of the City of New York, unless the plaintiff recovers $6,000 or more. CPLR 8102(1). Costs are not recoverable in an action brought in the Supreme Court in a county not within the City of New York, that could have been brought, except for the amount demanded, in any court of limited monetary jurisdiction in the county, unless the plaintiff recovers $500 or more. CPLR 8102(2). Nor can costs be recovered in an action brought in the county court, that could have been brought, except for the amount demanded, in any court of lesser monetary jurisdiction in the county, unless the plaintiff recovers $250 or more. CPLR 8102(3).

Because costs were unknown and not recoverable at common law, *Hayman v Morris* (1942, Sup) 37 NYS2d 884, settled 179 Misc 265, 38 NYS2d 782, costs may only be awarded pursuant to the provisions of some statute. *Conway v Bowe* (1952, Sup) 116 NYS2d 182. Costs and allowances awarded to the prevailing party belong to the client and not to the attorney. *Graham v Fisher* (1937) 251 AD 859, 297 NYS 199.

The granting or withholding of costs is discretionary with the trial court, and in the absence of a clear abuse thereof, should not be disturbed. *Govern & McDowell v McDowell & Walker, Inc.* (1980, 3d Dept) 75 AD2d 979, 428 NYS2d 367.

Where plaintiff satisfied his burden of establishing that the conduct of defendants constituted a constructive fraud, the difficult course plaintiff was forced to pursue justified an award of an additional allowance pursuant to CPLR 8303(a)(2). *Bagnall v Daharjon, Inc.* (1982, 2d Dept) 89 AD2d 612, 452 NYS2d 658.

Although the Workmen's Compensation carrier was entitled to recover a judgment against the claimant for amounts mistakenly paid to claimant, the judgment to be entered against defendant should not include interest or costs, because the error that necessitated the litigation was the plaintiff's and it would be unfair to charge defendant for it. *Liberty Mut. Ins. Co. v Newman* (1983, 2d Dept) 92 AD2d 613, 459 NYS2d 806.

It was error to award defendant costs in excess of the statutory maximum inasmuch as no request for a punitive award was made by defendant, and no reason for such award was stated by the court. *Scott v Hartford Fire Ins. Co.* (1985, 4th Dept) 115 AD2d 965, 497 NYS2d 535.

When an insurer wrongfully fails to defend, it will be held liable for reasonable legal fees incurred by the insured in defending the underlying action. *Sanabria v American Home Assurance Co.* (1985, 3d Dept) 113 AD2d 193, 495 NYS2d 533, revd on other grounds 68 NY2d 866, 508 NYS2d 416.

Although Debtor and Creditor Law § 276-a makes provision for attorneys' fees in actions or special proceedings to set aside a conveyance made with intent to defraud, it was held to be proper to deny such counsel fees to a wife who brought an action against her husband and against corporations that he controlled, and was awarded $100,000 in punitive damages, because her recovery went far beyond the mere recovery of the contingent half-interest in the corporation involved. *Keen v Keen* (1985, 3d Dept) 113 AD2d 964, 493 NYS2d 636, app dismd without op 67 NY2d 646, 499 NYS2d 683.

To recover counsel fees and punitive damages, it must be shown that malice was the gravamen of defendant's actions and that there was an intentional effort to inflict economic injury on the plaintiffs by forcing them to engage legal counsel; the damages must be shown to have been proximately related to the malicious acts, and the acts themselves must have been entirely motivated by a disinterested malevolence on defendant's part. *Brook Shopping Centers, Inc. v Bass* (1985, 1st Dept) 107 AD2d 615, 483 NYS2d 1021.

Counsel fees are not recoverable absent express statutory or contractual provisions therefor. *Hempstead General Hospital v Allstate Ins. Co.* (1984, 2d Dept) 106 AD2d 429, 482 NYS2d 523, affd 64 NY2d 958, 488 NYS2d 651. In an action against a bank to recover for money had and received, attorneys' fees were not recoverable in the absence of any allegation of malice. *Collision Plan Unlimited, Inc. v Bankers Trust Co.* (1984) 63 NY2d 827, 482 NYS2d 252.

Attorneys fees and disbursements are incidents of litigation and the prevailing party may not collect them from the loser unless an award is authorized by agreement between the parties or by a statute or court rule. *A. G. Ship Maintenance Corp. v Lezak* (1986) 69 NY2d 1, 511 NYS2d 216. Although the courts may proscribe frivolous litigation, sanctions cannot be imposed where at the time the petitioner instituted the proceedings there was neither a statute nor a court rule authorizing the imposition of sanctions for frivolous actions. *A.G. Ship Maintenance Corp. v Lezak, supra*.

The Supreme Court, which imposed sanctions of $3,000 for frivolous motion practice, lacked the inherent power to impose such sanctions, because there was no statutory provision or court rule permitting the imposition of sanctions. *Foxfire Enterprises, Inc. v Enterprise Holding Corp.* (1988, 2d Dept) 140 AD2d 581, 528 NYS2d 645.

Where it was determined that a lawsuit filed by an attorney was frivolous, the sanctions required pursuant to CPLR 8303-a are mandatory. *Mitchell v Herald Co.* (1988, 4th Dept) 137 AD2d 213, 529 NYS2d 602, app dismd without op 72 NY2d 952, 533 NYS2d 59. Where, however, it could not be said that the action of plaintiff's counsel in delaying his discontinuance of a medical malpractice action was taken in bad faith, solely to delay or prolong resolution of the litigation or harass or maliciously injure the defendant, and where it could not be said that the action was not promptly discontinued, the imposition of costs of the trial court would be vacated. *Narins v De Brovner* (1988, 1st Dept) 141 AD2d 381, 529 NYS2d 316.

An executor who brought a frivolous motion that sought to vacate a court order directing it to pay past due amounts of alimony obligations on the part of the decedent, on the asserted ground that it provided for an interlocutory judgment that could prevent a further appeal, had the effect of imposing an unnecessary burden on the judicial system. Accordingly, pursuant to Part 130 of the Rules of the Chief Administrator of the Courts, a sanction of $500 was imposed. *Hoeflich v Chemical Bank* (1989, 1st Dept) 149 AD2d 341, 539 NYS2d 916.

Before January 1, 1989, when rules were adopted that authorized the imposition of monetary sanctions for frivolous conduct in civil litigation, the court had no authority to impose sanctions against parties for what it believed to be frivolous conduct engaged in by parties in the course of jury selection, as there was at the time no statutory provision or court rule permitting such imposition. *Frerks v Iandoli* (1989, 2d Dept) 147 AD2d 672, 538 NYS2d 281.

Although the Court of Appeals has adopted new rules giving courts the discretion, in civil actions or proceedings, to award any party or attorney costs in the form of reimbursement for actual expenses reasonably incurred and reasonable attorney's fees resulting from frivolous conduct of an adversary, the rules did not take effect until January 1, 1989, and thus, at the time of petitioner's contempt motion, there was neither a statute nor a court rule authorizing the imposition of sanctions for frivolous actions, and sanctions could not be imposed. *Re Troni* (1989, 1st Dept) 147 AD2d 394, 537 NYS2d 817.

The Surrogate, who found that the beneficiary had made specious claims and baseless accusations, did not improvidently exercise his discretion in imposing a surcharge of 15% of all legal fees incurred. *Re Estate of Rappaport* (1989, 2d Dept) 150 AD2d 779, 542 NYS2d 215.

To the extent that 22 NYCRR subpart 130-1 allows for sanctions to be imposed for frivolous conduct, they are payable in the court's discretion, only through "the Clients' Security Fund" or to the "Clerk of the Court for transmittal to the Commissioner of Taxation and Finance;" therefore if sanctions, as opposed to costs, are awarded, they are not payable to respondents in the action. *Schulz v Washington County* (1990, 3d Dept) 157 AD2d 948, 550 NYS2d 446.

CPLR 8303-a, which permits imposition of costs upon frivolous claims in actions to recover damages for personal injury, injury to property or wrongful death, does not apply to an action for breach of employment agreement, which is essentially one for breach of contract. *Carver v Apple Rubber Products Corp.* (1990, 4th Dept) 163 AD2d 849, 558 NYS2d 379.

In a matrimonial action, the trial court properly denied defendant's request for sanctions pursuant to 22 NYCRR § 130-1.1, where the Appellate Division could not conclude on the record that plaintiff's cross-motion for temporary child support, counsel fees and an order preventing defendant from disposing of marital assets was frivolous. *Scheithauer v Scheithauer* (1990, 3d Dept) 162 AD2d 867, 557 NYS2d 770.

A court may, in its discretion, award costs to any party or attorney in the form of reimbursement or actual expenses reasonably incurred as a result of frivolous conduct. *Bronstein, Van Veen & Bronstein, P. C. v Taylor* (1990, 1st Dept) 161 AD2d 328, 555 NYS2d 93.

The imposition of $1,000 in sanctions pursuant to 22 NYCRR § 130 was amply justified after denial of the fifth motion in a chain reflecting a strategy of dilatory, frivolous avoidance of a 20-year-old student loan debt for two years of law school education. *Bell v New York Higher Educ. Assistance Corp.* (1990) 76

NY2d 930, 563 NYS2d 54, reh den, motion den 76 NY2d 1015, 565 NYS2d 764.

An action commenced and continued without any reasonable basis in law or fact, and without any good faith argument for an extension, modification or reversal of existing law, is frivolous, and the CPLR is mandatory in its terms: upon a determination of frivolousness, the matter must be remitted for the Supreme Court to determine the amount of costs and reasonable counsel fees, and whether they should be imposed against a plaintiff, counsel or both. *Grasso v Mathew* (1991, 3d Dept) 164 AD2d 476, 564 NYS2d 576, app dismd without op 77 NY2d 940, 569 NYS2d 613 and app den 78 NY2d 855.

Where, some 10 months after an appeal was perfected, the parties entered into a stipulation of settlement that resolved the issues raised in appellant's brief, the appellant's attorney in a subsequent communication with the Appellate Division refused to withdraw the appeal, conduct of the appellant and her attorney in maintaining the appeal after the stipulation must be characterized as frivolous because it was undertaken primarily to delay or prolong the resolution of the litigation or to harass or maliciously injure another, and accordingly the parties and their respective counsel were directed to appear before the Appellate Division to be heard on whether sanctions or costs should be imposed on the appellant and her attorney. *Leggio v Leggio* (1991, 2d Dept) 178 AD2d 513, 577 NYS2d 438.

The power to impose sanctions is part of a Housing Judge's dispute resolution authority. *Babigian v Wachtler* (1992, 1st Dept) 181 AD2d 640, 582 NYS2d 14.

Sanctions of $5,000 were imposed upon the plaintiffs and $5,000 on their attorney where the nature and repetition of plaintiffs' litigation tactics over a five-year period, resulting in four separate adjudications in the Court of Appeals, constituted a strategy of dilatory, abusive and frivolous conduct within the meaning of 22 NYCRR § 130-1.1(a) and (c). *Jason v Chusid* (1991) 78 NY2d 1099, 578 NYS2d 867.

Sanctions of $25,000 each were imposed upon the appellant and his attorney where the Court of Appeals had previously dismissed as untimely a motion by defendant for leave to appeal, and by a subsequent notice of motion, defendant moved for reargument, contending that the Court of Appeals had misapprehended the nature of the relief he sought; the subsequent motion was a frivolous one premised on a claim that the Court had mistakenly treated the initial motion as one for leave to appeal, rather than one for permission to make a motion out of time. *Intercontinental Credit Corp. Div. of Pan American Trade Dev. Corp. v Roth* (1991) 78 NY2d 306, 574 NYS2d 528.

An award of counsel fees and costs in the sum of $9,509 was warranted against a landowner who was sued by a plaintiff who sustained an injury when he slipped on a patch of ice in the landowner's parking lot and who commenced a third-party action against a contractor alleging that the contractor was responsible for the dangerous condition; the record supported the court's determination that a reasonable investigation by the landowner would have revealed that the contractor was not at fault and that the action was frivolous. *Jacobson v Chase Manhattan Bank, N.A.* (1991, 2d Dept) 174 AD2d 709, 571 NYS2d 559.

Sanctions were properly applied where plaintiff, a lessor, on three separate occasions sought to obtain a warrant of eviction, and was advised on each occasion that a warrant could not issue because the funds owed were on deposit with the court, and nevertheless sought a warrant of eviction for a fourth time. *Net Realty Holding Trust v Clerk of Dist. Court* (1992, 2d Dept) 186 AD2d 570, 588 NYS2d 373.

Where the first complaint was dismissed without leave to replead, and a second complaint was served that added nothing new of substance to distinguish it from the first, its service was frivolous and supported the award of sanctions. *Papa v Burrows* (1992, 1st Dept) 186 AD2d 375, 588 NYS2d 171, app den 81 NY2d 707, 597 NYS2d 937.

Plaintiff should have been accorded an opportunity to be heard prior to the imposition of sanctions. *Willer v 61 Jane St. Tenants Corp.* (1992, 1st Dept) 184 AD2d 225, 584 NYS2d 552.

The trial court properly granted partial summary judgment as to liability in plaintiff's favor and properly imposed a monetary sanction pursuant to CPLR 8303-a for the unjustified continuance of frivolous defenses where defendant driver admitted that

742

he momentarily took his eyes off the road and traffic ahead as he reached down to retrieve a package that had fallen off the seat, and when he looked back to the road, observing plaintiff's vehicle stopped for a red light, he was unable to stop and his vehicle struck the plaintiff's vehicle. *Aurnou v Craig* (1992, 4th Dept) 184 AD2d 1048, 584 NYS2d 249.

To the extent that the Supreme Court did not rule on the question of whether to impose sanctions, the failure to rule was deemed a denial. *State Farm Mut. Auto. Ins. Co. v Sanchez* (1994, 4th Dept) 201 AD2d 980, 607 NYS2d 838.

The refusal of the State Liquor Authority to dismiss charges against a bar owner, involving revocation of a liquor license, on the ground that the club in question had become a focal point for police activity, was not so egregious or frivolous that it warranted the imposition of sanctions. *Dawson v New York State Liquor Auth.* (1994, 3d Dept) 202 AD2d 787, 608 NYS2d 730.

Because the plaintiffs' causes of action for conversion, replevin and breach of contract were not barred by *res judicata,* collateral estoppel or any of the other numerous doctrines cited by defendants, the Supreme Court properly exercised its discretion in rejecting defendant's requests for equitable relief and an award of sanctions and attorney's fees against plaintiffs. *Miller v J. A. Keeffe, P.C.* (1993, 2d Dept) 198 AD2d 335, 604 NYS2d 571, related proceeding (2d Dept) 198 AD2d 339, 604 NYS2d 823.

An award of costs or imposition of sanctions may be upon a motion or by the court *sua sponte,* after a reasonable opportunity to be heard, but such award may only be made upon a written decision setting forth the offending conduct, why the court finds the conduct frivolous and why the amount awarded or imposed was appropriate, and it requires that the award of costs or the imposition of sanctions or both be entered as a judgment of the court. *Flaherty v Stavropoulos* (1993, 2d Dept) 199 AD2d 301, 605 NYS2d 99, motion den (2d Dept) 199 AD2d 302, 614 NYS2d 497.

§ 34:6 ALLOWANCE OF ATTORNEYS' FEES AS COSTS — It
is the general rule that attorneys' fees are incidents of litigation and a prevailing party may not collect from the loser unless an award is authorized by agreement between the parties, statute or

court rule. *Hooper Associates, Ltd. v AGS Computers, Inc.* (1989) 74 NY2d 487, 549 NYS2d 365; *Gottlieb v Kenneth D. Laub & Co.* (1993) 82 NY2d 457, 605 NYS2d 213, reconsideration den 83 NY2d 801, 611 NYS2d 136.

It was an abuse of discretion for Special Term to have awarded attorneys' fees under the guise of an additional allowance pursuant to CPLR 8303(a)(2). *Hoffliss Water Corp. v Arne* (1982, 2d Dept) 88 AD2d 989, 451 NYS2d 828.

Attorneys' fees should not be awarded by the court to the successful party, even though a principal witness for the defeated party was found by the court to have made an intentionally false statement on a material issue in an affidavit or on trial, that resulted in additional litigation expense to the successful party. *American Broadcasting Cos. v Engine Power Corp.* (1982, 1st Dept) 88 AD2d 842, 451 NYS2d 151.

Under Real Property Law § 234, when a clause contained in a residential lease allows a landlord, in an action against a tenant, to collect attorney's fees from the tenant, then a reciprocal right exists for the tenant to, in turn, collect such fees from the landlord, if the tenant is successful in an action against the landlord. *North Star Graphics, Inc. v Spitzer* (1987, 1st Dept) 135 AD2d 401, 521 NYS2d 699, app dismd without op 72 NY2d 841, 530 NYS2d 556.

A court has no inherent authority to impose attorney's fees or other monetary sanctions as a penalty for frivolous litigation; under the general rule, attorney's fees and disbursements are incidents of litigation and the prevailing party may not collect them from the loser unless an award is authorized by agreement between the parties or by statute or court rule. *Birnbaum v Birnbaum* (1987, 4th Dept) 135 AD2d 1116, 523 NYS2d 285.

In an action against a construction company that abandoned a construction project, although counsel fees were not available as an item of damage, in the absence of statutory or contractual authority, because the plaintiffs incurred legal expenses in order to re-bid the contract, attorneys' fees were recoverable expenditures directly occasioned and made necessary by the breach. *Elmira v Larry Walter, Inc.* (1989, 3d Dept) 150 AD2d 129, 546

NYS2d 183, app gr 75 NY2d 708, 554 NYS2d 833 and app den 75 NY2d 708, 554 NYS2d 833.

While counsel fees are not generally available as an item of damage in the absence of statutory and contractual authority, the trial court properly awarded attorneys' fees incurred by the plaintiff, a lessee of a parking garage, in obtaining a certificate of occupancy as an element of compensatory damages; these legal expenses were incurred by plaintiff in attempting by itself to fulfill defendants' obligations under the contract and were directly occasioned and made necessary by defendants' breach. *Aero Garage Corp. v Hirschfeld* (1992, 1st Dept) 185 AD2d 775, 586 NYS2d 611, app den 81 NY2d 701, 594 NYS2d 715.

§ 34:7   RELIEF FROM JUDGMENT OR ORDER — The court that rendered a judgment or order may relieve a party from it upon such terms as may be just, on a motion made by any interested person with such notice as the court may direct. CPLR 5015(a). The motion may be made on the grounds of: excusable default, if such motion is made within one year after service of a copy of the judgment or order with written notice of its entry upon the moving party, or if the moving party has entered a judgment or order, within one year after such entry, CPLR 5015(a)(1); newly discovered evidence which, if introduced at the trial, would probably have produced a different result and which could not have been discovered in time to move for a new trial under CPLR 4404, CPLR 5015(a)(2); upon the ground of fraud, misrepresentation, or other misconduct of an adverse party, CPLR 5015(a)(3); lack of jurisdiction to enter the judgment or order, CPLR 5015(a)(4); or reversal, modification or *vacatur* of a prior judgment or order upon which it is based. CPLR 5015(a)(5).

When a judgment or order is set aside, the court may direct and enforce restitution in a like manner and subject to the same conditions as when a judgment is reversed or modified on appeal. CPLR 5015(d).

RESEARCH REFERENCES

American Law Reports

14 ALR5th 557, Death of obligor parent as affecting decree for support of child

5 ALR5th 863, Authority of court, upon entering default judgment, to make orders for child custody or support which were not specifically requested in pleadings of prevailing party

5 ALR5th 422, Filing of notice of appeal as affecting jurisdiction of state trial court to consider motion to vacate judgment

4 ALR5th 753, Comparative negligence: judgment allocating fault in action against less than all potential defendants as precluding subsequent action against parties not sued in original action

3 ALR5th 237, Dismissal of state court action for plaintiffs failure or refusal to obey court order relating to pleadings or parties

80 ALR4th 707, Modern status of state court rules governing entry of judgment on multiple claims

73 ALR4th 938, Attorneys' fees: cost of services provided by paralegals or the like as compensable element of award in state court

68 ALR4th 343, Validity of law or rule requiring state court party who requests jury trial in civil case to pay costs associated with jury

53 ALR4th 414, Attorneys' fees in products liability suits

34 ALR4th 665, Priority between attorney's lien for fees against a judgment and lien of creditor against same judgment

31 ALR4th 706, Validity, construction, and application of Uniform Enforcement of Foreign Judgments Act

13 ALR4th 1109, Judgment of court of foreign country as entitled to enforcement or extraterritorial effect in state court

82 ALR3d 1199, Right of judgment creditor to demand that debtor's tender of payment be in cash or by certified check rather than by uncertified check

78 ALR3d 1119, Right of party who is attorney and appears for himself to award of attorney's fees against opposing party as element of costs

75 ALR3d 894, Right to a jury trial on motion to vacate judgment

ALR QUICK INDEX: Costs of Actions; Interest on Money; Judgments

American Jurisprudence 2d

46, 47 Am Jur 2d, Judgments §§ 1 et seq.

American Jurisprudence Pleading and Practice

15 Am Jur Pl & Pr Forms (Rev), Judgments, Forms 1 et seq.

American Jurisprudence Proof of Facts

24 Am Jur Proof of Facts 2d 705, "Excusable Neglect" Warranting Relief from Default Judgment

Other Resources

8, 9 Carmody-Wait 2d, Judgments §§ 63:1 et seq.

Auto-Cite®: Any case citation herein can be checked for form, parallel references, later history and annotation references through the Auto-Cite computer research system.

TABLE OF CASES

TABLE OF CASES

TABLE OF CASES

752

TABLE OF CASES

TABLE OF CASES

757

758

TABLE OF CASES

Chase Manhattan Bank, Nat'l Ass'n v
Federal Chandros, Inc. (1989, 2d
Dept) 148 AD2d 567, 539 NYS2d 36
13:12

Chen Yan Kao v Wang (1983, 2d Dept)
98 AD2d 709, 469 NYS2d 109 **33:2**

Cherney v Board of Education (1969,
2d Dept) 31 AD2d 764, 297 NYS2d
668 **24:1**

Cherno v Bank of Babylon (1967) 54
Misc 2d 277, 282 NYS2d 114, 4
UCCRS 505, affd (2d Dept) 29 AD2d
767, 288 NYS2d 862 **29:8**

Chertok v Effremoff (1929) 226 AD
388, 235 NYS 246, affd 253 NY 523,
171 NE 765 **1:1**

Chiesa v State (1974, 3d Dept) 43
AD2d 359, 351 NYS2d 735, affd 36
NY2d 21, 364 NYS2d 848 **29:22**

Chisholm v Eisenhuth (1902) 69 AD
134, 74 NYS 496 **25:5**

Chisholm v Mobil Oil Corp. (1974, 3d
Dept) 45 AD2d 776, 356 NYS2d 699
18:5

Chmielewski v Rosetti (1969) 59 Misc
2d 335, 298 NYS2d 875 **13:5**

Chong v New York City Transit
Authority (1981, 2d Dept) 83 AD2d
546, 441 NYS2d 24 **29:19**

Christian v New York City Transit
Authority (1980, 1st Dept) 74 AD2d
751, 425 NYS2d 586, affd 52 NY2d
920, 437 NYS2d 663 **7:4**

Christie v Mitchell (1960, 4th Dept) 10
AD2d 52, 197 NYS2d 206 **13:1**

Christopher v Great Atlantic & Pacific
Tea Co. (1990, AD 1st Dept) 161
Ad2d 274, 554 NYS2d 908, app
dismd 76 NY2d 1006,564 NYS2d
716 **31:6**

Cid v Bombardier Ltd. (1983, 1st Dept)
91 AD2d 913, 457 NYS2d 538 **33:2**

Cirasuolo v Cahill (1986, 4th Dept)
119 AD2d 986, 500 NYS2d 881 **33:8**

Cirino v St. John (1989, 3d Dept) 146
AD2d 912, 536 NYS2d 901 **2:2**

Citarella v Equitable Life Assurance
Soc. (1945, App Term) 59 NYS2d
215 **22:16**

Citibank Eastern, N.A. v Minbiole
(1975, 3d Dept) 50 AD2d 1052, 377

NYS2d 727 **25:16**

Citibank, N.A. v Liebowitz (1985, 2d
Dept) 110 AD2d 615, 487 NYS2d
368 **34:4**

City of New York v Estate of Levine
(1993, 2d Dept) 196 AD2d 654, 601
NYS2d 620, app dismd without op 84
NY2d 864, 618 NYS2d 8 **29:22**

Civil Service Employees Asso. v
Ontario County Health Facility
(1984, 4th Dept) 103 AD2d 1000,
478 NYS2d 380, later proceeding
(4th Dept) 103 AD2d 1001, 478
NYS2d 583, app dismd 64 NY2d
816, 486 NYS2d 926 **16:6**

Clark v Brooklyn H. R. Co. (1904) 177
NY 359, 69 NE 647 **19:2, 19:12**

Clark v Douglass (1896) 5 AD 547, 40
NYS 769 **22:25**

Clark v Iceland S.S. Co. (1958, 1st
Dept) 6 AD2d 544, 179 NYS2d 708,
reh and app den (1st Dept) 7 AD 837,
182 NYS2d 295 **22:4**

Clark v Rysedorph (1953) 281 AD 121,
118 NYS2d 103 **19:13**

Clark v Standard Rock Asphalt Corp.
(1931) 233 AD 536, 253 NYS 730,
affd (1932) 259 NY 595, 182 NE 195
7:8

Clark v State (1986, 3d Dept) 124
AD2d 879, 508 NYS2d 648 **28:6**

Clarke v New York City Transit
Authority (1992, 1st Dept) 174 AD2d
268, 580 NYS2d 221 **7:4**

Clarke v New York City Transit
Authority (1992, 1st Dept) 174 AD2d
268, 580 NYS2d 221 **23:10**

Clarke v New York City Transit
Authority (1992, 1st Dept) 174 AD2d
268, 580 NYS2d 221 **26:2**

Clarke v New York City Transit
Authority (1992, 1st Dept) 174 AD2d
268, 580 NYS2d 221 **31:6**

Clearview Concrete Products Corp. v S.
Charles Gherardi, Inc. (1982, 2d
Dept) 88 AD2d 461, 453 NYS2d 750
29:3

Cleary v John M. Maris Co. (1940) 173
Misc 954, 19 NYS2d 38 **17:6**

Clegg v Metropolitan S. R. Co. (1896) 1
AD 207, 37 NYS 130, affd 159 NY
550, 54 NE 1089 **19:11**

762

TABLE OF CASES

763

TABLE OF CASES

765

TABLE OF CASES

TABLE OF CASES

767

TABLE OF CASES

Diers v Heckelman (1958) 16 Misc 2d 872, 181 NYS2d 722, affd (2d Dept) 12 AD2d 952, 212 NYS2d 1010, app den 13 AD2d 799, 217 NYS2d 533 **12:2**

DiIorio v Gibson & Cushman, Inc. (1990, 1st Dept) 167 AD2d 267, 561 NYS2d 767, app dismd 77 NY2d 986, 571 NYS2d 909 and cert den 502 US 868, 116 L Ed 2d 156, 112 S Ct 196 **34:4**

Dillenbeck v Hess (1989) 73 NY2d 278, 539 NYS2d 707 **16:10**

DiMichel v South Buffalo Ry. Co. (1992) 80 NY2d 184, 590NYS2d 1, reconsideration den 81 NY2d 835, 595 NYS2d 397 and cert den (US) 126 L Ed 2d 37, 114 S Ct 68 **30:8**

Dimitroff v State (1939) 171 Misc 635, 13 NYS2d 458 **29:19**

Diodato v Rosetti (1959) 19 Misc 2d 780, 195 NYS2d 865 **14:8**

DiPasquale v Baker-Roos, Inc. (1989, 4th Dept) 156 AD2d 941, 548 NYS2d 827 **5:2**

Dirsa v Martuscello (1980, 3d Dept) 76 AD2d 1020, 429 NYS2d 483 **33:1**

Diston v Loucks (1941, Sup) 62 NYS2d 138, affd 264 AD 758, 35 NYS2d 715, app den 264 AD 838, 35 NYS2d 763 **13:2**

Dittmar Explosives, Inc. v A. E. Ottaviano, Inc. (1967) 20 NY2d 498, 285 NYS2d 55 **28:4**

Dixson v State (1968, 3d Dept) 30 AD2d 626, 290 NYS2d 682 **24:1**

Dlugosz v Exchange Mut. Ins. Co. (1991, 3d Dept) 176 AD2d 1011, 574 NYS2d 864 **24:1**

Dobro v Sloan (1975, 4th Dept) 48 AD2d 243, 368 NYS2d 621, app dismd 37 NY2d 804, 375 NYS2d 569 **29:19**

Dodge v Gallatin (1891) 130 NY 117, 29 NE 107 **21:13**

Doheny v Lacy (1901) 168 NY 213, 61 NE 255 **7:1**

Dolan v United Casualty Co. (1940) 259 AD 784, 18 NYS2d 387 **23:1**

Dole v Dow Chemical Co. (1972) 30 NY2d 143, 331 NYS2d 382, 53 ALR3d 175 **10:4, 33:1, 33:2**

Domermuth Petroleum Equipment & Maintenance Corp. v Herzog & Hopkins, Inc. (1985, 3d Dept) 111 AD2d 957, 490 NYS2d 54 **17:6**

Domestic Finance Corp. v Tinney Cadillac Corp. (1960) 23 Misc 2d 153, 197 NYS2d 693 **12:9**

Dominguez v Manhattan & Bronx Surface Transit Operating Authority (1979) 46 NY2d 528, 415 NYS2d 6341, on remand (1st Dept) 71 AD2d 555, 418 NYS2d 411 **10:4, 33:3**

Donaldson v Kilgore (1992, 4th Dept) 187 AD2d 1018, 590 NYS2d 364 **31:6**

Donnelly v United States (1913) 228 US 243, 57 L Ed 820, 33 S Ct 449, reh den 228 US 708, 57 L Ed 1035, 33 S Ct 1024 **23:1**

Donohue v Walter (1989, 1st Dept) 156 AD2d 149, 548 NYS2d 435, app den 75 NY2d 710, 556 NYS2d 532 **29:12**

Dontas v New York (1992, 2d Dept) 183 AD2d 868, 584 NYS2d 134 **29:19**

Dooley v Skodnek (1988, 2d Dept) 138 AD2d 102, 529 NYS2d 569 **28:3, 29:12**

Doolittle v T.E. Conklin Brass & Copper Co. (1984, 1st Dept) 103 AD2d 722, 478 NYS2d 625 **31:7**

Dore v Long I. R. R. Co. (1965, 2d Dept) 23 AD2d 502, 256 NYS2d 425 **33:1, 33:8**

Dorkin v Spodek (1994, 2d Dept) 201 AD2d 529, 607 NYS2d 951 **2:2**

Dorman v Broadway R. Co. (1889, City Ct) 5 NYS 769, revd on other grounds 117 NY 655, 23 NE 162 **4:2**

Dougherty v Braddock Automatic Music Corp. (1950) 277 AD 923, 98 NYS2d 514 **22:5**

Dougherty v Milliken (1900) 163 NY 527, 57 NE 757 **22:3**

Dougherty v Rye (1984) 63 NY2d 989, 483 NYS2d 999 **18:14**

Douglas v Adel (1935) 269 NY 144, 199 NE 35, remittitur den (1936) 271 NY 528 **3:4**

Douglas v Tomkins Realty Corp. (1960) 28 Misc 2d 192, 210 NYS2d 550 **29:8**

Douglass v Gibson (1995, 3d Dept) ___ AD2d ___, 630 NYS2d 401 **22:19**

769

770

TABLE OF CASES

Evans v Newark-Wayne Community
Hospital, Inc. (1970, 4th Dept) 35
AD2d 1071, 316 NYS2d 447 **1:1**

Evens v Denny's, Inc, (1985) 129 Misc
2d 767, 494 NYS2d 67 **25:15**

F

F. A. MacCluer, Inc. v Distribuidores
Industriales S. De R. L. (1947) 271
AD 987, 68 NYS2d 349 **28:2**

F. W. Woolworth Co. v Southbridge
Towers, Inc. (1984, 1st Dept) 101
AD2d 434, 476 NYS2d 299 **33:2**

Facci v General Elec. Co. (1993, 3d
Dept) 192 AD2d 991, 596 NYS2d
928 **25:5**

Fafard v Ajamian (1978, 2d Dept) 60
AD2d 853, 400 NYS2d 856 **29:5**

Fagan v Atlantic C. L. R. Co. (1917)
220 NY 301, 115 NE 704 **25:1**

Fagan v Pathe Industries, Inc. (1949)
274 AD 703, 86 NYS2d 859 **29:21**

Fahey v South Nassau Communities
Hospital (1950) 197 Misc 490, 95
NYS2d 842, affd 277 AD 774, 97
NYS2d 711 **33:11**

Fairchild v Union Ferry Co. (1923) 121
Misc 513, 201 NYS 295, affd 212 AD
823, 207 NYS 835, affd 240 NY 666,
148 NE 750 **21:13, 23:19**

Falcone v EDO Corp. (1988, 2d Dept)
141 AD2d 498, 529 NYS2d 123 **24:2**

Falcone v Joint Legislative Committee
(1957) 8 Misc 2d 693, 168 NYS2d
543 **9:4**

Fallon v American Sugar Refining Co.
(1953) 282 AD 910, 124 NYS2d 897
14:6

Fallon v Damianos (1993, 2d Dept)
192 AD2d 576, 596 NYS2d 134, app
den 83 NY2d 751, 611 NYS2d 133
33:9

Fallon v Mertz (1906) 110 AD 755, 97
NYS 417 **31:3**

Farina v Nastasi (1991, 2d Dept) 173
AD2d 520, 570 NYS2d 121 **24:2**

Farkas v Farkas (1965) 47 Misc 2d
827, 263 NYS2d 214 **2:7**

Farkas v Saary (1993, 1st Dept) 191
AD2d 178, 594 NYS2d 195 **22:19**

Farley v Patterson (1915) 166 AD 358,

152 NYS 59 **24:6**

Farmer v A & T Bus Co. (1983, 1st
Dept) 96 AD2d 783, 466 NYS2d 8
32:7

Farmer v Schneider (1945) 269 AD
1043, 58 NYS2d 587 **18:11**

Farmers' Loan & Trust Co. v Siefke
(1895) 144 NY 354, 39 NE 358 **31:8**

Farrar v Brooklyn Union Gas Co.
(1988) 73 NY2d 802, 537 NYS2d 26
29:19

Farrell v Labarbera (1992, 2d Dept)
181 AD2d 715, 581 NYS2d 226 **31:6**

Farrell v Lavine (1962) 37 Misc 2d
497, 236 NYS2d 323 **2:3, 28:2**

Farrell v Manhattan R. Co. (1903) 83
AD 393, 82 NYS 334, affd 178 NY
596, 70 NE 1098 **22:11**

Fasolino v Charming Stores, Inc.
(1991) 77 NY2d 847, 567 NYS2d
640 **7:3**

Fassett v Fassett (1984, 3d Dept) 101
AD2d 604, 475 NYS2d 154 **22:12**

Fata v Troyanos (1978, 2d Dept) 61
AD2d 828, 402 NYS2d 226 **25:16**

Feaster v New York City Transit
Authority (1991, 1st Dept) 172 AD2d
284, 568 NYS2d 380 **13:2, 22:33, 25:5**

Feblot v New York Times Co. (1973)
32 NY2d 486, 346 NYS2d 256, 63
ALR3d 881 **15:2**

Federal Brush Corp. v A. Zerega's Sons,
Inc. (1956, Co Ct) 149 NYS2d 374
25:16

Federal Chandros, Inc. v Silverite Constr. Co. (1990, 1st Dept) 167 AD2d
315, 562 NYS2d 64, app den 77
NY2d 893, 568 NYS2d 910 **13:16**

Federal Deposit Ins. Corp. v Salesmen
Unlimited Agency Corp.(1984, 2d
Dept) 101 AD2d 876, 475 NYS2d
1020, later proceeding (2d Dept) 101
AD2d 877, 475 NYS2d 1023 **3:5**

Feeley v Midas Properties, Inc. (1989,
2d Dept) 154 AD2d 505, 546 NYS2d
131 **28:3**

Feiden v Feiden (1989, 3d Dept) 151
AD2d 889, 542 NYS2d 860 **18:11**

Feinberg v Saks & Co. (1981, 2d Dept)
83 AD2d 952, 443 NYS2d 26, mod
56 NY2d 206, 451 NYS2d 677 **33:1**

TABLE OF CASES

TABLE OF CASES

TABLE OF CASES

TABLE OF CASES

TABLE OF CASES

Leib v Paparo (1981, 2d Dept) 84
AD2d 538, 443 NYS2d 98 **18:11**

Leighty v Brunn (1986, 2d Dept) 125
AD2d 648, 510 NYS2d 174 **29:1**

*Leiman v Long Island Jewish Hillside
Medical Center-South Shore Div.*
(1978, 2d Dept) 60 AD2d 908, 401
NYS2d 562 **22:18**

Leisman v Leisman (1994, 2d Dept)
208 AD2d 688, 617 NYS2d807 **16:5,
16:6**

Lemlich v Lemlich (1943) 266 AD 748,
41 NYS2d 81, app den 266 AD 787,
41 NYS2d 955 **12:1**

Leonard v Home Owners' Loan Corp.
(1946) 270 AD 363, 270 AD 785,
270 AD 867, 60 NYS2d 78, affd 297
NY 103 **13:2, 14:10**

Leone v Columbia Sussex Corp. (1994,
2d Dept) 203 AD2d 430, 610 NYS2d
586 **8:6**

Leone v Utica (1979, 4th Dept) 66
AD2d 463, 414 NYS2d 412, affd 49
NY2d 811, 426 NYS2d 980 **33:3**

Leonick v New York (1986, AD, 2d
Dept) 120 AD2d 573, 502 NYS2d 60
23:10

Leotta v Plessinger (1960) 8 NY2d 449,
209 NYS2d 304, remittitur amd 9
NY2d 686, 212 NYS2d 421 **25:12, 30:9**

Lerche v Brasher (1887) 104 NY 157,
10 NE 58 **12:3**

Lerner v Karageorgis Lines, Inc. (1985)
66 NY2d 479, 497 NYS2d 894 **17:2**

Lese v Lamprecht (1909) 196 NY 32,
89 NE 365 **25:16**

Lesniak v Chant (1957, 4th Dept) 4
AD2d 1007, 167 NYS2d 767 **29:1**

Lesocovich v 180 Madison Ave. Corp.
(1990, 3d Dept) 165 AD2d 963, 561
NYS2d 851, app den 77 NY2d 804,
568 NYS2d 912 **29:20**

Lessler v De Loynes (1912) 150 AD
868, 135 NYS 948, adhered to 153
AD 903, 138 NYS 503, affd 215 NY
745, 109 NE 1082 **26:4**

Levande v Dines (1989, 2d Dept) 153
AD2d 671, 544 NYS2d 864 **31:6**

Levatino v Rochester Sav. Bank (1942,
Sup) 38 NYS2d 182 **25:12, 27:4**

Levenson v Commonwealth Syndicate,

Inc. (1940, App Term) 24 NYS2d
781 **13:8**

Levin v Russell (1870) 42 NY 251 **26:4**

Levine v Joseph (1983, 2d Dept) 98
AD2d 712, 469 NYS2d 113 **34:4**

Levine v Levine (1981, 2d Dept) 83
AD2d 606, 441 NYS2d 299, revd 56
NY2d 42, 451 NYS2d 26 **9:6**

Levine v Morris (1990, 1st Dept) 157
AD2d 567, 550 NYS2d 289 **16:10**

Levine v Ross (1966) 25 AD2d 718,
269 NYS2d 682 **1:4, 18:8**

Levine v Threshman (1982, 3d Dept)
91 AD2d 789, 458 NYS2d 75 **23:11**

Levins v Bucholtz (1956, 1st Dept) 2
AD2d 351, 155 NYS2d 770 **23:4**

Levinson v Zipkin (1909) 65 Misc 203,
119 NYS 680 **32:8**

Levy v Bronx County Carting Co.
(1991, 1st Dept) 172 AD2d 356, 568
NYS2d 774 **29:8**

Levy v Corn (1920) 191 AD 56, 180
NYS 794 **32:5**

Lewis v Hynes (1975) 82 Misc 2d 256,
368 NYS2d 738, affd (2dDept) 51
AD2d 550, 379 NYS2d 374 **16:2**

*Lewis v New York City Housing
Authority* (1989, 1st Dept) 151 AD2d
237, 542 NYS2d 165, app den 75
NY2d 705, 552 NYS2d 927 **16:12**

Ley v State (1967, 3d Dept) 28 AD2d
943, 281 NYS2d 685, affd 25 NY2d
876, 303 NYS2d 887 **22:15**

Liberto v Worcester Mut. Ins. Co.
(1982, 2d Dept) 87 AD2d 477, 452
NYS2d 74 **25:10**

Liberty Mut. Ins. Co. v Newman
(1983, 2d Dept) 92 AD2d 613, 459
NYS2d 806 **34:5**

*Liberty Pipe & Boiler Covering Co. v
Zichlin & Fischer, Inc.* (1953, App
Tm) 127 NYS2d 83 **25:16**

Liddy v Frome (1981, 2d Dept) 85
AD2d 716, 445 NYS2d 841 **26:2**

Liebgott v City of New York (1995, 2d
Dept) 213 AD2d 606, 624 NYS2d
252 **31:5**

Liebman v County of Westchester
(1972) 71 Misc 2d 997, 337 NYS2d
164, revd (2d Dept) 41 AD2d 756,
341 NYS2d 567 **33:1**

793

TABLE OF CASES

Lopez v Yannotti (1965, 2d Dept) 24 AD2d 758, 263 NYS2d 523, motion to dismiss app den 17 NY2d 577, 268 NYS2d 334 and app dismd 17 NY2d 787, 270 NYS2d 637 **22:10**

Loschiavo v Port Authority of New York & New Jersey (1982, 2d Dept) 86 AD2d 624, 446 NYS2d 358, affd 58 NY2d 1040, 462 NYS2d 440 **23:20**

Loschiavo v Port Authority of New York & New Jersey (1983)58 NY2d 1040, 462 NYS2d 440 **24:2**

Losei Realty Corp. v New York (1930) 254 NY 41, 171 NE 899 **29:11**

Loughlin v Brassil (1907) 187 NY 128, 79 NE 854 **4:10**

Loughman v A.W. Flint Co. (1987, 1st Dept) 132 AD2d 507, 518 NYS2d 389, app den 70 NY2d 613, 524 NYS2d 432. **2:6**

Louis N. Picciano & Son v Olympic Constr. Co. (1985, 3d Dept) 112 AD2d 604, 492 NYS2d 476, app dismd 66 NY2d 854, 498 NYS2d 366 **34:4**

Love v State of New York (1991) 78 NY2d 540, 577 NYS2d 359 **34:4**

Lowe v State (1993, 3d Dept) 194 AD2d 898, 599 NYS2d 639 **29:12**

Lubin v One Gramercy Park, Inc. (1955, App Tm) 142 NYS2d 734 **22:16**

Luby v Hudson R. R. Co. (1858) 17 NY 131 **23:20**

Lucas v New York City Transit Authority (1990, 1st Dept) 163 AD2d 21, 557 NYS2d 919, app dismd 76 NY2d 933, 563 NYS2d 58 and app den 77 NY2d 807, 569 NYS2d 611 **29:12**

Luce v St. Peter's Hospital (1982, 3d Dept) 85 AD2d 194, 448 NYS2d 855 **14:3**

Lucisano v Paratore (1949) 195 Misc 45, 88 NYS2d 715, affd 198 Misc 193, 98 NYS2d 608 **25:7**

Lucivero v Long Island R. Co. (1960) 22 Misc 2d 674, 200 NYS2d 728 **29:19**

Ludlow's Sand & Gravel Co. v La Bella (1974) 80 Misc 2d 997, 364 NYS2d 669 **18:14**

Ludmerer v New York Life Ins. Co. (1940, Sup) 19 NYS2d 272 **24:9**

Lundgren v McColgin (1983, 4th Dept) 96 AD2d 706, 464 NYS2d 317, later proceeding (4th Dept) 96 AD2d 707, 464 NYS2d 701 and later proceeding (4th Dept) 96 AD2d 707, 464 NYS2d 701 **33:9**

Lunney v Graham (1982, 1st Dept) 91 AD2d 592, 457 NYS2d 282 **1:3**

Luppino v Busher (1986, 2d Dept) 119 AD2d 554, 500 NYS2d 557 **33:12**

Lusenskas v Axelrod (1992, 1st Dept) 183 AD2d 244, 592 NYS2d 685, app dismd, motion dismd 81 NY2d 300, 598 NYS2d 166 **7:3**

Lyman v Fidelity & Casualty Co. (1901) 65 AD 27, 72 NYS 498 **5:3**

Lynch v Figge (1922) 200 AD 92, 192 NYS 873 **31:6**

Lynch v Lynch (1986, 4th Dept) 122 AD2d 572, 505 NYS2d 739 **8:5**

Lynn v Lynn (1995, 1st Dept) ___ AD2d ___, 628 NYS2d 667 **7:4**

Lyon v Ricker (1894) 141 NY 225, 36 NE 189 **12:8**

Lyons v New York (1968, 1st Dept) 29 AD2d 923, 289 NYS2d 2,motion gr 23 NY2d 736, 296 NYS2d 567 and affd 25 NY2d 996, 305 NYS2d 509 **30:6**, **30:11**

M

M. S. R. Associates, Ltd. v Consolidated Mut. Ins. Co. (1977, 2d Dept) 58 AD2d 858, 396 NYS2d 684 **29:8**

M. Schottenfeld & Sons, Inc. v Kasabali (1956) 5 Misc 2d 562, 158 NYS2d 814 **6:4**

M. Viaggio & Sons, Inc. v New York (1985, 2d Dept) 114 AD2d 939, 495 NYS2d 680 **29:4**

M.C.D. Carbone, Inc. v Bedford (1983, 2d Dept) 98 AD2d 714, 469 NYS2d 117 **34:4**

MacArthur v Coxon Real Estate, Inc. (1967, 3d Dept) 28 AD2d 1191, 284 NYS2d 560 **29:16**

MacCormack v Brooklyn & Queens Transit Corp. (1943) 266 AD 735, 40 NYS2d 718 **6:4**

TABLE OF CASES

TABLE OF CASES

TABLE OF CASES

TABLE OF CASES

TABLE OF CASES

803

TABLE OF CASES

Pedro v Burns (1994, 3d Dept) 210 AD2d 782, 620 NYS2d 524 **23:2**

Peerless Ins. Co. v Casey (1993, 1st Dept) 194 AD2d 411, 599 NYS2d 542 **34:4**

Peerless Ins. Co. v Milloul (1988, 2d Dept) 140 AD2d 346, 527 NYS2d 838 **21:1**, **23:12**

Pekar v Tax (1974, 2d Dept) 43 AD2d 957, 352 NYS2d 39 **2:3**, **23:13**

Pellegrino v New York City Transit Authority (1991, 2d Dept) 177 AD2d 554, 576 NYS2d 154 **24:10**

Pellegrino v Walker Theatre, Inc. (1987, 2d Dept) 127 AD2d 574, 511 NYS2d 372 **8:6**

Pelletier v Brown Bros. Chevrolet & Oldsmobile, Inc. (1956, Sup) 164 NYS2d 249 **17:6**

Penn-Dixie Industries, Inc. v Castle (1980, 1st Dept) 77 AD2d 844, 431 NYS2d 34 **3:4**

Penn Yan Urban Renewal Agency v Penn Yan Realty Corp. (1968) 57 Misc 2d 1033, 294 NYS2d 66 **29:11**

Penrose v Arrow Constr. Co. (1958) 15 Misc 2d 512, 182 NYS2d 642 **29:17**

People ex rel. Barnes v Court of Sessions (1895) 147 NY 290, 41 NE 700 **3:4**

People ex rel. Blake v Charger (1974) 76 Misc 2d 577, 351 NYS2d 322 **12:1**

People ex rel. Bruckner v Wyner (1955) 207 Misc 673, 142 NYS2d 393 **21:1**, **21:3**

People ex rel. Choate v Barrett (1890) 56 Hun 351, 9 NYS 321, affd 121 NY 678, 24 NE 1095. **3:5**, **32:8**

People ex rel. Dailey v Livingston (1879) 79 NY 279 **31:5**

People ex rel. Davis v Sturtevant (1853) 9 NY 263 **3:5**

People ex rel. Hughes v Capoccia (1980, 3d Dept) 76 AD2d 1024, 429 NYS2d 494 **3:5**

People ex rel. McKinney v Richter (1943) 182 Misc 96, 43 NYS2d 114 **13:14**

People ex rel. Mooney v Sheriff of New York County (1936) 269 NY 291, 199 NE 415, 102 ALR 769 **16:1**, **16:15**

People ex rel. Munsell v Court of Oyer & Terminer (1886) 101 NY 245, 4 NE 259 **3:2**

People ex rel. Phelps v Court of Oyer & Terminer (1881) 83 NY 436 **6:2**

People ex rel. Quinlivan v Mendel (1960, 3d Dept) 10 AD2d 767, 197 NYS2d 484, app den (3d Dept) 11 AD2d 605, 204 NYS2d 110, reh and app den (3d Dept) 11 AD2d 962, 207 NYS2d 250 **24:1**

People ex rel. Roache v Hanbury (1914) 162 AD 337, 147 NYS 851 **3:4**

People ex rel. Rubin v Tax Com. of New York (1959, 3d Dept) 9 AD2d 47, 189 NYS2d 784, affd 8 NY2d 922, 204 NYS2d 165 **17:6**

People ex rel. Sassower v Sheriff of Suffolk County (1987, 2d Dept) 134 AD2d 641, 521 NYS2d 536 **3:3**

People ex rel. Walker v New York State Board of Parole (1983, 2d Dept) 98 AD2d 33, 469 NYS2d 780 **23:4**

People ex rel. Wallington Apartments, Inc. v Miller (1942) 288 NY 31, 141 ALR 1036, reh den 288 NY 672 **18:1**

People ex rel. Watchtower Bible & Tract Soc. v Mastin (1948) 191 Misc 899, 80 NYS2d 323 **7:2**

People ex rel. Woronoff v Mallon (1918) 222 NY 456, 119 NE 102, 4 ALR 463 **18:1**

People v Allen (1993, 3d Dept) 199 AD2d 781, 605 NYS2d 503, revd on other grounds (1995) 86 NY2d 101, 629 NYS2d 1003 **4:7**

People v Allman (1973, 2d Dept) 41 AD2d 325, 342 NYS2d 896 **16:3**

People v Anderson (1986, 1st Dept) 118 AD2d 488, 500 NYS2d 2 **4:14**

People v Arnette (1983) 58 NY2d 1104, 462 NYS2d 817 **3:5**

People v Bailey (1990, 3d Dept) 159 AD2d 862, 553 NYS2d 512 **14:3**

People v Bailey (1993, 2d Dept) 193 AD2d 689, 598 NYS2d 33, app den 81 NY2d 1069, 601 NYS2d 589 **15:1**

People v Beard (1993, 2d Dept) 197 AD2d 582, 602 NYS2d 430, app den 82 NY2d 891, 610 NYS2d 158 **16:3**

807

TABLE OF CASES

TABLE OF CASES

815

TABLE OF CASES

TABLE OF CASES

Re Public Beach (1936) 248 AD 902, 290 NYS 635, affd 274 NY 536 **29:22**

Re Public Beach at Rockaway Beach (1942) 288 NY 75 **29:22**

Re Purdy's Will (1947, Sur) 73 NYS2d 38, mod 275 AD 786, 88 NYS2d 2, affd 300 NY 688 **25:14**

Re Quintard Street & Additional Lands (1975, 2d Dept) 47 AD2d 644, 363 NYS2d 962 **29:22**

Re Radley's Will (1930) 228 AD 119, 239 NYS 44 **12:3**

Re Radus (1988, 2d Dept) 140 AD2d 348, 527 NYS2d 840 **12:8**

Re Reif's Will (1941, Sur Ct) 30 NYS2d 47 **25:16**

Re Rinchiuso's Estate (1964, 4th Dept) 20 AD2d 254, 246 NYS2d 798, affd 15 NY2d 865, 258 NYS2d 108 **23:22**

Re Rogers' Will (1937) 250 AD 26, 293 NYS 626 **18:12**

Re Saxe's Estate (1948, Sur) 82 NYS2d 738 **7:5**

Re Schlossman's Adm'x (1930) 136 Misc 893, 242 NYS 417 **13:2**

Re Seaman's Will (1949) 275 AD 484, 90 NYS2d 336, affd 300 NY 756 **21:3**

Re Seventh Judicial Dist. Asbestos Litig. (1993, 4th Dept) 190 AD2d 1068, 593 NYS2d 685 **29:8**

Re Seymour (1920) 113 Misc 421, 185 NYS 373 **18:9**

Re Shapolsky (1959, 1st Dept) 8 AD2d 122, 185 NYS2d 639 **3:5**

Re Shepard's Estate (1939) 257 AD 1031, 13 NYS2d 679, reh den 258 AD 779, 14 NYS2d 1010 **7:5**

Re Shirley C. (1987) 136 Misc 2d 843, 519 NYS2d 328 **17:6**

Re Site for City-Aided Low-Rent Housing Project, etc. (1949) 197 Misc 70, 89 NYS2d 855 **29:22**

Re Steinberg (1986, 1st Dept) 121 AD2d 872, 503 NYS2d 795 **22:19**

Re Taylor's Will (1947) 271 AD 947, 67 NYS2d 823 **2:7**

Re Tessitore's Estate (1950, Sur) 99 NYS2d 776 **13:9**

Re Tompkins' Estate (1923) 207 AD 166, 201 NYS 696 **18:7**

Re Troni (1989, 1st Dept) 147 AD2d 394, 537 NYS2d 817 **34:5**

Re Vanderbilt (1982) 57 NY2d 66, 453 NYS2d 662 **16:2**

Re Voges' Will (1950) 276 AD 982, 95 NYS2d 207, affd 301 NY 617 **25:14**

Re Walker (1949) 275 AD 688, 86 NYS2d 726, affd 299 NY 686 **3:5**

Re Webster (1905) 106 AD 360, 94 NYS 1050, affd 186 NY 549, 79 NE 1118 **21:13**

Re Wendel's Estate (1933) 146 Misc 260, 262 NYS 41 **19:10**

Re White's Will (1957) 2 NY2d 309, 160 NYS2d 841, 70 ALR2d 484 **14:1**, **23:6**

Re Will of Fuller (1959) 9 AD2d 565, 189 NYS2d 287, reh den (3d Dept) 9 AD2d 854, 194 NYS2d 454 **18:7**

Re Will of Kellum (1873, Sur Ct) 52 NY 517 **25:6**

Re Will of Lipsit (1966, Sur Ct) 50 Misc 2d 289, 269 NYS2d 989 **28:4**

Re Will of Miller (1974) 76 Misc 2d 1092, 353 NYS2d 379 **18:11**

Re Will of Mintzer (1968, 3d Dept) 29 AD2d 792, 286 NYS2d 879 **8:5**

Re Will of Nogueira (1961) 32 Misc 2d 446, 223 NYS2d 334 **22:6**

Re Will of Richards (1956, 3d Dept) 1 AD2d 502, 151 NYS2d 744 **28:3**

Re Will of Sheehan (1976, 4th Dept) 51 AD2d 645, 378 NYS2d 141 **12:3**

Re Will of Slade (1984, 4th Dept) 106 AD2d 914, 483 NYS2d 513 **22:18**

Re Will of Tomljenovich (1956, Sur) 154 NYS2d 327 **17:6**

Re Will of Wells (1973) 76 Misc 2d 458, 350 NYS2d 114 **24:6**

Re Will of Wilhelm (1978, 4th Dept) 62 AD2d 1155, 405 NYS2d 157, affd 46 NY2d 947, 415 NYS2d 413 **17:5**

Re v Beiny (1990, 1st Dept) 164 AD2d 233, 562 NYS2d 58, as amended (1990) 177 AD2d 463, 576 NYS2d 501 **3:3**

Realty Associates, Inc. v New York (1956, 2d Dept) 1 AD2d 1049, 152 NYS2d 766, reh den (2d Dept) 2 AD2d 812, 154 NYS2d 843 **29:21**

Redco v Oyster Bay (1990, 2d Dept) 160 AD2d 984, 554 NYS2d 705 **29:22**

820

TABLE OF CASES

TABLE OF CASES

TABLE OF CASES

Torres v State (1979, 4th Dept) 67 AD2d 814, 413 NYS2d 262 **33:2**

Torrillo v Command Bus Co. (1994, 2d Dept) 206 AD2d 520, 614 NYS2d 756. **2:6**

Tosto v Marra Bros., Inc. (1949) 275 AD 686, 86 NYS2d 549, affd 299 NY 700 **10:4**

Towli v Ford Motor Co. (1968, 1st Dept) 30 AD2d 319, 292 NYS2d 8 **31:8, 31:9**

Town Taxi Service Corp. v Green Cab & Brokerage Co. (1942, Sup) 38 NYS2d 529 **28:2**

Trafton v New York State Electric & Gas Corp. (1950) 277 AD 1013, 100 NYS2d 375 **4:9**

Trainor v Oasis Roller World, Inc. (1989, 1st Dept) 151 AD2d 323, 543 NYS2d 61 **31:6**

Trampusch v Kastner (1934) 242 AD 803, 274 NYS 771 **25:14**

Travelers Indem. Co. v Buffalo Motor & Generator Corp. (1977) 58 AD2d 978, 397 NYS2d 257 **25:7**

Trembley v Coca-Cola Bottling Co. (1955) 285 AD 539, 138 NYS2d 332 **25:7**

Triangle Publications, Inc. v Ferrare (1957, 3d Dept) 4 AD2d 591, 168 NYS2d 128 **13:10**

Trimarco v Klein (1982) 56 NY2d 98, 451 NYS2d 52 **25:7**

Triple A Auto Driving School, Inc. v Foschio (1985, 1st Dept) 107 AD2d 641, 484 NYS2d 566, affd 65 NY2d 755, 492 NYS2d 24 **23:4**

Trode v Omnetics, Inc. (1984, 3d Dept) 106 AD2d 808, 484 NYS2d 197 **22:12**

Troisi v Merit Oil Co. (1994, 2d Dept), 208 AD2d 615, 617 NYS2d 347 **18:5**

Trombetta v Conkling (1993) 82 NY2d 549, 605 NYS2d 678 **29:13**

Troy v Long Island Jewish-Hillside Medical Center (1982, 2d Dept) 86 AD2d 631, 446 NYS2d 347 **31:8**

Truck Rent-A-Center, Inc. v Puritan Farms 2nd, Inc. (1977) 41 NY2d 420, 393 NYS2d 365 **29:4**

Truden v Town of Oyster Bay (1994, 2d Dept) 204 AD2d 434, 611 NYS2d 647 **17:7**

Trump v Associated Transp. Inc. (1949) 275 AD 982, 90 NYS2d 154 **31:4**

Trump v Trump (1992, 1st Dept) 179 AD2d 201, 582 NYS2d 1008 **8:4**

Trustees of Columbia University v Mitchell/Giurgola Associates (1985, 1st Dept) 109 AD2d 449, 492 NYS2d 371 **33:2**

Trustees of Union College v Board of Assessment Review (1982, 3d Dept) 91 AD2d 713, 457 NYS2d 971 **8:5**

Trusts & Guarantee Co. v Barnhardt (1936) 270 NY 350 **18:9**

Tryon v Willbank (1932) 234 AD 335, 255 NYS 27 **14:8**

Tucker v Elimelech (1992, 2d Dept) 184 AD2d 636, 584 NYS2d 895 **22:18, 33:4**

Turcotte v Fell (1986) 68 NY2d 432, 510 NYS2d 49 **28:5**

Turner v Reynolds (1946) 271 AD 413, 66 NYS2d 339 **29:21**

Turner v Sunshine Taxi Corp. (1945) 269 AD 997, 58 NYS2d 422 **23:6, 23:7**

Turnure v Breitung (1921) 195 AD 200, 186 NYS 620, affd 233 NY 649, 135 NE 955 **22:25**

Twin Realty Corp. v Glens Falls Portland Cement Co. (1929) 225 AD 515, 234 NYS 217 **8:5**

Tynan Incinerator Co. v International Fidelity Ins. Co. (1986, 2d Dept) 117 AD2d 796, 499 NYS2d 118 **29:5**

U

Udell v Josephson (1939, Sup) 11 NYS2d 866 **29:23**

Uhler v Stix (1990, 2d Dept) 167 AD2d 388, 561 NYS2d 803 **9:4**

Underhill v Waite (1880) 9 NY Week Dig 438, 9 Daly 83 **19:15**

Underwriters' Laboratories, Inc. v Smith (1964) 41 Misc 2d 756, 246 NYS2d 436 **29:8**

Universal Carloading & Distribution Co. v Penn Cent. Transp. Co. (1984, 1st Dept) 101 AD2d 61, 474 NYS2d 502 **24:10**

834

TABLE OF CASES

TABLE OF CASES

TABLE OF STATUTES

TABLE OF STATUTES

TABLE OF RULES AND CODES

Constitutions

New York State Constitution

Policy Guidelines, Manuals, Handbooks

New York Pattern Jury Instructions

INDEX TO SUBJECTS

847

INDEX

INDEX

AIRCRAFT

Dead man statute applicable to accidents, § 12:1, 12:9

ALCOHOL AND DRUG ABUSE PROGRAMS

Confidential and privileged communications, § 16:17
Directed verdict, § 28:5

ALCOHOLIC BEVERAGES

Intoxicating Liquors (this index)

ALTERNATE JURORS

Generally, § 4:2, 4:11, 4:12

AMENDMENT OR MODIFICATION

Findings of fact, § 1:8
Pleadings (this index)
Verdict (this index)

AMNESIA

Presumptions and burden of proof, § 7:4

AMOUNT OR QUANTITY

Court costs, § 34:5
Damages (this index)
Judgment, § 34:3-34:6
Jury and Jury Trial (this index)

ANCIENT DOCUMENTS

Generally, § 23:19
Authentication, § 21:13

ANESTHESIA

Presumptions and burden of proof, § 7:3

ANESTHESIOLOGIST

Malpractice, burden of proof, § 7:2

ANIMALS

Closing arguments, § 30:11
Demonstrative and real evidence, § 19:7

ANNUITY AND MORTALITY TABLES

Generally, § 23:17

ANSWERS

Self-incrimination, § 13:18

ANTENUPTIAL AGREEMENTS

Dead man statute, application of, § 12:10
Parol or extrinsic evidence, § 25:16

ANXIETY

Damages, § 29:13

APARTMENT

Liquidated damages and penalties, § 29:4

APPEAL AND ERROR

Judicial notice by appellate courts, § 17:4-17:6

APPRAISERS

Expert and opinion evidence, § 22:16

APPROVAL

Consent or Approval (this index)

ARBITRATION

Hearsay rule, § 23:4
Punitive damages, § 29:8
Subpoenas, authority to issue, § 9:1

ARCHITECTS

Expert and opinion evidence, § 22:16

ARGUMENT OR COMMENT BY COUNSEL

Generally, § 1:5
Alibi witnesses, § 9:1
Closing Arguments (this index)
Criminal contempt, § 3:5
Damages (this index)
Opening Statements (this index)

849

INDEX

as grounds for challenge, § 4:4, 4:9

Libel action, damages recoverable in, § 29:23

Mistrial, § 2:4, 27:3

News media, restrictions on statements of counsel to, § 1:6

Presence of counsel, § 1:3, 2:4, 20:1, 20:2, 31:8, 32:3

Prior convictions. Impeachment of witness, supra

Pro se, § 1:3

Self-incrimination privilege in disciplinary proceedings, § 13:11

Sickness or illness of attorney, mistrial based on, § 2:4

Stipulations as binding on client, § 8:4

Subpoenas, authority to issue, § 9:1

Waiver

confidential and privileged communications, § 16:3

right to attorney, § 1:3

Witnesses

assistance by counsel, questions as to, § 13:6

competency of attorney as witness, § 11:5

conduct of counsel, § 1:5

Confidential and Privileged Communications (this index)

continuance where attorney is witness, § 2:4

disciplinary proceedings, supra

disobedience on advice of counsel, § 9:1

impeachment of witness, supra

qualification as expert witness, § 22:21

ATTORNEYS' FEES

Attorney and client privilege, § 16:5

Contempt of court, § 3:3

Costs, allowance as, § 34:6

Court costs, § 34:5

Damages, recovery as, § 29:26

Interest included in judgment, computation of, § 34:4

AUTHENTICATION

Generally, § 21:1 et seq.

Ancient documents, § 21:13

Attested documents, § 21:4

Corporate records, § 21:10

Dead man statute as applicable to books of account, § 12:10

Documentary evidence, § 21:10

Excusing of authentication, § 21:2

Family bible, § 21:12

Letters, § 21:11

Private writings, § 21:3, 21:11

Records and recordings, § 21:5, 21:8, 21:9, 21:12, 23:10

Signature on release or discharge, § 7:2

Statutes, § 21:6

AUTHOR'S INTERVIEWS

Privileged communication to journalist and newsmen, application of, § 16:15

AUTOMOBILES

Motor Vehicles (this index)

AUTOPSY REPORTS

Generally, § 23:10

Physician and patient privilege, § 16:10

BAILMENT

Burden of proof, § 7:8

Presumptions and burden of proof, § 7:9

BANKS AND BANKING

Admissions and declarations, § 24:12

Checks (this index)

Dead man or incompetent person statute, application of, § 12:9

Expert and opinion evidence, § 22:16

Self-serving declarations, § 25:14

BAPTISMAL RECORDS

Generally, § 21:12

BARS AND TAVERNS

Dramshop law, § 6:3

INDEX

BASTARDY PROCEEDINGS

Paternity and Legitimacy (this index)

BEST AND SECONDARY EVIDENCE

Family Bible, § 21:12
Prior or former trial, testimony at, § 23:9

BEYOND REASONABLE DOUBT

Reasonable Doubt (this index)

BIAS AND PREJUDICE

Conduct of trial, § 1:1 et seq.
Contempt proceeding, presiding judge in, § 3:4
Cross-examination, scope of, § 14:3, 14:10, 14:11
Directed verdict, amendment of pleadings to conform to evidence, §28:4
Expert and opinion evidence, § 22:17
Impeachment of witness, § 10:1-10:5
Interest in Action or Case (this index)
Jurors, § 4:3-4:5, 4:7, 4:9, 4:10, 4:14
Mistrial, § 27:1
New trial, § 2:4
Prejudicial or inflammable evidence, § 25:3

BIBLE

Family bible, entries in, § 21:12, 23:18

BIFURCATED TRIAL

Generally, § 1:2
Damages, § 6:2, 29:12 31:7
Interest included in judgment, computation of, § 34:4
Opening statements, § 1:2
Order of producing testimony, § 6:2

BILL OF PARTICULARS

Directed verdict, § 28:4
Directed verdict based on bill of particulars, § 28:2
Judicial admissions, § 24:5
Prior or former trial, § 23:9

BILLS AND INVOICES

Generally, § 8:3, 12:10, 23:10

BIRTH

Emotional injuries arising out of medical malpractice, § 29:13
Gestation period, § 17:6
Judicial notice
    gestation period, § 17:6
    records of birth, § 17:5
Pedigree evidence, § 23:16
Prenatal injuries, damages for, § 29:12, 29:19
Presumption as to age for child bearing, § 18:11
Records of birth, § 17:5, 23:11
Stillborn fetus, damages for "wrongful death" of, § 29:19

BLIND

Directed verdict, § 28:5

BLOOD RELATION

Consanguinity or *Affinity* (this index)

BLOOD TESTS

Generally, § 19:15
Blood grouping tests, § 18:11, 19:13, 19:15, 23:10
Intoxication test, § 19:15, 22:30, 25:8
Physical and mental examinations, § 25:15

BOARDS

Agencies, Boards, Commissions, and Departments (this index)

BOATING ACCIDENT

Dead man statute, application of, § 12:9
Liquidated damages and penalties, § 29:4

BREATHALYZER TEST

Generally, § 19:15, 22:30

BRIBERY

Admission, conduct as, § 24:9
    generally, § 24:9
    agents or employees, admissions by, § 24:2

Collateral issues, evidence on, § 25:4

Cross-examination of relatives as to gifts, § 14:10

Jurors, § 32:9

Presumption arising out of attempt to bribe witness, § 18:8

BRUTON CASE

Confession of nontestifying codefendant, admission of, § 13:19

BUILDING CODE

Expert testimony, § 22:15

BURDEN OF PROOF

Presumptions and Burden of Proof (this index)

BUSINESS RECORDS

Generally, § 21:13, 23:10

Authentication of records, § 21:8

Confrontation of witnesses, § 13:19

Documentary evidence, § 21:2

Expert and opinion evidence, § 22:35

Self-incrimination, privilege against, § 13:10, 13:11

BUSINESS RELATIONSHIPS

Jurors, § 4:3, 4:4, 4:5

CASTS

Models and Casts (this index)

CAUSE, CHALLENGES TO JURORS FOR

Jury and Jury Trial (this index)

CERTIFICATES AND CERTIFICATION

Authentication of document, § 21:2

Birth certificates, § 23:11

Court papers and records, § 21:9

Death certificates, § 23:11

Documentary evidence, § 21:7

Recorded documents, generally, § 21:5, 23:11

CHALLENGES TO JURORS

Jury and Jury Trial (this index)

CHARACTER AND REPUTATION

Generally, § 25:9 et seq.

Civil cases, generally, § 25:10

Cross-examination, § 14:1, 14:3, 14:10, 14:11

Libel and defamation, damages for, § 29:23

Materiality and relevancy of evidence, § 13:2

Rumors or reports, § 14:10

Truth and veracity, reputation for, § 10:1, 25:11

CHARTS

Diagrams, Charts, or Tables (this index)

CHECKS

Dead man statute, waiver of incompetency under, § 12:8

Expert and opinion evidence, § 22:16

Judicial notice, § 17:6

Self-serving declarations, § 25:14

CHIDREN AND MINORS

Closing arguments, § 30:11

CHILD ABUSE OR ENDANGERMENT

Confidential and Privileged Communications (this index)

Expert and opinion evidence, § 22:15, 22:26

Hearsay evidence, 23:24, § 23:24

Impeachment of witness, § 10:2

CHILDBIRTH

Birth (this index)

CHILD CUSTODY

Expert and opinion evidence, § 22:27

Psychologists and clients, privileged communications between, §16:13

Spouse, competency to testify for or against other spouse, § 11:4

INDEX

INDEX

INDEX

INDEX

INDEX

Personal property, damages to, § 29:17
Pleadings (this index)
Prenatal injuries, § 29:12, 29:19
Presumptions and burden of proof, § 7:2, 7:8, 29:1, 29:3, 29:5, 29:11
Prima facie tort, § 29:13
Punitive and Exemplary Damages (this index)
Real estate, damages to, § 29:21, 29:22
Relevancy of questions on direct examination, § 13:2
Self-incrimination, extent of privilege against, § 13:11
Special damages, § 29:10
Verdict (this index)
Speculative, § 29:1
Warranty, breach of, § 29:3
Witnesses, liability for failure to obey subpoena, § 9:1
Wrongful death actions, § 29:19

DANGEROUS OR UNSAFE CONDITION

Expert testimony, § 22:4

DAYLIGHT SAVING TIME

Judicial notice, § 17:6

DEAD MAN OR MENTALLY ILL PERSON STATUTE

Generally, § 11:1, 12:1-12:10
Administrator, § 12:2
Agents, § 12:3, 12:7
Aircraft accidents, § 12:1, 12:9
Bank officers, § 12:9
Competency of witness and testimony distinguished, § 12:4
Corporate officers and directors, § 12:5, 12:9
Corporate stockholders, § 12:3, 12:5, 12:9
Estates, claims against, § 7:5
Examination before trial, application of statute to, § 12:9
Exceptions, § 12:9
Executor, § 12:2
Joint contractors, § 12:6
Medical malpractice, § 12:8
Partners, § 12:6
Paternity or legitimacy, § 12:1, 12:3

Persons barred from testifying, generally, § 12:3
Persons entitled to protection, generally, § 12:2
Rules applied in determining incompetency, § 12:4
Testimony barred, § 12:10
Third persons hearing conversations, § 12:3, 12:10
Time in which incompetency is determined, § 12:5
Waiver of incompetency, § 12:8, 12:10

DEAF MUTE

Competency of witness, § 11:6

DEATH

Absence for three years, § 18:6
Autopsy Report (this index)
Closing arguments, § 30:8
Common disaster, persons dying in, § 18:14
Conspirators, admissions and declarations by, § 13:19
Dead Man or Mentally Ill Person Statute (this index)
Declarations against interest, § 23:23
Demonstrative and real evidence, § 19:2
Instructions to jury, § 31:6
Jurors replaced by alternate jurors, § 4:11
Mistrial, § 27:3, 27:4
Parties (this index)
Pedigree evidence, § 23:16
Presumptions, § 18:3, 18:4, 18:6, 18:11, 18:14
Prior or former trial, § 23:8
Prior or former trial, unavailability of witness, § 23:6
Public record, § 17:5, 23:11
Self-serving declarations of deceased person, § 25:14
Suicide (this index)
Witnesses (this index)
Wrongful Death (this index)

DECEDENTS' ESTATES

Estates (this index)

INDEX

DISMISSAL, DISCONTINUANCE, AND NONSUIT

Codefendant as deprived of right to pro rata liability, § 33:2
Default, § 2:8
Evidence, failure of, § 2:3, 28:2
Findings of fact, necessity of, § 1:8
Impeachment of witness by showing dismissal of criminal action, §10:5
Involuntary dismissal, § 2:8
Opening statement, dismissal on, § 5:2
Stipulations discontinuing third-party actions, § 8:5
Voluntary dismissal, § 2:7

DISORDERLY CONDUCT

Contempt of court, § 3:5
Impeachment of witness, § 10:5

DISPLAYS

Exhibits or Displays (this index)

DISTRICT OR PROSECUTING ATTORNEYS

Confidential and privileged communications, § 16:18
Self-incrimination, authority to grant immunity from, § 13:11

DIVORCE

Matrimonial Actions (this index)

DOCUMENTARY EVIDENCE

Generally, § 21:1 et seq.
Acknowledgement, § 21:2, 21:5
Administrative code of New York City, § 21:8
Ancient records, § 21:13
Attested documents, § 21:4
Authentication (this index)
Bills and invoices, § 8:3, 12:10, 23:10
Business Records (this index)
Certificates and certification, § 21:7
City clerk of New York City, § 21:8
Clerks, § 21:8
Code of New York City, § 21:8
Code of state, § 21:7
Copies, § 21:7

Corporate records, § 21:10
Directors of corporation, § 21:10
Expert and opinion testimony as to questioned documents, § 14:10, 22:25, 22:29
generally, § 14:10, 22:25, 22:29
Handwriting (this index)
Family bible, § 21:12, 23:18
Letters and Correspondence (this index)
Medical records, § 21:2
Minutes, § 21:10
Officers of corporation, § 21:10
Private writings, § 21:3, 21:11
Production of Evidence and Documents (this index)
Records and Recording (this index)
Regulaton of state, § 21:7
Rule of state, § 21:7
Secretary of state, § 21:7
Signature (this index)
Statutes, § 21:6
X-rays, § 21:2

DRAMSHOP LAW

Rebuttal testimony as to intoxication, § 6:3

DRAWINGS

Generally, § 19:9
Diagrams, Charts, or Tables (this index)
Maps and Plats (this index)

DRIVING WHILE INTOXICATED OR UNDER INFLUENCE

Blood test, § 22:30, 25:8
Breathalyzer test, § 19:15, 22:30, 25:8
Consent to take intoxication test, § 25:8
Evidence of intoxication, generally, § 25:8
Experiments and tests for intoxication, generally, § 22:30
Guilty plea as admissible in civil actions, § 24:4
Habits, proof of, § 25:6

INDEX

DRUG AND ALCOHOL ABUSE PROGRAMS

Confidential and privileged communications, § 16:17
Directed verdict, § 28:5

DRUGGISTS AND PHARMACISTS

Physician and patient privilege, § 16:10

DRUGS AND NARCOTICS

Competency of narcotic addict as witness, § 11:6
Cross-examination, § 14:12, 22:33
Druggists and Pharmacists (this index)
Expert testimony, § 22:15, 22:33
Impeachment of witness, § 10:2
Negligence, § 25:2
Physician and patient privilege, § 16:10
Prejudicial or inflammable evidence, § 25:3
Presumptions and burden of proof, § 7:3
Self-incrimination, refreshing testimony, § 13:20
Treatment program, physician and patient privilege as applicable to, § 16:10
Use of drugs, evidence of, § 25:2

DRUNKENNESS

Intoxication (this index)

DRUNKOMETER TEST

Expert and opinion evidence, § 22:30

DURESS OR COERCION

Burden of proof, § 7:2
Privileged communications between husband and wife, § 16:3
Relevancy of evidence, § 13:2

DYING DECLARATIONS

Hearsay evidence, § 23:5

EARNINGS

Expert and opinion evidence, § 22:35

EASEMENTS

Eminent domain, damages in taking by, § 29:22

ECONOMIC DISCRIMINATION

Jury selection, § 4:7

ECONOMIST

Expert testimony, § 22:18, 22:23, 29:12, 29:19

ELECTROENCEPHALOGRAM TEST

Generally, § 19:15

ELECTRONIC SURVEILLANCE

Eavesdropping and Electronic Surveillance (this index)

ELEVATOR ACCIDENTS

Presumptions and burden of proof, § 18:5

ELIGIBILITY

Qualification (this index)

EMERGENCIES

Instructions to jury, § 31:7

EMINENT DOMAIN

Damages, § 29:22
Relevancy of question, § 13:2

EMOTIONAL INJURIES

Damages, § 29:13

EMPLOYERS AND EMPLOYEES

Admissions by employee, § 24:2, 24:3
Attorney and client privilege as applicable to employees of attorney, § 16:5, 16:8
Closing arguments, § 30:11
Corporate Officers, Directors, and Employees (this index)

INDEX

INDEX

EXAMINATION BEFORE TRIAL

EXAMINATION OF WITNESSES

INDEX

INDEX

INDEX

Child protective proceedings, § 23:24
Church records, § 21:12, 23:18
Confessions (this index)
Conspirators, Admissions and Declarations of (this index)
Defined, § 23:2
Dying Declarations (this index)
Family bibles, § 23:18
Hotels, § 23:3
Insurance, § 23:3
Intent, § 23:3, 23:22, 23:23
Interest, declarations against, § 12:14, 23:23
Life insurance, § 23:3
Making of statement, evidence limited to showing, § 23:2, 23:3
Medical history, § 23:15
Mental state of mind, § 23:3, 23:13, 23:20, 23:22, 23:23
Mortality and annuity tables, § 23:17
Motor vehicles, § 23:15
Pedigree, § 21:12, 23:16, 23:18
Physicians, § 23:3, 23:15
Police, § 23:2
Prior Inconsistent Statements (this index)
Prior or former trial, testimony at. *Prior or Former Trial* (this index)
Products liability, § 23:3
Rape, § 23:3
Records and Recording (this index)
Refreshing Memory of Witnesses (this index)
Res Gestae and Spontaneous Declarations (this index)
Searches and Seizures (this index)
Self-serving declarations, § 23:4, 23:10, 25:14
Testing witness' knowledge, § 14:12
Wrongful death, § 23:1

HEIRS AND NEXT OF KIN

Judicial notice of public records, § 17:5
Pedigree evidence, § 21:12, 23:16
Presumption of death of unmarried person after three years' absence, § 18:6

HISTORICAL FACTS OR EVENTS

Judicial notice, § 17:6

HOME OR HOUSE

Constructive trusts arising out of relationship of husband and wife, § 7:7

HOSPITAL RECORDS

Generally, § 23:10
Cross-examination, scope of, § 14:10
Death certificate from hospital, § 23:11
Hearsay evidence, § 23:13
Physician and patient privilege, § 16:10

HOSPITALS

Damages for emotional injuries, § 29:13
Medical malpractice, burden of proof, § 7:2
Minimizing or mitigating damages, § 29:5
Records. *Hospital Records* (this index)
Release from patient while in hospital, § 7:2

HOSTILE JUROR

Generally, § 32:2

HOSTILE WITNESSES

Credibility of witnesses, § 10:5
Impeachment of witness, § 10:3
Leading questions, § 13:7
Medical malpractice, defendant as expert witness in, § 14:10
Presumptions and burden of proof, § 18:8, 18:16

HOTELS

Hearsay evidence, § 23:3

HOUSEHOLD FURNISHINGS

Expert and opinion evidence, § 22:12

HUMILIATION AND EMBARRASSMENT

Cross-examination, manner of, § 14:11

Damages for personal injuries, § 29:12-13

HUNTLEY HEARING

Confession, determining admissibility of, § 13:19

HUSBAND AND WIFE

Absence or presence, § 1:3

Admissions and declarations, § 24:12

Competency of spouse as witness, § 11:1, 11:4

Confidential and Privileged Communications (this index)

Constructive trusts as to proceeds of life insurance, § 7:7

Damages for loss of consortium, § 29:12, 29:20

Dead man statute, persons barred from testifying under, § 12:3, 12:10

Expert and opinion evidence, § 22:12, 22:16, 22:35

Interest included in judgment, computation of, § 34:4

Judicial admissions, § 24:4, 24:6

Marriage (this index)

Matrimonial Actions (this index)

Parol evidence, § 25:16

Presumptions and burden of proof, § 18:16

Prior or former trial, § 23:6

Relevancy of questions on direct examination, § 13:2

Wrongful death actions, § 29:19

HYPNOSIS

Self-incrimination, § 13:20

HYPOTHETICAL QUESTIONS

Expert witnesses, § 22:15, 22:31, 22:32

IDENTIFICATION

Cross-examination as to prior inconsistent statements, § 14:6

Dentist and patient privilege, § 16:11

Exhibit of person at trial, § 19:12, 19:14

Expert testimony, § 22:15

Husband and wife, privileged communications between, § 16:2

Models and casts used in identification of persons, § 19:10

Names and Addresses (this index)

Ownership, inferences arising out of, § 7:1

Voice Identification (this index)

IDENTIFICATION OF PERSONS

Demonstrative and real evidence, § 19:4

ILLEGITIMATE CHILDREN

Paternity and Legitimacy (this index)

ILLNESS

Sickness or Illness (this index)

IMMATERIALITY

Materiality and Relevancy of Evidence (this index)

IMMORALITY

Morality or Immorality (this index)

IMPEACHMENT OF WITNESSES

Generally, § 10:1-10:5

Admissions, § 10:3, 24:1

Attorneys (this index)

Church, expulsion from, § 14:11

Collateral issues, § 10:2

Conviction of crime, § 10:1, 10:2, 10:5, 11:1, 14:8

Dead man statute, application to claims under life insurance policy, § 12:2

Death certificates, admissibility of, § 23:11

Declarations against interest, § 23:23

Evidence of liability insurance, generally, § 25:12

Expert testimony as to tort settlement within policy limits, §22:15

Hearsay evidence, § 23:3

Interest included in judgment, computation of, § 34:4

Jurors
    challenges to favor, § 4:4
    mistrial for disclosure of liability insurance, § 2:4, 27:4
    questioning regarding insurance, § 4:4, 4:10

Mistrial for disclosure of liability insurance, § 2:4, 27:4

Motor Vehicles (this index)

Presumption arising out of delivery of letter, § 18:9

Relevancy of questions on direct examination, § 13:2

Suicide defense, § 16:11

Verdict on special interrogatories, § 33:8

Workers' Compensation Insurance (this index)

INTENT

Burden of proof, § 7:8, 25:2

Hearsay rule, § 23:3, 23:22, 23:23

Parol evidence, § 25:16

Prima facie tort, § 29:13

INTEREST, DECLARATIONS AGAINST

Generally, § 12:4, 23:23

INTEREST IN ACTION OR CASE

Competency of witness. *Witnesses* (this index)

Impeachment of witness, § 10:1-10:5

INTEREST INCLUDED IN JUDGMENT, COMPUTATION OF

Generally, § 34:4

INTEREST ON MONEY

Judgment, interest in, § 34:4

Parol evidence of usury, § 25:16

INTERPRETATION

Construction and Interpretation (this index)

INTERPRETER

Generally, § 9:7

Admissions made through interpreter, § 24:1

Hearsay statements, § 23:1

Jury and jury trial, § 4:18

INTERROGATORIES

Verdict on special interrogatories, § 33:7-33:10

INTERVIEWING OF WITNESSES

Generally, § 14:10

INTOXICATING LIQUORS

Intoxication (this index)

Jurors, purchase for, criminal contempt, § 3:5

INTOXICATION

Blood tests, § 22:30, 25:8

Breathalyzer test, § 19:15, 22:30, 25:8

Competency to testify, § 11:1

Cross-examination of witness as to prior alcoholism, § 14:10

Dramshop law, § 6:3

Driving While Intoxicated or Under Influence (this index)

Drunkometer test, § 22:30

Evidence or proof of intoxication, generally, § 25:8

Experiments and tests for intoxication, generally, § 22:30

Expert and opinion evidence, § 22:8, 22:30

Habits, proof of, § 25:6

Hospital records, admissibility of, § 23:13

Physician and patient privilege, § 16:10

Intoxication – contd.

Presumption arising from alcoholic content of blood, § 22:30

Prior convictions for purposes of impeachment of witness, § 14:8

INVERSE CONDEMNATION

Damages, § 29:22

INVOICES AND BILLS

Generally, § 8:3, 12:10, 23:10

JAILS

Prisons and Correctional Institutions (this index)

JEWELRY

Presumptions and burden of proof, § 7:9

JOINDER OF PARTIES

Verdicts, § 33:1

JOINT BANK ACCOUNTS

Constructive trusts, § 7:7

JOINT OR SEPARATE CAUSES OF ACTION

Verdict, § 33:1, 33:4

JOINT OR SEPARATE TRIALS

Bifurcated Trials (this index)

Confession of codefendant used in joint trial, § 13:19

Criminal trials, § 13:19

Dismissal depriving codefendant of right to pro rata liability, §33:2

New trial based on separable issues, § 2:6

Verdicts, § 33:1

JOINT OR SEVERAL COUNTS IN INDICTMENT

Verdict, § 33:1

JOINT TORTFEASORS

Payments received by plaintiff, dam-

ages affected by, § 29:27

Verdicts, apportionment of damages, § 33:1, 33:2

JOURNALISTS AND NEWSPAPERMEN

News Media (this index)

JUDGES

Absence or presence, § 4:8, 33:1

Competency as witness, § 11:5

Conduct and demeanor of judge, § 1:4

Jurors, private communications with, § 32:3, 32:8

Law, judge as determiner of, § 1:9

Prior or former trial, § 23:8

Subpoenas, authority to issue, § 9:1, 9:2

Transcribing of remarks and comments, § 1:6

Trial by Court (this index)

Witnesses (this index)

JUDGMENT DEBTOR

Self-incrimination, § 13:12

JUDGMENT DEBTORS

Criminal contempt for refusal to appear or be examined, § 3:4, 3:5

Impeachment by showing of unpaid judgments, § 10:5

JUDGMENTS AND DECREES

Generally, § 34:1-34:7

Advisory jury or referee, directing judgment on, § 2:5

Amount of judgment, § 34:3-34:6

Attorney's fees, § 34:6

Clerk of Court (this index)

Court costs, § 34:5, 34:6

Criminal contempt for failure to obey, § 3:4, 3:5

Default judgments, § 2:8, 24:4

Entry of judgment, § 34:1, 34:2

Interest included in judgment, § 34:4

Motion for judgment during trial, § 2:1, 2:3, 24:5

Post-trial motion for judgment, § 2:1

Relief from judgment, § 34:7

Res Judicata or Collateral Estoppel (this index)

Summary judgment, judicial admission in motion for, § 24:5

JUDICIAL ADMISSIONS

Generally, § 8:2, 24:4, 24:5
Children and minors, § 24:5
Husband and wife, § 24:4
Mental disability, § 24:5
Pleadings, § 8:1, 24:5
Res judicata or collateral estoppel, § 24:6
Stipulations as excusing proving facts, § 8:4

JUDICIAL NOTICE

Generally, § 17:1-17:7
Appeal, judicial notice on, § 17:4-17:6
Birth (this index)
Court, facts concerning, § 17:3
Government and political subdivisions, facts about, § 17:4
Motor vehicles, § 17:2, 17:6, 17:7
Pending actions, § 17:3, 17:4, 17:6
Proof of fact excused where judicially noticed, generally, § 17:1
Public officers and employees, facts about, § 17:4
Public record, matters of, § 17:5
Statutes and laws, § 17:2, 17:6, 21:6

JURISDICTION

Relief from judgment or order, § 34:7
Stipulations extending time to answer, § 8:5
Verdicts, revising to within jurisdictional limits of court, § 33:5
Waiver of defense of lack of jurisdiction, § 8:5

JURY AND JURY TRIAL

Absence from deliberation, § 32:2
Affidavits, § 32:10
Age
    cause, challenges for, § 4:14
    discrimination in selection of jurors, § 4:7

Alternate jurors, § 4:2, 4:11, 4:12
Amount, quantity, or number
    amount in controversy giving right to jury trial, § 4:5
    number of jurors, § 4:5, 4:15
    peremptory challenges, § 4:2, 4:12
    verdict, number of jurors, § 27:5
Appeal and error, § 4:14
Array, challenge to, § 4:14
Assault, § 32:9
Attorneys (this index)
Bias and prejudice, § 4:3 et seq.
Cause, challenges for
    generally, § 4:1, 4:3, 4:4, 4:14
    array, § 4:14
    favor, challenges to, § 4:1, 4:4, 4:14
    principal cause, § 4:1, 4:3, 4:14
    questions of law and fact, § 4:1, 4:3, 4:4
Challenges to jurors
    generally, § 4:1-4:4
    cause, challenges for, supra
    peremptory challenges, infra
    voir dire examination, § 4:8-4:10
Communications with jurors, § 32:3, 32:8, 32:9
Conduct of jury, generally, § 32:1 et seq.
Constitutional law
    generally, § 4:5
    discrimination in selection of jurors, § 4:7
Criminal contempt for misconduct, § 3:5
Damages, § 32:2
Deliberations, § 32:8 et seq.
    items taken by jury to jury room, § 32:5
Disability of juror, § 4:18
Discharge or dismissal of jury
    Mistrial (this index)
    reopening case for further testimony after discharge of jury, § 6:4
Discrimination because of sex, race, etc., § 4:7
Dismissal or discontinuance after submission of case to jury, § 2:7

INDEX

INDEX

MENTAL STATE OF MIND

Hearsay rule, § 23:3, 23:13, 23:20, 23:22, 23:23
Hospital records, § 23:13
Intent (this index)
Res gestae statements, § 23:20

MILEAGE

Witnesses, § 2:2, 9:5

MILITARY

Closing arguments, § 30:8

MINIMIZING OR MITIGATING DAMAGES

Generally, § 7:2, 29:5, 29:11

MINORS AND INFANTS

Admissions and declarations, § 24:2
Child Abuse or Endangerment (this index)
Childbirth. *Birth* (this index)
Child Custody (this index)
Child support, application of dead man statute, § 12:3
Closing arguments, § 30:8
Confidential and Privileged Communications (this index)
Damages, § 29:11
Dead man statute applicable to child support, § 12:3
Directed verdict, § 28:5
Expert and opinion evidence, § 22:4, 22:15, 22:16
Future damages, § 29:6
Guardian and Committee (this index)
Impeachment by proof prior violation of Children's Court Act, §14:8
Instructions to jury, § 31:6, 31:7
Judicial admissions, § 24:5
Judicial notice of facts, § 17:6
Juvenile Delinquency Proceedings (this index)
Presumptions, § 11:3, 18:2, 18:11
Sex Offenses (this index)
Variance between pleadings and proof, § 28:4
Witness

competency as witness, § 11:3, 11:6
corroboration of testimony, § 12:3
Wrongful death, damages, § 29:19

MINUTES

Documentary evidence, § 21:10
Prior or former trial, § 23:8

MIRANDA WARNINGS

Civil actions, § 24:1
Cross-examination, § 14:10
Tests and experiments, § 19:15

MISREPRESENTATION

Fraud and Deceit (this index)

MISTAKE, INADVERTENCE, OR ACCIDENT

Mutual Mistake (this index)
Rebuttal testimony, § 6:3
Stipulations, relief from terms of, § 8:5

MISTRIAL

Generally, § 2:1, 2:4
Arrest, § 27:1
Assault and battery, § 27:1
Attorneys (this index)
Bias or prejudice, § 27:1
Change in laws, § 27:3
Conduct of jurors, § 32:3
Death, § 27:3
Expert witness, § 27:3
Fraud, § 27:3
Grounds, generally, § 27:3
Inability of jury to arrive at verdict, § 27:5
Instructions to jury, § 27:1, 27:3
Liability insurance, disclosure to jurors of, 27:4, § 27:4
Medical malpractice, § 27:3
Prejudicial and reversible error, § 27:2
Prior acts and matters, § 27:3
Real property, § 27:3
Sickness or Illness (this index)
Variance between pleadings and proof, § 2:4
Verdict, § 2:4, 27:2
Waiver, § 27:2
Weight of prejudice, § 27:2

886

INDEX

Hearsay statements, § 23:2
Pedigree evidence, § 23:16

NEGATIVE INFERENCES

Self-incrimination, § 13:16

NEGLIGENCE

Admissions and declarations, § 24:2
Burden of proof, § 7:2-7:5, 7:8
Closing arguments, § 30:2, 30:9, 30:11
Comparative Negligence (this index)
Conditions before accident, § 13:4,
   14:3, 14:10
Contributory Negligence (this index)
Custom and usage, § 25:7
Demonstrative and real evidence, §
   19:4
Directed verdict, § 28:3
Drugs and narcotics, § 25:2
Expert and opinion evidence, § 22:3,
   22:14
Instructions to jury, § 31:4, 31:6, 31:7
Interest included in judgment, compu-
   tation of, § 34:4
Interest on judgment, § 34:4
Motor vehicle accidents, § 25:12,
   25:15
Objections and exceptions, § 26:2
Opinion evidence on ultimate issue, §
   22:5
Res ipsa loquitur, § 7:1, 17:2, 18:5
Similar acts or occurrences, evidence
   of, § 25:5
Variance between pleadings and proof,
   § 28:4
Verdict, § 33:1, 33:2, 33:7, 33:8

NEWLY DISCOVERED EVIDENCE

Relief from judgment or order, § 34:7

NEWS MEDIA

Confidential and privileged communications to journalists, § 16:1, 16:15
Constitutional law
   confidential and privileged commu-
      nications to journalists, § 16:15
   public trial, standing to object to
      denial of, § 1:6
Criminal contempt, § 3:4, 3:5

Privileged communications to journalist and newsmen, § 16:15
Publicity of proceedings, § 1:6
Public trial, standing to object to denial
   of, § 1:6
Redirect examination to explain statements to magazines, § 15:2

NEW TRIAL

Generally, § 2:6
Advisory jury or report of referee,
   action on, § 2:5
Bias and prejudice, § 2:4
Conduct of jurors, § 4:9, 32:2 et seq.
Insurance, questioning jurors as to, §
   4:4
Interest on judgment, time of compu-
   tation of, § 34:4
Newly discovered evidence, § 34:7
Trial (this index)

NO FAULT INSURANCE

Instructions to jury as to permanent
   injury, § 31:7

NO-KNOCK STATUTE

Generally, § 29:13

NOLO CONTENDERE

Judicial admissions, § 24:4

NOMINAL DAMAGES

Generally, § 29:3, 29:8

NONRESIDENTS

Compulsory process on nonresident
   witnesses, § 9:1
Depositions, use at trial, § 25:13
Former trial, admissibility of testi-
   mony at, § 23:6
Pedigree evidence, § 23:16
Privileges and immunities while
   attending proceedings, § 9:3

NONSUIT

*Dismissal, Discontinuance, and Non-
   suit* (this index)

INDEX

NOTATIONS

Demonstrative evidence, effect of notations on, § 19:11

NOTES

Dead man statute as applicable to promissory notes, § 12:3, 12:8, 12:10
Prior or former trial, § 23:8

NOTES AND MEMORANDA

Former trial, manner of proving testimony from, § 23:9
Judicial notice of government memorandum and regulations, § 17:4
Jury and Jury Trial (this index)
Physician, notes and memoranda of, § 23:14
Police and Law Enforcement Officers (this index)
Refreshing memory of witness, § 13:8, 14:10

NOTICE OR KNOWLEDGE

Admissions
    notice to admit, admissions made pursuant to, § 8:1
    personal knowledge as requirement, § 24:1
Civil contempt, § 3:1, 3:6
Common knowledge, matters of. *Judicial Notice* (this index)
Confessions (this index)
Contempt, § 3:4
Convicts or prisoners, compelling attendance of, § 9:2
Cross-examination to test knowledge, § 14:12
Declarations against interest, § 23:23
Judicial Notice (this index)
Physical and mental examination of party, § 25:15
Presumptions and burden of proof, § 7:1, 7:3, 18:9, 18:11, 18:12
Prior convictions to be used in impeachment of defendant, notice of, § 14:8
Reopening case for additional evidence, § 6:4

NUMBER

Amount or Quantity (this index)

NURSES

Confidential and privileged communications by client, § 16:1, 16:10
Expert and opinion evidence, § 22:16
Expert and opinion testimony of nurse, § 22:14

NURSING EXPENSES

Minimizing or mitigating damages, § 29:5

NURSING HOME

Demonstrative and real evidence, § 19:7
Records of home, § 13:11, 16:2

OATH OR AFFIRMATION

Interpreters, § 9:7
Jurors, swearing in. *Jury and Jury Trial* (this index)
Witnesses (this index)

OBJECTIONS AND EXCEPTIONS

Generally, § 26:1-26:5
Closing argument, § 30:4, 30:11
Cross-examination, § 26:2
Evidence or testimony, generally, § 26:1-26:5
Expert witness, § 26:2
Foundation objection, § 26:2
General or specific objections, § 26:4
Grounds for objection, stating of, § 26:4
Instructions to jury, § 26:2, 31:1, 31:4, 31:5
Medical expert, § 26:2
Necessity of objection to improper evidence, § 26:2
Negligence, § 26:2
Offer of proof, § 26:5
Photographs, § 26:2
Physician's records, § 26:2
Records, § 26:2
Timeliness of objection, § 26:3
Verdicts, § 33:2 et seq.

INDEX

INDEX

PARKING GARAGES AND LOTS

Agreements exempting tortfeasors from liability, § 8:6
Bailment, burden of proof for loss, § 7:8
Expert and opinion evidence, § 22:16
Instructions to jury, § 31:6
Presumptions and burden of proof, § 7:9

PAROL AND EXTRINSIC EVIDENCE

Generally, § 25:16
Agents, § 25:16
Custom and usage, § 25:7
Husband and wife, § 25:16
Impeachment of witness, § 10:2
Signature, § 25:16

PAROLE OR PROBATION

Confidential nature of interviews with prisoner or parolee, § 16:14

PARTIES

Absence or presence, § 1:3, 20:1, 20:2
Competency of party as witness, § 11:1
Credibility of parties as witnesses, § 10:4
Death of party
    deposition of party since deceased, § 25:13
    mistrial, § 27:4
    punitive damages, § 29:8
    self-servicing declarations of deceased person, § 25:14
Evidence of wrongdoing, § 25:17
Failure to testify, § 18:8
    generally, § 18:8
    accused. *Self-Incrimination* (this index)
Former trial, admissibility of testimony at, § 23:6
Juror, party acting as, § 4:14
Presumption arising from conduct, § 18:8
Prior inconsistent statements, § 14:7
Pro se appearance, § 1:1, 1:3

PARTNERS

Admissions by partner, § 24:2
Deceased partner, application of dead man statute, § 12:6
Expert and opinion evidence, § 22:15

PART OF TRANSACTION, STATEMENT, OR CONVERSATION

Confessions (this index)
Cross-examination, additional matters that are proper on, § 14:10
Depositions on trial, use of, § 25:13
Parol or extrinsic evidence, § 25:16
Redirect examination to explain or correct testimony, § 14:10, 15:2

PASSENGERS

Closing arguments, § 30:8

PASSERSBY

Presumptions and burden of proof, § 18:5

PATCH TEST

Generally, § 19:15

PATERNITY AND LEGITIMACY

Admissions by party, § 24:1
Blood tests, § 18:11, 19:13
Dead man statute, application of, § 12:1, 12:3
Exhibiting child, § 19:14
Pedigree evidence, § 23:16
Presumption of legitimacy of child, § 18:11
Public trial, § 1:6
Self-incrimination, waiver of, § 13:15

PEACE OFFICERS

Police and Law Enforcement Officers (this index)

PEDESTRIANS

Expert and opinion evidence, § 22:15

PEDIGREE EVIDENCE

Generally, § 21:12, 23:16, 23:18

INDEX

INDEX

INDEX

PUBLIC RECORDS

Records and Recording (this index)

PUBLIC TRIAL

Generally, § 1:6

PUNITIVE AND EXEMPLARY DAMAGES

Generally, § 29:8, 29:9
Court costs, § 34:5
Libel action, § 29:23
Opening statement, order of making, § 5:5

QUALIFICATIONS

Expert and opinion evidence, § 22:16, 22:17, 22:21, 22:33
Jurors, § 4:1
Mistrial, attorney disqualification, § 27:3

QUANTITY

Amount or Quantity (this index)

QUASH

Witnesses, § 9:4

QUASHING

Vacating or Setting Aside (this index)

QUESTIONS OF LAW AND FACT

Generally, 1:8, § 1:8
Competency of witness, § 11:1
Credibility of witnesses, § 10:4
Directed verdict, § 2:3, 28:3
Foreseeability of accident, § 7:2
Husband and wife, status of privileged communication between, §16:3
Jurors, challenges for cause, § 4:1, 4:3, 4:4
Spontaneous declarations, § 23:21

QUOTIENT VERDICTS

Generally, § 32:7, 33:1

RACE OR NATIONAL ORIGIN

Closing argument, improper remarks

in, 30:8, § 30:8
Cross-examination of witnesses, § 14:10, 14:11
Jurors, selection of, § 4:7

RADIO

News Media (this index)

RAILROAD CROSSING ACCIDENT

Negative evidence, admissibility of, § 13:3

RAPE

Communications with jurors, § 32:3
Hearsay evidence, § 23:3
Jury and jury trial, § 32:9
Public trial, § 1:6

READING TO JURY

Jury and Jury Trial (this index)

REAL ESTATE BROKER

Listings as constituting hearsay, § 23:3

REAL EVIDENCE

Demonstrative and Real Evidence (this index)

REAL PROPERTY

Admissions and declarations, § 24:12
Court costs, § 34:5
Damages to real estate, § 29:21, 29:22
Eminent Domain (this index)
Instructions to jury, § 31:6
Interest included in judgment, computation of, § 34:4
Mistrial, § 27:3
Taxation (this index)
Value (this index)
View by jury, § 20:1

REASONABLE DOUBT

Criminal contempt, § 3:4
Handwriting, genuineness of, § 22:25

REBUTTAL EVIDENCE OR TESTIMONY

Generally, § 6:3, 7:1

900

INDEX

INDEX

Instructions to jury in considering income taxes in determining award, § 31:8, 31:9

Relevancy of questions as to value, § 13:2

TAXICABS

Variance between pleadings and proof, § 28:4

TEACHERS

Disciplinary proceeding, stipulations in, § 8:5

TEACHERS' ASSOCIATION

Self-incrimination, application of privilege to records, § 13:11

TEETH OR BITE MARKS

Expert testimony as to identification, § 22:15

TELEGRAMS

Presumption of delivery of telegram, § 18:10

TELEPHONE

Jury and jury trial, § 32:2

TELEPHONE CONVERSATIONS

Confidential and privileged communications, § 16:7, 16:12

Direct examination of witnesses, § 13:19

Jurors, improper conduct of, § 32:8

TELEVISION

News Media (this index)

TERMS AND CONDITIONS

Conditions and Terms (this index)

TERRITORIES AND POSSESSIONS OF UNITED STATES

Judicial notice of statutes, § 21:6

TESTS

Experiments and Tests (this index)

TEXTBOOKS

Cross-examination of expert witness, § 22:33

THIRD PARTY ACTIONS

Apportionment of verdicts, § 33:2

Judicial admissions in pleadings, § 24:5

Stipulations discontinuing third-party actions, § 8:5

THIRD PERSONS

Confidential or privileged communications heard by third persons, § 11:4, 16:3, 16:7

Damages affected by payments received by plaintiff from third persons, § 29:27

Dead man's statute, persons barred from testifying, § 12:3, 12:10

Self-incrimination, standing to object to, § 13:10

Verdict, § 33:2

THREATS

Hearsay evidence, § 23:5a

Husband and wife, privileged communication between, § 16:3

TIME OR DATE

Dead man statute, time in which incompetency determined, § 12:5

Death after three years' absence, presumption of, § 18:6

Instructions to jury, request for, § 31:3

Interest included in judgment, computation of, § 34:4

Objections and exceptions to evidence, timeliness of, § 26:3

Per diem or unit of time measurement for damages, § 29:12, 29:16, 30:5, 30:8

Peremptory challenges, § 4:2

INDEX

INDEX

INDEX

INDEX

INDEX

NEW YORK PRACTICE LIBRARY

Trial Handbook for New York Lawyers Third Edition

by

Aaron J. Broder, Esq.

INSERT this new cumulative supplement into the pocket located on the inside back cover of your volume.

CUMULATIVE SUPPLEMENT
Issued March 1998

WEST GROUP

Bancroft-Whitney • Clark Boardman Callaghan
Lawyers Cooperative Publishing • WESTLAW® • West Publishing

TABLE OF CONTENTS

CHAPTER 1
THE CONDUCT OF THE TRIAL

CHAPTER 2
MOTIONS DURING TRIAL, DEFAULT AND DISMISSAL

CHAPTER 3
CONTEMPT OF COURT

CHAPTER 4
SELECTION OF JURY

CHAPTER 5
OPENING STATEMENTS

3

4

CHAPTER 12

DEAD MAN STATUTE

CHAPTER 13

EXAMINATION OF WITNESSES

CHAPTER 14

CROSS-EXAMINATION

CHAPTER 15

REDIRECT AND RECROSS EXAMINATION

CHAPTER 16

PRIVILEGED COMMUNICATIONS

6

CHAPTER 23
HEARSAY EVIDENCE

CHAPTER 24
ADMISSIONS

CHAPTER 25
ADMISSIBILITY OF OTHER TYPES OF EVIDENCE

Table of Contents

CHAPTER 1

THE CONDUCT OF THE TRIAL

§ 1:2 BIFURCATION—Bifurcation in a personal injury action is not appropriate where the nature of the injuries has an important bearing on the question of liability. Where, in a medical malpractice action, based on negligence in delivery and post-natal care alleged to have caused asphyxia, brain damage, and spastic quadriplegia, plaintiffs showed that it would be necessary for their medical experts to analyze the injuries to support their opinion that the injuries were caused by asphyxia, and defendants experts would also refer to the medical history to support their defense that the damage was caused by a subarachnoid hemorrhage, the defendants' motion to bifurcate was properly denied. *Mason v. Moore*, 226 A.D.2d 993, 641 N.Y.S.2d 195 (3d Dep't 1996).

Where some of plaintiff's injuries do have an important bearing on the issue of liability and others do not, the trial may be bifurcated with plaintiff being permitted to introduce evidence of the relevant injuries during the liability phase of the trial. *Faber v. New York City Housing Authority*, 227 A.D.2d 248, 642 N.Y.S.2d 279 (1st Dep't 1996).

§ 1:3 PRESENCE OF PARTIES AND COUNSEL—While the Family Court Act guarantees certain indigent persons the right to assistance of counsel, those persons are not guaranteed the right to choose their assigned counsel. Where the court refused to accede to a parent's demand that she be assigned the attorney of her choice, her decision to proceed pro se was not coerced, nor had the court deprived her of her right to counsel. *Child Welfare*

11

Admin. (John R.) v. Jennifer A., 218 A.D.2d 694, 630 N.Y.S.2d 379 (2d Dep't 1995).

Absent an express waiver or unusual circumstances, a party is entitled to be present at all stages of the trial; the stereotypical assumption that a party's disability will prejudice the jury is an insufficient ground for excluding that party from the courtroom. Where the infant plaintiff had sustained brain damage resulting in spastic quadriplegia, the trial court properly denied the defendants' motion to exclude him from the unified trial of liability and damages in his malpractice action. *Mason v. Moore,* 226 A.D.2d 993, 641 N.Y.S.2d 195 (3d Dep't 1996). (Compare: *Caputo v. Joseph J. Sarcona Trucking Co., Inc.,* 204 A.D.2d 507, 611 N.Y.S.2d 655 (2d Dep't 1994), main volume of Handbook, p. 6).

Except where otherwise provided by statute, the constitutional right to counsel does not extend to civil actions or administrative proceedings. Due process in such cases requires only that a party be afforded a reasonable opportunity to obtain counsel. Where a party to an administrative proceeding had at least seventeen days prior to the hearing to obtain counsel and failed to do so, the hearing officer's denial of a request for an adjournment did not deprive the party of due process. *Baywood Elec. Corp. v. New York State Dept. of Labor,* 232 A.D.2d 553, 649 N.Y.S.2d 28 (2d Dep't 1996). Similarly, the right to "effective assistance of counsel" does not generally apply in civil actions and administrative proceedings. *Siddiqui v. New York State Dept. of Health,* 228 A.D.2d 735, 644 N.Y.S.2d 64 (3d Dep't 1996).

Where the right to effective assistance of counsel does exist, such as in a permanent neglect proceedings, the denial thereof may be raised at any time, provided that the party demonstrates (1) that he or she was deprived of meaningful representation, and (2) that actual prejudice was suffered as a result of the claimed deficiencies in representation. *Matter of James R., Jr.,* 661 N.Y.S.2d 160 (App. Div. 4th Dep't 1997).

§ 1:4   **THE DEMEANOR OF THE JUDGE**—Although the trial court has broad authority to control the courtroom, rule on admission of evidence, elicit and clarify testimony, expedite the proceedings, and admonish counsel and witnesses where necessary, where the trial court questioned numerous witnesses, dictated the length of answers, at times suggested answers, and generally interjected himself into the proceedings, so that the jury was not allowed to review the case in the calm untrammeled spirit necessary to effect justice, the judgment was reversed and the case was remanded for new trial before a different judge, even though no bias or prejudice had been displayed. *Campbell v. Rogers & Wells*, 218 A.D.2d 576, 631 N.Y.S.2d 6 (1st Dep't 1995).

§ 1:5   CONDUCT OF COUNSEL—Although a party to a civil suit has the right to be represented by counsel, the additional right to effective assistance of counsel conferred by the Federal and State Constitutions, U.S. CONST. amend. VI; N.Y. CONST., art. I, § 6, does not generally extend to civil actions or administrative proceedings. Where a physician's license had been revoked in a disciplinary hearing before the Administrative Review Board for Professional Medical Conduct, his subsequent Article 78 proceeding to review the determination based, inter alia, on ineffective assistance of counsel was dismissed. *Siddiqui v. New York State Dept. of Health*, 228 A.D.2d 735, 644 N.Y.S.2d 64 (3d Dep't 1996).

§ 1:6   PUBLICITY OF PROCEEDINGS—New York recognizes a common law right of the press and public to attend civil and administrative proceedings that have historically been open to the public and there must be "compelling reasons" before that right will be abrogated. Where the petitioner had brought an Article 78 proceeding seeking prohibition to restrain the prosecutor from proceeding with a prosecution for murder after the prosecutor had disregarded an agreement not to prosecute petitioner for murder, petitioner had not made out a compelling showing of a substantial probability that his right to a fair trial would be prejudiced by publicity arising out of the Article 78 proceeding, and the petition was dismissed. *Whitehurst v. Kavanagh*, 167 Misc. 2d 86, 636 N.Y.S.2d 591 (Sup. Ct. 1995), order aff'd, 218 A.D.2d 366, 640 N.Y.S.2d 345 (3d Dep't 1996), leave to appeal dismissed in part on other grounds, denied, 88 N.Y.2d 873, 645 N.Y.S.2d 443, 668 N.E.2d 414 (1996).

RESEARCH REFERENCES

American Law Reports

Disqualification of judge for bias against counsel for litigant, 54 A.L.R.5th 575.

Power of successor judge taking office during term time to vacate, set aside or annul judgment entered by his or her predecessor, 51 A.L.R.5th 747.

Substitution of judge in state criminal trial, 45 A.L.R.5th 591.

Prejudicial effect of trial judge's remarks, during civil jury trial, disparaging litigants, witnesses, or subject matters of litigation—modern cases, 35 A.L.R.5th 1.

Prejudicial effect, in civil case, of communications between judges and jurors, 33 A.L.R.5th 205.

Failure or refusal of state court judge to have record made of bench conference with counsel in criminal proceeding, 31 A.L.R.5th 704.

Prejudicial effect, in civil case, of communications between court officials or attendants and jurors, 31 A.L.R.5th 572.

Disqualification of judge as affecting validity of decision in which other nondisqualified judges participated, 29 A.L.R.5th 722.

Profane or obscene language by party, witness, or observer during trial proceedings as basis for contempt citation, 29 A.L.R.5th 702.

Determination of indigency entitling accused in state criminal case to appointment of counsel on appeal, 26 A.L.R.5th 765.

When should jury's deliberation proceed from charged offense to lesser-included offense, 26 A.L.R.5th 603.

ALR Index: Bias or Prejudice; Conduct; Evidence Rules; Judges; Own Motion of Court; Publicity; Witnesses

American Jurisprudence 2d

81 Am Jur 2d, Witnesses §§ 50-58, 724-730

American Jurisprudence Pleading and Practice

23A Am Jur Pl & Pr Forms (Rev), Trial, Forms 76-103

8 Am Jur Pl & Pr Forms (Rev), Criminal Procedure §§ 193-199

Other Resources

KeyCite™/Insta-Cite®: Cases referred to herein can be further researched through the KeyCite™ and Insta-Cite® computer-assisted services. Use KeyCite or Insta-Cite to check citations for form, parallel references, and prior and later history. For comprehensive citator information, including citations to other decisions and secondary materials that have mentioned or discussed the cases cited, use KeyCite. ALR and ALR Fed Annotations referred to herein can be further researched through the WESTLAW® Find service.

CHAPTER 2

MOTIONS DURING TRIAL, DEFAULT AND DISMISSAL

§ 2:2.   Continuances
§ 2:3.   Motion for Judgment During Trial
§ 2:6.   Post-trial Motion for Judgment and New Trial
§ 2:8.   Default and Involuntary Dismissal

§ 2:2 CONTINUANCES—Where the defendant had at least five weeks' notice of the trial date, thereby providing him with ample time to retain new counsel if he was dissatisfied with his attorney, the trial court did not abuse its discretion in denying the eve-of-trial motion for an adjournment to obtain new counsel. *Rosato v. Macier*, 222 A.D.2d 865, 635 N.Y.S.2d 726 (3d Dep't 1995).

The trial court did not abuse its discretion in denying a defendant taxi owner's request for a continuance to produce the driver where (1) the driver's deposition testimony failed to refute the plaintiff pedestrian's allegations of negligence, and (2) the owner did not exercise due diligence to secure the driver's appearance. *Razzaque v. Krakow Taxi, Inc.*, 656 N.Y.S.2d 208 (App. Div. 1st Dep't 1997).

Although an application to adjourn a trial is a discretionary matter for the trial court, the denial of a request for a continuance of a few days was an improvident exercise of discretion where the defendant appeared in person and represented that he had retained new counsel who was out of town, and there was no indication that the request was a dilatory tactic. *Jadar Development Corp. v. Greenspan*, 230 A.D.2d 828, 646 N.Y.S.2d 828 (2d Dep't 1996).

Denial of a request for a continuance was not an abuse of discretion where a pro se litigant had initially waived the right to counsel, and did not request counsel until the hearing had already begun. *Croce v. Croce*, 236 A.D.2d 646, 653 N.Y.S.2d 188 (3d Dep't 1997).

§ 2:3 MOTION FOR JUDGMENT DURING TRIAL—The trial court properly granted plaintiff's motion for a directed verdict

17

in a dental negligence action. Although plaintiff's claim of negligence was established by expert testimony, the credibility of which is ordinarily for the jury, there was no rational view of the evidence that could have supported a jury finding in defendant's favor. *Guiton v. Gottlieb*, 236 A.D.2d 203, 653 N.Y.S.2d 553 (1st Dep't 1997).

§ 2:6 POST-TRIAL MOTION FOR JUDGMENT AND NEW TRIAL

—The trial court as no power to unconditionally modify a jury's findings as to damages in a personal injury action. Where the trial judge unconditionally increased the jury's verdict, the Appellate Division modified the judgment to reflect that a new trial would be granted unless the defendant stipulated to the increased amount. *Bensalem v. Royal-Pak Systems,* Inc., 228 A.D.2d 363, 644 N.Y.S.2d 271 (1st Dep't 1996).

§ 2:8 DEFAULT AND INVOLUNTARY DISMISSAL

—Although the trial court may grant a default judgment and direct an assessment of damages where a defendant fails to appear for trial, the defendant is then entitled to notice prior to the inquest. Where the inquest was conducted without such notice, and defendant's motion to vacate was denied, the order was modified to the extent of directing a new assessment of damages. The default, however, was not vacated, since defendant failed to demonstrate a meritorious defense. *Moore v. Copiers, Inc.*, 237 A.D.2d 585, 655 N.Y.S.2d 991 (2d Dep't 1997).

Where a defendant moved and failed to notify her attorney of her new address, and there was no contact for four years, and the trial court entered judgment against her, her contention that her attorney had failed to make diligent attempts to find her for trial did not amount to a reasonable excuse for her default. Denial of the motion to vacate the default was affirmed. *Dudley v. Steese*, 228 A.D.2d 931, 644 N.Y.S.2d 824 (3d Dep't 1996).

RESEARCH REFERENCES

American Law Reports

Dismissal of state court action for plaintiff's failure or refusal to obey court order relating to pleadings or parties, 3 A.L.R.5th 237.

American Jurisprudence 2d

75A Am Jur 2d, Trials § 854

75 Am Jur 2d, Trials §§ 440-446, 463-488

56 Am Jur 2d, Motions, Rules, and Orders §§ 2-19

American Jurisprudence Pleading and Practice

23 Am Jur Pl & Pr Forms (Rev), Trial, Forms 281-288

Other Resources

KeyCite™/Insta-Cite®: Cases referred to herein can be further researched through the KeyCite™ and Insta-Cite® computer-assisted services. Use KeyCite or Insta-Cite to check citations for form, parallel references, and prior and later history. For comprehensive citator information, including citations to other decisions and secondary materials that have mentioned or discussed the cases cited, use KeyCite. ALR and ALR Fed Annotations referred to herein can be further researched through the WESTLAW® Find service.

CHAPTER 3
CONTEMPT OF COURT

§ 3:1.   Power of Court to Punish for Contempt
§ 3:2.   Civil and Criminal Contempt
§ 3:3.   Procedure in Civil Contempt
§ 3:5.   Acts Constituting Criminal Contempt
§ 3:6.   Acts Constituting Civil Contempt

§ 3:1 POWER OF COURT TO PUNISH FOR CONTEMPT—A court order must be obeyed, no matter how erroneous it may be, so long as the court is possessed of jurisdiction and the order is not void on its face. Where an attorney for a party released funds in violation of orders of attachment, the subsequent vacatur of the attachment orders did not excuse disobedience nunc pro tunc. The Appellate Division ordered that the amount of the contempt award would await determination of a new action for damages against the same defendants. *Sigmoil Resources N.V. v. Fabbri*, 228 A.D.2d 335, 644 N.Y.S.2d 503 (1st Dep't 1996). See also, *Village of St. Johnsville v. Triumpho,* 220 A.D.2d 847, 632 N.Y.S.2d 263 (3d Dep't 1995).

A husband in default of a Florida matrimonial judgment was properly held in contempt in New York, where alternative means of enforcing the judgment would be ineffectual, and ample evidence of willfulness was shown. *Brand v. Brand,* 236 A.D.2d 229, 653 N.Y.S.2d 22 (1st Dep't 1997).

§ 3:2 CIVIL AND CRIMINAL CONTEMPT—A disbarred attorney was guilty of criminal contempt for failure to comply with the order of disbarment, which required him to file an affidavit of compliance with the disbarment order within ten days. The disbarred attorney had continued to deposit and distribute settlement proceeds of actions after his disbarment. However, there was no civil contempt, since there was no showing that his actions were calculated to or actually did defeat, impair, or prejudice the

rights or remedies of a party to a civil proceeding. *Matter of Greene*, 225 A.D.2d 273, 649 N.Y.S.2d 937 (2d Dep't 1996), appeal and leave to appeal dismissed, 89 N.Y.2d 938, 654 N.Y.S.2d 718, 677 N.E.2d 290 (1997). *See also, Matter of Sturm*, 225 A.D.2d 108, 648 N.Y.S.2d 662 (2d Dep't 1996).

§ 3:3 PROCEDURE IN CIVIL CONTEMPT—A hearing was not required on an application for criminal and civil contempt, where the opposing papers failed to raise any issue of triable fact. The fact that the decision which was violated was not embodied in an order did not preclude the finding of contempt. *Guiliano v. Carlisle*, 236 A.D.2d 364, 653 N.Y.S.2d 635 (2d Dep't 1997).

A finding of civil contempt for violation of an order should not be granted unless the court order violated is clear and explicit and the act complained of is clearly proscribed. Where there was a legitimate dispute as to the interpretation of a joint custody and visitation order, the finding of contempt was reversed. *Hoglund v. Hoglund*, 234 A.D.2d 794, 651 N.Y.S.2d 239 (3d Dep't 1996).

Where the defendant's wife was held in contempt for failure to comply with a subpoena in proceedings to enforce a judgment against her husband, the fine was properly set in the amount of the judgment. *Corpuel v. Galasso*, 659 N.Y.S.2d 65 (App. Div. 2d Dep't 1997).

§ 3:5 ACTS CONSTITUTING CRIMINAL CONTEMPT—A summary contempt finding for unjustified failure to answer the court's questions did not require that the party be found to have caused a disturbance or to have acted violently. Where the contumacious refusal to answer disrupted the orderly proceedings of the court and demonstrated a lack of respect for the authority of the court, petitioner's Article 78 proceedings to review the summary contempt finding was dismissed and the determination was confirmed. *Cimino v. Elliott*, 227 A.D.2d 986, 643 N.Y.S.2d 837 (4th Dep't 1996), appeal dismissed, 90 N.Y.2d 844, 660 N.Y.S.2d 869, 683 N.E.2d 775 (1997).

§ 3:6 ACTS CONSTITUTING CIVIL CONTEMPT—A civil contempt finding was affirmed against the bailees of an automobile

which the Surrogate had ordered them to turn over to the ancillary administrator; the bailees had contrived a competing claim to the property in an apparent attempt to acquire it for themselves, engaging the ancillary administrator in years of unnecessary and expensive litigation, and impairing the rights to possession of the car as unequivocally established by the underlying order. *Application of Re,* 659 N.Y.S.2d 3 (App. Div. 1st Dep't 1997).

A finding of civil contempt against a litigant was not justified, where the modest delay in compliance with a discovery order did not impede or prejudice the rights of any party. *Cherico, Stix & Associates v. Abramson,* 235 A.D.2d 515, 653 N.Y.S.2d 36 (2d Dep't 1997).

RESEARCH REFERENCES

American Law Reports

Propriety of publishing identity of sexual assault victim, 40 A.L.R.5th 787.

Vicarious liability of attorneys for acts of associated counsel, 35 A.L.R.5th 717.

Right of defendant in criminal contempt proceeding to obtain information by deposition, 33 A.L.R.5th 761.

Profane or obscene language by party, witness, or observer during trial proceedings as basis for contempt citation, 29 A.L.R.5th 702.

American Jurisprudence Pleading and Practice

7 Am Jur Pl & Pr Forms (Rev), Contempt, Form 53, Motion or Petition to Punish for Contempt

Other Resources

KeyCite™/Insta-Cite®: Cases referred to herein can be further researched through the KeyCite™ and Insta-Cite® computer-assisted services. Use KeyCite or Insta-Cite to check citations for form, parallel references, and prior and later history. For comprehensive citator information, including citations to other decisions and secondary materials that have mentioned or discussed the cases cited, use KeyCite. ALR and ALR Fed Annotations

referred to herein can be further researched through the
WESTLAW® Find service.

CHAPTER 4
SELECTION OF JURY

§ 4:2.   Peremptory Challenges
§ 4:5.   The Right to a Fair and Impartial Jury
§ 4:7.   Discrimination Because of Sex, Race, Etc.
§ 4:8.   Conduct of Voir Dire Examination

§ 4:2   PEREMPTORY CHALLENGES—In an action against two municipal defendants, a police department, and a vehicle operator, the defendants were not so united in interest that they had to be considered a single party; the trial court did not err in limiting plaintiff to three peremptory challenges. *Koperda v. Town of Whitestown*, 224 A.D.2d 944, 637 N.Y.S.2d 899 (4th Dep't 1996).

§ 4:5   THE RIGHT TO A FAIR AND IMPARTIAL JURY— The identities of expert witnesses in medical malpractice cases are generally immune from discovery until trial. CPLR § 3101(d)(1)(i). However, jury selection is not a pretrial stage, but is part of the trial, and parties are entitled to know whether the appearance of any witness will cause bias or prejudice. Thus, the trial court required experts' identities to be disclosed at the time of jury selection. *Draves v. Chua*, 168 Misc. 2d 314, 642 N.Y.S.2d 1022 (Sup. Ct. 1996).

§ 4:7   DISCRIMINATION BECAUSE OF SEX, RACE, ETC.— Prospective jurors' lack of familiarity with technical issues, which were properly related to specific issues presented in a case, were a sufficient race-neutral explanation to warrant defendant's peremptory challenges to the only two African-American women on the panel. *Superior Sales & Salvage, Inc. v. Time Release Sciences, Inc.*, 227 A.D.2d 987, 643 N.Y.S.2d 291 (4th Dep't 1996).

§ 4:8   CONDUCT OF VOIR DIRE EXAMINATION—Trial court's imposition of jury selection reform rules (now embodied in

25

22 NYCRR 202.33), limiting time for interrogation of jurors and requiring challenges to be exercised after each round of questioning, did not deprive the parties of proper legal representation or of the right to trial by a fair and impartial jury. The denial of the motion to set aside the verdict was affirmed. *Horton v. Associates in Obstetrics and Gynecology P.C.,* 229 A.D.2d 734, 645 N.Y.S.2d 354 (3d Dep't 1996).

RESEARCH REFERENCES

American Law Reports

Use of peremptory challenges to exclude ethnic and racial groups, other than black Americans, from criminal jury—post-Batson state cases, 20 A.L.R.5th 398.

ALR Index: Alternate Jurors; Challenges to Jury; Peremptory Challenges; Questions

American Jurisprudence Pleading and Practice

15 Am Jur Pl & Pr Forms (Rev), Jury, Forms 141-209, Impaneling, Examining, Challenging, and Swearing Jurors

American Jurisprudence Trials

52 Am Jur Trials 1, Civil Litigation

51 Am Jur Trials 1, Litigation Management

49 Am Jur Trials 407, Use of Jury Consultant in Civil Cases

30 Am Jur Trials 561, Jury Selection and Voir Dire in Criminal Cases

Other Resources

KeyCite™/Insta-Cite®: Cases referred to herein can be further researched through the KeyCite™ and Insta-Cite® computer-assisted services. Use KeyCite or Insta-Cite to check citations for form, parallel references, and prior and later history. For comprehensive citator information, including citations to other decisions and secondary materials that have mentioned or discussed the cases cited, use KeyCite. ALR and ALR Fed Annotations referred to herein can be further researched through the WESTLAW® Find service.

CHAPTER 5

OPENING STATEMENTS

§ 5:2.   Dismissal on the Opening Statement
§ 5:4.   Content of the Opening Statements

§ 5:2   DISMISSAL ON THE OPENING STATEMENT—The trial court is obligated to "accept as true" all of the facts stated in the opening, and resolve in plaintiff's favor all of the material facts in issue. Where plaintiff alleged that a manhole cover had been defectively installed, which would have obviated the need to prove written notice of the defect prior to the accident, the trial court's dismissal following opening statement, based upon speculation that the sidewalk might have been replaced by an abutting landowner at some time, violated the foregoing standard and placed a burden on plaintiff that went beyond her burden of proof. The dismissal was reversed. *Martinez v. City of New York*, 224 A.D.2d 242, 637 N.Y.S.2d 706 (1st Dep't 1996).

Dismissal upon plaintiff's opening statement is greatly disfavored. A cause of action may be dismissed after opening statements only where it can be determined either (1) that the complaint does not state a cause of action, or (2) that the cause of action is conclusively defeated by something interposed by way of defense and clearly admitted as fact, or (3) that counsel for the plaintiff, in the opening, by some admission or statement of facts, so completely ruined the case that the court is justified in granting nonsuit. *Schomaker v. Pecoraro*, 237 A.D.2d 424, 654 N.Y.S.2d 830 (2d Dep't 1997).

Where plaintiff's counsel admitted, in opening, that there was no prior written notice of the roadway defect, and failed to raise any exception to the "Pothole Law," the complaint was properly dismissed following the opening statement. *Sewell v. City of New York*, 656 N.Y.S.2d 916 (App. Div. 2d Dep't 1997).

§ 5:4   CONTENT OF THE OPENING STATEMENTS—Where opening statements were not transcribed, the Appellate Division

27

held that it could not review defendants' contention that plaintiff's counsel had made improper comments therein. *Wilcox v. Morrow*, 226 A.D.2d 1077, 641 N.Y.S.2d 774 (4th Dep't 1996).

RESEARCH REFERENCES

American Law Reports

Prejudicial effect of statement by prosecutor that verdict, recommendation of punishment, or other finding by jury is subject to review or correction by other authorities, 10 A.L.R.5th 700.

Propriety and prejudicial effect of trial counsel's reference or suggestion in medical malpractice case that defendant is insured, 71 A.L.R.4th 1025.

Propriety of trial court order limiting time for opening or closing argument in criminal case—state cases, 71 A.L.R.4th 200.

American Jurisprudence Pleading and Practice

9A Am Jur Pl & Pr Forms (Rev), Evidence, Form 22
8B Am Jur Pl & Pr Forms (Rev), Dismissal, Discontinuance, and Nonsuit § 250

American Jurisprudence Trials

52 Am Jur Trials 1, Commonsense Principles of Civil Litigation
51 Am Jur Trials 1, Litigation Management
5 Am Jur Trials 305, Opening Statement—Defense View
5 Am Jur Trials 285, Opening Statement—Plaintiff's View

Other Resources

KeyCite™/Insta-Cite®: Cases referred to herein can be further researched through the KeyCite™ and Insta-Cite® computer-assisted services. Use KeyCite or Insta-Cite to check citations for form, parallel references, and prior and later history. For comprehensive citator information, including citations to other decisions and secondary materials that have mentioned or discussed the cases cited, use KeyCite. ALR and ALR Fed Annotations

referred to herein can be further researched through the WESTLAW® Find service.

CHAPTER 6
ORDER OF PROOF

§ 6:3.   Rebuttal Testimony
§ 6:4.   Right to Introduce Testimony at Later Stage

§ 6:3   REBUTTAL TESTIMONY—Where the trial court permitted plaintiff to explain on rebuttal that he was undergoing medical treatment and taking medication which caused confusion and memory lapses, apparently to explain lapses in his direct case, the Appellate Division held that the probative value of the testimony outweighed its potential prejudice. The trial court's exercise of discretion, and the judgment for plaintiff, were affirmed. *Schonfeld v. Brody*, 220 A.D.2d 572, 632 N.Y.S.2d 797 (2d Dep't 1995).

The question whether to permit introduction of rebuttal evidence rests within the sound discretion of the trial court, and the court's decision in that regard should not be disturbed on appeal absent a clear abuse or improvident exercise of that discretion. In an action against a psychiatrist for malpractice based on an alleged sexual relationship with a patient, the trial court did not abuse its discretion in refusing to reopen the patient's case to allow plaintiff to call other former patients of the defendant for rebuttal after plaintiff stated that she had never seen scars above the psychiatrist's waist and the psychiatrist then exhibited surgical scars on his abdomen to the jury. While plaintiff contended that the witnesses would have testified that they had also had sex with the defendant and never saw the scars, plaintiff had already attempted to explain her lack of observation by stating that the defendant never removed his boxer shorts during their encounters. Judgment, on a verdict for the defendant, was affirmed. *Coopersmith v. Gold*, 223 A.D.2d 572, 636 N.Y.S.2d 399 (2d Dep't 1996), order aff'd, 89 N.Y.2d 957, 655 N.Y.S.2d 857, 678 N.E.2d 469 (1997), reargument dismissed, 90 N.Y.2d 889, 661 N.Y.S.2d 833, 684 N.E.2d 283 (1997).

The testimony of plaintiff's rebuttal witness was properly

received to show the hostility of a defense witness. *Marshall v. Handler*, 237 A.D.2d 158, 654 N.Y.S.2d 754 (1st Dep't 1997).

In a divorce action, the trial court properly limited the plaintiff's rebuttal case where the proposed testimony was redundant and could have been presented during plaintiff's direct case. *Petek v. Petek*, 657 N.Y.S.2d 738 (App. Div. 2d Dep't 1997).

§ 6:4   RIGHT TO INTRODUCE TESTIMONY AT LATER STAGE—The trial court abused its discretion in denying plaintiff's motion for leave to reopen his proof after the court concluded that the proof on plaintiff's direct case was insufficient to establish a causal connection between the accident in question and plaintiff's injuries, where: (1) any error in failing to establish the connection was inadvertent, (2) the motion was promptly brought, (3) plaintiff made an appropriate offer of proof by identifying the prospective witness and articulating the substance of his testimony, and (4) no prejudice to the defendant was shown. *Benjamin v. Desai*, 228 A.D.2d 764, 643 N.Y.S.2d 717 (3d Dep't 1996).

The trial court has discretion to permit reopening of the case, but such discretion should be sparingly exercised. The denial of a request to reopen evidence was not an abuse of discretion, where the party had failed, despite several opportunities during her direct case, to elicit the evidence at issue. *Ellis v. Ellis*, 235 A.D.2d 1002, 653 N.Y.S.2d 180 (3d Dep't 1997).

RESEARCH REFERENCES

American Law Reports

 ALR Index: Rebuttal; Witnesses

American Jurisprudence 2d

 75 Am Jur 2d, Trial §§ 354-394

Other Resources

 KeyCite™/Insta-Cite®: Cases referred to herein can be further researched through the KeyCite™ and Insta-Cite® computer-assisted services. Use KeyCite or Insta-Cite to check citations for form, parallel references, and prior and later history. For comprehensive citator information, including citations to other decisions and secondary materials that have mentioned or discussed the cases cited, use KeyCite. ALR and ALR Fed Annotations referred to herein can be further researched through the WESTLAW® Find service.

cited. use KeyCite, ALR and ALR Fed Annotations referred to herein can be further researched through the WESTLAW Pro

CHAPTER 7

BURDEN OF PROOF

§ 7:4. Burden of Proof in Wrongful Death Cases

§ 7:4 BURDEN OF PROOF IN WRONGFUL DEATH CASES—Although plaintiff in a wrongful death case has the burden of proof at trial on the issue of conscious pain and suffering of the decedent, a defendant moving for summary judgment on the pain and suffering cause of action has the initial burden of showing that the decedent did not endure conscious pain and suffering. Where the moving defendant failed to satisfy that threshold burden, and particularly where plaintiff submitted expert affidavits on the issue, an order granting summary judgment to defendant was reversed. *Massey v. New York City Housing Authority*, 230 A.D.2d 601, 646 N.Y.S.2d 105 (1st Dep't 1996).

RESEARCH REFERENCES

American Law Reports

ALR Index: Alibi; Criminal Law; Presumptions and Burden of Proof; Prima Facie Evidence

American Jurisprudence Pleading and Practice

16A Am Jur Pl & Pr Forms (Rev), Libel and Slander, Form 296, Proving Truth of Statements as Defense in Action for Defamation

Other Resources

KeyCite™/Insta-Cite®: Cases referred to herein can be further researched through the KeyCite™ and Insta-Cite® computer-assisted services. Use KeyCite or Insta-Cite to check citations for form, parallel references, and prior and later history. For comprehensive citator information, including citations to other decisions and secondary materials that have mentioned or discussed the cases cited, use KeyCite. ALR and ALR Fed Annotations referred to herein can be further researched through the WESTLAW® Find service.

CHAPTER 8

PROOF OF FACTS

§ 8:4. Use of Stipulations to Excuse Proving Facts
§ 8:5. Construction and Enforcement of Stipulations
§ 8:6. Agreements Exempting Certain Tortfeasors from Liability

§ 8:4 USE OF STIPULATIONS TO EXCUSE PROVING FACTS—Where the defendants, in an action alleging a defective sidewalk, stipulated before trial that they were responsible for the control, maintenance, and repair of the premises, the trial court properly excluded evidence of post-accident repairs. Judgment on a verdict for defendants was affirmed. *Blum v. Bregman*, 225 A.D.2d 324, 638 N.Y.S.2d 473 (1st Dep't 1996).

§ 8:5 CONSTRUCTION AND ENFORCEMENT OF STIPULATIONS—Non-party's agreement, in open court, to guarantee a party's agreement to pay was not enforceable as a stipulation, because only parties can enter into binding stipulations. CPLR 2104. However, the promise was enforceable under ordinary contract principles. *Jacobs v. Jacobs*, 229 A.D.2d 712, 645 N.Y.S.2d 342 (3d Dep't 1996) *(Compare, Wolf v Wolf* [1957, 2d Dept] 4 AD2d 952, see fn. 2, enforcing a stipulation against a party's parents, who were not parties to the action).

An oral stipulation made by counsel in open court will be strictly enforced, and a party will be relieved from the consequences thereof only where there is cause sufficient to invalidate a contract, such as fraud, collusion, mistake, or accident. Where counsel had stipulated that one of the plaintiffs in an automobile accident case would not pursue a claim for personal injuries, an order vacating the stipulation was reversed. There was no showing sufficient to invalidate a contract, or that the attorney, who had represented the client for over three years at the time of the stipulation, did not have at least apparent authority to enter the stipulation. *Javarone v. Pallone*, 234 A.D.2d 814, 651 N.Y.S.2d 664 (3d Dep't

1996), appeal dismissed, 89 N.Y.2d 1030, 658 N.Y.S.2d 245, 680 N.E.2d 619 (1997) and appeal dismissed, 90 N.Y.2d 884, 661 N.Y.S.2d 827, 684 N.E.2d 276 (1997).

§ 8:6 AGREEMENTS EXEMPTING CERTAIN TORTFEASORS FROM LIABILITY

—A general release may not be read to cover matters which the parties did not intend to cover. A release accompanied by a stipulation discontinuing an action should be read together therewith. Where the stipulation discontinued a specific cause of action, the release was determined not to be a defense to another claim. *Dillon v. Dean*, 236 A.D.2d 360, 653 N.Y.S.2d 639 (2d Dep't 1997).

RESEARCH REFERENCES

American Law Reports

Admissibility of statements made for purposes of medical diagnosis or treatment as hearsay exception under Rule 803(4) of the Uniform Rules of Evidence, 38 A.L.R.5th 433.

Applicability of rules of evidence to juvenile transfer, waiver, or certification hearings, 37 A.L.R.5th 703.

Admissibility in homicide prosecution of allegedly gruesome or inflammatory visual recording of crime scene, 37 A.L.R.5th 515.

Propriety of using prior conviction for drug dealing to impeach witness in criminal trial, 37 A.L.R.5th 319.

State statutes or ordinances requiring persons previously convicted of crime to register with authorities, 36 A.L.R.5th 161.

Right of defendant in criminal contempt proceeding to obtain information by deposition, 33 A.L.R.5th 761.

Liability for negligence of ambulance attendants, emergency medical technicians, and the like, rendering emergency medical care outside hospital, 16 A.L.R.5th 605.

American Jurisprudence 2d

75 Am Jur 2d, Trial §§ 354-394

29, 29A Am Jur 2d, Evidence §§ 396, 480, 465, 1432, 1433

American Jurisprudence Pleading and Practice

9A Am Jur Pl & Pr Forms (Rev), Evidence §§ 262-274

Other Resources

KeyCite™/Insta-Cite®: Cases referred to herein can be further researched through the KeyCite™ and Insta-Cite® computer-assisted services. Use KeyCite or Insta-Cite to check citations for form, parallel references, and prior and later history. For comprehensive citator information, including citations to other decisions and secondary materials that have mentioned or discussed the cases cited, use KeyCite. ALR and ALR Fed Annotations referred to herein can be further researched through the WESTLAW® Find service.

CHAPTER 9

WITNESSES

§ 9:3. Witnesses from Out of State
§ 9:4. Subpoena Duces Tecum
§ 9:5. Compensation of Witnesses

§ 9:3 WITNESSES FROM OUT OF STATE—The common law immunity from service of process for persons who voluntarily appear in New York to testify did not apply to a witness who appeared in New York in response to subpoena and not voluntarily. *People v. Calamia*, 169 Misc. 2d 1054, 648 N.Y.S.2d 226 (Sup. Ct. 1996).

§ 9:4 SUBPOENA DUCES TECUM—A subpoena duces tecum may not be used for the purpose of ascertaining the existence of evidence. Its purpose is to compel production of specific documents that are relevant and material to facts at issue in a pending judicial proceeding. Where the defendant in a criminal case sought a subpoena duces tecum for school records of psychological testing, but did not specifically recall whether such testing had occurred, his request was not for specific records, but rather to determine whether they existed, and the request was properly denied. *People v. Carpenter*, 658 N.Y.S.2d 542 (App. Div. 3d Dep't 1997), appeal denied, 90 N.Y.2d 902, 663 N.Y.S.2d 514, 686 N.E.2d 226 (1997).

Plaintiff's application for a subpoena duces tecum to the New York City Police Department, to produce all of its documents concerning the plaintiffs and the Department's investigation, was an improper attempt to engage in general discovery or a "fishing expedition" through the use of a subpoena, and was properly denied. *Oak Beach Inn Corp. v. Town of Babylon*, 658 N.Y.S.2d 72 (App. Div. 2d Dep't 1997).

Denial of a non-party examining physician's motion to quash a subpoena duces tecum for virtually all of his office records was reversed, where the issuing party admitted that the records were sought merely to gain material for collateral cross-examination as to the physician's credibility. *Pernice v. Devora,* 657 N.Y.S.2d 70 (App. Div. 2d Dep't 1997).

A subpoena duces tecum may not be used as part of a fishing expedition or to ascertain the existence of evidence. The party requesting that the court issue a subpoena duces tecum must make a preliminary showing that the record requested actually contains information that the party needs to obtain. A mere showing that the record may potentially uncover relevant evidence is insufficient, and it is necessary for the proponent to offer some factual predicate as to the likelihood that the record sought will contain the information sought. *Bostic v. State,* 232 A.D.2d 837, 649 N.Y.S.2d 200 (3d Dep't 1996).

§ 9:5 COMPENSATION OF WITNESSES—A witness cannot be punished for civil disobedience of a judicial subpoena where the requisite witness fee was not tendered when the subpoena was served or within a reasonable time thereafter. There is no basis for the court to waive the witness fee under the guise of substantial justice. Judgment holding the witness in contempt was reversed. *Hampton v. Annal Management Co., Ltd.,* 168 Misc. 2d 138, 646 N.Y.S.2d 227 (App. Term 1996).

RESEARCH REFERENCES

American Law Reports

Propriety of imposing capital punishment on mentally retarded individuals, 20 A.L.R.5th 177.

Other Resources

KeyCite™/Insta-Cite®: Cases referred to herein can be further researched through the KeyCite™ and Insta-Cite® computer-assisted services. Use KeyCite or Insta-Cite to check citations for form, parallel references, and prior and later history. For comprehensive citator information, including citations to other decisions and secondary materials that have mentioned or discussed the cases cited, use KeyCite. ALR and ALR Fed Annotations referred to herein can be further researched through the WESTLAW® Find service.

cited, use KeyCite, ALR and ALR fed. Annotations
referred to herein can be further researched through the
WESTLAW® Front screen.

CHAPTER 10

IMPEACHMENT OF WITNESSES

§ 10:1. The Impeachment of Witnesses, in General
§ 10:2. Impeachment on Collateral Issues
§ 10:5. Particular Matters Affecting Credibility

§ **10:1 THE IMPEACHMENT OF WITNESSES, IN GENER-AL**—Where plaintiff did not attack defendant's testimony as to the manner of the collision as a recent fabrication, the receipt of the investigating police officer's testimony as to defendant's consistent statement was prejudicial error. *Mooney v. Osowiecky,* 235 A.D.2d 603, 651 N.Y.S.2d 713 (3d Dep't 1997).

§ **10:2 IMPEACHMENT ON COLLATERAL ISSUES**—Although the cross-examiner is concluded by a witness' answer as to charges of immoral conduct, the witness may be confronted with a written statement of the charges to refresh his recollection as to details thereof. Where a plaintiff's treating physician has been asked about disciplinary charges by the cross-examiner, and the cross-examiner then referred to a disciplinary statement to refresh the witness recollection as to the specific charges, but the document was not received in evidence, the rule against impeachment on collateral matters with extrinsic evidence was not violated. *Spanier v. New York City Transit Authority,* 222 A.D.2d 219, 634 N.Y.S.2d 122 (1st Dep't 1995).

Bias or hostility of a witness are not collateral matters, and thus may be proved by extrinsic evidence. The plaintiff in a personal injury action was properly permitted to call a rebuttal witness to show the hostility of defendant's witness. *Marshall v. Handler,* 237 A.D.2d 158, 654 N.Y.S.2d 754 (1st Dep't 1997).

§ **10:5 PARTICULAR MATTERS AFFECTING CREDIBIL-ITY**—Evidence of a manufacturer's postmanufacture modification is admissible in a design defect case if the manufacturer contests the feasibility of that design modification. In a product liability action brought by an infant who lost his arm when it got caught in a combine's leveling auger, where the manufacturer's witnesses contended that tapering the auger to prevent injury would have defeated its function, plaintiffs were entitled to impeach them with evidence that the edges of the auger on a later model of the combine were tapered. *Doty v. Navistar Intern. Transp. Corp.,* 219 A.D.2d 32, 639 N.Y.S.2d 592 (4th Dep't 1996).

Prior settlement of an action by a witness may have an impact on the witness' credibility when called to testify on behalf of the formerly adverse party. Thus, an adverse witness may be shown to have settled a claim with the party calling him to show bias. Where plaintiff in a medical malpractice action called a nurse employed by a hospital, and the nurse gave testimony against a defendant physician, the physician should have been permitted to elicit that the witness employer had previously settled with plaintiff. Any adverse effects of such testimony on the jury's ability to award full damages could have been cured with a limiting instruction. *Hill v. Arnold,* 226 A.D.2d 232, 640 N.Y.S.2d 892 (1st Dep't 1996).

A witness whose employer sued for the witness alleged negligence is an interested witness, notwithstanding that (1) the witness was not sued individually, and (2) the cause of action against the employer has been settled. A nurse, employed by a hospital that had been sued but subsequently settled with plaintiff, who was alleged to have been an active tortfeasor, called by plaintiff to testify against the defendant physicians, is so interested that his testimony may be rejected even though it is not otherwise impeached or contradicted. *Hill v. Arnold,* 226 A.D.2d 232, 640 N.Y.S.2d 892 (1st Dep't 1996).

Impeachment of an expert witness with evidence that he had testified in over 100 cases was proper. *McClain v. Lockport Memorial Hosp.,* 236 A.D.2d 864, 653 N.Y.S.2d 774 (4th Dep't 1997).

A party to a civil case is permitted to utilize audio tapes of conversations with adverse parties and non-party witnesses for impeachment purposes. The fact that the conversations were recorded secretly does not require or authorize preclusion, and the trial court erred in precluding their use. *Breezy Point Co-op., Inc. v. Young,* 234 A.D.2d 409, 651 N.Y.S.2d 121 (2d Dep't 1996).

RESEARCH REFERENCES

American Jurisprudence Proof of Facts

21 Am Jur Proof of Facts 3d 629, Admission of Character Evidence and Evidence of Other Acts

American Jurisprudence Trials

49 Am Jur Trials 501, Examination of a Witness Based on a Prior Statement

Other Resources

KeyCite™/Insta-Cite®: Cases referred to herein can be further researched through the KeyCite™ and Insta-Cite® computer-assisted services. Use KeyCite or Insta-Cite to check citations for form, parallel references, and prior and later history. For comprehensive citator information, including citations to other decisions and secondary materials that have mentioned or discussed the cases cited, use KeyCite. ALR and ALR Fed Annotations referred to herein can be further researched through the WESTLAW® Find service.

CHAPTER 11

COMPETENCY OF A WITNESS TO TESTIFY

§ 11:3 COMPETENCY OF A CHILD TO TESTIFY—The Family Court did not err in receiving the sworn testimony of an eight year-old sodomy victim. The victim (1) indicated that she knew the difference between truth and lie, (2) understood that she had to promise not to tell any lies in court, (3) recognized that she would get into "big trouble" if she failed to tell the truth, and (4) candidly admitted when she did not remember or know an answer during her testimony. *Matter of Jason FF,* 224 A.D.2d 900, 638 N.Y.S.2d 226 (3d Dep't 1996).

§ 11:6 COMPETENCY OF ATHEIST, DEAF MUTE, OR INCOMPETENT TO TESTIFY—The trial court did not improvidently exercise its discretion in allowing a 15 year-old, autistic, and mentally retarded complaining witness to be sworn. Preliminary examination adequately demonstrated that he understood the nature of testifying under oath. *People v. Armenia,* 218 A.D.2d 747, 630 N.Y.S.2d 784 (2d Dep't 1995).

§ 11.1. Competency of a Child to Testify.
§ 11.2. Competency of Artificial, Deaf Mute, or Incompetent to Testify.

§ 11.1 COMPETENCY OF A CHILD TO TESTIFY.— The Family Court did not err in receiving the sworn testimony of eight-year-old sexual abuse victim. The victim (1) indicated that she knew the difference between truth and lie, (2) understood that she had to promise not to tell any lies in court, (3) recognized that she would get into trouble if she failed to tell the truth, and (4) candidly admitted when she did not remember or know answers during her testimony. Matter of Roman P., ___ A.D.2d 908, 908 N.Y.S.2d 226 (3d Dep't 1998).

§ 11.2 COMPETENCY OF ARTIFICIAL, DEAF MUTE, OR INCOMPETENT TO TESTIFY.— The trial court did not improvidently exercise its discretion in allowing a 19-year-old autistic and mentally retarded contaminating witness to be sworn. Plaintiff may establish frequently demonstrated that he understood the nature of testifying rather than. People v. Abraham, 711 N.Y.S.2d 833 (2d Dep't 1998).

CHAPTER 12

DEAD MAN STATUTE

§ 12:1 DISQUALIFICATION UNDER DEAD MAN STATUTE—Even if testimony is barred by the statute, it may be submitted to defeat a motion for summary judgment. *Lancaster v. 46 NYL Partners*, 228 A.D.2d 133, 651 N.Y.S.2d 440 (1st Dep't 1996).

Although testimony that would be excluded at trial may be considered in opposition to a motion for summary judgment, where the excludable evidence is the sole evidence proferred, such evidence is insufficient to defeat the motion. *Matter of Estate of Lockwood*, 234 A.D.2d 782, 651 N.Y.S.2d 224 (3d Dep't 1996).

§ 12:2 PERSONS ENTITLED TO PROTECTION OF DEAD MAN STATUTE—The defendants in a wrongful death action are not protected by the Dead Man Statute from testimony of claimed children of the decedent by which they seek to establish their pedigree, because the defendants are not interested in the decedent's estate. *Lancaster v. 46 NYL Partners*, 228 A.D.2d 133, 651 N.Y.S.2d 440 (1st Dep't 1996).

§ 12:3 PERSONS BARRED FROM TESTIFYING UNDER DEAD MAN STATUTE—The brother of the plaintiff in a personal injury action is not "interested in the event"; any general interest in the outcome would go to credibility but would not preclude his testimony under the statute. Where the defendant in a premises accident case admitted to the plaintiff's brother, shortly after the accident, that he had been aware of the dangerous condition before the accident, the plaintiff's brother was competent to testify as to the admission. *Smith v. Kuhn*, 221 A.D.2d 620, 634 N.Y.S.2d 167 (2d Dep't 1995).

§ 12:10 WHAT TESTIMONY IS BARRED—Note: *Poslock v. Teachers' Retirement Bd. of Teachers' Retirement System,* 209 A.D.2d 87, 624 N.Y.S.2d 574 (1st Dep't 1995), order aff'd, 88 N.Y.2d 146, 643 N.Y.S.2d 935, 666 N.E.2d 528 (1996).

In a proceeding for discharge of a mortgage based on an alleged tender of full payment, where the mortgagee is since deceased, the mortgagor was held incompetent to testify as to the alleged payment. *Matter of Goldin,* 227 A.D.2d 401, 641 N.Y.S.2d 731 (2d Dep't 1996).

RESEARCH REFERENCES

American Jurisprudence Pleading and Practice

   23A Am Jur Pl & Pr Forms (Rev), Forms 98, 99

Other Resources

   KeyCite™/Insta-Cite®: Cases referred to herein can be further researched through the KeyCite™ and Insta-Cite® computer-assisted services. Use KeyCite or Insta-Cite to check citations for form, parallel references, and prior and later history. For comprehensive citator information, including citations to other decisions and secondary materials that have mentioned or discussed the cases cited, use KeyCite. ALR and ALR Fed Annotations referred to herein can be further researched through the WESTLAW® Find service.

CHAPTER 13

EXAMINATION OF WITNESSES

§ 13:5. Competency of Questions Asked on Direct Examination
§ 13:7. Leading Questions
§ 13:8. Aiding a Witness by Refreshing Memory
§ 13:17. Use of Lie Detector (Polygraph) Tests

§ 13:5 COMPETENCY OF QUESTIONS ASKED ON DIRECT EXAMINATION—Evidence of prior, similar acts is inadmissible to prove that the defendant perpetrated the same act on a later, unrelated occasion. In an action brought against a psychiatrist by a patient who claimed that he had improperly engaged in a sexual relationship with her during her course of treatment, the testimony of several former patients of the psychiatrist, who claimed to have been sexually involved with the psychiatrist, was not admissible to prove that he perpetrated the same act on the occasion alleged in the action. *Coopersmith v. Gold*, 89 N.Y.2d 957, 655 N.Y.S.2d 857, 678 N.E.2d 469 (1997), reargument dismissed, 90 N.Y.2d 889, 661 N.Y.S.2d 833, 684 N.E.2d 283 (1997).

§ 13:7 LEADING QUESTIONS—Where an eight year sexual abuse victim was plainly reluctant to testify as to the details of the abuse, Family Court did not abuse its discretion in posing leading questions in order to clarify and expedite the victim's testimony. *Matter of Jason FF,* 224 A.D.2d 900, 638 N.Y.S.2d 226 (3d Dep't 1996).

§ 13:8 AIDING A WITNESS BY REFRESHING MEMORY—The documents or things that may be used to refresh a witness' recollection are not limited to writings. For example, an audiotape may serve the same purpose. *People v. Luchey*, 221 A.D.2d 936, 634 N.Y.S.2d 304 (4th Dep't 1995), appeal denied, 87 N.Y.2d 1021, 644 N.Y.S.2d 155, 666 N.E.2d 1069 (1996), on reconsideration, 88 N.Y.2d 988, 649 N.Y.S.2d 395, 672 N.E.2d 621 (1996).

§ 13:17 USE OF LIE DETECTOR (POLYGRAPH) TESTS—An Administrative Law Judge, in a hearing against the owner of taxi medallions charged with submitting fraudulent receipts, was not required to consider polygraph evidence submitted by the medallion owner, because of the unreliability of such evidence. *King Victor Taxi Corp. v. New York City Taxi and Limousine Com'n*, 236 A.D.2d 325, 654 N.Y.S.2d 358 (1st Dep't 1997) (*Compare: May v Shaw*, 79 A.D.2d 970, 434 N.Y.S.2d 284 (1981, 2d Dept) ¹3:17, main volume).

CHAPTER 14

CROSS-EXAMINATION

§ 14:3. The Scope of Cross-Examination
§ 14:10. Additional Matters Proper on Cross-Examination
§ 14:11. Manner of Conducting Cross-Examination

§ 14:3 THE SCOPE OF CROSS-EXAMINATION—Where the trial court had ruled that a witness could not testify as to the value of property on his direct examination, it was error to permit cross-examination on that issue. The cross-examination exceeded the scope of direct examination, and the witness was not qualified to render the opinion. *Town of Webb v. Sisters Realty North Corp.,* 229 A.D.2d 942, 645 N.Y.S.2d 233 (4th Dep't 1996).

In an action for injuries sustained in a fall on a staircase, the trial court properly permitted defense counsel to cross-examine plaintiff as to whether prior injuries affected plaintiff's ability to walk up and down stairs. The issue was relevant in determining whether plaintiff was comparatively negligent in light of her knowledge of the apparent danger in using the allegedly debris covered staircase. *Pierre-Louis v. Algoo,* 226 A.D.2d 441, 640 N.Y.S.2d 598 (2d Dep't 1996).

§ 14:10 ADDITIONAL MATTERS PROPER ON CROSS-EXAMINATION—The trial court erred in refusing to permit a defendant physician to cross-examine a nurse, who had given testimony critical of the physician, as to the prior settlement between the nurse's employer, a hospital, and plaintiff. The settlement goes to possible bias, and therefore to credibility. *Hill v. Arnold,* 226 A.D.2d 232, 640 N.Y.S.2d 892 (1st Dep't 1996).

§ 14:11 MANNER OF CONDUCTING CROSS-EXAMINATION—The trial court did not err in permitting a defense witness to go on vacation, and to conclude the last 45 minutes of his cross-examination by speakerphone, where (1) the witness' testimony

55

had been delayed by the actions of plaintiff's attorney, and (2) the jury had ample opportunity to observe the demeanor of the witness during the portion of the cross-examination in the courtroom. *Superior Sales & Salvage, Inc. v. Time Release Sciences, Inc.,* 227 A.D.2d 987, 643 N.Y.S.2d 291 (4th Dep't 1996).

Although the cross-examiner is concluded by a witness' answer as to charges of immoral conduct, the witness may be confronted with a written statement of the charges to refresh his recollection as to details thereof. Where a plaintiff's treating physician has been asked about disciplinary charges by the cross-examiner, and the cross-examiner then referred to a disciplinary statement to refresh the witness' recollection as to the specific charges, but the document was not received in evidence, the rule against impeachment on collateral matters with extrinsic evidence was not violated. *Spanier v. New York City Transit Authority,* 222 A.D.2d 219, 634 N.Y.S.2d 122 (1st Dep't 1995).

RESEARCH REFERENCES

American Law Reports

　ALR Index: Cross Examination; Questions; Prior Testimony or Statement

American Jurisprudence Trials

　59 Am Jur Trials 1, Persuasaive Cross-Examination
　50 Am Jur Trials 471, Use and Examination of Experts in Environmental Litigation

Other Resources

　KeyCite™/Insta-Cite®: Cases referred to herein can be further researched through the KeyCite™ and Insta-Cite® computer-assisted services. Use KeyCite or Insta-Cite to check citations for form, parallel references, and prior and later history. For comprehensive citator information, including citations to other decisions and secondary materials that have mentioned or discussed the cases cited, use KeyCite. ALR and ALR Fed Annotations referred to herein can be further researched through the WESTLAW® Find service.

CHAPTER 15
REDIRECT AND RECROSS EXAMINATION

§ 15:1 SCOPE OF REDIRECT EXAMINATION—The trial court has broad discretion in controlling the conduct of the trial, which includes limiting the scope of direct, cross, and redirect examination. The court properly acted within its discretion in limiting the redirect examination to the matters brought out on cross-examination. *Ingebretsen v. Manha*, 218 A.D.2d 784, 631 N.Y.S.2d 72 (2d Dep't 1995).

§ 15:2 EXPLAINING AND CORRECTING TESTIMONY ON REDIRECT EXAMINATION—In an action for medical malpractice in which plaintiff claimed that he had suffered the side effects of drugs prescribed following a misdiagnosis, defense counsel, during cross-examination of plaintiff, read a portion of plaintiff's deposition in an effort to prove that plaintiff had never made complaints of specific side effects. Plaintiff's counsel was properly permitted, on redirect examination, to read other portions of the deposition which demonstrated that plaintiff had made very specific complaints about the side effects of the medications. *Reape v. City of New York*, 228 A.D.2d 659, 645 N.Y.S.2d 499 (2d Dep't 1996).

§ 15:4 RECROSS EXAMINATION—Recross examination was properly limited to matters elicited on redirect, particularly where counsel had deliberately refrained from asking the subject questions on cross examination. *In re Morlin R.*, 236 A.D.2d 201, 653 N.Y.S.2d 331 (1st Dep't 1997).

RESEARCH REFERENCES
American Law Reports
  Propriety of questioning expert witness regarding specific

incidents or allegations of expert's unprofessional conduct or professional negligence, 11 A.L.R.5th 1.

Admissibility of evidence of other offense where record has been expunged or erased, 82 A.L.R.4th 913.

Impeachment or cross-examination of prosecuting witness in sexual offense trial by showing that similar charges were made against other persons, 71 A.L.R.4th 469.

Impeachment or cross-examination of prosecuting witness in sexual offense trial by showing that prosecuting witness threatened to make similar charges against other persons, 71 A.L.R.4th 448.

Admissibility of impeached witness' prior consistent statement—modern state civil cases, 59 A.L.R.4th 1000.

Admissibility of impeached witness' prior consistent statement—modern state criminal cases, 58 A.L.R.4th 1014.

Propriety of cross-examining expert witness regarding his status as "professional witness", 39 A.L.R.4th 742.

Use or admissibility of prior inconsistent statements of witness as substantive evidence of facts to which they relate in criminal case—modern state cases, 30 A.L.R.4th 414.

Cross-examination of character witness for accused with reference to particular acts or crimes—modern state rules, 13 A.L.R.4th 796.

Conviction by court-martial as proper subject of cross-examination for impeachment purposes, 7 A.L.R.4th 468.

American Jurisprudence Trials

59 Am Jur Trials 1, Persuasaive Cross-Examination

Other Resources

KeyCite™/Insta-Cite®: Cases referred to herein can be further researched through the KeyCite™ and Insta-Cite® computer-assisted services. Use KeyCite or Insta-Cite to check citations for form, parallel references, and prior and later history. For comprehensive citator information, including citations to other decisions and secondary materials that have mentioned or discussed the cases cited, use KeyCite. ALR and ALR Fed Annotations

referred to herein can be further researched through the
WESTLAW® Find service.

CHAPTER 16
PRIVILEGED COMMUNICATIONS

§ 16:2 COMMUNICATIONS BETWEEN HUSBAND AND WIFE—The statutory spousal privilege protects confidential communications between a "husband" and a "wife," "during marriage." CPLR 4502(b). The privilege does not protect communications between homosexual persons in a "spousal relationship." *Greenwald v. H & P 29th Street Associates,* 659 N.Y.S.2d 473 (App. Div. 1st Dep't 1997).

§ 16:6 EXISTENCE OF ATTORNEY AND CLIENT RELATIONSHIP—A family relationship between client and attorney does not vitiate the privilege. In a trust accounting proceeding, communications between remaindermen and attorney, who was the son of one remainderman and the nephew of the other, including documents prepared by the attorney for the purpose of protecting his family's legal rights, and provided to the remaindermen in confidence, were privileged. *Matter of Estate of Saxton,* 219 A.D.2d 85, 640 N.Y.S.2d 287 (3d Dep't 1996).

In a child custody proceeding, the child's communications to the law guardian, and to the social worker hired by the law guardian, implicated the attorney client privilege or the immunity from disclosure for attorney work product and material prepared for litigation. The subpoenas demanding the testimony of the law guardian and the social worker were properly quashed. *Renee B. v. Michael B.,* 227 A.D.2d 315, 642 N.Y.S.2d 685 (1st Dep't 1996).

§ 16:7 CONFIDENTIAL NATURE OF THE COMMUNICATION—The attorney-client privilege does not protect documents

61

that are not primarily of a legal character, even though they may be prepared by lawyers. Where an insurer retains an attorney to investigate whether a claim is covered, the investigation is part of the ordinary business of the insurer. Thus, communications and reports that occurred before the insurer had reasonable grounds to disclaim were not confidential communications, and were not protected from disclosure in the insured's action against the insurer for denying the claim. *Bertalo's Restaurant Inc. v. Exchange Ins. Co.,* 658 N.Y.S.2d 656 (App. Div. 2d Dep't 1997).

Fee arrangements between attorney and client do not ordinarily constitute "confidential communication" and are not privileged. Billing statements which are detailed in showing services, conversations and conferences between counsel and other others are protected; no such privilege attaches, however, to fee statements which do not provide detailed accounts of legal services provided. *Orange County Publications, Inc., a Div. of Ottaway Newspapers v. County of Orange,* 168 Misc. 2d 346, 637 N.Y.S.2d 596 (Sup. Ct. 1995).

§ 16:8 CLAIMING AND WAIVING THE ATTORNEY-CLIENT PRIVILEGE—A corporation's attorney-client privilege is controlled by the corporation's management, and the power to assert or waive the privilege is exercised by the corporation's officers and directors. Where a corporation is acquired in a merger, and the successor corporation continues to operate the business affairs of the preexisting business, the management of the successor corporation controls the privilege with respect to matters concerning the company's operations. *Tekni-Plex, Inc. v. Meyner and Landis,* 89 N.Y.2d 123, 651 N.Y.S.2d 954, 674 N.E.2d 663 (1996).

§ 16:10 EXISTENCE OF PHYSICIAN-PATIENT PRIVILEGE—The defendant physician in a medical malpractice action did not waive his own physician-patient privilege, where he had not affirmatively asserted his osteoarthritis condition either by counterclaim or to excuse the conduct alleged by plaintiff. Thus, the defendant's medical records were not subject to disclosure. *Manko v. Rees,* 228 A.D.2d 420, 643 N.Y.S.2d 229 (2d Dep't 1996).

The physician-patient privilege does not extend to optometrists. Thus, plaintiff could discover the defendant driver's optometrist's records, even though the defendant had not waived the medical privilege. *Robinson v. Meca*, 214 A.D.2d 246, 632 N.Y.S.2d 728 (3d Dep't 1995).

A defendant's testimony that he could not recall the accident, and that his doctor told him he had retrograde amnesia, did not place his medical condition in controversy so as to waive the privilege. The amnesia was not asserted as an excuse for his conduct at the time of the accident. *Casimiro v. Thayer*, 217 A.D.2d 951, 629 N.Y.S.2d 897 (4th Dep't 1995), appeal dismissed, 87 N.Y.2d 861, 639 N.Y.S.2d 313, 662 N.E.2d 794 (1995).

RESEARCH REFERENCES

American Law Reports

Attorney-client exception under state law making proceedings by public bodies open to the public, 34 A.L.R.5th 591.

Prejudicial effect, in civil case, of communications between court officials or attendants and jurors, 31 A.L.R.5th 572.

What persons or entities may assert or waive corporation's attorney-client privilege—modern cases, 28 A.L.R.5th 1.

What corporate communications are entitled to attorney-client privilege—modern cases, 27 A.L.R.5th 76.

Determination of whether a communication is from a corporate client for purposes of the attorney-client privilege—modern cases, 26 A.L.R.5th 628.

Liability in tort for interference with attorney-client relationship, 90 A.L.R.4th 621.

ALR Index: Evidence; Attorney-Client Privilege; Physician-Patient Privilege; Privileged and Confidential Matters

American Jurisprudence Pleading and Practice

25A Am Jur Pl & Pr Forms (Rev), Witnesses, Form 149

American Jurisprudence Proof of Facts

32 Am Jur Proof of Facts 3d 189, Proof of Waiver of Attorney-Client Privilege

24 Am Jur Proof of Facts 3d 123, Proof of Unauthorized
   Disclosure of Confidential Patient Information by a
   Psychotherapist

Other Resources

KeyCite™/Insta-Cite®: Cases referred to herein can be further researched through the KeyCite™ and Insta-Cite®
computer-assisted services. Use KeyCite or Insta-Cite to
check citations for form, parallel references, and prior
and later history. For comprehensive citator information, including citations to other decisions and secondary materials that have mentioned or discussed the cases
cited, use KeyCite. ALR and ALR Fed Annotations
referred to herein can be further researched through the
WESTLAW® Find service.

CHAPTER 17

JUDICIAL NOTICE

§ 17:2   JUDICIAL NOTICE OF LAWS—The trial court had discretion to take judicial notice of applicable foreign law, even though the request did not occur until after the time to move to strike the note of issue for trial had expired. *Burns v. Young*, 657 N.Y.S.2d 502 (App. Div. 3d Dep't 1997). *See also, Ekwunife v. Erike*, 171 Misc. 2d 554, 658 N.Y.S.2d 166 (App. Term 1997).

However, the court properly declined to apply foreign law where the party requesting it failed to provide sufficient information as required by CPLR 4511(b). *Lowy v. Heimann's Bus Tours*, Inc., 658 N.Y.S.2d 452 (App. Div. 2d Dep't 1997).

§ 17:3   JUDICIAL NOTICE OF FACTS CONCERNING THE COURT—A court may take judicial notice of its own records, including the files in cases decided previously. In determining whether the issues in a pending appeal were sufficiently identical to a previous appeal that had been decided against a party, the Appellate Division may review the record of the earlier case. *New York State Dam Ltd. Partnership v. Niagara Mohawk Power Corp.*, 222 A.D.2d 792, 634 N.Y.S.2d 830 (3d Dep't 1995), appeal dismissed in part on other grounds, 87 N.Y.2d 1041, 644 N.Y.S.2d 138, 666 N.E.2d 1051 (1996).

§ 17:6   OTHER FACTS JUDICIALLY NOTICED—An appellate court has discretion to take judicial notice, for the first time on appeal, of a fact which was not brought to the attention of the trial court, and may do so even for the purpose of reversing the judgment. In calculating the number of days for determination of a procedural issue, the Appellate Division reversed because a public holiday, Presidents' Day, provided an extra day for a step to be taken, even though the record contained no proof on the issue; respondent on the appeal could suggest no factual showing or legal counterstep that would have been made if the argument had been raised below. *Persing v. Coughlin*, 214 A.D.2d 145, 632 N.Y.S.2d 366 (4th Dep't 1995).

§ 17:7 FACTS NOT JUDICIALLY NOTICED—The court may only apply judicial notice to matters of common and general knowledge which are well-established and authoritatively settled, and are not doubtful or uncertain. The test is whether sufficient notoriety attaches to the fact to make it proper to assume its existence without proof. In a product liability action brought by the estates of shipyard workers who claimed that asbestos was used in the construction of a ship built in the yard, the trial court erred in taking judicial notice, on defendant's motion for summary judgment, that asbestos had not been used; even though evidence and government specifications in numerous other cases had established that asbestos had not been used, the deposition testimony of a witness that the product had been used precluded the taking of judicial notice on the issue. *Dollas v. W.R. Grace and Co.*, 225 A.D.2d 319, 639 N.Y.S.2d 323 (1st Dep't 1996).

In an action for personal injuries sustained when plaintiff was attacked by a German Shepherd, the trial court was not required to instruct the jury, by way of judicial notice, that German Shepherds are a vicious breed of dog. Although a certain amount of viciousness may be implied, the issue of vicious tendencies and the owner's notice thereof were questions for the jury. *Sorel v. Iacobucci*, 221 A.D.2d 852, 633 N.Y.S.2d 688 (3d Dep't 1995).

RESEARCH REFERENCES

American Jurisprudence 2d

75A Am Jur 2d, Trial § 811

Other Resources

KeyCite™/Insta-Cite®: Cases referred to herein can be fur-

ther researched through the KeyCite™ and Insta-Cite®
computer-assisted services. Use KeyCite or Insta-Cite to
check citations for form, parallel references, and prior
and later history. For comprehensive citator information, including citations to other decisions and secondary materials that have mentioned or discussed the cases
cited, use KeyCite. ALR and ALR Fed Annotations
referred to herein can be further researched through the
WESTLAW® Find service.

CHAPTER 18

PRESUMPTIONS

§ 18:4 INFERENCES—The mere fact that a floor is slippery because of its smoothness or polish does not raise an inference of negligence, and does not dispense with the need to present evidence of negligent application of the wax or polish. *Lathan v. NCAS Realty Management Corp.,* 658 N.Y.S.2d 436 (App. Div. 2d Dep't 1997).

Negligent inspection of an elevator by an elevator maintenance company may be inferred from evidence that (1) the doors opened when the elevator was not at the landing, and (2) the interlock system, which was designed to prevent such an occurrence, required replacement. *Alsaydi v. GSL Enterprises, Inc.,* 656 N.Y.S.2d 691 (App. Div. 2d Dep't 1997).

§ 18:5 RES IPSA LOQUITUR—Where an elevator company was contractually obligated to repair and maintain the elevator in plaintiff's residential building, its negligence in causing a misleveling malfunction was established through the application of the doctrine of *res ipsa loquitur.* The three to six inches of misleveling ordinarily would not occur in the absence of someone's negligence, the elevator was within the elevator company's exclusive control, and plaintiff did not in any way contribute to the misleveling. *Dickman v. Stewart Tenants Corp.,* 221 A.D.2d 158, 633 N.Y.S.2d 35 (1st Dep't 1995).

Where an elevator service contractor did not have a routine maintenance and inspection contract, but serviced the elevator only upon being called for specific problems, *res ipsa loquitur* did not supply an inference of negligence in causing the elevator door to malfunction. Since there was no evidence of negligence, the judgment upon a verdict for plaintiff was reversed, and the case was dismissed. *McMurray v. P.S. Elevator, Inc., 224 A.D.2d 668, 638 N.Y.S.2d 720 (2d Dep't 1996).*

Where the defendant has the duty to maintain and inspect an instrumentality under his exclusive control so as to invoke the *res ipsa loquitur* doctrine, proof of notice is not a prerequisite element of plaintiff's case. Thus, where plaintiff was injured when defendant's flatbed truck covering cap flew off and struck plaintiff, and plaintiff produced expert proof that the cap would not have come off if it had been properly secured and inspected, plaintiff was not required to prove that defendant had prior notice of the defective fastening. *Smith v. Moore, 227 A.D.2d 854, 642 N.Y.S.2d 393 (3d Dep't 1996).*

Although *res ipsa loquitur* usually creates a question of fact by permitting the jury to draw or reject the inference of negligence, where the inference is inescapable in the absence of evidence to rebut the inference, summary judgment is appropriately granted. Where plaintiff was struck by a flatbed covering cap, and (1) plaintiff's proof on a motion for summary judgment included an expert affidavit demonstrating that the cap would not have come off if it had been adequately secured and inspected, and (2) it was undisputed that the instrumentality had been under defendant's exclusive control, and (3) plaintiff was in no way responsible, the inference of defendant's negligence was inescapable, and summary judgment for plaintiff was affirmed. *Smith v. Moore, 227 A.D.2d 854, 642 N.Y.S.2d 393 (3d Dep't 1996).*

In order to avail themselves of doctrine of *res ipsa loquitur,* plaintiffs must establish that the injury was caused by an agency or instrumentality within the exclusive control of the defendant. The parents of an infant who was diagnosed with a fractured leg after delivery could not rely on the doctrine in their medical malpractice action against the hospital where there was no evidence of any event during the delivery which caused the fracture, and it appeared that the fracture might have occurred in utero. *Kruck v. St.*

John's Episcopal Hosp., 228 A.D.2d 565, 644 N.Y.S.2d 325 (2d Dep't 1996).

The element of exclusive control does not require plaintiff to show that there was no access by anyone other than defendant. Plaintiff need only show that the defendant's control was of sufficient exclusivity to fairly rule out the chance that the alleged defect was caused by someone other than the defendant. Where plaintiff was injured when a mirrored wall panel with shelves fell on her in defendant's store, sufficient exclusivity was shown. While the public might have touched the shelving, that did not explain the collapse of the entire panel, and the public did not have such unfettered access to the instrumentality that the store's control was insufficient to warrant submission of the case to the jury. Judgment dismissing the case at the close of plaintiff's evidence was reversed, and a new trial granted. *Bonventre v. August Max*, 229 A.D.2d 557, 645 N.Y.S.2d 867 (2d Dep't 1996).

In a medical malpractice action, where plaintiff's expert testified that (1) the occurrence, a catheter tip breaking off and remaining in plaintiff's chest, would not occur had proper technique been applied; (2) x-rays revealed that the tip had been bent into an unusual shape; (3) the missing tip should have been detected immediately by examination of the removed catheter and then retrieved, the case was properly submitted to the jury with a res ipsa charge. The mere fact that the patient was conscious and may have moved during the insertion did not bar the conclusion that the defendant was in exclusive control of the instrumentality that caused the injury, or that the true explanation of the event was more readily accessible to the physician than to the plaintiff. *Hawkins v. Brooklyn-Caledonian Hosp.*, 658 N.Y.S.2d 375 (App. Div. 2d Dep't 1997).

Where an 18-by-18 inch laparotomy pad was left in a patient during an abdominal hysterectomy, the trial court erred in refusing plaintiff's request to instruct the jury under res ipsa. Plaintiff was not required to conclusively eliminate all other possible causes. It was enough that plaintiff's evidence as to the three conditions for the charge — (1) that the event was of a kind that would not ordinarily occur in the absence of someone's negligence; (2) that it was caused by an instrumentality exclusively within the defendant's control; and (3) that it was not due to any voluntary act by the patient — afford a rational basis for concluding that it is more likely than not that the injury was caused by defendant's negligence. Defense testimony that the pads were carefully counted and that the patient might have eaten the pad, which was countered by plaintiff's expert witness' testimony that such pads are usually not accessible to patients, and that it was not anatomically possible to swallow the pad, or for a swallowed pad to reach the subject part of the body, did not defeat plaintiff's right to have the res ipsa charge given. *Kambat v. St. Francis Hosp.,* 89 N.Y.2d 489, 655 N.Y.S.2d 844, 678 N.E.2d 456 (1997).

A wheelchair bound passenger who was propelled from his wheelchair when it was lowered on a hydraulic lift on a van was properly given a res ipsa charge. The inference of negligence under res ipsa was inescapable on these facts. *Cunningham v. Vincent,* 234 A.D.2d 648, 650 N.Y.S.2d 850 (3d Dep't 1996).

Submission of the question of medical malpractice under a res ipsa theory was error, where (1) plaintiff attempted to prove specific acts of negligence, and (2) the medical issue as to which the inference was sought was beyond the knowledge of a lay jury. *Stanski v. Ezersky,* 228 A.D.2d 311, 644 N.Y.S.2d 220 (1st Dep't 1996).

§ 18:8　**PRESUMPTIONS ARISING FROM THE CONDUCT OF A PARTY**—Evidence that a driver fell asleep while driving creates a presumption of negligence that, if not explained or justified by the driver, requires a verdict for plaintiff. If the driver attempts to rebut the presumption of negligence, such as by showing circumstances demonstrating reasonable care or by introducing medical testimony of an illness such as narcolepsy, then a question of fact is created for the jury. The court's charge that the mere act of falling asleep was not sufficient to warrant a verdict of negligence required that the verdict for the defendant be set aside, and a new trial be conducted. *Kilburn v. Bush,* 223 A.D.2d 110, 646 N.Y.S.2d 429 (4th Dep't 1996).

§ 18:9　**PRESUMPTION OF DELIVERY OF LETTER**—Where a written notice of default was required to invoke a performance bond, the mailing presumption did not apply in the absence of testimony by a person with knowledge of claimant's regular office practice. The testimony of claimant's vice president that his secretary usually did what she was told was insufficient to establish a regular office practice as to mailing. *In re Liquidation of Union Indem. Ins. Co. of New York,* 220 A.D.2d 341, 633 N.Y.S.2d 21 (1st Dep't 1995).

The presumption of delivery arising from evidence of deposit in a United States Postal Service mailbox does not apply where a specific statute provides that registered or certified mailing will be prima facie evidence of delivery. *Dattilo v. Urbach,* 222 A.D.2d 28, 645 N.Y.S.2d 352 (3d Dep't 1996).

§ 18:11 PRESUMPTIONS ABOUT INDIVIDUALS—There is a presumption that every person has the capacity to manage his or her own affairs, especially regarding the course of his or her medical treatment. In a proceeding under § 81 of the MENTAL HYGIENE LAW for the appointment of a guardian, the presumption can be overcome only by clear and convincing evidence that "(1) the person cannot adequately understand and appreciate the nature and consequences of the person's particular inabilities; and (2) the person is likely to suffer harm because of these limitations and the inability to appreciate the consequences of the limitations." *Matter of Lula XX,* 224 A.D.2d 742, 637 N.Y.S.2d 234 (3d Dep't 1996).

§ 18:14 OTHER PRESUMPTIONS CREATED BY LAW— Property acquired during marriage is presumed to be marital property. Where one party claims that such property is separate, that party must bear the burden of disproving the presumption. *Cerretani v. Cerretani,* 221 A.D.2d 814, 634 N.Y.S.2d 228 (3d Dep't 1995).

Unwitnessed deaths that occur in the course of employment are presumed to arise out of that employment for purposes of workers' compensation. In order to overcome the heavy burden of the statutory presumption, employers must present substantial evidence to the contrary. *Onody v. County of Oswego Dept. of Public Works,* 223 A.D.2d 813, 636 N.Y.S.2d 180 (3d Dep't 1996).

Statutes are presumed to be constitutional. A party challenging the constitutionality of a statute bears the burden of demonstrating unconstitutionality beyond a reasonable doubt. *Trump v. Perlee*, 228 A.D.2d 367, 644 N.Y.S.2d 270 (1st Dep't 1996).

RESEARCH REFERENCES

American Law Reports
 ALR Index: Evidence

American Jurisprudence 2d
 81 Am Jur 2d, Witnesses § 1028
 75A Am Jur 2d, Trial §§ 748-750

American Jurisprudence Pleading and Practice
 23A Am Jur Pl & Pr Forms (Rev), Trial, Form 170

American Jurisprudence Proof of Facts
 32 Am Jur Proof of Facts 2d 253, Admission by Conduct or Silence

Other Resources
 KeyCite™/Insta-Cite®: Cases referred to herein can be further researched through the KeyCite™ and Insta-Cite® computer-assisted services. Use KeyCite or Insta-Cite to check citations for form, parallel references, and prior and later history. For comprehensive citator information, including citations to other decisions and secondary materials that have mentioned or discussed the cases cited, use KeyCite. ALR and ALR Fed Annotations referred to herein can be further researched through the WESTLAW® Find service.

CHAPTER 19

REAL AND DEMONSTRATIVE EVIDENCE

§ 19:2 TANGIBLE ARTICLES WITH SOME BEARING ON THE TRANSACTION IN QUESTION—Where plaintiff claimed neck injuries, the trial court did not abuse its discretion in receiving granite rocks of the type depicted in a surveillance videotape, and a common bathroom scale. The difference in size was readily observable to the jury, and the rocks were offered generally so that the jury could evaluate the significance of the tape showing plaintiff lifting granite boulders. *Krute v. Mosca*, 234 A.D.2d 622, 650 N.Y.S.2d 862 (3d Dep't 1996).

In an action to recover the sales price of hoppers used in scaffolding, the trial court properly excluded from evidence hoppers and photographs of hoppers offered by the purchaser, which were not in the same condition as, or a fair representation of, the hoppers at issue. *Saratoga Spa & Bath, Inc. v. Beeche Systems Corp.*, 230 A.D.2d 326, 656 N.Y.S.2d 787 (3d Dep't 1997).

§ 19:4 ADMISSIBILITY OF PHOTOGRAPHS—In order for photographs to be admissible as evidence of constructive notice of a defective condition, it must be shown that (1) the photographs were taken reasonably close to the time of the accident, and (2) the condition at the time of the accident was substantially as shown in the photographs. Where plaintiff, in an action for negligent failure to repair a crack in defendant's parking lot, relied exclusively on photographs that were taken six weeks after the accident, and could not recall whether the area had changed in the interim, and no other testimony on the issue was offered, the photographs

75

should not have been received. Judgment upon a verdict for plaintiff was reversed, and the complaint dismissed. *Truesdell v. Rite Aid of New York, Inc.,* 228 A.D.2d 922, 644 N.Y.S.2d 428 (3d Dep't 1996).

§ 19:7 ADMISSIBILITY OF VIDEOTAPE RECORD-INGS—In a product liability action against a motorcycle manufacturer, based on the failure of the side kickstand to retract upon contact with the ground during a turn, the trial court erred in receiving a videotaped demonstration where, although the same model was tested, plaintiff failed to show that the tests were performed under similar conditions, and the videotape was introduced during the testimony of a witness other than the expert who performed the demonstration. *Cramer v. Kuhns,* 213 A.D.2d 131, 630 N.Y.S.2d 128 (3d Dep't 1995), appeal dismissed, 87 N.Y.2d 860, 639 N.Y.S.2d 312, 662 N.E.2d 793 (1995).

§ 19:9 ADMISSION OF MAPS, DRAWINGS, DIAGRAMS, AND DISPLAYS—In an automobile accident case, the trial court erred in receiving the police report diagram of the accident, where one of the cars had been moved before the officer arrived; the diagram could not have been based on the officer's first-hand observations. *Mooney v. Osowiecky,* 235 A.D.2d 603, 651 N.Y.S.2d 713 (3d Dep't 1997).

§ 19:13 BLOOD TESTS IN PATERNITY CASES—In a proceeding to establish paternity, DNA tests are not admissible where they are not performed by "a duly qualified physician or by a laboratory duly approved for this purpose by the commissioner of health," as required by FAMILY COURT ACT § 532(a). *Lavis v. Clair,* 226 A.D.2d 535, 640 N.Y.S.2d 609 (2d Dep't 1996).

Where the court had ordered respondent to submit to HLA test, and laboratory gratuitously performed DNA test as well, the trial court properly excluded the DNA test results. *Tobi F. v. Bruce N.,* 229 A.D.2d 392, 645 N.Y.S.2d 65 (2d Dep't 1996).

RESEARCH REFERENCES

American Law Reports

Failure of police to preserve potentially exculpatory evidence as violating criminal defendant's rights under state constitution, 40 A.L.R.5th 113.

Admissibility in homicide prosecution of allegedly gruesome or inflammatory visual recording of crime scene, 37 A.L.R.5th 515.

Admissibility in evidence of composite picture or sketch produced by police to identify offender, 23 A.L.R.5th 672.

Admissibility of evidence of commission of similar crime by one other than accused, 22 A.L.R.5th 1.

ALR Index: Blackboard; Clothing; Diagrams, Charts, and Tables; Exhibits; Models

American Jurisprudence 2d

75A Am Jur 2d, Trial §§ 505-512
29A Am Jur 2d, Evidence §§ 934-1022

American Jurisprudence Proof of Facts

36 Am Jur Proof of Facts 3d 1, Proof of Criminal Identity or Paternity Through Polymerase Chain Reaction (PCR) Testing

30 Am Jur Proof of Facts 3d 307, Evidence of Subsequent Remedial Measures in Civil Cases

Other Resources

KeyCite™/Insta-Cite®: Cases referred to herein can be further researched through the KeyCite™ and Insta-Cite® computer-assisted services. Use KeyCite or Insta-Cite to check citations for form, parallel references, and prior and later history. For comprehensive citator information, including citations to other decisions and secondary materials that have mentioned or discussed the cases cited, use KeyCite. ALR and ALR Fed Annotations referred to herein can be further researched through the WESTLAW® Find service.

CHAPTER 20

THE VIEW

RESEARCH REFERENCES

American Law Reports

Unauthorized view of premises by juror or jury in criminal case as ground for reversal, new trial, or mistrial, 50 A.L.R.4th 995.

American Jurisprudence Pleading and Practice

23A Am Jur Pl & Pr Forms (Rev), Trial, Forms 126-133

Other Resources

KeyCite™/Insta-Cite®: Cases referred to herein can be further researched through the KeyCite™ and Insta-Cite® computer-assisted services. Use KeyCite or Insta-Cite to check citations for form, parallel references, and prior and later history. For comprehensive citator information, including citations to other decisions and secondary materials that have mentioned or discussed the cases cited, use KeyCite. ALR and ALR Fed Annotations referred to herein can be further researched through the WESTLAW® Find service.

CHAPTER 21

DOCUMENTARY EVIDENCE

§ 21:1.   Documentary Evidence, in General
§ 21:10. Authentication of Records of Corporations

§ 21:1 DOCUMENTARY EVIDENCE, IN GENERAL—An investigative report by the National Highway Traffic Safety Administration could not be received as a business record in a product liability action where no employee of the agency testified at trial. *Cramer v. Kuhns,* 213 A.D.2d 131, 630 N.Y.S.2d 128 (3d Dep't 1995), appeal dismissed, 87 N.Y.2d 860, 639 N.Y.S.2d 312, 662 N.E.2d 793 (1995).

§ 21:10 AUTHENTICATION OF RECORDS OF CORPORATIONS—The court erred in granting summary judgment to a bowling center in an action for personal injuries based on defendant's own accident report containing a purported admission by plaintiff. The report was neither signed by plaintiff, nor authenticated by defendant, and thus should not have been considered as part of defendant's prima facie showing of entitlement to judgment. *Wunsch v. AMF Bowling Center, Inc.,* 236 A.D.2d 467, 653 N.Y.S.2d 665 (2d Dep't 1997).

RESEARCH REFERENCES

American Law Reports

Failure of police to preserve potentially exculpatory evidence as violating criminal defendant's rights under state constitution, 40 A.L.R.5th 113.

Propriety of using prior conviction for drug dealing to impeach witness in criminal trial, 37 A.L.R.5th 319.

Pretermitted heir statutes: what constitutes sufficient testamentary reference to, or evidence of contemplation of, heir to render statute inapplicable, 83 A.L.R.4th 779.

Impeachment or cross-examination of prosecuting witness in sexual offense trial by showing that similar charges were made against other persons, 71 A.L.R.4th 469.

Impeachment or cross-examination of prosecuting witness in sexual offense trial by showing that prosecuting witness threatened to make similar charges against other persons, 71 A.L.R.4th 448.

Admissibility of impeached witness' prior consistent statement—modern state civil cases, 59 A.L.R.4th 1000.

Admissibility of evidence summaries under Uniform Evidence Rule 1006, 59 A.L.R.4th 971.

Admissibility of impeached witness' prior consistent statement—modern state criminal cases, 58 A.L.R.4th 1014.

Admissibility of school records under hearsay exceptions, 57 A.L.R.4th 1111.

Contingent fee informant testimony in state prosecutions, 57 A.L.R.4th 643.

Necessity or permissibility of mental examination to determine competency or credibility of complainant in sexual offense prosecution, 45 A.L.R.4th 310.

Use or admissibility of prior inconsistent statements of witness as substantive evidence of facts to which they relate in criminal case—modern state cases, 30 A.L.R.4th 414.

Permissibility of impeaching credibility of witness by showing verdict of guilty without judgment of sentence thereon, 28 A.L.R.4th 647.

Right to impeach witness in criminal case by inquiry or evidence as to witness' criminal activity for which witness was arrested or charged, but not convicted—modern state cases, 28 A.L.R.4th 505.

Admissibility of evidence as to other offense as affected by defendant's acquittal of that offense, 25 A.L.R.4th 934.

Right to impeach witness in criminal case by inquiry or evidence as to witness' criminal activity not having resulted in arrest or charge—modern state cases, 24 A.L.R.4th 333.

Impeachment of defense witness in criminal case by showing

witness' prior silence or failure or refusal to testify, 20 A.L.R.4th 245.

Admissibility of affidavit to impeach witness, 14 A.L.R.4th 828.

Admissibility of evidence concerning words spoken while declarant was asleep or unconscious, 14 A.L.R.4th 802.

Propriety of using otherwise inadmissible statement, taken in violation of Miranda rule, to impeach criminal defendant's credibility—state cases, 14 A.L.R.4th 676.

Cross-examination of character witness for accused with reference to particular acts or crimes—modern state rules, 13 A.L.R.4th 796.

Propriety of jury instruction regarding credibility of witness who has been convicted of a crime, 9 A.L.R.4th 897.

ALR Index: Best and Secondary Evidence

American Jurisprudence 2d

32B Am Jur 2d, Federal Rules of Evidence §§ 302-321

29A Am Jur 2d, Evidence §§ 1023-1429

American Jurisprudence Pleading and Practice

23A Am Jur Pl & Pr Forms (Rev), Trial, Forms 120-122

9A Am Jur Pl & Pr Forms (Rev), Evidence §§ 113-124

8A Am Jur Pl & Pr Forms (Rev), Depositions and Discovery §§ 586, 593, 595-613, 617, 618, 620-624, 627-637

Other Resources

KeyCite™/Insta-Cite®: Cases referred to herein can be further researched through the KeyCite™ and Insta-Cite® computer-assisted services. Use KeyCite or Insta-Cite to check citations for form, parallel references, and prior and later history. For comprehensive citator information, including citations to other decisions and secondary materials that have mentioned or discussed the cases cited, use KeyCite. ALR and ALR Fed Annotations referred to herein can be further researched through the WESTLAW® Find service.

CHAPTER 22

OPINION EVIDENCE

§ 22:3 ADMISSIBILITY OF OPINIONS IN GENERAL—In an action against a residential landlord for security negligence alleged to have caused plaintiff to be raped and robbed, the trial court erred in admitting the opinion of the investigating detective that plaintiff and her assailant were acquainted. The testimony was based on a hunch, and was not supported by any facts known to the witness or included in the record. The detective's testimony usurped the function of the jury by discrediting plaintiff's credibility while bolstering the testimony of defendant's witnesses, and the error was compounded when the trial court excluded contrary opinions by plaintiff's experts in the fields of rape trauma syndrome and clinical psychology. *Gomez by Gomez v. New York City Housing Authority,* 217 A.D.2d 110, 636 N.Y.S.2d 271 (1st Dep't 1995).

§ 22:5 OPINIONS ON THE ULTIMATE ISSUE IN NEGLIGENCE CASES—In an action for injuries sustained when plaintiff fell on a walkway to defendant's house, since the plaintiff did not

85

allege any violations of architectural standards or construction codes, ordinances, or the like, the maintenance of the walkway was not a subject calling for technical knowledge possessed by an expert and beyond the ken of the typical juror. The trial court properly excluded expert testimony, which would have usurped the jury's function. *Franco v. Muro*, 224 A.D.2d 579, 638 N.Y.S.2d 690 (2d Dep't 1996).

§ 22:7 WHEN OPINION EVIDENCE ON THE ULTIMATE ISSUE IS ADMISSIBLE—Whether expert testimony relates to the ultimate issue, or to questions of lesser significance, the opinion is admissible if it helps clarify an issue calling for professional or technical knowledge that is possessed by the expert, but is beyond the ken of the typical juror. Thus, in an action for personal injuries sustained in an elevator accident, plaintiff's expert witness was properly permitted to testify as to the adequacy of the elevator company's maintenance of the elevator. *Sanders v. Otis Elevator Co.*, 232 A.D.2d 327, 649 N.Y.S.2d 19 (1st Dep't 1996).

§ 22:15 MATTERS AS TO WHICH AN EXPERT WITNESS MAY OR MUST TESTIFY—Where jurors are competent to evaluate the evidence and draw inferences and conclusions, opinions of experts, which intrude on the province of the jury, are both unnecessary and improper. In an actions for injuries sustained when the infant plaintiff's foot was caught in a merry-go-round, given the testimony of fact witnesses regarding the condition of the playground and supervision of children, expert testimony regarding the lack of proper supervision of children or thorough inspection did not require professional or scientific knowledge or skill that was outside the range of ordinary training or intelligence, so that expert testimony was properly excluded. *Fortunato v. Dover Union Free School Dist.*, 224 A.D.2d 658, 638 N.Y.S.2d 727, 107 Ed. Law Rep. 930 (2d Dep't 1996).

Expert testimony as to constructive notice based on the condition of grapes on the floor in a supermarket was properly precluded. Any conclusion based on the condition of the grapes would not require professional or scientific knowledge or skill outside the range of the jurors' ordinary experience. *Rojas v.*

Supermarkets General Corp., 656 N.Y.S.2d 346 (App. Div. 2d Dep't 1997).

Although the admission of expert opinion generally rests within the trial court's discretion, an expert should be permitted to offer an opinion on an issue which involves professional or scientific knowledge or skill not within the range of the ordinary jurors' training or intelligence. Where plaintiff contended that the infant's injury in falling from a slide was caused by the absence of resilient material around the slide's base, the court erred in precluding the expert's opinion regarding resilient material. *Reale v. Herco, Inc.,* 231 A.D.2d 619, 647 N.Y.S.2d 533 (2d Dep't 1996).

§ **22:16 QUALIFICATIONS REQUIRED OF AN EXPERT WITNESS**—The trial court erred in refusing to qualify a board-certified psychiatrist as an expert for the purpose of establishing the severity and permanence of plaintiff's injuries, on the ground that the witness had not published in the field. Publication is not a *sine qua non* of expertise, and while a court's decision as to whether a witness should be qualified as an expert is largely discretionary, the range of allowable discretion is not so broad as to render sustainable a patently unreasonable refusal to recognize a witness as qualified. *Khatri v. Lazarus,* 225 A.D.2d 302, 639 N.Y.S.2d 1 (1st Dep't 1996).

A licensed engineer with experience in the electrical industry possessed the requisite skill, training, and knowledge to render an opinion regarding the proper insulation of power lines. Trapani v Rochester Gas and Electric Corp. (1996, 4th Dept) 229 A.D.2d 923, 645 N.Y.S.2d 229, affd 229 A.D.2d, 645 N.Y.S.2d 229, leave to appeal dismissed in part, denied in part, 89 N.Y.2d 937, 654 N.Y.S.2d 715 (1997).

§ **22:18 THE WEIGHT TO BE GIVEN EXPERT TESTI-MONY**—A party is not bound by the testimony of an expert. Such testimony does not constitute a formal judicial admission. Where plaintiff-estate claimed that decedent's death was caused by ingestion of unwholesome food at defendant's restaurant, and defendant moved for summary judgment, the statement of plaintiff's medical expert as to the incubation period was not conclusive against plaintiff. An affidavit of plaintiff's other expert, who was a Ph.D. in toxicology, to the effect that the fatal illness was caused by the food created a question of fact. *Edmiston v. Tony Rome's, Inc.,* 224 A.D.2d 941, 637 N.Y.S.2d 896 (4th Dep't 1996).

§ 22:19 MEDICAL EXPERTS—A nurse's opinion as to the type of post-surgery restraint that should have been ordered for the patient went beyond her professional and educational experience, and was not competent medical opinion to raise a question of fact on the defendant physicians motion for summary judgment. The affidavit of a surgeon, contending that certain restraints were required because plaintiff was a high risk patient with a history of prior falls, also failed to create a question of fact where no records to substantiate such a prior history were submitted. *Douglass v. Gibson,* 218 A.D.2d 856, 630 N.Y.S.2d 401 (3d Dep't 1995).

In a wrongful death action, based on decedent's development of aplastic anemia as an alleged result of exposure to creosote-treated railroad ties, decedent's former family physician was not qualified to testify as to the cause of the fatal disease. The physician was not the prime physician responsible for treatment of the anemia, and had no experience, education, or specialized training in hematology, toxicology, or industrial hygiene, and had not conducted any research on either aplastic anemia or creosote. *Corsetti v. Koppers Co. Inc.,* 226 A.D.2d 205, 640 N.Y.S.2d 556 (1st Dep't 1996).

A neurologist who had managed 200 to 300 cases of carpal tunnel injuries was competent to render an opinion as to the care rendered by orthopedic surgeons in a medical malpractice action. Any lack of experience went to the weight, rather than the admissibility, of the testimony. *Julien v. Physician's Hosp.,* 231 A.D.2d 678, 647 N.Y.S.2d 831 (2d Dep't 1996).

Although experts may rely on out of court materials generally relied on by experts in the field, there must be evidence to establish the reliability of such material. In an action for personal injuries including a herniated disk, the defense expert was improperly permitted to relate statistics as to percentages of people who have disk injuries and conditions unrelated to trauma. Neither the basis for, nor evidence as to the reliability of, these statistics was established. *Velez v. Svehla,* 229 A.D.2d 528, 645 N.Y.S.2d 842 (2d Dep't 1996).

Expert medical opinion that medications taken by a motorist could cause dizziness is too speculative to create a question of fact as to the motorist's conduct where there is no evidence that the motorist suffered any side effects. *Davis v. Pimm*, 228 A.D.2d 885, 644 N.Y.S.2d 401 (3d Dep't 1996).

A physician, although not a psychiatrist, was competent to diagnose conversion hysteria. The fact that the physician was not a psychiatrist went to the weight, but not the admissibility, of the testimony. *Smith v. City of New York*, 656 N.Y.S.2d 681 (App. Div. 2d Dep't 1997).

Where a physician's opinions as to a patient's condition are based only in part on x-rays or MRI's, but also on clinical observations and physical examinations, the failure to produce the films is not fatal to the expert's testimony. *Pegg v. Shahin*, 237 A.D.2d 271, 654 N.Y.S.2d 395 (2d Dep't 1997).

§ 22:20 EXPERT TESTIMONY ON MATTERS OF BUSINESS—In an action for libel, brought against owner of television and radio stations, receipt of expert testimony on journalistic standards and practices was within the trial court's discretion. *Prozeralik v. Capital Cities Communications, Inc.*, 222 A.D.2d 1020, 635 N.Y.S.2d 913 (4th Dep't 1995), appeal dismissed, 88 N.Y.2d 843, 644 N.Y.S.2d 683, 667 N.E.2d 334 (1996).

§ 22:22 TESTIMONY BY AN ACCIDENT RECONSTRUCTION EXPERT—Preclusion of defendant's accident reconstruction expert's testimony that plaintiff (1) was not wearing his seatbelt, and (2) would not have suffered facial injuries had he worn seatbelt, was error where it was sufficiently based on facts in the record. *Brullo v. Schiro*, 657 N.Y.S.2d 92 (App. Div. 2d Dep't 1997).

§ 22:23 EXPERT TESTIMONY BY AN ECONOMIST—Plaintiff's economic expert properly estimated future lost earnings. The expert did not base his calculations (1) upon an amount in excess of that which a high school graduate would have earned, accounting for inflation, or (2) upon hypothetical union benefits which the worker would have received had he joined union.

Hackworth v. WDW Development, Inc., 224 A.D.2d 265, 637 N.Y.S.2d 720 (1st Dep't 1996).

Notwithstanding that, pursuant to CPLR Articles 50-A and 50-B, 4% per year will be added to structured payments for future damages, plaintiff may present an expert economist's testimony as to the anticipated effect of inflation on any future damages claimed. *Schultz v. Harrison Radiator Div. General Motors Corp.*, 90 N.Y.2d 311, 660 N.Y.S.2d 685, 683 N.E.2d 307 (1997).

§ 22:28 EXPERT TESTIMONY BY A PSYCHOLOGIST—In a custody proceeding, the family court had a sound basis to credit a clinical psychologist's opinion that the psychological bond that had grown up between the mother and child should not be disrupted, and that disruption of the relationship could be detrimental to the child. The psychologist's conclusion was based on personal interviews with the mother, father, and child, and his review of materials each party had sent to him. *Lumbert v. Lumbert*, 229 A.D.2d 683, 645 N.Y.S.2d 164 (3d Dep't 1996).

§ 22:35 EXPERT TESTIMONY IN MATRIMONIAL CASES—Expert opinion as to the value of the husband's closely held business based on an accepted method, the discounted cash flow method, was properly received in a divorce action. *Ciaffone v. Ciaffone*, 228 A.D.2d 949, 645 N.Y.S.2d 549 (3d Dep't 1996).

RESEARCH REFERENCES

American Jurisprudence 2d

57A Am Jur 2d, Negligence § 463

American Jurisprudence Pleading and Practice

25A Am Jur Pl & Pr Forms (Rev), Witnesses, Forms 175-178

23A Am Jur Pl & Pr Forms (Rev), Trial, Forms 199-201

American Jurisprudence Proof of Facts

24 Am Jur Proof of Facts 3d 667, Identification of Handprinting and Numerals

Other Resources

KeyCite™/Insta-Cite®: Cases referred to herein can be fur-

ther researched through the KeyCite™ and Insta-Cite®
computer-assisted services. Use KeyCite or Insta-Cite to
check citations for form, parallel references, and prior
and later history. For comprehensive citator information, including citations to other decisions and secondary materials that have mentioned or discussed the cases
cited, use KeyCite. ALR and ALR Fed Annotations
referred to herein can be further researched through the
WESTLAW® Find service.

CHAPTER 23
HEARSAY EVIDENCE

§ 23:1 ADMISSIBILITY OF HEARSAY EVIDENCE—Written statements of the defendant and his witness, which were given to the investigating police officer following an automobile accident, were merely self-serving declarations, offered to bolster their trial testimony. Receipt of the written statements was error. *Hatton v. Gassler*, 219 A.D.2d 697, 631 N.Y.S.2d 757 (2d Dep't 1995).

A statement which is not offered to prove the truth of the facts asserted is not hearsay. In an action for injuries sustained when a store patron slipped on spilled liquid soap, the testimony of an eyewitness that an announcement had been made over the public address system directing an employee to clean up a spill in the subject aisle should have been received as proof of notice, notwithstanding that the identity of the declarant was unknown. *Stern v. Waldbaum, Inc.*, 234 A.D.2d 534, 651 N.Y.S.2d 187 (2d Dep't 1996).

§ 23:3 INAPPLICABILITY OF THE HEARSAY RULE TO CERTAIN SITUATIONS—The former rule that administrative determinations had to be supported by a "legal residuum" — that is, supported at least in part by legally admissible evidence — has been abandoned. Therefore, an administrative determination can now be based entirely on hearsay, provided that it is sufficiently believable, relevant, and probative. *Modern Medical Laboratory Inc. v. Dowling*, 232 A.D.2d 901, 648 N.Y.S.2d 820 (3d Dep't 1996).

In a custody proceeding, Family Court correctly permitted hearsay testimony concerning the child's complaints to the effect that the father had hurt her in the vaginal area, as mandated by FAMILY COURT ACT § 1046(a)(vi). *Hover v. Shear*, 232 A.D.2d 749, 648 N.Y.S.2d 718 (3d Dep't 1996), leave to appeal dismissed in part on other grounds, denied, 89 N.Y.2d 964, 655 N.Y.S.2d 883, 678 N.E.2d 495 (1997).

§ 23:10 BUSINESS RECORDS—In an action by an attorney to recover fees from a client, the attorney's detailed time records were properly admitted into evidence pursuant to the business records exception to the hearsay rule. *Shaw, Licitra, Eisenberg, Esernio and Schwartz, P.C. v. Gelb,* 221 A.D.2d 331, 633 N.Y.S.2d 212 (2d Dep't 1995).

Papers received and filed do not thereby become business records of the recipient. A letter from the injured plaintiff's attorney to a neurosurgeon who examined plaintiff was properly excluded from evidence. *Colonno v. Executive I Associates,* 228 A.D.2d 859, 644 N.Y.S.2d 105 (3d Dep't 1996).

§ 23:11 OFFICIAL RECORDS, GENERALLY—Admission of a National Highway Traffic Safety Administration investigative report under the public document exception to the hearsay rule is committed to the sound discretion of the trial court, and will hinge upon whether the report has sufficient independent indicia of reliability to justify admission, such as (1) timeliness of the investigation, (2) skill and/or experience of the investigator, (3) whether the report was based upon testimony at a hearing, and (4) possibility of bias. The results of a motorcycle safety study were not admissible in a products liability action against a motorcycle manufacturer where the study was preliminary in nature, was very brief, contained little detail as to the actual tests conducted, no public findings were released and no recalls issued, and the observations contained in the study were based in part on owner surveys and accident reports which were themselves not admissible. *Cramer v. Kuhns,* 213 A.D.2d 131, 630 N.Y.S.2d 128 (3d Dep't 1995), appeal dismissed, 87 N.Y.2d 860, 639 N.Y.S.2d 312, 662 N.E.2d 793 (1995).

§ 23:12 POLICE RECORDS—The conclusions of an investigating police officer, which were not based upon expert analysis of physical evidence, and statements of witnesses to the accident, who were under no business duty to provide information to the investigating officer, should have been redacted from the police report before it was received in evidence. *Hatton v. Gassler*, 219 A.D.2d 697, 631 N.Y.S.2d 757 (2d Dep't 1995).

§ 23:14 DOCTORS' RECORDS—A medical report interpreting MRI film, which was not a day-to-day business entry of a treating physician, was properly excluded from evidence. *Komar v. Showers*, 227 A.D.2d 135, 641 N.Y.S.2d 643 (1st Dep't 1996).

On a motion for summary judgment by defendant based on the absence of a "serious injury" under INSURANCE LAW § 5102, uncertified medical records and unsworn letters are of no probative value. *Parmisani v. Grasso*, 218 A.D.2d 870, 629 N.Y.S.2d 865 (3d Dep't 1995).

§ 23:15 MEDICAL HISTORY—Where plaintiff had undergone surgery under anesthesia, the history of drug and alcohol abuse contained in the hospital record was germane to treatment and therefore admissible in evidence. *Tirado v. 2188 Realty* Ltd., 216 A.D.2d 14, 627 N.Y.S.2d 364 (1st Dep't 1995).

RESEARCH REFERENCES

American Law Reports

ALR Index: Birth Certificates; Business Records; Death Certificate; Dying Declarations; Records and Recording; Res Gestae

American Jurisprudence Proof of Facts

16 Am Jur Proof of Facts 3d, Foundation for Contemporaneous Videotape Evidence

American Jurisprudence Trials

44 Am Jur Trials 171, Videotape Evidence

Other Resources

KeyCite™/Insta-Cite®: Cases referred to herein can be fur-

ther researched through the KeyCite™ and Insta-Cite®
computer-assisted services. Use KeyCite or Insta-Cite to
check citations for form, parallel references, and prior
and later history. For comprehensive citator information, including citations to other decisions and secondary materials that have mentioned or discussed the cases
cited, use KeyCite. ALR and ALR Fed Annotations
referred to herein can be further researched through the
WESTLAW® Find service.

CHAPTER 24

ADMISSIONS

§ 24:1 ADMISSIONS BY A PARTY OPPONENT—Post-accident design modification is admissible, in a product liability case, only to establish control, feasibility, or for impeachment purposes. The evidence is not received as an admission of negligence. When admitted for one of the permissible purposes, the evidence must be accompanied by a limiting instruction. *DePasquale v. Morbark Industries, Inc.*, 221 A.D.2d 409, 633 N.Y.S.2d 543 (2d Dep't 1995).

An admission of prior notice by a homeowner who died prior to trial was admissible, where the testimony as to the statement was given by a witness whose testimony was not barred by the Dead Man's Statute. *Smith v. Kuhn*, 221 A.D.2d 620, 634 N.Y.S.2d 167 (2d Dep't 1995).

Where a prior inconsistent statement of a party is offered in evidence on cross-examination of the party, no foundation is necessary. The party's statement is treated as an admission, and received as primary evidence against the party. *Viera v. New York City Transit Authority*, 221 A.D.2d 625, 634 N.Y.S.2d 168 (2d Dep't 1995).

§ 24:2 ADMISSION BY AGENT, EMPLOYEE, OR PARTNER OF PARTY—A supermarket manager's statement to an employee, admonishing the employee for failure to clean up a broken

97

bottle of lemon juice when previously told to do so, was not shown to have been made with the defendant owner's authority, and was thus inadmissible as evidence of notice. Note: the dissenting opinion points out that the manager did have the authority to reprimand the employee, and would have held that the statement was admissible. *Williams v. Waldbaums Supermarkets, Inc., 236 A.D.2d 605, 653 N.Y.S.2d 962 (2d Dep't 1997).*

§ 24:3   ADMISSIONS BY OTHERS—While the pre-trial statements of a defendant are admissible against him, they are not evidence against a co-defendant merely because they are joined as parties to the action. The trial court properly charged that the statements could not be considered in assessing the liability of the other defendants. *Morrissey v. City of New York*, 221 A.D.2d 607, 634 N.Y.S.2d 185 (2d Dep't 1995).

§ 24:4   JUDICIAL ADMISSIONS—In a premises accident case, an admission by counsel in an appellate brief on appeal of a discovery motion has been held to remove the question of control of the subject premises from the case. *Cleland v. 60-02 Woodside Corp.*, 221 A.D.2d 307, 633 N.Y.S.2d 529 (2d Dep't 1995).

Answers to plaintiff's interrogatories, handwritten by defendant who died prior to trial, were admissible against defendant's estate at trial. *Smith v. Kuhn*, 221 A.D.2d 620, 634 N.Y.S.2d 167 (2d Dep't 1995).

The declarations by counsel in affidavits and briefs in one case were admissible against the party, as informal judicial admissions, in another case. The statements were not conclusive, but constituted evidence of the facts admitted. *Matter of Liquidation of Union Indem. Ins. Co. of New York,* 89 N.Y.2d 94, 651 N.Y.S.2d 383, 674 N.E.2d 313 (1996).

Where a party to a matrimonial action fails to file a statement of net worth, the other party's statement is deemed admitted. *Miller-Glass v. Glass*, 237 A.D.2d 723, 653 N.Y.S.2d 982 (3d Dep't 1997).

§ 24:5   JUDICIAL ADMISSIONS IN PLEADINGS—In an action for breach of an employment contract by the alleged employer, the defendant's answer in a prior federal court action, which admitted the employment, was admissible as an informal judicial admission, and created a triable issue of fact when submitted in opposition to a motion for summary judgment. *Weichert v. Kimber*, 229 A.D.2d 998, 645 N.Y.S.2d 674 (4th Dep't 1996).

§ 24:7   SILENCE OF A PARTY AS AN ADMISSION IN CIVIL CASES—Where the record showed that plaintiff was present when her attorney agreed with the court's suggestion that matters should be submitted to a mediator or arbitrator, her failure to object defeated her subsequent claim that the stipulation her attorney entered into to so submit the matter was made without her authority. *Meyer v. Meyer*, 228 A.D.2d 955, 645 N.Y.S.2d 105 (3d Dep't 1996), leave to appeal dismissed in part on other grounds, denied, 88 N.Y.2d 1062, 651 N.Y.S.2d 404, 674 N.E.2d 334 (1996).

§ 24:8   FAILURE TO REPLY TO WRITTEN STATEMENTS AS AN ADMISSION—Where a notice to admit bears upon an ultimate issue in the case, the court may vacate the notice even though the other party failed to answer it. In an action for injuries sustained when plaintiff was struck by a tile that allegedly fell from defendant's school building, plaintiff's notice to admit that the tile fell from the defendant's building was properly vacated, and her motion for summary judgment was denied, there having been no other evidence that the tile came from defendant's building. *Ashkenazi v. City of New York*, 656 N.Y.S.2d 641 (App. Div. 1st Dep't 1997).

§ 24:10 OFFERS OF COMPROMISE AS ADMISSIONS—A party's settlement of another claim is not admissible as evidence of liability, where the settlement did not contain an express admission of fact. *Batavia Turf Farms, Inc. v. County of Genesee,* 659 N.Y.S.2d 681 (App. Div. 4th Dep't 1997).

RESEARCH REFERENCES

American Law Reports

Admissibility of statements made for purposes of medical diagnosis or treatment as hearsay exception under Rule

803(4) of the Uniform Rules of Evidence, 38 A.L.R.5th 433.

Propriety, under state constitutional provisions, of granting use or transactional immunity for compelled incriminating testimony—post-Kastigar cases, 29 A.L.R.5th 1.

Admissibility, in prosecution in another state's jurisdiction, of confession or admission made pursuant to plea bargain with state authorities, 90 A.L.R.4th 1133.

ALR Index: Self-Incrimination

American Jurisprudence 2d

29A Am Jur 2d, Evidence §§ 754-769, 785-793

American Jurisprudence Proof of Facts

30 Am Jur Proof of Facts 2d 307, Evidence of Subsequent Remedial Measures in Civil Cases

32 Am Jur Proof of Facts 2d 253, Admission by Conduct or Silence

23 Am Jur Proof of Facts 2d 713, Custodial Interrogation Under Miranda v Arizona

American Jurisprudence Trials

49 Am Jur Trials 501, Examination of a Witness Based on Prior Statement

42 Am Jur Trials 617, Invalidity of Suspect's Waiver of Miranda Rights

Other Resources

KeyCite™/Insta-Cite®: Cases referred to herein can be further researched through the KeyCite™ and Insta-Cite® computer-assisted services. Use KeyCite or Insta-Cite to check citations for form, parallel references, and prior and later history. For comprehensive citator information, including citations to other decisions and secondary materials that have mentioned or discussed the cases cited, use KeyCite. ALR and ALR Fed Annotations referred to herein can be further researched through the WESTLAW® Find service.

CHAPTER 25

ADMISSIBILITY OF OTHER TYPES OF EVIDENCE

§ 25:1. Admissibility of Circumstantial Evidence
§ 25:7. Custom and Usage
§ 25:16. Parol Evidence

§ 25:1 ADMISSIBILITY OF CIRCUMSTANTIAL EVIDENCE—In a product liability case where there is no proof of a specific defect, evidence that the product did not function as intended will constitute circumstantial evidence that the product was defective. If the defendant then comes forward with evidence that the accident was not necessarily attributable to a defect, plaintiff must produce direct evidence of a defect. Plaintiff is not required, however, to negate all other possible reasonable causes of the accident, such as user error, improper maintenance, or faulty repair. The existence of other contributing causes, including comparative fault, does not rule out that a defect may have been a proximate cause of injury. *Dubecky v. S2 Yachts, Inc.,* 234 A.D.2d 501, 651 N.Y.S.2d 602 (2d Dep't 1996).

An insured's motive to commit arson, such as financial difficulty, coupled with evidence that a fire was of incendiary origin, such as evidence that an accelerant was used, constitute sufficient circumstantial evidence of arson to create a triable issue in an insured's claim for fire loss made under a homeowner's policy. *Stone v. Continental Ins. Co.,* 234 A.D.2d 282, 650 N.Y.S.2d 772 (2d Dep't 1996).

§ 25:7 CUSTOM AND USAGE—Evidence of custom and industry practice is admissible as evidence of a standard of care in a negligence case. However, in a negligence action arising when a shopping mall patron allegedly tripped on an unmarked curb at the edge of the parking lot, expert testimony that it was the practice of three other area shopping malls to mark curbs with yellow paint, supported only by unintelligible photographs, could not es-

101

tablish a standard of care based on industry custom and usage. *Guldy v. Pyramid Corp.*, 222 A.D.2d 815, 634 N.Y.S.2d 788 (3d Dep't 1995).

Custom and usage are admissible to define contractual obligations only when such clarification is necessitated by an ambiguity in the agreement, but may not be used to create an ambiguity where none exists in the contract as made. Where the contract between the Unified Court System and the court reporters' unions provided that reporters would be paid for transcripts requested by judges at a rate to be set by the rules of the Chief Administrative Judge, and there was no provision for a higher rate for daily or expedited copy, parol evidence of a common practice by reporters to charge a higher rate for daily or expedited copy should not have been received. *Milonas v. Public Employment Relations Bd.*, 225 A.D.2d 57, 648 N.Y.S.2d 779 (3d Dep't 1996).

§ 25:16 PAROL EVIDENCE—The fact that a promissory note, in which the individual borrower promised to repay the loan, was on a printed letterhead of a corporation did not authorize extrinsic evidence that the intent was to create a corporate debt. *Struble v. Chapman*, 222 A.D.2d 856, 635 N.Y.S.2d 314 (3d Dep't 1995).

Where a written agreement contains an ambiguity, the court's authority to consider extrinsic evidence in construing the agreement is not vitiated because the agreement was one required to be in writing by the Statute of Frauds. *Smokes N Sweets Inc. v. West Lake Associates*, 227 A.D.2d 757, 642 N.Y.S.2d 358 (3d Dep't 1996).

The use of "etc." following an enumeration of types of wares a commercial tenant was permitted to sell under its lease, created an ambiguity that would be resolved by resort to extrinsic evidence. *Smokes N Sweets Inc. v. West Lake Associates*, 227 A.D.2d 757, 642 N.Y.S.2d 358 (3d Dep't 1996).

The question whether a contract term is ambiguous is one of law to be resolved by the court. The rules governing construction of an ambiguous contract are not triggered unless the court first finds an ambiguity. Where a written contract provided a price for "site cuts and fills," with "no blasting," plaintiff contractor should not have been permitted to introduce evidence that the cost of removing rock, by a method other than blasting, was not included in the contract price. *Marfurt v. College Park Associates,* 227 A.D.2d 913, 643 N.Y.S.2d 266 (4th Dep't 1996).

Where an employment contract is silent as to the duration of the employment, the employment is terminable at will by either party. The absence of a stated duration does not constitute an ambiguity, and parol evidence may not be received to show a promise that the employment would not be terminated until the employee's voluntary retirement, malfeasance, or death. *Bell v. Marine Midland Bank, Inc.,* 230 A.D.2d 758, 646 N.Y.S.2d 366 (2d Dep't 1996). See also, *Matter of Liquidation of New York Agency and Other Assets of Bank of Credit and Commerce Intern., S.A.,* 227 A.D.2d 145, 642 N.Y.S.2d 238 (1st Dep't 1996).

Extrinsic evidence is not generally admissible to contradict, supplement, add to, or explain municipal records, including minutes of a town board meeting. However, where it was undisputed that a resolution was inadvertently omitted from the board minutes by the Town Clerk, evidence that the resolution was adopted should have been received to show that the municipal contract at issue had been authorized. *Hubbard v. Onondaga County Dept. of Health, Div. of Environmental Health,* 219 A.D.2d 832, 632 N.Y.S.2d 370 (4th Dep't 1995).

Although parol evidence is not admissible to vary the terms of a clear writing, it may be used to show that a writing purporting to be a contract is not. Thus, defendant's testimony that a written lease was intended to be used only to defraud the owner's creditor into advancing additional money created a triable issue in the owner's action to recover rent. *Val-Ford Realty Corp. v. J.Z.'s Toy World, Inc.,* 231 A.D.2d 434, 647 N.Y.S.2d 488 (1st Dep't 1996).

Although specific disclaimers in a written contract may provide an effective defense against claims that one party relied on the other's oral representations, a general merger clause or "as is" clause will not preclude parol evidence of fraud in the inducement. *Schooley v. Mannion,* 659 N.Y.S.2d 374 (App. Div. 3d Dep't 1997).

CHAPTER 26

OBJECTIONS TO EVIDENCE

§ 26:2. Necessity for Objection to Improper Evidence

§ 26:2 NECESSITY FOR OBJECTION TO IMPROPER EVIDENCE—Where improper expert testimony on the ultimate issue of a driver's negligence, which invaded the jury's province on a subject not beyond the ken of the ordinary layman, was elicited from plaintiff's expert, and plaintiff failed to take a timely objection, appellate review of the issue whether plaintiff was prejudiced by receipt of the testimony was waived. *Ayala v. Kaestner*, 224 A.D.2d 266, 637 N.Y.S.2d 722 (1st Dep't 1996).

Where a jury instruction is fundamentally deficient in an important aspect of the case, the issue may be considered on appeal in the interest of justice. Where a partition action between former spouses was defended on the basis of adverse possession, and the case was given to the jury in a charge that did not comport with the requirements of the doctrine in that possession began in a permissive manner, the Appellate Division ordered a new trial notwithstanding plaintiff's failure to preserve the error at any stage of the trial. *Perez v. Perez*, 228 A.D.2d 161, 644 N.Y.S.2d 168 (1st Dep't 1996).

Where the defendant-employer in an action for breach of contract counterclaimed for the return of life insurance premiums, but failed to object to the omission of a verdict form question as to the counterclaim, the failure of the trial court to grant judgment on the counterclaim was not preserved for review. *Romano v. Basicnet, Inc.*, 661 N.Y.S.2d 135 (App. Div. 4th Dep't 1997).

Where a defendant's request to charge on damages consisted entirely of requests that the court charge specified Pattern Jury Instructions, review of the court's failure to expand on the pattern charges was precluded. *Guiton v. Gottlieb*, 236 A.D.2d 203, 653 N.Y.S.2d 553 (1st Dep't 1997).

RESEARCH REFERENCES

American Law Reports

Admissibility of evidence discovered in search of adult defendant's property or resident authorized by defendant's minor chile—state cases, 51 A.L.R.5th 425.

Propriety of execution of search warrant at nighttime, 41 A.L.R.5th 171.

Admissibility of statements made for purposes of medical diagnosis or treatment as hearsay exception under Rule 803(4) of the Uniform Rules of Evidence, 38 A.L.R.5th 433.

Admissibility in homicide prosecution of allegedly gruesome or inflammatory visual recording of crime scene, 37 A.L.R.5th 515.

Propriety of stop and search by law enforcement officers based solely on drug courier profile, 37 A.L.R.5th 1.

Propriety, under state constitutional provisions, of granting use or transactional immunity for compelled incriminating testimony—post-Kastigar cases, 29 A.L.R.5th 1.

Driving while intoxicated: subsequent consent to sobriety test as affecting initial refusal, 28 A.L.R.5th 459.

Necessity and sufficiency of showing, in criminal prosecution under "hit-and-run" statute, accused's knowledge of accident, injury, or damage, 26 A.L.R.5th 1.

American Jurisprudence 2d

75A Am Jur 2d, Trial §§ 705-713

American Jurisprudence Proof of Facts

36 Am Jur Proof of Facts 3d 331, Introduction of Evidence Over Parol Evidence Rule Objection

36 Am Jur Proof of Facts 3d 1, Proof of Criminal Identity or Paternity Through Polymerase Chain Reaction (PCR) Testing

American Jurisprudence Trials

49 Am Jur Trials 501, Examination of a Witness Based on a Prior Statement

Other Resources

KeyCite™/Insta-Cite®: Cases referred to herein can be fur-
    ther researched through the KeyCite™ and Insta-Cite®
    computer-assisted services. Use KeyCite or Insta-Cite to
    check citations for form, parallel references, and prior
    and later history. For comprehensive citator informa-
    tion, including citations to other decisions and second-
    ary materials that have mentioned or discussed the cases
    cited, use KeyCite. ALR and ALR Fed Annotations
    referred to herein can be further researched through the
    WESTLAW® Find service.

CHAPTER 27

MISTRIAL

§ 27:2.   Waiver of Right to Mistrial
§ 27:3.   Grounds for Declaring a Mistrial

§ 27:2   WAIVER OF RIGHT TO MISTRIAL—Where opening statements and summations were not transcribed, the Appellate Division could not review a party's contention that improper remarks therein influenced the verdict. *Wilcox v. Morrow,* 226 A.D.2d 1077, 641 N.Y.S.2d 774 (4th Dep't 1996).

§ 27:3   GROUNDS FOR DECLARING A MISTRIAL—In a premises accident case, where the trial court had sustained defendant's objections to references by plaintiff's counsel to dangerous conditions unrelated to the issues in the case, so that any possible prejudice was eliminated, the denial of a motion for a mistrial was not an abuse of discretion. *Wilcox v. Morrow,* 226 A.D.2d 1077, 641 N.Y.S.2d 774 (4th Dep't 1996).

Where the trial court questioned numerous witnesses, dictated the length of answers, at times suggested answers, and generally interjected himself into the proceedings, and where such misconduct interfered with the presentation of the evidence so that the jury was not allowed to review the case in the "calm untrammeled spirit necessary to effect justice," the verdict was set aside on appeal, even though no bias or prejudice was displayed by the trial justice. *Campbell v. Rogers & Wells,* 218 A.D.2d 576, 631 N.Y.S.2d 6 (1st Dep't 1995).

An isolated and unintentionally elicited reference made by a defendant, to a statement he provided to an insurance company representative for a co-defendant, was not so prejudicial as to warrant the granting of a mistrial. The jury verdict, which had been set aside upon the declaration of a mistrial, was reinstated on appeal. *Burlingame v. G & G Auto Repair,* 229 A.D.2d 511, 646 N.Y.S.2d 32 (2d Dep't 1996).

RESEARCH REFERENCES

American Law Reports

Disqualification of prosecuting attorney in state criminal case on account of relationship with accused, 42 A.L.R.5th 581.

Taking and use of trial notes by jury, 36 A.L.R.5th 255.

Prejudicial effect, in civil case, of communications between judges and jurors, 33 A.L.R.5th 205.

Failure or refusal of state court judge to have record made of bench conference with counsel in criminal proceeding, 31 A.L.R.5th 704.

Prejudicial effect, in civil case, of communications between court officials or attendants and jurors, 31 A.L.R.5th 572.

Threats of violence against juror in criminal trial as ground for mistrial or dismissal of juror, 3 A.L.R.5th 963.

Negative characterization or description of defendant, by prosecutor during summation of criminal trial, as ground for reversal, new trial, or mistrial—modern cases, 88 A.L.R.4th 8.

Other Resources

KeyCite™/Insta-Cite®: Cases referred to herein can be further researched through the KeyCite™ and Insta-Cite® computer-assisted services. Use KeyCite or Insta-Cite to check citations for form, parallel references, and prior and later history. For comprehensive citator information, including citations to other decisions and secondary materials that have mentioned or discussed the cases cited, use KeyCite. ALR and ALR Fed Annotations referred to herein can be further researched through the WESTLAW® Find service.

CHAPTER 28

DIRECTED VERDICT

§ 28:3 DETERMINING THE RIGHT TO A DIRECTED VERDICT—A defendant is entitled to a directed verdict only where, giving the plaintiff the benefit of every favorable inference, there is no rational basis on which the jury could reasonably find for the plaintiff. In an action for personal injury based on defendant's alleged negligence in failing to correct a condition of loose cork tiles on stairs, where plaintiff's proof would allow a jury to find that defendant had constructive notice based on its knowledge of a recurring problem elsewhere on the premises, the trial court did not err in denying defendant's motion for a directed verdict. *Gutz v. County of Monroe*, 221 A.D.2d 838, 634 N.Y.S.2d 776 (3d Dep't 1995).

Plaintiff's motion for a directed verdict on the question of defendant's negligent maintenance of property was properly granted, because defense counsel's admissions of negligence during his opening statement were "fatal" and "ruinous" to any defense on the issue, and were not refuted by any evidence presented. *Echavarria v. Cromwell Associates*, 232 A.D.2d 347, 648 N.Y.S.2d 600 (1st Dep't 1996).

The driver of a tractor-trailer that struck a slow moving pick-up truck from behind was negligent as a matter of law, where the tractor-trailer driver failed to offer any explanation for the accident other than his negligence, and photographic evidence showed that he had an unobstructed view. Directed verdict was properly granted to the plaintiff. *Atkinson v. Safety Kleen Corp.*, 659 N.Y.S.2d 132 (App. Div. 3d Dep't 1997).

Cases where expert testimony is a necessary element are not

111

excluded from the possibility of a directed verdict. Where plaintiff in a dental malpractice action introduced uncontroverted expert testimony that the defendant inserted fifteen unnecessary, ill-fitting crowns, and negligently performed a root canal, so that no rational jury could find for the defendant, directed verdict for the plaintiff was properly granted, even though the credibility of expert witnesses is normally a jury question. *Guiton v. Gottlieb*, 236 A.D.2d 203, 653 N.Y.S.2d 553 (1st Dep't 1997).

§ 28:5 NEGLIGENCE AND CONTRIBUTORY NEGLIGENCE AS QUESTIONS OF FACT—In a rear end collision case, where defendant testified that the vehicle in front of him came to a sudden stop, the question of the negligence of both drivers is for the jury. Judgment finding the defendant liable as a matter of law was reversed, and a new trial as to liability ordered. *Niemiec v. Jones*, 237 A.D.2d 267, 654 N.Y.S.2d 163 (2d Dep't 1997).

Where the plaintiff in a product liability action based on failure to provide warnings admitted that he was not looking for any warnings, there could be no proximate cause between the alleged failure to warn and the injuries sustained. Defendant's motion for judgment notwithstanding the verdict was properly granted. *Rodriguez v. Davis Equipment Corp.*, 235 A.D.2d 222, 651 N.Y.S.2d 528 (1st Dep't 1997).

§ 28:8 ASSUMPTION OF RISK—The doctrine of primary assumption of risk, as a complete bar to recovery for negligence, is limited to cases where injury is sustained during voluntary participation in sporting or entertainment activities. Where a delivery person was injured while using defective steps, his knowing use thereof would not bar his recovery, but would diminish his recovery in proportion to which his culpable conduct bore to the landowner's negligence. *Comeau v. Wray*, 659 N.Y.S.2d 347 (App. Div. 3d Dep't 1997).

RESEARCH REFERENCES

American Law Reports

Propriety of using prior conviction for drug dealing to impeach witness in criminal trial, 37 A.L.R.5th 319.

Propriety, under state constitutional provisions, of granting use or transactional immunity for compelled incriminating testimony—post-Kastigar cases, 29 A.L.R.5th 1.

Necessity and sufficiency of showing, in criminal prosecution under "hit-and-run" statute, accused's knowledge of accident, injury, or damage, 26 A.L.R.5th 1.

ALR Index: Striking Out Matter

American Jurisprudence 2d

75A Am Jur 2d, Trial §§ 907-1053

Other Resources

KeyCite™/Insta-Cite®: Cases referred to herein can be further researched through the KeyCite™ and Insta-Cite® computer-assisted services. Use KeyCite or Insta-Cite to check citations for form, parallel references, and prior and later history. For comprehensive citator information, including citations to other decisions and secondary materials that have mentioned or discussed the cases cited, use KeyCite. ALR and ALR Fed Annotations referred to herein can be further researched through the WESTLAW® Find service.

CHAPTER 29

DAMAGES

§ 29:2   AMOUNT DEMANDED IN COMPLAINT—Where plaintiff's original complaint sought $10,000 for personal injuries, her motion, made thirteen years later, to increase the ad damnum clause to $1 million and remove the case from Civil Court to Supreme Court was properly denied, since (1) the severity of the injuries had been known soon after commencement of the action, (2) there was no reasonable excuse for the delay in moving, and (3) the defendant would be prejudiced by having to defend against a claim so much greater than was originally made. *Morgan v MABSTOA* (1997, 1st Dept) — AD2d —, 656 NYS2d 273, *lv den.*, 90 NY2d 935, 664 NYS2d 273.

Plaintiff's motion to increase the ad damnum clause, based on a stroke which occurred six years after the accident, should have been denied with leave to renew on proper papers. The causation of the stroke was not undeniable, and plaintiff failed to supply medical proof of causation. *Clark v. Globe Business Furniture Inc., 237 A.D.2d 846, 655 N.Y.S.2d 184 (3d Dep't 1997).*

115

§ 29:4   LIQUIDATED DAMAGES AND PENALTIES—A liquidated damage clause in a lease would not be enforced where the amount was disproportionate to the damage actually sustained, and therefore constituted an unenforceable penalty. *Irving Tire Co., Inc. v. Stage II Apparel Corp.*, 230 A.D.2d 772, 646 N.Y.S.2d 528 (2d Dep't 1996).

§ 29:5   DUTY TO MINIMIZE DAMAGES—Leases are not subject to the mitigation of damages rule imposed on other contracts because, unlike executory contracts, leases have been historically recognized as the present transfer of an estate in real property. *Holy Properties Ltd., L.P. v. Kenneth Cole Productions, Inc.*, 87 N.Y.2d 130, 637 N.Y.S.2d 964, 661 N.E.2d 694 (1995).

In an action for injuries including a claimed herniated disk, the trial court properly charged that the jury could consider whether plaintiff had failed to mitigate his damage. Although there were risks in undergoing a myelogram, plaintiff's treating physician had recommended one on the basis that if surgery were indicated, it should be performed soon after the accident, and it was for the jury to determine whether plaintiff's refusal to have the myelogram and possible surgery was reasonable. *Van Guilder v. Sands Hecht Const. Corp.*, 659 N.Y.S.2d 439 (App. Div. 1st Dep't 1997).

In a personal injury action brought by a Jehovah's Witness, who declined surgery because the blood transfusions required would have demanded action against plaintiff's religious beliefs, the trial court erred in charging the jury to determine whether plaintiff had acted reasonably as a Jehovah's Witness. The religious distinction constituted an endorsement of religion that is prohibited by the First Amendment. *Williams v. Bright*, 230 A.D.2d 548, 658 N.Y.S.2d 910 (1st Dep't 1997), appeal dismissed, 90 N.Y.2d 935, 664 N.Y.S.2d 273, 686 N.E.2d 1368 (1997).

§ 29:8   LIABILITY FOR EXEMPLARY DAMAGES—In an action for personal injuries sustained when plaintiff was forced to leave a bar, (1) excessive force used by the bouncer supported an award of punitive damages against the bouncer personally where the bouncer slammed plaintiff's head into a wall twice, and shoved her out the door; (2) the evidence did not support employer liability for punitive damages based on the alleged failure to take reasonable measures to discover the employee's alleged propensity for violence, because the failure to perceive an alleged threat and take precautionary measures did not rise to a level of such conscious and deliberate disregard of the interests of others as to constitute willful or wanton conduct where there was evidence of only once instance in which the employee had used moderate force in what was characterized as self-defense; and (3) the verdict against the bouncer of $50,000 for punitive damages was reduced to $2,500, where plaintiff sustained a mild concussion. *Baume v. 212 E. 10 N.Y. Bar Ltd.*, 222 A.D.2d 211, 634 N.Y.S.2d 478 (1st Dep't 1995).

Where a statutory cause of action permits only pecuniary damages, punitive damages are unavailable. Punitive damages are also unavailable under general maritime law. *Public Adm'r of County of New York v. Frota Oceanica Brasileira, S.A.*, 222 A.D.2d 332, 635 N.Y.S.2d 606 (1st Dep't 1995).

Punitive damages are available only in those limited circumstances where it is necessary to deter the defendant and others like it from engaging in conduct that may be characterized as "gross" and "morally reprehensible," and of "such wanton dishonesty as to imply a criminal indifference to civil obligations." The pleading elements required to state a claim for punitive damages as an additional and exemplary remedy when the claim arises from a breach of contract are: (1) defendant's conduct must be actionable as an independent tort; (2) the tortious conduct must be of an egregious nature; (3) the egregious conduct must be directed to plaintiff; and (4) it must be part of a pattern directed at the public generally. In an action against an insurance company for breach of the policy, allegations that the carrier violated INSURANCE LAW § 2601, which prohibits unfair claim settlement practices, did not allege a tort independent of the breach of contract so as to state a claim for punitive damages. *New York University v. Continental Ins. Co.*, 87 N.Y.2d 308, 639 N.Y.S.2d 283, 662 N.E.2d 763, 108 Ed. Law Rep. 342 (1995).

Where a health center's complaint against a physician whose employment was terminated alleged that the defendant physician removed the medical records of hundreds of patients in need of

117

ongoing care, such conduct could be viewed as sufficiently egregious, reckless, or "undertaken with wanton disregard for the pubic safety," as would warrant an award of punitive damages. *Comprehensive Community Development Corp. v. Lehach*, 223 A.D.2d 399, 636 N.Y.S.2d 755 (1st Dep't 1996).

§ 29:9 THE AMOUNT OF EXEMPLARY DAMAGES—The award of $1,350,000 punitive damages against a Jewish funeral parlor for conduct which caused the wrongful autopsy of an Orthodox Jew was excessive, because it was not reasonably related to (1) the harm done, and (2) the flagrancy of the conduct, and was remitted to $650,000. *Liberman v. Riverside Memorial Chapel, Inc.*, 225 A.D.2d 283, 650 N.Y.S.2d 194 (1st Dep't 1996).

§ 29:13 DAMAGES FOR EMOTIONAL INJURIES—The negligence and destruction of a pet by a veterinarian will not support a claim for negligent infliction of emotional distress suffered by the owner. *Jason v. Parks*, 224 A.D.2d 494, 638 N.Y.S.2d 170 (2d Dep't 1996).

The erroneous report of a positive finding on an HIV blood analysis is a special circumstance that provides the assurance that a claim for negligent infliction of emotional distress is genuine and not spurious, so that the claim may be maintained against the parties who handled the blood sample and issued the erroneous report. Those defendants owed a duty of care to plaintiff, even in the absence of a direct relationship with him. However, no cause of action could be maintained against the defendants who had no connection with the vials of blood. *Schulman v. Prudential Ins. Co. of America*, 226 A.D.2d 164, 640 N.Y.S.2d 112 (1st Dep't 1996).

In an action for false imprisonment, assault, and negligent infliction of emotional distress, expert medical testimony was not needed to establish that emotional injuries allegedly suffered by the plaintiff and her young child were caused when police officers broke into plaintiff's apartment, held a gun to her head, and confined plaintiff and her child against a wall without explaining the reason for entering the apartment, and without displaying badges. The issue of causation did not require special knowledge or training, and plaintiffs could recover for their emotional injuries without proving a physical injury. *Allinger v. City of Utica*, 226 A.D.2d 1118, 641 N.Y.S.2d 959 (4th Dep't 1996).

Recovery for emotional distress may not be based on the observation of unintended damage to property. Where defendant's automobile came within inches of plaintiff when she was in front of her residence, but she did not see the vehicle until it hit her house, she could not recover for shock, anxiety, and mental distress. *Caprino v. Silsby*, 226 A.D.2d 1078, 642 N.Y.S.2d 120 (4th Dep't 1996).

Where the evidence did not establish permanency of emotional harm caused by neighbor's harassment and intimidation, awards of $600,000 for emotional distress, and $100,000 to spouse on derivative claim, were remitted to $250,000 and $50,000, respectively. *Stram v. Farrell*, 223 A.D.2d 260, 646 N.Y.S.2d 193 (3d Dep't 1996).

Since the virus that causes AIDS may take time to produce a positive HIV-antibody test, plaintiff's recovery for emotional distress during the first six months after exposure does not require scientific evidence of infection. However, the rational basis of fear of AIDS after the first six months will require plaintiff to show a positive HIV-antibody test. Upon showing such a test, plaintiff may recover for emotional suffering arising from fear of developing AIDS that is suffered during the latency period. *Brown v. New York City Health and Hospitals Corp.*, 225 A.D.2d 36, 648 N.Y.S.2d 880 (2d Dep't 1996).

Plaintiffs who were exposed to polychlorinated biphenyls (PCBs), a toxic substance, could not recover for emotional suffering or future monitoring costs; in the absence of evidence of PCB contamination, there was no rational basis for fear of development of disease. *Abusio v. Consolidated Edison Co. of New York, Inc.*, 656 N.Y.S.2d 371 (App. Div. 2d Dep't 1997).

Expert testimony is not essential for recovery of damages for mental anguish, which may be proved by the testimony of the victim alone. *Diaz Chemical Corp. v. New York State Div. of Human Rights*, 237 A.D.2d 932, 654 N.Y.S.2d 907 (4th Dep't 1997).

§ 29:15 DAMAGES FOR LOST EARNINGS—laintiff, who had received his paycheck while he was out of work and failed to prove any diminution in earnings capacity, was, as a matter of law, not entitled to any award for lost earnings; the award for lost earnings was vacated on appeal. *Bacigalupo v. Healthshield, Inc., 231 A.D.2d 538, 647 N.Y.S.2d 32 (2d Dep't 1996).*

The Appellate Division, Second Department, appears to have adopted a rule limiting lost earnings to an amount based on written documentation. Where the award exceeded the amount substantiated on plaintiff's tax return, the award was reduced to an amount based on previously reported salary income, notwithstanding her testimony that she earned a higher rate of pay working two jobs during the months preceding her accident. *Poturniak v. Rupcic, 232 A.D.2d 541, 648 N.Y.S.2d 668 (2d Dep't 1996).*

In a personal injury action, plaintiff has the burden of proving lost earnings with reasonable certainty. Where plaintiff's testimony was inconsistent as to the length of time he was disabled, and he offered no employment records, the jury's award of $3,000 for lost earnings was adequate. *Seargent v. Berben, 235 A.D.2d 1024, 652 N.Y.S.2d 904 (3d Dep't 1997).*

§ 29:16 COURT REVIEW OF DAMAGE AWARDS—An award of $375,000 to a 76 year old man who sustained a torn meniscus was remitted to $150,000. *Urquhart v. New York City Transit Authority, 221 A.D.2d 336, 633 N.Y.S.2d 206 (2d Dep't 1995).*

Total of $3.5 million, awarded to a psychiatric patient with suicidal tendencies in an action against the State for causing premature release from care, resulting in loss of both legs when he jumped in front of a subway train, was reduced to a total of $3 million. Plaintiff was not collaterally estopped by the jury award against non-State defendants where that judgment had been reversed. *Rodriguez v. State, 221 A.D.2d 277, 634 N.Y.S.2d 93 (1st Dep't 1995).*

An aggregate award of $2.8 million was not excessive, where the 27 year old plaintiff sustained injuries which required a fusion of two discs, leaving him permanently disabled. *Hackworth v. WDW Development, Inc., 224 A.D.2d 265, 637 N.Y.S.2d 720 (1st Dep't 1996).*

Awards of $2.5 million for past pain and suffering and $5 million for future pain and suffering were affirmed, for the amputation of plaintiff's leg six inches above the knee, the deterioration of parts of the surviving leg, numerous operations, consequential lifelong back pain, lifelong need to change the prosthesis on a regular basis and the need for constant adjustments and physical therapy, loss of a formerly athletic lifestyle, and a 42 year life expectancy. *Sladick v. Hudson General Corp.*, 226 A.D.2d 263, 641 N.Y.S.2d 270 (1st Dep't 1996).

An award of $250,000 would be reduced to $100,000, where plaintiff was eight months old when she sustained a supracondylar fracture of the femur, and evidence showed continuing pain when the child ran and when it rained. *Williams v. Williams*, 226 A.D.2d 710, 641 N.Y.S.2d 408 (2d Dep't 1996).

Awards of past and future pain and suffering, of $750,000 and $1 million, respectively, for serious personal injuries including a torn left rotator cuff, were reduced to $600,000 and $500,000. *Bernstein v. Red Apple Supermarkets*, 227 A.D.2d 264, 642 N.Y.S.2d 303 (1st Dep't 1996).

Awards to two plaintiffs for injuries sustained from gunshot wounds were not excessive. The plaintiff who received $4,059,500 received a gunshot wound to the abdomen that caused multiple perforations of the small bowel, requiring bowel resection; subsequent operations were performed, including removal of a growth in his nasal cavity that left a loss of sensation in the face and a permanent indentation in the cheek, a femoral neurolysis to repair nerve damage that left a severe limp, and repair of an incisional hernia. The second plaintiff, who was awarded $1,360,000, was struck by a bullet that fragmented upon entering the hip, causing a loss of pulse in the groin area and a fracture of the neck of the femur. He underwent three surgical procedures to remove bullet fragments, to graft a portion of bone and to insert a plate, wires and screws in the hip. His physical activities were greatly curtailed, and he was likely to require a hip replacement in the future. *Wyatt v. State*, 227 A.D.2d 283, 642 N.Y.S.2d 312 (1st Dep't 1996), appeal dismissed, 89 N.Y.2d 859, 653 N.Y.S.2d 276, 675 N.E.2d 1229 (1996) and appeal dismissed, 89 N.Y.2d 859, 653 N.Y.S.2d 276, 675 N.E.2d 1229 (1996).

Verdict of $750,000 for pain and suffering was remitted to $450,000, where the plaintiff sustained two herniated discs, and developed hypertrophic posterior spurs, causing pain and permanent disability in that plaintiff could not freely move his neck from side to side. *Adams v. Romero*, 227 A.D.2d 292, 642 N.Y.S.2d 673 (1st Dep't 1996).

Awards of $400,000 and $600,000 for past and future pain and suffering, respectively, were remitted to $300,000 and $100,000, where plaintiff firefighter was injured when scalding water and embers came in contact with his knees and shin as a result of an inadequate uniform. *Lyall v. City of New York*, 228 A.D.2d 566, 645 N.Y.S.2d 34 (2d Dep't 1996).

Total verdict of $3,750,000, for pain and suffering for the loss of one eye and a broken jaw, were remitted to $1,750,000. Although plaintiff would require plastic surgery and had not adjusted well to her injuries, she was able to maintain her job and did not continue to suffer pain. *Stiuso v. City of New York*, 228 A.D.2d 663, 645 N.Y.S.2d 314 (2d Dep't 1996).

Awards of $20,000 for past pain and suffering and $20,000 for future pain and suffering should be increased to $50,000 and $100,000, respectively, where plaintiff fractured the fibular shaft and medial malleolus of the right ankle, requiring open reductive surgery and the insertion of an orthopedic screw and pin, and it was uncontroverted that the ankle would continue to be painful and swollen, and that plaintiff would be unable to engage in the athletic activities he had enjoyed prior to the accident or to perform his job as an electrician without discomfort. *Murray v. Makey*, 229 A.D.2d 919, 645 N.Y.S.2d 680 (4th Dep't 1996).

Awards totaling $275,000 were conditionally increased to an aggregate of $1,350,000, where plaintiff, who was 72 years old at the time of trial, had been electrocuted, sustained internal injuries, and cervical spine injury, spent four months in the hospital with severe pain and multiple surgical procedures, and would continue to suffer pain and disability over a remaining eleven year statistical life expectancy. *Stedman v. Bouillon*, 234 A.D.2d 876, 651 N.Y.S.2d 685 (3d Dep't 1996).

Awards of $2.5 million for plaintiff's 4$1/2$ years of past pain and suffering, and $4 million for 25 years of future pain and suffering, were sustained on appeal where plaintiff, following a fall from a hospital window, underwent six surgical procedures, culminating in the amputation of both legs below the knee, endured constant pain, had to undergo four years of physical and mental rehabilitation, would require future psychiatric treatment, and would be unable to return to his former employment and recreations. *John v. City of New York*, 235 A.D.2d 210, 652 N.Y.S.2d 15 (1st Dep't 1997).

An order granting plaintiff's motion to set aside a damages verdict of $25,000 for past pain and suffering and no damages for future pain and suffering was affirmed, where the uncontroverted testimony of plaintiff's treating physician showed that plaintiff, whose face had been slammed into a wall, sustained crushing fractures of the eye sockets and sinus walls, ruptures sinus cavities, and fractures of other facial bones; multiple displaced fractures resulting in the misalignment of the cheek bones; underwent reconstructive surgery to reposition the facial bones; and continued to have persistent headaches, numbness of the cheek and nose, and pain upon sneezing and coughing. *Lagueux v. Hayes*, 661 N.Y.S.2d 86 (App. Div. 3d Dep't 1997).

Awards of $10,000 and $7,000 for past and future pain and suffering were conditionally increased to $175,000 and $125,000, respectively, where plaintiff sustained a herniated disk, required steroid injections and ultimately surgery, was rendered unable to lift heavy loads, and would require pain medication indefinitely. *Skow v. Jones, Lang & Wooton Corp.*, 657 N.Y.S.2d 709 (App. Div. 1st Dep't 1997).

Awards of $200,000 for past, and $200,000 for future pain and suffering were conditionally reduced to $60,000 and $90,000, respectively, where plaintiff sustained a bulging disk with resulting low back, neck, and leg pain, but no herniation. *Tariq v. Miller*, 657 N.Y.S.2d 769 (App. Div. 2d Dep't 1997).

Awards of past and future pain and suffering of $6,500 and $11,000, respectively, were conditionally increased to $125,000 and $50,000, where plaintiff, a 22 year old, caught her dominant hand in a door, and had her index finger severed just below the first knuckle. *Cecere v. 3950 Blackstone Associates*, 656 N.Y.S.2d 242 (App. Div. 1st Dep't 1997).

Awards aggregating $1,250,000 for pain and suffering were sustained, where plaintiff was assaulted, and her attacker repeatedly banged her head against a radiator, attempted to suffocate her, and slashed her with a knife about the hands, chest, face, and ankles. *Siler v. 146 Montague Associates,* 228 A.D.2d 33, 652 N.Y.S.2d 315 (2d Dep't 1997).

An award for loss of household services was vacated, where the services up to the time of trial had been performed gratuitously by relatives and friends. *Schultz v. Harrison Radiator Div. General Motors Corp.,* 90 N.Y.2d 311, 660 N.Y.S.2d 685, 683 N.E.2d 307 (1997).

§ 29:19 DAMAGES IN WRONGFUL DEATH ACTIONS—The mother of a deceased adult presented evidence of pecuniary loss arising from the assistance decedent provided in caring for a disabled brother who lived with the mother. However, in the absence of extensive services or financial contributions, the award of $1,205,051 was conditionally reduced to $150,000. *Abruzzo v City of New York* (1996, 2d Dept) 233 AD2d 278, 649 NYS2d 484.

Where decedent's conscious pain and suffering, including any preimpact terror, was limited to several seconds, the verdict of $1,500,000 was conditionally reduced to $100,000. The total of $850,000 for pecuniary loss to the 18 year old's parents was reduced to $250,000, notwithstanding that decedent worked in the family business, helped care for his younger sibling, and helped around the home. *Donofrio v. Montalbano,* 659 N.Y.S.2d 484 (App. Div. 2d Dep't 1997).

Awards of $1 million for loss of parental guidance to each of decedent's two children were conditionally reduced to $250,000 each. The award for loss of household services was also reduced from $380,000 to $100,000; and award for momentary preimpact terror was reduced from $115,000 to $50,000. *Klos v. New York City Transit Authority,* 659 N.Y.S.2d 97 (App. Div. 2d Dep't 1997).

§ 29:20 DAMAGES FOR LOSS OF CONSORTIUM—An award of $100,000 to the husband of the injured plaintiff who sustained serious injuries, including a torn rotator cuff, constituted reasonable compensation for loss of consortium. *Bernstein v. Red Apple Supermarkets,* 227 A.D.2d 264, 642 N.Y.S.2d 303 (1st Dep't 1996).

An award of $275,000 for past and future loss of services was reasonable, where plaintiff sustained numerous orthopedic and neurological injuries that resulted in the change from an active, vibrant person to one chronically depressed, pain-ridden, and inactive, and which required the wife to undertake all household services he had previously performed, in addition to raising their four children. *DeLeonibus v. Scognamillo*, 656 N.Y.S.2d 275 (App. Div. 2d Dep't 1997), leave to appeal dismissed in part on other grounds, denied, 90 N.Y.2d 978, 665 N.Y.S.2d 952, 688 N.E.2d 1034 (1997).

§ 29:21 DAMAGES FOR INJURY TO REAL ESTATE—
Plaintiff, seeking recovery for damage to realty, may prove the cost of repair; unless that cost is greater than the diminution in value, the repair costs may be recovered in full. However, where plaintiff proved the cost of repair, and the evidence was not refuted, and defendant did not present evidence of a lower diminution in value, the court erred in lowering the cost of repair based on a supposed lower diminution in value. *Prashant Enterprises, Inc. v. State*, 228 A.D.2d 144, 650 N.Y.S.2d 473 (3d Dep't 1996).

§ 29:24 DAMAGES IN CONTRACT ACTIONS—Where breach
of a construction contract by builders left houses partially unusable and unsafe, the damages were appropriately set at the market price of completing or correcting the contractor's performance. The defendants were not entitled to have the award limited to the diminution in value or least costly cost to cure. *Attardo v. Petosa*, 659 N.Y.S.2d 294 (App. Div. 2d Dep't 1997).

§ 29:27 TREATMENT OF OTHER PAYMENTS RECEIVED BY PLAINTIFF—CPLR 4545, authorizing the court in a personal
injury action to reduce an award by the amount of economic loss that will be recovered from collateral sources, is a statute enacted in derogation of common law and is to be strictly construed, in the narrowest sense that its words and underlying purposes permit. Where plaintiff received disability retirement pension benefits which were not paid in replacement of lost earnings and health benefits, those elements of damage would not be reduced; the award for lost ordinary pension benefits, which the disability retirement

pension did replace, would be offset thereby. *Oden v. Chemung County Indus. Development Agency,* 87 N.Y.2d 81, 637 N.Y.S.2d 670, 661 N.E.2d 142 (1995).

The burden of proving collateral source payments as a statutory setoff under CPLR § 4545 is on the defendant. Where the jury's verdict was itemized, and defendant failed to match the alleged collateral source payments to any item of damage that had been awarded, no reduction would be made. *Adamy v. Ziriakus,* 231 A.D.2d 80, 659 N.Y.S.2d 623 (4th Dep't 1997).

RESEARCH REFERENCES

American Law Reports

Excessiveness or adequacy of damages awarded for injuries causing mential or psychological damages, 52 A.L.R.5th 1.

Excessiveness or adequacy of damages awarded for injuries to head or brain, 50 A.L.R.5th 1.

Valuing damages in personal injury actions awarded for gratuitously rendered nursing and medical care, 49 A.L.R.5th 685.

Measure and elements of damages for lessee's breach of covenant as to repairs, 45 A.L.R.5th 251.

Collateral source rule: admissibility of evidence of availability to plaintiff of free public special education on issue of amount of damages recoverable from defendant, 41 A.L.R.5th 771.

Damages for wrongful termination of franchise other than automobile dealership contracts, 40 A.L.R.5th 57.

Recovery of punitive damages for injuries resulting from transport, handling, and storage of toxic or hazardous substances, 39 A.L.R.5th 763.

Allowance of punitive damages in medical malpractice action, 35 A.L.R.5th 145.

Intoxication of automobile driver as basis for awarding punitive damages, 33 A.L.R.5th 303.

Measure and elements of damages for injury to bridge, 31 A.L.R.5th 171.

Sufficiency of evidence to prove future medical expenses as result of injury to back, neck, or spine, 26 A.L.R.5th 401.

Validity, construction, and application of state statutory provisions limiting amount of recovery in medical malpractice claims, 26 A.L.R.5th 245.

Application of "fireman's rule" to preclude recovery by peace officer for injuries inflicted by defendant in resisting arrest, 25 A.L.R.5th 97.

American Jurisprudence Proof of Facts

36 Am Jur Proof of Facts 3d 439, Recovery of Damages for Injury to Landowners Property from Environmental Condition on Neighboring Land

35 Am Jur Proof of Facts 3d 161, Proving Damages Caused by Securities Brokers' Excessive, Unsuitable, or Unauthorized Trading

American Jurisprudence Trials

65 Am Jur Trials 261, Damages for Wrongful Death of, or Injury to, Child, 65 Am Jur Trials 261

59 Am Jur Trials 395, Presentation and Proof of Damages in Personal Injury Litigation

56 Am Jur Trials 369, Recovery of Damages for Property Devaluation Caused by Off-Site Environmental Hazards

54 Am Jur Trials 443, Punitive Damages in Products Liability Litigation

Other Resources

KeyCite™/Insta-Cite®: Cases referred to herein can be further researched through the KeyCite™ and Insta-Cite® computer-assisted services. Use KeyCite or Insta-Cite to check citations for form, parallel references, and prior and later history. For comprehensive citator information, including citations to other decisions and secondary materials that have mentioned or discussed the cases cited, use KeyCite. ALR and ALR Fed Annotations referred to herein can be further researched through the WESTLAW® Find service.

CHAPTER 30

CLOSING ARGUMENTS

§ 30:4. General Rules Governing Closing Argument
§ 30:8. Improper Remarks in Civil Cases
§ 30:11. Correcting Improper Conduct of Counsel

§ 30:4 GENERAL RULES GOVERNING CLOSING ARGU-MENT—Counsel must be permitted to comment within the four corners of the evidence during summation. Where counsel was prevented from commenting on certain medical insurance records which were received in evidence in a medical malpractice action, this was prejudicial error and a new trial was ordered. *Kasman v. Flushing Hosp. and Medical Center,* 224 A.D.2d 590, 638 N.Y.S.2d 687 (2d Dep't 1996).

§ 30:8 IMPROPER REMARKS IN CIVIL CASES—Where plaintiff's counsel, on summation in a personal injury action, (1) accused the defendants of illegal conduct, (2) acted as an unsworn witness on various subjects such as the manner in which bus drivers generally drive and the purpose of "no stopping" signs, (3) interjected his opinion of the evidence at trial, and (4) asked the jury to "provide" for plaintiff, discussing irrelevant evidence in an effort to appeal to the jury's passion and sympathy, the Appellate Division held that a new trial was required in the interests of justice, notwithstanding the failure of defense counsel to take timely objections. *Reynolds v. Burghezi,* 227 A.D.2d 941, 643 N.Y.S.2d 248 (4th Dep't 1996).

Where comments of counsel on summation exceeded the limits of appropriate comment, but had some evidentiary basis, the Appellate Division would not review these excesses in the absence of a timely objection. *Diaz v. Avis Rent A Car System Inc.,* 225 A.D.2d 390, 638 N.Y.S.2d 665 (1st Dep't 1996).

Plaintiff's counsel was properly precluded from arguing in his summation that the defendant could have subpoenaed a witness as

129

to whom the missing witness charge was given against the plaintiff. The witness was not under defendant's control, so that defendant's failure to call the witness could not be used to rebut the inference that the missing witness's testimony would not have favored plaintiff. *Jackson v. County of Sullivan,* 232 A.D.2d 954, 648 N.Y.S.2d 808 (3d Dep't 1996).

§ 30:11 CORRECTING IMPROPER CONDUCT OF COUN-SEL—Although aspects of counsel's summation were reprehensible, including irresponsible and unwarranted attacks on police witnesses, the trial court's prompt and thorough curative instructions were sufficient to assure that the adverse parties were not deprived of a fair trial, and averted reversible error. *Mena v. New York City Transit Authority,* 656 N.Y.S.2d 206 (App. Div. 1st Dep't 1997).

RESEARCH REFERENCES

American Law Reports

Prejudicial effect of statement by prosecutor that verdict, recommendation of punishment, or other finding by jury is subject to review or correction by other authorities, 10 A.L.R.5th 700.

Propriety and prejudicial effect of counsel's negative characterization or description of witness during summation of criminal trial—modern cases, 88 A.L.R.4th 209.

Negative characterization or description of defendant, by prosecutor during summation of criminal trial, as ground for reversal, new trial, or mistrial—modern cases, 88 A.L.R.4th 8.

American Jurisprudence Pleading and Practice

9A Am Jur Pl & Pr Forms (Rev), Evidence § 96

Other Resources

KeyCite™/Insta-Cite®: Cases referred to herein can be further researched through the KeyCite™ and Insta-Cite® computer-assisted services. Use KeyCite or Insta-Cite to check citations for form, parallel references, and prior and later history. For comprehensive citator information, including citations to other decisions and secondary materials that have mentioned or discussed the cases cited, use KeyCite. ALR and ALR Fed Annotations referred to herein can be further researched through the WESTLAW® Find service.

CHAPTER 31

INSTRUCTIONS TO THE JURY

§ 31:2. Pattern Jury Instructions
§ 31:5. Exceptions or Objections to Instructions
§ 31:7. Erroneous Instructions
§ 31:8. Other Rules Applicable to Instructions
§ 31:9. Correcting Erroneous Instructions

§ 31:2 PATTERN JURY INSTRUCTIONS—The trial judge is not required to track pattern jury instructions; as long as the charge adequately conveys the sum and substance of applicable law, departure from pattern instructions is not error. *Jackson v. County of Sullivan*, 232 A.D.2d 954, 648 N.Y.S.2d 808 (3d Dep't 1996).

§ 31:5 EXCEPTIONS OR OBJECTIONS TO INSTRUC-TIONS—The fact that an appellate decision, changing the applicable law in a manner that would control pending cases, is delivered after a verdict in a pending case does not excuse the failure to preserve the error by objecting to the charge. Where defendant Transit Authority withdrew its objection to the charge on common carrier liability, the Authority was precluded from seeking reversal based on an appellate decision six days after the verdict, which eviscerated the common carrier doctrine. *Kroupova v. Hill*, 661 N.Y.S.2d 218 (App. Div. 1st Dep't 1997).

§ 31:7 ERRONEOUS INSTRUCTIONS—Where a physician examined plaintiff on one occasion more than 13 years before trial, and plaintiff's counsel indicated that his efforts to locate that physician had been unsuccessful, plaintiff adequately established that the physician was not in plaintiff's control. The missing witness charge was an improvident exercise of discretion, and a new trial was ordered. *Kasman v. Flushing Hosp. and Medical Center*, 224 A.D.2d 590, 638 N.Y.S.2d 687 (2d Dep't 1996).

Where legal principles governing liability were adequately included in the charge as a whole, error in charging LABOR LAW § 200 against certain defendants was harmless, and the verdict would not be disturbed. *Maltese v Westinghouse Elec. Corp. (In re New York City Asbestos Litig.)* (1996, App Div, 1st Dept) 640 NYS2d 488, app gr 88 NY2d 809, 647 NYS2d 713, 670 NE2d 1345, order aff'd, 89 N.Y.2d 955, 655 N.Y.S.2d 855, 678 N.E.2d 467 (1997).

Even where the parties do not request the trial court to marshall the evidence, the court is obligated not merely to give the jury general legal principles, but to instruct the jury as to the application of the factual contentions of the parties to the legal principles charged. Where the trial court responded to repeated questions from the jury, during deliberations, by repeating general legal concepts and by giving the jury the written text of a portion of the charge, reversible error was committed. *Rivers v. Garden Way Inc.,* 231 A.D.2d 50, 660 N.Y.S.2d 893 (3d Dep't 1997).

Notwithstanding some potential for confusion where the questions on a verdict sheet adopt shorthand language which does not fully convey the legal principle involved, there is no error so long as the instruction itself adequately conveyed the legal principle; the propriety of the verdict sheet must be considered within the context of the charge as a whole. *Plunkett v. Emergency Medical Service of New York City,* 234 A.D.2d 162, 651 N.Y.S.2d 462 (1st Dep't 1996).

Where defendant, on the issue of damages in a personal injury action, presents evidence that plaintiff's injury is, in fact, not a new injury but rather the activation of a latent condition, the court is required, upon request by plaintiff, to instruct the jury that the defendant would be liable for any precipitation or activation of a latent condition that was caused by defendant's negligence. *Martin v. Volvo Cars of North America, Inc.,* 661 N.Y.S.2d 338 (App. Div. 4th Dep't 1997).

§ 31:8 OTHER RULES APPLICABLE TO INSTRUCTIONS—A party seeking a missing witness charge has the burden to promptly notify the court that the charge will be requested, so that the court may properly exercise its discretion and so that adverse counsel may adjust trial strategy. Thus, the trial court erred in its sua sponte decision to give the charge when it was too late for counsel to adjust trial strategy and avoid prejudice. *Spoto v. S.D.R. Const., Inc.,* 226 A.D.2d 202, 641 N.Y.S.2d 20 (1st Dep't 1996).

In a personal injury action, plaintiff was entitled to a missing witness charge with respect to a physician who examined plaintiff at defendants' request but was not called to testify at trial. Defendant's contention that the testimony would have merely been cumulative of the testimony of plaintiff's treating physicians was unavailing, because testimony may be considered cumulative only when both witnesses are testifying in favor of the same party. *Leahy v. Allen,* 221 A.D.2d 88, 644 N.Y.S.2d 388 (3d Dep't 1996).

Defendants' request for a missing witness charge was properly denied, where the testimony of plaintiff's treating physicians would have been cumulative. *Jones by Jones v. Anastasopoulos,* 229 A.D.2d 517, 645 N.Y.S.2d 840 (2d Dep't 1996).

The missing witness charge applies to expert as well as fact witnesses. Where the defendant gave notice of an expert's identity and the substance of the expert's proposed testimony, showing the expert's familiarity with the cause of the accident, and then chose not to call the expert, a missing witness charge was properly given. *Sanders v. Otis Elevator Co.,* 232 A.D.2d 327, 649 N.Y.S.2d 19 (1st Dep't 1996).

Where plaintiff claimed that his brother, an eyewitness, could not appear at trial because of a medical condition that prevented him from traveling from out of the state, the court erred in precluding plaintiff from offering the medical explanation to the jury to counteract the missing witness charge. *Minick v. Liquid Air Corp.,* 658 N.Y.S.2d 420 (App. Div. 2d Dep't 1997).

The missing witness charge was erroneously given as to several of plaintiff's treating or examining physicians where it appeared that their testimony would have been merely cumulative. *Austin v. Knowlton,* 234 A.D.2d 918, 651 N.Y.S.2d 795 (4th Dep't 1996). *See also, Dowling v. 257 Associates,* 235 A.D.2d 293, 652 N.Y.S.2d 736 (1st Dep't 1997).

§ 31:9 CORRECTING ERRONEOUS INSTRUCTIONS—If the trial judge accepts an exception to the charge, and then gives an adequate curative instruction, the original error will be deemed harmless. *Marek v. De Poalo & Son Bldg. Masonry Inc.*, 659 N.Y.S.2d 331 (App. Div. 3d Dep't 1997).

RESEARCH REFERENCES

American Law Reports

Right of defendant in prosecution for perjury to have the "two witnesses, or one witness and corroborating circumstances," rule included in charge to jury—state cases, 41 A.L.R.5th 1.

Prejudicial effect, in civil case, of communications between judges and jurors, 33 A.L.R.5th 205.

Prejudicial effect, in civil case, of communications between court officials or attendants and jurors, 31 A.L.R.5th 572.

When should jury's deliberation proceed from charged offense to lesser-included offense, 26 A.L.R.5th 603.

American Jurisprudence 2d

75B Am Jur 2d, Trial §§ 1228-1492

75A Am Jur 2d, Trial §§ 1077-1227

American Jurisprudence Pleading and Practice

25A Am Jur Pl & Pr Forms (Rev), Witnesses, Forms 158-187

Other Resources

KeyCite™/Insta-Cite®: Cases referred to herein can be further researched through the KeyCite™ and Insta-Cite® computer-assisted services. Use KeyCite or Insta-Cite to check citations for form, parallel references, and prior and later history. For comprehensive citator information, including citations to other decisions and secondary materials that have mentioned or discussed the cases cited, use KeyCite. ALR and ALR Fed Annotations referred to herein can be further researched through the WESTLAW® Find service.

CHAPTER 32

CONDUCT OF THE JURY

§ 32:8. Communications with Jurors During Deliberations
§ 32:9. Improper Conduct of Jurors
§ 32:10. Impeachment of Jury Verdicts

§ 32:8 COMMUNICATIONS WITH JURORS DURING DELIBERATIONS—Jurors' affidavits may not usually be used to impeach the verdict. However, where it appeared that (1) the jurors had informed a court officer that they were unable to reach a verdict, and the officer told them that they must continue deliberations until a verdict was reached, and (2) a juror thereupon changed her vote, producing a 5-1 verdict, the possible coercive effect of the officer's unauthorized communication required a new trial. The trial court should have conducted a hearing to determine the facts surrounding the officer's misconduct, and the effect it had on the jury's deliberations. However, because of the time between the verdict and the appeal, that was no longer feasible, and the likelihood of the communication having affected the verdict must be presumed. *Burtch v. Shah*, 230 A.D.2d 223, 661 N.Y.S.2d 118 (4th Dep't 1997).

§ 32:9 IMPROPER CONDUCT OF JURORS—Where a juror had held herself out as more knowledgeable than other jurors on the issue of personal injuries, and related information from an outside source which had a high probability of causing a verdict lower than it would have been based solely on the evidence, a new trial on damages was ordered. *Ryan v. Orange County Fair Speedway*, 227 A.D.2d 609, 643 N.Y.S.2d 211 (2d Dep't 1996).

§ 32:10 IMPEACHMENT OF JURY VERDICTS—Juries are not permitted to express an intent contrary to their verdict, except to correct clerical or ministerial mistakes. A jury's alleged error in reducing damages by the percentage attributed to plaintiff's comparative fault is not considered ministerial, and the trial court had no authority to reassemble the jury to fill out a new verdict sheet. However, the original verdict was set aside as inadequate, and a new trial on damages was ordered. *Alkinburgh v. Glessing,* 658 N.Y.S.2d 735 (App. Div. 3d Dep't 1997).

RESEARCH REFERENCES

American Law Reports

Taking and use of trial notes by jury, 36 A.L.R.5th 255.

Prejudicial effect, in civil case, of communications between court officials or attendants and jurors, 31 A.L.R.5th 572.

When should jury's deliberation proceed from charged offense to lesser-included offense, 26 A.L.R.5th 603.

Other Resources

KeyCite™/Insta-Cite®: Cases referred to herein can be further researched through the KeyCite™ and Insta-Cite® computer-assisted services. Use KeyCite or Insta-Cite to check citations for form, parallel references, and prior and later history. For comprehensive citator information, including citations to other decisions and secondary materials that have mentioned or discussed the cases cited, use KeyCite. ALR and ALR Fed Annotations referred to herein can be further researched through the WESTLAW® Find service.

CHAPTER 33

THE VERDICT

§ 33:2 APPORTIONMENT OF VERDICTS—Where the City's liability was for failure to promptly repair a stop sign, but the co-defendant drivers both failed to exercise the degree of care that conditions demanded, a verdict apportioning 90% against the City was against the weight of the evidence, and a new trial on the issue of apportionment was ordered. *Glassman v. City of New York*, 225 A.D.2d 658, 640 N.Y.S.2d 139 (2d Dep't 1996).

§ 33:3 VERDICTS AND WEIGHT OF EVIDENCE—In a rear-end collision case, defendant's sparse testimony concerning the wet condition of the roadway and a sudden stop by the vehicle in front was insufficient to rebut the presumption of negligence that arises in a rear-end collision with a stopped vehicle. The verdict for defendant was set aside as against the weight of the evidence, and a new trial ordered. *Hurley v. Cavitolo*, 658 N.Y.S.2d 90 (App. Div. 2d Dep't 1997).

§ 33:4 OBJECTIONS TO THE FORM OF A VERDICT—Where plaintiff failed to object to the omission of items of alleged damage from the itemized verdict sheet until after the jury had commenced deliberations, the issue would not be reviewed on appeal. *Figueroa v. Waldbaum's Inc.*, 222 A.D.2d 483, 635 N.Y.S.2d 251 (2d Dep't 1995).

§ 33:7 INCONSISTENT VERDICTS—A jury verdict which found defendant vehicle manufacturer liable for a "rollover" ac-

139

cident on a breach of warranty cause of action, but not on strict product liability, was not inconsistent. The finding could be reconciled under substantive law because while the vehicle might be unsuitable for ordinary use on the warranty claim, its benefits as an off-road vehicle might outweigh the dangers associated with rollover accidents on the strict liability claim. *Denny v. Ford Motor Co.,* 87 N.Y.2d 248, 639 N.Y.S.2d 250, 662 N.E.2d 730, 28 U.C.C. Rep. Serv. 2d (CBC) 15 (1995).

Where the trial court reinstructs the jury and directs continued deliberations as a result of inconsistent answers to jury interrogatories, the jury is free to substantially alter its answers to reflect the jury's true intentions; they are not bound to the original verdict, since it was not entered by the court. *Ryan v. Orange County Fair Speedway,* 227 A.D.2d 609, 643 N.Y.S.2d 211 (2d Dep't 1996).

When a party claims that, under the circumstances of a case, the jury verdict finding a party negligent, but also finding that such negligence was not a proximate cause of injury, is inconsistent, the failure to object before the jury is discharged operates as a failure to preserve the issue for appellate review. *Reynolds v. Burghezi,* 227 A.D.2d 941, 643 N.Y.S.2d 248 (4th Dep't 1996).

The trial court did not err in setting aside, as inconsistent and inadequate, a verdict which awarded substantial damages for future earnings, but nothing for future pain and suffering, and minimal damages for loss of services. *Schaefer v. RCP Associates,* 232 A.D.2d 286, 649 N.Y.S.2d 13 (1st Dep't 1996).

Where the verdict sheet incorrectly instructed the jury to proceed to an item of damages even though it found no negligence, and the foreperson explained that the jury merely followed the misdirection in proceeding to answer the damage question even though no negligence had been found, the trial court properly vacated the answer as to damages, and entered judgment for the defendant. *Peters v. Port Authority Trans-Hudson Corp.,* 234 A.D.2d 205, 651 N.Y.S.2d 500 (1st Dep't 1996).

Plaintiff fell at the entranceway to defendant's restaurant. The jury's verdict finding that defendant was negligent in allowing a dangerous condition to exist at the entranceway was inconsistent with the finding that the condition was not a proximate cause of the fall. Any inadvertence by plaintiff, while relevant to comparative fault, does not equate with a lack of proximate cause. *Brecht v. Copper Sands, Inc.,* 237 A.D.2d 907, 654 N.Y.S.2d 520 (4th Dep't 1997).

The trial court has a broad power to set aside a verdict where it is clearly a product of substantial confusion among the jurors. Where a jury interrogatory sheet contained a gratuitous comment that was inconsistent with the answers, demonstrating substantial confusion as to the burden and quantum of proof applied by the jury, the trial court acted within its discretion in ordering a new trial. *Provenzano v. Peters,* 661 N.Y.S.2d 41 (App. Div. 2d Dep't 1997).

In a personal injury action where the jury could not have reasonably concluded from the evidence that plaintiff's injuries would worsen over time, a verdict awarding zero for past pain and suffering and $200,000 for future pain and suffering reflected substantial jury confusion, and would be set aside as inconsistent. *Cadet v. City of New York,* 656 N.Y.S.2d 331 (App. Div. 2d Dep't 1997).

§ 33:9 SPECIAL INTERROGATORIES—In a motor vehicle accident case in which there is an issue whether plaintiff sustained a "serious injury" meeting the no-fault threshold, where several different theories to satisfy the requirement were charged, a separate interrogatory should have been submitted to the jury for each theory. Where the charge had blurred the distinctions among the several theories, and only one interrogatory was posed as to whether a serious injury had been sustained, these errors may have affected the verdict, and a new trial was ordered. *Velez v. Svehla,* 229 A.D.2d 528, 645 N.Y.S.2d 842 (2d Dep't 1996).

RESEARCH REFERENCES

American Law Reports

Taking and use of trial notes by jury, 36 A.L.R.5th 255.

Prejudicial effect, in civil case, of communications between court officials or attendants and jurors, 31 A.L.R.5th 572.

Disqualification of judge as affecting validity of decision in which other nondisqualified judges participated, 29 A.L.R.5th 722.

When should jury's deliberation proceed from charged offense to lesser-included offense, 26 A.L.R.5th 603.

American Jurisprudence Proof of Facts

24 Am Jur Proof of Facts 2d 633, Jury Misconduct Warranting New Trial

Other Resources

KeyCite™/Insta-Cite®: Cases referred to herein can be further researched through the KeyCite™ and Insta-Cite® computer-assisted services. Use KeyCite or Insta-Cite to check citations for form, parallel references, and prior and later history. For comprehensive citator information, including citations to other decisions and secondary materials that have mentioned or discussed the cases cited, use KeyCite. ALR and ALR Fed Annotations referred to herein can be further researched through the WESTLAW® Find service.

CHAPTER 34
THE JUDGMENT

§ 34:7.   Relief From Judgment or Order

§ 34:7   RELIEF FROM JUDGMENT OR ORDER—Future damages in tort actions are subject to the annuity provisions of Articles 50-A and 50-B of the CPLR. Where there is considerable delay before final judgment can be entered, such as may be caused by an intervening appeal, the trial court has discretion to make an immediate lump sum award for an appropriate portion of the future damages awarded, to be deducted from the annuity contract. *Williams v. Bright*, 230 A.D.2d 548, 658 N.Y.S.2d 910 (1st Dep't 1997), appeal dismissed, 90 N.Y.2d 935, 664 N.Y.S.2d 273, 686 N.E.2d 1368 (1997).

Relief from a judgment will be granted on the basis of newly discovered evidence that is material, not merely cumulative, not merely relevant for impeachment, and could not have been discovered earlier through the exercise of due diligence. Where plaintiff contractor's principal's testimony that the manner of performance of the contract had been approved by defendant's employee with responsibility for making the determination, but it later unfolded that defendant's official had been bribed by plaintiff's principal to approve the manner of performance, the judgment was reversed and a new trial ordered. *Prote Contracting Co., Inc. v. Board of Educ. of the City of New York*, 230 A.D.2d 32, 657 N.Y.S.2d 158, 118 Ed. Law Rep. 433 (1st Dep't 1997).

RESEARCH REFERENCES

American Law Reports

Propriety of applying cash bail to payment of fine, 42 A.L.R.5th 547.

Prejudicial effect of trial judge's remarks, during civil jury trial, disparaging litigants, witnesses, or subject matter of litigation—modern cases, 35 A.L.R.5th 1.

Disqualification of judge as affecting validity of decision in which other nondisqualified judges participated, 29 A.L.R.5th 722.

ALR Index: Judgment Notwithstanding Verdict; Judgment on Pleadings; Orders, and Decrees

American Jurisprudence 2d

75B Am Jur 2d, Trial §§ 1938-1941, 1953-1955

American Jurisprudence Proof of Facts

35 Am Jur Proof of Facts 3d 323, Entitlement to a Stay or Default Judgment Relief Under the Soldiers' and Sailors' Civil Relief Act

32 Am Jur Proof of Facts 2d 491, Modification of Spousal Support Award

American Jurisprudence Trials

56 Am Jur Trials 529, Strategies for Effective Management of Crossborder Recognition and Enforcement of American Money Judgments

Other Resources

KeyCite™/Insta-Cite®: Cases referred to herein can be further researched through the KeyCite™ and Insta-Cite® computer-assisted services. Use KeyCite or Insta-Cite to check citations for form, parallel references, and prior and later history. For comprehensive citator information, including citations to other decisions and secondary materials that have mentioned or discussed the cases cited, use KeyCite. ALR and ALR Fed Annotations referred to herein can be further researched through the WESTLAW® Find service.

Table of Cases

E

Echavarria v. Cromwell Associates, 232 A.D.2d 347, 648 N.Y.S.2d 600 (1st Dep't, 1996)—§ **28:3**

Edmiston v. Tony Rome's, Inc., 224 A.D.2d 941, 637 N.Y.S.2d 896 (4th Dep't, 1996)—§ **22:18**

Ekwunife v. Erike, 171 Misc. 2d 554, 658 N.Y.S.2d 166 (App. Term, 1997)—§ **17:2**

Ellis v. Ellis, 235 A.D.2d 1002, 653 N.Y.S.2d 180 (3d Dep't, 1997)—§ **6:4**

F

Faber v. New York City Housing Authority, 227 A.D.2d 248, 642 N.Y.S.2d 279 (1st Dep't, 1996)—§ **1:2**

Figueroa v. Waldbaum's Inc., 222 A.D.2d 483, 635 N.Y.S.2d 251 (2d Dep't, 1995)—§ **33:4**

Fortunato v. Dover Union Free School Dist., 224 A.D.2d 658, 638 N.Y.S.2d 727, 107 Ed. Law Rep. 930 (2d Dep't, 1996)—§ **22:15**

Franco v. Muro, 224 A.D.2d 579, 638 N.Y.S.2d 690 (2d Dep't, 1996)—§ **22:5**

G

Glassman v. City of New York, 225 A.D.2d 658, 640 N.Y.S.2d 139 (2d Dep't, 1996)—§ **33:2**

Goldin, Matter of, 227 A.D.2d 401, 641 N.Y.S.2d 731 (2d Dep't, 1996)—§ **12:10**

Gomez by Gomez v. New York City Housing Authority, 217 A.D.2d 110, 636 N.Y.S.2d 271 (1st Dep't, 1995)—§ **22:3**

Greene, Matter of, 225 A.D.2d 273, 649 N.Y.S.2d 937 (2d Dep't, 1996)—§ **3:2**

Greenwald v. H & P 29th Street Associates, 659 N.Y.S.2d 473 (App. Div. 1st Dep't, 1997)—§ **16:2**

Guiliano v. Carlisle, 236 A.D.2d 364, 653 N.Y.S.2d 635 (2d Dep't, 1997)—§ **3:3**

Guiton v. Gottlieb, 236 A.D.2d 203, 653 N.Y.S.2d 553 (1st Dep't, 1997)—§ **2:3, 26:2, 28:3**

Guldy v. Pyramid Corp., 222 A.D.2d 815, 634 N.Y.S.2d 788 (3d Dep't, 1995)—§ **25:7**

Gutz v. County of Monroe, 221 A.D.2d 838, 634 N.Y.S.2d 776 (3d Dep't, 1995)—§ **28:3**

H

Hackworth v. WDW Development, Inc., 224 A.D.2d 265, 637 N.Y.S.2d 720 (1st Dep't, 1996)—§ **22:23, 29:16**

Hampton v. Annal Management Co., Ltd., 168 Misc. 2d 138, 646 N.Y.S.2d 227 (App. Term, 1996)—§ **9:5**

Hatton v. Gassler, 219 A.D.2d 697, 631 N.Y.S.2d 757 (2d Dep't, 1995)—§ **23:1, 23:12**

Hawkins v. Brooklyn-Caledonian Hosp., 658 N.Y.S.2d 375 (App. Div. 2d Dep't, 1997)—§ **18:5**

Hill v. Arnold, 226 A.D.2d 232, 640 N.Y.S.2d 892 (1st Dep't, 1996)—§ **10:5, 14:10**

Hoglund v. Hoglund, 234 A.D.2d 794, 651 N.Y.S.2d 239 (3d Dep't, 1996)—§ **3:3**

Holy Properties Ltd., L.P. v. Kenneth Cole Productions, Inc., 87 N.Y.2d 130, 637 N.Y.S.2d 964, 661 N.E.2d 694 (1995)—§ **29:5**

Table of Cases

636 N.Y.S.2d 180 (3d Dep't, 1996)—§ **18:14**

Orange County Publications, Inc., a Div. of Ottaway Newspapers v. County of Orange, 168 Misc. 2d 346, 637 N.Y.S.2d 596 (Sup. Ct., 1995)—§ **16:7**

P

Parmisani v. Grasso, 218 A.D.2d 870, 629 N.Y.S.2d 865 (3d Dep't, 1995)—§ **23:14**

Pegg v. Shahin, 237 A.D.2d 271, 654 N.Y.S.2d 395 (2d Dep't, 1997)— § **22:19**

People v. Armenia, 218 A.D.2d 747, 630 N.Y.S.2d 784 (2d Dep't, 1995)—§ **11:6**

People v. Calamia, 169 Misc. 2d 1054, 648 N.Y.S.2d 226 (Sup. Ct., 1996)—§ **9:3**

People v. Carpenter, 658 N.Y.S.2d 542 (App. Div. 3d Dep't, 1997)—§ **9:4**

People v. Luchey, 221 A.D.2d 936, 634 N.Y.S.2d 304 (4th Dep't, 1995)—§ **13:8**

Perez v. Perez, 228 A.D.2d 161, 644 N.Y.S.2d 168 (1st Dep't, 1996)—§ **26:2**

Pernice v. Devora, 657 N.Y.S.2d 70 (App. Div. 2d Dep't, 1997)— § **9:4**

Persing v. Coughlin, 214 A.D.2d 145, 632 N.Y.S.2d 366 (4th Dep't, 1995)—§ **17:6**

Petek v. Petek, 657 N.Y.S.2d 738 (App. Div. 2d Dep't, 1997)— § **6:3**

Peters v. Port Authority Trans-Hudson Corp., 234 A.D.2d 205, 651 N.Y.S.2d 500 (1st Dep't, 1996)—§ **33:7**

Pierre-Louis v. Algoo, 226 A.D.2d 441, 640 N.Y.S.2d 598 (2d Dep't, 1996)—§ **14:3**

Plunkett v. Emergency Medical Service of New York City, 234 A.D.2d 162, 651 N.Y.S.2d 462 (1st Dep't, 1996)—§ **31:7**

Poslock v. Teachers' Retirement Bd. of Teachers' Retirement System, 209 A.D.2d 87, 624 N.Y.S.2d 574 (1st Dep't, 1995)—§ **12:10**

Poturniak v. Rupcic, 232 A.D.2d 541, 648 N.Y.S.2d 668 (2d Dep't, 1996)—§ **29:15**

Prashant Enterprises, Inc. v. State, 228 A.D.2d 144, 650 N.Y.S.2d 473 (3d Dep't, 1996)—§ **29:21**

Prote Contracting Co., Inc. v. Board of Educ. of the City of New York, 230 A.D.2d 32, 657 N.Y.S.2d 158, 118 Ed. Law Rep. 433 (1st Dep't, 1997)—§ **34:7**

Provenzano v. Peters, 661 N.Y.S.2d 41 (App. Div. 2d Dep't, 1997)— § **33:7**

Prozeralik v. Capital Cities Communications, Inc., 222 A.D.2d 1020, 635 N.Y.S.2d 913 (4th Dep't, 1995)—§ **22:20**

Public Adm'r of County of New York v. Frota Oceanica Brasileira, S.A., 222 A.D.2d 332, 635 N.Y.S.2d 606 (1st Dep't, 1995)—§ **29:8**

R

Razzaque v. Krakow Taxi, Inc., 656 N.Y.S.2d 208 (App. Div. 1st Dep't, 1997)—§ **2:2**

Re, Application of, 659 N.Y.S.2d 3 (App. Div. 1st Dep't, 1997)— § **3:6**

Table of Cases

Table of Cases

TABLE OF STATUTES

TABLE OF RULES AND CODES

CONSTITUTIONS

Index

INDEX